PRINCIPLES OF
CORPORATE FINANCE

ABOUT THE AUTHORS

Richard A. Brealey   Professor of Finance at the London Business School. He is the former president of the European Finance Association and a former director of the American Finance Association. He is a fellow of the British Academy and has served as a special adviser to the Governor of the Bank of England and director of a number of financial institutions. Other books written by Professor Brealey include *Introduction to Risk and Return from Common Stocks*.

Stewart C. Myers   Robert C. Merton (1970) Professor of Finance at MIT's Sloan School of Management. He is past president of the American Finance Association and a research associate of the National Bureau of Economic Research. His research has focused on financing decisions, valuation methods, the cost of capital, and financial aspects of government regulation of business. Dr. Myers is a director of Entergy Corporation and The Brattle Group, Inc. He is active as a financial consultant.

Franklin Allen   Nippon Life Professor of Finance at the Wharton School of the University of Pennsylvania. He is past president of the American Finance Association, Western Finance Association, and Society for Financial Studies. His research has focused on financial innovation, asset price bubbles, comparing financial systems, and financial crises. He is a scientific adviser at Sveriges Riksbank (Sweden's central bank).

Pitabas Mohanty   Professor of Finance at XLRI, Jamshedpur. He was a Fulbright Visiting Scholar at Stern School of Business, New York University during 2009-10. He teaches Corporate Finance, Company Valuation, and Financial Modeling. His research interests include asset pricing, mergers and acquisitions, corporate finance, and market efficiency.

PRINCIPLES OF
CORPORATE FINANCE

TENTH EDITION

Richard A. Brealey
Professor of Finance
London Business School

Stewart C. Myers
Robert C. Merton (1970) Professor of Finance
Sloan School of Management
Massachusetts Institute of Technology

Franklin Allen
Nippon Life Professor of Finance
The Wharton School
University of Pennsylvania

Pitabas Mohanty
Professor of Finance
Xavier Labour Relations Institute (XLRI)
Jamshedpur

Tata McGraw Hill Education Private Limited

NEW DELHI

McGraw-Hill Offices
New Delhi   New York   St Louis   San Francisco   Auckland   Bogotá   Caracas
Kuala Lumpur   Lisbon   London   Madrid   Mexico City   Milan   Montreal
San Juan   Santiago   Singapore   Sydney   Tokyo   Toronto

Tata McGraw-Hill

Principles of Corporate Finance, 10/e (SIE)

Indian Adaptation done by arrangement with The McGraw-Hill Companies, Inc., New York

Sales Territories: India, Pakistan, Nepal, Bangladesh, Sri Lanka and Bhutan

Tata McGraw-Hill Edition 2012

ISBN-13: 978-1-25-900465-0
ISBN-10: 1-25-900465-1

Vice President and Managing Director: *Ajay Shukla*
Head—Higher Education Publishing and Marketing: *Vibha Mahajan*
Publishing Manager—B&E/HSSL: *Tapas K Maji*
Deputy Manager (Sponsoring): *Surabhi Khare*
Development Editor: *Anirudh Sharan*
Senior Production Manager: *Manohar Lal*
Senior Production Executive: *Atul Gupta*
Marketing Manager—Higher Education: *Vijay Sarathi*
Assistant Product Manager: *Daisy Sachdeva*
Graphic Designer (Cover Design): *Meenu Raghav*
General Manager—Production: *Rajender P Ghansela*
Manager—Production: *Reji Kumar*

Published by the Tata McGraw Hill Education Private Limited, 7 west Patel Nagar, New Delhi 1100008 and typeset at The Composers, 260 C.A. Apt., Paschim Vihar, New Delhi 110 063, and printed at Sai Printo Pack Pvt. Ltd, A -102/4 Okhla Industrial Area, Phase II, New Delhi 110020

Cover Printed at: Sai Printo Pack

DLCYYRCHDDLRA

To Our Parents

PREFACE

information on the Indian edition of the book (more questions, more updates) from the website
google.com/site/acufin/profmohanty.

Chapter 1 is now called "Goals and Governance of the Firm." We introduce financial management
by recent examples of capital investment and financing decisions by several well-known corporations.
We explain why value maximisation makes sense as a financial objective. Finally we look at wh
governance and incentives ... how corporations encourage managers and employees to work c
to increase firm value and to behave ethically.

Chapter 2 combines Chapters 2 and 3 from the ninth edition. It goes directly into how presen
are calculated. We think that it is better organized and easier to understand in its new presenta

Chapter 3 introduces bond valuation. The material here has been reordered and simplified. Th
chapter focuses on default-free bonds, but also includes an introduction to corporate debt and default
risk. (We discuss corporate debt and default risk in more detail in Chapter 23.)

be used to value entire businesses as well as ind

Chapter 6 now includes an expanded treatment of this topic along with a new

Chapter 24 is now devoted

Chapter 29 co

Chapter 30 The discussion

suggested that the crisis dispro
was a wake-up call—call to remember basic principles, including the importance of good systems of
governance, proper management incentives, sensible capital structures, and effective risk management.
We have added examples and discussion of the crisis throughout
with a discussion of internal costs and the importance of good governance. Other chapters have
required important revisions to reflect
recent controversies. Chapter 13, where the topic of market effi

last three decades have also generated important changes in theory and practice. Research in finance

This book describes the theory and practice of corporate finance. We hardly need to explain why financial managers have to master the practical aspects of their job, but we should spell out why down-to-earth managers need to bother with theory.

Managers learn from experience how to cope with routine problems. But the best managers are also able to respond to change. To do so you need more than time-honored rules of thumb; you must understand *why* companies and financial markets behave the way they do. In other words, you need a *theory* of finance.

Does that sound intimidating? It shouldn't. Good theory helps you to grasp what is going on in the world around you. It helps you to ask the right questions when times change and new problems need to be analyzed. It also tells you which things you do *not* need to worry about. Throughout this book we show how managers use financial theory to solve practical problems.

Of course, the theory presented in this book is not perfect and complete—no theory is. There are some famous controversies where financial economists cannot agree. We have not glossed over these disagreements. We set out the arguments for each side and tell you where we stand.

Much of this book is concerned with understanding what financial managers do and why. But we also say what financial managers *should* do to increase company value. Where theory suggests that financial managers are making mistakes, we say so, while admitting that there may be hidden reasons for their actions. In brief, we have tried to be fair but to pull no punches.

This book may be your first view of the world of modern finance theory. If so, you will read first for new ideas, for an understanding of how finance theory translates into practice, and occasionally, we hope, for entertainment. But eventually you will be in a position to make financial decisions, not just study them. At that point you can turn to this book as a reference and guide.

CHANGES IN THE TENTH EDITION

We are proud of the success of previous editions of *Principles*, and we have done our best to make the tenth edition even better.

What is new in the tenth edition? First, we have rewritten and refreshed several basic chapters. Content remains much the same, but we think that the revised chapters are simpler and flow better. These chapters also contain more real-world examples both from India and from the other parts of the world. We have more examples from India, more Indian questions. You can also find more

information on the Indian edition of the book (more questions, more updates) from the website sites.
google.com/a/xlri.ac.in/profmohanty.

Chapter 1 is now titled "Goals and Governance of the Firm." We introduce financial management
by recent examples of capital investment and financing decisions by several well-known corporations.
We explain why value maximization makes sense as a financial objective. Finally, we look at why good
governance and incentive systems are needed to encourage managers and employees to work together
to increase firm value and to behave ethically.

Chapter 2 combines Chapters 2 and 3 from the ninth edition. It goes directly into how present values
are calculated. We think that it is better organized and easier to understand in its new presentation.

Chapter 3 introduces bond valuation. The material here has been reordered and simplified. The
chapter focuses on default-free bonds, but also includes an introduction to corporate debt and default
risk. (We discuss corporate debt and default risk in more detail in Chapter 23.)

Chapter 4 is devoted to the valuation of common stocks. A short illustration of how DCF models can
be used to value entire businesses as well as individual stocks has been added to this chapter.

Chapter 12 is concerned exclusively with agency problems and management incentives. A section on
the pressure for corporations to manage earnings has been added to further illustrate this topic.

Chapter 13 now includes an expanded treatment of this topic along with a new discussion on the
limits of arbitrage.

Chapter 19 presents the complications of valuing leveraged businesses.

Chapter 28 is now devoted to financial analysis, which should be more convenient to instructors who
wish to assign this topic early in their courses. We explain how the financial statements and ratios help
to reveal the value, profitability, efficiency, and financial strength of a real company (Lowe's).

Chapter 29 combines the ever-important topics of short-term and long-term financial planning.
Material on Working Capital has been re-arranged and includes an expanded section on inventory
management.

Chapter 30 The discussion of bank lending has been substantially rewritten. The chapter also offers
coverage on the effect of the crisis on money-market mutual funds.

The **credit crisis** that started in 2007 dramatically demonstrated the importance of a well-functioning financial system and the problems that occur when it ceases to function properly. Some have
suggested that the crisis disproved the lessons of modern finance. On the contrary, we believe that it
was a wake-up call—a call to remember basic principles, including the importance of good systems of
governance, proper management incentives, sensible capital structures, and effective risk management.

We have added **examples and discussion of the crisis throughout the book**, starting in Chapter
1 with a discussion of agency costs and the importance of good governance. Other chapters have
required significant revision as a result of the crisis. These include **Chapter 12**, which discusses
executive compensation; **Chapter 13**, where the review of market efficiency includes an expanded
discussion of asset price bubbles; **Chapter 14**, where the section on financial institutions covers the
causes and progress of the crisis; **Chapter 23**, where we discuss the AIG debacle; and **Chapter 30**,
where we note the effect of the crisis on money-market mutual funds.

The first edition of this book appeared in 1981. Basic principles are the same now as then, but the
last three decades have also generated important changes in theory and practice. Research in finance

has focused less on what financial managers should do, and more on understanding and interpreting what they do in practice. In other words, finance has become more positive and less normative. For example, we now have careful surveys of firms' capital investment practices and payout and financing policies. We review these surveys and look at how they cast light on competing theories.

Many financial decisions seem less clear-cut than they were 20 or 30 years ago. It no longer makes sense to ask whether high payouts are always good or always bad, or whether companies should always borrow less or more. The right answer is, "It depends." Therefore we set out pros and cons of different policies. We ask "What questions should the financial manager ask when setting financial policy?" You will, for example, see this shift in emphasis when we discuss payout decisions in **Chapter 16**.

This edition builds on other changes from earlier editions. We recognize that financial managers work more than ever in an international environment and therefore need to be familiar with international differences in financial management and in financial markets and institutions. **Chapters 27** (Managing International Risks) **and 33** (Governance and Corporate Control around the World) **are exclusively devoted to international issues**. We have also found more and more opportunities in other chapters to draw cross-border comparisons or use non-U.S. examples. We hope that this material will both provide a better understanding of the wider financial environment and be useful to our many readers around the world.

As every first-grader knows, it is easier to add than to subtract. To make way for new topics we have needed to make some judicious pruning. We will not tell you where we have cut out material, because we hope that the deletions will be invisible.

MAKING LEARNING EASIER

Each chapter of the book includes an introductory preview, a summary, and an annotated list of suggested further reading. The list of possible candidates for further reading is now voluminous. Rather than trying to list every important article, we have largely listed survey articles or general books. More specific references have been moved to footnotes.

Each chapter is followed by a set of **basic questions, intermediate questions** on both numerical and conceptual topics, and a few **challenge questions**. Answers to the odd-numbered basic questions appear in an appendix at the end of the book.

We have added a **Real-Time Data Analysis** section to chapters where it makes sense to do so. This section now houses some of the Web Projects you have seen in the previous edition, along with new Data Analysis problems. These exercises seek to familiarize the reader with some useful Web sites and to explain how to download and process data from the Web.

The book also contains 10 end-of-chapter **mini-cases**. These include specific questions to guide the case analyses. Answers to the mini-cases are available to instructors on the book's Web site.

Spreadsheet programs such as **Excel** are tailor-made for many financial calculations. Several chapters now include boxes that introduce **the most useful financial functions** and provide some short practice questions. We show how to use the Excel function key to locate the function and then enter the data. We think that this approach is much simpler than trying to remember the formula for each function.

Many tables in the text appear as spreadsheets. In these cases an equivalent "live" spreadsheet appears on the book's Web site. Readers can use these live spreadsheets to understand better the calculations behind the table and to see the effects of changing the underlying data. We have also linked end-of-chapter questions to the spreadsheets.

We conclude the book with a glossary of financial terms.

The 34 chapters in this book are divided into 11 parts. Parts 1 to 3 cover valuation and capital investment decisions, including portfolio theory, asset pricing models, and the cost of capital. Parts 4 to 8 cover payout policy, capital structure, options (including real options), corporate debt, and risk management. Part 9 covers financial analysis, planning, and working-capital management. Part 10 covers mergers and acquisitions, corporate restructuring, and corporate governance around the world. Part 11 concludes.

We realize that instructors will wish to select topics and may prefer a different sequence. We have therefore written chapters so that topics can be introduced in several logical orders. For example, there should be no difficulty in reading the chapters on financial analysis and planning before the chapters on valuation and capital investment.

ACKNOWLEDGMENTS

We have a long list of people to thank for their helpful criticism of earlier editions and for assistance in preparing this one. They include Faiza Arshad, Aleijda de Cazenove Balsan, Kedran Garrison, Robert Pindyck, Sara Salem, and Gretchen Slemmons at MIT; Elroy Dimson, Paul Marsh, Mike Staunton, and Stefania Uccheddu at London Business School; Lynda Borucki, Michael Barhum, Marjorie Fischer, Larry Kolbe, Michael Vilbert, Bente Villadsen, and Fiona Wang at The Brattle Group, Inc.; Alex Triantis at the University of Maryland; Adam Kolasinski at the University of Washington; Simon Gervais at Duke University; Michael Chui at The Bank for International Settlements; Pedro Matos at the University of Southern California; Yupana Wiwattanakantang at Hitotsubashi University; Nickolay Gantchev, Tina Horowitz, and Chenying Zhang at the University of Pennsylvania; Julie Wulf at Harvard University; Jinghua Yan at Tykhe Capital; Roger Stein at Moody's Investor Service; Bennett Stewart at EVA Dimensions; and James Matthews at Towers Perrin.

We want to express our appreciation to those instructors whose insightful comments and suggestions were invaluable to us during the revision process:

Neyaz Ahmed *University of Maryland*
Anne Anderson *Lehigh University*
Noyan Arsen *Koc University*
Anders Axvarn *Gothenburg University*
Jan Bartholdy *ASB, Denmark*
Penny Belk *Loughborough University*
Omar Benkato *Ball State University*
Eric Benrud *University of Baltimore*
Peter Berman *University of New Haven*
Tom Boulton *Miami University of Ohio*
Edward Boyer *Temple University*
Alon Brav *Duke University*
Jean Canil *University of Adelaide*
Celtin Ciner *University of North Carolina, Wilmington*
John Cooney *Texas Tech University*
Charles Cuny *Washington University, St. Louis*

John Davenport *Regent University*
Ray DeGennaro *University of Tennessee, Knoxville*
Adri DeRidder *Gotland University*
William Dimovski *Deakin University, Melbourne*
David Ding *Nanyang Technological University*
Robert Duvic *University of Texas at Austin*
Alex Edmans *University of Pennsylvania*
Susan Edwards *Grand Valley State University*
Robert Everett *Johns Hopkins University*
Frank Flanegin *Robert Morris University*
Zsuzsanna Fluck *Michigan State University*
Connel Fullenkamp *Duke University*
Mark Garmaise *University of California, Los Angeles*
Sharon Garrison *University of Arizona*

Christopher Geczy *University of Pennsylvania*
George Geis *University of Virginia*
Stuart Gillan *University of Delaware*
Felix Goltz *Edhec Business School*
Ning Gong *Melbourne Business School*
Levon Goukasian *Pepperdine University*
Gary Gray *Pennsylvania State University*
C. J. Green *Loughborough University*
Mark Griffiths *Thunderbird, American School of International Management*
Re-Jin Guo *University of Illinois, Chicago*
Ann Hackert *Idaho State University*
Winfried Hallerbach *Erasmus University, Rotterdam*
Milton Harris *University of Chicago*
Mary Hartman *Bentley College*
Glenn Henderson *University of Cincinnati*
Donna Hitscherich *Columbia University*
Ronald Hoffmeister *Arizona State University*
James Howard *University of Maryland, College Park*
George Jabbour *George Washington University*
Ravi Jagannathan *Northwestern University*
Abu Jalal *Suffolk University*
Nancy Jay *Mercer University*
Kathleen Kahle *University of Arizona*
Jarl Kallberg *NYU, Stern School of Business*
Ron Kaniel *Duke University*
Steve Kaplan *University of Chicago*
Arif Khurshed *Manchester Business School*
Ken Kim *University of Wisconsin, Milwaukee*
C. R. Krishnaswamy *Western Michigan University*
George Kutner *Marquette University*
Dirk Laschanzky *University of Iowa*
David Lins *University of Illinois, Urbana*
David Lovatt *University of East Anglia*
Debbie Lucas *Northwestern University*
Brian Lucey *Trinity College, Dublin*
Suren Mansinghka *University of California, Irvine*
Ernst Maug *Mannheim University*
George McCabe *University of Nebraska*
Eric McLaughlin *California State University, Pomona*
Joe Messina *San Francisco State University*

Dag Michalson *Bl, Oslo*
Franklin Michello *Middle Tennessee State University*
Peter Moles *University of Edinburgh*
Katherine Morgan *Columbia University*
Darshana Palkar *Minnesota State University, Mankato*
Claus Parum *Copenhagen Business School*
Dilip Patro *Rutgers University*
John Percival *University of Pennsylvania*
Birsel Pirim *University of Illinois, Urbana*
Latha Ramchand *University of Houston*
Rathin Rathinasamy *Ball State University*
Raghavendra Rau *Purdue University*
Joshua Raugh *University of Chicago*
Charu Reheja *Wake Forest University*
Thomas Rhee *California State University, Long Beach*
Tom Rietz *University of Iowa*
Robert Ritchey *Texas Tech University*
Michael Roberts *University of Pennsylvania*
Mo Rodriguez *Texas Christian University*
John Rozycki *Drake University*
Frank Ryan *San Diego State University*
Marc Schauten *Eramus University*
Brad Scott *Webster University*
Nejat Seyhun *University of Michigan*
Jay Shanken *Emory University*
Chander Shekhar *University of Melbourne*
Hamid Shomali *Golden Gate University*
Richard Simonds *Michigan State University*
Bernell Stone *Brigham Young University*
John Strong *College of William & Mary*
Avanidhar Subrahmanyam *University of California, Los Angeles*
Tim Sullivan *Bentley College*
Shrinivasan Sundaram *Ball State University*
Chu-Sheng Tai *Texas Southern University*
Stephen Todd *Loyola University, Chicago*
Walter Torous *University of California, Los Angeles*
Emery Trahan *Northeastern University*
Ilias Tsiakas *University of Warwick*
Narendar V. Rao *Northeastern University*
David Vang *St. Thomas University*
Steve Venti *Dartmouth College*

Joseph Vu *DePaul University*
John Wald *Rutgers University*
Chong Wang *Naval Postgraduate School*
Kelly Welch *University of Kansas*
Jill Wetmore *Saginaw Valley State University*
Patrick Wilkie *University of Virginia*
Matt Will *University of Indianapolis*
Art Wilson *George Washington University*
Shee Wong *University of Minnesota, Duluth*
Bob Wood *Tennessee Tech University*
Fei Xie *George Mason University*
Minhua Yang *University of Central Florida*
Chenying Zhang *University of Pennsylvania*
Uday Damodaran *XLRI School of Business and Human Resources Jamshedpur*
Ravi Anshuman *Indian Institute of Management Bangalore*

Pratap Biswal *MDI Gurgaon*
Shashidhar Murthy *Indian Institute of Management Bangalore*
Manoj Anand *Indian Institute of Management Lucknow*
Nalini Prava Tripathy *Indian Institute of Management Shillong*
Soumya Guha Deb *Xavier Institute of Management, Bhubaneswar*
Pankaj Madhani *ICFAI Business School, Ahmedabad*
Ashutosh Verma *Indian Institute of Forest Management, Bhopal*
Sathyanarayana S *M.P.Birla Institution of Management, Bangalore*

This list is surely incomplete. We know how much we owe to our colleagues at the London Business School, MIT's Sloan School of Management, and the University of Pennsylvania's Wharton School. In many cases, the ideas that appear in this book are as much their ideas as ours.

We would also like to thank all those at McGraw-Hill/Irwin who worked on the book, including Michele Janicek, Executive Editor; Lori Koetters, Managing Editor; Christina Kouvelis, Senior Developmental Editor; Melissa Caughlin, Senior Marketing Manager; Jennifer Jelinski, Marketing Specialist; Karen Fisher, Developmental Editor II; Laurie Entringer, Designer; Michael McCormick, Lead Production Supervisor; and Sue Lombardi Media Project Manager.

Finally, we record the continuing thanks due to our wives, Diana, Maureen, and Sally, who were unaware when they married us that they were also marrying the *Principles of Corporate Finance*.

Richard A. Brealey
Stewart C. Myers
Franklin Allen
Pitabas Mohanty

GUIDED TOUR

Pedagogical Features

CHAPTER OVERVIEW

Each chapter begins with a brief narrative and outline to explain the concepts that will be covered in more depth. Useful Web sites related to material for each Part are provided on the book's Web site at **www.mhhe.com/bmam10e.**

PART 1 VALUE

CHAPTER 1

GOALS AND GOVERNANCE OF THE FIRM

This book is about how corporations make financial decisions. We start by explaining what these decisions are and what they are seeking to accomplish.

There may be a few activities in which one can read a textbook and then just "do it," but financial management is not one of them. That is why finance is worth studying. Who wants to work in a field where there is no room for judgment, experience, creativity, and a pinch of luck? Although this book cannot guarantee any of these things, it does cover the concepts that govern good financial decisions, and it shows you how to use the tools of the trade of modern finance.

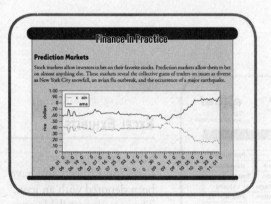

Finance In Practice

Prediction Markets

Stock markets allow investors to bet on their favorite stocks. Prediction markets allow them to bet on almost anything else. These markets reveal the collective guess of traders on issues as diverse as New York City snowfall, an avian flu outbreak, and the occurrence of a major earthquake.

FINANCE IN PRACTICE BOXES

Relevant news articles from financial publications appear in various chapters throughout the text. Aimed at bringing real-world flavor into the classroom, these boxes provide insight into the business world today.

NUMBERED EXAMPLES

New to this edition! Numbered and titled examples are called-out within chapters to further illustrate concepts. Students can learn how to solve specific problems step-by-step as well as gain insight into general principles by seeing how they are applied to answer concrete questions and scenarios.

EXAMPLE 2.3   Winning Big at the Lottery

When 13 lucky machinists from Ohio pooled their money to buy Powerball lottery tickets, they won a record ₹295.7 million. (A fourteenth member of the group pulled out at the last minute to put in his own numbers.) We suspect that the winners received unsolicited congratulations, good wishes, and requests for money from dozens of more or less worthy charities. In response, they could fairly point out that the prize wasn't really worth ₹295.7 million. That sum was to be repaid in 25 annual installments of ₹11.828 million each. Assuming that the first payment occurred at the end of one year, what was the present value of the prize? The interest rate at the time was 5.9%.

At an interest rate of 5.9%, the annuity factor is

$$\left[\frac{1}{.059} - \frac{1}{.059(1.059)^{25}} \right] = 12.9057$$

The present value of the cash payments is ₹11.828 × 12.9057 = ₹152.6 million, much below the well-trumpeted prize, but still not a bad day's haul.

Lottery operators generally make arrangements for winners with big spending plans to take an equivalent lump sum. In our example the winners could either take the ₹295.7 million spread over 25 years or receive ₹152.6 million up front. Both arrangements had the same present value.

Excel Treatment

USEFUL SPREADSHEET FUNCTIONS BOXES

New to this edition! These boxes provide detailed examples of how to use Excel spreadsheets when applying financial concepts. Questions that apply to the spreadsheet follow for additional practice.

Useful Spreadsheet Functions

Internal Rate of Return

Spreadsheet programs such as Excel provide built-in functions to solve for internal rates of return. You can find these functions by pressing *fx* on the Excel toolbar. If you then click on the function that you wish to use, Excel will guide you through the inputs that are required. At the bottom left of the function box there is a Help facility with an example of how the function is used.

Here is a list of useful functions for calculating internal rates of return, together with some points to remember when entering data:

- **IRR:** Internal rate of return on a series of regularly spaced cash flows.
- **XIRR:** The same as IRR, but for irregularly spaced flows.

TABLE 7.8 Calculating the variance of the market returns and the covariance between the returns on the market and those of Anchovy Queen. Beta is the ratio of the variance to the covariance (i.e., $\beta = \sigma_{im}/\sigma_m^2$).

eXcel
Visit us at
www.mhhe.com/bmam10e

(1)	(2)	(3)	(4)	(5)	(6)	(7)
						Product of
			Deviation	Deviation	Squared	deviations
			from	from average	deviation	from average
	Market	Anchovy Q	average	Anchovy Q	from average	returns
Month	return	return	market return	return	market return	(cols 4 × 5)
1	–8%	–11%	–10	–13	100	130
2	4	8	2	6	4	12
3	12	19	10	17	100	170
4	–6	–13	–8	–15	64	120
5	2	3	0	1	0	0
6	8	6	6	4	36	24
Average	2	2		Total	304	456
			Variance = σ_m^2 = 304/6 = 50.67			
			Covariance = σ_{im} = 456/6 = 76			

EXCEL EXHIBITS

Select exhibits are set as Excel spreadsheets and have been denoted with an icon. They are also available on the book's Web site at **www.mhhe.com/bmam10e.**

End-of-Chapter Features

PROBLEM SETS

New end-of-chapter problems are included for even more hands-on practice. We have separated the questions by level of difficulty: Basic, Intermediate, and Challenge. Answers to the odd-numbered basic questions are included at the back of the book.

BASIC

1. Read the following passage: "Companies usually buy (a) assets. These include both tangible assets such as (b) and intangible assets such as (c). To pay for these assets, they sell (d) assets such as (e). The decision about which assets to buy is usually termed the (f) or (g) decision. The decision about how to raise the money is usually termed the (h) decision." Now fit each of the following terms into the most appropriate space: *financing, real, bonds, investment, executive airplanes, financial, capital budgeting, brand names.*

2. Which of the following are real assets, and which are financial?
   a. A share of stock.
   b. A personal IOU.
   c. A trademark.
   d. A factory.
   e. Undeveloped land.
   f. The balance in the firm's checking account.
   g. An experienced and hardworking sales force.
   h. A corporate bond.

3. Vocabulary test. Explain the differences between:
   a. Real and financial assets.
   b. Capital budgeting and financing decisions.
   c. Closely held and public corporations.
   d. Limited and unlimited liability.

4. Which of the following statements always apply to corporations?
   a. Unlimited liability.
   b. Limited life.
   c. Ownership can be transferred without affecting operations.
   d. Managers can be fired with no effect on ownership.

5. Which of the following statements more accurately describe the treasurer than the controller?
   a. Responsible for investing the firm's spare cash.
   b. Responsible for arranging any issue of common stock.
   c. Responsible for the company's tax affairs.

INTERMEDIATE

6. In most large corporations, ownership and management are separated. What are the main implications of this separation?

7. F&H Corp. continues to invest heavily in a declining industry. Here is an excerpt from a rece

CHALLENGE

36. Here are two useful rules of thumb. The "Rule of 72" says that with discrete compounding the time it takes for an investment to double in value is roughly 72/interest rate (in percent). The "Rule of 69" says that with continuous compounding the time that it takes to double is exactly 69.3/interest rate (in percent).
   a. If the annually compounded interest rate is 12%, use the Rule of 72 to calculate roughly how long it takes before your money doubles. Now work it out exactly.
   b. Can you prove the Rule of 69?

EXCEL PROBLEMS

Most chapters contain problems, denoted by an icon, specifically linked to Excel templates that are available on the book's Web site at **www.mhhe.com/bmam10e.**

15. A 10-year German government bond (bund) has a face value of €100 and a coupon rate of 5% paid annually. Assume that the interest rate (in euros) is equal to 6% per year. What is the bond's PV?

16. A 10-year U.S. Treasury bond with a face value of $10,000 pays a coupon of 5.5% (2.75% of face value every six months). The semiannually compounded interest rate is 5.2% (a six-month discount rate of 5.2/2 = 2.6%).
   a. What is the present value of the bond?
   b. Generate a graph or table showing how the bond's present value changes for semiannually compounded interest rates between 1% and 15%.

17. A six-year government bond makes annual coupon payments of 5% and offers a yield of 3% annually compounded. Suppose that one year later

eXcel
Visit us at
www.mhhe.com/bmam10e

eXcel
Visit us at
www.mhhe.com/bmam10e

REAL-TIME DATA ANALYSIS
SECTION

Featured among select chapters, this section includes Web exercises as well as questions. The Web exercises give students the opportunity to explore financial Web sites on their own to gain familiarity and apply chapter concepts. These problems provide an easy method of including current, real-world data into the classroom.

REAL-TIME DATA ANALYSIS

You can download data for the following questions from the Standard & Poor's Market Insight Web site (www.mhhe.com/edumarketinsight)—see the "Monthly Adjusted Prices" spreadsheet —or from finance.yahoo.com. Refer to the useful Spreadsheet Functions box near the end of Chapter 9 for information on Excel functions.

1. Download the daily closing prices of HLL, Reliance and ITC from the website of the NSE (www.nseindia.com). Estimate the monthly returns from these data.   STANDARD &POOR'S
   a. Calculate the annual standard deviation of returns from each company, using the most recent three years of monthly returns. Use the Excel function STDEV. Multiply by the square root of 12 to convert to annual units.
   b. Use the Excel function CORREL to calculate the correlation coefficient between the monthly returns for each pair of stocks.
   c. Calculate the standard deviation of returns for a portfolio with equal investments in each of the three stocks.

2. Download to a spreadsheet the last five years of monthly adjusted stock prices for each of the companies in Table 7.6 and for the sensex.   STANDARD &POOR'S
   a. Calculate the monthly returns.
   b. Calculate beta for each stock using the Excel function SLOPE, where the "y" range refers to the stock return (the dependent variable) and the "x" range is the market return (the independent variable).
   c. How have the betas changed from those reported in Table 7.6?

3. A large mutual fund group such as Fidelity offers a variety of funds. They include *sector funds* that specialize in particular industries and *index funds* that simply invest in the market index. Log on to **www.fidelity.com** and find first the standard deviation of returns on the Fidelity Spartan 500 Index Fund, which replicates the S&P 500. Now find the standard deviations for different sector funds. Are they larger or smaller than the figure for the index fund? How do you interpret your findings?

REEBY SPORTS

Ten years ago, in 2001, George Reeby founded a small mail-order company selling high-quality sports equipment. Since those early days Reeby Sports has grown steadily and been consistently profitable. The company has issued 2 million shares, all of which are owned by George Reeby and his five children.

For some months George has been wondering whether the time has come to take the company public. This would allow him to cash in on part of his investment and would make it easier for the firm to raise capital should it wish to expand in the future.

But how much are the shares worth? George's first instinct is to look at the firm's balance sheet, which shows that the book value of the equity is $26.34 million, or $13.17 per share. A share price of $13.17 would put the stock on a P/E ratio of 6.6. That is quite a bit lower than the 13.1 P/E ratio of Reeby's larger rival, Molly Sports.

George suspects that book value is not necessarily a good guide to a share's market value. He thinks of his daughter Jenny, who works in an investment bank. She would undoubtedly know what the shares are worth. He decides to phone her after she finishes work that evening at 9 o'clock or before she starts the next day at 6.00 a.m.

Before phoning, George jots down some basic data on the company's profitability. After recovering from its early losses, the company has earned a return that is higher than its estimated 10% cost of capital. George is fairly confident that the company could continue to grow fairly steadily for the next six to eight years. In fact he feels that the company's growth has been somewhat held back in the last few ye...

MINI-CASES

To enhance concepts discussed within a chapter, mini-cases are included in select chapters so students can apply their knowledge to real-world scenarios.

SUPPLEMENTS

The solutions are provided for mini-cases as and where required.

In this edition, we have gone to great lengths to ensure that our supplements are equal in quality and
authority to the text itself.

FOR THE INSTRUCTOR

The following supplements are available to you via the book's Web site at
www.mhhe.com/bmam10e and are password protected for security:

Solutions Manual

The Solutions Manual contains solutions to all basic, intermediate, and challenge problems found at
the end of each chapter.

Instructor's Manual

The Instructor's Manual is extensively revised and updated. It contains an overview of each chapter,
teaching tips, learning objectives, challenge areas, key terms, and an annotated outline that provides
references to the PowerPoint slides.

Test Bank

The Test Bank has been updated to include hundreds of new multiple-choice and short answer/
discussion questions based on the revisions of the authors. The level of difficulty varies, as indicated
by the easy, medium, or difficult labels.

PowerPoint Presentations

The PowerPoint Presentations are inclusive of exhibits, outlines, key points, and summaries in a
visually stimulating collection of slides. Addition of Indian scenarios and concepts are provided as and
where required.

Minicase Solutions

The solutions are provided for mini-cases as and where required.

FOR THE STUDENT

Online Learning Center: www.mhhe.com/bmam10e
Find a wealth of information online! This site contains information about the book and the authors as well as teaching and learning materials for the student, including:

Online quizzes   These multiple-choice questions are provided as an additional testing and reinforcement tool for students. Each quiz is organized by chapter to test the specific concepts presented in that particular chapter. Immediate scoring of the quiz occurs upon submission and the correct answers are provided.

Excel templates   There are templates for select exhibits ("live" Excel), as well as various end-of-chapter problems that have been set as Excel spreadsheets — all denoted by an icon. They correlate with specific concepts in the text and allow students to work through financial problems and gain experience using spreadsheets. Also refer to the valuable Useful Spreadsheet Functions Boxes that are sprinkled throughout the text for some helpful prompts on working in Excel.

Interactive FinSims   This valuable asset consists of multiple simulations of key financial topics. Ideal for students to reinforce concepts and gain additional practice to strengthen skills.

BRIEF CONTENTS

CONTENTS

PART 1
VALUE

PART 2
RISK

PART 3
BEST PRACTICES IN CAPITAL BUDGETING

PART 5
PAYOUT POLICY AND CAPITAL STRUCTURE

PART 6
OPTIONS

PART 7
DEBT FINANCING

PART 8
RISK MANAGEMENT

PART 9
FINANCIAL PLANNING AND WORKING CAPITAL MANAGEMENT

PART 10
MERGERS, CORPORATE CONTROL, AND GOVERNANCE

Chapter 31 Mergers   841

PART 11
CONCLUSION

1

CHAPTER

GOALS AND GOVERNANCE OF THE FIRM

This book is about how corporations make financial decisions. We start by explaining what these decisions are and what they are seeking to accomplish.

Corporations invest in real assets, which generate cash inflows and income. Some of the assets are tangible assets such as plant and machinery; others are intangible assets such as brand names and patents. Corporations finance these assets by borrowing, by retaining and reinvesting cash flow, and by selling additional shares of stock to the corporation's shareholders. Thus the corporation's financial manager faces two broad financial questions: First, what investments should the corporation make? Second, how should it pay for those investments? The investment decision involves spending money; the financing decision involves raising it.

A large corporation may have hundreds of thousands of shareholders. These shareholders differ in many ways, such as their wealth, risk tolerance, and investment horizon. Yet we will see that they usually endorse the same financial goal: they want the financial manager to increase the value of the corporation and its current stock price.

Thus the secret of success in financial management is to increase value. That is easy to say, but not very helpful. Instructing the financial manager to increase value is like advising an investor in the stock market to "buy low, sell high." The problem is how to do it.

There may be a few activities in which one can read a textbook and then just "do it," but financial management is not one of them. That is why finance is worth studying. Who wants to work in a field where there is no room for judgment, experience, creativity, and a pinch of luck? Although this book cannot guarantee any of these things, it does cover the concepts that govern good financial decisions, and it shows you how to use the tools of the trade of modern finance.

We start this chapter by looking at a fundamental trade-off. The corporation can either invest in new assets or it can give the cash back to the shareholders, who can then invest that cash in the financial markets. Financial managers add value whenever the company can earn a higher return than shareholders can earn for themselves. The shareholders' investment opportunities *outside* the corporation set the standard for investments *inside* the corporation. Financial managers therefore refer to the *opportunity cost* of the capital that shareholders contribute to the firm.

The success of a corporation depends on how well it harnesses all its managers and employees to work to increase value. We therefore take a first look at how good systems of corporate governance, combined with appropriate incentives and compensation packages, encourage everyone to pull together to increase value.

Good governance and appropriate incentives also help block out temptations to increase stock price by illegal or unethical means. Thoughtful shareholders do not want the maximum possible stock price. They want the maximum honest stock price.

This chapter introduces three themes that return again and again, in various forms and circumstances, throughout the book:

1. Maximizing value.
2. The opportunity cost of capital.
3. The crucial importance of incentives and governance.

1-1 CORPORATE INVESTMENT AND FINANCING DECISIONS

To carry on business, a corporation needs an almost endless variety of **real assets.** These assets do not drop free from a blue sky; they need to be paid for. To pay for real assets, the corporation sells claims on the assets and on the cash flow that they will generate. These claims are called **financial assets** or **securities.** Take a bank loan as an example. The bank provides the corporation with cash in exchange for a financial asset, which is the corporation's promise to repay the loan with interest. An ordinary bank loan is not a security, however, because it is held by the bank and not sold or traded in financial markets.

Take a corporate bond as a second example. The corporation sells the bond to investors in exchange for the promise to pay interest on the bond and to pay off the bond at its maturity. The bond is a financial asset, and also a security, because it can be held by and traded among many investors in financial markets. Securities include bonds, shares of stock, and a dizzying variety of specialized instruments. We describe bonds in Chapter 3, stocks in Chapter 4, and other securities in later chapters.

This suggests the following definitions:

$$\text{Investment decision} = \text{purchase of real assets}$$
$$\text{Financing decision} = \text{sale of financial assets}$$

But these equations are too simple. The investment decision also involves managing assets already in place and deciding when to shut down and dispose of assets if profits decline. The corporation also has to manage and control the risks of its investments. The financing decision includes not just raising cash today but also meeting obligations to banks, bondholders, and stockholders that contributed financing in the past. For example, the corporation has to repay its debts when they become due. If it

TABLE 1.1 Examples of recent investment and financing decisions by major corporations.

Company (revenue)	Recent Investment Decision	Recent Financing Decision
Boeing ($61 billion)	Began production of its 787 Dreamliner aircraft, at a forecasted cost of more than $10 billion.	The cash flow from Boeing's operations allowed it to repay some of its debt and repurchase $2.8 billion of stock.
Royal Dutch Shell ($458 billion)	Invested in a $1.5 billion deepwater oil and gas field in the Gulf of Mexico.	In 2008 returned $13.1 billion of cash to its stockholders by buying back their shares.
Toyota (¥26,289 billion)	In 2008 opened new engineering and safety testing facilities in Michigan.	Returned ¥431 billion to shareholders in the form of dividends.
GlaxoSmithKline (£24 billion)	Spent £3.7 billion in 2008 on research and development of new drugs.	Financed R&D expenditures largely with reinvested cash flow generated by sales of pharmaceutical products.
Wal-Mart ($406 billion)	In 2008 announced plans to invest over a billion dollars in 90 new stores in Brazil.	In 2008 raised $2.5 billion by an issue of 5-year and 30-year bonds.
Union Pacific ($18 billion)	Acquired 315 new locomotives in 2007.	Largely financed its investment in locomotives by long-term leases.
Wells Fargo ($52 billion)	Acquired Wachovia Bank in 2008 for ₹15.1 billion.	Financed the acquisition by an exchange of shares.
LVMH (€17 billion)	Acquired the Spanish winery Bodega Numanthia Termes.	Issued a six-year bond in 2007, raising 300 million Swiss francs.
Lenovo ($16 billion)	Expanded its chain of retail stores to cover over 2,000 cities.	Borrowed $400 million for 5 years from a group of banks.
Indigo (₹26 billion)	In early 2011, placed order for 180 Airbus A320 aircraft, the largest single-firm order number for large jets in commercial aviation history.	Plans to finance this acquisition with an Initial Public Offer (IPO) and a Sale and Leaseback arrangement.

cannot do so, it ends up insolvent and bankrupt. Sooner or later the corporation will also want to pay out cash to its shareholders.[1]

Let's go to more specific examples. Table 1.1 lists nine corporations. Four are U.S. corporations. Five are foreign: GlaxoSmithKline's headquarters are in London, LVMH's in Paris,[2] Shell's in The Hague, Toyota's in Nagoya, and Lenovo's in Beijing and Indigo in India. We have chosen very large corporations that you are probably already familiar with. You probably have traveled on an Indigo flight, or used a Wells Fargo ATM, for example.

Investment Decisions

The second column of Table 1.1 shows an important recent investment decision for each corporation. These investment decisions are often referred to as **capital budgeting** or **capital expenditure**

---

[1] We have referred to the corporation's owners as "shareholders" and "stockholders." The two terms mean exactly the same thing and are used interchangeably. Corporations are also referred to casually as "companies," "firms," or "businesses." We also use these terms interchangeably.

[2] LVMH Moët Hennessy Louis Vuitton (usually abbreviated to LVMH) markets perfumes and cosmetics, wines and spirits, watches and other fashion and luxury goods. And, yes, we know what you are thinking, but LVMH really is short for Moët Hennessy Louis Vuitton.

(**CAPEX**) decisions, because most large corporations prepare an annual capital budget listing the major projects approved for investment. Some of the investments in Table 1.1, such as Indigo's flights or Wal-Mart's new stores or Union Pacific's new locomotives, involve the purchase of tangible assets—assets that you can touch and kick. Corporations also need to invest in intangible assets, however. These include research and development (R&D), advertising, and marketing. For example, GlaxoSmithKline and other major pharmaceutical companies invest billions every year on R&D for new drugs. These companies also invest to market their existing products.

Today's capital investments generate future returns. Often the returns come in the distant future. Boeing committed over $10 billion to design, test, and manufacture the Dreamliner. It did so because it expects that the plane will generate cash returns for 30 years or more after it first enters commercial service. Those cash returns must recover Boeing's huge initial investment and provide at least an adequate profit on that investment. The longer Boeing must wait for cash to flow back, the greater the profit that it requires. Thus the financial manager must pay attention to the timing of project returns, not just their cumulative amount. In addition, these returns are rarely certain. A new project could be a smashing success or a dismal failure.

Of course, not every investment has such distant payoffs as Boeing's Dreamliner. Some investments have only short-term consequences. For example, with the approach of the Christmas holidays, Wal-Mart spends about $40 billion to stock up its warehouses and retail stores. As the goods are sold over the following months, the company recovers this investment in inventories.

Financial managers do not make major investment decisions in solitary confinement. They may work as part of a team of engineers and managers from manufacturing, marketing, and other business functions. Also, do not think of the financial manager as making billion-dollar investments on a daily basis. Most investment decisions are smaller and simpler, such as the purchase of a truck, machine tool, or computer system. Corporations make thousands of these smaller investment decisions every year. The cumulative amount of small investments can be just as large as that of the occasional big investments, such as those shown in Table 1.1.

Financing Decisions

The third column of Table 1.1 lists a recent financing decision by each corporation. A corporation can raise money (cash) from lenders or from shareholders. If it borrows, the lenders contribute the cash, and the corporation promises to pay back the debt plus a fixed rate of interest. If the shareholders put up the cash, they get no fixed return, but they hold shares of stock and therefore get a fraction of future profits and cash flow. The shareholders are *equity investors,* who contribute *equity financing.* The choice between debt and equity financing is called the **capital structure** decision. *Capital* refers to the firm's sources of long-term financing.

The financing choices available to large corporations seem almost endless. Suppose the firm decides to borrow. Should it borrow from a bank or borrow by issuing bonds that can be traded by investors? Should it borrow for 1 year or 20 years? If it borrows for 20 years, should it reserve the right to pay off the debt early if interest rates fall? Should it borrow in Paris, receiving and promising to repay euros, or should it borrow dollars in New York? As Table 1.1 shows, the French company LVMH borrowed Swiss francs, but it could have borrowed dollars or euros instead.

Corporations raise equity financing in two ways. First, they can issue new shares of stock. The investors who buy the new shares put up cash in exchange for a fraction of the corporation's future cash flow and profits. Second, the corporation can take the cash flow generated by its existing assets and reinvest the cash in new assets. In this case the corporation is reinvesting on behalf of existing stockholders. No new shares are issued.

What happens when a corporation does not reinvest all of the cash flow generated by its existing assets? It may hold the cash in reserve for future investment, or it may pay the cash back to its shareholders. Table 1.1 shows that in 2008 Toyota paid cash dividends of ¥431 billion, equivalent to about $4.3 billion. In the same year Shell paid back $13.1 billion to its stockholders by repurchasing shares. This was in addition to $9.8 billion paid out as cash dividends. The decision to pay dividends or repurchase shares is called the *payout decision*. We cover payout decisions in Chapter 16.

In some ways financing decisions are less important than investment decisions. Financial managers say that "value comes mainly from the asset side of the balance sheet." In fact the most successful corporations sometimes have the simplest financing strategies. Take Infosys as an example. At the end of 2010, Infosys shares traded for ₹1684.6 each. There were about 571.3 million shares outstanding. Therefore, Infosys' overall market value – its *market capitalization* or *market cap* – was ₹1684.6 × 571.3 = ₹196.24 billion. Where did this market value come from? It came from Infosys' product development, from its brand name and worldwide customer base, from its research and development, and from its ability to make profitable future investments. The value did *not* come from sophisticated financing. Infosys' financial strategy is very simple: it carries no debt to speak of and finances almost all investment by retaining and reinvesting cash flow.

Financing decisions may not add much value, compared with good investment decisions, but they can destroy value if they are stupid or if they are ambushed by bad news. For example, when real estate mogul Sam Zell led a buyout of the *Chicago Tribune* in 2007, the newspaper took on about $8 billion of additional debt. This was not a stupid decision, but it did prove fatal. As advertising revenues fell away in the recession of 2008, the *Tribune* could no longer service its debt. In December 2008 it filed for bankruptcy with assets of $7.6 billion and debts of $12.9 billion.

Business is inherently risky. The financial manager needs to identify the risks and make sure they are managed properly. For example, debt has its advantages, but too much debt can land the company in bankruptcy, as the *Chicago Tribune* discovered. Companies can also be knocked off course by recessions, by changes in commodity prices, interest rates and exchange rates, or by adverse political developments. Some of these risks can be hedged or insured, however, as we explain in Chapters 26 and 27.

What Is a Corporation?

We have been referring to "corporations." Before going too far or too fast, we offer some basic definitions. Details follow as needed in later chapters.

A **corporation** is a legal entity. In the view of the law, it is a legal *person* that is owned by its shareholders. As a legal person, the corporation can make contracts, carry on a business, borrow or lend money, and sue or be sued. One corporation can make a takeover bid for another and then merge the two businesses. Corporations pay taxes—but cannot vote!

In India, corporations are formed under central law (The Companies Act, 1956), based on memorandum of association and articles of association that set out the purpose of the business and how it is to be governed and operated.[3] For example, the articles of incorporation specify the composition and role of the *board of directors*. A corporation's directors choose and advise top management and are required to sign off on some corporate actions, such as mergers and the payment of dividends to shareholders.

---

[3] In India, corporations are identified by the label "Company" "Limited" or "Ltd". The U.S. identifies public corporations by "Inc" (short for Incorporated), the U.K. identifies public corporations by "plc" (short for "Public Limited Corporation"). French corporations have the suffix "SA" ("Société Anonyme"). The corresponding labels in Germany are "GmbH" ("Gesellschaft mit beschränkter Haftung") or "AG" ("Aktiengesellschaft").

A corporation is owned by its shareholders but is legally distinct from them. Therefore the shareholders have **limited liability,** which means that shareholders cannot be held personally responsible for the corporation's debts. When the U.S. financial corporation Lehman Brothers failed in 2008, no one demanded that its stockholders put up more money to cover Lehman's massive debts. Shareholders can lose their entire investment in a corporation, but no more.

Corporations do not have to be prominent, multinational businesses like those listed in Table 1.1. You can organize a local plumbing contractor or barber shop as a corporation if you want to take the trouble.[4] But usually corporations are larger businesses or businesses that aspire to grow.

When a corporation is first established, its shares may be privately held by a small group of investors, perhaps the company's managers and a few backers. In this case the shares are not publicly traded and the company is *closely held.* Eventually, when the firm grows and new shares are issued to raise additional capital, its shares are traded in public markets such as the Mumbai Stock Exchange. Such corporations are known as *public companies.* Most well-known corporations in the U.S. are public companies with widely dispersed shareholdings. In other countries, it is more common for large corporations to remain in private hands, and many public companies may be controlled by just a handful of investors. The latter category includes such well-known names as Fiat, Porsche, Benetton, Bosch, IKEA, and the Swatch Group.

A large public corporation may have hundreds of thousands of shareholders, who own the business but cannot possibly manage or control it directly. This *separation of ownership and control* gives corporations permanence. Even if managers quit or are dismissed and replaced, the corporation survives. Today's stockholders can sell all their shares to new investors without disrupting the operations of the business. Corporations can, in principle, live forever, and in practice they may survive many human lifetimes. One of the oldest corporations is the Hudson's Bay Company, which was formed in 1670 to profit from the fur trade between northern Canada and England. The company still operates as one of Canada's leading retail chains.

The separation of ownership and control can also have a downside, for it can open the door for managers and directors to act in their own interests rather than in the stockholders' interest. We return to this problem later in the chapter.

1-2   THE ROLE OF THE FINANCIAL MANAGER AND THE OPPORTUNITY COST OF CAPITAL

What do financial managers do for a living? That simple question can be answered in several ways. We can start with financial managers' job titles. Most large corporations have a **chief financial officer (CFO),** who oversees the work of all financial staff. The CFO is deeply involved in financial policy and financial planning and is in constant contact with the Chief Executive Officer (CEO) and other top management. The CFO is the most important financial voice of the corporation, and explains earnings results and forecasts to investors and the media.

Below the CFO are usually a **treasurer** and a **controller.** The treasurer is responsible for short-term cash management, currency trading, financing transactions, and bank relationships. The controller manages the company's internal accounting systems and oversees preparation of its financial statements and tax returns. The largest corporations have dozens of more specialized financial managers, including tax lawyers and accountants, experts in planning and forecasting, and managers responsible for investing the money set aside for employee retirement plans.

---

[4] Single individuals doing business on their own behalf are called sole proprietorships. Smaller, local businesses can also be organized as partnerships or professional corporations (PCs). We cover these alternative forms of business organization in Chapter 14.

Financial decisions are not restricted to financial specialists. Top management must sign off on major investment projects, for example. But the engineer who designs a new production line is also involved, because the design determines the real assets that the corporation holds. The engineer also rejects many designs before proposing what he or she thinks is the best one. Those rejections are also investment decisions, because they amount to decisions *not* to invest in other types of real assets.

In this book we use the term *financial manager* to refer to anyone responsible for an investment or financing decision. Often we use the term collectively for all the managers drawn into such decisions.

Let's go beyond job titles. What is the essential role of the financial manager? Figure 1.1 gives one answer. The figure traces how money flows from investors to the corporation and back to investors again. The flow starts when cash is raised from investors (arrow 1 in the figure). The cash could come from banks or from securities sold to investors in financial markets. The cash is then used to pay for the real assets (investment projects) needed for the corporation's business (arrow 2). Later, as the business operates, the assets generate cash inflows (arrow 3). That cash is either reinvested (arrow 4a) or returned to the investors who furnished the money in the first place (arrow 4b). Of course, the choice between arrows 4a and 4b is constrained by the promises made when cash was raised at arrow 1. For example, if the firm borrows money from a bank at arrow 1, it must repay this money plus interest at arrow 4b.

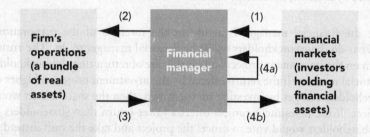

FIGURE 1.1

Flow of cash between financial markets and the firm's operations. Key: (1) Cash raised by selling financial assets to investors; (2) cash invested in the firm's operations and used to purchase real assets; (3) cash generated by the firm's operations; (4a) cash reinvested; (4b) cash returned to investors.

You can see examples of arrows 4a and 4b in Table 1.1. GlaxoSmithKline financed its drug research and development by reinvesting earnings (arrow 4a). Shell decided to return cash to shareholders by buying back its stock (arrow 4b). Shell could have chosen instead to pay the money out as additional cash dividends.

Notice how the financial manager stands between the firm and outside investors. On the one hand, the financial manager helps manage the firm's operations, particularly by helping to make good investment decisions. On the other hand, the financial manager deals with investors—not just with shareholders but also with financial institutions such as banks and with financial markets such as the Mumbai Stock Exchange.

The Investment Trade-off

Now look at Figure 1.2, which sets out the fundamental trade-off for corporate investment decisions. The corporation has a proposed investment project (a real asset). Suppose it has cash on hand sufficient to finance the project. The financial manager is trying to decide whether to invest in the project. If the financial manager decides not to invest, the corporation can pay out the cash to shareholders, say as an extra dividend. (The investment and dividend arrows in Figure 1.2 are arrows 2 and 4b in Figure 1.1.)

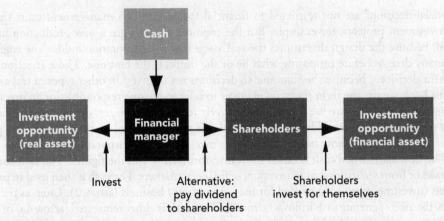

FIGURE 1.2

The firm can either keep and reinvest cash or return it to investors. (Arrows represent possible cash flows or transfers.) If cash is reinvested, the opportunity cost is the expected rate of return that shareholders could have obtained by investing in financial assets.

Assume that the financial manager is acting in the interests of the corporation's owners, its stockholders. What do these stockholders want the financial manager to do? The answer depends on the rate of return on the investment project and on the rate of return that the stockholders can earn by investing in financial markets. If the return offered by the investment project is higher than the rate of return that shareholders can get by investing on their own, then the shareholders would vote for the investment project. If the investment project offers a lower return than shareholders can achieve on their own, the shareholders would vote to cancel the project and take the cash instead.

Figure 1.2 could apply to Pantaloon Retail's decisions to invest in new retail stores, for example. Suppose Pantaloon has cash set aside to build 10 new stores in 2012. It could go ahead with the new stores, or it could choose to cancel the investment project and instead pay the cash out to its stockholders. If it pays out the cash, the stockholders could then invest for themselves.

Suppose that Pantaloon's new Big Bazaar stores project is just about as risky as the Indian stock market and that investment in the stock market offers a 10% expected rate of return. If the new stores offer a superior rate of return, say 20%, then Pantaloon shareholders would be happy to let Pantaloon keep the cash and invest it in the new stores. If the new stores offer only a 5% return, then the stockholders are better off with the cash and without the new stores; in that case, the financial manager should turn down the investment project.

As long as a corporation's proposed investments offer higher rates of return than its shareholders can earn for themselves in the stock market (or in other financial markets), its shareholders will applaud the investments and its stock price will increase. But if the company earns an inferior return, shareholders boo, stock price falls, and stockholders demand their money back so that they can invest on their own.

In our example, the minimum acceptable rate of return on Pantaloon's new stores is 10%. This minimum rate of return is called a *hurdle rate* or *cost of capital.* It is really an **opportunity cost of capital,** because it depends on the investment *opportunities* available to investors in financial markets. Whenever a corporation invests cash in a new project, its shareholders lose the opportunity to invest the cash on their own. Corporations increase value by accepting all investment projects that earn more than the opportunity cost of capital.

Notice that the opportunity cost of capital depends on the risk of the proposed investment project. Why? It's not just because shareholders are risk-averse. It's also because shareholders have to trade off risk against return when they invest on their own. The safest investments, such as Indian government securities, offer low rates of return. Investments with higher expected rates of return—the stock market, for example—are riskier and sometimes deliver painful losses. (The Indian stock market was down 52% in 2008, for example.) Other investments are riskier still. For example, high-tech growth stocks offer the prospect of higher rates of return, but are even more volatile.

Notice too that the opportunity cost of capital is generally *not* the interest rate that the company pays on a loan from a bank or on a bond. If the company is making a risky investment, the opportunity cost is the expected return that investors can achieve in financial markets at the same level of risk. The expected return on risky securities is normally well above the interest rate on corporate borrowing.

Managers look to the financial markets to measure the opportunity cost of capital for the firm's investment projects. They can observe the opportunity cost of capital for safe investments by looking up current interest rates on safe debt securities. For risky investments, the opportunity cost of capital has to be estimated. We start to tackle this task in Chapter 7.

Estimating the opportunity cost of capital is one of the hardest tasks in financial management, even when the stock, bond, and other financial markets are behaving normally. When these markets are misbehaving, precise estimates of the cost of capital can be temporarily out of the question.

Financial markets in the U.S. and most developed countries work well most of the time but just like the little girl in the poem, "When they are good, they are very good indeed, but when they are bad they are horrid."[5] In 2008 financial markets were horrid. Security prices bounced around like Tigger on stimulants, and for some types of investment the market temporarily disappeared. Financial markets no longer offered a good yardstick for a project's value or the opportunity cost of capital. That was a year in which financial managers really earned their keep.

We give more specific examples of investment decisions and the opportunity cost of capital at the start of the next chapter.

1-3 GOALS OF THE CORPORATION

Shareholders Want Managers to Maximize Market Value

Pantaloon Retail has over 27,000 shareholders. There is no way that Pantaloon's shareholders can be actively involved in management; it would be like trying to run Mumbai city by town meetings. Authority has to be delegated to professional managers. But how can Pantaloon's managers make decisions that satisfy all the shareholders? No two shareholders are exactly the same. They differ in age, tastes, wealth, time horizon, risk tolerance, and investment strategy. Delegating the operation of the firm to professional managers can work only if the shareholders have a common objective. Fortunately there is a natural financial objective on which almost all shareholders agree: Maximize the current market value of shareholders' investment in the firm.

---

[5] The poem is attributed to Longfellow:

> There was a little girl,
> Who had a little curl,
> Right in the middle of her forehead.
> When she was good,
> She was very good indeed,
> But when she was bad she was horrid.

A smart and effective manager makes decisions that increase the current value of the company's shares and the wealth of its stockholders. This increased wealth can then be put to whatever purposes the shareholders want. They can give their money to charity or spend it in glitzy nightclubs; they can save it or spend it now. Whatever their personal tastes or objectives, they can all do more when their shares are worth more.

Maximizing shareholder wealth is a sensible goal when the shareholders have access to well-functioning financial markets.[6] Financial markets allow them to share risks and transport savings across time. Financial markets give them the flexibility to manage their own savings and investment plans, leaving the corporation's financial managers with only one task: to increase market value.

A corporation's roster of shareholders usually includes both risk-averse and risk-tolerant investors. You might expect the risk-averse to say, "Sure, maximize value, but don't touch too many high-risk projects." Instead, they say, "Risky projects are OK, *provided* that expected profits are more than enough to offset the risks. If this firm ends up too risky for my taste, I'll adjust my investment portfolio to make it safer." For example, the risk-averse shareholders can shift more of their portfolios to safe assets, such as Indian government securities. They can also just say good-bye, selling shares of the risky firm and buying shares in a safer one. If the risky investments increase market value, the departing shareholders are better off than if the risky investments were turned down.

A Fundamental Result

The goal of maximizing shareholder value is widely accepted in both theory and practice. It's important to understand why. Let's walk through the argument step by step, assuming that the financial manager should act in the interests of the firm's owners, its stockholders.

1. Each stockholder wants three things:
    a. To be as rich as possible, that is, to maximize his or her current wealth.
    b. To transform that wealth into the most desirable time pattern of consumption either by borrowing to spend now or investing to spend later.
    c. To manage the risk characteristics of that consumption plan.
2. But stockholders do not need the financial manager's help to achieve the best time pattern of consumption. They can do that on their own, provided they have free access to competitive financial markets. They can also choose the risk characteristics of their consumption plan by investing in more- or less-risky securities.
3. How then can the financial manager help the firm's stockholders? There is only one way: by increasing their wealth. That means increasing the market value of the firm and the current price of its shares.

Economists have proved this value-maximization principle with great rigor and generality. After you have absorbed this chapter, take a look at its Appendix, which contains a further example. The example, though simple, illustrates how the principle of value maximization follows from formal economic reasoning.

We have suggested that shareholders want to be richer rather than poorer. But sometimes you hear managers speak as if shareholders have different goals. For example, managers may say that their job is to "maximize profits." That sounds reasonable. After all, don't shareholders want their company to

---

[6] Here we use "financial markets" as shorthand for the financial sector of the economy. Strictly speaking, we should say "access to well-functioning financial markets and institutions." Many investors deal mostly with financial institutions, for example, banks, insurance companies, or mutual funds. The financial institutions then engage in financial markets, including the stock and bond markets. The institutions act as financial intermediaries on behalf of individual investors.

be profitable? But taken literally, profit maximization is not a well-defined financial objective for at least two reasons:

1. Maximize profits? Which year's profits? A corporation may be able to increase current profits by cutting back on outlays for maintenance or staff training, but those outlays may have added long-term value. Shareholders will not welcome higher short-term profits if long-term profits are damaged.
2. A company may be able to increase future profits by cutting this year's dividend and investing the freed-up cash in the firm. That is not in the shareholders' best interest if the company earns less than the opportunity cost of capital.

Should Managers Look After the Interests of Their Shareholders?

We have described managers as the agent of shareholders, who want them to maximize their wealth. But perhaps this begs the question, Is it *desirable* for managers to act in the selfish interests of their shareholders? Does a focus on enriching the shareholders mean that managers must act as greedy mercenaries riding roughshod over the weak and helpless?

Most of this book is devoted to financial policies that increase value. None of these policies requires gallops over the weak and helpless. In most instances, there is little conflict between doing well (maximizing value) and doing good. Profitable firms are those with satisfied customers and loyal employees; firms with dissatisfied customers and a disgruntled workforce will probably end up with declining profits and a low stock price.

Most established corporations can add value by building long-term relationships with their customers and establishing a reputation for fair dealing and financial integrity. When something happens to undermine that reputation, the costs can be enormous. Here is an example.

The Market-Timing Scandal   In 2003 the mutual fund industry confronted a market-timing scandal. Market timing exploits the fact that stock markets in different parts of the world close at different times. For example, if there is a strong surge in U.S. stock prices while the Japanese market is closed, it is likely that Japanese prices will increase when markets open in Asia the next day. Traders who can buy mutual funds invested in Japanese stocks while their prices are frozen will be able to make substantial profits. U.S. mutual funds were not supposed to allow such trading, but some did. After it was disclosed that managers at Putnam Investments had allowed market-timing trades for some of its investors, the company was fined $100 million and obliged to pay $10 million in compensation. But the larger cost by far was Putnam's loss of reputation. When the scandal came to light, Putnam suffered huge withdrawals of funds. Putnam mutual funds suffered outflows of $30 billion in just two months. If Putnam's funds charged roughly 1% of invested assets as an annual management fee (about the industry average), this loss of assets cost the company $300 million of revenue per year.

When we say that the objective of the firm is to maximize shareholder wealth, we do not mean that anything goes. The law deters managers from making blatantly dishonest decisions, but most managers are not simply concerned with observing the letter of the law or with keeping to written contracts. In business and finance, as in other day-to-day affairs, there are unwritten rules of behavior. These rules make routine financial transactions feasible, because each party to the transaction has to trust the other to keep to his or her side of the bargain.[7]

---

[7] See L. Guiso, L. Zingales, and P. Sapienza, "Trusting the Stock Market," *Journal of Finance* 63 (December 2008), pp. 2557–600. The authors show that an individual's lack of trust is a significant impediment to participation in the stock market. "Lack of trust" means a subjective fear of being cheated.

Of course trust is sometimes misplaced. Charlatans and swindlers are often able to hide behind booming markets. It is only "when the tide goes out that you learn who's been swimming naked."[8] The tide went out in 2008 and a number of frauds were exposed. One notorious example was the Ponzi scheme run by the New York financier Bernard Madoff.[9] Individuals and institutions put about $65 billion in the scheme before it collapsed in 2008. (It's not clear what Madoff did with all this money, but much of it was apparently paid out to early investors in the scheme to create an impression of superior investment performance.) With hindsight, the investors should not have trusted Madoff or the financial advisers who steered money to Madoff.

Madoff's Ponzi scheme was (we hope) a once-in-a-lifetime event.[10] Most of the money lost by investors in the crisis of '08 was lost honestly. Few investors or investment managers saw the crisis coming. When it arrived, there was little they could do to get out of the way.

Should Firms Be Managed for Shareholders or All Stakeholders?

It is often suggested that companies should be managed on behalf of all *stakeholders*, not just shareholders. Other stakeholders include employees, customers, suppliers, and the communities where the firm's plants and offices are located.

Different countries take very different views on this question. In the U.S., U.K, and India, the idea of maximizing shareholder value is widely accepted as the chief financial goal of the firm.

In other countries, workers' interests are put forward much more strongly. In Germany, for example, workers in large companies have the right to elect up to half the directors to the companies' supervisory boards. As a result they have a significant role in the governance of the firm and less attention is paid to the shareholders.[11] In Japan managers usually put the interests of employees and customers on a par with, or even ahead of, the interests of shareholders. For example, Toyota's business philosophy is "to realize stable, long-term growth by working hard to strike a balance between the requirements of people and society, the global environment and the world economy . . . to grow with all of our stakeholders, including our customers, shareholders, employees, and business partners."[12]

Figure 1.3 summarizes the results of interviews with executives from large companies in five countries. Japanese, German, and French executives think that their firms should be run for all stakeholders, while U.S. and U.K. executives say that shareholders come first. When asked about the trade-off between job security and dividends, most U.S. and U.K. executives believe dividends should come first. By contrast, almost all Japanese executives and the majority of German and French executives believe that job security should come first.

As capital markets have become more global, there has been greater pressure for companies in all countries to adopt wealth creation for shareholders as a primary goal. Some German companies,

---

[8] The quotation is from Warren Buffett's annual letter to the shareholders of Berkshire Hathaway, March 2008.

[9] Ponzi schemes are named after Charles Ponzi who founded an investment company in 1920 that promised investors unbelievably high returns. He was soon deluged with funds from investors in New England, taking in ₹1 million during one three-hour period. Ponzi invested only about ₹30 of the money that he raised, but used part of the cash provided by later investors to pay generous dividends to the original investors. Within months the scheme collapsed and Ponzi started a five-year prison sentence.

[10] Ponzi schemes pop up frequently, but none has approached the scope and duration of Madoff's.

[11] The following quote from the German banker Carl Fürstenberg (1850–1933) offers an extreme version of how shareholders were once regarded by German managers: "Shareholders are stupid and impertinent—stupid because they give their money to somebody else without any effective control over what the person is doing with it and impertinent because they ask for a dividend as a reward for their stupidity." Quoted by M. Hellwig, "On the Economics and Politics of Corporate Finance and Corporate Control," in *Corporate Governance*, ed. X. Vives (Cambridge, U.K.: Cambridge University Press, 2000), p. 109.

[12] Toyota *Annual Report*, 2003, p. 10.

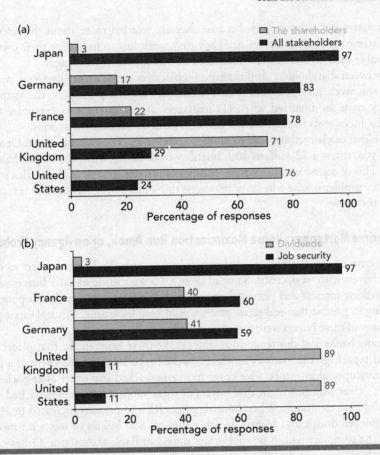

Figure 1.3

(*a*) Whose company is it? The views of 378 managers from five countries.

(*b*) Which is more important—job security for employees or shareholder dividends? The views of 399 managers from five countries.

Source: M. Yoshimori, "Whose Company Is It? The Concept of the Corporation in Japan and the West," *Long Range Planning*, 28 (August 1995), pp. 33–44. Copyright © 1995 with permission from Elsevier Science.

including Daimler and Deutsche Bank, have announced their primary goal as wealth creation for shareholders. In Japan there has been less movement in this direction. For example, the chairman of Toyota has suggested that it would be irresponsible to pursue shareholders' interests. On the other hand, the aggregate market value of Toyota's shares is significantly greater than the market values of GM's and Ford's. So perhaps there is not too much conflict between these goals in practice.

1-4 AGENCY PROBLEMS AND CORPORATE GOVERNANCE

We have emphasized the *separation of ownership and control* in public corporations. The owners (shareholders) cannot control what the managers do, except indirectly through the board of directors. This separation is necessary but also dangerous. You can see the dangers. Managers may be tempted to buy sumptuous corporate jets or to schedule business meetings at tony resorts. They may shy away from attractive but risky projects because they are worried more about the safety of their jobs than about maximizing shareholder value. They may work just to maximize their own bonuses, and therefore redouble their efforts to make and resell flawed subprime mortgages.

Conflicts between shareholders' and managers' objectives create *agency problems.* Agency problems arise when *agents* work for *principals.* The shareholders are the principals; the managers are their agents. **Agency costs** are incurred when (1) managers do not attempt to maximize firm value and (2) shareholders incur costs to monitor the managers and constrain their actions.

Agency problems can sometimes lead to outrageous behavior. For example, when Dennis Kozlowski, the CEO of Tyco, threw a $2 million 40th birthday bash for his wife, he charged half of the cost to the company. This of course was an extreme conflict of interest, as well as illegal. But more subtle and moderate agency problems arise whenever managers think just a little less hard about spending money when it is not their own.

Pushing Subprime Mortgages: Value Maximization Run Amok, or an Agency Problem?

The economic crisis of 2007–2009[13] started as a *subprime* crisis. "Subprime" refers to mortgage loans made to home buyers with weak credit. Some of these loans were made to naïve buyers who faced severe difficulties in making interest and principal payments. Some loans were made to opportunistic buyers who were willing to gamble that real estate prices would keep increasing. But real estate prices declined sharply, and many of these buyers were forced to default.

Why did many banks and mortgage companies make these loans in the first place? One reason is that they could repackage the loans as mortgage-backed securities and sell them at a profit to other banks and to institutional investors. (We cover mortgage-backed and other asset-backed securities in Chapter 24.) It's clear with hindsight that buyers of these subprime mortgage-backed securities were in turn naïve and paid too much. When housing prices fell and defaults increased in 2007, the prices of these securities fell drastically. Merrill Lynch wrote off $50 billion of losses on mortgage-backed securities, and the company had to be sold under duress to Bank of America. Other major financial institutions, such as Citigroup and Wachovia Bank, also recorded enormous losses.

There's lots more to say about the subprime crisis, which we discuss further in Chapters 13 and 14. But for now just think about the banks and mortgage companies that originated the subprime loans and made a profit by reselling them. With hindsight we see that they were selling defective products that would generate painful losses for their customers. Were these companies really pursuing value maximization? Perhaps they were trying to maximize value and just made a disastrous misjudgment about the course of house prices. But we think it is more likely that the companies were aware that a strategy of originating massive amounts of subprime was likely to end badly. Washington Mutual, one of the most aggressive players in the subprime market, quickly failed when the true risks of the subprime loans were revealed. Washington Mutual's shareholders would surely not have endorsed the company's strategy if they had understood it.

Although there is plenty of blame to pass around in the subprime crisis, some of it must go to the managers who actually promoted and resold the subprime mortgages. Were they acting in shareholders' interests, or were they acting in their own interests, trying to squeeze in one more, fat bonus before the game ended? We think that the managers would have thought much harder about their actions if they had not had a short-term selfish interest in promoting subprime mortgages. If so, the mess was largely an *agency problem,* not value maximization run amok. Agency problems occur when managers do *not* act in shareholders' interests, but in their own interests.

---

[13] We write this chapter in early 2009. We hope that the next edition of this book does *not* refer to the financial crisis of 2007–2010 or 2007–2011.

Agency Problems Are Mitigated by Good Systems of Corporate Governance

We return to agency problems and to how the problems are mitigated in practice later in the text. For example, Chapter 12 covers compensation schemes for top management, which can be designed to help align managers' and shareholders' interests. For now we list some of the characteristics of a good system of **corporate governance,** which ensures that the shareholders' pockets are close to the managers' hearts.

Legal and Regulatory Requirements Managers have a legal duty to act responsibly and in the interests of investors. For example, the Securities and Exchange Board of India (SEBI) sets accounting and reporting standards for public companies to ensure consistency and transparency. The SEBI also prohibits insider trading, that is, the purchase or sale of shares based on information that is not available to public investors.

Compensation Plans Managers are spurred on by incentive schemes that produce big returns if shareholders gain but are valueless if they do not. For example, Larry Ellison, CEO of the business software giant Oracle Corporation, received total compensation for 2007 estimated at between $60 and $70 million. Only a small fraction (a mere $1 million) of that amount was salary. A larger amount, a bit more than $6 million, was bonus and incentive pay, and the lion's share was in the form of stock and option grants. Those options will be worthless if Oracle's share price falls below its 2007 level, but will be highly valuable if the price rises. Moreover, as founder of Oracle, Ellison holds over 1 *billion* shares in the firm. No one can say for certain how hard Ellison would have worked with a different compensation package. But one thing is clear: He has a huge personal stake in the success of the firm—and in increasing its market value.

Board of Directors A company's board of directors is elected by the shareholders and has a duty to represent them. Boards of directors are sometimes portrayed as passive stooges who always champion the incumbent management. But response to past corporate scandals has tipped the balance toward greater independence. As per Clause 49 of the Listing Agreements, listed companies in India should have at least 50% independent directors, if the chairman is an executive director. If the chairman is not an executive director, then at least two-third directors of the board must consist of independent directors.

Monitoring The company's directors are not the only ones to be scrutinizing management's actions. Managers are also monitored by security analysts, who advise investors to buy, hold, or sell the company's shares, and by banks, which keep an eagle eye on the safety of their loans.

Takeovers Companies that consistently fail to maximize value are natural targets for takeovers by another company or by corporate raiders. "Raiders" are private investment funds that specialize in buying out and reforming poorly performing companies.

Takeovers are common in industries with slow growth and excess capacity. For example, at the end of the Cold War in 1990, it was clear that the defense industry would have to shrink drastically. A wave of consolidating mergers followed. We cover takeovers in Chapter 31 and buyouts in Chapter 32.

Shareholder Pressure If shareholders believe that the corporation is underperforming and that the board of directors is not holding managers to task, they can attempt to elect representatives to the board to make their voices heard. For example, in 2008 billionaire shareholder activist Carl Icahn felt that the directors of Yahoo! were not acting in shareholders' interest when they rejected a bid from Microsoft. He therefore invested $67 million in Yahoo! stock, and muscled himself and two like-minded friends onto the Yahoo! board.

Disgruntled stockholders also take the "Wall Street Walk" by selling out and moving on to other investments. The Wall Street Walk can send a powerful message. If enough shareholders bail out, the stock price tumbles. This damages top management's reputation and compensation. A large part of top managers' paychecks comes from stock options, which pay off if the stock price rises but are worthless if the price falls below a stated threshold. Thus a falling stock price has a direct impact on managers' personal wealth. A rising stock price is good for managers as well as stockholders.

We do not want to leave the impression that corporate life is a series of squabbles and endless micromanagement. It isn't, because practical corporate finance has evolved to reconcile personal and corporate interests—to keep everyone working together to increase the value of the whole pie, not merely the size of each person's slice. Few managers at the top of major U.S. corporations are lazy or inattentive to stockholders' interests. On the contrary, the pressure to perform can be intense.

We have given a brief overview of corporate governance in the U.S., U.K., and other "Anglo-Saxon" economies. Governance works differently in other countries, but we will not attempt a worldwide survey until Chapter 33. We will return to agency problems and governance many times in intermediate chapters, however.

SUMMARY

Corporations face two principal financial decisions. First, what investments should the corporation make? Second, how should it pay for the investments? The first decision is the investment decision; the second is the financing decision.

The stockholders who own the corporation want its managers to maximize its overall value and the current price of its shares. The stockholders can all agree on the goal of value maximization, so long as financial markets give them the flexibility to manage their own savings and investment plans. Of course, the objective of wealth maximization does not justify unethical behavior. Shareholders do not want the maximum possible stock price. They want the maximum honest share price.

How can financial managers increase the value of the firm? Mostly by making good investment decisions. Financing decisions can also add value, and they can surely destroy value if you screw them up. But it's usually the profitability of corporate investments that separates value winners from the rest of the pack.

Investment decisions force a trade-off. The firm can either invest cash or return it to shareholders, for example, as an extra dividend. When the firm invests cash rather than paying it out, shareholders forgo the opportunity to invest it for themselves in financial markets. The return that they are giving up is therefore called the opportunity cost of capital. If the firm's investments can earn a return higher than the opportunity cost of capital, shareholders cheer and stock price increases. If the firm invests at a return lower than the opportunity cost of capital, shareholders boo and stock price falls.

Managers are not endowed with a special value-maximizing gene. They will consider their own personal interests, which creates a potential conflict of interest with outside shareholders. This conflict is called a principal–agent problem. Any loss of value that results is called an agency cost.

Corporate governance helps to align managers' and shareholders' interests, so that managers pay close attention to the value of the firm. For example, managers are appointed by, and sometimes fired by, the board of directors, who are supposed to represent shareholders. The managers are spurred on by incentive schemes, such as grants of stock options, which pay off big only if the stock price increases. If the company performs poorly, it is more likely to be taken over. The takeover typically brings in a fresh management team.

Remember the following three themes, for you will see them again and again throughout this book:

1. Maximizing value.
2. The opportunity cost of capital.
3. The crucial importance of incentives and governance.

PROBLEM SETS

BASIC

1. Read the following passage: "Companies usually buy (*a*) assets. These include both tangible assets such as (*b*) and intangible assets such as (*c*). To pay for these assets, they sell (*d*) assets such as (*e*). The decision about which assets to buy is usually termed the (*f*) or (*g*) decision. The decision about how to raise the money is usually termed the (*h*) decision." Now fit each of the following terms into the most appropriate space: *financing, real, bonds, investment, executive airplanes, financial, capital budgeting, brand names.*

2. Which of the following are real assets, and which are financial?
   a. A share of stock.
   b. A personal IOU.
   c. A trademark.
   d. A factory.
   e. Undeveloped land.
   f. The balance in the firm's checking account.
   g. An experienced and hardworking sales force.
   h. A corporate bond.

3. Vocabulary test. Explain the differences between:
   a. Real and financial assets.
   b. Capital budgeting and financing decisions.
   c. Closely held and public corporations.
   d. Limited and unlimited liability.

4. Which of the following statements always apply to corporations?
   a. Unlimited liability.
   b. Limited life.
   c. Ownership can be transferred without affecting operations.
   d. Managers can be fired with no effect on ownership.

5. Which of the following statements more accurately describe the treasurer than the controller?
   a. Responsible for investing the firm's spare cash.
   b. Responsible for arranging any issue of common stock.
   c. Responsible for the company's tax affairs.

INTERMEDIATE

6. In most large corporations, ownership and management are separated. What are the main implications of this separation?

7. F&H Corp. continues to invest heavily in a declining industry. Here is an excerpt from a recent speech by F&H's CFO:

We at F&H have of course noted the complaints of a few spineless investors and uninformed security analysts about the slow growth of profits and dividends. Unlike those confirmed doubters, we have confidence in the long-run demand for mechanical encabulators, despite competing digital products. We are therefore determined to invest to maintain our share of the overall encabulator market. F&H has a rigorous CAPEX approval process, and we are confident of returns around 8% on investment. That's a far better return than F&H earns on its cash holdings.

The CFO went on to explain that F&H invested excess cash in short-term U.S. government securities, which are almost entirely risk-free but offered only a 4% rate of return.

a. Is a forecasted 8% return in the encabulator business necessarily better than a 4% safe return on short-term U.S. government securities? Why or why not?

b. Is F&H's opportunity cost of capital 4%? How in principle should the CFO determine the cost of capital?

8. We can imagine the financial manager doing several things on behalf of the firm's stockholders. For example, the manager might:

a. Make shareholders as wealthy as possible by investing in real assets.

b. Modify the firm's investment plan to help shareholders achieve a particular time pattern of consumption.

c. Choose high- or low-risk assets to match shareholders' risk preferences.

d. Help balance shareholders' checkbooks.

But in well-functioning capital markets, shareholders will vote for *only one* of these goals. Which one? Why?

9. Ms. Espinoza is retired and depends on her investments for her income. Mr. Liu is a young executive who wants to save for the future. Both are stockholders in Scaled Composites, LLC, which is building *SpaceShipOne* to take commercial passengers into space. This investment's payoff is many years away. Assume it has a positive NPV for Mr. Liu. Explain why this investment also makes sense for Ms. Espinoza.

10. If a financial institution is caught up in a financial scandal, would you expect its value to fall by more or less than the amount of any fines and settlement payments? Explain.

11. Why might one expect managers to act in shareholders' interests? Give some reasons.

12. Many firms have devised defenses that make it more difficult or costly for other firms to take them over. How might such defenses affect the firm's agency problems? Are managers of firms with formidable takeover defenses more or less likely to act in the shareholders' interests rather than their own? What would you expect to happen to the share price when management proposes to institute such defenses?

APPENDIX

FOUNDATIONS OF THE NET PRESENT VALUE RULE

We have suggested that well-functioning financial markets allow different investors to agree on the objective of maximizing value. This idea is sufficiently important that we need to pause and examine it more carefully.

How Financial Markets Reconcile Preferences for Current vs. Future Consumption   Suppose that there are two possible investors with entirely different preferences. Think of A as an ant, who wishes to save for the future, and of G as a grasshopper, who would prefer to spend all his wealth on some ephemeral frolic, taking no heed of tomorrow. Suppose that each has a nest egg of exactly ₹100,000 in cash. G chooses to spend all of it today, while A prefers to invest it in the financial market. If the interest rate is 10%, A would then have $1.10 \times ₹100,000 = ₹110,000$ to spend a year from now. Of course, there are many possible intermediate strategies. For example, A or G could choose to split the difference, spending ₹50,000 now and putting the remaining ₹50,000 to work at 10% to provide $1.10 \times ₹50,000 = ₹55,000$ next year. The entire range of possibilities is shown by the green line in Figure 1A.1.

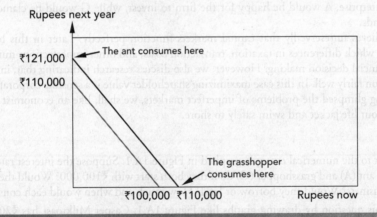

FIGURE 1A.1
The green line shows the possible spending patterns for the ant and grasshopper if they invest ₹100,000 in the capital market. The maroon line shows the possible spending patterns if they invest in their friend's business. Both are better off by investing in the business as long as the grasshopper can borrow against the future income.

In our example, A used the financial market to postpone consumption. But the market can also be used to bring consumption forward in time. Let's illustrate by assuming that instead of having cash on hand of ₹100,000, our two friends are due to receive ₹110,000 each at the end of the year. In this case A will be happy to wait and spend the income when it arrives. G will prefer to borrow against his future income and party it away today. With an interest rate of 10%, G can borrow and spend $₹110,000/1.10 = ₹100,000$. Thus the financial market provides a kind of time machine that allows people to separate the timing of their income from that of their spending. Notice that with an interest rate of 10%, A and G are equally happy with cash on hand of ₹100,000 or an income of ₹110,000 at the end of the year. They do not care about the timing of the cash flow; they just prefer the cash flow that has the highest value today (₹100,000 in our example).

Investing in Real Assets   In practice individuals are not limited to investing in financial markets; they may also acquire plant, machinery, and other real assets. For example, suppose that A and G are offered the opportunity to invest their ₹100,000 in a new business that a friend is founding. This will produce a one-off sure fire payment of ₹121,000 next year. A would clearly be happy to invest in the business. It will provide her with ₹121,000 to spend at the end of the year, rather than the ₹110,000 that she gets by investing her ₹100,000 in the financial market. But what about G, who wants money now, not in one year's time? He too is happy to invest, as long as he can borrow against the future payoff of the investment project. At an interest rate of 10%, G can borrow ₹110,000 and so will have an extra ₹10,000 to spend today. Both A and G are better off investing in their friend's venture. The investment increases their wealth. It moves them up from the green to the maroon line in Figure 1A.1.

A Crucial Assumption   The key condition that allows A and G to agree to invest in the new venture is that both have access to a well-functioning, competitive capital market, in which they can borrow and lend at the same rate. Whenever the corporation's shareholders have equal access to competitive capital markets, the goal of maximizing market value makes sense.

It is easy to see how this rule would be damaged if we did *not* have such a well-functioning capital market. For example, suppose that G could not easily borrow against future income. In that case he might well prefer to spend his cash today rather than invest it in the new venture. If A and G were shareholders in the same enterprise, A would be happy for the firm to invest, while G would be clamoring for higher current dividends.

No one believes unreservedly that capital markets function perfectly. Later in this book we discuss several cases in which differences in taxation, transaction costs, and other imperfections must be taken into account in financial decision making. However, we also discuss research indicating that, in general, capital markets function fairly well. In this case maximizing shareholder value is a sensible corporate objective. But for now, having glimpsed the problems of imperfect markets, we shall, like an economist in a shipwreck, simply *assume* our life jacket and swim safely to shore.

Questions

1. Look back to the numerical example graphed in Figure 1A.1. Suppose the interest rate is 20%. What would the ant (A) and grasshopper (G) do if they both start with ₹100,000? Would they invest in their friend's business? Would they borrow or lend? How much and when would each consume?

2. Answer this question by drawing graphs like Figure 1A.1. Casper Milktoast has ₹200,000 available to support consumption in periods 0 (now) and 1 (next year). He wants to consume *exactly* the same amount in each period. The interest rate is 8%. There is no risk.
   a. How much should he invest, and how much can he consume in each period?
   b. Suppose Casper is given an opportunity to invest up to ₹200,000 at 10% risk-free. The interest rate stays at 8%. What should he do, and how much can he consume in each period?

2

CHAPTER

How to Calculate Present Values

A corporation's shareholders want maximum value and the maximum honest share price. To reach this goal, the company needs to invest in real assets that are worth more than they cost. In this chapter we take the first steps toward understanding how assets are valued and capital investments are made.

There are a few cases in which it is not that difficult to estimate asset values. In real estate, for example, you can hire a professional appraiser to do it for you. Suppose you own a warehouse. The odds are that your appraiser's estimate of its value will be within a few percent of what the building would actually sell for. After all, there is continuous activity in the real estate market, and the appraiser's stock-in-trade is knowledge of the prices at which similar properties have recently changed hands. Thus the problem of valuing real estate is simplified by the existence of an active market in which all kinds of properties are bought and sold.[1] No formal theory of value is needed. We can take the market's word for it.

But we need to go deeper than that. First, it is important to know how asset values are reached in an active market. Even if you can take the appraiser's word for it, it is important to understand *why* that warehouse is worth, say, ₹2 million and not a higher or lower figure. Second, the market for most corporate assets is pretty thin. Look in the classified advertisements in *The Economic Times*: it is not often that you see a blast furnace for sale.

Companies are always searching for assets that are worth more to them than to others. That warehouse is worth more to you if you can manage it better than others can. But in that case, the price of similar

[1] Needless to say, there are some properties that appraisers find nearly impossible to value—for example, nobody knows the potential selling price of the Taj Mahal, the Parthenon, or Windsor Castle.

buildings may not tell you what the warehouse is worth under your management. You need to know how asset values are determined.

In the first section of this chapter we work through a simple numerical example: Should you invest in a new office building in the hope of selling it at a profit next year? You should do so if net present value is positive, that is, if the new building's value today exceeds the investment that is required. A positive net present value implies that the rate of return on your investment is higher than your opportunity cost of capital, that is, higher than you could earn by investing in financial markets.

Next we introduce shortcut formulas for calculating present values. We show how to value an investment that delivers a steady stream of cash flows forever (a *perpetuity*) and one that produces a steady stream for a limited period (an *annuity*). We also look at investments that produce growing cash flows. We illustrate the formulas by applications to some personal financial decisions.

The term *interest rate* sounds straightforward enough, but rates can be quoted in various ways. We conclude the chapter by explaining the difference between the quoted rate and the true or effective interest rate.

By then you will deserve some payoff for the mental investment you have made in learning how to calculate present values. Therefore, in the next two chapters we try out these new tools on bonds and stocks. After that we tackle capital investment decisions at a practical level of detail.

For simplicity, every problem in this chapter is set out in dollars, but the concepts and calculations are identical in euros, yen, or any other currency.

2-1 FUTURE VALUES AND PRESENT VALUES

Calculating Future Values

Money can be invested to earn interest. So, if you are offered the choice between ₹100 today and ₹100 next year, you naturally take the money now to get a year's interest. Financial managers make the same point when they say that money has a *time value* or when they quote the most basic principle of finance: *a rupee today is worth more than a rupee tomorrow.*

Suppose you invest ₹100 in a bank account that pays interest of $r = 7\%$ a year. In the first year you will earn interest of $.07 \times ₹100 = ₹7$ and the value of your investment will grow to ₹107:

$$\text{Value of investment after 1 year} = ₹100 \times (1 + r) = 100 \times 1.07 = ₹107$$

By investing, you give up the opportunity to spend ₹100 today and you gain the chance to spend ₹107 next year.

If you leave your money in the bank for a second year, you earn interest of $.07 \times ₹107 = ₹7.49$ and your investment will grow to ₹114.49:

$$\text{Value of investment after 2 years} = ₹107 \times 1.07 = ₹100 \times 1.07^2 = ₹114.49$$

Today		Year 2
₹100	$\times 1.07^2$	₹114.49

Notice that in the second year you earn interest on both your initial investment (₹100) and the previous year's interest (₹7). Thus your wealth grows at a *compound rate* and the interest that you earn is called **compound interest.**

If you invest your ₹100 for t years, your investment will continue to grow at a 7% compound rate to ₹100 × $(1.07)^t$. For any interest rate r, the future value of your ₹100 investment will be

$$\text{Future value of } ₹100 = ₹100 \times (1 + r)^t$$

The higher the interest rate, the faster your savings will grow. Figure 2.1 shows that a few percentage points added to the interest rate can do wonders for your future wealth. For example, by the end of 20 years ₹100 invested at 10% will grow to ₹100 × $(1.10)^{20}$ = ₹672.75. If it is invested at 5%, it will grow to only ₹100 × $(1.05)^{20}$ = ₹265.33.

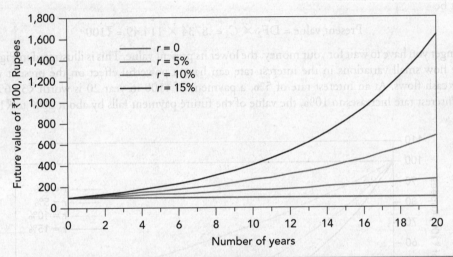

FIGURE 2.1
How an investment of ₹100 grows with compound interest at different interest rates.

Calculating Present Values

We have seen that ₹100 invested for two years at 7% will grow to a future value of 100 × 1.07^2 = ₹114.49. Let's turn this around and ask how much you need to invest *today* to produce ₹114.49 at the end of the second year. In other words, what is the **present value (PV)** of the ₹114.49 payoff?

You already know that the answer is ₹100. But, if you didn't know or you forgot, you can just run the future value calculation in reverse and divide the future payoff by $(1.07)^2$:

$$\text{Present value} = PV = \frac{₹114.49}{(1.07)^2} = ₹100$$

Today		Year 2
₹100	÷ 1.07²	₹114.49

In general, suppose that you will receive a cash flow of C_t rupees at the end of year t. The present value of this future payment is

$$\text{Present value} = PV = \frac{C_t}{(1 + r)^t}$$

You sometimes see this present value formula written differently. Instead of *dividing* the future payment by $(1 + r)^t$, you can equally well *multiply* the payment by $1/(1 + r)^t$. The expression $1/(1 + r)^t$ is called the **discount factor.** It measures the present value of one rupee received in year t. For example, with an interest rate of 7% the two-year discount factor is

$$DF_2 = 1/(1.07)^2 = .8734$$

Investors are willing to pay ₹.8734 today for delivery of ₹1 at the end of two years. If each rupee received in year 2 is worth ₹.8734 today, then the present value of your payment of ₹114.49 in year 2 must be

$$\text{Present value} = DF_2 \times C_2 = .8734 \times 114.49 = ₹100$$

The longer you have to wait for your money, the lower its present value. This is illustrated in Figure 2.2. Notice how small variations in the interest rate can have a powerful effect on the present value of distant cash flows. At an interest rate of 5%, a payment of ₹100 in year 20 is worth ₹37.69 today. If the interest rate increases to 10%, the value of the future payment falls by about 60% to ₹14.86.

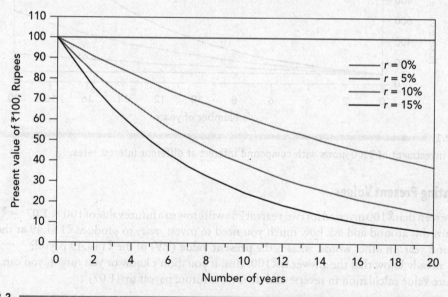

FIGURE 2.2

Present value of a future cash flow of ₹100. Notice that the longer you have to wait for your money, the less it is worth today.

Calculating the Present Value of an Investment Opportunity

How do you decide whether an investment opportunity is worth undertaking? Suppose you own a small company that is contemplating construction of an office block. The total cost of buying the land and constructing the building is ₹370,000, but your real estate adviser forecasts a shortage of office space a year from now and predicts that you will be able sell the building for ₹420,000. For simplicity, we will assume that this ₹420,000 is a sure thing.

You should go ahead with the project if the present value (PV) of the cash inflows is greater than the ₹370,000 investment. Suppose that the rate of interest on the Indian government securities is $r = 5\%$ per year. Then, the present value of your office building is:

$$PV = \frac{420,000}{1.05} = ₹400,000$$

The rate of return r is called the **discount rate, hurdle rate,** or **opportunity cost of capital.** It is an opportunity cost because it is the return that is foregone by investing in the project rather than investing in financial markets. In our example the opportunity cost is 5%, because you could earn a safe 5% by investing in the Indian government securities. Present value was found by *discounting* the future cash flows by this opportunity cost.

Suppose that as soon as you have bought the land and paid for the construction, you decide to sell your project. How much could you sell it for? That is an easy question. If the venture will return a surefire ₹420,000, then your property ought to be worth its PV of ₹400,000 today. That is what investors would need to pay to get the same future payoff. If you tried to sell it for more than ₹400,000, there would be no takers, because the property would then offer an expected rate of return lower than the 5% available on government securities. Of course, you could always sell your property for less, but why sell for less than the market will bear? The ₹400,000 present value is the only feasible price that satisfies both buyer and seller. Therefore, the present value of the property is also its market price.

Net Present Value

The office building is worth ₹400,000 today, but that does not mean you are ₹400,000 better off. You invested ₹370,000, so the **net present value (NPV)** is ₹30,000. Net present value equals present value minus the required investment:

$$NPV = PV - investment = 400,000 - 370,000 = ₹30,000$$

In other words, your office development is worth more than it costs. It makes a *net* contribution to value and increases your wealth. The formula for calculating the NPV of your project can be written as:

$$NPV = C_0 + C_1/(1 + r)$$

Remember that C_0, the cash flow at time 0 (that is, today) is usually a negative number. In other words, C_0 is an investment and therefore a cash outflow. In our example, $C_0 = -₹370,000$.

When cash flows occur at different points in time, it is often helpful to draw a time line showing the date and value of each cash flow. Figure 2.3 shows a time line for your office development. It sets out the present value calculations assuming that the discount rate r is 5%.

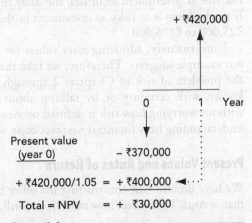

FIGURE 2.3

Calculation showing the NPV of the office development.

Risk and Present Value

We made one unrealistic assumption in our discussion of the office development: Your real estate adviser cannot be certain about the profitability of an office building. Those future cash flows represent the best forecast, but they are not a sure thing.

If the cash flows are uncertain, your calculation of NPV is wrong. Investors could achieve those cash flows with certainty by buying ₹400,000 worth of U.S. government securities, so they would not buy your building for that amount. You would have to cut your asking price to attract investors' interest.

Here we can invoke a second basic financial principle: *a safe rupee is worth more than a risky rupee.* Most investors avoid risk when they can do so without sacrificing return. However, the concepts of present value and the opportunity cost of capital still make sense for risky investments. It is still proper to discount the payoff by the rate of return offered by a risk-equivalent investment in financial markets. But we have to think of *expected* payoffs and the *expected* rates of return on other investments.[2]

Not all investments are equally risky. The office development is more risky than a government security but less risky than a start-up biotech venture. Suppose you believe the project is as risky as investment in the stock market and that stocks offer a 12% expected return. Then 12% is the opportunity cost of capital. That is what you are giving up by investing in the office building and *not* investing in equally risky securities.

Now recompute NPV with $r = .12$:

$$PV = \frac{420,000}{1.12} = ₹375,000$$

$$NPV = PV - 370,000 = ₹5,000$$

The office building still makes a net contribution to value, but the increase in your wealth is smaller than in our first calculation, which assumed that the cash flows from the project were risk-free.

The value of the office building depends, therefore, on the timing of the cash flows and their risk. The ₹420,000 payoff would be worth just that if you could get it today. If the office building is as risk-free as government securities, the delay in the cash flow reduces value by ₹20,000 to ₹400,000. If the building is as risky as investment in the stock market, then the risk further reduces value by ₹25,000 to ₹375,000.

Unfortunately, adjusting asset values for both time and risk is often more complicated than our example suggests. Therefore, we take the two effects separately. For the most part, we dodge the problem of risk in Chapters 2 through 6, either by treating all cash flows as if they were known with certainty or by talking about expected cash flows and expected rates of return without worrying how risk is defined or measured. Then in Chapter 7 we turn to the problem of understanding how financial markets cope with risk.

Present Values and Rates of Return

We have decided that constructing the office building is a smart thing to do, since it is worth more than it costs. To discover how much it is worth, we asked how much you would need to invest directly

---

[2] We define "expected" more carefully in Chapter 9. For now think of expected payoff as a realistic forecast, neither optimistic nor pessimistic. Forecasts of expected payoffs are correct on average.

in securities to achieve the same payoff. That is why we discounted the project's future payoff by the rate of return offered by these equivalent-risk securities—the overall stock market in our example.

We can state our decision rule in another way: your real estate venture is worth undertaking because its rate of return exceeds the opportunity cost of capital. The rate of return is simply the profit as a proportion of the initial outlay:

$$\text{Return} = \frac{\text{profit}}{\text{investment}} = \frac{420,000 - 370,000}{370,000} = .135, \text{ or } 13.5\%$$

The cost of capital is once again the return foregone by *not* investing in financial markets. If the office building is as risky as investing in the stock market, the return foregone is 12%. Since the 13.5% return on the office building exceeds the 12% opportunity cost, you should go ahead with the project.

Here, then, we have two equivalent decision rules for capital investment:[3]

- *Net present value rule.* Accept investments that have positive net present values.
- *Rate of return rule.* Accept investments that offer rates of return in excess of their opportunity costs of capital.[4]

Calculating Present Values When There Are Multiple Cash Flows

One of the nice things about present values is that they are all expressed in current rupees—so you can add them up. In other words, the present value of cash flow (A + B) is equal to the present value of cash flow A plus the present value of cash flow B.

Suppose that you wish to value a stream of cash flows extending over a number of years. Our rule for adding present values tells us that the *total* present value is:

$$PV = \frac{C_1}{(1+r)} + \frac{C_2}{(1+r)^2} + \frac{C_3}{(1+r)^3} + \cdots + \frac{C_T}{(1+r)^T}$$

This is called the **discounted cash flow** (or **DCF**) formula. A shorthand way to write it is

$$PV = \sum_{t=1}^{T} \frac{C_t}{(1+r)^t}$$

where Σ refers to the sum of the series. To find the *net* present value (NPV) we add the (usually negative) initial cash flow:

$$NPV = C_0 + PV = C_0 + \sum_{t=1}^{T} \frac{C_t}{(1+r)^t}$$

EXAMPLE 2.1   Present Values with Multiple Cash Flows

Your real estate adviser has come back with some revised forecasts. He suggests that you rent out the building for two years at ₹20,000 a year, and predicts that at the end of that time you will be able to sell the building for ₹400,000. Thus there are now two future cash flows—a cash flow of

---

[3] You might check for yourself that these are equivalent rules. In other words, if the return of ₹50,000/₹370,000 is greater than *r*, then the net present value − ₹370,000 + [₹420,000/(1 + *r*)] *must* be greater than 0.

[4] The two rules can conflict when there are cash flows at more than two dates. We address this problem in Chapter 5.

$C_1 = ₹20,000$ at the end of one year and a further cash flow of $C_2 = (20,000 + 400,000) = ₹420,000$ at the end of the second year.

The present value of your property development is equal to the present value of C_1 plus the present value of C_2. Figure 2.4 shows that the value of the first year's cash flow is $C_1/(1 + r) = 20,000/1.12 = ₹17,900$ and the value of the second year's flow is $C_2/(1 + r)^2 = 420,000/1.12^2 = ₹334,800$. Therefore our rule for adding present values tells us that the *total* present value of your investment is

$$PV = \frac{C_1}{1 + r} + \frac{C_2}{(1 + r)^2} = \frac{20,000}{1.12} + \frac{420,000}{1.12^2} = 17,900 + 334,800 = ₹352,700$$

Sorry, but your office building is now worth less than it costs. NPV is negative:

$$NPV = ₹352,700 - ₹370,000 = -₹17,300$$

Perhaps you should revert to the original plan of selling in year 1.

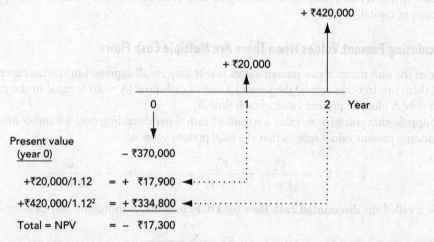

FIGURE 2.4

Calculation showing the NPV of the revised office project.

Your two-period calculations in Example 2.1 required just a few keystrokes on a calculator. Real problems can be much more complicated, so financial managers usually turn to financial calculators especially programmed for present value calculations or to computer spreadsheet programs. A box near the end of the chapter introduces you to some useful Excel functions that can be used to solve discounting problems. In addition, the Web site for this book (**www.mhhe.com/bmam10e**) contains appendixes to help get you started using financial calculators and Excel spreadsheets. It also includes tables that can be used for a variety of discounting problems.

The Opportunity Cost of Capital

By investing in the office building you gave up the opportunity to earn an expected return of 12% in the stock market. The opportunity cost of capital is therefore 12%. When you discount the expected cash flows by the opportunity cost of capital, you are asking how much investors in the financial markets are prepared to pay for a security that produces a similar stream of future cash flows. Your calculations showed that investors would need to pay only ₹352,700 for an investment that produces cash flows of ₹20,000 at year 1 and ₹420,000 at year 2. Therefore, they won't pay any more than that for your office building.

Confusion sometimes sneaks into discussions of the cost of capital. Suppose a banker approaches. "Your company is a fine and safe business with few debts," she says. "My bank will lend you the ₹370,000 that you need for the office block at 8%." Does this mean that the cost of capital is 8%? If so, the project would be worth doing. At an 8% cost of capital, PV would be $20,000/1.08 + 420,000/1.08^2 = ₹378,600$ and NPV = $₹378,600 - ₹370,000 = + ₹8,600$.

But that can't be right. First, the interest rate on the loan has nothing to do with the risk of the project: it reflects the good health of your existing business. Second, whether you take the loan or not, you still face the choice between the office building and an equally risky investment in the stock market. The stock market investment could generate the same expected payoff as your office building at a lower cost. A financial manager who borrows ₹370,000 at 8% and invests in an office building is not smart, but stupid, if the company or its shareholders can borrow at 8% and invest the money at an even higher return. That is why the 12% expected return on the stock market is the opportunity cost of capital for your project.

2-2 LOOKING FOR SHORTCUTS—PERPETUITIES AND ANNUITIES

How to Value Perpetuities

Sometimes there are shortcuts that make it easy to calculate present values. Let us look at some examples.

On occasion, the British and the French have been known to disagree and sometimes even to fight wars. At the end of some of these wars the British consolidated the debt they had issued during the war. The securities issued in such cases were called consols. Consols are **perpetuities.** These are bonds that the government is under no obligation to repay but that offer a fixed income for each year to perpetuity. The British government is still paying interest on consols issued all those years ago. The annual rate of return on a perpetuity is equal to the promised annual payment divided by the present value:[5]

$$\text{Return} = \frac{\text{cash flow}}{\text{present value}}$$

$$r = \frac{C}{PV}$$

---

[5] You can check this by writing down the present value formula

$$PV = \frac{C}{1+r} + \frac{C}{(1+r)^2} + \frac{C}{(1+r)^3} + \cdots$$

Now let $C/(1 + r) = a$ and $1/(1 + r) = x$. Then we have (1) $PV = a(1 + x + x^2 + \cdots)$.
Multiplying both sides by x, we have (2) $PVx = a(x + x^2 + \cdots)$.
Subtracting (2) from (1) gives us $PV(1 - x) = a$. Therefore, substituting for a and x,

$$PV\left(1 - \frac{1}{1+r}\right) = \frac{C}{1+r}$$

Multiplying both sides by $(1 + r)$ and rearranging gives

$$PV = \frac{C}{r}$$

We can obviously twist this around and find the present value of a perpetuity given the discount rate r and the cash payment C:

$$PV = \frac{C}{r}$$

The year is 2030. You have been fabulously successful and are now a billionaire many times over. It was fortunate indeed that you took that finance course all those years ago. You have decided to follow in the footsteps of two of your heroes, Bill Gates and Warren Buffet. Malaria is still a scourge and you want to help eradicate it and other infectious diseases by endowing a foundation to combat these diseases. You aim to provide ₹1 billion a year in perpetuity, starting next year. So, if the interest rate is 10%, you are going to have to write a check today for

$$\text{Present value of perpetuity} = \frac{C}{r} = \frac{₹1 \text{ billion}}{.1} = ₹10 \text{ billion}$$

Two warnings about the perpetuity formula. First, at a quick glance you can easily confuse the formula with the present value of a single payment. A payment of ₹1 at the end of one year has a present value of $1/(1 + r)$. The perpetuity has a value of $1/r$. These are quite different.

Second, the perpetuity formula tells us the value of a regular stream of payments starting one period from now. Thus your ₹10 billion endowment would provide the foundation with its first payment in one year's time. If you also want to provide an up-front sum, you will need to lay out an extra ₹1 billion.

Sometimes you may need to calculate the value of a perpetuity that does not start to make payments for several years. For example, suppose that you decide to provide ₹1 billion a year with the first payment four years from now. We know that in year 3 this endowment will be an ordinary perpetuity with payments starting in one year. So our perpetuity formula tells us that in year 3 the endowment will be worth $₹1/r = 1/.1 = ₹10$ billion. But it is not worth that much now. To find *today's* value we need to multiply by the three-year discount factor $1/(1 + r)^3 = 1/(1.1)^3 = .751$. Thus, the "delayed" perpetuity is worth ₹10 billion $\times$ .751 = ₹7.51 billion. The full calculation is

$$PV = ₹1 \text{ billion} \times \frac{1}{r} \times \frac{1}{(1+ r)^3} = ₹1 \text{ billion} \times \frac{1}{.10} \times \frac{1}{(1.10)^3} = ₹7.51 \text{ billion}$$

How to Value Annuities

An **annuity** is an asset that pays a fixed sum each year for a specified number of years. The equal-payment house mortgage or installment credit agreement are common examples of annuities. So are interest payments on most bonds, as we see in the next chapter.

Figure 2.5 illustrates a simple trick for valuing annuities. It shows the payments and values of three investments.

Row 1 The investment in the first row provides a perpetual stream of ₹1 starting at the end of the first year. We have already seen that this perpetuity has a present value of $1/r$.

Row 2 Now look at the investment shown in the second row. It also provides a perpetual stream of ₹1 payments, but these payments don't start until year 4. This investment is identical to the delayed

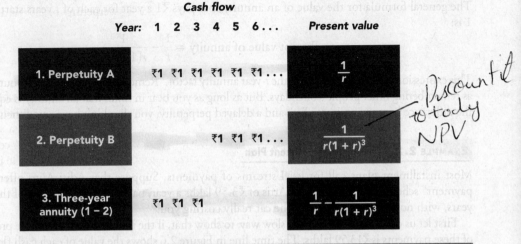

FIGURE 2.5

An annuity that makes payments in each of years 1 through 3 is equal to the difference between two perpetuities.

perpetuity that we have just valued. In year 3, the investment will be an ordinary perpetuity with payments starting in one year and will be worth $1/r$ in year 3. Its value today is, therefore,

$$PV = \frac{1}{r(1+r)^3}$$

Row 3 The perpetuities in rows 1 and 2 both provide a cash flow from year 4 onward. The only difference between the two investments is that the first one also provides a cash flow in each of years 1 through 3. In other words, the difference between the two perpetuities is an annuity of three years. Row 3 shows that the present value of this annuity is equal to the value of the row 1 perpetuity less the value of the delayed perpetuity in row 2:[6]

$$PV \text{ of 3-year annuity} = \frac{1}{r} - \frac{1}{r(1+r)^3}$$

---

[6] Again we can work this out from first principles. We need to calculate the sum of the finite geometric series (1) $PV = a(1 + x + x^2 + \cdots + x^{t-1})$, where $a = C/(1+r)$ and $x = 1/(1+r)$.

Multiplying both sides by x, we have (2) $PVx = a(x + x^2 + \cdots + x^t)$.

Subtracting (2) from (1) gives us $PV(1-x) = a(1-x^t)$.

Therefore, substituting for a and x,

$$PV\left(1 - \frac{1}{1+r}\right) = C\left[\frac{1}{1+r} - \frac{1}{(1+r)^{t+1}}\right]$$

Multiplying both sides by $(1+r)$ and rearranging gives

$$PV = C\left[\frac{1}{r} - \frac{1}{r(1+r)^t}\right]$$

The general formula for the value of an annuity that pays ₹1 a year for each of t years starting in year 1 is:

$$\text{Present value of annuity} = \frac{1}{r} - \frac{1}{r(1+r)^t}$$

This expression is generally known as the t-year annuity factor.[7] Remembering formulas is about as difficult as remembering other people's birthdays. But as long as you bear in mind that an annuity is equivalent to the difference between an immediate and a delayed perpetuity, you shouldn't have any difficulty.

EXAMPLE 2.2   Costing an Installment Plan

Most installment plans call for level streams of payments. Suppose that Aditi Auto offers an "easy payment" scheme on a new Toyota Attis of ₹3.59 lakhs a year, paid at the end of each of the next five years, with no cash down. What is the car really costing you?

First let us do the calculations the slow way, to show that, if the interest rate is 10%, the present value of these payments is ₹13.59 lakhs. The time line in Figure 2.6 shows the value of each cash flow and the total present value. The annuity formula, however, is generally quicker:

$$PV = 3.59 \left[\frac{1}{0.1} - \frac{1}{0.1(1.1)^5} \right] = 3.59 \times 3.79 = ₹13.59 \text{ lakhs}$$

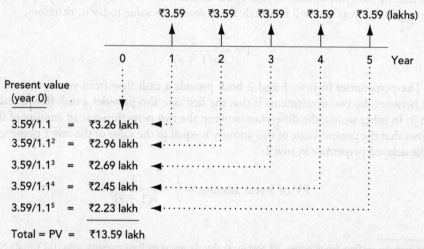

FIGURE 2.6

Calculations showing the year-by-year present value of the installment payments.

---

[7] Some people find the following equivalent formula more intuitive:

$$\text{Present value of annuity} = \frac{1}{r} \left[1 - \frac{1}{(1+r)^t} \right]$$

perpetuity formula   ₹1 starting next year   minus ₹1 starting at $t+1$

EXAMPLE 2.3   Winning Big at the Lottery

When 13 lucky machinists from Ohio pooled their money to buy Powerball lottery tickets, they won a record $295.7 million. (A fourteenth member of the group pulled out at the last minute to put in his own numbers.) We suspect that the winners received unsolicited congratulations, good wishes, and requests for money from dozens of more or less worthy charities. In response, they could fairly point out that the prize wasn't really worth $295.7 million. That sum was to be repaid in 25 annual installments of $11.828 million each. Assuming that the first payment occurred at the end of one year, what was the present value of the prize? The interest rate at the time was 5.9%.

These payments constitute a 25-year annuity. To value this annuity we simply multiply ₹11.828 million by the 25-year annuity factor:

$$PV = 11.828 \times \text{25-year annuity factor}$$

$$= 11.828 \times \left[\frac{1}{r} - \frac{1}{r(1+r)^{25}} \right]$$

At an interest rate of 5.9%, the annuity factor is

$$\left[\frac{1}{.059} - \frac{1}{.059(1.059)^{25}} \right] = 12.9057$$

The present value of the cash payments is $11.828 \times 12.9057 = $152.6 million, much below the well-trumpeted prize, but still not a bad day's haul.

Lottery operators generally make arrangements for winners with big spending plans to take an equivalent lump sum. In our example the winners could either take the $295.7 million spread over 25 years or receive $152.6 million up front. Both arrangements had the same present value.

PV Annuities Due

When we used the annuity formula to value the Powerball lottery prize in Example 2.3, we presupposed that the first payment was made at the end of one year. In fact, the first of the 25 yearly payments was made immediately. How does this change the value of the prize?

If we discount each cash flow by one less year, the present value is increased by the multiple $(1 + r)$. In the case of the lottery prize the value becomes $152.6 \times (1 +,r) = 152.6 \times 1.059 = $161.6 million.

A level stream of payments starting immediately is called an **annuity due.** An annuity due is worth $(1 + r)$ times the value of an ordinary annuity.

Calculating Annual Payments

Annuity problems can be confusing on first acquaintance, but you will find that with practice they are generally straightforward. In Example 2.4, you will need to use the annuity formula to find the amount of the payment given the present value.

EXAMPLE 2.4 **Finding Mortgage Payments**

Suppose that you take out a ₹5,000,000 house mortgage from a bank. The bank requires you to repay the mortgage in equal annual installments over the next 30 years. It must set the annual payments so that they have a present value of ₹5,000,000. Thus,

PV = mortgage payment × 30-year annuity factor = ₹5,000,000

Mortgage payment = ₹5,000,000/30-year annuity factor

Suppose that the interest rate is 12% a year. Then

$$30\text{-year annuity factor} = \left[\frac{1}{.12} - \frac{1}{.12(1.12)^{30}}\right] = 8.055$$

and

$$\text{Mortgage payment} = 5,000,000/8.055 = ₹620,732.46$$

The mortgage loan is an example of an *amortizing loan.* "Amortizing" means that part of the regular payment is used to pay interest on the loan and part is used to reduce the amount of the loan.

Table 2.1 illustrates another amortizing loan. This time it is a four-year loan of ₹1,000 with an interest rate of 10% and annual payments. The annual payment needed to repay the loan is ₹315.47. In other words, ₹1,000 divided by the four-year annuity factor is ₹315.47. At the end of the first year, the interest charge is 10% of ₹1,000, or ₹100. So ₹100 of the first payment is absorbed by interest, and the remaining ₹215.47 is used to reduce (or "amortize") the loan balance to ₹784.53.

Next year, the outstanding balance is lower, so the interest charge is only ₹78.45. Therefore ₹315.47 − ₹78.45 = ₹237.02 can be applied to amortization. Because the loan is progressively paid off, the fraction of each payment devoted to interest steadily falls over time, while the fraction used to reduce the loan increases. By the end of year 4 the amortization is just enough to reduce the balance of the loan to zero.

TABLE 2.1 An example of an amortizing loan. If you borrow ₹1,000 at an interest rate of 10%, you would need to make an annual payment of ₹315.47 over four years to repay that loan with interest.

Year	Beginning-of-Year Balance	Year-end Interest on Balance	Total Year-end Payment	Amortization of Loan	End-of-Year Balance
1	₹1,000.00	₹100.00	₹315.47	₹215.47	₹784.53
2	784.53	78.45	315.47	237.02	547.51
3	547.51	54.75	315.47	260.72	286.79
4	286.79	28.68	315.47	286.79	0

Future Value of an Annuity

Sometimes you need to calculate the *future* value of a level stream of payments.

EXAMPLE 2.5   Saving to Buy a Mercedes

Perhaps your ambition is to buy a Mercedes. But that means some serious savings. You estimate that once you start work, you could save ₹500,000 a year of your income and earn a return of 8% on these savings. How much will you be able to spend after five years?

We are looking here at a level stream of cash flows—an annuity. We have seen that there is a shortcut formula to calculate the *present* value of an annuity. So there ought to be a similar formula for calculating the *future value* of a level stream of cash flows.

Think first how much your savings are worth today. You will set aside ₹500,000 in each of the next five years. The present value of this five-year annuity is therefore equal to

$$PV = ₹500,000 \times \text{5-year annuity factor}$$

$$= ₹500,000 \times \left[\frac{1}{.08} - \frac{1}{.08(1.08)^5} \right] = ₹1,996,355$$

Now think how much you would have after five years if you invested ₹1,996,355 today. Simple! Just multiply by $(1.08)^5$:

$$\text{Value at end of year 5} = ₹1,996,355 \times 1.08^5 = ₹2,933,300$$

That is not enough to buy a Mercedes. Either you need to save more or wait for some time to buy one.

In Example 2.5 we calculated the future value of an annuity by first calculating its present value and then multiplying by $(1 + r)^t$. The general formula for the future value of a level stream of cash flows of ₹1 a year for t years is, therefore,

$$\text{Future value of annuity} = \text{present value of annuity of ₹1 a year} \times (1 + r)^t$$

$$= \left[\frac{1}{r} - \frac{1}{r(1 + r)^t} \right] \times (1 + r)^t = \frac{(1 + r)^t - 1}{r}$$

2-3   MORE SHORTCUTS—GROWING PERPETUITIES AND ANNUITIES

Growing Perpetuities

You now know how to value level streams of cash flows, but you often need to value a stream of cash flows that grows at a constant rate. For example, think back to your plans to donate ₹10 billion to fight malaria and other infectious diseases. Unfortunately, you made no allowance for the growth in salaries and other costs, which will probably average about 4% a year starting in year 1. Therefore, instead of providing ₹1 billion a year in perpetuity, you must provide ₹1 billion in year 1, 1.04 × ₹1 billion in year 2, and so on. If we call the growth rate in costs g, we can write down the present value of this stream of cash flows as follows:

$$PV = \frac{C_1}{1 + r} + \frac{C_2}{(1 + r)^2} + \frac{C_3}{(1 + r)^3} + \cdots$$

$$= \frac{C_1}{1 + r} + \frac{C_1(1 + g)}{(1 + r)^2} + \frac{C_1(1 + g)^2}{(1 + r)^3} + \cdots$$

Fortunately, there is a simple formula for the sum of this geometric series.[8] If we assume that r is greater than g, our clumsy-looking calculation simplifies to

$$\text{Present value of growing perpetuity} = \frac{C_1}{r - g}$$

Therefore, if you want to provide a perpetual stream of income that keeps pace with the growth rate in costs, the amount that you must set aside today is

$$PV = \frac{C_1}{r - g} = \frac{\text{₹1 billion}}{.10 - .04} = \text{₹16.667 billion}$$

You will meet this perpetual-growth formula again in Chapter 4, where we use it to value the stock of mature, slowly growing companies.

Growing Annuities

You are contemplating membership in the local Golf Club. The annual membership dues for the coming year are ₹5,000, but you can make a single payment of ₹12,750, which will provide you with membership for the next three years. In each case no payments are due until the end of the first year. Which is the better deal? The answer depends on how rapidly membership fees are likely to increase over the three-year period. For example, suppose that fees are payable at the end of each year and are expected to increase by 6% per annum. The discount rate is 10%.

The problem is to calculate the value of a three-year stream of cash flows that grows at the rate of $g = .06$ each year. Of course, you could calculate each year's cash flow and discount it at 10%. The alternative is to employ the same trick that we used to find the formula for an ordinary annuity. This is illustrated in Figure 2.7. The first row shows the value of a perpetuity that produces a cash flow of ₹1 in year 1, ₹1 × (1 + g) in year 2, and so on. It has a present value of

$$PV = \frac{\text{₹1}}{(r - g)}$$

The second row shows a similar growing perpetuity that produces its first cash flow of ₹1 × (1 + g)³ in year 4. It *will* have a present value of ₹1 × (1 + g)³/(r − g) in year 3 and therefore has a value today of

$$PV = \frac{\text{₹1}}{(r - g)} \times \frac{(1 + g)^3}{(1 + r)^3}$$

The third row in the figure shows that the difference between the two sets of cash flows consists of a three-year stream of cash flows beginning with ₹1 in year 1 and growing each year at the rate of g. Its value is equal to the difference between our two growing perpetuities:

$$PV = \frac{\text{₹1}}{(r - g)} - \frac{\text{₹1}}{(r - g)} \times \frac{(1 + g)^3}{(1 + r)^3}$$

---

[8] We need to calculate the sum of an infinite geometric series PV = $a(1 + x + x^2 + \cdots)$ where $a = C_1/(1 + r)$ and $x = (1 + g)/(1 + r)$. In footnote 5 we showed that the sum of such a series is $a/(1 - x)$. Substituting for a and x in this formula,

$$PV = \frac{C_1}{r - g}$$

Cash flow							
Year:	1	2	3	4	5	6 . . .	**Present value**
1. Growing perpetuity A	₹1	₹1 x (1 + g)	₹1 x $(1 + g)^2$	₹1 x $(1 + g)^3$	₹1 x $(1 + g)^4$	₹1 x $(1 + g)^5$ . . .	$\frac{1}{r-g}$
2. Growing perpetuity B				₹1 x $(1 + g)^3$	₹1 x $(1 + g)^4$	₹1 x $(1 + g)^5$ . . .	$\frac{(1+g)^3}{(r-g)(1+r)^3}$
3. Growing 3-year annuity (1 − 2)	₹1	₹1 x (1 + g)	₹1 x $(1 + g)^2$				$\frac{1}{r-g} - \frac{(1+g)^3}{(r-g)(1+r)^3}$

FIGURE 2.7

A three-year stream of cash flows that grows at the rate g is equal to the difference between two growing perpetuities.

In our golf club example, the present value of the three annual membership dues would be:

$$\text{PV} = [1/(.10 - .06) - (1.06)^3/(.10 - .06)(1.10)^3] \times ₹5{,}000$$

$$= 2.629 \times ₹5{,}000 = ₹13{,}146$$

If you can find the cash, you would be better off paying now for a three-year membership.

Too many formulas are bad for the digestion. So we will stop at this point and spare you any more of them. The formulas discussed so far appear in Table 2.2.

TABLE 2.2 Some useful shortcut formulas.

Cash Flow, ₹							
Year:	**0**	**1**	**2 . . .**	**. . . t − 1**	**t**	**t + 1 . . .**	**Present Value**
Perpetuity		1	1 . . .	1	1	1 . . .	$\frac{1}{r}$
t-period annuity		1	1 . . .	1	1		$\frac{1}{r} - \frac{1}{r(1+r)^t}$
t-period annuity due	1	1	1 . . .	1			$(1+r)\left(\frac{1}{r} - \frac{1}{r(1+r)^t}\right)$
Growing perpetuity		1	1 × (1 + g) . . .	1 × $(1 + g)^{t-2}$	1 × $(1 + g)^{t-1}$	1 × $(1 + g)^t$ . . .	$\frac{1}{r-g}$
t-period growing annuity		1	1 × (1 + g) . . .	1 × $(1 + g)^{t-2}$	1 × $(1 + g)^{t-1}$		$\frac{1}{r-g} - \frac{1}{r-g} \times \frac{(1+g)^t}{(1+r)^t}$

2-4 HOW INTEREST IS PAID AND QUOTED

In our examples we have assumed that cash flows occur only at the end of each year. This is sometimes the case. For example, in France and Germany the government pays interest on its bonds annually. However, in India, U.S. and Britain, government bonds pay interest semiannually. So if the interest rate on a Indian Government Security is quoted as 10%, the investor in practice receives interest of 5% every six months.

If the first interest payment is made at the end of six months, you can earn an additional six months' interest on this payment. For example, if you invest ₹100 in a bond that pays interest of 10% compounded semiannually, your wealth will grow to $1.05 \times ₹100 = ₹105$ by the end of six months and to $1.05 \times ₹105 = ₹110.25$ by the end of the year. In other words, an interest rate of 10% compounded semiannually is equivalent to 10.25% compounded annually. The *effective annual interest rate* on the bond is 10.25%.

Let's take another example. Suppose a bank offers you an automobile loan at an **annual percentage rate,** or **APR,** of 12% with interest to be paid monthly. This means that each month you need to pay one-twelfth of the annual rate, that is, $12/12 = 1\%$ a month. Thus the bank is *quoting* a rate of 12%, but the effective annual interest rate on your loan is $1.01^{12} - 1 = .1268$, or 12.68%.[9]

Our examples illustrate that you need to distinguish between the *quoted* annual interest rate and the *effective* annual rate. The quoted annual rate is usually calculated as the total annual payment divided by the number of payments in the year. When interest is paid once a year, the quoted and effective rates are the same. When interest is paid more frequently, the effective interest rate is higher than the quoted rate.

In general, if you invest ₹1 at a rate of r per year compounded m times a year, your investment at the end of the year will be worth $[1 + (r/m)]^m$ and the effective interest rate is $[1 + (r/m)]^m - 1$. In our automobile loan example $r = .12$ and $m = 12$. So the effective annual interest rate was $[1 + .12/12]^{12} - 1 = .1268$, or 12.68%.

Continuous Compounding

Instead of compounding interest monthly or semiannually, the rate could be compounded weekly ($m = 52$) or daily ($m = 365$). In fact there is no limit to how frequently interest could be paid. One can imagine a situation where the payments are spread evenly and continuously throughout the year, so the interest rate is continuously compounded.[10] In this case m is infinite.

It turns out that there are many occasions in finance when continuous compounding is useful. For example, one important application is in option pricing models, such as the Black–Scholes model that we introduce in Chapter 21. These are continuous time models. So you will find that most computer programs for calculating option values ask for the continuously compounded interest rate.

It may seem that a lot of calculations would be needed to find a continuously compounded interest rate. However, think back to your high school algebra. You may recall that as m approaches infinity

---

[9] In the U.S., truth-in-lending laws oblige the company to quote an APR that is calculated by multiplying the payment each period by the number of payments in the year. APRs are calculated differently in other countries. For example, in the European Union APRs must be expressed as annually compounded rates, so consumers know the effective interest rate that they are paying.

[10] When we talk about *continuous* payments, we are pretending that money can be dispensed in a continuous stream like water out of a faucet. One can never quite do this. For example, instead of paying out ₹1 billion every year to combat malaria, you could pay out about ₹1 million every 8¾ hours or ₹10,000 every 5¼ minutes or ₹10 every 3⅙ seconds but you could not pay it out *continuously*. Financial managers *pretend* that payments are continuous rather than hourly, daily, or weekly because (1) it simplifies the calculations and (2) it gives a very close approximation to the NPV of frequent payments.

$[1 + (r/m)]^m$ approaches $(2.718)^r$. The figure 2.718—or e, as it is called—is the base for natural logarithms. Therefore, $1 invested at a continuously compounded rate of r will grow to $e^r = (2.718)^r$ by the end of the first year. By the end of t years it will grow to $e^{rt} = (2.718)^{rt}$.

Example 1 Suppose you invest ₹1 at a continuously compounded rate of 11% ($r = .11$) for one year ($t = 1$). The end-year value is $e^{.11}$, or ₹1.116. In other words, investing at 11% a year *continuously* compounded is exactly the same as investing at 11.6% a year *annually* compounded.

Example 2 Suppose you invest ₹1 at a continuously compounded rate of 11% ($r = .11$) for two years ($t = 2$). The final value of the investment is $e^{rt} = e^{.22}$, or $1.246.

Sometimes it may be more reasonable to assume that the cash flows from a project are spread evenly over the year rather than occurring at the year's end. It is easy to adapt our previous formulas to handle this. For example, suppose that we wish to compute the present value of a perpetuity of C dollars a year. We already know that if the payment is made at the end of the year, we divide the payment by the *annually* compounded rate of r:

$$PV = \frac{C}{r}$$

If the same total payment is made in an even stream throughout the year, we use the same formula but substitute the *continuously* compounded rate.

Example 3 Suppose the annually compounded rate is 18.5%. The present value of a ₹100 perpetuity, with each cash flow received at the end of the year, is $100/.185 = ₹540.54$. If the cash flow is received continuously, we must divide ₹100 by 17%, because 17% continuously compounded is equivalent to 18.5% annually compounded ($e^{.17} = 1.185$). The present value of the continuous cash flow stream is $100/.17 = ₹588.24$. Investors are prepared to pay more for the continuous cash payments because the cash starts to flow in immediately.

For any other continuous payments, we can always use our formula for valuing annuities. For instance, suppose that you have thought again about your donation and have decided to fund a vaccination program in emerging countries, which will cost ₹1 billion a year, starting immediately, and spread evenly over 20 years. Previously, we used the annually compounded rate of 10%; now we must use the continuously compounded rate of $r = 9.53\%$ ($e^{.0953} = 1.10$). To cover such an expenditure, then, you need to set aside the following sum:[11]

$$PV = C \left(\frac{1}{r} - \frac{1}{r} \times \frac{1}{e^{rt}} \right)$$

$$= ₹1 \text{ billion} \left(\frac{1}{.0953} - \frac{1}{.0953} \times \frac{1}{6.727} \right) = ₹1 \text{ billion} \times 8.932 = ₹8.932 \text{ billion}$$

---

[11] Remember that an annuity is simply the difference between a perpetuity received today and a perpetuity received in year t. A continuous stream of C dollars a year in perpetuity is worth C/r, where r is the continuously compounded rate. Our annuity, then, is worth

$$PV = \frac{C}{r} - \text{present value of } \frac{C}{r} \text{ received in year } t$$

Since r is the continuously compounded rate, C/r received in year t is worth $(C/r) \times (1/e^{rt})$ today. Our annuity formula is therefore

$$PV = \frac{C}{r} - \frac{C}{r} \times \frac{1}{e^t}$$

sometimes written as

$$\frac{C}{r}(1 - e^{-rt})$$

Useful Spreadsheet Functions

Discounting Cash Flows

Spreadsheet programs such as Excel provide built-in functions to solve discounted-cash-flow (DCF) problems. You can find these functions by pressing *fx* on the Excel toolbar. If you then click on the function that you wish to use, Excel asks you for the inputs that it needs. At the bottom left of the function box there is a Help facility with an example of how the function is used.

Here is a list of useful functions for DCF problems and some points to remember when entering data:

- **FV:** Future value of single investment or annuity.
- **PV:** Present value of single future cash flow or annuity.
- **RATE:** Interest rate (or rate of return) needed to produce given future value or annuity.
- **NPER:** Number of periods (e.g., years) that it takes an investment to reach a given future value or series of future cash flows.
- **PMT:** Amount of annuity payment with a given present or future value.
- **NPV:** Calculates the value of a stream of negative and positive cash flows. (When using this function, note the warning below.)
- **XNPV:** Calculates the net present value of a series of unequal cash flows at the date of the first cash flow.
- **EFFECT:** The effective annual interest rate, given the quoted rate (APR) and number of interest payments in a year.
- **NOMINAL:** The quoted interest rate (APR) given the effective annual interest rate.

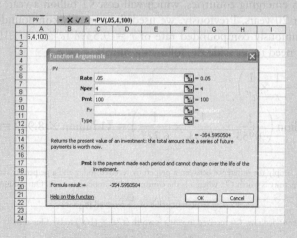

All the inputs in these functions can be entered directly as numbers or as the addresses of cells that contain the numbers. Three warnings:

1. PV is the amount that needs to be invested today to produce a given future value. It should therefore be entered as a negative number. Entering both PV and FV with the same sign when solving for RATE results in an error message.
2. Always enter the interest or discount rate as a decimal value.
3. Use the NPV function with care. It gives the value of the cash flows one period *before* the first cash flow and not the value at the date of the first cash flow.

Spreadsheet Questions

The following questions provide opportunities to practice each of the Excel functions.

2.1 (FV) In 1880 five aboriginal trackers were each promised the equivalent of 100 Australian dollars for helping to capture the notorious outlaw Ned Kelly. One hundred and thirteen years later the granddaughters of two of the trackers claimed that this reward had not been paid. If the interest rate over this period averaged about 4.5%, how much would the A\$100 have accumulated to?

2.2 (PV) Your company can lease a truck for ₹10,000 a year (paid at the end of the year) for six years, or it can buy the truck today for ₹50,000. At the end of the six years the truck will be worthless. If the interest rate is 6%, what is the present value of the lease payments? Is the lease worthwhile?

2.3 (RATE) Ford Motor stock was one of the victims of the 2008 credit crisis. In June 2007, Ford stock price stood at \$9.42. Eighteen months later it was \$2.72. What was the annual rate of return over this period to an investor in Ford stock?

2.4 (NPER) An investment adviser has promised to double your money. If the interest rate is 7% a year, how many years will she take to do so?

2.5 (PMT) You need to take out a home mortgage for ₹200,000. If payments are made annually over 30 years and the interest rate is 8%, what is the amount of the annual payment?

2.6 (XNPV) Your office building requires an initial cash outlay of \$370,000. Suppose that you plan to rent it out for three years at \$20,000 a year and then sell it for \$400,000. If the cost of capital is 12%, what is its net present value?

2.7 (EFFECT) First National Bank pays 6.2% interest compounded annually. Second National Bank pays 6% interest compounded monthly. Which bank offers the higher effective annual interest rate?

2.8 (NOMINAL) What monthly compounded interest rate would Second National Bank need to pay on savings deposits to provide an effective rate of 6.2%?

If you look back at our earlier discussion of annuities, you will notice that the present value of ₹1 billion paid at the *end* of each of the 20 years was ₹8.514 billion. Therefore, it costs you ₹418 million—or 5%—more to provide a continuous payment stream.

Often in finance we need only a ballpark estimate of present value. An error of 5% in a present value calculation may be perfectly acceptable. In such cases it doesn't usually matter whether we assume that cash flows occur at the end of the year or in a continuous stream. At other times precision matters, and we do need to worry about the exact frequency of the cash flows.

Firms can best help their shareholders by accepting all projects that are worth more than they cost. In other words, they need to seek out projects with positive net present values. To find net present value we first calculate present value. Just discount future cash flows by an appropriate rate r, usually called the *discount rate, hurdle rate*, or *opportunity cost of capital*:

$$\text{Present value (PV)} = \frac{C_1}{(1 + r)} + \frac{C_2}{(1 + r)^2} + \frac{C_3}{(1 + r)^3} + \cdots$$

Net present value is present value plus any immediate cash flow:

$$\text{Net present value (NPV)} = C_0 + \text{PV}$$

Remember that C_0 is negative if the immediate cash flow is an investment, that is, if it is a cash outflow.

The discount rate r is determined by rates of return prevailing in capital markets. If the future cash flow is absolutely safe, then the discount rate is the interest rate on safe securities such as Indian government debt. If the future cash flow is uncertain, then the expected cash flow should be discounted at the expected rate of return offered by equivalent-risk securities. (We talk more about risk and the cost of capital in Chapters 7 to 9.)

Cash flows are discounted for two simple reasons: because (1) a rupee today is worth more than a rupee tomorrow and (2) a safe rupee is worth more than a risky one. Formulas for PV and NPV are numerical expressions of these ideas.

Financial markets, including the bond and stock markets, are the markets where safe and risky future cash flows are traded and valued. That is why we look to rates of return prevailing in the financial markets to determine how much to discount for time and risk. By calculating the present value of an asset, we are estimating how much people will pay for it if they have the alternative of investing in the capital markets.

You can always work out any present value using the basic formula, but shortcut formulas can reduce the tedium. We showed how to value an investment that makes a level stream of cash flows forever (a *perpetuity*) and one that produces a level stream for a limited period (an *annuity*). We also showed how to value investments that produce growing streams of cash flows.

When someone offers to lend you a rupee at a quoted interest rate, you should always check how frequently the interest is to be paid. For example, suppose that a ₹100 loan requires six-month payments of ₹3. The total yearly interest payment is ₹6 and the interest will be quoted as a rate of 6% compounded semiannually. The equivalent *annually compounded rate* is $(1.03)^2 - 1 = .061$, or 6.1%. Sometimes it is convenient to assume that interest is paid evenly over the year, so that interest is quoted as a continuously compounded rate.

BASIC

1. At an interest rate of 12%, the six-year discount factor is .507. How many rupees is ₹.507 worth in six years if invested at 12%?
2. If the PV of ₹139 is ₹125, what is the discount factor?
3. If the cost of capital is 9%, what is the PV of ₹374 paid in year 9?
4. A project produces a cash flow of ₹432 in year 1, ₹137 in year 2, and ₹797 in year 3. If the cost of capital is 15%, what is the project's PV?
5. If you invest ₹100 at an interest rate of 15%, how much will you have at the end of eight years?
6. An investment costs ₹1,548 and pays ₹138 in perpetuity. If the interest rate is 9%, what is the NPV?

7. A common stock will pay a cash dividend of ₹4 next year. After that, the dividends are expected to increase indefinitely at 4% per year. If the discount rate is 14%, what is the PV of the stream of dividend payments?

8. The interest rate is 10%.
   a. What is the PV of an asset that pays ₹1 a year in perpetuity?
   b. The value of an asset that appreciates at 10% per annum approximately doubles in seven years. What is the approximate PV of an asset that pays ₹1 a year in perpetuity beginning in year 8?
   c. What is the approximate PV of an asset that pays ₹1 a year for each of the next seven years?
   d. A piece of land produces an income that grows by 5% per annum. If the first year's income is ₹10,000, what is the value of the land?

9. a. The cost of a new automobile is ₹600,000. If the interest rate is 5%, how much would you have to set aside now to provide this sum in five years?
   b. You have to pay ₹600,000 a year in school fees at the end of each of the next six years. If the interest rate is 8%, how much do you need to set aside today to cover these bills?
   c. You have invested ₹3,000,000 at 8%. After paying the above school fees, how much would remain at the end of the six years?

10. The continuously compounded interest rate is 12%.
    a. You invest ₹1,000 at this rate. What is the investment worth after five years?
    b. What is the PV of ₹5 million to be received in eight years?
    c. What is the PV of a continuous stream of cash flows, amounting to ₹2,000 per year, starting immediately and continuing for 15 years?

11. You are quoted an interest rate of 6% on an investment of ₹10 million. What is the value of your investment after four years if interest is compounded:
    a. Annually?
    b. Monthly? or
    c. Continuously?

INTERMEDIATE

12. What is the PV of ₹100 received in:
    a. Year 10 (at a discount rate of 1%)?
    b. Year 10 (at a discount rate of 13%)?
    c. Year 15 (at a discount rate of 25%)?
    d. Each of years 1 through 3 (at a discount rate of 12%)?

13. a. If the one-year discount factor is .905, what is the one-year interest rate?
    b. If the two-year interest rate is 10.5%, what is the two-year discount factor?
    c. Given these one- and two-year discount factors, calculate the two-year annuity factor.
    d. If the PV of ₹10 a year for three years is ₹24.65, what is the three-year annuity factor?
    e. From your answers to (c) and (d), calculate the three-year discount factor.

14. A factory costs ₹4,000,000. You reckon that it will produce an inflow after operating costs of ₹900,000 a year for 10 years. If the opportunity cost of capital is 14%, what is the net present value of the factory? What will the factory be worth at the end of five years?

15. A machine costs ₹20,000,000 and is expected to produce the following cash flows:

Year	1	2	3	4	5	6	7	8	9	10
Cash flow (₹000s)	2500	2850	3750	4000	4250	4600	4600	4000	3400	2500

eXcel

Visit us at
www.mhhe.com/bmam10e

If the cost of capital is 12%, what is the machine's NPV?

16. Aditya is 30 years of age and his salary next year will be ₹900,000. Aditya forecasts that his salary will increase at a steady rate of 8% per annum until his retirement at age 60.
    a. If the discount rate is 8%, what is the PV of these future salary payments?
    b. If Aditya saves 5% of his salary each year and invests these savings at an interest rate of 8%, how much will he have saved by age 60?
    c. If Aditya plans to spend these savings in even amounts over the subsequent 20 years, how much can he spend each year?

17. A factory costs ₹20,000,000. It will produce an inflow after operating costs of ₹5,000,000 in year 1, ₹10,000,000 in year 2, and ₹15,000,000 in year 3. The opportunity cost of capital is 15%. Calculate the NPV.

18. Halcyon Lines is considering the purchase of a new bulk carrier for $8 million. The forecasted revenues are $5 million a year and operating costs are $4 million. A major refit costing $2 million will be required after both the fifth and tenth years. After 15 years, the ship is expected to be sold for scrap at $1.5 million. If the discount rate is 8%, what is the ship's NPV?

Visit us at
www.mhhe.com/bmam10e

19. As winner of a breakfast cereal competition, you can choose one of the following prizes:
    a. ₹100,000 now.
    b. ₹180,000 at the end of five years.
    c. ₹11,400 a year forever.
    d. ₹19,000 for each of 10 years.
    e. ₹6,500 next year and increasing thereafter by 5% a year forever.

    If the interest rate is 12%, which is the most valuable prize?

20. Parminder Kaur is 65 years of age and has a life expectancy of 12 more years. She wishes to invest ₹10 lakh in an annuity that will make a level payment at the end of each year until her death. If the interest rate is 9.5%, what income can Mrs. Kaur expect to receive each year?

21. David and Helen Zhang are saving to buy a boat at the end of five years. If the boat costs $20,000 and they can earn 10% a year on their savings, how much do they need to put aside at the end of years 1 through 5?

22. Kangaroo Autos is offering free credit on a new $10,000 car. You pay $1,000 down and then $300 a month for the next 30 months. Turtle Motors next door does not offer free credit but will give you $1,000 off the list price. If the rate of interest is 10% a year, (about .83% a month) which company is offering the better deal?

23. Recalculate the NPV of the office building venture in Section 2.1 at interest rates of 5, 10, and 15%. Plot the points on a graph with NPV on the vertical axis and the discount rates on the horizontal axis. At what discount rate (approximately) would the project have zero NPV? Check your answer.

24. If the interest rate is 7%, what is the value of the following three investments?
    a. An investment that offers you ₹100 a year in perpetuity with the payment at the *end* of each year.
    b. A similar investment with the payment at the *beginning* of each year.
    c. A similar investment with the payment spread evenly over each year.

25. Refer back to Sections 2.2–2.4. If the rate of interest is 8% rather than 10%, how much would you need to set aside to provide each of the following?
    a. ₹1 billion at the end of each year in perpetuity.
    b. A perpetuity that pays ₹1 billion at the end of the first year and that grows at 4% a year.

c. ₹1 billion at the end of each year for 20 years.

d. ₹1 billion a year spread evenly over 20 years.

26. How much will you have at the end of 20 years if you invest ₹100 today at 15% *annually* compounded? How much will you have if you invest at 15% *continuously* compounded?

27. You have just read an advertisement stating, "Pay us ₹100 a year for 10 years and we will pay you ₹100 a year thereafter in perpetuity." If this is a fair deal, what is the rate of interest?

28. Which would you prefer?
   a. An investment paying interest of 12% compounded annually.
   b. An investment paying interest of 11.7% compounded semiannually.
   c. An investment paying 11.5% compounded continuously.
   Work out the value of each of these investments after 1, 5, and 20 years.

29. A leasing contract calls for an immediate payment of ₹100,000 and nine subsequent ₹100,000 semiannual payments at six-month intervals. What is the PV of these payments if the *annual* discount rate is 8%?

30. Several years ago *The Wall Street Journal* reported that the winner of the Massachusetts State Lottery prize had the misfortune to be both bankrupt and in prison for fraud. The prize was $9,420,713, to be paid in 19 equal annual installments. (There were 20 installments, but the winner had already received the first payment.) The bankruptcy court judge ruled that the prize should be sold off to the highest bidder and the proceeds used to pay off the creditors.

Visit us at
www.mhhe.com/bmam10e

   a. If the interest rate was 8%, how much would you have been prepared to bid for the prize?
   b. Enhance Reinsurance Company was reported to have offered $4.2 million. Use Excel to find the return that the company was looking for.

31. A mortgage requires you to pay ₹70,000 at the end of each of the next eight years. The interest rate is 8%.
   a. What is the present value of these payments?
   b. Calculate for each year the loan balance that remains outstanding, the interest payment on the loan, and the reduction in the loan balance.

32. You estimate that by the time you retire in 35 years, you will have accumulated savings of ₹2 million. If the interest rate is 8% and you live 15 years after retirement, what annual level of expenditure will those savings support?

   Unfortunately, inflation will eat into the value of your retirement income. Assume a 4% inflation rate and work out a spending program for your retirement that will allow you to increase your expenditure in line with inflation.

33. The *annually* compounded discount rate is 5.5%. You are asked to calculate the present value of a 12-year annuity with payments of ₹50,000 per year. Calculate PV for each of the following cases.
   a. The annuity payments arrive at one-year intervals. The first payment arrives one year from now.
   b. The first payment arrives in six months. Following payments arrive at one-year intervals (i.e., at 18 months, 30 months, etc.).

34. Dear Financial Adviser,
   My spouse and I are each 62 and hope to retire in three years. After retirement we will receive $7,500 per month after taxes from our employers' pension plans and $1,500 per month after taxes from Social Security. Unfortunately our monthly living expenses are $15,000. Our social obligations preclude further economies.

We have $1,000,000 invested in a high-grade, tax-free municipal-bond mutual fund. The return on the fund is 3.5% per year. We plan to make annual withdrawals from the mutual fund to cover the difference between our pension and Social Security income and our living expenses. How many years before we run out of money?

Sincerely,
Luxury Challenged
Marblehead, MA

You can assume that the withdrawals (one per year) will sit in a checking account (no interest). The couple will use the account to cover the monthly shortfalls.

35. Your firm's geologists have discovered a small oil field in New York's Westchester County. The field is forecasted to produce a cash flow of $C_1 = \$2$ million in the first year. You estimate that you could earn an expected return of $r = 12\%$ from investing in stocks with a similar degree of risk to your oil field. Therefore, 12% is the opportunity cost of capital.

What is the present value? The answer, of course, depends on what happens to the cash flows after the first year. Calculate present value for the following cases:

a. The cash flows are forecasted to continue forever, with no expected growth or decline.

b. The cash flows are forecasted to continue for 20 years only, with no expected growth or decline during that period.

c. The cash flows are forecasted to continue forever, increasing by 3% per year because of inflation.

d. The cash flows are forecasted to continue for 20 years only, increasing by 3% per year because of inflation.

CHALLENGE

36. Here are two useful rules of thumb. The "Rule of 72" says that with discrete compounding the time it takes for an investment to double in value is roughly 72/interest rate (in percent). The "Rule of 69" says that with continuous compounding the time that it takes to double is exactly 69.3/interest rate (in percent).

a. If the annually compounded interest rate is 12%, use the Rule of 72 to calculate roughly how long it takes before your money doubles. Now work it out exactly.

b. Can you prove the Rule of 69?

37. Use Excel to construct your own set of annuity tables showing the annuity factor for a selection of interest rates and years.

eXcel

Visit us at
www.mhhe.com/bmam10e

38. You own an oil pipeline that will generate a $2 million cash return over the coming year. The pipeline's operating costs are negligible, and it is expected to last for a very long time. Unfortunately, the volume of oil shipped is declining, and cash flows are expected to decline by 4% per year. The discount rate is 10%.

a. What is the PV of the pipeline's cash flows if its cash flows are assumed to last forever?

b. What is the PV of the cash flows if the pipeline is scrapped after 20 years?

REAL-TIME DATA ANALYSIS

There are dozens of Web sites that provide calculators to help with personal financial decisions. Two good examples are **www.smartmoney.com** and **finance.yahoo.com**. (*Note:* for both calculators the annual rate of interest is quoted as 12 times the monthly rate.)

1. **Amortizing loans** Suppose that you take out a 30-year mortgage loan of ₹200,000 at an interest rate of 10%.
   a. What is your total monthly payment?
   b. How much of the first month's payment goes to reduce the size of the loan?
   c. How much of the payment after two years goes to reduce the size of the loan?
   You can check your answers by logging on to the personal finance page of **www.smartmoney.com** and using the mortgage calculator.

2. **Retirement planning** You need to have accumulated savings of ₹5 crore by the time you retire in 30 years. You currently have savings of ₹10 lakh. How much do you need to save each year to meet your goal? Find the savings calculator on **finance.yahoo.com** to check your answer.

3. In 2006 the State of Indiana sold a 75-year concession to operate and maintain the East-West Toll Road. Before doing so, it commissioned a consulting report that estimated the value of the concession. You can access this report at **www.in.gov/ifa/files/TollRoadFinancialAnalysis. pdf.** Download the spreadsheet of the forecasted cash flows from the toll road from this book's Web site at **www.mhhe.com/bmam10e** to answer the following questions. (*Note:* Cash flows are reported only for each 10-year block. Except where more information is available, we have arbitrarily assumed cash flows are spread evenly during those 10 years.)
   a. Calculate the present value of the concession using a discount rate of 6%. (*Note:* Your figure will differ slightly from that in the consultant's report because we do not have exact cash flow forecasts for each year.)
   b. The consultant chose this discount rate because it was the interest rate that the state paid on its bonds. Do you think that this was the correct criterion? Why or why not?
   c. How does the value of the concession change if you use a higher discount rate?

3

CHAPTER

VALUING BONDS

Investment in new plant and equipment requires money—often a lot of money. Sometimes firms can retain and accumulate earnings to cover the cost of investment, but often they need to raise extra cash from investors. If they choose not to sell additional shares of common stock, the cash has to come from borrowing. If cash is needed for only a short while, firms may borrow from a bank. If they need cash for long-term investments, they generally issue bonds, which are simply long-term loans.

Companies are not the only bond issuers. Municipalities also raise money by selling bonds. So do national governments. There is always some risk that a company or municipality will not be able to come up with the cash to repay its bonds, but investors in government bonds can generally be confident that the promised payments will be made in full and on time.

We start our analysis of the bond market by looking at the valuation of government bonds and at the interest rate that the government pays when it borrows. Do not confuse this interest rate with the cost of capital for a corporation. The projects that companies undertake are almost invariably risky and investors demand higher prospective returns from these projects than from safe government bonds. (In Chapter 7 we start to look at the additional returns that investors demand from risky assets.)

The markets for government bonds are huge. At the end of March 2011, investors held ₹13,47,435 crore of Indian government securities. The bond markets are also sophisticated. Bond traders make massive trades motivated by tiny price discrepancies. This book is not for professional bond traders, but if you are to be involved in managing the company's debt, you will have to get beyond the simple mechanics of bond valuation. Financial managers need to understand the bond pages in the financial press and know what bond dealers mean when they quote spot rates or yields to maturity. They realize why short-term rates are usually lower (but sometimes higher) than long-term rates and why the longest-term bond prices are most sensitive to fluctuations in interest rates. They can distinguish real (inflation-adjusted) interest rates and nominal (money) rates and anticipate how future inflation can affect interest rates. We cover all these topics in this chapter.

Companies can't borrow at the same low interest rates as governments. The interest rates on government bonds are benchmarks for all interest rates, however. When government interest rates go up or down, corporate rates follow more or less proportionally. Therefore, financial managers had better understand how the government rates are determined and what happens when they change.

Corporate bonds are more complex securities than government bonds. A corporation may not be able to come up with the money to pay its debts, so investors have to worry about default risk. Corporate bonds are also less liquid than government bonds: they are not as easy to buy or sell, particularly in large quantities or on short notice. Some corporate bonds give the borrower an option to repay early; others can be exchanged for the company's common stock. All of these complications affect the "spread" of corporate bond rates over interest rates on government bonds of similar maturities.

This chapter only introduces corporate debt. We take a more detailed look in Chapters 23 and 24.

3-1 USING THE PRESENT VALUE FORMULA TO VALUE BONDS

If you own a bond, you are entitled to a fixed set of cash payoffs. Every year until the bond matures, you collect regular interest payments. At maturity, when you get the final interest payment, you also get back the **face value** of the bond, which is called the bond's **principal.**

A Short Trip to Paris to Value a Government Bond

Why are we going to Paris, apart from the cafés, restaurants, and sophisticated nightlife? Because we want to start with the simplest type of bond, one that makes payments just once a year.

French government bonds, known as OATs (short for Obligations Assimilables du Trésor), pay interest and principal in euros (€). Suppose that in December 2010 you decide to buy €100 face value of the 8.5% OAT maturing in December 2014. Each December until the bond matures you are entitled to an interest payment of $.085 \times 100 = €8.50$. This amount is the bond's **coupon.**[1] When the bond matures in 2014, the government pays you the final €8.50 interest, plus the principal payment of the €100 face value. Your first coupon payment is in one year's time, in December 2011. So the cash payments from the bond are as follows:

Cash Payments (€)			
2011	**2012**	**2013**	**2014**
€8.50	€8.50	€8.50	€108.50

What is the present value of these payments? It depends on the opportunity cost of capital, which in this case equals the rate of return offered by other government debt issues denominated in euros. In

---

[1] Bonds used to come with coupons attached, which had to be clipped off and presented to the issuer to obtain the interest payments. This is still the case with *bearer bonds*, where the only evidence of indebtedness is the bond itself. In many parts of the world bearer bonds are still issued and are popular with investors who would rather remain anonymous. The alternative is *registered bonds*, where the identity of the bond's owner is recorded and the coupon payments are sent automatically. OATs are registered bonds.

December 2010, other medium-term French government bonds offered a return of about 3.0%. That is what you were giving up when you bought the 8.5% OATs. Therefore, to value the 8.5% OATs, you must discount the cash flows at 3.0%:

$$PV = \frac{8.50}{1.03} + \frac{8.50}{1.03^2} + \frac{8.50}{1.03^3} + \frac{108.50}{1.03^4} = €120.44$$

Bond prices are usually expressed as a percentage of face value. Thus the price of your 8.5% OAT was quoted as 120.44%.

You may have noticed a shortcut way to value this bond. Your OAT amounts to a package of two investments. The first investment gets the four annual coupon payments of €8.50 each. The second gets the €100 face value at maturity. You can use the annuity formula from Chapter 2 to value the coupon payments and then add on the present value of the final payment.

PV(bond) = PV(annuity of coupon payments) + PV(final payment of principal)

= (coupon × 4-year annuity factor) + (final payment × discount factor)

$$= 8.50 \left[\frac{1}{.03} - \frac{1}{.03(1.03)^4} \right] + \frac{100}{(1.03)^4} = 31.59 + 88.85 = €120.44$$

Thus the bond can be valued as a package of an annuity (the coupon payments) and a single, final payment (the repayment of principal).[2]

We just used the 3% interest rate to calculate the present value of the OAT. Now we turn the valuation around: If the price of the OAT is 120.44%, what is the interest rate? What return do investors get if they buy the bond? To answer this question, you need to find the value of the variable y that solves the following equation:

$$120.44 = \frac{8.50}{1+y} + \frac{8.50}{(1+y)^2} + \frac{8.50}{(1+y)^3} + \frac{108.50}{(1+y)^4}$$

The rate of return y is called the bond's **yield to maturity.** In this case, we already know that the present value of the bond is €120.44 at a 3% discount rate, so the yield to maturity must be 3.0%. If you buy the bond at 120.44% and hold it to maturity, you will earn a return of 3.0% per year.

Why is the yield to maturity less than the 8.5% coupon payment? Because you are paying €120.44 for a bond with a face value of only €100. You lose the difference of €20.44 if you hold the bond to maturity. On the other hand, you get four annual cash payments of €8.50. (The immediate, *current yield* on your investment is 8.50/120.44 = .071, or 7.1%.) The yield to maturity blends the return from the coupon payments with the declining value of the bond over its remaining life.

The only general procedure for calculating the yield to maturity is trial and error. You guess at an interest rate and calculate the present value of the bond's payments. If the present value is greater than the actual price, your discount rate must have been too low, and you need to try a higher rate. The more practical solution is to use a spreadsheet program or a specially programmed calculator to calculate the yield. At the end of this chapter, you will find a box which lists the Excel function for calculating yield to maturity plus several other useful functions for bond analysts.

---

[2] You could also value a three-year annuity of €8.50 plus a final payment of €108.50.

Back to India: Semiannual Coupons and Bond Prices

Just like the French government, the Reserve Bank of India (on behalf of the Indian Government) raises money by regular auctions of new bond known as Government Securities or G-Secs issues. Some of these issues do not mature for 20 or 30 years. The RBI also issues short-term debt maturing in a year or less. These short-term securities are known as *Treasury bills.* Government securities and bills are traded in the *fixed-income market.*

Let's look at an example of an Indian Government security. In 2010, the RBI issued 8.28% securities maturing in 2032. These securities are called "8.28%GS, 2032". These Government securities have face values of ₹100, so if you own the 8.28% Government Security, the RBI will give you back ₹100 at maturity. You can also look forward to a regular coupon but, in contrast to our French bond, coupons on G-Secs are mostly paid semiannually.[3] Thus, the above G-Sec will provide a coupon of 8.28/2 = 4.14% of face value every six months.

The prices at which you can buy or sell Government Securities are shown each day in the financial press and on the Web. Figure 3.1 is taken from the website of the National Stock Exchange of India and it shows the prices of a small sample of Government Securities. Look at the entry for the 7.49% 2017 bond. The last traded price was ₹97.68. This is the price at which the last transaction took place. Since the face value is ₹100, each G-Sec costs ₹97.68.[4]

Maturity	Coupon	Last Traded Price	Weighted YTM
2013	7.27%	99.07	7.69%
2015	7.17%	97.2	7.96%
2017	**7.49%**	**97.68**	**7.98%**
2017	7.99%	99.95	8.00%
2022	8.08%	99.65	8.12%
2022	8.13%	100.15	8.11%
2025	7.95%	96.45	8.39%
2027	8.26%	99.12	8.36%
2040	8.30%	99.05	8.39%

FIGURE 3.1

Sample government securities.

Source: Website of National Stock Exchange of India.

The last column shows the weighted yield to maturity of the security. Because interest is semiannual, yields on Indian G-Secs are usually quoted as semiannually compounded yields. Thus, if you buy the 7.49% security and hold it till maturity, you earn a semiannual compounded return of 7.98%. This means that every six months you earn a return of 7.89/2 = 3.945%.

---

[3] The frequency of interest payments varies from country to country. For example, most euro bonds pay interest annually, while most bonds in the U.K., Canada, and Japan pay interest semiannually.

[4] The quoted bond price is known as the *flat* (or *clean*) price. The price that the bond buyer actually pays (sometimes called the *full* or *dirty* price) is equal to the flat price *plus* the interest that the seller has already earned on the bond since the last interest payment. The precise method for calculating this *accrued interest* varies from one type of bond to another. We use the flat price to calculate the yield.

You can now repeat the present value calculations that we did for the French government bond. You just need to recognize that government securities in India have a face value of ₹100, that their coupons are paid semiannually, and that the quoted yield is a semiannually compounded rate.

Here are the cash payments from the above government security:

Cash Payments (₹)					
Sept. 2011	Mar. 2012	Sept. 2012	Mar. 2013	—	Mar. 2017
₹3.75	₹3.75	₹3.75	₹3.75	—	₹103.75

If investors demand a semiannual return of 3.945%, then the present value of these cash flows is

$$PV = \frac{3.745}{(1+3.945\%)} + \frac{3.745}{(1+3.945\%)^2} + ... + \frac{3.745}{(1+3.945\%)^{11}} + \frac{103.745}{(1+3.945\%)^{12}} = ₹98.12$$

Each security is worth ₹98.12. You can see that there is a slight difference between this price and the last traded price mentioned in Figure 3.1. That is because in this calculation, we assumed that the next coupon of ₹3.745 is exactly six months away.

Again we could turn the valuation around: given the price, what's the yield to maturity? Try it, and you'll find (no surprise) that the yield to maturity is $y = 0.03945$. This is the semiannual rate of return that you can earn over the six remaining half-year periods until the note matures. Take care to remember that the yield is *reported* as an annual rate, calculated as $2 \times .03945 = .0789$, or 7.89%. If you see a reported yield to maturity of $R\%$, you have to remember to use $y = R/2\%$ as the semiannual rate for discounting cash flows received every six months.

3-2 HOW BOND PRICES VARY WITH INTEREST RATES[5]

Figure 3.2 plots the yield to maturity on 10-year Indian Government Securities from 1976 to 2010. Notice how much the rate fluctuates. For example, the rates climbed sharply after 1993, when the RBI increased the interest rate to control the high growth in money supply (exceeded 20%) and the high inflation of 15%. Within 2 years, the interest rate on 10-year government securities increased from around 9.44% in 1992 to 13.3% in 1994. Contrast this with 2005, when due to excess liquidity (due to large FII inflows and foreign direct investments), the RBI kept the interest rate at just above 5%.

As interest rates change, so do bond prices. For example, suppose that investors demanded a semiannual return of 6% on the 2027 G-Sec, rather than the 3.945% return we used above. In that case the price would be

$$PV = \frac{3.745}{(1+6\%)} + \frac{3.745}{(1+6\%)^2} + ... + \frac{3.745}{(1+6\%)^{11}} + \frac{103.745}{(1+6\%)^{12}} = ₹81.09$$

---

[5] From this point forward, we will just say "bonds," and not distinguish notes from bonds unless we are referring to a specific security. Note also that bonds with long maturities end up with short maturities when they approach the final payment date. Thus you will encounter 30-year bonds trading 20 years later at the same prices as new 10-year notes (assuming equal coupons).

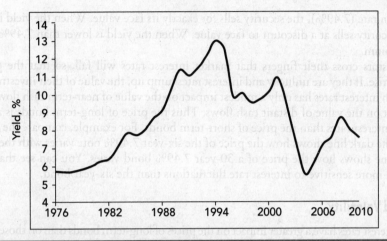

FIGURE 3.2

The interest rate on 10-year Indian Government Securities

The higher interest rate results in a lower price.

Bond prices and interest rates *must* move in opposite directions. The yield to maturity, our measure of the interest rate on a bond, is *defined* as the discount rate that explains the bond price. When bond prices fall, interest rates (that is, yields to maturity) must rise. When interest rates rise, bond prices must fall. We recall a hapless TV pundit who intoned, "The recent decline in long-term interest rates suggests that long-term bond prices may rise over the next week or two." Of course the bond prices had already gone up. We are confident that you won't make the pundit's mistake.

The solid green line in Figure 3.3 shows the value of our 7.49% security for different interest rates. As the yield to maturity falls, the bond price increases. When the annual yield is equal to the note's

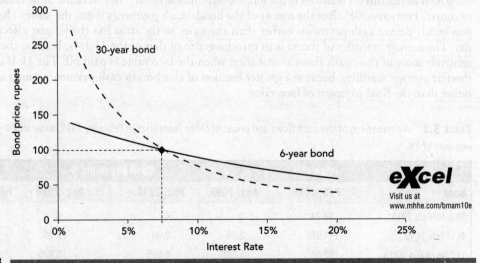

FIGURE 3.3

Plot of bond prices as a function of the interest rate. The price of long-term bonds is more sensitive to changes in the interest rate than is the price of short-term bonds.

annual coupon rate (7.49%), the security sells for exactly its face value. When the yield is higher than 7.49%, the security sells at a discount to face value. When the yield is lower than 7.49%, the security sells at a premium.

Bond investors cross their fingers that market interest rates will fall, so that the price of their securities will rise. If they are unlucky and interest rates jump up, the value of their investment declines.

A change in interest rates has only a modest impact on the value of near-term cash flows but a much greater impact on the value of distant cash flows. Thus the price of long-term bonds is affected more by changing interest rates than the price of short-term bonds. For example, compare the two curves in Figure 3.3. The dark line shows how the price of the six-year 7.49% note varies with the interest rate. The dotted line shows how the price of a 30-year 7.49% bond varies. You can see that the 30-year bond is much more sensitive to interest rate fluctuations than the six-year bond.

Duration and Volatility

Changes in interest rates have a greater impact on the prices of long-term bonds than on those of short-term bonds. But what do we mean by "long-term" and "short-term"? A coupon bond that matures in year 30 makes payments in *each* of years 1 through 30. It's misleading to describe the bond as a 30-year bond; the average time to each cash payment is less than 30 years.

EXAMPLE 3.1   **Which Is the Longest-Term Bond?**

A strip is a special type of Treasury bond that repays principal at maturity, but makes no coupon payments along the way. Strips are also called *zero-coupon* bonds. (We cover strips in more detail in the next section.)

Consider a strip maturing in February 2015 in the U.S. and two coupon bonds maturing on the same date. Table 3.1 calculates the prices of these three Treasuries, assuming a yield to maturity of 2% per year. Take a look at the time pattern of each bond's cash payments and review how the prices are calculated.

Which of the three Treasuries is the longest-term investment? They have the same final maturity, of course, February 2015. But the *timing* of the bonds' cash payments is not the same. The two coupon bonds deliver cash payments earlier than the strip, so the strip has the longest effective maturity. The *average* maturity of the 4s is in turn longer than that of the 11 1/4s, because the 4s deliver relatively more of their cash flows at maturity, when the face value is paid off. The 11 1/4s have the shortest average maturity, because a greater fraction of this bond's cash payments comes as coupons rather than the final payment of face value.

TABLE 3.1   A comparison of the cash flows and prices of three Treasuries in February 2009, assuming a yield to maturity of 2%.

	Price (%)		Cash payments %		
Bond	Feb. 2009	Aug. 2009	Feb. 2010...	...Aug. 2014	Feb. 2015
Strip for Feb. 2015	88.74	0	0...	...0	100.00
4s of Feb. 2015	111.26	2.00	2.00...	...2.00	102.00
11 1/4s of Feb. 2015	152.05	5.625	5.625...	...5.625	105.625

Note: All three securities mature in February 2015.

Investors and financial managers calculate a bond's average maturity by its **duration.** They keep track of duration because it measures the exposure of the bond's price to fluctuations in interest rates. Duration is often called *Macaulay duration* after its inventor.

Duration is the weighted average of the times when the bond's cash payments are received. The times are the future years 1, 2, 3, etc., extending to the final maturity date, which we call T. The weight for each year is the present value of the cash flow received at that time divided by the total present value of the bond.

$$\text{Duration} = \frac{1 \times \text{PV}(C_1)}{\text{PV}} + \frac{2 \times \text{PV}(C_2)}{\text{PV}} + \frac{3 \times \text{PV}(C_3)}{\text{PV}} + \cdots + \frac{T \times \text{PV}(C_T)}{\text{PV}}$$

Table 3.2 shows how to compute duration for the French OATs maturing in 2012. First, we value each of the three annual coupon payments of €8.50 and the final payment of coupon plus face value of €108.50. Of course the present values of these payments add up to the bond price of €120.44. Then we calculate the fraction of the price accounted for by each cash flow and multiply each fraction by the year of the cash flow. The results sum across to a duration of 3.60 years.

TABLE 3.2 Calculating duration for the French OATs maturing in 2012. The yield to maturity is 3% per year.

Year (t)	1	2	3	4	
Cash payment (C_t)	€8.50	€8.50	€8.50	€108.50	
PV(C_t) at 3%	€8.25	€8.01	€7.78	€96.40	PV = €120.44
Fraction of total value [PV(C_t)/PV]	0.069	0.067	0.065	0.800	
Year × Fraction of total value [$t \times$ PV(C_t)/PV]	0.069	0.133	0.194	3.202	Total = duration = 3.60

Table 3.3 shows the same calculation for the 11¼% U.S. Treasury bond maturing in February 2015. The present value of each cash payment is calculated using a 2% yield to maturity. Again we calculate the fraction of the price accounted for by each cash flow and multiply each fraction by the year. The calculations look more formidable than in Table 3.2, but only because the final maturity date is 2016 rather than 2012 and coupons are paid semiannually. Thus in Table 3.3 we have to track 12 dates rather than 4. The duration of the 11 1/4s equals 4.83 years.

We leave it to you to calculate durations for the other two bonds in Table 3.1. You will find that duration increases to 5.43 years for the 4s of 2015. The duration of the strip is six years exactly, the same as its maturity. Because there are no coupons, 100% of the strip's value comes from payment of principal in year 6.

We mentioned that investors and financial managers track duration because it measures how bond prices change when interest rates change. For this purpose it's best to use *modified duration* or *volatility,* which is just duration divided by one plus the yield to maturity:

$$\text{Modified duration} = \text{volatility (\%)} = \frac{\text{duration}}{1 + \text{yield}}$$

TABLE 3.3 Calculating the duration of the 11¼% Treasuries of 2015. The yield to maturity is 2%.

Date	Aug. 2009	Feb. 2010	Aug. 2010	Feb. 2011	...	Aug. 2013	Feb. 2014	Aug. 2014	Feb. 2015	
Year (t)	0.5	1.0	1.5	2.0	...	4.5	5.0	5.5	6.0	
Cash payment (C_t)	5.63	5.63	5.63	5.63	...	5.63	5.63	5.63	105.625	
PV(C_t) at 2%	5.57	5.51	5.46	5.41	...	5.14	5.09	5.04	93.74	PV = 152.05
fraction of total value [PV(C_t)/PV]	0.0366	0.0363	0.0359	0.0355	...	0.0338	0.0335	0.0332	0.6165	
Year × fraction of total value [t × PV(C_t)/PV]	0.0183	0.0363	0.0539	0.0711	...	0.1522	0.1674	0.1824	3.6988	Total = duration = 4.83
Duration (years) = 4.83										

Modified duration measures the percentage change in bond price for a 1 percentage-point change in yield.[6] .Let's try out this formula for the OAT bond in Table 3.2. The bond's modified duration is duration/(1 + yield) = 3.60/1.03 = 3.49%. This means that a 1% change in the yield to maturity should change the bond price by 3.49%.

Let's check that prediction. Suppose the yield to maturity either increases or declines by .5%:

Yield to Maturity	Price	Change (%)
3.5%	118.37	− 1.767
3.0	120.44	—
2.5	122.57	+ 1.726

The total difference between price at 2.5% and 3.5% is 1.767 + 1.726 = 3.49%. Thus a 1% change in interest rates means a 3.49% change in bond price, just as predicted.

The modified duration for the 1/1¼% U.S. Treasury in Table 3.3 is 4.83/1.02 = 4.74%. In other words, a 1% change in yield to maturity results in a 4.74% change in the bond's price. Modified durations for the other bonds in Table 3.1 are larger, which means more exposure of price to changes in interest rates. For example, the modified duration of the strip is 6/1.02 = 5.88%.

You can see why duration (or modified duration) is a handy measure of interest-rate risk. For example, investment managers regularly monitor the duration of their bond portfolios to ensure that they are not running undue risk.[7]

---

[6] In other words, the derivative of the bond price with respect to a change in yield to maturity is $dPV/dy = -\text{duration}/(1 + y) = -\text{modified duration}$.

[7] The portfolio duration is a weighted average of the durations of the bonds in the portfolio. The weight for each bond is the fraction of the portfolio invested in that bond. Note that as time passes and interest rates change, the portfolio manager needs to recalculate duration.

3-3   THE TERM STRUCTURE OF INTEREST RATES

When we explained in Chapter 2 how to calculate present values, we used the same discount rate to calculate the value of each period's cash flow. A single yield to maturity y can also be used to discount all future cash payments from a bond. For many purposes, using a single discount rate is a perfectly acceptable approximation, but there are also occasions when you need to recognize that short-term interest rates are different from long-term rates.

The relationship between short- and long-term interest rates is called the **term structure of interest rates.** Look for example at Figure 3.4, which shows the term structure in India at two different points of time. Notice that the term structure sloped downward towards the end of June 2008; long-term interest rates were lower than short-term rates. In the earlier part of 2008, the pattern was reversed and long-term bonds offered a higher interest rate than short-term bonds. You now need to learn how to measure the term structure and understand why long- and short-term rates differ.

Consider a simple loan that pays ₹1 at the end of one year. To find the present value of this loan you need to discount the cash flow by the one-year rate of interest rate, r_1:

$$PV = 1/(1 + r_1)$$

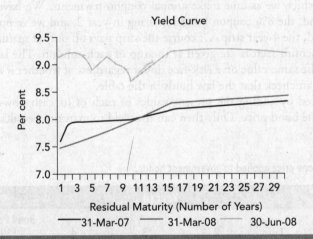

Yield Curve

Residual Maturity (Number of Years)

——— 31-Mar-07   ——— 31-Mar-08   ——— 30-Jun-08

FIGURE 3.4

Short- and long-term interest rates do not always move in parallel.

Source: RBI Bulletin, April 14, 2008.

This rate, r_1 is called the one-year **spot rate.** To find the present value of a loan that pays ₹1 at the end of two years, you need to discount by the two-year spot rate, r_2:

$$PV = 1/(1 + r_2)^2$$

The first year's cash flow is discounted at today's one-year spot rate and the second year's flow is discounted at today's two-year spot rate. The series of spot rates $r_1, r_2, \ldots, r_t, \ldots$ traces out the term structure of interest rates.

Now suppose you have to value ₹1 paid at the end of years 1 *and* 2. If the spot rates are different, say $r_1 = 3\%$ and $r_2 = 4\%$, then we need two discount rates to calculate present value:

$$PV = \frac{1}{1.03} + \frac{1}{1.04^2} = 1.895$$

Once we know that PV = 1.895, we can go on to calculate a single discount rate that would give the right answer. That is, we could calculate the yield to maturity by solving for y in the following equation:

$$PV = 1.895 = \frac{1}{(1+y)} + \frac{1}{(1+y)^2}$$

This gives a yield to maturity of 3.66%. Once we have the yield, we could use it to value other two-year annuities. But we can't get the yield to maturity until we know the price. The price is determined by the spot interest rates for dates 1 and 2. Spot rates come first. Yields to maturity come later, after bond prices are set. That is why professionals identify spot interest rates and discount each cash flow at the spot rate for the date when the cash flow is received.

Spot Rates, Bond Prices, and the Law of One Price

The *law of one price* states that the same commodity must sell at the same price in a well-functioning market. Therefore, all safe cash payments delivered on the same date must be discounted at the same spot rate.

Table 3.4 illustrates how the law of one price applies to the U.S. government bonds. It lists four government bonds, which we assume make annual coupon payments. We have put at the top the shortest-duration bond, the 8% coupon bond maturing in year 2, and we've put at the bottom the longest-duration bond, the 4-year strip. Of course the strip pays off only at maturity.

Spot rates and discount factors are given at the top of each column. The law of one price says that investors place the same value on a risk-free dollar regardless of whether it is provided by bond A, B, C, or D. You can check that the law holds in the table.

Each bond is priced by adding the present values of each of its cash flows. Once total PV is calculated, we have the bond price. Only then can the yield to maturity be calculated.

e𝕏cel

Visit us at
www.mhhe.com/bmam10e

TABLE 3.4 The law of one price applied to government bonds.

	Year (t)				Bond Price (PV)	Yield to Maturity (y, %)
	1	2	3	4		
Spot rates	.035	.04	.042	.044		
Discount factors	.9662	.9246	.8839	.8418		
Bond A (8% coupon):						
Payment (C_t)	$80	1,080				
PV(C_t)	$77.29	998.52			$1,075.82	3.98
Bond B (11% coupon):						
Payment (C_t)	$110	110	1,110			
PV(C_t)	$106.28	101.70	981.11		$1,189.10	4.16
Bond C (6% coupon):						
Payment (C_t)	$60	60	60	1,060		
PV(C_t)	$57.97	55.47	53.03	892.29	$1,058.76	4.37
Bond D (strip):						
Payment (C_t)				$1,000		
PV(C_t)				$841.78	$841.78	4.40

Notice how the yield to maturity increases as bond maturity increases. The yields increase with maturity because the term structure of spot rates is upward-sloping. Yields to maturity are complex averages of spot rates.

Financial managers who want a quick, summary measure of interest rates bypass spot interest rates and look in the financial press at yields to maturity. They may refer to the *yield curve*, which plots yields to maturity, instead of referring to the term structure, which plots spot rates. They may use the yield to maturity on one bond to value another bond with roughly the same coupon and maturity. They may speak with a broad brush and say, "Ampersand Bank will charge us 6% on a three-year loan," referring to a 6% yield to maturity.

Throughout this book, we too use the yield to maturity to summarize the return required by bond investors. But you also need to understand the measure's limitations when spot rates are not equal.

Measuring the Term Structure

You can think of the spot rate, r_t, as the rate of interest on a bond that makes a single payment at time t. Such simple bonds do exist—we have already seen examples. They are known as **stripped bonds,** or **strips.** On request the U.S. Treasury will split a normal coupon bond into a package of mini-bonds, each of which makes just one cash payment. Our 4.875% notes of 2012 could be exchanged for six semiannual coupon strips, each paying $24.375, and a principal strip paying $1,000. In February 2009 this package of coupon strips would have cost $143.83 and the principal strip would have cost $964.42, making a total cost of $1,108.25, just a few cents more than it cost to buy one 4.875% note. That should be no surprise. Because the two investments provide identical cash payments, they must sell for very close to the same price.

We can use the prices of strips to measure the term structure of interest rates. For example, in February 2009 a 10-year strip cost $714.18. In return, investors could look forward to a single payment of $1,000 in February 2019. Thus investors were prepared to pay $.71418 for the promise of $1 at the end of 10 years. The 10-year discount factor was $DF_{10} = 1/(1 + r_{10})^{10} = .71418$, and the 10-year spot rate was $r_{10} = (1/.71418)^{.10} - 1 = .0342$, or 3.42%. In Figure 3.5 we use the prices of strips with different maturities to plot the term structure of spot rates from 1 to 10 years. You can see that in 2009 investors required a somewhat higher interest rate for lending for 10 years rather than for 1.

In India, the RBI allowed stripping of government securities from 1 April 2010. To begin with, bonds with coupon or maturity dates of January 2 or July 2, irrespective of the year of maturity, are eligible for stripping. Thus, for example, if the coupon date of a particular security is January 2 (or July 2), then it is eligible for stripping. Each strip will have a face value of ₹100. To begin with, the RBI has allowed trading of STRIPS in the OTC market only.

Why the Discount Factor Declines As Futurity Increases—and a Digression on Money Machines

In Chapter 2 we saw that the longer you have to wait for your money, the less is its present value. In other words, the two-year discount factor $DF_2 = 1/(1 + r_2)^2$ is less than the one-year discount factor $DF_1 = (1 + r_1)$. But is this *necessarily* the case when there can be a different spot interest rate for each period?

Suppose that the one-year spot rate of interest is $r_1 = 20\%$, and the two-year spot rate is $r_2 = 7\%$. In this case the one-year discount factor is $DF_1 = 1/1.20 = .833$ and the two-year discount factor is

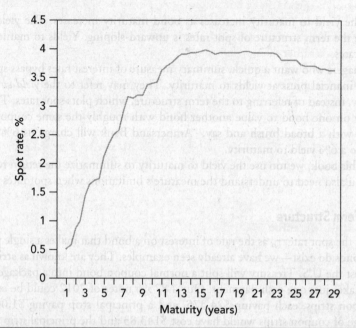

FIGURE 3.5

Spot rates on U.S. Treasury strips, February 2009.

$DF_2 = 1/1.07^2 = .873$. Apparently a dollar received the day after tomorrow is *not* necessarily worth less than a dollar received tomorrow.

But there is something wrong with this example. Anyone who could borrow and invest at these interest rates could become a millionaire overnight. Let us see how such a "money machine" would work. Suppose the first person to spot the opportunity is Hermione Kraft. Ms. Kraft first buys a one-year Treasury strip for $.833 \times \$1,000 = \$833$. Now she notices that there is a way to earn an *immediate* surefire profit on this investment. She reasons as follows. Next year the strip will pay off $1,000 that can be reinvested for a further year. Although she does not know what interest rates will be at that time, she does know that she can always put the money in a checking account and be certain of having $1,000 at the end of year 2. Her next step, therefore, is to go to her bank and borrow the present value of this $1,000. At 7% interest the present value is $PV = 1000/(1.07)^2 = \$873$.

So Ms. Kraft borrows $873, invests $830, and walks away with a profit of $43. If that does not sound like very much, notice that by borrowing more and investing more she can make much larger profits. For example, if she borrows $21,778,584 and invests $20,778,584, she would become a millionaire.[8]

Of course this story is completely fanciful. Such an opportunity would not last long in well-functioning capital markets. Any bank that allowed you to borrow for two years at 7% when the one-year interest rate was 20% would soon be wiped out by a rush of small investors hoping to become millionaires and a rush of millionaires hoping to become billionaires. There are, however, two

---

[8] We exaggerate Ms. Kraft's profits. There are always costs to financial transactions, though they may be very small. For example, Ms. Kraft could use her investment in the one-year strip as security for the bank loan, but the bank would need to charge more than 7% on the loan to cover its costs.

lessons to our story. The first is that a dollar tomorrow *cannot* be worth less than a dollar the day after tomorrow. In other words, the value of a dollar received at the end of one year (DF_1) cannot be less than the value of a dollar received at the end of two years (DF_2). There must be some extra gain from lending for two periods rather than one: $(1 + r_2)^2$ cannot be less than $1 + r_1$.

Our second lesson is a more general one and can be summed up by this precept: "There is no such thing as a surefire money machine." The technical term for money machine is **arbitrage.** In well-functioning markets, where the costs of buying and selling are low, arbitrage opportunities are eliminated almost instantaneously by investors who try to take advantage of them.

Later in the book we invoke the *absence* of arbitrage opportunities to prove several useful properties about security prices. That is, we make statements like, "The prices of securities X and Y must be in the following relationship—otherwise there would be potential arbitrage profits and capital markets would not be in equilibrium."

3-4 EXPLAINING THE TERM STRUCTURE

The term structure that we showed in Figure 3.5 was upward-sloping. Long-term rates of interest in February 2009 were more than 3.5%; short-term rates were 1% or less. Why then didn't everyone rush to buy long-term bonds? Who were the (foolish?) investors who put their money into the short end of the term structure?

Suppose that you held a portfolio of one-year U.S. Treasuries in February 2009. Here are three possible reasons why you might decide to hold on to them, despite their low rate of return:

1. You believe that short-term interest rates will be higher in the future.
2. You worry about the greater exposure of long-term bonds to changes in interest rates.
3. You worry about the risk of higher future inflation.

We review each of these reasons now.

Expectations Theory of the Term Structure

Recall that you own a portfolio of one-year Treasuries. A year from now, when the Treasuries mature, you can reinvest the proceeds for another one-year period and enjoy whatever interest rate the bond market offers then. The interest rate for the second year may be high enough to offset the first year's low return. You often see an upward-sloping term structure when future interest rates are expected to rise.

EXAMPLE 3.2   Expectations and the Term Structure

Suppose that the one-year interest rate, r_1, is 5%, and the two-year rate, r_2, is 7%. If you invest $100 for one year, your investment grows to $100 \times 1.05 = \$105$; if you invest for two years, it grows to $100 \times 1.07^2 = \$114.49$. The *extra* return that you earn for that second year is $1.07^2/1.05 - 1 = .090$, or 9.0%.[9]

Would you be happy to earn that extra 9% for investing for two years rather than one? The answer depends on how you expect interest rates to change over the coming year. If you are confident that

---

[9] The extra return for lending for one more year is termed the *forward rate of interest*. In our example the forward rate is 9.0%. In Ms. Kraft's arbitrage example, the forward interest rate was negative. In real life, forward interest rates can't be negative. At the lowest they are zero.

in 12 months' time one-year bonds will yield more than 9.0%, you would do better to invest in a one-year bond and, when that matured, reinvest the cash for the next year at the higher rate. If you forecast that the future one-year rate is exactly 9.0%, then you will be indifferent between buying a two-year bond or investing for one year and then rolling the investment forward at next year's short-term interest rate.

If everyone is thinking as you just did, then the two-year interest rate has to adjust so that everyone is equally happy to invest for one year or two. Thus the two-year rate will incorporate both today's one-year rate and the consensus forecast of next year's one-year rate.

We have just illustrated (in Example 3.2) the **expectations theory** of the term structure. It states that in equilibrium investment in a series of short-maturity bonds must offer the same expected return as an investment in a single long-maturity bond. Only if that is the case would investors be prepared to hold both short- and long-maturity bonds.

The expectations theory implies that the *only* reason for an upward-sloping term structure is that investors expect short-term interest rates to rise; the *only* reason for a declining term structure is that investors expect short-term rates to fall.

If short-term interest rates are significantly lower than long-term rates, it is tempting to borrow short-term rather than long-term. The expectations theory implies that such naïve strategies won't work. If short-term rates are lower than long-term rates, then investors must be expecting interest rates to rise. When the term structure is upward-sloping, you are likely to make money by borrowing short only if investors are *overestimating* future increases in interest rates.

Even at a casual glance the expectations theory does not seem to be the complete explanation of term structure. For example, if we look back over the period 1900–2008, we find that the return on long-term U.S. Treasury bonds was on average 1.5 percentage points higher than the return on short-term Treasury bills. Perhaps short-term interest rates stayed lower than investors expected, but it seems more likely that investors wanted some extra return for holding long bonds and that on average they got it. If so, the expectations theory is only a first step.

These days the expectations theory has few strict adherents. Nevertheless, most economists believe that expectations about future interest rates have an important effect on the term structure. For example, you will hear market commentators remark that the six-month interest rate is higher than the three-month rate and conclude that the market is expecting the Federal Reserve Board to raise interest rates. There is good evidence for this type of reasoning. Suppose that every month from 1950 to 2008 you used the extra return from lending for six months rather than three to predict the likely change in interest rates. You would have found on average that the steeper the term structure, the more that interest rates subsequently rose. So it looks as if the expectations theory has some truth to it even if it is not the whole truth.

Introducing Risk

What does the expectations theory leave out? The most obvious answer is "risk." If you are confident about the future level of interest rates, you will simply choose the strategy that offers the highest return. But, if you are not sure of your forecasts, you may well opt for a less risky strategy even if it means giving up some return.

Remember that the prices of long-duration bonds are more volatile than prices of short-duration bonds. A sharp increase in interest rates can knock 30% or 40% off the price of long-term bonds.

For some investors, this extra volatility of long-duration bonds may not be a concern. For example, pension funds and life insurance companies have fixed long-term liabilities, and may prefer to lock in future returns by investing in long-term bonds. However, the volatility of long-term bonds *does* create extra risk for investors who do not have such long-term obligations. These investors will be prepared to hold long bonds only if they offer the compensation of a higher return. In this case the term structure will be upward-sloping more often than not. Of course, if interest rates are expected to fall, the term structure could be downward-sloping and still reward investors for lending long. But the additional reward for risk offered by long bonds would result in a less dramatic downward slope.

Inflation and Term Structure

Suppose you are saving for your retirement 20 years from now. Which of the following strategies is more risky? Invest in a succession of one-year Treasuries, rolled over annually, or invest once in 20-year strips? The answer depends on how confident you are about future inflation.

If you buy the 20-year strips, you know exactly how much money you will have at year 20, but you don't know what that money will buy. Inflation may seem benign now, but who knows what it will be in 10 or 15 years? This uncertainty about inflation may make it uncomfortably risky for you to lock in one 20-year interest rate by buying the strips. This was a problem facing investors in 2009, when no one could be sure whether the country was facing the prospect of prolonged deflation or whether the high levels of government borrowing would prompt rapid inflation.

You can reduce exposure to inflation risk by investing short-term and rolling over the investment. You do not know future short-term interest rates, but you do know that future interest rates will adapt to inflation. If inflation takes off, you will probably be able to roll over your investment at higher interest rates.

If inflation is an important source of risk for long-term investors, borrowers must offer some extra incentive if they want investors to lend long. That is why we often see a steeply upward-sloping term structure when inflation is particularly uncertain.

3-5 REAL AND NOMINAL RATES OF RETURN

It is now time to review more carefully the relation between inflation and interest rates. Suppose you invest ₹1,000 in a one-year bond that makes a single payment of ₹1,100 at the end of the year. Your cash flow is certain, but the government makes no promises about what that money will buy. If the prices of goods and services increase by more than 10%, you will lose ground in terms of purchasing power.

Several indices are used to track the general level of prices. The best known is the Consumer Price Index (CPI), which measures the number of dollars that it takes to pay for a typical family's purchases. The change in the CPI from one year to the next measures the rate of inflation.

Figure 3.6 shows the rate of inflation in India since 1970. Inflation touched a peak of 34.6% in 1974, prior to the emergency. However, this figure pales into insignificance compared with the hyperinflation in Zimbabwe in 2008. Prices there rose so fast that a Z$50 trillion bill was barely enough to buy a loaf of bread.

Prices can fall as well as rise. India experienced severe *deflation* in 1976 during emergency, when prices fell by 13%. More recently, consumer prices in Hong Kong fell by nearly 15% in the six years from 1999 to 2004.

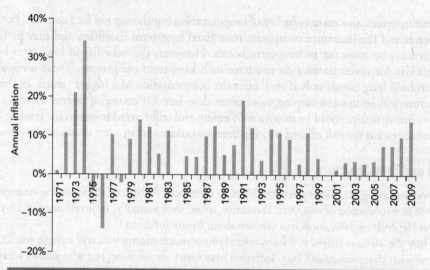

FIGURE 3.6

Annual rates of inflation in India from 1970–2009.

Source: www.rbi.org.in

The *average* Indian inflation rate from 1970 to 2009 was 7.57%. As you can see from Figure 3.7, among major economies the U.S. has been almost top of the class in holding inflation in check. Countries torn by war have generally experienced much higher inflation. For example, in Italy and Japan, inflation since 1900 has averaged about 11% a year.

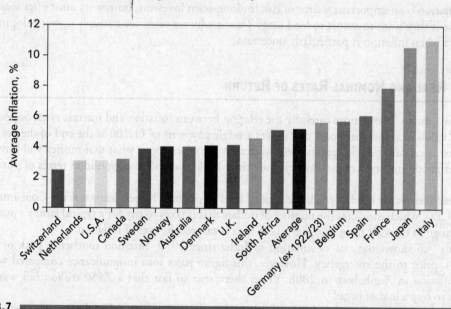

FIGURE 3.7

Average rates of inflation in 17 countries from 1900–2008.

Source: E. Dimson, P. R. Marsh, and M. Staunton, *Triumph of the Optimists: 101 Years of Investment Returns* (Princeton, NJ: Princeton University Press, 2002), with updates provided by the authors.

Economists and financial managers refer to current, or *nominal*, rupees versus constant, or *real*, rupees. For example, the nominal cash flow from your one-year bond is ₹1,100. But if prices rise over the year by 6%, then each rupee will buy you 6% less next year than it does today. So at the end of the year ₹1,100 has the same purchasing power as 1,100/1.06 = ₹1,037.74 today. The nominal payoff on the bond is ₹1,100, but the real payoff is only ₹1,037.74.

The formula for converting nominal cash flows in a future period *t* to real cash flows today is

$$\text{Real cash flow at date } t = \frac{\text{Nominal cash flow at date } t}{(1 + \text{inflation rate})^t}$$

For example, suppose you invest in a 20-year strip, but inflation over the 20 years averages 6% per year. The strip pays ₹1,000 in year 20, but the real value of that payoff is only $1,000/1.06^{20} = ₹311.80$. In this example, the purchasing power of ₹1 today declines to just over ₹.31 after 20 years.

These examples show you how to get from nominal to real cash flows. The journey from nominal to real interest rates is similar. When a bond dealer says that your bond yields 10%, she is quoting a nominal interest rate. That rate tells you how rapidly your money will grow, say over one year:

Invest Current Rupees	Receive Rupees in Year 1	Result
₹1,000 →	₹1,100	10% *nominal* rate of return

However, with an expected inflation rate of 6%, you are only 3.774% better off at the end of the year than at the start:

Invest Current Rupees	Expected Real Value of Rupees in Year 1	Result
₹1,000 →	₹1,037.74 (= 1,100/1.06)	3.774% expected *real* rate of return

Thus, we could say, "The bond offers a 10% nominal rate of return," or "It offers a 3.774% expected real rate of return."

The formula for calculating the real rate of return is:

$$1 + r_{\text{real}} = (1 + r_{\text{nominal}})/(1 + \text{inflation rate})$$

In our example, $1 + r_{\text{real}} = 1.10/1.06 = 1.03774$.[10]

Indexed Bonds and the Real Rate of Interest

Most bonds are like Indian Treasury bonds; they promise you a fixed *nominal* rate of interest. The *real* interest rate that you receive is uncertain and depends on inflation. If the inflation rate turns out to be higher than you expected, the real return on your bonds will be lower.

You *can* nail down a real return, however. You do so by buying an *indexed bond* that makes cash payments linked to inflation. Indexed bonds have been around in many other countries for decades, but they were almost unknown in India until 1997, when the RBI issued the Capital Index Bond

---

[10] A common rule of thumb states that $r_{\text{real}} = r_{\text{nominal}} - \text{inflation rate}$. In our example this gives $r_{\text{real}} = .10 - .06 = .04$, or 4%. This is not a bad approximation to the true real interest rate of 3.774%. But when inflation is high, it pays to use the full formula.

2002. In this bond, however, only the principal amount was indexed to the inflation rate. RBI plans to launch the inflation indexed bonds in India for the second time sometime in 2011, where both the interest and principal will be indexed to the inflation rate.

Inflation indexed bonds were also relatively new in the U.S. where the U.S. Treasury began to issue inflation-indexed bonds (better known as TIPS or Treasury Inflation-Protected Securities) in 1997.[11]

The real cash flows on TIPS are fixed, but the nominal cash flows (interest and principal) increase as the CPI increases.[12] For example, suppose that the U.S. Treasury issues 3% 20-year TIPS at a price equal to its face value of $1,000. If during the first year the CPI rises by 10%, then the coupon payment on the bond increases by 10% from $30 to 30 × 1.10 = $33. The amount that you will be paid at maturity also increases to $1,000 × 1.10 = $1,100. The purchasing power of the coupon and face value remain constant at $33/1.10 = $30 and $1,100/1.10 = $1,000. Thus, an investor who buys the bond at the issue price earns a real interest rate of 3%.

Long-term TIPS offered a yield of about 1.7% in February 2009. This is a *real* yield to maturity. It measures the extra goods and services your investment will allow you to buy. The 1.7% yield on TIPS was about 1.0% less than the nominal yield on ordinary Treasury bonds. If the annual inflation rate turns out to be higher than 1.0%, investors will earn a higher return by holding long-term TIPS; if the inflation rate turns out to be less than 1.0%, they would have been better off with nominal bonds.

What Determines the Real Rate of Interest?

The real rate of interest depends on people's willingness to save (the supply of capital)[13] and the opportunities for productive investment by governments and businesses (the demand for capital). For example, suppose that investment opportunities generally improve. Firms have more good projects, so they are willing to invest more than previously at the current real interest rate. Therefore, the rate has to rise to induce individuals to save the additional amount that firms want to invest.[14] Conversely, if investment opportunities deteriorate, there will be a fall in the real interest rate.

Thus the real rate of interest depends on the balance of saving and investment in the overall economy.[15] A high aggregate willingness to save may be associated with high aggregate wealth (because wealthy people usually save more), an uneven distribution of wealth (an even distribution would mean fewer rich people who do most of the saving), and a high proportion of middle-aged people (the young don't need to save and the old don't want to—"You can't take it with you"). A high propensity to invest may be associated with a high level of industrial activity or major technological advances.

---

[11] Indexed bonds were not completely unknown in the United States before 1997. For example, in 1780 American Revolutionary soldiers were compensated with indexed bonds that paid the value of "five bushels of corn, 68 pounds and four-seventh parts of a pound of beef, ten pounds of sheep's wool, and sixteen pounds of sole leather."

[12] The reverse happens if there is deflation. In this case the coupon payment and principal amount are adjusted downward. However, the U.S. government guarantees that when the bond matures it will not pay less than its original face value.

[13] Some of this saving is done indirectly. For example, if you hold 100 shares of Tata Motors stock, and Tata Motors retains and reinvests earnings of ₹1.00 a share, Tata Motors is saving ₹100 on your behalf. The government may also oblige you to save by raising taxes to invest in roads, hospitals, etc.

[14] We assume that investors save more as interest rates rise. It doesn't have to be that way. Suppose that 20 years hence you will need ₹300,000 in today's rupee terms for your children's college tuition. How much will you have to set aside today to cover this obligation? The answer is the present value of a real expenditure of ₹300,000 after 20 years, or $300,000/(1 + \text{real interest rate})^{20}$. The higher the real interest rate, the lower the present value and the less you have to set aside.

[15] Short- and medium-term real interest rates are also affected by the monetary policy of central banks. For example, sometimes central banks keep short-term nominal interest rates low despite significant inflation. The resulting real rates can be negative. Nominal interest rates cannot be negative, however, because investors can simply hold cash. Cash always pays zero interest, which is better than negative interest.

Real interest rates do change but they do so gradually. We can see this by looking at the U.K., where the government has issued indexed bonds since 1982. The green line in Figure 3.8 shows that the real yield to maturity on these bonds has fluctuated within a relatively narrow range, while the yield on nominal government bonds (the brown line) has declined dramatically.

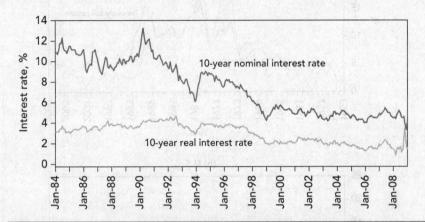

FIGURE 3.8

The green line shows the real yield on long-term indexed bonds issued by the U.K. government. The brown line shows the yield on long-term nominal bonds. Notice that the real yield has been much more stable than the nominal yield.

Inflation and Nominal Interest Rates

How does the inflation outlook affect the nominal rate of interest? Here is how economist Irving Fisher answered the question. Suppose that consumers are equally happy with 100 apples today or 103 apples in a year's time. In this case the real or "apple" interest rate is 3%. If the price of apples is constant at (say) ₹1 each, then we will be equally happy to receive ₹100 today or ₹103 at the end of the year. That extra ₹3 will allow us to buy 3% more apples at the end of the year than we could buy today.

But suppose now that the apple price is expected to increase by 5% to ₹1.05 each. In that case we would *not* be happy to give up ₹100 today for the promise of ₹103 next year. To buy 103 apples in a year's time, we will need to receive $1.05 \times ₹103 = ₹108.15$. In other words, the nominal rate of interest must increase by the expected rate of inflation to 8.15%.

This is Fisher's theory: A change in the expected inflation rate causes the same proportionate change in the *nominal* interest rate; it has no effect on the required real interest rate. The formula relating the nominal interest rate and expected inflation is

$$1 + r_{normal} = (1 + r_{real})(1 + i)$$

where r_{real} is the real interest rate that consumers require and i is the expected inflation rate. In our example, the prospect of inflation causes $1 + r_{nominal}$ to rise to $1.03 \times 1.05 = 1.0815$.

Not all economists would agree with Fisher that the real rate of interest is unaffected by the inflation rate. For example, if changes in prices are associated with changes in the level of industrial activity, then in inflationary conditions I might want more or less than 103 apples in a year's time to compensate me for the loss of 100 today.

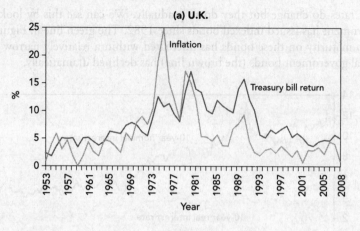

FIGURE 3.9

The return on Treasury bills and the rate of inflation in the U.K., U.S., and Germany, 1953–2008.

Source: E. Dimson, P. R. Marsh, and M. Staunton, *Triumph of the Optimists: 101 Years of Investment Returns* (Princeton, NJ: Princeton University Press, 2002), with updates provided by the authors.

We wish we could show you the past behavior of interest rates and *expected* inflation. Instead we have done the next best thing and plotted in Figure 3.9 the return on Treasury bills (short-term government debt) against *actual* inflation for the U.S., U.K., and Germany. Notice that since 1953 the return on Treasury bills has generally been a little above the rate of inflation. Investors in each country earned an average real return of between 1% and 2% during this period.

Look now at the relationship between the rate of inflation and the Treasury bill rate. Figure 3.9 shows that investors have for the most part demanded a higher rate of interest when inflation was high. So it looks as if Fisher's theory provides a useful rule of thumb for financial managers. If the expected inflation rate changes, it is a good bet that there will be a corresponding change in the interest rate. In other words, a strategy of rolling over short-term investments affords some protection against uncertain inflation.

We show the movement of the inflation rate and the yield on short-term government securities from 1975 in Figure 3.9(a). The dark line represents the year-to-year movement of the inflation rate (rate of increase in the Consumer Price Index) and the dotted line represents the yield on the short-term government securities. We see that the yield on the G-Sec is now always greater than the inflation rate. The average real rate of return during this time period is 1.23%.

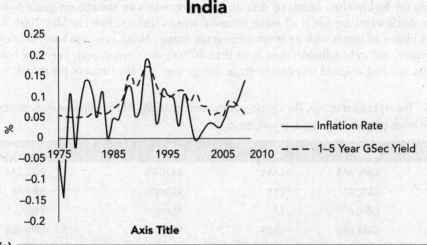

FIGURE 3.9(A)
The inflation rate and the yield on short-term government securities from 1975–2010.

3-6 CORPORATE BONDS AND THE RISK OF DEFAULT

Our focus so far has been on Indian Government securities and U.S. Treasury bonds. But these are not the only issuer of bonds. State governments and, public sector units borrow by selling bonds.[16] So do the companies in the private sector. Indian companies also borrow dollars and other foreign currencies by selling bonds outside India. They may even issue dollar bonds in London that are then sold to investors throughout the world.

---

[16] These *municipal bonds* enjoy a special tax advantage, because investors are exempt from federal income tax on the coupon payments on state and local government bonds. As a result, investors accept lower pretax yields on "munis."

National governments don't go bankrupt—they just print more money. But they can't print money of other countries.[17] Therefore, when a foreign government borrows dollars, investors worry that in some future crisis the government may not be able to come up with enough dollars to repay the debt. This worry shows up in bond prices and yields to maturity. For example, in 2008 a collapse in the Ukrainian exchange rate raised the cost of servicing the country's foreign debts. Despite a bailout from the International Monetary Fund, bondholders worried that the Ukrainian government would not be able to service the dollar bonds that it had issued. By early 2009, the promised yield on Ukrainian government debt had climbed to 25 percentage points above the yield on U.S. Treasuries.

Corporations that get into financial distress may also be forced to default on their bonds. Thus the payments promised to corporate bondholders represent a best-case scenario: The firm will never pay more than the promised cash flows, but in hard times it may pay less.

The safety of most CRISIL, ICRA, CARE, FITCH India and Brickwork Ratings. Table 3.5 lists the possible bond ratings in declining order of quality. For example, the bonds that receive the highest CRISIL AAA rating are known as AAA (or "triple A") bonds. Then come AA (double A), A, BBB bonds, and so on. Bonds rated BBB and above are called **investment grade,** while those with a rating of BB or below are referred to as *speculative grade, high-yield,* or **junk bonds.**

It is rare for highly rated bonds to default. However, when an investment-grade bond does go under, the shock waves are felt in all major financial centers. For example, in May 2001 WorldCom sold $11.8 billion of bonds with an investment-grade rating. About one year later, WorldCom filed for bankruptcy, and its bondholders lost more than 80% of their investment. For those bondholders, the agencies that had assigned investment-grade ratings were not the flavor of the month.

TABLE 3.5 The key to bond ratings. The highest-quality bonds rated BAA/BBB or above are investment grade. Lower-rated bonds are called high-yield, or junk, bonds.

CRISIL	CARE	ICRA	FITCH	BRICKWORKS
AAA	CARE AAA	LAAA	AAA(Ind)	BWR AAA
AA	CARE AA	LAA	AA(Ind)	BWR AA
A	CARE A	LA	A(Ind)	BWRA
BBB	CARE BBB	LBBB	BBB(Ind)	BWR BBB
BB	CARE BB	LBB	BB(Ind)	BWR BB
B	CARE B	LB	B(Ind)	BWR B
C	CARE C	LC	CCC(Ind), CC(Ind), C(Ind)	BWR C
D	CARE D	LD	D(Ind)	BWRD

As you would expect, yields on corporate bonds vary with the bond rating. Figure 3.10 shows the yield spread of corporate bonds against U.S. Treasuries. Notice how spreads widen as safety falls off.

The credit crunch that began in 2008 saw a dramatic widening in yield spreads. Look at Table 3.6, which shows the prices and yields in December 2008 for a sample of corporate bonds

[17] The U.S. government can print dollars and the Japanese government can print yen. But governments in the Eurozone don't even have the luxury of being able to print their own currency. For example, during the 2008 credit crisis, investors worried that the Greek government would not be able to service its euro debts. At one point Greek bonds yielded 3% more than equivalent German government bonds.

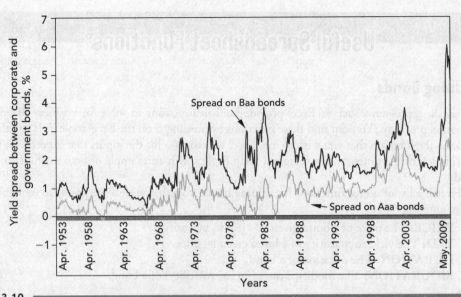

FIGURE 3.10

Yield spreads between corporate and 10-year Treasury bonds.

TABLE 3.6   Prices and yields of a sample of corporate bonds, December 2008.

Source: Bond transactions reported on FINRA's TRACE service: **http://cxa.marketwatch.com/finra/BondCenter**.

Issuer	Coupon	Maturity	S&P Rating	Price, % of Face Value	Yield to Maturity
Pfizer	4.65%	2018	AAA	104.00%	4.12%
Wal-Mart	6.75	2023	AA	111.45	5.60
DuPont	6	2018	A	101.97	5.73
ConAgra	9.75	2021	BBB	111.00	8.30
Woolworth	8.50	2022	BB	93.99	9.30
Eastman Kodak	9.20	2021	B	70.00	14.46
General Motors	8.8	2021	CCC	16.66	56.78

ranked by Standard & Poor's rating. The yield on General Motors bonds exceeded 50%. That may seem like a mouth-watering rate of return, but investors foresaw that GM was likely to go bankrupt and that bond investors would not get their money back.

The yields to maturity reported in Table 3.6 depend on the probability of default, the amount recovered by the bondholder in the event of default, and also on *liquidity*. Corporate bonds are less liquid than Treasuries: they are more difficult and expensive to trade, particularly in large quantities or on short notice. Many investors value liquidity and will demand a higher interest rate on a less liquid bond. Lack of liquidity accounts for some of the spread between yields on corporate and Treasury bonds.

Useful Spreadsheet Functions

Valuing Bonds

Spreadsheet programs such as Excel provide built-in functions to solve for a variety of bond valuation problems. You can find these functions by pressing *fx* on the Excel toolbar. If you then click on the function that you wish to use, Excel will ask you for the inputs that it needs. At the bottom left of the function box there is a Help facility with an example of how the function is used.

Here is a list of useful functions for valuing bonds, together with some points to remember when entering data:

- **PRICE:** The price of a bond given its yield to maturity.
- **YLD:** The yield to maturity of a bond given its price.
- **DURATION:** The duration of a bond.
- **MDURATION:** The modified duration (or volatility) of a bond.

Note:

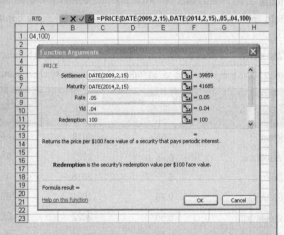

- You can enter all the inputs in these functions directly as numbers or as the addresses of cells that contain the numbers.
- You must enter the yield and coupon as decimal values, for example, for 3% you would enter .03.
- Settlement is the date that payment for the security is made. Maturity is the maturity date. You can enter these dates directly using the Excel date function, for example, you would enter 15 Feb 2009 as DATE(2009,02,15). Alternatively, you can enter these dates in a cell and then enter the cell address in the function.
- In the functions for PRICE and YLD you need to scroll down in the function box to enter the frequency of coupon payments. Enter 1 for annual payments or 2 for semiannual.
- The functions for PRICE and YLD ask for an entry for "basis." We suggest you leave this blank. (See the Help facility for an explanation.)

Spreadsheet Questions

The following questions provide an opportunity to practice each of these functions.

3.1 (PRICE) In March 2011, 8.08% GS of 2022 yielded 8.12% (See Figure 3.1). What was their price? If the yield rose to 9%, what would happen to the price?

3.2 (YLD) On the same day 8.13% GS of 2022 was priced at ₹100.15 (see Figure 3.1). What was their yield to maturity? Suppose that the price was ₹110. What would happen to the yield?

3.3 (DURATION) What was the duration of the 7.17% GS of 2015? How would the duration change, if the yield rose to 8.5%? Can you explain why?

3.4 (MDURATION) What was the modified duration of the above security? How would modified duration differ if the coupon were only 4%?

Corporate Bonds Come in Many Forms

Most corporate bonds are similar to the government bonds that we have analyzed in this chapter. In other words, they promise to make a fixed nominal coupon payment for each year until maturity, at which point they also promise to repay the face value. However, you will find that corporate bonds offer far greater variety than governments. Here are just two examples.

Floating-Rate Bonds   Some corporate bonds are *floating rate*. They make coupon payments that are tied to some measure of current market rates. The rate might be reset once a year to the current short-term Treasury rate plus a spread of 2%, for example. So if the Treasury bill rate at the start of the year is 6%, the bond's coupon rate over the next year is set at 8%. This arrangement means that the bond's coupon rate always approximates current market interest rates.

Convertible Bonds   If you buy a convertible bond, you can choose later to exchange it for a specified number of shares of common stock. For example, a convertible bond that is issued at a face value of ₹1,000 may be convertible into 50 shares of the firm's stock. Because convertible bonds offer the opportunity to participate in any price appreciation of the company's stock, convertibles can be issued at lower coupon rates than plain-vanilla bonds.

We have only skimmed the differences between government and corporate bonds. More detail follows in several later chapters, including Chapters 23 and 24. But you have a sufficient start for now.

SUMMARY

Bonds are simply long-term loans. If you own a bond, you are entitled to a regular interest (or *coupon*) payment and at maturity you get back the bond's face value (or *principal*). In India, coupons are normally paid every six months, but in other countries they may be paid annually.

The value of any bond is equal to its cash payments discounted at the spot rates of interest. For example, the present value of a 10-year bond with a 5% coupon paid annually equals

$$\text{PV}(\% \text{ of face value}) = \frac{5}{(1+r_1)} + \frac{5}{(1+r_2)^2} + \cdots + \frac{105}{(1+r_{10})^{10}}$$

This calculation uses a different spot rate of interest for each period. A plot of spot rates by maturity shows the term structure of interest rates.

Spot interest rates are most conveniently calculated from the prices of strips, which are bonds that make a single payment of face value at maturity, with zero coupons along the way. The price of a strip maturing in a future date t reveals the discount factor and spot rate for cash flows at that date. All other safe cash payments on that date are valued at that same spot rate.

Investors and financial managers use the yield to maturity on a bond to summarize its prospective return. To calculate the yield to maturity on the 10-year 5s, you need to solve for y in the following equation:

$$PV(\% \text{ of face value}) = \frac{5}{(1+y)} + \frac{5}{(1+y)^2} + \cdots + \frac{105}{(1+y)^{10}}$$

The yield to maturity discounts all cash payments at the same rate, even if spot rates differ. Notice that the yield to maturity for a bond can't be calculated until you know the bond's price or present value.

A bond's maturity tells you the date of its final payment, but it is also useful to know the *average* time to each payment. This is called the bond's *duration*. Duration is important because there is a direct relationship between the duration of a bond and the exposure of its price to changes in interest rates. A change in interest rates has a greater effect on the price of long-duration bonds.

The term structure of interest rates is upward-sloping more often than not. This means that long-term spot rates are higher than short-term spot rates. But it does *not* mean that investing long is more profitable than investing short. The *expectations theory* of the term structure tells us that bonds are priced so that an investor who holds a succession of short bonds can expect the same return as another investor who holds a long bond. The expectations theory predicts an upward-sloping term structure only when future short-term interest rates are expected to rise.

The expectations theory cannot be a complete explanation of term structure if investors are worried about risk. Long bonds may be a safe haven for investors with long-term fixed liabilities. But other investors may not like the extra volatility of long-term bonds or may be concerned that a sudden burst of inflation may largely wipe out the real value of these bonds. These investors will be prepared to hold long-term bonds only if they offer the compensation of a higher rate of interest.

Bonds promise fixed nominal cash payments, but the *real* interest rate that they provide depends on inflation. The best-known theory about the effect of inflation on interest rates was suggested by Irving Fisher. He argued that the nominal, or money, rate of interest is equal to the required real rate plus the expected rate of inflation. If the expected inflation rate increases by 1%, so too will the money rate of interest. During the past 50 years Fisher's simple theory has not done a bad job of explaining changes in short-term interest rates.

When you buy an Indian Government Security, you can be confident that you will get your money back. When you lend to a company, you face the risk that it will go belly-up and will not be able to repay its bonds. Defaults are rare for companies with investment-grade bond ratings, but investors worry nevertheless. Companies need to compensate investors for default risk by promising to pay higher rates of interest.

FURTHER READING

A good general text on debt markets is:

S. Sundaresan, *Fixed Income Markets and Their Derivatives,* 3rd ed. (San Diego, CA: Academic Press, 2009).

Schaefer's paper is a good review of duration and how it is used to hedge fixed liabilities:

A.M. Schaefer, "Immunisation and Duration: A Review of Theory, Performance and Application," in *The Revolution in Corporate Finance,* ed. J. M. Stern and D. H. Chew, Jr. (Oxford: Basil Blackwell, 1986).

BASIC

1. A 10-year bond is issued with a face value of ₹1,000, paying interest of ₹60 a year. If market yields increase shortly after the T-bond is issued, what happens to the bond's
   a. Coupon rate?
   b. Price?
   c. Yield to maturity?
2. The following statements are true. Explain why.
   a. If a bond's coupon rate is higher than its yield to maturity, then the bond will sell for more than face value.
   b. If a bond's coupon rate is lower than its yield to maturity, then the bond's price will increase over its remaining maturity.
3. In March 2011, 8.3%–2040 G-Secs offered a semiannually compounded yield of 8.38%. Recognizing that coupons are paid semiannually, calculate the security's price.

eXcel
Visit us at
www.mhhe.com/bmam10e

4. Here are the prices of three bonds with 10-year maturities:

eXcel
Visit us at
www.mhhe.com/bmam10e

Bond Coupon (%)	Price (%)
2	81.62
4	98.39
8	133.42

   If coupons are paid annually, which bond offered the highest yield to maturity? Which had the lowest? Which bonds had the longest and shortest durations?
5. Construct some simple examples to illustrate your answers to the following:
   a. If interest rates rise, do bond prices rise or fall?
   b. If the bond yield is greater than the coupon, is the price of the bond greater or less than 100?
   c. If the price of a bond exceeds 100, is the yield greater or less than the coupon?
   d. Do high-coupon bonds sell at higher or lower prices than low-coupon bonds?
   e. If interest rates change, does the price of high-coupon bonds change proportionately more than that of low-coupon bonds?
6. Which comes first in the market for U.S. Treasury bonds:
   a. Spot interest rates or yields to maturity?
   b. Bond prices or yields to maturity?
7. Look again at Table 3.4. Suppose that spot interest rates all change to 4%—a "flat" term structure of interest rates.
   a. What is the new yield to maturity for each bond in the table?
   b. Recalculate the price of bond A.

eXcel
Visit us at
www.mhhe.com/bmam10e

8. a. What is the formula for the value of a two-year, 5% bond in terms of spot rates?
   b. What is the formula for its value in terms of yield to maturity?
   c. If the two-year spot rate is higher than the one-year rate, is the yield to maturity greater or less than the two-year spot rate?
9. The following table shows the prices of a sample of U.S. Treasury strips in August 2009. Each strip makes a single payment of $1,000 at maturity.
   a. Calculate the annually compounded, spot interest rate for each year.
   b. Is the term structure upward- or downward-sloping, or flat?
   c. Would you expect the yield on a coupon bond maturing in August 2013 to be higher or lower than the yield on the 2013 strip?

Maturity	Price (%)
August 2010	99.423
August 2011	97.546
August 2012	94.510
August 2013	90.524

10. a.   An 8%, five-year bond yields 6%. If the yield remains unchanged, what will be its price one year hence? Assume annual coupon payments.

b. What is the total return to an investor who held the bond over this year?

c. What can you deduce about the relationship between the bond return over a particular period and the yields to maturity at the start and end of that period?

11. True or false? Explain.

a. Longer-maturity bonds necessarily have longer durations.

b. The longer a bond's duration, the lower its volatility.

c. Other things equal, the lower the bond coupon, the higher its volatility.

d. If interest rates rise, bond durations rise also.

12. Calculate the durations and volatilities of securities A, B, and C. Their cash flows are shown below. The interest rate is 8%.

Visit us at
www.mhhe.com/bmam10e

	Period 1	Period 2	Period 3
A	40	40	40
B	20	20	120
C	10	10	110

13. The one-year spot interest rate is $r_1 = 5\%$ and the two-year rate is $r_2 = 6\%$. If the expectations theory is correct, what is the expected one-year interest rate in one year's time?

14. The two-year interest rate is 10% and the expected annual inflation rate is 5%.

a. What is the expected real interest rate?

b. If the expected rate of inflation suddenly rises to 7%, what does Fisher's theory say about how the real interest rate will change? What about the nominal rate?

INTERMEDIATE

15. A 10-year German government bond (bund) has a face value of €100 and a coupon rate of 5% paid annually. Assume that the interest rate (in euros) is equal to 6% per year. What is the bond's PV?

Visit us at
www.mhhe.com/bmam10e

16. A 10-year U.S. Treasury bond with a face value of $10,000 pays a coupon of 5.5% (2.75% of face value every six months). The semiannually compounded interest rate is 5.2% (a six-month discount rate of $5.2/2 = 2.6\%$).

Visit us at
www.mhhe.com/bmam10e

a. What is the present value of the bond?

b. Generate a graph or table showing how the bond's present value changes for semiannually compounded interest rates between 1% and 15%.

17. A six-year government bond makes annual coupon payments of 5% and offers a yield of 3% annually compounded. Suppose that one year later the bond still yields 3%. What return has the bondholder earned over the

Visit us at
www.mhhe.com/bmam10e

12-month period? Now suppose that the bond yields 2% at the end of the year. What return would the bondholder earn in this case?

18. A 6% six-year bond yields 12% and a 10% six-year bond yields 8%. Calculate the six-year spot rate. Assume annual coupon payments. (*Hint:* What would be your cash flows if you bought 1.2 10% bonds?)

Visit us at
www.mhhe.com/bmam10e

19. Is the yield on high-coupon bonds more likely to be higher than that on low-coupon bonds when the term structure is upward-sloping or when it is downward-sloping? Explain.

20. You have estimated spot rates as follows:
$r_1 = 5.00\%$, $r_2 = 5.40\%$, $r_3 = 5.70\%$, $r_4 = 5.90\%$, $r_5 = 6.00\%$.

Visit us at
www.mhhe.com/bmam10e

   a. What are the discount factors for each date (that is, the present value of $1 paid in year t)?
   b. Calculate the PV of the following bonds assuming annual coupons: **(i)** 5%, two-year bond; **(ii)** 5%, five-year bond; and **(iii)** 10%, five-year bond.
   c. Explain intuitively why the yield to maturity on the 10% bond is less than that on the 5% bond.
   d. What should be the yield to maturity on a five-year zero-coupon bond?
   e. Show that the correct yield to maturity on a five-year annuity is 5.75%.
   f. Explain intuitively why the yield on the five-year bonds described in part (c) must lie between the yield on a five-year zero-coupon bond and a five-year annuity.

21. Calculate durations and modified durations for the 4% coupon bond and the strip in Table 3.1. The answers for the strip will be easy. For the 4% bond, you can follow the procedure set out in Table 3.3 for the 11¼% coupon bonds. Confirm that modified duration predicts the impact of a 1% change in interest rates on the bond prices.

Visit us at
www.mhhe.com/bmam10e

22. Find the "live" spreadsheet for Table 3.3 on this book's Web site, **www. mhhe.com/bmam10e**. Show how duration and volatility change if (a) the bond's coupon is 8% of face value and (b) the bond's yield is 6%. Explain your finding.

Visit us at
www.mhhe.com/bmam10e

23. The formula for the duration of a perpetual bond that makes an equal payment each year in perpetuity is (1 + yield)/yield. If each bond yields 5%, which has the longer duration—a perpetual bond or a 15-year zero-coupon bond? What if the yield is 10%?

Visit us at
www.mhhe.com/bmam10e

24. Look up prices of 5 Indian Government securities with different coupons and different maturities. Calculate how their prices would change if their yields to maturity increased by 1 percentage point. Are long- or short-term bonds most affected by the change in yields? Are high- or low-coupon bonds most affected?

Visit us at
www.mhhe.com/bmam10e

25. Look again at Table 3.4. Suppose the spot interest rates change to the following *downward-sloping* term structure: $r_1 = 4.6\%$, $r_2 = 4.4\%$, $r_3 = 4.2\%$, and $r_4 = 4.0\%$. Recalculate discount factors, bond prices, and yields to maturity for each of the bonds listed in the table.

Visit us at
www.mhhe.com/bmam10e

26. Look at the spot interest rates shown in Problem 25. Suppose that someone told you that the five-year spot interest rate was 2.5%. Why would you not believe him? How could you make money if he was right? What is the minimum sensible value for the five-year spot rate?

27. Look again at the spot interest rates shown in Problem 25. What can you deduce about the one-year spot interest rate in three years if . . .

    a. The expectations theory of term structure is right?

    b. Investing in long-term bonds carries additional risks?

28. Suppose that you buy a two-year 8% bond at its face value.

    a. What will be your nominal return over the two years if inflation is 3% in the first year and 5% in the second? What will be your real return?

    b. Now suppose that the bond is a TIPS. What will be your real and nominal returns?

29. A bond's credit rating provides a guide to its price. As we write this in March 2011, AAA bonds yield 5.41% and BAA bonds yield 8.47%. If some bad news causes a 10% five-year bond to be unexpectedly downrated from AAA to BAA, what would be the effect on the bond price? (Assume annual coupons.)

CHALLENGE

30. Write a spreadsheet program to construct a series of bond tables that show the present value of a bond given the coupon rate, maturity, and yield to maturity. Assume that coupon payments are semiannual and yields are compounded semiannually.

31. Find the arbitrage opportunity (opportunities?). Assume for simplicity that coupons are paid annually. In each case the face value of the bond is ₹1,000.

Bond	Maturity (years)	Coupon, ₹	Price, ₹
A	3	0	751.30
B	4	50	842.30
C	4	120	1,065.28
D	4	100	980.57
E	3	140	1,120.12
F	3	70	1,001.62
G	2	0	834.00

32. The duration of a bond that makes an equal payment each year in perpetuity is $(1 + \text{yield})/\text{yield}$. Prove it.

33. What is the duration of a common stock whose dividends are expected to grow at a constant rate in perpetuity?

34. a. What spot and forward rates are embedded in the following Treasury bonds? The price of one-year strips is 93.46%. Assume for simplicity that bonds make only annual payments. (*Hint:* Can you devise a mixture of long and short positions in these bonds that gives a cash payoff only in year 2? In year 3?)

Maturity (years)	Coupon (%)	Price (%)
4	2	94.92
8	3	103.64

    b. A three-year bond with a 4% coupon is selling at 95.00%. Is there a profit opportunity here? If so, how would you take advantage of it?

35. Look one more time at Table 3.4.
   a. Suppose you knew the bond prices but not the spot interest rates. Explain how you would calculate the spot rates. (*Hint:* You have four unknown spot rates, so you need four equations.)
   b. Suppose that you could buy bond C in large quantities at $1,040 rather than at its equilibrium price of $1,058.76. Show how you could make a zillion dollars without taking on any risk.

REAL-TIME DATA ANALYSIS

1. The Web sites of *The Wall Street Journal* (**www.wsj.com**) and the *Financial Times* (**www.ft.com**) are wonderful sources of market data. You should become familiar with them. Use **www.wsj.com** to answer the following questions:
   a. Find the prices of coupon strips. Use these prices to plot the term structure. If the expectations theory is correct, what is the expected one-year interest rate three years hence?
   b. Find a three- or four-year bond and construct a package of coupon and principal strips that provides the same cash flows. The law of one price predicts that the cost of the package should be very close to that of the bond. Is it?
   c. Find a long-term Treasury bond with a low coupon and calculate its duration. Now find another bond with a similar maturity and a higher coupon. Which has the longer duration?
   d. Look up the yields on 10-year nominal Treasury bonds and on TIPS. If you are confident that inflation will average 2% a year, which bond will provide the higher real return?
2. Log on to **www.smartmoney.com** and find the Living Yield Curve, which shows a picture of the yield curve. How does today's yield curve compare with yield curves in the past? Do short-term interest rates move more than long rates?

4

CHAPTER

THE VALUE OF COMMON STOCKS

We should warn you that being a financial expert has its occupational hazards. One is being cornered at cocktail parties by people who are eager to explain their system for making creamy profits by investing in common stocks. One of the few good things about a financial crisis is that these bores tend to disappear, at least temporarily.

We may exaggerate the perils of the trade. The point is that there is no easy way to ensure superior investment performance. Later in the book we show that in well-functioning capital markets it is impossible to predict changes in security prices. Therefore, in this chapter, when we use the concept of present value to price common stocks, we are not promising you a key to investment success; we simply believe that the idea can help you to understand why some investments are priced higher than others.

Why should you care? If you want to know the value of a firm's stock, why can't you look up the stock price in the newspaper? Unfortunately, that is not always possible. For example, you may be the founder of a successful business. You currently own all the shares but are thinking of going public by selling off shares to other investors. You and your advisers need to estimate the price at which those shares can be sold.

There is also another, deeper reason why managers need to understand how shares are valued. If a firm acts in its shareholders' interest, it should accept those investments that increase the value of their stake in the firm. But in order to do this, it is necessary to understand what determines the shares' value.

We begin with a look at how stocks are traded. Then we explain the basic principles of share valuation and the use of discounted-cash-flow (DCF) models to estimate expected rates of return.

These principles lead us to the fundamental difference between growth and income stocks. A growth stock doesn't just grow; its future investments are also expected to earn rates of return that are higher than the cost of capital. It's the *combination* of growth and superior returns that generates high price–earnings ratios for growth stocks. We explain why price–earnings ratios may differ for growth and income stocks. Finally we show how DCF models can be extended to value entire businesses rather than individual shares.

Still another warning: Everybody knows that common stocks are risky and that some are more risky than others. Therefore, investors will not commit funds to stocks unless the expected rates of return are commensurate with the risks. But we say next to nothing in this chapter about the linkages between risk and expected return. A more careful treatment of risk starts in Chapter 7.

4-1 How Common Stocks Are Traded

Infosys has about 571.3 million shares outstanding and at last count these shares were owned by about 403,000 shareholders. They included large pension funds and insurance companies that each own several million shares, as well as individuals who own a handful of shares. If you owned one Infosys share, you would own 0.000000175041% of the company and have a claim on the same tiny fraction of Infosys' profits. Of course, the more shares you own, the larger your "share" of the company.

If Infosys wishes to raise new capital, it can do so either by borrowing or by selling new shares to investors. Sales of shares to raise new capital are said to occur in the *primary market*. However, such sales occur relatively infrequently and most trades in Infosys take place on the stock exchange, where investors buy and sell existing Infosys shares. Stock exchanges are really markets for secondhand shares, but they prefer to describe themselves as *secondary markets,* which sounds more important.

The two principal stock exchanges in India are the National Stock Exchange of India and the Bombay Stock Exchange (BSE). Both compete vigorously for business. The volume of business that they handle is immense. For example, on an average day the NSE trades around 706 million shares in some 1500 companies.

Suppose that Ms. Kamiya, a longtime Infosys shareholder, no longer wishes to hold her shares in the company. She can sell them via the BSE to Mr. Karthik, who wants to increase his stake in the company. The transaction merely transfers partial ownership of the firm from one investor to another. No new shares are created, and Infosys will not care to know that the trade has taken place.

Ms. Kamiya and Mr. Karthik do not trade the Infosys shares directly. Instead, their orders must go through a brokerage firm. Ms. Kamiya, who is anxious to sell, might give her broker a market order to sell stock at the best available price. On the other hand, Mr. Karthik might state a price limit at which he is willing to buy Infosys stock. If his limit order cannot be executed immediately, it is recorded in the exchange's limit order book until it can be executed.

The prices at which stocks trade are summarized in the daily press. Here, for example, is how The *Business Standard's* Web site (**www.business-standard.com/stockpage**) recorded a day's trading in Infosys in March 2011.

52 week High	52 week Low	Closing Price	Day High	Day Low	P/E	Market Cap	Volume
₹3499	₹2510.1	₹3135.35	₹3157.9	₹3109.75	27.41	₹180006.71 crores	95884

You can see that on this day investors traded a total of about 96,000 shares of Infosys stock. By the close of the day, the stock traded at ₹3135.35 a share. Since there were 571 million shares outstanding, investors were placing a total value of ₹180,000 crore on the stock.

Buying stock is a risky occupation. Infosys's stock picked at about ₹3454 in mid-2010. By March 2011, an investor who had bought in at ₹3454 would have lost 8% of his or her investment. Infosys stock traded at ₹3.36 in 1993 (adjusted for all the bonus issues and stock split). Had any fortunate investor bought the share at this price, he would have made a whopping 94,600% return in the 19-year interval. Another unfortunate investor would have lost close to about 50% of his investment had he invested in 2006 and sold in 2008.

4-2 HOW COMMON STOCKS ARE VALUED

Finding the value of Infosys stock may sound like a simple problem. Each quarter, the company publishes a balance sheet, which lists the value of the firm's assets and liabilities. At the end of 2010, the book value of all Infosys' assets—plant and machinery, cash and bank balances, investments, and so on—was ₹27,736 crore. Infosys' liabilities—money that it owes the banks, taxes that are due to be paid, and the like—amounted to ₹4,687 crores. The difference between the value of the assets and the liabilities was ₹23,049 crore. This was the book value of Infosys' equity.

Book value is a reassuringly definite number. Each year, BSR & Co, a member firm of KPMG, gives its opinion that Infosys' financial statements present fairly in all material respects the company's financial position, in conformity with Indian generally accepted accounting principles (commonly called GAAP). However, the book value of Infosys' assets measures their original (or "historical") cost less an allowance for depreciation. This may not be a good guide to what those assets are worth today. When Infosys raised money to invest in various projects, its shares should sell for more than their book value.

Valuation by Comparables

When financial analysts need to value a business, they often start by identifying a sample of similar firms. They then examine how much investors in these companies are prepared to pay for each dollar of assets or earnings. This is often called *valuation by comparables*. Look, for example, at Table 4.1. The first column of numbers shows for some well-known companies the ratio of the market value of the equity to its book value. Notice that market value is generally higher than book value. There are two exceptions; Both HPCL and RCom were selling for less than the book.

The second column of numbers shows the market-to-book ratio for competing firms. For example, you can see from the first row of the table that the stock of the typical large pharmaceutical firm sells for 3.38 times its book value. Therefore, if you did not have the market price of Dr. Reddy's Labs, you might estimate that it would also sell at three times book value. This would give you a stock price of ₹1326, about ₹200 lower than the actual market price.

An alternative would be to look at how much investors in other pharmaceutical stocks are prepared to pay for each rupee of earnings. The first row of Table 4.1 shows that the typical price-earnings (*P/E*) ratio for these stocks is 33.8. If you assumed that Dr. Reddy's Lab should sell at a similar multiple of earnings, you would get a value for the stock of ₹2022, about ₹700 higher than its actual market price in March 2011.

Valuation by comparables would not always give a price that is closer to the actual market price. Look at Reliance Power. It was trading at 140 times its earnings per share (about ₹0.88 per share). If you naively assumed that Reliance Power would sell at similar ratios to comparable power companies, you would have been out by a wide margin. Both the market-to-book ratio and the price–earnings ratio can vary considerably from stock to stock even for firms that are in the same line of business. To understand why this is so, we need to dig deeper and look at what determines a stock's market value.

TABLE 4.1 Market-to-book-value ratios and price–earnings ratios for selected companies and their principal competitors, March 2011.

	Market-to-Book-Value Ratio		Price-Earnings Ratio	
	Company	Competitors*	Company	Competitors*
Bajaj Auto Ltd.	8.21	6.94	16.18	16.22
Dr. Reddy's Laboratories Ltd.	3.95	3.38	25.9	33.8
Bharti Airtel Ltd.	3.02	1.62	16.08	28.41
Reliance Power Ltd.	2.37	1.9	140.67	22.34
Tata Steel Ltd.	1.26	1.87	8.04	13.73
Hindustan Petroleum Corpn. Ltd.	0.96	2,08	9.52	15.78
Reliance Communications Ltd.	0.45	1.62	–21.86	28.41

Source: Prowess Database
* Figures are average ratios for competing companies.

The Determinants of Stock Prices

Think back to Chapter 2, where we described how to value future cash flows. The discounted-cash-flow (DCF) formula for the present value of a stock is just the same as it is for the present value of any other asset. We just discount the cash flows by the return that can be earned in the capital market on securities of comparable risk. Shareholders receive cash from the company in the form of a stream of dividends. So

$$PV(stock) = PV(expected\ future\ dividends)$$

At first sight this statement may seem surprising. When investors buy stocks, they usually expect to receive a dividend, but they also hope to make a capital gain. Why does our formula for present value say nothing about capital gains? As we now explain, there is no inconsistency.

Today's Price

The cash payoff to owners of common stocks comes in two forms: (1) cash dividends and (2) capital gains or losses. Suppose that the current price of a share is P_0, that the expected price at the end of a year is P_1, and that the expected dividend per share is DIV_1. The rate of return that investors expect from this share over the next year is defined as the expected dividend per share DIV_1 plus the expected price appreciation per share $P_1 - P_0$, all divided by the price at the start of the year P_0:

$$Expected\ return = r = \frac{DIV_1 + P_1 - P_0}{P_0}$$

Suppose Fledgling Electronics stock is selling for ₹100 a share ($P_0 = 100$). Investors expect a ₹5 cash dividend over the next year ($DIV_1 = 5$). They also expect the stock to sell for ₹110 a year hence ($P_1 = 110$). Then the expected return to the stockholders is 15%:

$$r = \frac{5 + 110 - 100}{100} = .15, \text{ or } 15\%$$

On the other hand, if you are given investors' forecasts of dividend and price and the expected return offered by other equally risky stocks, you can predict today's price:

$$\text{Price} = P_0 = \frac{DIV_1 + P_1}{1 + r}$$

For Fledgling Electronics $DIV_1 = 5$ and $P_1 = 110$. If r, the expected return for Fledgling is 15%, then today's price should be ₹100:

$$P_0 = \frac{5 + 110}{1.15} = ₹100$$

What exactly is the discount rate, r, in this calculation? It's called the **market capitalization rate** or **cost of equity capital,** which are just alternative names for the opportunity cost of capital, defined as the expected return on other securities with the same risks as Fledgling shares.

Many stocks will be safer than Fledgling, and many riskier. But among the thousands of traded stocks there will be a group with essentially the same risks. Call this group Fledgling's *risk class*. Then all stocks in this risk class have to be priced to offer the same expected rate of return.

Let's suppose that the other securities in Fledgling's risk class all offer the same 15% expected return. Then ₹100 per share has to be the right price for Fledgling stock. In fact it is the only possible price. What if Fledgling's price were above $P_0 = ₹100$? In this case investors would shift their capital to the other securities and in the process would force down the price of Fledgling stock. If P_0 were less than ₹100, the process would reverse. Investors would rush to buy, forcing the price up to ₹100. Therefore at each point in time *all securities in an equivalent risk class are priced to offer the same expected return.* This is a condition for equilibrium in well-functioning capital markets. It is also common sense.

But What Determines Next Year's Price?

We have managed to explain today's stock price P_0 in terms of the dividend DIV_1 and the expected price next year P_1. Future stock prices are not easy things to forecast directly. But think about what determines next year's price. If our price formula holds now, it ought to hold then as well:

$$P_1 = \frac{DIV_2 + P_2}{1 + r}$$

That is, a year from now investors will be looking out at dividends in year 2 and price at the end of year 2. Thus we can forecast P_1 by forecasting DIV_2 and P_2, and we can express P_0 in terms of DIV_1, DIV_2, and P_2:

$$P_0 = \frac{1}{1 + r}(DIV_1 + P_1) = \frac{1}{1 + r}\left(DIV_1 + \frac{DIV_2 + P_2}{1 + r}\right) = \frac{DIV_1}{1 + r} + \frac{DIV_2 + P_2}{(1 + r)^2}$$

Take Fledgling Electronics. A plausible explanation for why investors expect its stock price to rise by the end of the first year is that they expect higher dividends and still more capital gains in the second. For example, suppose that they are looking today for dividends of ₹5.50 in year 2 and a subsequent price of ₹121. That implies a price at the end of year 1 of

$$P_1 = \frac{5.50 + 121}{1.15} = ₹110$$

Today's price can then be computed either from our original formula

$$P_0 = \frac{DIV_1 + P_1}{1 + r} = \frac{5.00 + 110}{1.15} = ₹100$$

or from our expanded formula

$$P_0 = \frac{DIV_1}{1 + r} + \frac{DIV_2 + P_2}{(1 + r)^2} = \frac{5.00}{1.15} + \frac{5.50 + 121}{(1.15)^2} = ₹100$$

We have succeeded in relating today's price to the forecasted dividends for two years (DIV_1 and DIV_2) plus the forecasted price at the end of the *second* year (P_2). You will not be surprised to learn that we could go on to replace P_2 by $(DIV_3 + P_3)/(1 + r)$ and relate today's price to the forecasted dividends for three years (DIV_1, DIV_2, and DIV_3) plus the forecasted price at the end of the *third* year (P_3). In fact we can look as far out into the future as we like, removing Ps as we go. Let us call this final period H. This gives us a general stock price formula:

$$P_0 = \frac{DIV_1}{1 + r} + \frac{DIV_2}{(1 + r)^2} + \cdots + \frac{DIV_H + P_H}{(1 + r)^H}$$

$$= \sum_{t=1}^{H} \frac{DIV_t}{(1 + r)^t} + \frac{P_H}{(1 + r)^H}$$

The expression $\sum_{t=1}^{H}$ indicates the sum of the discounted dividends from year 1 to year H.

Table 4.2 continues the Fledgling Electronics example for various time horizons, assuming that the dividends are expected to increase at a steady 10% compound rate. The expected price P_t increases at the same rate each year. Each line in the table represents an application of our general formula for a different value of H. Figure 4.1 is a graph of the table. Each column shows the present value of the dividends up to the time horizon and the present value of the price at the horizon. As the horizon recedes, the dividend stream accounts for an increasing proportion of present value, but the *total* present value of dividends plus terminal price always equals ₹100.

How far out could we look? In principle, the horizon period H could be infinitely distant. Common stocks do not expire of old age. Barring such corporate hazards as bankruptcy or acquisition, they are immortal. As H approaches infinity, the present value of the terminal price ought to approach zero, as it does in the final column of Figure 4.1. We can, therefore, forget about the terminal price entirely and express today's price as the present value of a perpetual stream of cash dividends. This is usually written as

$$P_0 = \sum_{t=1}^{\infty} \frac{DIV_t}{(1 + r)^t}$$

where ∞ indicates infinity.

TABLE 4.2 Applying the stock valuation formula to Fledgling Electronics.

Assumptions:
1. Dividends increase at 10% per year, compounded.
2. Capitalization rate is 15%.

Horizon Period (H)	Expected Future Values		Present Values		
	Dividend (DIV$_t$)	Price (P$_t$)	Cumulative Dividends	Future Price	Total
0	—	100	—	—	100
1	5.00	110	4.35	95.65	100
2	5.50	121	8.51	91.49	100
3	6.05	133.10	12.48	87.52	100
4	6.66	146.41	16.29	83.71	100
10	11.79	259.37	35.89	64.11	100
20	30.58	672.75	58.89	41.11	100
50	533.59	11,739.09	89.17	10.83	100
100	62,639.15	1,378,061.23	98.83	1.17	100

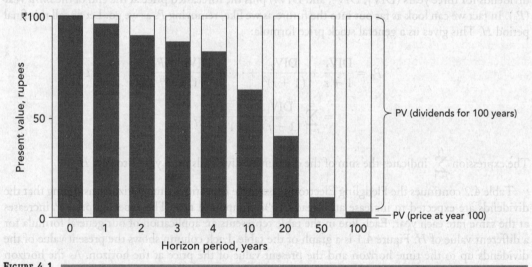

FIGURE 4.1

As your horizon recedes, the present value of the future price (shaded area) declines but the present value of the stream of dividends (unshaded area) increases. The total present value (future price and dividends) remains the same.

This discounted-cash-flow (DCF) formula for the present value of a stock is just the same as it is for the present value of any other asset. We just discount the cash flows—in this case the dividend stream—by the return that can be earned in the capital market on securities of equivalent risk. Some find the DCF formula implausible because it seems to ignore capital gains. But we know that the formula was *derived* from the assumption that price in any period is determined by expected dividends *and* capital gains over the next period.

Notice that it is *not* correct to say that the value of a share is equal to the sum of the discounted stream of earnings per share. Earnings are generally larger than dividends because part of those earnings is reinvested in new plant, equipment, and working capital. Discounting earnings would recognize the rewards of that investment (a higher *future* dividend) but not the sacrifice (a lower dividend *today*). The correct formulation states that share value is equal to the discounted stream of dividends per share.

These days many growth companies do not pay dividends. Any cash that is not plowed back into the company is used to buy back stock. Take Bharti Telecom, for example. Bharti Telecom has never paid a dividend. Yet it is a successful company with a market capitalization of ₹132,078 crore. How can this be consistent with the dividend discount model?

If it were the case that Bharti's shareholders could *never* look forward to receiving a cash dividend or being bought out by another company,[1] then it would indeed be difficult to explain the price of the stock. But sometime in the future profitable investment opportunities for Cisco are likely to become less plentiful, releasing cash that can be paid out as dividends. It is this prospect that accounts for the ₹132,078 crore that shareholders are prepared to pay for the company.

4-3 ESTIMATING THE COST OF EQUITY CAPITAL

In Chapter 2 we encountered some simplified versions of the basic present value formula. Let us see whether they offer any insights into stock values. Suppose, for example, that we forecast a constant growth rate for a company's dividends. This does not preclude year-to-year deviations from the trend: It means only that *expected* dividends grow at a constant rate. Such an investment would be just another example of the growing perpetuity that we valued in Chapter 2. To find its present value we must divide the first year's cash payment by the difference between the discount rate and the growth rate:

$$P_0 = \frac{DIV_1}{r - g}$$

Remember that we can use this formula only when g, the anticipated growth rate, is less than r, the discount rate. As g approaches r, the stock price becomes infinite. Obviously r must be greater than g if growth really is perpetual.

Our growing perpetuity formula explains P_0 in terms of next year's expected dividend DIV_1, the projected growth trend g, and the expected rate of return on other securities of comparable risk r. Alternatively, the formula can be turned around to obtain an estimate of r from DIV_1, P_0, and g:

$$r = \frac{DIV_1}{P_0} + g$$

The expected return equals the **dividend yield** (DIV_1/P_0) plus the expected rate of growth in dividends (g).

These two formulas are much easier to work with than the general statement that "price equals the present value of expected future dividends."[2] Here is a practical example.

---

[1] If Bharti were taken over, any cash payment to Bharti's shareholders would be equivalent to a bumper dividend.

[2] These formulas were first developed in 1938 by Williams and were rediscovered by Gordon and Shapiro. See J. B. Williams, *The Theory of Investment Value* (Cambridge, MA: Harvard University Press, 1938); and M. J. Gordon and E. Shapiro, "Capital Equipment Analysis: The Required Rate of Profit," *Management Science* 3 (October 1956), pp. 102–110.

Using the DCF Model to Set Gas and Electricity Prices

In the United States the prices charged by local electric and gas utilities are regulated by state commissions. The regulators try to keep consumer prices down but are supposed to allow the utilities to earn a fair rate of return. But what is fair? It is usually interpreted as r, the market capitalization rate for the firm's common stock. In other words the fair rate of return on equity for a public utility ought to be the cost of equity, that is, the rate offered by securities that have the same risk as the utility's common stock.[3]

Small variations in estimates of this return can have large effects on the prices charged to the customers and on the firm's profits. So both utilities and regulators work hard to estimate the cost of equity accurately. They've noticed that utilities are mature, stable companies that are tailor-made for application of the constant-growth DCF formula.[4]

Suppose you wished to estimate the cost of equity for Northwest Natural Gas, a local natural gas distribution company. Its stock was selling for $42.45 per share at the start of 2009. Dividend payments for the next year were expected to be $1.68 a share. Thus it was a simple matter to calculate the first half of the DCF formula:

$$\text{Dividend yield} = \frac{\text{DIV}_1}{P_0} = \frac{1.68}{42.45} = .040, \text{ or } 4.0\%$$

The hard part is estimating g, the expected rate of dividend growth. One option is to consult the views of security analysts who study the prospects for each company. Analysts are rarely prepared to stick their necks out by forecasting dividends to kingdom come, but they often forecast growth rates over the next five years, and these estimates may provide an indication of the expected long-run growth path. In the case of Northwest, analysts in 2009 were forecasting an annual growth of 6.1%.[5] This, together with the dividend yield, gave an estimate of the cost of equity capital:

$$r = \frac{\text{DIV}_1}{P_0} + g = .040 + .061 = .101, \text{ or } 10.1$$

An alternative approach to estimating long-run growth starts with the **payout ratio,** the ratio of dividends to earnings per share (EPS). For Northwest, this was forecasted at 60%. In other words, each year the company was plowing back into the business about 40% of earnings per share:

$$\text{Plowback ratio} = 1 - \text{payout ratio} = 1 - \frac{\text{DIV}}{\text{EPS}} = 1 - .60 = .40$$

---

[3] This is the accepted interpretation of the U.S. Supreme Court's directive in 1944 that "the returns to the equity owner [of a regulated business] should be commensurate with returns on investments in other enterprises having corresponding risks." *Federal Power Commission v. Hope Natural Gas Company,* 302 U.S. 591 at 603.

[4] There are many exceptions to this statement. For example, Pacific Gas & Electric (PG&E), which serves northern California, used to be a mature, stable company until the California energy crisis of 2000 sent wholesale electric prices sky-high. PG&E was not allowed to pass these price increases on to retail customers. The company lost more than $3.5 billion in 2000 and was forced to declare bankruptcy in 2001. PG&E emerged from bankruptcy in 2004, but we may have to wait a while before it is again a suitable subject for the constant-growth DCF formula.

[5] In this calculation we're assuming that earnings and dividends are forecasted to grow forever at the same rate g. We show how to relax this assumption later in this chapter. The growth rate was based on the average earnings growth forecasted by Value Line and IBES. IBES compiles and averages forecasts made by security analysts. Value Line publishes its own analysts' forecasts.

Also, Northwest's ratio of earnings per share to book equity per share was about 11%. This is its **return on equity,** or **ROE:**

$$\text{Return on equity} = \text{ROE} = \frac{\text{EPS}}{\text{book equity per share}} = .11$$

If Northwest earns 11% of book equity and reinvests 40% of income, then book equity will increase by $.40 \times .11 = .044$, or 4.4%. Earnings and dividends per share will also increase by 4.4%:

$$\text{Dividend growth rate} = g = \text{plowback ratio} \times \text{ROE} = .40 \times .11 = .044$$

That gives a second estimate of the market capitalization rate:

$$r = \frac{\text{DIV}_1}{P_0} + g = .040 + .044 = .084, \text{ or } 8.4\%$$

Although these estimates of Northwest's cost of equity seem reasonable, there are obvious dangers in analyzing any single firm's stock with the constant-growth DCF formula. First, the underlying assumption of regular future growth is at best an approximation. Second, even if it is an acceptable approximation, errors inevitably creep into the estimate of g.

Remember, Northwest's cost of equity is not its personal property. In well-functioning capital markets investors capitalize the dividends of all securities in Northwest's risk class at exactly the same rate. But any estimate of r for a single common stock is "noisy" and subject to error. Good practice does not put too much weight on single-company estimates of the cost of equity. It collects samples of similar companies, estimates r for each, and takes an average. The average gives a more reliable benchmark for decision making.

The next-to-last column of Table 4.3 gives DCF cost-of-equity estimates for Northwest and seven other gas distribution companies. These are all stable, mature companies for which the constant-growth DCF formula *ought* to work. Notice the variation in the cost-of-equity estimates. Some of the variation may reflect differences in the risk, but some is just noise. The average estimate is 10.2%.

TABLE 4.3 Cost-of-equity estimates for local gas distribution companies at the start of 2009. The long-term growth rate is based on security analysts' forecasts. In the multistage DCF model, growth after five years is assumed to adjust gradually to the estimated long-term growth rate of Gross Domestic Product (GDP).

Company	Dividend Yield	Long-Term Growth Rate	DCF Cost of Equity	Multistage DCF Cost of Equity*
AGL Resources Inc	6.8%	5.0%	11.8%	11.9%
Laclede Group Inc	4.2	2.2	6.4	8.6
Nicor	6.1	5.2	11.3	11.2
Northwest Natural Gas Co	4.0	6.1	10.1	9.2
Piedmont Natural Gas Co	4.6	6.9	11.5	10.1
South Jersey Industries Inc	3.7	7.4	11.1	9.2
Southwest Gas Corp	4.7	6.6	11.3	10.1
WGL Holdings Inc	4.6	3.5	8.0	9.2
		Average:	10.2%	9.9%

* Long-term GDP growth forecasted at 4.9%.
Source: The Brattle Group, Inc.

Table 4.4 gives another example of DCF cost-of-equity estimates, this time for U.S. railroads in 2009.

TABLE 4.4   Cost-of-equity estimates for U.S. railroads mid-2009. The long-term growth rate is based on security analysts' forecasts. In the multistage DCF model, growth after five years is assumed to adjust gradually to the estimated long-term growth rate of Gross Domestic Product (GDP).

Company	Dividend Yield	Long-Term Growth Rate	DCF Cost of Equity	Multistage DCF Cost of Equity*
Burlington Northern Santa Fe	2.2%	11.0%	13.2%	7.9%
CSX	2.4	14.9	17.3	8.9
Norfolk Southern	3.4	12.1	15.5	9.7
Union Pacific	2.1	12.2	14.2	7.9
		Average:	15.1%	8.6%

* Long-term GDP growth forecasted at 4.9%.
Source: The Brattle Group, Inc.

Estimates of this kind are only as good as the long-term forecasts on which they are based. For example, several studies have observed that security analysts are subject to behavioral biases and their forecasts tend to be over-optimistic. If so, such DCF estimates of the cost of equity should be regarded as upper estimates of the true figure.

Dangers Lurk in Constant-Growth Formulas

The simple constant-growth DCF formula is an extremely useful rule of thumb, but no more than that. Naive trust in the formula has led many financial analysts to silly conclusions.

We have stressed the difficulty of estimating r by analysis of one stock only. Try to use a large sample of equivalent-risk securities. Even that may not work, but at least it gives the analyst a fighting chance, because the inevitable errors in estimating r for a single security tend to balance out across a broad sample.

In addition, resist the temptation to apply the formula to firms having high current rates of growth. Such growth can rarely be sustained indefinitely, but the constant-growth DCF formula assumes it can. This erroneous assumption leads to an overestimate of r.

DCF Valuation with Varying Growth Rates   Consider Growth-Tech, Inc., a firm with $DIV_1 = ₹.50$ and $P_0 = ₹50$. The firm has plowed back 80% of earnings and has had a return on equity (ROE) of 25%. This means that *in the past*

$$\text{Dividend growth rate} = \text{plowback ratio} \times \text{ROE} = .80 \times .25 = .20$$

The temptation is to assume that the future long-term growth rate g also equals .20. This would imply

$$r = \frac{.50}{50.00} + .20 = .21$$

But this is silly. No firm can continue growing at 20% per year forever, except possibly under extreme inflationary conditions. Eventually, profitability will fall and the firm will respond by investing less.

In real life the return on equity will decline gradually over time, but for simplicity let's assume it suddenly drops to 16% at year 3 and the firm responds by plowing back only 50% of earnings. Then g drops to $.50 \times .16 = .08$.

Table 4.5 shows what's going on. Growth-Tech starts year 1 with book equity of ₹10.00 per share. It earns ₹2.50, pays out 50 cents as dividends, and plows back ₹2. Thus it starts year 2 with book equity of ₹10 + 2 = ₹12. After another year at the same ROE and payout, it starts year 3 with equity of ₹14.40. However, ROE drops to .16, and the firm earns only ₹2.30. Dividends go up to ₹1.15, because the payout ratio increases, but the firm has only ₹1.15 to plow back. Therefore subsequent growth in earnings and dividends drops to 8%.

TABLE 4.5 Forecasted earnings and dividends for Growth-Tech. Note the changes in year 3: ROE and earnings drop, but payout ratio increases, causing a big jump in dividends. However, subsequent growth in earnings and dividends falls to 8% per year. Note that the increase in equity equals the earnings not paid out as dividends.

	Year			
	1	2	3	4
Book equity	10.00	12.00	14.40	15.55
Earnings per share, EPS	2.50	3.00	2.30	2.49
Return on equity, ROE	.25	.25	.16	.16
Payout ratio	.20	.20	.50	.50
Dividends per share, DIV	.50	.60	1.15	1.24
Growth rate of dividends (%)	—	20	92	8

Now we can use our general DCF formula:

$$P_0 = \frac{DIV_1}{1+r} + \frac{DIV_2}{(1+r)^2} + \frac{DIV_3 + P_3}{(1+r)^3}$$

Investors in year 3 will view Growth-Tech as offering 8% per year dividend growth. So we can use the constant-growth formula to calculate P_3:

$$P_3 = \frac{DIV_4}{r - .08}$$

$$P_0 = \frac{DIV_1}{1+r} + \frac{DIV_2}{(1+r)^2} + \frac{DIV_3}{(1+r)^3} + \frac{1}{(1+r)^3} \times \frac{DIV_4}{r - .08}$$

$$= \frac{.50}{1+r} + \frac{.60}{(1+r)^2} + \frac{1.15}{(1+r)^3} + \frac{1}{(1+r)^3} \times \frac{1.24}{r - .08}$$

We have to use trial and error to find the value of r that makes P_0 equal ₹50. It turns out that the r implicit in these more realistic forecasts is approximately .099, quite a difference from our "constant-growth" estimate of .21.

Our present value calculations for Growth-Tech used a *two-stage* DCF valuation model. In the first stage (years 1 and 2), Growth-Tech is highly profitable (ROE = 25%), and it plows back 80% of earnings. Book equity, earnings, and dividends increase by 20% per year. In the second stage, starting in year 3, profitability and plowback decline, and earnings settle into long-term growth at 8%. Dividends jump up to ₹1.15 in year 3, and then also grow at 8%.

Growth rates can vary for many reasons. Sometimes growth is high in the short run not because the firm is unusually profitable, but because it is recovering from an episode of *low* profitability. Table 4.6 displays projected earnings and dividends for Phoenix Corp., which is gradually regaining financial health after a near meltdown. The company's equity is growing at a moderate 4%. ROE in year 1 is only 4%, however, so Phoenix has to reinvest all its earnings, leaving no cash for dividends. As profitability increases in years 2 and 3, an increasing dividend can be paid. Finally, starting in year 4, Phoenix settles into steady-state growth, with equity, earnings, and dividends all increasing at 4% per year.

TABLE 4.6 Forecasted earnings and dividends for Phoenix Corp. The company can initiate and increase dividends as profitability (ROE) recovers. Note that the increase in book equity equals the earnings not paid out as dividends.

	Year			
	1	**2**	**3**	**4**
Book equity at start of year	10.00	10.40	10.82	11.25
Earnings per share, EPS	.40	.73	1.08	1.12
Return on equity, ROE	.04	.07	.10	.10
Dividends per share, DIV	0	.31	.65	.67
Growth rate of dividends (%)	—	—	110	4

Assume the cost of equity is 10%. Then Phoenix shares should be worth ₹9.13 per share:

$$P_0 = \underbrace{\frac{0}{1.1} + \frac{.31}{(1.1)^2} + \frac{.65}{(1.1)^3}}_{\text{PV (first-stage dividends)}} + \underbrace{\frac{1}{(1.1)^3} \times \frac{.67}{(.10 - .04)}}_{\text{PV (second-stage dividends)}} = \$9.13$$

You could go on to valuation models with three or more stages. For example, the far right columns of Tables 4.3 and 4.4 present multistage DCF estimates of the cost of equity for our local gas distribution companies and railroads. In this case the long-term growth rates reported in the table do not continue forever. After five years, each company's growth rate gradually adjusts to an estimated long-term growth rate for Gross Domestic Product (GDP). The resulting cost-of-equity estimates for the gas distribution companies are fairly similar to the estimates from the simple, perpetual-growth model. The estimates for the railroads are substantially different.

We must leave you with two more warnings about DCF formulas for valuing common stocks or estimating the cost of equity. First, it's almost always worthwhile to lay out a simple spreadsheet, like Table 4.5 or 4.6, to ensure that your dividend projections are consistent with the company's earnings and required investments. Second, be careful about using DCF valuation formulas to test whether the market is correct in its assessment of a stock's value. If your estimate of the value is different from that of the market, it is probably because you have used poor dividend forecasts. Remember what we said at the beginning of this chapter about simple ways of making money on the stock market: there aren't any.

4-4 THE LINK BETWEEN STOCK PRICE AND EARNINGS PER SHARE

Investors separate *growth stocks* from *income stocks*. They buy growth stocks primarily for the expectation of capital gains, and they are interested in the future growth of earnings rather than in next year's dividends. They buy income stocks primarily for the cash dividends. Let us see whether these distinctions make sense.

Imagine first the case of a company that does not grow at all. It does not plow back any earnings and simply produces a constant stream of dividends. Its stock would resemble the perpetual bond described in Chapter 2. Remember that the return on a perpetuity is equal to the yearly cash flow divided by the present value. So the expected return on our share would be equal to the yearly dividend divided by the share price (i.e., the dividend yield). Since all the earnings are paid out as dividends, the expected return is also equal to the earnings per share divided by the share price (i.e., the earnings–price ratio). For example, if the dividend is ₹10 a share and the stock price is ₹100, we have

$$\text{Expected return} = \text{dividend yield} = \text{earnings–price ratio}$$

$$= \frac{DIV_1}{P_0} \qquad = \frac{EPS_1}{P_0}$$

$$= \frac{10.00}{100} \qquad = .10$$

The price equals

$$P_0 = \frac{DIV_1}{r} = \frac{EPS_1}{r} = \frac{10.00}{.10} = 100$$

The expected return for *growing* firms can also equal the earnings–price ratio. The key is whether earnings are reinvested to provide a return equal to the market capitalization rate. For example, suppose our monotonous company suddenly hears of an opportunity to invest ₹10 a share next year. This would mean no dividend at $t = 1$. However, the company expects that in each subsequent year the project would earn ₹1 per share, and therefore the dividend could be increased to ₹11 a share.

Let us assume that this investment opportunity has about the same risk as the existing business. Then we can discount its cash flow at the 10% rate to find its net present value at year 1:

$$\text{Net present value per share at year 1} = -10 + \frac{1}{.10} = 0$$

Thus the investment opportunity will make no contribution to the company's value. Its prospective return is equal to the opportunity cost of capital.

What effect will the decision to undertake the project have on the company's share price? Clearly none. The reduction in value caused by the nil dividend in year 1 is exactly offset by the increase in value caused by the extra dividends in later years. Therefore, once again the market capitalization rate equals the earnings–price ratio:

$$r = \frac{EPS_1}{P_0} = \frac{10}{100} = .10$$

Table 4.7 repeats our example for different assumptions about the cash flow generated by the new project. Note that the earnings–price ratio, measured in terms of EPS_1, next year's expected earnings,

TABLE 4.7   Effect on stock price of investing an additional ₹10 in year 1 at different rates of return. Notice that the earnings–price ratio overestimates r when the project has negative NPV and underestimates it when the project has positive NPV.

Project Rate of Return	Incremental Cash Flow, C	Project NPV in Year 1[a]	Project's Impact on Share Price in Year 0[b]	Share Price in Year 0, P_0	$\dfrac{EPS_1}{P_0}$	r
.05	₹ .50	−₹5.00	−₹4.55	₹ 95.45	.105	.10
.10	1.00	0	0	100.00	.10	.10
.15	1.50	+ 5.00	+ 4.55	104.55	.096	.10
.20	2.00	+ 10.00	+ 9.09	109.09	.092	.10

[a] Project costs ₹10.00 (EPS_1). NPV = $-10 + C/r$, where r = .10.
[b] NPV is calculated at year 1. To find the impact on P_0, discount for one year at r = .10.

equals the market capitalization rate (r) *only* when the new project's NPV = 0. This is an extremely important point—managers frequently make poor financial decisions because they confuse earnings–price ratios with the market capitalization rate.

In general, we can think of stock price as the capitalized value of average earnings under a no-growth policy, plus **PVGO**, the **net present value of growth opportunities**:

$$P_0 = \frac{EPS_1}{r} + PVGO$$

The earnings–price ratio, therefore, equals

$$\frac{EPS}{P_0} = r\left(1 - \frac{PVGO}{P_0}\right)$$

It will underestimate r if PVGO is positive and overestimate it if PVGO is negative. The latter case is less likely, since firms are rarely forced to take projects with negative net present values.

Calculating the Present Value of Growth Opportunities for Fledgling Electronics

In our last example both dividends and earnings were expected to grow, but this growth made no net contribution to the stock price. The stock was in this sense an "income stock". Be careful not to equate firm performance with the growth in earnings per share. A company that reinvests earnings at below the market capitalization rate r may increase earnings but will certainly reduce the share value.

Now let us turn to that well-known growth stock, Fledgling Electronics. You may remember that Fledgling's market capitalization rate, r, is 15%. The company is expected to pay a dividend of ₹5 in the first year, and thereafter the dividend is predicted to increase indefinitely by 10% a year. We can use the simplified constant-growth formula to work out Fledgling's price:

$$P_0 = \frac{DIV_1}{r - g} = \frac{5}{.15 - .10} = ₹100$$

Suppose that Fledgling has earnings per share of EPS_1 = ₹8.33. Its payout ratio is then

$$\text{Payout ratio} = \frac{DIV_1}{EPS_1} = \frac{5.00}{8.33} = .6$$

In other words, the company is plowing back $1 - .6$, or 40% of earnings. Suppose also that Fledgling's ratio of earnings to book equity is ROE $= .25$. This explains the growth rate of 10%:

$$\text{Growth rate} = g = \text{plowback ratio} \times \text{ROE} = .4 \times .25 = .10$$

The capitalized value of Fledgling's earnings per share if it had a no-growth policy would be

$$\frac{\text{EPS}_1}{r} = \frac{8.33}{.15} = ₹55.56$$

But we know that the value of Fledgling stock is ₹100. The difference of ₹44.44 must be the amount that investors are paying for growth opportunities. Let's see if we can explain that figure.

Each year Fledgling plows back 40% of its earnings into new assets. In the first year Fledgling invests ₹3.33 at a permanent 25% return on equity. Thus the cash generated by this investment is $.25 \times 3.33 = ₹.83$ per year starting at $t = 2$. The net present value of the investment as of $t = 1$ is

$$\text{NPV}_1 = -3.33 + \frac{.83}{.15} = ₹2.22$$

Everything is the same in year 2 except that Fledgling will invest ₹3.67, 10% more than in year 1 (remember $g = .10$). Therefore at $t = 2$ an investment is made with a net present value of

$$\text{NPV}_2 = -3.67 + \frac{.83 \times 1.10}{.15} = ₹2.44$$

Thus the payoff to the owners of Fledgling Electronics stock can be represented as the sum of (1) a level stream of earnings, which could be paid out as cash dividends if the firm did not grow, and (2) a set of tickets, one for each future year, representing the opportunity to make investments having positive NPVs. We know that the first component of the value of the share is

$$\text{Present value of level stream of earnings} = \frac{\text{EPS}_1}{r} = \frac{8.33}{.15} = ₹55.56$$

The first ticket is worth ₹2.22 in $t = 1$, the second is worth $₹2.22 \times 1.10 = ₹2.44$ in $t = 2$, the third is worth $₹2.44 \times 1.10 = ₹2.69$ in $t = 3$. These are the forecasted cash values of the tickets. We know how to value a stream of future cash values that grows at 10% per year: Use the constant-growth DCF formula, replacing the forecasted dividends with forecasted ticket values:

$$\text{Present value of growth opportunities} = \text{PVGO} = \frac{\text{NPV}_1}{r - g} = \frac{2.22}{.15 - .10} = ₹44.44$$

Now everything checks:

$$\text{Share price} = \text{present value of level stream of earnings}$$
$$+ \text{present value of growth opportunities}$$
$$= \frac{\text{EPS}_1}{r} + \text{PVGO}$$
$$= ₹55.56 + ₹44.44$$
$$= ₹100$$

Why is Fledgling Electronics a growth stock? Not because it is expanding at 10% per year. It is a growth stock because the net present value of its future investments accounts for a significant fraction (about 44%) of the stock's price.

Today's stock price reflects investor expectations about the earning power of the firm's current and *future* assets. Take Google, for example. All its earnings are plowed back into new investments and the stock sells at 26 times current earnings of $13.31 a share. Suppose that the earnings from Google's existing business are expected to stay constant in real terms. In this case the value of the business is equal to the real earnings divided by an estimated 7.4% real cost of equity:

$$\text{PV assets in place} = 13.31/.074 = ₹180$$

But, as we write this, Google's stock price is $344. So it looks as if investors are valuing Google's future investment opportunities at 344 − 180 = $164. Google is a growth stock because roughly 50% of the stock price comes from the value that investors place on its future investment opportunities.

4-5   VALUING A BUSINESS BY DISCOUNTED CASH FLOW

Investors routinely buy and sell shares of common stock. Companies frequently buy and sell entire businesses or major stakes in businesses. For example, in 2009 *The New York Times* announced that it had retained Goldman Sachs to explore the possible sale of its interest in the Boston Red Sox baseball team. You can be sure that *The New York Times,* Goldman Sachs, and potential purchasers all burned a lot of midnight oil to estimate the value of the business.

Do the discounted-cash-flow formulas we presented in this chapter work for entire businesses as well as for shares of common stock? Sure: It doesn't matter whether you forecast dividends per share or the total free cash flow of a business. Value today always equals future cash flow discounted at the opportunity cost of capital.

Valuing the Concatenator Business

Rumor has it that Establishment Industries is interested in buying your company's concatenator manufacturing operation. Your company is willing to sell if it can get the full value of this rapidly growing business. The problem is to figure out what its true present value is.

Table 4.8 gives a forecast of **free cash flow** (FCF) for the concatenator business. Free cash flow is the amount of cash that a firm can pay out to investors after paying for all investments necessary for growth. As we will see, free cash flow can be negative for rapidly growing businesses.

Table 4.8 is similar to Table 4.5, which forecasted earnings and dividends per share for Growth-Tech, based on assumptions about Growth-Tech's equity per share, return on equity, and the growth of its business. For the concatenator business, we also have assumptions about assets, profitability—in this case, after-tax operating earnings relative to assets—and growth. Growth starts out at a rapid 20% per year, then falls in two steps to a moderate 6% rate for the long run. The growth rate determines the net additional investment required to expand assets, and the profitability rate determines the earnings thrown off by the business.[6]

Free cash flow, the next to last line in Table 4.8, is equal to the firm's earnings less any new investment expenditures. Free cash flow is negative in years 1 through 6. The concatenator business is paying a negative dividend to the parent company; it is absorbing more cash than it is throwing off.

Is that a bad sign? Not really: The business is running a cash deficit not because it is unprofitable, but because it is growing so fast. Rapid growth is good news, not bad, so long as the business is earning

---

[6]Table 4.8 shows *net* investment, which is total investment less depreciation. We are assuming that investment for replacement of existing assets is covered by depreciation and that net investment is devoted to growth.

TABLE 4.8 Forecasts of free cash flow, in ₹ millions, for the Concatenator Manufacturing Division. Rapid expansion in years 1–6 means that free cash flow is negative, because required additional investment outstrips earnings. Free cash flow turns positive when growth slows down after year 6.

	Year									
	1	**2**	**3**	**4**	**5**	**6**	**7**	**8**	**9**	**10**
Asset value	10.00	12.00	14.40	17.28	20.74	23.43	26.47	28.05	29.73	31.51
Earnings	1.20	1.44	1.73	2.07	2.49	2.81	3.18	3.36	3.57	3.78
Net investment	2.00	2.40	2.88	3.46	2.69	3.04	1.59	1.68	1.78	1.89
Free cash flow	−.80	−.96	−1.15	−1.39	−.20	−.23	1.59	1.68	1.79	1.89
Earnings growth from previous period (%)	20	20	20	20	20	13	13	6	6	6

Notes:
1. Starting asset value is ₹10 million. Assets required for the business grow initially at 20% per year, then at 13%, and finally at 6%.
2. Profitability (earnings/asset values) is constant at 12%.
3. Free cash flow equals earnings minus net investment. Net investment equals total capital expenditures less depreciation. Note that earnings are also calculated net of depreciation.

more than the opportunity cost of capital. Your company, or Establishment Industries, will be happy to invest an extra ₹800,000 in the concatenator business next year, so long as the business offers a superior rate of return.

Valuation Format

The value of a business is usually computed as the discounted value of free cash flows out to a *valuation horizon (H),* plus the forecasted value of the business at the horizon, also discounted back to present value. That is,

$$PV = \underbrace{\frac{FCF_1}{1 + r} + \frac{FCF_2}{(1 + r)^2} + \cdots + \frac{FCF_H}{(1 + r)^H}}_{PV(\text{free cash flow})} + \underbrace{\frac{PV_H}{(1 + r)^H}}_{PV(\text{horizon value})}$$

Of course, the concatenator business will continue after the horizon, but it's not practical to forecast free cash flow year by year to infinity. PV_H stands in for free cash flow in periods $H + 1, H + 2$, etc.

Valuation horizons are often chosen arbitrarily. Sometimes the boss tells everybody to use 10 years because that's a round number. We will try year 6, because growth of the concatenator business seems to settle down to a long-run trend after year 7.

Estimating Horizon Value

There are several common formulas or rules of thumb for estimating horizon value. First, let us try the constant-growth DCF formula. This requires free cash flow for year 7, which we have from Table 4.8; a long-run growth rate, which appears to be 6%; and a discount rate, which some high-priced consultant has told us is 10%. Therefore,

$$PV \text{ (horizon value)} = \frac{1}{(1.1)^6}\left(\frac{1.59}{.10 - .06}\right) = 22.4$$

The present value of the near-term free cash flows is

$$\text{PV(cash flows)} = -\frac{.80}{1.1} - \frac{.96}{(1.1)^2} - \frac{1.15}{(1.1)^3} - \frac{1.39}{(1.1)^4} - \frac{.20}{(1.1)^5} - \frac{.23}{(1.1)^6}$$

$$= -3.6$$

and, therefore, the present value of the business is

$$\text{PV(business)} = \text{PV(free cash flow)} + \text{PV(horizon value)}$$
$$= -3.6 \qquad\qquad + 22.4$$
$$= \$18.8 \text{ million}$$

Now, are we done? Well, the mechanics of this calculation are perfect. But doesn't it make you just a little nervous to find that 119% of the value of the business rests on the horizon value? Moreover, a little checking shows that the horizon value can change dramatically in response to apparently minor changes in assumptions. For example, if the long-run growth rate is 8% rather than 6%, the value of the business increases from ₹18.8 to ₹26.3 million.[7]

In other words, it's easy for a discounted-cash-flow business valuation to be mechanically perfect and practically wrong. Smart financial managers try to check their results by calculating horizon value in different ways.

Horizon Value Based on P/E Ratios   Suppose you can observe stock prices for mature manufacturing companies whose scale, risk, and growth prospects today roughly match those projected for the concatenator business in year 6. Suppose further that these companies tend to sell at price—earnings ratios of about 11. Then you could reasonably guess that the price—earnings ratio of a mature concatenator operation will likewise be 11. That implies:

$$\text{PV(horizon value)} = \frac{1}{(1.1)^6}(11 \times 3.18) = 19.7$$

$$\text{PV (business)} = -3.6 + 19.7 = ₹16.1 \text{ million}$$

Horizon Value Based on Market–Book Ratios   Suppose also that the market–book ratios of the sample of mature manufacturing companies tend to cluster around 1.4. If the concatenator business market–book ratio is 1.4 in year 6,

$$\text{PV(horizon value)} = \frac{1}{(1.1)^6}(1.4 \times 23.43) = 18.5$$

$$\text{PV (business)} = -3.6 + 18.5 = ₹14.9 \text{ million}$$

It's easy to poke holes in these last two calculations. Book value, for example, is often a poor measure of the true value of a company's assets. It can fall far behind actual asset values when there

---

[7] If long-run growth is 8% rather than 6%, an extra 2% of period-7 assets will have to be plowed back into the concatenator business. This reduces free cash flow by ₹.53 million to ₹1.06 million. So,

$$\text{PV(horizon value)} = \frac{1}{(1.1)^6}\left(\frac{1.06}{.10 - .08}\right) = ₹29.9$$

$$\text{PV(business)} = -3.6 + 29.9 = ₹26.3 \text{ million}$$

is rapid inflation, and it often entirely misses important intangible assets, such as your patents for concatenator design. Earnings may also be biased by inflation and a long list of arbitrary accounting choices. Finally, you never know when you have found a sample of truly similar companies.

But remember, the purpose of discounted cash flow is to estimate market value—to estimate what investors would pay for a stock or business. When you can *observe* what they actually pay for similar companies, that's valuable evidence. Try to figure out a way to use it. One way to use it is through valuation by comparables, based on price–earnings or market–book ratios. Valuation rules of thumb, artfully employed, sometimes beat a complex discounted-cash-flow calculation hands down.

A Further Reality Check

Here is another approach to valuing a business. It is based on what you have learned about price–earnings ratios and the present value of growth opportunities.

Suppose the valuation horizon is set not by looking for the first year of stable growth, but by asking when the industry is likely to settle into competitive equilibrium. You might go to the operating manager most familiar with the concatenator business and ask:

Sooner or later you and your competitors will be on an equal footing when it comes to major new investments. You may still be earning a superior return on your core business, but you will find that introductions of new products or attempts to expand sales of existing products trigger intense resistance from competitors who are just about as smart and efficient as you are. Give a realistic assessment of when that time will come.

"That time" is the horizon after which PVGO, the net present value of subsequent growth opportunities, is zero. After all, PVGO is positive only when investments can be expected to earn more than the cost of capital. When your competition catches up, that happy prospect disappears.

We know that present value in any period equals the capitalized value of next period's earnings, plus PVGO:

$$PV_t = \frac{\text{earnings}_{t+1}}{r} + PVGO$$

But what if PVGO = 0? At the horizon period H, then,

$$PV_H = \frac{\text{earnings}_{H+1}}{r}$$

In other words, when the competition catches up, the price–earnings ratio equals $1/r$, because PVGO disappears.[8]

---

[8] In other words, we can calculate horizon value *as if* earnings will not grow after the horizon date, because growth will add no value. But what does "no growth" mean? Suppose that the concatenator business maintains its assets and earnings in real (inflation-adjusted) terms. Then nominal earnings will growth at the inflation rate. This takes us back to the constant-growth formula: earnings in period H + 1 should be valued by dividing by r − g, where g in this case equals the inflation rate.

We have simplified the concatenator example. In real-life valuations, with big bucks involved, be careful to track growth from inflation as well as growth from investment. For guidance see M. Bradley and G. Jarrell, "Expected Inflation and the Constant-Growth Valuation Model," *Journal of Applied Corporate Finance* 20 (Spring 2008), pp. 66–78.

Suppose that competition is expected to catch up in period 9. Then we can calculate the horizon value at period 8 as the present value of a level stream of earnings starting in period 9 and continuing indefinitely. The resulting value for the concatenator business is:[9]

$$PV(\text{horizon value}) = \frac{1}{(1+r)^8}\left(\frac{\text{earnings in period 9}}{r}\right)$$

$$= \frac{1}{(1.1)^8}\left(\frac{3.57}{.10}\right)$$

$$= ₹16.7 \text{ million}$$

$$PV(\text{business}) = -2.0 + 16.7 = ₹14.7 \text{ million}$$

We now have four estimates of what Establishment Industries ought to pay for the concatenator business. The estimates reflect four different methods of estimating horizon value. There is no best method, although in many cases we put most weight on the last method, which sets the horizon date at the point when management expects PVGO to disappear. The last method forces managers to remember that sooner or later competition catches up.

Our calculated values for the concatenator business range from ₹14.7 to ₹18.8 million, a difference of about ₹4 million. The width of the range may be disquieting, but it is not unusual. Discounted-cash-flow formulas only estimate market value, and the estimates change as forecasts and assumptions change. Managers cannot know market value for sure until an actual transaction takes place.

SUMMARY

In this chapter we have used our newfound knowledge of present values to examine the market price of common stocks. The value of a stock is equal to the stream of cash payments discounted at the rate of return that investors expect to receive on other securities with equivalent risks.

Common stocks do not have a fixed maturity; their cash payments consist of an indefinite stream of dividends. Therefore, the present value of a common stock is

$$PV = \sum_{t=1}^{\infty} \frac{DIV_t}{(1+r)^t}$$

However, we did not just *assume* that investors purchase common stocks solely for dividends. In fact, we began with the assumption that investors have relatively short horizons and invest for both dividends and capital gains. Our fundamental valuation formula is, therefore,

$$P_0 = \frac{DIV_1 + P_1}{1+r}$$

This is a condition of market equilibrium. If it did not hold, the share would be overpriced or underpriced, and investors would rush to sell or buy it. The flood of sellers or buyers would force the price to adjust so that the fundamental valuation formula holds.

---

[9] Three additional points about this calculation: First, the PV of free cash flow before the horizon improves to −₹2.0 million because inflows in years 7 and 8 are now included. Second, if competition really catches up by year 9, then the earnings shown for year 10 in Table 4.8 are too high, since they include a 12% return on the investment in year 9. Competition would allow only the 10% cost of capital. Third, we assume earnings in year 9 of ₹3.57, 12% on assets of ₹29.73. But competition might force down the rate of return on existing assets in addition to returns on new investment. That is, earnings in year 9 could be only ₹2.97 (10% of ₹29.73). Problem 26 explores these possibilities.

We also made use of the formula for a growing perpetuity presented in Chapter 2. If dividends are expected to grow forever at a constant rate of g, then

$$P_0 = \frac{DIV_1}{r - g}$$

It is often helpful to twist this formula around and use it to estimate the market capitalization rate r, given P_0 and estimates of DIV_1 and g:

$$r = \frac{DIV_1}{P_0} + g$$

Remember, however, that this formula rests on a *very* strict assumption: constant dividend growth in perpetuity. This may be an acceptable assumption for mature, low-risk firms, but for many firms, near-term growth is unsustainably high. In that case, you may wish to use a *two-stage* DCF formula, where near-term dividends are forecasted and valued, and the constant-growth DCF formula is used to forecast the value of the shares at the start of the long run. The near-term dividends and the future share value are then discounted to present value.

The general DCF formula can be transformed into a statement about earnings and growth opportunities:

$$P_0 = \frac{EPS_1}{r} + PVGO$$

The ratio EPS_1/r is the capitalized value of the earnings per share that the firm would generate under a no-growth policy. PVGO is the net present value of the investments that the firm will make in order to grow. A growth stock is one for which PVGO is large relative to the capitalized value of EPS. Most growth stocks are stocks of rapidly expanding firms, but expansion alone does not create a high PVGO. What matters is the profitability of the new investments.

The same formulas that we used to value common shares can also be used to value entire businesses. In that case, we discount not dividends per share but the entire free cash flow generated by the business. Usually a two-stage DCF model is deployed. Free cash flows are forecasted out to a horizon and discounted to present value. Then a horizon value is forecasted, discounted, and added to the value of the free cash flows. The sum is the value of the business.

Valuing a business is simple in principle but not so easy in practice. Forecasting reasonable horizon values is particularly difficult. The usual assumption is moderate long-run growth after the horizon, which allows use of the growing-perpetuity DCF formula at the horizon. Horizon values can also be calculated by assuming "normal" price–earnings or market-to-book ratios at the horizon date.

In earlier chapters you should have acquired—we hope painlessly—a knowledge of the basic principles of valuing assets and a facility with the mechanics of discounting. Now you know something of how common stocks are valued and market capitalization rates estimated. In Chapter 5 we can begin to apply all this knowledge in a more specific analysis of capital budgeting decisions.

FURTHER READING

For a comprehensive review of company valuation, see:

T. Koller, M. Goedhart, and D. Wessels, *Valuation: Measuring and Managing the Value of Companies,* 4th ed. (New York: Wiley, 2005).

Leibowitz and Kogelman call PVGO the "franchise factor." They analyze it in detail in:

M.L. Leibowitz and S. Kogelman, "Inside the P/E Ratio: The Franchise Factor," *Financial Analysts Journal* 46 (November–December 1990), pp. 17–35.

PROBLEM SETS

BASIC

1. True or false?
   a. All stocks in an equivalent-risk class are priced to offer the same expected rate of return.
   b. The value of a share equals the PV of future dividends per share.

2. Respond briefly to the following statement:
   "You say stock price equals the present value of future dividends? That's crazy! All the investors I know are looking for capital gains."

3. Company X is expected to pay an end-of-year dividend of ₹5 a share. After the dividend its stock is expected to sell at ₹110. If the market capitalization rate is 8%, what is the current stock price?

4. Company Y does not plow back any earnings and is expected to produce a level dividend stream of ₹5 a share. If the current stock price is ₹40, what is the market capitalization rate?

5. Company Z's earnings and dividends per share are expected to grow indefinitely by 5% a year. If next year's dividend is ₹10 and the market capitalization rate is 8%, what is the current stock price?

6. Company Z-prime is like Z in all respects save one: Its growth will stop after year 4. In year 5 and afterward, it will pay out all earnings as dividends. What is Z-prime's stock price? Assume next year's EPS is ₹15.

7. If company Z (see Problem 5) were to distribute all its earnings, it could maintain a level dividend stream of ₹15 a share. How much is the market actually paying per share for growth opportunities?

8. Consider three investors:
   a. Mr. Single invests for one year.
   b. Ms. Double invests for two years.
   c. Mrs. Triple invests for three years.
   Assume each invests in company Z (see Problem 5). Show that each expects to earn a rate of return of 8% per year.

9. True or false? Explain.
   a. The value of a share equals the discounted stream of future earnings per share.
   b. The value of a share equals the PV of earnings per share assuming the firm does not grow, plus the NPV of future growth opportunities.

10. Under what conditions does r, a stock's market capitalization rate, equal its earnings–price ratio EPS_1/P_0?

11. What do financial managers mean by "free cash flow"? How is free cash flow calculated? Briefly explain.

12. What is meant by the "horizon value" of a business? How can it be estimated?

13. Suppose the horizon date is set at a time when the firm will run out of positive-NPV investment opportunities. How would you calculate the horizon value? (*Hint:* What is the *P*/EPS ratio when PVGO = 0?)

INTERMEDIATE

14. Look in a recent issue of *The Business Standard* at www.business_standard.com/stockpage.
    a. What is the latest price of Bharti Airtel?
    b. What are the annual dividend payment and the dividend yield on Bharti stock?
    c. What is the P/E on Bharti stock?
    d. Use the P/E to calculate Bharti's earnings per share.
    e. Is Bharti's P/E higher or lower than that of Colgate?
    f. What are the possible reasons for the difference in P/E?

15. Rework Table 4.2 under the assumption that the dividend on Fledgling Electronics is ₹10 next year and that it is expected to grow by 5% a year. The capitalization rate is 15%.

eXcel

Visit us at
www.mhhe.com/bmam10e

16. Consider the following three stocks:
    a. Stock A is expected to provide a dividend of ₹10 a share forever.
    b. Stock B is expected to pay a dividend of ₹5 next year. Thereafter, dividend growth is expected to be 4% a year forever.
    c. Stock C is expected to pay a dividend of ₹5 next year. Thereafter, dividend growth is expected to be 20% a year for five years (i.e., until year 6) and zero thereafter.
    If the market capitalization rate for each stock is 10%, which stock is the most valuable? What if the capitalization rate is 7%?

17. Pharmecology is about to pay a dividend of ₹1.35 per share. It's a mature company, but future EPS and dividends are expected to grow with inflation, which is forecasted at 2.75% per year.
    a. What is Pharmecology's current stock price? The nominal cost of capital is 9.5%.
    b. Redo part (a) using forecasted real dividends and a real discount rate.

18. Company Q's current return on equity (ROE) is 14%. It pays out one-half of earnings as cash dividends (payout ratio = .5). Current book value per share is ₹50. Book value per share will grow as Q reinvests earnings.
    Assume that the ROE and payout ratio stay constant for the next four years. After that, competition forces ROE down to 11.5% and the payout ratio increases to 0.8. The cost of capital is 11.5%.
    a. What are Q's EPS and dividends next year? How will EPS and dividends grow in years 2, 3, 4, 5, and subsequent years?
    b. What is Q's stock worth per share? How does that value depend on the payout ratio and growth rate after year 4?

19. Mexican Motors stock sells for 200 pesos per share and next year's dividend is 8.5 pesos. Security analysts are forecasting earnings growth of 7.5% per year for the next five years.
    a. Assume that earnings and dividends are expected to grow at 7.5% in perpetuity. What rate of return are investors expecting?

b. Mexican Motors has generally earned about 12% on book equity (ROE = .12) and paid out 50% of earnings as dividends. Suppose it maintains the same ROE and payout ratio in the long-run future. What is the implication for g? For r? Should you revise your answer to part (a) of this question?

20. Phoenix Corp. faltered in the recent recession but has recovered since. EPS and dividends have grown rapidly since 2017.

	2017	2018	2019	2020	2021
EPS	₹.75	2.00	2.50	2.60	2.65
Dividends	₹ 0	1.00	2.00	2.30	2.65
Dividend growth	—	—	100%	15%	15%

The figures for 2020 and 2021 are of course forecasts. Phoenix's stock price today in 2019 is ₹21.75. Phoenix's recovery will be complete in 2021, and there will be *no further growth* in EPS or dividends.

A security analyst forecasts *next year's* rate of return on Phoenix stock as follows:

$$r = \frac{DIV}{P} + g = \frac{2.30}{21.75} + .15 = .256, \text{ about } 26\%$$

What's wrong with the security analyst's forecast? What is the actual expected rate of return over the next year?

21. Each of the following formulas for determining shareholders' required rate of return can be right or wrong depending on the circumstances:

a. $r = \dfrac{DIV_1}{P_0} + g$

b. $r = \dfrac{EPS_1}{P_0}$

For each formula construct a *simple* numerical example showing that the formula can give wrong answers and explain why the error occurs. Then construct another simple numerical example for which the formula gives the right answer.

22. Alpha Corp's earnings and dividends are growing at 15% per year. Beta Corp's earnings and dividends are growing at 8% per year. The companies' assets, earnings, and dividends per share are now (at date 0) exactly the same. Yet PVGO accounts for a greater fraction of Beta Corp's stock price. How is this possible? (*Hint:* There is more than one possible explanation.)

23. Look again at the financial forecasts for Growth-Tech given in Table 4.5. This time assume you *know* that the opportunity cost of capital is $r = .12$ (discard the .099 figure calculated in the text). Assume you do *not* know Growth-Tech's stock value. Otherwise follow the assumptions given in the text.
    a. Calculate the value of Growth-Tech stock.
    b. What part of that value reflects the discounted value of P_3, the price forecasted for year 3?
    c. What part of P_3 reflects the present value of growth opportunities (PVGO) after year 3?
    d. Suppose that competition will catch up with Growth-Tech by year 4, so that it can earn only its cost of capital on any investments made in year 4 or subsequently. What is Growth-Tech stock worth now under this assumption? (Make additional assumptions if necessary.)

24. Compost Science, Inc. (CSI), is in the business of converting Boston's sewage sludge into fertilizer. The business is not in itself very profitable. However, to induce CSI to remain in business, the Metropolitan District Commission (MDC) has agreed to pay whatever amount is necessary to yield CSI a 10% book return on equity. At the end of the year CSI is expected to pay a $4 dividend. It has been reinvesting 40% of earnings and growing at 4% a year.

   a. Suppose CSI continues on this growth trend. What is the expected long-run rate of return from purchasing the stock at $100? What part of the $100 price is attributable to the present value of growth opportunities?

   b. Now the MDC announces a plan for CSI to treat Cambridge sewage. CSI's plant will, therefore, be expanded gradually over five years. This means that CSI will have to reinvest 80% of its earnings for five years. Starting in year 6, however, it will again be able to pay out 60% of earnings. What will be CSI's stock price once this announcement is made and its consequences for CSI are known?

25. Permian Partners (PP) produces from aging oil fields in west Texas. Production is 1.8 million barrels per year in 2009, but production is declining at 7% per year for the foreseeable future. Costs of production, transportation, and administration add up to $25 per barrel. The average oil price was $65 per barrel in 2009.

   PP has 7 million shares outstanding. The cost of capital is 9%. All of PP's net income is distributed as dividends. For simplicity, assume that the company will stay in business forever and that costs per barrel are constant at $25. Also, ignore taxes.

   a. What is the PV of a PP share? Assume that oil prices are expected to fall to $60 per barrel in 2010, $55 per barrel in 2011, and $50 per barrel in 2012. After 2012, assume a long-term trend of oil-price increases at 5% per year.

   b. What is PP's EPS/P ratio and why is it not equal to the 9% cost of capital?

26. Construct a new version of Table 4.8, assuming that competition drives down profitability (on existing assets as well as new investment) to 11.5% in year 6, 11% in year 7, 10.5% in year 8, and 8% in year 9 and all later years. What is the value of the concatenator business?

Visit us at
www.mhhe.com/bmam10e

CHALLENGE

27. The constant-growth DCF formula:

$$P_0 = \frac{DIV_1}{r - g}$$

is sometimes written as:

$$P_0 = \frac{ROE(1 - b)BVPS}{r - bROE}$$

where BVPS is book equity value per share, b is the plowback ratio, and ROE is the ratio of earnings per share to BVPS. Use this equation to show how the price-to-book ratio varies as ROE changes. What is price-to-book when $ROE = r$?

28. Portfolio managers are frequently paid a proportion of the funds under management. Suppose you manage a ₹100 million equity portfolio offering a dividend yield (DIV_1/P_0) of 5%. Dividends and portfolio value are expected to grow at a constant rate. Your annual fee for managing this portfolio is .5% of portfolio value and is calculated at the end of each year. Assuming that you will continue to manage the portfolio from now to eternity, what is the present value of the management contract? How would the contract value change if you invested in stocks with a 4% yield?

29. Suppose the concatenator division, which we valued based on Table 4.8, is spun off as an independent company, Concatco, with 1 million shares of common stock outstanding. What would each share sell for? Before answering, notice the negative free cash flows for years 1 to 6. The PV of these cash flows is −₹3.6 million. Assume that this shortfall will have to be financed by additional shares issued in the near future. Also assume for simplicity that the ₹3.6 million earns interest at 10% and is sufficient to cover the negative free cash flows in Table 4.8. Concatco will pay no dividends in years 1 to 6, but will pay out all free cash flow starting in year 7.

Now calculate the value of each of the 1 million existing Concatco shares. Briefly explain your answer. *Hints:* Suppose the existing stockholders, who own 1 million shares, buy newly issued shares to cover the ₹3.6 million financing requirement. In other words, the ₹3.6 million comes directly out of existing stockholders' wallets. What's the value per share? Now suppose instead that the ₹3.6 million comes from new investors, who buy shares at a fair price. Does your answer change?

REAL-TIME DATA ANALYSIS

The major stock exchanges have wonderful Web sites. Look at both the NYSE site (**www.nyse.com**) and the Nasdaq site (**www.nasdaq.com**). You will find plenty of material on their trading systems, and you can also access quotes and other data.

1. Go to **www.nyse.com**. Find *NYSE MarkeTrac* and click on the DJIA ticker tape, which shows trades for the stocks in the Dow Jones Industrial Averages. Stop the tape at GE. What are the latest price, dividend yield, and P/E ratio?

Use data from the Standard & Poor's Market Insight Database at www.mhhe.com/ edumarketinsight or from finance.yahoo.com to answer the following questions.

2. Look up General Mills, Inc., and Kellogg Co. The companies' ticker symbols are GIS and K.

STANDARD &POOR'S

   a. What are the current dividend yield and price–earnings ratio (P/E) for each company? How do the yields and P/Es compare with the average for the food industry and for the stock market as a whole? (The stock market is represented by the S & P 500 index.)

   b. What are the growth rates of earnings per share (EPS) and dividends for each company over the last five years? Do these growth rates appear to reflect a steady trend that could be projected for the long-run future?

   c. Would you be confident in applying the constant-growth DCF valuation model to these companies' stocks? Why or why not?

3. Look up Intel (INTC), Dell Computer (DELL), Dow Chemical (DOW), Harley-Davidson (HOG), and Pfizer, Inc. (PFE). Look at "Financial Highlights" and "Company Profile" for each company. You will note wide differences in these companies' price–earnings ratios. What are the possible explanations for these differences? Which would you classify as growth (high-PVGO) stocks and which as income stocks?

STANDARD &POOR'S

REEBY SPORTS

Ten years ago, in 2001, George Reeby founded a small mail-order company selling high-quality sports equipment. Since those early days Reeby Sports has grown steadily and been consistently profitable. The company has issued 2 million shares, all of which are owned by George Reeby and his five children.

For some months George has been wondering whether the time has come to take the company public. This would allow him to cash in on part of his investment and would make it easier for the firm to raise capital should it wish to expand in the future.

But how much are the shares worth? George's first instinct is to look at the firm's balance sheet, which shows that the book value of the equity is $26.34 million, or $13.17 per share. A share price of $13.17 would put the stock on a P/E ratio of 6.6. That is quite a bit lower than the 13.1 P/E ratio of Reeby's larger rival, Molly Sports.

George suspects that book value is not necessarily a good guide to a share's market value. He thinks of his daughter Jenny, who works in an investment bank. She would undoubtedly know what the shares are worth. He decides to phone her after she finishes work that evening at 9 o'clock or before she starts the next day at 6.00 a.m.

Before phoning, George jots down some basic data on the company's profitability. After recovering from its early losses, the company has earned a return that is higher than its estimated 10% cost of capital. George is fairly confident that the company could continue to grow fairly steadily for the next six to eight years. In fact he feels that the company's growth has been somewhat held back in the last few years by the demands from two of the children for the company to make large dividend payments. Perhaps, if the company went public, it could hold back on dividends and plow more money back into the business.

There are some clouds on the horizon. Competition is increasing and only that morning Molly Sports announced plans to form a mail-order division. George is worried that beyond the next six or so years it might become difficult to find worthwhile investment opportunities.

George realizes that Jenny will need to know much more about the prospects for the business before she can put a final figure on the value of Reeby Sports, but he hopes that the information is sufficient for her to give a preliminary indication of the value of the shares.

	2002	2003	2004	2005	2006	2007	2008	2009	2010	2011E
Earnings per share, $	−2.10	−0.70	0.23	0.81	1.10	1.30	1.52	1.64	2.00	2.03
Dividend, $	0.00	0.00	0.00	0.20	0.20	0.30	0.30	0.60	0.60	0.80
Book value per share, $	9.80	7.70	7.00	7.61	8.51	9.51	10.73	11.77	13.17	14.40
ROE, %	−27.10	−7.1	3.0	11.6	14.5	15.3	16.0	15.3	17.0	15.4

Questions

1. Help Jenny to forecast dividend payments for Reeby Sports and to estimate the value of the stock. You do not need to provide a single figure. For example, you may wish to calculate two figures, one on the assumption that the opportunity for further profitable investment is reduced in year 6 and another on the assumption that it is reduced in year 8.

2. How much of your estimate of the value of Reeby's stock comes from the present value of growth opportunities?

5

NET PRESENT VALUE AND OTHER INVESTMENT CRITERIA

A company's shareholders prefer to be rich rather than poor. Therefore, they want the firm to invest in every project that is worth more than it costs. The difference between a project's value and its cost is its *net present value (NPV)*. Companies can best help their shareholders by investing in all projects with a positive NPV and rejecting those with a negative NPV.

We start this chapter with a review of the net present value rule. We then turn to some other measures that companies may look at when making investment decisions. The first two of these measures, the project's payback period and its book rate of return, are little better than rules of thumb, easy to calculate and easy to communicate. Although there is a place for rules of thumb in this world, an engineer needs something more accurate when designing a 100-story building, and a financial manager needs more than a rule of thumb when making a substantial capital investment decision.

Instead of calculating a project's NPV, companies often compare the expected rate of return from investing in the project with the return that shareholders could earn on equivalent-risk investments in the capital market. The company accepts those projects that provide a higher return than shareholders could earn for themselves. If used correctly, this rate of return rule should always identify projects that increase firm value. However, we shall see that the rule sets several traps for the unwary.

We conclude the chapter by showing how to cope with situations when the firm has only limited capital. This raises two problems. One is computational. In simple cases we just choose those projects that give the highest NPV per rupee invested, but more elaborate techniques are sometimes needed to sort through the possible alternatives. The other problem is to decide whether capital rationing really exists and whether it invalidates the net present value rule. Guess what? NPV, properly interpreted, wins out in the end.

5-1 A REVIEW OF THE BASICS

Vegetron's chief financial officer (CFO) is wondering how to analyze a proposed ₹1 million investment in a new venture called project X. He asks what you think.

Your response should be as follows: "First, forecast the cash flows generated by project X over its economic life. Second, determine the appropriate opportunity cost of capital (r). This should reflect both the time value of money and the risk involved in project X. Third, use this opportunity cost of capital to discount the project's future cash flows. The sum of the discounted cash flows is called present value (PV). Fourth, calculate *net* present value (NPV) by subtracting the ₹1 million investment from PV. If we call the cash flows C_0, C_1, and so on, then

$$\text{NPV} = C_0 + \frac{C_1}{1 + r} + \frac{C_2}{(1 + r)^2} + \cdots$$

We should invest in project X if its NPV is greater than zero."

However, Vegetron's CFO is unmoved by your sagacity. He asks why NPV is so important.

Your reply: "Let us look at what is best for Vegetron stockholders. They want you to make their Vegetron shares as valuable as possible.

"Right now Vegetron's total market value (price per share times the number of shares outstanding) is ₹10 million. That includes ₹1 million cash we can invest in project X. The value of Vegetron's other assets and opportunities must therefore be ₹9 million. We have to decide whether it is better to keep the ₹1 million cash and reject project X or to spend the cash and accept the project. Let us call the value of the new project PV. Then the choice is as follows:

	Market Value (₹ millions)	
Asset	**Reject Project X**	**Accept Project X**
Cash	1	0
Other assets	9	9
Project X	0	PV
	10	9 + PV

"Clearly project X is worthwhile if its present value, PV, is greater than ₹1 million, that is, if net present value is positive."

CFO: "How do I know that the PV of project X will actually show up in Vegetron's market value?"

Your reply: "Suppose we set up a new, independent firm X, whose only asset is project X. What would be the market value of firm X?

"Investors would forecast the dividends that firm X would pay and discount those dividends by the expected rate of return of securities having similar risks. We know that stock prices are equal to the present value of forecasted dividends.

"Since project X is the only asset, the dividend payments we would expect firm X to pay are exactly the cash flows we have forecasted for project X. Moreover, the rate investors would use to discount firm X's dividends is exactly the rate we should use to discount project X's cash flows.

"I agree that firm X is entirely hypothetical. But if project X is accepted, investors holding Vegetron stock will really hold a portfolio of project X and the firm's other assets. We know the other assets are worth ₹9 million considered as a separate venture. Since asset values add up, we can easily figure out the portfolio value once we calculate the value of project X as a separate venture.

"By calculating the present value of project X, we are replicating the process by which the common stock of firm X would be valued in capital markets."

CFO: "The one thing I don't understand is where the discount rate comes from."

Your reply: "I agree that the discount rate is difficult to measure precisely. But it is easy to see what we are *trying* to measure. The discount rate is the opportunity cost of investing in the project rather than in the capital market. In other words, instead of accepting a project, the firm can always return the cash to the shareholders and let them invest it in financial assets.

"You can see the trade-off (Figure 5.1). The opportunity cost of taking the project is the return shareholders could have earned had they invested the funds on their own. When we discount the project's cash flows by the expected rate of return on financial assets, we are measuring how much investors would be prepared to pay for your project."

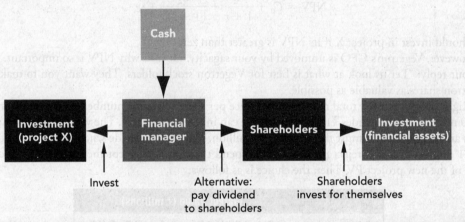

FIGURE 5.1

The firm can either keep and reinvest cash or return it to investors. (Arrows represent possible cash flows or transfers.) If cash is reinvested, the opportunity cost is the expected rate of return that shareholders could have obtained by investing in financial assets.

"But which financial assets?" Vegetron's CFO queries. "The fact that investors expect only 12% on IBM stock does not mean that we should purchase Fly-by-Night Electronics if it offers 13%."

Your reply: "The opportunity-cost concept makes sense only if assets of equivalent risk are compared. In general, you should identify financial assets that have the same risk as your project, estimate the expected rate of return on these assets, and use this rate as the opportunity cost."

Net Present Value's Competitors

When you advised the CFO to calculate the project's NPV, you were in good company. These days 65% of firms always, or almost always, calculate net present value when deciding on investment projects. However, as you can see from Figure 5.2, NPV is not the only investment criterion that companies use, and firms often look at more than one measure of a project's attractiveness.

About three-quarters of firms calculate the project's internal rate of return (or IRR); that is roughly the same proportion as use NPV. The IRR rule is a close relative of NPV and, when used properly, it will give the same answer. You therefore need to understand the IRR rule and how to take care when using it.

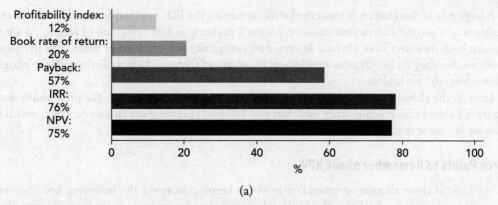

(a)

Source: Reprinted from J. R. Graham and C. R. Harvey, "The Theory and Practice of Finance: Evidence from the Field," *Journal of Financial Economics* 61 (2001), pp. 187–243, © 2001 with permission from Elsevier Science.

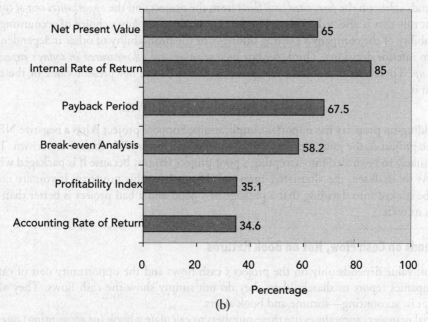

(b)

Source: Anand, M., 2002, "Corporate Finance Practices in India: A Survey", Vikalpa, October–December, Vol. 27, No. 4, pp 29-56. Reprinted with permission

FIGURE 5.2

(a) Survey evidence on the percentage of CFOs who always, or almost always, use a particular technique for evaluating investment projects.

(b) Survey Evidence on the percentage of Indian CFOs who use a particular technique for evaluating investment projects.

A large part of this chapter is concerned with explaining the IRR rule, but first we look at two other measures of a project's attractiveness—the project's payback and its book rate of return. As we will explain, both measures have obvious defects. Few companies rely on them to make their investment decisions, but they do use them as supplementary measures that may help to distinguish the marginal project from the no-brainer.

Later in the chapter we also come across one further investment measure, the profitability index. Figure 5.2 shows that it is not often used, but you will find that there are circumstances in which this measure has some special advantages.

Three Points to Remember about NPV

As we look at these alternative criteria, it is worth keeping in mind the following key features of the net present value rule. First, the NPV rule recognizes that *a rupee today is worth more than a rupee tomorrow,* because the rupee today can be invested to start earning interest immediately. Any investment rule that does not recognize the *time value of money* cannot be sensible. Second, net present value depends solely on the *forecasted cash flows* from the project and the *opportunity cost of capital.* Any investment rule that is affected by the manager's tastes, the company's choice of accounting method, the profitability of the company's existing business, or the profitability of other independent projects will lead to inferior decisions. Third, *because present values are all measured in today's rupees, you can add them up.* Therefore, if you have two projects A and B, the net present value of the combined investment is

$$NPV(A + B) = NPV(A) + NPV(B)$$

This adding-up property has important implications. Suppose project B has a negative NPV. If you tack it onto project A, the joint project (A + B) must have a lower NPV than A on its own. Therefore, you are unlikely to be misled into accepting a poor project (B) just because it is packaged with a good one (A). As we shall see, the alternative measures do not have this property. If you are not careful, you may be tricked into deciding that a package of a good and a bad project is better than the good project on its own.

NPV Depends on Cash Flow, Not on Book Returns

Net present value depends only on the project's cash flows and the opportunity cost of capital. But when companies report to shareholders, they do not simply show the cash flows. They also report book—that is, accounting—income and book assets.

Financial managers sometimes use these numbers to calculate a book (or accounting) rate of return on a proposed investment. In other words, they look at the prospective book income as a proportion of the book value of the assets that the firm is proposing to acquire:

$$\text{Book rate of return} = \frac{\text{book income}}{\text{book assets}}$$

Cash flows and book income are often very different. For example, the accountant labels some cash outflows as *capital investments* and others as *operating expenses.* The operating expenses are, of course, deducted immediately from each year's income. The capital expenditures are put on the firm's balance sheet and then depreciated. The annual depreciation charge is deducted from each year's income. Thus the book rate of return depends on which items the accountant treats as capital investments and how rapidly they are depreciated.[1]

Now the merits of an investment project do not depend on how accountants classify the cash flows[2] and few companies these days make investment decisions just on the basis of the book rate of return. But managers know that the company's shareholders pay considerable attention to book measures of profitability and naturally they think (and worry) about how major projects would affect the company's book return. Those projects that would reduce the company's book return may be scrutinized more carefully by senior management.

You can see the dangers here. The company's book rate of return may not be a good measure of true profitability. It is also an *average* across all of the firm's activities. The average profitability of past investments is not usually the right hurdle for new investments. Think of a firm that has been exceptionally lucky and successful. Say its average book return is 24%, double shareholders' 12% opportunity cost of capital. Should it demand that all *new* investments offer 24% or better? Clearly not: That would mean passing up many positive-NPV opportunities with rates of return between 12 and 24%.

We will come back to the book rate of return in Chapters 12 and 28, when we look more closely at accounting measures of financial performance.

5-2 PAYBACK

We suspect that you have often heard conversations that go something like this: "We are spending ₹200 every week, or ₹100,000 a year, on hiring a cab to go to office. If we bought a car for ₹300,000, it would pay for itself within three years. That's well worth it." You have just encountered the payback rule.

A project's **payback period** is found by counting the number of years it takes before the cumulative cash flow equals the initial investment. For the washing machine the payback period was just under three years. The **payback *rule*** states that a project should be accepted if its payback period is less than some specified cutoff period. For example, if the cutoff period is four years, the washing machine makes the grade; if the cutoff is two years, it doesn't.

EXAMPLE 5.1   The Payback Rule

Consider the following three projects:

Project	C_0	C_1	C_2	C_3	Payback Period (years)	NPV at 10%
			Cash Flows (₹)			
A	−2,000	500	500	5,000	3	+2,624
B	−2,000	500	1,800	0	2	−58
C	−2,000	1,800	500	0	2	+50

---

[1] This chapter's mini-case contains simple illustrations of how book rates of return are calculated and of the difference between accounting income and project cash flow. Read the case if you wish to refresh your understanding of these topics. Better still, do the case calculations.

[2] Of course, the depreciation method used for tax purposes does have cash consequences that should be taken into account in calculating NPV. We cover depreciation and taxes in the next chapter.

Project A involves an initial investment of ₹2,000 ($C_0 = -2,000$) followed by cash inflows during the next three years. Suppose the opportunity cost of capital is 10%. Then project A has an NPV of +₹2,624:

$$NPV(A) = -2,000 + \frac{500}{1.10} + \frac{500}{1.10^2} + \frac{5,000}{1.10^3} = +₹2,624$$

Project B also requires an initial investment of ₹2,000 but produces a cash inflow of ₹500 in year 1 and ₹1,800 in year 2. At a 10% opportunity cost of capital project B has an NPV of −₹58:

$$NPV(B) = -2,000 + \frac{500}{1.10} + \frac{1,800}{1.10^2} = -₹58$$

The third project, C, involves the same initial outlay as the other two projects but its first-period cash flow is larger. It has an NPV of +₹50.

$$NPV(C) = -2,000 + \frac{1,800}{1.10} + \frac{500}{1.10^2} = +₹50$$

The net present value rule tells us to accept projects A and C but to reject project B.

Now look at how rapidly each project pays back its initial investment. With project A you take three years to recover the ₹2,000 investment; with projects B and C you take only two years. If the firm used the *payback rule* with a cutoff period of two years, it would accept only projects B and C; if it used the payback rule with a cutoff period of three or more years, it would accept all three projects. Therefore, regardless of the choice of cutoff period, the payback rule gives different answers from the net present value rule.

You can see why payback can give misleading answers as illustrated in Example 5.1:

1. *The payback rule ignores all cash flows after the cutoff date.* If the cutoff date is two years, the payback rule rejects project A regardless of the size of the cash inflow in year 3.

2. *The payback rule gives equal weight to all cash flows before the cutoff date.* The payback rule says that projects B and C are equally attractive, but because C's cash inflows occur earlier, C has the higher net present value at any discount rate.

In order to use the payback rule, a firm has to decide on an appropriate cutoff date. If it uses the same cutoff regardless of project life, it will tend to accept many poor short-lived projects and reject many good long-lived ones.

We have had little good to say about the payback rule. So why do many companies continue to use it? Senior managers don't truly believe that all cash flows after the payback period are irrelevant. We suggest three explanations. First, payback may be used because it is the simplest way to *communicate* an idea of project profitability. Investment decisions require discussion and negotiation between people from all parts of the firm, and it is important to have a measure that everyone can understand. Second, managers of larger corporations may opt for projects with short paybacks because they believe that quicker profits mean quicker promotion. That takes us back to Chapter 1 where we discussed the need to align the objectives of managers with those of shareholders. Finally, owners of family firms with limited access to capital may worry about their future ability to raise capital. These worries may lead them to favor rapid payback projects even though a longer-term venture may have a higher NPV.

Discounted Payback

Occasionally companies discount the cash flows before they compute the payback period. The discounted cash flows for our three projects are as follows:

		Discounted Cash Flows (₹)			Discounted Payback Period (years)	NPV at 20%
Project	C_0	C_1	C_2	C_3		
A	−2,000	500/1.10 = 455	500/1.10² = 413	5,000/1.10³ = 3,757	3	+2,624
B	−2,000	500/1.10 = 455	1,800/1.10² = 1,488		—	−58
C	−2,000	1,800/1.10 = 1,636	500/1.10² = 413		2	+50

The *discounted payback rule* asks, How many years does the project have to last in order for it to make sense in terms of net present value? You can see that the value of the cash inflows from project B never exceeds the initial outlay and would always be rejected under the discounted payback rule. Thus the discounted payback rule will never accept a negative-NPV project. On the other hand, it still takes no account of cash flows after the cutoff date, so that good long-term projects such as A continue to risk rejection.

Rather than automatically rejecting any project with a long discounted payback period, many managers simply use the measure as a warning signal. These managers don't unthinkingly reject a project with a long discounted-payback period. Instead, they check that the proposer is not unduly optimistic about the project's ability to generate cash flows into the distant future. They satisfy themselves that the equipment has a long life and that competitors will not enter the market and eat into the project's cash flows.

5-3 INTERNAL (OR DISCOUNTED-CASH-FLOW) RATE OF RETURN

Whereas payback and return on book are ad hoc measures, internal rate of return has a much more respectable ancestry and is recommended in many finance texts. If, therefore, we dwell more on its deficiencies, it is not because they are more numerous but because they are less obvious.

In Chapter 2 we noted that the net present value rule could also be expressed in terms of rate of return, which would lead to the following rule: "Accept investment opportunities offering rates of return in excess of their opportunity costs of capital." That statement, properly interpreted, is absolutely correct. However, interpretation is not always easy for long-lived investment projects.

There is no ambiguity in defining the true rate of return of an investment that generates a single payoff after one period:

$$\text{Rate of return} = \frac{\text{payoff}}{\text{investment}} - 1$$

Alternatively, we could write down the NPV of the investment and find the discount rate that makes NPV = 0.

$$\text{NPV} = C_0 + \frac{C_1}{1 + \text{discount rate}} = 0$$

implies

$$\text{Discount rate} = \frac{C_1}{-C_0} - 1$$

Of course C_1 is the payoff and $-C_0$ is the required investment, and so our two equations say exactly the same thing. *The discount rate that makes NPV = 0 is also the rate of return.*

How do we calculate return when the project produces cash flows in several periods? Answer: we use the same definition that we just developed for one-period projects—*the project rate of return is the discount rate that gives a zero NPV.* This discount rate is known as the **discounted-cash-flow (DCF) rate of return** or **internal rate of return (IRR).** The internal rate of return is used frequently in finance. It can be a handy measure, but, as we shall see, it can also be a misleading measure. You should, therefore, know how to calculate it and how to use it properly.

Calculating the IRR

The internal rate of return is defined as the rate of discount that makes NPV = 0. So to find the IRR for an investment project lasting T years, we must solve for IRR in the following expression:

$$\text{NPV} = C_0 + \frac{C_1}{1 + \text{IRR}} + \frac{C_2}{(1 + \text{IRR})^2} + \cdots + \frac{C_T}{(1 + \text{IRR})^T} = 0$$

Actual calculation of IRR usually involves trial and error. For example, consider a project that produces the following flows:

Cash Flows (₹)		
C_0	C_1	C_2
−4,000	+2,000	+4,000

The internal rate of return is IRR in the equation

$$\text{NPV} = -4,000 + \frac{2,000}{1 + \text{IRR}} + \frac{4,000}{(1 + \text{IRR})^2} = 0$$

Let us arbitrarily try a zero discount rate. In this case NPV is not zero but +₹2,000:

$$\text{NPV} = -4,000 + \frac{2,000}{1.0} + \frac{4,000}{(1.0)^2} = +₹2,000$$

The NPV is positive; therefore, the IRR must be greater than zero. The next step might be to try a discount rate of 50%. In this case net present value is −₹889:

$$\text{NPV} = -4,000 + \frac{2,000}{1.50} + \frac{4,000}{(1.50)^2} = -₹889$$

The NPV is negative; therefore, the IRR must be less than 50%. In Figure 5.3 we have plotted the net present values implied by a range of discount rates. From this we can see that a discount rate of 28% gives the desired net present value of zero. Therefore IRR is 28%.

The easiest way to calculate IRR, if you have to do it by hand, is to plot three or four combinations of NPV and discount rate on a graph like Figure 5.3, connect the points with a smooth line, and read off the discount rate at which NPV = 0. It is of course quicker and more accurate to use a computer spreadsheet or a specially programmed calculator, and in practice this is what financial managers do. The Useful Spreadsheet Functions box near the end of the chapter presents Excel functions for doing so.

Some people confuse the internal rate of return and the opportunity cost of capital because both appear as discount rates in the NPV formula. The internal rate of return is a *profitability measure* that depends solely on the amount and timing of the project cash flows. The opportunity cost of capital is a *standard of profitability* that we use to calculate how much the project is worth. The opportunity cost of capital is established in capital markets. It is the expected rate of return offered by other assets with the same risk as the project being evaluated.

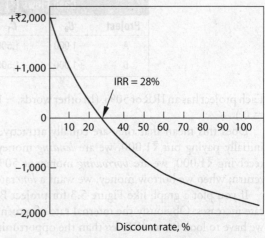

Net present value, dollars

IRR = 28%

Discount rate, %

FIGURE 5.3

This project costs ₹4,000 and then produces cash inflows of ₹2,000 in year 1 and ₹4,000 in year 2. Its internal rate of return (IRR) is 28%, the rate of discount at which NPV is zero.

The IRR Rule

The internal rate of return rule is to accept an investment project if the opportunity cost of capital is less than the internal rate of return. You can see the reasoning behind this idea if you look again at Figure 5.3. If the opportunity cost of capital is less than the 28% IRR, then the project has a *positive* NPV when discounted at the opportunity cost of capital. If it is equal to the IRR, the project has a *zero* NPV. And if it is greater than the IRR, the project has a *negative* NPV. Therefore, when we compare the opportunity cost of capital with the IRR on our project, we are effectively asking whether our project has a positive NPV. This is true not only for our example. The rule will give the same answer as the net present value rule *whenever the NPV of a project is a smoothly declining function of the discount rate.*

Many firms use internal rate of return as a criterion in preference to net present value. We think that this is a pity. Although, properly stated, the two criteria are formally equivalent, the internal rate of return rule contains several pitfalls.

Pitfall 1—Lending or Borrowing?

Not all cash-flow streams have NPVs that decline as the discount rate increases. Consider the following projects A and B:

Cash Flows (₹)				
Project	C_0	C_1	IRR	NPV at 10%
A	−1,000	+1,500	+50%	+364
B	+1,000	−1,500	+50%	−364

Each project has an IRR of 50%. (In other words, $−1,000 + 1,500/1.50 = 0$ *and* $+1,000 − 1,500/1.50 = 0$.)

Does this mean that they are equally attractive? Clearly not, for in the case of A, where we are initially paying out ₹1,000, we are *lending* money at 50%, in the case of B, where we are initially receiving ₹1,000, we are *borrowing* money at 50%. When we lend money, we want a *high* rate of return; when we borrow money, we want a *low* rate of return.

If you plot a graph like Figure 5.3 for project B, you will find that NPV increases as the discount rate increases. Obviously the internal rate of return rule, as we stated it above, won't work in this case; we have to look for an IRR *less* than the opportunity cost of capital.

Pitfall 2—Multiple Rates of Return

Helmsley Iron is proposing to develop a new strip mine in Western Australia. The mine involves an initial investment of A$3 billion and is expected to produce a cash inflow of A$1 billion a year for the next nine years. At the end of that time the company will incur A$6.5 billion of cleanup costs. Thus the cash flows from the project are:

Cash Flows (billions of Australian dollars)				
C_0	C_1	...	C_9	C_{10}
−3	1		1	−6.5

Helmsley calculates the project's IRR and its NPV as follows:

IRR (%)	NPV at 10%
+3.50 *and* 19.54	₹A253 million

Note that there are *two* discount rates that make NPV = 0. That is, *each* of the following statements holds:

$$NPV = −3 + \frac{1}{1.035} + \frac{1}{1.035^2} + \cdots + \frac{1}{1.035^9} − \frac{6.5}{1.035^{10}} = 0$$

$$NPV = −3 + \frac{1}{1.1954} + \frac{1}{1.1954^2} + \cdots + \frac{1}{1.1954^9} − \frac{6.5}{1.1954^{10}} = 0$$

In other words, the investment has an IRR of both 3.50 *and* 19.54%. Figure 5.4 shows how this comes about. As the discount rate increases, NPV initially rises and then declines. The reason for this is the double change in the sign of the cash-flow stream. There can be as many internal rates of return for a project as there are changes in the sign of the cash flows.[3]

---

[3] By Descartes's "rule of signs" there can be as many different solutions to a polynomial as there are changes of sign.

NPV, A$billions

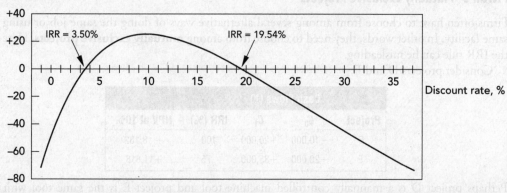

FIGURE 5.4

Helmsley Iron's mine has two internal rates of return. NPV = 0 when the discount rate is +3.50% *and* when it is +19.54%.

Decommissioning and clean-up costs can sometimes be huge. Phillips Petroleum has estimated that it will need to spend $1 billion to remove its Norwegian offshore oil platforms. It can cost over $300 million to decommission a nuclear power plant. These are obvious instances where cash flows go from positive to negative, but you can probably think of a number of other cases where the company needs to plan for later expenditures. Ships periodically need to go into dry dock for a refit, hotels may receive a major face-lift, machine parts may need replacement, and so on.

Whenever the cash-flow stream is expected to change sign more than once, the company typically sees more than one IRR.

As if this is not difficult enough, there are also cases in which *no* internal rate of return exists. For example, project C has a positive net present value at all discount rates:

| Project | Cash Flows ($) | | | IRR (%) | NPV at 10% |
	C_0	C_1	C_2		
C	+1,000	−3,000	+2,500	None	+339

A number of adaptations of the IRR rule have been devised for such cases. Not only are they inadequate, but they also are unnecessary, for the simple solution is to use net present value.[4]

---

[4] Companies sometimes get around the problem of multiple rates of return by discounting the later cash flows back at the cost of capital until there remains only one change in the sign of the cash flows. A *modified internal rate of return* (MIRR) can then be calculated on this revised series. In our example, the MIRR is calculated as follows:

1. Calculate the present value in year 5 of all the subsequent cash flows:

$$\text{PV in year 5} = 1/1.1 + 1/1.1^2 + 1/1.1^3 + +1/1.1^4 - 6.5/1.1^5 = -.866$$

2. Add to the year 5 cash flow the present value of subsequent cash flows:

$$C_5 + \text{PV(subsequent cash flows)} = 1 - .866 = .134$$

3. Since there is now only one change in the sign of the cash flows, the revised series has a unique rate of return, which is 13.7%

$$\text{NPV} = 1/1.137 + 1/1.137^2 + 1/1.137^3 + 1/1.137^4 + .134/1.137^5 = 0$$

Since the MIRR of 13.7% is greater than the cost of capital (and the initial cash flow is negative), the project has a positive NPV when valued at the cost of capital.

Of course, it would be much easier in such cases to abandon the IRR rule and just calculate project NPV.

Pitfall 3—Mutually Exclusive Projects

Firms often have to choose from among several alternative ways of doing the same job or using the same facility. In other words, they need to choose from among **mutually exclusive projects.** Here too the IRR rule can be misleading.

Consider projects D and E:

Cash Flows (₹)				
Project	C_0	C_1	IRR (%)	NPV at 10%
D	−10,000	+20,000	100	+ 8,182
E	−20,000	+35,000	75	+11,818

Perhaps project D is a manually controlled machine tool and project E is the same tool with the addition of computer control. Both are good investments, but E has the higher NPV and is, therefore, better. However, the IRR rule seems to indicate that if you have to choose, you should go for D since it has the higher IRR. If you follow the IRR rule, you have the satisfaction of earning a 100% rate of return; if you follow the NPV rule, you are ₹11,818 richer.

You can salvage the IRR rule in these cases by looking at the internal rate of return on the *incremental* flows. Here is how to do it: First, consider the smaller project (D in our example). It has an IRR of 100%, which is well in excess of the 10% opportunity cost of capital. You know, therefore, that D is acceptable. You now ask yourself whether it is worth making the additional ₹10,000 investment in E. The incremental flows from undertaking E rather than D are as follows:

Cash Flows (₹)				
Project	C_0	C_1	IRR (%)	NPV at 10%
E − D	−10,000	+15,000	50	+3,636

The IRR on the incremental investment is 50%, which is also well in excess of the 10% opportunity cost of capital. So you should prefer project E to project D.[5]

Unless you look at the incremental expenditure, IRR is unreliable in ranking projects of different scale. It is also unreliable in ranking projects that offer different patterns of cash flow over time. For example, suppose the firm can take project F *or* project G but not both (ignore H for the moment):

Cash Flows (₹)								
Project	C_0	C_1	C_2	C_3	C_4	C_5	Etc.	IRR (%)	NPV at 10%
F	−9,000	+6,000	+5,000	+4,000	0	0	. . .	33	3,592
G	−9,000	+1,800	+1,800	+1,800	+1,800	+1,800	. . .	20	9,000
H		−6,000	+1,200	+1,200	+1,200	+1,200	. . .	20	6,000

Project F has a higher IRR, but project G, which is a perpetuity, has the higher NPV. Figure 5.5 shows why the two rules give different answers. The green line gives the net present value of project F at different rates of discount. Since a discount rate of 33% produces a net present value of zero, this is the

[5] You may, however, find that you have jumped out of the frying pan into the fire. The series of incremental cash flows may involve several changes in sign. In this case there are likely to be multiple IRRs and you will be forced to use the NPV rule after all.

internal rate of return for project F. Similarly, the brown line shows the net present value of project G at different discount rates. The IRR of project G is 20%. (We assume project G's cash flows continue indefinitely.) Note, however, that project G has a higher NPV as long as the opportunity cost of capital is less than 15.6%.

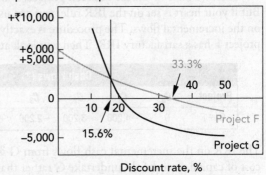

FIGURE 5.5

The IRR of project F exceeds that of project G, but the NPV of project F is higher *only* if the discount rate is greater than 15.6%.

The reason that IRR is misleading is that the total cash inflow of project G is larger but tends to occur later. Therefore, when the discount rate is low, G has the higher NPV; when the discount rate is high, F has the higher NPV. (You can see from Figure 5.5 that the two projects have the *same* NPV when the discount rate is 15.6%.) The internal rates of return on the two projects tell us that at a discount rate of 20% G has a zero NPV (IRR = 20%) and F has a positive NPV. Thus, if the opportunity cost of capital were 20%, investors would place a higher value on the shorter-lived project F. However, in our example, the opportunity cost of capital is not 20%, but 10%. So investors will pay a relatively high price for the longer-lived project. At a 10% cost of capital, an investment in G has an NPV of ₹9,000 and an investment in F has an NPV of only ₹3,592.[6]

This is a favorite example of ours. We have gotten many businesspeople's reaction to it. When asked to choose between F and G, many choose F. The reason seems to be the rapid payback generated by project F. In other words, they believe that if they take F, they will also be able to take a later project like H (note that H can be financed using the cash flows from F), whereas if they take G, they won't have money enough for H. In other words they implicitly assume that it is a *shortage of capital* that forces the choice between F and G. When this implicit assumption is brought out, they usually admit that G is better if there is no capital shortage.

But the introduction of capital constraints raises two further questions. The first stems from the fact that most of the executives preferring F to G work for firms that would have no difficulty raising more capital. Why would a manager at IBM, say, choose F on the grounds of limited capital? IBM can raise plenty of capital and can take project H regardless of whether F or G is chosen; therefore H should not affect the choice between F and G. The answer seems to be that large firms usually impose capital budgets on divisions and subdivisions as a part of the firm's planning and control system. Since the system is complicated and cumbersome, the budgets are not easily altered, and so they are perceived as real constraints by middle management.

The second question is this. If there is a capital constraint, either real or self-imposed, should IRR be used to rank projects? The answer is no. The problem in this case is to find the package of investment projects that satisfies the capital constraint and has the largest net present value. The IRR rule will not identify this package. As we will show in the next section, the only practical and general way to do so is to use the technique of linear programming.

---

[6] It is often suggested that the choice between the net present value rule and the internal rate of return rule should depend on the probable reinvestment rate. This is wrong. The prospective return on another *independent* investment should *never* be allowed to influence the investment decision.

When we have to choose between projects F and G, it is easiest to compare the net present values. But if your heart is set on the IRR rule, you can use it as long as you look at the internal rate of return on the incremental flows. The procedure is exactly the same as we showed above. First, you check that project F has a satisfactory IRR. Then you look at the return on the incremental cash flows from G.

Cash Flows (₹)									
Project	C_0	C_1	C_2	C_3	C_4	C_5	Etc.	IRR (%)	NPV at 10%
G − F	0	−4,200	−3,200	−2,200	+1,800	+1,800	...	15.6	+5,408

The IRR on the incremental cash flows from G is 15.6%. Since this is greater than the opportunity cost of capital, you should undertake G rather than F.[7]

Pitfall 4—What Happens When There Is More than One Opportunity Cost of Capital?

We have simplified our discussion of capital budgeting by assuming that the opportunity cost of capital is the same for all the cash flows, C_1, C_2, C_3, etc. Remember our most general formula for calculating net present value:

$$\text{NPV} = C_0 + \frac{C_1}{1 + r_1} + \frac{C_2}{(1 + r_2)^2} + \frac{C_3}{(1 + r_3)^3} + \cdots$$

In other words, we discount C_1 at the opportunity cost of capital for one year, C_2 at the opportunity cost of capital for two years, and so on. The IRR rule tells us to accept a project if the IRR is greater than the opportunity cost of capital. But what do we do when we have several opportunity costs? Do we compare IRR with r_1, r_2, r_3, . . .? Actually we would have to compute a complex weighted average of these rates to obtain a number comparable to IRR.

What does this mean for capital budgeting? It means trouble for the IRR rule whenever there is more than one opportunity cost of capital. Many firms use the IRR, thereby implicitly assuming that there is no difference between short-term and long-term discount rates. They do this for the same reason that we have so far finessed the issue: simplicity.[8]

The Verdict on IRR

We have given four examples of things that can go wrong with IRR. We spent much less space on payback or return on book. Does this mean that IRR is worse than the other two measures? Quite the contrary. There is little point in dwelling on the deficiencies of payback or return on book. They are clearly ad hoc measures that often lead to silly conclusions. The IRR rule has a much more respectable ancestry. It is less easy to use than NPV, but, used properly, it gives the same answer.

Nowadays few large corporations use the payback period or return on book as their primary measure of project attractiveness. Most use discounted cash flow or "DCF," and for many companies DCF means IRR, not NPV. For "normal" investment projects with an initial cash outflow followed

---

[7] Because F and G had the same 10% cost of capital, we could choose between the two projects by asking whether the IRR on the incremental cash flows was greater or less than 10%. But suppose that F and G had different risks and therefore different costs of capital. In that case there would be no simple yardstick for assessing whether the IRR on the incremental cash flows was adequate.

[8] In Chapter 9 we look at some other cases in which it would be misleading to use the same discount rate for both short-term and long-term cash flows.

by a series of cash inflows, there is no difficulty in using the internal rate of return to make a simple accept/reject decision. However, we think that financial managers need to worry more about Pitfall 3. Financial managers never see all possible projects. Most projects are proposed by operating managers. A company that instructs nonfinancial managers to look first at project IRRs prompts a search for those projects with the highest IRRs rather than the highest NPVs. It also encourages managers to *modify* projects so that their IRRs are higher. Where do you typically find the highest IRRs? In short-lived projects requiring little up-front investment. Such projects may not add much to the value of the firm.

We don't know why so many companies pay such close attention to the internal rate of return, but we suspect that it may reflect the fact that management does not trust the forecasts it receives. Suppose that two plant managers approach you with proposals for two new investments. Both have a positive NPV of ₹1,400 at the company's 8% cost of capital, but you nevertheless decide to accept project A and reject B. Are you being irrational?

The cash flows for the two projects and their NPVs are set out in the table below. You can see that, although both proposals have the same NPV, project A involves an investment of ₹9,000, while B requires an investment of ₹9 million. Investing ₹9,000 to make ₹1,400 is clearly an attractive proposition, and this shows up in A's IRR of nearly 16%. Investing ₹9 million to make ₹1,400 might also be worth doing if you could be *sure* of the plant manager's forecasts, but there is almost no room for error in project B. You could spend time and money checking the cash-flow forecasts, but is it really worth the effort? Most managers would look at the IRR and decide that, if the cost of capital is 8%, a project that offers a return of 8.01% is not worth the worrying time.

Alternatively, management may conclude that project A is a clear winner that is worth undertaking right away, but in the case of project B it may make sense to wait and see whether the decision looks more clear-cut in a year's time.[9] Management postpones the decision on projects such as B by setting a hurdle rate for the IRR that is higher than the cost of capital.

Cash Flows (₹ thousands)						
Project	C_0	C_1	C_2	C_3	NPV at 8%	IRR (%)
A	−9.0	2.9	4.0	5.4	1.4	15.58
B	−9,000	2,560	3,540	4,530	1.4	8.01

5-4 CHOOSING CAPITAL INVESTMENTS WHEN RESOURCES ARE LIMITED

Our entire discussion of methods of capital budgeting has rested on the proposition that the wealth of a firm's shareholders is highest if the firm accepts *every* project that has a positive net present value. Suppose, however, that there are limitations on the investment program that prevent the company from undertaking all such projects. Economists call this *capital rationing*. When capital is rationed, we need a method of selecting the package of projects that is within the company's resources yet gives the highest possible net present value.

[9] In Chapter 22 we discuss when it may pay a company to delay undertaking a positive-NPV project. We will see that when projects are "deep-in-the-money" (project A), it generally pays to invest right away and capture the cash flows. However, in the case of projects that are close-to-the-money (project B) it makes more sense to wait and see.

An Easy Problem in Capital Rationing

Let us start with a simple example. The opportunity cost of capital is 10%, and our company has the following opportunities:

	Cash Flows (₹ millions)			
Project	C_0	C_1	C_2	NPV at 10%
A	−10	+30	+5	21
B	−5	+5	+20	16
C	−5	+5	+15	12

All three projects are attractive, but suppose that the firm is limited to spending ₹10 million. In that case, it can invest *either* in project A *or* in projects B and C, but it cannot invest in all three. Although individually B and C have lower net present values than project A, when taken together they have the higher net present value. Here we cannot choose between projects solely on the basis of net present values. When funds are limited, we need to concentrate on getting the biggest bang for our buck. In other words, we must pick the projects that offer the highest net present value per dollar of initial outlay. This ratio is known as the **profitability index**:[10]

$$\text{Profitability index} = \frac{\text{net present value}}{\text{investment}}$$

For our three projects the profitability index is calculated as follows:[11]

Project	Investment (₹ millions)	NPV (₹ millions)	Profitability Index
A	10	21	2.1
B	5	16	3.2
C	5	12	2.4

Project B has the highest profitability index and C has the next highest. Therefore, if our budget limit is ₹10 million, we should accept these two projects.[12]

Unfortunately, there are some limitations to this simple ranking method. One of the most serious is that it breaks down whenever more than one resource is rationed.[13] For example, suppose that the firm

---

[10] If a project requires outlays in two or more periods, the denominator should be the present value of the outlays. A few companies do not discount the benefits or costs before calculating the profitability index. The less said about these companies the better.

[11] Sometimes the profitability index is defined as the ratio of the present value to initial outlay, that is, as PV/investment. This measure is also known as the *benefit–cost ratio*. To calculate the benefit–cost ratio, simply add 1.0 to each profitability index. Project rankings are unchanged.

[12] If a project has a positive profitability index, it must also have a positive NPV. Therefore, firms sometimes use the profitability index to select projects when capital is *not* limited. However, like the IRR, the profitability index can be misleading when used to choose between mutually exclusive projects. For example, suppose you were forced to choose between (1) investing ₹100 in a project whose payoffs have a present value of ₹200 or (2) investing ₹1 million in a project whose payoffs have a present value of ₹1.5 million. The first investment has the higher profitability index; the second makes you richer.

[13] It may also break down if it causes some money to be left over. It might be better to spend all the available funds even if this involves accepting a project with a slightly lower profitability index.

can raise only ₹10 million for investment in *each* of years 0 and 1 and that the menu of possible projects is expanded to include an investment next year in project D:

Cash Flows (₹ millions)					
Project	C_0	C_1	C_2	NPV at 10%	Profitability Index
A	−10	+30	+5	21	2.1
B	−5	+5	+20	16	3.2
C	−5	+5	+15	12	2.4
D	0	−40	+60	13	0.4

One strategy is to accept projects B and C; however, if we do this, we cannot also accept D, which costs more than our budget limit for period 1. An alternative is to accept project A in period 0. Although this has a lower net present value than the combination of B and C, it provides a ₹30 million positive cash flow in period 1. When this is added to the ₹10 million budget, we can also afford to undertake D next year. A and D have *lower* profitability indexes than B and C, but they have a *higher* total net present value.

The reason that ranking on the profitability index fails in this example is that resources are constrained in each of two periods. In fact, this ranking method is inadequate whenever there is *any* other constraint on the choice of projects. This means that it cannot cope with cases in which two projects are mutually exclusive or in which one project is dependent on another.

For example, suppose that you have a long menu of possible projects starting this year and next. There is a limit on how much you can invest in each year. Perhaps also you can't undertake both project alpha and beta (they both require the same piece of land), and you can't invest in project gamma unless you invest in delta (gamma is simply an add-on to delta). You need to find the package of projects that satisfies all these constraints and gives the highest NPV.

One way to tackle such a problem is to work through all possible combinations of projects. For each combination you first check whether the projects satisfy the constraints and then calculate the net present value. But it is smarter to recognize that linear programming (LP) techniques are specially designed to search through such possible combinations.[14]

Uses of Capital Rationing Models

Linear programming models seem tailor-made for solving capital budgeting problems when resources are limited. Why then are they not universally accepted either in theory or in practice? One reason is that these models can turn out to be very complex. Second, as with any sophisticated long-range planning tool, there is the general problem of getting good data. It is just not worth applying costly, sophisticated methods to poor data. Furthermore, these models are based on the assumption that all future investment opportunities are known. In reality, the discovery of investment ideas is an unfolding process.

Our most serious misgivings center on the basic assumption that capital is limited. When we come to discuss company financing, we shall see that most large corporations do not face capital rationing and can raise large sums of money on fair terms. Why then do many company presidents

---

[14] On our Web site at www.mhhe.com/bmam10e we show how linear programming can be used to select from the four projects in our earlier example.

tell their subordinates that capital is limited? If they are right, the capital market is seriously imperfect. What then are they doing maximizing NPV?[15] We might be tempted to suppose that if capital is not rationed, they do not *need* to use linear programming and, if it is rationed, then surely they *ought* not to use it. But that would be too quick a judgment. Let us look at this problem more deliberately.

Soft Rationing   Many firms' capital constraints are "soft." They reflect no imperfections in capital markets. Instead they are provisional limits adopted by management as an aid to financial control.

Some ambitious divisional managers habitually overstate their investment opportunities. Rather than trying to distinguish which projects really are worthwhile, headquarters may find it simpler to impose an upper limit on divisional expenditures and thereby force the divisions to set their own priorities. In such instances budget limits are a rough but effective way of dealing with biased cash-flow forecasts. In other cases management may believe that very rapid corporate growth could impose intolerable strains on management and the organization. Since it is difficult to quantify such constraints explicitly, the budget limit may be used as a proxy.

Because such budget limits have nothing to do with any inefficiency in the capital market, there is no contradiction in using an LP model in the division to maximize net present value subject to the budget constraint. On the other hand, there is not much point in elaborate selection procedures if the cash-flow forecasts of the division are seriously biased.

Even if capital is not rationed, other resources may be. The availability of management time, skilled labor, or even other capital equipment often constitutes an important constraint on a company's growth.

Hard Rationing   Soft rationing should never cost the firm anything. If capital constraints become tight enough to hurt—in the sense that projects with significant positive NPVs are passed up—then the firm raises more money and loosens the constraint. But what if it *can't* raise more money—what if it faces *hard* rationing?

Hard rationing implies market imperfections, but that does not necessarily mean we have to throw away net present value as a criterion for capital budgeting. It depends on the nature of the imperfection.

Karnataka Horticulture Limited (HCL), borrows as much as the banks will lend it, yet it still has good investment opportunities. This is not hard rationing so long as HCL can issue stock. But perhaps it can't. Perhaps the founder and majority shareholder vetoes the idea from fear of losing control of the firm. Perhaps a stock issue would bring costly red tape or legal complications.[16]

This does not invalidate the NPV rule. HCL's *shareholders* can borrow or lend, sell their shares, or buy more. They have free access to security markets. The type of portfolio they hold is independent of HCL's financing or investment decisions. The only way HCL can help its shareholders is to make them richer. Thus HCL should invest its available cash in the package of projects having the largest aggregate net present value.

A barrier between the firm and capital markets does not undermine net present value so long as the barrier is the *only* market imperfection. The important thing is that the firm's *shareholders* have free access to well-functioning capital markets.

The net present value rule *is* undermined when imperfections restrict shareholders' portfolio choice. Suppose that Udupi Horticulture, is solely owned by its founder, Mr. Narayan Bhatt. Mr. Bhatt has no cash or credit remaining, but he is convinced that expansion of his operation is a high-NPV investment. He has tried to sell stock but has found that prospective investors, skeptical

[15] Don't forget that in Chapter 1 we had to assume perfect capital markets to derive the NPV rule.

[16] A majority owner who is "locked in" and has much personal wealth tied up in AAI may be effectively cut off from capital markets. The NPV rule may not make sense to such an owner, though it will to the other shareholders.

Useful Spreadsheet Functions

Internal Rate of Return

Spreadsheet programs such as Excel provide built-in functions to solve for internal rates of return. You can find these functions by pressing *fx* on the Excel toolbar. If you then click on the function that you wish to use, Excel will guide you through the inputs that are required. At the bottom left of the function box there is a Help facility with an example of how the function is used.

Here is a list of useful functions for calculating internal rates of return, together with some points to remember when entering data:

- **IRR:** Internal rate of return on a series of regularly spaced cash flows.
- **XIRR:** The same as IRR, but for irregularly spaced flows.

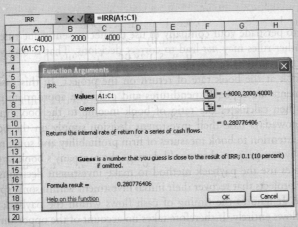

Note the following:

- For these functions, you must enter the addresses of the cells that contain the input values.
- The IRR functions calculate only one IRR even when there are multiple IRRs.

Spreadsheet Questions

The following questions provide an opportunity to practice each of the above functions:

1. (IRR) Check the IRRs on projects F and G in Section 5-3.
2. (IRR) What is the IRR of a project with the following cash flows:

C_0	C_1	C_2	C_3
−₹5,000	+₹2,200	+₹4,650	+₹3,330

3. (IRR) Now use the function to calculate the IRR on Helmsley Iron's mining project in Section 5-3. There are really two IRRs to this project (why?). How many IRRs does the function calculate?

4. (XIRR) What is the IRR of a project with the following cash flows:

C_0	C_4	C_5	C_6
$-₹215,000$ ...	$+₹185,000$ ...	$+₹85,000$ ...	$+₹43,000$

(All other cash flows are 0.)

of prospects for fish farming in the desert, offer him much less than he thinks his firm is worth. For Mr. Bhatt, capital markets hardly exist. It makes little sense for him to discount prospective cash flows at a market opportunity cost of capital.

SUMMARY

If you are going to persuade your company to use the net present value rule, you must be prepared to explain why other rules may *not* lead to correct decisions. That is why we have examined three alternative investment criteria in this chapter.

Some firms look at the book rate of return on the project. In this case the company decides which cash payments are capital expenditures and picks the appropriate rate to depreciate these expenditures. It then calculates the ratio of book income to the book value of the investment. Few companies nowadays base their investment decision simply on the book rate of return, but shareholders pay attention to book measures of firm profitability and some managers therefore look with a jaundiced eye on projects that would damage the company's book rate of return.

Some companies use the payback method to make investment decisions. In other words, they accept only those projects that recover their initial investment within some specified period. Payback is an ad hoc rule. It ignores the timing of cash flows within the payback period, and it ignores subsequent cash flows entirely. It therefore takes no account of the opportunity cost of capital.

The internal rate of return (IRR) is defined as the rate of discount at which a project would have zero NPV. It is a handy measure and widely used in finance; you should therefore know how to calculate it. The IRR rule states that companies should accept any investment offering an IRR in excess of the opportunity cost of capital. The IRR rule is, like net present value, a technique based on discounted cash flows. It will therefore give the correct answer if properly used. The problem is that it is easily misapplied. There are four things to look out for:

1. *Lending or borrowing?* If a project offers positive cash flows followed by negative flows, NPV can *rise* as the discount rate is increased. You should accept such projects if their IRR is *less* than the opportunity cost of capital.
2. *Multiple rates of return.* If there is more than one change in the sign of the cash flows, the project may have several IRRs or no IRR at all.
3. *Mutually exclusive projects.* The IRR rule may give the wrong ranking of mutually exclusive projects that differ in economic life or in scale of required investment. If you insist on using IRR to rank mutually exclusive projects, you must examine the IRR on each incremental investment.
4. *The cost of capital for near-term cash flows may be different from the cost for distant cash flows.* The IRR rule requires you to compare the project's IRR with the opportunity cost of capital. But sometimes there is an opportunity cost of capital for one-year cash flows, a different cost of capital

for two-year cash flows, and so on. In these cases there is no simple yardstick for evaluating the IRR of a project.

In developing the NPV rule, we assumed that the company can maximize shareholder wealth by accepting every project that is worth more than it costs. But, if capital is strictly limited, then it may not be possible to take every project with a positive NPV. If capital is rationed in only one period, then the firm should follow a simple rule: Calculate each project's profitability index, which is the project's net present value per dollar of investment. Then pick the projects with the highest profitability indexes until you run out of capital. Unfortunately, this procedure fails when capital is rationed in more than one period or when there are other constraints on project choice. The only general solution is linear programming.

Hard capital rationing always reflects a market imperfection—a barrier between the firm and capital markets. If that barrier also implies that the firm's shareholders lack free access to a well-functioning capital market, the very foundations of net present value crumble. Fortunately, hard rationing is rare for corporations in the United States. Many firms do use soft capital rationing, however. That is, they set up self-imposed limits as a means of financial planning and control.

FURTHER READING

For a survey of capital budgeting procedures, see:

J. Graham and C. Harvey, "How CFOs Make Capital Budgeting and Capital Structure Decisions," *Journal of Applied Corporate Finance* 15 (spring 2002), pp. 8–23.

PROBLEM SETS

BASIC

1. a. What is the payback period on each of the following projects?

	Cash Flows (₹)				
Project	C_0	C_1	C_2	C_3	C_4
A	−5,000	+1,000	+1,000	+3,000	0
B	−1,000	0	+1,000	+2,000	+3,000
C	−5,000	+1,000	+1,000	+3,000	+5,000

  b. Given that you wish to use the payback rule with a cutoff period of two years, which projects would you accept?

  c. If you use a cutoff period of three years, which projects would you accept?

d. If the opportunity cost of capital is 10%, which projects have positive NPVs?

e. "If a firm uses a single cutoff period for all projects, it is likely to accept too many short-lived projects." True or false?

f. If the firm uses the discounted-payback rule, will it accept any negative-NPV projects? Will it turn down positive-NPV projects? Explain.

2. Write down the equation defining a project's internal rate of return (IRR). In practice how is IRR calculated?

3. a. Calculate the net present value of the following project for discount rates of 0, 50, and 100%:

Cash Flows (₹)		
C_0	C_1	C_2
−6,750	+4,500	+18,000

b. What is the IRR of the project?

4. You have the chance to participate in a project that produces the following cash flows:

Cash Flows (₹)		
C_0	C_1	C_2
+5,000	+4,000	−11,000

The internal rate of return is 13%. If the opportunity cost of capital is 10%, would you accept the offer?

5. Consider a project with the following cash flows:

C_0	C_1	C_2
−100	+200	−75

a. How many internal rates of return does this project have?

b. Which of the following numbers is the project IRR:
   (i) −50%; (ii) −12%; (iii) +5%; (iv) +50%?

c. The opportunity cost of capital is 20%. Is this an attractive project? Briefly explain.

6. Consider projects Alpha and Beta:

Cash Flows (₹)				
Project	C_0	C_1	C_2	IRR (%)
Alpha	−400,000	+241,000	+293,000	21
Beta	−200,000	+131,000	+172,000	31

The opportunity cost of capital is 8%.

Suppose you can undertake Alpha or Beta, but not both. Use the IRR rule to make the choice. (*Hint:* What's the incremental investment in Alpha?)

7. Suppose you have the following investment opportunities, but only ₹90,000 available for investment. Which projects should you take?

Project	NPV	Investment
1	5,000	10,000
2	5,000	5,000
3	10,000	90,000
4	15,000	60,000
5	15,000	75,000
6	3,000	15,000

INTERMEDIATE

8. Consider the following projects:

	Cash Flows (₹)					
Project	C_0	C_1	C_2	C_3	C_4	C_5
A	−1,000	+1,000	0	0	0	0
B	−2,000	+1,000	+1,000	+4,000	+1,000	+1,000
C	−3,000	+1,000	+1,000	0	+1,000	+1,000

a. If the opportunity cost of capital is 10%, which projects have a positive NPV?
b. Calculate the payback period for each project.
c. Which project(s) would a firm using the payback rule accept if the cutoff period were three years?
d. Calculate the discounted payback period for each project.
e. Which project(s) would a firm using the discounted payback rule accept if the cutoff period were three years?

9. Respond to the following comments:
a. "I like the IRR rule. I can use it to rank projects without having to specify a discount rate."
b. "I like the payback rule. As long as the minimum payback period is short, the rule makes sure that the company takes no borderline projects. That reduces risk."

10. Calculate the IRR (or IRRs) for the following project:

eXcel

Visit us at
www.mhhe.com/bmam10e

C_0	C_1	C_2	C_3
−3,000	+3,500	+4,000	−4,000

For what range of discount rates does the project have positive NPV?

11. Consider the following two mutually exclusive projects:

	Cash Flows (₹)			
Project	C_0	C_1	C_2	C_3
A	−100	+60	+60	0
B	−100	0	0	+140

a. Calculate the NPV of each project for discount rates of 0, 10, and 20%. Plot these on a graph with NPV on the vertical axis and discount rate on the horizontal axis.

b. What is the approximate IRR for each project?

c. In what circumstances should the company accept project A?

d. Calculate the NPV of the incremental investment (B − A) for discount rates of 0, 10, and 20%. Plot these on your graph. Show that the circumstances in which you would accept A are also those in which the IRR on the incremental investment is less than the opportunity cost of capital.

12. Mr. Gopi Mittal, the president of Giant Enterprises, has to make a choice between two possible investments:

		Cash Flows (₹ thousands)		
Project	C_0	C_1	C_2	IRR (%)
A	−400	+250	+300	23
B	−200	+140	+179	36

The opportunity cost of capital is 9%. Mr. Mittal is tempted to take B, which has the higher IRR.

a. Explain to Mr. Mittal why this is not the correct procedure.

b. Show him how to adapt the IRR rule to choose the best project.

c. Show him that this project also has the higher NPV.

13. The Titanic Shipbuilding Company has a noncancelable contract to build a small cargo vessel. Construction involves a cash outlay of $250,000 at the end of each of the next two years. At the end of the third year the company will receive payment of $650,000. The company can speed up construction by working an extra shift. In this case there will be a cash outlay of $550,000 at the end of the first year followed by a cash payment of $650,000 at the end of the second year. Use the IRR rule to show the (approximate) range of opportunity costs of capital at which the company should work the extra shift.

eXcel

Visit us at
www.mhhe.com/bmam10e

14. Look again at projects D and E in Section 5.3. Assume that the projects are mutually exclusive and that the opportunity cost of capital is 10%.

a. Calculate the profitability index for each project.

b. Show how the profitability-index rule can be used to select the superior project.

15. Pipli Pharmaceuticals has ₹1 million allocated for capital expenditures. Which of the following projects should the company accept to stay within the ₹1 million budget? How much does the budget limit cost the company in terms of its market value? The opportunity cost of capital for each project is 11%.

Project	Investment (₹ thousands)	NPV (₹ thousands)	IRR (%)
1	300	66	17.2
2	200	−4	10.7
3	250	43	16.6
4	100	14	12.1
5	100	7	11.8
6	350	63	18.0
7	400	48	13.5

CHALLENGE

16. Some people believe firmly, even passionately, that ranking projects on IRR is OK if each project's cash flows can be reinvested at the project's IRR. They also say that the NPV rule "assumes that cash flows are reinvested at the opportunity cost of capital." Think carefully about these statements. Are they true? Are they helpful?

17. Look again at the project cash flows in Problem 10. Calculate the modified IRR as defined in Footnote 4 in Section 5.3. Assume the cost of capital is 12%.

    Now try the following variation on the MIRR concept. Figure out the fraction x such that x times C_1 and C_2 has the same present value as (minus) C_3.

    $$xC_1 + \frac{xC_2}{1.12} = -\frac{C_3}{1.12^2}$$

    Define the modified project IRR as the solution of

    $$C_0 + \frac{(1-x)C_1}{1+\text{IRR}} + \frac{(1-x)C_2}{(1+\text{IRR})^2} = 0$$

    Now you have two MIRRs. Which is more meaningful? If you can't decide, what do you conclude about the usefulness of MIRRs?

18. Consider the following capital rationing problem:

Project	C_0	C_1	C_2	NPV
W	−10,000	−10,000	0	+6,700
X	0	−20,000	+5,000	+9,000
Y	−10,000	+5,000	+5,000	+0
Z	−15,000	+5,000	+4,000	−1,500
Financing available	20,000	20,000	20,000	

Set up this problem as a linear program and solve it.

You can allow partial investments, that is, $0 \leq x \leq 1$. Calculate and interpret the shadow prices[17] on the capital constraints.

VEGETRON'S CFO CALLS AGAIN

(The first episode of this story was presented in Section 5.1.)

Later that afternoon, Vegetron's CFO bursts into your office in a state of anxious confusion. The problem, he explains, is a last-minute proposal for a change in the design of the fermentation tanks that

---

[17] A shadow price is the marginal change in the objective for a marginal change in the constraint.

Vegetron will build to extract hydrated zirconium from a stockpile of powdered ore. The CFO has brought a printout (Table 5.1) of the forecasted revenues, costs, income, and book rates of return for the standard, low-temperature design. Vegetron's engineers have just proposed an alternative high-temperature design that will extract most of the hydrated zirconium over a shorter period, five instead of seven years. The forecasts for the high-temperature method are given in Table 5.2.[18]

CFO: Why do these engineers always have a bright idea at the last minute? But you've got to admit the high-temperature process looks good. We'll get a faster payback, and the rate of return beats Vegetron's 9% cost of capital in every year except the first. Let's see, income is ₹30,000 per year. Average investment is half the ₹400,000 capital outlay, or ₹200,000, so the average rate of return is 30,000/200,000, or 15%—a lot better than the 9% hurdle rate. The average rate of return for the low-temperature process is not that good, only 28,000/200,000, or 14%. Of course we might get a higher rate of return for the low-temperature proposal if we depreciated the investment faster—do you think we should try that?

TABLE 5.1 Income statement and book rates of return for low-temperature extraction of hydrated zirconium (₹ thousands).

	Year						
	1	2	3	4	5	6	7
1. Revenue	140	140	140	140	140	140	140
2. Operating costs	55	55	55	55	55	55	55
3. Depreciation*	57	57	57	57	57	57	57
4. Net income	28	28	28	28	28	28	28
5. Start-of-year book value†	400	343	286	229	171	114	57
6. Book rate of return (4 ÷ 5)	7%	8.2%	9.8%	12.2%	16.4%	24.6%	49.1%

* Rounded. Straight-line depreciation over seven years is 400/7 = 57.14, or ₹57,140 per year.
† Capital investment is ₹400,000 in year 0.

TABLE 5.2 Income statement and book rates of return for high-temperature extraction of hydrated zirconium (₹ thousands).

	Year				
	1	2	3	4	5
1. Revenue	180	180	180	180	180
2. Operating costs	70	70	70	70	70
3. Depreciation*	80	80	80	80	80
4. Net income	30	30	30	30	30
5. Start-of-year book value†	400	320	240	160	80
6. Book rate of return (4 ÷ 5)	7.5%	9.4%	12.5%	18.75%	37.5%

* Straight-line depreciation over five years is 400/5 = 80, or ₹80,000 per year.
† Capital investment is ₹400,000 in year 0.

[18] For simplicity we have ignored taxes. There will be plenty about taxes in Chapter 6.

You: Let's not fixate on book accounting numbers. Book income is not the same as cash flow to Vegetron or its investors. Book rates of return don't measure the true rate of return.

CFO: But people use accounting numbers all the time. We have to publish them in our annual report to investors.

You: Accounting numbers have many valid uses, but they're not a sound basis for capital investment decisions. Accounting changes can have big effects on book income or rate of return, even when cash flows are unchanged.

Here's an example. Suppose the accountant depreciates the capital investment for the low-temperature process over six years rather than seven. Then income for years 1 to 6 goes down, because depreciation is higher. Income for year 7 goes up because the depreciation for that year becomes zero. But there is no effect on year-to-year cash flows, because depreciation is not a cash outlay. It is simply the accountant's device for spreading out the "recovery" of the up-front capital outlay over the life of the project.

CFO: So how do we get cash flows?

You: In these cases it's easy. Depreciation is the only noncash entry in your spreadsheets (Tables 5.1 and 5.2), so we can just leave it out of the calculation. Cash flow equals revenue minus operating costs. For the high-temperature process, annual cash flow is:

$$\text{Cash flow} = \text{revenue} - \text{operating cost} = 180 - 70 = 110, \text{ or } ₹110,000$$

CFO: In effect you're adding back depreciation, because depreciation is a noncash accounting expense.

You: Right. You could also do it that way:

$$\text{Cash flow} = \text{net income} + \text{depreciation} = 30 + 80 = 110, \text{ or } ₹110,000$$

CFO: Of course. I remember all this now, but book returns seem important when someone shoves them in front of your nose.

You: It's not clear which project is better. The high-temperature process appears to be less efficient. It has higher operating costs and generates less total revenue over the life of the project, but of course it generates more cash flow in years 1 to 5.

CFO: Maybe the processes are equally good from a financial point of view. If so we'll stick with the low-temperature process rather than switching at the last minute.

You: We'll have to lay out the cash flows and calculate NPV for each process.

CFO: OK, do that. I'll be back in a half hour—and I also want to see each project's true, DCF rate of return.

Questions

1. Are the book rates of return reported in Tables 5.1 and 5.2 useful inputs for the capital investment decision?

2. Calculate NPV and IRR for each process. What is your recommendation? Be ready to explain to the CFO.

6

Making Investment Decisions with the Net Present Value Rule

In late 2003 Boeing announced its intention to produce and market the 787 Dreamliner. The decision committed Boeing and its partners to a $10 billion capital investment, involving 3 million square feet of additional facilities. If the technical glitches that have delayed production can be sorted out, it looks as if Boeing will earn a good return on this investment. As we write this in August 2009, Boeing has booked orders for 865 Dreamliners, making it one of the most successful aircraft launches in history.

How does a company, such as Boeing, decide to go ahead with the launch of a new airliner? We know the answer in principle. The company needs to forecast the project's cash flows and discount them at the opportunity cost of capital to arrive at the project's NPV. A project with a positive NPV increases shareholder value.

But those cash flow forecasts do not arrive on a silver platter. First, the company's managers need answers to a number of basic questions. How soon can the company get the plane into production? How many planes are likely to be sold each year and at what price? How much does the firm need to invest in new production facilities, and what is the likely production cost? How long will the model stay in production, and what happens to the plant and equipment at the end of that time?

These predictions need to be checked for completeness and accuracy, and then pulled together to produce a single set of cash-flow forecasts. That requires careful tracking of taxes, changes in working capital, inflation, and the end-of-project salvage values of plant, property, and equipment. The financial manager must also ferret out hidden cash flows and take care to reject accounting entries that look like cash flows but truly are not.

Our first task in this chapter is to look at how to develop a set of project cash flows. We will then work through a realistic and comprehensive example of a capital investment analysis.

We conclude the chapter by looking at how the financial manager should apply the present value rule when choosing between investment in plant and equipment with different economic lives. For example, suppose you must decide between machine Y with a 5-year useful life and Z with a 10-year life. The present value of Y's lifetime investment and operating costs is naturally less than Z's because Z will last twice as long. Does that necessarily make Y the better choice? Of course not. You will find that, when you are faced with this type of problem, the trick is to transform the present value of the cash flow into an *equivalent annual* flow, that is, the total cash per year from buying and operating the asset.

6-1 APPLYING THE NET PRESENT VALUE RULE

Many projects require a heavy initial outlay on new production facilities. But often the largest investments involve the acquisition of intangible assets. Consider, for example, the expenditure by major banks on information technology. These projects can soak up hundreds of millions of rupees. Yet much of the expenditure goes to intangibles such as system design, programming, testing, and training. Think also of the huge expenditure by pharmaceutical companies on research and development (R&D). Pfizer, one of the largest pharmaceutical companies, spent ₹7.9 billion on R&D in 2008. The R&D cost of bringing *one* new prescription drug to market has been estimated at ₹800 million.

Expenditures on intangible assets such as IT and R&D are investments just like expenditures on new plant and equipment. In each case the company is spending money today in the expectation that it will generate a stream of future profits. Ideally, firms should apply the same criteria to all capital investments, regardless of whether they involve a tangible or intangible asset.

We have seen that an investment in any asset creates wealth if the discounted value of the future cash flows exceeds the up-front cost. But up to this point we have glossed over the problem of *what* to discount. When you are faced with this problem, you should stick to three general rules:

1. Only cash flow is relevant.
2. Always estimate cash flows on an incremental basis.
3. Be consistent in your treatment of inflation.

We discuss each of these rules in turn.

Rule 1: Only Cash Flow Is Relevant

The first and most important point: Net present value depends on future cash flows. Cash flow is the simplest possible concept; it is just the difference between cash received and cash paid out. Many people nevertheless confuse cash flow with accounting income.

Income statements are intended to show how well the company is performing. Therefore, accountants *start* with "rupees in" and "rupees out," but to obtain accounting income they adjust these inputs in two ways. First, they try to show profit as it is *earned* rather than when the company and its customers get around to paying their bills. Second, they sort cash outflows into two categories:

current expenses and capital expenses. They deduct current expenses when calculating income but do not deduct capital expenses. There is a good reason for this. If the firm lays out a large amount of money on a big capital project, you do not conclude that the firm is performing poorly, even though a lot of cash is going out the door. Therefore, the accountant does not deduct capital expenditure when calculating the year's income but, instead, depreciates it over several years.

As a result of these adjustments, income includes some cash flows and excludes others, and it is reduced by depreciation charges, which are not cash flows at all. It is not always easy to translate the customary accounting data back into actual rupees—rupees you can buy beer with. If you are in doubt about what is a cash flow, simply count the rupees coming in and take away the rupees going out. Don't assume without checking that you can find cash flow by routine manipulations of accounting data.

Always estimate cash flows on an after-tax basis. Some firms do not deduct tax payments. They try to offset this mistake by discounting the cash flows before taxes at a rate higher than the opportunity cost of capital. Unfortunately, there is no reliable formula for making such adjustments to the discount rate.

You should also make sure that cash flows are recorded *only when they occur* and not when work is undertaken or a liability is incurred. For example, taxes should be discounted from their actual payment date, not from the time when the tax liability is recorded in the firm's books.

Rule 2: Estimate Cash Flows on an Incremental Basis

The value of a project depends on *all* the additional cash flows that follow from project acceptance. Here are some things to watch for when you are deciding which cash flows to include:

Do Not Confuse Average with Incremental Payoffs   Most managers naturally hesitate to throw good money after bad. For example, they are reluctant to invest more money in a losing division. But occasionally you will encounter turnaround opportunities in which the *incremental* NPV from investing in a loser is strongly positive.

Conversely, it does not always make sense to throw good money after good. A division with an outstanding past profitability record may have run out of good opportunities. You would not pay a large sum for a 20-year-old horse, sentiment aside, regardless of how many races that horse had won or how many champions it had sired.

Here is another example illustrating the difference between average and incremental returns: Suppose that a railroad bridge is in urgent need of repair. With the bridge the railroad can continue to operate; without the bridge it can't. In this case the payoff from the repair work consists of all the benefits of operating the railroad. The incremental NPV of such an investment may be enormous. Of course, these benefits should be net of all other costs and all subsequent repairs; otherwise the company may be misled into rebuilding an unprofitable railroad piece by piece.

Include All Incidental Effects   It is important to consider a project's effects on the remainder of the firm's business. For example, suppose Sony proposes to launch PlayStation 4, a new version of its video game console. Demand for the new product will almost certainly cut into sales of Sony's existing consoles. This incidental effect needs to be factored into the incremental cash flows. Of course, Sony may reason that it needs to go ahead with the new product because its existing product line is likely to come under increasing threat from competitors. So, even if it decides not to produce the new PlayStation, there is no guarantee that sales of the existing consoles will continue at their present level. Sooner or later they will decline.

Sometimes a new project will *help* the firm's existing business. Suppose that you are the financial manager of an airline that is considering opening a new short-haul route from Jamshedpur to Kolkata. When considered in isolation, the new route may have a negative NPV. But once you allow for the additional business that the new route brings to your other traffic out of Jamshedpur, it may be a very worthwhile investment.

Forecast Sales Today and Recognize After-Sales Cash Flows to Come Later   Financial managers should forecast all incremental cash flows generated by an investment. Sometimes these incremental cash flows last for decades. When GE commits to the design and production of a new jet engine, the cash inflows come first from the sale of engines and then from service and spare parts. A jet engine will be in use for 30 years. Over that period revenues from service and spare parts will be roughly seven times the engine's purchase price. GE's revenue in 2008 from commercial engine services was $6.8 billion versus $5.2 billion from commercial engine sales.[1]

Many manufacturing companies depend on the revenues that come *after* their products are sold. The consulting firm Accenture estimates that services and parts typically account for about 25% of revenues and 50% of profits for industrial companies.

Do Not Forget Working Capital Requirements   Net working capital (often referred to simply as *working capital*) is the difference between a company's short-term assets and liabilities. The principal short-term assets are accounts receivable (customers' unpaid bills) and inventories of raw materials and finished goods. The principal short-term liabilities are accounts payable (bills that *you* have not paid). Most projects entail an additional investment in working capital. This investment should, therefore, be recognized in your cash-flow forecasts. By the same token, when the project comes to an end, you can usually recover some of the investment. This is treated as a cash inflow. We supply a numerical example of working-capital investment later in this chapter.

Include Opportunity Costs   The cost of a resource may be relevant to the investment decision even when no cash changes hands. For example, suppose a new manufacturing operation uses land that could otherwise be sold for ₹100,000. This resource is not free: It has an opportunity cost, which is the cash it could generate for the company if the project were rejected and the resource were sold or put to some other productive use.

This example prompts us to warn you against judging projects on the basis of "before versus after." The proper comparison is "with or without." A manager comparing before versus after might not assign any value to the land because the firm owns it both before and after:

Before	Take Project	After	Cash Flow, Before versus After
Firm owns land	→	Firm still owns land	0

The proper comparison, with or without, is as follows:

With	Take Project	After	Cash Flow, with Project
Firm owns land	→	Firm still owns land	0

---

[1] P. Glader, "GE's Focus on Services Faces Test," *The Wall Street Journal*, March 3, 2009, p. B1. The following estimate from Accenture also comes from this article.

Without	Do Not Take Project	After	Cash Flow, without Project
	→	Firm sells land for ₹100,000	₹100,000

Comparing the two possible "afters," we see that the firm gives up ₹100,000 by undertaking the project. This reasoning still holds if the land will not be sold but is worth ₹100,000 to the firm in some other use.

Sometimes opportunity costs may be very difficult to estimate; however, where the resource can be freely traded, its opportunity cost is simply equal to the market price. Why? It cannot be otherwise. If the value of a parcel of land to the firm is less than its market price, the firm will sell it. On the other hand, the opportunity cost of using land in a particular project cannot exceed the cost of buying an equivalent parcel to replace it.

Forget Sunk Costs   Sunk costs are like spilled milk: They are past and irreversible outflows. Because sunk costs are bygones, they cannot be affected by the decision to accept or reject the project, and so they should be ignored.

For example, when Lockheed sought a federal guarantee for a bank loan to continue development of the TriStar airplane, the company and its supporters argued it would be foolish to abandon a project on which nearly ₹1 billion had already been spent. Some of Lockheed's critics countered that it would be equally foolish to continue with a project that offered no prospect of a satisfactory return on that ₹1 billion. Both groups were guilty of the *sunk-cost fallacy;* the ₹1 billion was irrecoverable and, therefore, irrelevant.

Beware of Allocated Overhead Costs   We have already mentioned that the accountant's objective is not always the same as the investment analyst's. A case in point is the allocation of overhead costs. Overheads include such items as supervisory salaries, rent, heat, and light. These overheads may not be related to any particular project, but they have to be paid for somehow. Therefore, when the accountant assigns costs to the firm's projects, a charge for overhead is usually made. Now our principle of incremental cash flows says that in investment appraisal we should include only the *extra* expenses that would result from the project. A project may generate extra overhead expenses; then again, it may not. We should be cautious about assuming that the accountant's allocation of overheads represents the true extra expenses that would be incurred.

Remember Salvage Value   When the project comes to an end, you may be able to sell the plant and equipment or redeploy the assets elsewhere in the business. If the equipment is sold, you must pay tax on the difference between the sale price and the book value of the asset. The salvage value (net of any taxes) represents a positive cash flow to the firm.

Some projects have significant shut-down costs, in which case the final cash flows may be *negative*. For example, the mining company, FCX, has earmarked over ₹430 million to cover the future reclamation and closure costs of its New Mexico mines.

Rule 3: Treat Inflation Consistently

As we pointed out in Chapter 3, interest rates are usually quoted in *nominal* rather than *real* terms. For example, if you buy an 8% Government security, the government promises to pay you ₹80 interest each year, but it does not promise what that ₹80 will buy. Investors take inflation into account when they decide what is an acceptable rate of interest.

If the discount rate is stated in nominal terms, then consistency requires that cash flows should also be estimated in nominal terms, taking account of trends in selling price, labor and materials costs, etc. This calls for more than simply applying a single assumed inflation rate to all components of cash flow. Labor costs per hour of work, for example, normally increase at a faster rate than the consumer price index because of improvements in productivity. Tax savings from depreciation do *not* increase with inflation; they are constant in nominal terms because tax law in India allows only the original cost of assets to be depreciated.

Of course, there is nothing wrong with discounting real cash flows at a real discount rate. In fact this is standard procedure in countries with high and volatile inflation. Here is a simple example showing that real and nominal discounting, properly applied, always give the same present value.

Suppose your firm usually forecasts cash flows in nominal terms and discounts at a 15% nominal rate. In this particular case, however, you are given project cash flows in real terms, that is, current rupees:

Real Cash Flows (₹ thousands)			
C_0	C_1	C_2	C_3
−100	+35	+50	+30

It would be inconsistent to discount these real cash flows at the 15% nominal rate. You have two alternatives: Either restate the cash flows in nominal terms and discount at 15%, or restate the discount rate in real terms and use it to discount the real cash flows.

Assume that inflation is projected at 10% a year. Then the cash flow for year 1, which is ₹35,000 in current rupees, will be $35,000 \times 1.10 =$ ₹38,500 in year-1 rupees. Similarly the cash flow for year 2 will be $50,000 \times (1.10)^2 =$ ₹60,500 in year-2 rupees, and so on. If we discount these nominal cash flows at the 15% nominal discount rate, we have

$$\text{NPV} = -100 + \frac{38.5}{1.15} + \frac{60.5}{(1.15)^2} + \frac{39.9}{(1.15)^3} = 5.5, \text{ or } ₹5,500$$

Instead of converting the cash-flow forecasts into nominal terms, we could convert the discount rate into real terms by using the following relationship:

$$\text{Real discount rate} = \frac{1 + \text{nominal discount rate}}{1 + \text{inflation rate}} - 1$$

In our example this gives

$$\text{Real discount rate} = \frac{1.15}{1.10} - 1 = .045, \text{ or } 4.5\%$$

If we now discount the real cash flows by the real discount rate, we have an NPV of ₹5,500, just as before:

$$\text{NPV} = -100 + \frac{35}{1.045} + \frac{50}{(1.045)^2} + \frac{30}{(1.045)^3} = 5.5, \text{ or } ₹5,500$$

The message of all this is quite simple. Discount nominal cash flows at a nominal discount rate. Discount real cash flows at a real rate. *Never* mix real cash flows with nominal discount rates or nominal flows with real rates.

6-2 EXAMPLE—IM&C'S FERTILIZER PROJECT

As the newly appointed financial manager of International Mulch and Compost Company (IM&C), you are about to analyze a proposal for marketing guano as a garden fertilizer. (IM&C's planned advertising campaign features a rustic gentleman who steps out of a vegetable patch singing, "All my troubles have guano way.")[2]

You are given the forecasts shown in Table 6.1.[3] The project requires an investment of ₹10 million in plant and machinery (line 1). This machinery can be dismantled and sold for net proceeds estimated at ₹4 million in year 7 (line 1, column 7). This amount is your forecast of the plant's *salvage value*.

TABLE 6.1   IM&C's guano project—projections (₹ thousand) reflecting inflation and assuming WDV straight-line depreciation.

eXcel

Visit us at
www.mhhe.com/bmam10e

		Period							
		0	1	2	3	4	5	6	7
1.	Capital investment	10,000							−4,000[a]
2.	Accumulated depn.		1,500	2,775	3,859	4,780	5,563	6,229	
3.	Year-end book value	10,000	8,500	7,225	6,141	5,220	4,437	3,771	
4.	Working capital		550	1,289	3,261	4,890	3,583	2,002	0
5.	Total book value (3 + 4)		9,050	8,514	9,402	10,110	8,020	5,773	0
6.	Sales		523	12,887	32,610	48,901	35,834	19,717	
7.	Cost of goods sold[b]		837	7,729	19,552	29,345	21,492	11,830	
8.	Other costs[c]	4,000	2,200	1,210	1,331	1,464	1,611	1,772	
9.	Depreciation		1,500	1,275	1,084	921	783	666	
10.	Pretax profits (6 − 7 − 8 − 9)	−4,000	−4,014	2,673	10,643	17,171	11,948	5,449	229
11.	Tax	−1,360	−1,364	909	3,618	5,836	4,061	1,852	78
12.	Profit after tax (10 − 11)	−2,640	−2,650	1,764	7,026	11,334	7,887	3,597	151

[a] Salvage value.
[b] We have departed from the usual income-statement format by *not* including depreciation in cost of goods sold. Instead, we break out depreciation separately (see line 9).
[c] Start-up costs in years 0 and 1, and general and administrative costs in years 1 to 6.
[d] The difference between the salvage value and the ending book value of ₹3,771 is a taxable profit.

Whoever prepared Table 6.1 depreciated the capital investment over six years using 15%[4] as the depreciation rate. The estimated salvage value of the plant and machinery (₹3.771 million) is lower than your forecasted salvage value of ₹4 million. Since the Income Tax Act in India prescribes written down value (WDV) method to depreciate assets, we have used WDV method here[5]. Under this

---

[2] Sorry

[3] "Live" Excel versions of Tables 6.1, 6.2, 6.4, 6.5, 6.6, and 6.8 are available on the book's website, www.mhhe.com/bmam10e8e. However, in this book, we have re-estimated the depreciation figures by using WDV (rather than SLM, as has been assumed in the US edition of the book) and hence you will find some difference between the figures given in the book and the ones given in the website.

[4] The depreciation rate on plant and machinery in India has been reduced to 15% (from 25%) after the 2005 Budget.

[5] From the assessment year 1998–99, a business unit engaged in generation and distribution of power has the option of claiming depreciation using straight line method for any asset acquired after March 31, 1997.

method annual depreciation equals a constant proportion of the written down value of the asset at the beginning of the year. The WDV depreciation in year t is

Depreciation in year t = Beginning of the year t (same as close of year $t-1$) Book Value of the Asset × Depreciation Rate

Thus for example, in year 2, the depreciation is 15% of beginning of year-2 book value (₹8.5 million), that is, ₹1.275 million.

Lines 6 through 12 in Table 6.1 show a simplified profit and loss account for the guano project[6]. This will be our starting point for estimating cash flow. All the entries in the table are nominal amounts. In other words, IM&C's managers have taken into account the likely effect of inflation on prices and costs.

Table 6.2 derives cash-flow forecasts from the investment and income data given in Table 6.1. The project's net cash flow is the sum of three elements:

$$\text{Net cash flow} = \text{cash flow from capital investment and disposal}$$
$$+ \text{cash flow from changes in working capital}$$
$$+ \text{operating cash flow}$$

eXcel

Visit us at
www.mhhe.com/bmam10e

TABLE 6.2 IM&C's guano project—initial cash-flow analysis (₹ thousand).

		Period							
		0	1	2	3	4	5	6	7
1.	Capital investment and disposable	−10,000	0	0	0	0	0	0	3,922[a]
2.	Change in working capital		−550	−739	−1,972	−1,629	1,307	1,581	2,002
3.	Sales	0	523	12,887	32,610	48,901	35,834	19,717	0
4.	Cost of goods sold	0	837	7,729	19,552	29,345	21,492	11,830	0
5.	Other costs	4,000	2,200	1,210	1,331	1,464	1,611	1,772	0
6.	Tax	−1,360	−1,364	909	3,618	5,836	4,061	1,852	0
7.	Operating cash flow (3 − 4 − 5 − 6)	−2,640	−1,150	3,039	8,109	12,256	8,670	4,263	0
8.	Net cash flow (1 + 2 + 7)	−12,640	−1,700	2,300	6,137	10,627	9,977	5,844	5,924
9.	Present value @ 20%	−12,640	−1,416	1,598	3,552	5,125	4,009	1,957	1,653
10.	Net present value =	3,837	(sum of 9)						

[a] Salvage value of ₹4000 less tax of ₹78 on the difference between salvage value and ending book value.

Each of these items is shown in the table. Row 1 shows the initial capital investment and the estimated salvage value of the equipment when the project comes to an end. If, as you expect, the salvage value is higher than the depreciated value of the machinery, you will have to pay tax on the difference. So the salvage value in row 1 is shown after payment of this tax. Row 2 of the table shows the changes in working capital, and the remaining rows calculate the project's operating cash flows.

[6] We have departed from the usual profit and loss account format by separating depreciation from costs of goods sold.

Notice that in calculating the operating cash flows we did not deduct depreciation. Depreciation is an accounting entry. It affects the tax that the company pays, but the firm does not send anyone a check for depreciation. The operating cash flow is simply the rupees coming in less the rupees going out:[7]

$$\text{Operating cash flow} = \text{revenue} - \text{cash expenses} - \text{taxes}$$

For example, in year 6 of the guano project:

$$\text{Operating cash flow} = 19,717 - (11,830 + 1,772) - 1,852 = 4,263$$

IM&C estimates the nominal opportunity cost of capital for projects of this type as 20%. When all cash flows are added up and discounted, the guano project is seen to offer a net present value of about ₹3.9 million:

$$NPV = -12,600 - \frac{1,416}{1.20} + \frac{1,598}{(1.20)^2} + \frac{3,552}{(1.20)^3} + \frac{5,125}{(1.20)^4} + \frac{4,009}{(1.20)^5}$$

$$+ \frac{1,957}{(1.20)^6} + \frac{1,653}{(1.20)^7} = +3,837 \text{ or } ₹3,837,000$$

Separating Investment and Financing Decisions

Our analysis of the guano project takes no notice of how that project is financed. It may be that IM&C will decide to finance partly by debt, but if it does we will not subtract the debt proceeds from the required investment, nor will we recognize interest and principal payments as cash outflows. We analyze the project as if it were all-equity-financed, treating all cash outflows as coming from stockholders and all cash inflows as going to them.

We approach the problem in this way so that we can separate the analysis of the investment decision from the financing decision. But this does not mean that the financing decision can be ignored. We explain in Chapter 19 how to recognize the effect of financing choices on project values.

Investments in Working Capital

Now here is an important point. You can see from line 2 of Table 6.2 that working capital increases in the early and middle years of the project. What is working capital, you may ask, and why does it increase?

---

[7] There are several alternative ways to calculate operating cash flow. For example, you can add depreciation back to the after-tax profit:

$$\text{Operating cash flow 5 after-tax profit 1 depreciation}$$

Thus, in year 6 of the guano project:

$$\text{Operating cash flow} = 3,597 + 666 = 4,263$$

Another alternative is to calculate after-tax profit assuming *no* depreciation, and then to add back the tax saving provided by the depreciation allowance:

$$\text{Operating cash flow} = (\text{revenues} - \text{expenses}) \times (1 - \text{tax rate}) + (\text{depreciation} \times \text{tax rate})$$

Thus, in year 6 of the guano project:

$$\text{Operating cash flow} = (19,717 - 11,830 - 1,772) \times (1 - 0.3399) + (666 \times 0.3399) = 4,263$$

Working capital summarizes the net investment in short-term assets associated with a firm, business, or project. Its most important components are *inventory, accounts receivable,* and *accounts payable.* The guano project's requirements for working capital in year 2 might be as follows:

$$\text{Working capital} = \text{inventory} + \text{accounts receivable} - \text{accounts payable}$$
$$₹1,289 = 635 \quad\quad +1,030 \quad\quad\quad -376$$

Why does working capital increase? There are several possibilities:

1. Sales recorded on the income statement overstate actual cash receipts from guano shipments because sales are increasing and customers are slow to pay their bills. Therefore, accounts receivable increase.
2. It takes several months for processed guano to age properly. Thus, as projected sales increase, larger inventories have to be held in the aging sheds.
3. An offsetting effect occurs if payments for materials and services used in guano production are delayed. In this case accounts payable will increase.

The additional investment in working capital from year 2 to 3 might be

$$
\begin{array}{ccccccc}
\text{Additional} & & & & \text{increase in} & & \text{increase in} \\
\text{investment in} & = & \text{increase in} & + & \text{accounts} & - & \text{accounts} \\
\text{working capital} & & \text{inventory} & & \text{receivable} & & \text{payable} \\
₹1,972 & = & 972 & + & 1,500 & - & 500
\end{array}
$$

A more detailed cash-flow forecast for year 3 would look like Table 6.3.

TABLE 6.3 Details of cash-flow forecast for IM&C's guano project in year 3 (₹ thousands).

Cash Flows		Data from Forecasted P & L Account		Working-Capital Changes
Cash inflow	=	Sales	−	Increase in accounts receivable
₹31,110	=	32,610		1,500
Cash outflow	=	Cost of goods sold, other costs, and taxes	+	Increase in inventory net of increase in accounts payable
₹24,973	=	(19,552 + 1,331 + 3617.640675)	+	(972 − 500)
		Net cash flow = cash inflow − cash outflow		
		₹6,137 = 31,110 − 24,973		

Working capital is one of the most common sources of confusion in estimating project cash flows. Here are the most common mistakes:

1. *Forgetting about working capital entirely.* We hope you never fall into that trap.
2. *Forgetting that working capital may change during the life of the project.* Imagine that you sell ₹100,000 of goods one year and that customers pay six months late. You will therefore have ₹50,000 of unpaid bills. Now you increase prices by 10%, so revenues increase to ₹110,000. If customers continue to pay six months late, unpaid bills increase to ₹55,000, and therefore you need to make an *additional* investment in working capital of ₹5,000.

3. *Forgetting that working capital is recovered at the end of the project.* When the project comes to an end, inventories are run down, any unpaid bills are paid off (you hope) and you recover your investment in working capital. This generates a cash *inflow*.

There is an alternative to worrying about changes in working capital. You can estimate cash flow directly by counting the dollars coming in from customers and deducting the rupees going out to suppliers. You would also deduct all cash spent on production, including cash spent for goods held in inventory. In other words,

1. If you replace each year's sales with that year's cash payments received from customers, you don't have to worry about accounts receivable.

2. If you replace cost of goods sold with cash payments for labor, materials, and other costs of production, you don't have to keep track of inventory or accounts payable.

However, you would still have to construct a projected income statement to estimate taxes.

We discuss the links between cash flow and working capital in much greater detail in Chapter 30.

A Further Note on Depreciation

Depreciation is a noncash expense; it is important only because it reduces taxable income. It provides an annual *tax shield* equal to the product of depreciation and the marginal tax rate. Thus, for example, in our case, the tax shield in year 1 is given by:

$$\text{Tax shield} = \text{depreciation} \times \text{tax rate}$$
$$= 1{,}500 \times 0.3399 = 509.85, \text{ or } ₹509{,}850$$

The present value of the tax shields (for all the six years put together) is ₹1,272,722 at a 20% discount rate.

Now if IM&C could just get those tax shields sooner, they would be worth more, right? If a company is allowed to use a higher depreciation rate in the initial part of the life of the asset, then it will get the tax shields sooner. In the U.S., the tax laws allow accelerated depreciation, whereby a company can compute depreciation at a higher rate in the initial part of the life of the asset.

In India, a company can (on top of normal depreciation) claim additional depreciation under certain situations. The Finance Act 2005 amended Section 32 of the Income Tax Act in India to increase the rate of additional depreciation to 20 percent (from 15%) on new plant and machinery (other than ships and aircraft), acquired and installed after 31 March 2005. Prior to this amendment, only new undertakings were granted the additional depreciation. The Finance Act, 2005, however, reduced the normal depreciation rate on plant and machinery to 15% (from 25%).[8]

Let's assume that the guano project qualifies for the additional depreciation of 20%. IM&C can claim this additional depreciation in the first year. Therefore, IM&C can write off 35% of the depreciable investment in year 1, as soon as the assets are placed in service, then 15% of the written-down value from year 2 till year 6. Here are the tax shields for the guano project.

The present value of the tax shields is ₹1, 639, 730 about ₹367, 010 higher than the earlier estimate we get by ignoring additional depreciation.

---

[8] See http://incometaxindia.gov.in/Notifications/IncomeTaxAct/2005/Notification672005.pdf *for the depreciation rates for the different types of assets in India.*

TABLE 6.4 Estimation of depreciation tax shield (₹thousands) when additional depreciation is allowed.

	Year					
	1	2	3	4	5	6
Normal depreciation	1500.00	975.00	828.75	704.44	598.77	508.96
Additional depreciation	2000.00	0.00	0.00	0.00	0.00	0.00
Total tax depreciation	3500	975	829	704	599	509
Tax shield (tax depreciation: tax rate, $t = 0.3399$)	1,190	331	282	239	204	173
Book value	10000.00	6500.00	5525.00	4696.25	3991.81	3393.04

Table 6.5 recalculates the guano project's impact on IM&C's future tax bills, and Table 6.6 shows revised after-tax cash flows and present value. This time, we have incorporated realistic assumptions about taxes. We of course, arrive at a higher NPV than in Table 6.2, because that table ignored the additional present value of additional depreciation.

TABLE 6.5 Tax Payments on IM&C's guano project (₹ thousands)

All the figures are from Table 6.1. A negative tax payment means a cash inflow, assuming IM&C can use the tax loss on its guano project to shield income from other projects.

		Period							
		0	1	2	3	4	5	6	7
1.	Capital investment	10,000	0	0	0	0	0	0	−4,000
2.	Accumulated Depreciation		3,500	4,475	5,304	6,008	6,607	7,116	0
3.	Year-end book value	10,000	6,500	5,525	4,696	3,992	3,393	2,884	0
4.	Working Capital		550	1,289	3,261	4,890	3,583	2,002	0
5.	Total book value (3 + 4)		7,050	6,814	7,957	8,882	6,976	4,886	0
6.	Sales		523	12,887	32,610	48,901	35,834	19,717	
7.	Cost of Goods Sold		837	7,729	19,552	29,345	21,492	11,830	
8.	Other costs	4000	2,200	1,210	1,331	1,464	1,611	1,772	
9.	Depreciation		3,500	975	829	704	599	509	0
10.	Pre-tax Profits (6 − 7 − 8 − 9)	−4,000	−6,014	2,973	10,898	17,388	12,132	5,606	1,116
11.	Tax at 33.99%	−1,360	−2,044	1,011	3,704	5,910	4,124	1,905	379
12.	Profit after tax (10 − 11)	−2,640	−3,970	1,962	7,194	11,478	8,008	3,701	737

There is one possible additional problem lurking in the woodwork behind Table 6.5: It is the *minimum alternate tax (MAT)*[9], which can limit or defer the tax shields of additional depreciation or other tax preference items. As per Section 115JB of the Income Tax Act in India, if tax payable by a company (ignoring the provisions of Section 115JB of the Income Tax Act) is lower than 18% of the book profit, then the effective tax liability of the company will be 18% of the *book profit*. The effective minimum alternate tax rate comes out to 20.008% in 2011. For the purpose of MAT, *book profit* is

---

[9] Refer to Section 115JB of the Income Tax Act of India, 1961.

TABLE 6.6   IM&C's guano project – revised cash flow analysis (₹ thousands)

		\multicolumn{8}{c}{Period}
		0	1	2	3	4	5	6	7
1.	Sales	0	523	12,887	32,610	48,901	35,834	19,717	0
2.	Cost of goods sold	0	837	7,729	19,552	29,345	21,492	11,830	0
3.	Other costs	4,000	2,200	1,210	1,331	1,464	1,611	1,772	0
4.	Tax	−1,360	−2,044	1,011	3,704	5,910	4,124	1,905	379
5.	Cash flow from operations (1 − 2 − 3 − 4)	−2,640	−470	2,937	8,023	12,182	8,607	4,210	−379
6.	Change working capital		−550	−739	−1,972	−1,629	1,307	1,581	2,002
7.	Capital investment and disposal	−10,000	0	0	0	0	0	0	4,000
8.	Net cash flow (5 + 6 + 7)	−12,640	−1,020	2,198	6,051	10,553	9,914	5,791	5,623
9.	Present value	−12,640	−850	1,527	3,502	5,089	3,984	1,939	1,569
10.	Net present value =	4,120	(sum of 9)						

estimated from the *net profit* (as reported to the shareholders) after making certain adjustments. One of the adjustments requires adding back the excess depreciation to the net profit of the company. In a few cases, this can partially neutralize the benefits of having additional depreciation. We will discuss about MAT in Chapter 26, rather than here. So make a mental note not to sign off on a capital budgeting analysis without checking whether your company is subject to the minimum alternative tax.

A Final Comment on Taxes

In India, depreciation is normally computed on the written down value of the block of assets. Here a 'block of assets' refers to a group of similar assets (belonging to the same class) and having the same rate of depreciation. Thus for example, as per the Income Tax Act in India, all the furniture and fittings (including electrical fittings) form one block of assets with a WDV depreciation rate of 10 percent. Similarly certain types of plant and equipment will form another block of assets with WDV depreciation rate of 15%, and so on.

In the guano example, we simplified by assuming that when IM&C sells the asset at a gain, it has to pay tax on the difference between the sale proceeds and the written down value of the asset. In India, the tax authorities follow a different system however. Section 50 of the Income Tax Act, 1961 prescribes the following procedure to determine the tax implications of sale of assets.[10]

Step 1: Determine the net consideration (sale proceeds) by deducting any expense incurred while selling (or transferring) the asset from the actual consideration received while selling the asset. Thus, for example, in the guano project, we assumed that IM&C will receive ₹4 million by selling the asset after the sixth year. If we further assume that IM&C will incur an additional cost of ₹1 lakh to sell the asset, then the net consideration will be ₹3.9 million.

Step 2: Determine the short term capital gain by deducting the written down value of the block of assets from the net consideration. Here, it is important to understand that we subtract the written

[10] Source: http://incometaxindia.gov.in/publications/4_Compute_Your_Capital_Gains/Chapter4.asp

down value of the block of assets (and not the asset sold) from the net consideration to derive the short term capital gains.

To illustrate, in the guano example, the written down value of the asset at the end of year 6 was ₹2.88 million (Table 6.5). Suppose, this asset is part of a block, whose written down value at the time was more than ₹4 million. Then the difference between ₹4 million (or ₹3.9 million, if one considers the cost incurred while selling the asset) and ₹2.88 million will not be treated as capital gains. If this happens, then the cash flow in year 7 (in both Table 6.1, and Table 6.5) will be higher by the tax that IM&C does not have to pay. The NPV of the project will accordingly be higher by the present value of the excess tax computed.

All large Indian corporations keep two separate sets of books, one for stockholders and one for the Income Tax Department. It is common to use straight-line depreciation (using the rates provided in the Schedule XIV of the Companies Act) on the stockholder books and written down value rates on the tax books. The Income Tax Department does not object to this as it is perfectly legal to do so, and it makes the firm's reported earnings higher, if written down value method were used everywhere.[11] There are many other differences between tax books and shareholder books. This separation of tax accounts from shareholder accounts is not found worldwide. In Japan, for example, taxes reported to shareholders must equal taxes paid to the government; ditto for France and many other European countries.

Project Analysis

Let us review. Several pages ago, you embarked on an analysis of IM&C's guano project. You started with a simplified statement of assets and income for the project that you used to develop a series of cash-flow forecasts. Then you remembered accelerated depreciation and had to recalculate cash flows and NPV.

You were lucky to get away with just two NPV calculations. In real situations, it often takes several tries to purge all inconsistencies and mistakes. Then you may want to analyze some alternatives. For example, should you go for a larger or smaller project? Would it be better to market the fertilizer through wholesalers or directly to the consumer? Should you build 90,000-square-foot aging sheds for the guano in northern South Dakota rather than the planned 100,000-square-foot sheds in southern North Dakota? In each case your choice should be the one offering the highest NPV. Sometimes the alternatives are not immediately obvious. For example, perhaps the plan calls for two costly high-speed packing lines. But, if demand for guano is seasonal, it may pay to install just one high-speed line to cope with the base demand and two slower but cheaper lines simply to cope with the summer rush. You won't know the answer until you have compared NPVs.

You will also need to ask some "what if" questions. How would NPV be affected if inflation rages out of control? What if technical problems delay start-up? What if gardeners prefer chemical fertilizers to your natural product? Managers employ a variety of techniques to develop a better understanding of how such unpleasant surprises could damage NPV. For example, they might undertake a *sensitivity analysis,* in which they look at how far the project could be knocked off course by bad news about one of the variables. Or they might construct different *scenarios* and estimate the effect of each on NPV. Another technique, known as *break-even analysis,* is to explore how far sales could fall short of forecast before the project went into the red.

---

[11] Thus for example, Schedule XIV of the Companies Act recommends a straight line rate of 4.75% (single shift) for plant and machinery against the WDV rate of 15% prescribed by the Income Tax Act.

In Chapter 10 we practice using each of these "what if" techniques. You will find that project analysis is much more than one or two NPV calculations.[12]

Calculating NPV in Other Countries and Currencies

Our guano project was undertaken in India by an Indian company. But the principles of capital investment are the same worldwide. For example, suppose that you are the financial manager of the German company, K.G.R. Ökologische Naturdüngemittel GmbH (KGR), that is faced with a similar opportunity to make a €10 million investment in Germany. What changes?

1. KGR must also produce a set of cash-flow forecasts, but in this case the project cash flows are stated in euros, the Eurozone currency.
2. In developing these forecasts, the company needs to recognize that prices and costs will be influenced by the German inflation rate.
3. Profits from KGR's project are liable to the German rate of corporate tax.
4. KGR must use the German system of depreciation allowances. In common with many other countries, Germany allows firms to choose between two methods of depreciation—the straight-line system and the declining-balance system. KGR opts for the declining-balance method and writes off 30% of the depreciated value of the equipment each year (the maximum allowed under current German tax rules). Thus, in the first year KGR writes off $.30 \times 10 = €3$ million and the written-down value of the equipment falls to $10 - 3 = €7$ million. In year 2, KGR writes off $.30 \times 7 = €2.1$ million and the written-down value is further reduced to $7 - 2.1 = €4.9$ million. In year 4 KGR observes that depreciation would be higher if it could switch to straight-line depreciation and write off the balance of €3.43 million over the remaining three years of the equipment's life. Fortunately, German tax law allows it to do this. Therefore, KGR's depreciation allowance each year is calculated as follows:

	Year					
	1	**2**	**3**	**4**	**5**	**6**
Written-down value, start of year (€ millions)	10	7	4.9	3.43	2.29	1.14
Depreciation (€ millions)	$.3 \times 10$ = 3	$.3 \times 7$ = 2.1	$.3 \times 4.9$ = 1.47	3.43/3 = 1.14	3.43/3 = 1.14	3.43/3 = 1.14
Written-down value, end of year (€ millions)	$10 - 3$ = 7	$7 - 2.1$ = 4.9	$4.9 - 1.47$ = 3.43	$3.43 - 1.14$ = 2.29	$2.29 - 1.14$ = 1.14	$1.14 - 1.14$ = 0

Notice that KGR's depreciation deduction declines for the first few years and then flattens out. That is also the case with the Indian system of depreciation. In fact, MACRS is just another example of the declining-balance method with a later switch to straight-line.

---

[12] In the meantime you might like to get ahead of the game by viewing the live spreadsheets for the guano project and seeing how NPV would change with a shortfall in sales or an unexpected rise in costs.

6-3 INVESTMENT TIMING

The fact that a project has a positive NPV does not mean that it is best undertaken now. It might be even more valuable if undertaken in the future.

The question of optimal timing is not difficult when the cash flows are certain. You must first examine alternative start dates (t) for the investment and calculate the net *future* value at each of these dates. Then, to find which of the alternatives would add most to the firm's *current* value, you must discount these net future values back to the present:

$$\text{Net present value of investment if undertaken at date } t = \frac{\text{Net future value at date } t}{(1 + r)^t}$$

For example, suppose you own a large tract of inaccessible timber. To harvest it, you have to invest a substantial amount in access roads and other facilities. The longer you wait, the higher the investment required. On the other hand, lumber prices will rise as you wait, and the trees will keep growing, although at a gradually decreasing rate.

Let us suppose that the net present value of the harvest at different *future* dates is as follows:

	Year of Harvest					
	0	**1**	**2**	**3**	**4**	**5**
Net *future* value (₹ thousands)	50	64.4	77.5	89.4	100	109.4
Change in value from previous year (%)		+28.8	+20.3	+15.4	+11.9	+9.4

As you can see, the longer you defer cutting the timber, the more money you will make. However, your concern is with the date that maximizes the net *present* value of your investment, that is, its contribution to the value of your firm *today*. You therefore need to discount the net future value of the harvest back to the present. Suppose the appropriate discount rate is 10%. Then, if you harvest the timber in year 1, it has a net *present* value of ₹58,500:

$$\text{NPV if harvested in year 1} = \frac{64.4}{1.10} = 58.5, \text{ or } ₹58,500$$

The net present value for other harvest dates is as follows:

	Year of Harvest					
	0	**1**	**2**	**3**	**4**	**5**
Net present value (₹ thousands)	50	58.5	64.0	67.2	68.3	67.9

The optimal point to harvest the timber is year 4 because this is the point that maximizes NPV.

Notice that before year 4 the net future value of the timber increases by more than 10% a year: The gain in value is greater than the cost of the capital tied up in the project. After year 4 the gain in value is still positive but less than the cost of capital. So delaying the harvest further just reduces shareholder wealth.[13]

The investment-timing problem is much more complicated when you are unsure about future cash flows. We return to the problem of investment timing under uncertainty in Chapters 10 and 22.

6-4 EQUIVALENT ANNUAL CASH FLOWS

When you calculate NPV, you transform future, year-by-year cash flows into a lump-sum value expressed in today's dollars (or euros, or other relevant currency). But sometimes it's helpful to reverse the calculation, transforming an investment today into an equivalent stream of future cash flows. Consider the following example.

Investing to Produce Reformulated Gasoline at California Refineries

In the early 1990s, the California Air Resources Board (CARB) started planning its "Phase 2" requirements for reformulated gasoline (RFG). RFG is gasoline blended to tight specifications designed to reduce pollution from motor vehicles. CARB consulted with refiners, environmentalists, and other interested parties to design these specifications.

As the outline for the Phase 2 requirements emerged, refiners realized that substantial capital investments would be required to upgrade California refineries. What might these investments mean for the retail price of gasoline? A refiner might ask: "Suppose my company invests $400 million to upgrade our refinery to meet Phase 2. How much extra revenue would we need every year to recover that cost?" Let's see if we can help the refiner out.

Assume $400 million of capital investment and a real (inflation-adjusted) cost of capital of 7%. The new equipment lasts for 25 years, and does not change raw-material and operating costs.

How much additional revenue does it take to cover the $400 million investment? The answer is simple: Just find the 25-year annuity payment with a present value equal to $400 million.

$$PV \text{ of annuity} = \text{annuity payment} \times 25\text{-year annuity factor}$$

At a 7% cost of capital, the 25-year annuity factor is 11.65.

$$\$400 \text{ million} = \text{annuity payment} \times 11.65$$
$$\text{Annuity payment} = \$34.3 \text{ million per year}^{[14]}$$

---

[13] Our timber-cutting example conveys the right idea about investment timing, but it misses an important practical point: The sooner you cut the first crop of trees, the sooner the second crop can start growing. Thus, the value of the second crop depends on when you cut the first. The more complex and realistic problem can be solved in one of two ways:

1. Find the cutting dates that maximize the present value of a series of harvests, taking into account the different growth rates of young and old trees.

2. Repeat our calculations, counting the future market value of cut-over land as part of the payoff to the first harvest. The value of cut-over land includes the present value of all subsequent harvests.

The second solution is far simpler if you can figure out what cut-over land will be worth.

[14] For simplicity we have ignored taxes. Taxes would enter this calculation in two ways. First, the $400 million investment would generate depreciation tax shields. The easiest way to handle these tax shields is to calculate their PV and subtract it from the initial outlay. For example, if the PV of depreciation tax shields is $83 million, equivalent annual cost would be calculated on an after-tax investment base of $400 − 83 = $317 million. Second, our annuity payment is after-tax. To actually achieve after-tax revenues of, say, $34.3 million, the refiner would have to achieve pretax revenue sufficient to pay tax and have $34.3 million left over. If the tax rate is 35%, the required pretax revenue is 34.3/(1 − .35) = $52.8 million. Note how the after-tax figure is "grossed up" by dividing by one minus the tax rate.

This annuity is called an **equivalent annual cash flow.** It is the annual cash flow sufficient to recover a capital investment, including the cost of capital for that investment, over the investment's economic life. In our example the refiner would need to generate an extra ₹34.3 million for each of the next 25 years to recover the initial investment of ₹400 million.

Equivalent annual cash flows are handy—and sometimes essential—tools of finance. Here is a further example.

Choosing between Long- and Short-Lived Equipment

Suppose the firm is forced to choose between two machines, A and B. The two machines are designed differently but have identical capacity and do exactly the same job. Machine A costs ₹15,000 and will last three years. It costs ₹5,000 per year to run. Machine B is an economy model costing only ₹10,000, but it will last only two years and costs ₹6,000 per year to run. These are real cash flows: the costs are forecasted in rupees of constant purchasing power.

Because the two machines produce exactly the same product, the only way to choose between them is on the basis of cost. Suppose we compute the present value of cost:

Machine	C_0	C_1	C_2	C_3	PV at 6% (₹ thousands)
			Costs (₹ thousands)		
A	+15	+5	+5	+5	28.37
B	+10	+6	+6		21.00

Should we take machine B, the one with the lower present value of costs? Not necessarily, because B will have to be replaced a year earlier than A. In other words, the timing of a future investment decision depends on today's choice of A or B.

So, a machine with total PV(costs) of ₹21,000 spread over three years (0, 1, and 2) is not necessarily better than a competing machine with PV(costs) of ₹28,370 spread over four years (0 through 3). We have to convert total PV(costs) to a cost per year, that is, to an equivalent annual cost. For machine A, the annual cost turns out to be 10.61, or ₹10,610 per year:

Machine	C_0	C_1	C_2	C_3	PV at 6% (₹ thousands)
			Costs (₹ thousands)		
Machine A	+15	+5	+5	+5	28.37
Equivalent annual cost		+10.61	+10.61	+10.61	28.37

We calculated the equivalent annual cost by finding the three-year annuity with the same present value as A's lifetime costs.

$$PV \text{ of annuity} = PV \text{ of A's costs} = 28.37$$
$$= \text{annuity payment} \times \text{3-year annuity factor}$$

The annuity factor is 2.673 for three years and a 6% real cost of capital, so

$$\text{Annuity payment} = \frac{28.37}{2.673} = 10.61$$

A similar calculation for machine B gives:

	Costs (₹ thousands)			
	C_0	C_1	C_2	PV at 6% (₹ thousands)
Machine B	+10	+6	+6	21.00
Equivalent annual cost		+11.45	+11.45	21.00

Machine A is better, because its equivalent annual cost is less (₹10,610 versus ₹11,450 for machine B).

You can think of the equivalent annual cost of machine A or B as an annual rental charge. Suppose the financial manager is asked to *rent* machine A to the plant manager actually in charge of production. There will be three equal rental payments starting in year 1. The three payments must recover both the original cost of machine A in year 0 and the cost of running it in years 1 to 3. Therefore the financial manager has to make sure that the rental payments are worth ₹28,370, the total PV(costs) of machine A. You can see that the financial manager would calculate a fair rental payment equal to machine A's equivalent annual cost.

Our rule for choosing between plant and equipment with different economic lives is, therefore, to select the asset with the lowest fair rental charge, that is, the lowest equivalent annual cost.

Equivalent Annual Cash Flow and Inflation

The equivalent annual costs we just calculated are *real* annuities based on forecasted *real* costs and a 6% *real* discount rate. We could, of course, restate the annuities in nominal terms. Suppose the expected inflation rate is 5%; we multiply the first cash flow of the annuity by 1.05, the second by $(1.05)^2 = 1.1025$, and so on.

		C_0	C_1	C_2	C_3
A	Real annuity		10.61	10.61	10.61
	Nominal cash flow		11.14	11.70	12.28
B	Real annuity		11.45	11.45	
	Nominal cash flow		12.02	12.62	

Note that B is still inferior to A. Of course the present values of the nominal and real cash flows are identical. Just remember to discount the real annuity at the real rate and the equivalent nominal cash flows at the consistent nominal rate.[15]

When you use equivalent annual costs simply for comparison of costs per period, as we did for machines A and B, we strongly recommend doing the calculations in real terms.[16] But if you actually rent out the machine to the plant manager, or anyone else, be careful to specify that the rental payments be "indexed" to inflation. If inflation runs on at 5% per year and rental payments do not increase

---

[15] The nominal discount rate is

$$r_{nominal} = (1 + r_{real})(1 + \text{inflation rate}) - 1$$
$$= (1.06)(1.05) - 1 = .113, \text{ or } 11.3\%$$

Discounting the nominal annuities at this rate gives the same present values as discounting the real annuities at 6%.

[16] Do *not* calculate equivalent annual cash flows as level *nominal* annuities. This procedure can give incorrect rankings of true equivalent annual flows at high inflation rates. See Challenge Question 32 at the end of this chapter for an example.

proportionally, then the real value of the rental payments must decline and will not cover the full cost of buying and operating the machine.

Equivalent Annual Cash Flow and Technological Change

So far we have the following simple rule: Two or more streams of cash outflows with different lengths or time patterns can be compared by converting their present values to equivalent annual cash flows. Just remember to do the calculations in real terms.

Now any rule this simple cannot be completely general. For example, when we evaluated machine A versus machine B, we implicitly assumed that their fair rental charges would *continue* at ₹10,610 versus ₹11,450. This will be so only if the *real* costs of buying and operating the machines stay the same.

Suppose that this is not the case. Suppose that thanks to technological improvements new machines each year cost 20% less in real terms to buy and operate. In this case future owners of brand-new, lower-cost machines will be able to cut their rental cost by 20%, and owners of old machines will be forced to match this reduction. Thus, we now need to ask: if the real level of rents declines by 20% a year, how much will it cost to rent each machine?

If the rent for year 1 is $rent_1$, rent for year 2 is $rent_2 = .8 \times rent_1$. $Rent_3$ is $.8 \times rent_2$, or $.64 \times rent_1$. The owner of each machine must set the rents sufficiently high to recover the present value of the costs. In the case of machine A,

$$\text{PV of renting machine A} = \frac{rent_1}{1.06} + \frac{rent_2}{(1.06)^2} + \frac{rent_3}{(1.06)^3} = 28.37$$

$$= \frac{rent_1}{1.06} + \frac{.8(rent_1)}{(1.06)^2} + \frac{.64(rent_1)}{(1.06)^3} = 28.37$$

$$rent_1 = 12.94, \text{ or } \$12,940$$

For machine B,

$$\text{PV of renting machine B} = \frac{rent_1}{1.06} + \frac{.8(rent_1)}{(1.06)^2} = 21.00$$

$$rent_1 = 12.69, \text{ or } ₹12,690$$

The merits of the two machines are now reversed. Once we recognize that technology is expected to reduce the real costs of new machines, then it pays to buy the shorter-lived machine B rather than become locked into an aging technology with machine A in year 3.

You can imagine other complications. Perhaps machine C will arrive in year 1 with an even lower equivalent annual cost. You would then need to consider scrapping or selling machine B at year 1 (more on this decision below). The financial manager could not choose between machines A and B in year 0 without taking a detailed look at what each machine could be replaced with.

Comparing equivalent annual cash flow should never be a mechanical exercise; always think about the assumptions that are implicit in the comparison. Finally, remember why equivalent annual cash flows are necessary in the first place. The reason is that A and B will be replaced at different future dates. The choice between them therefore affects future investment decisions. If subsequent decisions are not affected by the initial choice (for example, because neither machine will be replaced) then we do *not need to take future decisions into account.*[17]

Equivalent Annual Cash Flow and Taxes We have not mentioned taxes. But you surely realized that machine A and B's lifetime costs should be calculated after-tax, recognizing that operating costs are tax-deductible and that capital investment generates depreciation tax shields.

Deciding When to Replace an Existing Machine

The previous example took the life of each machine as fixed. In practice the point at which equipment is replaced reflects economic considerations rather than total physical collapse. *We* must decide when to replace. The machine will rarely decide for us.

Here is a common problem. You are operating an elderly machine that is expected to produce a net cash *inflow* of ₹4,000 in the coming year and ₹4,000 next year. After that it will give up the ghost. You can replace it now with a new machine, which costs ₹15,000 but is much more efficient and will provide a cash inflow of ₹8,000 a year for three years. You want to know whether you should replace your equipment now or wait a year.

We can calculate the NPV of the new machine and also its *equivalent annual cash flow,* that is, the three-year annuity that has the same net present value:

Cash Flows (₹ thousands)					
	C_0	C_1	C_2	C_3	NPV at 6% (₹ thousands)
New machine	−15	+8	+8	+8	6.38
Equivalent annual cash flow		+2.387	+2.387	+2.387	6.38

In other words, the cash flows of the new machine are equivalent to an annuity of ₹2,387 per year. So we can equally well ask at what point we would want to replace our old machine with a new one producing ₹2,387 a year. When the question is put this way, the answer is obvious. As long as your old machine can generate a cash flow of ₹4,000 a year, who wants to put in its place a new one that generates only ₹2,387 a year?

It is a simple matter to incorporate salvage values into this calculation. Suppose that the current salvage value is ₹8,000 and next year's value is ₹7,000. Let us see where you come out next year if you wait and then sell. On one hand, you gain ₹7,000, but you lose today's salvage value *plus* a year's return on that money. That is, $8,000 \times 1.06 = ₹8,480$. Your net loss is $8,480 - 7,000 = ₹1,480$, which only partly offsets the operating gain. You should not replace yet.

Remember that the logic of such comparisons requires that the new machine be the best of the available alternatives and that it in turn be replaced at the optimal point.

Cost of Excess Capacity Any firm with a centralized information system (computer servers, storage, software, and telecommunication links) encounters many proposals for using it. Recently installed systems tend to have excess capacity, and since the immediate marginal costs of using them seem to be negligible, management often encourages new uses. Sooner or later, however, the load on a system

---

[17] However, if neither machine will be replaced, then we have to consider the extra revenue generated by machine A in its third year, when will be operating but B will not.

increases to the point at which management must either terminate the uses it originally encouraged or invest in another system several years earlier than it had planned. Such problems can be avoided if a proper charge is made for the use of spare capacity.

Suppose we have a new investment project that requires heavy use of an existing information system. The effect of adopting the project is to bring the purchase date of a new, more capable system forward from year 4 to year 3. This new system has a life of five years, and at a discount rate of 6% the present value of the cost of buying and operating it is ₹500,000.

We begin by converting the ₹500,000 present value of the cost of the new system to an equivalent annual cost of ₹118,700 for each of five years.[18] Of course, when the new system in turn wears out, we will replace it with another. So we face the prospect of future information-system expenses of ₹118,700 a year. If we undertake the new project, the series of expenses begins in year 4; if we do not undertake it, the series begins in year 5. The new project, therefore, results in an *additional* cost of ₹118,700 in year 4. This has a present value of $118,700/(1.06)^4$, or about ₹94,000. This cost is properly charged against the new project. When we recognize it, the NPV of the project may prove to be negative. If so, we still need to check whether it is worthwhile undertaking the project now and abandoning it later, when the excess capacity of the present system disappears.

SUMMARY

By now present value calculations should be a matter of routine. However, forecasting project cash flows will never be routine. Here is a checklist that will help you to avoid mistakes:

1. Discount cash flows, not profits.
   a. Remember that depreciation is not a cash flow (though it may affect tax payments).
   b. Concentrate on cash flows after taxes. Stay alert for differences between tax depreciation and depreciation used in reports to shareholders.
   c. Exclude debt interest or the cost of repaying a loan from the project cash flows. This enables you to separate the investment from the financing decision.
   d. Remember the investment in working capital. As sales increase, the firm may need to make additional investments in working capital, and as the project comes to an end, it will recover those investments.
   e. Beware of allocated overhead charges for heat, light, and so on. These may not reflect the incremental costs of the project.
2. Estimate the project's incremental cash flows—that is, the difference between the cash flows with the project and those without the project.
   a. Include all indirect effects of the project, such as its impact on the sales of the firm's other products.
   b. Forget sunk costs.
   c. Include *opportunity costs,* such as the value of land that you would otherwise sell.
3. Treat inflation consistently.
   a. If cash flows are forecasted in nominal terms, use a nominal discount rate.
   b. Discount real cash flows at a real rate.

These principles of valuing capital investments are the same worldwide, but inputs and assumptions vary by country and currency. For example, cash flows from a project in Germany would be in euros, not dollars, and would be forecasted after German taxes.

---

[18] The present value of ₹118,700 a year for five years discounted at 6% is ₹500,000.

When we assessed the guano project, we transformed the series of future cash flows into a single measure of their present value. Sometimes it is useful to reverse this calculation and to convert the present value into a stream of annual cash flows. For example, when choosing between two machines with unequal lives, you need to compare equivalent annual cash flows. Remember, though, to calculate equivalent annual cash flows in real terms and adjust for technological change if necessary.

BASIC

1. Which of the following should be treated as incremental cash flows when deciding whether to invest in a new manufacturing plant? The site is already owned by the company, but existing buildings would need to be demolished.
   a. The market value of the site and existing buildings.
   b. Demolition costs and site clearance.
   c. The cost of a new access road put in last year.
   d. Lost earnings on other products due to executive time spent on the new facility.
   e. A proportion of the cost of leasing the president's jet airplane.
   f. Future depreciation of the new plant.
   g. The reduction in the corporation's tax bill resulting from tax depreciation of the new plant.
   h. The initial investment in inventories of raw materials.
   i. Money already spent on engineering design of the new plant.

2. Ms. Chhavi Varma will be paid ₹100,000 one year hence. This is a nominal flow, which she discounts at an 8% nominal discount rate:

$$PV = \frac{100,000}{1.08} = ₹92,593$$

   The inflation rate is 4%.

   Calculate the PV of Ms. Varma payment using the equivalent *real* cash flow and *real* discount rate. (You should get exactly the same answer as she did.)

3. True or false?
   a. A project's depreciation tax shields depend on the actual future rate of inflation.
   b. Project cash flows should take account of interest paid on any borrowing undertaken to finance the project.
   c. In India, income reported to the tax authorities must equal income reported to shareholders.
   d. Accelerated depreciation reduces near-term project cash flows and therefore reduces project NPV.

4. How does the PV of depreciation tax shields vary if (i) the additional depreciation is allowed throughout the life of the asset rather than only in the first year of its operation, and if (ii) the normal depreciation rate is 25% and there is no additional depreciation?

5. The following table tracks the main components of working capital over the life of a four-year project.

	2010	2011	2012	2013	2014
Accounts receivable	0	150,000	225,000	190,000	0
Inventory	75,000	130,000	130,000	95,000	0
Accounts payable	25,000	50,000	50,000	35,000	0

Calculate net working capital and the cash inflows and outflows due to investment in working capital.

6. When appraising mutually exclusive investments in plant and equipment, financial managers calculate the investments' equivalent annual costs and rank the investments on this basis. Why is this necessary? Why not just compare the investments' NPVs? Explain briefly.

7. Air conditioning for a college dormitory will cost ₹1.5 million to install and ₹200,000 per year to operate. The system should last 25 years. The real cost of capital is 5%, and the college pays no taxes. What is the equivalent annual cost?

8. Machines A and B are mutually exclusive and are expected to produce the following real cash flows:

Cash Flows (₹ thousands)			
Machine	C_0	C_1	C_2	C_3
A	−100	+110	+121	
B	−120	+110	+121	+133

The real opportunity cost of capital is 10%.
a. Calculate the NPV of each machine.
b. Calculate the equivalent annual cash flow from each machine.
c. Which machine should you buy?

9. Machine C was purchased five years ago for ₹200,000 and produces an annual real cash flow of ₹80,000. It has no salvage value but is expected to last another five years. The company can replace machine C with machine B (see Problem 8) *either* now *or* at the end of five years. Which should it do?

INTERMEDIATE

10. Restate the net cash flows in Table 6.6 in real terms. Discount the restated cash flows at a real discount rate. Assume a 20% *nominal* rate and 10% expected inflation. NPV should be unchanged at +4,120, or ₹4,120,000.

11. CSC is evaluating a new project to produce encapsulators. The initial investment in plant and equipment is $500,000. Sales of encapsulators in year 1 are forecasted at $200,000 and costs at $100,000. Both are expected to increase by 10% a year in line with inflation. Profits are taxed at 35%.

Visit us at
www.mhhe.com/bmam10e

Working capital in each year consists of inventories of raw materials and is forecasted at 20% of sales in the following year.

The project will last five years and the equipment at the end of this period will have no further value. For tax purposes the equipment can be depreciated straight-line over these five years. If the nominal discount rate is 15%, show that the net present value of the project is the same whether calculated using real cash flows or nominal flows.

12. In 1898 Simon North announced plans to construct a funeral home on land he owned and rented out as a storage area for railway carts. (A local newspaper commended Mr. North for not putting the cart before the hearse.) Rental income from the site barely covered real estate taxes, but the site was valued at $45,000. However, Mr. North had refused several offers for the land and planned to continue renting it out if for some reason the funeral home was not built. Therefore he did not include the value of the land as an outlay in his NPV analysis of the funeral home. Was this the correct procedure? Explain.

13. Each of the following statements is true. Explain why they are consistent.
a. When a company introduces a new product, or expands production of an existing product, investment in net working capital is usually an important cash outflow.

b. Forecasting changes in net working capital is not necessary if the timing of *all* cash inflows and outflows is carefully specified.

14. Mrs. Malhotra, the treasurer of Ideal Pune, has a problem. The company has just ordered a new kiln for ₹40 lakh. Of this sum, ₹5 lakh is described by the supplier as an installation cost. Mrs. Malhotra does not know whether the Income Tax Department will permit the company to treat this as a tax-deductible current expense, or as a capital investment. In the latter case, the company could depreciate ₹5 lakh by using 15% as the WDV depreciation rate over a period of 5 years. In this case, Mrs. Malhotra can also charge the written down value of the kiln at the end of the fifth year as depreciation in the sixth year. How will the IT Department's decision affect the after-tax cost of the kiln? The tax rate is 33.66% and the opportunity cost of capital is 15%.

eXcel
Visit us at
www.mhhe.com/bmam10e

15. After spending ₹3 million on research, Better Mousetraps has developed a new trap. The project requires an initial investment in plant and equipment of ₹6 million. This investment will be depreciated straight-line over five years to a value of zero, but, when the project comes to an end in five years, the equipment can in fact be sold for ₹500,000. The firm believes that working capital at each date must be maintained at 10% of next year's forecasted sales. Production costs are estimated at ₹1.50 per trap and the traps will be sold for ₹4 each. (There are no marketing expenses.) Sales forecasts are given in the following table. The firm pays tax at 35% and the required return on the project is 12%. What is the NPV?

eXcel
Visit us at
www.mhhe.com/bmam10e

Year:	0	1	2	3	4	5
Sales (millions of traps)	0	.5	.6	1.0	1.0	.6

16. A project requires an initial investment of ₹10,00,000 and is expected to produce a cash inflow before tax of ₹2,60,000 per year for five years. Company A has substantial accumulated tax losses and is unlikely to pay taxes in the foreseeable future. Company B pays corporate taxes at a rate of 33.66% and can depreciate the investment for tax purposes using a WDV depreciation rate of 15% in the first four years. Company B can change the entire written-down value of the project as depreciation in the fifth year. Suppose the opportunity cost of capital is 8%. Ignore inflation.

eXcel
Visit us at
www.mhhe.com/bmam10e

a. Calculate project NPV for each company.
b. What is the IRR of the after-tax cash flows for each company? What does comparison of the IRRs suggest is the effective corporate tax rate?

17. Go back to the guano project again and answer the following questions.

eXcel
Visit us at
www.mhhe.com/bmam10e

a. How does the guano project's NPV change if IM&C is forced to depreciate the asset by using 10% as the depreciation rate?
b. New engineering estimates raise the possibility that capital investment will be more than ₹10 million, perhaps as much as ₹15 million. On the other hand, you believe that the 20% cost of capital is unrealistically high and that the true cost of capital is about 11%. Is the project still attractive under these alternative assumptions?
c. Continue with the assumed $15 million capital investment and the 11% cost of capital. What if sales, cost of goods sold, and net working capital are each 10% higher in every year? Recalculate NPV. (*Note:* Enter the revised sales, cost, and working-capital forecasts in the spreadsheet for Table 6.1.)

Assume that IM&G does not have to pay any tax in year 7, following Section 50 of the Income Tax Act in India. Re-estimate the NPV of the project.

18. A widget manufacturer currently produces 200,000 units a year. It buys widget lids from an outside supplier at a price of ₹2 a lid. The plant manager believes that it would be cheaper to make these lids rather than buy them. Direct production costs are estimated to be only ₹1.50 a lid. The necessary machinery would cost ₹150,000 and would last 10 years. This investment could be written off for tax purposes using the seven-year tax depreciation schedule. The plant manager estimates that the operation would require additional working capital of ₹30,000 but argues that this sum can be ignored since it is recoverable at the end of the 10 years. If the company pays tax at a rate of 35% and the opportunity cost of capital is 15%, would you support the plant manager's proposal? State clearly any additional assumptions that you need to make.

19. Reliable Electric is considering a proposal to manufacture a new type of industrial electric motor which would replace most of its existing product line. A research breakthrough has given Reliable a two-year lead on its competitors. The project proposal is summarized in Table 6.7 on the next page.
    a. Read the notes to the table carefully. Which entries make sense? Which do not? Why or why not?
    b. What additional information would you need to construct a version of Table 6.7 that makes sense?
    c. Construct such a table and recalculate NPV. Make additional assumptions as necessary.

20. Marsha Jones has bought a used Mercedes horse transporter for her Connecticut estate. It cost $35,000. The object is to save on horse transporter rentals.

    Marsha had been renting a transporter every other week for $200 per day plus $1.00 per mile. Most of the trips are 80 or 100 miles in total. Marsha usually gives the driver a $40 tip. With the new transporter she will only have to pay for diesel fuel and maintenance, at about $.45 per mile. Insurance costs for Marsha's transporter are $1,200 per year.

    The transporter will probably be worth $15,000 (in real terms) after eight years, when Marsha's horse Nike will be ready to retire. Is the transporter a positive-NPV investment? Assume a nominal discount rate of 9% and a 3% forecasted inflation rate. Marsha's transporter is a personal outlay, not a business or financial investment, so taxes can be ignored.

21. United Pigpen is considering a proposal to manufacture high-protein hog feed. The project would make use of an existing warehouse, which is currently rented out to a neighboring firm. The next year's rental charge on the warehouse is $100,000, and thereafter the rent is expected to grow in line with inflation at 4% a year. In addition to using the warehouse, the proposal envisages an investment in plant and equipment of $1.2 million. This could be depreciated for tax purposes straight-line over 10 years. However, Pigpen expects to terminate the project at the end of eight years and to resell the plant and equipment in year 8 for $400,000. Finally, the project requires an initial investment in working capital of $350,000. Thereafter, working capital is forecasted to be 10% of sales in each of years 1 through 7.

    Year 1 sales of hog feed are expected to be $4.2 million, and thereafter sales are forecasted to grow by 5% a year, slightly faster than the inflation rate. Manufacturing costs are expected to be 90% of sales, and profits are subject to tax at 35%. The cost of capital is 12%. What is the NPV of Pigpen's project?

22. Hindustan Motors has been producing its Ambassador car in India since 1948. As the company's Web site explains, the Ambassador's "dependability, spaciousness and comfort factor have made it the most preferred car for generations of Indians." Hindustan is now considering producing the car in China. This

TABLE 6.7 Cash flows and present value of Reliable Electric's proposed investment (₹ thousands). See Problem 19.

	2009	2010	2011	2012–2019
1. Capital expenditure	−10,400			
2. Research and development	−2,000			
3. Working capital	−4,000			
4. Revenue		8,000	16,000	40,000
5. Operating costs		−4,000	−8,000	−20,000
6. Overhead		−800	−1,600	−4,000
7. Depreciation		−1,040	−1,040	−1,040
8. Interest		−2,160	−2,160	−2,160
9. Income	−2,000	0	3,200	12,800
10. Tax	0	0	420	4,480
11. Net cash flow	−16,400	0	2,780	8,320
12. Net present value = +13,932				

Notes:

1. *Capital expenditure:* ₹8 million for new machinery and ₹2.4 million for a warehouse extension. The full cost of the extension has been charged to this project, although only about half of the space is currently needed. Since the new machinery will be housed in an existing factory building, no charge has been made for land and building.
2. *Research and development:* ₹1.82 million spent in 2008. This figure was corrected for 10% inflation from the time of expenditure to date. Thus $1.82 \times 1.1 = ₹2$ million.
3. *Working capital:* Initial investment in inventories.
4. *Revenue:* These figures assume sales of 2,000 motors in 2010, 4,000 in 2011, and 10,000 per year from 2012 through 2019. The initial unit price of ₹4,000 is forecasted to remain constant in real terms.
5. *Operating costs:* These include all direct and indirect costs. Indirect costs (heat, light, power, fringe benefits, etc.) are assumed to be 200% of direct labor costs. Operating costs per unit are forecasted to remain constant in real terms at ₹2,000.
6. *Overhead:* Marketing and administrative costs, assumed equal to 10% of revenue.
7. *Depreciation:* Straight-line for 10 years.
8. *Interest:* Charged on capital expenditure and working capital at Reliable's current borrowing rate of 15%.
9. *Income:* Revenue less the sum of research and development, operating costs, overhead, depreciation, and interest.
10. *Tax:* 35% of income. However, income is negative in 2009. This loss is carried forward and deducted from taxable income in 2011.
11. *Net cash flow:* Assumed equal to income less tax.
12. *Net present value:* NPV of net cash flow at a 15% discount rate.

will involve an initial investment of RMB 4 billion.[19] The plant will start production after one year. It is expected to last for five years and have a salvage value at the end of this period of RMB 500 million in real terms. The plant will produce 100,000 cars a year. The firm anticipates that in the first year it will be able to sell each car for RMB 65,000, and thereafter the price is expected to increase by 4% a year. Raw materials for each car are forecasted to cost RMB 18,000 in the first year and these costs are predicted to increase by 3% annually. Total labor costs for the plant are expected to be RMB 1.1 billion in the first year and thereafter will increase by 7% a year. The land on which the plant is built can be rented for five years at a fixed cost of RMB 300 million a year payable at the *beginning* of each year. Hindustan's discount rate

[19] The Renminbi (RMB) is the Chinese currency.

for this type of project is 12% (nominal). The expected rate of inflation is 5%. The plant can be depreciated straight-line over the five-year period and profits will be taxed at 25%. Assume all cash flows occur at the end of each year except where otherwise stated. What is the NPV of the plant?

23. In the International Mulch and Compost example (Section 6.2), we assumed that losses on the project could be used to offset taxable profits elswhere in the corporation. Suppose that the losses had to be carried forward and offset against future taxable profits from the project. How would the project NPV change? What is the value of the company's ability to use the tax deductions immediately?

24. As a result of improvements in product engineering, United Automation is able to sell one of its two milling machines. Both machines perform the same function but differ in age. The newer machine could be sold today for $50,000. Its operating costs are $20,000 a year, but in five years the machine will require a $20,000 overhaul. Thereafter operating costs will be $30,000 until the machine is finally sold in year 10 for $5,000.

*e**X**cel*
Visit us at
www.mhhe.com/bmam10e

The older machine could be sold today for $25,000. If it is kept, it will need an immediate $20,000 overhaul. Thereafter operating costs will be $30,000 a year until the machine is finally sold in year 5 for $5,000.

Both machines are fully depreciated for tax purposes. The company pays tax at 35%. Cash flows have been forecasted in real terms. The real cost of capital is 12%. Which machine should United Automation sell? Explain the assumptions underlying your answer.

25. Low-energy lightbulbs cost $3.50, have a life of nine years, and use about $1.60 of electricity a year. Conventional lightbulbs cost only $.50, but last only about a year and use about $6.60 of energy. If the real discount rate is 5%, what is the equivalent annual cost of the two products?

26. Hayden Inc. has a number of copiers that were bought four years ago for $20,000. Currently maintenance costs $2,000 a year, but the maintenance agreement expires at the end of two years and thereafter the annual maintenance charge will rise to $8,000. The machines have a current resale value of $8,000, but at the end of year 2 their value will have fallen to $3,500. By the end of year 6 the machines will be valueless and would be scrapped.

*e**X**cel*
Visit us at
www.mhhe.com/bmam10e

Hayden is considering replacing the copiers with new machines that would do essentially the same job. These machines cost $25,000, and the company can take out an eight-year maintenance contract for $1,000 a year. The machines will have no value by the end of the eight years and will be scrapped.

Both machines are depreciated by using seven-year MACRS, and the tax rate is 35%. Assume for simplicity that the inflation rate is zero. The real cost of capital is 7%. When should Hayden replace its copiers?

27. Return to the start of Section 6-4, where we calculated the equivalent annual cost of producing reformulated gasoline in California. Capital investment was $400 million. Suppose this amount can be depreciated for tax purposes on the 10-year MACRS schedule from Table 6.4. The marginal tax rate, including California taxes, is 39%, the cost of capital is 7%, and there is no inflation. The refinery improvements have an economic life of 25 years.

*e**X**cel*
Visit us at
www.mhhe.com/bmam10e

  a. Calculate the after-tax equivalent annual cost. (*Hint:* It's easiest to use the PV of depreciation tax shields as an offset to the initial investment).
  b. How much extra would retail gasoline customers have to pay to cover this equivalent annual cost? (*Note:* Extra income from higher retail prices would be taxed.)

28. The Borstal Company has to choose between two machines that do the same job but have different lives. The two machines have the following costs:

Visit us at
www.mhhe.com/bmam10e

Year	Machine A	Machine B
0	₹40,000	₹50,000
1	10,000	8,000
2	10,000	8,000
3	10,000 + replace	8,000
4		8,000 + replace

These costs are expressed in real terms.

a. Suppose you are Borstal's financial manager. If you had to buy one or the other machine and rent it to the production manager for that machine's economic life, what annual rental payment would you have to charge? Assume a 6% real discount rate and ignore taxes.

b. Which machine should Borstal buy?

c. Usually the rental payments you derived in part (a) are just hypothetical—a way of calculating and interpreting equivalent annual cost. Suppose you actually do buy one of the machines and rent it to the production manager. How much would you actually have to charge in each future year if there is steady 8% per year inflation? (*Note:* The rental payments calculated in part (a) are real cash flows. You would have to mark up those payments to cover inflation.)

29. Look again at your calculations for Problem 28 above. Suppose that technological change is expected to reduce costs by 10% per year. There will be new machines in year 1 that cost 10% less to buy and operate than A and B. In year 2 there will be a second crop of new machines incorporating a further 10% reduction, and so on. How does this change the equivalent annual costs of machines A and B?

Visit us at
www.mhhe.com/bmam10e

30. The president's executive jet is not fully utilized. You judge that its use by other officers would increase direct operating costs by only $20,000 a year and would save $100,000 a year in airline bills. On the other hand, you believe that with the increased use the company will need to replace the jet at the end of three years rather than four. A new jet costs $1.1 million and (at its current low rate of use) has a life of six years. Assume that the company does not pay taxes. All cash flows are forecasted in real terms. The real opportunity cost of capital is 8%. Should you try to persuade the president to allow other officers to use the plane?

CHALLENGE

31. One measure of the effective tax rate is the difference between the IRRs of pretax and after-tax cash flows, divided by the pretax IRR. Consider, for example, an investment I generating a perpetual stream of pretax cash flows C. The pretax IRR is C/I, and the after-tax IRR is $C(1 - T_C)/I$, where T_C is the statutory tax rate. The effective rate, call it T_E, is

$$T_E = \frac{C/I - C(1 - T_c)/I}{C/I} = T_c$$

In this case the effective rate equals the statutory rate.

a. Calculate T_E for the guano project in Section 6.2.

b. How does the effective rate depend on the tax depreciation schedule? On the inflation rate?

c. Consider a project where all of the up-front investment is treated as an expense for tax purposes. For example, R&D and marketing outlays are always expensed in the United States. They create no tax depreciation. What is the effective tax rate for such a project?

32. We warned that equivalent annual costs should be calculated in real terms. We did not fully explain why. This problem will show you.

Look back to the cash flows for machines A and B (in "Choosing between Long- and Short-Lived Equipment"). The present values of purchase and operating costs are 28.37 (over three years for A) and 21.00 (over two years for B). The real discount rate is 6% and the inflation rate is 5%.

a. Calculate the three- and two-year *level nominal* annuities which have present values of 28.37 and 21.00. Explain why these annuities are *not* realistic estimates of equivalent annual costs. (*Hint:* In real life machinery rentals increase with inflation.)

b. Suppose the inflation rate increases to 25%. The real interest rate stays at 6%. Recalculate the level nominal annuities. Note that the *ranking* of machines A and B appears to change. Why?

33. In December 2005 Mid-American Energy brought online one of the largest wind farms in the world. It cost an estimated $386 million and the 257 turbines have a total capacity of 360.5 megawatts (mW). Wind speeds fluctuate and most wind farms are expected to operate at an average of only 35% of their rated capacity. In this case, at an electricity price of $55 per megawatt-hour (mWh), the project will produce revenues in the first year of $60.8 million (i.e., .35 × 8,760 hours × 360.5 mW × $55 per mWh). A reasonable estimate of maintenance and other costs is about $18.9 million in the first year of operation. Thereafter, revenues and costs should increase with inflation by around 3% a year.

e**X**cel

Visit us at
www.mhhe.com/bmam10e

Conventional power stations can be depreciated using 20-year MACRS, and their profits are taxed at 35%. Suppose that the project will last 20 years and the cost of capital is 12%. To encourage renewable energy sources, the government offers several tax breaks for wind farms.

a. How large a tax break (if any) was needed to make Mid-American's investment a positive-NPV venture?

b. Some wind farm operators assume a capacity factor of 30% rather than 35%. How would this lower capacity factor alter project NPV?

MINI-CASE

NEW ECONOMY TRANSPORT (A)

The New Economy Transport Company (NETCO) was formed in 1955 to carry cargo and passengers between ports in the Pacific Northwest and Alaska. By 2008 its fleet had grown to four vessels, including a small dry-cargo vessel, the *Vital Spark*.

The *Vital Spark* is 25 years old and badly in need of an overhaul. Peter Handy, the finance director, has just been presented with a proposal that would require the following expenditures:

Overhaul engine and generators	$340,000
Replace radar and other electronic equipment	75,000
Repairs to hull and superstructure	310,000
Painting and other repairs	95,000
	$820,000

Mr. Handy believes that all these outlays could be depreciated for tax purposes in the seven-year MACRS class.
NETCO's chief engineer, McPhail, estimates the postoverhaul operating costs as follows:

Fuel	$ 450,000
Labor and benefits	480,000
Maintenance	141,000
Other	110,000
	$1,181,000

These costs generally increase with inflation, which is forecasted at 2.5% a year.

The *Vital Spark* is carried on NETCO's books at a net depreciated value of only $100,000, but could probably be sold "as is," along with an extensive inventory of spare parts, for $200,000. The book value of the spare parts inventory is $40,000. Sale of the *Vital Spark* would generate an immediate tax liability on the difference between sale price and book value.

The chief engineer also suggests installation of a brand-new engine and control system, which would cost an extra $600,000.[20] This additional equipment would not substantially improve the *Vital Spark*'s performance, but would result in the following reduced annual fuel, labor, and maintenance costs:

Fuel	$ 400,000
Labor and benefits	405,000
Maintenance	105,000
Other	110,000
	$1,020,000

Overhaul of the *Vital Spark* would take it out of service for several months. The overhauled vessel would resume commercial service next year. Based on past experience, Mr. Handy believes that it would generate revenues of about $1.4 million next year, increasing with inflation thereafter.

But the *Vital Spark* cannot continue forever. Even if overhauled, its useful life is probably no more than 10 years, 12 years at the most. Its salvage value when finally taken out of service will be trivial.

NETCO is a conservatively financed firm in a mature business. It normally evaluates capital investments using an 11% cost of capital. This is a nominal, not a real, rate. NETCO's tax rate is 35%.

Question

1. Calculate the NPV of the proposed overhaul of the *Vital Spark,* with and without the new engine and control system. To do the calculation, you will have to prepare a spreadsheet table showing all costs

---

[20] This additional outlay would also qualify for tax depreciation in the seven-year MACRS class.

after taxes over the vessel's remaining economic life. Take special care with your assumptions about depreciation tax shields and inflation.

NEW ECONOMY TRANSPORT (B)

There is no question that the *Vital Spark* needs an overhaul soon. However, Mr. Handy feels it unwise to proceed without also considering the purchase of a new vessel. Cohn and Doyle, Inc., a Wisconsin shipyard, has approached NETCO with a design incorporating a Kort nozzle, extensively automated navigation and power control systems, and much more comfortable accommodations for the crew. Estimated annual operating costs of the new vessel are:

Fuel	$380,000
Labor and benefits	330,000
Maintenance	70,000
Other	105,000
	$885,000

The crew would require additional training to handle the new vessel's more complex and sophisticated equipment. Training would probably cost $50,000 next year.

The estimated operating costs for the new vessel assume that it would be operated in the same way as the *Vital Spark*. However, the new vessel should be able to handle a larger load on some routes, which could generate additional revenues, net of additional out-of-pocket costs, of as much as $100,000 per year. Moreover, a new vessel would have a useful service life of 20 years or more.

Cohn and Doyle offered the new vessel for a fixed price of $3,000,000, payable half immediately and half on delivery next year.

Mr. Handy stepped out on the foredeck of the *Vital Spark* as she chugged down the Cook Inlet. "A rusty old tub," he muttered, "but she's never let us down. I'll bet we could keep her going until next year while Cohn and Doyle are building her replacement. We could use up the spare parts to keep her going. We might even be able to sell or scrap her for book value when her replacement arrives.

"But how do I compare the NPV of a new ship with the old *Vital Spark*? Sure, I could run a 20-year NPV spreadsheet, but I don't have a clue how the replacement will be used in 2023 or 2028. Maybe I could compare the overall *cost* of overhauling and operating the *Vital Spark* to the cost of buying and operating the proposed replacement."

Questions

1. Calculate and compare the equivalent annual costs of (a) overhauling and operating the *Vital Spark* for 12 more years, and (b) buying and operating the proposed replacement vessel for 20 years. What should Mr. Handy do if the replacement's annual costs are the same or lower?

2. Suppose the replacement's equivalent annual costs are higher than the *Vital Spark*'s. What additional information should Mr. Handy seek in this case?

7

INTRODUCTION TO RISK AND RETURN

We have managed to go through six chapters without directly addressing the problem of risk, but now the jig is up. We can no longer be satisfied with vague statements like "The opportunity cost of capital depends on the risk of the project." We need to know how risk is defined, what the links are between risk and the opportunity cost of capital, and how the financial manager can cope with risk in practical situations.

In this chapter we concentrate on the first of these issues and leave the other two to Chapters 8 and 9. We start by summarizing more than 100 years of evidence on rates of return in capital markets. Then we take a first look at investment risks and show how they can be reduced by portfolio diversification. We introduce you to beta, the standard risk measure for individual securities.

The themes of this chapter, then, are portfolio risk, security risk, and diversification. For the most part, we take the view of the individual investor. But at the end of the chapter we turn the problem around and ask whether diversification makes sense as a corporate objective.

7-1 OVER A CENTURY OF CAPITAL MARKET HISTORY IN THE U.S. IN ONE EASY LESSON

Financial analysts are blessed with an enormous quantity of data. There are comprehensive databases of the prices of U.S. stocks, bonds, options, and commodities, as well as huge amounts of data for securities in other countries. We focus on a study by Dimson, Marsh, and Staunton that measures the historical performance of three portfolios of U.S. securities:[1]

---

[1] See E. Dimson, P. R. Marsh, and M. Staunton, *Triumph of the Optimists: 101 Years of Investment Returns* (Princeton, NJ: Princeton University Press, 2002).

1. A portfolio of Treasury bills, that is, U.S. government debt securities maturing in less than one year.[2]
2. A portfolio of U.S. government bonds.
3. A portfolio of U.S. common stocks.

These investments offer different degrees of risk. Treasury bills are about as safe an investment as you can make. There is no risk of default, and their short maturity means that the prices of Treasury bills are relatively stable. In fact, an investor who wishes to lend money for, say, three months can achieve a perfectly certain payoff by purchasing a Treasury bill maturing in three months. However, the investor cannot lock in a *real* rate of return: There is still some uncertainty about inflation.

By switching to long-term government bonds, the investor acquires an asset whose price fluctuates as interest rates vary. (Bond prices fall when interest rates rise and rise when interest rates fall.) An investor who shifts from bonds to common stocks shares in all the ups and downs of the issuing companies.

Figure 7.1 shows how your money would have grown if you had invested $1 at the start of 1900 and reinvested all dividend or interest income in each of the three portfolios.[3] Figure 7.2 is identical except that it depicts the growth in the *real* value of the portfolio. We focus here on nominal values.

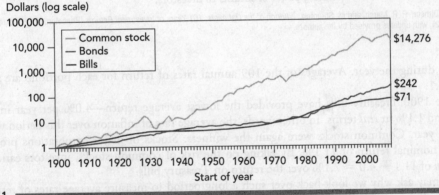

FIGURE 7.1

How an investment of $1 at the start of 1900 would have grown by the end of 2008, assuming reinvestment of all dividend and interest payments.

Source: E. Dimson, P. R. Marsh, and M. Staunton, *Triumph of the Optimists: 101 Years of Investment Returns* (Princeton, NJ: Princeton University Press, 2002), with updates provided by the authors.

Investment performance coincides with our intuitive risk ranking. A dollar invested in the safest investment, Treasury bills, would have grown to $71 by the end of 2008, barely enough to keep up with inflation. An investment in long-term Treasury bonds would have produced $242. Common stocks were in a class by themselves. An investor who placed a dollar in the stocks of large U.S. firms would have received $14,276.

We can also calculate the rate of return from these portfolios for each year from 1900 to 2008. This rate of return reflects both cash receipts—dividends or interest—and the capital gains or losses

---

[2] Treasury bills were not issued before 1919. Before that date the interest rate used is the commercial paper rate.

[3] Portfolio values are plotted on a log scale. If they were not, the ending values for the common stock portfolio would run off the top of the page.

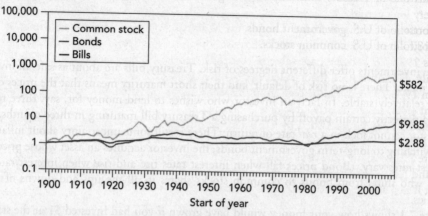

FIGURE 7.2

How an investment of $1 at the start of 1900 would have grown in real terms by the end of 2008, assuming reinvestment of all dividend and interest payments. Compare this plot with Figure 7.1, and note how inflation has eroded the purchasing power of returns to investors.

Source: E. Dimson, P. R. Marsh, and M. Staunton, *Triumph of the Optimists: 101 Years of Investment Returns* (Princeton, NJ: Princeton University Press, 2002), with updates provided by the authors.

realized during the year. Averages of the 109 annual rates of return for each portfolio are shown in Table 7.1.

Since 1900 Treasury bills have provided the lowest average return—4.0% per year in *nominal* terms and 1.1% in *real* terms. In other words, the average rate of inflation over this period was about 3% per year. Common stocks were again the winners. Stocks of major corporations provided an average nominal return of 11.1%. By taking on the risk of common stocks, investors earned a *risk premium* of 11.1 − 4.0 = 7.1% over the return on Treasury bills.

You may ask why we look back over such a long period to measure average rates of return. The reason is that annual rates of return for common stocks fluctuate so much that averages taken over

TABLE 7.1   Average rates of return on U.S. Treasury bills, government bonds, and common stocks, 1900–2008 (figures in % per year).

	Average Annual Rate of Return		
	Nominal	**Real**	**Average Risk Premium (Extra Return versus Treasury Bills)**
Treasury bills	4.0	1.1	0
Government bonds	5.5	2.6	1.5
Common stocks	11.1	8.0	7.1

Source: E. Dimson, P. R. Marsh, and M. Staunton, *Triumph of the Optimists: 101 Years of Investment Returns*, (Princeton, NJ: Princeton University Press, 2002), with updates provided by the authors.

short periods are meaningless. Our only hope of gaining insights from historical rates of return is to look at a very long period.[4]

What about evidence from India? Though the Mumbai Stock Exchange started functioning from as early as 1875, it started compiling the BSE sensitivity index (Sensex) only from 1986. The base-year of sensex is 1978–79 and the base value is 100. The website of the Reserve Bank of India contains the monthly data on sensex (back-calculated) from 1978–79.[5] We estimate the yearly returns on sensex from 1978-79 by using the data from this website. We also obtain estimates of yields on 1-year government securities, popularly known as G-Secs (a proxy for risk free rate of return) and the average return offered by the bonds issued by DFIs (a proxy for AAA rated corporate bond rate) from the website of RBI.

In Figure 7.3, we show how your money would have grown if you had invested ₹100 at the start of 1978–79 and reinvested the dividend and interest income in these portfolios.[6] Figure 7.4 is identical except that it depicts the growth in the real value of the portfolio.

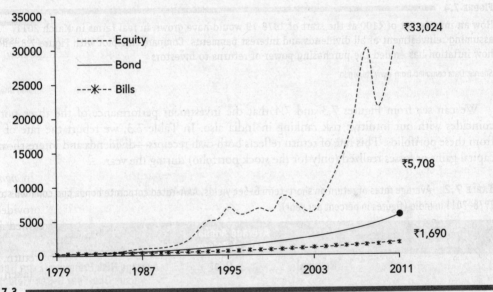

FIGURE 7.3

How an investment of ₹100 at the start of 1978–79 would have grown in March 2011, assuming reinvestment of all the dividend and interest income)

Source: Data compiled from www.rbi.org.in

---

[4] We cannot be sure that this period is truly representative and that the average is not distorted by a few unusually high or low returns. The reliability of an estimate of the average is usually measured by its *standard error*. For example, the standard error of our estimate of the average risk premium on common stocks is 1.9%. There is a 95% chance that the *true* average is within plus or minus 2 standard errors of the 7.1% estimate. In other words, if you said that the true average was between 3.3 and 10.9%, you would have a 95% chance of being right. *Technical note:* The standard error of the average is equal to the standard deviation divided by the square root of the number of observations. In our case the standard deviation is 20.2%, and therefore the standard error is $20.2/\sqrt{109} = 1.9\%$.

[5] See http://www.rbi.org.in/scripts/Statistics.

[6] While computing sensex, BSE adjusts for rights issue, bonus issue, mergers, spin-offs, conversion of debentures, buyback of shares and other corporate restructurings. It however makes no adjustment for dividend. We assume that the dividend yield on sensex is a constant 2.85 percent during 1979–2011. This has been the average dividend yield on sensex during 1979–2005.

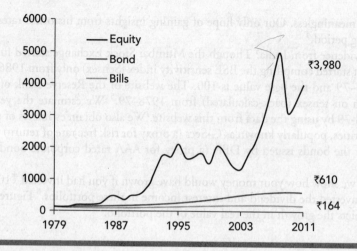

FIGURE 7.4

How an investment of ₹100 at the start of 1978-79 would have grown in real terms in March 2011, assuming reinvestment of all dividends and interest payments. Compare this plot with Figure 7.3, and note how inflation has eroded the purchasing power of returns to investors

Source: Data compiled from www.rbi.org.in

We can see from Figures 7.3 and 7.4 that the investment performance of the three portfolios coincides with our intuitive risk ranking in India also. In Table 7.3, we report the rate of return from these portfolios. This rate of return reflects both cash receipts—dividends and interest—and the capital gains or losses realized (only for the stock portfolio) during the year.

TABLE 7.2   Average rates of return on short-term G-Sec yields, AAA-rated corporate bonds and common stocks, 1978–2011 in India (figures in percent per year).

	Average Annual Rate of Return		
	Nominal	**Real**	**Average Risk Premium (Extra Return versus One-Year G-Sec Yields)**
One-Year G-Sec Yield	9.29	1.71	0.00
AAA-Rated Corporate Bonds	13.50	6.35	4.21
Common Stocks	22.89	15.98	13.61

Source: Compiled from www.rbi.org.in

Since 1979–80, the one-year government securities in India have provided the lowest average return, 9.29 percent per year, in nominal terms and 1.71 percent in real terms. In other words, the average rate of inflation over this period was about 7.58 percent per year. Common stocks were clearly the winners. Stocks of the sensex 30 corporations provided an average nominal return of 22.9 percent. By taking on the risk of common stocks, investors earned a risk premium of 13.61 percent over the return on one-year G-Secs.[7]

---

[7] If we consider only the 2000–2011 period, the market risk premium was 10.5%. It was 10.55% during 1990–2011.

Arithmetic Averages and Compound Annual Returns

Notice that the average returns shown in Tables 7.1 and 7.2 are arithmetic averages. Thus, for example, in Table 7.2, we simply added thirty-two annual returns and divided by 32. The arithmetic average is higher than the compound annual return over the period. The 109-year compound annual return for the S&P index was 9.2 percent.[8] The 32-year compound annual return for the Sensex was 19.87 percent.

The proper uses of arithmetic and compound rates of return from past investments are often misunderstood. Therefore, we call a brief time-out for a clarifying example.

Suppose that the price of Big Oil's common stock is ₹100. There is an equal chance that at the end of the year the stock will be worth ₹90, ₹110, or ₹130. Therefore, the return could be −10%, +10%, or +30% (we assume that Big Oil does not pay a dividend). The *expected* return is $\frac{1}{3}(-10 + 10 + 30) = +10\%$.

If we run the process in reverse and discount the expected cash flow by the expected rate of return, we obtain the value of Big Oil's stock:

$$PV = \frac{110}{1.10} = ₹100$$

The expected return of 10% is therefore the correct rate at which to discount the expected cash flow from Big Oil's stock. It is also the opportunity cost of capital for investments that have the same degree of risk as Big Oil.

Now suppose that we observe the returns on Big Oil stock over a large number of years. If the odds are unchanged, the return will be −10% in a third of the years, +10% in a further third, and +30% in the remaining years. The arithmetic average of these yearly returns is

$$\frac{-10 + 10 + 30}{3} = +10\%$$

Thus the arithmetic average of the returns correctly measures the opportunity cost of capital for investments of similar risk to Big Oil stock.[9]

The average compound annual return[10] on Big Oil stock would be

$$(.9 \times 1.1 \times 1.3)^{1/3} - 1 = .088, \text{ or } 8.8\%.$$

which is *less* than the opportunity cost of capital. Investors would not be willing to invest in a project that offered an 8.8% expected return if they could get an expected return of 10% in the capital markets. The net present value of such a project would be

---

[8] This was calculated from $(1 + r)^{109} = 14{,}276$, which implies $r = .092$. *Technical note:* For lognormally distributed returns the annual compound return is equal to the arithmetic average return minus half the variance. For example, the annual standard deviation of returns on the U.S. market was about .20, or 20%. Variance was therefore $.20^2$, or .04. The compound annual return is about $.04/2 = .02$, or 2 percentage points less than the arithmetic average.

[9] You sometimes hear that the arithmetic average correctly measures the opportunity cost of capital for one-year cash flows, but not for more distant ones. Let us check. Suppose that you expect to receive a cash flow of ₹121 in year 2. We know that one year hence investors will value that cash flow by discounting at 10% (the arithmetic average of possible returns). In other words, at the end of the year they will be willing to pay $PV_1 = 121/1.10 = ₹110$ for the expected cash flow. But we already know how to value an asset that pays off ₹110 in year 1—just discount at the 10% opportunity cost of capital. Thus $PV_0 = PV_1/1.10 = 110/1.1 = ₹100$. Our example demonstrates that the arithmetic average (10% in our example) provides a correct measure of the opportunity cost of capital regardless of the timing of the cash flow.

[10] The compound annual return is often referred to as the *geometric average* return.

$$NPV = -100 + \frac{108.8}{1.1} = -1.1$$

Moral: If the cost of capital is estimated from historical returns or risk premiums, use arithmetic averages, not compound annual rates of return.[11]

Using Historical Evidence to Evaluate Today's Cost of Capital

Suppose there is an investment project that you *know*—don't ask how—has the same risk as sensex. We will say that it has the same risk as the *market portfolio,* although this is speaking somewhat loosely, because the index does not include all risky securities. What rate should you use to discount this project's forecasted cash flows?

Clearly you should use the currently expected rate of return on the market portfolio; that is the return investors would forgo by investing in the proposed project. Let us call this market return r_m. One way to estimate r_m is to assume that the future will be like the past and that today's investors expect to receive the same "normal" rates of return revealed by the averages shown in Table 7.2. In this case, you would set r_m at 21.5%, the average of past market returns.

Unfortunately, this is *not* the way to do it; r_m is not likely to be stable over time. Remember that it is the sum of the risk-free interest rate r_f and a premium for risk. We know that r_f varies. For example, in 1991–92, the yield on 1-year G-Sec was 17.3%. May be in that year, investors were content to hold common stocks offering an expected return of only 22.9%.

If you need to estimate the return that investors expect to receive, a more sensible procedure is to take the 1-year G-Sec yield and add 13.6%, the average *risk premium* shown in Table 7.3. For example, as we write this in early 2011, the 1-year G-Sec yield is about 7.23%. Adding on the average risk premium, therefore, gives

$$r_m(2011) = r_f(2011) + \text{normal risk premium}$$
$$= 0.0723 + 0.1361 = 0.2084, \text{ or about } 20.84\%$$

The crucial assumption here is that there is a normal, stable risk premium on the market portfolio, so that the expected *future* risk premium can be measured by the average past risk premium.

Even with 32 years of data, we can't estimate the market risk premium exactly[12]; nor can we be sure that investors today are demanding the same reward for risk that they were 10 or 20 years ago. All this leaves plenty of room for argument about what the risk premium *really* is.[13]

Many financial managers and economists believe that long-run historical returns are the best measure available. Others have a gut instinct that investors don't need such a large risk premium to

---

[11] Our discussion above assumed that we *knew* that the returns of −10, +10, and +30% were equally likely. For an analysis of the effect of uncertainty about the expected return see I. A. Cooper, "Arithmetic Versus Geometric Mean Estimators: Setting Discount Rates for Capital Budgeting," *European Financial Management* 2 (July 1996), pp. 157–167; and E. Jaquier, A. Kane, and A. J. Marcus, "Optimal Estimation of the Risk Premium for the Long Run and Asset Allocation: A Case of Compounded Estimation Risk," *Journal of Financial Econometrics* 3 (2005), pp. 37–55. When future returns are forecasted to distant horizons, the historical arithmetic means are upward-biased. This bias would be small in most corporate-finance applications, however.

[12] Even with more than 100 years of data for the US, we cannot estimate the expected market risk premium in the US exactly.

[13] Some of the disagreements simply reflect the fact that the risk premium is sometimes defined in different ways. Some measure the average difference between stock returns and the returns (or yields) on long-term bonds. Others measure the difference between the compound rate of growth on stocks and the interest rate. As we explained above, this is not an appropriate measure of the cost of capital.

persuade them to hold common stocks.[14] For example, two recent surveys of financial economists in the US revealed that they expect a market risk premium that is several percentage points below the historical average.[15]

If you believe that the expected market risk premium is less than the historical average, you probably also believe that history has been unexpectedly kind to investors in the United States and that their good luck is unlikely to be repeated. Here are two reasons that history *may* overstate the risk premium that investors demand today.

Reason 1   Since 1900 the United States has been among the world's most prosperous countries. Other economies have languished or been wracked by war or civil unrest. By focusing on equity returns in the United States, we may obtain a biased view of what investors expected. Perhaps the historical averages miss the possibility that the United States could have turned out to be one of these less-fortunate countries.[16]

Figure 7.5 sheds some light on this issue. It is taken from a comprehensive study by Dimson, Marsh, and Staunton of market returns in 17 countries and shows the average risk premium in each country between 1900 and 2008. There is no evidence here that U.S. investors have been particularly fortunate; the U.S. was just about average in terms of returns.

In Figure 7.5 Danish stocks come bottom of the league; the average risk premium in Denmark was only 4.3%. The clear winner was Italy with a premium of 10.2%. Some of these differences between countries may reflect differences in risk. For example, Italian stocks have been particularly variable and investors may have required a higher return to compensate. But remember how difficult it is to make precise estimates of what investors expected. You probably would not be too far out if you concluded that the *expected* risk premium was the same in each country.[17]

Reason 2   Stock prices in the United States have for some years outpaced the growth in company dividends or earnings. For example, between 1950 and 2000 dividend yields in the United States fell from 7.2% to 1.1%. It seems unlikely that investors *expected* such a sharp decline in yields, in which case some part of the actual return during this period was *unexpected.*

What about the market risk premium in India? As we saw, sensex has registered an excess return of 13.6 percent over the yield on one-year G-Sec (our proxy for risk-free rate in India) over the last 32

---

[14] There is some theory behind this instinct. The high risk premium earned in the market seems to imply that investors are extremely risk-averse. If that is true, investors ought to cut back their consumption when stock prices fall and wealth decreases. But the evidence suggests that when stock prices fall, investors spend at nearly the same rate. This is difficult to reconcile with high risk aversion and a high market risk premium. There is an active research literature on this "equity premium puzzle." See R. Mehra, "The Equity Premium Puzzle: A Review," *Foundations and Trends in Finance*® 2 (2006), pp. 11–81, and R. Mehra, ed., *Handbook of the Equity Risk Premium* (Amsterdam: Elsevier Handbooks in Finance Series, 2008).

[15] It is difficult to interpret the responses to such surveys precisely. The best known is conducted every quarter by Duke University and *CFO* magazine and reported on at **www.cfosurvey.org**. On average since inception CFOs have predicted a 10-year return on U.S. equities of 3.7% in excess of the return on 10-year Treasury bonds. However, respondents appear to have interpreted the question as asking for their forecast of the *compound* annual return. In this case the comparable *expected* (arithmetic average) premium over *bills* is probably 2 or 3 percentage points higher at about 6%. For a description of the survey data, see J. R. Graham and C. Harvey, "The Long-Run Equity Risk Premium," *Finance Research Letters* 2 (2005), pp. 185–194.

[16] This possibility was suggested in P. Jorion and W. N. Goetzmann, "Global Stock Markets in the Twentieth Century," *Journal of Finance* 54 (June 1999), pp. 953–980.

[17] We are concerned here with the difference between the nominal market return and the nominal interest rate. Sometimes you will see *real* risk premiums quoted—that is, the difference between the *real* market return and the *real* interest rate. If the inflation rate is i, then the real risk premium is $(r_m - r_f)/(1 + i)$. For countries such as Italy that have experienced a high degree of inflation, this real risk premium may be significantly lower than the nominal premium.

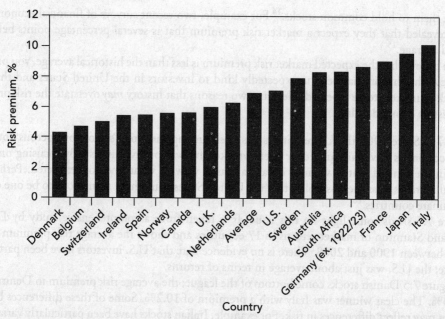

FIGURE 7.5

Average market risk premiums (nominal return on stocks minus nominal return on bills), 1900–2008.

Source: E. Dimson, P. R. Marsh, and M. Staunton, *Triumph of the Optimists: 101 Years of Investment Returns* (Princeton, NJ: Princeton University Press, 2002), with updates provided by the authors.

years. Given the high volatility observed in the stock market, we certainly need much more than 32 years of data to estimate the equity risk premium with some confidence.

The dividend yield on the sensex 30 companies has fallen from 8.38%[18] (in 1979–80) to 1.46% in 2010–11. It is unlikely that investors expected such a sharp decline in yields, and hence part of the actual return during this period was unexpected.

Some believe that the low dividend yields at the turn of the century reflected optimism that the new economy would lead to a golden age of prosperity and surging profits. Others attribute the low yield to a reduction in risk premiums. The growth in mutual funds has made it easier for the individual investors in India to diversify the risk. Similarly, now the mutual funds are allowed to invest outside India (with certain restrictions)[19] and hence, can reduce their risk by investing outside India. If these investors can eliminate more of their risk than in the past, they may become content with a lower return.

To see how a rise in stock prices can stem from a fall in the risk premium, suppose that a stock is expected to pay a dividend next year of ₹12 ($DIV_1 = 12$). The stock yields 3% and the dividend is expected to grow indefinitely by 7% a year ($g = .07$). Therefore the total return that investors expect is $r = 3 + 7 = 10\%$. We can find the stock's value by plugging these numbers into the constant-growth formula that we used in Chapter 4 to value stocks:

$$PV = DIV_1/(r - g) = 12/(.10 - .07) = ₹400$$

---

[18] This has happened despite the fact that some of the low dividend-paying companies like SAIL, Arvind Mills, Hindustan Motors, and Premier Auto have been replaced with high dividend-paying stocks like Infosys, Hero Honda, and Wipro in Sensex.

[19] See http://www.indiainbusiness.nic.in/invest-abroad/inv-guidelines.htm for details of the restrictions that apply.

Imagine that investors now revise downward their required return to $r = 9\%$. The dividend yield falls to 2% and the value of the stock rises to

$$PV = DIV_1/(r - g) = 12/(.09 - .07) = ₹600$$

Thus a fall from 10% to 9% in the required return leads to a 50% rise in the stock price. If we include this price rise in our measures of past returns, we will be doubly wrong in our estimate of the risk premium. First, we will overestimate the return that investors required in the past. Second, we will fail to recognize that the return investors require in the future is lower than they needed in the past.

Dividend Yields and the Risk Premium

If there has been a downward shift in the return that investors have required, then past returns will provide an overestimate of the risk premium. We can't wholly get around this difficulty, but we can get another clue to the risk premium by going back to the constant-growth model that we discussed in Chapter 2. If stock prices are expected to keep pace with the growth in dividends, then the expected market return is equal to the dividend yield plus the expected dividend growth—that is, $r = DIV_1/P_0 + g$. Since 1979–80, dividend yield on sensex has averaged 2.85[20] percent and the annual growth rate in dividends has been 11.33 percent. It seems the expected market return over this period was 14.18 percent, about 4.9 percent above the yield on the G-Secs. This is 8.7 percent lower than the realized risk premium reported in Table 7.3. In the US, a similar research shows that the difference between the realized and the actual risk premium is 1.5%.[21]

Dividend yields have averaged 2.85% since 1980, but as you can see from Figure 7.6, they have fluctuated quite sharply. At the end of 1980, stocks were offering a yield of 8.4%; by 2011 the yield had plunged to 1.46%.

You sometimes hear financial managers suggest that in years such as 2000, when dividend yields were low, capital was relatively cheap. Is there any truth to this? Should companies be adjusting their cost of capital to reflect these fluctuations in yield?

Notice that there are only two possible reasons for the yield changes in Figure 7.4. One is that in some years investors were unusually optimistic or pessimistic about g, the future growth in dividends. The other is that r, the required return, was unusually high or low. Economists who have studied the behavior of dividend yields have concluded that very little of the variation is related to the subsequent rate of dividend growth. If they are right, the level of yields ought to be telling us something about the return that investors require.

This in fact appears to be the case. A reduction in the dividend yield seems to herald a reduction in the risk premium that investors can expect over the following few years. So, when yields are relatively low, companies may be justified in shaving their estimate of required returns over the next year or so. However, changes in the dividend yield tell companies next to nothing about the expected risk premium over the next 10 or 20 years. It seems that, when estimating the discount rate for longer term investments, a firm can safely ignore year-to-year fluctuations in the dividend yield.

---

[20] If we exclude the pre-1991 period, the average dividend yield on Sensex 1.52 percent and the growth rate in dividends is 16.91 percent.

[21] See E. F. Fama and K. R. French, "The Equity Premium," *Journal of Finance* 57 (April 2002), pp. 637–659. Fama and French quote even lower estimates of the risk premium, particularly for the second half of the period. The difference partly reflects the fact that they define the risk premium as the difference between market returns and the commercial paper rate. Except for the years 1900–1918, the interest rates used in Table 7.1 are the rates on U.S. Treasury bills.

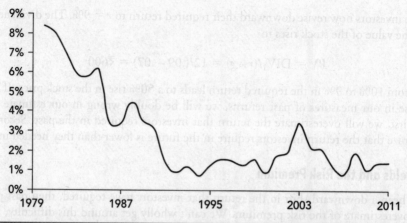

FIGURE 7.6

Dividend Yields on Sensex 1980–2011.

Out of this debate only one firm conclusion emerges: do not trust anyone who claims to *know* what returns investors expect. History contains some clues, but ultimately we have to judge whether investors on average have received what they expected. Many financial economists rely on the evidence of history and therefore work with a risk premium of about 7.5% in the US and 13.6% in India. The remainder generally uses a somewhat lower figure. If we consider the post-1991 period, then the risk premium is about 3 percent lower than the historical average of 13.61 percent. Many analysts would be happy to ignore the pre-1991 period because liberalization in the capital market in India started after 1991. We have no official position on the issue, but we believe that a range of 9 to 13 percent is reasonable for the risk premium in India.

Time Period	Sensex Return	Average G-Sec Yield	Market Risk Premium
1979–2011	22.89%	9.29%	13.61%
1991–2011	20.37	9.82%	10.55%

7-2 MEASURING PORTFOLIO RISK

You now have a couple of benchmarks. You know the discount rate for safe projects, and you have an estimate of the rate for average-risk projects. But you *don't* know yet how to estimate discount rates for assets that do not fit these simple cases. To do that, you have to learn (1) how to measure risk and (2) the relationship between risks borne and risk premiums demanded.

Figure 7.7 shows the 32 years of return of Indian common stocks (we use sensex as a proxy for this). The fluctuations in year-to-year returns are remarkably wide. The highest annual return was 88% in 1985–86. In four of the last 32 years, the returns on sensex exceeded 50 percent. However, there were negative returns in seven of the last 32 years, the worst being -28 percent in 2008–09.

Another way of presenting these data is by a histogram or frequency distribution. This is done in Figure 7.8, where the variability of year-to-year returns shows up in the wide "spread" of outcomes.

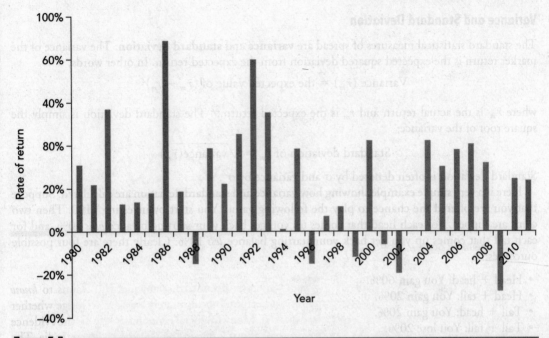

FIGURE 7.7

The stock market has been a profitable but extremely variable investment.

Source: Compiled from www.rbi.org.in

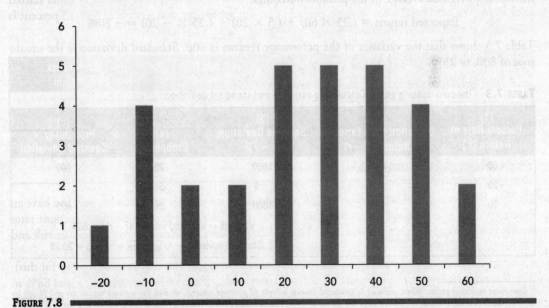

FIGURE 7.8

Histogram of the annual rates of return from the stock market in India, 1979-80 to 2010-11, showing the wide spread of returns from investment in common stocks.

Source: Compiled from www.rbi.org.in

Variance and Standard Deviation

The standard statistical measures of spread are **variance** and **standard deviation.** The variance of the market return is the expected squared deviation from the expected return. In other words,

$$\text{Variance } (\tilde{r}_m) = \text{the expected value of } (\tilde{r}_m - r_m)^2$$

where $\tilde{r}_m$ is the actual return and r_m is the expected return.[22] The standard deviation is simply the square root of the variance:

$$\text{Standard deviation of } \tilde{r}_m = \sqrt{\text{variance}(\tilde{r}_m)}$$

Standard deviation is often denoted by σ and variance by σ^2.

Here is a very simple example showing how variance and standard deviation are calculated. Suppose that you are offered the chance to play the following game. You start by investing ₹100. Then two coins are flipped. For each head that comes up you get back your starting balance *plus* 30%, and for each tail that comes up you get back your starting balance *less* 10%. Clearly there are four possible outcomes:

- Head + head: You gain 60%.
- Head + tail: You gain 20%.
- Tail + head: You gain 20%.
- Tail + tail: You lose 20%.

There is a chance of 1 in 4, or .25, that you will make 60%; a chance of 2 in 4, or .5, that you will make 20%; and a chance of 1 in 4, or .25, that you will lose 20%. The game's expected return is, therefore, a weighted average of the possible outcomes:

$$\text{Expected return} = (.25 \times 60) + (.5 \times 20) + (.25 \times - 20) = +20\%$$

Table 7.3 shows that the variance of the percentage returns is 800. Standard deviation is the square root of 800, or 28%.

TABLE 7.3   The coin-tossing game: Calculating variance and standard deviation.

(1) Percent Rate of Return ($\tilde{r}$)	(2) Deviation from Expected Return ($\tilde{r} - r$)	(3) Squared Deviation ($\tilde{r} - r)^2$	(4) Probability	(5) Probability × Squared Deviation
+60	+40	1600	.25	400
+20	0	0	.5	0
−20	−40	1600	.25	400

Variance = expected value of $(\tilde{r} - r)^2 = 800$

Standard deviation = $\sqrt{\text{variance}} = \sqrt{800} = 28.28$

---

[22] One more technical point. When variance is estimated from a sample of *observed* returns, we add the squared deviations and divide by $N - 1$, where N is the number of observations. We divide by $N - 1$ rather than N to correct for what is called *the loss of a degree of freedom.* The formula is

$$\text{Variance } (\tilde{r}_m) = \frac{1}{N - 1}\sum_{t=1}^{N}(\tilde{r}_{mt} - r_m)^2$$

where $\tilde{r}_{mt}$ is the market return in period t and r_m is the mean of the values of $\tilde{r}_{mt}$.

One way of defining uncertainty is to say that more things can happen than will happen. The risk of an asset can be completely expressed, as we did for the coin-tossing game, by writing all possible outcomes and the probability of each. In practice this is cumbersome and often impossible. Therefore we use variance or standard deviation to summarize the spread of possible outcomes.[23]

These measures are natural indexes of risk.[24] If the outcome of the coin-tossing game had been certain, the standard deviation would have been zero. The actual standard deviation is positive because we *don't* know what will happen.

Or think of a second game, the same as the first except that each head means a 50% gain and each tail means a 30% loss. Again, there are four possible outcomes:

- Head + head: You gain 100%.
- Head + tail: You gain 20%.
- Tail + head: You gain 20%.
- Tail + tail: You lose 60%.

For this game the expected return is 20%, the same as that of the first game. But its standard deviation is double that of the first game, 56% versus 28%. By this measure, the second game is twice as risky as the first.

Measuring Variability

In principle, you could estimate the variability of any portfolio of stocks or bonds by the procedure just described. You would identify the possible outcomes, assign a probability to each outcome, and grind through the calculations. But where do the probabilities come from? You can't look them up in the newspaper; newspapers seem to go out of their way to avoid definite statements about prospects for securities. We once saw an article headlined "Bond Prices Possibly Set to Move Sharply Either Way." Stockbrokers are much the same. Yours may respond to your query about possible market outcomes with a statement like this:

> The market currently appears to be undergoing a period of consolidation. For the intermediate term, we would take a constructive view, provided economic recovery continues. The market could be up 20% a year from now, perhaps more if inflation continues low. On the other hand, . . .

The Delphic oracle gave advice, but no probabilities.

Most financial analysts start by observing past variability. Of course, there is no risk in hindsight, but it is reasonable to assume that portfolios with histories of high variability also have the least predictable future performance.

The annual standard deviations and variances observed for our three portfolios over the period 1979–2011 were:[25]

---

[23] Which of the two we use is solely a matter of convenience. Since standard deviation is in the same units as the rate of return, it is generally more convenient to use standard deviation. However, when we are talking about the *proportion* of risk that is due to some factor, it is less confusing to work in terms of the variance.

[24] As we explain in Chapter 8, standard deviation and variance are the correct measures of risk if the returns are normally distributed.

[25] In discussing the riskiness of *bonds,* be careful to specify the time period and whether you are speaking in real or nominal terms. The *nominal* return on a long-term government bond is absolutely certain to an investor who holds on until maturity; in other words, it is risk-free if you forget about inflation. After all, the government can always print money to pay off its debts. However, the real return on Treasury securities is uncertain because no one knows how much each future dollar will buy.

The bond returns were measured annually. The returns reflect year-to-year changes in bond prices as well as interest received. The *one-year* returns on long-term bonds are risky in *both* real and nominal terms.

Portfolio	Standard Deviation (σ)	Variance (σ^2)
Short- term Government securities	3	9
Common stocks	27.4	753

As expected, government securities were the least variable security, and common stocks were the most variable.

You may find it interesting to compare the coin-tossing game and the stock market as alternative investments. The stock market generated an average annual return of 23% with a standard deviation of 27.4%. The game offers 20% and 28.28%, respectively. Your gambling friends may have come up with a crude representation of the stock market.

Figure 7.9 compares the standard deviation of stock market returns in 17 countries over the same 109-year period. Canada occupies low field with a standard deviation of 17.0%, but most of the other countries cluster together with percentage standard deviations in the low 20s. It is interesting to note that Indian stock market is as volatile as the Japanese stock market.

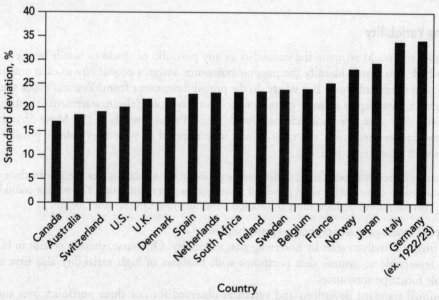

FIGURE 7.9

The risk (standard deviation of annual returns) of markets around the world, 1900–2008.

Source: E. Dimson, P. R. Marsh, and M. Staunton, *Triumph of the Optimists: 101 Years of Global Investment Returns* (Princeton, NJ: Princeton University Press, 2002), with updates provided by the authors.

Of course, there is no reason to suppose that the market's variability should stay the same over more than a century. For example, Germany, Italy, and Japan now have much more stable economies and markets than they did in the years leading up to and including the Second World War. As you can see from the following table, standard deviation in India has remained quite stable in the last 30 years (excepting for the 1985–90 period).

Time Period	Variability
1980–85	16.68%
1985–90	37.84%
1991–95	28.79%
1995–00	23.13%
2000–05	26.04%
2005–10	28.30%

Figure 7.10 does not suggest a long-term upward or downward trend in the volatility of Indian stock market.[26] Instead, there have been periods of both calm and turbulence. In 2005, an unusually tranquil year, the standard deviation of returns was only about 15%, almost half of the average standard deviation. The standard deviation in early 1993 was about three times higher at 48%.

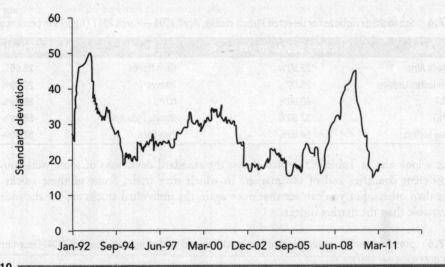

FIGURE 7.10

Annualized standard deviation of the preceding 52 weekly changes in sensex, 1991–2011

Market turbulence over shorter daily, weekly, or monthly periods can be amazingly high. Sensex fell by more than 16.5 percent during two trading days (14 and 17 May)[27] after the 2004 Parliament election results were announced. The standard deviation of the market for the week surrounding these two days was equivalent to 117 percent per year. Fortunately, volatility dropped to 30 percent in the next week itself.

---

[26] These standard deviations are calculated from weekly data. The weekly variance is converted to an annual variance by multiplying by 52. That is, the variance of the weekly return is one-fifty-second of the annual variance. The longer you hold a security or portfolio, the more risk you have to bear.

This conversion assumes that successive weekly returns are statistically independent. This is, in fact, a good assumption, as we will show in Chapter 13.

Because variance is approximately proportional to the length of time interval over which a security or portfolio return is measured, standard deviation is proportional to the square root of the interval.

[27] 15th and 16th of May were holidays.

Volatility again increased to mid-40s in September and October, 2009. However, in early 2011, it had fallen back to about 16%.

How Diversification Reduces Risk

We can calculate our measures of variability equally well for individual securities and portfolios of securities. Of course, the level of variability over 100 years is less interesting for specific companies than for the market portfolio—it is a rare company that faces the same business risks today as it did a century ago.

Table 7.4 presents estimated standard deviations for 10 well-known common stocks for a recent five-year period.[28] Do these standard deviations look high to you? They should. Remember that the market portfolio's standard deviation was about 29.6 percent during the same five-year period. The standard deviation of about six of the stocks was pretty close to this. Tata Steel was almost twice as volatile as the market.

TABLE 7.4   Standard deviations for selected Indian stocks, April 2006 – March 2011 (figures in percent per year)

Stock	Standard Deviation (σ)	Stock	Standard Deviation (σ)
Bharti Airtel	33.50%	Hero Honda	28.80%
Hindustan Unilever	28.60%	Infosys	29.20%
L&T	46.90%	NTPC	30.00%
ONGC	37.30%	Sterlite Industries	59.60%
Tata Motors	54.80%	Tata Steel	62.30%

Take a look also at Table 7.5, which shows the standard deviations of some well-known stocks from different countries and of the markets in which they trade. Some of these stocks are more variable than others, but you can see that once again the individual stocks are for the most part are more variable than the market indexes.

TABLE 7.5   Standard deviations for selected foreign stocks and market indexes, January 2004–December 2008 (figures in percent per year).

	Standard Deviation (σ)			Standard Deviation (σ)	
	Stock	Market		Stock	Market
BP	20.7	16.0	LVMH	20.6	18.3
Deutsche Bank	28.9	20.6	Nestlé	14.6	13.7
Fiat	35.7	18.9	Nokia	31.6	25.8
Heineken	21.0	20.8	Sony	33.9	16.6
Iberia	35.4	20.4	Telefonica de Argentina	58.6	40.0

This raises an important question: The market portfolio is made up of individual stocks, so why doesn't its variability reflect the average variability of its components? The answer is that *diversification reduces variability.*

---

[28] These standard deviations are calculated from monthly data.

Even a little diversification can provide a substantial reduction in variability. Suppose you calculate and compare the standard deviations between 2002 and 2007 of one-stock portfolios, two-stock portfolios, five-stock portfolios, etc. However, you can see from Figure 7.11 that diversification can cut the variability of US returns about in half. Notice also that you can get most of this benefit with relatively few stocks: The improvement is much smaller when the number of securities is increased beyond, say, 20 or 30.[29] Obaidullah (1994)[30] also reports similar findings from India. The author finds that almost half of the risk of an individual security is non-systematic risk and is eliminated by diversification.

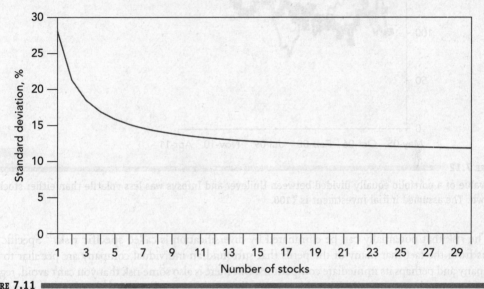

FIGURE 7.11

Average risk (standard deviation) of portfolios containing different numbers of stocks. The stocks were selected randomly from stocks traded on the New York Exchange from 2002 through 2007. Notice that diversification reduces risk rapidly at first, then more slowly.

Diversification works because prices of different stocks do not move exactly together. Statisticians make the same point when they say that stock price changes are less than perfectly correlated. Look, for example, at Figure 7.12, which plots the prices of Hindustan Unilever Limited and Infosys for the 60-month period ending March 2011. As we showed in Table 7.4, during this period the standard deviation of the monthly returns of both stocks was about 30%. Although the two stocks enjoyed a fairly bumpy ride, they did not move in exact lockstep. Sometimes, a decline in the value of Hindustan Unilever was offset by a rise in the price of Infosys. So, if you had split your portfolio between the two stocks, you could have reduced the monthly fluctuations in the value of your investment. You can see from the dashed line in Figure 7.12 that if your portfolio had been evenly divided between Hindustan Unilever Limited and Infosys, there would have been many more months when the return was just middling and far fewer cases of extreme returns. By diversifying between the two stocks, you would have reduced the standard deviation of the returns to about 20% a year.

---

[29] There is some evidence that in recent years stocks have become individually more risky but have moved less closely together. Consequently, the benefits of diversification have increased. See J. Y. Campbell, M. Lettau, B. C. Malkiel, and Y. Xu, "Have Individual Stocks Become More Volatile? An Empirical Exploration of Idiosyncratic Risk," *Journal of Finance 56* (February 2001), pp. 1–43.

[30] M Obaidullah, 1994, Indian Stock Market: Theories and Evidence, ICFAI Publication, Hyderabad, India. The sample period for this study was 1986-90.

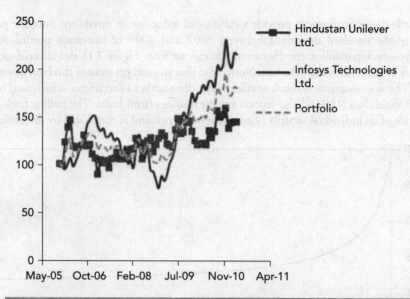

FIGURE 7.12

The value of a portfolio equally divided between Unilever and Infosys was less volatile than either stock on its own. The assumed initial investment is ₹100.

The risk that potentially can be eliminated by diversification is called **specific risk.**[31] Specific risk stems from the fact that many of the perils that surround an individual company are peculiar to that company and perhaps its immediate competitors. But there is also some risk that you can't avoid, regardless of how much you diversify. This risk is generally known as **market risk.**[32] Market risk stems from the fact that there are other economywide perils that threaten all businesses. That is why stocks have a tendency to move together. And that is why investors are exposed to market uncertainties, no matter how many stocks they hold.

In Figure 7.13 we have divided risk into its two parts—specific risk and market risk. If you have only a single stock, specific risk is very important; but once you have a portfolio of 20 or more stocks, diversification has done the bulk of its work. For a reasonably well-diversified portfolio, only market risk matters. Therefore, the predominant source of uncertainty for a diversified investor is that the market will rise or plummet, carrying the investor's portfolio with it.

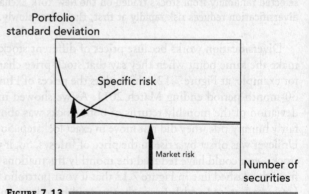

FIGURE 7.13

Diversification eliminates specific risk. But there is some risk that diversification *cannot* eliminate. This is called *market risk.*

---

[31] Specific risk may be called *unsystematic risk, residual risk, unique risk,* or *diversifiable risk.*

[32] Market risk may be called *systematic risk* or *undiversifiable risk.*

7-3 CALCULATING PORTFOLIO RISK

We have given you an intuitive idea of how diversification reduces risk, but to understand fully the effect of diversification, you need to know how the risk of a portfolio depends on the risk of the individual shares.

Suppose that 62% of your portfolio is invested in Bharti and the remainder is invested in Tata Motors. You expect that over the coming year Bharti Airtel will give a return of 14% and Tata Motors, 17%. The expected return on your portfolio is simply a weighted average of the expected returns on the individual stocks:[33]

$$\text{Expected portfolio return} = (.62 \times 14) + (.38 \times 17) = 15.14\%$$

Calculating the expected portfolio return is easy. The hard part is to work out the risk of your portfolio. In the past the standard deviation of returns was 33.5% for Bharti Airtel and 54.8% for Tata Motors. You believe that these figures are a good representation of the spread of possible *future* outcomes. At first you may be inclined to assume that the standard deviation of the portfolio is a weighted average of the standard deviations of the two stocks, that is, $(.62 \times 33.5) + (.38 \times 54.8) = 41.59\%$. That would be correct *only* if the prices of the two stocks moved in perfect lockstep. In any other case, diversification reduces the risk below this figure.

The exact procedure for calculating the risk of a two-stock portfolio is given in Figure 7.14. You need to fill in four boxes. To complete the top-left box, you weight the variance of the returns on stock 1 (σ_1^2) by the *square* of the proportion invested in it (x_1^2). Similarly, to complete the bottom-right box, you weight the variance of the returns on stock 2 (σ_1^2) by the *square* of the proportion invested in stock 2 (x_2^2).

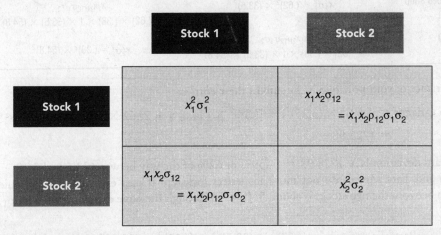

FIGURE 7.14

The variance of a two-stock portfolio is the sum of these four boxes. x_1, x_2 = proportions invested in stocks 1 and 2; $\sigma_1{}^2$, $\sigma_2{}^2$ = variances of stock returns; σ_{12} = covariance of returns $(\rho_{12}\sigma_1\sigma_2)$; ρ_{12} = correlation between returns on stocks 1 and 2.

---

[33] Let's check this. Suppose you invest ₹62 in Bharti and ₹38 in Tata Motors. The expected rupee return on your Bharti holding is $0.14 \times 62 = $ ₹8.68, and on Tata Motors, it is $0.17 \times 38 = $ ₹6.46. The expected rupee return on your portfolio is ₹8.68 + ₹6.46 = ₹15.14. The portfolio *rate* of return is ₹15.14/100 = 15.14, or 15.14 percent.

The entries in these diagonal boxes depend on the variances of stocks 1 and 2; the entries in the other two boxes depend on their **covariance.** As you might guess, the covariance is a measure of the degree to which the two stocks "covary." The covariance can be expressed as the product of the correlation coefficient ρ_{12} and the two standard deviations:[34]

$$\text{Covariance between stocks 1 and 2} = \sigma_{12} = \rho_{12}\rho_1\rho_2$$

For the most part stocks tend to move together. In this case the correlation coefficient ρ_{12} is positive, and therefore the covariance σ_{12} is also positive. If the prospects of the stocks were wholly unrelated, both the correlation coefficient and the covariance would be zero; and if the stocks tended to move in opposite directions, the correlation coefficient and the covariance would be negative. Just as you weighted the variances by the square of the proportion invested, so you must weight the covariance by the *product* of the two proportionate holdings x_1 and x_2.

Once you have completed these four boxes, you simply add the entries to obtain the portfolio variance:

$$\text{Portfolio variance} = x_1^2\sigma_1^2 + x_2^2\sigma_2^2 + 2(x_1x_2\rho_{12}\sigma_1\sigma_2)$$

The portfolio standard deviation is, of course, the square root of the variance.

Now you can try putting in some figures for Bharti and Tata Motors. We said earlier that if the two stocks were perfectly correlated, the standard deviation of the portfolio would lie 62% of the way between the standard deviations of the two stocks. Let us check this out by filling in the boxes with $\rho_{12} = +1$.

	Campbell Soup	Boeing
Campbell Soup	$x_1^2\sigma_1^2 = (.62)^2 \times (33.5)^2$	$x_1x_2\rho_{12}\sigma_1\sigma_2$ $= (.62) \times (.38) \times 1 \times (33.5) \times (54.8)$
Boeing	$x_1x_2\rho_{12}\sigma_1\sigma_2$ $= (.62) \times (.38) \times 1 \times (33.5) \times (54.8)$	$x_2^2\sigma_2^2 = (.38)^2 \times (54.8)^2$

The variance of your portfolio is the sum of these entries:

$$\text{Portfolio variance} = [(.62)^2 \times (33.5)^2] + [(.38)^2 \times (54.8)^2] + 2(.62 \times .38 \times 1 \times 33.5 \times 54.8)$$
$$= 1728.98$$

The standard deviation is $\sqrt{1728.98} = 41.59\%$ or 62% of the way between 33.5 and 54.8.

Bharati and Tata Motors do not move in perfect lockstep. If past experience is any guide, the correlation between the two stocks is about .5. If we go through the same exercise again with $\rho_{12} = .5$, we find

$$\text{Portfolio variance} = [(.62)^2 \times (33.5)^2] + [(.38)^2 \times (54.8)^2]$$
$$+ 2(.62 \times .38 \times .5 \times 33.5 \times 54.8) = 1296.73$$

---

[34] Another way to define the covariance is as follows:

$$\text{Covariance between stocks 1 and 2} = \sigma_{12} = \text{expected value of } (\tilde{r}_1 - r_1) \times (\tilde{r}_2 - r_2)$$

Note that any security's covariance with itself is just its variance:

$$\sigma_{11} = \text{expected value of } (\tilde{r}_1 - r_1) \times (\tilde{r}_1 - r_1)$$
$$= \text{expected value of } (\tilde{r}_1 - r_1)^2 = \text{variance of stock 1} = \sigma_1^2$$

The standard deviation is $\sqrt{1296.73} = 36.01\%$. The risk is now less than 62% of the way between 33.5 and 54.8. In fact, it is less than the risk of investing in Tata Motors alone.

The greatest payoff to diversification comes when the two stocks are negatively correlated. Unfortunately, this almost never occurs, but just for illustration, let us assume it for Bharti and Tata Motors. And as long as we are being unrealistic, we might as well go whole hog and assume perfect negative correlation ($\rho_{12} = -1$). In this case,

$$\text{Portfolio variance} = [(.62)^2 \times (33.5)^2] + [(.38)^2 \times (54.8)^2]$$
$$+ 2(.62 \times .38 \times (-1) \times 33.5 \times 54.8) = 0$$

When there is perfect negative correlation, there is always a portfolio strategy (represented by a particular set of portfolio weights) that will completely eliminate risk.[35] It's too bad perfect negative correlation doesn't really occur between common stocks.

General Formula for Computing Portfolio Risk

The method for calculating portfolio risk can easily be extended to portfolios of three or more securities. We just have to fill in a larger number of boxes. Each of those down the diagonal—the shaded boxes in Figure 7.15—contains the variance weighted by the square of the proportion invested. Each of the other boxes contains the covariance between that pair of securities, weighted by the product of the proportions invested.[36]

Limits to Diversification

Did you notice in Figure 7.15 how much more important the covariances become as we add more securities to the portfolio? When there are just two securities, there are equal numbers of variance boxes and of covariance boxes. When there are many securities, the number of covariances is much larger than the number of variances. Thus the variability of a well-diversified portfolio reflects mainly the covariances.

Suppose we are dealing with portfolios in which equal investments are made in each of N stocks. The proportion invested in each stock is, therefore, $1/N$. So in each variance box we have $(1/N)^2$ times the variance, and in each covariance box we have $(1/N)^2$ times the covariance. There are N variance boxes and $N^2 - N$ covariance boxes. Therefore,

$$\text{Portfolio variance} = N\left(\frac{1}{N}\right)^2 \times \text{average variance}$$

$$+ (N^2 - N)\left(\frac{1}{N}\right)^2 \times \text{average covariance}$$

$$= \frac{1}{N} \times \text{average variance} + \left(1 - \frac{1}{N}\right) \times \text{average covariance}$$

[35] Since the standard deviation of Bharti is (33.5/54.8) times that of Tata Motors, you need to invest (37/33) times more in Grasim to eliminate risk in this two-stock portfolio.

[36] The formal equivalent to "add up all the boxes" is

$$\text{Portfolio variance} = \sum_{i=1}^{N}\sum_{j=1}^{N} x_i x_j \sigma_{ij}$$

Notice that when $i = j$, σ_{ij} is just the variance of stock i.

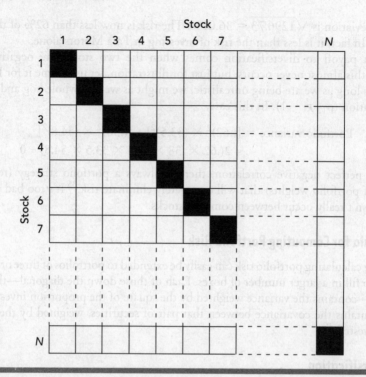

FIGURE 7.15

To find the variance of an N-stock portfolio, we must add the entries in a matrix like this. The diagonal cells contain variance terms ($x^2 \sigma^2$) and the off-diagonal cells contain covariance terms ($x_i x_j \sigma_{ij}$).

Notice that as N increases, the portfolio variance steadily approaches the average covariance. If the average covariance were zero, it would be possible to eliminate *all* risk by holding a sufficient number of securities. Unfortunately common stocks move together, not independently. Thus most of the stocks that the investor can actually buy are tied together in a web of positive covariances that set the limit to the benefits of diversification. Now we can understand the precise meaning of the market risk portrayed in Figure 7.13. It is the average covariance that constitutes the bedrock of risk remaining after diversification has done its work.

7-4 HOW INDIVIDUAL SECURITIES AFFECT PORTFOLIO RISK

We presented earlier some data on the variability of 10 individual Indian stocks. Tata Steel had the highest standard deviation and Hindustan Unilever had the lowest. If you had held Tata Steel on its own, the spread of possible returns would have been more than two times greater than if you had held Hindustan Unilever on its own. But that is not a very interesting fact. Wise investors do not put all their eggs into just one basket: They reduce their risk by diversification. They are therefore interested in the effect that each stock will have on the risk of their portfolio.

This brings us to one of the principal themes of this chapter. *The risk of a well-diversified portfolio depends on the market risk of the securities included in the portfolio.* Tattoo that statement on your forehead if you can't remember it any other way. It is one of the most important ideas in this book.

Market Risk Is Measured by Beta

If you want to know the contribution of an individual security to the risk of a well-diversified portfolio, it is no good thinking about how risky that security is if held in isolation—you need to measure its *market risk,* and that boils down to measuring how sensitive it is to market movements. This sensitivity is called **beta** (β).

Stocks with betas greater than 1.0 tend to amplify the overall movements of the market. Stocks with betas between 0 and 1.0 tend to move in the same direction as the market, but not as far. Of course, the market is the portfolio of all stocks, so the "average" stock has a beta of 1.0. Table 7.5 reports betas for the 10 well-known common stocks we referred to earlier.

Over the five years from April 2006 to March 2011, Tata Steel had a beta of 1.77. If the future resembles the past, this means that *on average* when the market rises an extra 1%, Tata Steel's stock price will rise by an extra 1.77%. When the market falls an extra 2%, Tata Steel's stock prices will fall an extra $2 \times 1.77 = 3.54\%$. Thus a line fitted to a plot of Tata Steel's returns versus market returns has a slope of 1.77. See Figure 7.16.

Of course Tata Steel's stock returns are not

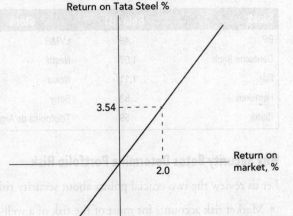

FIGURE 7.16

The return on Tata Steel's stock changes on average by 1.77% for each additional 1% change in the market return. Beta is therefore 1.77.

perfectly correlated with market returns. The company is also subject to specific risk, so the actual returns will be scattered about the line in Figure 7.16. Sometimes Tata Steel's will head south while the market goes north, and vice versa.

Of the 10 stocks in Table 7.6 Tata Steel's has one of the highest betas. Hindustan Unilever is at the other extreme. A line fitted to a plot of Hindustan Unilever's returns versus market returns would be less steep: Its slope would be only .41. Notice that many of the stocks that have high standard deviations also have high betas. But that is not always so. For example, ONGC, which has a relatively high standard deviation, has relatively Lower beta. It seems that while ONGC is a risky investment if held on its own, it makes a relatively low contribution to the risk of a diversified portfolio.

TABLE 7.6   Betas for selected Indian common stocks, April 2006–March 2011

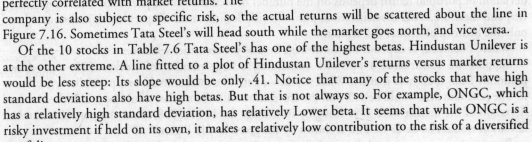

Stock	Beta (β)	Stock	Beta (β)
Bharti Airtel	0.76	Hero Honda	0.57
Hindustan Unilever	0.41	Infosys	0.55
L&T	1.38	NTPC	0.72
ONGC	0.95	Sterlite Industries	1.66
Tata Motors	1.48	Tata Steel	1.77

Just as we can measure how the returns of a an Indian stock are affected by fluctuations in the Indian market, so we can measure how stocks in other countries are affected by movements in *their* markets. Table 7.7 shows the betas for the sample of stocks from other countries.

TABLE 7.7 Betas for selected foreign stocks, January 2004–December 2008 (beta is measured relative to the stock's home market).

Stock	Beta (β)	Stock	Beta (β)
BP	.49	LVMH	.86
Deutsche Bank	1.07	Nestlé	.35
Fiat	1.11	Nokia	1.07
Heineken	.53	Sony	1.32
Iberia	.59	Telefonica de Argentina	.42

Why Security Betas Determine Portfolio Risk

Let us review the two crucial points about security risk and portfolio risk:

- Market risk accounts for most of the risk of a well-diversified portfolio.
- The beta of an individual security measures its sensitivity to market movements.

It is easy to see where we are headed: In a portfolio context, a security's risk is measured by beta. Perhaps we could just jump to that conclusion, but we would rather explain it. Here is an intuitive explanation. We provide a more technical one in footnote 38.

Explanation 1: Where's the Bedrock? Look back to Figure 7.13, which shows how the standard deviation of portfolio return depends on the number of securities in the portfolio. With more securities, and therefore better diversification, portfolio risk declines until all specific risk is eliminated and only the bedrock of market risk remains.

Where's bedrock? It depends on the average beta of the securities selected.

Suppose we constructed a portfolio containing a large number of stocks—500, say—drawn randomly from the whole market. What would we get? The market itself, or a portfolio *very* close to it. The portfolio beta would be 1.0, and the correlation with the market would be 1.0. If the standard deviation of the market were 27% (roughly its average for 1900–2008), then the portfolio standard deviation would also be 27%. This is shown by the green line in Figure 7.17.

But suppose we constructed the portfolio from a large group of stocks with an average beta of 1.5. Again we would end up with a 500-stock portfolio with virtually no specific risk—a portfolio that moves almost in lockstep with the market. However, *this* portfolio's standard deviation would be 40%, 1.5 times that of the market.[37] A well-diversified portfolio with a beta of 1.5 will amplify every market move by 50% and end up with 150% of the market's risk. The upper red line in Figure 7.17 shows this case.

Of course, we could repeat the same experiment with stocks with a beta of .5 and end up with a well-diversified portfolio half as risky as the market. You can see this also in Figure 7.17.

---

[37] A 500-stock portfolio with β = 1.5 would still have some specific risk because it would be unduly concentrated in high-beta industries. Its actual standard deviation would be a bit higher than 40%. If that worries you, relax; we will show you in Chapter 8 how you can construct a fully diversified portfolio with a beta of 1.5 by borrowing and investing in the market portfolio.

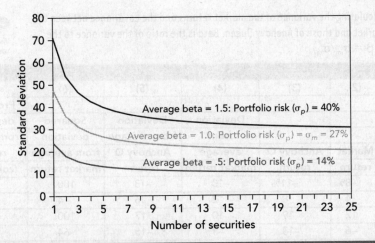

FIGURE 7.17

The green line shows that a well-diversified portfolio of randomly selected stocks ends up with $\beta = 1$ and a standard deviation equal to the market's—in this case 27%. The upper red line shows that a well-diversified portfolio with $\beta = 1.5$ has a standard deviation of about 40%—1.5 times that of the market. The lower brown line shows that a well-diversified portfolio with $\beta = .5$ has a standard deviation of about 14%—half that of the market.

The general point is this: The risk of a well-diversified portfolio is proportional to the portfolio beta, which equals the average beta of the securities included in the portfolio. This shows you how portfolio risk is driven by security betas.

Calculating Beta   A statistician would define the beta of stock i as

$$\beta_i = \sigma_{im}/\sigma_m^2$$

where σ_{im} is the *covariance* between the stock returns and the market returns and σ_m^2 is the variance of the returns on the market. It turns out that this ratio of covariance to variance measures a stock's contribution to portfolio risk.[38]

Here is a simple example of how to do the calculations. Columns 2 and 3 in Table 7.8 show the returns over a particular six-month period on the market and the stock of the Anchovy Queen restaurant chain. You can see that, although both investments provided an average return of 2%,

---

[38] To understand why, skip back to Figure 7.15. Each row of boxes in Figure 7.15 represents the contribution of that particular security to the portfolio's risk. For example, the contribution of stock 1 is

$$x_1 x_1 \sigma_{11} + x_1 x_2 \sigma_{12} + \cdots = x_1(x_1 \sigma_{11} + x_2 \sigma_{12} + \cdots)$$

where x_i is the proportion invested in stock i, and σ_{ij} is the covariance between stocks i and j (note: σ_{ii} is equal to the variance of stock i). In other words, the contribution of stock 1 to portfolio risk is equal to the relative size of the holding (x_1) times the average covariance between stock 1 and all the stocks in the portfolio. We can write this more concisely by saying that the contribution of stock 1 to portfolio risk is equal to the holding size (x_1) times the covariance between stock 1 and the entire portfolio (σ_{1p}).

To find stock 1's *relative* contribution to risk we simply divide by the portfolio variance to give $x_1(\sigma_{1p}/\sigma_p^2)$. In other words, it is equal to the holding size (x_1) times the beta of stock 1 relative to the portfolio (σ_{1p}/σ_p^2).

We can calculate the beta of a stock relative to *any* portfolio by simply taking its covariance with the portfolio and dividing by the portfolio's variance. If we wish to find a stock's beta *relative to the market portfolio* we just calculate its covariance with the market portfolio and divide by the variance of the market:

$$\text{Beta relative to market portfolio} = \frac{\text{covariance with the market}}{\text{variance of market}} = \frac{\sigma_{im}}{\sigma_m^2}$$
$$\text{(or, more simply, beta)}$$

TABLE 7.8 Calculating the variance of the market returns and the covariance between the returns on the market and those of Anchovy Queen. Beta is the ratio of the variance to the covariance (i.e., $\beta = \sigma_{im}/\sigma_m^2$).

eXcel

Visit us at
www.mhhe.com/bmam10e

(1)	(2)	(3)	(4)	(5)	(6)	(7)
						Product of deviations from average returns
			Deviation from	Deviation from average	Squared deviation	
	Market	Anchovy Q	average	Anchovy Q	from average	
Month	return	return	market return	return	market return	(cols 4 × 5)
1	–8%	–11%	–10	–13	100	130
2	4	8	2	6	4	12
3	12	19	10	17	100	170
4	–6	–13	–8	–15	64	120
5	2	3	0	1	0	0
6	8	6	6	4	36	24
Average	2	2		Total	304	456
			Variance = σ_m^2 = 304/6 = 50.67			
			Covariance = σ_{im} = 456/6 = 76			
			Beta (β) = σ_{im}/σ_m^2 = 76/50.67 = 1.5			

Anchovy Queen's stock was particularly sensitive to market movements, rising more when the market rises and falling more when the market falls.

Columns 4 and 5 show the deviations of each month's return from the average. To calculate the market variance, we need to average the squared deviations of the market returns (column 6). And to calculate the covariance between the stock returns and the market, we need to average the product of the two deviations (column 7). Beta is the ratio of the covariance to the market variance, or $76/50.67 = 1.50$. A diversified portfolio of stocks with the same beta as Anchovy Queen would be one-and-a-half times as volatile as the market.

7-5   DIVERSIFICATION AND VALUE ADDITIVITY

We have seen that diversification reduces risk and, therefore, makes sense for investors. But does it also make sense for the firm? Is a diversified firm more attractive to investors than an undiversified one? If it is, we have an *extremely* disturbing result. If diversification is an appropriate corporate objective, each project has to be analyzed as a potential addition to the firm's portfolio of assets. The value of the diversified package would be greater than the sum of the parts. So present values would no longer add.

Diversification is undoubtedly a good thing, but that does not mean that firms should practice it. If investors were *not* able to hold a large number of securities, then they might want firms to diversify for them. But investors *can* diversify.[39] In many ways they can do so more easily than firms. Individuals can invest in the steel industry this week and pull out next week. A firm cannot do that. To be sure, the individual would have to pay brokerage fees on the purchase and sale of steel company shares, but think of the time and expense for a firm to acquire a steel company or to start up a new steel-making operation.

---

[39] One of the simplest ways for an individual to diversify is to buy shares in a mutual fund that holds a diversified portfolio.

You can probably see where we are heading. If investors can diversify on their own account, they will not pay any *extra* for firms that diversify. And if they have a sufficiently wide choice of securities, they will not pay any *less* because they are unable to invest separately in each factory. Therefore, in countries like the United States and India which have large and competitive capital markets, diversification does not add to a firm's value or subtract from it. The total value is the sum of its parts.

This conclusion is important for corporate finance, because it justifies adding present values. The concept of *value additivity* is so important that we will give a formal definition of it. If the capital market establishes a value PV(A) for asset A and PV(B) for B, the market value of a firm that holds only these two assets is

$$PV(AB) = PV(A) + PV(B)$$

A three-asset firm combining assets A, B, and C would be worth PV(ABC) = PV(A) + PV(B) + PV(C), and so on for any number of assets.

We have relied on intuitive arguments for value additivity. But the concept is a general one that can be proved formally by several different routes.[40] The concept seems to be widely accepted, for thousands of managers add thousands of present values daily, usually without thinking about it.

SUMMARY

Our review of capital market history showed that the returns to investors have varied according to the risks they have borne. At one extreme, very safe securities like Short-term government securities have provided an average return of 9.29% over 32 years. The riskiest securities that we looked at were common stocks. The stock market provided an average return of 22.89%, a premium of 13.61% over the safe rate of interest.

This gives us two benchmarks for the opportunity cost of capital. If we are evaluating a safe project, we discount at the current risk-free rate of interest. If we are evaluating a project of average risk, we discount at the expected return on the average common stock. Historical evidence suggests that this return is 13.61% above the risk-free rate, but many financial managers and economists opt for a lower figure. That still leaves us with a lot of assets that don't fit these simple cases. Before we can deal with them, we need to learn how to measure risk.

Risk is best judged in a portfolio context. Most investors do not put all their eggs into one basket: They diversify. Thus the effective risk of any security cannot be judged by an examination of that security alone. Part of the uncertainty about the security's return is diversified away when the security is grouped with others in a portfolio.

Risk in investment means that future returns are unpredictable. This spread of possible outcomes is usually measured by standard deviation. The standard deviation of the *market portfolio*, generally represented by the Mumbai Stock Exchange's Sensitivity Index (Sensex), is around 25% to 30% a year.

Most individual stocks have higher standard deviations than this, but much of their variability represents *specific* risk that can be eliminated by diversification. Diversification cannot eliminate *market* risk. Diversified portfolios are exposed to variation in the general level of the market.

A security's contribution to the risk of a well-diversified portfolio depends on how the security is liable to be affected by a general market decline. This sensitivity to market movements is known as *beta* (β). Beta measures the amount that investors expect the stock price to change for each additional 1% change in the market. The average beta of all stocks is 1.0. A stock with a beta greater than 1

---

[40] You may wish to refer to the Appendix to Chapter 31, which discusses diversification and value additivity in the context of mergers.

is unusually sensitive to market movements; a stock with a beta below 1 is unusually insensitive to market movements. The standard deviation of a well-diversified portfolio is proportional to its beta. Thus a diversified portfolio invested in stocks with a beta of 2.0 will have twice the risk of a diversified portfolio with a beta of 1.0.

One theme of this chapter is that diversification is a good thing *for the investor*. This does not imply that *firms* should diversify. Corporate diversification is redundant if investors can diversify on their own account. Since diversification does not affect the value of the firm, present values add even when risk is explicitly considered. Thanks to *value additivity*, the net present value rule for capital budgeting works even under uncertainty.

In this chapter we have introduced you to a number of formulas. They are reproduced in the endpapers to the book. You should take a look and check that you understand them.

Near the end of Chapter 9 we list some Excel functions that are useful for measuring the risk of stocks and portfolios.

FURTHER READING

For international evidence on market returns since 1900, see:

E. Dimson, P. R. Marsh, and M. Staunton, *Triumph of the Optimists: 101 Years of Investment Returns* (Princeton, NJ: Princeton University Press, 2002). More recent data is available in The Credit Suisse Global Investment Returns Yearbook at **www.tinyurl.com/DMSyearbook**.

The Ibbotson Yearbook is a valuable record of the performance of U.S. securities since 1926:

Ibbotson Stocks, Bonds, Bills, and Inflation 2009 Yearbook (Chicago, IL: Morningstar, Inc., 2009).

Useful books and reviews on the equity risk premium include:

B. Cornell, *The Equity Risk Premium: The Long-Run Future of the Stock Market* (New York: Wiley, 1999).

W. Goetzmann and R. Ibbotson, *The Equity Risk Premium: Essays and Explorations* (Oxford University Press, 2006).

R. Mehra (ed.), *Handbook of Investments: Equity Risk Premium 1* (Amsterdam, North-Holland, 2007).

R. Mehra and E. C. Prescott, "The Equity Risk Premium in Prospect," in *Handbook of the Economics of Finance*, eds. G. M. Constantinides, M. Harris, and R. M. Stulz (Amsterdam, North-Holland, 2003).

PROBLEM SETS

BASIC

1. A game of chance offers the following odds and payoffs. Each play of the game costs ₹100, so the net profit per play is the payoff less ₹100.

Probability	Payoff	Net Profit
.10	₹500	₹400
.50	100	0
.40	0	−100

What are the expected cash payoff and expected rate of return? Calculate the variance and standard deviation of this rate of return.

2. The following table shows the nominal returns on the Indian stocks and the rate of inflation.

eXcel

Visit us at
www.mhhe.com/bmam10e

   a. What was the standard deviation of the market returns?
   b. Calculate the average real return.

Year	Nominal Return (%)	Inflation (%)
2006	+37.9	+3.8
2007	+40.3	+7.4
2008	+31.9	+7.4
2009	−28.2	+9.6
2010	+24.5	+13.1

3. Mr. Rakesh Sabharwal, ace mutual fund manager, produced the following percentage rates of return from 1999 to 2003. Rates of return on sensex are given for comparison.

	1998-99	1999-00	2000-01	2001-02	2002-03
Mr. Rakesh Sabharwal	−6.20%	48.07%	−1.50%	−6.91%	−1.10%
Sensex	−12.0%	42.3%	−6.6%	−19.9%	−0.3%

Calculate the average return and standard deviation of Mr. Sabharwal's mutual fund. Did he do better or worse than sensex by these measures?

4. True or false?
   a. Investors prefer diversified companies because they are less risky.
   b. If stocks were perfectly positively correlated, diversification would not reduce risk.
   c. Diversification over a large number of assets completely eliminates risk.
   d. Diversification works only when assets are uncorrelated.
   e. A stock with a low standard deviation always contributes less to portfolio risk than a stock with a higher standard deviation.
   f. The contribution of a stock to the risk of a well-diversified portfolio depends on its market risk.
   g. A well-diversified portfolio with a beta of 2.0 is twice as risky as the market portfolio.
   h. An undiversified portfolio with a beta of 2.0 is less than twice as risky as the market portfolio.

5. In which of the following situations would you get the largest reduction in risk by spreading your investment across two stocks?
   a. The two shares are perfectly correlated.
   b. There is no correlation.
   c. There is modest negative correlation.
   d. There is perfect negative correlation.

6. To calculate the variance of a three-stock portfolio, you need to add nine boxes:

Use the same symbols that we used in this chapter; for example, x_1 = proportion invested in stock 1 and σ_{12} = covariance between stocks 1 and 2. Now complete the nine boxes.

7. Suppose the standard deviation of the market return is 27%.
   a. What is the standard deviation of returns on a well-diversified portfolio with a beta of 1.3?
   b. What is the standard deviation of returns on a well-diversified portfolio with a beta of 0?
   c. A well-diversified portfolio has a standard deviation of 15%. What is its beta?
   d. A poorly diversified portfolio has a standard deviation of 20%. What can you say about its beta?

8. A portfolio contains equal investments in 10 stocks. Five have a beta of 1.2; the remainder have a beta of 1.4. What is the portfolio beta?
   a. 1.3.
   b. Greater than 1.3 because the portfolio is not completely diversified.
   c. Less than 1.3 because diversification reduces beta.

9. What is the beta of each of the stocks shown in Table 7.9?

TABLE 7.9 See Problem 9.

Stock	Stock Return if Market Return Is:	
	−10%	**+10%**
A	0	+20
B	−20	+20
C	−30	0
D	+15	+15
E	+10	−10

INTERMEDIATE

10. Here are inflation rates and U.S. stock market and Treasury bill returns between 1929 and 1933:

Year	Inflation	Stock Market Return	T-Bill Return
1929	−.2	−14.5	4.8
1930	−6.0	−28.3	2.4
1931	−9.5	−43.9	1.1
1932	−10.3	−9.9	1.0
1933	.5	57.3	.3

eXcel

Visit us at
www.mhhe.com/bmam10e

   a. What was the real return on the stock market in each year?
   b. What was the average real return?
   c. What was the risk premium in each year?
   d. What was the average risk premium?
   e. What was the standard deviation of the risk premium?

11. Each of the following statements is dangerous or misleading. Explain why.
   a. A long-term Indian government security is always absolutely safe.
   b. All investors should prefer stocks to bonds because stocks offer higher long-run rates of return.

   c. The best practical forecast of future rates of return on the stock market is a 5- or 10-year average of historical returns.

12. Hippique s.a., which owns a stable of racehorses, has just invested in a mysterious black stallion with great form but disputed bloodlines. Some experts in horseflesh predict the horse will win the coveted Prix de Bidet; others argue that it should be put out to grass. Is this a risky investment for Hippique shareholders? Explain.

13. Lonesome Gulch Mines has a standard deviation of 42% per year and a beta of $+.10$. Amalgamated Copper has a standard deviation of 31% a year and a beta of $+.66$. Explain why Lonesome Gulch is the safer investment for a diversified investor.

14. Kamia invests 60% of her funds in stock I and the balance in stock J. The standard deviation of returns on I is 10%, and on J it is 20%. Calculate the variance of portfolio returns, assuming

   a. The correlation between the returns is 1.0.

   b. The correlation is .5.

   c. The correlation is 0.

15. a. How many variance terms and how many covariance terms do you need to calculate the risk of a 100-share portfolio?

   b. Suppose all stocks had a standard deviation of 30% and a correlation with each other of .4. What is the standard deviation of the returns on a portfolio that has equal holdings in 50 stocks?

   c. What is the standard deviation of a fully diversified portfolio of such stocks?

16. Suppose that the standard deviation of returns from a typical share is about .40 (or 40%) a year. The correlation between the returns of each pair of shares is about .3.

   a. Calculate the variance and standard deviation of the returns on a portfolio that has equal investments in 2 shares, 3 shares, and so on, up to 10 shares.

   b. Use your estimates to draw a graph like Figure 7.13. How large is the underlying market risk that cannot be diversified away?

   c. Now repeat the problem, assuming that the correlation between each pair of stocks is zero.

17. Table 7.10 shows standard deviations and correlation coefficients for eight stocks from different countries. Calculate the variance of a portfolio with equal investments in each stock.

18. Your eccentric aunt Mrs. Sharma has left you ₹500,000 in Tata Motors shares plus ₹500,000 cash. Unfortunately her will requires that the Tata Motors shares cannot be sold for one year and the ₹500,000 cash must be entirely invested in one of the stocks shown in Table 7.9. Which is the safest attainable portfolio under these restrictions?

19. There are few, if any, real companies with negative betas. But suppose you found one with $\beta = -.25$.

   a. How would you expect this stock's rate of return to change if the overall market rose by an extra 5%? What if the market fell by an extra 5%?

   b. You have ₹1 million invested in a well-diversified portfolio of stocks. Now you receive an additional ₹200,000 bequest. Which of the following actions will yield the safest overall portfolio return?

     i. Invest ₹200,000 in Treasury bills (which have $\beta = 0$).

     ii. Invest ₹200,000 in stocks with $\beta = 1$.

     iii. Invest ₹200,000 in the stock with $\beta = -.25$.

     Explain your answer.

TABLE 7.10 Standard deviations of returns and correlation coefficients for a sample of eight stocks.

Note: Correlations and standard deviations are calculated using returns in each country's own currency; in other words, they assume that the investor is protected against exchange risk.

	BP	Canadian Pacific	Deutsche Bank	Fiat	Heineken	LVMH	Nestlé	Tata Motors	Standard Deviation
				Correlation Coefficients					
BP	1	0.19	0.23	0.20	0.34	0.30	0.16	0.09	22.2%
Canadian Pacific		1	0.43	0.31	0.39	0.34	0.17	0.40	23.9
Deutsche Bank			1	0.74	0.73	0.73	0.49	0.68	29.2
Fiat				1	0.66	0.64	0.47	0.53	35.7
Heineken					1	0.64	0.51	0.50	18.9
LVMH						1	0.52	0.60	20.8
Nestlé							1	0.43	15.4
Tata Motors								1	43.0

20. You can form a portfolio of two assets, A and B, whose returns have the following characteristics:

Stock	Expected Return	Standard Deviation	Correlation
A	10%	20%	.5
B	15	40	

If you demand an expected return of 12%, what are the portfolio weights? What is the portfolio's standard deviation?

CHALLENGE

21. Here are some historical data on the risk characteristics of ICICI Bank and ITC:

	ICICI Bank	ITC
β (beta)	1.34	.44
Yearly standard deviation of return (%)	47	28

Assume the standard deviation of the return on the market was 27%.

a. The correlation coefficient of ICICI's return versus ITC's is 0.15. What is the standard deviation of a portfolio invested half in ICICI Bank and half in ITC?

b. What is the standard deviation of a portfolio invested one-third in ICICI Bank, one-third in ITC and one-third in risk-free Treasury bills?

c. What is the standard deviation if the portfolio is split evenly between ICICI Bank and ITC and is financed at 50% margin, i.e. the investor puts up only 50% of the total amount and borrows the balance from the broker?

d. What is the approximate standard deviation of a portfolio composed of 100 stocks with betas of 1.34 like ICICI Bank? How about 100 stocks like ITC? (Hint: Part (d) should not require anything but the simplest arithmetic to answer.)

22. Suppose that Treasury bills offer a return of about 6% and the expected market risk premium is 8.5%. The standard deviation of Treasury-bill returns is zero and the standard deviation of market returns is 20%. Use the formula for portfolio risk to calculate the standard deviation of portfolios with different proportions in Treasury bills and the market. (*Note:* The covariance of two rates of return must be zero when the standard deviation of one return is zero.) Graph the expected returns and standard deviations.

23. Calculate the beta of each of the stocks in Table 7.9 relative to a portfolio with equal investments in each stock.

Visit us at
www.mhhe.com/bmam10e

You can download data for the following questions from the Standard & Poor's Market Insight Web site (www.mhhe.com/edumarketinsight)—see the "Monthly Adjusted Prices" spreadsheet —or from finance.yahoo.com. Refer to the useful Spreadsheet Functions box near the end of Chapter 9 for information on Excel functions.

1. Download the daily closing prices of HLL, Reliance and ITC from the website of the NSE (www.nseindia.com). Estimate the monthly returns from these data.

    STANDARD &POOR'S

    a. Calculate the annual standard deviation of returns from each company, using the most recent three years of monthly returns. Use the Excel function STDEV. Multiply by the square root of 12 to convert to annual units.

    b. Use the Excel function CORREL to calculate the correlation coefficient between the monthly returns for each pair of stocks.

    c. Calculate the standard deviation of returns for a portfolio with equal investments in each of the three stocks.

2. Download to a spreadsheet the last five years of monthly adjusted stock prices for each of the companies in Table 7.6 and for the sensex.

    STANDARD &POOR'S

    a. Calculate the monthly returns.

    b. Calculate beta for each stock using the Excel function SLOPE, where the "y" range refers to the stock return (the dependent variable) and the "x" range is the market return (the independent variable).

    c. How have the betas changed from those reported in Table 7.6?

3. A large mutual fund group such as Fidelity offers a variety of funds. They include *sector funds* that specialize in particular industries and *index funds* that simply invest in the market index. Log on to **www.fidelity.com** and find first the standard deviation of returns on the Fidelity Spartan 500 Index Fund, which replicates the S&P 500. Now find the standard deviations for different sector funds. Are they larger or smaller than the figure for the index fund? How do you interpret your findings?

8

CHAPTER

PORTFOLIO THEORY AND THE CAPITAL ASSET PRICING MODEL

In Chapter 7 we began to come to grips with the problem of measuring risk. Here is the story so far.

The stock market is risky because there is a spread of possible outcomes. The usual measure of this spread is the standard deviation or variance. The risk of any stock can be broken down into two parts. There is the *specific* or *diversifiable risk* that is peculiar to that stock, and there is the *market risk* that is associated with marketwide variations. Investors can eliminate specific risk by holding a well-diversified portfolio, but they cannot eliminate market risk. *All* the risk of a fully diversified portfolio is market risk.

A stock's contribution to the risk of a fully diversified portfolio depends on its sensitivity to market changes. This sensitivity is generally known as *beta*. A security with a beta of 1.0 has average market risk—a well-diversified portfolio of such securities has the same standard deviation as the market index. A security with a beta of .5 has below-average market risk—a well-diversified portfolio of these securities tends to move half as far as the market moves and has half the market's standard deviation.

In this chapter we build on this newfound knowledge. We present leading theories linking risk and return in a competitive economy, and we show how these theories can be used to estimate the returns required by investors in different stock-market investments. We start with the most widely used theory, the capital asset pricing model, which builds directly on the ideas developed in the last chapter. We will also look at another class of models, known as arbitrage pricing or factor models. Then in Chapter 9 we show how these ideas can help the financial manager cope with risk in practical capital budgeting situations.

8-1 HARRY MARKOWITZ AND THE BIRTH OF PORTFOLIO THEORY

Most of the ideas in Chapter 7 date back to an article written in 1952 by Harry Markowitz.[1] Markowitz drew attention to the common practice of portfolio diversification and showed exactly how an investor can reduce the standard deviation of portfolio returns by choosing stocks that do not move exactly together. But Markowitz did not stop there; he went on to work out the basic principles of portfolio construction. These principles are the foundation for much of what has been written about the relationship between risk and return.

We begin with Figure 8.1, which shows a histogram of the daily returns on Grasim Industries. On this histogram we have superimposed a bell-shaped normal distribution. The result is typical: When measured over a short interval, the past rates of return on any stock conform fairly closely to a normal distribution.[2]

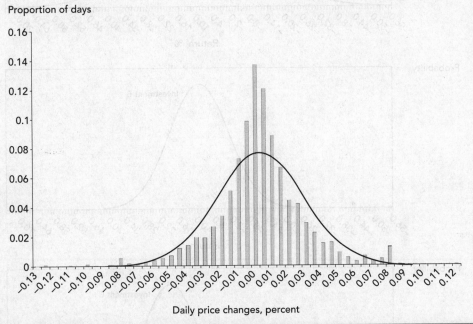

Proportion of days

Daily price changes, percent

FIGURE 8.1

Daily price changes for Grasim Industries are approximately normally distributed. This plot spans November 1994 to March 2006

Normal distributions can be completely defined by two numbers. One is the average or expected return; the other is the variance or standard deviation. Now you can see why in Chapter 7 we discussed the calculation of expected return and standard deviation. They are not just arbitrary measures: if

---

[1] H. M. Markowitz, "Portfolio Selection," *Journal of Finance 7* (March 1952), pp. 77–91.

[2] If you were to measure returns over *long* intervals, the distribution would be skewed. For example, you would encounter returns greater than 100% but none less than −100%. The distribution of returns over periods of, say, one year would be better approximated by a *lognormal* distribution. The lognormal distribution, like the normal, is completely specified by its mean and standard deviation.

returns are normally distributed, expected return and standard deviation are the *only* two measures that an investor need consider.

Figure 8.2 pictures the distribution of possible returns from three investments. A and B offer an expected return of 10%, but A has the much wider spread of possible outcomes. Its standard deviation

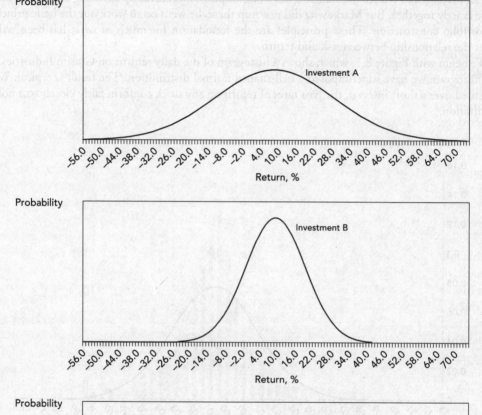

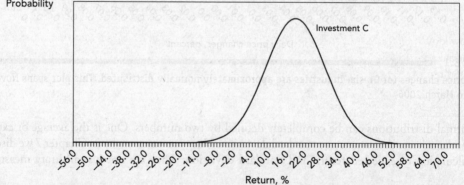

FIGURE 8.2

Investments A and B both have an *expected* return of 10%, but because investment A has the greater spread of *possible* returns, it is more risky than B. We can measure this spread by the standard deviation. Investment A has a standard deviation of 15%; B, 7.5%. Most investors would prefer B to A. Investments B and C both have the same standard deviation, but C offers a higher expected return. Most investors would prefer C to B.

is 15%; the standard deviation of B is 7.5%. Most investors dislike uncertainty and would therefore prefer B to A.

Now compare investments B and C. This time both have the *same* standard deviation, but the expected return is 20% from stock C and only 10% from stock B. Most investors like high expected return and would therefore prefer C to B.

Combining Stocks into Portfolios

Suppose that you are wondering whether to invest in the shares of Bharti Airtel or Tata Motors. You decide that Bharti offers an expected return of 14% and Tata Motors offers an expected return of 17%. After looking back at the past variability of the two stocks, you also decide that the standard deviation of returns is 33.5% for Bharti and 54.8% for Tata Motors. Tata Motors offers the higher expected return, but it is more risky.

Now there is no reason to restrict yourself to holding only one stock. For example, in Section 7-3 we analyzed what would happen if you invested 62% of your money in Bharti and 38% in Tata Motors. The expected return on this portfolio is about 15.14%, simply a weighted average of the expected returns on the two holdings. What about the risk of such a portfolio? We know that thanks to diversification the portfolio risk is less than the average of the risks of the separate stocks. In fact, on the basis of past experience the standard deviation of this portfolio is 36.01%.[3]

The thick line in Figure 8.3 shows the expected return and risk that you could achieve by different combinations of the two stocks. Which of these combinations is the best? That depends on your stomach. If you want to stake all on getting rich quickly, you will do the best to put all your money in Tata Motors. If you want a more peaceful life, you should invest most of your money in Bharti, but you should keep at least a small investment in Tata Motors.[4]

In practice, you are not limited to investing in just two stocks. For example, you could decide to choose a portfolio from the 10 stocks listed in the first column of Table 8.1. After analyzing the prospects for each firm, you come up with forecasts of their returns. You are most optimistic about the outlook for Tata Steel, and forecast that it will provide a return of 25%. At the other end, you are cautious about the prospects for Infosys and predict a return of 7%. You use data for the past five years to estimate the risk of each stock and the correlation between the returns on each pair of stocks.[5]

Now look at Figure 8.4. Each diamond marks the combination of risk and return offered by a different individual security. For example, Tata Steel has both the highest standard deviation and the highest expected return. It is represented by the upper-right diamond in the figure.

---

[3] We pointed out in Section 7-3 that the correlation between the returns of Bharti and Tata Motors is .5. The variance of a portfolio which is invested 62% in Bharti and 38% in Tata Motors is

$$\text{Variance} = x_1^2\sigma_1^2 + x_2^2\sigma_2^2 + 2x_1x_2\rho_{12}\sigma_1\sigma_2$$
$$= [(.62)^2 \times (33.5)^2] + [(.38)^2 \times (54.8)^2] + 2(.62 \times .38 \times .5 \times 33.5 \times 54.8)$$
$$= 1296.73$$

The portfolio standard deviation is $\sqrt{1296.73} = 36.01\%$.

[4] The portfolio with the minimum risk has 91% in Bharti. We assume in Figure 8.4 that you may not take negative positions in either stock, i.e., we rule out short sales.

[5] There are 45 different correlation coefficients, so we have not listed them in Table 8.1.

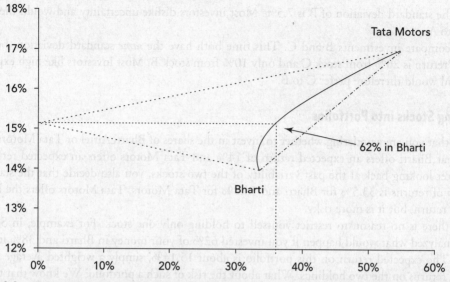

FIGURE 8.3

The curved line illustrates how expected return and standard deviation change as you hold different combinations of two stocks. For example, if you invest 38 percent of your money in Tata Motors and the remaining in Bharti, your expected return is 15.14 percent, which is 38 percent of the way between the expected returns on the two stocks. The standard deviation is 36.01 percent, which is less than 40 percent of the way between the standard deviations between the two stocks. This is because diversification reduces risk.

TABLE 8.1   Examples of efficient portfolios chosen from 10 stocks.

Stock	Expected Return	Standard Deviation	Efficient Portfolios – Percentages Allocated to Each Stock		
			A	B	C
Bharti	14.0%	33.5%		10.5%	11.0%
Hero Honda	9.9%	28.8%		0.8%	19.1%
HUL	9.9%	28.6%		10.6%	26.3%
Infosys	7.0%	29.2%			30.2%
L&T	22.8%	46.9%		20.1%	
NTPC	16.0%	30.0%		42.0%	13.5%
ONGC	18.0%	37.3%		12.7%	
Sterlite	19.0%	59.6%			
Tata Motors	17.0%	54.8%			
Tata Steel	25.0%	62.3%	100.00%	3.3%	
Expected Portfolio Return			25.00%	17.00%	10.28%
Portfolio Standard Deviation			62.30%	29.09%	20.68%

Note: Standard deviations and the correlations between stock returns were estimated from monthly stock returns, April 2006–March 2011. Efficient portfolios are calculated assuming that short sales are prohibited.

By holding different proportions of the 10 securities, you can obtain an even wider selection of risk and return: in fact, *anywhere* in the shaded area in Figure 8.4. But where in the shaded area is best? Well, what is your goal? Which direction do you want to go? The answer should be obvious: you want to go up (to increase expected return) and to the left (to reduce risk). Go as far as you can, and you will end up with one of the portfolios that lies along the heavy solid line. Markowitz called them **efficient portfolios.** They offer the highest expected return for any level of risk.

We will not calculate this set of efficient portfolios here, but you may be interested in how to do it. Think back to the capital rationing problem in Section 5-4. There we wanted to deploy a limited amount of capital investment in a mixture of projects to give the highest NPV. Here we want to deploy an investor's funds to give the highest expected return for a given standard deviation. In principle, both problems can be solved by hunting and pecking—but only in principle. To solve the capital rationing problem, we can employ linear programming; to solve the portfolio problem, we would turn to a variant of linear programming known as *quadratic programming*. Given the expected return and standard deviation for each stock, as well as the correlation between each pair of stocks, we could use a standard quadratic computer program to calculate the set of efficient portfolios.

Three of these efficient portfolios are marked in Figure 8.4. Their compositions are summarized in Table 8.1. Portfolio B is invested entirely in one stock, Tata Steel. Portfolio C offers the minimum risk; you can see from Table 8.1 that it has large holdings in Infosys, Hindustan Unilever and Hero Honda, which have the lowest standard deviations.

Table 8.1 also shows the compositions of a third efficient portfolio with intermediate levels of risk and expected return.

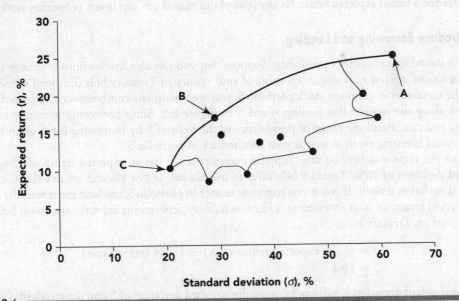

FIGURE 8.4
Each shaded box marked "•" shows the expected return and the standard deviation of 1 of the 10 stocks in Table 8.1. The area between the dark and the thin line shows the possible combinations of expected return and standard deviation from investing in a mixture of these stocks. If you like high expected returns and dislike high standard deviations, you will prefer portfolios along the heavy line. These are efficient portfolios. We have marked the three efficient portfolios described in Table 8.1 (A, B, and C).

Of course, large investment funds can choose from thousands of stocks and thereby achieve a wider choice of risk and return. This choice is represented in Figure 8.5 by the shaded, broken-egg-shaped area. The set of efficient portfolios is again marked by the heavy curved line.

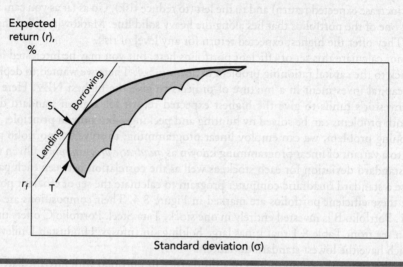

FIGURE 8.5

Lending and borrowing extend the range of investment possibilities. If you invest in portfolio S and lend or borrow at the risk-free interest rate, r_f, you can achieve any point along the straight line from r_f through S. This gives you a higher expected return for any level of risk than if you just invest in common stocks.

We Introduce Borrowing and Lending

Now we introduce yet another possibility. Suppose that you can also lend or borrow money at some risk-free rate of interest r_f. If you invest some of your money in Treasury bills (i.e., lend money) and place the remainder in common stock portfolio S, you can obtain any combination of expected return and risk along the straight line joining r_f and S in Figure 8.5. Since borrowing is merely negative lending, you can extend the range of possibilities to the right of S by borrowing funds at an interest rate of r_f and investing them as well as your own money in portfolio S.

Let us put some numbers on this. Suppose that portfolio S has an expected return of 15% and a standard deviation of 16%. Treasury bills offer an interest rate (r_f) of 5% and are risk-free (i.e., their standard deviation is zero). If you invest half your money in portfolio S and lend the remainder at 5%, the expected return on your investment is likewise halfway between the expected return on S and the interest rate on Treasury bills:

$$r = (\tfrac{1}{2} \times \text{expected return on S}) + (\tfrac{1}{2} \times \text{interest rate})$$
$$= 10\%$$

And the standard deviation is halfway between the standard deviation of S and the standard deviation of Treasury bills:[6]

---

[6] If you want to check this, write down the formula for the standard deviation of a two-stock portfolio:

$$\text{Standard deviation} = \sqrt{x_1^2 \sigma_1^2 + x_2^2 \sigma_2^2 + 2x_1 x_2 \rho_{12} \sigma_1 \sigma_2}$$

Now see what happens when security 2 is riskless, i.e., when $\sigma_2 = 0$.

$$\sigma = (\tfrac{1}{2} \times \text{standard deviation of S}) + (\tfrac{1}{2} \times \text{standard deviation of bills})$$
$$= 8\%$$

Or suppose that you decide to go for the big time: You borrow at the Treasury bill rate an amount equal to your initial wealth, and you invest everything in portfolio S. You have twice your own money invested in S, but you have to *pay* interest on the loan. Therefore your expected return is

$$r = (2 \times \text{expected return on S}) - (1 \times \text{interest rate})$$
$$= 25\%$$

And the standard deviation of your investment is

$$\sigma = (2 \times \text{standard deviation of S}) - (1 \times \text{standard deviation of bills})$$
$$= 32\%$$

You can see from Figure 8.5 that when you lend a portion of your money, you end up partway between r_f and S; if you can borrow money at the risk-free rate, you can extend your possibilities beyond S. You can also see that regardless of the level of risk you choose, you can get the highest expected return by a mixture of portfolio S and borrowing or lending. S is the *best* efficient portfolio. There is no reason ever to hold, say, portfolio T.

If you have a graph of efficient portfolios, as in Figure 8.5, finding this best efficient portfolio is easy. Start on the vertical axis at r_f and draw the steepest line you can to the curved heavy line of efficient portfolios. That line will be tangent to the heavy line. The efficient portfolio at the tangency point is better than all the others. Notice that it offers the highest *ratio* of risk premium to standard deviation. This ratio of the risk premium to the standard deviation is called the *Sharpe ratio:*

$$\text{Sharpe ratio} = \frac{\text{Risk premium}}{\text{Standard deviation}} = \frac{r - r_f}{\sigma}$$

Investors track Sharpe ratios to measure the risk-adjusted performance of investment managers. (Take a look at the mini-case at the end of this chapter.)

We can now separate the investor's job into two stages. First, the best portfolio of common stocks must be selected—S in our example. Second, this portfolio must be blended with borrowing or lending to obtain an exposure to risk that suits the particular investor's taste. Each investor, therefore, should put money into just two benchmark investments—a risky portfolio S and a risk-free loan (borrowing or lending).

What does portfolio S look like? If you have better information than your rivals, you will want the portfolio to include relatively large investments in the stocks you think are undervalued. But in a competitive market you are unlikely to have a monopoly of good ideas. In that case there is no reason to hold a different portfolio of common stocks from anybody else. In other words, you might just as well hold the market portfolio. That is why many professional investors invest in a market-index portfolio and why most others hold well-diversified portfolios.

8-2 THE RELATIONSHIP BETWEEN RISK AND RETURN

In Chapter 7 we looked at the returns on selected investments. The least risky investment was the 1-year government security. Since the return on G-Sec is fixed, it is unaffected by what happens to the market. In other words, G-Secs have a beta of zero. We also considered a much riskier investment, the market portfolio of common stocks. This has the average market risk: its beta is 1.0.

Wise investors don't take risks just for fun. They are playing with real money. Therefore, they require a higher return from the market portfolio than from the Treasury bills. The difference between the return on the market and the interest rate is termed the *market risk premium*. Since 1978–79 the market risk premium ($r_m - r_f$) has averaged 13.61% a year in India.

In Figure 8.6 we have plotted the risk and expected return from Treasury bills and the market portfolio. You can see that Treasury bills have a beta of 0 and a risk premium of 0.[7] The market portfolio has a beta of 1 and a risk premium of $r_m - r_f$. This gives us two benchmarks for the expected risk premium. But what is the expected risk premium when beta is not 0 or 1?

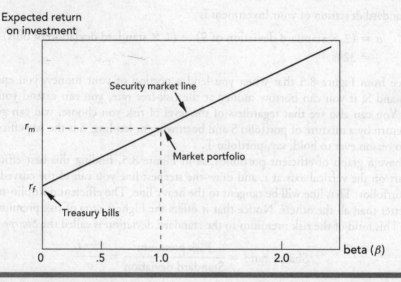

FIGURE 8.6

The capital asset pricing model states that the expected risk premium on each investment is proportional to its beta. This means that each investment should lie on the sloping security market line connecting Treasury bills and the market portfolio.

In the mid-1960s three economists—William Sharpe, John Lintner, and Jack Treynor—produced an answer to this question.[8] Their answer is known as the **capital asset pricing model,** or **CAPM.** The model's message is both startling and simple. In a competitive market, the expected risk premium varies in direct proportion to beta. This means that in Figure 8.6 all investments must plot along the sloping line, known as the **security market line.** The expected risk premium on an investment with a beta of .5 is, therefore, *half* the expected risk premium on the market; the expected risk premium on an investment with a beta of 2 is *twice* the expected risk premium on the market. We can write this relationship as

Expected risk premium on stock = beta × expected risk premium on market

$$r - r_f = \beta(r_m - r_f)$$

---

[7] Remember that the risk premium is the difference between the investment's expected return and the risk-free rate. For Treasury bills, the difference is zero.

[8] W. F. Sharpe, "Capital Asset Prices: A Theory of Market Equilibrium under Conditions of Risk," *Journal of Finance* 19 (September 1964), pp. 425–442; and J. Lintner, "The Valuation of Risk Assets and the Selection of Risky Investments in Stock Portfolios and Capital Budgets," *Review of Economics and Statistics* 47 (February 1965), pp. 13–37. Treynor's article has not been published.

Some Estimates of Expected Returns

Before we tell you where the formula comes from, let us use it to figure out what returns investors are looking for from particular stocks. To do this, we need three numbers: β, r_f, and $r_m - r_f$. We gave you estimates of the betas of 10 stocks in Table 7.5. In March 2011, the yield on G-Sec was about 7.40%.

How about the market risk premium? As we pointed out in the last chapter, we can't measure $r_m - r_f$ with precision. From past evidence it appears to be 13.61%, although many economists and financial managers would forecast a slightly lower figure. Let us use 13% in this example.

Table 8.2 puts these numbers together to give an estimate of the expected return on each stock. The stock with the highest beta in our example is Tata Steel. Our estimate of the expected return from Tata Steel is 30.41%. The stock with the lowest beta is Hindustan Unilever. Our estimate of its expected return is 12.73%, 5.33% more than the yield on 1-year government securities.

TABLE 8.2 These estimates of the returns expected by investors in March 2011 were based on the capital asset pricing model. We assumed 7.4% for the risk free rate r_f and 13% for the expected risk premium $r_m - r_f$.

Stock	Beta (β)	Expected Return $[r_f + \beta(r_m - r_f)]$
Bharti	0.76	17.28
Hero Honda	0.57	14.81
HUL	0.41	12.73
Infosys	0.55	14.55
L&T	1.38	25.34
NTPC	0.72	16.76
ONGC	0.95	19.75
Sterlite	1.66	28.98
Tata Motors	1.48	26.64
Tata Steel	1.77	30.41

You can also use the capital asset pricing model to find the discount rate for a new capital investment. For example, suppose that you are analyzing a proposal by Hero Honda to expand its capacity. At what rate should you discount the forecasted cash flows? According to Table 8.2, investors are looking for a return of 14.81% from businesses with the risk of Hero Honda. So the cost of capital for a further investment in the same business is 14.81%.[9]

In practice, choosing a discount rate is seldom so easy. (After all, you can't expect to be paid a fat salary just for plugging numbers into a formula.) For example, you must learn how to adjust the expected return for the extra risk caused by company borrowing. Also you need to consider the difference between short- and long-term interest rates. In 2011 short-term rate was about 1.1% lower than the long-term rate. It is possible that investors were content with the prospect of quite modest equity returns in the short run, but they almost certainly required higher long-run returns than the figures shown in Table 8.2.[10] If that is so, a cost of capital based on short-term rates may be inappropriate for long-term capital investments. But these refinements can wait until later.

---

[9] Remember that instead of investing in plant and machinery, the firm could return the money to the shareholders. The opportunity cost of investing is the return that shareholders could expect to earn by buying financial assets. This expected return depends on the market risk of the assets.

[10] The estimates in Table 8.2 may also be too low for the *short term* if investors required a higher risk premium in the short term to compensate for the unusual market volatility in 2011.

Review of the Capital Asset Pricing Model

Let us review the basic principles of portfolio selection:

1. Investors like high expected return and low standard deviation. Common stock portfolios that offer the highest expected return for a given standard deviation are known as *efficient portfolios.*
2. If the investor can lend or borrow at the risk-free rate of interest, one efficient portfolio is better than all the others: the portfolio that offers the highest ratio of risk premium to standard deviation (that is, portfolio S in Figure 8.5). A risk-averse investor will put part of his money in this efficient portfolio and part in the risk-free asset. A risk-tolerant investor may put all her money in this portfolio or she may borrow and put in even more.
3. The composition of this best efficient portfolio depends on the investor's assessments of expected returns, standard deviations, and correlations. But suppose everybody has the same information and the same assessments. If there is no superior information, each investor should hold the same portfolio as everybody else; in other words, everyone should hold the market portfolio.

Now let us go back to the risk of individual stocks:

4. Do not look at the risk of a stock in isolation but at its contribution to portfolio risk. This contribution depends on the stock's sensitivity to changes in the value of the portfolio.
5. A stock's sensitivity to changes in the value of the *market* portfolio is known as *beta.* Beta, therefore, measures the marginal contribution of a stock to the risk of the market portfolio.

Now if everyone holds the market portfolio, and if beta measures each security's contribution to the market portfolio risk, then it is no surprise that the risk premium demanded by investors is proportional to beta. That is what the CAPM says.

What If a Stock Did Not Lie on the Security Market Line?

Imagine that you encounter stock A in Figure 8.7. Would you buy it? We hope not[11]—if you want an investment with a beta of .5, you could get a higher expected return by investing half your money in Treasury bills and half in the market portfolio. If everybody shares your view of the stock's prospects, the price of A will have to fall until the expected return matches what you could get elsewhere.

What about stock B in Figure 8.7? Would you be tempted by its high return? You wouldn't if you were smart. You could get a higher expected return for the same beta by borrowing 50 cents for every dollar of your own money and investing in the market portfolio. Again, if everybody agrees with your assessment, the price of stock B cannot hold. It will have to fall until the expected return on B is equal to the expected return on the combination of borrowing and investment in the market portfolio.[12]

We have made our point. An investor can always obtain an expected risk premium of $\beta(r_m - r_f)$ by holding a mixture of the market portfolio and a risk-free loan. So in well-functioning markets nobody will hold a stock that offers an expected risk premium of *less* than $\beta(r_m - r_f)$. But what about the other possibility? Are there stocks that offer a higher expected risk premium? In other words, are there any that lie above the security market line in Figure 8.7? If we take all stocks together, we have the market portfolio. Therefore, we know that stocks *on average* lie on the line. Since none lies *below* the line, then there also can't be any that lie *above* the line. Thus each and every stock must lie on the security market line and offer an expected risk premium of

$$r - r_f = \beta(r_m - r_f)$$

---

[11] Unless, of course, we were trying to sell it.

[12] Investing in A or B only would be stupid; you would hold an undiversified portfolio.

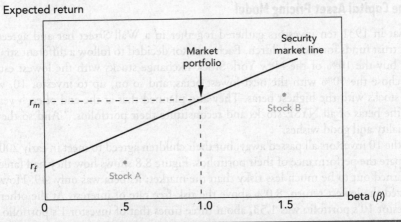

FIGURE 8.7

In equilibrium no stock can lie below the security market line. For example, instead of buying stock A, investors would prefer to lend part of their money and put the balance in the market portfolio. And instead of buying stock B, they would prefer to borrow and invest in the market portfolio.

8-3   VALIDITY AND ROLE OF THE CAPITAL ASSET PRICING MODEL

Any economic model is a simplified statement of reality. We need to simplify in order to interpret what is going on around us. But we also need to know how much faith we can place in our model.

Let us begin with some matters about which there is broad agreement. First, few people quarrel with the idea that investors require some extra return for taking on risk. That is why common stocks have given on average a higher return than the risk free assets in India. Who would want to invest in risky common stocks if they offered only the *same* expected return as bills? We would not, and we suspect you would not either.

Second, investors do appear to be concerned principally with those risks that they cannot eliminate by diversification. If this were not so, we should find that stock prices increase whenever two companies merge to spread their risks. And we should find that investment companies which invest in the shares of other firms are more highly valued than the shares they hold. But we do not observe either phenomenon. Mergers undertaken just to spread risk do not increase stock prices, and investment companies are no more highly valued than the stocks they hold.

The capital asset pricing model captures these ideas in a simple way. That is why financial managers find it a convenient tool for coming to grips with the slippery notion of risk and why nearly three-quarters of them use it to estimate the cost of capital.[13] It is also why economists often use the capital asset pricing model to demonstrate important ideas in finance even when there are other ways to prove these ideas. But that does not mean that the capital asset pricing model is ultimate truth. We will see later that it has several unsatisfactory features, and we will look at some alternative theories. Nobody knows whether one of these alternative theories is eventually going to come out on top or whether there are other, better models of risk and return that have not yet seen the light of day.

---

[13] See J. R. Graham and C. R. Harvey, "The Theory and Practice of Corporate Finance: Evidence from the Field," *Journal of Financial Economics* 61 (2001), pp. 187–243. A number of the managers surveyed reported using more than one method to estimate the cost of capital. Seventy-three percent used the capital asset pricing model, while 39% stated they used the average historical stock return and 34% used the capital asset pricing model with some extra risk factors.

Tests of the Capital Asset Pricing Model

Imagine that in 1931 ten investors gathered together in a Wall Street bar and agreed to establish investment trust funds for their children. Each investor decided to follow a different strategy. Investor 1 opted to buy the 10% of the New York Stock Exchange stocks with the lowest estimated betas; investor 2 chose the 10% with the next-lowest betas; and so on, up to investor 10, who proposed to buy the stocks with the highest betas. They also planned that at the end of each year they would reestimate the betas of all NYSE stocks and reconstitute their portfolios.[14] And so they parted with much cordiality and good wishes.

In time the 10 investors all passed away, but their children agreed to meet in early 2009 in the same bar to compare the performance of their portfolios. Figure 8.8 shows how they had fared. Investor 1's portfolio turned out to be much less risky than the market; its beta was only .49. However, investor 1 also realized the lowest return, 8.0% above the risk-free rate of interest. At the other extreme, the beta of investor 10's portfolio was 1.53, about three times that of investor 1's portfolio. But investor 10 was rewarded with the highest return, averaging 14.3% a year above the interest rate. So over this 77-year period returns did indeed increase with beta.

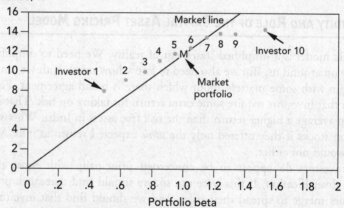

Average risk premium, 1931–2008, %

FIGURE 8.8

The capital asset pricing model states that the expected risk premium from any investment should lie on the security market line. The dots show the actual average risk premiums from portfolios with different betas. The high-beta portfolios generated higher average returns, just as predicted by the CAPM. But the high-beta portfolios plotted below the market line, and the low-beta portfolios plotted above. A line fitted to the 10 portfolio returns would be "flatter" than the market line.

Source: F. Black, "Beta and Return," *Journal of Portfolio Management* 20 (Fall 1993), pp. 8–18. © 1993 Institutional Investor. Used with permission. We are grateful to Adam Kolasinski for updating the calculations.

As you can see from Figure 8.8, the market portfolio over the same 77-year period provided an average return of 11.8% above the interest rate[15] and (of course) had a beta of 1.0. The CAPM predicts

---

[14] Betas were estimated using returns over the previous 60 months.

[15] In Figure 8.8 the stocks in the "market portfolio" are weighted equally. Since the stocks of small firms have provided higher average returns than those of large firms, the risk premium on an equally weighted index is higher than on a value-weighted index. This is one reason for the difference between the 11.8% market risk premium in Figure 8.8 and the 7.1% premium reported in Table 7.1.

that the risk premium should increase in proportion to beta, so that the returns of each portfolio should lie on the upward-sloping security market line in Figure 8.8. Since the market provided a risk premium of 11.8%, investor 1's portfolio, with a beta of .49, should have provided a risk premium of 5.8% and investor 10's portfolio, with a beta of 1.53, should have given a premium of 18.1%. You can see that, while high-beta stocks performed better than low-beta stocks, the difference was not as great as the CAPM predicts.

Although Figure 8.8 provides broad support for the CAPM, critics have pointed out that the slope of the line has been particularly flat in recent years. For example, Figure 8.9 shows how our 10 investors fared between 1966 and 2008. Now it is less clear who is buying the drinks: returns are pretty much in line with the CAPM with the important exception of the two highest-risk portfolios. Investor 10, who rode the roller coaster of a high-beta portfolio, earned a return that was below that of the market. Of course, before 1966 the line was correspondingly steeper. This is also shown in Figure 8.9.

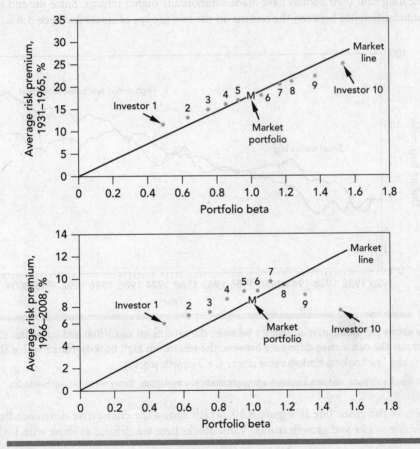

FIGURE 8.9

The relationship between beta and actual average return has been weaker since the mid-1960s. Stocks with the highest betas have provided poor returns.

Source: F. Black, "Beta and Return," *Journal of Portfolio Management* 20 (Fall 1993), pp. 8–18. © 1993 Institutional Investor. Used with permission. We are grateful to Adam Kolasinski for updating the calculations.

What is going on here? It is hard to say. Defenders of the capital asset pricing model emphasize that it is concerned with *expected* returns, whereas we can observe only *actual* returns. Actual stock returns reflect expectations, but they also embody lots of "noise"—the steady flow of surprises that conceal whether on average investors have received the returns they expected. This noise may make it impossible to judge whether the model holds better in one period than another.[16] Perhaps the best that we can do is to focus on the longest period for which there is reasonable data. This would take us back to Figure 8.8, which suggests that expected returns do indeed increase with beta, though less rapidly than the simple version of the CAPM predicts.[17]

The CAPM has also come under fire on a second front: although return has not risen with beta in recent years, it has been related to other measures. For example, the red line in Figure 8.10 shows the cumulative difference between the returns on small-firm stocks and large-firm stocks. If you had bought the shares with the smallest market capitalizations and sold those with the largest capitalizations, this is how your wealth would have changed. You can see that small-cap stocks did not always do well, but over the long haul their owners have made substantially higher returns. Since the end of 1926 the average annual difference between the returns on the two groups of stocks has been 3.6%.

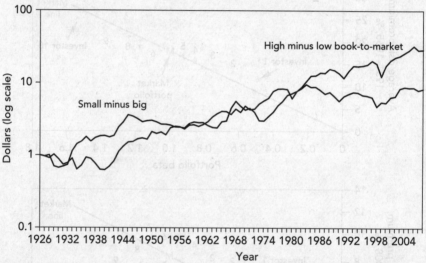

FIGURE 8.10

The red line shows the cumulative difference between the returns on small-firm and large-firm stocks. The green line shows the cumulative difference between the returns on high book-to-market-value stocks (i.e., value stocks) and low book-to-market-value stocks (i.e., growth stocks).

Source: Kenneth French's Web site, **mba.tuck.dartmouth.edu/pages/faculty/ken.french/data_library.html**. Used with permission.

Now look at the green line in Figure 8.10, which shows the cumulative difference between the returns on value stocks and growth stocks. Value stocks here are defined as those with high ratios of

---

[16] A second problem with testing the model is that the market portfolio should contain all risky investments, including stocks, bonds, commodities, real estate—even human capital. Most market indexes contain only a sample of common stocks.

[17] We say "simple version" because Fischer Black has shown that if there are borrowing restrictions, there should still exist a positive relationship between expected return and beta, but the security market line would be less steep as a result. See F. Black, "Capital Market Equilibrium with Restricted Borrowing," *Journal of Business* 45 (July 1972), pp. 444–455.

book value to market value. Growth stocks are those with low ratios of book to market. Notice that value stocks have provided a higher long-run return than growth stocks.[18] Since 1926 the average annual difference between the returns on value and growth stocks has been 5.2%.

Figure 8.10 does not fit well with the CAPM, which predicts that beta is the *only* reason that expected returns differ. It seems that investors saw risks in "small-cap" stocks and value stocks that were not captured by beta.[19] Take value stocks, for example. Many of these stocks may have sold below book value because the firms were in serious trouble; if the economy slowed unexpectedly, the firms might have collapsed altogether. Therefore, investors, whose jobs could also be on the line in a recession, may have regarded these stocks as particularly risky and demanded compensation in the form of higher expected returns. If that were the case, the simple version of the CAPM cannot be the whole truth.

Again, it is hard to judge how seriously the CAPM is damaged by this finding. The relationship among stock returns and firm size and book-to-market ratio has been well documented. However, if you look long and hard at past returns, you are bound to find some strategy that just by chance would have worked in the past. This practice is known as "data-mining" or "data snooping." Maybe the size and book-to-market effects are simply chance results that stem from data snooping. If so, they should have vanished once they were discovered. There is some evidence that this is the case. For example, if you look again at Figure 8.10, you will see that in the past 25 years small-firm stocks have underperformed just about as often as they have overperformed.

There is no doubt that the evidence on the CAPM is less convincing than scholars once thought. But it will be hard to reject the CAPM beyond all reasonable doubt. Since data and statistics are unlikely to give final answers, the plausibility of the CAPM *theory* will have to be weighed along with the empirical "facts."

Assumptions behind the Capital Asset Pricing Model

The capital asset pricing model rests on several assumptions that we did not fully spell out. For example, we assumed that investment in U.S. Treasury bills is risk-free. It is true that there is little chance of default, but bills do not guarantee a *real* return. There is still some uncertainty about inflation. Another assumption was that investors can *borrow* money at the same rate of interest at which they can lend. Generally borrowing rates are higher than lending rates.

It turns out that many of these assumptions are not crucial, and with a little pushing and pulling it is possible to modify the capital asset pricing model to handle them. The really important idea is that investors are content to invest their money in a limited number of benchmark portfolios. (In the basic CAPM these benchmarks are Treasury bills and the market portfolio.)

In these modified CAPMs expected return still depends on market risk, but the definition of market risk depends on the nature of the benchmark portfolios. In practice, none of these alternative capital asset pricing models is as widely used as the standard version.

---

[18] Fama and French calculated the returns on portfolios designed to take advantage of the size effect and the book-to-market effect. See E. F. Fama and K. R. French, "The Cross-Section of Expected Stock Returns," *Journal of Financial Economics* 47 (June 1992), pp. 427–465. When calculating the returns on these portfolios, Fama and French control for differences in firm size when comparing stocks with low and high book-to-market ratios. Similarly, they control for differences in the book-to-market ratio when comparing small- and large-firm stocks. For details of the methodology and updated returns on the size and book-to-market factors see Kenneth French's Web site (**mba.tuck.dartmouth.edu/pages/faculty/ken.french/data_library.html**).

[19] An investor who bought small-company stocks and sold large-company stocks would have incurred some risk. Her portfolio would have had a beta of .28. This is not nearly large enough to explain the difference in returns. There is no simple relationship between the return on the value- and growth-stock portfolios and beta.

8-4 SOME ALTERNATIVE THEORIES

The capital asset pricing model pictures investors as solely concerned with the level and uncertainty o' their future wealth. But this could be too simplistic. For example, investors may become accustomec to a particular standard of living, so that poverty tomorrow may be particularly difficult to bear if you were wealthy yesterday. Behavioral psychologists have also observed that investors do not focus solely on the *current* value of their holdings, but look back at whether their investments are showing a profit A gain, however small, may be an additional source of satisfaction. The capital asset pricing mode does not allow for the possibility that investors may take account of the price at which they purchasec stock and feel elated when their investment is in the black and depressed when it is in the red.[20]

Arbitrage Pricing Theory

The capital asset pricing theory begins with an analysis of how investors construct efficient portfolios Stephen Ross's **arbitrage pricing theory,** or **APT,** comes from a different family entirely. It does no' ask which portfolios are efficient. Instead, it starts by *assuming* that each stock's return depends partly on pervasive macroeconomic influences or "factors" and partly on "noise"—events that are unique tc that company. Moreover, the return is assumed to obey the following simple relationship:

$$\text{Return} = a + b_1(r_{\text{factor 1}}) + b_2(r_{\text{factor 2}}) + b_3(r_{\text{factor 3}}) + \cdots + \text{noise}$$

The theory does not say what the factors are: there could be an oil price factor, an interest-rate factor and so on. The return on the market portfolio *might* serve as one factor, but then again it might not.

Some stocks will be more sensitive to a particular factor than other stocks. Exxon Mobil would be more sensitive to an oil factor than, say, Coca-Cola. If factor 1 picks up unexpected changes in oi prices, b_1 will be higher for Exxon Mobil.

For any individual stock there are two sources of risk. First is the risk that stems from the pervasive macroeconomic factors. This cannot be eliminated by diversification. Second is the risk arising from possible events that are specific to the company. Diversification eliminates specific risk, and diversifiec investors can therefore ignore it when deciding whether to buy or sell a stock. The expected risk premium on a stock is affected by factor or macroeconomic risk; it is *not* affected by specific risk.

Arbitrage pricing theory states that the expected risk premium on a stock should depend on the expected risk premium associated with each factor and the stock's sensitivity to each of the factor: (b_1, b_2, b_3, etc.). Thus the formula is[21]

$$\text{Expected risk premium} = r - r_f$$
$$= b_1(r_{\text{factor 1}} - r_f) + b_2(r_{\text{factor 2}} - r_f) + \cdots$$

Notice that this formula makes two statements:

1. If you plug in a value of zero for each of the b's in the formula, the expected risk premium i zero. A diversified portfolio that is constructed to have zero sensitivity to each macroeconomic

---

[20] We discuss aversion to loss again in Chapter 13. The implications for asset pricing are explored in S. Benartzi and R. Thaler, "Myopic Los Aversion and the Equity Premium Puzzle," *Quarterly Journal of Economics* 110 (1995), pp. 75–92; and in N. Barberis, M. Huang, and T Santos, "Prospect Theory and Asset Prices," *Quarterly Journal of Economics* 116 (2001), pp. 1–53.

[21] There may be some macroeconomic factors that investors are simply not worried about. For example, some macroeconomists believe tha money supply doesn't matter and therefore investors are not worried about inflation. Such factors would not command a risk premium. The would drop out of the APT formula for expected return.

factor is essentially risk-free and therefore must be priced to offer the risk-free rate of interest. If the portfolio offered a higher return, investors could make a risk-free (or "arbitrage") profit by borrowing to buy the portfolio. If it offered a lower return, you could make an arbitrage profit by running the strategy in reverse; in other words, you would *sell* the diversified zero-sensitivity portfolio and *invest* the proceeds in U.S. Treasury bills.

2. A diversified portfolio that is constructed to have exposure to, say, factor 1, will offer a risk premium, which will vary in direct proportion to the portfolio's sensitivity to that factor. For example, imagine that you construct two portfolios, A and B, that are affected only by factor 1. If portfolio A is twice as sensitive as portfolio B to factor 1, portfolio A must offer twice the risk premium. Therefore, if you divided your money equally between U.S. Treasury bills and portfolio A, your combined portfolio would have exactly the same sensitivity to factor 1 as portfolio B and would offer the same risk premium.

   Suppose that the arbitrage pricing formula did *not* hold. For example, suppose that the combination of Treasury bills and portfolio A offered a higher return. In that case investors could make an arbitrage profit by selling portfolio B and investing the proceeds in the mixture of bills and portfolio A.

The arbitrage that we have described applies to well-diversified portfolios, where the specific risk has been diversified away. But if the arbitrage pricing relationship holds for all diversified portfolios, it must generally hold for the individual stocks. Each stock must offer an expected return commensurate with its contribution to portfolio risk. In the APT, this contribution depends on the sensitivity of the stock's return to unexpected changes in the macroeconomic factors.

A Comparison of the Capital Asset Pricing Model and Arbitrage Pricing Theory

Like the capital asset pricing model, arbitrage pricing theory stresses that expected return depends on the risk stemming from economywide influences and is not affected by specific risk. You can think of the factors in arbitrage pricing as representing special portfolios of stocks that tend to be subject to a common influence. If the expected risk premium on each of these portfolios is proportional to the portfolio's market beta, then the arbitrage pricing theory and the capital asset pricing model will give the same answer. In any other case they will not.

How do the two theories stack up? Arbitrage pricing has some attractive features. For example, the market portfolio that plays such a central role in the capital asset pricing model does not feature in arbitrage pricing theory.[22] So we do not have to worry about the problem of measuring the market portfolio, and in principle we can test the arbitrage pricing theory even if we have data on only a sample of risky assets.

Unfortunately you win some and lose some. Arbitrage pricing theory does not tell us what the underlying factors are—unlike the capital asset pricing model, which collapses *all* macroeconomic risks into a well-defined *single* factor, the return on the market portfolio.

The Three-Factor Model

Look back at the equation for APT. To estimate expected returns, you first need to follow three steps:

Step 1: Identify a reasonably short list of macroeconomic factors that could affect stock returns.

---

[22] Of course, the market portfolio *may* turn out to be one of the factors, but that is not a necessary implication of arbitrage pricing theory.

Step 2: Estimate the expected risk premium on each of these factors ($r_{\text{factor 1}} - r_f$, etc.).

Step 3: Measure the sensitivity of each stock to the factors (b_1, b_2, etc.).

One way to shortcut this process is to take advantage of the research by Fama and French, which showed that stocks of small firms and those with a high book-to-market ratio have provided above-average returns. This could simply be a coincidence. But there is also some evidence that these factors are related to company profitability and therefore may be picking up risk factors that are left out of the simple CAPM.[23]

If investors do demand an extra return for taking on exposure to these factors, then we have a measure of the expected return that looks very much like arbitrage pricing theory:

$$r - r_f = b_{\text{market}}(r_{\text{market factor}}) + b_{\text{size}}(r_{\text{size factor}}) + b_{\text{book-to-market}}(r_{\text{book-to-market factor}})$$

This is commonly known as the Fama–French three-factor model. Using it to estimate expected returns is the same as applying the arbitrage pricing theory. Here is an example.[24]

Step 1: Identify the Factors   Fama and French have already identified the three factors that appear to determine expected returns. The returns on each of these factors are

Factor	Measured by
Market factor	Return on market index *minus* risk-free interest rate
Size factor	Return on small-firm stocks *less* return on large-firm stocks
Book-to-market factor	Return on high book-to-market-ratio stocks *less* return on low book-to-market-ratio stocks

Step 2: Estimate the Risk Premium for Each Factor   We will keep to our figure of 7% for the market risk premium. History may provide a guide to the risk premium for the other two factors. As we saw earlier, between 1926 and 2008 the difference between the annual returns on small and large capitalization stocks averaged 3.6% a year, while the difference between the returns on stocks with high and low book-to-market ratios averaged 5.2%.

Step 3: Estimate the Factor Sensitivities   Some stocks are more sensitive than others to fluctuations in the returns on the three factors. You can see this from the first three columns of numbers in Table 8.3, which show some estimates of the factor sensitivities of 10 industry groups for the 60 months ending in December 2008. For example, an increase of 1% in the return on the book-to-market factor *reduces* the return on computer stocks by .87% but *increases* the return on utility stocks by .77%. In other words, when value stocks (high book-to-market) outperform growth stocks (low book-to-market), computer stocks tend to perform relatively badly and utility stocks do relatively well.

Once you have estimated the factor sensitivities, it is a simple matter to multiply each of them by the expected factor return and add up the results. For example, the expected risk premium on computer stocks is $r - r_f = (1.43 \times 7) + (.22 \times 3.6) - (.87 \times 5.2) = 6.3\%$. To calculate the return

---

[23] E. F. Fama and K. R. French, "Size and Book-to-Market Factors in Earnings and Returns," *Journal of Finance* 50 (1995), pp. 131–155.

[24] The three-factor model was first used to estimate the cost of capital for different industry groups by Fama and French. See E. F. Fama and K. R. French, "Industry Costs of Equity," *Journal of Financial Economics* 43 (1997), pp. 153–193. Fama and French emphasize the imprecision in using either the CAPM or an APT-style model to estimate the returns that investors expect.

TABLE 8.3 Estimates of expected equity returns for selected industries using the Fama–French three-factor model and the CAPM.

	Three-Factor Model Factor Sensitivities				CAPM
	b_{market}	b_{size}	$b_{book-to-market}$	Expected Return[*]	Expected Return[**]
Autos	1.51	.07	.91	15.7	7.9
Banks	1.16	−.25	.72	11.1	6.2
Chemicals	1.02	−.07	.61	10.2	5.5
Computers	1.43	.22	−.87	6.5	12.8
Construction	1.40	.46	.98	16.6	7.6
Food	.53	−.15	.47	5.8	2.7
Oil and gas	.85	−.13	.54	8.5	4.3
Pharmaceuticals	.50	−.32	−.13	1.9	4.3
Telecoms	1.05	−.29	−.16	5.7	7.3
Utilities	.61	−.01	.77	8.4	2.4

[*] The expected return equals the risk-free interest rate plus the factor sensitivities multiplied by the factor risk premiums, that is, $r_f + (b_{market} \times 7) + (b_{size} \times 3.6) + (b_{book-to-market} \times 5.2)$.

[**] Estimated as $r_f + \beta(r_m − r_f)$, that is, $r_f + \beta \times 7$. Note that we used *simple* regression to estimate β in the CAPM formula. This beta may, therefore, be different from b_{market} that we estimated from a *multiple* regression of stock returns on the three factors.

that investors expected in 2008 we need to add on the risk-free interest rate of about .2%. Thus the three-factor model suggests that expected return on computer stocks in 2008 was .2 + 6.3 = 6.5%.

Compare this figure with the expected return estimate using the capital asset pricing model (the final column of Table 8.3). The three-factor model provides a substantially lower estimate of the expected return for computer stocks. Why? Largely because computer stocks are growth stocks with a low exposure (−.87) to the book-to-market factor. The three-factor model produces a lower expected return for growth stocks, but it produces a higher figure for value stocks such as those of auto and construction companies which have a high book-to-market ratio.

In India, researchers have found very similar evidences, albeit by using data for a much smaller period. Obaidullah (1993), Ray (1994), and Mohanty (2002) find evidence against CAPM in the Indian capital market. Connor and Sehgal (2001) and Mohanty (2002) find evidence of Fama-French factors in the Indian context.[25]

---

[25] See Obaidullah, M., "Does the CAPM Explain Actual Price behavior", Chartered Financial Analyst, November 1993, Ray, S., Capital Asset pricing Model: The Indian Context, Unpublished Doctoral Dissertation, 1994, Indian Institute of Management, Bangalore. Connor, G., and S Sehgal, Tests of Fama and French Model in India, May 2001. Paper can be downloaded from www.lse.ac.uk/collections/accountingAndFinance/staff/connor/files/Fama%26FrenchIndia and Mohanty, P., Efficiency of the Market for Small Stock, NSE Research Initiative, April 2001.

SUMMARY

The basic principles of portfolio selection boil down to a commonsense statement that investors try to increase the expected return on their portfolios and to reduce the standard deviation of that return. A portfolio that gives the highest expected return for a given standard deviation, or the lowest standard deviation for a given expected return, is known as an *efficient portfolio*. To work out which portfolios are efficient, an investor must be able to state the expected return and standard deviation of each stock and the degree of correlation between each pair of stocks.

Investors who are restricted to holding common stocks should choose efficient portfolios that suit their attitudes to risk. But investors who can also borrow and lend at the risk-free rate of interest should choose the *best* common stock portfolio *regardless* of their attitudes to risk. Having done that, they can then set the risk of their overall portfolio by deciding what proportion of their money they are willing to invest in stocks. The best efficient portfolio offers the highest ratio of forecasted risk premium to portfolio standard deviation.

For an investor who has only the same opportunities and information as everybody else, the best stock portfolio is the same as the best stock portfolio for other investors. In other words, he or she should invest in a mixture of the market portfolio and a risk-free loan (i.e., borrowing or lending).

A stock's marginal contribution to portfolio risk is measured by its sensitivity to changes in the value of the portfolio. The marginal contribution of a stock to the risk of the *market portfolio* is measured by *beta*. That is the fundamental idea behind the capital asset pricing model (CAPM), which concludes that each security's expected risk premium should increase in proportion to its beta:

$$\text{Expected risk premium} = \text{beta} \times \text{market risk premium}$$
$$r - r_f = \beta(r_m - r_f)$$

The capital asset pricing theory is the best-known model of risk and return. It is plausible and widely used but far from perfect. Actual returns are related to beta over the long run, but the relationship is not as strong as the CAPM predicts, and other factors seem to explain returns better since the mid-1960s. Stocks of small companies, and stocks with high book values relative to market prices, appear to have risks not captured by the CAPM.

The arbitrage pricing theory offers an alternative theory of risk and return. It states that the expected risk premium on a stock should depend on the stock's exposure to several pervasive macroeconomic factors that affect stock returns:

$$\text{Expected risk premium} = b_1(r_{\text{factor 1}} - r_f) + b_2(r_{\text{factor 2}} - r_f) + \cdots$$

Here b's represent the individual security's sensitivities to the factors, and $r_{\text{factor}} - r_f$ is the risk premium demanded by investors who are exposed to this factor.

Arbitrage pricing theory does not say what these factors are. It asks for economists to hunt for unknown game with their statistical toolkits. Fama and French have suggested three factors:

- The return on the market portfolio less the risk-free rate of interest.
- The difference between the return on small- and large-firm stocks.
- The difference between the return on stocks with high book-to-market ratios and stocks with low book-to-market ratios.

In the Fama–French three-factor model, the expected return on each stock depends on its exposure to these three factors.

Each of these different models of risk and return has its fan club. However, all financial economists agree on two basic ideas: (1) Investors require extra expected return for taking on risk, and (2) they appear to be concerned predominantly with the risk that they cannot eliminate by diversification.

Near the end of Chapter 9 we list some Excel Functions that are useful for measuring the risk of stocks and portfolios.

A number of textbooks on portfolio selection explain both Markowitz's original theory and some ingenious simplified versions. See, for example:

E. J. Elton, M. J. Gruber, S. J. Brown, and W. N. Goetzmann: *Modern Portfolio Theory and Investment Analysis,* 7th ed. (New York: John Wiley & Sons, 2007).

The literature on the capital asset pricing model is enormous. There are dozens of published tests of the capital asset pricing model. Fisher Black's paper is a very readable example. Discussions of the theory tend to be more uncompromising. Two excellent but advanced examples are Campbell's survey paper and Cochrane's book.

F. Black, "Beta and Return," *Journal of Portfolio Management* 20 (Fall 1993), pp. 8–18.

J. Y. Campbell, "Asset Pricing at the Millennium," *Journal of Finance* 55 (August 2000), pp. 1515–1567.

J. H. Cochrane, *Asset Pricing,* revised ed. (Princeton, NJ: Princeton University Press, 2004).

FURTHER READING

PROBLEM SETS

BASIC

1. Here are returns and standard deviations for four investments.

	Return	Standard Deviation
Treasury bills	6 %	0%
Stock P	10	14
Stock Q	14.5	28
Stock R	21	26

Calculate the standard deviations of the following portfolios.
   a. 50% in Treasury bills, 50% in stock P.
   b. 50% each in Q and R, assuming the shares have
   • perfect positive correlation
   • perfect negative correlation
   • no correlation
   c. Plot a figure like Figure 8.3 for Q and R, assuming a correlation coefficient of .5.
   d. Stock Q has a lower return than R but a higher standard deviation. Does that mean that Q's price is too high or that R's price is too low?

2. For each of the following pairs of investments, state which would always be preferred by a rational investor (assuming that these are the *only* investments available to the investor):

   a. Portfolio A $r = 18\%$ $\sigma = 20\%$
          Portfolio B $r = 14\%$ $\sigma = 20\%$

   b. Portfolio C $r = 15\%$ $\sigma = 18\%$
          Portfolio D $r = 13\%$ $\sigma = 8\%$

   c. Portfolio E $r = 14\%$ $\sigma = 16\%$
          Portfolio F $r = 14\%$ $\sigma = 10\%$

3. Use the long-term data on security returns in Sections 7-1 and 7-2 to calculate the historical level of the Sharpe ratio of the market portfolio.

4. Figure 8.11 below purports to show the range of attainable combinations of expected return and standard deviation.
   a. Which diagram is incorrectly drawn and why?
   b. Which is the efficient set of portfolios?
   c. If r_f is the rate of interest, mark with an X the optimal stock portfolio.

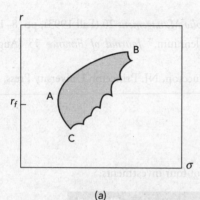 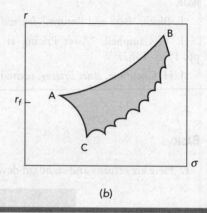

(a)   (b)

FIGURE 8.11

See Problem 4.

5. a. Plot the following risky portfolios on a graph:

				Portfolio				
	A	**B**	**C**	**D**	**E**	**F**	**G**	**H**
Expected return (r), %	10	12.5	15	16	17	18	18	20
Standard deviation (σ), %	23	21	25	29	29	32	35	45

   b. Five of these portfolios are efficient, and three are not. Which are *inefficient* ones?
   c. Suppose you can also borrow and lend at an interest rate of 12%. Which of the above portfolios has the highest Sharpe ratio?
   d. Suppose you are prepared to tolerate a standard deviation of 25%. What is the maximum expected return that you can achieve if you cannot borrow or lend?
   e. What is your optimal strategy if you can borrow or lend at 12% and are prepared to tolerate a standard deviation of 25%? What is the maximum expected return that you can achieve with this risk?

6. Suppose that the Treasury bill rate were 5% and the expected return on the market is 17%. Use the betas in Table 8.2.
   a. Calculate the expected return from Sterlite.
   b. Find the highest expected return that is offered by one of these stocks.
   c. Find the lowest expected return that is offered by one of these stocks.
   d. Would NTPC offer a higher or lower expected return if the interest rate was 6% rather than 5%? Assume that the expected market return stays at 17%.
   e. Would Tata Steel offer a higher or lower return if the interest rate was 6% rather than 5%.

7. True or false?
   a. The CAPM implies that if you could find an investment with a negative beta, its expected return would be less than the interest rate.
   b. The expected return on an investment with a beta of 2.0 is twice as high as the expected return on the market.
   c. If a stock lies below the security market line, it is undervalued.

8. Consider a three-factor APT model. The factors and associated risk premiums are

Factor	Risk Premium
Change in GNP	5%
Change in energy prices	−1
Change in long-term interest rates	+2

Calculate expected rates of return on the following stocks. The risk-free interest rate is 7%.
   a. A stock whose return is uncorrelated with all three factors.
   b. A stock with average exposure to each factor (i.e., with $b = 1$ for each).
   c. A pure-play energy stock with high exposure to the energy factor ($b = 2$) but zero exposure to the other two factors.
   d. An aluminum company stock with average sensitivity to changes in interest rates and GNP, but negative exposure of $b = -1.5$ to the energy factor. (The aluminum company is energy-intensive and suffers when energy prices rise.)

INTERMEDIATE

9. True or false? Explain or qualify as necessary.
   a. Investors demand higher expected rates of return on stocks with more variable rates of return.
   b. The CAPM predicts that a security with a beta of 0 will offer a zero expected return.
   c. An investor who puts ₹10,000 in Treasury bills and ₹20,000 in the market portfolio will have a beta of 2.0.
   d. Investors demand higher expected rates of return from stocks with returns that are highly exposed to macroeconomic risks.
   e. Investors demand higher expected rates of return from stocks with returns that are very sensitive to fluctuations in the stock market.

10. Look back at the calculation of Bharti and Tata Motors in Section 8.1. Recalculate the expected portfolio return and standard deviation for different values of x_1 and x_2, assuming the correlation coefficient $\rho_{12} = 0$. Plot the range of possible combinations of expected return and standard deviation as in Figure 8.4. Repeat the problem for $\rho_{12} = -1$.

11. Mark Harrywitz proposes to invest in two shares, X and Y. He expects a return of 12% from X and 8% from Y. The standard deviation of returns is 8% for X and 5% for Y. The correlation coefficient between the returns is .2.

    Visit us at
    www.mhhe.com/bmam10e

   a. Compute the expected return and standard deviation of the following portfolios:

Portfolio	Percentage in X	Percentage in Y
1	50	50
2	25	75
3	75	25

b. Sketch the set of portfolios composed of X and Y.

c. Suppose that Mr. Harrywitz can also borrow or lend at an interest rate of 5%. Show on your sketch how this alters his opportunities. Given that he can borrow or lend, what proportions of the common stock portfolio should be invested in X and Y?

12. Ebenezer Scrooge has invested 60% of his money in share A and the remainder in share B. He assesses their prospects as follows:

	A	B
Expected return (%)	15	20
Standard deviation (%)	20	22
Correlation between returns		.5

a. What are the expected return and standard deviation of returns on his portfolio?

b. How would your answer change if the correlation coefficient were 0 or −.5?

c. Is Mr. Scrooge's portfolio better or worse than one invested entirely in share A, or is it not possible to say?

13. Look back at Problem 3 in Chapter 7. The risk-free interest rate in each of these years was as follows:

	1998-99	1999-00	2000-01	2001-02	2002-03
Interest rate%	11.09	8.74	10.8	8.14	8.05

a. Calculate the average return and standard deviation of returns for Ms. Sabharwal's portfolio and for the market. Use these figures to calculate the Sharpe ratio for the portfolio and the market. On this measure did Ms. Sabharwal perform better or worse than the market?

b. Now calculate the average return that you could have earned over this period if you had held a combination of the market and a risk-free loan. Make sure that the combination has the same beta as Ms. Sabharwal's portfolio. Would your average return on this portfolio have been higher or lower?

Explain your results.

14. Look back at Table 7.5.

a. What is the beta of a portfolio that has 40% invested in Sterlite and 60% in ONGC?

b. Would you invest in this portfolio if you had no superior information about the prospects for these stocks? Devise an alternative portfolio with the same expected return and less risk.

c. Now repeat parts (a) and (b) with a portfolio that has 40% invested in L&T and 60% in Infosys.

15. The Treasury bill rate is 4%, and the expected return on the market portfolio is 12%. Using the capital asset pricing model:

a. Draw a graph similar to Figure 8.6 showing how the expected return varies with beta.

b. What is the risk premium on the market?

c. What is the required return on an investment with a beta of 1.5?

d. If an investment with a beta of .8 offers an expected return of 9.8%, does it have a positive NPV?

e. If the market expects a return of 11.2% from stock X, what is its beta?

16. Sumit Chand has ₹100 million invested in long-term corporate bonds. This bond portfolio's expected annual rate of return is 9%, and the annual standard deviation is 10%.

Anand Desai, Sumit's financial adviser, recommends that Sumit consider investing in an index fund that closely tracks the S&P CNX Nifty index. The index has an expected return of 15%, and its standard deviation is 20%.

a. Suppose Sumit puts all his money in a combination of the index fund and Treasury bills. Can he thereby improve his expected rate of return without changing the risk of his portfolio? The Treasury bill yield is 6%.

b. Could Sumit do better by investing equal amounts in the corporate bond portfolio and the index fund? The correlation between the bond portfolio and the index fund is +.2.

17. Epsilon Corp. is evaluating an expansion of its business. The cash-flow forecasts for the project are as follows:

Years	Cash Flow (₹ millions)
0	−100
1–10	+15

The firm's existing assets have a beta of 1.4. The risk-free interest rate is 4% and the expected return on the market portfolio is 12%. What is the project's NPV?

18. Some true or false questions about the APT:
a. The APT factors cannot reflect diversifiable risks.
b. The market rate of return cannot be an APT factor.
c. There is no theory that specifically identifies the APT factors.
d. The APT model could be true but not very useful, for example, if the relevant factors change unpredictably.

19. Consider the following simplified APT model:

Factor	Expected Risk Premium
Market	6.4%
Interest rate	−.6
Yield spread	5.1

Calculate the expected return for the following stocks. Assume $r_f = 5\%$.

	Factor Risk Exposures		
	Market	Interest Rate	Yield Spread
Stock	(b_1)	(b_2)	(b_3)
P	1.0	−2.0	−.2
P^2	1.2	0	.3
P^3	.3	.5	1.0

20. Look again at Problem 19. Consider a portfolio with equal investments in stocks P, P^2, and P^3.
a. What are the factor risk exposures for the portfolio?
b. What is the portfolio's expected return?

21. The following table shows the sensitivity of four stocks to the three Fama–French factors. Estimate the expected return on each stock assuming that the interest rate is 6%, the expected risk premium on the market is 10%, the expected risk premium on the size factor is 6%, and the expected risk premium on the book-to-market factor is 5%.

Factor Sensitivities				
Factor	**Bharat Forge Ltd.**	**Madras Petro Chem Ltd.**	**Priyadarshini Cement Ltd.**	**Wimco Ltd.**
Market	0.354	0.453	0.640	0.598
Size	0.182	0.047	0.252	−0.075
Book-to-Market	0.363	−0.007	−0.595	−0.051

CHALLENGE

22. In footnote 4 we noted that the minimum-risk portfolio contained an investment of 91% in Bharti Soup and 9% in Tata Motors. Prove it. (*Hint:* You need a little calculus to do so.)

23. Look again at the set of the three efficient portfolios that we calculated in Section 8.1.
    a. If the interest rate is 10%, which of the four efficient portfolios should you hold?
    b. What is the beta of each holding relative to that portfolio? (*Hint:* Note that if a portfolio is efficient, the expected risk premium on each holding must be proportional to the beta of the stock *relative to that portfolio.*)
    c. How would your answers to (a) and (b) change if the interest rate were 5%?

24. The following question illustrates the APT. Imagine that there are only two pervasive macroeconomic factors. Investments X, Y, and Z have the following sensitivities to these two factors:

Investment	b_1	b_2
X	1.75	.25
Y	−1.00	2.00
Z	2.00	1.00

We assume that the expected risk premium is 4% on factor 1 and 8% on factor 2. Treasury bills obviously offer zero risk premium.

   a. According to the APT, what is the risk premium on each of the three stocks?
   b. Suppose you buy ₹200 of X and ₹50 of Y and sell ₹150 of Z. What is the sensitivity of your portfolio to each of the two factors? What is the expected risk premium?
   c. Suppose you buy $80 of X and $60 of Y and sell $40 of Z. What is the sensitivity of your portfolio to each of the two factors? What is the expected risk premium?
   d. Finally, suppose you buy $160 of X and $20 of Y and sell $80 of Z. What is your portfolio's sensitivity now to each of the two factors? And what is the expected risk premium?
   e. Suggest two possible ways that you could construct a fund that has a sensitivity of .5 to factor 1 only. (*Hint:* One portfolio contains an investment in Treasury bills.) Now compare the risk premiums on each of these two investments.
   f. Suppose that the APT did *not* hold and that X offered a risk premium of 8%, Y offered a premium of 14%, and Z offered a premium of 16%. Devise an investment that has zero sensitivity to each factor and that has a positive risk premium.

You can download data for the following questions from the Standard & Poor's Market Insight Web site (www.mhhe.com/edumarketinsight)—see the "Monthly Adjusted Prices" spread-sheet—or from finance.yahoo.com.

Note: When we calculated the efficient portfolios in Table 8.1, we assumed that the investor could not hold short positions (i.e., have negative holdings). The book's Web site (**www.mhhe.com/bmam10e**) contains an Excel program for calculating the efficient frontier with short sales. (We are grateful to Simon Gervais for providing us with a copy of this program.) Excel functions SLOPE, STDEV, and COR-REL are especially useful for answering the following questions.

STANDARD &POOR'S

1. a. Look at the efficient portfolios constructed from the 10 stocks in Table 8.1. How does the possibility of short sales improve the choices open to the investor?
    b. Now download daily stock prices from www.nseindia.com and estimate monthly returns from that. Enter the past returns into the Excel program. Enter some plausible figures for the expected return on each stock and find the set of efficient portfolios.

2. Go to the website of www.nseindia.com and find a low risk income stock. Estimate the company's beta to confirm that it well below 1.0. use monthly rates of return for the most recent three years. For the same period, estimate the annual standard deviation for the stock, the standard deviation of Nifty, and the correlation coefficient between returns on the stock and the Nifty. Forecast the expected rate of return for the stock, assuming the CAPM holds, with a market return of 17 percent and a risk-free rate of 6 percent.
    a. Plot a graph like Figure 8.5 showing the combinations of risk and return from a portfolio invested in your low-risk stock and the market. Vary the fraction invested in the stock from 0 to 100%.
    b. Suppose that you can borrow or lend at 5%. Would you invest in some combination of your low-risk stock and the market, or would you simply invest in the market? Explain.
    c. Suppose that you forecasted a return on the stock that is 5 percentage points higher than the CAPM return used in part (b). Redo parts (a) and (b) with the higher forecasted return.
    d. Find a high-risk stock and redo parts (a) and (b).

3. Recalculate the betas for the stocks in Table 8.2 using the latest 60 monthly returns. You can get the data for the companies in Table 8.2 from www.in.finance.yahoo.com. Recalculate expected rates of return from the CAPM formula, using a current risk-free rate and a market risk premium of 13%. How have the expected returns changed from figure reported in Table 8.2?

4. Download daily stock prices for Tata Motors and Hindustan Unilever from www.nseindia.com. Use the Excel function SLOPE to calculate beta for each company.
    a. Suppose the market index falls unexpectedly by 5%. By how much would you expect Tata Motors and HUL to fall?
    b. Which is the riskier company for the well-diversified investor? How much riskier?
    c. Suppose the Treasury bill rate is 5% and the expected return on Nifty is 16%. Use the CAPM to forecast the expected rate of return on each stock.

5. Download the monthly stock prices for Reliance Industries and Infosys from www.in.finance. yahoo.com.
    a. Calculate the annual standard deviation for each company, using the most recent three years of monthly returns. Use the Excel function STDEV. Multiply by the square root of 12 to convert to annual basis.
    b. Use the Excel function CORREL to calculate the correlation coefficient between the stocks' monthly returns.

     c. Use the CAPM to estimate expected rates of return. Calculate betas, or download the beta estimates from www.nseindia.com. Use the current Treasury bill rate (download from www.fimmda.org) and a reasonable estimate of the market risk premium?

     d. Construct a graph like Figure 8.3. What combination of Reliance and Infosys has the lowest portfolio risk? What is the expected return for this minimum-risk portfolio?

JOHN AND MARSHA ON PORTFOLIO SELECTION

The scene: John and Marsha hold hands in a cozy French restaurant in downtown Manhattan, several years before the mini-case in Chapter 9. Marsha is a futures-market trader. John manages a $125 million common-stock portfolio for a large pension fund. They have just ordered tournedos financiere for the main course and flan financiere for dessert. John reads the financial pages of *The Wall Street Journal* by candlelight.

John: Wow! Potato futures hit their daily limit. Let's add an order of gratin dauphinoise. Did you manage to hedge the forward interest rate on that euro loan?

Marsha: John, please fold up that paper. (*He does so reluctantly.*) John, I love you. Will you marry me?

John: Oh, Marsha, I love you too, but . . . there's something you must know about me—something I've never told anyone.

Marsha (concerned): John, what is it?

John: I think I'm a closet indexer.

Marsha: What? Why?

John: My portfolio returns always seem to track the S&P 500 market index. Sometimes I do a little better, occasionally a little worse. But the correlation between my returns and the market returns is over 90%.

Marsha: What's wrong with that? Your client wants a diversified portfolio of large-cap stocks. Of course your portfolio will follow the market.

John: Why doesn't my client just buy an index fund? Why is he paying *me*? Am I really adding value by active management? I try, but I guess I'm just an . . . indexer.

Marsha: Oh, John, I know you're adding value. You were a star security analyst.

John: It's not easy to find stocks that are truly over- or undervalued. I have firm opinions about a few, of course.

Marsha: You were explaining why Pioneer Gypsum is a good buy. And you're bullish on Global Mining.

John: Right, Pioneer. (*Pulls handwritten notes from his coat pocket.*) Stock price $87.50. I estimate the expected return as 11% with an annual standard deviation of 32%.

Marsha: Only 11%? You're forecasting a market return of 12.5%.

John: Yes, I'm using a market risk premium of 7.5% and the risk-free interest rate is about 5%. That gives 12.5%. But Pioneer's beta is only .65. I was going to buy 30,000 shares this morning, but I lost my nerve. I've got to stay diversified.

Marsha: Have you tried modern portfolio theory?

John: MPT? Not practical. Looks great in textbooks, where they show efficient frontiers with 5 or 10 stocks. But I choose from hundreds, maybe thousands, of stocks. Where do I get the inputs for 1,000 stocks? That's a million variances and covariances!

Marsha: Actually only about 500,000, dear. The covariances above the diagonal are the same as the covariances below. But you're right, most of the estimates would be out-of-date or just garbage.

John: To say nothing about the expected returns. Garbage in, garbage out.

Marsha: But John, you don't need to solve for 1,000 portfolio weights. You only need a handful. Here's the trick: Take your benchmark, the S&P 500, as security 1. That's what you would end up with as an indexer. Then consider a few securities you really know something about. Pioneer could be security 2, for example. Global, security 3. And so on. Then you could put your wonderful financial mind to work.

John: I get it: active management means selling off some of the benchmark portfolio and investing the proceeds in specific stocks like Pioneer. But how do I decide whether Pioneer really improves the portfolio? Even if it does, how much should I buy?

Marsha: Just maximize the Sharpe ratio, dear.

John: I've got it! The answer is yes!

Marsha: What's the question?

John: You asked me to marry you. The answer is yes. Where should we go on our honeymoon?

Marsha: How about Australia? I'd love to visit the Sydney Futures Exchange.

Questions

1. Table 8.4 reproduces John's notes on Pioneer Gypsum and Global Mining. Calculate the expected return, risk premium, and standard deviation of a portfolio invested partly in the market and partly in Pioneer. (You can calculate the necessary inputs from the betas and standard deviations given in the table.) Does adding Pioneer to the market benchmark improve the Sharpe ratio? How much should John invest in Pioneer and how much in the market?

2. Repeat the analysis for Global Mining. What should John do in this case? Assume that Global accounts for .75% of the S&P index.

TABLE 8.4 John's notes on Pioneer Gypsum and Global Mining.

	Pioneer Gypsum	Global Mining
Expected return	11.0%	12.9%
Standard deviation	32%	20%
Beta	.65	1.22
Stock price	$87.50	$105.00

9

CHAPTER

RISK AND THE COST OF CAPITAL

Long before the development of modern theories linking risk and return, smart financial managers adjusted for risk in capital budgeting. They knew that risky projects are, other things equal, less valuable than safe ones—that is just common sense. Therefore they demanded higher rates of return from risky projects, or they based their decisions about risky projects on conservative forecasts of project cash flows.

Today most companies start with the *company cost of capital* as a benchmark risk-adjusted discount rate for new investments. The company cost of capital is the right discount rate only for investments that have the same risk as the company's overall business. For riskier projects the opportunity cost of capital is greater than the company cost of capital. For safer projects it is less.

The company cost of capital is usually estimated as a weighted-average cost of capital, that is, as the average rate of return demanded by investors in the company's debt and equity. The hardest part of estimating the weighted-average cost of capital is figuring out the cost of equity, that is, the expected rate of return to investors in the firm's common stock. Many firms turn to the capital asset pricing model (CAPM) for an answer. The CAPM states that the expected rate of return equals the risk-free interest rate plus a risk premium that depends on beta and the market risk premium.

We explained the CAPM in the last chapter, but didn't show you how to estimate betas. You can't look up betas in a newspaper or see them clearly by tracking a few day-to-day changes in stock price. But you can get useful statistical estimates from the history of stock and market returns.

Now suppose you're responsible for a specific investment project. How do you know if the project is average risk or above- or below-average risk? We suggest you check whether the project's cash flows are more or less sensitive to the business cycle than the average project. Also check whether the project has higher or lower fixed operating costs (higher or lower operating leverage) and whether it requires large future investments.

Remember that a project's cost of capital depends only on market risk. Diversifiable risk can affect project cash flows but does not increase the cost of capital. Also don't be tempted to add arbitrary fudge factors to discount rates. Fudge factors are too often added to discount rates for projects in unstable parts of the world, for example.

Risk varies from project to project. Risk can also vary over time for a given project. For example, some projects are riskier in youth than in old age. But financial managers usually assume that project risk will be the same in every future period, and they use a single risk-adjusted discount rate for all future cash flows. We close the chapter by introducing certainty equivalents, which illustrate how risk can change over time.

9-1 COMPANY AND PROJECT COSTS OF CAPITAL

The **company cost of capital** is defined as the expected return on a portfolio of all the company's existing securities. It is the opportunity cost of capital for investment in the firm's assets, and therefore the appropriate discount rate for the firm's average-risk projects.

If the firm has no debt outstanding, then the company cost of capital is just the expected rate of return on the firm's stock. Many large, successful companies pretty well fit this special case. Here, we consider the case of Infosys, which has no debt outstanding as of March 2011. In Table 8.2 we estimated that investors require a return of 14.55% from Infosys' common stock. If Infosys is contemplating an expansion of its existing business, it would make sense to discount the forecasted cash flows at 14.55%.[1]

The company cost of capital is *not* the correct discount rate if the new projects are more or less risky than the firm's existing business. Each project should in principle be evaluated at its *own* opportunity cost of capital. This is a clear implication of the value-additivity principle introduced in Chapter 7. For a firm composed of assets A and B, the firm value is

$$\text{Firm value} = PV(AB) = PV(A) + PV(B)$$
$$= \text{sum of separate asset values}$$

Here PV(A) and PV(B) are valued just as if they were mini-firms in which stockholders could invest directly. Investors would value A by discounting its forecasted cash flows at a rate reflecting the risk of A. They would value B by discounting at a rate reflecting the risk of B. The two discount rates will, in general, be different. If the present value of an asset depended on the identity of the company that bought it, present values would *not* add up, and we know they do add up. (Consider a portfolio of ₹1 million invested in Infosys and ₹1 million invested in Tata Motors. Would any reasonable investor say that the portfolio is worth anything more or less than ₹2 million?)

If the firm considers investing in a third project C, it should also value C as if C were a mini-firm. That is, the firm should discount the cash flows of C at the expected rate of return that investors would demand if they could make a separate investment in C. *The opportunity cost of capital depends on the use to which that capital is put.*

---

[1] The long-term rates are higher in 2011, and Infosys would use a higher discount rate for cash flows spread out over many future years. We return to this distinction later in the chapter. The market value debt-equity ratio for Infosys is 0.

Perhaps we're saying the obvious. Think of Infosys: it is a large IT company that offers software products primarily for the banking industry, with ₹261,950 million of revenue in the 12 months ending December 2010. It provides software development and engineering to corporate clients. It also provides data management, systems integration, project management, support, and maintenance services. It also invests in research and development of processes, frameworks, methodologies to effectively capture customer requirements and to iron out common critical issues during a project life cycle.[2] Do you think that investment in research & development has the same cost of capital as investment made in opening a BPO centre? We don't, though we admit that estimating the cost of capital for the BPO centre could be challenging.

Suppose we measure the risk of each project by its beta. Then Infosys should accept any project lying above the upward sloping security market line that links expected return to risk in Figure 9.1. If the project is high-risk, Infosys needs a higher prospective return than if the project is low-risk. That

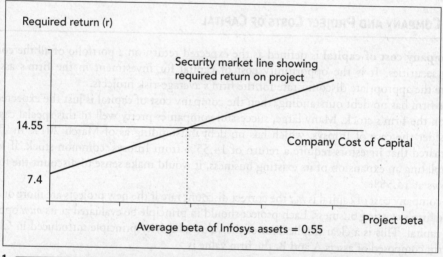

FIGURE 9.1

A comparison between the company cost of capital rule and the required return from the capital asset pricing model. Infosys' company cost of capital is about 14.55%. This is the correct discount rate only if the project beta is .55. In general, the correct discount rate increases as project beta increases. Infosys should accept projects with rates of return above the security market line relating required return to beta.

is different from the company cost of capital rule, which accepts any project *regardless of its risk* as long as it offers a higher return than the *company's* cost of capital. The rule tells Infosys to accept any project above the horizontal cost of capital line in Figure 9.1, that is, any project offering a return of more than 3.8%.

It is clearly silly to suggest that Infosys should demand the same rate of return from a very safe project as from a very risky one. If Infosys used the company cost of capital rule, it would reject many good low-risk projects and accept many poor high-risk projects. It is also silly to suggest that just because another company has a low company cost of capital, it is justified in accepting projects that Infosys would reject.

---

[2] Source: www.en.wikipedia.org

Perfect Pitch and the Cost of Capital

The true cost of capital depends on project risk, not on the company undertaking the project. So why is so much time spent estimating the company cost of capital?

There are two reasons. First, many (maybe most) projects can be treated as average risk, that is, neither more nor less risky than the average of the company's other assets. For these projects the company cost of capital is the right discount rate. Second, the company cost of capital is a useful starting point for setting discount rates for unusually risky or safe projects. It is easier to add to, or subtract from, the company cost of capital than to estimate each project's cost of capital from scratch.

There is a good musical analogy here. Most of us, lacking perfect pitch, need a well-defined reference point, like middle C, before we can sing on key. But anyone who can carry a tune gets *relative* pitches right. Businesspeople have good intuition about *relative* risks, at least in industries they are used to, but not about absolute risk or required rates of return. Therefore, they set a companywide cost of capital as a benchmark. This is not the right discount rate for everything the company does, but adjustments can be made for more or less risky ventures.

That said, we have to admit that many large companies use the company cost of capital not just as a benchmark, but also as an all-purpose discount rate for every project proposal. Measuring differences in risk is difficult to do objectively, and financial managers shy away from intracorporate squabbles. (You can imagine the bickering: "My projects are safer than yours! I want a lower discount rate!" "No they're not! Your projects are riskier than a naked call option!")[3]

When firms force the use of a single company cost of capital, risk adjustment shifts from the discount rate to project cash flows. Top management may demand extra-conservative cash-flow forecasts from extra-risky projects. They may refuse to sign off on an extra-risky project unless NPV, computed at the company cost of capital, is well above zero. Rough-and-ready risk adjustments are better than none at all.

Debt and the Company Cost of Capital

We defined the company cost of capital as "the expected return on a portfolio of all the company's existing securities." That portfolio usually includes debt as well as equity. Thus the cost of capital is estimated as a blend of the *cost of debt* (the interest rate) and the *cost of equity* (the expected rate of return demanded by investors in the firm's common stock).

Suppose the company's market-value balance sheet looks like this:

Asset value	100	Debt	$D = 30$ at 7.5%
		Equity	$E = 70$ at 15%
Asset value	100	Firm value	$V = 100$

The values of debt and equity add up to overall firm value ($D + E = V$) and firm value V equals asset value. These figures are all market values, not book (accounting) values. The market value of equity is often much larger than the book value, so the market debt ratio D/V is often much lower than a debt ratio computed from the book balance sheet.

The 7.5% cost of debt is the opportunity cost of capital for the investors who hold the firm's debt. The 15% cost of equity is the opportunity cost of capital for the investors who hold the firm's

---

[3] A "naked" call option is an option purchased with no offsetting (hedging) position in the underlying stock or in other options. We discuss options in Chapter 20.

shares. Neither measures the *company* cost of capital, that is, the opportunity cost of investing in the firm's *assets*. The cost of debt is less than the company cost of capital, because debt is safer than the assets. The cost of equity is greater than the company cost of capital, because the equity of a firm that borrows is riskier than the assets. Equity is not a direct claim on the firm's free cash flow. It is a residual claim that stands behind debt.

The company cost of capital is not equal to the cost of debt or to the cost of equity but is a blend of the two. Suppose you purchased a portfolio consisting of 100% of the firm's debt and 100% of its equity. Then you would own 100% of its assets lock, stock, and barrel. You would not share the firm's free cash flow with anyone; every rupee that the firm pays out would be paid to you.

The expected rate of return on your hypothetical portfolio is the company cost of capital. The expected rate of return is just a weighted average of the cost of debt ($r_D = 7.5\%$) and the cost of equity ($r_E = 15\%$). The weights are the relative market values of the firm's debt and equity, that is, $D/V = 30\%$ and $E/V = 70\%$.[4]

$$\text{Company cost of capital} = r_D D/V + r_E E/V$$
$$= 7.5 \times .30 + 15 \times .70 = 12.75\%$$

This blended measure of the company cost of capital is called the **weighted-average cost of capital** or **WACC** (pronounced "whack"). Calculating WACC is a bit more complicated than our example suggests, however. For example, interest is a tax-deductible expense for corporations, so the after-tax cost of debt is $(1 - T_c)r_D$, where T_c is the marginal corporate tax rate. Suppose $T_c = 35\%$. Then *after-tax WACC* is

$$\text{After-tax WACC} = (1 - T_c)r_D D/V + r_E E/V$$
$$= (1 - .35) \times 7.5 \times .30 + 15 \times .70 = 12.0\%$$

We give another example of the after-tax WACC later in this chapter, and we cover the topic in much more detail in Chapter 19. But now we turn to the hardest part of calculating WACC, estimating the cost of equity.

9-2 MEASURING THE COST OF EQUITY

To calculate the weighted-average cost of capital, you need an estimate of the cost of equity. You decide to use the capital asset pricing model (CAPM). Here you are in good company: as we saw in the last chapter, most large U.S. companies do use the CAPM to estimate the cost of equity, which is the expected rate of return on the firm's common stock.[5] The CAPM says that

$$\text{Expected stock return} = r_f + \beta (r_m - r_f)$$

Now you have to estimate beta. Let us see how that is done in practice.

---

[4] Recall that the 30% and 70% weights in your hypothetical portfolio are based on market, not book, values. Now you can see why. If the portfolio were constructed with different book weights, say 50-50, then the portfolio returns could not equal the asset returns.

[5] The CAPM is not the last word on risk and return, of course, but the principles and procedures covered in this chapter work just as well with other models such as the Fama–French three-factor model. See Section 8-4.

Estimating Beta

In principle we are interested in the future beta of the company's stock, but lacking a crystal ball, we turn first to historical evidence. For example, look at the scatter diagram at the top left of Figure 9.2. Each dot represents the return on HUL stock and the return on the market in a particular month. The plot starts in April 2001 and runs to March 2006, so there are 60 dots in all.

The second diagram on the left shows a similar plot for the returns on Tata Motors stock, and the third shows a plot for Bharti Airtel Stock. In each case we have fitted a line through the points. The slope of this line[6] is an estimate of beta.[7] It tells us how much on average the stock price changed when the market return was 1% higher or lower.

The right-hand diagrams show similar plots for the same three stocks during the subsequent period ending in March 2011. Although the slopes varied from the first period to the second, there is little doubt that HUL's beta is much less than Tata Motors' or that Bharti's beta falls somewhere between the two. If you had used the past beta of each stock to predict its future beta, you would not have been too far off, for Bharti and Tata Motors, although you missed on HUL's beta, which decreased from 0.77 to 0.44 in the later period.

Only a small portion of each stock's total risk comes from movements in the market. The rest is firm-specific, diversifiable risk, which shows up in the scatter of points around the fitted lines in Figure 9.2. *R-squared* (R^2) measures the proportion of the total variance in the stock's returns that can be explained by market movements. For example, from 2001 to 2006, the R^2 of Tata Motors was 0.52. In other words, only about one-half of Tata Motors' risk was market risk and the remaining half was unique risk. The variance of returns on Tata Motors stock was 1100.66[8]. So we could say that the variance in stock returns that was due to the market was $0.52 \times 1100.66 = 568.92$, and the variance of unique returns was 531.75.

The estimates of beta shown in Figure 9.2 are just that. They are based on the stocks' returns in 60 (55 for Bharti) particular months. The noise in the returns can obscure the true beta.[9] Therefore, statisticians calculate the *standard error* of the estimated beta to show the extent of possible mismeasurement. Then they set up a *confidence interval* of the estimated value plus or minus two standard errors. For example, the standard error of HUL's estimated beta is .07 for the period 2006-11. Thus the confidence interval for HUL's beta is .41 plus or minus $1.96 \times .07$. If you state that the *true* beta for HUL is between .27 and .55, you have a 95% chance of being right. Notice that we can be equally confident of our estimate of HUL's beta, but much less confident of Tata Motors'.

Usually you will have more information (and thus more confidence) than this simple, and somewhat depressing, calculation suggests. For example, you know that HUL's estimated beta was well below 1 in the previous period, while Tata Motors' estimated beta was well above. Nevertheless, there is always a large margin for error when estimating the beta for individual stocks.

---

[6] We have used Excel to draw these scatter plots. Excel automatically scales the axes and hence you will not be able to guess the slope of the best-fit line by merely looking at the lines.

[7] Notice that to estimate beta you must regress the *returns* on the stock on the market *returns*. You would get a very similar estimate if you simply used the percentage *changes* in the stock price and the market index. But sometimes people make the mistake of regressing the stock price *level* on the *level* of the index and obtain nonsense results.

[8] This is an annual figure; we annualized the monthly variance by multiplying by 12. The standard deviation was $\sqrt{1100.66} = 33.17\%$.

[9] Estimates of beta may be distorted if there are extreme returns in one or two months. This is a potential problem in our estimates for 2004–2008, since you can see in Figure 9.2 that there was one month (October 2008) when the market fell by over 16%. The performance of each stock that month has an excessive effect on the estimated beta. In such cases statisticians may prefer to give less weight to the extreme observations or even to omit them entirely.

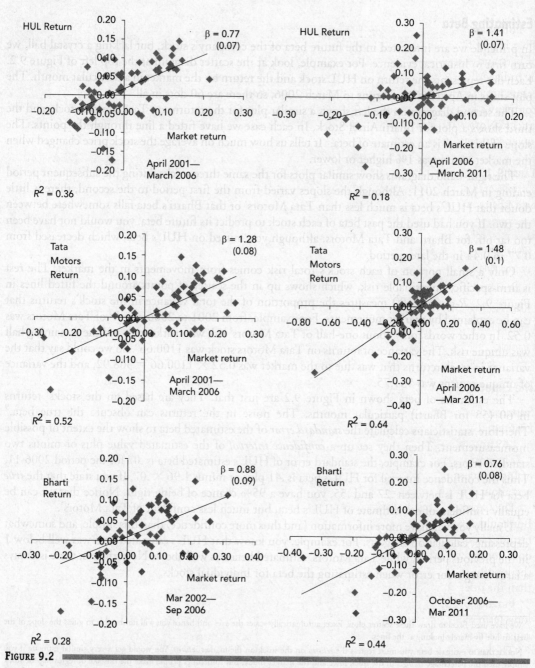

FIGURE 9.2

We have used past returns to estimate the betas of three stocks for the periods April 2001 to March 2006 (March 2002 to September 2006 for Bharti) for the left-hand diagrams and April 2006 to March 2011 (October 2006 to March 2011 for Bharti) right-hand diagrams. Notice that in both periods Tata Motors had the highest beta and HUL the lowest. Standard errors are in parentheses below the betas. The standard error shows the range of possible error in the beta estimate. We also report the proportion of total risk that is due to market movements (R^2).

Fortunately, the estimation errors tend to cancel out when you estimate betas of *portfolios*.[10] That is why financial managers often turn to *industry betas*. For example, Table 9.1 shows estimates of beta and the standard errors of these estimates for the common stocks of five airline companies in India. All the standard errors are higher than what we saw in Figure 9.2. Four of the standard errors are greater than 0.15, large enough to preclude a precise estimate of any particular cement company's beta. However, the table also shows the estimated beta for a portfolio of all five airline stocks. Notice that the estimated industry beta is somewhat more reliable. This shows up in the lower standard error.

TABLE 9.1 Estimated betas and standard errors for a sample of large cement manufacturing companies and for a portfolio of these companies, based on monthly returns from January 2001 to May 2006. The precision of the portfolio beta is better than that of the betas of the individual companies—note the lower standard error for the portfolio.

	Beta	Standard Error
Global Vectra Helicorp Ltd.	1.50	0.15
Jagson Airlines Ltd.	1.19	0.19
Jet Airways (India) Ltd.	1.89	0.15
Kingfisher Airlines Ltd.	2.08	0.14
Spicejet Ltd.	1.67	0.16
Portfolio	1.67	0.11

The Expected Return on Jet Airways' Common Stock

Suppose that in early 2011 you have been asked to estimate the company cost of capital of Jet Airways Limited. Table 9.1 provides two clues about the true beta of Jet Airways' stock: the direct estimate of 1.89 and the average estimate for the industry of 1.67. We will use the industry average of 1.67.[11]

The next issue is what value to use for the risk-free interest rate. In March 2011, the Reserve Bank of India increased the interest rate for the eighth time since March 2010. The yield on 1-year G-Sec was about 7.4%. The yields on longer-maturity G-Secs was higher at 8.4% on 30-year G-Secs.

The CAPM is a short-term model. It works period by period and calls for a short-term interest rate. But could the one-year risk-free rate give the right discount rate for cash flows 10 or 20 years in the future? Here, the difference between the 1-year and 30-year rate is just about 1%. So one may say, it does not make a big difference. But as of March 2011, the difference between the short-term rate and the long-term rate is greater than 4% in the U.S. It does matter, if you decide to use one rate rather than the other.

Financial managers muddle through this problem in one of two ways. The first way simply uses a long-term risk-free rate in the CAPM formula. If this short-cut is used, then the market risk premium must be restated as the average difference between market returns and returns on *long-term* Treasuries.[12]

The second way retains the usual definition of the market risk premium as the difference between

---

[10] If the observations are independent, the standard error of the estimated mean beta declines in proportion to the square root of the number of stocks in the portfolio.

[11] Comparing the beta of Jet Airways with those of the other airline companies would be misleading as Jet Airways had a marginally higher debt ratio.

[12] This approach gives a security market line with a higher intercept and a lower market risk premium. Using a "flatter" security market line is perhaps a better match to the historical evidence, which shows that the slope of average returns against beta is not as steeply upward-sloping as the CAPM predicts. See Figures 8.8 and 8.9.

market returns and returns on *short-term* Treasury bill rates. But now you have to forecast the expected return from holding Treasury bills over the life of the project. In Chapter 3 we observed that investors require a risk premium for holding long-term bonds rather than bills. The average risk premium over the 1975–2010 period is around 1.5%. So to get a rough, but reasonable estimate of the expected long-term return from investing in Treasury bills, we need to subtract 1.5% from the currents yield on long-term bonds. Since the difference between the short-term and long-term G-Sec in India is only 1% now, we do not use this approach here. But when one finds the current spread to be substantially different from the long-term average premium, one should use this approach.

Returning to our Jet Airways example, suppose you decide to use a market risk premium of 12% and a risk-free rate of 7.4%. Then the resulting estimate for Jet Airways' cost of equity is about 27.4%:

$$\text{Cost of equity} = \text{expected return} = r_f + \beta(r_m - r_f)$$
$$= 7.4 + 1.67 \times 12 = 27.44\%$$

Now you can calculate Jet Airways' after-tax WACC in March 2011. The company's cost of debt was about 14%. With a 34% corporate tax rate, the after-tax cost of debt was $r_D(1 - T_c) = 14 \times (1 - 0.34) = 9.24\%$. The ratio of debt to overall company value was $D/V = 77\%$. Therefore:

$$\text{After-tax WACC} = (1 - T_c)r_D D/V + r_E E/V$$
$$= (1 - 0.34) \times 14 \times 0.77 + 27.44 \times 0.23 = 13.21\%$$

Jet Airways should set its overall cost of capital to 13.21%, assuming that its CFO agrees with the estimates.

Warning   The cost of debt is always less than the cost of equity. The WACC formula blends the two costs. The formula is dangerous, however, because it suggests that the average cost of capital could be reduced by substituting cheap debt for expensive equity. It doesn't work that way! As the debt ratio D/V increases, the cost of the remaining equity also increases, offsetting the apparent advantage of more cheap debt. We show how and why this offset happens in Chapter 17.

Debt does have a tax advantage, however, because interest is a tax-deductible expense. That is why we use the after-tax cost of debt in the after-tax WACC. We cover debt and taxes in much more detail in Chapters 18 and 19.

Jet Airways' Asset Beta

The after-tax WACC depends on the average risk of the company's assets, but it also depends on taxes and financing. It's easier to think about project risk if you measure it directly. The direct measure is called the **asset beta.**

We calculate the asset beta as a blend of the separate betas of debt (β_D) and equity (β_E). For Jet Airways we have $\beta_E = 1.67$, and we'll assume $\beta_D = .0.55$.[13] The weights are the fractions of debt and equity financing, $D/V = .77$ and $E/V = .23$:

$$\text{Asset beta} = \beta_A = \beta_D(D/V) + \beta_E(E/V)$$
$$\beta_A = .55 \times .77 + 1.67 \times .23 = .81$$

Calculating an asset beta is similar to calculating a weighted-average cost of capital. The debt

---

[13] Why is the debt beta positive? Two reasons: First, debt investors worry about the risk of default. Corporate bond prices fall, relative to Treasury-bond prices, when the economy goes from expansion to recession. The risk of default is therefore partly a macroeconomic and market risk. Second, all bonds are exposed to uncertainty about interest rates and inflation. Even Treasury bonds have positive betas when long-term interest rates and inflation are volatile and uncertain.

and equity weights D/V and E/V are the same. The logic is also the same: Suppose you purchased a portfolio consisting of 100% of the firm's debt and 100% of its equity. Then you would own 100% of its assets lock, stock, and barrel, and the beta of your portfolio would equal the beta of the assets. The portfolio beta is of course just a weighted average of the betas of debt and equity.

This asset beta is an estimate of the average risk of Jet Airways' airlines business. It is a useful benchmark, but it can take you only so far. Not all airline investments are average risk.

How can you make informed judgments about costs of capital for projects or lines of business when you suspect that risk is *not* average? That is our next topic.

9-3 ANALYZING PROJECT RISK

Suppose that a coal-mining corporation wants to assess the risk of investing in commercial real estate, for example, in a new company headquarters. The asset beta for coal mining is not helpful. You need to know the beta of real estate. Fortunately, portfolios of commercial real estate are traded. For example, you could estimate asset betas from returns on Real Estate Investment Trusts (REITs) specializing in commercial real estate.[14] The REITs would serve as traded *comparables* for the proposed office building. You could also turn to indexes of real estate prices and returns derived from sales and appraisals of commercial properties.[15]

A company that wants to set a cost of capital for one particular line of business typically looks for *pure plays* in that line of business. Pure-play companies are public firms that specialize in one activity. For example, suppose that Johnson & Johnson wants to set a cost of capital for its pharmaceutical business. It could estimate the average asset beta or cost of capital for pharmaceutical companies that have *not* diversified into consumer products like Band-Aid® bandages or baby powder.

Overall company costs of capital are almost useless for *conglomerates*. Conglomerates diversify into several unrelated industries, so they have to consider industry-specific costs of capital. They therefore look for pure plays in the relevant industries. Take Hindustan Unilever as an example. HUL operates in soaps and detergents, personal care products, beverages, foods, ice cream and others. We cannot use the overall cost of capital of HUL for the personal care division, for example. Fortunately, there are many pure-play personal care companies, and pure-play food processing companies. The trick is picking the comparables with business risks that are most similar to the Unilever's divisions.

Sometimes good comparables are not available or not a good match to a particular project. Then the financial manager has to exercise his or her judgment. Here we offer the following advice:

1. *Think about the determinants of asset betas.* Often the characteristics of high- and low-beta assets can be observed when the beta itself cannot be.
2. *Don't be fooled by diversifiable risk.*
3. *Avoid fudge factors.* Don't give in to the temptation to add fudge factors to the discount rate to offset things that could go wrong with the proposed investment. Adjust cash-flow forecasts first.

[14] REITs are investment funds that invest in real estate. You would have to be careful to identify REITs investing in commercial properties similar to the proposed office building. There are also REITs that invest in other types of real estate, including apartment buildings, shopping centers, and timberland.

[15] See Chapter 23 in D. Geltner, N. G. Miller, J. Clayton, and P. Eichholtz, *Commercial Real Estate Analysis and Investments,* 2nd ed. (South-Western College Publishing, 2006).

What Determines Asset Betas?

Cyclicality   Many people's intuition associates risk with the variability of earnings or cash flow. But much of this variability reflects diversifiable risk. Lone prospectors searching for gold look forward to extremely uncertain future income, but whether they strike it rich is unlikely to depend on the performance of the market portfolio. Even if they do find gold, they do not bear much market risk. Therefore, an investment in gold prospecting has a high standard deviation but a relatively low beta.

What really counts is the strength of the relationship between the firm's earnings and the aggregate earnings on all real assets. We can measure this either by the *earnings beta* or by the *cash-flow beta*. These are just like a real beta except that changes in earnings or cash flow are used in place of rates of return on securities. We would predict that firms with high earnings or cash-flow betas should also have high asset betas.

This means that cyclical firms—firms whose revenues and earnings are strongly dependent on the state of the business cycle—tend to be high-beta firms. Thus you should demand a higher rate of return from investments whose performance is strongly tied to the performance of the economy. Examples of cyclical businesses include airlines, luxury resorts and restaurants, construction, and steel. (Much of the demand for steel depends on construction and capital investment.) Examples of less-cyclical businesses include food and tobacco products and established consumer brands such as J&J's baby products. MBA programs are another example, because spending a year or two at a business school is an easier choice when jobs are scarce. Applications to top MBA programs increase in recessions.

Operating Leverage   A production facility with high fixed costs, relative to variable costs, is said to have high *operating leverage*. High operating leverage means a high asset beta. Let us see how this works.

The cash flows generated by an asset can be broken down into revenue, fixed costs, and variable costs:

$$\text{Cash flow} = \text{revenue} - \text{fixed cost} - \text{variable cost}$$

Costs are variable if they depend on the rate of output. Examples are raw materials, sales commissions, and some labor and maintenance costs. Fixed costs are cash outflows that occur regardless of whether the asset is active or idle, for example, property taxes or the wages of workers under contract.

We can break down the asset's present value in the same way:

$$\text{PV(asset)} = \text{PV(revenue)} - \text{PV(fixed cost)} - \text{PV(variable cost)}$$

Or equivalently

$$\text{PV(revenue)} = \text{PV(fixed cost)} + \text{PV(variable cost)} + \text{PV(asset)}$$

Those who *receive* the fixed costs are like debtholders in the project; they simply get a fixed payment. Those who receive the net cash flows from the asset are like holders of common stock; they get whatever is left after payment of the fixed costs.

We can now figure out how the asset's beta is related to the betas of the values of revenue and costs. The beta of PV(revenue) is a weighted average of the betas of its component parts:

$$\beta_{\text{revenue}} = \beta_{\text{fixed cost}} \frac{\text{PV(fixed cost)}}{\text{PV(revenue)}}$$

$$+ \beta_{\text{variable cost}} \frac{\text{PV(variable cost)}}{\text{PV(revenue)}} + \beta_{\text{assets}} \frac{\text{PV(asset)}}{\text{PV(revenue)}}$$

The fixed-cost beta should be about zero; whoever receives the fixed costs receives a fixed stream of cash flows. The betas of the revenues and variable costs should be approximately the same, because they respond to the same underlying variable, the rate of output. Therefore we can substitute β_{revenue} for $\beta_{\text{variable cost}}$ and solve for the asset beta. Remember, we are assuming $\beta_{\text{fixed cost}} = 0$. Also, PV(revenue) − PV(variable cost) = PV(asset) + PV(fixed cost).[16]

$$\beta_{\text{assets}} = \beta_{\text{revenue}} \frac{\text{PV(revenue)} - \text{PV(variable cost)}}{\text{PV(asset)}}$$

$$= \beta_{\text{revenue}} \left[1 + \frac{\text{PV(fixed cost)}}{\text{PV(asset)}} \right]$$

Thus, given the cyclicality of revenues (reflected in β_{revenue}), the asset beta is proportional to the ratio of the present value of fixed costs to the present value of the project.

Now you have a rule of thumb for judging the relative risks of alternative designs or technologies for producing the same project. Other things being equal, the alternative with the higher ratio of fixed costs to project value will have the higher project beta. Empirical tests confirm that companies with high operating leverage actually do have high betas.[17]

We have interpreted fixed costs as costs of production, but fixed costs can show up in other forms, for example, as future investment outlays. Suppose that an electric utility commits to build a large electricity-generating plant. The plant will take several years to build, and the cost is fixed. Our operating leverage formula still applies, but with PV(future investment) included in PV(fixed costs). The commitment to invest therefore increases the plant's asset beta. Of course PV(future investment) decreases as the plant is constructed and disappears when the plant is up and running. Therefore the plant's asset beta is only temporarily high during construction.

Other Sources of Risk   So far we have focused on cash flows. Cash-flow risk is not the only risk. A project's value is equal to the expected cash flows discounted at the risk-adjusted discount rate r. If either the risk-free rate or the market risk premium changes, then r will change and so will the project value. A project with very long-term cash flows is more exposed to such shifts in the discount rate than one with short-term cash flows. This project will, therefore, have a high beta even though it may not have high operating leverage and cyclicality.[18]

You cannot hope to estimate the relative risk of assets with any precision, but good managers examine any project from a variety of angles and look for clues as to its riskiness. They know that high market risk is a characteristic of cyclical ventures, of projects with high fixed costs and of projects that are sensitive to marketwide changes in the discount rate. They think about the major uncertainties affecting the economy and consider how projects are affected by these uncertainties.

Don't Be Fooled by Diversifiable Risk

In this chapter we have defined risk as the asset beta for a firm, industry, or project. But in everyday usage, "risk" simply means "bad outcome." People think of the risks of a project as a list of things that can go wrong. For example,

---

[16] In Chapter 10 we describe an accounting measure of the degree of operating leverage (DOL), defined as DOL = 1 + fixed costs/profits. DOL measures the percentage change in profits for a 1% change in revenue. We have derived here a version of DOL expressed in PVs and betas.

[17] See B. Lev, "On the Association between Operating Leverage and Risk," *Journal of Financial and Quantitative Analysis* 9 (September 1974), pp. 627–642; and G. N. Mandelker and S. G. Rhee, "The Impact of the Degrees of Operating and Financial Leverage on Systematic Risk of Common Stock," *Journal of Financial and Quantitative Analysis* 19 (March 1984), pp. 45–57.

[18] See J. Y. Campbell and J. Mei, "Where Do Betas Come From? Asset Price Dynamics and the Sources of Systematic Risk," *Review of Financial Studies* 6 (Fall 1993), pp. 567–592. Cornell discusses the effect of duration on project risk in B. Cornell, "Risk, Duration and Capital Budgeting: New Evidence on Some Old Questions," *Journal of Business* 72 (April 1999), pp. 183–200.

- A geologist looking for oil worries about the risk of a dry hole.
- A pharmaceutical-company scientist worries about the risk that a new drug will have unacceptable side effects.
- A plant manager worries that new technology for a production line will fail to work, requiring expensive changes and repairs.
- A telecom CFO worries about the risk that a communications satellite will be damaged by space debris. (This was the fate of an Iridium satellite in 2009, when it collided with Russia's defunct Cosmos 2251. Both were blown to smithereens.)

Notice that these risks are all diversifiable. For example, the Iridium-Cosmos collision was definitely a zero-beta event. These hazards do not affect asset betas and should not affect the discount rate for the projects.

Sometimes financial managers increase discount rates in an attempt to offset these risks. This makes no sense. Diversifiable risks should not increase the cost of capital.

EXAMPLE 9.1   Allowing for Possible Bad Outcomes

Project Z will produce just one cash flow, forecasted at ₹1 million at year 1. It is regarded as average risk, suitable for discounting at a 10% company cost of capital:

$$PV = \frac{C_1}{1 + r} = \frac{1,000,000}{1.1} = ₹909,100$$

But now you discover that the company's engineers are behind schedule in developing the technology required for the project. They are confident it will work, but they admit to a small chance that it will not. You still see the *most likely* outcome as ₹1 million, but you also see some chance that project Z will generate *zero* cash flow next year.

Now the project's prospects are clouded by your new worry about technology. It must be worth less than the ₹909,100 you calculated before that worry arose. But how much less? There is *some* discount rate (10% plus a fudge factor) that will give the right value, but we do not know what that adjusted discount rate is.

We suggest you reconsider your original ₹1 million forecast for project Z's cash flow. Project cash flows are supposed to be *unbiased* forecasts that give due weight to all possible outcomes, favorable and unfavorable. Managers making unbiased forecasts are correct on average. Sometimes their forecasts will turn out high, other times low, but their errors will average out over many projects.

If you forecast a cash flow of ₹1 million for projects like Z, you will overestimate the average cash flow, because every now and then you will hit a zero. Those zeros should be "averaged in" to your forecasts.

For many projects, the most likely cash flow is also the unbiased forecast. If there are three possible outcomes with the probabilities shown below, the unbiased forecast is ₹1 million. (The unbiased forecast is the sum of the probability-weighted cash flows.)

Possible Cash Flow	Probability	Probability-Weighted Cash Flow	Unbiased Forecast
1.2	.25	.3	
1.0	.50	.5	1.0, or ₹1 million
.8	.25	.2	

This might describe the initial prospects of project Z. But if technological uncertainty introduces a 10% chance of a zero cash flow, the unbiased forecast could drop to ₹900,000:

Possible Cash Flow	Probability	Probability-Weighted Cash Flow	Unbiased Forecast
1.2	.225	.27	
1.0	.45	.45	.90, or ₹900,000
.8	.225	.18	
0	.10	.0	

The present value is

$$PV = \frac{.90}{1.1} = .818, \text{ or } ₹818,000$$

Managers often work out a range of possible outcomes for major projects, sometimes with explicit probabilities attached. We give more elaborate examples and further discussion in Chapter 10. But even when outcomes and probabilities are not explicitly written down, the manager can still consider the good and bad outcomes as well as the most likely one. When the bad outcomes outweigh the good, the cash-flow forecast should be reduced until balance is regained.

Step 1, then, is to do your best to make unbiased forecasts of a project's cash flows. Unbiased forecasts incorporate all risks, including diversifiable risks as well as market risks. Step 2 is to consider whether *diversified* investors would regard the project as more or less risky than the average project. In this step only market risks are relevant.

Avoid Fudge Factors in Discount Rates

Think back to our example of project Z, where we reduced forecasted cash flows from ₹1 million to ₹900,000 to account for a possible failure of technology. The project's PV was reduced from ₹909,100 to ₹818,000. You could have gotten the right answer by adding a fudge factor to the discount rate and discounting the original forecast of ₹1 million. But you have to think through the possible cash flows to get the fudge factor, and once you forecast the cash flows correctly, you don't need the fudge factor.

Fudge factors in discount rates are dangerous because they displace clear thinking about future cash flows. Here is an example.

EXAMPLE 9.2   **Correcting for Optimistic Forecasts**

The CFO of EZ² Corp. is disturbed to find that cash-flow forecasts for its investment projects are almost always optimistic. On average they are 10% too high. He therefore decides to compensate by adding 10% to EZ²'s WACC, increasing it from 12% to 22%.[19]

Suppose the CEO is right about the 10% upward bias in cash-flow forecasts. Can he just add 10% to the discount rate?

Project ZZ has level forecasted cash flows of $1,000 per year lasting for 15 years. The first two lines of Table 9.2 show these forecasts and their PVs discounted at 12%. Lines 3 and 4 show the corrected

---

[19] The CFO is ignoring Brealey, Myers, and Allen's Second Law, which we cover in the next chapter.

TABLE 9.2 The original cash-flow forecasts for the ZZ project (line 1) are too optimistic. The forecasts and PVs should be reduced by 10% (lines 3 and 4). But adding a 10% fudge factor to the discount rate reduces PVs by far more than 10% (line 6). The fudge factor overcorrects for bias and would penalize long-lived projects.

Year:	1	2	3	4	5	...	10	...	15
1. Original cash-flow forecast	₹1,000.00	₹1,000.00	₹1,000.00	₹1,000.00	₹1,000.00	...	₹1,000.00	...	₹1,000.00
2. PV at 12%	₹892.90	₹797.20	₹711.80	₹635.50	₹567.40	...	₹322.00	...	₹182.70
3. Corrected cash-flow forecast	₹900.00	₹900.00	₹900.00	₹900.00	₹900.00	...	₹900.00	...	₹900.00
4. PV at 12%	₹803.60	₹717.50	₹640.60	₹572.00	₹510.70	...	₹289.80	...	₹164.40
5. PV correction	−10.0%	−10.0%	−10.0%	−10.0%	−10.0%	...	−10.0%	...	−10.0%
6. Original forecast discounted at 22%	₹819.70	₹671.90	₹550.70	₹451.40	₹370.00	...	₹136.90	...	₹50.70
7. PV "correction" at 22% discount rate	−8.2%	−15.7%	−22.6%	−29.0%	−34.8%	...	−57.5%	...	−72.3%

forecasts, each reduced by 10%, and the corrected PVs, which are (no surprise) also reduced by 10% (line 5). Line 6 shows the PVs when the uncorrected forecasts are discounted at 22%. The final line 7 shows the percentage reduction in PVs at the 22% discount rate, compared to the unadjusted PVs in line 2.

Line 5 shows the correct adjustment for optimism (10%). Line 7 shows what happens when a 10% fudge factor is added to the discount rate. The effect on the first year's cash flow is a PV "haircut" of about 8%, 2% less than the CFO expected. But later present values are knocked down by much more than 10%, because the fudge factor is compounded in the 22% discount rate. By years 10 and 15, the PV haircuts are 57% and 72%, far more than the 10% bias that the CFO started with.

Did the CFO really think that bias accumulated as shown in line 7 of Table 9.2? We doubt that he ever asked that question. If he was right in the first place, and the true bias is 10%, then adding a 10% fudge factor to the discount rate understates PV. The fudge factor also makes long-lived projects look much worse than quick-payback projects.[20]

Discount Rates for International Projects

In this chapter we have concentrated on investments in India. In Chapter 27 we say more about investments made internationally. Here we simply warn against adding fudge factors to discount rates for projects in developing economies. Such fudge factors are too often seen in practice.

It's true that markets are more volatile in developing economies, but much of that risk is diversifiable for investors in the U.S., Europe, and other developed countries. It's also true that more things can go wrong for projects in developing economies, particularly in countries that are unstable politically.

---

[20] The optimistic bias could be worse for distant than near cash flows. If so, the CFO should make the time-pattern of bias explicit and adjust the cash-flow forecasts accordingly.

Expropriations happen. Sometimes governments default on their obligations to international investors. Thus it's especially important to think through the downside risks and to give them weight in cash-flow forecasts.

Some international projects are at least partially protected from these downsides. For example, an opportunistic government would gain little or nothing by expropriating the local IBM affiliate, because the affiliate would have little value without the IBM brand name, products, and customer relationships. A privately owned toll road would be a more tempting target, because the toll road would be relatively easy for the local government to maintain and operate.

9-4 CERTAINTY EQUIVALENTS—ANOTHER WAY TO ADJUST FOR RISK

In practical capital budgeting, a single risk-adjusted rate is used to discount all future cash flows. This assumes that project risk does not change over time, but remains constant year-in and year-out. We know that this cannot be strictly true, for the risks that companies are exposed to are constantly shifting. We are venturing here onto somewhat difficult ground, but there is a way to think about risk that can suggest a route through. It involves converting the expected cash flows to **certainty equivalents.** First we work through an example showing what certainty equivalents are. Then, as a reward for your investment, we use certainty equivalents to uncover what you are really assuming when you discount a series of future cash flows at a single risk-adjusted discount rate. We also value a project where risk changes over time and ordinary discounting fails. Your investment will be rewarded still more when we cover options in Chapters 20 and 21 and forward and futures pricing in Chapter 26. Option-pricing formulas discount certainty equivalents. Forward and futures prices *are* certainty equivalents.

Valuation by Certainty Equivalents

Think back to the simple real estate investment that we used in Chapter 2 to introduce the concept of present value. You are considering construction of an office building that you plan to sell after one year for ₹420,000. That cash flow is uncertain with the same risk as the market, so $\beta = 1$. Given $r_f = 5\%$ and $r_m - r_f = 7\%$, you discount at a risk-adjusted discount rate of $5 + 1 \times 7 = 12\%$ rather than the 5% risk-free rate of interest. This gives a present value of $420,000/1.12 = ₹375,000$.

Suppose a real estate company now approaches and offers to fix the price at which it will buy the building from you at the end of the year. This guarantee would remove any uncertainty about the payoff on your investment. So you would accept a lower figure than the uncertain payoff of ₹420,000. But how much less? If the building has a present value of ₹375,000 and the interest rate is 5%, then

$$PV = \frac{\text{Certain cash flow}}{1.05} = 375,000$$

$$\text{Certain cash flow} = ₹393,750$$

In other words, a certain cash flow of ₹393,750 has exactly the same present value as an expected but uncertain cash flow of $420,000. The cash flow of ₹393,750 is therefore known as the *certainty-equivalent cash flow.* To compensate for both the delayed payoff and the uncertainty in real estate prices, you need a return of $420,000 - 375,000 = ₹45,000$. One part of this difference compensates for the time value of money. The other part $(₹420,000 - 393,750 = ₹26,250)$ is a markdown or haircut to compensate for the risk attached to the forecasted cash flow of ₹420,000.

Our example illustrates two ways to value a risky cash flow:

Method 1: Discount the risky cash flow at a *risk-adjusted discount rate* r that is greater than r_f.[21] The risk-adjusted discount rate adjusts for both time and risk. This is illustrated by the clockwise route in Figure 9.3.

Method 2: Find the certainty-equivalent cash flow and discount at the risk-free interest rate r_f. When you use this method, you need to ask, What is the smallest *certain* payoff for which I would exchange the risky cash flow? This is called the *certainty equivalent,* denoted by CEQ. Since CEQ is the value equivalent of a safe cash flow, it is discounted at the risk-free rate. The certainty-equivalent method makes *separate* adjustments for risk and time. This is illustrated by the counterclockwise route in Figure 9.3.

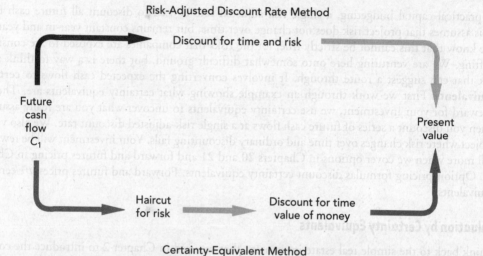

FIGURE 9.3

Two ways to calculate present value. "Haircut for risk" is financial slang referring to the reduction of the cash flow from its forecasted value to its certainty equivalent.

We now have two identical expressions for the PV of a cash flow at period 1:[22]

$$PV = \frac{C_1}{1 + r} = \frac{CEQ_1}{1 + r_f}$$

For cash flows two, three, or t years away,

$$PV = \frac{C_t}{(1 + r)^t} = \frac{CEQ_t}{(1 + r_f)^t}$$

---

[21] The discount rate r can be less than r_f for assets with negative betas. But actual betas are almost always positive.

[22] CEQ_1 can be calculated directly from the capital asset pricing model. The certainty-equivalent form of the CAPM states that the certainty-equivalent value of the cash flow C_1 is $C_1 - \lambda \, cov(\tilde{C}_1, \tilde{r}_m)$. Cov$(\tilde{C}_1, \tilde{r}_m)$ is the covariance between the uncertain cash flow, and the return on the market, $\tilde{r}_m$. Lambda, λ, is a measure of the market price of risk. It is defined as $(r_m - r_f)/\sigma_m^2$. For example, if $r_m - r_f = .08$ and the standard deviation of market returns is $\sigma_m = .20$, then lambda $= .08/.20^2 = 2$. We show on our Web site (**www.mhhe.com/bmam10e**) how the CAPM formula can be restated in this certainty-equivalent form.

When to Use a Single Risk-Adjusted Discount Rate for Long-Lived Assets

We are now in a position to examine what is implied when a constant risk-adjusted discount rate is used to calculate a present value.

Consider two simple projects. Project A is expected to produce a cash flow of ₹100 million for each of three years. The risk-free interest rate is 6%, the market risk premium is 8%, and project A's beta is .75. You therefore calculate A's opportunity cost of capital as follows:

$$r = r_f + \beta(r_m - r_f)$$
$$= 6 + .75(8) = 12\%$$

Discounting at 12% gives the following present value for each cash flow:

Project A		
Year	Cash Flow	PV at 12%
1	100	89.3
2	100	79.7
3	100	71.2
	Total PV	240.2

Now compare these figures with the cash flows of project B. Notice that B's cash flows are lower than A's; but B's flows are safe, and therefore they are discounted at the risk-free interest rate. The *present value* of each year's cash flow is identical for the two projects.

Project B		
Year	Cash Flow	PV at 6%
1	94.6	89.3
2	89.6	79.7
3	84.8	71.2
	Total PV	240.2

In year 1 project A has a risky cash flow of 100. This has the same PV as the safe cash flow of 94.6 from project B. Therefore 94.6 is the certainty equivalent of 100. Since the two cash flows have the same PV, investors must be willing to give up $100 - 94.6 = 5.4$ in expected year-1 income in order to get rid of the uncertainty.

In year 2 project A has a risky cash flow of 100, and B has a safe cash flow of 89.6. Again both flows have the same PV. Thus, to eliminate the uncertainty in year 2, investors are prepared to give up $100 - 89.6 = 10.4$ of future income. To eliminate uncertainty in year 3, they are willing to give up $100 - 84.8 = 15.2$ of future income.

To value project A, you discounted each cash flow at the same risk-adjusted discount rate of 12%. Now you can see what is implied when you did that. By using a constant rate, you effectively made a larger deduction for risk from the later cash flows:

Year	Forecasted Cash Flow for Project A	Certainty-Equivalent Cash Flow	Deduction for Risk
1	100	94.6	5.4
2	100	89.6	10.4
3	100	84.8	15.2

The second cash flow is riskier than the first because it is exposed to two years of market risk. The third cash flow is riskier still because it is exposed to three years of market risk. This increased risk is reflected in the certainty equivalents that decline by a constant proportion each period.

Therefore, use of a constant risk-adjusted discount rate for a stream of cash flows assumes that risk accumulates at a constant rate as you look farther out into the future.

A Common Mistake

You sometimes hear people say that because distant cash flows are riskier, they should be discounted at a higher rate than earlier cash flows. That is quite wrong: We have just seen that using the same risk-adjusted discount rate for each year's cash flow implies a larger deduction for risk from the later cash flows. The reason is that the discount rate compensates for the risk borne *per period*. The more distant the cash flows, the greater the number of periods and the larger the *total* risk adjustment.

When You Cannot Use a Single Risk-Adjusted Discount Rate for Long-Lived Assets

Sometimes you will encounter problems where the use of a single risk-adjusted discount rate will get you into trouble. For example, later in the book we look at how options are valued. Because an option's risk is continually changing, the certainty-equivalent method needs to be used.

Here is a disguised, simplified, and somewhat exaggerated version of an actual project proposal that one of the authors was asked to analyze. The scientists at Vegetron have come up with an electric mop, and the firm is ready to go ahead with pilot production and test marketing. The preliminary phase will take one year and cost ₹125,000. Management feels that there is only a 50% chance that pilot production and market tests will be successful. If they are, then Vegetron will build a ₹1 million plant that would generate an expected annual cash flow in perpetuity of ₹250,000 a year after taxes. If they are not successful, the project will have to be dropped.

The expected cash flows (in thousands of dollars) are

$$C_0 = -125$$
$$C_1 = 50\% \text{ chance of } -1{,}000 \text{ and } 50\% \text{ chance of } 0$$
$$= .5(-1{,}000) + .5(0) = -500$$
$$C_t \text{ for } t = 2,3, \ldots = 50\% \text{ chance of } 250 \text{ and } 50\% \text{ chance of } 0$$
$$= .5(250) + .5(0) = 125$$

Management has little experience with consumer products and considers this a project of extremely high risk.[23] Therefore management discounts the cash flows at 25%, rather than at Vegetron's normal 10% standard:

$$\text{NPV} = -125 - \frac{500}{1.25} + \sum_{t=2}^{\infty} \frac{125}{(1.25)^t} = -125, \text{ or } -₹125{,}000$$

---

[23] We will assume that they mean high *market risk* and that the difference between 25% and 10% is *not* a fudge factor introduced to offset optimistic cash-flow forecasts.

Useful Spreadsheet Functions

Estimating Stock and Market Risk

Spreadsheets such as Excel have some built-in statistical functions that are useful for calculating risk measures. You can find these functions by pressing *fx* on the Excel toolbar. If you then click on the function that you wish to use, Excel will ask you for the inputs that it needs. At the bottom left of the function box there is a Help facility with an example of how the function is used.

Here is a list of useful functions for estimating stock and market risk. You can enter the inputs for all these functions as numbers or as the addresses of cells that contain the numbers.

1. **VARP** and **STDEVP**: Calculate variance and standard deviation of a series of numbers, as shown in Section 7-2.
2. **VAR** and **STDEV**: Footnote 15 on page 154 noted that when variance is estimated from a sample of observations (the usual case), a correction should be made for the loss of a degree of freedom. VAR and STDEV provide the corrected measures. For any large sample VAR and VARP will be similar.
3. **SLOPE**: Useful for calculating the beta of a stock or portfolio.
4. **CORREL**: Useful for calculating the correlation between the returns on any two investments.
5. **RSQ**: R-squared is the square of the correlation coefficient and is useful for measuring the proportion of the variance of a stock's returns that can be explained by the market.
6. **AVERAGE**: Calculates the average of any series of numbers.

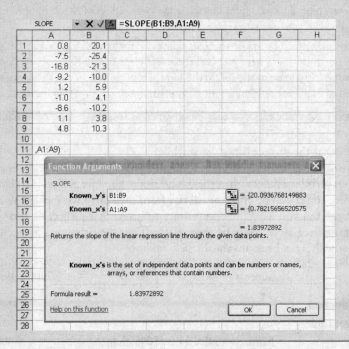

If, say, you need to know the standard error of your estimate of beta, you can obtain more detailed statistics by going to the *Tools* menu and clicking on *Data Analysis* and then on *Regression*.

Spreadsheet Questions

The following questions provide opportunities to practice each of the Excel functions.

1. (VAR and STDEV) Choose two well-known stocks and download the latest 61 months of adjusted prices from **finance.yahoo.com**. Calculate the monthly returns for each stock. Now find the variance and standard deviation of the returns for each stock by using VAR and STDEV. Annualize the variance by multiplying by 12 and the standard deviation by multiplying by the square root of 12.

2. (AVERAGE, VAR, and STDEV) Now calculate the annualized variance and standard deviation for a portfolio that each month has equal holdings in the two stocks. Is the result more or less than the average of the standard deviations of the two stocks? Why?

3. (SLOPE) Download the Standard & Poor's index for the same period (its symbol is ^GSPC). Find the beta of each stock and of the portfolio. (*Note:* You need to enter the stock returns as the Y-values and market returns as the X-values.) Is the beta of the portfolio more or less than the average of the betas of the two stocks?

4. (CORREL) Calculate the correlation between the returns on the two stocks. Use this measure and your earlier estimates of each stock's variance to calculate the variance of a portfolio that is evenly divided between the two stocks. (You may need to reread Section 7-3 to refresh your memory of how to do this.) Check that you get the same answer as when you calculated the portfolio variance directly.

5. (RSQ) For each of the two stocks calculate the proportion of the variance explained by the market index. Do the results square with your intuition?

6. Use the *Regression* facility under the *Data Analysis* menu to calculate the beta of each stock and of the portfolio (beta here is called the coefficient of the X-variable). Look at the standard error of the estimate in the cell to the right. How confident can you be of your estimates of the betas of each stock? How about your estimate of the portfolio beta?

This seems to show that the project is not worthwhile.

Management's analysis is open to criticism if the first year's experiment resolves a high proportion of the risk. If the test phase is a failure, then there is no risk at all—the project is *certain* to be worthless. If it is a success, there could well be only normal risk from then on. That means there is a 50% chance that in one year Vegetron will have the opportunity to invest in a project of *normal* risk, for which the *normal* discount rate of 10% would be appropriate. Thus the firm has a 50% chance to invest ₹1 million in a project with a net present value of ₹1.5 million:

$$\text{Success} \to \text{NPV} = -1{,}000 + \frac{250}{.10} = +1{,}500 \text{ (50\% chance)}$$

Pilot production and market tests

$$\text{Failure} \to \text{NPV} = 0 \text{ (50\% chance)}$$

Thus we could view the project as offering an expected payoff of $.5(1,500) + .5(0) = 750$, or ₹750,000, at $t = 1$ on a ₹125,000 investment at $t = 0$. Of course, the certainty equivalent of the payoff is less than ₹750,000, but the difference would have to be very large to justify rejecting the project. For example, if the certainty equivalent is half the forecasted cash flow (an extremely large cash-flow haircut) and the risk-free rate is 7%, the project is worth ₹225,500:

$$NPV = C_0 + \frac{CEQ_1}{1 + r}$$

$$= -125 + \frac{.5(750)}{1.07} = 225.5, \text{ or } ₹225,500$$

This is not bad for a ₹125,000 investment—and quite a change from the negative-NPV that management got by discounting all future cash flows at 25%.

SUMMARY

In Chapter 8 we set out the basic principles for valuing risky assets. This chapter shows you how to apply those principles when valuing capital investment projects.

Suppose the project has the same market risk as the company's existing assets. In this case, the project cash flows can be discounted at the *company cost of capital*. The company cost of capital is the rate of return that investors require on a portfolio of all of the company's outstanding debt and equity. It is usually calculated as an after-tax *weighted-average cost of capital* (after-tax WACC), that is, as the weighted average of the after-tax cost of debt and the cost of equity. The weights are the relative market values of debt and equity. The cost of debt is calculated after tax because interest is a tax-deductible expense.

The hardest part of calculating the after-tax WACC is estimation of the cost of equity. Most large, public corporations use the capital asset pricing model (CAPM) to do this. They generally estimate the firm's equity beta from past rates of return for the firm's common stock and for the market, and they check their estimate against the average beta of similar firms.

The after-tax WACC is the correct discount rate for projects that have the same market risk as the company's existing business. Many firms, however, use the after-tax WACC as the discount rate for all projects. This is a dangerous procedure. If the procedure is followed strictly, the firm will accept too many high-risk projects and reject too many low-risk projects. It is *project* risk that counts: the true cost of capital depends on the use to which the capital is put.

Managers, therefore, need to understand why a particular project may have above- or below-average risk. You can often identify the characteristics of a high- or low-beta project even when the beta cannot be estimated directly. For example, you can figure out how much the project's cash flows are affected by the performance of the entire economy. Cyclical projects are generally high-beta projects. You can also look at operating leverage. Fixed production costs increase beta.

Don't be fooled by diversifiable risk. Diversifiable risks do not affect asset betas or the cost of capital, but the possibility of bad outcomes should be incorporated in the cash-flow forecasts. Also be careful not to offset worries about a project's future performance by adding a fudge factor to the discount rate. Fudge factors don't work, and they may seriously undervalue long-lived projects.

There is one more fence to jump. Most projects produce cash flows for several years. Firms generally use the same risk-adjusted rate to discount each of these cash flows. When they do this, they are implicitly assuming that cumulative risk increases at a constant rate as you look further into the future. That assumption is usually reasonable. It is precisely true when the project's future beta will be constant, that is, when risk *per period* is constant.

But exceptions sometimes prove the rule. Be on the alert for projects where risk clearly does not increase steadily. In these cases, you should break the project into segments within which the same discount rate can be reasonably used. Or you should use the certainty-equivalent version of the DCF model, which allows separate risk adjustments to each period's cash flow.

The nearby box (on page 251) provides useful spreadsheet functions for estimating stock and market risk.

FURTHER READING

Michael Brennan provides a useful, but quite difficult, survey of the issues covered in this chapter:

M. J. Brennan, "Corporate Investment Policy," *Handbook of the Economics of Finance, Volume 1A, Corporate Finance,* eds. G. M. Constantinides, M. Harris, and R. M. Stulz (Amsterdam: Elsevier BV, 2003).

PROBLEM SETS

BASIC

1. Suppose a firm uses its company cost of capital to evaluate all projects. Will it underestimate or overestimate the value of high-risk projects?

2. A company is 40% financed by risk-free debt. The interest rate is 10%, the expected market risk premium is 8%, and the beta of the company's common stock is .5. What is the company cost of capital? What is the after-tax WACC, assuming that the company pays tax at a 35% rate?

3. Look back to the top-right panel of Figure 9.2. What proportion of HUL's returns was explained by market movements? What proportion was unique or diversifiable risk? How does the unique risk show up in the plot? What is the range of possible errors in the beta estimate?

4. Define the following terms:
   a. Cost of debt
   b. Cost of equity
   c. After-tax WACC
   d. Equity beta
   e. Asset beta
   f. Pure-play comparable
   g. Certainty equivalent

5. EZCUBE Corp. is 50% financed with long-term bonds and 50% with common equity. The debt securities have a beta of .15. The company's equity beta is 1.25. What is EZCUBE's asset beta?

6. Many investment projects are exposed to diversifiable risks. What does "diversifiable" mean in this context? How should diversifiable risks be accounted for in project valuation? Should they be ignored completely?

7. John Barleycorn estimates his firm's after-tax WACC at only 8%. Nevertheless he sets a 15% companywide discount rate to offset the optimistic biases of project sponsors and to impose "discipline" on the capital-budgeting process. Suppose Mr. Barleycorn is correct about the project sponsors, who are in fact optimistic by 7% on average. Will the increase in the discount rate from 8% to 15% offset the bias?

8. Which of these projects is likely to have the higher asset beta, other things equal? Why?
   a. The sales force for project A is paid a fixed annual salary. Project B's sales force is paid by commissions only.
   b. Project C is a first-class-only airline. Project D is a well-established line of breakfast cereals.

9. True or false?
   a. The company cost of capital is the correct discount rate for all projects, because the high risks of some projects are offset by the low risk of other projects.
   b. Distant cash flows are riskier than near-term cash flows. Therefore long-term projects require higher risk-adjusted discount rates.
   c. Adding fudge factors to discount rates undervalues long-lived projects compared with quick-payoff projects.

10. A project has a forecasted cash flow of ₹110 in year 1 and ₹121 in year 2. The interest rate is 5%, the estimated risk premium on the market is 10%, and the project has a beta of .5. If you use a constant risk-adjusted discount rate, what is
    a. The PV of the project?
    b. The certainty-equivalent cash flow in year 1 and year 2?
    c. The ratio of the certainty-equivalent cash flows to the expected cash flows in years 1 and 2?

INTERMEDIATE

11. The total market value of the common stock of the Okefenokee Real Estate Company is $6 million, and the total value of its debt is $4 million. The treasurer estimates that the beta of the stock is currently 1.5 and that the expected risk premium on the market is 6%. The Treasury bill rate is 4%. Assume for simplicity that Okefenokee debt is risk-free and the company does not pay tax.
    a. What is the required return on Okefenokee stock?
    b. Estimate the company cost of capital.
    c. What is the discount rate for an expansion of the company's present business?
    d. Suppose the company wants to diversify into the manufacture of rose-colored spectacles. The beta of unleveraged optical manufacturers is 1.2. Estimate the required return on Okefenokee's new venture.

12. Nero Violins has the following capital structure:

Security	Beta	Total Market Value (₹ millions)
Debt	0	₹100
Preferred stock	.20	40
Common stock	1.20	299

   a. What is the firm's asset beta? (*Hint:* What is the beta of a portfolio of all the firm's securities?)
   b. Assume that the CAPM is correct. What discount rate should Nero set for investments that expand the scale of its operations without changing its asset beta? Assume a risk-free interest rate of 5% and a market risk premium of 6%.

13. The following table shows estimates of the risk of two well-known Canadian stocks:

	Standard Deviation, %	R^2	Beta	Standard Error of Beta
Toronto Dominion Bank	25	.25	.82	.18
Canadian Pacific	28	.30	1.04	.20

  a. What proportion of each stock's risk was market risk, and what proportion was specific risk?
  b. What is the variance of Toronto Dominion? What is the specific variance?
  c. What is the confidence interval on Canadian Pacific's beta?
  d. If the CAPM is correct, what is the expected return on Toronto Dominion? Assume a risk-free interest rate of 5% and an expected market return of 12%.
  e. Suppose that next year the market provides a zero return. Knowing this, what return would you expect from Toronto Dominion?

14. You are given the following information for Golden Fleece Financial:

Long-term debt outstanding:	₹300,000
Current yield to maturity (r_{debt}):	8%
Number of shares of common stock:	10,000
Price per share:	₹50
Book value per share:	₹25
Expected rate of return on stock (r_{equity}):	15%

  Calculate Golden Fleece's company cost of capital. Ignore taxes.

15. Look again at Table 9.1. This time we will concentrate on Kingfisher Airlines.
  a. Calculate Kingfisher Airlines' cost of equity from the CAPM using its own beta estimate and the industry beta estimate. How different are your answers? Assume a risk-free rate of return of 6 percent and a market risk premium of 10 percent.
  b. Can you be confident that Kingfisher Airlines' true beta is *not* the industry beta?
  c. Under what circumstances might you advise Kingfisher Airlines to calculate its cost of equity based on its own beta estimate?

16. What types of firms need to estimate industry asset betas? How would such a firm make the estimate? Describe the process step by step.

17. Binomial Tree Farm's financing includes ₹5 million of bank loans. Its common equity is shown in Binomial's *Annual Report* at ₹6.67 million. It has 500,000 shares of common stock outstanding, which trade on the Wichita Stock Exchange at ₹18 per share. What debt ratio should Binomial use to calculate its WACC or asset beta? Explain.

18. You run a perpetual encabulator machine, which generates revenues averaging $20 million per year. Raw material costs are 50% of revenues. These costs are variable—they are always proportional to revenues. There are no other operating costs. The cost of capital is 9%. Your firm's long-term borrowing rate is 6%.

  Now you are approached by Studebaker Capital Corp., which proposes a fixed-price contract to supply raw materials at $10 million per year for 10 years.

  a. What happens to the operating leverage and business risk of the encabulator machine if you agree to this fixed-price contract?

b. Calculate the present value of the encabulator machine with and without the fixed-price contract.

19. Mom and Pop Groceries has just dispatched a year's supply of groceries to the government of the Central Antarctic Republic. Payment of $250,000 will be made one year hence after the shipment arrives by snow train. Unfortunately there is a good chance of a coup d'état, in which case the new government will not pay. Mom and Pop's controller therefore decides to discount the payment at 40%, rather than at the company's 12% cost of capital.
    a. What's wrong with using a 40% rate to offset political risk?
    b. How much is the $250,000 payment really worth if the odds of a coup d'état are 25%?

20. An oil company is drilling a series of new wells on the perimeter of a producing oil field. About 20% of the new wells will be dry holes. Even if a new well strikes oil, there is still uncertainty about the amount of oil produced: 40% of new wells that strike oil produce only 1,000 barrels a day; 60% produce 5,000 barrels per day.
    a. Forecast the annual cash revenues from a new perimeter well. Use a future oil price of $50 per barrel.
    b. A geologist proposes to discount the cash flows of the new wells at 30% to offset the risk of dry holes. The oil company's normal cost of capital is 10%. Does this proposal make sense? Briefly explain why or why not.

21. A project has the following forecasted cash flows:

Cash Flows, ₹ Thousands			
C_0	C_1	C_2	C_3
−100	+40	+60	+50

    The estimated project beta is 1.5. The market return r_m is 16%, and the risk-free rate r_f is 7%.
    a. Estimate the opportunity cost of capital and the project's PV (using the same rate to discount each cash flow).
    b. What are the certainty-equivalent cash flows in each year?
    c. What is the ratio of the certainty-equivalent cash flow to the expected cash flow in each year?
    d. Explain why this ratio declines.

22. The McGregor Whisky Company is proposing to market diet scotch. The product will first be test-marketed for two years in southern California at an initial cost of ₹500,000. This test launch is not expected to produce any profits but should reveal consumer preferences. There is a 60% chance that demand will be satisfactory. In this case McGregor will spend ₹5 million to launch the scotch nationwide and will receive an expected annual profit of ₹700,000 in perpetuity. If demand is not satisfactory, diet scotch will be withdrawn.

    Once consumer preferences are known, the product will be subject to an average degree of risk, and, therefore, McGregor requires a return of 12% on its investment. However, the initial test-market phase is viewed as much riskier, and McGregor demands a return of 20% on this initial expenditure.

    What is the NPV of the diet scotch project?

CHALLENGE

23. Suppose you are valuing a future stream of high-risk (high-beta) cash *outflows*. High risk means a high discount rate. But the higher the discount rate, the less the present value. This seems to say that the higher the risk of cash outflows, the less you should worry about them! Can that be right? Should the sign of the cash flow affect the appropriate discount rate? Explain.

24. An oil company executive is considering investing $10 million in one or both of two wells: well 1 is expected to produce oil worth $3 million a year for 10 years; well 2 is expected to produce $2 million for 15 years. These are *real* (inflation-adjusted) cash flows.

    The beta for *producing wells* is .9. The market risk premium is 8%, the nominal risk-free interest rate is 6%, and expected inflation is 4%.

    The two wells are intended to develop a previously discovered oil field. Unfortunately there is still a 20% chance of a dry hole in each case. A dry hole means zero cash flows and a complete loss of the $10 million investment.

    Ignore taxes and make further assumptions as necessary.
    a. What is the correct real discount rate for cash flows from developed wells?
    b. The oil company executive proposes to add 20 percentage points to the real discount rate to offset the risk of a dry hole. Calculate the NPV of each well with this adjusted discount rate.
    c. What do *you* say the NPVs of the two wells are?
    d. Is there any *single* fudge factor that could be added to the discount rate for developed wells that would yield the correct NPV for both wells? Explain.

1. Look again at the companies listed in Table 8.2. Download the daily closing prices of the stocks for the last four years from www.nseindia.com. Download the daily closing level of Nifty from the website for the same period. Estimate monthly returns from the data. From the respective companies' websites obtain data on dividend paid, bonus issue and stock split. Estimate the adjusted monthly returns from this. What percentage of the variance of each company's return is explained by the index? Use the excel function RSQ, which calculates R^2.
2. Identify a sample of chemical companies listed in India. Obtain the daily closing prices data from www.nseindia.com.
    a. Estimate beta and R^2 for each company by using the monthly returns data. The Excel functions are SLOPE and RSQ.
    b. Calculate an industry beta. Here is the best procedure: First calculate the monthly returns on an equally weighted portfolio of the stocks in your sample. Then calculate the industry beta using these portfolio returns. How does the R^2 of this portfolio compare to the average R^2 of the individual stocks?
    c. Use the CAPM to calculate an average cost of equity (r_{equity}) for the chemicals industry. Use current interest rates (from www.fimmda.org) and a reasonable estimate of the market risk premium.

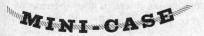

THE JONES FAMILY, INCORPORATED

The Scene: Early evening in an ordinary family room in Manhattan. Modern furniture, with old copies of *The Wall Street Journal* and the *Financial Times* scattered around. Autographed photos of Alan Greenspan and George Soros are prominently displayed. A picture window reveals a distant view of lights on the Hudson River. John Jones sits at a computer terminal, glumly sipping a glass of chardonnay and putting on a carry trade in Japanese yen over the Internet. His wife Marsha enters.

Marsha: Hi, honey. Glad to be home. Lousy day on the trading floor, though. Dullsville. No volume. But I did manage to hedge next year's production from our copper mine. I couldn't get a good quote on the right package of futures contracts, so I arranged a commodity swap.

John doesn't reply.

Marsha: John, what's wrong? Have you been selling yen again? That's been a losing trade for weeks.

John: Well, yes. I shouldn't have gone to Goldman Sachs's foreign exchange brunch. But I've got to get out of the house somehow. I'm cooped up here all day calculating covariances and efficient risk-return trade-offs while you're out trading commodity futures. You get all the glamour and excitement.

Marsha: Don't worry, dear, it will be over soon. We only recalculate our most efficient common stock portfolio once a quarter. Then you can go back to leveraged leases.

John: You trade, and I do all the worrying. Now there's a rumor that our leasing company is going to get a hostile takeover bid. I knew the debt ratio was too low, and you forgot to put on the poison pill. And now you've made a negative-NPV investment!

Marsha: What investment?

John: That wildcat oil well. Another well in that old Sourdough field. It's going to cost $5 million! Is there any oil down there?

Marsha: That Sourdough field has been good to us, John. Where do you think we got the capital for your yen trades? I bet we'll find oil. Our geologists say there's only a 30% chance of a dry hole.

John: Even if we hit oil, I bet we'll only get 150 barrels of crude oil per day.

Marsha: That's 150 barrels day in, day out. There are 365 days in a year, dear.

John and Marsha's teenage son Johnny bursts into the room.

Johnny: Hi, Dad! Hi, Mom! Guess what? I've made the junior varsity derivatives team! That means I can go on the field trip to the Chicago Board Options Exchange. (*Pauses.*) What's wrong?

John: Your mother has made another negative-NPV investment. A wildcat oil well, way up on the North Slope of Alaska.

Johnny: That's OK, Dad. Mom told me about it. I was going to do an NPV calculation yesterday, but I had to finish calculating the junk-bond default probabilities for my corporate finance homework. (*Grabs a financial calculator from his backpack.*) Let's see: 150 barrels a day times 365 days per year times $50 per barrel when delivered in Los Angeles . . . that's $2.7 million per year.

John: That's $2.7 million *next* year, assuming that we find any oil at all. The production will start declining by 5% every year. And we still have to pay $10 per barrel in pipeline and tanker charges to ship the oil from the North Slope to Los Angeles. We've got some serious operating leverage here.

Marsha: On the other hand, our energy consultants project increasing oil prices. If they increase with inflation, price per barrel should increase by roughly 2.5% per year. The wells ought to be able to keep pumping for at least 15 years.

Johnny: I'll calculate NPV after I finish with the default probabilities. The interest rate is 6%. Is it OK if I work with the beta of .8 and our usual figure of 7% for the market risk premium?

Marsha: I guess so, Johnny. But I am concerned about the fixed shipping costs.

John: (*Takes a deep breath and stands up.*) Anyway, how about a nice family dinner? I've reserved our usual table at the Four Seasons.

Everyone exits.

Announcer: Is the wildcat well really negative-NPV? Will John and Marsha have to fight a hostile takeover? Will Johnny's derivatives team use Black–Scholes or the binomial method? Find out in the next episode of The Jones Family, Incorporated.

You may not aspire to the Jones family's way of life, but you will learn about all their activities, from futures contracts to binomial option pricing, later in this book. Meanwhile, you may wish to replicate Johnny's NPV analysis.

Questions

1. Calculate the NPV of the wildcat oil well, taking account of the probability of a dry hole, the shipping costs, the decline in production, and the forecasted increase in oil prices. How long does production have to continue for the well to be a positive-NPV investment? Ignore taxes and other possible complications.

2. Now consider operating leverage. How should the shipping costs be valued, assuming that output is known and the costs are fixed? How would your answer change if the shipping costs were proportional to output? Assume that unexpected fluctuations in output are zero-beta and diversifiable. (*Hint:* The Jones's oil company has an excellent credit rating. Its long-term borrowing rate is only 7%.)

10

PROJECT ANALYSIS

Having read our earlier chapters on capital budgeting, you may have concluded that the choice of which projects to accept or reject is a simple one. You just need to draw up a set of cash-flow forecasts, choose the right discount rate, and crank out net present value. But finding projects that create value for the shareholders can never be reduced to a mechanical exercise. We therefore devote the next three chapters to ways in which companies can stack the odds in their favor when making investment decisions.

Investment proposals may emerge from many different parts of the organization. So companies need procedures to ensure that every project is assessed consistently. Our first task in this chapter is to review how firms develop plans and budgets for capital investments, how they authorize specific projects, and how they check whether projects perform as promised.

When managers are presented with investment proposals, they do not accept the cash flow forecasts at face value. Instead, they try to understand what makes a project tick and what could go wrong with it. Remember Murphy's law, "if anything can go wrong, it will," and O'Reilly's corollary, "at the worst possible time."

Once you know what makes a project tick, you may be able to reconfigure it to improve its chance of success. And if you understand why the venture could fail, you can decide whether it is worth trying to rule out the possible causes of failure. Maybe further expenditure on market research would clear up those doubts about acceptance by consumers, maybe another drill hole would give you a better idea of the size of the ore body, and maybe some further work on the test bed would confirm the durability of those welds.

If the project really has a negative NPV, the sooner you can identify it, the better. And even if you decide that it is worth going ahead without further analysis, you do not want to be caught by surprise if things go wrong later. You want to know the danger signals and the actions that you might take.

Our second task in this chapter is to show how managers use *sensitivity analysis, break-even analysis,* and *Monte Carlo simulation* to identify the crucial assumptions in investment proposals and to explore what can go wrong. There is no magic in these techniques, just computer-assisted common sense. You do not need a license to use them.

Discounted-cash-flow analysis commonly assumes that companies hold assets passively, and it ignores the opportunities to expand the project if it is successful or to bail out if it is not. However, wise managers recognize these opportunities when considering whether to invest. They look for ways to capitalize on success and to reduce the costs of failure, and they are prepared to pay up for projects that give them this flexibility. Opportunities to modify projects as the future unfolds are known as *real options*. In the final section of the chapter we describe several important real options, and we show how to use *decision trees* to set out the possible future choices.

10-1 THE CAPITAL INVESTMENT PROCESS

Senior management needs some forewarning of future investment outlays. So for most large firms, the investment process starts with the preparation of an annual **capital budget,** which is a list of investment projects planned for the coming year.

Most firms let project proposals bubble up from plants for review by divisional management and then from divisions for review by senior management and their planning staff. Of course middle managers cannot identify all worthwhile projects. For example, the managers of plants A and B cannot be expected to see the potential economies of closing their plants and consolidating production at a new plant C. Divisional managers would propose plant C. But the managers of divisions 1 and 2 may not be eager to give up their own computers to a corporation-wide information system. That proposal would come from senior management, for example, the company's chief information officer.

Inconsistent assumptions often creep into expenditure plans. For example, suppose the manager of your furniture division is bullish on housing starts, but the manager of your appliance division is bearish. The furniture division may push for a major investment in new facilities, while the appliance division may propose a plan for retrenchment. It would be better if both managers could agree on a common estimate of housing starts and base their investment proposals on it. That is why many firms begin the capital budgeting process by establishing consensus forecasts of economic indicators, such as inflation and growth in national income, as well as forecasts of particular items that are important to the firm's business, such as housing starts or the prices of raw materials. These forecasts are then used as the basis for the capital budget.

Preparation of the capital budget is not a rigid, bureaucratic exercise. There is plenty of give-and-take and back-and-forth. Divisional managers negotiate with plant managers and fine-tune the division's list of projects. The final capital budget must also reflect the corporation's strategic planning. Strategic planning takes a top-down view of the company. It attempts to identify businesses where the company has a competitive advantage. It also attempts to identify businesses that should be sold or allowed to run down.

A firm's capital investment choices should reflect both bottom-up and top-down views of the business—capital budgeting and strategic planning, respectively. Plant and division managers, who do most of the work in bottom-up capital budgeting, may not see the forest for the trees. Strategic planners may have a mistaken view of the forest because they do not look at the trees one by one. (We return to the links between capital budgeting and corporate strategy in the next chapter.)

Project Authorizations—and the Problem of Biased Forecasts

Once the capital budget has been approved by top management and the board of directors, it is the official plan for the ensuing year. However, it is not the final sign-off for specific projects. Most companies require **appropriation requests** for each proposal. These requests include detailed forecasts, discounted-cash-flow analyses, and back-up information.

Many investment projects carry a high price tag; they also determine the shape of the firm's business 10 or 20 years in the future. Hence final approval of appropriation requests tends to be reserved for top management. Companies set ceilings on the size of projects that divisional managers can authorize. Often these ceilings are surprisingly low. For example, a large company, investing ₹500 crore per year, might require top management to approve all projects over ₹2,00,000.

This centralized decision making brings its problems: Senior management can't process detailed information about hundreds of projects and must rely on forecasts put together by project sponsors. A smart manager quickly learns to worry whether these forecasts are realistic.

Even when the forecasts are not consciously inflated, errors creep in. For example, most people tend to be overconfident when they forecast. Events they think are almost certain to occur may actually happen only 80% of the time, and events they believe are impossible may happen 20% of the time. Therefore project risks are understated. Anyone who is keen to get a project accepted is also likely to look on the bright side when forecasting the project's cash flows. Such overoptimism seems to be a common feature in financial forecasts. Overoptimism afflicts governments too, probably more than private businesses. How often have you heard of a new dam, highway, or military aircraft that actually cost *less* than was originally forecasted?

You can expect plant or divisional managers to look on the bright side when putting forward investment proposals. That is not altogether bad. Psychologists stress that optimism and confidence are likely to increase effort, commitment, and persistence. The problem is that hundreds of appropriation requests may reach senior management each year, all essentially sales documents presented by united fronts and designed to persuade. Alternative schemes have been filtered out at earlier stages.

It is probably impossible to eliminate bias completely, but senior managers should take care not to encourage it. For example, if managers believe that success depends on having the largest division rather than the most profitable one, they will propose large expansion projects that they do not truly believe have positive NPVs. Or if new plant managers are pushed to generate increased earnings right away, they will be tempted to propose quick-payback projects even when NPV is sacrificed.

Sometimes senior managers try to offset bias by increasing the hurdle rate for capital expenditure. Suppose the true cost of capital is 10%, but the CFO is frustrated by the large fraction of projects that don't earn 10%. She therefore directs project sponsors to use a 15% discount rate. In other words, she adds a 5% fudge factor in an attempt to offset forecast bias. But it doesn't work; it *never* works. Brealey, Myers, and Allen's Second Law[1] explains why. The law states: *The proportion of proposed projects having positive NPVs at the corporate hurdle rate is independent of the hurdle rate.*

The law is not a facetious conjecture. It was tested in a large oil company where staff kept careful statistics on capital investment projects. About 85% of projects had positive NPVs. (The remaining 15% were proposed for other reasons, for example, to meet environmental standards.) One year, after several quarters of disappointing earnings, top management decided that more financial discipline was called for and increased the corporate hurdle rate by several percentage points. But in the following year the fraction of projects with positive NPVs stayed rock-steady at 85%.

---

[1] There is no First Law. We think "Second Law" sounds better. There is a Third Law, but that is for another chapter.

If you're worried about bias in forecasted cash flows, the only remedy is careful analysis of the forecasts. *Do not add fudge factors to the cost of capital.*[2]

Postaudits

Most firms keep a check on the progress of large projects by conducting **postaudits** shortly after the projects have begun to operate. Postaudits identify problems that need fixing, check the accuracy of forecasts, and suggest questions that should have been asked before the project was undertaken. Postaudits pay off mainly by helping managers to do a better job when it comes to the next round of investments. After a postaudit the controller may say, "We should have anticipated the extra training required for production workers." When the next proposal arrives, training will get the attention it deserves.

Postaudits may not be able to measure all of a project's costs and benefits. It may be impossible to split the project away from the rest of the business. Suppose that you have just taken over a trucking firm that operates a delivery service for local stores. You decide to improve service by installing custom software to keep track of packages and to schedule trucks. You also construct a dispatching center and buy five new diesel trucks. A year later you try a postaudit of the investment in software. You verify that it is working properly and check actual costs of purchase, installation, and operation against projections. But how do you identify the incremental cash inflows? No one has kept records of the extra diesel fuel that *would have been* used or the extra shipments that *would have been* lost absent the software. You may be able to verify that service is better, but how much of the improvement comes from the new trucks, how much from the dispatching center, and how much from the software? The only meaningful measures of success are for the delivery business as a whole.

10-2 SENSITIVITY ANALYSIS

Uncertainty means that more things can happen than will happen. Whenever you are confronted with a cash-flow forecast, you should try to discover what else can happen.

Put yourself in the well-heeled shoes of the treasurer of the Otobai Company in Osaka, Japan. You are considering the introduction of an electrically powered motor scooter for city use. Your staff members have prepared the cash-flow forecasts shown in Table 10.1. Since NPV is positive at the 10% opportunity cost of capital, it appears to be worth going ahead.

$$\text{NPV} = -15 + \sum_{t=1}^{10} \frac{3}{(1.10)^t} = +¥3.43 \text{ billion}$$

Before you decide, you want to delve into these forecasts and identify the key variables that determine whether the project succeeds or fails. It turns out that the marketing department has estimated revenue as follows:

---

[2] Adding a fudge factor to the cost of capital also favors quick-payback projects and penalizes longer-lived projects, which tend to have lower rates of return but higher NPVs. Adding a 5% fudge factor to the discount rate is roughly equivalent to reducing the forecast and present value of the first year's cash flow by 5%. The impact on the present value of a cash flow 10 years in the future is much greater, because the fudge factor is compounded in the discount rate. The fudge factor is not too much of a burden for a 2- or 3-year project, but an enormous burden for a 10- or 20-year project.

$$\text{Unit sales} = \text{new product's share of market} \times \text{size of scooter market}$$
$$= .1 \times 1 \text{ million} = 100,000 \text{ scooters}$$
$$\text{Revenue} = \text{unit sales} \times \text{price per unit}$$
$$= 100,000 \times 375,000 = ¥37.5 \text{ billion}$$

The production department has estimated variable costs per unit as ¥300,000. Since projected volume is 100,000 scooters per year, total variable cost is ¥30 billion. Fixed costs are ¥3 billion per year. The initial investment can be depreciated on a straight-line basis over the 10-year period, and profits are taxed at a rate of 50%.

These seem to be the important things you need to know, but look out for unidentified variables. Perhaps there are patent problems, or perhaps you will need to invest in service stations that will recharge the scooter batteries. The greatest dangers often lie in these *unknown* unknowns, or "unk-unks," as scientists call them.

Having found no unk-unks (no doubt you will find them later), you conduct a **sensitivity analysis** with respect to market size, market share, and so on. To do this, the marketing and production staffs are asked to give optimistic and pessimistic estimates for the underlying variables. These are set out in the left-hand columns of Table 10.2. The right-hand side shows what happens to the project's net present value if the variables are set *one at a time* to their optimistic and pessimistic values. Your project appears to be by no means a sure thing. The most dangerous variables are market share and unit variable cost. If market share is only .04 (and all other variables are as expected), then the project has an NPV of −¥10.4 billion. If unit variable cost is ¥360,000 (and all other variables are as expected), then the project has an NPV of −¥15 billion.

TABLE 10.1 Preliminary cash-flow forecasts for Otobai's electric scooter project (figures in ¥ billions).

Assumptions:
1. Investment is depreciated over 10 years straight-line.
2. Income is taxed at a rate of 50%.

"Live" Excel versions of Tables 10.1 to 10.5 are available on the book's Web site, www.mhhe.com/bmam10e.

Visit us at www.mhhe.com/bmam10e

		Year 0	Years 1–10
1	Investment	15	
2	Revenue		37.5
3	Variable cost		30
4	Fixed cost		3
5	Depreciation		1.5
6	Pretax profit		3
7	Tax		1.5
8	Net profit		1.5
	Operating cash flow		3
	Net cash flow	−15	3

TABLE 10.2 To undertake a sensitivity analysis of the electric scooter project, we set each variable in turn at its most pessimistic or optimistic value and recalculate the NPV of the project.

Visit us at www.mhhe.com/bmam10e

	Range			NPV, ¥ billions		
Variable	Pessimistic	Expected	Optimistic	Pessimistic	Expected	Optimistic
Market size, million	0.9	1	1.1	1.1	3.4	5.7
Market share	0.04	0.10	0.16	−10.4	3.4	17.3
Unit price, yen	350,000	375,000	380,000	−4.2	3.4	5.0
Unit variable cost, yen	360,000	300,000	275,000	−15.0	3.4	11.1
Fixed cost, ¥ billions	4	3	2	0.4	3.4	6.5

Value of Information

Now you can check whether you could resolve some of the uncertainty *before* your company parts with the ¥15 billion investment. Suppose that the pessimistic value for unit variable cost partly reflects the production department's worry that a particular machine will not work as designed and that the operation will have to be performed by other methods at an extra cost of ¥20,000 per unit. The chance that this will occur is only 1 in 10. But, if it does occur, the extra ¥20,000 unit cost will reduce after-tax cash flow by

$$\text{Unit sales} \times \text{additional unit cost} \times (1 - \text{tax rate})$$
$$= 100,000 \times 20,000 \times .50 = \text{¥1 billion}$$

It would reduce the NPV of your project by

$$\sum_{t=1}^{10} \frac{1}{(1.10)^t} = \text{¥6.14 billion,}$$

putting the NPV of the scooter project underwater at $+3.43 - 6.14 = -\text{¥}2.71$ billion. It is possible that a relatively small change in the scooter's design would remove the need for the new machine. Or perhaps a ¥10 million pretest of the machine will reveal whether it will work and allow you to clear up the problem. It clearly pays to invest ¥10 million to avoid a 10% probability of a ¥6.14 billion fall in NPV. You are ahead by $-10 + .10 \times 6,140 = +\text{¥}604$ million.

On the other hand, the value of additional information about market size is small. Because the project is acceptable even under pessimistic assumptions about market size, you are unlikely to be in trouble if you have misestimated that variable.

Limits to Sensitivity Analysis

Sensitivity analysis boils down to expressing cash flows in terms of key project variables and then calculating the consequences of misestimating the variables. It forces the manager to identify the underlying variables, indicates where additional information would be most useful, and helps to expose inappropriate forecasts.

One drawback to sensitivity analysis is that it always gives somewhat ambiguous results. For example, what exactly does *optimistic* or *pessimistic* mean? The marketing department may be interpreting the terms in a different way from the production department. Ten years from now, after hundreds of projects, hindsight may show that the marketing department's pessimistic limit was exceeded twice as often as the production department's; but what you may discover 10 years hence is no help now. Of course, you could specify that, when you use the terms "pessimistic" and "optimistic," you mean that there is only a 10% chance that the actual value will prove to be worse than the pessimistic figure or better than the optimistic one. However, it is far from easy to extract a forecaster's notion of the true probabilities of possible outcomes.[3]

Another problem with sensitivity analysis is that the underlying variables are likely to be interrelated. What sense does it make to look at the effect in isolation of an increase in market size? If market size exceeds expectations, it is likely that demand will be stronger than you anticipated and unit prices will

---

[3] If you doubt this, try some simple experiments. Ask the person who repairs your dishwasher to state a numerical probability that it will work for at least one more year. Or construct your own subjective probability distribution of the number of telephone calls you will receive next week. That ought to be easy. Try it.

be higher. And why look in isolation at the effect of an increase in price? If inflation pushes prices to the upper end of your range, it is quite probable that costs will also be inflated.

Sometimes the analyst can get around these problems by defining underlying variables so that they are roughly independent. But you cannot push *one-at-a-time* sensitivity analysis too far. It is impossible to obtain expected, optimistic, and pessimistic values for total *project* cash flows from the information in Table 10.2.

Scenario Analysis

If the variables are interrelated, it may help to consider some alternative plausible scenarios. For example, perhaps the company economist is worried about the possibility of another sharp rise in world oil prices. The direct effect of this would be to encourage the use of electrically powered transportation. The popularity of compact cars after the oil price increases in 2007 leads you to estimate that an immediate 20% rise in the price of oil would enable you to capture an extra 3% of the scooter market. On the other hand, the economist also believes that higher oil prices would prompt a world recession and at the same time stimulate inflation. In that case, market size might be in the region of .8 million scooters and both prices and cost might be 15% higher than your initial estimates. Table 10.3 shows that this scenario of higher oil prices and recession would on balance help your new venture. Its NPV would increase to ¥6.4 billion.

Managers often find **scenario analysis** helpful. It allows them to look at different but *consistent* combinations of variables. Forecasters generally prefer to give an estimate of revenues or costs under a particular scenario than to give some absolute optimistic or pessimistic value.

e**X**cel

Visit us at
www.mhhe.com/bmam10e

TABLE 10.3   How the NPV of the electric scooter project would be affected by higher oil prices and a world recession.

Cash Flows, Years 1-10, ¥ billions				
	Base Case	**High Oil Prices and Recession Case**		
1. Revenue	37.5		44.9	
2. Variable cost	30		35.9	
3. Fixed cost	3		3.5	
4. Depreciation	1.5		1.5	
5. Pretax profit	3		4.0	
6. Tax	1.5		2.0	
7. Net profit	1.5		2.0	
8. Net cash flow	3		3.5	
PV of cash flows	18.4		21.4	
NPV	3.4		6.4	

	Assumptions		
	Base Case	**High Oil Prices and Recession Case**	
Market size, million	1	0.8	
Market share	0.10	0.13	
Unit price, yen	375,000	431,300	
Unit variable cost, yen	300,000	345,000	
Fixed cost, ¥ billions	3	3.5	

Break-Even Analysis

When we undertake a sensitivity analysis of a project or when we look at alternative scenarios, we are asking how serious it would be if sales or costs turned out to be worse than we forecasted. Managers sometimes prefer to rephrase this question and ask how bad sales can get before the project begins to lose money. This exercise is known as **break-even analysis.**

In the left-hand portion of Table 10.4 we set out the revenues and costs of the electric scooter project under different assumptions about annual sales.[4] In the right-hand portion of the table we discount these revenues and costs to give the *present value* of the inflows and the *present value* of the outflows. Net present value is of course the difference between these numbers.

TABLE 10.4 NPV of electric scooter project under different assumptions about unit sales (figures in ¥ billions except as noted).

eXcel
Visit us at
www.mhhe.com/bmam10e

| | Inflows | | Outflows | | | | | | |
| | | Year 0 | Years 1-10 | | | | | | |
Unit Sales, Thousands	Revenues, Years 1-10	Investment	Variable Costs	Fixed Costs	Taxes	PV Inflows	PV Outflows	NPV
0	0	15	0	3	−2.25	0	19.6	−19.6
100	37.5	15	30	3	1.5	230.4	227.0	3.4
200	75.0	15	60	3	5.25	460.8	434.4	26.5

You can see that NPV is strongly negative if the company does not produce a single scooter. It is just positive if (as expected) the company sells 100,000 scooters and is strongly positive if it sells 200,000. Clearly the *zero*-NPV point occurs at a little under 100,000 scooters.

In Figure 10.1 we have plotted the present value of the inflows and outflows under different assumptions about annual sales. The two lines cross when sales are 85,000 scooters. This is the point at which the project has zero NPV. As long as sales are greater than 85,000, the project has a positive NPV.[5]

Managers frequently calculate break-even points in terms of accounting profits rather than present values. Table 10.5 shows Otobai's after-tax profits at three levels of scooter sales. Figure 10.2 once again plots revenues and costs against sales. But the story this time is different. Figure 10.2, which is based on accounting profits, suggests a breakeven of 60,000 scooters. Figure 10.1, which is based on present values, shows a breakeven at 85,000 scooters. Why the difference?

TABLE 10.5 The electric scooter project's accounting profit under different assumptions about unit sales (figures in ¥ billions except as noted).

eXcel
Visit us at
www.mhhe.com/bmam10e

Unit Sales, Thousands	Revenues Years 1-10	Variable Costs	Fixed Costs	Depreciation	Taxes	Total Costs	Profit after Tax
0	0	0	3	1.5	−2.25	2.25	−2.25
100	37.5	30	3	1.5	1.5	36.0	1.5
200	75.0	60	3	1.5	5.25	69.75	5.25

When we work in terms of accounting profit, we deduct depreciation of ¥1.5 billion each year to cover the cost of the initial investment. If Otobai sells 60,000 scooters a year, revenues will be

---

[4] Notice that if the project makes a loss, this loss can be used to reduce the tax bill on the rest of the company's business. In this case the project produces a tax saving—the tax outflow is negative.

[5] We could also calculate break-even sales by plotting equivalent annual costs and revenues. Of course, the break-even point would be identical at 85,000 scooters.

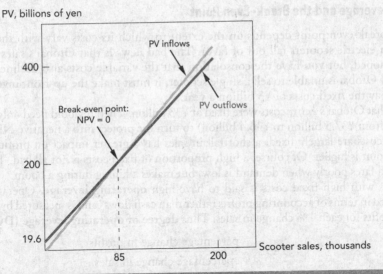

FIGURE 10.1

A break-even chart showing the present values of Otobai's cash inflows and outflows under different assumptions about unit sales. NPV is zero when sales are 85,000.

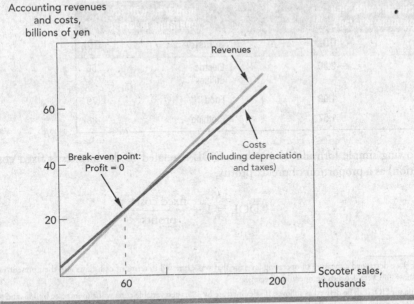

FIGURE 10.2

Sometimes break-even charts are constructed in terms of accounting numbers. After-tax profit is zero when sales are 60,000.

sufficient both to pay operating costs and to recover the initial outlay of ¥15 billion. But they will *not* be sufficient to repay the *opportunity cost of capital* on that ¥15 billion. A project that breaks even in accounting terms will surely have a negative NPV.

Operating Leverage and the Break-Even Point

A project's break-even point depends on the extent to which its costs vary with the level of sales. Suppose that electric scooters fall out of favor. The bad news is that Otobai's sales revenue is less than you'd hoped, but you have the consolation that the variable costs also decline. On the other hand, even if Otobai is unable to sell a single scooter, it must make the up-front investment of ¥15 billion and pay the fixed costs of ¥3 billion a year.

Suppose that Otobai's *entire* costs were fixed at ¥33 billion. Then it would need only a 3% shortfall in revenues (from ¥37.5 billion to ¥36.4 billion) to turn the project into a negative-NPV investment. Thus, when costs are largely fixed, a shortfall in sales has a greater impact on profitability and the break-even point is higher. Of course, a high proportion of fixed costs is not all bad. The firm whose costs are fixed fares poorly when demand is low, but makes a killing during a boom.

A business with high fixed costs is said to have high **operating leverage.** Operating leverage is usually defined in terms of accounting profits rather than cash flows[6] and is measured by the percentage change in profits for each 1% change in sales. Thus **degree of operating leverage (DOL)** is

$$DOL = \frac{\text{percentage change in profits}}{\text{percentage change in sales}}$$

TABLE 10.6   Estimated degree of operating leverage (DOL) for large U.S. companies by industry.

Note: DOL is estimated as the median ratio of the change in profits to the change in sales for firms in Standard & Poor's index, 1998–2008.

Industries with high operating leverage		Industries with low operating leverage	
Industry	DOL	Industry	DOL
Steel	2.20	Electric utilities	.56
Railroads	1.99	Food	.79
Autos	1.57	Clothing	.88

The following simple formula[7] shows how DOL is related to the business's fixed costs (including depreciation) as a proportion of pretax profits:

$$DOL = 1 + \frac{\text{fixed costs}}{\text{profits}}$$

---

[6] In Chapter 9 we developed a measure of operating leverage that was expressed in terms of cash flows and their present values. We used this measure to show how beta depends on operating leverage.

[7] This formula for DOL can be derived as follows. If sales increase by 1%, then variable costs will also increase by 1%, and profits will increase by .01 × (sales − variable costs) = .01 × (pretax profits + fixed costs). Now recall the definition of DOL:

$$DOL = \frac{\text{percentage change in profits}}{\text{percentage change in sales}} = \frac{(\text{change in profits})/(\text{level of profits})}{.01}$$

$$= 100 \times \frac{\text{change in profits}}{\text{level of profits}} = 100 \times \frac{.01 \times (\text{profits} + \text{fixed costs})}{\text{level of profits}}$$

$$= 1 + \frac{\text{fixed costs}}{\text{profits}}$$

In the case of Otobai's scooter project

$$DOL = 1 + \frac{(3 + 1.5)}{3} = 2.5$$

A 1% shortfall in the scooter project's revenues would result in a 2.5% shortfall in profits.

Look now at Table 10.6, which shows how much the profits of some large U.S. companies have typically changed as a proportion of the change in sales. For example, notice that each 1% drop in sales has reduced steel company profits by 2.20%. This suggests that steel companies have an estimated operating leverage of 2.20. You would expect steel stocks therefore to have correspondingly high betas and this is indeed the case.

10-3   MONTE CARLO SIMULATION

Sensitivity analysis allows you to consider the effect of changing one variable at a time. By looking at the project under alternative scenarios, you can consider the effect of a *limited number* of plausible combinations of variables. **Monte Carlo simulation** is a tool for considering *all* possible combinations. It therefore enables you to inspect the entire distribution of project outcomes.

Imagine that you are a gambler at Monte Carlo. You know nothing about the laws of probability (few casual gamblers do), but a friend has suggested to you a complicated strategy for playing roulette. Your friend has not actually tested the strategy but is confident that it will *on the average* give you a 2½% return for every 50 spins of the wheel. Your friend's optimistic estimate for any series of 50 spins is a profit of 55%; your friend's pessimistic estimate is a loss of 50%. How can you find out whether these really are the odds? An easy but possibly expensive way is to start playing and record the outcome at the end of each series of 50 spins. After, say, 100 series of 50 spins each, plot a frequency distribution of the outcomes and calculate the average and upper and lower limits. If things look good, you can then get down to some serious gambling.

An alternative is to tell a computer to simulate the roulette wheel and the strategy. In other words, you could instruct the computer to draw numbers out of its hat to determine the outcome of each spin of the wheel and then to calculate how much you would make or lose from the particular gambling strategy.

That would be an example of Monte Carlo simulation. In capital budgeting we replace the gambling strategy with a model of the project, and the roulette wheel with a model of the world in which the project operates. Let us see how this might work with our project for an electrically powered scooter.

Simulating the Electric Scooter Project

Step 1: Modeling the Project   The first step in any simulation is to give the computer a precise model of the project. For example, the sensitivity analysis of the scooter project was based on the following implicit model of cash flow:

Cash flow = (revenues − costs − depreciation) × (1 − tax rate) + depreciation
Revenues = market size × market share × unit price
Costs = (market size × market share × variable unit cost) + fixed cost

This model of the project was all that you needed for the simpleminded sensitivity analysis that we described above. But if you wish to simulate the whole project, you need to think about how the variables are interrelated.

For example, consider the first variable—market size. The marketing department has estimated a market size of 1 million scooters in the first year of the project's life, but of course you do not know how things will work out. Actual market size will exceed or fall short of expectations by the amount of the department's forecast error:

$$\text{Market size, year 1} = \text{expected market size, year 1} \times (1 + \text{forecast error, year 1})$$

You *expect* the forecast error to be zero, but it could turn out to be positive or negative. Suppose, for example, that the actual market size turns out to be 1.1 million. That means a forecast error of 10%, or +.1:

$$\text{Market size, year 1} = 1 \times (1 + .1) = 1.1 \text{ million}$$

You can write the market size in the second year in exactly the same way:

$$\text{Market size, year 2} = \text{expected market size, year 2} \times (1 + \text{forecast error, year 2})$$

But at this point you must consider how the expected market size in year 2 is affected by what happens in year 1. If scooter sales are below expectations in year 1, it is likely that they will continue to be below in subsequent years. Suppose that a shortfall in sales in year 1 would lead you to revise down your forecast of sales in year 2 by a like amount. Then

$$\text{Expected market size, year 2} = \text{actual market size, year 1}$$

Now you can rewrite the market size in year 2 in terms of the actual market size in the previous year plus a forecast error:

$$\text{Market size, year 2} = \text{market size, year 1} \times (1 + \text{forecast error, year 2})$$

In the same way you can describe the expected market size in year 3 in terms of market size in year 2 and so on.

This set of equations illustrates how you can describe interdependence between different *periods*. But you also need to allow for interdependence between different *variables*. For example, the price of electrically powered scooters is likely to increase with market size. Suppose that this is the only uncertainty and that a 10% addition to market size would lead you to predict a 3% increase in price. Then you could model the first year's price as follows:

$$\text{Price, year 1} = \text{expected price, year 1} \times (1 + .3 \times \text{error in market size forecast, year 1})$$

Then, if variations in market size exert a permanent effect on price, you can define the second year's price as

$$\text{Price, year 2} = \text{expected price, year 2} \times (1 + .3 \times \text{error in market size forecast, year 2})$$
$$= \text{actual price, year 1} \times (1 + .3 \times \text{error in market size forecast, year 2})$$

Notice how we have linked each period's selling price to the *actual* selling prices (including forecast error) in all previous periods. We used the same type of linkage for market size. These linkages mean that forecast errors accumulate; they do not cancel out over time. Thus, uncertainty *increases* with time: The farther out you look into the future, the more the actual price or market size may depart from your original forecast.

The complete model of your project would include a set of equations for each of the variables: market size, price, market share, unit variable cost, and fixed cost. Even if you allowed for only a few interdependencies between variables and across time, the result would be quite a complex list of equations.[8] Perhaps that is not a bad thing if it forces you to understand what the project is all about. Model building is like spinach: You may not like the taste, but it is good for you.

Step 2: Specifying Probabilities   Remember the procedure for simulating the gambling strategy? The first step was to specify the strategy, the second was to specify the numbers on the roulette wheel, and the third was to tell the computer to select these numbers at random and calculate the results of the strategy:

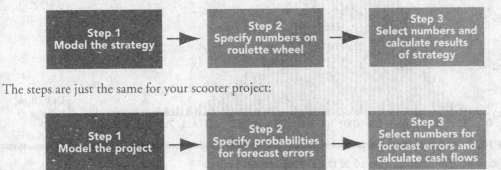

The steps are just the same for your scooter project:

Think about how you might go about specifying your possible errors in forecasting market size. You *expect* market size to be 1 million scooters. You obviously don't think that you are underestimating or overestimating, so the expected forecast error is zero. On the other hand, the marketing department has given you a range of possible estimates. Market size could be as low as .85 million scooters or as high as 1.15 million scooters. Thus the forecast error has an expected value of 0 and a range of plus or minus 15%. If the marketing department has in fact given you the lowest and highest possible outcomes, actual market size should fall somewhere within this range with near certainty.[9]

That takes care of market size; now you need to draw up similar estimates of the possible forecast errors for each of the other variables that are in your model.

Step 3: Simulate the Cash Flows   The computer now *samples* from the distribution of the forecast errors, calculates the resulting cash flows for each period, and records them. After many iterations you begin to get accurate estimates of the probability distributions of the project cash flows—accurate, that is, only to the extent that your model and the probability distributions of the forecast errors are accurate. Remember the GIGO principle: "Garbage in, garbage out."

Figure 10.3 shows part of the output from an actual simulation of the electric scooter project.[10] Note the positive skewness of the outcomes—very large outcomes are more likely than very small

---

[8] Specifying the interdependencies is the hardest and most important part of a simulation. If all components of project cash flows were unrelated, simulation would rarely be necessary.

[9] Suppose "near certainty" means "99% of the time." If forecast errors are normally distributed, this degree of certainty requires a range of plus or minus three standard deviations.

Other distributions could, of course, be used. For example, the marketing department may view any market size between .85 and 1.15 million scooters as *equally likely*. In that case the simulation would require a uniform (rectangular) distribution of forecast errors.

[10] These are actual outputs from Crystal Ball™ software. The simulation assumed annual forecast errors were normally distributed and ran through 10,000 trials. We thank Christopher Howe for running the simulation. An Excel program to simulate the Otobai project was kindly provided by Marek Jochec and is available on the Web site, **www.mhhe.com/bma**.

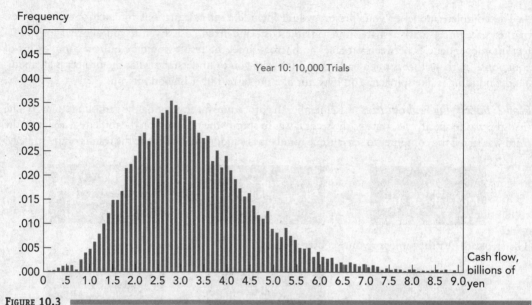

Figure 10.3

Simulation of cash flows for year 10 of the electric scooter project.

ones. This is common when forecast errors accumulate over time. Because of the skewness the average cash flow is somewhat higher than the most likely outcome; in other words, a bit to the right of the peak of the distribution.[11]

Step 4: Calculate Present Value

The distributions of project cash flows should allow you to calculate the expected cash flows more accurately. In the final step you need to discount these expected cash flows to find present value.

Simulation, though complicated, has the obvious merit of compelling the forecaster to face up to uncertainty and to interdependencies. Once you have set up your simulation model, it is a simple matter to analyze the principal sources of uncertainty in the cash flows and to see how much you could reduce this uncertainty by improving the forecasts of sales or costs. You may also be able to explore the effect of possible modifications to the project.

Simulation may sound like a panacea for the world's ills, but, as usual, you pay for what you get. Sometimes you pay for more than you get. It is not just a matter of the time spent in building the model. It is extremely difficult to estimate interrelationships between variables and the underlying probability distributions, even when you are trying to be honest. But in capital budgeting, forecasters are seldom completely impartial and the probability distributions on which simulations are based can be highly biased.

In practice, a simulation that attempts to be realistic will also be complex. Therefore the decision maker may delegate the task of constructing the model to management scientists or consultants. The danger here is that, even if the builders understand their creation, the decision maker cannot and therefore does not rely on it. This is a common but ironic experience.

---

[11] When you are working with cash-flow forecasts, bear in mind the distinction between the expected value and the most likely (or modal) value. Present values are based on *expected* cash flows—that is, the probability-weighted average of the possible future cash flows. If the distribution of possible outcomes is skewed to the right as in Figure 10.3, the expected cash flow will be greater than the most likely cash flow.

10-4   REAL OPTIONS AND DECISION TREES

When you use discounted cash flow (DCF) to value a project, you implicitly assume that the firm will hold the assets passively. But managers are not paid to be dummies. After they have invested in a new project, they do not simply sit back and watch the future unfold. If things go well, the project may be expanded; if they go badly, the project may be cut back or abandoned altogether. Projects that can be modified in these ways are more valuable than those that do not provide such flexibility. The more uncertain the outlook, the more valuable this flexibility becomes.

That sounds obvious, but notice that sensitivity analysis and Monte Carlo simulation do not recognize the opportunity to modify projects.[12] For example, think back to the Otobai electric scooter project. In real life, if things go wrong with the project, Otobai would abandon to cut its losses. If so, the worst outcomes would not be as devastating as our sensitivity analysis and simulation suggested.

Options to modify projects are known as **real options.** Managers may not always use the term "real option" to describe these opportunities; for example, they may refer to "intangible advantages" of easy-to-modify projects. But when they review major investment proposals, these option intangibles are often the key to their decisions.

The Option to Expand

Long-haul airfreight businesses such as FedEx need to move a massive amount of goods each day. Therefore, when Airbus announced delays to its A380 superjumbo freighter, FedEx turned to Boeing and ordered 15 of its 777 freighters to be delivered between 2009 and 2011. If business continues to expand, FedEx will need more aircraft. But rather than placing additional firm orders, the company secured a place in Boeing's production line by acquiring *options* to buy a further 15 aircraft at a predetermined price. These options did not commit FedEx to expand but gave it the flexibility to do so.

Figure 10.4 displays FedEx's expansion option as a simple **decision tree.** You can think of it as a game between FedEx and fate. Each square represents an action or decision by the company. Each circle represents an outcome revealed by fate. In this case there is only one outcome—when fate reveals the airfreight demand and FedEx's capacity needs. FedEx then decides whether to exercise its options and buy additional 777s. Here the future decision is easy: Buy the airplanes only if demand is high and the company can operate them profitably. If demand is low, FedEx walks away and leaves Boeing with the problem of finding another customer for the planes that were reserved for FedEx.

You can probably think of many other investments that take on added value because of the further options they provide. For example,

- When launching a new product, companies often start with a pilot program to iron out possible design problems and to test the market. The company can evaluate the pilot project and then decide whether to expand to full-scale production.
- When designing a factory, it can make sense to provide extra land or floor space to reduce the future cost of a second production line.
- When building a four-lane highway, it may pay to build six-lane bridges so that the road can be converted later to six lanes if traffic volumes turn out to be higher than expected.

---

[12] Some simulation models *do* recognize the possibility of changing policy. For example, when a pharmaceutical company uses simulation to analyze its R&D decisions, it allows for the possibility that the company can abandon the development at each phase.

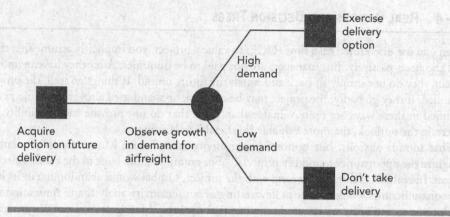

FIGURE 10.4

FedEx's expansion option expressed as a simple decision tree.

- When building production platforms for offshore oil and gas fields, companies usually allow ample vacant deck space. The vacant space costs more up front but reduces the cost of installing extra equipment later. For example, vacant deck space could provide an option to install water-flooding equipment if oil or gas prices turn out high enough to justify this investment.

Expansion options do not show up on accounting balance sheets, but managers and investors are well aware of their importance. For example, in Chapter 4 we showed how the present value of growth opportunities (PVGO) contributes to the value of a company's common stock. PVGO equals the forecasted total NPV of future investments. But it is better to think of PVGO as the value of the firm's *options* to invest and expand. The firm is not obliged to grow. It can invest more if the number of positive-NPV projects turns out high or slow down if that number turns out low. The flexibility to adapt investment to future opportunities is one of the factors that makes PVGO so valuable.

The Option to Abandon

If the option to expand has value, what about the decision to bail out? Projects do not just go on until assets expire of old age. The decision to terminate a project is usually taken by management, not by nature. Once the project is no longer profitable, the company will cut its losses and exercise its option to abandon the project.

Some assets are easier to bail out of than others. Tangible assets are usually easier to sell than intangible ones. It helps to have active secondhand markets, which really exist only for standardized items. Real estate, airplanes, trucks, and certain machine tools are likely to be relatively easy to sell. On the other hand, the knowledge accumulated by a software company's research and development program is a specialized intangible asset and probably would not have significant abandonment value. (Some assets, such as old mattresses, even have *negative* abandonment value; you have to pay to get rid of them. It is costly to decommission nuclear power plants or to reclaim land that has been strip-mined.)

EXAMPLE 10.1   Bailing Out of the Outboard-Engine Project

Managers should recognize the option to abandon when they make the initial investment in a new project or venture. For example, suppose you must choose between two technologies for production of a Wankel-engine outboard motor.

1. Technology A uses computer-controlled machinery custom-designed to produce the complex shapes required for Wankel engines in high volumes and at low cost. But if the Wankel outboard does not sell, this equipment will be worthless.

2. Technology B uses standard machine tools. Labor costs are much higher, but the machinery can be sold for ₹17 million if demand turns out to be low.

Just for simplicity, assume that the initial capital outlays are the same for both technologies. If demand in the first year is buoyant, technology A will provide a payoff of ₹24 million. If demand is sluggish, the payoff from A is ₹16 million. Think of these payoffs as the project's cash flow in the first year of production plus the value in year 1 of all future cash flows. The corresponding payoffs to technology B are ₹22.5 million and ₹15 million:

	Payoffs from Producing Outboard (₹ millions)	
	Technology A	Technology B
Buoyant demand	₹24.0	₹22.5
Sluggish demand	16.0	15.0*

*Composed of a cash flow of ₹1.5 million and a PV in year 1 of 13.5 million.

Technology A looks better in a DCF analysis of the new product because it was designed to have the lowest possible cost at the planned production volume. Yet you can sense the advantage of the flexibility provided by technology B if you are unsure whether the new outboard will sink or swim in the marketplace. If you adopt technology B and the outboard is not a success, you are better off collecting the first year's cash flow of ₹1.5 million and then selling the plant and equipment for ₹17 million.

Figure 10.5 summarizes Example 10.1 as a decision tree. The abandonment option occurs at the right-hand boxes for technology B. The decisions are obvious: continue if demand is buoyant, abandon otherwise. Thus the payoffs to technology B are

Buoyant demand → continue production → payoff of ₹22.5 million

Sluggish demand → exercise option to sell assets → payoff of 1.5 + 17 = ₹18.5 million

Technology B provides an insurance policy: If the outboard's sales are disappointing, you can abandon the project and receive ₹18.5 million. The total value of the project with technology B is its DCF value, assuming that the company does not abandon, *plus* the value of the option to sell the assets for ₹17 million. When you value this abandonment option, you are placing a value on flexibility.

Production Options

When companies undertake new investments, they generally think about the possibility that at a later stage they may wish to modify the project. After all, today everybody may be demanding round pegs, but, who knows, tomorrow square ones may be all the rage. In that case you need a plant that provides

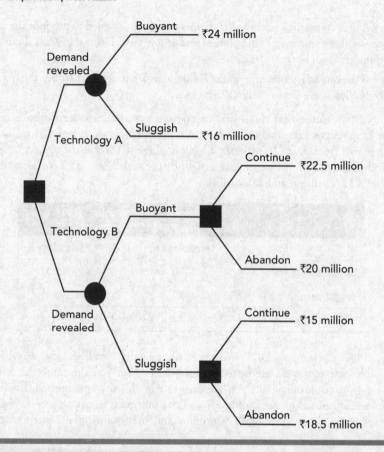

FIGURE 10.5

Decision tree for the Wankel outboard motor project. Technology B allows the firm to abandon the project and recover ₹18.5 million if demand is sluggish.

the flexibility to produce a variety of peg shapes. In just the same way, it may be worth paying up front for the flexibility to vary the inputs. For example in Chapter 22 we will describe how electric utilities often build in the option to switch between burning oil and burning natural gas. We refer to these opportunities as *production options*.

Timing Options

The fact that a project has a positive NPV does not mean that it is best undertaken now. It might be even more valuable to delay.

Timing decisions are fairly straightforward under conditions of certainty. You need to examine alternative dates for making the investment and calculate its net future value at each of these dates. Then, to find which of the alternatives would add most to the firm's *current* value, you must discount these net future values back to the present:

$$\text{Net present value of investment if undertaken at time } t = \frac{\text{Net future value at date } t}{(1 + r)^t}$$

The optimal date to undertake the investment is the one that maximizes its contribution to the value of your firm today. This procedure should already be familiar to you from Chapter 6, where we worked out when it was best to cut a tract of timber.

In the timber-cutting example we assumed that there was no uncertainty about the cash flows, so that you knew the optimal time to exercise your option. When there is uncertainty, the timing option is much more complicated. An opportunity not taken at $t = 0$ might be more or less attractive at $t = 1$; there is rarely any way of knowing for sure. Perhaps it is better to strike while the iron is hot even if there is a chance that it will become hotter. On the other hand, if you wait a bit you might obtain more information and avoid a bad mistake. That is why you often find that managers choose not to invest today in projects where the NPV is only marginally positive and there is much to be learned by delay.

More on Decision Trees

We will return to all these real options in Chapter 22, after we have covered the theory of option valuation in Chapters 20 and 21. But we will end this chapter with a closer look at decision trees.

Decision trees are commonly used to describe the real options imbedded in capital investment projects. But decision trees were used in the analysis of projects years before real options were first explicitly identified. Decision trees can help to understand project risk and how future decisions will affect project cash flows. Even if you never learn or use option valuation theory, decision trees belong in your financial toolkit.

The best way to appreciate how decision trees can be used in project analysis is to work through a detailed example.

EXAMPLE 10.2 A Decision Tree for Pharmaceutical R&D

Drug development programs may last decades. Usually hundreds of thousands of compounds may be tested to find a few with promise. Then these compounds must survive several stages of investment and testing to gain approval from the Food and Drug Administration (FDA). Only then can the drug be sold commercially. The stages are as follows:

1. *Phase I clinical trials.* After laboratory and clinical tests are concluded, the new drug is tested for safety and dosage in a small sample of humans.

2. *Phase II clinical trials.* The new drug is tested for efficacy (Does it work as predicted?) and for potentially harmful side effects.

3. *Phase III clinical trials.* The new drug is tested on a larger sample of humans to confirm efficacy and to rule out harmful side effects.

4. *Prelaunch.* If FDA approval is gained, there is investment in production facilities and initial marketing. Some clinical trials continue.

5. *Commercial launch.* After making a heavy initial investment in marketing and sales, the company begins to sell the new drug to the public.

Once a drug is launched successfully, sales usually continue for about 10 years, until the drug's patent protection expires and competitors enter with generic versions of the same chemical compound. The drug may continue to be sold off-patent, but sales volume and profits are much lower.

The commercial success of FDA-approved drugs varies enormously. The PV of a "blockbuster" drug at launch can be 5 or 10 times the PV of an average drug. A few blockbusters can generate most of a large pharmaceutical company's profits.[13]

No company hesitates to invest in R&D for a drug that it *knows* will be a blockbuster. But the company will not find out for sure until after launch. Sometimes a company thinks it has a blockbuster, only to discover that a competitor has launched a better drug first.

Sometimes the FDA approves a drug but limits its scope of use. Some drugs, though effective, can only be prescribed for limited classes of patients; other drugs can be prescribed much more widely. Thus the manager of a pharmaceutical R&D program has to assess the odds of clinical success and the odds of commercial success. A new drug may be abandoned if it fails clinical trials—for example, because of dangerous side effects—or if the outlook for profits is discouraging.

Figure 10.6 is a decision tree that illustrates these decisions. We have assumed that a new drug has passed phase I clinical trials with flying colors. Now it requires an investment of $18 million for phase II trials. These trials take two years. The probability of success is 44%.

If the trials are successful, the manager learns the commercial potential of the drug, which depends on how widely it can be used. Suppose that the forecasted PV at launch depends on the scope of use allowed by the FDA. These PVs are shown at the far right of the decision tree: an upside outcome of NPV = $700 million if the drug can be widely used, a most likely case with NPV = $300 million, and a downside case of NPV = $100 million if the drug's scope is greatly restricted.[14] The NPVs are the payoffs at launch after investment in marketing. Launch comes three years after the start of phase III if the drug is approved by the FDA. The probabilities of the upside, most likely, and downside outcomes are 25%, 50%, and 25%, respectively.

A further R&D investment of $130 million is required for phase III trials and for the prelaunch period. (We have combined phase III and prelaunch for simplicity.) The probability of FDA approval and launch is 80%.

Now let's value the investments in Figure 10.6. We assume a risk-free rate of 4% and market risk premium of 7%. If FDA-approved pharmaceutical products have asset betas of .8, the opportunity cost of capital is $4 + .8 \times 7 = 9.6\%$.

We work back through the tree from right to left. The NPVs at the start of phase III trials are:

$$\text{NPV(upside)} \quad = -130 + .8 \times \frac{700}{(1.096)^3} = +\$295 \text{ million}$$

$$\text{NPV(most likely)} = -130 + .8 \times \frac{300}{(1.096)^3} = +\$52 \text{ million}$$

$$\text{NPV(downside)} \quad = -130 + .8 \times \frac{100}{(1.096)^3} = -\$69 \text{ million}$$

Since the downside NPV is negative at −$69 million, the $130 million investment at the start of phase III should *not* be made in the downside case. There is no point investing $130 million for an 80% chance of a $100 million payoff three years later. Therefore the value of the R&D program at this point in the decision tree is not −$69 million, but zero.

---

[13] The Web site of the Tufts Center for the Study of Drug Development (**http://csdd.tufts.edu**) provides a wealth of information about the costs and risks of pharmaceutical R&D.

[14] The most likely case is not the average outcome, because PVs in the pharmaceutical business are skewed to the upside. The average PV is .25 × 700 + .5 × 300 + .25 × 100 = $350 million.

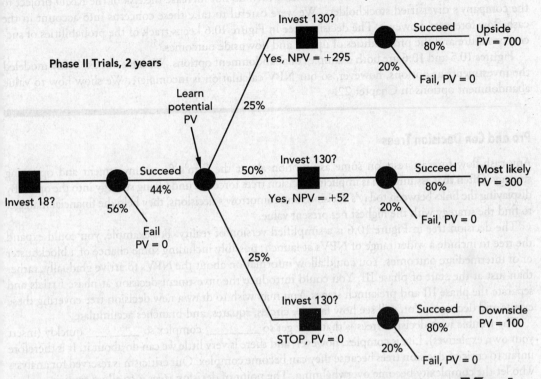

FIGURE 10.6

A simplified decision tree for pharmaceutical R&D. A candidate drug requires an $18 million investment for phase II clinical trials. If the trials are successful (44% probability), the company learns the drug's scope of use and updates its forecast of the drug's PV at commercial launch. The investment required for the phase III trials and prelaunch outlays is $130 million. The probability of success in phase III and prelaunch is 80%.

Now calculate the NPV at the initial investment decision for phase II trials. The payoff two years later depends on whether the drug delivers on the upside, most likely, or downside: a 25% chance of NPV = +$295 million, a 50% chance of NPV = +$52 million, and a 25% chance of cancellation and NPV = 0. These NPVs are achieved only if the phase II trials are successful: there is a 44% chance of success and a 56% chance of failure. The initial investment is $18 million. Therefore NPV is

$$\text{NPV} = -18 + .44 \times \frac{.25 \times 295 + .5 \times 52 + .25 \times 0}{(1.096)^2} = -18 + 37 = +19 \text{ million}$$

Thus the phase II R&D is a worthwhile investment, even though the drug has only a 33% chance of making it to launch (.44 × .75 = .33, or 33%).

Notice that we did not increase the 9.6% discount rate to offset the risks of failure in clinical trials or the risk that the drug will fail to generate profits. Concerns about the drug's efficacy, possible side effects, and scope of use are diversifiable risks, which do not increase the risk of the R&D project to the company's diversified stockholders. We were careful to take these concerns into account in the cash-flow forecasts, however. The decision tree in Figure 10.6 keeps track of the probabilities of success or failure and the probabilities of upside and downside outcomes.[15]

Figures 10.5 and 10.6 are both examples of abandonment options. We have not explicitly modeled the investments as options, however, so our NPV calculation is incomplete. We show how to value abandonment options in Chapter 22.

Pro and Con Decision Trees

Any cash-flow forecast rests on some assumption about the firm's future investment and operating strategy. Often that assumption is implicit. Decision trees force the underlying strategy into the open. By displaying the links between today's decisions and tomorrow's decisions, they help the financial manager to find the strategy with the highest net present value.

The decision tree in Figure 10.6 is a simplified version of reality. For example, you could expand the tree to include a wider range of NPVs at launch, possibly including some chance of a blockbuster or of intermediate outcomes. You could allow information about the NPVs to arrive gradually, rather than just at the start of phase III. You could introduce the investment decision at phase I trials and separate the phase III and prelaunch stages. You may wish to draw a new decision tree covering these events and decisions. You will see how fast the circles, squares, and branches accumulate.

The trouble with decision trees is that they get so _____ complex so _____ quickly (insert your own expletives). Life is complex, however, and there is very little we can do about it. It is therefore unfair to criticize decision trees because they can become complex. Our criticism is reserved for analysts who let the complexity become overwhelming. The point of decision trees is to allow explicit analysis of possible future events and decisions. They should be judged not on their comprehensiveness but on whether they show the most important links between today's and tomorrow's decisions. Decision trees used in real life will be more complex than Figure 10.6, but they will nevertheless display only a small fraction of possible future events and decisions. Decision trees are like grapevines: They are productive only if they are vigorously pruned.

---

[15] The market risk attaching to the PVs at launch is recognized in the 9.6% discount rate.

SUMMARY

Earlier chapters explained how companies calculate a project's NPV by forecasting the cash flows and discounting them at a rate that reflects project risk. The end result is the project's contribution to shareholder wealth. Understanding discounted-cash-flow analysis is important, but there is more to good capital budgeting practice than an ability to discount.

First, companies need to establish a set of capital budgeting procedures to ensure that decisions are made in an orderly manner. Most companies prepare an annual capital budget, which is a list of investment projects planned for the coming year. Inclusion of a project in the capital budget does not constitute final approval for the expenditure. Before the plant or division can go ahead with a proposal, it will usually need to submit an appropriation request that includes detailed forecasts, a discounted-cash-flow analysis, and back-up information.

Sponsors of capital investment projects are tempted to overstate future cash flows and understate risks. Therefore firms need to encourage honest and open discussion. They also need procedures to ensure that projects fit in with the company's strategic plans and are developed on a consistent basis.

(These procedures should *not* include fudge factors added to project hurdle rates in an attempt to offset optimistic forecasts.) Later, after a project has begun to operate, the firm can follow up with a postaudit. Postaudits identify problems that need fixing and help the firm learn from its mistakes.

Good capital budgeting practice also tries to identify the major uncertainties in project proposals. An awareness of these uncertainties may suggest ways that the project can be reconfigured to reduce the dangers, or it may point out some additional research that will confirm whether the project is worthwhile.

There are several ways in which companies try to identify and evaluate the threats to a project's success. The first is *sensitivity analysis.* Here the manager considers in turn each forecast or assumption that drives cash flows and recalculates NPV at optimistic and pessimistic values of that variable. The project is "sensitive to" that variable if the resulting range of NPVs is wide, particularly on the pessimistic side.

Sensitivity analysis often moves on to *break-even analysis,* which identifies break-even values of key variables. Suppose the manager is concerned about a possible shortfall in sales. Then he or she can calculate the sales level at which the project just breaks even (NPV = 0) and consider the odds that sales will fall that far. Break-even analysis is also done in terms of accounting income, although we do not recommend this application.

Sensitivity analysis and break-even analysis are easy, and they identify the forecasts and assumptions that really count for the project's success or failure. The important variables do not change one at a time, however. For example, when raw material prices are higher than forecasted, it's a good bet that selling prices will be higher too. The logical response is *scenario analysis,* which examines the effects on NPV of changing several variables at a time.

Scenario analysis looks at a limited number of combinations of variables. If you want to go whole hog and look at all possible combinations, you will have to turn to *Monte Carlo simulation.* In that case, you must build a financial model of the project and specify the probability distribution of each variable that determines cash flow. Then you ask the computer to draw random values for each variable and work out the resulting cash flows. In fact you ask the computer to do this thousands of times, in order to generate complete distributions of future cash flows. With these distributions in hand, you can get a better handle on expected cash flows and project risks. You can also experiment to see how the distributions would be affected by altering project scope or the ranges for any of the variables.

Elementary treatises on capital budgeting sometimes create the impression that, once the manager has made an investment decision, there is nothing to do but sit back and watch the cash flows unfold. In practice, companies are constantly modifying their operations. If cash flows are better than anticipated, the project may be expanded; if they are worse, it may be contracted or abandoned altogether. Options to modify projects are known as *real options.* In this chapter we introduced the main categories of real options: *expansion* options, *abandonment* options, *timing* options, and options providing *flexibility in production.*

Good managers take account of real options when they value a project. One convenient way to summarize real options and their cash-flow consequences is to create a *decision tree.* You identify the things that could happen to the project and the main counteractions that you might take. Then, working back from the future to the present, you can consider which action you *should* take in each case.

Decision trees can help to identify the possible impact of real options on project cash flows, but we largely skirted the issue of how to value real options. We return to this topic in Chapter 22, after we have covered option-valuation methods in the previous two chapters.

FURTHER READING

Three not-too-technical references on real options are listed below. Additional references follow Chapter 22.

A. Dixit and R. Pindyck, "The Options Approach to Capital Investment," *Harvard Business Review* 73 (May–June 1995), pp. 105–115.

W. C. Kester, "Today's Options for Tomorrow's Growth," *Harvard Business Review* 62 (March–April 1984), pp. 153–160.

A. Triantis and A. Borison, "Real Options: State of the Practice," *Journal of Applied Corporate Finance* 14 (Summer 2001), pp. 8 –24.

PROBLEM SETS

BASIC

1. True or false?
   a. The approval of a capital budget allows managers to go ahead with any project included in the budget.
   b. Capital budgets and project authorizations are mostly developed "bottom up." Strategic planning is a "top-down" process.
   c. Project sponsors are likely to be overoptimistic.

2. Explain how each of the following actions or problems can distort or disrupt the capital budgeting process.
   a. Overoptimism by project sponsors.
   b. Inconsistent forecasts of industry and macroeconomic variables.
   c. Capital budgeting organized solely as a bottom-up process.

3. Define and briefly explain each of the following terms or procedures:
   a. Sensitivity analysis
   b. Scenario analysis
   c. Break-even analysis
   d. Monte Carlo simulation
   e. Decision tree
   f. Real option
   g. Abandonment value
   h. Expansion value

4. True or false?
   a. Sensitivity analysis is unnecessary for projects with asset betas that are equal to 0.
   b. Sensitivity analysis can be used to identify the variables most crucial to a project's success.
   c. If only one variable is uncertain, sensitivity analysis gives "optimistic" and "pessimistic" values for project cash flow and NPV.
   d. The break-even sales level of a project is higher when *breakeven* is defined in terms of NPV rather than accounting income.
   e. Risk is reduced when a high proportion of costs are fixed.
   f. Monte Carlo simulation can be used to help forecast cash flows.

5. Suppose a manager has already estimated a project's cash flows, calculated its NPV, and done a sensitivity analysis like the one shown in Table 10.2. List the additional steps required to carry out a Monte Carlo simulation of project cash flows.

6. True or false?
   a. Decision trees can help identify and describe real options.
   b. The option to expand increases PV.
   c. High abandonment value decreases PV.
   d. If a project has positive NPV, the firm should always invest immediately.

7. Explain why setting a higher discount rate is not a cure for upward-biased cash-flow forecasts.

INTERMEDIATE

8. Draw up an outline or flowchart tracing the capital budgeting process from the initial idea for a new investment project to the completion of the project and the start of operations. Assume the idea for a new obfuscator machine comes from a plant manager in the Deconstruction Division of the Modern Language Corporation.

   Here are some questions your outline or flowchart should consider: Who will prepare the original proposal? What information will the proposal contain? Who will evaluate it? What approvals will be needed, and who will give them? What happens if the machine costs 40% more to purchase and install than originally forecasted? What will happen when the machine is finally up and running?

9. Look back to the cash flows for projects F and G in Section 5-3. The cost of capital was assumed to be 10%. Assume that the forecasted cash flows for projects of this type are overstated by 8% on average. That is, the forecast for each cash flow from each project should be reduced by 8%. But a lazy financial manager, unwilling to take the time to argue with the projects' sponsors, instructs them to use a discount rate of 18%.
   a. What are the projects' true NPVs?
   b. What are the NPVs at the 18% discount rate.
   c. Are there any circumstances in which the 18% discount rate would give the correct NPVs?
      (*Hint:* Could upward bias be more severe for more-distant cash flows?)

10. What is the NPV of the electric scooter project under the following scenario?

Market size	1.1 million
Market share	.1
Unit price	¥400,000
Unit variable cost	¥360,000
Fixed cost	¥2 billion

eXcel

Visit us at www.mhhe.com/bmam10e

11. Otobai's staff (see Section 10-2) has come up with the following revised estimates for the electric scooter project:

	Pessimistic	Expected	Optimistic
Market size	.8 million	1.0 million	1.2 million
Market share	.04	.1	.16
Unit price	¥300,000	¥375,000	¥400,000
Unit variable cost	¥350,000	¥300,000	¥275,000
Fixed cost	¥5 billion	¥3 billion	¥1 billion

Conduct a sensitivity analysis using the "live" spreadsheets (available at **www.mhhe.com bmam10e**). What are the principal uncertainties in the project?

12. Otobai is considering still another production method for its electric scooter (see Section 10 2). It would require an additional investment of ¥15 billion but would reduce variable costs by ¥40,000 per unit. Other assumptions follow Table 10.1.

    a. What is the NPV of this alternative scheme?
    b. Draw break-even charts for this alternative scheme along the lines of Figure 10.1.
    c. Explain how you would interpret the break-even figure.
    d. Now suppose Otobai's management would like to know the figure for variable cost per unit at which the electric scooter project in Section 10.1 would break even. Calculate the level of costs at which the project would earn zero profit and at which it would have zero NPV. Assume that the initial investment is ¥15 billion.
    e. Recalculate DOL.

13. The Rustic Welt Company is proposing to replace its old welt-making machinery with more modern equipment. The new equipment costs ₹9 million (the existing equipment has zero salvage value). The attraction of the new machinery is that it is expected to cut manufacturing costs from their current level of ₹8 a welt to ₹4. However, as the following table shows, there is some uncertainty both about future sales and about the performance of the new machinery:

Visit us at
www.mhhe.com/bmam10e

	Pessimistic	Expected	Optimistic
Sales, millions of welts	.4	.5	.7
Manufacturing cost with new machinery, dollars per welt	6	4	3
Economic life of new machinery, years	7	10	13

Conduct a sensitivity analysis of the replacement decision, assuming a discount rate of 12%. Rustic Welt does not pay taxes.

14. Suppose that the expected variable costs of Otobai's project are ¥33 billion a year and that fixed costs are zero. How does this change the degree of operating leverage? Now recompute the operating leverage assuming that the entire ¥33 billion of costs are fixed.

Visit us at
www.mhhe.com/bmam10e

15. Operating leverage is often measured as the percentage increase in pretax profits after depreciation for a 1% increase in sales.

    a. Calculate the operating leverage for the electric scooter project assuming unit sales are 100,000 (see Section 10-2).
    b. Now show that this figure is equal to 1 + (fixed costs including depreciation divided by pretax profits).
    c. Would operating leverage be higher or lower if sales were 200,000 scooters?

16. Look back at the Vegetron electric mop project in Section 9-4. Assume that if tests fail and Vegetron continues to go ahead with the project, the ₹1 million investment would generate only ₹75,000 a year. Display Vegetron's problem as a decision tree.

17. Our Web site (**www.mhhe.com/bma**) contains an Excel program for simulating the cash flows from the Otobai project. Use this program to examine which are the principal uncertainties surrounding the project. Suppose that some more analysis could effectively remove uncertainty about *one* of the variables. Suggest where it could be most usefully applied.

Visit us at
www.mhhe.com/bmam10e

18. Describe the real option in each of the following cases:
    a. Deutsche Metall postpones a major plant expansion. The expansion has positive NPV on a discounted-cash-flow basis but top management wants to get a better fix on product demand before proceeding.
    b. Western Telecom commits to production of digital switching equipment specially designed for the European market. The project has a negative NPV, but it is justified on strategic grounds by the need for a strong market position in the rapidly growing, and potentially very profitable, market.
    c. Western Telecom vetoes a fully integrated, automated production line for the new digital switches. It relies on standard, less-expensive equipment. The automated production line is more efficient overall, according to a discounted-cash-flow calculation.
    d. Mount Fuji Airways buys a jumbo jet with special equipment that allows the plane to be switched quickly from freight to passenger use or vice versa.

19. Look again at the decision tree in Figure 10.6. Expand the possible outcomes as follows:

    • Blockbuster: PV = $1.5 billion with 5% probability.
    • Above average: PV = $700 million with 20% probability.
    • Average: PV = $300 million with 40% probability.
    • Below average: PV = $100 million with 25% probability.
    • "Dog": PV = $40 million with 10% probability.

    Redraw the decision tree. Is the $18 million investment in phase II trials still positive NPV?

20. Look again at the example in Figure 10.6. The R&D team has put forward a proposal to invest an extra $20 million in expanded phase II trials. The object is to prove that the drug can be administered by a simple inhaler rather than as a liquid. If successful, the scope of use is broadened and the upside PV increases to $1 billion. The probabilities of success are unchanged. Go to the "live" Excel spreadsheet version of Table 10.6 at **www.mhhe.com/ bmam10e**. Is the extra $20 million investment worthwhile? Would your answer change if the probability of success in the phase III trials falls to 75%?

CHALLENGE

21. Air Coromondal is a new corporation formed by Rajesh Talwar to provide an executive flying service for the southeastern India. The founder thinks there will be a ready demand from businesses that cannot justify a full-time company plane but nevertheless need one from time to time. However, the venture is not a sure thing. There is a 40% chance that demand in the first year will be low. If it is low, there is a 60% chance that it will remain low in subsequent years. On the other hand, if the initial demand is high, there is an 80% chance that it will stay high. The immediate problem is to decide what kind of plane to buy. A turboprop costs ₹25,000,000. A piston-engine plane costs only $250,000 but has less capacity. Moreover, the piston-engine plane is an old design and likely to depreciate rapidly. Mr. Rajesh thinks that next year secondhand piston aircraft will be available for only ₹5,000,000.

    Table 10.7 shows how the payoffs in years 1 and 2 from both planes depend on the pattern of demand. You can see, for example, that if demand is high in both years, the turbo will provide a payoff of ₹45,000,000 in year 2. If demand is high in year 1 but low in year 2, the turbo's payoff in the second year is only ₹9,000,000. Think of the payoffs in the second year as the cash flow that year plus the year-2 value of any subsequent cash flows. Also think of these cash flows as certainty equivalents, which can therefore be discounted at the risk-free interest rate of 10%.

Mr. Rajesh now has an idea: Why not start out with one piston plane. If demand is low in the first year, Air Coromondal can sit tight with this one relatively inexpensive aircraft. On the other hand, if demand is high in the first year he can buy a second piston-engine plane for only ₹6,000,000. In this case, if demand continues to be high, the payoff in year 2 from the two piston planes will be ₹36,000,000. However, if demand in year 2 were to decline, the payoff would be only ₹5,000,000.

TABLE 10.7   The possible payoffs from Mr. Talwar's flying service. (All figures are in thousands. Probabilities are in parentheses.)

Payoffs from the Turboprop				
Year 1 demand	High (.6)		Low (.4)	
Year 1 payoff	₹7,500		₹1,500	
Year 2 demand	High (.8)	Low (.2)	High (.4)	Low (.6)
Year 2 payoff	₹4,600	₹10,000	₹45,000	₹6,500
Payoffs from the Piston Engine				
Year 1 demand	High (.6)		Low (.4)	
Year 1 payoff	₹5,000		₹2,500	
Year 2 demand	High (.8)	Low (.2)	High (.4)	Low (.6)
Year 2 payoff	₹20,000	₹8,500	₹10,500	₹5,000

a. Draw a decision tree setting out Air Coromondal's choices.
b. If Air Coromondal buys a piston plane, should it expand if demand turns out to be high in the first year?
c. Given your answer to b, would you recommend that Ms. Magna buys the turboprop or the piston-engine plane today?
d. What would be the NPV of an investment in a piston plane if there were no option to expand? How much extra value is contributed by the option to expand?

22. Look back at the guano project in Section 6-2. Use the Crystal Ball™ software to simulate how uncertainty about inflation could affect the project's cash flows.

MINI-CASE

WALDO COUNTY

Waldo County, the well-known real estate developer, worked long hours, and he expected his staff to do the same. So George Chavez was not surprised to receive a call from the boss just as George was about to leave for a long summer's weekend.

Mr. County's success had been built on a remarkable instinct for a good site. He would exclaim "Location! Location! Location!" at some point in every planning meeting. Yet finance was not his strong suit. On this occasion he wanted George to go over the figures for a new $90 million outlet mall designed to intercept tourists heading downeast toward Maine. "First thing Monday will do just fine," he said as he handed George the file. "I'll be in my house in Bar Harbor if you need me."

George's first task was to draw up a summary of the projected revenues and costs. The results are shown in Table 10.8. Note that the mall's revenues would come from two sources: The company would charge retailers an annual rent for the space they occupied and in addition it would receive 5% of each store's gross sales.

TABLE 10.8 Projected revenues and costs in real terms for the Downeast Tourist Mall (figures in $ millions).

	Year					
	0	1	2	3	4	5–17
Investment:						
Land	30					
Construction	20	30	10			
Operations:						
Rentals				12	12	12
Share of retail sales				24	24	24
Operating and maintenance costs	2	4	4	10	10	10
Real estate taxes	2	2	3	4	4	4

Construction of the mall was likely to take three years. The construction costs could be depreciated straight-line over 15 years starting in year 3. As in the case of the company's other developments, the mall would be built to the highest specifications and would not need to be rebuilt until year 17. The land was expected to retain its value, but could not be depreciated for tax purposes.

Construction costs, revenues, operating and maintenance costs, and real estate taxes were all likely to rise in line with inflation, which was forecasted at 2% a year. The company's tax rate was 35% and the cost of capital was 9% in nominal terms.

George decided first to check that the project made financial sense. He then proposed to look at some of the things that might go wrong. His boss certainly had a nose for a good retail project, but he was not infallible. The Salome project had been a disaster because store sales had turned out to be 40% below forecast. What if that happened here? George wondered just how far sales could fall short of forecast before the project would be underwater.

Inflation was another source of uncertainty. Some people were talking about a zero long-term inflation rate, but George also wondered what would happen if inflation jumped to, say, 10%.

A third concern was possible construction cost overruns and delays due to required zoning changes and environmental approvals. George had seen cases of 25% construction cost overruns and delays up to 12 months between purchase of the land and the start of construction. He decided that he should examine the effect that this scenario would have on the project's profitability.

"Hey, this might be fun," George exclaimed to Mr. Waldo's secretary, Fifi, who was heading for Old Orchard Beach for the weekend. "I might even try Monte Carlo."

"Waldo went to Monte Carlo once," Fifi replied. "Lost a bundle at the roulette table. I wouldn't remind him. Just show him the bottom line. Will it make money or lose money? That's the bottom line."

"OK, no Monte Carlo," George agreed. But he realized that building a spreadsheet and running scenarios was not enough. He had to figure out how to summarize and present his results to Mr. County.

Questions

1. What is the project's NPV, given the projections in Table 10.8?
2. Conduct a sensitivity and a scenario analysis of the project. What do these analyses reveal about the project's risks and potential value?

11
CHAPTER

INVESTMENT, STRATEGY, AND ECONOMIC RENTS

Why is a manager who has learned about discounted cash flows (DCF) like a baby with a hammer? Answer: Because to a baby with a hammer, everything looks like a nail.

Our point is that you should not focus on the arithmetic of DCF and thereby ignore the forecasts that are the basis of every investment decision. Senior managers are continuously bombarded with requests for funds for capital expenditures. All these requests are supported with detailed DCF analyses showing that the projects have positive NPVs.[1] How, then, can managers distinguish the NPVs that are truly positive from those that are merely the result of forecasting errors? We suggest that they should ask some probing questions about the possible sources of economic gain.

To make good investment decisions, you need to understand your firm's competitive advantages. This is where corporate strategy and finance come together. Good strategy positions the firm to generate the most value from its assets and growth opportunities. The search for good strategy starts with understanding how your firm stacks up versus your competitors, and how they will respond to your initiatives. Are your cash-flow forecasts realistic in your competitive environment? What effects will your competitors' actions have on the NPVs of your investments?

The first section in this chapter reviews certain common pitfalls in capital budgeting, notably the tendency to apply DCF when market values are already available and no DCF calculations are needed. The second section covers the *economic rents* that underlie all positive-NPV investments. The third section presents a case study describing how Marvin Enterprises, the gargle blaster company, analyzed the introduction of a radically new product.

---

[1] Here is another riddle. Are projects proposed because they have positive NPVs, or do they have positive NPVs because they are proposed? No prizes for the correct answer.

11-1 LOOK FIRST TO MARKET VALUES

Let us suppose that you have persuaded all your project sponsors to give honest forecasts. Although those forecasts are unbiased, they are still likely to contain errors, some positive and others negative. The average error will be zero, but that is little consolation because you want to accept only projects with *truly* superior profitability.

Think, for example, of what would happen if you were to jot down your estimates of the cash flows from operating various lines of business. You would probably find that about half *appeared* to have positive NPVs. This may not be because you personally possess any superior skill in operating jumbo jets or running a chain of laundromats but because you have inadvertently introduced large errors into your estimates of the cash flows. The more projects you contemplate, the more likely you are to uncover projects that *appear* to be extremely worthwhile.

What can you do to prevent forecast errors from swamping genuine information? We suggest that you begin by looking at market values.

The Cadillac and the Movie Star

The following parable should help to illustrate what we mean. Your local Cadillac dealer is announcing a special offer. For $55,001 you get not only a brand-new Cadillac but also the chance to shake hands with your favorite movie star. You wonder how much you are paying for that handshake.

There are two possible approaches to the problem. You could evaluate the worth of the Cadillac's overhead camshafts, disappearing windshield wipers, and other features and conclude that the Cadillac is worth $56,000. This would seem to suggest that the dealership is willing to pay $999 to have a movie star shake hands with you. Alternatively, you might note that the market price for Cadillacs is $55,000, so that you are paying $1 for the handshake. As long as there is a competitive market for Cadillacs, the latter approach is more appropriate.

Security analysts face a similar problem whenever they value a company's stock. They must consider the information that is already known to the market about a company, *and* they must evaluate the information that is known only to them. The information that is known to the market is the Cadillac; the private information is the handshake with the movie star. Investors have already evaluated the information that is generally known. Security analysts do not need to evaluate this information again. They can *start* with the market price of the stock and concentrate on valuing their private information.

While lesser mortals would instinctively accept the Cadillac's market value of $55,000, the financial manager is trained to enumerate and value all the costs and benefits from an investment and is therefore tempted to substitute his or her own opinion for the market's. Unfortunately this approach increases the chance of error. Many capital assets are traded in a competitive market, so it makes sense to *start* with the market price and then ask why these assets should earn more in your hands than in your rivals'.

EXAMPLE 11.1   Investing in a New Department Store

We encountered a department store chain that estimated the present value of the expected cash flows from each proposed store, including the price at which it could eventually sell the store. Although the firm took considerable care with these estimates, it was disturbed to find that its conclusions were heavily influenced by the forecasted selling price of each store. Management disclaimed any particular real estate expertise, but it discovered that its investment decisions were unintentionally dominated by its assumptions about future real estate prices.

Once the financial managers realized this, they always checked the decision to open a new store by asking the following question: "Let us assume that the property is fairly priced. What is the evidence that it is best suited to one of our department stores rather than to some other use?" In other words, *if an asset is worth more to others than it is to you, then beware of bidding for the asset against them.*

Let us take the department store problem a little further. Suppose that the new store costs ₹100 million.[2] You forecast that it will generate after-tax cash flow of ₹8 million a year for 10 years. Real estate prices are estimated to grow by 3% a year, so the expected value of the real estate at the end of 10 years is $100 \times (1.03)^{10}$ = ₹134 million. At a discount rate of 10%, your proposed department store has an NPV of ₹1 million:

$$\text{NPV} = -100 + \frac{8}{1.10} + \frac{8}{(1.10)^2} + \cdots + \frac{8 + 134}{(1.10)^{10}} = ₹1 \text{ million}$$

Notice how sensitive this NPV is to the ending value of the real estate. For example, an ending value of ₹120 million implies an NPV of –₹5 million.

It is helpful to imagine such a business as divided into two parts—a real estate subsidiary that buys the building and a retailing subsidiary that rents and operates it. Then figure out how much rent the real estate subsidiary would have to charge, and ask whether the retailing subsidiary could afford to pay the rent.

In some cases a fair market rental can be estimated from real estate transactions. For example, we might observe that similar retail space recently rented for ₹10 million a year. In that case we would conclude that our department store was an unattractive use for the site. Once the site had been acquired, it would be better to rent it out at ₹10 million than to use it for a store generating only ₹8 million.

Suppose, on the other hand, that the property could be rented for only ₹7 million per year. The department store could pay this amount to the real estate subsidiary and still earn a net operating cash flow of 8 − 7 = ₹1 million. It is therefore the best *current* use for the real estate.[3]

Will it also be the best *future* use? Maybe not, depending on whether retail profits keep pace with any rent increases. Suppose that real estate prices and rents are expected to increase by 3% per year. The real estate subsidiary must charge 7×1.03 = ₹7.21 million in year 2, 7.21×1.03 = ₹7.43 million in year 3, and so on.[4] Figure 11.1 shows that the store's income fails to cover the rental after year 5.

If these forecasts are right, the store has only a five-year economic life; from that point on the real estate is more valuable in some other use. If you stubbornly believe that the department store is the best long-term use for the site, you must be ignoring potential growth in income from the store.[5]

---

[2] For simplicity we assume the ₹100 million goes entirely to real estate. In real life there would also be substantial investments in fixtures, information systems, training, and start-up costs.

[3] The fair market rent equals the profit generated by the real estate's *second*-best use.

[4] This rental stream yields a 10% rate of return to the real estate subsidiary. Each year it gets a 7% "dividend" and 3% capital gain. Growth at 3% would bring the value of the property to ₹134 million by year 10.

The present value (at r = .10) of the growing stream of rents is

$$\text{PV} = \frac{7}{r-g} = \frac{7}{.10 - .03} = ₹100 \text{ million}$$

This PV is the initial market value of the property.

[5] Another possibility is that real estate rents and values are expected to grow at less than 3% a year. But in that case the real estate subsidiary would have to charge more than ₹7 million rent in year 1 to justify its ₹100 million real estate investment (see footnote 4). That would make the department store even less attractive.

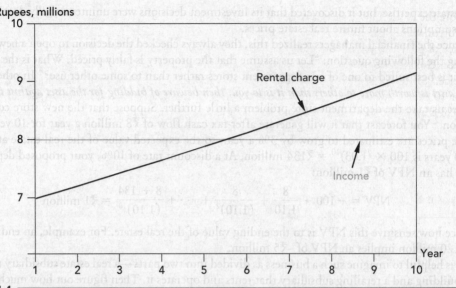

FIGURE 11.1
Beginning in year 6, the department store's income fails to cover the rental charge.

There is a general point here as illustrated in Example 11.1. Whenever you make a capital investment decision, think what bets you are placing. Our department store example involved at least two bets—one on real estate prices and another on the firm's ability to run a successful department store. But that suggests some alternative strategies. For instance, it would be foolish to make a lousy department store investment just because you are optimistic about real estate prices. You would do better to buy real estate and rent it out to the highest bidders. The converse is also true. You shouldn't be deterred from going ahead with a profitable department store because you are pessimistic about real estate prices. You would do better to sell the real estate and *rent* it back for the department store. We suggest that you separate the two bets by first asking, "Should we open a department store on this site, assuming that the real estate is fairly priced?" and then deciding whether you also want to go into the real estate business.

Here is another example of how market prices can help you make better decisions, see below.

EXAMPLE 11.2   Opening a Gold Mine

Kingsley Solomon is considering a proposal to open a new gold mine. He estimates that the mine will cost $400 million to develop and that in each of the next 10 years it will produce .1 million ounces of gold at a cost, after mining and refining, of $480 an ounce. Although the extraction costs can be predicted with reasonable accuracy, Mr. Solomon is much less confident about future gold prices. His best guess is that the price will rise by 5% per year from its current level of $800 an ounce. At a discount rate of 10%, this gives the mine an NPV of –$70 million:

$$\text{NPV} = -400 + \frac{.1(840 - 480)}{1.10} + \frac{.1(882 - 480)}{(1.10)^2} + \cdots + \frac{.1(1303 - 480)}{(1.10)^{10}}$$

$$= -\$70 \text{ million}$$

'herefore the gold mine project is rejected.

Unfortunately, Mr. Solomon did not look at what the market was telling him. What is the PV of n ounce of gold? Clearly, if the gold market is functioning properly, it is the current price—$800 n ounce. Gold does not produce any income, so $800 is the discounted value of the expected future old price.[6] Since the mine is expected to produce a total of 1 million ounces (.1 million ounces per ear for 10 years), the present value of the revenue stream is $1 \times 800 = \$800$ million.[7] We assume nat 10% is an appropriate discount rate for the relatively certain extraction costs. Thus

$$NPV = -\text{initial investment} + \text{PV revenues} - \text{PV costs}$$

$$= -400 + 800 - \sum_{t=1}^{10} \frac{.1 \times 480}{(1.10)^t} = \$105 \text{ million}$$

: looks as if Kingsley Solomon's mine is not such a bad bet after all.[8]

Mr. Solomon's gold, in Example 11.2, was just like anyone else's gold. So there was no point in rying to value it separately. By taking the PV of the gold sales as given, Mr. Solomon was able to focus n the crucial issue: Were the extraction costs sufficiently low to make the venture worthwhile? That rings us to another of those fundamental truths: If others are producing a good or service profitably nd (like Mr. Solomon) you can make it more cheaply, then you don't need any NPV calculations to now that you are probably onto a good thing.

Investing in an ounce of gold is like investing in a stock that pays no dividends: The investor's return comes entirely as capital gains. Look ack at Section 4-2, where we showed that P_0, the price of the stock today, depends on DIV_1 and P_1, the expected dividend and price for next ear, and the opportunity cost of capital r:

$$P_0 = \frac{DIV_1 + P_1}{1 + r}$$

ut for gold DIV1 = 0, so

$$P_0 = \frac{P_1}{1 + r}$$

n words, *today's price is the present value of next year's price*. Therefore, we don't have to know either P_1 or r to find the present value. Also since $DIV_2 = 0$,

$$P_1 = \frac{P_2}{1 + r}$$

nd we can express P_0 as

$$P_0 = \frac{P_1}{1 + r} = \frac{1}{1 + r}\left(\frac{P_2}{1 + r}\right) = \frac{P_2}{(1 + r)^2}$$

n general,

$$P_0 = \frac{P_t}{(1 + r)^t}$$

'his holds for any asset that pays no dividends, is traded in a competitive market, and costs nothing to store. Storage costs for gold or common tocks are very small compared to asset value.

We also assume that guaranteed future delivery of gold is just as good as having gold in hand today. This is not quite right. As we will see n Chapter 26, gold in hand can generate a small "convenience yield."

We assume that the extraction rate does not vary. If it can vary, Mr. Solomon has a valuable operating option to increase output when gold rices are high or to cut back when prices fall. Option pricing techniques are needed to value the mine when operating options are important. ee Chapter 22.

As in the case of our department store example, Mr. Solomon is placing two bets: one on his ability to mine gold at a low cost and the other n the price of gold. Suppose that he really does believe that gold is overvalued. That should not deter him from running a low-cost gold mine s long as he can place separate bets on gold prices. For example, he might be able to enter into a long-term contract to sell the mine's output r he could sell gold futures. (We explain *futures* in Chapter 26.)

We confess that our example of Kingsley Solomon's mine is somewhat special. Unlike gold, most commodities are not kept solely for investment purposes, and therefore you cannot automatically assume that today's price is equal to the present value of the future price.[9]

However, here is another way that you may be able to tackle the problem. Suppose that you are considering investment in a new copper mine and that someone offers to buy the mine's future output at a fixed price. If you accept the offer—and the buyer is completely creditworthy—the revenue from the mine are certain and can be discounted at the risk-free interest rate.[10] That takes us to Chapter 9, where we explained that there are two ways to calculate PV:

- Estimate the expected cash flows and discount at a rate that reflects the risk of those flows.
- Estimate what sure-fire cash flows would have the same values as the risky cash flows. Then discount these *certainty-equivalent* cash flows at the risk-free interest rate.

When you discount the fixed-price revenues at the risk-free rate, you are using the certainty-equivalent method to value the mine's output. By doing so, you gain in two ways: You don't need to estimate future mineral prices, and you don't need to worry about the appropriate discount rate for risky cash flows.

But here's the question: What is the minimum fixed price at which you could agree today to sell your future output? In other words, what is the certainty-equivalent price? Fortunately, for many commodities there is an active market in which firms fix today the price at which they will buy or sell copper and other commodities in the future. This market is known as the *futures market,* which we will cover in Chapter 26. Futures prices are certainty equivalents, and you can look them up in the daily newspaper. So you don't need to make elaborate forecasts of copper prices to work out the PV of the mine's output. The market has already done the work for you; you simply calculate future revenues using the price in the newspaper of copper futures and discount these revenues at the risk-free interest rate.

Of course, things are never as easy as textbooks suggest. Trades in organized futures exchanges are largely confined to deliveries over the next year or so, and therefore your newspaper won't show the price at which you could sell output beyond this period. But financial economists have developed techniques for using the prices in the futures market to estimate the amount that buyers would agree to pay for more-distant deliveries.[11]

Our two examples of gold and copper producers are illustrations of a universal principle of finance:

When you have the market value of an asset, *use it,* at least as a starting point in your analysis.

11-2   ECONOMIC RENTS AND COMPETITIVE ADVANTAGE

Profits that more than cover the cost of capital are known as *economic rents*. Economics 101 teaches us that in the long run competition eliminates economic rents. That is, in a long-run competitive equilibrium, no competitor can expand and earn more than the cost of capital on the investment

---

[9] A more general guide to the relationship of current and future commodity prices was proposed by Hotelling, who pointed out that if there are constant returns to scale in mining any mineral, the expected rise in the price of the mineral *less* extraction costs should equal the cost of capital. If the expected growth were faster, everyone would want to postpone extraction; if it were slower, everyone would want to exploit the resource today. For a review of Hotelling's principle, see S. Devarajan and A. C. Fisher, "Hotelling's 'Economics of Exhaustible Resources': Fifty Years Later," *Journal of Economic Literature* 19 (March 1981), pp. 65–73.

[10] We assume that the *volume* of output is certain (or does not have any market risk).

[11] After reading Chapter 26, check out E. S. Schwartz, "The Stochastic Behavior of Commodity Prices: Implications for Valuation and Hedging," *Journal of Finance* 52 (July 1997), pp. 923–973; and A. J. Neuberger, "Hedging Long-Term Exposures with Multiple Short-Term Contracts," *Review of Financial Studies* 12 (1999), pp. 429–459.

Economic rents are earned when an industry has not settled down to equilibrium or when your firm has something valuable that your competitors don't have.

Suppose that demand takes off unexpectedly and that your firm is well-placed to expand production capacity quicker and cheaper than your competitors. This stroke of luck is pretty sure to generate economic rents, at least temporarily as other firms struggle to catch up.

Some competitive advantages are longer lived. They include patents or proprietary technology; reputation, embodied in respected brand names, for example; economies of scale that customers can't match; protected markets that competitors can't enter; and strategic assets that competitors can't easily duplicate.

Here's an example of strategic assets. Think of the difference between railroads and trucking companies. It's easy to enter the trucking business but nearly impossible to build a brand-new, long-haul railroad.[12] The interstate lines operated by U.S. railroads are strategic assets. With these assets in place, railroads were able to increase revenues and profits rapidly from 2005 to 2007, when shipments surged and energy prices increased. The high cost of diesel fuel was more burdensome for trucks, which are less fuel efficient than railroads. Thus high energy prices actually handed the railroads a competitive advantage.

Corporate strategy aims to find and exploit sources of competitive advantage. The problem, as always, is how to do it. John Kay advises firms to pick out distinctive capabilities—existing strengths, not just ones that would be nice to have—and then to identify the product markets where the capabilities can generate the most value added. The capabilities may come from durable relationships with customers or suppliers, from the skills and experience of employees, from brand names and reputation, and from the ability to innovate.[13]

Michael Porter identifies five aspects of industry structure (or "five forces") that determine which industries are able to provide sustained economic rents.[14] These are the rivalry among existing competitors, the likelihood of new competition, the threat of substitutes, and the bargaining power both of suppliers and customers.

With increasing global competition, firms cannot rely so easily on industry structure to provide high returns. Therefore, managers also need to ensure that the firm is positioned *within* its industry so as to secure a competitive advantage. Michael Porter suggests three ways that this can be done—by cost leadership, by product differentiation, and by focus on a particular market niche.[15]

In today's world successful strategies that combine different mixes of cost leadership, product differentiation, and focus appear to be the key to developing a unique position in an industry.[16] Think, for example, Maruti Udyog Limited. It blends elements of all the three strategies. It is one of the low-cost manufacturers of passenger cars in India. It differentiates itself from its competitors by its distinct Japanese design. It provides insurance with delivery to customers. It makes funds available in the showrooms so that customers buying its cars can get instant credit. It also provides third and fourth year warranty on its cars. It has a clear focus on a group of customers, who belong to the middle class and are price-conscious.

You can see how business strategy and finance reinforce each other. Managers who have a clear understanding of their firm's competitive strengths are better placed to separate those projects that truly

---

[12] The Dakota, Minnesota & Eastern Railroad is proposing to build a new line to transport coal from Wyoming to the Midwest U.S., but construction would require government subsidies.

[13] John Kay, *Why Firms Succeed* (New York: Oxford University Press, 1995).

[14] See M. E. Porter, *Competitive Strategy: Techniques for Analyzing Industries and Competitors* (New York: The Free Press, 1980).

[15] See M. E. Porter, *Competitive Advantage: Creating and Sustaining Superior Advantage* (New York: The Free Press, 1985).

[16] R. M. Grant, *Contemporary Strategy Analysis,* 4th ed. (Oxford: Blackwell, 2002), p. 248.

have a positive NPV from those that do not. Therefore when you are presented with a project that appears to have a positive NPV, do not just accept the calculations at face value. They may reflect simple estimation errors in forecasting cash flows. Probe behind the cash-flow estimates, and *try to identify the source of economic rents.* A positive NPV for a new project is believable only if you believe that your company has some special advantage.

Thinking about competitive advantage can also help ferret out negative-NPV calculations that are negative by mistake. For example, if you are the lowest-cost producer of a profitable product in a growing market, then you should invest to expand along with the market. If your calculations show a negative NPV for such an expansion, then you have probably made a mistake.

We will work through shortly an extended example that shows how a firm's analysis of its competitive position confirmed that its investment had a positive NPV. But first we look at an example in which the analysis helped a firm to ferret out a negative-NPV transaction and avoid a costly mistake.

EXAMPLE 11.3   How One Company Avoided a $100 Million Mistake

A U.S. chemical producer was about to modify an existing plant to produce a specialty product, poly-zone, which was in short supply on world markets.[17] At prevailing raw material and finished-product prices the expansion would have been strongly profitable. Table 11.1 shows a simplified version of management's analysis. Note the assumed constant spread between selling price and the cost of raw materials. Given this spread, the resulting NPV was about $64 million at the company's 8% real cost of capital—not bad for a $100 million outlay.

TABLE 11.1 NPV calculation for proposed investment in polyzone production by a U.S. chemical company (figures in $ millions except as noted).

eXcel
Visit us at
www.mhhe.com/bmam10e

	Year 0	Year 1	Year 2	Years 3–10
Investment	100			
Production, millions of pounds per year[a]	0	0	40	80
Spread, $ per pound	1.20	1.20	1.20	1.20
Net revenues	0	0	48	96
Production costs[b]	0	0	30	30
Transport[c]	0	0	4	8
Other costs	0	20	20	20
Cash flow	−100	−20	−6	38
NPV (at $r = 8\%$) = $63.56 million				

Note: For simplicity, we assume no inflation and no taxes. Plant and equipment have no salvage value after 10 years.
[a]Production capacity is 80 million pounds per year.
[b]Production costs are $.375 per pound after start up ($.75 per pound in year 2, when production is only 40 million pounds).
[c]Transportation costs are $.10 per pound to European ports.

Then doubt began to creep in. Notice the outlay for transportation costs. Some of the project's raw materials were commodity chemicals, largely imported from Europe, and much of the polyzone production would be exported back to Europe. Moreover, the U.S. company had no long-run technological edge over potential European competitors. It had a head start perhaps, but was that really enough to generate a positive NPV?

---
[17]This is a true story, but names and details have been changed to protect the innocent.

Notice the importance of the price spread between raw materials and finished product. The analysis in Table 11.1 forecasted the spread at a constant $1.20 per pound of polyzone for 10 years. That had to be wrong: European producers, who did not face the U.S. company's transportation costs, would see an even larger NPV and expand capacity. Increased competition would almost surely squeeze the spread. The U.S. company decided to calculate the *competitive* spread—the spread at which a European competitor would see polyzone capacity as zero NPV. Table 11.2 shows management's analysis. The resulting spread of about $.95 per pound was the best *long-run* forecast for the polyzone market, other things constant of course.

TABLE 11.2   What is the competitive spread to a European producer? About $.95 per pound of polyzone. Note that European producers face no transportation costs. Compare Table 11.1 (figures in $ millions except as noted).

	Year 0	Year 1	Year 2	Years 3–10
Investment	100			
Production, millions of pounds per year	0	0	40	80
Spread, $ per pound	.95	.95	.95	.95
Net revenues	0	0	38	76
Production costs	0	0	30	30
Transport	0	0	0	0
Other costs	0	20	20	20
Cash flow	−100	−20	−12	+26
NPV (at $r = 8\%$) = 0				

How much of a head start did the U.S. producer have? How long before competitors forced the spread down to $.95? Management's best guess was five years. It prepared Table 11.3, which is identical to Table 11.1 except for the forecasted spread, which would shrink to $.95 by the start of year 5. Now the NPV was negative.

TABLE 11.3   Recalculation of NPV for polyzone investment by U.S. company (figures in $ millions except as noted). If expansion by European producers forces competitive spreads by year 5, the U.S. producer's NPV falls to −$9.8 million. Compare Table 11.1.

	Year 0	Year 1	Year 2	Year 3	Year 4	Years 5–10
Investment	100					
Production, millions of pounds per year	0	0	40	80	80	80
Spread, $ per pound	1.20	1.20	1.20	1.20	1.10	0.95
Net revenues	0	0	48	96	88	76
Production costs	0	0	30	30	30	30
Transport	0	0	4	8	8	8
Other costs	0	20	20	20	20	20
Cash flow	−100	−20	−6	38	30	18
NPV (at $r = 8\%$) = −9.8						

The project might have been saved if production could have been started in year 1 rather than 2 or if local markets could have been expanded, thus reducing transportation costs. But these changes were not feasible, so management canceled the project, albeit with a sigh of relief that its analysis had not stopped at Table 11.1.

This is a perfect example of the importance of thinking through sources of economic rents. Positive NPVs are suspect without some long-run competitive advantage. When a company contemplates investing in a new product or expanding production of an existing product, it should specifically identify its advantages or disadvantages over its most dangerous competitors. It should calculate NPV from those competitors' points of view. If competitors' NPVs come out strongly positive, the company had better expect decreasing prices (or spreads) and evaluate the proposed investment accordingly.

11-3   MARVIN ENTERPRISES DECIDES TO EXPLOIT A NEW TECHNOLOGY—AN EXAMPLE

To illustrate some of the problems involved in predicting economic rents, let us leap forward several years and look at the decision by Marvin Enterprises to exploit a new technology.[18]

One of the most unexpected developments of these years was the remarkable growth of a completely new industry. By 2032 annual sales of gargle blasters totaled $1.68 billion, or 240 million units. Although it controlled only 10% of the market, Marvin Enterprises was among the most exciting growth companies of the decade. Marvin had come late into the business, but it had pioneered the use of integrated microcircuits to control the genetic engineering processes used to manufacture gargle blasters. This development had enabled producers to cut the price of gargle blasters from $9 to $7 and had thereby contributed to the dramatic growth in the size of the market. The estimated demand curve in Figure 11.2 shows just how responsive demand is to such price reductions.

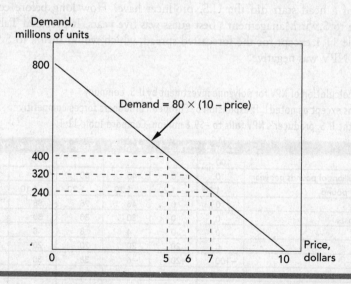

FIGURE 11.2

The demand "curve" for gargle blasters shows that for each $1 cut in price there is an increase in demand of 80 million units.

---

[18] We thank Stewart Hodges for permission to adapt this example from a case prepared by him, and we thank the BBC for permission to use the term *gargle blasters*.

Table 11.4 summarizes the cost structure of the old and new technologies. While companies with the new technology were earning 20% on their initial investment, those with first-generation equipment had been hit by the successive price cuts. Since all Marvin's investment was in the 2028 technology, it had been particularly well placed during this period.

TABLE 11.4   Size and cost structure of the gargle blaster industry before Marvin announced its expansion plans.

Technology	Capacity, Millions of Units		Capital Cost per Unit ($)	Manufacturing Cost per Unit ($)	Salvage Value per Unit ($)
	Industry	Marvin			
First generation (2020)	120	—	17.50	5.50	2.50
Second generation (2028)	120	24	17.50	3.50	2.50

Note: Selling price is $7 per unit. One unit means one gargle blaster.

Rumors of new developments at Marvin had been circulating for some time, and the total market value of Marvin's stock had risen to $460 million by January 2033. At that point Marvin called a press conference to announce another technological breakthrough. Management claimed that its new third-generation process involving mutant neurons enabled the firm to reduce capital costs to $10 and manufacturing costs to $3 per unit. Marvin proposed to capitalize on this invention by embarking on a huge $1 billion expansion program that would add 100 million units to capacity. The company expected to be in full operation within 12 months.

Before deciding to go ahead with this development, Marvin had undertaken extensive calculations on the effect of the new investment. The basic assumptions were as follows:

1. The cost of capital was 20%.
2. The production facilities had an indefinite physical life.
3. The demand curve and the costs of each technology would not change.
4. There was no chance of a fourth-generation technology in the foreseeable future.
5. The corporate income tax, which had been abolished in 2023, was not likely to be reintroduced.

Marvin's competitors greeted the news with varying degrees of concern. There was general agreement that it would be five years before any of them would have access to the new technology. On the other hand, many consoled themselves with the reflection that Marvin's new plant could not compete with an existing plant that had been fully depreciated.

Suppose that you were Marvin's financial manager. Would you have agreed with the decision to expand? Do you think it would have been better to go for a larger or smaller expansion? How do you think Marvin's announcement is likely to affect the price of its stock?

You have a choice. You can go on *immediately* to read *our* solution to these questions. But you will learn much more if you stop and work out your own answer first. Try it.

Forecasting Prices of Gargle Blasters

Up to this point in any capital budgeting problem we have always given you the set of cash-flow forecasts. In the present case you have to *derive* those forecasts.

The first problem is to decide what is going to happen to the price of gargle blasters. Marvin's new venture will increase industry capacity to 340 million units. From the demand curve in Figure 11.2, you can see that the industry can sell this number of gargle blasters only if the price declines to $5.75:

$$\text{Demand} = 80 \times (10 - \text{price})$$
$$= 80 \times (10 - 5.75) = 340 \text{ million units}$$

If the price falls to $5.75, what will happen to companies with the 2020 technology? They also have to make an investment decision: Should they stay in business, or should they sell their equipment for its salvage value of $2.50 per unit? With a 20% opportunity cost of capital, the NPV of staying in business is

$$\text{NPV} = -\text{investment} + \text{PV}(\text{price} - \text{manufacturing cost})$$
$$= -2.50 + \frac{5.75 - 5.50}{.20} = -\$1.25 \text{ per unit}$$

Smart companies with 2020 equipment will, therefore, see that it is better to sell off capacity. No matter what their equipment originally cost or how far it is depreciated, it is more profitable to sell the equipment for $2.50 per unit than to operate it and lose $1.25 per unit.

As capacity is sold off, the supply of gargle blasters will decline and the price will rise. An equilibrium is reached when the price gets to $6. At this point 2020 equipment has a zero NPV:

$$\text{NPV} = -2.50 + \frac{6.00 - 5.50}{.20} = \$0 \text{ per unit}$$

How much capacity will have to be sold off before the price reaches $6? You can check that by going back to the demand curve:

$$\text{Demand} = 80 \times (10 - \text{price})$$
$$= 80 \times (10 - 6) = 320 \text{ million units}$$

Therefore Marvin's expansion will cause the price to settle down at $6 a unit and will induce first-generation producers to withdraw 20 million units of capacity.

But after five years Marvin's competitors will also be in a position to build third-generation plants. As long as these plants have positive NPVs, companies will increase their capacity and force prices down once again. A new equilibrium will be reached when the price reaches $5. At this point, the NPV of new third-generation plants is zero, and there is no incentive for companies to expand further:

$$\text{NPV} = -10 + \frac{5.00 - 3.00}{.20} = \$0 \text{ per unit}$$

Looking back once more at our demand curve, you can see that with a price of $5 the industry can sell a total of 400 million gargle blasters:

$$\text{Demand} = 80 \times (10 - \text{price}) = 80 \times (10 - 5) = 400 \text{ million units}$$

The effect of the third-generation technology is, therefore, to cause industry sales to expand from 240 million units in 2032 to 400 million five years later. But that rapid growth is no protection against failure. By the end of five years any company that has only first-generation equipment will no longer be able to cover its manufacturing costs and will be *forced* out of business.

The Value of Marvin's New Expansion

We have shown that the introduction of third-generation technology is likely to cause gargle blaster prices to decline to $6 for the next five years and to $5 thereafter. We can now set down the expected cash flows from Marvin's new plant:

	Year 0 (Investment)	Years 1–5 (Revenue – Manufacturing Cost)	Year 6, 7, 8, . . . (Revenue – Manufacturing Cost)
Cash flow per unit ($)	–10	6 – 3 = 3	5 – 3 = 2
Cash flow, 100 million units ($ millions)	–1,000	600 – 300 = 300	500 – 300 = 200

Discounting these cash flows at 20% gives us

$$\text{NPV} = -1,000 + \sum_{t=1}^{5}\frac{300}{(1.20)^t} + \frac{1}{(1.20)^5}\left(\frac{200}{.20}\right) = \$299 \text{ million}$$

It looks as if Marvin's decision to go ahead was correct. But there is something we have forgotten. When we evaluate an investment, we must consider *all* incremental cash flows. One effect of Marvin's decision to expand is to reduce the value of its existing 2028 plant. If Marvin decided not to go ahead with the new technology, the $7 price of gargle blasters would hold until Marvin's competitors started to cut prices in five years' time. Marvin's decision, therefore, leads to an immediate $1 cut in price. This reduces the present value of its 2028 equipment by

$$24 \text{ million} \times \sum_{t=1}^{5}\frac{1.00}{(1.20)^t} = \$72 \text{ million}$$

Considered in isolation, Marvin's decision has an NPV of $299 million. But it also reduces the value of existing plant by $72 million. The net present value of Marvin's venture is, therefore, 299 – 72 = $227 million.

Alternative Expansion Plans

Marvin's expansion has a positive NPV, but perhaps Marvin would do better to build a larger or smaller plant. You can check that by going through the same calculations as above. First you need to estimate how the additional capacity will affect gargle blaster prices. Then you can calculate the net present value of the new plant and the change in the present value of the existing plant. The total NPV of Marvin's expansion plan is

Total NPV = NPV of new plant + change in PV of existing plant

We have undertaken these calculations and plotted the results in Figure 11.3. You can see how total NPV would be affected by a smaller or larger expansion.

When the new technology becomes generally available in 2038, firms will construct a total of 280 million units of new capacity.[19] But Figure 11.3 shows that it would be foolish for Marvin to go that far. If Marvin added 280 million units of new capacity in 2033, the discounted value of the cash flows from the new plant would be zero *and* the company would have reduced the value of its old plant by

---

[19] Total industry capacity in 2038 will be 400 million units. Of this, 120 million units are second-generation capacity, and the remaining 280 million units are third-generation capacity.

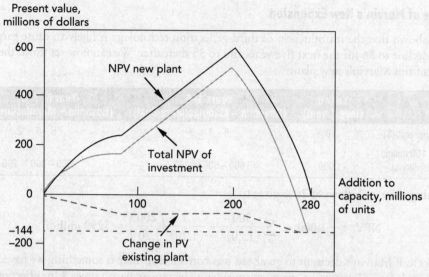

FIGURE 11.3

Effect on net present value of alternative expansion plans. Marvin's 100-million-unit expansion has a total NPV of $227 million (total NPV = NPV new plant + change in PV existing plant = 299 − 72 = 227). Total NPV is maximized if Marvin builds 200 million units of new capacity. If Marvin builds 280 million units of new capacity, total NPV is −$144 million.

$144 million. To maximize NPV, Marvin should construct 200 million units of new capacity and set the price just below $6 to drive out the 2020 manufacturers. Output is, therefore, less and price is higher than either would be under free competition.[20]

The Value of Marvin Stock

Let us think about the effect of Marvin's announcement on the value of its common stock. Marvin has 24 million units of second-generation capacity. In the absence of any third-generation technology, gargle blaster prices would hold at $7 and Marvin's existing plant would be worth

$$PV = 24 \text{ million} \times \frac{7.00 - 3.50}{.20}$$
$$= \$420 \text{ million}$$

Marvin's new technology reduces the price of gargle blasters initially to $6 and after five years to $5. Therefore the value of existing plant declines to

$$PV = 24 \text{ million} \times \left[\sum_{t=1}^{5} \frac{6.00 - 3.50}{(1.20)^t} + \frac{5.00 - 3.50}{.20 \times (1.20)^5} \right]$$
$$= \$252 \text{ million}$$

---

[20] Notice that we are assuming that all customers have to pay the same price for their gargle blasters. If Marvin could charge each customer the maximum price that that customer would be willing to pay, output would be the same as under free competition. Such direct price discrimination is illegal and in any case difficult to enforce. But firms do search for indirect ways to differentiate between customers. For example, stores often offer free delivery, which is equivalent to a price discount for customers who live at an inconvenient distance.

But the *new* plant makes a net addition to shareholders' wealth of $299 million. So after Marvin's announcement its stock will be worth

$$252 + 299 = \$551 \text{ million}^{21}$$

Now here is an illustration of something we talked about in Chapter 4: Before the announcement, Marvin's stock was valued in the market at $460 million. The difference between this figure and the value of the existing plant represented the present value of Marvin's growth opportunities (PVGO). The market valued Marvin's ability to stay ahead of the game at $40 million even before the announcement. After the announcement PVGO rose to $299 million.[22]

The Lessons of Marvin Enterprises

Marvin Enterprises may be just a piece of science fiction, but the problems that it confronts are very real. Whenever Intel considers developing a new microprocessor or Genzyme considers developing a new drug, these firms must face up to exactly the same issues as Marvin. We have tried to illustrate the *kind* of questions that you should be asking when presented with a set of cash-flow forecasts. Of course, no economic model is going to predict the future with accuracy. Perhaps Marvin can hold the price above $6. Perhaps competitors will not appreciate the rich pickings to be had in the year 2038. In that case, Marvin's expansion would be even more profitable. But would you want to bet $1 billion on such possibilities? We don't think so.

Investments often turn out to earn far more than the cost of capital because of a favorable surprise. This surprise may in turn create a temporary opportunity for further investments earning more than the cost of capital. But anticipated and more prolonged rents will naturally lead to the entry of rival producers. That is why you should be suspicious of any investment proposal that predicts a stream of economic rents into the indefinite future. Try to estimate *when* competition will drive the NPV down to zero, and think what that implies for the price of your product.

Many companies try to identify the major growth areas in the economy and then concentrate their investment in these areas. But the sad fate of first-generation gargle blaster manufacturers illustrates how rapidly existing plants can be made obsolete by changes in technology. It is fun being in a growth industry when you are at the forefront of the new technology, but a growth industry has no mercy on technological laggards.

Therefore, do not simply follow the herd of investors stampeding into high-growth sectors of the economy. Think of the fate of the dot.com companies in the "new economy" of the late 1990s. Optimists argued that the information revolution was opening up opportunities for companies to grow at unprecedented rates. The pessimists pointed out that competition in e-commerce was likely to be intense and that competition would ensure that the benefits of the information revolution would go largely to consumers. The Finance in Practice Box, which contains an extract from an article by Warren Buffett, emphasizes that rapid growth is no guarantee of superior profits.

We do not wish to imply that good investment opportunities don't exist. For example, good opportunities frequently arise because the firm has invested money in the past, which gives it the

---

[21] To finance the expansion, Marvin is going to have to sell $1,000 million of new stock. Therefore the *total* value of Marvin's stock will rise to $1,551 million. But investors who put up the new money will receive shares worth $1,000 million. The value of Marvin's old shares after the announcement is therefore $551 million.

[22] The market value of Marvin stock will be greater than $551 million if investors expect the company to expand again within the five-year period. In other words, PVGO after the expansion may still be positive. Investors may expect Marvin to stay one step ahead of its competitors or to successfully apply its special technology in other areas.

Finance In Practice

Warren Buffett on Growth and Profitability

I thought it would be instructive to go back and look at a couple of industries that transformed this country much earlier in this century: automobiles and aviation. Take automobiles first: I have here one page, out of 70 in total, of car and truck manufacturers that have operated in this country. At one time, there was a Berkshire car and an Omaha car. Naturally I noticed those. But there was also a telephone book of others.

All told, there appear to have been at least 2,000 car makes, in an industry that had an incredible impact on people's lives. If you had foreseen in the early days of cars how this industry would develop, you would have said, "Here is the road to riches." So what did we progress to by the 1990s? After corporate carnage that never let up, we came down to three U.S. car companies—themselves no lollapaloozas for investors. So here is an industry that had an enormous impact on America—and also an enormous impact, though not the anticipated one, on investors. Sometimes, incidentally, it's much easier in these transforming events to figure out the losers. You could have grasped the importance of the auto when it came along but still found it hard to pick companies that would make you money. But there was one obvious decision you could have made back then—it's better sometimes to turn these things upside down—and that was to short horses. Frankly, I'm disappointed that the Buffett family was not short horses through this entire period. And we really had no excuse: Living in Nebraska, we would have found it super-easy to borrow horses and avoid a "short squeeze."

U.S. Horse Population
1900: 21 million
1998: 5 million

The other truly transforming business invention of the first quarter of the century, besides the car, was the airplane—another industry whose plainly brilliant future would have caused investors to salivate. So I went back to check out aircraft manufacturers and found that in the 1919–39 period, there were about 300 companies, only a handful still breathing today. Among the planes made then—we must have been the Silicon Valley of that age—were both the Nebraska and the Omaha, two aircraft that even the most loyal Nebraskan no longer relies upon.

Move on to failures of airlines. Here's a list of 129 airlines that in the past 20 years filed for bankruptcy. Continental was smart enough to make that list twice. As of 1992, in fact—though the picture would have improved since then—the money that had been made since the dawn of aviation by all of this country's airline companies was zero. Absolutely zero.

Sizing all this up, I like to think that if I'd been at Kitty Hawk in 1903 when Orville Wright took off, I would have been farsighted enough, and public-spirited enough—I owed this to future capitalists—to shoot him down. I mean, Karl Marx couldn't have done as much damage to capitalists as Orville did.

I won't dwell on other glamorous businesses that dramatically changed our lives but concurrently failed to deliver rewards to U.S. investors: the manufacture of radios and televisions, for example. But I will draw a lesson from these businesses: The key to investing is not assessing how much an industry is going to affect society, or how much it will grow, but rather determining the competitive advantage of any given company and, above all, the durability of that advantage. The products or services that have wide, sustainable moats around them are the ones that deliver rewards to investors.

Source: C. Loomis, "Mr. Buffett on the Stock Market," *Fortune* (November 22, 1999), pp. 110–115. © 1999 Time Inc. All rights reserved.

option to expand cheaply in the future. Perhaps the firm can increase its output just by adding an extra production line, whereas its rivals would need to construct an entirely new factory.

Marvin also reminds us to include a project's impact on the rest of the firm when estimating incremental cash flows. By introducing the new technology immediately, Marvin reduced the value of its existing plant by $72 million.

Sometimes the losses on existing plants may completely offset the gains from a new technology. That is why we may see established, technologically advanced companies deliberately slowing down the rate at which they introduce new products. But this can be a dangerous game to play if it opens up opportunities for competitors. For example, for many years Bausch & Lomb was the dominant producer of contact lenses and earned large profits from glass contact lenses that needed to be sterilized every night. Because its existing business generated high returns, the company was slow to introduce disposable lenses. This delay opened up an opportunity for competitors and enabled Johnson & Johnson to introduce disposable lenses.

Marvin's economic rents were equal to the difference between its costs and those of the marginal producer. The costs of the marginal 2020-generation plant consisted of the manufacturing costs plus the opportunity cost of not selling the equipment. Therefore, if the salvage value of the 2020 equipment were higher, Marvin's competitors would incur higher costs and Marvin could earn higher rents. We took the salvage value as given, but it in turn depends on the cost savings from substituting outdated gargle blaster equipment for some other asset. In a well-functioning economy, assets will be used so as to minimize the *total* cost of producing the chosen set of outputs. The economic rents earned by any asset are equal to the total extra costs that would be incurred if that asset were withdrawn.

When Marvin announced its expansion plans, many owners of first-generation equipment took comfort in the belief that Marvin could not compete with their fully depreciated plant. Their comfort was misplaced. Regardless of past depreciation policy, it paid to scrap first-generation equipment rather than keep it in production. Do not expect that numbers in your balance sheet can protect you from harsh economic reality.

SUMMARY

All good financial managers want to find and undertake positive-NPV projects. They calculate NPVs carefully. But NPVs can be positive for two reasons: (1) The company really can expect to earn economic rents, or (2) there are biases or errors in cash-flow forecasts. Good managers are wary of these "false positives" and try to keep the odds stacked in their favor by investing in areas where the company has clear competitive advantages. They give careful attention to corporate strategy, which attempts to identify distinct capabilities and deploy them in markets where economic rents can be generated. They avoid expansion where competitive advantages are absent and economic rents are unlikely. They do not project favorable current product prices into the future without checking whether entry or expansion by competitors will drive future prices down.

Our story of Marvin Enterprises illustrates the origin of rents and how they determine a project's cash flows and net present value.

Any present value calculation, including our calculation for Marvin Enterprises, is subject to error. That's life: There's no other sensible way to value most capital investment projects. But some assets, such as gold, real estate, crude oil, ships, and airplanes, as well as financial assets, such as stocks and bonds, are traded in reasonably competitive markets. When you have the market value of such an asset, *use it,* at least as a starting point for your analysis.

FURTHER READING

The following papers discuss capital investment and strategy:

P. Barwise, P. Marsh, and R. Wensley, "Must Finance and Strategy Clash?" *Harvard Business Review,* September–October 1989, pp. 2–7.

M. Porter, "What Is Strategy?" *Harvard Business Review,* November–December 1996, pp. 61–78.

S. C. Myers, "Finance Theory and Financial Strategy," *Midland Corporate Finance Journal* 5 (Spring 1987), pp. 6–13. Reprinted from *Interfaces* (January–February 1984).

The following book describes how to identify economic rents and positive NPVs:

S. Woolley, *Sources of Value,* Cambridge University Press, 2009.

PROBLEM SETS

BASIC

1. True or false?
   a. A firm that earns the opportunity cost of capital is earning economic rents.
   b. A firm that invests in positive-NPV ventures expects to earn economic rents.
   c. Financial managers should try to identify areas where their firms can earn economic rents, because it is there that positive-NPV projects are likely to be found.
   d. Economic rent is the equivalent annual cost of operating capital equipment.

2. Demand for concave utility meters is expanding rapidly, but the industry is highly competitive. A utility meter plant costs ₹50 million to set up, and it has an annual capacity of 500,000 meters. The production cost is ₹5 per meter, and this cost is not expected to change. The machines have an indefinite physical life and the cost of capital is 10%. What is the competitive price of a utility meter?
   a. ₹5
   b. ₹10
   c. ₹15

3. Your brother-in-law wants you to join him in purchasing a building on the outskirts of town. You and he would then develop and run a Taco Palace restaurant. Both of you are extremely optimistic about future real estate prices in this area, and your brother-in-law has prepared a cash-flow forecast that implies a large positive NPV. This calculation assumes sale of the property after 10 years.
   What further calculations should you do before going ahead?

4. On the London Metals Exchange the price for copper to be delivered in one year is $3,450 a ton. (*Note:* Payment is made when the copper is delivered.) The risk-free interest rate is .5% and the expected market return is 8%.
   a. Suppose that you expect to produce and sell 100,000 tons of copper next year. What is the PV of this output? Assume that the sale occurs at the end of the year.
   b. If copper has a beta of 1.2, what is the expected price of copper at the end of the year? What is the certainty-equivalent price?
5. New-model commercial airplanes are much more fuel-efficient than older models. How is it possible for airlines flying older models to make money when its competitors are flying newer planes? Explain briefly.

INTERMEDIATE

6. Suppose that you are considering investing in an asset for which there is a reasonably good secondary market. Specifically, your company is Jet Airways, and the asset is a Boeing 757—a widely used airplane. How does the presence of a secondary market simplify your problem in principle? Do you think these simplifications could be realized in practice? Explain.
7. There is an active, competitive leasing (i.e., rental) market for most standard types of commercial jets. Many of the planes flown by the major domestic and international airlines are not owned by them but leased for periods ranging from a few months to several years.

   Coromondal Airlines, however, owns two long-range DC-11s just withdrawn from Singapore operations. Coromondal is considering using these planes to develop the potentially lucrative new route from Jamshedpur to Bangalore. A considerable investment in terminal facilities, training, and advertising will be required. Once committed, Coromondal will have to operate the route for at least three years. One further complication: The manager of Coromondal's international division is opposing commitment of the planes to the Jamshedpur–Bangalore route because of anticipated future growth in traffic through Coromondal's new hub in Bangkok.

   How would you evaluate the proposed Jamshedpur–Bangalore project? Give a detailed list of the necessary steps in your analysis. Explain how the airplane leasing market would be taken into account. If the project is attractive, how would you respond to the manager of the international division?
8. Suppose the current price of gold is ₹22,000 per 10 grams. Yellow-Gold Consultants advises you that gold prices will increase at an average rate of 12% for the next two years. After that the growth rate will fall to a long-run trend of 3% per year. What is the price of 1 kg of gold produced in eight years? Assume that gold prices have a beta of 0 and that the risk-free rate is 6.2%.
9. We characterized the interstate rail lines owned by major U.S. railroads as "strategic assets" that generated increased profits from 2005 to 2007. In what conditions would you expect these assets to generate economic rents? Keep in mind that railroads compete with trucking companies as well as other railroads. Trucking companies have some advantages, including flexibility.
10. Thanks to acquisition of a key patent, your company now has exclusive production rights for barkelgassers (BGs) in India. Production facilities for 200,000 BGs per year will require a ₹25 million immediate capital expenditure. Production costs are estimated at ₹65 per BG. The BG marketing manager is confident that all 200,000 units can be sold for ₹100 per unit (in real terms) until the patent runs out five years hence. After that the marketing manager hasn't a clue about what the selling price will be.

    *e***X***cel*

    Visit us at
    www.mhhe.com/bmam10e

    What is the NPV of the BG project? Assume the real cost of capital is 9%. To keep things simple, also make the following assumptions:

- The technology for making BGs will not change. Capital and production costs will stay the same in real terms.
- Competitors know the technology and can enter as soon as the patent expires, that is, in year 6.
- If your company invests immediately, full production begins after 12 months, that is, in year 1.
- There are no taxes.
- BG production facilities last 12 years. They have no salvage value at the end of their useful life.

11. How would your answer to Problem 10 change if technological improvements reduce the cost of new BG production facilities by 3% per year? Thus a new plant built in year 1 would cost only 25 (1 – .03) = ₹24.25 million; a plant built in year 2 would cost ₹23.52 million; and so on. Assume that production costs per unit remain at ₹65.

Visit us at
www.mhhe.com/bmam10e

12. Go to the "live" Excel spreadsheets versions of Tables 11.1–11.3 at **www.mhhe.com/bmam10e**. Reevaluate the NPV of the proposed polyzone project under each of the following assumptions. What's the right management decision in each case?

Visit us at
www.mhhe.com/bmam10e

   a. Spread in year 4 holds at $1.20 per pound.
   b. The U.S. chemical company can start up polyzone production at 40 million pounds in year 1 rather than year 2.
   c. The U.S. company makes a technological advance that reduces its annual production costs to $25 million. Competitors' production costs do not change.

13. Photographic laboratories recover and recycle the silver used in photographic film. Riverside Photo is considering purchase of improved equipment for their laboratory at Kolkata. Here is the information they have:

Visit us at
www.mhhe.com/bmam10e

   - The equipment costs ₹1,000,000 and will cost ₹800,000 per year to run.
   - It has an economic life of 10 years but can be depreciated over five years by the written-down value method (see Section 6-2).
   - It will recover an additional 5,000 grams of silver per year.
   - Silver is selling for ₹72,500 per kg. Over the past 10 years, the price of silver has appreciated by 4.5% per year in real terms. Silver is traded in an active, competitive market.
   - The marginal tax rate is 34%. Assume Indian tax law.
   - The company cost of capital is 8% in real terms.
   - The nominal interest rate is 6.2%.
   What is the NPV of the new equipment? Make additional assumptions as necessary.

14. The Dracula Dramatic Association has come up with a unique prize for its December (2012) fund-raising ball: Twenty door prizes will be distributed, each one a ticket entitling the bearer to receive a cash award from its association on December 31, 2013. The cash award is to be determined by calculating the ratio of the level of S&P CNX Nifty Index of stock prices on December 31, 2013, to its level on June 30, 2014, and multiplying by $100. Thus, if the index turns out to be 1,000 on June 30, 2013, and 1,200 on December 31, 2013, the payoff will be 1000 × (1,200/1,000) = ₹1200.

   After the ball, a black market springs up in which the tickets are traded. What will the tickets sell for on January 1, 2013? On June 30, 2013? Assume the risk-free interest rate is 10% per year. Also assume that the Dracula Dramatic Association will be solvent at year-end 2014 and will, in fact, pay off on the tickets. Make other assumptions as necessary.

Would ticket values be different if the tickets' payoffs depended on sensex rather than on Nifty?

15. You are asked to value a large building in northern New Jersey. The valuation is needed for a bankruptcy settlement. Here are the facts:
    - The settlement *requires* that the building's value equal the PV of the *net cash proceeds* the railroad would receive if it cleared the building and sold it for its highest and best nonrailroad use, which is as a warehouse.
    - The building has been appraised at $1 million. This figure is based on actual recent selling prices of a sample of similar New Jersey buildings used as, or available for use as, warehouses.
    - If rented today as a warehouse, the building could generate $80,000 per year. This cash flow is calculated *after* out-of-pocket operating expenses and *after* real estate taxes of $50,000 per year:

Gross rents	$180,000
Operating expenses	50,000
Real estate taxes	50,000
Net	$80,000

Gross rents, operating expenses, and real estate taxes are uncertain but are expected to grow with inflation.
    - However, it would take one year and $200,000 to clear out the railroad equipment and prepare the building for use as a warehouse. The $200,000 would have to be invested immediately.
    - The property will be put on the market when ready for use as a warehouse. Your real estate adviser says that properties of this type take, on average, one year to sell after they are put on the market. However, the railroad could rent the building as a warehouse while waiting for it to sell.
    - The opportunity cost of capital for investment in real estate is 8% in *real* terms.
    - Your real estate adviser notes that selling prices of comparable buildings in northern New Jersey have declined, in real terms, at an average rate of 2% per year over the last 10 years.
    - A 5% sales commission would be paid by the railroad at the time of the sale.
    - The railroad pays no income taxes. It would have to pay property taxes.

CHALLENGE

16. The manufacture of polysyllabic acid is a competitive industry. Most plants have an annual output of 100,000 tons. Operating costs are $.90 a ton, and the sales price is $1 a ton. A 100,000-ton plant costs $100,000 and has an indefinite life. Its current scrap value of $60,000 is expected to decline to $57,900 over the next two years.

Visit us at
www.mhhe.com/bmam10e

Phlogiston, Inc., proposes to invest $100,000 in a plant that employs a new low-cost process to manufacture polysyllabic acid. The plant has the same capacity as existing units, but operating costs are $.85 a ton. Phlogiston estimates that it has two years' lead over each of its rivals in use of the process but is unable to build any more plants itself before year 2. Also it believes that demand over the next two years is likely to be sluggish and that its new plant will therefore cause temporary overcapacity.

You can assume that there are no taxes and that the cost of capital is 10%.

a. By the end of year 2, the prospective increase in acid demand will require the construction of several new plants using the Phlogiston process. What is the likely NPV of such plants?

b. What does that imply for the price of polysyllabic acid in year 3 and beyond?

c. Would you expect existing plant to be scrapped in year 2? How would your answer differ if scrap value were $40,000 or $80,000?

d. The acid plants of United Alchemists, Inc., have been fully depreciated. Can it operate them profitably after year 2?

e. Acidosis, Inc., purchased a new plant last year for $100,000 and is writing it down by $10,000 a year. Should it scrap this plant in year 2?

f. What would be the NPV of Phlogiston's venture?

17. The world airline system is composed of the routes X and Y, each of which requires 10 aircraft. These routes can be serviced by three types of aircraft—A, B, and C. There are 5 type A aircraft available, 10 type B, and 10 type C. These aircraft are identical except for their operating costs, which are as follows:

Aircraft Type	Annual Operating Cost ($ millions)	
	Route X	Route Y
A	1.5	1.5
B	2.5	2.0
C	4.5	3.5

The aircraft have a useful life of five years and a salvage value of $1 million.

The aircraft owners do not operate the aircraft themselves but rent them to the operators. Owners act competitively to maximize their rental income, and operators attempt to minimize their operating costs. Airfares are also competitively determined. Assume the cost of capital is 10%.

a. Which aircraft would be used on which route, and how much would each aircraft be worth?

b. What would happen to usage and prices of each aircraft if the number of type A aircraft increased to 10?

c. What would happen if the number of type A aircraft increased to 15?

d. What would happen if the number of type A aircraft increased to 20?

State any additional assumptions you need to make.

18. Taxes are a cost, and, therefore, changes in tax rates can affect consumer prices, project lives, and the value of existing firms. The following problem illustrates this. It also illustrates that tax changes that appear to be "good for business" do not always increase the value of existing firms. Indeed, unless new investment incentives increase consumer demand, they can work only by rendering existing equipment obsolete.

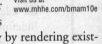

Visit us at
www.mhhe.com/bmam10e

The manufacture of bucolic acid is a competitive business. Demand is steadily expanding, and new plants are constantly being opened. Expected cash flows from an investment in a new plant are as follows:

	0	1	2	3
1. Initial investment	100			
2. Revenues		100	100	100
3. Cash operating costs		50	50	50
4. Tax depreciation		33.33	33.33	33.33
5. Income pretax		16.67	16.67	16.67
6. Tax at 40%		6.67	6.67	6.67
7. Net income		10	10	10
8. After-tax salvage				15
9. Cash flow (7 + 8 + 4 – 1)	–100	+43.33	+43.33	+58.33

NPV at 20% = 0

Assumptions:
1. Tax depreciation is straight-line over three years.
2. Pretax salvage value is 25 in year 3 and 50 if the asset is scrapped in year 2.
3. Tax on salvage value is 40% of the difference between salvage value and depreciated investment.
4. The cost of capital is 20%.

a. What is the value of a one-year-old plant? Of a two-year-old plant?
b. Suppose that the government now changes tax depreciation to allow a 100% writeoff in year 1. How does this affect the value of existing one- and two-year-old plants? Existing plants must continue using the original tax depreciation schedule.
c. Would it now make sense to scrap existing plants when they are two rather than three years old?
d. How would your answers change if the corporate income tax were abolished entirely?

~~~MINI-CASE~~~

ECSY-COLA[23]

Libby Flannery, the regional manager of Ecsy-Cola, the international soft drinks empire, was reviewing her investment plans for Central Asia. She had contemplated launching Ecsy-Cola in the ex-Soviet republic of Inglistan in 2013. This would involve a capital outlay of $20 million in 2012 to build a bottling plant and set up a distribution system there. Fixed costs (for manufacturing, distribution, and marketing) would then be $3 million per year from 2012 onward. This would be sufficient to make and sell 200 million liters per year—enough for every man, woman, and child in Inglistan to drink four bottles per week! But there would be few savings from building a smaller plant, and import tariffs and transport costs in the region would keep all production within national borders.

The variable costs of production and distribution would be 12 cents per liter. Company policy requires a rate of return of 25% in nominal dollar terms, after local taxes but before deducting any costs of financing. The sales revenue is forecasted to be 35 cents per liter.

Bottling plants last almost forever, and all unit costs and revenues were expected to remain constant in nominal terms. Tax would be payable at a rate of 30%, and under the Inglistan corporate tax code, capital expenditures can be written off on a straight-line basis over four years.

All these inputs were reasonably clear. But Ms. Flannery racked her brain trying to forecast sales. Ecsy-Cola found that the "1–2–4" rule works in most new markets. Sales typically double in the second year, double again in the third year, and after that remain roughly constant. Libby's best guess was that, if she went ahead immediately, initial sales in Inglistan would be 12.5 million liters in 2014, ramping up to 50 million in 2016 and onward.

Ms. Flannery also worried whether it would be better to wait a year. The soft drink market was developing rapidly in neighboring countries, and in a year's time she should have a much better idea whether Ecsy-Cola would be likely to catch on in Inglistan. If it didn't catch on and sales stalled below 20 million liters, a large investment probably would not be justified.

Ms. Flannery had assumed that Ecsy-Cola's keen rival, Sparky-Cola, would not also enter the market. But last week she received a shock when in the lobby of the Kapitaliste Hotel she bumped into her opposite number at Sparky-Cola. Sparky-Cola would face costs similar to Ecsy-Cola. How would Sparky-Cola respond if Ecsy-Cola entered the market? Would it decide to enter also? If so, how would that affect the profitability of Ecsy-Cola's project?

Ms. Flannery thought again about postponing investment for a year. Suppose Sparky-Cola were interested in the Inglistan market. Would that favor delay or immediate action?

Maybe Ecsy-Cola should announce its plans before Sparky-Cola had a chance to develop its own proposals. It seemed that the Inglistan project was becoming more complicated by the day.

Questions

1. Calculate the NPV of the proposed investment, using the inputs suggested in this case. How sensitive is this NPV to future sales volume?

2. What are the pros and cons of waiting for a year before deciding whether to invest? (*Hint:* What happens if demand turns out high and Sparky-Cola also invests? What if Ecsy-Cola invests right away and gains a one-year head start on Sparky-Cola?)

---

[23] We thank Anthony Neuberger for suggesting this topic.

12

CHAPTER

AGENCY PROBLEMS, COMPENSATION, AND PERFORMANCE MEASUREMENT

So far we've concentrated on criteria and procedures for identifying capital investments with positive NPVs. If a firm takes all (and only) positive-NPV projects, it maximizes the firm's value. But do the firm's managers want to maximize value?

Managers have no special gene that automatically aligns their personal interests with outside investors' financial objectives. So how do shareholders ensure that top managers do not feather their own nests or grind their own axes? And how do top managers ensure that middle managers and employees try as hard as they can to find positive-NPV projects?

Here we circle back to the principal–agent problems first raised in Chapter 1. Shareholders are the ultimate principals; top managers are the stockholders' agents. But middle managers and employees are in turn agents of top management. Thus senior managers, including the chief financial officer, are simultaneously agents vis-à-vis shareholders and principals vis-à-vis the rest of the firm. The problem is to get everyone working together to maximize value.

This chapter summarizes how corporations grapple with that problem. The two main topics we cover are:

- **Incentives:** Making sure that managers and employees are rewarded appropriately when they add value to the firm.

- **Performance measurement:** You can't reward value added unless you can measure it. Since you get what you reward, and reward what you measure, you get what you measure.

We describe alternative performance measures, including economic value added. We uncover the biases lurking in standard accounting income and rates of return. Finally, we confront a disturbing fact: some, maybe most, public corporations seem willing to sacrifice NPV to maintain or increase short-run earnings per share.

12-1   INCENTIVES AND COMPENSATION

Top management, including the CFO, must try to ensure that managers and employees have the right incentives to find and invest in positive-NPV projects. We will soon see how difficult it is to get incentives right throughout a large corporation. Why not bypass these difficulties, and let the CFO and his or her immediate staff make the important investment decisions?

The bypass won't work, for at least five reasons. First, top management would have to analyze thousands of projects every year. There's no way to know enough about each one to make intelligent choices. Top management must rely on analysis done at lower levels.

Second, the *design* of a capital investment project involves investment decisions that top managers do not see. Think of a proposal to build a new factory. The managers who developed the plan for the factory had to decide its location. Suppose they chose a more expensive site to get closer to a pool of skilled workers. That's an investment decision: additional investment to generate extra cash flow from access to these workers' skills. (Outlays for training could be lower, for example.) Does the additional investment generate additional NPV, compared to building the factory at a cheaper but remote site? How is the CFO to know? He or she can't afford the time to investigate every alternative that was considered but rejected by the project's sponsors.

Third, many capital investments don't appear in the capital budget. These include research and development, worker training, and marketing outlays designed to expand a market or lock in satisfied customers.

Fourth, *small decisions add up.* Operating managers make investment decisions every day. They may carry extra inventories of raw materials so they won't have to worry about being caught short. Managers at the steel plant in Bokaro may decide they need one more forklift. They may hold on to an idle machine tool or an empty warehouse that could have been sold. These are not big decisions (₹5,00,000 here, ₹6,00,000 there) but thousands of such decisions add up to real money.

Fifth, the CFO may be subject to the same kinds of temptations that afflict lower layers of management.

We now consider incentives and agency problems in capital investment.

Agency Problems in Capital Budgeting

As you have surely guessed, there is no perfect system of incentives. But it's easy to see what *won't* work. Suppose shareholders decide to pay the financial managers a fixed salary—no bonuses, no stock options, just ₹X per month. The manager, as the stockholders' agent, is instructed to find and invest in all positive-NPV projects open to the firm. The manager may sincerely try to do so, but will face various tempting alternatives:

Reduced effort. Finding and implementing investment in truly valuable projects is a high-effort, high-pressure activity. The financial manager will be tempted to slack off.

Perks. Our hypothetical financial manager gets no bonuses. Only ₹X per month. But he or she may take a bonus anyway, not in cash, but in tickets to sporting events, lavish office accommodations, planning meetings scheduled at luxury resorts, and so on. Economists refer to these nonpecuniary rewards as *private benefits*. Ordinary people call them *perks* (short for perquisites).[1]

Empire building. Other things equal, managers prefer to run large businesses rather than small ones. Getting from small to large may not be a positive-NPV undertaking. Managers are also reluctant to dismantle their empires. That is, they are reluctant to disinvest.

Entrenching investment. Suppose manager Q considers two expansion plans. One plan will require a manager with special skills that manager Q just happens to have. The other plan requires only a general-purpose manager. Guess which plan Q will favor. Projects designed to require or reward the skills of existing managers are called *entrenching investments*.[2]

Entrenching investments and empire building are typical symptoms of overinvestment, that is, investing beyond the point where NPV falls to zero. The temptation to overinvest is highest when the firm has plenty of cash but limited investment opportunities. Michael Jensen calls this the *free-cash-flow* problem.[3]

Avoiding risk. If the manager receives only a fixed salary, she cannot share in the upside of risky projects. But, if the risky project turns out to be a loser, her job may be on the line. In this case safe projects are from the manager's viewpoint better than risky ones.[4] But risky projects can sometimes have large, positive NPVs.

A manager on a fixed salary could hardly avoid all these temptations all of the time. The resulting loss in value is an agency cost.

Monitoring

Agency costs can be reduced by monitoring a manager's efforts and actions and by intervening when the manager veers off course.

Monitoring can prevent the more obvious agency costs, such as blatant perks. It can confirm that the manager is putting sufficient time on the job. But monitoring requires time and money. Some monitoring is almost always worthwhile, but a limit is soon reached at which an extra rupee spent on monitoring would not return an extra rupee of value from reduced agency costs. Like all investments, monitoring encounters diminishing returns.

---

[1] But don't assume that all perks are unwarranted and inefficient. That corporate jet can be a good investment if it saves three or four hours a week that the CEO and CFO would otherwise waste in airports. Also, some large companies require the CEO to fly in the corporate jet for security reasons. Rajan and Wulf argue that it is *not* correct to treat all perks as managerial excess. See R. Rajan and J. Wulf, "Are Perks Purely Managerial Excess?" *Journal of Financial Economics* 79 (January 2006), pp. 1–33.

[2] A. Shleifer and R. W. Vishny, "Management Entrenchment: The Case of Manager-Specific Investments," *Journal of Financial Economics* 25 (November 1989), pp. 123–140.

[3] M. C. Jensen, "Agency Costs of Free Cash Flow, Corporate Finance and Takeovers," *American Economic Review* 76 (May 1986), pp. 323–329.

[4] Sometimes managers can be tempted to take *too much risk*. Suppose that a regional office suffers unexpected losses. The regional manager's job is on the line, and in response he or she tries a risky strategy that offers a small probability of a big, quick payoff. If the strategy pays off, the manager's job is safe. If it fails, nothing is lost, because the manager would have been fired anyway.

Some agency costs can't be prevented even with the most thorough monitoring. Suppose a share holder undertakes to monitor capital investment decisions. How could he or she ever know for sure whether a capital budget approved by top management includes (1) *all* the positive-NPV opportunities open to the firm and (2) *no* projects with negative NPVs due to empire-building or entrenching investments? The managers obviously know more about the firm's prospects than outsiders ever can. If the shareholder could list all projects and their NPVs, then the managers would hardly be needed!

Who actually does the monitoring? Ultimately it is the shareholders' responsibility, but in large, public companies, monitoring is *delegated* to the board of directors, who are elected by shareholders and are supposed to represent their interests. The board meets regularly, both formally and informally, with top management. Attentive directors come to know a great deal about the firm's prospects and performance and the strengths and weaknesses of its top management.

The board also hires independent accountants to audit the firm's financial statements. If the audit uncovers no problems, the auditors issue an opinion that the financial statements fairly represent the company's financial condition and are consistent with Generally Accepted Accounting Principles (GAAP).

If problems are found, the auditors will negotiate changes in assumptions or procedures. Managers almost always agree, because if acceptable changes are not made, the auditors will issue a *qualified opinion*, which is bad news for the company and its shareholders. A qualified opinion suggests that managers are covering something up and undermines investors' confidence.

A qualified audit opinion may be bad news, but when investors learn of accounting irregularities that have escaped detection, there can be hell to pay. In January 2004 Adecco, the giant Swiss employment agency, announced that it had discovered material accounting irregularities in its North American operations. The next day Adecco's share price fell by 40%, wiping $5 billion off the market value of the company.

Lenders also monitor. If a company takes out a large bank loan, the bank will track the company's assets, earnings, and cash flow. By monitoring to protect its loan, the bank protects shareholders' interests also.[5]

Delegated monitoring is especially important when ownership is widely dispersed. If there is a dominant shareholder, he or she will generally keep a close eye on top management. But when the number of stockholders is large, and each stockholding is small, individual investors cannot justify much time and expense for monitoring. Each is tempted to leave the task to others, taking a free ride on others' efforts. But if everybody prefers to let somebody else do it, then it will not get done; that is, monitoring by shareholders will not be strong or effective. Economists call this the *free-rider problem*.[6]

If the free-rider problem is severe, delegated monitoring may be the only solution. But delegation brings its own agency problems. For example, many board members may be long-standing friends of the CEO and may be indebted to the CEO for help or advice. Understandably, they may be reluctant to fire the CEO or enquire too deeply into his or her conduct. Auditing firms may also have conflicts of interest. For example, many believed that Enron's auditors, Arthur Andersen, might have been tougher on the company had it not also earned substantial fees from providing Enron with consulting services. If monitors are likely to have their own agenda, then we have Dr. Seuss's bee-watching problem:

---

[5] Lenders' and shareholders' interests are not always aligned—see Chapter 18. But a company's ability to satisfy lenders is normally good news for stockholders, particularly when lenders are well placed to monitor. See C. James "Some Evidence on the Uniqueness of Bank Loans," *Journal of Financial Economics* 19 (December 1987), pp. 217–235.

[6] The free-rider problem might seem to drive out all monitoring by dispersed shareholders. But investors have another reason to investigate: They want to make money on their common stock portfolios by buying undervalued companies and selling overvalued ones. To do this they must investigate companies' performance.

Oh, the jobs people work at!
Out west, near Hawtch-Hawtch,
there's a Hawtch-Hawtcher Bee Watcher.
His job is to watch . . .
is to keep both his eyes on the lazy town bee.
A bee that is watched will work harder you see!

Well . . . he watched and he watched
But, in spite of his watch,
that bee didn't work any harder. Not mawtch.

So then somebody said,
"Our bee-watching man
just isn't bee-watching as hard as he can.
He ought to be watched by another Hawtch-Hawtcher!!
The thing that we need
is a Bee-Watcher-Watcher!"[7]

In response to the Enron debacle, the Sarbanes-Oxley Act set up a bee-watcher-watcher, called the Public Company Oversight Board, to monitor the activities of auditors. It also prohibited an auditing firm from providing both auditing and consulting services to the same company.[8]

Management Compensation

Because monitoring is necessarily imperfect, compensation plans must be designed to attract competent managers and to give them the right incentives.

Figure 12.1 compares the level of compensation in different countries[9] and Figure 12.2 shows the growth of CEO compensation in the U.S. Three features stand out.

1. The U.S. has unusually high levels of executive pay. CEOs in the States receive over 3 times the pay of German CEOs and almost 10 times the pay of Japanese CEOs.
2. Although CEO compensation in the U.S. fell in 2001 after the end of the dot.com boom and probably again during the 2008–2009 credit crisis, there has for the most part been a strong upward trend.
3. A large and increasing fraction of CEO compensation in the U.S. comes from variable bonuses, stock options, and other long-term incentives.

We look first at the size of the pay package. Then we turn to its contents.

High levels of CEO pay undoubtedly encourage CEOs to work hard and (perhaps more important) offer an attractive carrot to lower-level managers who hope to become CEOs. But there has been widespread concern about "excessive" pay, especially pay for mediocre performance. For example,

---

[7] Dr. Seuss, *Did I Ever Tell You How Lucky You Are?* (New York: Random House, 1973), pp. 26–28.

[8] The Sarbanes-Oxley Act forbids auditing firms from providing their clients with fairness opinions, actuarial services, investment banking services, management functions, legal services, or any other services proscribed by the Public Company Accounting Oversight Board.

[9] Since the CEOs of most of the companies belonging to the Indian business groups are promoter-shareholders of the company, it is very difficult to compare the compensation of Indian CEOs with their counterparts elsewhere. As per a Hewitt survey done in 2010, the variable pay (as a percentage of total pay) has been increasing in India and is around 25% in 2010 (based on a survey of 465 companies).

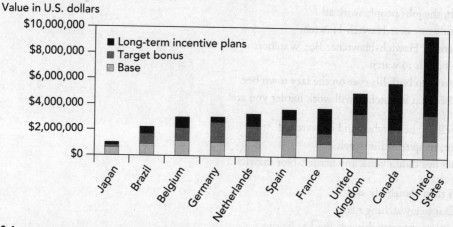

FIGURE 12.1

Median CEO compensation in 2008 for large companies. Compensation in the U.S. is relatively high and is heavily dependent on performance. We are grateful to Towers Perrin for providing these data.

Source: Towers Perrin's proprietary data.

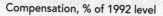

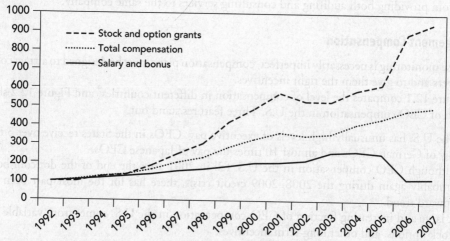

FIGURE 12.2

Growth in CEO compensation in the U.S. The growth has come largely from grants of stock and options.

Source: Execucomp.

eXcel

Visit us at
www.mhhe.com/bmam10e

Robert Nardelli received a $210 million severance package on leaving The Home Depot and Henry McKinnell received almost $200 million on leaving Pfizer. Both CEOs left behind troubled and underperforming companies. You can imagine the newspaper headlines.

Those headlines got a lot bigger in 2008 when it was revealed that generous bonuses were to be paid to the senior management of banks that had been bailed out by the government. Merrill Lynch hurried through $3.6 billion in bonuses, including $121 million to just four executives, only days before Bank of America finalized its deal to buy the collapsing firm with the help of taxpayer money. "Bonuses for Boneheads" was the headline in *Forbes* magazine.

The widespread view that taxpayer money was being used to pay bonuses to bankers whose greed had brought about the credit crisis led to demands that governments curb bankers' compensation. In France President Sarkozy announced that there would be no bonuses in 2009 at banks that had received state aid. The German government set a €500,000 ($630,000) limit on executive pay at rescued banks. In the U.S., the Obama administration appointed a "pay czar" to oversee the salaries of top executives at companies receiving "exceptional assistance" from the government. The U.S. Congress also set restrictions on the pay of top executives in banks who accepted bail-out funds. Incentive compensation was limited to one-third of total pay, and was to be paid only in the form of stock that could not be cashed in as long as the company remained in receipt of government aid. The banks were also prohibited from giving big handouts to departing executives.

These restrictions ensured that banks taking government aid did not pay "excessive" compensation. Putting compensation in a Congressional straightjacket is dangerous, however. How can it make sense to require that two-thirds of executive pay *not* be related to performance? Why should all incentive compensation be in restricted stock?

It is easy to point to cases where poorly performing managers have received unjustifiably large payouts. But is there a more general problem? Perhaps high levels of pay simply reflect a shortage of talent. After all, CEOs are not alone in earning large sums. The earnings of top professional athletes are equally mouthwatering. In 2007 the New York Yankees' Jason Giambi, Derek Jeter, and Alex Rodriguez were each paid more than $20 million. The Yankees must have believed that it was worth paying up for stars that would win games and fill up the ballpark.

If star managers are as rare as star baseball players, corporations may need to pay up for CEO talent. Suppose that a superior CEO can add 1% to the value and stock price of a large corporation with a market capitalization of $10 billion. One percent on a stock-market value of $10 billion is $100 million. If the CEO can really deliver, then a pay package of, say, $20 million per year sounds like a bargain.[10]

There is also a less charitable explanation of managerial pay. This view stresses the close links between the CEO and the other members of the board of directors. If directors are too chummy with the CEO, they may find it difficult to get tough when it comes to setting compensation packages. Sometimes directors approve extra payments that provide shareholders with little or no prospective benefit. Take the example of the German company, Mannesmann, which was acquired in a $200 billion takeover. After the deal was finalized, Mannesmann's board of directors voted an ex gratia payment of $74 million to the company's executives. German Federal prosecutors charged six of the directors with breach of their fiduciary duty and failure to preserve the company's assets. Although the case was eventually settled out of court, it highlighted the danger that directors may be tempted to act as lords of the manor, rather than as stewards of the estate, when they set compensation levels.

In most firms executive pay is the responsibility of a compensation committee of the board of directors. This committee does not operate in a vacuum; it usually places significant weight on average compensation in peer companies. The problem is that few boards are prepared to approve

---

[10] Gabaix and Landier argue that high CEO pay is a natural consequence of steadily increasing firm values and the competition for management talent. See X. Gabaix and A. Landier, "Why Has CEO Pay Increased So Much?" *Quarterly Journal of Economics* 123 (February 2008), pp. 49–100.

a compensation package that is below average. But, if every firm wants its CEO to have above-average compensation, the average will ratchet upward.[11]

The danger that CEOs may have undue influence over their compensation has prompted some countries, such as the U.K., Sweden, Australia, and the Netherlands, to give shareholders a vote on executive pay. In most cases the vote is nonbinding,[12] but when shareholders of the pharmaceutical giant GlaxoSmithKline voted against a new compensation package for its chief executive, three members of the board's remuneration committee were replaced and the pay package was renegotiated. Shareholders voted against compensation packages at several other U.K. companies, including Royal Dutch Shell and the Royal Bank of Scotland Group.

So we have two views of the level of managerial pay. One is that it results from arms-length contracting in a tight market for managerial talent. The other is that poor governance and weak boards allow excessive pay. There is evidence for and against both views. For example, CEOs are not the only group to have seen their compensation increase rapidly in recent years. Corporate lawyers, sports stars, and celebrity entertainers have all increased their share of national income, even though their compensation is determined by arms-length negotiation.[13] However, the shortage-of-talent argument cannot account for wide disparities in pay. For example, compare the CEO of GM (compensation of $16 million in 2007, two years before GM's bankruptcy) to the CEO of Toyota (compensation about $1 million) or to General Petraeus, the former U.S. military commander in Iraq (about $180,000). It is difficult to argue that GM's CEO delivered the most value or had the most difficult and important job.

Incentive Compensation

The amount of compensation may be less important than how it is structured. The compensation package should encourage managers to maximize shareholder wealth.

Compensation could be based on input (for example, the manager's effort) or on output (income or value added as a result of the manager's decisions). But input is difficult to measure. How can outside investors observe effort? They can check that the manager clocks in on time, but hours worked does not measure true effort. (Is the manager facing up to difficult and stressful choices, or is he or she just burning time with routine meetings, travel, and paperwork?)

Because effort is not observable, compensation must be based on output, that is, on verifiable results. Trouble is, results depend not just on the manager's contribution, but also on events outside the manager's control. Unless you can separate out the manager's contribution, you face a difficult trade-off. You want to give the manager high-powered incentives, so that he or she does very well when the firm does very well and poorly when the firm underperforms. But suppose the firm is a cyclical business that always struggles in recessions. Then high-powered incentives will force the manager to bear business cycle risk that is not his or her fault.

There are limits to the risks that managers can be asked to bear. So the result is a compromise. Firms do link managers' pay to performance, but fluctuations in firm value are shared by managers

---

[11] Bizjak, Lemmon, and Naveen found that most firms set pay levels at or above the median of the peer group, and some go much higher. For example, Coca-Cola and IBM consistently aim for pay levels in the upper quartile of their peers. See J. M. Bizjak, M. L. Lemmon, and L. Naveen, "Has the Use of Peer Groups Contributed to Higher Pay and Less Efficient Compensation?" *Journal of Financial Economics* 90 (November 2008), pp. 152–168.

[12] The Netherlands gives shareholders a binding vote.

[13] See S. N. Kaplan and J. D. Rauh, "Wall Street and Main Street: What Contributes to the Rise in the Highest Incomes?" *Review of Financial Studies,* forthcoming.

and shareholders. Managers bear some of the risks that are beyond their control and shareholders bear some of the agency costs if managers fail to maximize firm value. Thus some agency costs are inevitable.

Most major companies around the world now link part of their executive pay to the stock-price performance.[14] This compensation is generally in one of three forms: stock options, restricted stock (stock that must be retained for several years), or performance shares (shares awarded only if the company meets an earnings or other target).

Stock options give managers the right (but not the obligation) to buy their company's shares in the future at a fixed exercise price. Usually the exercise price is set equal to the company's stock price on the day when the options are granted. If the company performs well and stock price increases, the manager can buy shares and cash in on the difference between the stock price and the exercise price. If the stock price falls, the manager leaves the options unexercised and hopes for a stock price recovery or compensation through another channel. (If the stock price doesn't recover, the manager may be granted a new batch of options or given a lower exercise price on the original options.)

The popularity of stock options was encouraged by U.S. accounting rules, which allowed companies to grant stock options without recognizing any immediate compensation expense. The rules allowed companies to value options at the excess of the stock price over the exercise price on the grant date. But the exercise price was almost always set equal to the stock price on that date. Thus the excess was zero and the stock options were valued at zero. (We show how to calculate the actual value of options in Chapters 20 and 21.) So companies could grant lots of options at no recorded cost and with no reduction in accounting earnings. Naturally accountants and investors were concerned, because earnings were more and more overstated as the volume of option grants increased. After years of controversy, the accounting rules were changed in 2006. U.S. corporations are now required to value executive stock options more realistically and to deduct these values as a compensation expense.

Options also have a tax advantage in the U.S. Compensation of more than $1 million has since 1994 been considered unreasonable and is not a tax-deductible expense. However, there is no restriction on compensation in the form of stock options.[15]

You can see the advantages of tying compensation to stock price. When a manager works hard to maximize firm value, she helps both the stockholders and herself. But compensation via options or restricted stock also has at least four imperfections. First, the payoffs depend on the absolute change in stock price, not the change relative to the market or to stock prices of other firms in the same industry. Thus they force the manager to bear market or industry risks, which are outside the manager's control. Compensation based on relative stock-price performance makes logical sense but is rarely seen in practice.

Here is a second difficult issue. Because a company's stock price depends on investors' expectations of future earnings, rates of return depend on how well the company performs relative to expectations. Suppose a company announces the appointment of an outstanding new manager. The stock price leaps up in anticipation of improved performance. If the new manager then delivers exactly the good performance that investors expected, the stock will earn only a normal rate of return. In this case a compensation scheme linked to the stock return after the manager starts would fail to recognize the manager's special contribution.

---

[14] The major exceptions are in China, Japan, India, and South Korea, where such incentive schemes are still used by a minority of large firms. See Towers Perrin, *Equity Incentives Around the World*, 2008, **www.towersperrin.com**.

[15] ESOPs do not enjoy as much of tax benefit in India. The 2007 Finance Bill brought ESOPs under the ambit of Fringe Benefit Taxes (FBT) in India. The FBT rate (30% plus 3% education cess) is marginally lower than the effective corporate tax rate of 33.99%). The FBT will be paid on the value of exercise of the option and not on the date of vesting.

Third, incentive plans may tempt managers to withhold bad news or manipulate earnings to pump up stock prices. They may also be tempted to defer valuable investment projects if the projects would depress earnings in the short run. We return to this point at the end of the chapter.

Fourth, some compensation schemes encourage excessive risk-taking. Suppose a possible deal comes up that could make or lose ₹100 million. You are about to reject it, but then you think of your stock options and realize that you can't lose. If the deal comes off, the stock price will rise and your options will be worth a packet. If it doesn't, there is nothing lost; you just wait for the next deal to surface.

In Chapter 1 we suggested that the subprime crisis was largely an agency problem, where bank CEOs were encouraged by poorly designed incentive schemes to bet the shop. The solution is not to move away from incentive compensation but to ensure that managers bear more of the cost of poor decisions. For example, in 2008 the Swiss bank UBS adopted a new pay system to deal with this problem. Incentive payments are to be retained by the bank for up to five years. If, in the meantime, the manager or trader underperforms, the previously agreed payments will be forfeited.

12-2   MEASURING AND REWARDING PERFORMANCE: RESIDUAL INCOME AND EVA

Almost all top executives of firms with publicly traded shares have compensation packages that depend in part on their firms' stock price performance. But their compensation also includes a bonus that depends on increases in earnings or on other accounting measures of performance. For lower-level managers, compensation packages usually depend more on accounting measures and less on stock returns.

Accounting measures of performance have two advantages:

1. They are based on absolute performance, rather than on performance relative to investors' expectations.
2. They make it possible to measure the performance of junior managers whose responsibility extends to only a single division or plant.

Tying compensation to accounting profits also creates some obvious problems. First, accounting profits are partly within the control of management. For example, managers whose pay depends on near-term earnings may cut maintenance or staff training. This is not a recipe for adding value, but an ambitious manager hoping for a quick promotion will be tempted to pump up short-term profits, leaving longer-run problems to his or her successors.

Second, accounting earnings and rates of return can be severely biased measures of true profitability. We ignore this problem for now, but return to it in the next section.

Third, growth in earnings does not necessarily mean that shareholders are better off. Any investment with a positive rate of return (1% or 2% will do) will eventually increase earnings. Therefore, if managers are told to maximize growth in earnings, they will dutifully invest in projects offering 1% or 2% rates of return—projects that destroy value. But shareholders do not want growth in earnings for its own sake, and they are not content with 1% or 2% returns. They want positive-NPV investments, and *only* positive-NPV investments. They want the company to invest only if the expected rate of return exceeds the cost of capital.

Look at Table 12.1, which contains a simplified income statement and balance sheet for your company's Quayle City confabulator plant. There are two methods for judging whether the plant's returns are higher than the cost of capital.

TABLE 12.1 Simplified statements of income and assets for the Quayle City confabulator plant (figures in millions).

Income		Assets	
Sales	₹550	Net working capital[†]	₹80
Cost of goods sold*	275	Property, plant, and equipment investment	1,170
Selling, general, and administrative expenses	75	*Less* cumulative depreciation	360
	200	Net investment	810
Taxes at 35%	70	Other assets	110
Net income	₹130	Total assets	₹1,000

* Includes depreciation expense.
† Current assets less current liabilities.

Net Return on Investment   Book return on investment (ROI) is just the ratio of after-tax operating income to the net (depreciated) book value of assets.[16] In Chapter 5 we rejected book ROI as a capital investment criterion, and in fact few companies now use it for that purpose. However, managers frequently assess the performance of a division or a plant by comparing its ROI with the cost of capital.

Suppose you need to assess the performance of the Quayle City plant. As you can see from Table 12.1, the corporation has ₹1,000 million invested in the plant, which is generating earnings of ₹130 million. Therefore the plant is earning an ROI of 130/1,000 = .13, or 13%.[17] If the cost of capital is (say) 10%, then the plant's activities are adding to shareholder value. The *net* return is 13 − 10 = 3%. If the cost of capital is (say) 20%, then shareholders would have been better off investing ₹1 billion somewhere else. In this case the net return is negative, at 13 − 20 = −7%.

Residual Income or Economic Value Added (EVA®)[18]   The second method calculates a net rupees return to shareholders. It asks, What are earnings after deducting a charge for the cost of capital?

When firms calculate income, they start with revenues and then deduct costs, such as wages, raw material costs, overhead, and taxes. But there is one cost that they do not commonly deduct: the cost of capital. True, they allow for depreciation, but investors are not content with a return of their investment; they also demand a return *on* that investment. As we pointed out in Chapter 10, a business that breaks even in terms of accounting profits is really making a loss; it is failing to cover the cost of capital.

To judge the net contribution to value, we need to deduct the cost of capital contributed to the plant by the parent company and its stockholders. Suppose again that the cost of capital is 10%. Then

[16] Notice that investment includes the net working capital (current assets minus current liabilities) required to operate the plant. The investment shown is also called net assets or the net capital invested in the plant. We say "ROI," but you will also hear "return on capital" (ROC). "Return on assets" (ROA) sometimes refers to return on assets defined to include net working capital, as in Table 12.1, but sometimes to return on total assets, where current assets are included but current liabilities are not subtracted. It's prudent to check definitions when reviewing reported ROIs, ROCs, or ROAs.

[17] Notice that earnings are calculated after tax but with no deductions for interest paid. The plant is evaluated as if it were all-equity-financed. This is standard practice (see Chapter 6). It helps to separate investment and financing decisions. The tax advantages of debt financing supported by the plant are picked up not in the plant's earnings or cash flows but in the discount rate. The cost of capital is the after-tax weighted-average cost of capital, or WACC. WACC was briefly introduced in Chapter 9 and will be further explained in Chapters 17 and 19.

[18] EVA is the term used by the consulting firm Stern–Stewart, which has done much to popularize and implement this measure of residual income. With Stern–Stewart's permission, we omit the copyright symbol in what follows.

the rupees cost of capital for the Quayle City plant is .10 × ₹1,000 = ₹100 million. The net gain is therefore ₹130 − 100 = ₹30 million. This is the addition to shareholder wealth due to management's hard work (or good luck).

Net income after deducting the rupee return required by investors is called *residual income* or *economic value added (EVA)*. The formula is

$$\text{EVA} = \text{residual income} = \text{income earned} - \text{income required}$$
$$= \text{income earned} - \text{cost of capital} \times \text{investment}$$

For our example, the calculation is

$$\text{EVA} = \text{residual income} = 130 - (.10 \times 1,000) = +₹30 \text{ million}$$

But if the cost of capital were 20%, EVA would be negative by ₹70 million.

Net return on investment and EVA are focusing on the same question. When return on investment equals the cost of capital, net return and EVA are both zero. But the net return is a percentage and ignores the scale of the company. EVA recognizes the amount of capital employed and the number of dollars of additional wealth created.

The term *EVA* has been popularized by the consulting firm Stern–Stewart. But the concept of residual income has been around for some time,[19] and many companies that are not Stern–Stewart clients use this concept to measure and reward managers' performance.

Other consulting firms have their own versions of residual income. McKinsey & Company uses *economic profit (EP)*, defined as capital invested multiplied by the spread between return on investment and the cost of capital. This is another way to measure residual income. For the Quayle City plant, with a 10% cost of capital, economic profit is the same as EVA:

$$\text{Economic profit (EP)} = (\text{ROI} - r) \times \text{capital invested}$$
$$= (.13 - .10) \times 1,000 = ₹30 \text{ million}$$

In Chapter 28 we take a look at EVAs calculated for some well-known companies. But EVA's most valuable contributions happen inside companies. EVA encourages managers and employees to concentrate on increasing value, not just on increasing earnings.

Pros and Cons of EVA

Let us start with the pros. EVA, economic profit, and other residual income measures are clearly better than earnings or earnings growth for measuring performance. A plant that is generating lots of EVA should generate accolades for its managers as well as value for shareholders. EVA may also highlight parts of the business that are not performing up to scratch. If a division is failing to earn a positive EVA, its management is likely to face some pointed questions about whether the division's assets could be better employed elsewhere.

EVA sends a message to managers: Invest if and only if the increase in earnings is enough to cover the cost of capital. This is an easy message to grasp. Therefore EVA can be used down deep in the organization as an incentive compensation system. It is a substitute for explicit monitoring by top management. Instead of *telling* plant and divisional managers not to waste capital and then trying o figure out whether they are complying, EVA rewards them for careful investment decisions. Of course, if you tie junior managers' compensation to their economic value added, you must also give them power over those decisions that affect EVA. Thus the use of EVA implies delegated decision making.

EVA makes the cost of capital *visible* to operating managers. A plant manager can improve EVA by (a) increasing earnings or (b) *reducing* capital employed. Therefore underutilized assets tend to be flushed out and disposed of.

Introduction of residual income measures often leads to surprising reductions in assets employed—not from one or two big capital disinvestment decisions, but from many small ones. Ehrbar quotes a sewing machine operator at Herman Miller Corporation:

> [EVA] lets you realize that even assets have a cost. . . . we used to have these stacks of fabric sitting here on the tables until we needed them. . . . We were going to use the fabric anyway, so who cares that we're buying it and stacking it up there? Now no one has excess fabric. They only have the stuff we're working on today. And it's changed the way we connect with suppliers, and we're having [them] deliver fabric more often.[20]

If you propose to tie a manager's remuneration to her business's profitability, it is clearly better to use EVA than accounting income which takes no account of the cost of the capital employed. But what are the limitations of EVA? Here we return to the same question that bedevils stock-based measures of performance. How can you judge whether a low EVA is a consequence of bad management or of factors outside the manager's control? The deeper you go in the organization, the less independence that managers have and therefore the greater the problem in measuring their contribution.

The second limitation with any accounting measure of performance lies in the data on which it is based. We explore this issue in the next section.

12-3   BIASES IN ACCOUNTING MEASURES OF PERFORMANCE

Anyone using accounting measures of performance had better hope that the accounting numbers are accurate. Unfortunately, they are often not accurate, but biased. Applying EVA or any other accounting measure of performance therefore requires adjustments to the income statements and balance sheets.

For example, think of the difficulties in measuring the profitability of a pharmaceutical research program, where it typically takes 10 to 12 years to bring a new drug from discovery to final regulatory approval and the drug's first revenues. That means 10 to 12 years of guaranteed losses, even if the managers in charge do everything right. Similar problems occur in start-up ventures, where there may be heavy capital outlays but low or negative earnings in the first years of operation. This does not imply negative NPV, so long as operating earnings and cash flows are sufficiently high later on. But EVA and ROI would be negative in the start-up years, even if the project were on track to a strong positive NPV.

The problem in these cases is not with EVA or ROI, but with the accounting data. The pharmaceutical R&D program may be showing accounting losses, because generally accepted accounting principles require that outlays for R&D be written off as current expenses. But from an economic point of view, those outlays are an investment, not an expense. If a proposal for a new business predicts accounting losses during a start-up period, but the proposal nevertheless shows a positive NPV, then the start-up

---

[20] A. Ehrbar, *EVA: The Real Key to Creating Wealth* (New York: John Wiley & Sons, Inc., 1998), pp. 130–131.

losses are really an investment—cash outlays made to generate larger cash inflows when the busines hits its stride.

Example: Measuring the Profitability of the Ranchi Supermarket

Supermarket chains invest heavily in building and equipping new stores. The regional manager of a chain is about to propose investing ₹1 million in a new store in Ranchi. Projected cash flows are

	Year						
	1	**2**	**3**	**4**	**5**	**6**	**after 6**
Cash flow (₹ thousands)	100	200	250	298	298	297	0

Of course, real supermarkets last more than six years. But these numbers are realistic in one important sense: It may take two or three years for a new store to build up a substantial, habitual clientele. Thus cash flow is low for the first few years even in the best locations.

We will assume the opportunity cost of capital is 10%. The Ranchi store's NPV at 10% is zero. It is an acceptable project, but not an unusually good one:

$$NPV = -1{,}000 + \frac{100}{1.10} + \frac{200}{(1.10)^2} + \frac{250}{(1.10)^3} + \frac{298}{(1.10)^4} + \frac{298}{(1.10)^5} + \frac{297}{(1.10)^6} = 0$$

With NPV = 0, the true (internal) rate of return of this cash-flow stream is also 10%.

Table 12.2 shows the store's forecasted *book* profitability, assuming straight-line depreciation over its six-year life. The book ROI is lower than the true return for the first two years and higher afterward.[21] EVA also starts negative for the first two years, then turns positive and grows steadily to year 6. These are typical outcomes, because accounting income is too low when a project or business is young and too high as it matures.

TABLE 12.2   Forecasted book income, ROI, and EVA for the proposed Ranchi store. Book ROI and EVA are underestimated for the first two years and overestimated thereafter.

eXcel
Visit us at
www.mhhe.com/bmam10e

	Year					
	1	**2**	**3**	**4**	**5**	**6**
Cash flow	100	200	250	298	298	297
Book value at start of year	1,000	834	667	500	333	167
Book value at end of year	834	667	500	333	167	0
Book depreciation	167	167	167	167	167	167
Book income	−67	33	83	131	131	130
Book ROI	−0.067	0.040	0.125	0.263	0.394	0.782
EVA	−167	−50	17	81	98	114

Note: There are minor rounding errors in some annual figures.

---

[21] The errors in book ROI always catch up with you in the end. If the firm chooses a depreciation schedule that overstates a project's return in some years, it must also understate the return in other years. In fact, you can think of a project's IRR as a kind of average of the book returns. It is not a simple average, however. The weights are the project's book values discounted at the IRR. See J. A. Kay, "Accountants, Too, Could Be Happy in a Golden Age: The Accountant's Rate of Profit and the Internal Rate of Return," *Oxford Economic Papers* 28 (1976), pp. 447–460.

At this point the regional manager steps up on stage for the following soliloquy:

> The Ranchi store's a decent investment. But if we go ahead, I won't look very good at next year's performance review. And what if I also go ahead with the new stores in Dhanbad, Jamshedpur, and Kharagpur? Their cash-flow patterns are pretty much the same. I could actually appear to lose money next year. The stores I've got won't earn enough to cover the initial losses on four new ones.
>
> Of course, everyone knows new supermarkets lose money at first. The loss would be in the budget. My boss will understand—I think. But what about her boss? What if the board of directors starts asking pointed questions about profitability in my region? I'm under a lot of pressure to generate better earnings. Kamia Saxena, the upstate manager, got a bonus for generating a positive EVA. She didn't spend much on expansion.

The regional manager is getting conflicting signals. On the one hand, he is told to find and propose good investment projects. *Good* is defined by discounted cash flow. On the other hand, he is also urged to seek high book income. But the two goals conflict because book income does not measure true income. The greater the pressure for immediate book profits, the more the regional manager is tempted to forgo good investments or to favor quick-payback projects over longer-lived projects, even if the latter have higher NPVs.

Measuring Economic Profitability

Let us think for a moment about how profitability should be measured in principle. It is easy enough to compute the true, or economic, rate of return for a common stock that is continuously traded. We just record cash receipts (dividends) for the year, add the change in price over the year, and divide by the beginning price:

$$\text{Rate of return} = \frac{\text{cash receipts} + \text{change in price}}{\text{beginning price}}$$

$$= \frac{C_1 + (P_1 - P_0)}{P_0}$$

The numerator of the expression for rate of return (cash flow plus change in value) is called **economic income:**

$$\text{Economic income} = \text{cash flow} + \text{change in present value}$$

Any reduction in present value represents **economic depreciation;** any increase in present value represents *negative* economic depreciation. Therefore

$$\text{Economic income} = \text{cash flow} - \text{economic depreciation}$$

The concept works for any asset. Rate of return equals cash flow plus change in value divided by starting value:

$$\text{Rate of return} = \frac{C_1 + (\text{PV}_1 - \text{PV}_0)}{\text{PV}_0}$$

where PV_0 and PV_1 indicate the present values of the business at the ends of years 0 and 1.

The only hard part in measuring economic income is calculating present value. You can observe market value if the asset is actively traded, but few plants, divisions, or capital projects have shares traded in the stock market. You can observe the present market value of *all* the firm's assets but not of any one of them taken separately.

Accountants rarely even attempt to measure present value. Instead they give us net book value (BV), which is original cost less depreciation computed according to some arbitrary schedule. If book depreciation and economic depreciation are different (they are rarely the same), then book earnings will not measure true earnings. (In fact, it is not clear that accountants should even *try* to measure true profitability. They could not do so without heavy reliance on subjective estimates of value. Perhaps they should stick to supplying objective information and leave the estimation of value to managers and investors.)

It is not hard to *forecast* economic income and rate of return for the Ranchi store. Table 12.3 shows the calculations. From the cash-flow forecasts we can forecast present value at the start of periods 1 to 6. Cash flow minus economic depreciation equals economic income. Rate of return equals economic income divided by start-of-period value.

TABLE 12.3 Forecasted economic income, rate of return, and EVA for the proposed Ranchi store. Economic income equals cash flow minus economic depreciation. Rate of return equals economic income divided by value at start of year. EVA equals income minus cost of capital times value at start of year.

	Year					
	1	2	3	4	5	6
Cash flow	100	200	250	298	298	297
PV at start of year	1,000	1,000	900	740	516	270
PV at end of year	1,000	900	740	516	270	0
Economic depreciation	0	100	160	224	246	270
Economic income	100	100	90	74	52	27
Rate of return	0.10	0.10	0.10	0.10	0.10	0.10
EVA	0.00	0.00	0.00	0.00	0.00	0.00

Note: There are minor rounding errors in some annual figures.

Of course, these are forecasts. Actual future cash flows and values will be higher or lower. Table 12.3 shows that investors *expect* to earn 10% in each year of the store's six-year life. In other words, investors expect to earn the opportunity cost of capital each year from holding this asset.

Notice that EVA calculated using present value and economic income is zero in each year of the Ranchi project's life. For year 2, for example,

$$EVA = 100 - (.10 \times 1,000) = 0$$

EVA *should* be zero, because the project's true rate of return is only equal to the cost of capital. EVA will always give the right signal if book income equals economic income and asset values are measured accurately.

Do the Biases Wash Out in the Long Run?

Even if the forecasts for the Ranchi store turn out to be correct, ROI and EVA will be biased. That might not be a serious problem if the errors wash out in the long run, when the region settles down to a steady state with an even mix of old and new stores.

It turns out that the errors do not wash out in the steady state. Table 12.4 shows steady-state book ROIs and forecasted EVAs for the supermarket chain if it opens one store a year. For simplicity we assume that the company starts from scratch and that each store's cash flows are carbon copies of the Ranchi store. The true rate of return on each store is, therefore, 10% and the true EVA is zero. But as Table 12.4 demonstrates, steady-state book ROI and estimated EVA *overstate* the true profitability.

TABLE 12.4   Book ROI for a group of stores like the Ranchi store. The steady-state book ROI overstates the 10% *economic rate* of return. The steady-state EVA is also biased upward.

eXcel

Visit us at
www.mhhe.com/bmam10e

	Year					
	1	**2**	**3**	**4**	**5**	**6**
Book income for store[a]						
1	−67	33	83	131	131	130
2		−67	33	83	131	131
3			−67	33	83	131
4				−67	33	83
5					−67	33
6						−67
Total book income	−67	−33	50	181	312	443
Book value for store						
1	1,000	834	667	500	333	167
2		1,000	834	667	500	333
3			1,000	834	667	500
4				1,000	834	667
5					1,000	834
6						1,000
Total book value	1,000	1,834	2,501	3,001	3,334	3,501
Book ROI for all stores	−0.067	−0.018	0.020	0.060	0.094	0.126[b]
EVA	−166.73	−216.79	−200.19	−118.91	−20.96	92.66[c]
						▲
						Steady state

[a] Book income = cash flow − book depreciation.
[b] Steady-state book ROI.
[c] Steady-state EVA.
Note: There are minor rounding errors in some annual figures.

Thus we still have a problem even in the long run. The extent of the error depends on how fast the business grows. We have just considered one steady state with a zero growth rate. Think of another firm with a 5% steady-state growth rate. Such a firm would invest ₹1,000 the first year, ₹1,050 the second, ₹1,102.50 the third, and so on. Clearly the faster growth means more new projects relative to old ones. The greater weight given to young projects, which have low book ROIs and negative apparent EVAs, the lower the business's apparent profitability.[22]

What Can We Do about Biases in Accounting Profitability Measures?

The dangers in judging profitability by accounting measures are clear from these examples. To be forewarned is to be forearmed. But we can say something beyond just "be careful."

It is natural for firms to set a standard of profitability for plants or divisions. Ideally that standard should be the opportunity cost of capital for investment in the plant or division. That is the whole point of EVA: to compare actual profits with the cost of capital. But if performance is measured by return on investment or EVA, then these measures need to recognize accounting biases. Ideally, the

---

[22] We could repeat the steady-state analysis in Table 12.4 for different growth rates. It turns out that book income will overstate economic income if the growth rate is less than the internal rate of return and understate economic income if the growth rate exceeds the internal rate of return. Biases disappear if the growth rate and internal rate of return are exactly equal.

financial manager should identify and eliminate accounting biases before calculating EVA or net ROI. The managers and consultants that implement these measures work hard to adjust book income closer to economic income. For example, they may record R&D as an investment rather than an expense and construct alternative balance sheets showing R&D as an asset.

Accounting biases are notoriously hard to get rid of, however. Thus, many firms end up asking not "Did the widget division earn more than its cost of capital last year?" but "Was the widget division's book ROI typical of a successful firm in the widget industry?" The underlying assumptions are that (1) similar accounting procedures are used by other widget manufacturers and (2) successful widget companies earn their cost of capital.

There are some simple accounting changes that could reduce biases in performance measures. Remember that the biases all stem from *not* using economic depreciation. Therefore why not switch to economic depreciation? The main reason is that each asset's present value would have to be reestimated every year. Imagine the confusion if this were attempted. You can understand why accountants set up a depreciation schedule when an investment is made and then stick to it. But why restrict the choice of depreciation schedules to the old standbys, such as straight-line? Why not specify a depreciation pattern that at least matches *expected* economic depreciation? For example, the Ranchi store could be depreciated according to the expected economic depreciation schedule shown in Table 12.3. This would avoid any systematic biases. It would break no law or accounting standard. This step seems so simple and effective that we are at a loss to explain why firms have not adopted it.[23]

Earnings and Earnings Targets

The biases that we have just described do not come from creative accounting. They are built into GAAP. Of course we should worry about creative accounting also. We have already noted how stock options have tempted managers to fiddle with accounting choices to make reported earnings look good and prop up stock price.

But perhaps there is a deeper problem. CEOs of public companies face constant scrutiny. Much of that scrutiny focuses on earnings. Security analysts forecast earnings per share (EPS) and investors, security analysts, and professional portfolio managers wait to see whether the company can meet or beat the forecasts. *Not* meeting the forecasts can be a big disappointment.

Monitoring by security analysts and portfolio managers can help constrain agency problems. But CEOs complain about the "tyranny of EPS" and the apparent short-sightedness of the stock market. (The British call it *short-termism.*) Of course the stock market is not systematically short-sighted. If it were, growth companies would not sell at the high price–earnings ratios observed in practice.[24] Nevertheless, the pressure on CEOs to generate steady, predictable growth in earnings is real.

CEOs complain about this pressure, but do they do anything about it? Unfortunately the answer appears to be yes, according to Graham, Harvey, and Rajgopal, who surveyed about 400 senior managers.[25] Most of the managers said that accounting earnings were the single most important number reported to investors. Most admitted to adjusting their firms' operations and investments

---

[23] This procedure has been suggested by several authors, for example by Zvi Bodie in "Compound Interest Depreciation in Capital Investment," *Harvard Business Review* 60 (May–June 1982), pp. 58–60.

[24] Recall from Chapter 4 that the price–earnings ratio equals $1/r_E$, where r_E is the cost of equity, *unless* the firm has valuable growth opportunities (PVGO). The higher the PVGO, the lower the earnings–price ratio and the higher the price–earnings ratio. Thus the high price–earnings ratios observed for growth companies (much higher than plausible estimates of $1/r_E$) imply that investors forecast large PVGOs. But PVGO depends on investments made many years in the future. If investors see significant PVGOs, they can't be systematically short-sighted.

[25] J. R. Graham, C. R. Harvey, and S. Rajgopal, "The Economic Implications of Corporate Financial Reporting," *Journal of Accounting and Economics* 40 (2005), pp. 3–73.

to manage earnings. For example, 80% were willing to decrease discretionary spending in R&D, advertising, or maintenance if necessary to meet earnings targets. Many managers were also prepared to defer or reject investment projects with positive NPVs. There is a good deal of evidence that firms do indeed manage their earnings. For example, DeGeorge, Patel, and Zeckhauser studied a large sample of earnings announcements.[26] With remarkable regularity, earnings per share either met or beat security analysts' forecasts, but only by a few cents. CFOs appeared to report conservatively in good times, building a stockpile of earnings that could be reported later. The rule, it seems, is *Make sure that you report sufficiently good results to keep analysts happy, and, if possible, keep something back for a rainy day.*[27]

How much value was lost because of such adjustments? For a healthy, profitable company, spending a little more on advertising or deferring a project start for a few months may cause no significant damage. But we cannot endorse any sacrifice of fundamental shareholder value done just to manage earnings.

We may condemn earnings management, but in practice it's hard for CEOs and CFOs to break away from the crowd. Graham and his coauthors explain it this way:[28]

> The common belief is that a well-run and stable firm should be able to "produce the numbers"... even in a year that is somewhat down. Because the market expects firms to be able to hit or slightly exceed earnings targets, and on average firms do just this, problems can arise when a firm does not deliver. ... The market might assume that not delivering [reveals] potentially serious problems (because the firm is apparently so near the edge that it cannot produce the dollars to hit earnings ...). As one CFO put it, "if you see one cockroach, you immediately assume that there are hundreds behind the walls."

Thus we have a cockroach theory explaining why stock prices sometimes fall sharply when a company's earnings fall short, even if the shortfall is only a penny or two.

Of course private firms do not have to worry about earnings management—which could help explain the increasing number of firms that have been bought out and returned to private ownership. (We discuss "going private" in Chapters 32 and 33.) Firms in some other countries, where quarterly earnings reports are not required and governance is more relaxed, may find it easier to invest for the long run. But such firms will also accumulate more agency problems. We wish there were simple answers to these trade-offs.

---

[26] F. Degeorge, J. Patel, and R. Zeckhauser, "Earnings Management to Exceed Thresholds," *The Journal of Business* 72 (January 1999), pp. 1–33.

[27] Sometimes, instead of adjusting their operations, companies meet their target earnings by bending the accounting rules. For example, in August 2009 GE was fined $50 million for creative accounting in earlier years. The SEC said that GE had met or exceeded analysts' profit targets in every quarter from 1995 through 2004, but that its top accountants signed off on improper decisions to make its numbers look better and to avoid missing analysts' earnings expectations.

[28] Graham, Harvey, and Rajgopal, *op. cit.,* p. 29.

SUMMARY

Capital investment decisions must be decentralized to a large extent. Consequently, agency problems are inevitable. Plant or divisional managers may be tempted to slack off, to avoid risk, or to propose empire-building or entrenching investments. Of course, top management is also exposed to similar temptations.

Agency problems are mitigated by a combination of monitoring and incentives. For example, shareholders delegate the task of monitoring top management to the board of directors and to the accountants who audit the company's books.

To encourage managers to maximize shareholder value, a large part of their compensation is usually tied to company performance. Typically, this performance-related pay consists of a mixture of stock or stock options and bonuses that depend on accounting measures of profitability. The U.S is unusual both in the high levels of compensation for top executives and the extent to which pay is performance-related.

If you want to align the interests of the manager and the shareholder, it makes sense to give the manager common stock or stock options. But this is not a complete solution, for at least three reasons. First, stock prices depend on market and industry developments, not just on firm-specific performance. Thus compensation by stock or options exposes managers to risks that are outside their control. Second, today's stock price already reflects managers' expected future performance. Therefore, superior performance if it is expected, will not be rewarded with a superior stock-market return. Third, tying too much of management compensation to stock prices tempts managers to pump up stock prices, for example, by manipulating reported earnings per share.

The further you go down in a company, the more tenuous the link between the stock price and a manager's effort and decisions. Therefore a higher fraction of pay depends on accounting income. Increasing accounting income is not the same thing as increasing value, because accountants do not recognize the cost of capital as an expense. Many companies therefore tie compensation to net return on investment (net ROI) or to Economic Value Added (EVA). Net ROI is the difference between ordinary ROI and the cost of capital. EVA and other residual income measures subtract a charge for capital employed. This charge pushes managers and employees to let go of unneeded assets and to acquire new ones only if the additional earnings exceed the cost of capital.

Of course, any accounting measure of profitability, such as EVA or the book return on investment (ROI), depends on accurate measures of earnings and capital employed. Unless adjustments are made to accounting data, these measures may underestimate the true profitability of new assets and overestimate that of old assets.

In principle, the solution is easy. EVA and ROI should be calculated using true or economic income. Economic income is equal to the cash flow less economic depreciation (that is, the decline in the present value of the asset). Unfortunately, we can't ask accountants to recalculate each asset's present value each time income is calculated. But it does seem fair to ask why they don't at least try to match book depreciation schedules to typical patterns of economic depreciation.

The more pressing problem is that CEOs and CFOs seem to pay too much attention to earnings, at least in the short run, to maintain smooth growth and to meet earnings targets. They manage earnings, not with improper accounting, but by tweaking operating and investment plans. For example, they may defer a positive-NPV project for a few months to move the project's up-front expenses into the next fiscal year. It's not clear how much value is lost by this kind of behavior, but any value loss is unfortunate.

FURTHER READING

Current practices in management remuneration are discussed in:

K. J. Murphy, "Executive Compensation," in O. Ashenfelter and D. Cards (eds.), *Handbook of Labor Economics* (North-Holland, 1999).

R.K. Aggarwal, "Executive Compensation and Incentives," in B. E Eckbo (ed.), *Handbook of Empirical Corporate Finance* (Amsterdam: Elsevier/North-Holland, 2007), Chapter 7.

B. J. Hall and K. J. Murphy, "The Trouble with Stock Options," *Journal of Economic Perspectives* 17 (Summer 2003), pp. 49–70.

The following surveys argue that executive compensation has been excessive, owing partly to weaknesses in corporate governance:

L. Bebchuk and J. Fried, *Pay without Performance: The Unfulfilled Promise of Executive Compensation* (Cambridge, MA: Harvard University Press, 2005).

M. C. Jensen, K. J. Murphy, and E. G. Wruck, "Remuneration: Where We've Been, How We Got to Here, What Are the Problems, and How to Fix Them," 2004, at www.ssrn.com, posted July 12, 2004.

The Fall 2005 issue of the Journal of Applied Corporate Finance *focuses on executive pay and corporate governance.*

The following article is worth reading for survey evidence on earnings and corporate reporting:

J. R. Graham, C. R. Harvey, and S. Rajgopal, "The Economic Implications of Corporate Financial Reporting," *Journal of Accounting and Economics* 40 (2005), pp. 3–73.

For easy-to-read descriptions of EVA, see:

A. Ehrbar, *EVA: The Real Key to Creating Wealth* (New York: John Wiley & Sons, 1998).

J. M. Stern and J. S. Shiely, *The EVA Challenge—Implementing Value-added Change in an Organization* (New York: John Wiley & Sons, 2001).

PROBLEM SETS

BASIC

1. True or false?
   a. U.S. CEOs are paid much more than CEOs in other countries.
   b. A large fraction of compensation for U.S. CEOs comes from stock-option grants.
   c. Stock-option grants give the manager a certain number of shares delivered at annual intervals, usually over five years.
   d. U.S. accounting rules now require recognition of the value of stock-option grants as a compensation expense.

2. Define the following: (a) Agency costs in capital investment, (b) private benefits, (c) empire building, (d) free-rider problem, (e) entrenching investment, (f) delegated monitoring.

3. Monitoring alone can never completely eliminate agency costs in capital investment. Briefly explain why.

4. Here are several questions about economic value added or EVA.
   a. Is EVA expressed as a percentage or a rupee amount?
   b. Write down the formula for calculating EVA.
   c. What is the difference, if any, between EVA and residual income?
   d. What is the point of EVA? Why do firms use it?
   e. Does the effectiveness of EVA depend on accurate measures of accounting income and assets?

5. The Modern Language Corporation earned ₹1.6 million on net assets of ₹20 million. The cost of capital is 11.5%. Calculate the net ROI and EVA.

6. Fill in the blanks:
   "A project's economic income for a given year equals the project's _____ less its _____ depreciation. New projects may take several years to reach full profitability. In these cases book income is _____ than economic income early in the project's life and _____ than economic income later in its life."

7. How in practice do managers of public firms meet short-run earnings targets? By creative accounting?

INTERMEDIATE

8. Compare typical compensation and incentive arrangements for (a) top management, for example, the CEO or CFO, and (b) plant or division managers. What are the chief differences? Can you explain them?

9. Suppose all plant and division managers were paid only a fixed salary—no other incentives or bonuses.
   a. Describe the agency problems that would appear in capital investment decisions.
   b. How would tying the managers' compensation to EVA alleviate these problems?
10. We noted that management compensation must in practice rely on results rather than on effort. Why? What problems are introduced by not rewarding effort?
11. Here are a few questions about compensation schemes that tie top management's compensation to the rate of return earned on the company's common stock.
    a. Today's stock price depends on investors' expectations of future performance. What problems does this create?
    b. Stock returns depend on factors outside the managers' control, for example, changes in interest rates or prices of raw materials. Could this be a serious problem? If so, can you suggest a partial solution?
    c. Compensation schemes that depend on stock returns do *not* depend on accounting data. Is that an advantage? Why or why not?
12. You chair the compensation committee of the board of directors of Nasik Copper. A consultant suggests two stock-option packages for the CEO:
    a. A conventional stock-option plan, with the exercise price fixed at today's stock price.
    b. An alternative plan in which the exercise price depends on the future market value of a portfolio of the stocks of *other* copper-mining companies. This plan pays off for the CEO only if Androscoggin's stock price performs better than its competitors'.

    The second plan sets a higher hurdle for the CEO, so the number of shares should be higher than in the conventional plan. Assume that the number of shares granted under each plan has been calibrated so that the present values of the two plans are the same.

    Which plan would you vote for? Explain.
13. Table 12.5 shows a condensed income statement and balance sheet for Nasik Copper's Shirdi smelting plant.
    a. Calculate the plant's EVA. Assume the cost of capital is 9%.
    b. As Table 12.5 shows, the plant is carried on Androscoggin's books at ₹48.32 million. However, it is a modern design, and could be sold to another copper company for $95 million. How should this fact change your calculation of EVA?

TABLE 12.5 Condensed financial statements for the Shirdi smelting plant. See Problem 14 (figures in ₹ millions).

Income Statement for 2011		Assets, December 31, 2011	
Revenue	₹56.66	Net working capital	₹ 7.08
Raw materials cost	18.72		
Operating cost	21.09	Investment in plant and equipment	69.33
Depreciation	4.50	*Less* accumulated depreciation	21.01
Pretax income	12.35	Net plant and equipment	48.32
Tax at 35%	4.32		
Net income	₹ 8.03	Total assets	₹55.40

14. Herbal Resources is a small but profitable producer of dietary supplements for pets. This is not a high-tech business, but Herbal's earnings have averaged around ₹1.2 million after tax, largely on the strength of its patented enzyme for making cats nonallergenic. The patent has eight years to run, and Herbal has been offered ₹4 million for the patent rights.

Herbal's assets include ₹2 million of working capital and ₹8 million of property, plant, and equipment. The patent is not shown on Herbal's books. Suppose Herbal's cost of capital is 15%. What is its EVA?

15. True or false? Explain briefly.
   a. Book profitability measures are biased measures of true profitability for individual assets. However, these biases "wash out" when firms hold a balanced mix of old and new assets.
   b. Systematic biases in book profitability would be avoided if companies used depreciation schedules that matched expected economic depreciation. However, few, if any, firms have done this.

16. Consider the following project:

	Period			
	0	**1**	**2**	**3**
Net cash flow	−100	0	78.55	78.55

The internal rate of return is 20%. The NPV, assuming a 20% opportunity cost of capital, is exactly zero. Calculate the expected *economic* income and economic depreciation in each year.

17. Calculate the year-by-year book and economic profitability for investment in polyzone production, as described in Chapter 11. Use the cash flows and competitive spreads shown in Table 11.2, and assume straight-line depreciation over 10 years.

Visit us at
www.mhhe.com/bmam10e

What is the steady-state book rate of return (ROI) for a mature company producing polyzone? Assume no growth and competitive spreads.

18. The Web site www.mhhe.com/bmam10e contains an Excel program for calculating the profitability of the Ranchi project. Now suppose that the cash flows from Ranchi's new supermarket are as follows:

Visit us at
www.mhhe.com/bmam10e

	Year						
	0	**1**	**2**	**3**	**4**	**5**	**6**
Cash flows ($ thousands)	−1,000	+298	+298	+298	+138	+138	+140

   a. Recalculate economic depreciation. Is it accelerated or decelerated?
   b. Rework Tables 12.2 and 12.3 to show the relationship between (i) the "true" rate of return and book ROI and (ii) true EVA and forecasted EVA in each year of the project's life.

19. The Web site www.mhhe.com/bmam10e contains an Excel program for measuring the profitability of the Ranchi project. Reconstruct Table 12.4 assuming a steady-state growth rate of 10% per year. Your answer will illustrate a fascinating theorem, namely, that book rate of return equals the economic rate of return when the economic rate of return and the steady-state growth rate are the same.

Visit us at
www.mhhe.com/bmam10e

CHALLENGE

20. Consider an asset with the following cash flows:

Visit us at
www.mhhe.com/bmam10e

	Year			
	0	**1**	**2**	**3**
Cash flows (₹ millions)	−12	+5.20	+4.80	+4.40

The firm uses straight-line depreciation. Thus, for this project, it writes off $4 million per year in years 1, 2, and 3. The discount rate is 10%.

a. Show that economic depreciation equals book depreciation.

b. Show that the book rate of return is the same in each year.

c. Show that the project's book profitability is its true profitability.

You've just illustrated another interesting theorem. If the book rate of return is the same in each year of a project's life, the book rate of return equals the IRR.

21. In our Ranchi example, true depreciation was decelerated. That is not always the case. For instance, Table 12.6 shows how on average the market value of a Boeing 737 has varied with its age[29] and the cash flow needed in each year to provide a 10% return. (For example, if you bought a 737 for $19.69 million at the start of year 1 and sold it a year later, your total profit would be $17.99 + 3.67 - 19.69 = \$1.97$ million , 10% of the purchase cost.)

eXcel
Visit us at
www.mhhe.com/bmam10e

Many airlines write off their aircraft straight-line over 15 years to a salvage value equal to 20% of the original cost.

a. Calculate economic and book depreciation for each year of the plane's life.

b. Compare the true and book rates of return in each year.

c. Suppose an airline invested in a fixed number of Boeing 737s each year. Would steady-state book return overstate or understate true return?

TABLE 12.6 Estimated market values of a Boeing 737 in January 1987 as a function of age, plus the cash flows needed to provide a 10% true rate of return (figures in $ millions).

Start of Year	Market Value	Cash Flow
1	19.69	
2	17.99	$3.67
3	16.79	3.00
4	15.78	2.69
5	14.89	2.47
6	14.09	2.29
7	13.36	2.14
8	12.68	2.02
9	12.05	1.90
10	11.46	1.80
11	10.91	1.70
12	10.39	1.61
13	9.91	1.52
14	9.44	1.46
15	9.01	1.37
16	8.59	1.32

[29] We are grateful to Mike Staunton for providing us with these estimates.

13

CHAPTER

EFFICIENT MARKETS AND BEHAVIORAL FINANCE

Up to this point we have concentrated almost exclusively on the left-hand side of the balance sheet—the firm's capital investment decision. Now we move to the right-hand side and to the problems involved in financing the capital investments. To put it crudely, you've learned how to spend money, now learn how to raise it.

Of course we haven't totally ignored financing in earlier chapters. We introduced the weighted-average cost of capital, for example. But in most places we have looked past financing issues and used estimates of the opportunity cost of capital to discount future cash flows. We didn't ask how the cost of capital might be affected by financing.

Now we are turning the problem around. We take the firm's present portfolio of real assets and its future investment strategy as given, and then we determine the best financing strategy. For example,

- Should the firm reinvest most of its earnings in the business, or distribute the cash to shareholders?
- If the firm needs more money, should it issue more stock or should it borrow?
- Should it borrow short term or long term?
- Should it borrow by issuing a normal long-term bond or a convertible bond (a bond which can be exchanged for stock by the bondholders)?

There are countless other financing trade-offs, as you will see.

The purpose of holding the firm's capital investment decision constant is to separate that decision from the financing decision. Strictly speaking, this assumes that investment and financing decisions are *independent*. In many circumstances this is a reasonable assumption. The firm is generally free to change its capital structure by repurchasing one security and issuing another. In that case there is no need to associate a particular investment project with a particular source of cash. The firm can think, first, about which projects to accept and, second, about how they should be financed.

Sometimes decisions about capital structure depend on project choice or vice versa, and in those cases the investment and financing decisions have to be considered jointly. However, we defer discussion of such interactions of financing and investment decisions until Chapter 19.

We start this chapter by contrasting investment and financing decisions. The objective in each case is the same—to maximize NPV. However, it may be harder to find positive-NPV financing opportunities. The reason it is difficult to add value by clever financing decisions is that capital markets are usually efficient. By this we mean that fierce competition between investors eliminates profit opportunities and causes debt and equity issues to be fairly priced. If you think that sounds like a sweeping statement, you are right. That is why we have devoted this chapter to explaining and evaluating the efficient-market hypothesis.

You may ask why we start our discussion of financing issues with this conceptual point, before you have even the most basic knowledge about securities and issue procedures. We do it this way because financing decisions seem overwhelmingly complex if you don't learn to ask the right questions. We are afraid you might flee from confusion to the myths that often dominate popular discussion of corporate financing. You need to understand the efficient-market hypothesis not because it is *universally* true but because it leads you to ask the right questions.

We define the efficient-market hypothesis more carefully in Section 13-2. The hypothesis comes in different strengths, depending on the information available to investors. Sections 13-2 through 13-4 review the evidence for and against efficient markets. The evidence "for" is considerable, but over the years a number of puzzling anomalies have accumulated.

Advocates for rational and efficient markets also have a hard time explaining *bubbles*. Every decade seems to find its own bubble: the 1980s real estate and stock market bubble in Japan, the 1990s technology stock bubble, and the recent real estate bubble that triggered the subprime crisis. Part of the blame for bubbles goes to the incentive and agency problems that can plague even the most rational people, particularly when they are investing other people's money. But bubbles may also reflect patterns of irrational behavior that have been well documented by behavioral psychologists. We describe the main features of *behavioral finance* and the challenge that it poses to the efficient-market hypothesis.

The chapter closes with the six lessons of market efficiency.

13-1   WE ALWAYS COME BACK TO NPV

Although it is helpful to separate investment and financing decisions, there are basic similarities in the criteria for making them. The decisions to purchase a machine tool and to sell a bond each involve valuation of a risky asset. The fact that one asset is real and the other is financial doesn't matter. In both cases we end up computing net present value.

The phrase *net present value of borrowing* may seem odd to you. But the following example should help to explain what we mean: As part of its policy of encouraging industrialization in Tamil Nadu, the Government of Tamil Nadu allows the companies to defer the payment of sales tax (with certain exceptions, of course[1]) to the State Government for a period of 14 years. That is the companies can collect the sales tax from the customers at the time of sale and retain the sales tax collected as an

---

[1] See http://www.indiainbusiness.nic.in/indian-states/tamilnadu/ITPol.htm for details.

interest-free loan from the government for a period of 14 years. The sales tax deferred in year 1 will be repayable in five equal annual instalments from year 15 to 19; sales tax deferred in year 2 will be repayable in five equal annual instalments from year 16 to 20, and so on and finally the sales tax collected in year 14 will be repayable in five equal annual instalments from year 28 to 32.

Let's assume that your company sets up a new plant in Tamil Nadu and that you expect to collect ₹5 million of sales tax every year. This means that for each of the next 14 years, your company will receive ₹5 million as an interest-free loan from the Tamil Nadu Government. In year 15, the company will refund ₹1 million; In Year 16, the company will refund ₹2 million (1 million from year 1 and 1 million from year 2), and so on and so forth. We show the repayment schedule in the below table. Should you accept the offer?

Total Sales tax >>>	Deferred Sales Tax Example — Payments Made in Year-														Total Collections
	1	2	3	4	5	6	7	8	9	10	11	12	13	14	
	5	5	5	5	5	5	5	5	5	5	5	5	5	5	
15	1														1
16	1	1													2
17	1	1	1												3
18	1	1	1	1											4
19	1	1	1	1	1										5
20		1	1	1	1	1									5
21			1	1	1	1	1								5
22				1	1	1	1	1							5
23					1	1	1	1	1						5
24						1	1	1	1	1					5
25							1	1	1	1	1				5
26								1	1	1	1	1			5
27									1	1	1	1	1		5
28										1	1	1	1	1	5
29											1	1	1	1	4
30												1	1	1	3
31													1	1	2
32														1	1

We can compute the NPV of the loan agreement in the usual way. The one difference is that the first few cash flows are *positive* and the subsequent cash flows are *negative*.

$$\text{NPV} = \text{sales tax collected} - \text{present value of sales tax payments}[2]$$

$$= \sum_{t=1}^{14} \frac{5}{(1+r)^t} - \frac{1}{(1+r)^{15}} - \frac{2}{(1+r)^{16}} - \frac{3}{(1+r)^{17}} - \frac{4}{(1+r)^{18}}$$

$$- \sum_{t=19}^{28} \frac{5}{(1+r)^t} - \frac{4}{(1+r)^{29}} - \frac{3}{(1+r)^{30}} - \frac{2}{(1+r)^{31}} - \frac{1}{(1+r)^{32}}$$

---

[2] Here, we assume that the entire sales tax will be paid at the end of the year. Actually, Tamil Nadu Government expects you to pay the money in four equal quarterly instalments. We ignore that here.

The only missing variable is r, the opportunity cost of capital. You need that to value the liability created by this deferred sales tax benefits. We reason this way: The deferred sales tax benefit to you is a financial asset: a piece of paper representing your promise to pay the sales tax collected back to the government after the 14th year. How much would that paper sell for if freely traded in the capital market? It would sell for the present value of those cash flows, discounted at r, the rate of return offered by other securities issued by your firm. All you have to do to determine r is to answer the question, what interest rate would my firm have to pay to borrow money directly from the capital markets rather than the government?

Suppose that this rate is 10 percent. Then

$$NPV = \sum_{t=1}^{14} \frac{5}{(1+0.1)^t} - \frac{1}{(1+0.1)^{15}} - \frac{2}{(1+0.1)^{16}} - \frac{3}{(1+0.1)^{17}} - \frac{4}{(1+0.1)^{18}}$$
$$- \sum_{t=19}^{28} \frac{5}{(1+0.1)^t} - \frac{4}{(1+0.1)^{29}} - \frac{3}{(1+0.1)^{30}} - \frac{2}{(1+0.1)^{31}} - \frac{1}{(1+0.1)^{32}}$$

$$= ₹\, 28.74 \text{ million.}$$

Of course, you do not need any arithmetic to tell that getting an interest-free loan for 14 years is a good deal when the fair rate is 10 percent. But the NPV calculations tell you just how much that opportunity is worth (₹28.74 million)[3]. It also brings out the essential similarity of investment and financing decisions.

Differences between Investment and Financing Decisions

In some ways investment decisions are simpler than financing decisions. The number of different securities and financing strategies is well into the hundreds (we have stopped counting). You will have to learn the major families, genera, and species. You will also need to become familiar with the vocabulary of financing. You will learn about such matters as red herrings, greenshoes, and bookrunners; behind each of these terms lies an interesting story.

There are also ways in which financing decisions are much easier than investment decisions. First, financing decisions do not have the same degree of finality as investment decisions. They are easier to reverse. That is, their abandonment value is higher. Second, it's harder to make money by smart financing strategies. The reason is that financial markets are more competitive than product markets. This means it is more difficult to find positive-NPV financing strategies than positive-NPV investment strategies.

When the firm looks at capital investment decisions, it does *not* assume that it is facing perfect, competitive markets. It may have only a few competitors that specialize in the same line of business in the same geographical area. And it may own some unique assets that give it an edge over its competitors. Often these assets are intangible, such as patents, expertise, or reputation. All this opens up the opportunity to make superior profits and find projects with positive NPVs.

In financial markets your competition is all other corporations seeking funds, to say nothing of the state, local, and central governments that go to Mumbai, New York, London, and other financial centers to raise money. The investors who supply financing are comparably numerous, and they are smart: Money attracts brains. The financial amateur often views capital markets as *segmented,* that is, broken down into distinct sectors. But money moves between those sectors, and it usually moves fast.

---

[3] We ignore here any tax consequences of borrowing. These are discussed in Chapter 18.

In general, as we shall see, firms should assume that the securities they issue are fairly priced. That takes us into the main topic of this chapter: efficient capital markets.

13-2 WHAT IS AN EFFICIENT MARKET?

A Startling Discovery: Price Changes Are Random

As is so often the case with important ideas, the concept of efficient capital markets stemmed from a chance discovery. In 1953 Maurice Kendall, a British statistician, presented a controversial paper to the Royal Statistical Society on the behavior of stock and commodity prices.[4] Kendall had expected to find regular price cycles, but to his surprise they did not seem to exist. Each series appeared to be "a 'wandering' one, almost as if once a week the Demon of Chance drew a random number . . . and added it to the current price to determine the next week's price." In other words, the prices of stocks and commodities seemed to follow a *random walk*.

If you are not sure what we mean by "random walk," you might like to think of the following example: You are given ₹100 to play a game. At the end of each week a coin is tossed. If it comes up heads, you win 3% of your investment; if it is tails, you lose 2.5%. Therefore, your capital at the end of the first week is either ₹103.00 or ₹97.50. At the end of the second week the coin is tossed again. Now the possible outcomes are:

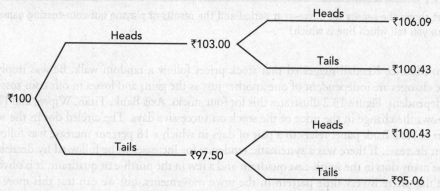

This process is a random walk with a positive drift of .25% per week.[5] It is a random walk because successive changes in value are independent. That is, the odds each week are the same, regardless of the value at the start of the week or of the pattern of heads and tails in the previous weeks.

If you find it difficult to believe that there are no patterns in share price changes, look at the two charts in Figure 13.1. One of these charts shows the outcome from playing our game for five years; the other shows the actual performance of the sensex index for a five-year period. Can you tell which one is which?[6]

---

[4] See M. G. Kendall, "The Analysis of Economic Time Series, Part I. Prices," *Journal of the Royal Statistical Society* 96 (1953), pp. 11–25. Kendall's idea was not wholly new. It had been proposed in an almost forgotten thesis written 53 years earlier by a French doctoral student, Louis Bachelier. Bachelier's accompanying development of the mathematical theory of random processes anticipated by five years Einstein's famous work on the random Brownian motion of colliding gas molecules. See L. Bachelier, *Théorie de la Speculation* (Paris: Gauthiers-Villars, 1900). Reprinted in English (A. J. Boness, trans.) in P. H. Cootner (ed.), *The Random Character of Stock Market Prices* (Cambridge, MA: MIT Press, 1964), pp. 17–78.

[5] The drift is equal to the expected outcome: $(1/2)(3) + (1/2)(-2.5) = .25\%$.

[6] The bottom chart (from left) in Figure 13.1 shows the real sensex for April 2006 to March 2011; the top chart is a series of cumulated random numbers. Of course, 50% of you are likely to have guessed right, but we bet it was just a guess.

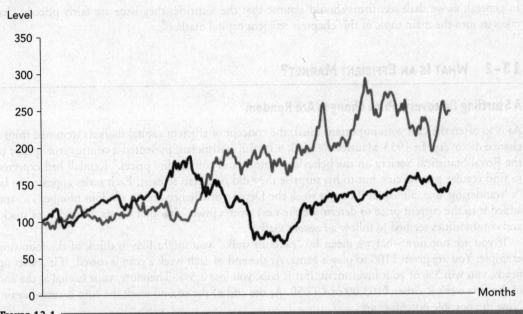

FIGURE 13.1

This chart shows the sensex for a five-year period and the results of playing our coin-tossing game for five years. Can you tell which line is which?

When Maurice Kendall suggested that stock prices follow a random walk, he was implying that the price changes are independent of one another just as the gains and losses in our coin-tossing game were independent. Figure 13.2 illustrates this for four stocks, Axis Bank, Titan, Wipro, and ITC. Each panel shows the change in the price of the stock on successive days. The circled dot in the south-east quadrant of Axis Bank panel refers to a pair of days in which a 18 percent increase was followed by a 7 percent decrease. If there was a systematic tendency for increases to be followed by decreases, there would be many dots in the south-east quadrant and a few in the north-east quadrant. It is obvious from a glance that there is very little pattern in the price movements, but we can test this more precisely by calculating the coefficient of correlation between each day's price change and the next. If price movements persisted, the correlation would be positive; if there was no relationship, it would be 0. In our example, the correlation between successive price changes in Axis Bank stock was -0.001; there was a negligible tendency for price rises to be followed by subsequent price decreases.[7]

Figure 13.2 suggests that successive price changes of all four stocks were effectively uncorrelated. Today's price change gave investors almost no clue as to the likely change tomorrow. Does that surprise you? If so, imagine that it were not the case and that changes in Titan's stock price were expected to persist for several months. Figure 13.3 provides an example of such a predictable cycle. You can see that an upswing in Titan's stock price started last month, when the price was ₹4200, and it is expected to carry the price to ₹5000 next month. What will happen when investors perceive this bonanza? Since Titan's stock is a bargain at ₹4700 investors will rush to buy. They will stop buying only when the

---

[7] The correlation coefficient between successive observations is known as the *autocorrelation coefficient*. An autocorrelation of –0.001 implies that, if Axis Bank price rose by 1 percent more than average yesterday, your best forecast of today's price change would be an increase of 0.1 percent less than average.

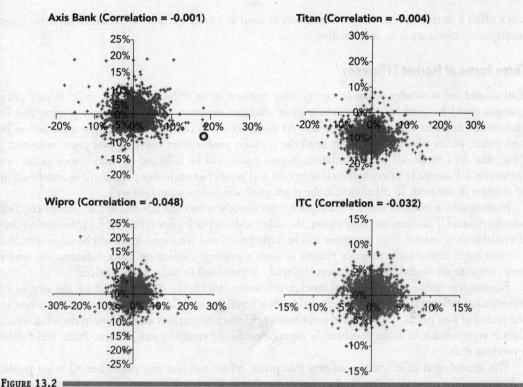

FIGURE 13.2

Each dot shows a pair of returns for a stock on two successive days between January 2002 and March 2011. The circled dot for Axis Bank records a daily return of +18% and then −7% on the next day. The scatter diagram shows no significant relationship between returns on successive days.

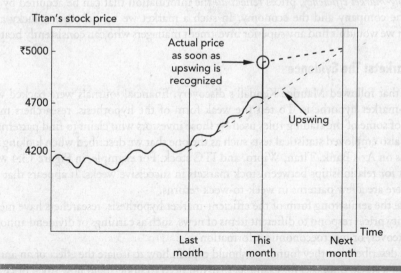

FIGURE 13.3

Cycles self-destruct as soon as they are recognized by investors. The stock price instantaneously jumps to the present value of the expected future price.

stock offers a normal rate of return. Therefore, as soon as a cycle becomes apparent to investors, they immediately eliminate it by their trading.

Three Forms of Market Efficiency

You should see now why prices in competitive markets must follow a random walk. If past price changes could be used to predict future price changes, investors could make easy profits. But in competitive markets easy profits don't last. As investors try to take advantage of the information in past prices, prices adjust immediately until the superior profits from studying past price movements disappear. As a result, all the information in past prices will be reflected in *today's* stock price, not tomorrow's. Patterns in prices will no longer exist and price changes in one period will be independent of changes in the next. In other words, the share price will follow a random walk.

In competitive markets today's stock price must already reflect the information in past prices. But why stop there? If markets are competitive, shouldn't today's stock price reflect *all* the information that is available to investors? If so, securities will be fairly priced and security returns will be unpredictable. No one earns consistently superior returns in such a market. Collecting more information won't help, because all available information is already impounded in today's stock prices.

Economists define three levels of market efficiency, which are distinguished by the degree of information reflected in security prices. In the first level, prices reflect the information contained in the record of past prices. This is called *weak market efficiency*. If markets are efficient in the weak sense, then it is impossible to make consistently superior profits by studying past returns. Prices will follow a random walk.

The second level of efficiency requires that prices reflect not just past prices but all other public information, for example, from the Internet or the financial press. This is known as *semistrong market efficiency*. If markets are semistrong efficient, then prices will adjust immediately to public information such as the announcement of the last quarter's earnings, a new issue of stock, or a proposal to merge two companies.

With *strong-market efficiency*, prices reflect *all* the information that can be acquired by painstaking analysis of the company and the economy. In such a market we would observe lucky and unlucky investors, but we wouldn't find any superior investment managers who can consistently beat the market.

Efficient Markets: The Evidence

In the years that followed Maurice Kendall's discovery, financial journals were packed with tests of the efficient-market hypothesis. To test the weak form of the hypothesis, researchers measured the profitability of some of the trading rules used by those investors who claim to find patterns in security prices. They also employed statistical tests such as the one that we described when looking for patterns in the returns on Axis Bank, Titan, Wipro, and ITC stock. For example, in Figure 13.4 we have used the same test for relationships between stock markets in successive weeks. It appears that throughout the world there are a few patterns in week-to-week returns.

To analyze the semistrong form of the efficient-market hypothesis, researchers have measured how rapidly security prices respond to different items of news, such as earnings or dividend announcements, news of a takeover, or macroeconomic information.

Before we describe what they found, we should explain how to isolate the effect of an announcement on the price of a stock. Suppose, for example, that you need to understand how stock prices of takeover targets respond when the takeovers are first announced. As a first stab, you could simply calculate the average return on target-company stocks in the days leading up to the announcement and immediately

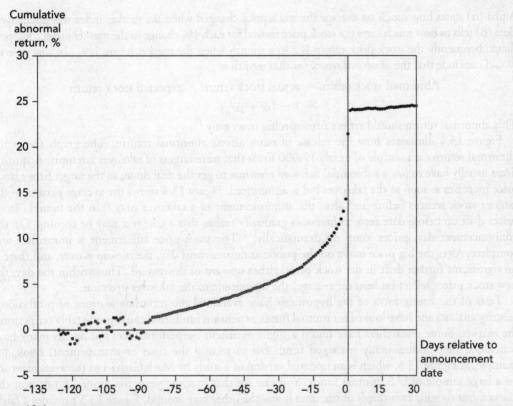

FIGURE 13.4

The performance of the stocks of target companies compared with that of the market. The prices of target stocks jump up on the announcement day, but from then on, there are no unusual price movements. The announcement of the takeover attempt seems to be fully reflected in the stock price on the announcement day.

Source: A. Keown and J. Pinkerton, "Merger Announcements and Insider Trading Activity," *Journal of Finance* 36 (September 1981), pp. 855–869. © 1981. Reprinted with permission of Blackwell Publishers Journal Rights. We are grateful to Jinghua Yan for updating the calculations to the period 1979–2004.

after it. With daily returns on a large sample of targets, the average announcement effect should be clear. There won't be too much contamination from movements in the overall market around the announcement dates, because daily market returns average out to a very small number.[8] The potential contamination increases for weekly or monthly returns, however. Thus you will usually want to adjust for market movements. For example, you can simply subtract out the return on the market:

$$\text{Adjusted stock return} = \text{return on stock} - \text{return on market index}$$

Chapter 8 suggests a refined adjustment based on betas. (Just subtracting the market return assumes that target-firm betas equal 1.0.) This adjustment is called the *market model:*

$$\text{Expected stock return} = \alpha + \beta \times \text{return on market index}$$

---

[8] Suppose, for example, that the market return is 12% per year. With 250 trading days in the year, the average daily return is $(1.12)^{1/250} - 1$ = .00045, or .045%.

Alpha (α) states how much on average the stock price changed when the market index was unchanged. Beta (β) tells us how much *extra* the stock price moved for each 1% change in the market index.[9] Suppose that subsequently the stock price return is $\tilde{r}$ in a month when the market return is $\tilde{r}_m$. In that case we would conclude that the *abnormal return* for that month is

$$\text{Abnormal stock return} = \text{actual stock return} - \text{expected stock return}$$
$$= \tilde{r} - (\alpha + \beta\tilde{r}_m)$$

This abnormal return should reflect firm-specific news only.[10]

Figure 13.4 illustrates how the release of news affects abnormal returns. The graph shows the abnormal return on a sample of nearly 17,000 firms that were targets of takeover attempts. Acquiring firms usually have to pay a substantial *takeover premium* to get the deal done, so the target firm's stock price increases as soon as the takeover bid is announced. Figure 13.4 shows the average pattern of the target's stock returns before and after the announcement of a takeover (day 0 in the figure). Stock prices drift up before date zero, as investors gradually realize that a takeover may be coming. On the announcement day, prices jump up dramatically.[11] The stock-price adjustment is immediate and complete. After the big price move on the public announcement day, the run-up is over, and there is no significant further drift in the stock price, either upward or downward. Thus within the day, the new stock prices reflect (at least on average) the magnitude of the takeover premium.

Tests of the strong form of the hypothesis have examined the recommendations of professional security analysts and have looked for mutual funds or pension funds that could predictably outperform the market. Some researchers have found a slight persistent outperformance, but just as many have concluded that professionally managed funds fail to recoup the costs of management. Look, for example, at Figure 13.5, which is an updated version of a study by Mark Carhart of the average return on a large sample of U.S. mutual funds. You can see that in some years the mutual funds beat the market, but roughly two-thirds of the time it was the other way around. Figure 13.5 provides a fairly crude comparison, for mutual funds have tended to specialize in particular sectors of the market, such as low-beta stocks or large-firm stocks, that may have given below-average returns. To control for such differences, each fund needs to be compared with a benchmark portfolio of similar securities. The study by Mark Carhart did this, but the message was unchanged: The funds earned a lower return than the benchmark portfolios *after* expenses and roughly matched the benchmarks *before* expenses.

It would be surprising if some managers were not smarter than others and could earn superior returns. But it seems difficult to spot the smart ones, and the top-performing managers one year have about an average chance of falling on their faces the next year.[12]

The evidence on efficient markets has convinced many professional and individual investors to give up pursuit of superior performance. They simply "buy the index," which maximizes diversification

---

[9] It is important when estimating α and β that you choose a period in which you believe that the stock behaved normally. If its performance was abnormal, then estimates of α and β cannot be used to measure the returns that investors expected. As a precaution, ask yourself whether your estimates of expected returns look sensible. Methods for estimating abnormal returns are analyzed in A. C. MacKinlay, "Event Studies in Economics and Finance," *Journal of Economic Literature* 35 (1997), pp. 13–39; and also S. P. Kothari and J. B. Warner, "Econometrics of Event Studies," in B. E. Eckbo (ed.), *The Handbook of Empirical Corporate Finance* (Amsterdam: Elsevier/North-Holland, 2007), Chapter 1.

[10] Abnormal returns are also often calculated using the Fama-French three-factor model, which we discussed in Chapter 8. The stock return is adjusted for the market return, the difference between small- and large-stock returns, and the difference between returns on high and low book-to-market firms.

[11] Big profits await if you can identify target firms before the takeover announcement. Purchases based on confidential inside information are illegal, however, and could land you in jail.

[12] See, for example, B. G. Malkiel, "Returns from Investing in Equity Mutual Funds 1971 to 1991," *Journal of Finance* 50 (June 1995), pp. 549–572. Some contrary evidence that good performance does persist is provided in R. Kosowski, A. Timmerman, R. Wermers, and H. White, "Can Mutual Fund 'Stars' Really Pick Stocks? New Evidence from a Bootstrap Analysis," *Journal of Finance* 61 (December 2006), pp. 2551–2595. See also M. J. Gruber, "Another Puzzle: The Growth in Actively Managed Mutual Funds," *Journal of Finance* 51 (July 1996), pp. 783–810.

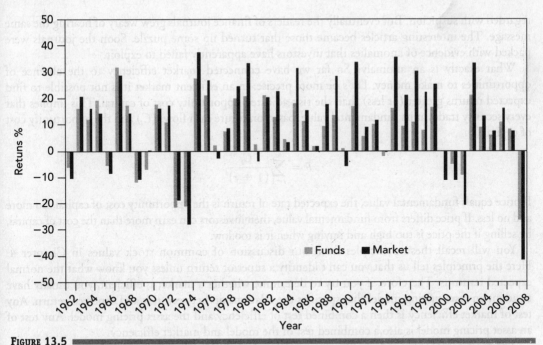

FIGURE 13.5

Average annual returns on a large sample of U.S. mutual funds and the market index, 1962–2008. Notice that mutual funds underperform the market in approximately two-thirds of the years.

Source: M. M. Carhart, "On Persistence in Mutual Fund Performance," *Journal of Finance* 52 (March 1997), pp. 57–82. © 1997 Blackwell Publishers. We are grateful to Jinghua Yan for updating the calculations.

and cuts costs to the bone. Individual investors can buy *index funds,* which are mutual funds that track stock market indexes. There is no active management, so costs are very low. For example, management fees for the Vanguard 500 Index Fund, which tracks the S&P 500 Index, were .18% per year in 2009 (.09% per year for investments over $100,000). The size of this fund was $73 billion.

How far could indexing go? Not to 100%: If all investors hold index funds then nobody will be collecting information and prices will not respond to new information when it arrives. An efficient market needs some smart investors who gather information and attempt to profit from it. To provide incentives to gather costly information, prices cannot reflect *all* information.[13] There must be some profits available to allow the costs of information to be recouped. But if the costs are small, relative to the total market value of traded securities, then the financial market can still be close to perfectly efficient.

13-3   THE EVIDENCE AGAINST MARKET EFFICIENCY

Almost without exception, early researchers concluded that the efficient-market hypothesis was a remarkably good description of reality. So powerful was the evidence that any dissenting research was

---

[13] See S. J. Grossman and J. E. Stiglitz, "On the Impossibility of Informationally Efficient Markets," *American Economic Review* 70 (June 1980), pp. 393–408.

regarded with suspicion. But eventually the readers of finance journals grew weary of hearing the same message. The interesting articles became those that turned up some puzzle. Soon the journals were packed with evidence of anomalies that investors have apparently failed to exploit.

What exactly is an anomaly? So far we have connected market efficiency to the absence of opportunities to make money. Let's be more precise: in an efficient market it is not possible to find expected returns greater (or less) than the risk-adjusted opportunity cost of capital. This implies that every security trades at its fundamental value, based on future cash flows (C_t) and the opportunity cost of capital (r):

$$P = \sum_{t=1}^{\infty} \frac{C_t}{(1 + r)^t}$$

If price equals fundamental value, the expected rate of return is the opportunity cost of capital, no more and no less. If price differs from fundamental value, then investors can earn more than the cost of capital, by selling if the price is too high and buying when it is too low.

You will recall these principles from our discussion of common stock values in Chapter 4. Here the principles tell us that you can't identify a superior return unless you know what the normal expected return is. Therefore, if you try to determine whether a market is efficient, you usually have to adopt an asset pricing model that specifies the relationship between risk and expected return. Any test of market efficiency is then a combined test of efficiency and the asset pricing model. Any test of an asset pricing model is also a combined test of the model and market efficiency.

The most commonly used asset pricing model is the CAPM. Chapter 8 pointed to some apparent violations of the CAPM, including the abnormally high returns on the stocks of small firms. For example, look back at Figure 8.10, which shows the cumulative difference between the returns on small-firm stocks and large-firm stocks. You can see that since 1926 the stocks of the firms with the lowest market capitalizations have performed substantially better than those with the highest capitalizations.

Now this may mean one (or more) of several things. First, it could be that investors have demanded a higher expected return from small firms to compensate for some extra risk factor that is not captured in the simple capital asset pricing model.

Second, the superior performance of small firms could simply be a coincidence, a finding that stems from the efforts of many researchers to find interesting patterns in the data. There is evidence for and against the coincidence theory. Those who believe that the small-firm effect is a pervasive phenomenon can point to the fact that small-firm stocks have provided a higher return in many other countries. On the other hand, you can see from Figure 8.10 that the small-firm effect seems to have disappeared as soon as it was first documented in 1981. Perhaps investors did underestimate the returns on small firms before 1981, but then bid up the firms' stock prices as soon as the mispricing was identified.

Third, the small-firm effect could be an important exception to the efficient-market theory, an exception that gave investors the opportunity for consistently superior returns over a period of several decades. If these anomalies offer easy pickings, you would expect to find a number of investors eager to take advantage of them. It turns out that, while many investors do try to exploit such anomalies, it is surprisingly difficult to get rich by doing so. For example, Professor Richard Roll, who probably knows as much as anyone about market anomalies, confesses

> Over the past decade, I have attempted to exploit many of the seemingly most promising "inefficiencies" by actually trading significant amounts of money according to a trading rule suggested

by the "inefficiencies" . . . I have never yet found one that worked in practice, in the sense that it returned more after cost than a buy-and-hold strategy.[14]

Do Investors Respond Slowly to New Information?

We have dwelt on the small-firm effect, but there is no shortage of other puzzles and anomalies. Some of them relate to the short-term behavior of stock prices. For example, returns appear to be higher in January than in other months, they seem to be lower on a Monday than on other days of the week, and most of the daily return comes at the beginning and end of the day.

To have any chance of making money from such short-term patterns, you need to be a professional trader, with one eye on the computer screen and the other on your annual bonus. If you are a corporate financial manager, these short-term patterns in stock prices may be intriguing conundrums, but they are unlikely to change the major financial decisions about which projects to invest in and how they should be financed.

Corporate financial managers should be more concerned about mispricing that lasts months or years. Here are two examples of possible longer-lasting inefficiency.

The Earnings Announcement Puzzle The earnings announcement puzzle is summarized in Figure 13.6, which shows stock performance following the announcement of unexpectedly good or bad earnings during the years 1972 to 2001 in the U.S. The 10% of the stocks of firms with the best

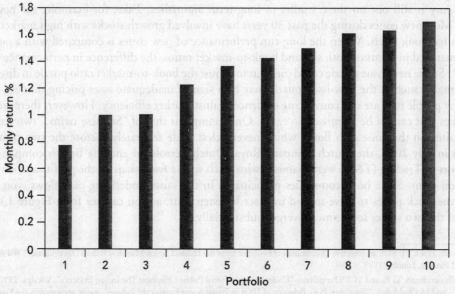

FIGURE 13.6

The average return 1972–2001 on stocks of firms over the six months following an announcement of quarterly earnings. The 10% of stocks with the best earnings news (portfolio 10) outperformed those with the worst news (portfolio1) by about 1% per month.

Source: T. Chordia and L. Shivakumar, "Inflation Illusion and the Post-earnings Announcement Drift," *Journal of Accounting Research* 43 (2005), pp. 521–556.

---

[14] R. Roll, "What Every CFO Should Know about Scientific Progress in Financial Economics: What Is Known and What Remains to Be Resolved," *Financial Management* 23 (Summer 1994), pp. 69–75.

earnings news outperform those with the worst news by about 1% per month over the six-month period following the announcement. It seems that investors underreact to the earnings announcement and become aware of the full significance only as further information arrives. Using data for 90 stocks for the sample period January 1990 to March 1996, Prof. Hari Om Chaturvedi[15] reports similar results from India. Within a span of 40 days after the announcement of the earnings, the 20% of the stocks of firms with the best earnings news outperform those with the worst news by 26%.

The New-Issue Puzzle   When firms issue stock to the public, investors typically rush to buy. On average those lucky enough to receive stock receive an immediate capital gain. However, researchers have found that these early gains often turn into losses. For example, suppose that you bought stock immediately following each initial public offering (IPO) and then held that stock for five years. Over the period 1970–2007 your average annual return would have been 3.8% less than the return on a portfolio of similar-sized stocks in the U.S. Madhusoodanan and Thiripalraju, and Baral and Obaidullah report positive abnormal return on the first day of listing of IPOs in India[16]. Both the studies also report negative *risk-adjusted returns* in the one-year period after the listing of IPOs. The study by Baral and Obaidullah document another interesting results about the Indian IPOs. They find the average return form the day of listing till the 20th day after listing is 11.5%. This means even if an investor does not apply (or does not get the allotment) for the IPOs, he can still make excess return by buying on the day of listing and selling it on the 20th day. However, the same study also documents lower liquidity on the first day of the listing.

The jury is still out on these studies of long-term anomalies. Take, for example, the new-issue puzzle. Most new issues during the past 30 years have involved growth stocks with high market values and limited book assets. When the long-run performance of new issues is compared with a portfolio that is matched in terms of both size and book-to-market ratios, the difference in performance almost halves.[17] So the new-issue puzzle could turn out to be just the book-to-market ratio puzzle in disguise.[18]

Anomalies such as the new-issue puzzle may be a sign of inadequate asset pricing models, and so for many people they are not convincing evidence against market efficiency. However, there are other anomalies that cannot be dismissed so easily. One example is that of "Siamese twins," two securities with claims on the same cash flows, which nevertheless trade separately. Before the two companies merged in July 2005, the Dutch company Royal Dutch Petroleum and the British company Shell Transport & Trading (T&T) were Siamese twins, each with a fixed share in the profits and dividends of the oil giant. Since both companies participated in the same underlying cash flows, you would expect the stock prices to have moved in exact lockstep. But, as you can see from Figure 13.7, the prices of the two shares sometimes diverged substantially.[19]

---

[15] Chaturvedi, H. O., "Is SUE an Effective Discriminator? Evidence from the Indian Capital Market – It does Discriminate!", ICFAI Journal of Applied Finance, January, 1999.

[16] See Madhusoodanan, T. P., and M T Thiripalraju, "Underpricing in Initial Public Offerings: The Indian Evidence", Vikalpa, 1997. See also Baral, S K., and M Obaidullah, "Short-run Price Behavior of IPOs in India: Some Empirical Findings", paper presented in the First Capital Markets Conference held at the Indian Institute of Capital Markets, 1997.

[17] The long-run underperformance of new issues was documented in R. Loughran and J. R. Ritter, "The New Issues Puzzle," *Journal of Finance* 50 (1995), pp. 23–51. The figures are updated on Jay Ritter's Web site, where IPO returns are compared with those of a portfolio that is matched in terms of size and book-to-market ratio. (See **bear.cba.ufl.edu/ritter**.)

[18] There may be still other reasons for the poor long-term performance of IPOs, including tax effects. Portfolios of IPOs generate many extreme winners and losers. Investors can sell the losers, deducting the losses against other capital gains, and hold the winners, thus deferring taxes. IPO stocks are a good venue for this tax strategy, so tax-savvy investors may have bid up IPO stock prices.

[19] For evidence on the pricing of Siamese twins see K. A. Froot and E. Dabora, "How Are Stock Prices Affected by the Location of Trade?" *Journal of Financial Economics* 53 (August 1999), pp. 189–216, and, for more recent data, A. De Jong, L. Rosenthal, and M. A. Van Dijk, "The Risk and Return of Arbitrage in Dual-Listed Companies," *Review of Finance* 13 (2009), pp. 495–520.

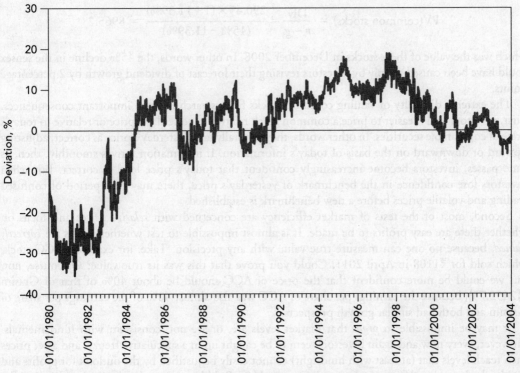

FIGURE 13.7

Log deviations from Royal Dutch Shell/Shell T&T parity.

Source: Mathijs van Dijk Web site **www.mathijsavandijk.com/dual-listed-companies**. Used with permission.

Bubbles and Market Efficiency

Cases such as the Siamese twins suggest that there are occasions when prices of individual stocks can get out of line. But are there also cases in which prices as a whole can no longer be justified by fundamentals? We will look at the evidence in a moment, but first we should note how difficult it is to value common stocks and to determine whether their prices are irrational.

For example, imagine that in December 2007 you wanted to check whether the stocks forming sensex were fairly valued. As a first stab, you might use the constant-growth formula that we introduced in Chapter 4. In 2007 the annual weighted dividends (the actual dividend multiplied with the weight in the index) paid by the companies in the index came to about ₹290.45. Suppose that these dividends were expected to grow at a steady rate of 13.36% and that investors required a return of 15%. Then the constant-growth formula gives a value for the common stocks of

$$PV(\text{common stocks}) = \frac{\text{Div}}{r-g} = \frac{290.45 \times (1+13.36\%)}{(15\% - 13.36\%)} = 20{,}030.8$$

which was roughly the value of sensex in December 2007 (20,030.83). But how confident could anyone have been about these figures? Perhaps the likely dividend growth was only 11.39% per year. In that case the value of the common stocks would decline to

$$PV(\text{common stocks}) = \frac{\text{Div}}{r-g} = \frac{290.45 \times (1+11.39\%)}{(15\% - 11.39\%)} = 8965.2$$

which was the value of these stocks in December 2008. In other words, the 45% decline in the sensex could have been caused simply by investors revising their forecast of dividend growth by 2 percentage points.

The extreme difficulty of valuing common stocks from scratch has two important consequences. First, investors find it easier to price a common stock relative to yesterday's price or relative to today's price of comparable securities. In other words, they generally take yesterday's price as correct, adjusting upward or downward on the basis of today's information. If information arrives smoothly, then, as time passes, investors become increasingly confident that today's price level is correct. But when investors lose confidence in the benchmark of yesterday's price, there may be a period of confused trading and volatile prices before a new benchmark is established.

Second, most of the tests of market efficiency are concerned with *relative* prices and focus on whether there are easy profits to be made. It is almost impossible to test whether stocks are *correctly valued*, because no one can measure true value with any precision. Take, for example, ACC stock, which sold for ₹1108 in April 2011. Could you prove that this was its true value? Of course, not, but we could be more confident that the price of ACC should be about 40% of that of Grasim (₹2452.75), because the earnings per share of ACC was also almost 40% of the earnings per share of Grasim and both had similar growth prospects.

It may be impossible to *prove* that market levels are, or are not, consistent with fundamentals. However, every now and again investors seem to be caught up in a speculative frenzy, and asset prices then reach levels that (at least with hindsight) cannot easily be justified by the outlook for profits and dividends. Investors refer to such occasions as *bubbles*. Bubbles can result when prices rise rapidly, and more and more investors join the game on the assumption that prices will *continue* to rise. These bubbles can be self-sustaining for a while. It can be rational to jump on the bandwagon as long as you are sure that there will be greater fools that you can sell out to. But remember that lots of money will be lost, perhaps by you, when the bubble bursts.[20]

The Japanese bubble is a good example. The Nikkei 225 Index rose about 300% between the start of 1985 and December 1989. After a sharp increase in interest rates at the beginning of 1990, stock prices began to fall. By October the Nikkei had sunk to about half its peak. In March 2009, the Nikkei was still down 80% from its peak 19 years before.

The boom in Japanese stock prices was matched by an even greater explosion in land prices. For example, Ziemba and Schwartz document that the few hundred acres of land under the Emperor's Palace in Tokyo, evaluated at neighborhood land prices, was worth as much as all the land in Canada or California.[21] But then the real estate bubble also burst. By 2005 land prices in the six major Japanese cities had slumped to just 13% of their peak.

Such bubbles are not confined to Japan. Toward the end of the twentieth century investors in technology stocks saw a remarkable run-up in the value of their holdings. The sensex, for example, which has a heavy weighting in technology stocks, rose 60% from the start of 1995 to its high in February 2000. Then, as rapidly as it began, the boom ended, and by October 2002 the sensex had fallen 55%. During the same period, the Nasdaq Composite index rose 580% points before falling by 78%.

---

[20] Bubbles are not necessarily irrational. See M. Brunnermeier, *Asset Pricing under Asymmetric Information: Bubbles, Crashes, Technical Analysis and Herding* (Oxford: Oxford University Press, 2001).

[21] See W. T. Ziemba and S. L. Schwartz, *Invest Japan* (Chicago, IL: Probus Publishing Co., 1992), p. 109.

Some of the largest gains and losses were experienced by dot.com stocks. For example, Yahoo! shares, which began trading in April 1996, appreciated by 1,400% in four years. In these heady days some companies found that they could boost their stock price simply by adding "dot.com" to the company name.[22]

Looking back at the Japanese and dot.com bubbles, it seems difficult to believe that future cash flows could ever have been sufficient to provide investors with a reasonable return.[23] If that is the case, we have two important exceptions to the theory of efficient markets.

13-4 BEHAVIORAL FINANCE

Why might prices depart from fundamental values? Some believe that the answer lies in behavioral psychology. People are not 100% rational 100% of the time. This shows up in investors' attitudes to risk and the way they assess probabilities.

1. *Attitudes toward risk.* Psychologists have observed that, when making risky decisions, people are particularly loath to incur losses. It seems that investors do not focus solely on the current value of their holdings, but look back at whether their investments are showing a profit or a loss. For example, if I sell my holding of HUL stock for ₹50,000, I may gain considerable satisfaction, if the stock only cost me ₹25,000, but I will be much less happy if it had cost ₹75,000. This observation is the basis for *prospect theory.*[24] Prospect theory states that (a) the value investors place on a particular outcome is determined by the gains or losses that they have made since the asset was acquired or the holding last reviewed, and (b) investors are particularly averse to the possibility of even a very small loss and need a high return to compensate for it.

   The pain of loss seems also to depend on whether it comes on the heels of earlier losses. Once investors have suffered a loss, they may be even more concerned not to risk a further loss. Conversely, just as gamblers are known to be more willing to make large bets when they are ahead, so investors may be more prepared to run the risk of a stock market dip after they have enjoyed a run of unexpectedly high returns.[25] If they do then suffer a small loss, they at least have the consolation of still being ahead for the year.

   When we discussed portfolio theory in Chapters 7 and 8, we pictured investors as forward-looking only. Past gains or losses were not mentioned. All that mattered was the investor's current wealth and the expectation and risk of future wealth. We did not allow for the possibility that Nicholas would be elated because his investment is in the black, while Nicola with an equal amount of wealth would be despondent because hers is in the red.

2. *Beliefs about probabilities.* Most investors do not have a Ph.D. in probability theory and may make systematic errors in assessing the probability of uncertain events. Psychologists have found that, when judging possible future outcomes, individuals tend to look back at what happened in a few

---

[22] P. R. Rau, O. Dimitrov, and M. Cooper, "A Rose.com by Any Other Name," *Journal of Finance* 56 (2001), pp. 2371–2388.

[23] For an analysis of Japanese stock prices, see K. French and J. M. Poterba, "Were Japanese Stock Prices Too High?" *Journal of Financial Economics* 29 (October 1991), pp. 337–364. For more on dot.com stock prices, see E. Ofek and M. Richardson, "The Valuation and Market Rationality of Internet Stock Prices," *Oxford Review of Economic Policy* 18 (Autumn 2002), pp. 265–287.

[24] Prospect theory was first set out in D. Kahneman and A. Tversky, "Prospect Theory: An Analysis of Decision under Risk," *Econometrica* 47 (1979), pp. 263–291.

[25] The effect is described in R. H. Thaler and E. J. Johnson, "Gambling with the House Money and Trying to Break Even: The Effects of Prior Outcomes on Risky Choice," *Management Science* 36 (1990), pp. 643–660. The implications of prospect theory for stock returns are explored in N. Barberis, M. Huang, and T. Santos, "Prospect Theory and Asset Prices," *Quarterly Journal of Economics* 116 (February 2001), pp. 1–53.

similar situations. As a result, they are led to place too much weight on a small number of recent events. For example, an investor might judge that an investment manager is particularly skilled because he has "beaten the market" for three years in a row, or that three years of rapidly rising prices are a good indication of future profits from investing in the stock market. The investor may not stop to reflect on how little one can learn about expected returns from three years' experience.

Most individuals are also too *conservative,* that is, too slow to update their beliefs in the face of new evidence. People tend to update their beliefs in the correct direction but the magnitude of the change is less than rationality would require.

Another systematic bias is *overconfidence.* Most of us believe that we are better-than-average drivers and most investors think they are better-than-average stock pickers. Two speculators who trade with each other cannot both make money, but may be prepared to continue trading because each is confident that the other is the patsy. Overconfidence also shows up in the certainty that people express about their judgments. They consistently overestimate the odds that the future will turn out as they say and underestimate the chances of unlikely events.

You can see how these behavioral characteristics may help to explain the Japanese and dot.com bubbles. As prices rose, they generated increased optimism about the future and stimulated additional demand. The more that investors racked up profits, the more confident they became in their views and the more willing they became to bear the risk that next month might not be so good.

Limits to Arbitrage

It is not difficult to believe that amateur investors may sometimes be caught up in a scatty whirl of irrational exuberance.[26] But there are plenty of hard-headed professional investors managing huge sums of money. Why don't these investors bail out of overpriced stocks and force their prices down to fair value? One reason is that there are *limits to arbitrage,* that is, limits on the ability of the rational investors to exploit market inefficiencies.

Strictly speaking, *arbitrage* means an investment strategy that guarantees superior returns without any risk. In practice, arbitrage is defined more casually as a strategy that exploits market inefficiency and generates superior returns if and when prices return to fundamental values. Such strategies can be very rewarding, but they are rarely risk-free.

In an efficient market, if prices get out of line, then arbitrage forces them back. The arbitrageur buys the underpriced securities (pushing up their prices) and sells the overpriced securities (pushing down their prices). The arbitrageur earns a profit by buying low and selling high and waiting for prices to converge to fundamentals. Thus arbitrage trading is often called *convergence trading.*

In practice arbitrage is harder than it looks. Trading costs can be significant and some trades are difficult to execute. For example, suppose that you identify an overpriced security that is *not* in your existing portfolio. You want to "sell high," but how do you sell a stock that you don't own? It can be done, but you have to *sell short.*

To sell a stock short, you borrow shares from another investor's portfolio, sell them, and then wait hopefully until the price falls and you can buy the stock back for less than you sold it for. If you're wrong and the stock price increases, then sooner or later you will be forced to repurchase the stock at a higher price (therefore at a loss) to return the borrowed shares to the lender. But if you're right and the price does fall, you repurchase, pocket the difference between the sale and repurchase prices, and

---

[26] The term "irrational exuberance" was coined by Alan Greenspan, former chairman of the Federal Reserve Board, to describe the dot.com boom. It was also the title of a book by Robert Shiller that examined the boom. See R. Shiller, *Irrational Exuberance* (New York: Broadway Books, 2001).

return the borrowed shares. Sounds easy, once you see how short selling works, but there are costs and fees to be paid, and in some cases you will not be able to find shares to borrow.[27]

The perils of selling short were dramatically illustrated in 2008. Given the gloomy outlook for the automobile industry, a number of hedge funds decided to sell Volkswagen (VW) shares short in the expectation of buying them back at a lower price. Then in a surprise announcement Porsche revealed that it had effectively gained control of 74% of VW's shares. Since a further 20% was held by the state of Lower Saxony, there was not enough stock available for the short sellers to buy back. As they scrambled to cover their positions, the price of VW stock rose in just two days from €209 to a high of €1005, making VW the most highly valued company in the world. Although the stock price drifted rapidly down, those short-sellers who were caught in the *short squeeze* suffered large losses.

The VW example illustrates that the most important limit to arbitrage is the risk that prices will diverge even further before they converge. Thus an arbitrageur has to have the guts and resources to hold on to a position that may get much worse before it gets better. Take another look at the relative prices of Royal Dutch and Shell T&T in Figure 13.7. Suppose that you were a professional money manager in 1980, when Royal Dutch was about 12% below parity. You decided to buy Royal Dutch, sell Shell T&T short, and wait confidently for prices to converge to parity. It was a long wait. The first time you would have seen any profit on your position was in 1983. In the meantime the mispricing got worse, not better. Royal Dutch fell to more than 30% below parity in mid-1981. Therefore, you had to report a substantial loss on your "arbitrage" strategy in that year. You were fired and took up a new career as a used-car salesman.

The demise in 1998 of Long Term Capital Management (LTCM) provides another example of the problems with convergence trades. LTCM, one of the largest and most profitable hedge funds of the 1990s, believed that interest rates in the different euro zone countries would converge when the euro replaced the countries' previous currencies. LTCM had taken massive positions to profit from this convergence, as well as massive positions designed to exploit other pricing discrepancies. After the Russian government announced a moratorium on some of its debt payments in August 1998, there was great turbulence in the financial markets, and many of the discrepancies that LTCM was betting on suddenly got much larger.[28] LTCM was losing hundreds of millions of dollars daily. The fund's capital was nearly gone when the Federal Reserve Bank of New York arranged for a group of LTCM's creditor banks to take over LTCM's remaining assets and shut down what was left in an orderly fashion.

LTCM's sudden meltdown has not prevented rapid growth in the hedge fund industry in the 2000s. If hedge funds can push back the limits to arbitrage and avoid the kinds of problems that LTCM ran into, markets will be more efficient going forward. But asking for complete efficiency is probably asking too much. Prices can get out of line and stay out if the risks of an arbitrage strategy outweigh the expected returns.

Incentive Problems and the Subprime Crisis

The limits to arbitrage open the door to individual investors with built-in biases and misconceptions that can push prices away from fundamental values. But there can also be incentive problems that get

---

[27] Investment and brokerage firms identify shares eligible for lending and arrange to make them available to short-sellers. The supply of shares that can be borrowed is limited. You are charged a fee for borrowing the stock, and you are required to put up collateral to protect the lender in case the share price rises and the short-seller is unable to repurchase and return the shares. Putting up collateral is costless if the short-seller gets a market interest rate, but sometimes only lower interest rates are offered.

[28] The Russian debt moratorium was unexpected and unusual, because the debt had only recently been issued and was denominated in *roubles*. The government preferred to default rather than to print roubles to service the debt.

in the way of a rational focus on fundamentals. We illustrate with a brief look at the subprime crisis in the United States.

Few U.S. homeowners foresaw a collapse in the price of their home. After all, the average house price in the U.S. had not fallen since the Great Depression of the 1930s. But in 2005 *The Economist* surveyed the widespread increase in property prices and warned:

> [T]he total value of the residential property in developed economies rose by more than $30 trillion over the past five years to over $70 trillion, an increase equivalent to 100% of those countries' combined GDPs. Not only does this dwarf any previous house-price boom, it is larger than the global stock market bubble in the late 1920s (55% of GDP). In other words it looks like the biggest bubble in history.[29]

Shortly afterward the bubble burst. By March 2009, U.S. house prices had fallen by nearly a third from their peak in 2006.[30]

How could such a boom and crash arise? In part because banks, credit rating agencies, and other financial institutions all had distorted incentives. Purchases of real estate are generally financed with mortgage loans from banks. In most parts of the U.S., borrowers can default on their mortgages with relatively small penalties. If property prices fall, they can simply walk away. But, if prices rise, they make money. Thus borrowers may be willing to take large risks, especially if the fraction of the purchase price financed with their own money is small.

Why, then, are banks willing to lend money to people who are bound to default if property prices fall significantly? Since the borrowers benefited most of the time, they were willing to pay attractive up-front fees to banks to get mortgage loans. But the banks could pass on the default risk to somebody else by packaging and reselling the mortgages as mortgage-backed securities (MBSs). Many MBS buyers assumed that they were safe investments, because the credit rating agencies said so. As it turned out, the credit ratings were a big mistake. (The rating agencies introduced another agency problem, because issuers paid the agencies to rate the MBS issues, and the agencies consulted with issuers over how MBS issues should be structured.)

The "somebody else" was also the government. Many subprime mortgages were sold to FNMA and FMAC ("Fannie Mae" and "Freddie Mac"). These were private corporations with a special advantage: government credit backup. (The backup was implicit, but quickly became explicit when Fannie and Freddie got into trouble in 2008. The U.S. Treasury had to take them over.) Thus these companies were able to borrow at artificially low rates, channeling money into the mortgage market.

The government was also on the hook because large banks that held subprime MBSs were "too big to fail" in a financial crisis. So the original incentive problem—the temptation of home buyers to take out a large mortgage and hope for higher real estate prices—was never corrected. The government could have cut its exposure by reining in Fannie and Freddie before the crisis but did not do so.

Agency and incentive problems do not arise just in real estate. They are widespread in the financial services industry. In the U.S. and many other countries, people engage financial institutions such as pension funds and mutual funds to invest their money. These institutions are the investors' agents, but the agents' incentives do not always match the investors' interests. Just as with real estate, these agency relationships can lead to mispricing, and potentially bubbles.[31]

---

[29] "In come the waves," *The Economist*, June 16, 2005.

[30] Investors who did foresee that the fall in house prices would lead to the subprime debacle were able to earn high profits. For example, John Paulson, the hedge fund manager, earned $3.7 billion in 2007 as a result (*Financial Times*, January 15, 2008, and June 18, 2008).

[31] See F. Allen, "Do Financial Institutions Matter?" *Journal of Finance* 56 (2001), pp. 1165–1175.

13-5   THE SIX LESSONS OF MARKET EFFICIENCY

The efficient-market hypothesis emphasizes that arbitrage will rapidly eliminate any profit opportunities and drive market prices back to fair value. Behavioral-finance specialists may concede that there are no easy profits, but argue that arbitrage is costly and sometimes slow-working, so that deviations from fair value may persist.

Sorting out the puzzles will take time, but we suggest that financial managers should assume, at least as a starting point, that there are no free lunches to be had on Wall Street.

The "no free lunch" principle gives us the following six lessons of market efficiency. After reviewing these lessons, we consider what market *in* efficiency can mean for the financial manager.

Lesson 1: Markets Have No Memory

The weak form of the efficient-market hypothesis states that the sequence of past price changes contains no information about future changes. Economists express the same idea more concisely when they say that the market has no memory. Sometimes financial managers *seem* to act as if this were not the case. For example, after an abnormal market rise, managers prefer to issue equity rather than debt.[32] The idea is to catch the market while it is high. Similarly, they are often reluctant to issue stock after a fall in price. They are inclined to wait for a rebound. But we know that the market has no memory and the cycles that financial managers seem to rely on do not exist.[33]

Sometimes a financial manager will have inside information indicating that the firm's stock is overpriced or underpriced. Suppose, for example, that there is some good news that the market does not know but you do. The stock price will rise sharply when the news is revealed. Therefore, if your company sells shares at the current price, it would offer a bargain to new investors at the expense of present stockholders.

Naturally, managers are reluctant to sell new shares when they have favorable inside information. But such information has nothing to do with the history of the stock price. Your firm's stock could be selling at half its price of a year ago, and yet you could have special information suggesting that it is *still* grossly overvalued. Or it may be undervalued at twice last year's price.

Lesson 2: Trust Market Prices

In an efficient market you can trust prices, for they impound all available information about the value of each security. This means that in an efficient market, there is no way for most investors to achieve consistently superior rates of return. To do so, you not only need to know more than *anyone* else; you also need to know more than *everyone* else. This message is important for the financial manager who is responsible for the firm's exchange-rate policy or for its purchases and sales of debt. If you operate on the basis that you are smarter than others at predicting currency changes or interest-rate moves, you will trade a consistent financial policy for an elusive will-o'-the-wisp.

The company's assets may also be directly affected by management's faith in its investment skills. For example, one company may purchase another simply because its management thinks that the

---

[32] See, for example, P. Asquith and D. W. Mullins, Jr., "Equity Issues and Offering Dilution," *Journal of Financial Economics* 15 (January–February 1986), pp. 16–89; and (for the U.K.) P. R. Marsh, "The Choice between Debt and Equity: An Empirical Study," *Journal of Finance* 37 (March 1982), pp. 121–144.

[33] If high stock prices signal expanded investment opportunities and the need to finance these new investments, we would expect to see firms raise more money *in total* when stock prices are historically high. But this does not explain why firms prefer to raise the extra cash at these times by an issue of equity rather than debt.

stock is undervalued. On approximately half the occasions the stock of the acquired firm will with hindsight turn out to be undervalued. But on the other half it will be overvalued. On average the value will be correct, so the acquiring company is playing a fair game except for the costs of the acquisition.

Lesson 3: Read the Entrails

If the market is efficient, prices impound all available information. Therefore, if we can only learn to read the entrails, security prices can tell us a lot about the future. For example, in Chapter 23 we show how information in a company's financial statements can help the financial manager to estimate the probability of bankruptcy. But the market's assessment of the company's securities can also provide important information about the firm's prospects. Thus, if the company's bonds are trading at low prices, you can deduce that the firm is probably in trouble.

Here is another example: Suppose that investors are confident that interest rates are set to rise over the next year. In that case, they will prefer to wait before they make long-term loans, and any firm that wants to borrow long-term money today will have to offer the inducement of a higher rate of interest. In other words, the long-term rate of interest will have to be higher than the one-year rate. Differences between the long-term interest rate and the short-term rate tell you something about what investors expect to happen to short-term rates in the future.

The nearby box shows how market prices reveal opinions about issues as diverse as a presidential election, the weather, or the demand for a new product.

Lesson 4: There Are No Financial Illusions

In an efficient market there are no financial illusions. Investors are unromantically concerned with the firm's cash flows and the portion of those cash flows to which they are entitled. However, there are occasions on which managers seem to assume that investors suffer from financial illusion.

For example, some firms devote considerable ingenuity to the task of manipulating earnings reported to stockholders. This is done by "creative accounting," that is, by choosing accounting methods that stabilize and increase reported earnings. Presumably firms go to this trouble because management believes that stockholders take the figures at face value.[34]

One way that companies can affect their reported earnings is through the way that they cost the goods taken out of inventory. As per the Accounting Standard 2 (AS 2) prescribed by ICAI, India, companies can choose between two methods. Under the FIFO (first-in, first-out) method, the firm deducts the cost of the first goods to have been placed in the inventory. Under the weighted-average cost method companies deduct the weighted average cost of the latest goods to arrive in the warehouse. When inflation is high, the cost of the goods that were brought first is likely to be lower than the cost of those that were brought last (and hence likely to be lower than the weighted average cost). So earnings calculated by FIFO appear higher than those calculated under the weighted average cost method.

Now, if it were just a matter of presentation, there would be no harm in switching from weighted average cost method to FIFO. Section 145A of the Income Tax does not prescribe any method of inventory valuation. It merely states that the valuation of inventory shall be in accordance with the method of accounting regularly employed by the company. In an inflationary environment, the weighted average cost method will reduce the tax liability of a company. So the lower apparent earnings from using the weighted average cost method also bring lower immediate tax payments.

---

[34] For a discussion of the evidence that investors are not fooled by earnings manipulation, see R. Watts, "Does It Pay to Manipulate EPS?" in J. M. Stern and D. H. Chew, Jr. (eds.), *The Revolution in Corporate Finance* (Oxford: Basil Blackwell, 1992).

Finance In Practice

Prediction Markets

Stock markets allow investors to bet on their favorite stocks. Prediction markets allow them to bet on almost anything else. These markets reveal the collective guess of traders on issues as diverse as New York City snowfall, an avian flu outbreak, and the occurrence of a major earthquake.

Prediction markets are conducted on the major futures exchanges and on a number of smaller online exchanges such as Intrade (**www.intrade.com**) and the Iowa Electronic Markets (**www.biz. uiowa.edu/iem**). Take the 2008 presidential race as an example. On the Iowa Electronic Markets you could bet that Barack Obama would win by buying one of his contracts. Each Obama contract paid $1 if he won the presidency and nothing if he lost. If you thought that the probability of an Obama victory was 55% (say), you would have been prepared to pay up to $.55 for his contract. Someone who was relatively pessimistic about Obama's chances would have been happy to *sell* you such a contract, for that sale would turn a profit if Obama were to lose. With many participants buying and selling, the market price of a contract revealed the collective wisdom of the crowd.

Take a look at the accompanying figure from the Iowa Electronic Markets. It shows the contract prices for the two contenders for the White House between June and November 2008. Following the Republican convention at the start of September, the price of a McCain contract reached a maximum of $.47. From then on the market suggested a steady fall in the probability of a McCain victory.

Participants in prediction markets are putting their money where their mouth is. So the forecasting accuracy of these markets compares favorably with those of major polls. Some businesses have also formed internal prediction markets to survey the views of their staff. For example, Google operates an internal market to forecast product launch dates, the number of Gmail users, and other strategic questions.*

---

*Google's experience is analyzed in B. Cowgill, J. Wolfers, and E. Zitzewitz, "Using Prediction Markets to Track Information Flows: Evidence from Google," Working paper, Dartmouth College, January 2009.

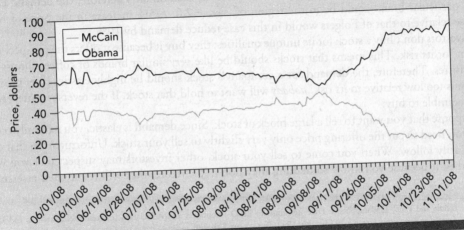

Though AS 2 in India does not allow LIFO, the US GAAP accepts LIFO as a legitimate way of valuing inventories. Under LIFO (last-in, last-out), a firm reports still lower earnings as compared to FIFO and weighted-average cost method under inflationary environment. In the U.S., the IRS insists that the same method that is used to report to shareholders also be used to calculate the firm's taxes.

If markets are efficient, investors should welcome a change to LIFO accounting, even though it reduces earnings. Biddle and Lindahl, who studied the matter, concluded that this is exactly what happens, so that the move to LIFO is associated with an abnormal rise in the stock price.[35] It seems that shareholders look behind the figures and focus on the amount of the tax savings.

Lesson 5: The Do-It-Yourself Alternative

In an efficient market investors will not pay others for what they can do equally well themselves. As we shall see, many of the controversies in corporate financing center on how well individuals can replicate corporate financial decisions. For example, companies often justify mergers on the grounds that they produce a more diversified and hence more stable firm. But if investors can hold the stocks of both companies why should they thank the companies for diversifying? It is much easier and cheaper for them to diversify than it is for the firm.

The financial manager needs to ask the same question when considering whether it is better to issue debt or common stock. If the firm issues debt, it will create financial leverage. As a result, the stock will be more risky and it will offer a higher expected return. But stockholders can obtain financial leverage without the firm's issuing debt; they can borrow on their own accounts. The problem for the financial manager is, therefore, to decide whether the company can issue debt more cheaply than the individual shareholder.

Lesson 6: Seen One Stock, Seen Them All

The elasticity of demand for any article measures the percentage change in the quantity demanded for each percentage addition to the price. If the article has close substitutes, the elasticity will be strongly negative; if not, it will be near zero. For example, coffee, which is a staple commodity, has a demand elasticity of about $-.2$. This means that a 5% increase in the price of coffee changes sales by $-.2 \times .05 = -.01$; in other words, it reduces demand by only 1%. Consumers are likely to regard different *brands* of coffee as much closer substitutes for each other. Therefore, the demand elasticity for a particular brand could be in the region of, say, -2.0. A 5% increase in the price of Maxwell House relative to that of Folgers would in this case reduce demand by 10%.

Investors don't buy a stock for its unique qualities; they buy it because it offers the prospect of a fair return for its risk. This means that stocks should be like *very* similar brands of coffee, almost perfect substitutes. Therefore, the demand for a company's stock should be highly elastic. If its prospective return is too low relative to its risk, *nobody* will want to hold that stock. If the reverse is true, *everybody* will scramble to buy.

Suppose that you want to sell a large block of stock. Since demand is elastic, you naturally conclude that you need to cut the offering price only very slightly to sell your stock. Unfortunately, that doesn't necessarily follow. When you come to sell your stock, other investors may suspect that you want to get rid of it because you know something they don't. Therefore, they will revise their assessment of

---

[35] G. C. Biddle and F. W. Lindahl, "Stock Price Reactions to LIFO Adoptions: The Association between Excess Returns and LIFO Tax Savings," *Journal of Accounting Research* 20 (Autumn 1982, Part 2), pp. 551–588.

the stock's value downward. Demand is still elastic, but the whole demand curve moves down. Elastic demand does not imply that stock prices never change when a large sale or purchase occurs; it *does* imply that you can sell large blocks of stock at close to the market price *as long as you can convince other investors that you have no private information.*

Here again we encounter an apparent contradiction with practice. State and federal regulatory commissions, which set the prices charged by local telephone companies, electric companies, and other utilities, have sometimes allowed significantly higher earnings to compensate the firm for price "pressure." This pressure is the decline in the firm's stock price that is supposed to occur when new shares are offered to investors. Yet Paul Asquith and David Mullins, who searched for evidence of pressure, found that new stock issues by utilities drove down their stock prices on average by only .9%.[36] We come back to the subject of pressure when we discuss stock issues in Chapter 15.

What If Markets Are Not Efficient? Implications for the Financial Manager

Our six lessons depend on efficient markets. What should financial managers do when markets are *not* efficient? The answer depends on the nature of the inefficiency.

Trading Opportunities—Are They Really There for Nonfinancial Corporations?   Suppose that the treasurer's staff in your firm notices mispricing in fixed-income or commodities markets, the kind of mispricing that a hedge fund would attempt to exploit in a convergence trade. Should the treasurer authorize the staff to undertake a similar convergence trade? In most cases, the answer should be *no.* First, the corporation faces the same limits to arbitrage that afflict hedge funds and other investors. Second, the corporation probably has no competitive edge in the convergence-trade business.

Procter & Gamble (P&G) supplied a costly example of this point in early 1994, when it lost $102 million in short order. It seems that in 1993 P&G's treasury staff believed that interest rates would be stable and decided to act on this belief to reduce P&G's borrowing costs. They committed P&G to deals with Bankers Trust designed to do just that. Of course there was no free lunch. In exchange for a reduced interest rate, P&G agreed to compensate Bankers Trust if interest rates rose sharply. Rates did increase dramatically in early 1994, and P&G was on the hook.

Then P&G accused Bankers Trust of misrepresenting the transactions—an embarrassing allegation, since P&G was hardly investing as a widow or orphan—and sued Bankers Trust.

We take no stand on the merits of this litigation, which was eventually settled. But think of P&G's competition when it traded in the fixed-income markets. Its competition included the trading desks of all the major investment banks, hedge funds like LTCM, and fixed-income portfolio managers. P&G had no special insights or competitive advantages on the fixed-income playing field. There was no evident reason to expect positive NPV on the trades it committed to. Why was it trading at all? P&G would never invest to enter a new consumer market if it had no competitive advantage in that market.

In Chapter 11 we argued that a corporation should not invest unless it can identify a competitive advantage and a source of economic rents. Market inefficiencies may offer economic rents from convergence trades, but few corporations have a competitive edge in pursuing these rents. As a general rule, nonfinancial corporations gain nothing, on average, by speculation in financial markets. They should not try to imitate hedge funds.[37]

---

[36] See P. Asquith and D. W. Mullins, "Equity Issues and Offering Dilution," *Journal of Financial Economics* 15 (January–February 1986), pp. 61–89.

[37] There are of course some likely exceptions. Hershey and Nestlé are credible traders in cocoa futures markets. The major oil companies probably have special skills and knowledge relevant to energy markets.

What If Your Company's Shares Are Mispriced? The financial manager may not have special information about future interest rates, but definitely has special information about the value of his or her own company's shares. The strong form of market efficiency does not always hold, so the financial manager will often have information that outside investors do not have. Or investors may have the same information as management, but be slow in reacting to that information or may be infected with behavioral biases.

Sometimes you hear managers thinking out loud like this:

> Great! Our stock is clearly overpriced. This means we can raise capital cheaply and invest in Project X. Our high stock price gives us a big advantage over our competitors who could not possibly justify investing in Project X.

But that doesn't make sense. If your stock is truly overpriced, you can help your current shareholders by selling additional stock and using the cash to invest in other capital market securities. But you should *never* issue stock to invest in a project that offers a lower rate of return than you could earn elsewhere in the capital market. Such a project would have a negative NPV. You can always do better than investing in a negative-NPV project: Your company can go out and buy common stocks. In an efficient market, such purchases are always *zero* NPV.

What about the reverse? Suppose you know that your stock is *underpriced*. In that case, it certainly would not help your current shareholders to sell additional "cheap" stock to invest in other fairly priced stocks. If your stock is sufficiently underpriced, it may even pay to forgo an opportunity to invest in a positive-NPV project rather than to allow new investors to buy into your firm at a low price. Financial managers who believe that their firm's stock is underpriced may be justifiably reluctant to issue more stock, but they may instead be able to finance their investment program by an issue of debt. In this case the market inefficiency would affect the firm's choice of financing but not its real investment decisions. In Chapter 15 we will have more to say about the financing choice when managers believe their stock is mispriced.

What If Your Firm Is Caught in a Bubble?

Once in a lifetime, your company's stock price may be swept up in a bubble like the dot.com boom of the late 1990s. Bubbles can be exhilarating. It's hard not to join in the enthusiasm of the crowds of investors bidding up your firm's stock price.[38] On the other hand, financial management *inside* a bubble poses difficult personal and ethical challenges. Managers don't want to "talk down" a high-flying stock price, especially when bonuses and stock-option payoffs depend on it. The temptation to cover up bad news or manufacture good news can be very strong. But the longer a bubble lasts, the greater the damage when it finally bursts. When it does burst, there will be lawsuits and possibly jail time for managers who have resorted to tricky accounting or misleading public statements in an attempt to sustain the inflated stock price.

When a firm's stock price is swept upward in a bubble, CEOs and financial managers are tempted to acquire another firm using the stock as currency. One extreme example where this arguably happened is AOL's acquisition of Time Warner at the height of the dot.com bubble in 2000. AOL was a classic dot.com company. Its stock rose from $2.34 at the end of 1995 to $75.88 at the end of 1999. Time Warner's stock price also increased during this period, but only from $18.94 to $72.31. AOL's total market capitalization was a small fraction of Time Warner's in 1995, but overtook Time Warner's in 1998. By the end of 1999 AOL's outstanding shares were worth $173 billion, compared with Time Warner's $95 billion. AOL managed to complete the acquisition before the Internet bubble burst.

---

[38] See J. C. Stein, "Rational Capital Budgeting in an Irrational World," *Journal of Business* 69 (October 1996), pp. 429–455.

AOL-Time Warner's stock then plummeted, but not by nearly as much as the stocks of dot.com companies that had not managed to find and acquire safer partners.[39]

---

[39] Pavel Savor and Qi Lu provide evidence that many other firms were able to benefit from stock acquisitions. See "Do Stock Mergers Create Value for Acquirers?" *Journal of Finance*, 64 (June 2009), pp. 1061–1097.

SUMMARY

The patron saint of the Bolsa (stock exchange) in Barcelona, Spain, is Nuestra Señora de la Esperanza—Our Lady of Hope. She is the perfect patroness, for we all hope for superior returns when we invest. But competition between investors will tend to produce an efficient market. In such a market, prices will rapidly impound any new information, and it will be difficult to make consistently superior returns. We may indeed hope, but all we can rationally *expect* in an efficient market is a return just sufficient to compensate us for the time value of money and for the risks we bear.

The efficient-market hypothesis comes in three different flavors. The weak form of the hypothesis states that prices efficiently reflect all the information in the past series of stock prices. In this case it is impossible to earn superior returns simply by looking for patterns in stock prices; in other words, price changes are random. The semistrong form of the hypothesis states that prices reflect all published information. That means it is impossible to make consistently superior returns just by reading the newspaper, looking at the company's annual accounts, and so on. The strong form of the hypothesis states that stock prices effectively impound all available information. It tells us that superior information is hard to find because in pursuing it you are in competition with thousands, perhaps millions, of active, intelligent, and greedy investors. The best you can do in this case is to assume that securities are fairly priced and to hope that one day Nuestra Señora will reward your humility.

During the 1960s and 1970s every article on the topic seemed to provide additional evidence that markets are efficient. But then readers became tired of hearing the same message and wanted to read about possible exceptions. During the 1980s and 1990s more and more anomalies and puzzles were uncovered. Bubbles, including the dot.com bubble of the 1990s and the real estate bubble of the 2000s, cast doubt on whether markets were always and everywhere efficient.

Limits to arbitrage can explain why asset prices may get out of line with fundamental values. Behavioral finance, which relies on psychological evidence to interpret investor behavior, is consistent with many of the deviations from market efficiency. Behavioral finance says that investors are averse to even small losses, especially when recent investment returns have been disappointing. Investors may rely too much on a few recent events in predicting the future. They may be overconfident in their predictions and may be sluggish in reacting to new information.

There are plenty of quirks and biases in human behavior, so behavioral finance has plenty of raw material. But if every puzzle or anomaly can be explained by some recipe of quirks, biases, and hindsight, what have we learned? Research in behavioral finance literature is informative and intriguing, but not yet at the stage where a few parsimonious models can account for most of the deviations from market efficiency.

For the corporate treasurer who is concerned with issuing or purchasing securities, the efficient-market theory has obvious implications. In one sense, however, it raises more questions than it answers. The existence of efficient markets does not mean that the financial manager can let financing take care of itself. It provides only a starting point for analysis. It is time to get down to details about securities and issue procedures. We start in Chapter 14.

FURTHER READING

Malkiel's book is an-easy-to-read book on market efficiency. Fama has written two classic review article on the topic:

B. G. Malkiel, *A Random Walk Down Wall Street,* 8th ed. (New York: W.W. Norton, 2004).

E. F. Fama, "Efficient Capital Markets: A Review of Theory and Empirical Work," *Journal of Finance* 25 (May 1970), pp. 383–417.

E. F. Fama, "Efficient Capital Markets: II," *Journal of Finance* 46 (December 1991), pp. 1575–1617

There are several useful surveys of behavioral finance:

N. Barberis and R. H. Thaler, "A Survey of Behavioral Finance," in G. M. Constantinides, M. Harris, and R. M. Stulz (eds.), *Handbook of the Economics of Finance* (Amsterdam: Elsevier Science, 2003).

M. Baker, R. S. Ruback, and J. Wurgler, "Behavioral Corporate Finance," in B. E. Eckbo (ed.), *The Handbook of Empirical Corporate Finance* (Amsterdam: Elsevier/North-Holland, 2007), Chapter 4.

R. J. Shiller, "Human Behavior and the Efficiency of the Financial System," in J. B. Taylor and M. Woodford (eds.), *Handbook of Macroeconomics* (Amsterdam: North-Holland, 1999).

A. Shleifer, *Inefficient Markets: An Introduction to Behavioral Finance* (Oxford: Oxford University Press, 2000).

R. H. Thaler (ed.), *Advances in Behavioral Finance* (New York: Russell Sage Foundation, 1993).

Some conflicting views on market efficiency are provided by:

G. W. Schwert, "Anomalies and Market Efficiency," in G. M. Constantinides, M. Harris, and R. M. Stulz (eds.), *Handbook of the Economics of Finance* (Amsterdam: Elsevier Science, 2003).

M. Rubinstein, "Rational Markets: Yes or No? The Affirmative Case?" *Financial Analysts Journal* 57 (May–June 2001), pp. 15–29.

B. G. Malkiel, "The Efficient Market Hypothesis and Its Critics," *Journal of Economic Perspectives* 17 (Winter 2003), pp. 59–82.

R. J. Shiller, "From Efficient Markets Theory to Behavioral Finance," *Journal of Economic Perspectives* 17 (Winter 2003), pp. 83–104.

E. F. Fama and K. R. French, "Dissecting Anomalies," *Journal of Finance* 63 (August 2008), pp. 1653–1678.

Bubbles are discussed in:

M. Brunnermeier, *Asset Pricing under Asymmetric Information: Bubbles, Crashes, Technical Analysis, and Herding* (Oxford: Oxford University Press, 2001).

R. J. Shiller, *Irrational Exuberance,* 2nd ed. (Princeton, NJ: Princeton University Press, 2005).

PROBLEM SETS

BASIC

1. Which (if any) of these statements are true? Stock prices appear to behave as though successive values (a) are random numbers, (b) follow regular cycles, (c) differ by a random number.

2. Supply the missing words:

"There are three forms of the efficient-market hypothesis. Tests of randomness in stock returns provide evidence for the _____ form of the hypothesis. Tests of stock price reaction to well-publicized news provide evidence for the _____ form, and tests of the performance of professionally managed funds provide evidence for the _____ form. Market efficiency results from competition between investors. Many investors search for new information about the company's business that would help them to value the stock more accurately. Such research helps to ensure that prices reflect all available information; in other words, it helps to keep the market efficient in the _____ form. Other investors study past stock prices for recurrent patterns that would allow them to make superior profits. Such research helps to ensure that prices reflect all the information contained in past stock prices; in other words, it helps to keep the market efficient in the _____ form."

3. True or false? The efficient-market hypothesis assumes that
   a. There are no taxes.
   b. There is perfect foresight.
   c. Successive price changes are independent.
   d. Investors are irrational.
   e. There are no transaction costs.
   f. Forecasts are unbiased.

4. True or false?
   a. Financing decisions are less easily reversed than investment decisions.
   b. Tests have shown that there is almost perfect negative correlation between successive price changes.
   c. The semistrong form of the efficient-market hypothesis states that prices reflect all publicly available information.
   d. In efficient markets the expected return on each stock is the same.

5. Analysis of 60 monthly rates of return on ITC common stock indicates a beta of .83 and an alpha of 1.49% per month. A month later, the market is up by 5%, and ITC is up by 6%. What is ITC's abnormal rate of return?

6. True or false?
   a. Analysis by security analysts and investors helps keep markets efficient.
   b. Psychologists have found that, once people have suffered a loss, they are more relaxed about the possibility of incurring further losses.
   c. Psychologists have observed that people tend to put too much weight on recent events when forecasting.
   d. If the efficient-market hypothesis is correct, managers will not be able to increase stock prices by creative accounting that boosts reported earnings.

7. Geothermal Corporation has just received good news: its earnings increased by 20% from last year's value. Most investors are anticipating an increase of 25%. Will Geothermal's stock price increase or decrease when the announcement is made?

8. Here again are the six lessons of market efficiency. For each lesson give an example showing the lesson's relevance to financial managers.
   a. Markets have no memory.
   b. Trust market prices.
   c. Read the entrails.
   d. There are no financial illusions.
   e. The do-it-yourself alternative.
   f. Seen one stock, seen them all.

9. Give two or three examples of research results or events that raise doubts about market efficiency. Briefly explain why.

INTERMEDIATE

10. How would you respond to the following comments?
    a. "Efficient market, my eye! I know lots of investors who do crazy things."
    b. "Efficient market? Balderdash! I know at least a dozen people who have made a bundle in the stock market."

c. "The trouble with the efficient-market theory is that it ignores investors' psychology."

d. "Despite all the limitations, the best guide to a company's value is its written-down book value. It is much more stable than market value, which depends on temporary fashions."

11. Respond to the following comments:

a. "The random-walk theory, with its implication that investing in stocks is like playing roulette, is a powerful indictment of our capital markets."

b. "If everyone believes you can make money by charting stock prices, then price changes won't be random."

c. "The random-walk theory implies that events are random, but many events are not random. If it rains today, there's a fair bet that it will rain again tomorrow."

12. Which of the following observations *appear* to indicate market inefficiency? Explain whether the observation appears to contradict the weak, semistrong, or strong form of the efficient-market hypothesis.

a. Tax-exempt municipal bonds offer lower pretax returns than taxable government bonds.

b. Managers make superior returns on their purchases of their company's stock.

c. There is a positive relationship between the return on the market in one quarter and the change in aggregate profits in the next quarter.

d. There is disputed evidence that stocks that have appreciated unusually in the recent past continue to do so in the future.

e. The stock of an acquired firm tends to appreciate in the period before the merger announcement.

f. Stocks of companies with unexpectedly high earnings appear to offer high returns for several months after the earnings announcement.

g. Very risky stocks on average give higher returns than safe stocks.

13. Here are alphas and betas for HUL and Bharti Airtel for the 60 months ending April 2011. Alpha is expressed as a percent per month.

	Alpha	Beta
HUL	−.003	.38
Bharti	−.001	.75

Explain how these estimates would be used to calculate an abnormal return.

14. "If the efficient-market hypothesis is true, the pension fund manager might as well select a portfolio with a pin." Explain why this is not so.

15. Two financial managers, Alpha and Beta, are contemplating a chart showing the actual performance of the Standard and Poor's Composite Index over a five-year period. Each manager's company needs to issue new shares of common stock sometime in the next year.

Alpha: My company's going to issue right away. The stock market cycle has obviously topped out, and the next move is almost surely down. Better to issue now and get a decent price for the shares.

Beta: You're too nervous; we're waiting. It's true that the market's been going nowhere for the past year or so, but the figure clearly shows a basic upward trend. The market's on the way up to a new plateau.

What would you say to Alpha and Beta?

16. What does the efficient-market hypothesis have to say about these two statements?

a. "I notice that short-term interest rates are about 1% below long-term rates. We should borrow short-term."

b. "I notice that interest rates in Japan are lower than rates in India. We would do better to borrow Japanese yen rather than Indian rupees."

17. Fama and French show that average stock returns on firms with small market capitalizations have been significantly higher than average returns for "large-cap" firms. What are the possible explanations for this result? Does the result disprove market efficiency? Explain briefly.

18. Column (A) in Table 13.1 on the following page shows the monthly return on sensex from September 2009 through April 2011. Columns (B) and (C) show returns on the stocks of two firms—Reliance Industries Limited and TCS Limited. Both firms announced their earnings towards the end of March 2011. Calculate the average abnormal return of the two stocks during the month of the earnings announcement.

eXcel

Visit us at
www.mhhe.com/bmam10e

TABLE 13.1 See Problem 18. Rates of return in percent per month:

Year	(A) Sensex Return	(B) Reliance Industries Return	(C) TCS Return
Sep-09	0.09	0.10	0.18
Oct-09	−0.07	−0.12	0.01
Nov-09	0.06	0.10	0.10
Dec-09	0.03	0.03	0.09
Jan-10	−0.06	−0.04	−0.02
Feb-10	0.00	−0.07	0.03
Mar-10	0.07	0.10	0.03
Apr-10	0.00	−0.04	−0.02
May-10	−0.03	0.01	−0.03
Jun-10	0.04	0.04	0.01
Jul-10	0.01	−0.07	0.12
Aug-10	0.01	−0.09	0.00
Sep-10	0.12	0.07	0.09
Oct-10	0.00	0.11	0.14
Nov-10	−0.03	−0.10	0.02
Dec-10	0.05	0.07	0.08
Jan-11	−0.11	−0.13	−0.01
Feb-11	−0.03	0.05	−0.04
Mar-11	0.09	0.09	0.06
Apr-11	0.00	-0.01	0.00

19. On May 15, 1997, the government of Kuwait offered to sell 170 million BP shares, worth about $2 billion. Goldman Sachs was contacted after the stock market closed in London and given one hour to decide whether to bid on the stock. They decided to offer 710.5 pence ($11.59) per share, and Kuwait accepted. Then Goldman Sachs went looking for buyers. They lined up 500 institutional and individual investors worldwide, and resold all the shares at 716

pence ($11.70). The resale was complete before the London Stock Exchange opened the next morning. Goldman Sachs made $15 million overnight.[40]

What does this deal say about market efficiency? Discuss.

20. Explain how incentive and agency problems can contribute to mispricing of securities or to bubbles. Give examples.

21. Many commentators have blamed the subprime crisis on "irrational exuberance." What is your view? Explain briefly.

CHALLENGE

22. "The strong-form of the efficient-market hypothesis is nonsense. Look at mutual fund X; it has had superior performance for each of the last 10 years." Does the speaker have a point? Suppose that there is a 50% probability that X will obtain superior performance in any year simply by chance.

   a. If X is the only fund, calculate the probability that it will have achieved superior performance for each of the past 10 years.

   b. Now recognize that there are over 4,000 mutual funds in India. What is the probability that by chance there is at least 1 out of 4,000 funds that obtained 10 successive years of superior performance?

23. Some extreme bubbles are obvious with hindsight, *after* they burst. But how would you *define* a bubble? There are many examples of good news and rising stock prices, followed by bad news and falling stock prices. Can you set out rules and procedures to distinguish bubbles from the normal ups and downs of stock prices?

REAL-TIME DATA ANALYSIS

From the website of NSE (www.nseindia.com) download daily prices for five stocks for the recent 12 months period. Avoid any stock that has announced a bonus issue, stock split or rights issue in the last 12 months period. For each stock, construct a scatter diagram of successive returns as in Figure 13.2. Then calculate the correlation coefficient between the returns on successive days. Do you find any consistent patterns?

---

[40] "Goldman Sachs Earns a Quick $15 Million Sale of BP Shares," *The Wall Street Journal,* May 16, 1997, p. A4.

14

CHAPTER

AN OVERVIEW OF CORPORATE FINANCING

We now begin our analysis of long-term financing decisions—an undertaking we will not complete until Chapter 25. This chapter provides an introduction to corporate financing. It reviews with a broad brush several topics that will be explored more carefully later on.

We start the chapter by looking at aggregate data on the sources of financing for Indian corporations. Much of the money for new investments comes from profits that companies retain and reinvest. The remainder comes from selling new debt or equity securities. These financing patterns raise several interesting questions. Do companies rely too heavily on internal financing rather than on external equality financing? Are debt ratios of Indian corporations dangerously high? How do patterns of financing differ across the major industrialized and emerging economies?

Our second task in the chapter is to review some of the essential features of debt and equity. Lenders and stockholders have different *cash flow rights* and also different *control rights*. The lenders have first claim on cash flow, because they are promised definite cash payments for interest and principal. The stockholder receives whatever cash is left over after the lenders are paid. Stockholders, on the other hand, have complete control of the firm, providing that they keep their promises to lenders. As owners of the business, stockholders have the ultimate control over what assets the company buys, how the assets are financed, and how they are used. Of course, in large public corporations the stockholders delegate these decisions to the board of directors, who in turn appoint senior management. In these cases *effective* control often ends up with the company's management.

The simple division of cash flow among debt and equity glosses over the many different types of debt that companies issue. Therefore, we close our discussion of debt and equity with a brief canter through the main categories of debt. We also pause to describe certain less common forms of equity, particularly preferred stock.

The financial crisis that started in the summer of 2007 demonstrated the importance of healthy financial markets and institutions. We will review the crisis, introduce you to the major financial institutions, and look at the roles that financial institutions play in corporate financing and in the economy at large.

14-1 PATTERNS OF CORPORATE FINANCING

Corporations invest in long-term assets (primarily property, plant, and equipment) and in net working capital (current assets minus current liabilities). Figure 14.1 shows where Indian corporations get the cash to pay for these investments. Most of the cash is generated internally. That is, it comes from cash flow allocated to depreciation and from retained earnings (earnings not paid out as cash dividends).[1] Shareholders are happy to plow this cash back into the firm, provided that investments are positive NPV. Every positive-NPV outlay increases shareholder value.

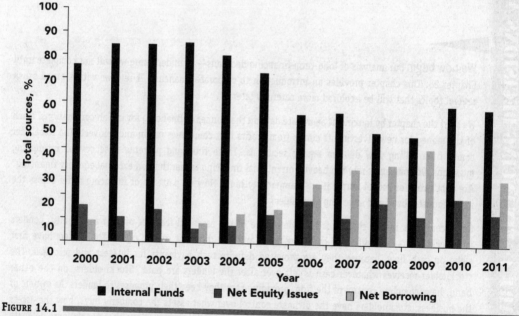

FIGURE 14.1

Sources of funds for Indian nonfinancial corporations expressed as a fraction of the total.

Source: Data compiled from Prowess Database of CMIE. The figures are based on a sample size of 2009 companies.

Indian corporations are not alone in relying mostly on internally generated cash. For example, internal cash flow makes up more than two-thirds of corporate financing in the U.S., Germany, Japan, and the U.K.

---

[1] In Figure 14.1, internally generated cash was calculated by adding depreciation to retained earnings. Depreciation is a noncash expense. Thus, retained earnings understate the cash flow available for reinvestment.

Sometimes internal cash flow more than covers investment. More often it does not, and the company faces a financial deficit. To cover the deficit, the company must cut back on dividends in order to increase retained earnings, or it must raise new debt or equity capital from outside investors. So there are two basic financing decisions. First, what fraction of profits should be plowed back into the business rather than paid out to shareholders? Second, what fraction of the financial deficit should be met with debt rather than equity? Thus the firm needs a payout policy (Chapter 16) and a debt policy (Chapters 17 and 18).

Take a look at Indian equity issues in Figure 14.1. After 2002, net equity issues were the lowest in each year. However, the net equity issues were positive in each year. This means that the cash paid out to shareholders by repurchase of previously outstanding shares was less than the cash raised by issue of shares. The choice between cash dividends and repurchases is another aspect of payout policy.

Stock repurchases are usually large in countries like the U.S., where the net equity issue is usually negative for most companies. However, repurchase of shares is not as high in India and that explains why the net equity issue is positive in each year in the last decade.

Do Firms Rely Too Much on Internal Funds?

We have seen that on average internal funds (retained earnings plus depreciation) cover most of the cash needed for investment. It seems that internal financing is more convenient than external financing by stock and debt issues. But some observers worry that managers have an irrational or self-serving aversion to external finance. A manager seeking comfortable employment could be tempted to forego a risky but positive-NPV project if it involved launching a new stock issue and facing awkward questions from potential investors. Perhaps managers take the line of least resistance and dodge the "discipline of capital markets."

We do not mean to paint managers as loafers. There are also some good reasons for relying on internally generated funds. The cost of issuing new securities is avoided, for example. Moreover, the announcement of a new equity issue is usually bad news for investors, who worry that the decision signals lower future profits or higher risk.[2] If issues of shares are costly and send a bad-news signal to investors, companies may be justified in looking more carefully at those projects that would require a new stock issue.

How Much Do Firms Borrow?

The mix of debt and equity financing varies widely from industry to industry and from firm to firm. Debt ratios also vary over time for particular firms. These variations are a fact of life: there is no constant, God-given debt ratio, and if there were, it would change. But a few aggregate statistics will do no harm.

Table 14.1 shows the aggregate balance sheet of all Indian manufacturing corporations. If all these businesses were merged into a single gigantic firm, Table 14.1 would be its balance sheet. Assets and liabilities in the table are entered at book values, that is, accounting values. These do not generally equal market values. The numbers are nevertheless instructive. Notice that firms had long-term debt of ₹4,57,272 crore and equity of ₹7,19,468 crore. The ratio of debt to long-term debt plus equity was, therefore, ₹4,57,272/(₹4,57,272 + ₹7,19,468) = .39.[3]

---

[2] Managers do have insiders' insights and naturally are tempted to issue stock when the price looks good to them, that is, when they are less optimistic than outside investors. The outside investors realize this and will buy a new issue only at a discount from the pre-announcement price. More on stock issues in Chapter 15.

[3] This debt ratio may be understated, because "Other long-term liabilities" probably include some debt-equivalent claims. We will not pause to sort through these other liabilities, however.

TABLE 14.1   Aggregate balance sheet for manufacturing corporations in India, as on 31 March, 2011.

Assets	₹ Crores	Liabilities		₹ Crores
Current assets	6,78,060	**Current Liabilities**		4,57,376
Inventories	2,45,107	**Secured & Unsecured Loans**		4,57,272
Receivables	2,70,729	**Shareholders' Equity**		7,19,468
Loans and Advances	58,498	Share Capital	43,989	
Cash	1,03,727	Reserves & Surpluses	6,75,479	
Gross fixed assets	9,81,062			
Less: Depreciation	3,24,834			
Net fixed assets	6,56,227			
Investments	2,86,765			
Other assets	13,064			
Total assets	16,34,116	**Total Liabilities**		16,34,116

Source: Data compiled from (about 11,000 manufacturing companies) Prowess Database of CMIE.

Table 14.1 is of course only a snapshot. Is there a long-term trend to more debt and less equity? The answer depends partly on how you measure the debt ratio, as Figure 14.2 demonstrates. In book value terms, the debt ratio started declining since 1993 as firms opted to pay down debt. The picture is somewhat different in terms of market values. Booming stock prices in 1992 and again in 2004-07 ensured that the amount of long-term debt grew less rapidly than the market value of equity, but this trend reversed during 2008-09 when the stock market declined.

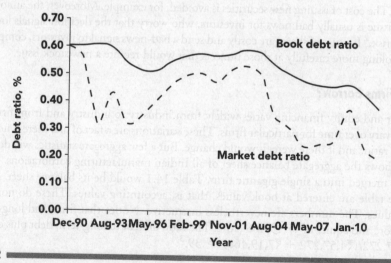

FIGURE 14.2

The ratio of debt to debt plus equity for the manufacturing corporate sector, India.

Source: Data compiled from Prowess database

Should we take solace from the fact that book debt ratios are lower today than they were 20 years ago? It is true that lower debt ratios mean that fewer companies will fall into financial distress when a serious recession hits the economy. But all companies live with this risk to some degree, and it does not follow that less risk is better. Finding the optimal debt ratio is like finding the optimal speed limit. We can agree that accidents at 30 miles per hour are generally less dangerous than accidents at 60 miles per hour, but we do not therefore set the speed limit on all roads at 30. Speed has benefits as well as risks. So does debt, as we see in Chapter 18.

International Comparisons   International comparisons of corporate debt ratios are muddied by differences in accounting standards. However, by comparing Indian debt ratio with the debt ratios of the other countries, we can at least get a rough indication of where India ranks in the debt-ratio league. Figure 14.3 compares the average ratio of total liabilities to total liabilities plus equity for manufacturing industry in a sample of countries. The debt-ratio of the U.S. (not given in Figure 14.3) is 0.39. You can see that the debt ratio in all the countries is greater than that of India.

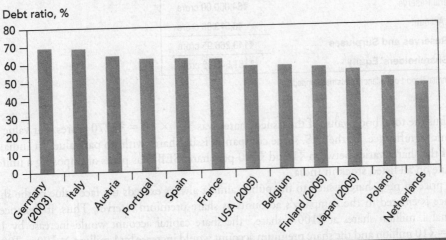

FIGURE 14.3

Ratios of total liabilities to total liabilities plus equity for manufacturing industry, 2006.

Source: European Union *Bach* database of harmonized company accounts. © European Communities, 1995–2006.

14-2   COMMON STOCK

Now we take a brief tour of the debt and equity securities issued by corporations. We start with Table 14.2, which shows how the common stock (ordinary shares) of Reliance Industries Limited is recorded on its books.

The maximum number of shares that can be issued is known as the *authorized share capital;* for Reliance it was 500 crore shares. If management wishes to increase the number of authorized shares, it needs the agreement of shareholders to do so.[4] By March 2011, Reliance had already issued only 327 crore shares, so it could issue 163 crore shares more without further shareholder approval.

These shares are said to be issued and subscribed (or outstanding). The issued shares are entered into the company's books at their face value (or par value). Each Reliance share has a par value of

---

[4] The memorandum of association of a company mentions the authorized capital. If a company wants to increase the authorized capital, then it needs shareholders' permission to amend the capital clause in the memorandum of association.

TABLE 14.2 Book value of common shareholders' equity of Reliance Industries Limited, March 31, 2011.

Authorized Shares (₹10 face value per share)	
500 crore equity shares	₹5000 crore
Issued, Subscribed and paid-up	
327.337 crore shares	₹3273.37 crore
Reserves & Surpluses	
Revaluation Reserve	₹5,467.00 crore
Capital Reserve	₹291.28 crore
Securities Premium Account	₹50,878.24 crore
Debenture Redemption Reserve	₹1,116.57 crore
General Reserve	₹84,000.00 crore
P&L Account	₹6,513.86 crore
Total Reserves and Surpluses	₹148,266.95 crore
Total Shareholders' Equity	₹151,540.32 crore

Source: Annual Report of Reliance Industries Limited.

₹10. Thus the total book value of the issued shares was 327 × 10 = ₹3270 crores. Par value has little economic significance. In the U.S. some companies issue shares with no par value. In India, the face value of the shares varies between ₹1 and ₹100 per share. SEBI has plans of imposing a uniform face value rule on all listed stock in India.

The price of new shares issued to the public almost always exceeds the face value of the share. The difference is entered in the company's accounts as share premium reserves. Thus, if Reliance sold an additional 1 million shares at ₹100 a share,[5] the share capital account would increase by 1 million × ₹10 = ₹10 million and the share premium account would increase by 1 million × ₹90 = ₹90 million.

Reliance distributed part of its earnings as dividends. The remainder was retained in the business and used to finance new investments. The cumulative amount of retained earnings (that was not transferred to general reserve) was ₹1,48,267 crore.

Reliance shares had a book value (also known as net worth) in March 2011 of ₹151,540 crore. That works out to 151,540/327.3 = ₹463 per share. But in March 2011, Reliance's shares were priced at about ₹1,048 each. So the market value of the outstanding shares was 327.3 crores × ₹1,048 = ₹343010 crore, over ₹191470 crore higher than book.

Ownership of the Corporation

A corporation is owned by its ordinary shareholders. Some of this ordinary shares are held directly by individual investors, and promoters. The remaining shares are held by the institutional investors including financial institutions, mutual funds, foreign institutional investors, pension funds, and the banks. For example, look at Figure 14.4. You can see that in India about 50% of the total shares are held by the promoters. The individual investors hold 15% of the total shares. Private corporate bodies hold 23% of the total shares. The remaining shares are held by the institutional investors.

---

[5] We will be more than happy to buy the shares at this price!

The institutional investors usually avoid the illiq-uid stocks. If we consider the 30 companies that are part of BSE sensex, then we will observe that about 27% of the shares are owned by the institutional investors. The promoters own 57% of the shares. If we consider the 500 stocks that are part of the BSE 500 index, then the stake of the institutional investors drops to 21%, whereas the stake of the promoters increases to 61%.

What do we mean when we say that these stockholders *own* the corporation? The answer is obvious if the company has issued no other securities. Consider the simplest possible case of a corporation financed solely by common stock, all of which is owned by the firm's chief executive officer (CEO). This lucky owner-manager receives all the cash flows and makes all investment and operating decisions. She has complete *cash-flow rights* and also complete *control rights.*

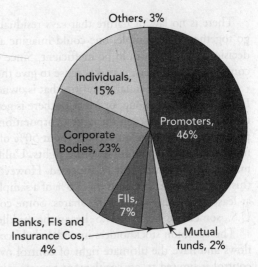

FIGURE 14.4

Holdings of Ordinary shares in India, 2006

Source: Compiled from prowess database based on a sample of 10015 companies. Data Updated as on 10 May, 2006

These rights are split up and reallocated as soon as the company borrows money. If it takes out a bank loan, it enters into a contract with the bank promising to pay interest and eventually repay the principal. The bank gets a privileged, but limited, right to cash flows; the residual cash-flow rights are left with the stockholder. Thus common stock is a *residual claim* on the firm's assets and cash flow.

The bank typically protects its claim by imposing restrictions on what the firm can or cannot do. For example, it may require the firm to limit future borrowing, and it may forbid the firm to sell off assets or to pay excessive dividends. The stockholders' control rights are thereby limited. However, the contract with the bank can never restrict or determine all the operating and investment decisions necessary to run the firm efficiently. (No team of lawyers, no matter how long they scribbled, could ever write a contract covering all possible contingencies.)[6] The owner of the common stock retains the residual rights of control over these decisions. For example, she may choose to increase the selling price of the firm's products, to hire temporary rather than permanent employees, or to construct a new plant in Goa Beach rather than Gujrat.[7]

Ownership of the firm can of course change. If the firm fails to make the promised payments to the bank, it may be forced into bankruptcy. Once the firm is under the "protection" of a bankruptcy court, shareholders' cash-flow and control rights are tightly restricted and may be extinguished altogether. Unless some rescue or reorganization plan can be implemented, the bank will become the new owner of the firm and will acquire the cash-flow and control rights of ownership. (We discuss bankruptcy in Chapter 32.)

---

[6] Theoretical economists therefore stress the importance of *incomplete contracts.* Their point is that contracts pertaining to the management of the firm *must* be incomplete and that someone must exercise residual rights of control. See O. Hart, *Firms, Contracts, and Financial Structure* (Oxford: Oxford University Press, 1995).

[7] Of course, the bank manager may suggest that a particular decision is unwise, or even threaten to cut off future lending, but the bank does not have any *right* to make these decisions.

There is no law of nature that says residual cash-flow rights and residual control rights have to go together. For example, one could imagine a situation where the debtholder gets to make all the decisions. But this would be inefficient. Since the benefits of good decisions are felt mainly by the common stockholders, it makes sense to give them control over how the firm's assets are used.

We have focused so far on a firm that is owned by a single stockholder. However, in countries like India, Italy, Hong Kong, or Mexico, there is generally a dominant shareholder who controls 20% or more of the votes of even the largest corporations. In India, this dominant shareholder (known as the promoter) controls on an average about 50% of the votes. In Reliance, the promoters control a little more than 44% of the total voting rights. Unlike in India, in the United States, ownership of most major corporations is widely dispersed. However, recent research by Clifford Holderness shows that this is not the case. He finds that 96% of a sample of U.S. public corporations have block holders with at least 5% of the outstanding shares. Some countries have more concentrated ownership than the U.S., some have less. The U.S. lies in the middle of the pack.[8]

The common stockholders in widely held corporations still have the residual rights over the cash flows and have the ultimate right of control over the company's affairs. In practice, however, their control is limited to an entitlement to vote, either in person or by proxy, on appointments to the *board of directors,* and on other crucial matters such as the decision to merge. Many shareholders do not bother to vote. They reason that, since they own so few shares, their vote will have little impact on the outcome. The problem is that, if all shareholders think in the same way, they cede effective control and management gets a free hand to look after its own interests.

Voting Procedures

According to Section 255 of the Companies Act, the shareholders must appoint directors in a general meeting. Of the total number of directors, a maximum of 33% of the directors can be permanent directors. However, the articles of association of a company can provide for all directors to be rotational. At an annual meeting, one-third of the rotational directors retire and elections take place in the general meeting. In India, most of the time, the rotational directors contest the election again and re-elect themselves.

Usually, the articles of associations provide for election of directors by a simple majority (also known as *majority voting* system). As per the majority voting system, all the directors of a company can be elected by a simple majority and the minority shareholders will not be able to elect a single director. Let's assume that the promoter of a company has 51% of the shares. Then the promoter, under the majority voting system, can elect all the directors. Even with the remaining 49% shares, the minority shareholders will not be able to appoint a single director. According to Section 265 of the Companies Act, a company can however provide for the system of proportional representation (also known as the *cumulative voting system*) in its articles of association. Under this system, the minority shareholders may be able to elect a director to the board, provided they act intelligently. Let's assume that in the above case, there are five directors to be elected to the board. Then the promoter has $51 \times 5 = 255$ votes and the minority shareholder has $49 \times 5 = 245$ votes. Then the minority shareholders (with 49% stake) can elect two members by casting 123 votes for the first candidate and 122 votes for the second.

The issues on which stockholders are asked to vote are rarely contested, particularly in the case of large, publicly traded firms. Occasionally, there are *proxy contests* in which the firm's existing

[8] See R. La Porta, F. Lopez-de-Silanes, and A. Shleifer, "Corporate Ownership around the World," *Journal of Finance* 54 (1999), pp. 471–517; and C. Holderness, "The Myth of Diffuse Ownership in the United States," *Review of Financial Studies* 22 (April 2009), pp. 1377–1408.

management and directors compete with outsiders for effective control of the corporation. But the odds are stacked against the outsiders, for the insiders can get the firm to pay all the costs of presenting their case and obtaining votes.

Dual-Class Shares and Private Benefits

Usually companies have one class of common stock and each share has one vote. The Companies Amendment Act, 2000 has, however, allowed companies in India to issue shares with differential rights. This Act came into effect on 9 March, 2001. Usually, differential shares have different voting rights. However, the Companies Amendment Act, 2000 allows companies to issue shares with differential rights to vote, dividends, or otherwise, provided they satisfy certain conditions. We find many instances of companies based in the U.S. to issue shares with differential voting rights. For example, when Google made its first issue of common stock, the founders were reluctant to give up control of the company. Therefore, the company created two classes of shares. The A shares, which were sold to the public, had 1 vote each, while the B shares, which were owned by the founders, had 10 votes each. Both classes of share had the same cash-flow rights, but they had different control rights.

When there are two classes of stock, shareholders with the extra voting power may sometimes use it to toss out bad management or to force management to adopt policies that enhance shareholder value. But, as long as both classes of share have identical cash-flow rights, all shareholders benefit equally from such changes. So here is the question: if everyone gains equally from better management, why do shares with superior voting power typically sell at a premium? The only plausible reason is that there are *private benefits* captured by the owners of these shares. For example, a holder of a block of voting shares might be able to obtain a seat on the board of directors or access to perquisites provided by the company. (How about a ride to Bermuda on the corporate jet?) The shares might have extra bargaining power in an acquisition. Or they might be held by another company, which could use its voting power and influence to secure a business advantage. These are some of the reasons why shares with more votes usually sell for a higher price.

These private benefits of control seem to be much larger in some countries than others. For example, Tatiana Nenova has looked at a number of countries in which firms may have two classes of stock.[9] In the United States the premium that an investor needed to pay to gain voting control amounted to only 2% of firm value, but in Italy it was over 29% and in Mexico it was 36%. It appears that in these two countries majority investors are able to secure large private benefits. The Finance in the News box describes a major dispute in Switzerland over the value of superior voting rights.

Even when there is only one class of shares, minority stockholders may be at a disadvantage; the company's cash flow and potential value may be diverted to management or to one or a few dominant stockholders holding large blocks of shares. In the U.S., the law protects minority stockholders from exploitation, but minority shareholders in other countries (including India) do not always fare so well.[10]

Financial economists sometimes refer to the exploitation of minority shareholders as *tunneling;* the majority shareholder tunnels into the firm and acquires control of the assets for himself. Let us look at tunneling Russian-style.

---

[9] T. Nenova, "The Value of Corporate Voting Rights and Control: A Cross-Country Analysis," *Journal of Financial Economics* 68 (June 2003) pp. 325–352.

[10] International differences in the opportunities for dominant shareholders to exploit their position are discussed in S. Johnson et al., "Tunnelling," *American Economic Review* 90 (May 2000), pp. 22–27.

Finance In The News

A Contest Over Voting Rights

w "Not so long ago," wrote *The Economist* magazine, "shareholder friendly companies in Switzerland were as rare as Swiss admirals. Safe behind anti-takeover defences, most managers treated their shareholders with disdain." However, *The Economist* perceived one encouraging sign that these attitudes were changing. This was a proposal by the Union Bank of Switzerland (UBS) to change the rights of its equity-holders.

UBS had two classes of shares—bearer shares, which are anonymous, and registered shares, which are not. In Switzerland, where anonymity is prized, bearer shares usually traded at a premium. UBS's bearer shares had sold at a premium for many years. However, there was another important distinction between the two share classes. The registered shares carried five times as many votes as an equivalent investment in the bearer shares. Presumably attracted by this feature, an investment company, BK Vision, began to accumulate a large position in the registered shares, and its price rose to a 38% premium over the bearer shares.

At this point UBS announced its plan to merge the two classes of shares, so that the registered shares would become bearer shares and would lose their superior voting rights. Since all UBS's shares would then sell for the same price, UBS's announcement led to a rise in the price of the bearer shares and a fall in the price of the registered.

Martin Ebner, the president of BK Vision, objected to the change, complaining that it stripped the registered shareholders of some of their voting rights without providing compensation. The dispute highlighted the question of the value of superior voting stock. If the votes are used to secure benefits for *all* shareholders, then the stock should not sell at a premium. However, a premium would arise if holders of the superior voting stock expected to secure benefits for themselves alone.

To many observers UBS's proposal was a welcome attempt to prevent one group of shareholders from profiting at the expense of others and to unite all shareholders in the common aim of maximizing firm value. To others it represented an attempt to take away their rights. In any event, the debate over the proposal was never fully resolved, for UBS shortly afterward agreed to merge with SBC, another Swiss bank.

EXAMPLE 14.1   **Raiding the Minority Shareholders**

To grasp how the scam works, you first need to understand *reverse stock splits*. These are often used by companies with a large number of low-priced shares. The company making the reverse split simply combines its existing shares into a smaller, more convenient, number of new shares. For example, the shareholders might be given 2 new shares in place of the 3 shares that they currently own. As long as all shareholdings are reduced by the same proportion, nobody gains or loses by such a move.

However, the majority shareholder of one Russian company realized that the reverse stock split could be used to loot the company's assets. He therefore proposed that existing shareholders receive 1 new share in place of every 136,000 shares they currently held.[11]

---

[11] Since a reverse stock split required only the approval of a simple majority of the shareholders, the proposal was voted through.

Why did the majority shareholder pick the number "136,000"? Answer: because the two minority shareholders owned less than 136,000 shares and therefore did not have the right to *any* shares. Instead they were simply paid off with the par value of their shares and the majority shareholder was left owning the entire company. The majority shareholders of several other companies were so impressed with this device that they also proposed similar reverse stock splits to squeeze out their minority shareholders.

Equity in Disguise

Common stocks are issued by corporations. But a few equity securities are issued not by corporations but by partnerships or trusts. We will give some brief examples.

Partnerships   Plains All American Pipeline LP is a *master limited partnership* that owns crude oil pipelines in the United States and Canada. You can buy "units" in this partnership on the New York Stock Exchange, thus becoming a *limited partner* in Plains All American. The most the limited partners can lose is their investment in the company.[12] In this and most other respects, the partnership units are just like the shares in an ordinary corporation. They share in the profits of the business and receive cash distributions (like dividends) from time to time.

Partnerships avoid corporate income tax; any profits or losses are passed straight through to the partners' tax returns. Offsetting this tax advantage are various limitations of partnerships. For example, the law regards a partnership merely as a voluntary association of individuals; like its partners, it is expected to have a limited life. A corporation, on the other hand, is an independent legal "person" that can, and often does, outlive all its original shareholders.

Trusts and REITs   Would you like to own a part of the oil in the Prudhoe Bay field on the north slope of Alaska? Just call your broker and buy a few units of the Prudhoe Bay Royalty Trust. BP set up this trust and gave it a royalty interest in production from BP's share of the Prudhoe Bay revenues. As the oil is produced, each trust unit gets its share of the revenues.

This trust is the passive owner of a single asset: the right to a share of the revenues from BP's Prudhoe Bay production. Operating businesses, which cannot be passive, are rarely organized as trusts, though there are exceptions, notably *real estate investment trusts,* or *REITs* (pronounced "reets").

REITs were created to facilitate public investment in commercial real estate; there are shopping center REITs, office building REITs, apartment REITs, and REITs that specialize in lending to real estate developers. REIT "shares" are traded just like common stocks. The REITs themselves are not taxed, so long as they distribute at least 95% of earnings to the REITs' owners, who must pay whatever taxes are due on the dividends. However, REITs are tightly restricted to real estate investment. You cannot set up a widget factory and avoid corporate taxes by calling it a REIT.

In India, there is no law yet to establish a REIT. SEBI drafted draft regulations for the establishment of REITs in India in December 2007. However, the legislation is yet to be enacted in India as of now.

---

[12] A partnership can offer limited liability *only* to its limited partners. The partnership must also have one or more general partners, who have unlimited liability. However, general partners can be corporations. This puts the corporation's shield of limited liability between the partnership and the human beings who ultimately own the general partner.

Preferred Stock

Usually when investors talk about equity or stock, they are referring to what is known as common stock or ordinary shares. But some companies also issue preferred stock or preference shares. Thus for example, Tata Consultancy Services has issued ₹100 crore of preference shares, and this is usually considered as part of the equity of the company. Despite its name, preferred stock provides only a small part of most companies' cash needs and it will occupy less time in later chapters. However, it can be a useful method of financing in mergers and certain other special situations.

Like debt, preferred stock offers a series of fixed payments to the investor. The company can choose *not* to pay a preferred dividend, but in that case it may not pay a dividend to its common stockholders. Most issues of preferred are known as *cumulative preferred stock.* This means that the firm must pay *all* past preferred dividends before common stockholders get a cent. If the company does miss a preferred dividend, the preferred stockholders generally gain some voting rights, so that the common stockholders are obliged to share control of the company with the preferred holders. Directors are also aware that failure to pay the preferred dividend earns the company a black mark with investors, so they do not take such a decision lightly.

14-3   DEBT

When companies borrow money, they promise to make regular interest payments and to repay the principal. However, this liability is limited. Stockholders have the right to default on the debt if they are willing to hand over the corporation's assets to the lenders. Clearly, they will choose to do this only if the value of the assets is less than the amount of the debt.[13]

Because lenders are not considered to be owners of the firm, they do not normally have any voting power. The company's payments of interest are regarded as a cost and are deducted from taxable income. Thus interest is paid from *before-tax* income, whereas dividends on common and preferred stock are paid from *after-tax* income. Therefore the government provides a tax subsidy for debt that it does not provide for equity. We discuss debt and taxes in detail in Chapter 18.

We have seen that financial institutions (including insurance companies, banks, and mutual funds) own a substantial portion of the total equity of the Indian companies. Figure 14.5 shows that this is also true of the company's bonds. In fact, in 2011 they owned majority of the debt instruments issued by the companies. The promoters contributed hardly 0.3% of the total debt of the Indian companies.[14]

Debt Comes in Many Forms

The financial manager is faced with an almost bewildering choice of debt securities. For example, look at Table 14.3, which shows the many ways that H.J. Heinz and the U.S. has borrowed money. Honeywell has also entered into a number of other arrangements that are not shown on the balance sheet. For example, it has arranged lines of credit that allow it to take out further short-term bank loans. Also it has entered into a swap that converts some of its fixed-rate debt into floating-rate debt.

---

[13] In practice this handover of assets is far from straightforward. Sometimes there may be thousands of lenders with different claims on the firm. Administration of the handover is usually left to the bankruptcy court (see Chapter 32).

[14] Figure 14.5 does not include shorter-term debt such as bank loans. Almost all short-term debt issued by corporations is held by financial institutions.

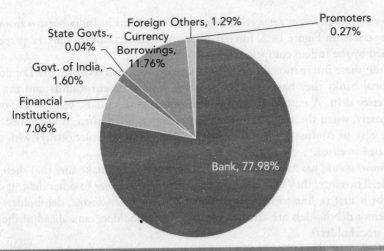

FIGURE 14.5

Holdings of different debt securities issued in India by different non-finance companies in 2005.

Source: Compiled from Prowess Database of CMIE.

You are probably wondering what a swap or floating-rate debt is. Relax—later in the book we explain the various features of corporate debt. For the moment, simply notice that the mixture of debt securities that each company issues reflects the financial manager's response to a number of questions:

1. *Should the company borrow short-term or long-term?* If your company simply needs to finance a temporary increase in inventories ahead of the holiday season, then it may make sense to take out a short-term bank loan. But suppose that the cash is needed to pay for expansion of an oil refinery. Refinery facilities can operate more or less continuously for 15 or 20 years. In that case it would be more appropriate to issue a long-term bond.[15]

   Some loans are repaid in a steady, regular way; in other cases the entire loan is repaid at maturity. Occasionally either the borrower or the lender has the option to terminate the loan early and to demand that it be repaid immediately.

2. *Should the debt be fixed or floating rate?* The interest payment, or coupon, on long-term bonds is commonly fixed at the time of issue. If a ₹1,000 bond is issued when long-term interest rates are 10%, the firm continues to pay ₹100 per year regardless of how interest rates fluctuate.

   Most bank loans and some bonds offer a variable, or *floating,* rate. For example, the interest rate in each period may be set at 1% above MIBOR (Mumbai Interbank Offered Rate), which is the interest rate at which major international banks lend rupees to each other. When MIBOR changes, the interest rate on your loan also changes.

TABLE 14.3 Large firms issue many different securities. This table shows some of the debt securities on Honeywell's balance sheet in December 2008.

Bank loans
Commercial paper
Notes
Unsecured debentures
Floating-rate bonds
Zero-coupon bonds
Money multiplier notes
Industrial development bonds

---

[15] A company might choose to finance a long-term project with short-term debt if it wished to signal its confidence in the future. Investors would deduce that, if the company anticipated declining profits, it would not take the risk of being unable to take out a fresh loan when the first one matured. See D. Diamond, "Debt Maturity Structure and Liquidity Risk," *Quarterly Journal of Economics* 106 (1991), pp. 709–737.

3. *Should you borrow rupees or some other currency?* Many firms in India borrow from within India. As can be seen from Figure 14.5, foreign currency loans account for only 12 percent of the total loans issued by the Indian companies.

Because these international bonds have usually been marketed by the London branches of international banks they have traditionally been known as **eurobonds** and the debt is called **eurocurrency** debt. A eurobond may be denominated in dollars, yen, or any other currency. Unfortunately, when the single European currency was established, it was called the *euro*. It is, therefore, easy to confuse a *eurobond* (a bond that is sold internationally) with a bond that is denominated in euros.

4. *What promises should you make to the lender?* Lenders want to make sure that their debt is as safe as possible. Therefore, they may demand that their debt is *senior* to other debt. If default occurs, senior debt is first in line to be repaid. The *junior,* or *subordinated,* debtholders are paid only after all senior debtholders are satisfied (though all debtholders rank ahead of the preferred and common stockholders).

The firm may also set aside some of its assets specifically for the protection of particular creditors. Such debt is said to be *secured* and the assets that are set aside are known as *collateral.* Thus a retailer might offer inventory or accounts receivable as collateral for a bank loan. If the retailer defaults on the loan, the bank can seize the collateral and use it to help pay off the debt.

Usually the firm also provides assurances to the lender that it will not take unreasonable risks. For example, a firm that borrows in moderation is less likely to get into difficulties than one that is up to its gunwales in debt. So the borrower may agree to limit the amount of extra debt that it can issue. Lenders are also concerned that, if trouble occurs, others will push ahead of them in the queue. Therefore, the firm may agree not to create new debt that is senior to existing debtholders or to put aside assets for other lenders.

5. *Should you issue straight or convertible bonds?* Companies often issue securities that give the owner an option to convert them into other securities. These options may have a substantial effect on value. The most dramatic example is provided by a **warrant,** which is *nothing but* an option. The owner of a warrant can purchase a set number of the company's shares at a set price before a set date. Warrants and bonds are often sold together as a package.

A **convertible bond** gives its owner the option to exchange the bond for a predetermined number of shares. The convertible bondholder hopes that the issuing company's share price will zoom up so that the bond can be converted at a big profit. But if the shares zoom down, there is no obligation to convert; the bondholder remains a bondholder.

A Debt by Any Other Name

The word *debt* sounds straightforward, but companies make a number of promises that look suspiciously like debt but are treated differently in the accounts. Some of these disguised debts are easily spotted. For example, accounts payable are simply obligations to pay for goods that have already been delivered and are therefore like short-term debt.

Other arrangements are less obvious. For example, instead of borrowing to buy new equipment, the company may rent or **lease** it on a long-term basis. In this case, the firm promises to make a series of lease payments to the owner of the equipment. This is just like the obligation to make payments on an outstanding loan. If the firm gets into deep water, it can't choose to miss out on its debt interest, and it can't choose to skip those lease payments.

Here is another example of a disguised debt. At the end of 2008 Honeywell had promised its employees postretirement health care and life insurance benefits valued at $17 billion. However, Honeywell had set aside only $8.5 billion to help meet this obligation. The *unfunded* obligation amounted to $8.5 billion.

There is nothing underhand about any of these obligations. They are all clearly shown on the balance sheet or explained in the notes to the accounts. Sometimes, however, companies go to considerable lengths to ensure that investors do *not* know how much the companies have borrowed. For example, Enron was able to borrow $658 million by setting up *special-purpose entities (SPEs)*, which raised cash by a mixture of equity and debt and then used these debts to help fund the parent company. None of this debt showed up on Enron's balance sheet.

Variety's the Very Spice of Life

We have indicated several dimensions along which corporate securities can be classified. That gives the financial manager plenty of choice in designing securities. As long as you can convince investors of its attractions, you can issue a convertible, subordinated, floating-rate bond denominated in Swedish kronor. Rather than combining features of existing securities, you may create an entirely new one. We can imagine a coal mining company issuing convertible bonds on which the payment fluctuates with coal prices. We know of no such security, but it is perfectly legal to issue it—and who knows?—it might generate considerable interest among investors.

Given the enormous variety of corporate securities, it's no surprise to find hybrids that incorporate features of both debt and equity. The dividing line between debt and equity is sometimes hard to locate. For example, monthly income preferred stock (MIPS) in the U.S. is subordinated debt that is repackaged as preferred stock. MIPS is treated as equity on the issuing company's balance sheet, but the Internal Revenue Service treats the preferred dividends as tax-deductible interest.[16] MIPS is debt for tax purposes, equity otherwise.

Financial managers don't care what a security is called; they care how it works. ("What's in a name? That which we call a rose by any other name would smell as sweet.")[17] But a security's classification as debt or equity does matter for accounting and tax purposes. Classification can sometimes be challenging. It doesn't help to say that "Debt is safe, equity is risky," because there are plenty of examples of safe equity (preferred stock issued by a blue-chip corporation, for example) and risky debt (junk bonds). It does help to remember that equity is a *residual claim* that participates in the upsides and downsides of the business after debt claims are satisfied. Equity has residual cash-flow rights and residual control rights. Debt has first claim on cash flows, but its claim is limited. It does not participate in the upsides of the business. Debt has no control rights unless the firm defaults or violates debt covenants.

14-4 FINANCIAL MARKETS AND INSTITUTIONS

That completes our tour of corporate securities. You may feel like the tourist who has just seen 12 cathedrals in five days. But there will be plenty of time in later chapters for reflection and analysis. It is now time to move on and to look briefly at the markets in which the firm's securities are traded and at the financial institutions that hold them.

---

[16] See P. Irvine and J. Rosenfeld, "Raising Capital Using Monthly Income Preferred Stock: Market Reaction and Implications for Capital Structure Theory," *Financial Management* 29 (Summer 2000), pp. 5–20.

[17] *Romeo and Juliet*, Act II, Scene 2.

We have explained that corporations raise money by selling financial assets such as stocks and bonds. This increases the amount of cash held by the company and the amount of stocks and bonds held by the public. These issues are known as *primary issues* that are sold in the **primary market.** But in addition to helping companies to raise cash, financial markets also allow investors to trade stocks or bonds among themselves. For example, Ms. Sundarrajan might decide to raise some cash by selling her ACC stock at the same time that Mr. Sharma invests his savings in ACC. So they make a trade. The result is simply a transfer of ownership from one person to another, which has no effect on the company's cash, assets, or operations. Such purchases and sales are known as *secondary transactions* and they take place in the **secondary market.**

Some financial assets have less active secondary markets than others. For example, when a company borrows money from a bank, the bank acquires a financial asset (the company's promise to repay the loan with interest). Banks do sometimes sell packages of loans to other banks, but generally they retain the loan until it is repaid by the borrower. Other financial assets are regularly traded. Some of these assets, such as shares of stock, are traded on organized exchanges like the Mumbai, New York, London, or Tokyo stock exchanges. In other cases there is no organized exchange, and the assets are traded by a network of dealers. Such markets are known as *over-the-counter (OTC)* markets. For example, most government and corporate bonds are traded OTC.

Some financial markets are not used to raise cash but instead help firms to manage their risks. In these markets firms can buy or sell derivatives, whose payoffs depend on the prices of other securities or commodities. For example, if a chocolate producer is worried about rising cocoa prices, it can use the derivatives markets to fix the price at which it buys its future cocoa requirements.

The Financial Crisis of 2007–2009

The financial crisis of 2007–2009[18] raised many questions, but it settled one question conclusively: Yes, financial markets and institutions are important. When financial markets and institutions ceased to operate properly, the world was pushed deeper into a global recession.

For the U.S., the recession was the worst since the Great Depression of the 1930s. But financial crises have hit many other countries. Carmen Reinhart and Kenneth Rogoff examined 18 postwar financial crises in the developed world, several crises in developing economies, and two earlier historical episodes.[19] They found that systemic banking crises are typically preceeded by credit booms and asset price bubbles. The crises result, on average, in a 35% real drop in housing prices spread over a period of six years. Stock prices fall 55% over three and a half years. Output falls by 9% over two years, and unemployment rises 7% over four years. Government debt rises 86% from its precrisis level.

Crises always come as nasty surprises. Perhaps managers, investors, and policymakers ignore the many prior crises. ("Those who cannot remember the past are condemned to repeat it.")[20] Perhaps they believe that their country is different or this time is different.

The crisis of 2007–2009 cannot be blamed on any short list of economic events. We can note a few of the many contributing factors, however. We start with easy-money policies adopted by the U.S. Federal Reserve and other central banks after the collapse of the technology stock bubble in 2000. At

---

[18] We write this chapter in July 2009. We hope that "2007–2009" is not overly optimistic.

[19] C. Reinhart and K. Rogoff, "The Aftermath of Financial Crises," *American Economic Review* 99 (May 2009), pp. 466–472. Among the 18 postwar crises in developed countries, they put particular emphasis on "the big five" (Spain 1977, Norway 1987, Finland 1991, Sweden 1991, and Japan 1992). The emerging market episodes are the 1997—1998 Asian Crisis (Indonesia, Malaysia, and the Philippines), Colombia 1998, and Argentina 2001. The historical episodes are Norway 1899 and the U.S. 1929.

[20] This maxim appears in many versions. We have quoted the American philosopher George Santayana.

the same time, large balance-of-payments surpluses in Asian economies were invested back into U.S. Treasuries and other debt securities. This also contributed to lax credit.

Low interest rates and easy credit helped fuel a dramatic increase in housing prices in the U.S. and several other countries, including the U.K., Ireland, and Spain. Housing prices reached a peak in 2006, but then started to fall.

Many subprime mortgages had been packaged together and resold to banks. As house prices fell, investors became increasingly worried about the losses that these banks were suffering. By August banks had become wary about lending to each other for more than a few days, and central banks were forced to inject massive liquidity. Lenders demanded more and more collateral for what were ordinarily safe, routine transactions.

During the fall of 2007 prices of debt that was backed by subprime mortgages continued to decline. In March 2008, the Federal Reserve bailed out Bear Sterns through an arranged merger with J.P. Morgan. Public money and guarantees were required to induce J.P. Morgan to engage in the transaction.

Although the financial system, particularly banks, came under tremendous pressure during 2008, the real economy was not much affected. That changed in September 2008, when Lehman Brothers was *not* bailed out by the government. Lehman's bankruptcy meant major losses for investors and other financial institutions. More important, the investors and institutions now feared that new risks could be lurking in every balance sheet. Many of those fears were justified. For example, AIG, once an AAA-rated insurance company, turned out to have massive exposure from insuring bonds against default. Bailing out AIG cost the U.S. Treasury about $85 billion.

By first quarter of 2009, economic activity in the U.S. and many other countries was declining rapidly. Unemployment rose dramatically. As international trade fell away, export-based economies such as Japan and Germany were hit particularly badly. It was the worst worldwide crisis since the Great Depression.

Fortunately, the economic crisis did not affect India as much as it did the rest of the world. India's GDP grew at more than 6% throughout this period, when many developed countries registered negative growth rate in GDP. India is not as dependent on global flows of trade and capital as are many other countries. Exports contribute to about 20% of India's GDP. The Indian banks follow a rather conservative style of investment and did not invest in the mortgage backed securities as much as most of the non-Indian banks did. India's exports did fall during this time period. However, that did not bring down the overall growth rate substantially. The decline in the world-wide stock market led to an outflow of foreign currency in 2008-09 due to portfolio investment. Foreign portfolio investment was -$13,618 millions in 2008-09. Foreign portfolio investment, however, increased to $153,516 millions in 2009-10. These data show that even the international investors had faith in India's growth story during the period of global economic crisis.

The Role of Financial Institutions

We have described some of the consequences when financial institutions don't work as designed. We should say more about how they should work. What functions are they supposed to serve?

Financial institutions act as *financial intermediaries* that gather the savings of many individuals and reinvest them in loans or in the financial markets. For example, banks raise money by taking deposits and by selling debt and common stock to investors. They then lend the money to companies and individuals. Of course banks must charge sufficient interest to cover their costs and to compensate depositors and other investors.

Banks are the most familiar intermediaries. But there are many others, such as financial institutions, insurance companies, and mutual funds. In the United States, insurance companies are more important than banks for the long-term financing of business. Prior to 1990s, the Development Financial Institutions (DFIs) were the main financers of the long-term financing to the corporate sector in India. The DFIs had access to low-cost funds. They were allowed to issue bonds with government guarantee, and were given funds through budgetary allocations. IDBI, the largest DFI, was also allocated a sizeable portion of RBI's National Industrial Credit (Long Term Operations) funds.[21] The interest rate on the long-term finance was also kept lower as compared to the working capital loans provided by the commercial banks. The commercial banks were not allowed to provide the long-term finance to the corporate sector. The corporate sector also did not have any incentive in financing long-term projects by issuing bonds because of three reasons. The interest rates on bonds were much higher than the interest charged by the DFIs. The Finance Ministry never allowed companies to go for bond issues when the debt-equity ratio (after the bond issue) exceeded 2:1. However, the DFIs were allowed to extend long-term finance that raised the debt-equity ratio to 3:1. Finally, the state governments used to charge high stamp duties on the secondary market transactions in bonds. These factors ensured that the DFIs remained virtually the only source of funds for the companies in India till the early 1990s.

However, after the liberalization process started, the DFIs started loosing their importance. After 1991, they had to compete with the commercial banks while extending long-term finances to the companies. While the commercial banks had access to cheaper sources of funds, the DFIs stopped getting budgetary support and were not allowed to issue bonds with government guarantee. Both ICICI and IDBI got merged with their own banking subsidiaries. So after the late 1990s, the banks started dominating the long-term finance market. In 2010-11, banks provided 78% of the total debt requirement of manufacturing companies in India as against 7% provided by the development financial institutions.

Why are financial intermediaries different from a manufacturing corporation? First, the financial intermediary may raise money in special ways, for example, by taking deposits or by selling insurance policies. Second, the financial intermediary invests in *financial assets,* such as stocks, bonds, or loans to businesses or individuals. By contrast, the manufacturing company's main investments are in *real* assets, such as plant and equipment. Thus the intermediary receives cash flows from its investment in one set of financial assets (stocks, bonds, etc.) and repackages those flows as a different set of financial assets (bank deposits, insurance policies, etc.). The intermediary hopes that investors will find the cash flows on this new package more attractive than those provided by the original security.

Financial intermediaries contribute in many ways to our individual well-being and the smooth functioning of the economy. Here are some examples.

The Payment Mechanism   Think how inconvenient life would be if all payments had to be made in cash. Fortunately, checking accounts, credit cards, and electronic transfers allow individuals and firms to send and receive payments quickly and safely over long distances. Banks are the obvious providers of payments services, but they are not alone. For example, if you buy shares in a money-market mutual fund, your money is pooled with that of other investors and is used to buy safe, short-term securities. You can then write checks on this mutual fund investment, just as if you had a bank deposit.

Borrowing and Lending   Almost all financial institutions are involved in channeling savings toward those who can best use them. Thus, if Ms. Jones has more money now than she needs and wishes to

---

[21] See Patil, R.H., "Broadbasing and Deepening the Bond Market in India", Wharton Financial Institutions Centre, University of Pennsylvania, 2001.

save for a rainy day, she can put the money in a bank savings deposit. If Mr. Smith wants to buy a car now and pay for it later, he can borrow money from the bank. Both the lender and borrower are happier than if they were forced to spend cash as it arrived. Of course, individuals are not alone in needing to raise cash. Companies with profitable investment opportunities may wish to borrow from the bank, or they may raise the finance by selling new shares or bonds. Governments also often run at a deficit, which they fund by issuing large quantities of debt.

In principle, individuals or firms with cash surpluses could take out newspaper advertisements or surf the Net looking for those with cash shortages. But it can be cheaper and more convenient to use a financial intermediary, such as a bank, to link up the borrower and lender. For example, banks are equipped to check out the would-be borrower's creditworthiness and to monitor the use of cash lent out. Would you lend money to a stranger contacted over the Internet? You would be safer lending the money to the bank and letting the bank decide what to do with it.

Notice that banks promise their checking account customers instant access to their money and at the same time make long-term loans to companies and individuals. This mismatch between the liquidity of the bank's liabilities (the deposits) and most of its assets (the loans) is possible only because the number of depositors is sufficiently large that the bank can be fairly sure that they will not all want to withdraw their money simultaneously.

Pooling Risk Financial markets and institutions allow firms and individuals to pool their risks. For instance, insurance companies make it possible to share the risk of an automobile accident or a household fire. Here is another example. Suppose that you have only a small sum to invest. You could buy the stock of a single company, but then you would be wiped out if that company went belly-up. It is generally better to buy shares in a mutual fund that invests in a diversified portfolio of common stocks or other securities. In this case you are exposed only to the risk that security prices as a whole will fall.

The basic functions of financial markets are the same the world over. So it is not surprising that similar institutions have emerged to perform these functions. In almost every country you will find banks accepting deposits, making loans, and looking after the payments system. You will also encounter insurance companies offering life insurance and protection against accident. If the country is relatively prosperous, other institutions, such as pension funds and mutual funds, will also have been established to help manage people's savings.

Of course there are differences in institutional structure. Take banks, for example. In many countries where securities markets are relatively undeveloped, banks play a much more dominant role in financing industry. Often the banks undertake a wider range of activities than they do in the United States. For example, they may take large equity stakes in industrial companies; this would not generally be allowed in the United States. In India banks control 4% of the total equity shares of the non-financial companies.

SUMMARY

Financial managers are faced with two broad financing decisions:

1. How much of internally generated cash flow should be plowed back into the business? How much should be paid out to shareholders by cash dividends or share repurchases?
2. To what extent should the firm use debt rather than equity financing?

The answers to these questions depend on the firm's payout policy and debt policy.

Figure 14.1 summarizes how U.S. corporations raise and spend money. Have another look at it and try to get a feel for the numbers. Notice that internally generated cash is the major source of financing for investment. Borrowing is also significant. Net equity issues have been negative, however—that is, share repurchases have been larger than share issues.

Common stock is the simplest form of finance. The common stockholders own the corporation. They get all of the cash flow and assets that are left over after the firm's debts have been paid. Common stock is therefore a residual claim that participates in the upsides and downsides of the business. Debt has first claim on cash flows, but its claim is limited. Debt has no control rights unless the firm defaults or violates debt covenants.

Preferred stock is another form of equity financing. Preferreds promise a fixed dividend, but if the board of directors decides to skip the dividend, holders of the preferred have no recourse. The firm must pay the preferred dividends before it pays any dividends on common stock, however.

Debt is the most important source of external financing. Holders of bonds and other corporate debt are promised interest payments and return of principal. If the company cannot make these payments, the debt investors can sue for payment or force bankruptcy. Bankruptcy usually means that the debt holders take over and either sell the company's assets or continue to operate them under new management.

Note that the tax authorities treat interest payments as a cost and therefore the company can deduct interest when calculating its taxable income. Interest is paid from pretax income, whereas dividends and retained earnings come from after-tax income. That is one reason why preferred stock is a less important source of financing than debt. Preferred dividends are not tax-deductible.

Book debt ratios in the United States have generally increased over the post–World War II period. However, they are not appreciably higher than the ratios in the other major industrialized countries.

The variety of debt instruments is almost endless. The instruments differ by maturity, interest rate (fixed or floating), currency, seniority, security, and whether the debt can be converted into equity.

The majority of the firm's debt and equity is owned by financial institutions—notably banks, insurance companies, pension funds, and mutual funds. The crisis of 2007–2009 dramatized the crucial role that these institutions play. They finance much of corporate investment, as well as investment in real estate and other assets. They run the payments mechanism, help individuals diversify and manage their portfolios, and help companies manage risk.

FURTHER READING

A useful article for comparing financial structure in the United States and other major industrial countries is:

R. G. Rajan and L. Zingales, "What Do We Know about Capital Structure? Some Evidence from International Data," *Journal of Finance* 50 (December 1995), pp. 1421–1460.

For a discussion of the allocation of control rights and cash-flow rights between stockholders and debt holders, see:

O. Hart, *Firms, Contracts, and Financial Structure* (Oxford: Oxford University Press, 1995).

Robert Merton gives an excellent overview of the functions of financial institutions in:

R. Merton, "A Functional Perspective of Financial Intermediation," *Financial Management* 24 (Summer 1995), 23–41.

The Winter 2009 issue of the Journal of Financial Perspectives *contains several articles on the crisis of 2007–2009. See also:*

V. V. Acharya and M. W. Richardson, eds., *Restoring Financial Stability* (Hoboken, NJ: John Wiley & Sons, 2009).

The following works cover financial crises more generally:

F. Allen and D. Gale, *Understanding Financial Crises* (Oxford: Oxford University Press, 2007).

C. Reinhart and K. Rogoff, "The Aftermath of Financial Crises," *American Economic Review* 99 (May 2009), pp. 466–472.

C. M. Reinhart and K. Rogoff, *This Time Is Different: Eight Centuries of Financial Folly* (Princeton: Princeton University Press, 2009).

PROBLEM SETS

Quiz

1. *True* or *false?*
   a. Net stock issues by Indian nonfinancial corporations are in most years small but positive.
   b. Most capital investment by Indian companies is funded by retained earnings and reinvested depreciation.
   c. Debt ratios in India have generally increased in the last five years.

2. The authorized share capital of Hindustan Unilever Limited is ₹2,250,000,000 equity shares. The equity is currently shown in the company's books as on 31 March, 2011 as follows:

Ordinary Shares (₹1 face value)	₹215.95 crores
Share Premium Account	₹0.86 crores
Profit and Loss Account Balances	₹1235.6 crores
Other Reserves	₹1181.51 crores
Net Worth	₹2633.92 crores

   a. How many shares are issued?
   b. How many are outstanding?
   c. When will your answers to (a) and (b) above will be different?
   d. How many more equity shares can be issued without the approval of shareholders?
   e. What is the book value per share?
   f. Suppose that HUL issues 1 million equity shares at ₹230, each. What will be the book value per equity share?
   g. How will the book value per share change, if HUL buys back 1 million equity shares by paying ₹220 per share?

3. There are 10 directors to be elected. A shareholder owns 80 shares. What is the maximum number of votes that he or she can cast for a favorite candidate under (a) majority voting? (b) cumulative voting?

4. Fill in the blanks, using the following terms: floating rate, common stock, convertible, subordinated, preferred stock, senior, warrant.
   a. If a lender ranks behind the firm's general creditors in the event of default, his or her loan is said to be _____.
   b. Interest on many bank loans is based on a _____ of interest.
   c. A(n) _____ bond can be exchanged for shares of the issuing corporation.
   d. A(n) _____ gives its owner the right to buy shares in the issuing company at a predetermined price.
   e. Dividends on _____ cannot be paid unless the firm has also paid any dividends on its _____.

5. True or false?

   a. In India, most ordinary shares are owned by individual investors.

   b. An insurance company is a financial intermediary.

INTERMEDIATE

6. In 2008 Pfizer had 12,000 million shares of common stock authorized, 8,863 million in issue, and 6,746 million outstanding (figures rounded to the nearest million). Its equity account was as follows:

Common stock	$ 443
Additional paid-in capital	70,283
Retained earnings	44,148
Treasury shares	(57,391)

   a. What was the par value of each share?

   b. What was the average price at which shares were sold?

   c. How many shares had been repurchased?

   d. What was the average price at which the shares were repurchased?

   e. What was the net book value of Pfizer's common equity?

7. Inbox Software was founded in 2011. Its founder put up ₹20 million for 2 million ordinary shares. Each stock has a face value of ₹10.

   a. Construct an equity account (like the one in Table 14.2) for Inbox on the day after its founding. Ignore any legal or administrative costs of setting up the company.

   b. After two years of operation, Inbox generated earnings of ₹0.12 million and paid no dividends. What was the equity account at this point?

   c. After three years the company sold 1 million additional shares for ₹50 per share. It earned ₹0.25 million during the year and paid no dividends. What was the equity account?

8. Look back at Table 14.2.

   a. Suppose that Reliance issued an additional 50 million shares at ₹700 a share. Rework Table 14.2 to show the company's equity after the issue.

   b. Suppose that Reliance *subsequently* repurchased 20 million shares at ₹750 a share. Rework Table 14.2 to show the effect of this further change.

9. Suppose that East Corporation has issued voting and nonvoting stock. Investors hope that holders of the voting stock will use their power to vote out the company's incompetent management. Would you expect the voting stock to sell for a higher price? Explain.

10. In 2007 Beta Corporation earned gross profits of ₹760,000.

   a. Suppose that it is financed by a combination of common stock and ₹1 million of debt. The interest rate on the debt is 10%, and the corporate tax rate is 35%. How much profit is available for common stockholders after payment of interest and corporate taxes?

   b. Now suppose that instead of issuing debt Beta is financed by a combination of common stock and ₹1 million of preferred stock. The dividend yield on the preferred is 8% and the corporate tax rate is still 35%. How much profit is now available for common stockholders after payment of preferred dividends and corporate taxes?

11. Look up the financial statements for an Indian company on the Internet and construct a table like Table 14.3 showing the types of debt that the company has issued. What arrangements has it made that would allow it to borrow more in the future? (*Hint:* You will need to look at the notes to the accounts to answer this.)

12. Which of the following features would increase the value of a corporate bond? Which would reduce its value?
    a. The borrower has the option to repay the loan before maturity.
    b. The bond is convertible into shares.
    c. The bond is secured by a mortgage on real estate.
    d. The bond is subordinated.
13. Construct a time line of the important events in the financial crisis that started in the summer of 2007. When do you think the crisis ended? You will probably want to review some of the entries under Further Reading before you answer.
14. We mention several causes of the financial crisis. What other causes can you identify? You will probably want to review some of the entries under Further Reading before you answer.

CHALLENGE

15. The shareholders of the Pickwick Paper Company need to elect five directors. There are 200,000 shares outstanding. How many shares do you need to own to *ensure* that you can elect at least one director if (a) the company has majority voting? (b) it has cumulative voting?

REAL-TIME DATA ANALYSIS

1. Use data from the Standard & Poor's market insight database at **www.mhhe.com/ed-umarketinsight** to work out the financing proportions given in Figure 14.1 for a particular industrial company for some recent year.
2. The Web site www.federalreserve.gov/releases/z1/current/default.htm provides data on sources of funds and an aggregate balance sheet for nonfarm nonfinancial corporations. Look at Table F.102 for the latest year. What proportion of the cash that companies needed was generated internally and how much had to be raised on the financial markets? Is this the usual pattern? Now look at "new equity issues." Were companies on average issuing new equity or buying their shares back?

    STANDARD &POOR'S

3. An aggregate balance sheet for U.S. manufacturing corporations can be found on www.census.gov/econ/qfr. Find the balance sheet for the latest year. What was the ratio of long-term debt to long-term debt plus equity? What about the ratio of all long-term liabilities to long-term liabilities plus equity?

15

CHAPTER

How Corporations Issue Securities

In Chapter 11 we encountered Marvin Enterprises, one of the most remarkable growth companies of the twenty-first century. It was founded by George and Mildred Marvin, two high-school dropouts, together with their chum Charles P. (Chip) Norton. To get the company off the ground the three entrepreneurs relied on their own savings together with personal loans from a bank. However, the company's rapid growth meant that they had soon borrowed to the hilt and needed more equity capital. Equity investment in young private companies is generally known as *venture capital*. Such venture capital may be provided by investment institutions or by wealthy individuals who are prepared to back an untried company in return for a piece of the action. In the first part of this chapter we will explain how companies like Marvin go about raising venture capital.

Venture capital organizations aim to help growing firms over that awkward adolescent period before they are large enough to go public. For a successful firm such as Marvin, there is likely to come a time when it needs to tap a wider source of capital and therefore decides to make its first public issue of common stock. The next section of the chapter describes what is involved in such an issue in the United States. We explain the process for registering the offering with the Securities and Exchange Board of India and we introduce you to the underwriters who buy the issue and resell it to the public. We also see that new issues are generally sold below the price at which they subsequently trade. To understand why that is so, we need to make a brief sortie into the field of auction procedures.

A company's first issue of stock is seldom its last. In Chapter 14 we saw that corporations face a persistent financial deficit that they meet by selling securities. We therefore look at how established corporations go about raising more capital. In the process we encounter another puzzle: When companies announce a new issue of stock, the stock price generally falls. We suggest that the explanation lies in the information that investors read into the announcement.

If a stock or bond is sold publicly, it can then be traded on the securities markets. But sometimes investors intend to hold on to their securities and are not concerned about whether they can sell them. In these cases there is little advantage to a public issue, and the firm may prefer to place the securities directly with one or two financial institutions. At the end of this chapter we explain how companies arrange a private placement.

15-1 VENTURE CAPITAL

On April 1, 2022, George and Mildred Marvin met with Chip Norton in their research lab (which also doubled as a bicycle shed) to celebrate the incorporation of Marvin Enterprises. The three entrepreneurs had raised $100,000 from savings and personal bank loans and had purchased one million shares in the new company. At this *zero-stage* investment, the company's assets were $90,000 in the bank ($10,000 had been spent for legal and other expenses of setting up the company), plus the *idea* for a new product, the household gargle blaster. George Marvin was the first to see that the gargle blaster, up to that point an expensive curiosity, could be commercially produced using microgenetic refenestrators.

Marvin Enterprises' bank account steadily drained away as design and testing proceeded. Local banks did not see Marvin's idea as adequate collateral, so a transfusion of equity capital was clearly needed. Preparation of a *business plan* was a necessary first step. The plan was a confidential document describing the proposed product, its potential market, the underlying technology, and the resources (time, money, employees, and plant and equipment) needed for success.

Most entrepreneurs are able to spin a plausible yarn about their company. But it is as hard to convince a venture capitalist that your business plan is sound as to get a first novel published. Marvin's managers were able to point to the fact that they were prepared to put their money where their mouths were. Not only had they staked all their savings in the company but they were mortgaged to the hilt. This *signaled* their faith in the business.

First Meriam Venture Partners was impressed with Marvin's presentation and agreed to buy one million new shares for $1 each. After this *first-stage* financing, the company's market-value balance sheet looked like this:

Marvin Enterprises' First-Stage Balance Sheet (Market Values in $ Millions)

Cash from new equity	$1	$1	New equity from venture capital
Other assets, mostly intangible	1	1	Original equity held by entrepreneurs
Value	$2	$2	Value

By agreeing to pay $1 a share for Marvin's stock, First Meriam placed a value of $1 million on the entrepreneurs' original shareholdings. This was First Meriam's estimate of the value of the entrepreneurs' original idea and their commitment to the enterprise. If the estimate was right, the entrepreneurs could congratulate themselves on a $900,000 paper gain over their original $100,000 investment. In exchange, the entrepreneurs gave up half their company and accepted First Meriam's representatives to the board of directors.[1]

---

[1] Venture capital investors do not necessarily demand a majority on the board of directors. Whether they do depends, for example, on how mature the business is and on what fraction they own. A common compromise gives an equal number of seats to the founders and to outside investors; the two parties then agree to one or more additional directors to serve as tie-breakers in case a conflict arises. Regardless of whether they have a majority of directors, venture capital companies are seldom silent partners; their judgment and contacts can often prove useful to a relatively inexperienced management team.

The success of a new business depends critically on the effort put in by the managers. Therefore venture capital firms try to structure a deal so that management has a strong incentive to work hard. That takes us back to Chapters 1 and 12, where we showed how the shareholders of a firm (who are the principals) need to provide incentives for the managers (who are their agents) to work to maximize firm value.

If Marvin's management had demanded watertight employment contracts and fat salaries, they would not have found it easy to raise venture capital. Instead the Marvin team agreed to put up with modest salaries. They could cash in only from appreciation of their stock. If Marvin failed they would get nothing, because First Meriam actually bought *preferred* stock designed to convert automatically into common stock when and if Marvin Enterprises succeeded in an initial public offering or consistently generated more than a target level of earnings. But if Marvin Enterprises had failed, First Meriam would have been first in line to claim any salvageable assets. This raised even further the stakes for the company's management.[2]

Venture capitalists rarely give a young company up front all the money it will need. At each stage they give enough to reach the next major checkpoint. Thus in spring 2024, having designed and tested a prototype, Marvin Enterprises was back asking for more money for pilot production and test marketing. Its *second-stage* financing was $4 million, of which $1.5 million came from First Meriam, its original backers, and $2.5 million came from two other venture capital partnerships and wealthy individual investors. The balance sheet just after the second stage was as follows:

Marvin Enterprises' Second-Stage Balance Sheet (Market Values in $ Millions)

Cash from new equity	$4	$4	New equity, second stage
Fixed assets	1	5	Equity from first stage
Other assets, mostly intangible	9	5	Original equity held by entrepreneurs
Value	$14	$14	Value

Now the after-the-money valuation was $14 million. First Meriam marked up its original investment to $5 million, and the founders noted an additional $4 million paper gain.

Does this begin to sound like a (paper) money machine? It was so only with hindsight. At stage 1 it wasn't clear whether Marvin would ever get to stage 2; if the prototype hadn't worked, First Meriam could have refused to put up more funds and effectively closed down the business.[3] Or it could have advanced stage 2 money in a smaller amount on less favorable terms. The board of directors could also have fired George, Mildred, and Chip and gotten someone else to try to develop the business.

In Chapter 14 we pointed out that stockholders and lenders differ in their cash-flow rights and control rights. The stockholders are entitled to whatever cash flows remain after paying off the other security holders. They also have control over how the company uses its money, and it is only if the company defaults that the lenders can step in and take control of the company. When a new business raises venture capital, these cash-flow rights and control rights are usually negotiated separately. The venture capital firm will want a say in how that business is run and will demand representation on the board and a significant number of votes. The venture capitalist may agree that it will relinquish some of these rights if the business subsequently performs well. However, if performance turns out to be

---

[2] Notice the trade-off here. Marvin's management is being asked to put all its eggs into one basket. That creates pressure for managers to work hard, but it also means that they take on risk that could have been diversified away.

[3] If First Meriam had refused to invest at stage 2, it would have been an exceptionally hard sell convincing another investor to step in in its place. The other outside investors knew they had less information about Marvin than First Meriam and would have read its refusal as a bad omen for Marvin's prospects.

poor, the venture capitalist may automatically get a greater say in how the business is run and whether the existing management should be replaced.

For Marvin, fortunately, everything went like clockwork. Third-stage *mezzanine financing* was arranged,[4] full-scale production began on schedule, and gargle blasters were acclaimed by music critics worldwide. Marvin Enterprises went public on February 3, 2028. Once its shares were traded, the paper gains earned by First Meriam and the company's founders turned into fungible wealth. Before we go on to this initial public offering, let us look briefly at the venture capital markets today.

The Venture Capital Market

Most new companies rely initially on family funds and bank loans. Some of them continue to grow with the aid of equity investment provided by wealthy individuals known as *angel investors*. However, like Marvin, many adolescent companies raise capital from specialist venture-capital firms, which pool funds from a variety of investors, seek out fledgling companies to invest in, and then work with these companies as they try to grow. In addition, some large technology firms, such as Intel and Johnson & Johnson, act as *corporate venturers* by providing equity capital to new innovative companies.

The Indian Government issued the guidelines to legalize the operations of the venture capital in November 1988.[5] More or less, at the same time, four state-owned financial institutions established venture capital subsidiaries including Technology Development and Information Company of India[6] (now ICICI Ventures), subsidiary of ICICI, with the active help of the World Bank. In 1996, international and private domestic venture capitalists started investing in India. Draper International, Walden International Investment Group, etc entered India in 1996. Walden International Investment Group of U.S. and Nikko Capital of Japan started the first VC fund, named, Walden-Nikko India Fund. As of now, there are multiple legal bodies that monitor the activities of the venture capitalists in India. The Department of Economic Affairs (in Ministry of Finance), the Central Board of Direct Taxes, and the Security Exchange Board of India are the three regulators that regulate the different activities of the venture capitalists in India. On the top of it, the foreign venture capitalists are also monitored by two additional regulatory bodies, namely the Foreign Investment Promotion Board and the Reserve Bank of India.

Figure 15.1 shows the changing level of venture capital investment in India. In 2007, funds invested over $21 billion, but during the period of financial crisis, venture capital investments slumped. During 2007-09, the foreign venture capital investors reduced their investments in India by almost $17 billion.

In the U.S. most venture capital funds are organized as limited private partnerships with a fixed life of about 10 years. In India, the regulations, however, do not recognize limited life funds. Since it is easier to terminate a trust in India, most funds were set up as trusts. However, when a trust is closed, the entire firm was closed rather than a particular fund within the firm. So, initially each fund was created as a trust.

You will find that these venture capital firms are often lumped together with similar firms that provide funds for companies in distress or that buy out whole companies or divisions of companies and then take them private. The general term for these activities is *private equity investing*.

---

[4] Mezzanine financing does not necessarily come in the third stage; there may be four or five stages. The point is that mezzanine investors come in late, in contrast to venture capitalists who get in on the ground floor.

[5] For an excellent discussion on the history of venture capital financing in India, read Dossani and Kenney (2002), "Creating an Environment: Developing Venture Capital in India", Berkeley Roundtable on International Economy, Working paper No. 143.

[6] Actually TDICI was set up in August 1988.

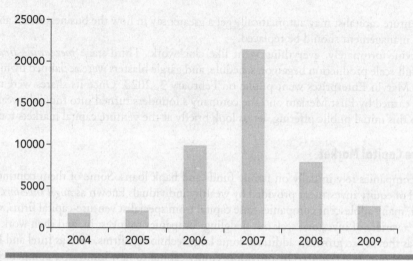

FIGURE 15.1

Venture capital and private equity investments in India (Figures in $ millions)

Source: India Venture Capital and Private Equity Report 2010

Venture capital firms are not passive investors. They tend to specialize in young high-tech firms that are difficult to evaluate and they monitor these firms closely. They also provide ongoing advice to the firms that they invest in and often play a major role in recruiting the senior management team. Their judgment and contacts can be valuable to a business in its early years and can help the firm to bring its products more quickly to market.[7]

Venture capitalists may cash in on their investment in two ways. Generally, once the new business has established a track record, it may be sold out to a larger firm. However, many entrepreneurs do not fit easily into a corporate bureaucracy and would prefer instead to remain the boss. In this case, the company may decide, like Marvin, to go public and so provide the original backers with an opportunity to "cash out," selling their stock and leaving the original entrepreneurs in control. A thriving venture capital market therefore needs an active stock exchange, such as Nasdaq, that specializes in trading the shares of young, rapidly growing firms.[8]

During the late 1990s the venture capital market in Europe was helped by the formation of new European stock exchanges that modeled themselves on Nasdaq and specialized in trading the stocks of young fast-growing firms. In three years the Neuer Markt exchange in Frankfurt listed over 300 new companies, more than half of which were backed by venture capital firms. But then the exchange was hit by scandal as one high-tech firm, Comroad, revealed that most of its claimed $94 million of revenue was fictitious. As the dot.com boom fizzled out, stock prices on the Neuer Markt fell by 95% and the exchange was finally closed down.

Very few new businesses make it big, but venture capitalists keep sane by forgetting about the many failures and reminding themselves of the success stories—the investors who got in on the ground floor

---

[7] For evidence on the role of venture capitalists in assisting new businesses, see T. Hellman and M. Puri, "The Interaction between Product Market and Financial Strategy: The Role of Venture Capital," *Review of Financial Studies* 13 (2000), pp. 959–984; and S. N. Kaplan and P. Stromberg, "Contracts, Characteristics and Actions: Evidence from Venture Capitalist Analyses," *Journal of Finance* 59 (October 2004), pp. 2177–2210.

[8] This argument is developed in B. Black and R. Gilson, "Venture Capital and the Structure of Capital Markets: Banks versus Stock Markets," *Journal of Financial Economics* 47 (March 1998), pp. 243–277.

of firms like Federal Express, Genentech, and Intel. For every 10 first-stage venture capital investments, only two or three may survive as successful, self-sufficient businesses. From these statistics come two rules for success in venture capital investment. First, don't shy away from uncertainty; accept a low probability of success. But don't buy into a business unless you can see the *chance* of a big, public company in a profitable market. There's no sense taking a long shot unless it pays off handsomely if you win. Second, cut your losses; identify losers early, and if you can't fix the problem—by replacing management, for example—throw no good money after bad.

How successful is venture capital investment? Since you can't look up the value of new start-up businesses in *Economic Times*, it is difficult to say with confidence. However, *Venture Economics*, which tracks the performance of a large sample of venture capital funds in the U.S., calculated that in the 20 years to the end of 2008 investors in these funds would have earned an average annual return of 17% after expenses.[9] That is nearly 10% more a year than they would have earned from investing in the stocks of large public corporations. We do not know whether this compensates for the extra risks of investing in venture capital.

15-2 THE INITIAL PUBLIC OFFERING

There comes a stage in the life of many young companies when they decide to make an **initial public offering** of stock, or **IPO.** This may be a *primary* offering, in which new shares are sold to raise additional cash for the company. Or it may be a *secondary* offering, where the existing shareholders decide to cash in by selling part of their holdings.

Secondary offerings are not confined to small, immature businesses. For example, in 1998 Du Pont sold off a large part of its holding in Conoco for $4.4 billion. The biggest secondary offerings occur when governments sell their shareholdings in companies. For example, the Indian government raised ₹994 crores while selling 7.94 crores shares in Maruti Udyog Limited. Similarly, the British government raised $9 billion from its sale of British Gas stock, while the 1985 initial offering by the Japanese government of a 12.5% stake in NTT brought in $15 billion. Even these two issues were dwarfed by the 2006 IPO of the state-owned Industrial and Commercial Bank of China, which raised $22 billion.

We have seen that companies may make an IPO to raise new capital or to enable shareholders to cash out, but, as you can see from Figure 15.2, there may be other benefits to going public. For example, the company's stock price provides a readily available yardstick of performance, and allows the firm to reward the management team with stock options. And, because information about the company becomes more widely available, the company can diversify its sources of finance and reduce its borrowing cost.

While there are advantages to having a market for your shares, we should not give the impression that firms everywhere aim to go public. In many countries it is common for large businesses to remain privately owned. For example, Italy has only about a tenth as many listed companies as the U.K. although the economies are roughly similar in size.

Even in the United States, some very large companies, such as Bechtel, Cargill, and Levi Strauss, have chosen to remain private. In India, most of the successful unlisted (though not necessarily private) companies are either group holding companies like Tata Sons and TV Sundaram Iyengar & Sons or public sector units like Bharat Sanchar Nigam Limited. Tata Consultancy Services, one of the most

---

[9] Gompers and Lerner, who studied the period 1979–1997, found somewhat higher returns. P. A. Gompers and J. Lerner, "Risk and Reward in Private Equity Investments: The Challenge of Performance Assessment," *Journal of Private Equity*, Winter 1997, pp. 5–12.

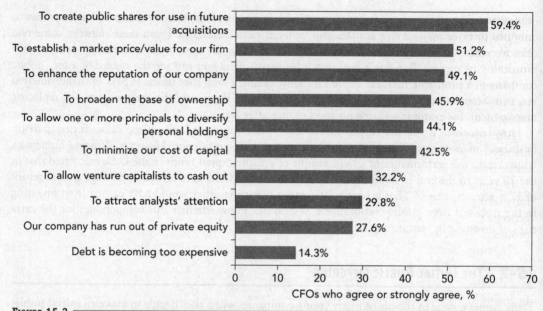

FIGURE 15.2

Survey evidence on the motives for going public.

Source: J. C. Brau and S. E. Fawcett, "Evidence on What CFOs Think about the IPO Process: Practice, Theory and Managerial Implications," *Journal of Applied Corporate Finance* 18 (Summer 2006), pp. 107–117. © 2006 Blackwell Publishers.

successful IT companies in India was unlisted till 2004. In certain other countries, it is more common for large businesses to remain privately owned. For example, in Italy, there are only about 250 listed companies. The U.K. has almost 10 times that number and the USA nearly 20 times. By April 2006, in India, about 4800 companies' stocks were listed in BSE alone.

Public firms in the U.S. often go into the reverse process of IPO and return to being privately owned. For a somewhat extreme example, consider the food service company, Aramark. It began life in 1936 as a private company and went public in 1960. In 1984 a management buyout led to the company going private and it remained private until 2001, when it had its second public offering. But the experiment did not last long, for five years later Aramark was once again the object of a buyout that took the company private again.

Managers often chafe at the red tape involved in running a public company and at the costs of communicating with shareholders. These complaints have become more vocal since the passage of the Sarbanes-Oxley Act. This act sought to prevent a repeat of the corporate scandals that brought about the collapse of Enron and WorldCom, but, as the nearby box suggests, a consequence has been an increased reporting burden on small public companies and an apparent increase in their readiness to go private.[10]

Arranging an Initial Public Offering

Let us now look at how Marvin arranged to go public. By 2028 the company had grown to the point at which it needed still more capital to implement its second-generation production technology. At

---

[10] There has also been an increase in the number of firms that have reduced the regulatory and reporting burden by "going dark." In this case the company must have less than 300 shareholders and must not be listed on a public exchange.

the same time the company's founders were looking to sell some of their shares.[11] In the previous few months there had been a spate of IPOs by high-tech companies and the shares had generally sold like hotcakes. So Marvin's management hoped that investors would be equally keen to buy the company's stock.

Management's first task was to select the *underwriters.* Underwriters act as financial midwives to a new issue. Usually they play a triple role: First they provide the company with procedural and financial advice, then they buy the issue, and finally they resell it to the public.

After some discussion Marvin settled on Klein Merrick as the managing underwriter and Goldman Stanley as the comanager. Klein Merrick then formed a syndicate of underwriters who would buy the entire issue and reoffer it to the public.

In choosing Klein Merrick to manage its IPO, Marvin was influenced by Merrick's proposals for making an active market in the stock in the weeks after the issue.[12] Merrick also planned to generate continuing investor interest in the stock by distributing a major research report on Marvin's prospects.[13] Marvin hoped that this report would encourage investors to hold its stock.

Together with Klein Merrick and firms of lawyers and accountants, Marvin prepared a **registration statement** for the approval of the Securities and Exchange Commission (SEC).[14] This statement is a detailed and somewhat cumbersome document that presents information about the proposed financing and the firm's history, existing business, and plans for the future.

The most important sections of the registration statement are distributed to investors in the form of a **prospectus.** In the appendix to this chapter we have reproduced the prospectus for Marvin's first public issue of stock. Real prospectuses would go into much more detail on each topic, but this example should give you some feel for the mixture of valuable information and redundant qualification that characterizes these documents. The Marvin prospectus also illustrates how the SEC insists that investors' eyes are opened to the dangers of purchase (see "Certain Considerations" of the prospectus). Some investors have joked that if they read each prospectus carefully, they would not dare buy any new issue.

In addition to registering the issue with the SEC, Marvin needed to check that the issue complied with the so-called *blue-sky laws* of each state that regulate sales of securities within the state.[15] It also arranged for its newly issued shares to be traded on the Nasdaq exchange.

---

[11] First Meriam also wanted to cash in on its investment, but venture capital companies usually believe that selling out at the time of the IPO would send a bad signal to investors. Therefore First Meriam planned to wait until well after the IPO and then either sell its holding or distribute its shares in Marvin to the investors in the First Meriam fund.

[12] On average the managing underwriter accounts for 40% to 60% of trading volume in the stock during the first 60 days after an IPO. See K. Ellis, R. Michaely, and M. O'Hara, "When the Underwriter Is the Market Maker: An Examination of Trading in the IPO Aftermarket," *Journal of Finance* 55 (June 2000), pp. 1039–1074.

[13] The 40 days after the offer are designated as a *quiet period.* Merrick is obliged to wait until after this period before commenting on the valuation of the company. Survey evidence suggests that, in choosing an underwriter, firms place considerable importance on its ability to provide follow-up research reports. See L. Krigman, W. H. Shaw, and K. L. Womack, "Why Do Firms Switch Underwriters?" *Journal of Financial Economics* 60 (May–June 2001), pp. 245–284.

[14] The rules governing the sale of securities derive principally from the Securities Act of 1933. The SEC is concerned solely with disclosure and it has no power to prevent an issue as long as there has been proper disclosure. Some public issues are exempt from registration. These include issues by small businesses and loans maturing within nine months.

[15] In 1980, when Apple Computer Inc. went public, the Massachusetts state government decided the offering was too risky and barred the sale of the shares to individual investors in the state. The state relented later after the issue was out and the price had risen. Needless to say, this action was not acclaimed by Massachusetts investors.

States do not usually reject security issues by honest firms through established underwriters. We cite the example to illustrate the potential power of state securities laws and to show why underwriters keep careful track of them.

Finance In The News

The Urge to Go Private

Recent years have seen a boom in U.S. companies choosing to go private. The following passage from *The Wall Street Journal* argues that the boom was accentuated by more burdensome regulation of public companies:

> At least part of the strength of private equity is a direct result of the problems besetting public markets. Public-to-private deals are in fact lengthy, costly and can lead to unpleasantness with shareholders—often via lawsuits. The fact that so many companies have nonetheless been willing to take the plunge speaks volumes about how eager they are to escape the increasing burdens of public-company regulation.
>
> Sarbanes-Oxley has been the last straw for some, with its auditing and reporting requirements imposing major new costs, especially on smaller companies. The Securities and Exchange Commission is promising Sarbox reform, though its recent noises suggest it won't exempt smaller companies from the rules. It might want to consider International Strategy & Investment Group data showing that 191 public companies—worth $146 billion in deal value—have gone private since June 30, 2002, shortly before Sarbox went into effect. Daniel Clifton, executive director of the American Shareholders Association, notes that the big spike came right after Sarbox's implementation, yet the dollar amount of the deals didn't rise equivalently—suggesting it was mainly smaller firms doing the exiting.
>
> Mr. Clifton has also been studying the surging costs of regulation for public companies and has found that, while in 1999 regulatory costs were about 4.8% of market capitalization, by 2002 the ratio was 9.9%. It has fallen some since. But these costs are a double whammy for smaller companies, which have fewer resources to devote to compliance costs and "it is also money that they can't use for the investments that they need make grow," says Mr. Clifton.
>
> The relentless pressure of quarterly earnings is also a tyranny that some managers would prefer to avoid. Such targets have their uses in holding managers accountable. But even capable executives who fail to meet Wall Street expectations, or suffer an unexpected bump in the road, have to worry that they'll get hit with shareholder suits for even a temporary stock price dip. It may not be a coincidence that, according to a recent survey from Booz Allen Hamilton, 15.3% of CEOs at the world's 2,500 largest public companies left office in 2005, many of them fleeing to private companies that can afford the luxury of a longer-run view.*

*"Hot Topic: Going Private," *The Wall Street Journal,* June 3, 2006, p. A.7. © 2006 Dow Jones & Company, Inc.

The Sale of Marvin Stock

While the registration statement was awaiting approval, Marvin and its underwriters began to firm up the issue price. First they looked at the price–earnings ratios of the shares of Marvin's principal competitors. Then they worked through a number of discounted-cash-flow calculations like the ones we described in Chapters 4 and 11. Most of the evidence pointed to a market price in the region of $74 to $76 a share and the company therefore included this provisional figure in the preliminary version of the prospectus.[16]

---

[16] The company is allowed to circulate a preliminary version of the prospectus (known as a *red herring*) before the SEC has approved the registration statement.

Marvin and Klein Merrick arranged a *road show* to talk to potential investors. Mostly these were institutional investors, such as managers of mutual funds and pension funds. The investors gave their reactions to the issue and indicated to the underwriters how much stock they wished to buy. Some stated the maximum price that they were prepared to pay, but others said that they just wanted to invest so many dollars in Marvin at whatever issue price was chosen. These discussions with fund managers allowed Klein Merrick to build up a book of potential orders.[17] Although the managers were not bound by their responses, they knew that, if they wanted to keep in the underwriters' good books, they should be careful not to go back on their expressions of interest. The underwriters also were not obliged to treat all investors equally. Some investors who were keen to buy Marvin stock were disappointed in the allotment that they subsequently received.

Immediately after it received clearance from the SEC, Marvin and the underwriters met to fix the issue price. Investors had been enthusiastic about the story that the company had to tell and it was clear that they were prepared to pay more than $76 for the stock. Marvin's managers were tempted to go for the highest possible price, but the underwriters were more cautious. Not only would they be left with any unsold stock if they overestimated investor demand but they also argued that some degree of underpricing was needed to tempt investors to buy the stock. Marvin and the underwriters therefore compromised on an issue price of $80. Potential investors were encouraged by the fact that the offer price was higher than the $74 to $76 proposed in the preliminary prospectus and decided that the underwriters must have encountered considerable enthusiasm for the issue.

Although Marvin's underwriters were committed to buy only 900,000 shares from the company, they chose to sell 1,035,000 shares to investors. This left the underwriters short of 135,000 shares or 15% of the issue. If Marvin's stock had proved unpopular with investors and traded below the issue price, the underwriters could have bought back these shares in the marketplace. This would have helped to stabilize the price and would have given the underwriters a profit on these extra shares that they sold. As it turned out, investors fell over themselves to buy Marvin stock and by the end of the first day the stock was trading at $105. The underwriters would have incurred a heavy loss if they had been obliged to buy back the shares at $105. However, Marvin had provided underwriters with a *greenshoe* option that allowed them to buy an additional 135,000 shares from the company. This ensured that the underwriters were able to sell the extra shares to investors without fear of loss.

The Underwriters

Marvin's underwriters were prepared to enter into a firm commitment to buy the stock and then offer it to the public. Thus they took the risk that the issue might flop and they would be left with unwanted stock. Occasionally, where the sale of common stock is regarded as particularly risky, the underwriters may be prepared to handle the sale only on a best-efforts basis. In this case the underwriters promise to sell as much of the issue as possible but do not guarantee to sell the entire amount.[18]

Successful underwriting requires financial muscle and considerable experience. The names of Marvin's underwriters are of course fictitious, but Table 15.1 shows that underwriting is dominated by the major investment banks and large commercial banks. Foreign players are also heavily involved in underwriting securities that are sold internationally.

---

[17] The managing underwriter is therefore often known as the *bookrunner*.

[18] The alternative is to enter into an *all-or-none* arrangement. In this case, either the entire issue is sold at the offering price or the deal is called off and the issuing company receives nothing.

TABLE 15.1 The top managing underwriters, January–December 2008. Values include global debt and equity issues.

	Value of Issues ($ billions)	Number of Issues
J.P. Morgan	$455	1,210
Barclays Capital	401	1,041
Citigroup	309	986
Deutsche Bank	309	807
Merrill Lynch	241	852
Goldman Sachs	228	584
Morgan Stanley	220	661
RBS	214	712
Credit Suisse	205	682
UBS	204	867

Source: Thomson Reuters (**www.thomsonreuters.com**). © 2008 Thomson Reuters.

Underwriting is not always fun. In April 2008 the British bank, HBOS, offered its shareholders two new shares at a price of £2.75 for each five shares that they currently held.[19] The underwriters to the issue, Morgan Stanley and Dresdner Kleinwort, guaranteed that at the end of eight weeks they would buy any new shares that the stockholders did not want. At the time of the offer HBOS shares were priced at about £5, so the underwriters felt confident that they would not have to honor their pledge. Unfortunately, they reckoned without the turbulent market in bank shares that year. The bank's shareholders worried that the money they were asked to provide would largely go to bailing out the bondholders and depositors. By the end of the eight weeks the price of HBOS stock had slumped below the issue price, and the underwriters were left with 932 million unwanted shares worth £3.6 billion.

Companies get to make only one IPO, but underwriters are in the business all the time. Wise underwriters, therefore, realize that their reputation is on the line and will not handle an issue unless they believe the facts have been presented fairly to investors. So, when a new issue goes wrong, the underwriters may be blamed for overhyping the issue and failing in their "due diligence." For example, in December 1999 the software company Va Linux went public at $30 a share. The next day trading opened at $299 a share, but then the price began to sag. Within two years it had fallen below $2. Disgruntled Va Linux investors sued the underwriters, complaining that the prospectus was "materially false." These underwriters had plenty of company, for following the collapse of the dot.com stocks in 2000, investors in many other high-tech IPOs sued the underwriters. As the nearby box explains, there was further embarrassment when it emerged that several well-known underwriters had engaged in "spinning"—that is, allocating stock in popular new issues to managers of their important corporate clients. The underwriter's seal of approval for a new issue no longer seemed as valuable as it once had.

In India, for the normal public issues, underwriting is not compulsory. However, underwriting is mandatory, if the issue price is determined by the book-building method. In India, the underwriter comes to picture after the issue is over. If the issue devolves, then the underwriter buys the unsubscribed portion of the shares (up to the underwriting obligations limit). Thus for example, when the Hindalco

---

[19] This arrangement is known as a *rights issue*. We describe rights issues later in the chapter.

rights issue devolved in October 2008, ABN Amro Asia Equities (India) Limited, ABN Amro Securities (Private) Limited, Citigroup Global Markets India Pvt Ltd, Deutsche Equities India Pvt. Ltd, DSP Merrill Lynch Ltd, and the State Bank of India were asked to pick up the unsubscribed part of the issue (around 34% of the issue amount of ₹5000 crores). If the company does not receive 90 percent of the net offer including the devolvement of underwriters within 60 days from the date of closure of the issue, the company has to return the entire money collected from the investors.

Costs of a New Issue

We have described Marvin's underwriters as filling a triple role—providing advice, buying the new issue, and reselling it to the public. In return they received payment in the form of a *spread*[20]; that is, they were allowed to buy the shares for less than the *offering price* at which the shares were sold to investors.[21] Klein Merrick as syndicate manager kept 20% of this spread. A further 25% of the spread was used to pay those underwriters who bought the issue. The remaining 55% went to the firms that provided the salesforce.

The underwriting spread on the Marvin issue amounted to 7% of the total sum raised from investors. Since many of the costs incurred by underwriters are fixed, you would expect that the percentage spread would decline with issue size. This in part is what we find. For example, a $5 million IPO might carry a spread of 10%, while the spread on a $300 million issue might be only 5%. However, Chen and Ritter found that for almost every IPO between $20 and $80 million the spread was exactly 7%.[22] Since it is difficult to believe that there are no scale economies, this clustering at 7% is a puzzle.[23]

In addition to the underwriting fee, Marvin's new issue entailed substantial administrative costs. Preparation of the registration statement and prospectus involved management, legal counsel, and accountants, as well as the underwriters and their advisers. In addition, the firm had to pay fees for registering the new securities, printing and mailing costs, and so on. You can see from the first page of the Marvin prospectus (see this chapter's appendix) that these administrative costs totaled $820,000 or just over 1% of the proceeds.

Underpricing of IPOs

Marvin's issue was costly in yet another way. Since the offering price was less than the true value of the issued securities, investors who bought the issue got a bargain at the expense of the firm's original shareholders.

These costs of *underpricing* are hidden but nevertheless real. For IPOs they generally exceed all other issue costs. Whenever any company goes public, it is very difficult to judge how much investors will be prepared to pay for the stock. Sometimes the underwriters misjudge dramatically. For example, when the prospectus for the IPO of eBay was first published, the underwriters indicated that the company would sell 3.5 million shares at a price between $14 and $16 each. However, the enthusiasm

---

[20] In India, underwriters typically receive their payment in the form of a commission, based on the issue price and the amount underwritten.

[21] In the more risky cases the underwriter usually receives some extra noncash compensation, such as warrants to buy additional common stock in the future.

[22] H. C. Chen and J. R. Ritter, "The Seven Percent Solution," *Journal of Finance* 55 (June 2000), pp. 1105–1132.

[23] Chen and Ritter argue that the fixed spread suggests the underwriting market is not competitive and the Justice Department was led to investigate whether the spread constituted evidence of price-fixing. Robert Hansen disagrees that the market is not competitive. Among other things, he provides evidence that the 7% spread is not abnormally profitable and argues that it is part of a competitive and efficient market. See R. Hansen, "Do Investment Banks Compete in IPOs?: The Advent of the 7% Plus Contract," *Journal of Financial Economics* 59 (2001) pp. 313–346.

Finance In The News

How Scandal Hit the Investment Banking Industry

Nineteen ninety-nine looked to be a wonderful year for investment banks. Not only did they underwrite a near-record number of IPOs, but the stocks that they sold leapt by an average of 72% on their first day of trading, earning the underwriters some very grateful clients. Just three years later the same investment banks were in disgrace. Probing by New York State Attorney General Eliot Spitzer uncovered a chronicle of unethical and shameful behavior during the boom years.

As the dot.com stock market boom developed, investment banking analysts had begun to take on the additional role of promoters of the shares that they analyzed, in the process becoming celebrities with salaries to match. The early run-up in the stock price of dot.com IPOs therefore owed much to hype by the underwriters' analysts, who strongly promoted stocks that they sometimes privately thought were overpriced. One superstar Internet analyst was revealed in internal e-mails to have believed that stocks he was peddling to investors were "junk" and "piece[s] of crap." In many cases the stocks were indeed junk, and the underwriters who had puffed the IPOs soon found themselves sued by disgruntled investors who had bought at the inflated prices.

The underwriters' troubles deepened further when it was disclosed that in a number of cases they had allocated stock in hot new issues to the personal brokerage accounts of the CEOs of major corporate clients. This stock could then be sold, or "spun," for quick profits. Five senior executives of leading telecom companies were disclosed to have received a total of $28 million in profits from their allocation of stocks in IPOs underwritten by one bank. Over the same period the bank was awarded over $100 million of business from these five companies. Eliot Spitzer argued that such lucrative perks were really attempts by the banks to buy future business and that the profits therefore belonged to the companies' shareholders rather than the executives. Soon top executives of several other companies were facing demands from disgruntled shareholders that they return to their companies the profits that they had pocketed from hot initial public offerings.

These scandals that engulfed the investment banking industry resulted in a $1.4 billion payout by the banks and an agreement to separate investment banking and research departments, hire independent consultants, and select independent research providers. But the revelations also raised troubling questions about ethical standards and the pressures that can lead employees to unscrupulous behavior.

for eBay's Web-based auction system was such that the underwriters increased the issue price to $18. The next morning dealers were flooded with orders to buy eBay; over 4.5 million shares traded and the stock closed the day at a price of $47.375.

We admit that the eBay issue was unusual.[24] But researchers have found that investors who buy at the issue price on average realize very high returns over the following days. For example, one study of nearly 12,000 U.S. IPOs from 1960 to 2008 found average underpricing of 16.9%.[25]

---

[24] It does not, however, hold the record. That honor goes to Va Linux.

[25] Our figure is an equally weighted average of first-day returns and is calculated from data on **bear.cba.ufl.edu/ritter**. As we saw in Chapter 13, there is some evidence that these early gains are not maintained and in the five years following an IPO the shares underperform the market.

Figure 15.3 shows that the United States is not the only country in which IPOs are underpriced. In China the gains from buying IPOs have averaged 165%.[26]

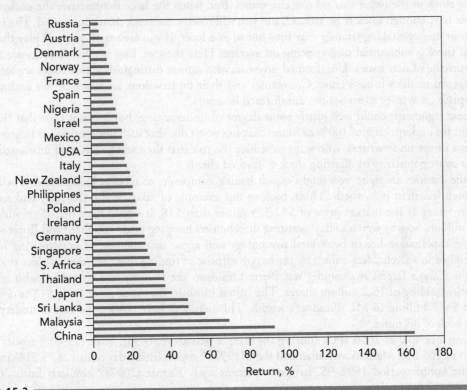

FIGURE 15.3

Average initial returns from investing in IPOs in different countries.

Source: T. Loughran, J. R. Ritter, and K. Rydqvist, "Initial Public Offerings: International Insights," *Pacific Basin Finance Journal* 2 (1994), pp. 165–199, extended and updated on **bear.cba.ufl.edu/ritter**. © 1994 Elsevier Science. Reprinted with permission.

You might think that shareholders would prefer not to sell stock in their company for less than its market price, but many investment bankers and institutional investors argue that underpricing is in the interests of the issuing firm. They say that a low offering price on an IPO raises the price when it is subsequently traded in the market and enhances the firm's ability to raise further capital.

There is another possible reason that it may make sense to underprice new issues. Suppose that you successfully bid for a painting at an art auction. Should you be pleased? It is true that you now own the painting, which was presumably what you wanted, but everybody else at the auction apparently thought that the painting was worth less than you did. In other words, your success suggests that you may have overpaid. This problem is known as the *winner's curse*. The highest bidder in an auction is most likely to have overestimated the object's value and, unless bidders recognize this in their bids, the buyer will on average overpay. If bidders are aware of the danger, they are likely to adjust their bids down correspondingly.

---

[26] The Chinese returns are for A shares, which are traded only domestically.

The same problem arises when you apply for a new issue of securities. For example, suppose that you decide to apply for every new issue of common stock. You will find that you have no difficulty in getting stock in the issues that no one else wants. But, when the issue is attractive, the underwriters will not have enough stock to go around, and you will receive less stock than you wanted. The result is that your money-making strategy may turn out to be a loser. If you are smart, you will play the game only if there is substantial underpricing on average. Here then we have a possible rationale for the underpricing of new issues. Uninformed investors who cannot distinguish which issues are attractive are exposed to the winner's curse. Companies and their underwriters are aware of this and need to underprice on average to attract the uninformed investors.[27]

These arguments could well justify some degree of underpricing, but it is not clear that they can account for underpricing of 100% or more. Skeptics point out that such underpricing is largely in the interests of the underwriters, who want to reduce the risk that they will be left with unwanted stock and to court popularity by allotting stock to favored clients.

If the skeptics are right, you might expect issuing companies to rebel at being asked to sell stock for much less than it is worth. Think back to our example of eBay. If the company had sold 3.5 million shares at the market price of $47.375 rather than $18, it would have netted an additional $103 million. So why weren't eBay's existing shareholders hopping mad? Loughran and Ritter suggest that the explanation lies in behavioral psychology and argue that the cost of underpricing may be outweighed in shareholders' minds by the happy surprise of finding that they are wealthier than they thought. EBay's largest shareholder was Pierre Omidyar, the founder and chairman, who retained his entire holding of 15.2 million shares. The initial jump in the stock price from $18 to $47.375 added $447 million to Mr. Omidyar's wealth. This may well have pushed the cost of underpricing to the back of his mind.[28]

Using a sample of 2056 IPOs (during the sample period 1991–95), Shah (1995)[29] report initial returns of 105.6%. Madhusoodhanan and Raju (1997)[30] report listing day return of 75.21% in India over the sample period 1992–95. In a more recent stydy Kumar (2007)[31] similarly finds 26.35% return on the listing day.

Hot New-Issue Periods

Figure 15.4 shows that the degree of underpricing fluctuates sharply from year to year. In 1999, around the peak of the dot.com boom, new issues raised $65 billion and the average first-day return on IPOs was 72%. Nearly $37 billion was left on the table that year. But, as the number of new issues slumped, so did the amount of underpricing. The year 2008 saw just 21 IPOs and the average first-day return was a measly 6.4%.

Some observers believe that these hot new-issue periods arise because investors are prone to periods of excessive optimism and would-be issuers time their IPOs to coincide with these periods. Other observers stress the fact that a fall in the cost of capital or an improvement in the economic outlook

---

[27] Notice that the winner's curse would disappear if only investors knew what the market price was going to be. One response is to allow trading in a security before it has been issued. This is known as a *gray market* and in the U.S. is most common for debt issues. Investors can observe the price in the gray market and can be more confident that they are not overbidding when the actual issue takes place.

[28] T. Loughran and J. Ritter, "Why Don't Issuers Get Upset about Leaving Money on the Table in IPOs?" *Review of Financial Studies* 15 (2002), pp. 413–443.

[29] Shah, A., "The Indian IPO Market: Empirical Facts, technical Report", Centre for Monitoring Indian Economy, 1995.

[30] Madhusoodhanan, T. P. and T. M. Raju, "Underpricing in IPOs: The Indian Evidence", Vikalpa (1997), p 17–30.

[31] Kumar, S.S.S., "Short and Long-run Performance of Bookbuilt IPOs in India", International Journal of Management Practices and Contemporary Thoughts, (2007), pp. 19–29.

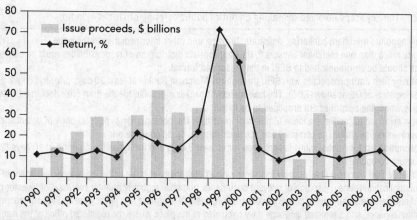

FIGURE 15.4

IPO proceeds in the United States and average first-day returns, 1990–2008.

Source: J. R. Ritter, "Some Factoids about the 2008 IPO Market," February 6, 2009, **bear.cba.ufl.edu/ritter**.

may mean that a number of new or dormant projects suddenly become profitable. At such times, many entrepreneurs rush to raise new cash to invest in these projects.[32]

15-3 ALTERNATIVE ISSUE PROCEDURES FOR IPOs

Table 15.2 summarizes the main steps involved in making an initial public offering of stocks in India. Of late, most IPOs in India use the *bookbuilding* method in which the book runner builds a book of likely orders and uses this information to set the issue price.[33]

The bookbuilding method is in some ways like an auction, since potential buyers indicate how many shares they are prepared to buy at given prices. However, these indications are not binding, and are used only as a guide to fix the price of the issue. The advantage of the bookbuilding method is that it allows underwriters to give preference to those investors whose bids are most helpful in setting the issue price and to offer them a reward in the shape of underpricing.[34] Critics of bookbuilding point to the abuses of the 1990s, and emphasize the dangers of allowing the underwriter to decide who is allotted stock.

Bookbuilding has rapidly gained popularity throughout the world, but it is not the only way to sell new stock. One alternative is to conduct an open auction. In this case investors are invited to submit their bids, stating how many shares they wish to buy and the price. The securities are then sold to the highest bidders. Most governments, including India Treasury, sell their bonds by auction. In the United States auctions of common stock have accounted for only 1% of IPOs in the 10 years to 2009. However, in 2004, Google simultaneously raised eyebrows and $1.7 billion in the world's largest initial public offering to be sold by auction.[35]

---

for examples of these explanations, see A. P. Ljungqvist, V. Nanda, and R. Singh, "Hot Markets, Investor Sentiment, and IPO Pricing," *Journal of Business* 79 (July 2006), pp. 1667–1702; and L. Pastor and P. Veronesi, "Rational IPO Waves," *Journal of Finance* 60 (2005), pp. 1713–1757.

Out of the 274 IPOs that came out between January 2007 and September 2011 period in India, only 21 have used the fixed price route.

See L. M. Benveniste and P. A. Spindt, "How Investment Bankers Determine the Offer Price and Allocation of New Issues," *Journal of Financial Economics* 24 (1989), pp. 343–362; and F. Cornelli and D. Goldreich, "Bookbuilding and Strategic Allocation," *Journal of Finance* (December 2001), pp. 2337–2369.

Google's issue was followed in 2005 by a $140 million auction of stock by Morningstar.

TABLE 15.2 The key steps involved in making an initial public offering of stocks in India.

1. Company appoints merchant banker(s), registrars, brokers, and other intermediaries to the issue.
2. If there are more than one merchant bankers[36], then appropriate distribution of responsibilities must be carried out and the same should be communicated to SEBI in the prescribed format.
3. The company files draft prospectus with SEBI through the Merchant Banker at least 30 days prior to filing of prospectus with the Registrar of Companies (ROC). The lead merchant banker must also file the draft offer document with the stock exchanges where the securities are proposed to be listed.
4. Roadshow arranged to market the issue to potential investors. The book runner(s) build(s) book of potential demand.
5. SEBI approves registration. The company and the book runners agree on issue price.
6. The subscription list for public issues is kept open for at least 3 days and for a maximum period of 10 days (21 days for infrastructure companies).
7. The post-issue lead manager shall actively associate himself with the post-issue activities, namely, allotment of shares, refund of application money, dispatch of relevant documents, and shall regularly monitor redressal of investor grievances. It should also release an ad (giving details of subscription, basis of allotment, etc.) in at least an English national daily, one Hindi national paper, and a regional language daily circulated at the place where the registered office of the issuer company is located.
8. In case there is devolvement on the underwriters, the lead merchant banker shall ensure that the underwriters honor their commitments within 60 days from the date of closure of the issue.
9. In August 2003, SEBI introduced the system of Green Shoe option in India. An issuing company can avail of this facility to stabilize the post-listing prices of its shares. It must appoint one of the issue managers as the stabilization agent (SA), who will be responsible for the price stabilization process.

Source: www.sebi.gov.in

Fans of auctions often point to countries such as France, Israel, and Japan, where auctions were once commonly used to sell new issues of stock. Japan is a particularly interesting case, for the bookbuilding method was widely used until it was revealed that investment banks had been allocating shares in hot IPOs to government officials. In 1989 the finance ministry responded to this scandal by ruling that in the future all IPOs were to be auctioned. This resulted in a sharp fall in underpricing. However, in 1997 the restrictions were lifted, bookbuilding returned to favor, and the level of underpricing increased.[37]

Types of Auction: A Digression

Suppose that a government wishes to auction four million bonds and three would-be buyers submit bids. Investor A bids ₹1,020 each for one million bonds, B bids ₹1,000 for three million bonds, and C bids ₹980 for two million bonds. The bids of the two highest bidders (A and B) absorb all the bonds on offer and C is left empty-handed. What price do the winning bidders, A and B, pay?

The answer depends on whether the sale is a *discriminatory auction* or a *uniform-price auction*. In a discriminatory auction every winner is required to pay the price that he or she bid. In this case A would pay ₹1,020 and B would pay ₹1,000. In a uniform-price auction both would pay ₹1,000, which is the price of the lowest winning bidder (investor B).

It might seem from our example that the proceeds from a uniform-price auction would be lower than from a discriminatory auction. But this ignores the fact that the uniform-price auction provides better protection against the winner's curse. Wise bidders know that there is little cost to overbidding in a uniform-price auction, but there is potentially a very high cost to doing so in a discriminatory

---

[36] In case the issue price is determined by the book-building route, then the merchant bankers also play the role of the book runners and hence are called the book-running lead managers (BRLMs).

[37] T. Kaneko and R. Pettway, "Auctions versus Bookbuilding of Japanese IPOs," *Pacific Basin Journal* 11 (2003), pp. 439–462.

uction.[38] Economists therefore often argue that the uniform-price auction should result in higher roceeds.[39]

In India, both types of auctions are used by the RBI for the issue of G-Secs. The Reserve Bank of ndia announces in the notification of the auction itself whether the auction is a uniform price auction r discriminatory auction.

Sales of bonds by the U.S. Treasury used to take the form of discriminatory auctions so that uccessful buyers paid their bid. However, in 1998 the government switched to a uniform-price uction.[40]

5-4 SECURITY SALES BY PUBLIC COMPANIES

company's first public issue of stock is seldom its last. As the firm grows, it is likely to make further sues of debt and equity. Public companies can issue securities either by offering them to investors large or by making a rights issue that is limited to existing stockholders. We begin by describing eneral cash offers, which are now used for almost all debt and equity issues in the United States. We en describe rights issues, which are widely used in other countries for issues of common stock.

eneral Cash Offers

/hen a corporation makes a general cash offer of debt or equity in India, it goes through much the me procedure as when it first went public. In other words, it registers the issue with the SEBI and en the issue remains open for the specified time period. If the issue price is determined through the ookbuilding route, then the lead book runner builds up a book of likely demand for the securities.

In the U.S., the SEC allows large companies to file a single registration statement covering financing lans for up to two years into the future. In India, SEBI has extended this facility only to the public ctor banks, scheduled commercial banks and public financial institutions. The bank or institution roposing to take advantage of this has to first file, what is known as a *shelf prospectus* with SEBI. he shelf prospectus must disclose, among other things, the aggregate amount proposed to be raised rough all the stages of offers of securities made under the shelf prospectus. Once the shelf prospectus filed and approved, the actual issue can then be done with scant additional paperwork, whenever ne firm needs the cash or thinks it can issue securities at an attractive price. This is known as *shelf gistration*—the registration statement is "put on the shelf", to be taken down and used as needed.

Think of how you as a financial manager might use shelf registration. Suppose your company likely to need up to ₹200 million of new long-term debt over the next year or so. It can file a gistration statement for that amount. It then has prior approval to issue up to ₹200 million of debt, ut it isn't obligated to issue a paise. Nor is it required to work through any particular underwriters; ne registration statement may name one or more underwriters the firm thinks it may work with, but hers can be substituted later.

In addition, the price in the uniform-price auction depends not only on the views of B but also on those of A (for example, if A had bid $990 ther than $1,020, then both A and B would have paid $990 for each bond). Since the uniform-price auction takes advantage of the views of th A and B, it reduces the winner's curse.

Sometimes auctions reduce the winner's curse by allowing uninformed bidders to enter noncompetitive bids, whereby they submit a quantity it not a price. In India, noncompetitive bids up to 5 percent of the notified amount are accepted in the auction of dated G-Secs.

Experience in the United States with uniform-price auctions suggests that they do indeed reduce the winner's curse problem and realize gher prices for the seller. See D. Goldreich, "Underpricing in Discriminatory and Uniform-Price Auctions, "*Journal of Financial and Quan- ative Analysis* 42 (June 2007), pp. 443–466.

Now you can sit back and issue debt as needed, in bits and pieces if you like. Suppose Citibank comes across an insurance company with ₹10 million ready to invest in corporate bonds. Your phone rings. It's Citibank offering to buy ₹10 million of your bonds, priced to yield, say, 8½%. If you think that's a good price, you say OK and the deal is done, subject only to a little additional paperwork. Citibank then resells the bonds to the insurance company, it hopes at a higher price than it paid for them, thus earning an intermediary's profit.

Here is another possible deal: Suppose that you perceive a window of opportunity in which interest rates are temporarily low. You invite bids for ₹100 million of bonds. Some bids may come from large investment banks acting alone; others may come from ad hoc syndicates. But that's not your problem: if the price is right, you just take the best deal offered.[41]

Not all companies eligible for shelf registration actually use it for all their public issues. Sometimes they believe they can get a better deal by making one large issue through traditional channels, especially when the security to be issued has some unusual feature or when the firm believes that it needs the investment banker's counsel or stamp of approval on the issue. Consequently, shelf registration is less often used for issues of common stock or convertible securities than for garden-variety corporate bonds. In India, prior to November 2007, shelf-registration could be used only for the issue of debt securities. However, now it can be used by the banks, financial institutions and PSUs for the issue of any type of security.

International Security Issues

Instead of borrowing in their local market, companies often issue bonds in another country's domestic market, in which case the issue will be governed by the rules of that country.

A second alternative is to make an issue of *eurobonds,* which is underwritten by a group of international banks and offered simultaneously to investors in a number of countries. The borrower must provide a prospectus or offering circular that sets out the detailed terms of the issue. The underwriters will then build up a book of potential orders, and finally the issue will be priced and sold. Very large debt issues may be sold as *global bonds,* with one part sold internationally in the eurobond market and the remainder sold in the company's domestic market.

Equity issues too may be sold overseas. In fact some companies' stocks do not trade at all in their home country. For example, in 2009 Changyou.com, the Chinese online game company, raised $120 million by an IPO in the United States. Its stock was not traded in China. Presumably, the company thought it could get a better price and more active follow-on trading by listing overseas.

In May 1992, Reliance Industries raised $150 million in the first-ever GDR issue by any Indian company. Most of the Indian companies that have issued GDRs prefer Luxembourg stock exchange because it is very fast to close the deal at Luxembourg. In fact, the highest number of foreign companies listed in Luxembourg exchange are of Indian origin. Till 1999, Indian companies used to prefer the GDR route mainly because of the stringent disclosure requirements (and adherence to US Accounting Standards) required in case of ADR issues. BPL Cellular is the first Indian company to have issued its ADRs in the US and it got its shares listed in NASDAQ in May 1997.[42] In December 1996, BPL cellular attempted to issue ADRs. However, the company pulled out the issue hours before it were on offer. It was difficult for the lead underwriters to find enough takers at the initially-proposed issue

---

[41] These two deals are examples of *accelerated underwritings.* For a good description of such issues, see B. Bortolotti, W. Megginson, and B. Smart, "The Rise of Accelerated Seasoned Equity Underwritings," *Journal of Applied Corporate Finance,* 20 (Summer 2008), pp. 35–57.

[42] ICICI is the first Indian company to list on NYSE through an issue of ADRs.

rice of $16. Even when the underwriters reduced the price to $10, there was not enough interest in he stock and hence BPL Cellular had to pull out the issue in the last moment. VSNL also had to go hrough two failed attempts in 1994 before successfully issuing its GDRs in March 1997.

he Costs of a General Cash Offer

Whenever a firm makes a cash offer of securities, it incurs substantial administrative costs. The expenses nclude fees payable to lead managers and co-lead managers (if any), fees payable to co-managers and other merchant bankers, fees payable to registrars to the issue, fees payable to issue advisors, fees payable to bankers to the issue, fees payable to trustees (in case of debenture issues), underwriting ommissions, brokerage commissions and selling commissions. Table 15.3 lists issue expenses for a ew issues in 2011.

In the U.S., since the issuing company directly sells to the underwriters, it compensates the underwriters by selling them securities below the price (the difference is known as underwriting spreads) hat they expect to receive from investors. The underwriting spreads for debt securities and rights ssues are lower than for initial public issues of stocks. Larger issues tend to have lower spreads than maller issues.[43]

ABLE 15.3 Issue expenses as percentage of total issue size of selected issue

Type of Issue	Company	Issue Amount (₹ Millions)	Issue Expenses	%
Common Stock:				
Public	Indo Thai Securities	296	16.59	5.60%
Public	Taksheel Solutions	825	57.84	7.01%
Public	Flexituff International	1046.25	64.83	6.20%
Public	Onelife Capital Advisors	368.5	15.96	4.33%
Public	RDB Rasayans	355.5	30.48	8.57%
Rights	Bajaj Hindustan	16441.71	487.4	2.96%
Rights	Atul Auto	43.89	1.5	3.42%
Rights	Velan Hotels	614.96	6	0.98%
Rights	Arvind International	113.6	3.45	3.04%
Rights	E L Forge	129.44	5	3.86%
Debt:				
8.5% Non-Convertible Debentures, 2016	Power Finance Coporation	2000	63.6	3.18%
12% Non-convertible debenture, 2016	Religare Finvest	8000	228.42	2.86%
11.85% Non-convertible debentures, 2016	Shriram City Union Finance	7500	273.9	3.65%
11.6% Non-Convertible Debenture, 2016	Shriram Transport Finance Company	50000	268.2	0.54%

Source: www.sebi.gov.in

Figure 15.5 summarizes a study of total issue costs (spreads plus administrative costs) for several housand issues between 2004 and 2008.

---

[43] This point is emphasized in O. Altinkilic and R. S. Hansen, "Are There Economies of Scale in Underwriting Fees? Evidence of Rising External Financing Costs," *Review of Financial Studies* 13 (Spring 2000), pp. 191–218.

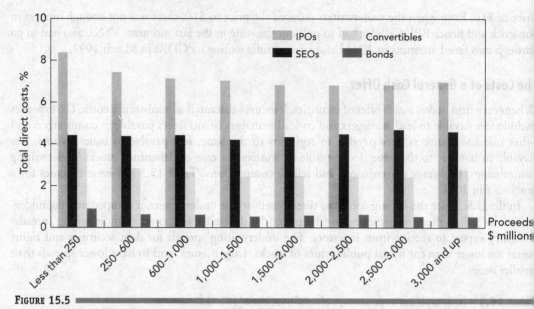

FIGURE 15.5

Total direct costs as a percentage of gross proceeds. The total direct costs for initial public offerings (IPOs) seasoned equity offerings (SEOs), convertible bonds, and straight bonds are composed of underwriter spreads and other direct expenses.

Source: We are grateful to Nickolay Gantchev for undertaking these calculations, which update tables in I. Lee, S. Lochhead, J. R. Ritter, and Q. Zhao, "The Costs of Raising Capital," *Journal of Financial Research* 19 (Spring 1996), pp. 59–74.

Market Reaction to Stock Issues

Economists who have studied seasoned issues of common stock have generally found tha announcement of the issue results in a decline in the stock price. For industrial issues in the Unite States this decline amounts to about 3%. While this may not sound overwhelming, the fall in marke value is equivalent, on average, to nearly a third of the new money raised by the issue.

What's going on here? One view is that the price of the stock is simply depressed by the prospect of the additional supply. On the other hand, there is little sign that the extent of the price fall increase with the size of the stock issue. There is an alternative explanation that seems to fit the facts better.

Suppose that the CFO of a restaurant chain is strongly optimistic about its prospects. From he point of view, the company's stock price is too low. Yet the company wants to issue shares to financ expansion into the new state of Northern California.[44] What is she to do? All the choices have draw backs. If the chain sells common stock, it will favor new investors at the expense of old shareholder When investors come to share the CFO's optimism, the share price will rise, and the bargain price t the new investors will be evident.

If the CFO could convince investors to accept her rosy view of the future, then new shares could b sold at a fair price. But this is not so easy. CEOs and CFOs always take care to *sound* upbeat, so ju announcing "I'm optimistic" has little effect. But supplying detailed information about business plar and profit forecasts is costly and is also of great assistance to competitors.

---

[44] Northern California seceded from California and became the fifty-second state in 2016.

The CFO could scale back or delay the expansion until the company's stock price recovers. That too is costly, but it may be rational if the stock price is severely undervalued and a stock issue is the only source of financing.

If a CFO knows that the company's stock is *over*valued, the position is reversed. If the firm sells new shares at the high price, it will help existing shareholders at the expense of the new ones. Managers might be prepared to issue stock even if the new cash was just put in the bank.

Of course, investors are not stupid. They can predict that managers are more likely to issue stock when they think it is overvalued and that optimistic managers may cancel or defer issues. Therefore, when an equity issue is announced, they mark down the price of the stock accordingly. Thus the decline in the price of the stock at the time of the new issue may have nothing to do with the increased supply but simply with the information that the issue provides.[45]

Cornett and Tehranian devised a natural experiment that pretty much proves this point.[46] They examined a sample of stock issues by commercial banks. Some of these issues were necessary to meet capital standards set by banking regulators. The rest were ordinary, voluntary stock issues designed to raise money for various corporate purposes. The necessary issues caused a much smaller drop in stock prices than the voluntary ones, which makes perfect sense. If the issue is outside the manager's discretion, announcement of the issue conveys no information about the manager's view of the company's prospects.[47]

Most financial economists now interpret the stock price drop on equity issue announcements as an information effect and not a result of the additional supply.[48] But what about an issue of preferred stock or debt? Are they equally likely to provide information to investors about company prospects? A pessimistic manager might be tempted to get a debt issue out before investors become aware of the bad news, but how much profit can you make for your shareholders by selling overpriced debt? Perhaps 1% or 2%. Investors know that a pessimistic manager has a much greater incentive to issue equity rather than preferred stock or debt. Therefore, when companies announce an issue of preferred or debt, there is a barely perceptible fall in the stock price.[49]

There is, however, at least one puzzle left. As we saw in Chapter 13, it appears that the long-run performance of companies that issue shares is substandard. Investors who bought these companies' shares *after* the stock issue earned lower returns than they would have if they had bought into similar companies. This result holds for both IPOs and seasoned issues.[50] It seems that investors fail to appreciate fully the issuing companies' information advantage. If so, we have an exception to the efficient-market theory.

This explanation was developed in S. C. Myers and N. S. Majluf, "Corporate Financing and Investment Decisions When Firms Have Information That Investors Do Not Have," *Journal of Financial Economics* 35 (1998), pp. 99–122.

M. M. Cornett and H. Tehranian, "An Examination of Voluntary versus Involuntary Issuances by Commercial Banks," *Journal of Financial Economics* 35 (1994), pp. 99–122.

The "involuntary issuers" did make a choice: they could have foregone the stock issue and run the risk of failing to meet the regulatory capital standards. The banks that were more concerned with this risk were more likely to issue. Thus it is no surprise that Cornett and Tehranian found some drop in stock price even for the involuntary issues.

There is another possible information effect. Just as an unexpected increase in the dividend suggests to investors that the company is generating more cash than they thought, the announcement of a new issue may have the reverse implication. However, this effect cannot explain why the announcement of an issue of debt does not result in a similar fall in the stock price.

See L. Shyam-Sunder, "The Stock Price Effect of Risky vs. Safe Debt," *Journal of Financial and Quantitative Analysis* 26 (December 1991), pp. 549–558.

See, for example, T. Loughran and J. R. Ritter, "The New Issues Puzzle," *Journal of Finance* 50 (March 1995), pp. 23–51; and Jay Ritter's web site: **bear.cba.ufl.edu/ritter**.

Rights Issues

Instead of making an issue of stock to investors at large, companies sometimes give their existing shareholders the right of first refusal. In India, when a company wants to make further issue of equity shares, Sec 81 of the Companies Act of India makes it mandatory for the companies to offer the shares to the existing equity shareholders. However, as per Sec 81(1A) of the Companies Act, a company can issue new shares to outsiders to the total exclusion of the existing shareholders, if the company has passed a special resolution to this effect. Alternatively, after passing a general resolution, the Board of Directors of a company can directly appeal to the Central Government and issue additional shares to outsiders. Indian law with regard to rights issue is very similar to the practice followed by the European countries, where seasoned issues of common stock (a non-IPO public issue) must generally be sold by rights. In the United States, however, rights issues are largely confined to closed-end investment companies.

Here is an example of rights issue. In March 2011, Krypton Industries needed to raise ₹109.6 crores of new equity. It did so by offering to its existing shareholders the right to buy 17 shares for every 10 that they currently held. The new shares were prices at ₹15 each (₹10 face value + ₹5 premium per share), some 25 percent below the pre-announcement price of ₹20.

Imagine that you hold 10 shares of Krypton just prior to the rights issue. Your holding is worth ₹200. Krypton gives you the opportunity to buy 17 additional shares for ₹15 each. If you buy the new share, your holding increases to 27 shares, and the value of your holding increases by the extra cash to 200 + (17 × 15) = ₹455. Therefore, after the issue, the value of each share is no longer ₹20 but lower at ₹16.85.

How much is the right to buy each new share for ₹15 worth? The answer is ₹16.85 − ₹15.00 = ₹1.85. An investor who could buy a share worth ₹16.85 for ₹15 would be willing to pay ₹1.85 for the privilege.[51]

It should be clear on reflection that Krypton could have raised the same amount of money on a variety of terms. For example, instead of a 17-for-10 at ₹15, it could have made a 34-for-10 issue at ₹7.5. In this case it would have sold twice as many shares at half the price. If you held 10 shares of Krypton before the issue, you could subscribe for 34 new shares at ₹7.5 each. This could give you 44 shares in total worth 200 + (34 × 7.5) = ₹455. After the issue, the value of each share would be 455/44 = ₹10.34. This is less than in the case of the 17-for-10 issue, but then you would have the compensation of owning 44 rather than 27 shares. Suppose that you wanted to sell your right to buy one new share for ₹7.5. Investors would be prepared to pay you ₹2.84 for this right. They would then pay ₹7.5 to Krypton and receive a share worth ₹10.34.

Our example illustrates that, as long as the company successfully sells the new shares, the issue price in a rights offering is irrelevant. That is not the case in a general cash offer. If the company sells stock to new shareholders for less than the market will bear, the buyer makes a profit at the expense of existing shareholders. General cash offers are typically sold at a small discount of about 3% on the

---

[51] There is a minor, but potentially confusing, difference between U.S. and European rights issues. In the Xstrata issue shareholders were offered two rights for each share held. Each right allowed them to buy one new share. A similar issue in the United States would provide the shareholder with four rights for each share held. However, the shareholder would need two rights to buy one new share and each right would therefore be worth correspondingly less. You may often encounter formulas for the value of a right. Remember to check whether it is referring to a U.S. or a European issue.

previous day's closing price,[52] so underpricing is not a major worry. But, since this cost can be avoided completely by using a rights issue, we are puzzled by the apparent preference of companies for general cash offers.

15-5 PRIVATE PLACEMENTS AND PUBLIC ISSUES

As we saw earlier, public issue of shares is a costly affair. A company could avoid this costly process by selling the securities privately. All private placements are governed by Section 81 (1A) of the Companies Act, SEBI guidelines and RBI Guidelines (in case of private placement of shares with the FIIs). As per the SEBI guidelines, the securities issued under the private placement route will be subject to a 1-year lock-in period from the date of their allotment.[53]

An Indian company can also make what is known as *Qualified Institutions Placement* (private placement of shares with qualified institutional buyers) if its shares are listed on a stock exchange having nation-wide trading terminals and if it has got the prescribed minimum shareholding requirement of the listing agreement.[54] As per the SEBI guidelines, a minimum of 10% of the total issue should be reserved for the mutual funds.

The company should file a placement document (containing all material information regarding the issue) with SEBI within 30 days of the allotment of the securities. As per the SEBI guidelines, if the issue size is less than or equal to ₹250 crores, then there must be at least 2 allottees of the securities. Else the minimum number of allottees is 5.[55] This issue, like a public issue, is also managed by a merchant banker.

One of the drawbacks of a private placement is that the investor cannot easily resell the security. However, institutions such as life insurance companies invest huge amounts in corporate debt for the long haul and are less concerned about its marketability. Consequently, an active private placement market has evolved for corporate debt.

As you would expect, it costs less to arrange a private placement than to make a public issue. This is a particular advantage for companies making smaller issues.

In 1990 the SEC adopted Rule 144A, which relaxed its restrictions on who can buy and trade unregistered securities. The rule allows large financial institutions (known as *qualified institutional buyers*) to trade unregistered securities among themselves. Rule 144A was intended to increase liquidity and reduce interest rates and issue costs for private placements. It was aimed largely at foreign corporations deterred by registration requirements in the United States. The SEC argued that such firms would welcome the opportunity to issue unregistered stocks and bonds that could then be freely traded by large U.S. financial institutions.

Rule 144A issues have proved very popular, particularly with foreign issuers. There has also been an increasing volume of secondary trading in Rule 144A issues.

---

[52] ee S. A. Corwin, "The Determinants of Underpricing for Seasoned Equity Offers," *Journal of Finance* 58 (October 1993), pp. 2249–2279; and S. Mola and T. Loughran, "Discounting and Clustering in Seasoned Equity Offering Price," *Journal of Financial and Quantitative Analysis* 39 (March 2004), pp. 1–23.

[53] If a company makes preferential allotment of shares to the promoters of the company under the private placement route, then the shares shall be subject to a 3-year lock-in period.

[54] This is very similar to Rule 144a of SEC.

[55] In the U.S. the SEC has insisted that the security should be sold to no more than 35 knowledgeable investors.

SUMMARY

In this chapter we have summarized the various procedures for issuing corporate securities. We first looked at how infant companies raise venture capital to carry them through to the point at which they can make their first public issue of stock. We then looked at how companies can make further public issues of securities by a general cash offer. Finally, we reviewed the procedures for a private placement.

It is always difficult to summarize a summary. Instead we will remind you of some of the most important implications for the financial manager who must decide how to raise financing.

- **Larger is cheaper.** There are economies of scale in issuing securities. It is cheaper to go to the market once for $100 million than to make two trips for $50 million each. Consequently firms bunch security issues. That may often mean relying on short-term financing until a large issue is justified. Or it may mean issuing more than is needed at the moment in order to avoid another issue later.
- **Watch out for underpricing.** Underpricing is often a serious hidden cost to the existing shareholders.
- **The winner's curse may be a serious problem with IPOs.** Would-be investors in an initial public offering (IPO) do not know how other investors will value the stock and they worry that they are likely to receive a larger allocation of the overpriced issues. Careful design of issue procedure may reduce the winner's curse.
- **New stock issues may depress the price.** The extent of this price pressure varies, but for industrial issues in the United States the fall in the value of the existing stock may amount to a significant proportion of the money raised. This pressure is due to the information that the market reads into the company's decision to issue stock.
- **Shelf registration often makes sense for debt issues by blue-chip firms.** Shelf registration reduces the time taken to arrange a new issue, it increases flexibility, and it may cut underwriting costs. It seems best suited for debt issues by large firms that are happy to switch between investment banks. It seems less suited for issues of unusually risky or complex securities or for issues by small companies that are likely to benefit from a close relationship with an investment bank.

FURTHER READING

Metrick, Megginson, Gompers, and Gompers and Lerner provide an overview of the venture capital industry, while Sahlman looks at the form of the venture capital contract:

A. Metrick, *Venture Capital and the Finance of Innovation* (New York: John Wiley & Sons, 2006).

W. L. Megginson, "Toward a Global Model of Venture Capital?" *Journal of Applied Corporate Finance* 16 (Winter 2004), pp. 89–107.

P. Gompers, "Venture Capital," in B. E. Eckbo (ed.), *Handbook of Corporate Finance: Empirical Corporate Finance* (Amsterdam: Elsevier/North Holland, 2007).

P. Gompers and J. Lerner, "The Venture Capital Revolution," *Journal of Economic Perspectives* 15 (Spring 2001), pp. 145–168.

W. A. Sahlman, "Aspects of Financial Contracting in Venture Capital," *Journal of Applied Corporate Finance* (Summer 1988), pp. 23–26.

Here are four comprehensive surveys of the literature on new issues:

B. E. Eckbo, R. W. Masulis, and Ø. Norli, "Security Offerings: A Survey," in B. E. Eckbo (ed.), *Handbook of Corporate Finance: Empirical Corporate Finance* (Amsterdam: Elsevier/North-Holland, 2007).

A. P. Ljungqvist, "IPO Underpricing," in B. E. Eckbo (ed.), *Handbook of Corporate Finance: Empirical Corporate Finance* (Amsterdam: Elsevier/North-Holland, 2007).

J. R. Ritter, "Investment Banking and Securities Issuance," in G. M. Constantinides, M. Harris, and R. Stulz (eds.), *Handbook of the Economics of Finance* (Amsterdam: Elsevier Science, 2003).

T. Jenkinson and A. P. Ljungqvist, *Going Public: The Theory and Evidence on How Companies Raise Equity Finance,* 2nd ed. (Oxford: Oxford University Press, 2001).

Two useful articles on IPOs are:

R. G. Ibbotson, J. L. Sindelar, and J. R. Ritter, "The Market's Problems with the Pricing of Initial Public Offerings," *Journal of Applied Corporate Finance* 7 (Spring 1994), pp. 66–74.

L. M. Benveniste and W. J. Wilhelm, Jr., "Initial Public Offerings: Going by the Book," *Journal of Applied Corporate Finance* 10 (Spring 1997) pp. 98–108.

A useful introduction to the design of auctions is:

P. Milgrom, "Auctions and Bidding: A Primer," *Journal of Economic Perspectives* 2 (1989), pp. 3–22.

PROBLEM SETS

BASIC

1. After each of the following issue methods we have listed two types of issue. Choose the one more likely to employ that method.
   a. Rights issue (*initial public offer/further sale of an already publicly traded stock*)
   b. Rule 144A issue (*international bond issue/U.S. bond issue by a foreign corporation*)
   c. Private placement (*issue of existing stock/bond issue by an industrial company*)
   d. Shelf registration (*initial public offer/bond issue by a large financial institution*)

2. Each of the following terms is associated with one of the events beneath. Can you match them up?
   a. Bookbuilding
   b. Shelf registration
   c. Rule 144A
   Events:
   A. Investors indicate to the underwriter how many shares they would like to buy in a new issue and these indications are used to help set the price.
   B. Some issues are not registered but can be traded freely among qualified institutional buyers.
   C. Several tranches of the same security may be sold under the same registration. (A "tranche" is a batch, a fraction of a larger issue.)

3. Explain what each of the following terms or phrases means:
   a. Venture capital
   b. Book building
   c. Underwriting spread
   d. Winner's curse

4. For each of the following pairs of issues, which is likely to involve the lower proportionate underwriting and administrative costs?
   a. A large issue/a small issue.
   b. A bond issue/a common stock issue.
   c. Initial public offering/subsequent issue of stock.
   d. A small private placement of bonds/a small general cash offer of bonds.

5. True or false?
   a. Venture capitalists typically provide first-stage financing sufficient to cover all development expenses. Second-stage financing is provided by stock issued in an IPO.
   b. Underpricing in an IPO is only a problem when the original investors are selling part of their holdings.

c. Stock price generally falls when the company announces a new issue of shares. This is attributable to the information released by the decision to issue.

6. You need to choose between making a public offering and arranging a private placement. In each case the issue involves ₹10 million face value of 10-year debt. You have the following data for each:

   • *A public issue:* The interest rate on the debt would be 8.5%, and the debt would be issued at face value. The underwriting spread would be 1.5%, and other expenses would be ₹80,000.

   • *A private placement:* The interest rate on the private placement would be 9%, but the total issuing expenses would be only ₹30,000.

   a. What is the difference in the proceeds to the company net of expenses?
   b. Other things being equal, which is the better deal?
   c. What other factors beyond the interest rate and issue costs would you wish to consider before deciding between the two offers?

7. Associated Breweries is planning to market unleaded beer. To finance the venture it proposes to make a rights issue at ₹10 of one new share for each two shares held. (The company currently has outstanding 100,000 shares priced at ₹40 a share.) Assuming that the new money is invested to earn a fair return, give values for the following:

   a. Number of new shares.
   b. Amount of new investment.
   c. Total value of company after issue.
   d. Total number of shares after issue.
   e. Stock price after the issue.
   f. Price of the right to buy one new share.

INTERMEDIATE

8. Here is a further vocabulary quiz. Briefly explain each of the following:

   a. Zero-stage vs. first- or second-stage financing.
   b. Carried interest.
   c. Rights issue.
   d. Road show.
   e. Best-efforts offer.
   f. Qualified institutional buyer.
   g. Greenshoe option.

9. a. "A signal is credible only if it is costly." Explain why management's willingness to invest in Marvin's equity was a credible signal. Was its willingness to accept only part of the venture capital that would eventually be needed also a credible signal?

   b. "When managers take their reward in the form of increased leisure or executive jets, the cost is borne by the shareholders." Explain how First Meriam's financing package tackled this problem.

10. In some U.K. IPOs any investor may be able to apply to buy shares. Mr. Bean has observed that on average these stocks are underpriced by about 9% and for some years has followed a policy of applying for a constant proportion of each issue. He is therefore disappointed and puzzled to find that this policy has not resulted in a profit. Explain to him why this is so.

11. Why are the costs of debt issues less than those of equity issues? List the possible reasons.

12. There are three reasons that a common stock issue might cause a fall in price: (a) the price fall is needed to absorb the extra supply, (b) the issue causes temporary price pressure until it has been

digested, and (c) management has information that stockholders do not have. Explain these reasons more fully. Which do you find most plausible? Is there any way that you could seek to test whether you are right?

13. Construct a simple example to show the following:
    a. Existing shareholders are made worse off when a company makes a cash offer of new stock below the market price.
    b. Existing shareholders are not made worse off when a company makes a rights issue of new stock below the market price even if the new stockholders do not wish to take up their rights.

14. In 2001 the Pandora Box Company made a rights issue at ₹5 a share of one new share for every four shares held. Before the issue there were 10 million shares outstanding and the share price was ₹6.
    a. What was the total amount of new money raised?
    b. What was the value of the right to buy one new share?
    c. What was the prospective stock price after the issue?
    d. How far could the total value of the company fall before shareholders would be unwilling to take up their rights?

15. Problem 14 contains details of a rights offering by Pandora Box. Suppose that the company had decided to issue new stock at ₹4. How many new shares would it have needed to sell to raise the same sum of money? Recalculate the answers to questions (b) to (d) in Problem 14. Show that the shareholders are just as well off if the company issues the shares at ₹4 rather than ₹5.

16. Suppose that instead of having a rights issue of new stock at ₹4 (see Problem 15), Pandora decided to make a general cash offer at ₹4. Would existing shareholders still be just as well off? Explain.

17. Refer to the Marvin Prospectus Appendix at the end of this chapter to answer the following questions.
    a. If there is unexpectedly heavy demand for the issue, how many extra shares can the underwriter buy?
    b. How many shares are to be sold in the primary offering? How many will be sold in the secondary offering?
    c. One day post-IPO, Marvin shares traded at $105. What was the degree of underpricing? How does that compare with the average degree of underpricing for IPOs in the United States?
    d. There are three kinds of cost to Marvin's new issue—underwriting expense, administrative costs, and underpricing. What was the *total* dollar cost of the Marvin issue?
    e. Suppose that the management of Marvin want to issue Indian Depository Receipts (IDRs) in India rather than in the U.S.[56] What are the differences in the public issue procedures between India and U.S.? Do you think it has made any difference to Marvin?

18. Find the prospectus for a recent Indian IPO. How do the issue costs compare with those shown in Table 15.3? Can you suggest reasons for the differences?

CHALLENGE

19. a. Why do venture capital companies prefer to advance money in stages? If you were the management of Marvin Enterprises, would you have been happy with such an arrangement? With the benefit of hindsight did First Meriam gain or lose by advancing money in stages?
    b. The price at which First Meriam would invest more money in Marvin was not fixed in advance. But Marvin could have given First Meriam an *option* to buy more shares at a preset price. Would this have been better?
    c. At the second stage Marvin could have tried to raise money from another venture capital company in preference to First Meriam. To protect themselves against this, venture capital firms sometimes demand first refusal on new capital issues. Would you recommend this arrangement?

---

[56] Visit www.sebi.gov.in to know the details of IDR issue.

20. Explain the difference between a uniform-price auction and a discriminatory auction. Why might you prefer to sell securities by one method rather than another?

21. Here is recent financial data on Pisa Construction, Inc.

Stock price	₹40	Market value of firm	₹400,000
Number of shares	10,000	Earnings per share	₹4
Book net worth	₹500,000	Return on investment	8%

Pisa has not performed spectacularly to date. However, it wishes to issue new shares to obtain ₹80,000 to finance expansion into a promising market. Pisa's financial advisers think a stock issue is a poor choice because, among other reasons, "sale of stock at a price below book value per share can only depress the stock price and decrease shareholders' wealth." To prove the point they construct the following example: "Suppose 2,000 new shares are issued at ₹40 and the proceeds are invested. (Neglect issue costs.) Suppose return on investment does not change. Then

Book net worth = ₹580,000

Total earnings = .08(580,000) = ₹46,400

Earnings per share = $\frac{46,400}{12,000}$ = ₹3.87

Thus, EPS declines, book value per share declines, and share price will decline proportionally to ₹38.70."

Evaluate this argument with particular attention to the assumptions implicit in the numerical example.

Look up a recent IPO on www.sebi.gov.in. Download the final prospectus from the site. Compare the IPO with that of Marvin. For example, Who were the existing shareholders? Was the company raising more capital or were existing shareholders selling? Were existing shareholders prevented by a lock-up agreement from selling more shares? How did the underwriting and other costs compare with those of Marvin? Did the underwriters have a greenshoe option? Did the issue turn out to be underpriced? (The Yahoo! Web site should help here.) If so, how much money was left on the table?

APPENDIX

MARVIN'S NEW-ISSUE PROSPECTUS[57]

PROSPECTUS
900,000 Shares
Marvin Enterprises Inc.
Common Stock ($.10 par value)

Of the 900,000 shares of Common Stock offered hereby, 500,000 shares are being sold by the Company and 400,000 shares are being sold by the Selling Stockholders. See "Principal and Selling Stockholders." The Company will not receive any of the proceeds from the sale of shares by the Selling Stockholders.

Before this offering there has been no public market for the Common Stock. **These securities involve a high degree of risk. See "Certain Considerations."**

THESE SECURITIES HAVE NOT BEEN APPROVED OR DISAPPROVED BY THE SECURITIES AND EXCHANGE COMMISSION NOR HAS THE COMMISSION PASSED ON THE ACCURACY OR ADEQUACY OF THIS PROSPECTUS. ANY REPRESENTATION TO THE CONTRARY IS A CRIMINAL OFFENSE.

	Price to Public	Underwriting Discount	Proceeds to Company[1]	Proceeds to Selling Stockholders[1]
Per share	$80.00	$5.60	$74.40	$74.40
Total[2]	$72,000,000	$5,040,000	$37,200,000	$29,760,000

[1] Before deducting expenses payable by the Company estimated at $820,000, of which $455,555 will be paid by the Company and $364,445 will be paid by the Selling Stockholders.

[2] The Company and the selling shareholders have granted to the Underwriters an option to purchase up to an additional 135,000 shares at the initial public offering price, less the underwriting discount, solely to cover overallotment.

The Common Stock is offered subject to receipt and acceptance by the Underwriters, to prior sale, and to the Underwriters' right to reject any order in whole or in part and to withdraw, cancel, or modify the offer without notice.

Klein Merrick Inc.   February 3, 2028

No person has been authorized to give any information or to make any representations, other than as contained therein, in connection with the offer contained in this Prospectus, and, if given or made, such information or representations must not be relied upon. This Prospectus does not constitute an offer of any securities other than the registered securities to which it relates or an offer to any person in any jurisdiction where such an offer would be unlawful. The delivery of this Prospectus at any time does not imply that information herein is correct as of any time subsequent to its date.

IN CONNECTION WITH THIS OFFERING, THE UNDERWRITERS MAY OVERALLOT OR EFFECT TRANSACTIONS WHICH STABILIZE OR MAINTAIN THE MARKET PRICE OF THE COMMON STOCK OF THE COMPANY AT A LEVEL ABOVE THAT WHICH MIGHT OTHERWISE PREVAIL IN THE OPEN MARKET. SUCH STABILIZING, IF COMMENCED, MAY BE DISCONTINUED AT ANY TIME.

---

[57] Most prospectuses have content similar to that of the Marvin prospectus but go into considerably more detail. Also we have omitted Marvin's financial statements.

Prospectus Summary

The following summary information is qualified in its entirety by the detailed information and financial statements appearing elsewhere in this Prospectus.

The Offering

Common Stock offered by the Company ....500,000 shares

Common Stock offered by the Selling Stockholders ....400,000 shares

Common Stock to be outstanding after this offering..4,100,000 shares

Use of Proceeds

For the construction of new manufacturing facilities and to provide working capital.

The Company

Marvin Enterprises Inc. designs, manufactures, and markets gargle blasters for domestic use. Its manufacturing facilities employ integrated nanocircuits to control the genetic engineering processes used to manufacture gargle blasters.

The Company was organized in Delaware in 2022.

Use of Proceeds

The net proceeds of this offering are expected to be $36,744,445. Of the net proceeds, approximately $27.0 million will be used to finance expansion of the Company's principal manufacturing facilities. The balance will be used for working capital.

Certain Considerations

Investment in the Common Stock involves a high degree of risk. The following factors should be carefully considered in evaluating the Company:

Substantial Capital Needs The Company will require additional financing to continue its expansion policy. The Company believes that its relations with its lenders are good, but there can be no assurance that additional financing will be available in the future.

Licensing The expanded manufacturing facilities are to be used for the production of a new imploding gargle blaster. An advisory panel to the U.S. Food and Drug Administration (FDA) has recommended approval of this product for the U.S. market but no decision has yet been reached by the full FDA committee.

Dividend Policy

The company has not paid cash dividends on its Common Stock and does not anticipate that dividends will be paid on the Common Stock in the foreseeable future.

Management

The following table sets forth information regarding the Company's directors, executive officers, and key employees.

Name	Age	Position
George Marvin	32	President, Chief Executive Officer, & Director
Mildred Marvin	28	Treasurer & Director
Chip Norton	30	General Manager

George Marvin—George Marvin established the Company in 2022 and has been its Chief Executive Officer since that date. He is a past president of the Institute of Gargle Blasters and has recently been inducted into the Confrérie des Gargarisateurs.

Mildred Marvin—Mildred Marvin has been employed by the Company since 2022.

Chip Norton—Mr. Norton has been General Manager of the Company since 2022. He is a former vice-president of Amalgamated Blasters, Inc.

Executive Compensation

The following table sets forth the cash compensation paid for services rendered for the year 2027 by the executive officers:

Name	Capacity	Cash Compensation
George Marvin	President and Chief Executive Officer	$300,000
Mildred Marvin	Treasurer	220,000
Chip Norton	General Manager	220,000

Certain Transactions

At various times between 2023 and 2026 First Meriam Venture Partners invested a total of $8.5 million in the Company. In connection with this investment, First Meriam Venture Partners was granted certain rights to registration under the Securities Act of 1933, including the right to have their shares of Common Stock registered at the Company's expense with the Securities and Exchange Commission.

Principal and Selling Stockholders

The following table sets forth certain information regarding the beneficial ownership of the Company's voting Common Stock as of the date of this prospectus by (i) each person known by the Company to be the beneficial owner of more than 5 percent of its voting Common Stock, and (ii) each director of the Company who beneficially owns voting Common Stock. Unless otherwise indicated, each owner has sole voting and dispositive power over his or her shares.

	Common Stock				
	Shares Beneficially Owned Prior to Offering			Shares Beneficially Owned After Offer[1]	
Name of Beneficial Owner	Number	Percent	Shares to Be Sold	Number	Percent
George Marvin	375,000	10.4	60,000	315,000	7.7
Mildred Marvin	375,000	10.4	60,000	315,000	7.7
Chip Norton	250,000	6.9	80,000	170,000	4.1
First Meriam Venture Partners	1,700,000	47.2	—	1,700,000	41.5
TFS Investors	260,000	7.2	—	260,000	6.3
Centri-Venture Partnership	260,000	7.2	—	260,000	6.3
Henry Pobble	180,000	5.0	—	180,000	4.4
Georgina Sloberg	200,000	5.6	200,000	—	—

[1] Assuming no exercise of the Underwriters' overallotment option.

Lock-up Agreements

The holders of the common stock have agreed with the underwriters not to sell, pledge, or otherwise dispose of their shares, other than as specified in this prospectus, for a period of 180 days after the date of the prospectus without the prior consent of Klein Merrick.

Description of Capital Stock

The Company's authorized capital stock consists of 10,000,000 shares of voting Common Stock.

As of the date of this Prospectus, there are 10 holders of record of the Common Stock.

Under the terms of one of the Company's loan agreements, the Company may not pay cash dividends on Common Stock except from net profits without the written consent of the lender.

Underwriting

Subject to the terms and conditions set forth in the Underwriting Agreement, the Company has agreed to sell to each of the Underwriters named below, and each of the Underwriters, for whom Klein Merrick Inc. are acting as Representatives, has severally agreed to purchase from the Company, the number of shares set forth opposite its name below.

Underwriters	Number of Shares to Be Purchased
Klein Merrick, Inc.	300,000
Goldman Stanley	300,000
Medici Bank	100,000
Canary Wharf Securities	100,000
Bank of New England	100,000

In the Underwriting Agreement, the several Underwriters have agreed, subject to the terms and conditions set forth therein, to purchase all shares offered hereby if any such shares are purchased. In the event of a default by any Underwriter, the Underwriting Agreement provides that, in certain circumstances, purchase commitments of the nondefaulting Underwriters may be increased or the Underwriting Agreement may be terminated.

There is no public market for the Common Stock. The price to the public for the Common Stock was determined by negotiation between the Company and the Underwriters and was based on, among other things, the Company's financial and operating history and condition, its prospects and the prospects for its industry in general, the management of the Company, and the market prices of securities for companies in businesses similar to that of the Company.

Legal Matters

The validity of the shares of Common Stock offered by the Prospectus is being passed on for the Company by Dodson and Fogg and for the Underwriters by Kenge and Carboy.

Experts

The consolidated financial statements of the Company have been so included in reliance on the reports of Hooper Firebrand, independent accountants, given on the authority of that firm as experts in auditing and accounting.

Financial Statements

[*Text and tables omitted.*]

16

CHAPTER

PAYOUT POLICY

Corporations can return cash to their shareholders by paying a dividend or by repurchasing shares. In this chapter we explain how financial managers decide on the amount and form of payout, and we discuss the controversial question of how payout policy affects shareholder value.

Suppose you own stock in a corporation that has ₹1 per share of unneeded cash. It can hold on to the cash or it can pay an extra cash dividend of ₹1 per share. Does the decision matter? Your first instinct should be to say no. The dividend puts ₹1 per share in your pocket but, at the same time, each share should be worth ₹1 less. Your wealth should be unaffected.

But corporations usually hold cash for a reason. What if that ₹1 per share is not redundant money? Suppose that it was set aside for capital investment. Then paying the extra dividend could mean cancelation of investment projects. The payout decision could also be an investment decision.

Suppose the firm pays out ₹1 per share, but replaces the cash by borrowing. Then the payout decision would also be a borrowing decision.

To fully understand payout policy, we must separate payout decisions from investment and borrowing decisions. If we hold investment and borrowing fixed, changes in cash dividends must be offset by issues or retirements of shares. For example, a company might pay generous cash dividends, knowing that it will have to schedule stock issues to raise cash for investment. Another company might pay no dividends, but instead use cash to repurchase shares.

Therefore we will take care to analyze the trade-off between higher or lower cash dividends and the issue or repurchase of common stock. The trade-off is more interesting than you might at first think, for at least three reasons. First, changes in dividends convey information about the firm's profitability to investors. Second, dividends in most countries are taxed at higher rates than capital gains. In India, the dividend distribution tax rate is higher the long-term capital gains tax rate (which in most cases is zero). Third, investors worry that cash-cow corporations will run out of positive-NPV investments and waste cash on perks or poor projects. Generous cash payouts are one way of relieving such worries.

We start the chapter with facts about payout and a description of how dividends and repurchases happen.

16-1 FACTS ABOUT PAYOUT

Corporations can pay out cash to their shareholders in two ways. They can pay a dividend or they can buy back some of the outstanding shares. In recent years dividend payments and stock repurchases have amounted to a high proportion of earnings.

Although dividends remain the principal channel for returning cash to shareholders, many corporations pay no dividends at all. Till 1998, dividends were the principal way that corporate India returned cash to shareholders. Dividends continue to remain as the pre-dominant form of cash distribution even after share buybacks were legalized in India. Nevertheless, Reddy (2002) finds that only about a third of companies paid dividends in India in 2001. Some of the remainder had paid dividends in the past, but they fell on hard times and were forced to conserve cash. A large part of the non-dividend paying companies never paid any dividends. According to Reddy, 34 percent of the companies in his sample never paid any dividends. The percentage of dividend-paying firms in India fell from 24% in 2001 to almost 16% in 2009 before increasing to 19% in 2010[1]. In the U.S., some of the growth companies like Sun Microsystems, Cisco, and Oracle do not pay any dividends and invest their total profit in the business itself.

Figure 16.1 shows that, before 2004 stock repurchases were fairly rare, but since then have become somewhat common. Indian companies were allowed to buyback shares from 1998[2]. In 2011, a total of 9 companies went ahead with buyback of shares. Among them were Amrutanjan Health Care (₹9.6 crores), Piramal Healthcare (₹2508 crores), and Lakshmi Machine Works (₹225.5 crores). Once the Board of Directors approves the company's decision to buyback shares, the companies inform SEBI of the decision. However, it is always possible that the company does not actually buy back any share even after filing a copy of the resolution passed by the Board with SEBI. Reliance Energy wanted to buyback shares worth ₹350 crores at a maximum share price of ₹525 each and informed SEBI of its decision on 16 June 2004. However, on 27 June 2005, it informed SEBI that during the buyback period it did not buyback any share.

16-2 DIVIDEND PAYMENTS AND STOCK REPURCHASES

Before we look at the choice between dividends and stock repurchases, we need to review how these payments to shareholders take place.

---

[1] The proportion of dividend payers among U.S. industrial companies is even lower. See E. Fama and K. French, "Disappearing Dividends: Changing Firm Characteristics or Lower Propensity to Pay?" *Journal of Financial Economics* 60 (2001), pp. 3–43. In Europe the decline in the proportion of dividend payers has been particularly marked in Germany. See D. J. Denis and I. Osobov, "Why Do Firms Pay Dividends? International Evidence on the Determinants of Dividend Policy," *Journal of Financial Economics* 89 (July 2008), pp. 62–82.

[2] Share Buyback in India is regulated by Sec 77A, 77AA, and 77B of the Companies Act and SEBI (Buy-Back of Securities) Regulations, 1998. The three sections in the Companies Act were inserted by the Companies (Amendment) Act in 1999 and apply with retrospective effect from 31 October, 1998.

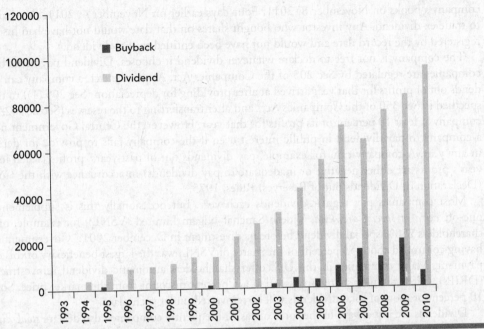

FIGURE 16.1

Dividends and stock repurchases in India 1993–2010 (figures in ₹ crores).

Source: Prowess Database of CMIE.

How Dividends are Paid

A company's dividend is set by the board of directors. The announcement of the dividend states that the payment will be made to all stockholders who are registered on a particular *record date*. Then a week or so later dividend checks are mailed to stockholders. Stocks are normally bought or sold *with dividend* (or *cum dividend*) until two business days before the record date, and then they trade *ex dividend*. If you buy stock on the ex-dividend date, your purchase will not be entered on the company's books before the record date and you will not be entitled to the dividend.

Figure 16.2 illustrates this sequence of events. On October 31, 2011, the Board of Directors of Hindustan Unilever Limited (HUL) declared an interim dividend of ₹3.50 per share. The dividend was credited on November 22, 2011 to the account of all shareholders who were registered on the

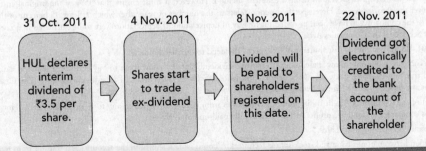

FIGURE 16.2

An illustration of how dividends are paid.

company's books on November 8, 2011. Four days earlier on November 4, 2011, the shares began to trade ex-dividend. Any investor who bought shares on that date would not have had his purchase registered by the record date and would not have been entitled to that dividend.

The company is not free to declare whatever dividend it chooses. Dividend payments by Indian companies are regulated by Sec 205 of the Companies Act. As per the Act, a company can pay dividends out of profits for that year arrived at after providing for depreciation (Sec 205 (1)) to the extent specified in Sec 350 of the Companies Act[3] and after transferring to the reserves (Sec 205 (2A)) of the company at least 10 percent of its profits for that year. However, the Central Government may allow a company to pay dividend in public interest even if the company fails to provide for depreciation in any year. A company can, for example, pay dividends out of past years' profits (when its current year's profits are either negative or inadequate to pay dividends) in accordance with the Companies (Declaration of Dividends out of Reserves) Rules, 1975.

Most companies pay regular dividends each year, but occasionally this is supplemented by a one-off *extra* or *special dividend*. Videsh Sanchar Nigam Limited (VSNL), for example, offered its shareholders 750% special dividend before its divestment in December 2001.[4] Government of India, having controlled about 53 percent of the shares of VSNL, was the largest beneficiary of this dividend payment. Many companies in the U.S. offer shareholders automatic dividend reinvestment plans (DRIPs). Often the new shares are issued at a 5 percent discount from the market price. Sometimes 10 percent or more of total dividends will be reinvested under such plans.[5]

Dividends are not always in the form of cash[6]. Frequently companies also declare *stock dividends*[7]. For example, if a company announces a 1:2 bonus issue (50% stock dividends), it sends each shareholder 1 extra share for every 2 shares currently held. Practically a bonus issue is equivalent to a stock split. Both increase the number of shares but do not affect the company's assets, profits, or total value. So, both reduce value *per share*[8]. Our focus in this chapter will be on cash dividends.

Importance of Bonus Issues in India

Bonus issues (stock dividends) used to play a vital role in India. Prior to April 2009, Indian companies used to declare dividend as a percentage of the face value per share. Thus, for example, companies used to announce 100% dividend when they were in fact paying ₹2 per share as dividend on a stock with a face value of ₹2. Mohanty finds that Indian companies do not reduce the dividend rate proportionately after the bonus issues[9]. During the 1982-96 sample period, only 9 percent of the companies reduced the dividend proportionately (or more than proportionately) after a bonus issue. In the remaining 91 percent of the cases, the shareholders received higher dividends from the companies.

---

[3] A company can also charge depreciation using a different method. However, it must ensure that 95% of the original cost of the asset is depreciated over the *specified period*. Here, specified period refers to the number of years after which at least 95 percent of the original cost of that asset to the company will have been provided for by way of depreciation, if depreciation were to be calculated in accordance with the provisions of Sec 350 of the Companies Act.

[4] IN July 2001, VSNL had already distributed a 400% special dividend to the shareholders.

[5] Sometimes companies not only allow shareholders to reinvest dividends but also allow them to buy additional shares at a discount. For an amusing and true rags-to-riches story, see M. S. Scholes and M. A. Wolfson, "Decentralized Investment Banking: The Case of Dividend-Reinvestment and Stock-Purchase Plans," *Journal of Financial Economics* 24 (September 1989), pp. 7–36.

[6] Sec 205 (3) of the Companies Act in India prohibits companies from paying dividends in any form other than cash. However, the same section allows companies to capitalize profits and reserves as fully paid-up bonus shares.

[7] This is the same as issue of bonus shares.

[8] The distinction between bonus issue and stock split is technical. A bonus issue is shown in the accounts as a transfer from retained earnings to share capital, whereas a split is shown as a reduction in the par value of each share.

[9] Mohanty, P., 1999, Dividend and Bonus Policies of Indian Companies: An Analysis, Vikalpa, pp 35-42.

In April 2009, SEBI made it mandatory for the Indian companies to announce the dividend on a per share basis.

How Firms Repurchase (Buyback) Stock

Instead of paying a dividend to its stockholders, the firm can use the cash to repurchase stock. As per SEBI (Buyback of Securities) Regulations, 1998, a company can buyback its shares by the tender offer (on a proportionate basis), from open market either through the bookbuilding process or stock exchanges, or from odd-lot holders. Companies in India mostly use the open market route to buyback shares. Out of the 160 buyback offers made by the Indian companies during 2004-11 (for which information is available in the website of SEBI), only 67 offers are tender offers. The remaining 93 offers have been made through the open market route. In the U.S., a company is also allowed to buy back shares by employing Dutch auction. In this case, the firm states a series of prices at which it is prepared to repurchase stock.

Shareholders submit offers declaring how many shares they wish to sell at each price and the company calculates the lowest price at which it can buy the desired number of shares.[10] A company cannot buyback shares through negotiated deals. However, in the U.S., a company can buyback shares by direct negotiation with a major shareholder.

16-3 HOW DO COMPANIES DECIDE ON PAYOUTS?

In 2004 a survey of senior executives asked about their firms' dividend policies.[11] Figure 16.3 paraphrases the executives' responses. Three features stand out:

1. Managers are reluctant to make dividend changes that may have to be reversed. They are particularly worried about having to rescind a dividend increase and, if necessary, would choose to raise new funds to maintain the payout.
2. To avoid the risk of a reduction in payout, managers "smooth" dividends. Consequently, dividend changes follow shifts in long-run sustainable earnings. Transitory earnings changes are unlikely to affect dividend payouts.
3. Managers focus more on dividend changes than on absolute levels. Thus paying a $2.00 dividend is an important financial decision if last year's dividend was $1.00, but no big deal if last year's dividend was $2.00.

While stock repurchases are like bumper dividends, they do not typically *substitute* for dividends. Over 98% of the companies in India that repurchased stocks in 2004–2011 also paid dividends. Firms are likely to buyback stock when they have accumulated a large amount of unwanted cash or wish to change their capital structure by replacing equity with debt.

Unlike a stock repurchase, dividends are not regarded as an appropriate way to pay out transitory earnings. Therefore, many firms that repurchase stock would not contemplate using the cash to raise the dividend and so incur a commitment to maintain the payout.[12]

---

[10] This is another example of the uniform-price auction described in Section 15.3.

[11] See A. Brav, J. R. Graham, C. R. Harvey, and R. Michaely, "Payout Policy in the 21st Century," *Journal of Financial Economics* 77 (September 2005), pp. 483–527. This paper revisits an earlier classic series of interviews on dividend policy described in J. Lintner, "Distribution of Incomes of Corporations among Dividends, Retained Earnings, and Taxes," *American Economic Review* 46 (May 1956), pp. 97–113.

[12] See, for example, R. Dittmar and A. Dittmar, "Stock Repurchase Waves: An Examination of the Trends in Aggregate Corporate Payout Policy," working paper, University of Michigan at Ann Arbor, February 2004.

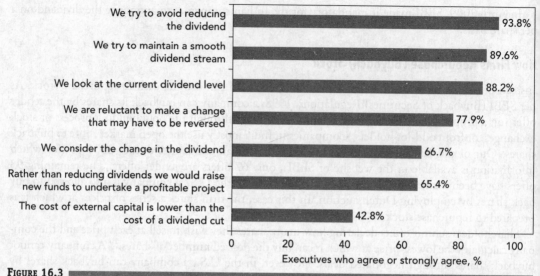

FIGURE 16.3

A 2004 survey of financial executives suggested that their firms were reluctant to cut the dividend and tried to maintain a smooth series of payments.

Source: A. Brav, J. R. Graham, C. R. Harvey, and R. Michaely, "Payout Policy in the 21st Century," *Journal of Financial Economics* 77 (September 2005), pp. 483–527. © 2005 Elsevier Science, used with permission.

Given these differences in the way that dividends and repurchases are used, it is not surprising to find that repurchases are much more volatile than dividends. Repurchases generally mushroom during boom times as firms accumulate excess cash but wither in recessions.

Until recently many countries (just like India) banned or severely restricted the use of stock repurchases. As a result, firms that had amassed large amounts of cash were tempted to invest it at very low rates of return rather than hand it back to shareholders, who could have reinvested it in firms that were short of cash. But many of these limitations have now been removed. For example, Japan permitted repurchases in 1995 and Sweden in 2000, while Germany relaxed its restrictions in 1998.[13] Many multinational giants now repurchase huge amounts of stock. For example, in 2007 the Spanish bank BBVA, BP, Royal Dutch Shell, and Glaxo Smith Kline all spent huge sums on buying back their stock.

16-4 THE INFORMATION IN DIVIDENDS AND STOCK REPURCHASES

In some countries you cannot rely on the information that companies provide. Passion for secrecy and a tendency to construct multilayered corporate organizations produce asset and earnings figures that are next to meaningless.

How does an investor in such a world separate marginally profitable firms from the real money makers? One clue is dividends. Investors can't read managers' minds, but they can learn from managers' actions. They know that a firm that reports good earnings and pays a generous dividend is putting its

---

[13] For a survey of repurchase practices in different countries, see International Organization of Securities Commissions (IOSCO), "Report on Stock Repurchase Programs," February 2004, www.iosco.org.

money where its mouth is. We can understand, therefore, why investors would value the *information content of dividends* and would refuse to believe a firm's reported earnings unless they were backed up by an appropriate dividend policy.

Of course, firms can cheat in the short run by overstating earnings and scraping up cash to pay a generous dividend. But it is hard to cheat in the long run, for a firm that is not making enough money will not have enough cash to pay out. If a firm chooses a high dividend payout without the cash flow to back it up, that firm will ultimately have to reduce its investment plans or turn to investors for additional debt or equity financing. All of these consequences are costly. Therefore, most managers don't increase dividends until they are confident that sufficient cash will flow in to pay them.

Do dividend changes convey information about future as well as current profitability to predict future earnings? Reddy finds that Indian companies that paid dividends for the first time in four years, had positive and increasing past earnings. These companies also experienced 216 percent growth in standardized earnings in the year the dividend was paid. Healey and Palepu similarly find that companies in the U.S. that paid dividends for the first time, experience an increase of 43 percent earnings growth in the year a dividend was paid. If management thought that this was a temporary windfall, they might have been cautious about committing themselves to paying out cash. But it looks as if these managers had good reason to be confident about prospects, for earnings continued to rise in the following years.[14]

Investors certainly appear to take comfort from an increase in dividends. When the increase is announced, analysts generally up their forecast of the current year's earnings.[15] It is no surprise, therefore, to find that a higher dividend prompts a rise in the stock price, whereas a dividend cut results in a fall in price. For example, in the case of the dividend initiations studied by Healy and Palepu, the dividend announcement resulted in a 4% stock-price increase on average.[16]

Notice that investors do not get excited about the *level* of a company's dividend; they worry about the *change*, which they view as an important indicator of the sustainability of earnings.

It seems that in some other countries investors are less preoccupied with dividend changes. For example, in Japan there is a much closer relationship between corporations and major stockholders, and therefore information may be more easily shared with investors. Consequently, Japanese corporations are more prone to cut their dividends when there is a drop in earnings, but investors do not mark the stocks down as sharply as in the U.S.[17]

Do not assume that all dividend cuts are bad news, however. The nearby box explains how investors endorsed a drastic dividend cut announced in 2009 by J.P. Morgan.

The Information Content of Share Repurchases

Share repurchases, like dividends, are a way to hand cash back to shareholders. But unlike dividends, share repurchases are frequently a one-off event. So a company that announces a repurchase program is

---

[14] P. Healy and K. Palepu, "Earnings Information Conveyed by Dividend Initiations and Omissions," *Journal of Financial Economics* 21 (1988), pp. 149–175. For an example of a study that finds no information in dividend changes, see G. Grullon, R. Michaely, and B. Swaminathan, "Are Dividend Changes a Sign of Firm Maturity?" *Journal of Business* 75 (July 2002), pp. 387–424.

[15] A. R. Ofer and D. R. Siegel, "Corporate Financial Policy, Information, and Market Expectations: An Empirical Investigation of Dividends," *Journal of Finance* 42 (September 1987), pp. 889–911.

[16] The 4% average return was adjusted for market returns. Healy and Palepu also looked at companies that *stopped* paying a dividend. In this case the stock price on average declined by 9.5% on the announcement and earnings fell over the next four quarters.

[17] The dividend policies of Japanese *keiretsus* are analyzed in K. L. Dewenter and V. A. Warther, "Dividends, Asymmetric Information, and Agency Conflicts: Evidence from a Comparison of the Dividend Policies of Japanese and U.S. Firms," *Journal of Finance* 53 (June 1998), pp. 879–904.

Finance In Practice

Good News: J.P. Morgan Cuts Its Dividend to a Nickel

On February 23, 2009, J.P. Morgan cut its quarterly dividend from 38¢ to a nickel (5¢) per share. The cut was a surprise to investors, but the bank's share price *increased* by about 5%.

Usually dividend cuts or omissions are bad news, because investors infer trouble. Investors take the cut as a signal of a cash or earnings shortfall—and they are usually right. Managers know that cuts will be treated as bad news, so they usually put off cuts until enough bad news accumulates to force them to act. For example, General Motors, which lost $39 billion in 2007 and $31 billion in 2008, continued paying quarterly dividends of 25¢ per share until June 2008, when it cut its dividend to zero.

J.P. Morgan Chase, however, acted from a position of relative strength. It remained profitable when other large U.S. banks were announcing horrific losses. Its CEO James Dimon explained that the dividend cut would save $5 billion a year and prepare it for a worst-case recession. It would also "put the bank in a position to pay back more quickly the $25 billion that it took from the government under the Troubled Asset Relief Program." J.P. Morgan has said it was encouraged to take the money and didn't need it.

Thus investors interpreted the dividend cut as a signal of confidence, not of distress.

Source: R. Sidel and M. Rieker, "J.P. Morgan Makes 87% Cut in its Dividend to a Nickel," *The New York Times*, February 24, 2009, pp. C1, C3.

not making a long-term commitment to distribute more cash. The information in the announcement of a share repurchase program is therefore different from the information in a dividend payment.

Corporations repurchase shares when they have accumulated excess cash or when they want to substitute debt for equity. Shareholders applaud payout of excess cash when they worry that the firm would otherwise fritter the money away on perks or unprofitable empire building. Shareholders also know that firms with large quantities of debt to service are less likely to squander cash. A study by Comment and Jarrell, who looked at the announcements of open-market repurchase programs, found that on average they resulted in an abnormal price rise of 2%.[18]

Stock repurchases may also be used to signal a manager's confidence in the future. Suppose that you, the manager, believe that your stock is substantially undervalued. You announce that the company is prepared to buy back a fifth of its stock at a price that is 20% above the current market price. But (you say) you are certainly not going to sell any of your own stock at that price. Investors jump to the obvious conclusion—you must believe that the stock is a good value even at 20% above the current price.

---

[18] R. Comment and G. Jarrell, "The Relative Signalling Power of Dutch-Auction and Fixed Price Self-Tender Offers and Open-Market Share Repurchases," *Journal of Finance* 46 (September 1991), pp. 1243–1271. There is also evidence of continuing superior performance during the years following a repurchase announcement. See D. Ikenberry, J. Lakonishok, and T. Vermaelen, "Market Underreaction to Open Market Share Repurchases," *Journal of Financial Economics* 39 (October 1995), pp. 181–208.

When companies offer to repurchase their stock at a premium, senior management and directors usually commit to hold on to their stock.[19] So it is not surprising that researchers have found that announcements of offers to buy back shares above the market price have prompted a larger rise in the stock price, averaging about 11%.[20]

16-5 THE PAYOUT CONTROVERSY

We have seen that a change in payout may provide information about management's confidence in the future and so affect the stock price. But eventually this change in the stock price would happen anyway as information seeps out through other channels. But does payout policy change the value of the firm's common stock, rather than just sending a signal about value?

One endearing feature of economics is its ability to accommodate not just two, but three, opposing points of view. And so it is with payout policy. On the right, a conservative group argues that investors prefer higher dividend payouts. On the left, another group argues that higher dividends decrease value, because dividends are taxed more heavily than capital gains. And in the center, there is a middle-of-the-road party that claims that payout policy makes no difference.

Dividend Policy Is Irrelevant in Perfect Capital Markets

The middle-of-the-road party was founded in 1961 by Miller and Modigliani (always referred to as "MM"), when they published a proof that dividend policy is irrelevant in a world without taxes, transaction costs, or other market imperfections.[21] MM argued as follows. Suppose your firm has settled on its investment program. You have a plan to finance the investments with cash on hand, additional borrowing, and reinvestment of future earnings. Any surplus cash is to be paid out as dividends.

Now think what happens if you want to increase the total payout by upping the dividend without also changing the investment and financing policy. The extra money must come from somewhere. If the firm fixes its borrowing, the only way it can finance the extra dividend is to print some more shares and sell them. The new stockholders are going to part with their money only if you can offer them shares that are worth as much as they cost. But how can the firm sell more shares when its assets, earnings, investment opportunities, and, therefore, market value are all unchanged? The answer is that there must be a *transfer of value* from the old to the new stockholders. The new ones get the newly printed shares, each one worth less than before the dividend change was announced, and the old ones suffer a capital loss on their shares. The capital loss borne by the old shareholders just offsets the extra cash dividend they receive.

Figure 16.4 shows how this transfer of value occurs. Our hypothetical company pays out a third of its total value as a dividend and it raises the money to do so by selling new shares. The capital loss suffered by the old stockholders is represented by the reduction in the size of the red boxes. But that capital loss is exactly offset by the fact that the new money raised (the black boxes) is paid over to them as dividends.

---

[19] Not only do managers hold on to their stock; on average they also add to their holdings *before* the announcement of a repurchase. See D. S. Lee, W. Mikkelson, and M. M. Partch, "Managers' Trading around Stock Repurchases," *Journal of Finance* 47 (December 1992), pp. 1947–1961.

[20] See R. Comment and G. Jarrell, *op. cit.*

[21] M. H. Miller and F. Modigliani, "Dividend Policy, Growth and the Valuation of Shares," *Journal of Business* 34 (October 1961), pp. 411–433. MM's arguments were anticipated in 1938 in J. B. Williams, *The Theory of Investment Value* (Cambridge, MA: Harvard University Press, 1938). Also, a proof similar to MM's was developed in J. Lintner, "Dividends, Earnings, Leverage and Stock Prices and the Supply of Capital to Corporations," *Review of Economics and Statistics* 44 (August 1962), pp. 243–269.

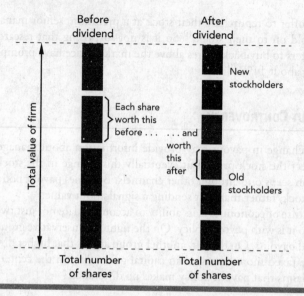

Before dividend After dividend

Total value of firm

New stockholders

Each share worth this before . . .   . . . and worth this after

Old stockholders

Total number of shares Total number of shares

FIGURE 16.4

This firm pays out a third of its worth as a dividend and raises the money by selling new shares. The transfer of value to the new stockholders is equal to the dividend payment. The total value of the firm is unaffected.

Does it make any difference to the old stockholders that they receive an extra dividend payment plus an offsetting capital loss? It might if that were the only way they could get their hands on cash. But as long as there are efficient capital markets, they can raise the cash by selling shares. Thus the old shareholders can cash in either by persuading the management to pay a higher dividend or by selling some of their shares. In either case there will be a transfer of value from old to new shareholders. The only difference is that in the former case this transfer is caused by a dilution in the value of each of the firm's shares, and in the latter case it is caused by a reduction in the number of shares held by the old shareholders. The two alternatives are compared in Figure 16.5.

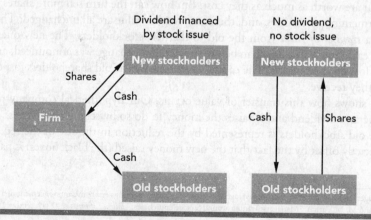

Dividend financed by stock issue   No dividend, no stock issue

New stockholders   New stockholders

Shares

Cash

Firm   Cash   Shares

Cash

Old stockholders   Old stockholders

FIGURE 16.5

Two ways of raising cash for the firm's original shareholders. In each case the cash received is offset by a decline in the value of the old stockholders' claim on the firm. If the firm pays a dividend, each share is worth less because more shares have to be issued against the firm's assets. If the old stockholders sell some of their shares, each share is worth the same but the old stockholders have fewer shares.

Because investors do not need dividends to get their hands on cash, they will not pay higher prices for the shares of firms with high payouts. Therefore firms ought not to worry about dividend policy. They can let dividends fluctuate as a by-product of their investment and financing decisions.

Dividend Irrelevance—An Illustration

Consider the case of Rational Demiconductor, which at this moment has the following balance sheet:

Rational Demiconductor's Balance Sheet (Market Values)

Cash (₹1,000 held for investment)	1,000	0	Debt
Fixed assets	9,000	10,000 + NPV	Equity
Investment opportunity (₹1,000 investment required)	NPV		
Total asset value	₹10,000 + NPV	₹10,000 + NPV	Value of firm

Rational Demiconductor has ₹1,000 cash earmarked for a project requiring a ₹1,000 investment. We do not know how attractive the project is, and so we enter it at NPV; after the project is undertaken it will be worth ₹1,000 + NPV. Note that the balance sheet is constructed with market values; equity equals the market value of the firm's outstanding shares (price per share times number of shares outstanding). It is not necessarily equal to their book value.

Now Rational Demiconductor uses the cash to pay a ₹1,000 dividend to its stockholders. The benefit to them is obvious: ₹1,000 of spendable cash. It is also obvious that there must be a cost. The cash is not free.

Where does the money for the dividend come from? Of course, the immediate source of funds is Rational Demiconductor's cash account. But this cash was earmarked for the investment project. Since we want to isolate the effects of dividend policy on shareholders' wealth, we assume that the company *continues* with the investment project. That means that ₹1,000 in cash must be raised by new financing. This could consist of an issue of either debt or stock. Again, we just want to look at dividend policy for now, and we defer discussion of the debt-equity choice until Chapters 17 and 18. Thus Rational Demiconductor ends up financing the dividend with a ₹1,000 stock issue.

Now we examine the balance sheet after the dividend is paid, the new stock is sold, and the investment is undertaken. Because Rational Demiconductor's investment and borrowing policies are unaffected by the dividend payment, its *overall* market value must be unchanged at ₹10,000 + NPV.[22] We know also that if the new stockholders pay a fair price, their stock is worth ₹1,000. That leaves us with only one missing number—the value of the stock held by the original stockholders. It is easy to see that this must be

$$\text{Value of original stockholders' shares} = \text{value of company} - \text{value of new shares}$$
$$= (10,000 + \text{NPV}) - 1,000$$
$$= \$9,000 + \text{NPV}$$

The old shareholders have received a ₹1,000 cash dividend and incurred a ₹1,000 capital loss. Dividend policy doesn't matter.

---

[22] All other factors that might affect Rational Demiconductor's value are assumed constant. This is not a necessary assumption, but it simplifies the proof of MM's theory.

By paying out ₹1,000 with one hand and taking it back with the other, Rational Demiconductor is recycling cash. To suggest that this makes shareholders better off is like advising a cook to cool the kitchen by leaving the refrigerator door open.

Of course, our proof ignores taxes, issue costs, and a variety of other complications. We turn to those items in a moment. The really crucial assumption in our proof is that the new shares are sold at a fair price. The shares sold to raise ₹1,000 must actually be *worth* ₹1,000.[23] In other words, we have assumed efficient capital markets.

Calculating Share Price

We have assumed that Rational Demiconductor's new shares can be sold at a fair price, but what is that price and how many new shares are issued?

Suppose that before this dividend payout the company had 1,000 shares outstanding and that the project had an NPV of ₹2,000. Then the old stock was worth in total ₹10,000 + NPV = ₹12,000, which works out at ₹12,000/1,000 = ₹12 per share. After the company has paid the dividend and completed the financing, this old stock is worth ₹9,000 + NPV = ₹11,000. That works out at ₹11,000/1,000 = ₹11 per share. In other words, the price of the old stock falls by the amount of the ₹1 per share dividend payment.

Now let us look at the new stock. Clearly, after the issue this must sell at the same price as the rest of the stock. In other words, it must be valued at ₹11. If the new stockholders get fair value, the company must issue ₹1,000/₹11 or 91 new shares in order to raise the ₹1,000 that it needs.

Stock Repurchase

We have seen that any increased cash dividend payment must be offset by a stock issue if the firm's investment and borrowing policies are held constant. In effect the stockholders finance the extra dividend by selling off part of their ownership of the firm. Consequently, the stock price falls by just enough to offset the extra dividend.

This process can also be run backward. With investment and borrowing policy given, any *reduction* in dividends must be balanced by a reduction in the number of shares issued or by repurchase of previously outstanding stock. But if the process has no effect on stockholders' wealth when run forward, it must likewise have no effect when run in reverse. We will confirm this by another numerical example.

Suppose that a technical discovery reveals that Rational Demiconductor's new project is not a positive-NPV venture but a sure loser. Management announces that the project is to be discarded and that the ₹1,000 earmarked for it will be paid out as an extra dividend of ₹1 per share. After the dividend payout, the balance sheet is

Rational Demiconductor's Balance Sheet (Market Values)

Cash	₹ 0	₹ 0	Debt
Existing fixed assets	9,000	9,000	Equity
New project	0		
Total asset value	₹ 9,000	₹ 9,000	Total firm value

---

[23] The "old" shareholders get all the benefit of the positive-NPV project. The new shareholders require only a fair rate of return. They are making a zero-NPV investment.

Since there are 1,000 shares outstanding, the stock price is ₹10,000/1,000 = ₹10 before the dividend payment and ₹9,000/1,000 = ₹9 *after* the payment.

What if Rational Demiconductor uses the ₹1,000 to repurchase stock instead? As long as the company pays a fair price for the stock, the ₹1,000 buys ₹1,000/₹10 = 100 shares. That leaves 900 shares worth 900 × ₹10 = ₹9,000.

As expected, we find that switching from cash dividends to share repurchase has no effect on shareholders' wealth. They forgo a ₹1 cash dividend but end up holding shares worth ₹10 instead of ₹9.

Note that when shares are repurchased the transfer of value is in favor of those stockholders who do not sell. They forgo any cash dividend but end up owning a larger slice of the firm. In effect they are using their share of Rational Demiconductor's ₹1,000 distribution to buy out some of their fellow shareholders.

Stock Repurchase and Valuation

Valuing the equity of a firm that repurchases its own stock can be confusing. Let's work through a simple example.

Company X has 100 shares outstanding. It earns ₹1,000 a year, all of which is paid out as a dividend. The dividend per share is, therefore, ₹1,000/100 = ₹10. Suppose that investors expect the dividend to be maintained indefinitely and that they require a return of 10%. In this case the value of each share is PV_{share} = ₹10/.10 = ₹100. Since there are 100 shares outstanding, the *total* market value of the equity is PV_{equity} = 100 × ₹100 = ₹10,000. Note that we could reach the same conclusion by discounting the *total* dividend payments to shareholders (PV_{equity} = ₹1,000/.10 = ₹10,000).[24]

Now suppose the company announces that instead of paying a cash dividend in year 1, it will spend the same money repurchasing its shares in the open market. The total expected cash flows to shareholders (dividends and cash from stock repurchase) are unchanged at ₹1,000. So the total value of the equity also remains at ₹1,000/.10 = $10,000. This is made up of the value of the ₹1,000 received from the stock repurchase in year 1 ($PV_{repurchase}$ = ₹1,000/1.1 = ₹909.1) and the value of the $1,000-a-year dividend starting in year 2 [$PV_{dividends}$ = ₹1,000/(.10 × 1.1) = ₹9,091]. Each share continues to be worth $10,000/100 = $100 just as before.

Think now about those shareholders who plan to sell their stock back to the company. They will demand a 10% return on their investment. So the expected price at which the firm buys back shares must be 10% higher than today's price, or $110. The company spends ₹1,000 buying back its stock, which is sufficient to buy $1,000/$110 = 9.09 shares.

The company starts with 100 shares, it buys back 9.09, and therefore 90.91 shares remain outstanding. Each of these shares can look forward to a dividend stream of ₹1,000/90.91 = ₹11 per share. So after the repurchase shareholders have 10% fewer shares, but earnings and dividends per share are 10% higher. An investor who owns one share today that is not repurchased will receive no dividends in year 1 but can look forward to $11 a year thereafter. The value of each share is therefore 11/(.1 × 1.1) = ₹100.

Our example illustrates several points. First, other things equal, company value is unaffected by the decision to repurchase stock rather than to pay a cash dividend. Second, when valuing the entire equity you need to include both the cash that is paid out as dividends and the cash that is used to repurchase stock. Third, when calculating the cash flow *per share,* it is double counting to include both

---

[24] When valuing the entire equity, remember that if the company is expected to issue additional shares in the future, we should include the dividend payments on these shares only if we also include the amount that investors pay for them. See Chapter 19.

the forecasted dividends per share *and* the cash received from repurchase (if you sell back your share, you don't get any subsequent dividends). Fourth, a firm that repurchases stock instead of paying dividends reduces the number of shares outstanding but produces an offsetting increase in subsequent earnings and dividends per share.

16-6 THE RIGHTISTS

MM said that dividend policy is irrelevant because it does not affect shareholder value. MM did not say that payout should be random or erratic; for example, it may change over the life cycle of the firm. A young growth firm pays out little or nothing, to maximize the cash flow available for investment. As the firm matures, positive-NPV investment opportunities are harder to come by and growth slows down. There is cash available for payout to shareholders. At some point the firm commits to pay a regular dividend. It may also repurchase shares. In old age, profitable growth opportunities disappear, and payout may become much more generous.

Of course MM assumed absolutely perfect and efficient capital markets. In MM's world, everyone is a rational optimizer. The right-wing payout party points to real-world imperfections that could make high dividend payout ratios better than low ones. There is a natural clientele for high-payout stocks, for example. Some financial institutions in the U.S. are legally restricted from holding stocks lacking established dividend records.[25] In India, the Insurance Regulatory and Development Authority (IRDA) has not specified any clear guidelines about the stocks in which an insurance company can invest. However, it has made its apparent bias towards dividend paying companies clear when its prudential norms for debentures recommend insurance companies to buy only those fully and partly convertible debentures where dividends are likely to be received.

There is also a natural clientele of investors, such as the elderly, who look to their stock portfolios for a steady source of cash to live on.[26] In principle, this cash could be easily generated from stocks paying no dividends at all; the investor could just sell off a small fraction of his or her holdings from time to time. But it is simpler and cheaper for the company to send a quarterly check than for its shareholders to sell, say, one share every three months. Regular dividends relieve many of its shareholders of transaction costs and considerable inconvenience.[27]

Some observers have appealed to behavioral psychology to explain why we may prefer to receive those regular dividends rather than sell small amounts of stock.[28] We are all, they point out, liable to succumb to temptation. Some of us may hanker after fattening foods, while others may be dying for a drink. We could seek to control these cravings by willpower, but that can be a painful struggle. Instead, it may be easier to set simple rules for ourselves ("cut out chocolate," or "wine with meals only"). In just the same way, we may welcome the self-discipline that comes from spending only dividend income, and thereby sidestep the difficult decision of how much we should dip into capital.

---

[25] Most colleges and universities are legally free to spend capital gains from their endowments, but they usually restrict spending to a moderate percentage that can be covered by dividends and interest receipts.

[26] See, for example, J. R. Graham and A. Kumar, "Do Dividend Clienteles Exist? Evidence on Dividend Preferences of Retail Investors," *Journal of Finance* 61 (June 2006), pp. 1305–1336; and M. Baker, S. Nagel and J. Wurgler, "The Effect of Dividends on Consumption," *Brookings Papers on Economic Activites* (2007), pg 277–291.

[27] Those advocating generous dividends might go on to argue that a regular cash dividend relieves stockholders of the risk of having to sell shares at "temporarily depressed" prices. Of course, the firm will have to issue shares eventually to finance the dividend, but (the argument goes) the firm can pick the *right time* to sell. If firms really try to do this and if they are successful—two big *ifs*—then stockholders of high-payout firms might indeed get something for nothing.

[28] See H. Shefrin and M. Statman, "Explaining Investor Preference for Cash Dividends," *Journal of Financial Economics* 13 (June 1984), pp. 253–282.

Finance In Practice

Microsoft's Payout Bonanza

There is a point at which hoarding money becomes embarrassing. . . . Microsoft, which grew into the world's largest software company . . . and which has been generating cash at the rate of $1 billion a month passed that point years ago. On July 20th, it finally addressed the issue.

Its solution was to give back to its shareholders, in various forms, an unprecedented $75 billion. One dollop, to the tune of $32 billion, will be a one-time dividend to be paid in December. Another will be share buybacks worth $30 billion over four years. The third will be a doubling of Microsoft's ongoing dividend to 32 cents a share annually, payable in quarterly instalments. Not bad for a company that has not even turned 30 yet, and that only declared its first dividend in January 2003.

The decision is impressive for the mature analysis by Microsoft of its role in the industry and the prospects for the future that it implies.

Source: "An End to Growth?" *The Economist*, July 24, 2004, p. 61. © 2004 The Economist Newspaper Group, Inc. Reprinted with permission. Further reproduction prohibited (**www.economist.com**).

Payout Policy, Investment Policy, and Management Incentives

Perhaps the most persuasive argument in favor of the rightist position is that paying out funds to shareholders prevents managers from misusing or wasting funds.[29] Suppose a company has plenty of free cash flow but few profitable investment opportunities. Shareholders may not trust the managers to spend retained earnings wisely and may fear that the money will be plowed back into building a larger empire rather than a more profitable one. In such cases investors may demand higher dividends or a stock repurchase not because these are valuable in themselves, but because they encourage a more careful, value-oriented investment policy.

The nearby box describes how Microsoft announced the largest cash distribution in corporate history. By 2004 the company's investment opportunities had diminished, and investors were, therefore, happy to see Microsoft distribute its cash mountain.

Microsoft paid out its gigantic special dividend willingly. Other cash-cow corporations may let go of cash grudgingly under pressure from investors. Stock price falls when investors sense excessive perks or empire building. The threat of a falling stock price is an excellent motivator, particularly for top managers holding valuable stock options.

The willingness of mature corporations to make generous payouts shows that corporate governance works in the U.S. and other developed economies. But governance is less effective in many emerging economies, and managers' and stockholders' interests are not as closely aligned. Payout ratios are smaller where governance is weak.[30]

---

[29] See M. Rozeff, "Growth, Beta and Agency Costs as Determinants of Dividend Payout Ratios," *Journal of Financial Research* 5 (1982), pp. 249–259; F. Easterbrook, "Two Agency Cost Explanations of Dividends," *American Economic Review* 74 (1984), pp. 650–659; and especially M. Jensen, "Agency Costs of Free Cash Flow, Corporate Finance, and Takeovers," *American Economic Review* 76 (May 1986), pp. 323–329.

[30] See R. La Porta, F. Lopez-de-Silanes, A. Shleifer, and R. W. Vishny, "Agency Problems and Dividend Policies around the World," *Journal of Finance* 55 (February 2000), pp. 1–34.

16-7 TAXES AND THE RADICAL LEFT

The left-wing dividend creed is simple: Whenever dividends are taxed more heavily than capital gains, firms should pay the lowest cash dividend they can get away with. Available cash should be retained or used to repurchase shares.

By shifting their distribution policies in this way, corporations can transmute dividends into capital gains. If this financial alchemy results in lower taxes, it should be welcomed by any taxpaying investor. That is the basic point made by the leftist party when it argues for low-dividend payout.

If dividends are taxed more heavily than capital gains, investors should pay more for stocks with low dividend yields. In other words, they should accept a lower *pretax* rate of return from securities offering returns in the form of capital gains rather than dividends. Table 16.1 illustrates this. The stocks of firms A and B are equally risky. Investors expect A to be worth ₹112.50 per share next year. The share price of B is expected to be only ₹102.50, but a ₹10 dividend is also forecasted, and so the total pretax payoff is the same, ₹112.50.

TABLE 16.1 Effects of a shift in dividend policy when dividends are taxed more heavily than capital gains. The high-payout stock (firm B) must sell at a lower price to provide the same after-tax return.

	Firm A (No Dividend)	Firm B (High Dividend)
Next year's price	₹112.50	₹102.50
Dividend	₹0	₹10.00
Total pretax payoff	₹112.50	₹112.50
Today's stock price	₹100	₹97.78
Capital gain	₹12.50	₹4.72
Before-tax rate of return	$100 \times \left(\dfrac{12.5}{100}\right) = 12.5\%$	$100 \times \left(\dfrac{9.78}{97.78}\right) = 10.0\%$
Tax on dividend at 40%	₹0	$.40 \times 10 = ₹4.00$
Tax on capital gains at 20%	$.20 \times 12.50 = ₹2.50$	$.20 \times 4.72 = ₹.94$
Total after-tax income (dividends plus capital gains less taxes)	$(0 + 12.50) - 2.50 = ₹10.00$	$(10.00 + 4.72) - (4.00 + .94) = ₹9.78$
After-tax rate of return	$100 \times \left(\dfrac{10}{100}\right) = 10.0\%$	$P_0 = \dfrac{DIV}{r - g} = \dfrac{2}{.12 - .08} = 50$

Yet we find B's stock selling for less than A's and therefore offering a higher pretax rate of return. The reason is obvious: Investors prefer A because its return comes in the form of capital gains. Table 16.1 shows that A and B are equally attractive to investors who, we assume, pay a 40% tax on dividends and a 20% tax on capital gains. Each offers a 10% return after all taxes. The difference between the stock prices of A and B is exactly the present value of the extra taxes the investors face if they buy B.[31]

---

[31] Michael Brennan has modeled what happens when you introduce taxes into an otherwise perfect market. He found that the capital asset pricing model continues to hold, but on an *after-tax* basis. Thus, if A and B have the same beta, they should offer the same after-tax rate of return. The spread between pretax and post-tax returns is determined by a weighted average of investors' tax rates. See M. J. Brennan, "Taxes, Market Valuation and Corporate Financial Policy," *National Tax Journal* 23 (December 1970), pp. 417–427.

The management of B could save these extra taxes by eliminating the ₹10 dividend and using the released funds to repurchase stock instead. Its stock price should rise to ₹100 as soon as the new policy is announced.

Dividend Tax Policy in India

In India, when a company announces dividends, it also pays the *dividend distribution tax* directly to the Government of India and the shareholders do not have to pay any tax on the dividends they receive. Before the introduction of the dividend distribution tax in India in 1997, dividends were taxed in the hands of the shareholders[32]. Shareholders used to disclose the dividend income under the head 'Income from Other Sources' and then used to pay tax on dividend at a rate that depended on their individual tax bracket. The Finance Act 1997 introduced the dividend distribution tax for the first time in India and under this system, the companies used to pay dividend distribution tax directly at the rate of 10 percent. Such dividend was exempt in the hands of the shareholders and this benefited those shareholders who fell in the higher-than-10-percent tax bracket.

The 2002-03 Budget reverted back to the earlier system for one year where dividends were again taxed in the hands of the shareholders. However, the 2003-04 Budget reintroduced the dividend distribution tax rate in India (albeit at a higher rate of 12.5 percent plus the surcharges). It was further hiked to 15% by the Union Budget of 2007. Currently the effective dividend distribution tax rate in India works out to 16.609 percent.

The Finance Bill No 22 in 2004 introduced a securities transaction tax (STT) of 0.025% on the total turnover and removed the long-term capital gains tax on sell of shares listed in recognized stock exchanges altogether. As of now (2011), the STT is 0.125% for delivery based purchase of shares. (The STT got further reduced to 0.1% in the 2012 Budget). The short term capital gains tax rate (on sell of equity shares) was reduced to 10 percent in the same bill. The 2008-09 Union Budget further increased the short term capital gains tax rate on sale transactions of equity shares to 15%.

Why Pay Any Dividends at All?

So the current tax system in India favors low dividend payments by the companies. This raises a very interesting question: If dividends attract more tax than capital gains, why should any firm ever pay a cash dividend? If cash is to be distributed to stockholders, isn't share repurchase always the best channel for doing so?

The answer is 'yes'. Buyback transactions are not recognized as taxable securities transactions because they do not take place in a recognized stock exchange. Secondly, as per Section 2(22)(iv) of the Income Tax Act, any payment by a company on payment of its own shares from a shareholder does *not* amount to dividend. So, in case of buyback, the normal capital gains tax rates apply.[33]

So, if an Indian company pays more dividends, then the company pays 16.609 percent dividend distribution tax. If the company buys back shares instead, then individual investors pay 10 percent capital gains tax[34] (assuming they sell the shares back after a year of purchase and hence are subject

---

[32] The actual system was very complicated where the companies used to deduct taxes directly and issue a withholding tax certificate to the shareholders. The shareholders used to pay taxes on this dividend using the applicable rate and claim credit based on the withholding tax certificates provided by the company.

[33] The capital gain is computed as the difference between the consideration received by the shareholder and the indexed cost of acquisition of the share. The tax will be computed at 20% with the indexation benefits or 10% without the indexation benefits (whichever is lower).

[34] For individuals, the long term capital gains tax rate is (for transactions happening outside the stock exchange) 20% with indexation benefits or 10% without indexation benefits (whichever is lower). So the maximum long capital gains tax rate can be taken as 10%.

to long-term capital gains tax) whereas the FIIs (investing from favorable treaty jurisdictions like Mauritius or Cyprus) do not have to pay any capital gains tax[35]. For the other FIIs, the long term capital gains tax rate is 10%.

Empirical Evidence on Dividends and Taxes

It is hard to deny that taxes are important to investors. You can see that in the bond market. In 2003, the RBI issued two types of relief bonds in India. In the first type of bond, the interest rate was 6.5 percent and interest was tax free; in the second type of bond, the interest rate was 8 percent and interest was taxable. It does not seem likely that investors in bonds just forget about taxes when they enter the stock market.

There is some evidence that in the past taxes have affected U.S. investors' choice of stocks.[36] Lightly taxed institutional investors have tended to hold high-yield stocks and retail investors have preferred low-yield stocks. Moreover, this preference for low-yield stocks has been somewhat more marked for high-income individuals. Nevertheless, it seems that taxes have been only a secondary consideration with these investors, and have not deterred individuals in high-tax brackets from holding substantial amounts of dividend-paying stocks.

If investors are concerned about taxes, we might also expect that, when the tax penalty on dividends is high, companies would think twice about increasing the payout. Only about a fifth of U.S. financial managers cite investor taxes as an important influence when the firm makes its dividend decision. On the other hand, firms have sometimes responded to major shifts in the way that investors are taxed. For example, when Australia introduced a tax change in 1987 that effectively eliminated the tax penalty on dividends for Australian investors, firms became more willing to increase their payout.[37]

If tax considerations are important, we would expect to find a historical tendency for high-dividend stocks to sell at lower prices and therefore to offer higher returns, just as in Table 16.1. Unfortunately, there are difficulties in measuring this effect. For example, suppose that stock A is priced at ₹100 and is expected to pay a ₹5 dividend. The *expected* yield is, therefore, 5/100 = .05, or 5%. The company now announces bumper earnings and a $10 dividend. Thus with the benefit of hindsight, A's *actual* dividend yield is 10/100 = .10, or 10%. If the unexpected increase in earnings causes a rise in A's stock price, we will observe that a high actual yield is accompanied by a high actual return. But that would not tell us anything about whether a high *expected* yield was accompanied by a high *expected* return. To measure the effect of dividend policy, we need to estimate the dividends that investors expected.

A second problem is that nobody is quite sure what is meant by high dividend yield. Did the high dividend stocks have a high yield all year, or only in months or on days that dividends were paid? Perhaps for most of the year, they had zero yields and were perfect holdings for the highly taxed individuals.

A number of researchers have attempted to tackle these problems and to measure whether investors demand a higher return from high-yielding stocks. Their findings offer some limited comfort to the dividends-are-bad school, for most of the researchers have suggested that high-yielding stocks have provided higher returns. However, the estimated tax rates differ substantially from one study to another. For example, while Litzenberger and Ramaswamy concluded that investors have priced

[35] The India-Mauritius double taxation avoidance agreement (DTAA) provides that capital gains are taxable in the country of residence of the shareholder. Thus FIIs entering through the Mauritius route do not pay any capital gains tax as the capital gains tax rate in Mauritius is 0.

[36] See, for example, Y. Grinstein and R. Michaely, "Institutional Holdings and Payout Policy," *Journal of Finance* 60 (June 2005), pp. 1389–1426; and J. R. Graham and A. Kumar, "Do Dividend Clienteles Exist? Evidence on Dividend Preferences of Retail Investors," *Journal of Finance* 61 (June 2006), pp. 1305–1336.

[37] K. Pattenden and G. Twite, "Taxes and Dividend Policy under Alternative Tax Regimes," *Journal of Corporate Finance* 14 (2008), pp. 1–16.

stocks as if dividend income attracted an extra 14% to 23% rate of tax, Miller and Scholes used a different methodology and came up with a negligible 4% difference in the rate of tax.[38] In India, Narasimhan and Asha find that after the change in dividend tax system in India in 1998, investors demand changed in favor of the high payout companies.[39]

Here, we have assumed that the companies will adopt that dividend policy that reduces the tax liability of their investors. But do the companies care? Reddy finds that the tax regime changes have not influenced the dividend behavior of Indian corporate firms in the post-1997 period.

Alternative Tax System

In India, shareholders' returns are taxed twice. They are taxed at the corporate level, both when the company earns profit (corporate tax) and when it distributes dividend (dividend distribution tax). These two tiers of tax are illustrated in Table 16.2, which shows the after-tax return to the shareholder, if the company distributes all its income as dividends. We assume the company earns ₹100 a share before tax and therefore pays corporate tax of $0.3399 \times 100 = ₹33.99$. This leaves ₹66.01 a share to be paid out as dividend, which is then subject to second layer of tax. Since the effective dividend distribution tax rate is India is 16. 609 percent, the company can at best give ₹56.61 a share as dividends. This dividend will be subject to a dividend distribution tax of ₹9.4 a share. Instead of distribution ₹66.01 as dividends, the company can buyback shares worth ₹66.01. In that case, the individual shareholders will have to pay capital gains tax on the difference between ₹66.01 and the cost of acquisition of the proportionate number of shares. Even if we take the cost of acquiring the necessary number of shares (that the company is able to buy back today by offering ₹66.01) as 0, the shareholder will have to pay capital gains tax equal to $0.1 \times (₹66.01 - 0) = ₹6.1$. So the net payoff to the shareholder will be $₹66.01 - ₹6.1 = ₹59.41$. This is higher than what the individual shareholder receives, if the company pays off the entire income as dividends.

TABLE 16.2 In India, returns to shareholders are taxed twice. This example assumes dividends are distributed in such a manner that the dividends and the dividend distribution tax exhaust the total after-tax income.

Operating Income	100	
Corporate tax at 33.99%	33.99	◄———— Corporate tax
After-tax income	66.01	
Distributed as dividends	56.61	
Dividends distribution tax paid	9.4	◄———— Dividend distribution tax paid by companies

Of course, dividends are regularly paid by companies that operate under very different tax systems. In fact, the two-tier Indian system (or for that matter the U.S. system) is relatively rare. Some Countries partly compensate the investors for the corporate layer of tax by levying income tax on only half an individual's dividend income.

---

[38] See R. H. Litzenberger and K. Ramaswamy, "The Effects of Dividends on Common Stock Prices: Tax Effects or Information Effects," *Journal of Finance* 37 (May 1982), pp. 429–443; and M. H. Miller and M. Scholes, "Dividends and Taxes: Some Empirical Evidence," *Journal of Political Economy* 90 (1982), pp. 1118–1141. Merton Miller provides a broad review of the empirical literature in "Behavioral Rationality in Finance: The Case of Dividends," *Journal of Business* 59 (October 1986), pp. S451–S468.

[39] See Narasirhan, M.S. and C. Asha, 1997, "Implications of Dividend Tax on Corporate Financial Policies," The ICFAI Journal of Applied Finance, July, pp. 11–28.

In some other countries, such as Australia and New Zealand, shareholders' returns are not taxed twice. For example, in Australia shareholders are taxed on dividends, but they may deduct from this tax bill their share of the corporate tax that the company has paid. This is known as an *imputation tax system*. Table 16.3 shows how the imputation system works. Suppose that an Australian company earns pretax profits of A\$100 a share. After it pays corporate tax at 30%, the profit is A\$70 a share. The company now declares a net dividend of A\$70 and sends each shareholder a check for this amount. This dividend is accompanied by a tax credit saying that the company has already paid A\$30 of tax on the shareholder's behalf. Thus shareholders are treated as if each received a total, or gross, dividend of $70 + 30 = A\$100$ and paid tax of A\$30. If the shareholder's tax rate is 30%, there is no more tax to pay and the shareholder retains the net dividend of A\$70. If the shareholder pays tax at the top personal rate of 45%, then he or she is required to pay an additional \$15 of tax; if the tax rate is 15% (the rate at which Australian pension funds are taxed), then the shareholder receives a *refund* of $30 - 15 = A\$15$.[40]

TABLE 16.3   Under imputation tax systems, such as that in Australia, shareholders receive a tax credit for the corporate tax that the firm has paid (figures in Australian dollars per share).

	Rate of Income Tax		
	15%	**30%**	**45%**
Operating income	100	100	100
Corporate tax (T_c = .30)	30	30	30
After-tax income	70	70	70
Grossed-up dividend	100	100	100
Income tax	15	30	45
Tax credit for corporate payment	−30	−30	−30
Tax due from shareholder	−15	0	15
Available to shareholder	85	70	55

Under an imputation tax system, millionaires have to cough up the extra personal tax on dividends. If this is more than the tax that they would pay on capital gains, then millionaires would prefer that the company does not distribute earnings. If it is the other way around, they would prefer dividends.[41] Investors with low tax rates have no doubts about the matter. If the company pays a dividend, these investors receive a check from the revenue service for the excess tax that the company has paid, and therefore they prefer high payout rates.

Look once again at Table 16.3 and think what would happen if the corporate tax rate were zero. The shareholder with a 15% tax rate would still end up with A\$85, and the shareholder with the 45% rate would still receive A\$55. Thus, under an imputation tax system, when a company pays out all its earnings, there is effectively only one layer of tax—the tax on the shareholder. The revenue service collects this tax through the company and then sends a demand to the shareholder for any excess tax or makes a refund for any overpayment.[42]

---

[40] In Australia, shareholders receive a credit for the full amount of corporate tax that has been paid on their behalf. In other countries the tax credit is less than the corporate tax rate. You can think of the tax system in these countries as lying between the Australian and U.S. systems.

[41] In the case of Australia the tax rate on capital gains is the same as the tax rate on dividends. However, for securities that are held for more than 12 months only half of the gain is taxed.

[42] This is only true for earnings that are paid out as dividends. Retained earnings are subject to corporate tax. Shareholders get the benefit of retained earnings in the form of capital gains.

16-8   THE MIDDLE-OF-THE-ROADERS

The middle-of-the-road party, which is principally represented by Miller, Black, and Scholes,[43] maintains that a company's value is not affected by its dividend policy. Unlike the other two parties, they emphasize that the supply of dividends is free to adjust to the demand. Therefore, if companies could increase their stock price by changing their dividend payout, they would surely have done so. Presumably, dividends are where they are because no company believes that it could add value simply by upping or reducing its dividend payout.

This "supply argument" is not inconsistent with the existence of a clientele of investors who prefer low-payout stocks. If necessary, these investors would be prepared to pay a premium for low-payout stocks. But perhaps they do not have to. Enough firms may have already noticed the existence of this clientele and switched to low-payout policies. If so, there is no incentive for *additional* firms to switch to low-payout policies. Similarly, there may well be some investors who prefer high dividends, but these investors too already have a wide choice of suitable stocks. A third group of investors, such as pension funds and other tax-exempt institutions, may have no reason to prefer dividends to capital gains. These investors will be happy to hold both low- and high-payout stocks, and the value that they place on each stock will be unaffected by the company's dividend policy. In that case we are back in an MM world where dividend policy does not affect value.[44]

The middle-of-the-roaders stress that companies would not supply such a large quantity of dividends unless they believed that this was what investors wanted. But that still leaves a puzzle. Even in the days when there was a large tax disadvantage to dividends, in the U.S., many investors were apparently happy to hold high-payout stocks. Why? The response of the middle-of-the-roaders has been to argue that there are always plenty of wrinkles in the tax system that shareholders can use to avoid paying taxes on dividends. For example, instead of investing directly in common stocks, they can do so through a pension fund or insurance company, which receives more favorable tax treatment. However, it is not clear that this is the whole story, for a high proportion of dividends is regularly paid out to wealthy individuals and included in their taxable income.[45]

There is another possible reason that U.S. companies may pay dividends even when these dividends result in higher tax bills. Companies that pay *low* dividends will be more attractive to highly taxed individuals; those that pay *high* dividends will have a greater proportion of pension funds or other tax-exempt institutions as their stockholders. These financial institutions are sophisticated investors; they monitor carefully the companies that they invest in and they bring pressure on poor managers to perform. Successful, well-managed companies are happy to have financial institutions as investors, but their poorly managed brethren would prefer unsophisticated and more docile stockholders.

You can probably see now where the argument is heading. Well-managed companies want to signal their worth. They can do so by having a high proportion of demanding institutions among their stockholders. How do they achieve this? By paying high dividends. Those shareholders who pay tax do not object to these high dividends as long as the effect is to encourage institutional investors who are prepared to put the time and effort into monitoring the management.[46]

---

[43] F. Black and M. S. Scholes, "The Effects of Dividend Yield and Dividend Policy on Common Stock Prices and Returns," *Journal of Financial Economics* 1 (May 1974), pp. 1–22; M. H. Miller and M. S. Scholes, "Dividends and Taxes," *Journal of Financial Economics* 6 (December 1978), pp. 333–364; and M. H. Miller, "Behavioral Rationality in Finance: The Case of Dividends," *Journal of Business* 59 (October 1986), pp. S451–S468.

[44] Baker and Wurgler argue that the demand for dividends may change. When this is reflected in stock prices, firms adjust their dividend policy to cater for the shift in demand. Thus a shift in clienteles shows up in a change in firms' propensity to pay dividends. See M. Baker and J. Wurgler, "A Catering Theory of Dividends," *Journal of Finance* 59 (June 2004), pp. 1125–1165.

[45] See, for example, F. Allen and R. Michaely, "Payout Policy," in *Handbook of the Economics of Finance: Corporate Finance*, G. Constantinides, M. Harris, and R. Stulz, (eds.), (Amsterdam: North-Holland, 2003).

[46] This signaling argument is developed in F. Allen, A. E. Bernardo, and I. Welch, "A Theory of Dividends Based on Tax Clienteles," *Journal of Finance* 55 (December 2000), pp. 2499–2536.

Payout Policy and the Life Cycle of the Firm

MM said that dividend policy does not affect shareholder value. Shareholder value is driven by the firm's investment policy, including its future growth opportunities. Financing policy, including the choice between debt and equity, can also affect value, as we will see in Chapter 18.

In MM's analysis, payout is a residual, a by-product of other financial policies. The firm should make investment and financing decisions, and then pay out whatever cash is left over. Therefore payout should change over the life cycle of the firm.

MM assumed a perfect and rational world, but many of the complications discussed in this chapter actually reinforce the life cycle of payout. Let's review the life-cycle story.[47]

Young growth firms have plenty of profitable investment opportunities. During this time it is efficient to retain and reinvest all operating cash flow. Why pay out cash to investors if the firm then has to replace the cash by borrowing or issuing more shares? Retaining cash avoids costs of issuing securities and minimizes shareholders' taxes. Investors are not worried about wasteful overinvestment, because investment opportunities are good, and managers' compensation is tied to stock price.

As the firm matures, positive-NPV projects become scarcer relative to cash flow. The firm begins to accumulate cash. Now investors begin to worry about overinvestment or excessive perks. The investors pressure management to start paying out cash. Sooner or later, managers comply—otherwise stock price stagnates. The payout may come as share repurchases, but initiating a regular cash dividend sends a stronger and more reassuring signal of financial discipline. The commitment to financial discipline can outweigh the tax costs of dividends. (The middle-of-the-road party argues that the tax costs of paying cash dividends may not be that large, particularly in recent years, when U.S. personal tax rates on dividends and capital gains have been low.) Regular dividends may also be attractive to some types of investors, for example, retirees who depend on dividends for living expenses.

As the firm ages, more and more payout is called for. The payout may come as higher dividends or large repurchases. Sometimes the payout comes as the result of a takeover. Shareholders are bought out, and the firm's new owners generate cash by selling assets and restructuring operations. We discuss takeovers in Chapter 32.

SUMMARY

When managers decide on the dividend, their primary concern seems to be to give shareholders a "fair" payment on their investment. However, most managers are very reluctant to reduce dividends and will not increase the payout unless they are confident it can be maintained.

As an alternative to dividend payments, the company can repurchase its own stock. In recent years companies have bought back their stock in large quantities, but repurchases do not generally substitute for dividends. Instead they are used to return unwanted cash to shareholders or to retire equity and replace it with debt.

If we hold the company's investment decision and capital structure constant, then payout policy is a trade-off between cash dividends and the issue or repurchase of common stock. Should firms retain whatever earnings are necessary to finance growth and pay out any residual as cash dividends? Or should they increase dividends and then (sooner or later) issue stock to make up the shortfall of equity capital? Or should they reduce dividends and use the released cash to repurchase stock?

If we lived in an ideally simple and perfect world, there would be no problem, for the choice would have no effect on market value. The controversy centers on the effects of dividend policy in our

---

[47] Here we are following a life-cycle theory set out in H. DeAngelo, L. DeAngelo, and D. Skinner, "Corporate Payout Policy," *Foundations and Trends in Finance* 3 (2008), pp. 95–287.

flawed world. Many investors believe that a high dividend payout enhances share price. Perhaps they welcome the self-discipline that comes from spending only dividend income rather than having to decide whether they should dip into capital. We suspect also that investors often pressure companies to increase dividends when they do not trust management to spend free cash flow wisely. In this case a dividend increase may lead to a rise in the stock price not because investors like dividends as such but because they want managers to run a tighter ship.

The most obvious and serious market imperfection has been the different tax treatment of dividends and capital gains. Dividends in India are taxed at about 16.6% whereas the long-term capiatal gains tax rate is 10% (excluding surcharges). If dividends are more heavily taxed, highly taxed investors should hold mostly low-payout stocks, and we would expect high-payout stocks to offer investors the compensation of greater pretax returns.

This view has a respectable theoretical basis. It is supported by some evidence that, when dividends were at a significant tax disadvantage in the U.S., gross returns did reflect the tax differential. The weak link is the theory's silence on the question of why companies continued to distribute such large dividends when they landed investors with such large tax bills.

The third view of dividend policy starts with the notion that the actions of companies do reflect investors' preferences; thus the fact that companies pay substantial dividends is the best evidence that investors want them. If the supply of dividends exactly meets the demand, no single company could improve its market value by changing its payout policy.

It is difficult to be dogmatic over these controversies. If investment policy and borrowing are held constant, then the arguments over payout policy are largely about shuffling money from one pocket to another. Unless there are substantial tax consequences to these shuffles, it is unlikely that firm value is greatly affected either by the total amount of the payout or the choice between dividends and repurchase. Investors' concern with payout decisions seems to stem mainly from the information that they read into managers' actions.

The bottom-line conclusion, if there is one, is that payout varies over the life cycle of the firm. Young growth firms pay no cash dividends and rarely repurchase stock. These firms have profitable investment opportunities. They finance these investments as much as possible from internally generated cash flow. As firms mature, profitable investment opportunities shrink relative to cash flow. The firm comes under pressure from investors, because investors worry that managers will overinvest if there is too much idle cash available. The threat of a lagging stock price pushes managers to distribute cash by repurchases or cash dividends. Committing to a regular cash dividend sends the more credible signal of financial discipline.

For comprehensive reviews of the literature on payout policy, see:

F. Allen and R. Michaely, "Payout Policy," in G. Constantinides, M. Harris, and R. Stulz, (eds.), *Handbook of the Economics of Finance: Corporate Finance* (Amsterdam: North-Holland, 2003).

H. DeAngelo, L. DeAngelo, and D. Skinner, "Corporate Payout Policy," *Foundations and Trends in Finance* 3 (2008), pp. 95–287.

For a recent survey of managers' attitudes to the payout decision, see:

A. Kalay and M. Lemmon, "Payout Policy," in B. E. Eckbo (ed.), *Handbook of Empirical Corporate Finance* (Amsterdam: Elsevier/North-Holland, 2007), Chapter 10.

A. Brav, J. R. Graham, C. R. Harvey, and R. Michaely, "Payout Policy in the 21st Century," *Journal of Financial Economics* 77 (September 2005), pp. 483–527.

BASIC

1. In 2012 SMR Limited paid a regular quarterly dividend of ₹.35 a share.
   a. Match each of the following sets of dates:

(A1) 17 July 2009	(B1) Record date
(A2) 11 August 2009	(B2) Payment date
(A3) 12 August 2009	(B3) Ex-dividend date
(A4) 14 August 2009	(B4) Last with-dividend date
(A5) 1 September 2009	(B5) Declaration date

   b. On one of these dates the stock price is likely to fall by about the value of the dividend. Which date? Why?
   c. SMR Limited's stock price in August 2009 was $52. What was the dividend yield?
   d. If earnings per share for 2009 are $4.56, what is the percentage payout rate?
   e. Suppose that in 2009 the company paid a 10% stock dividend. What would be the expected fall in price?

2. Here are several "facts" about typical corporate dividend policies. Which are true and which false?
   a. Companies decide each year's dividend by looking at their capital expenditure requirements and then distributing whatever cash is left over.
   b. Managers and investors seem more concerned with dividend changes than with dividend levels.
   c. Managers often increase dividends temporarily when earnings are unexpectedly high for a year or two.
   d. Companies undertaking substantial share repurchases usually finance them with an offsetting reduction in cash dividends.

3. a. Wotan owns 1,000 shares of a firm that has just announced an increase in its dividend from $2.00 to $2.50 a share. The share price is currently $150. If Wotan does not wish to spend the extra cash, what should he do to offset the dividend increase?
   b. Brunhilde owns 1,000 shares of a firm that has just announced a dividend cut from $8.00 a share to $5.00. The share price is currently $200. If Brunhilde wishes to maintain her consumption, what should she do to offset the dividend cut?

4. Patriot Games has 5 million shares outstanding. The president has proposed that, given the firm's large cash holdings, the annual dividend should be increased from ₹6.00 a share to ₹8.00. If you agree with the president's plans for investment and capital structure, what else must the company do as a consequence of the dividend increase?

5. House of Haddock has 5,000 shares outstanding and the stock price is $140. The company expected to pay a dividend of $20 per share next year and thereafter the dividend is expected to grow indefinitely by 5% a year. The President, George Mullet, now makes a surprise announcement: He says that the company will henceforth distribute half the cash in the form of dividends and the remainder will be used to repurchase stock.
   a. What is the total value of the company before and after the announcement? What is the value of one share?
   b. What is the expected stream of dividends per share for an investor who plans to retain his shares rather than sell them back to the company? Check your estimate of share value by discounting this stream of dividends per share.

6. Here are key financial data for House of Herring, Inc.:

Earnings per share for 2015	$5.50
Number of shares outstanding	40 million
Target payout ratio	50%
Planned dividend per share	$2.75
Stock price, year-end 2015	$130

House of Herring plans to pay the entire dividend early in January 2016. All corporate and personal taxes were repealed in 2014.
   a. Other things equal, what will be House of Herring's stock price after the planned dividend payout?
   b. Suppose the company cancels the dividend and announces that it will use the money saved to repurchase shares. What happens to the stock price on the announcement date? Assume that investors learn nothing about the company's prospects from the announcement. How many shares will the company need to repurchase?
   c. Suppose the company increases dividends to $5.50 per share and then issues new shares to recoup the extra cash paid out as dividends. What happens to the with- and ex-dividend share prices? How many shares will need to be issued? Again, assume investors learn nothing from the announcement about House of Herring's prospects.

7. Answer the following question twice, once assuming current tax law and once assuming that dividends are taxed at the hands of the shareholders at the rate of 30% and the capital gains tax rate is 10%.

   Suppose all investments offered the same expected return before tax. Consider two equally risky shares, Hi and Lo. Hi shares pay a generous dividend and offer low expected capital gains. Lo shares pay low dividends and offer high expected capital gains. Which of the following investors would prefer Lo shares? Which would prefer the Hi shares? Which should not care? (Assume that any stock purchased will be sold after one year.)
   a. A high net worth individual
   b. An FII
   c. LIC
   d. An NRI
   e. An MNC
   f. An Indian company

8. Find out an Indian company that has announced an interim dividend recently.
   a. How frequently does the company pay a regular dividend?
   b. What is the amount of the dividend?
   c. By what amount must your stock be registered for you to receive the dividend? (Visit the website of any of the online brokerage houses to get this information)
   d. How many weeks later is the dividend paid?
   e. Look up the stock price and calculate the annual yield on the stock.

9. Which types of companies would you expect to distribute a relatively high or low proportion of current earnings? Which would you expect to have a relatively high or low price–earnings ratio?
   a. High-risk companies.
   b. Companies that have experienced an unexpected decline in profits.
   c. Companies that *expect* to experience a decline in profits.
   d. Growth companies with valuable future investment opportunities.

10. Little Oil has outstanding 1 million shares with a total market value of ₹20 million. The firm is expected to pay ₹1 million of dividends next year, and thereafter the amount paid out is expected to grow by 5% a year in perpetuity. Thus the expected dividend is ₹1.05 million in year 2, ₹1.105 million in year 3, and so on. However, the company has heard that the value of a share depends on the flow of dividends, and therefore it announces that next year's dividend will be increased to ₹2 million and that the extra cash will be raised immediately by an issue of shares. After that, the total amount paid out each year will be as previously forecasted, that is, ₹1.105 million in year 2 and increasing by 5% in each subsequent year.

     a. At what price will the new shares be issued in year 1?

     b. How many shares will the firm need to issue?

     c. What will be the expected dividend payments on these new shares, and what therefore will be paid out to the *old* shareholders after year 1?

     d. Show that the present value of the cash flows to current shareholders remains ₹20 million.

11. We stated in Section 16-5 that MM's proof of dividend irrelevance assumes that new shares are sold at a fair price. Look back at problem 10. Assume that new shares are issued in year 1 at ₹1 a share. Show who gains and who loses. Is dividend policy still irrelevant? Why or why not?

12. Respond to the following comment: "It's all very well saying that I can sell shares to cover cash needs, but that may mean selling at the bottom of the market. If the company pays a regular cash dividend, investors avoid that risk."

13. Refer to the first balance sheet prepared for Rational Demiconductor in Section 16-5. Again it uses cash to pay a ₹1,000 cash dividend, planning to issue stock to recover the cash required for investment. But this time catastrophe hits before the stock can be issued. A new pollution control regulation increases manufacturing costs to the extent that the value of Rational Demiconductor's existing business is cut in half, to ₹4,500. The NPV of the new investment opportunity is unaffected, however. Show that dividend policy is still irrelevant.

14. "Many companies use stock repurchases to increase earnings per share. For example, suppose that a company is in the following position:

Net profit	₹10 million
Number of shares before repurchase	1 million
Earnings per share	₹10
Price–earnings ratio	20
Share price	₹200

The company now repurchases 200,000 shares at ₹200 a share. The number of shares declines to 800,000 shares and earnings per share increase to ₹12.50. Assuming the price–earnings ratio stays at 20, the share price must rise to ₹250." Discuss.

15. Hors d'Age Cheeseworks has been paying a regular cash dividend of $4 per share each year for over a decade. The company is paying out all its earnings as dividends and is not expected to grow. There are 100,000 shares outstanding selling for $80 per share. The company has sufficient cash on hand to pay the next annual dividend.

     Suppose that Hors d'Age decides to cut its cash dividend to zero and announces that it will repurchase shares instead.

     a. What is the immediate stock price reaction? Ignore taxes, and assume that the repurchase program conveys no information about operating profitability or business risk.

     b. How many shares will Hors d'Age purchase?

     c. Project and compare future stock prices for the old and new policies. Do this for at least years 1, 2, and 3.

16. An article on stock repurchase in the *Los Angeles Times* noted: "An increasing number of companies are finding that the best investment they can make these days is in themselves." Discuss this view. How is the desirability of repurchase affected by company prospects and the price of its stock?

17. Comment briefly on each of the following statements:

    a. "Unlike American firms, which are always being pressured by their shareholders to increase dividends, Japanese companies pay out a much smaller proportion of earnings and so enjoy a lower cost of capital."

    b. "Unlike new capital, which needs a stream of new dividends to service it, retained earnings have zero cost."

    c. "If a company repurchases stock instead of paying a dividend, the number of shares falls and earnings per share rise. Thus stock repurchase must always be preferred to paying dividends."

18. Formaggio Vecchio has just announced its regular quarterly cash dividend of $1 per share.

    a. When will the stock price fall to reflect this dividend payment—on the record date, the ex-dividend date, or the payment date?

    b. Assume that there are no taxes. By how much is the stock price likely to fall?

    c. Now assume that *all* investors pay tax of 30% on dividends and nothing on capital gains. What is the likely fall in the stock price?

    d. Suppose, finally, that everything is the same as in part (c), except that security dealers pay tax on *both* dividends and capital gains. How would you expect your answer to (c) to change? Explain.

19. Refer back to Problem 18. Assume no taxes and a stock price immediately after the dividend announcement of $100.

    a. If you own 100 shares, what is the value of your investment? How does the dividend payment affect your wealth?

    b. Now suppose that Formaggio Vecchio cancels the dividend payment and announces that it will repurchase 1% of its stock at $100. Do you rejoice or yawn? Explain.

20. The shares of A and B both sell for ₹100 and offer a pretax return of 10%. However, in the case of company A the return is entirely in the form of dividend yield (the company pays a regular annual dividend of ₹10 a share), while in the case of B the return comes entirely as capital gain (the shares appreciate by 10% a year). Suppose that dividends and capital gains are both taxed at 30%. What is the after-tax return on share A? What is the after-tax return on share B to an investor who sells after two years? What about an investor who sells after 10 years?

21. a. The Horner Pie Company pays a quarterly dividend of $1. Suppose that the stock price is expected to fall on the ex-dividend date by $.90. Would you prefer to buy on the with-dividend date or the ex-dividend date if you were (i) a tax-free investor, (ii) an investor with a marginal tax rate of 40% on income and 16% on capital gains?

    b. In a study of ex-dividend behavior, Elton and Gruber[48] estimated that the stock price fell on the average by 85% of the dividend. Assuming that the tax rate on capital gains was 40% of the rate on income tax, what did Elton and Gruber's result imply about investors' marginal rate of income tax?

    c. Elton and Gruber also observed that the ex-dividend price fall was different for high-payout stocks and for low-payout stocks. Which group would you expect to show the larger price fall as a proportion of the dividend?

---

[48] E. J. Elton and M. J. Gruber, "Marginal Stockholders' Tax Rates and the Clientele Effect," *Review of Economics and Statistics* 52 (1970), pp. 68–74.

    d. Would the fact that investors can trade stocks freely around the ex-dividend date alter you interpretation of Elton and Gruber's study?

    e. Suppose Elton and Gruber repeated their tests for 2009, when the tax rate was the same or dividends and capital gains. How would you expect their results to have changed?

22. The middle-of-the-road party holds that dividend policy doesn't matter because the *suppl* of high-, medium-, and low-payout stocks has already adjusted to satisfy investors' demands Investors who like generous dividends hold stocks that give them all the dividends that they want. Investors who want capital gains see ample low-payout stocks to choose from. Thus high-payout firms cannot gain by transforming to low-payout firms, or vice versa.

    Suppose the government reduces the tax rate on dividends. Suppose that before this change the supply of dividends matched investor needs. How would you expect the tax change to affect the total cash dividends paid by Indian corporations and the proportion of high-versu low-payout companies? Would dividend policy still be irrelevant after any dividend supply adjustments are completed? Explain.

CHALLENGE

23. Consider the following two statements: "Dividend policy is irrelevant," and "Stock price is the present value of expected future dividends." (See Chapter 4.) They *sound* contradictory. Thi question is designed to show that they are fully consistent.

    The current price of the shares of Charles River Mining Corporation is ₹50. Next year' earnings and dividends per share are ₹4 and ₹2, respectively. Investors expect perpetual growth at 8% per year. The expected rate of return demanded by investors is $r = 12\%$.

    We can use the perpetual-growth model to calculate stock price:

$$P_0 = \frac{\text{DIV}}{r - g} = \frac{2}{.12 - .08} = 50$$

    Suppose that Charles River Mining announces that it will switch to a 100% payout policy issuing shares as necessary to finance growth. Use the perpetual-growth model to show tha current stock price is unchanged.

24. "If a company pays a dividend, the investor is liable for tax on the total value of the dividend. I instead the company distributes the cash by stock repurchase, the investor is liable for tax only on any capital gain rather than on the entire amount. Therefore, even if the tax rates on divi dend income and capital gains are the same, stock repurchase is always preferable to a dividend payment." Explain with a simple example why this is not the case. (Ignore the fact that capital gains may be postponed.)

25. Adherents of the "dividends-are-good" school sometimes point to the fact that stocks with high yields tend to have above-average price–earnings multiples. Is this evidence convincing Discuss.

26. Suppose that there are just three types of investors with the following tax rates:

	Individuals	Corporations	Institutions
Dividends	50%	5%	0%
Capital gains	15	35	0

Individuals invest a total of ₹80 billion in stock and corporations invest ₹10 billion. The remaining stock is held by the institutions. All three groups simply seek to maximize their after-tax income.

These investors can choose from three types of stock offering the following pretax payouts:

	Low Payout	Medium Payout	High Payout
Dividends	₹5	₹5	₹30
Capital gains	15	5	0

These payoffs are expected to persist in perpetuity. The low-payout stocks have a total market value of ₹100 billion, the medium-payout stocks have a value of ₹50 billion, and the high-payout stocks have a value of ₹120 billion.

a. Who are the marginal investors that determine the prices of the stocks?

b. Suppose that this marginal group of investors requires a 12% after-tax return. What are the prices of the low-, medium-, and high-payout stocks?

c. Calculate the after-tax returns of the three types of stock for each investor group.

d. What are the dollar amounts of the three types of stock held by each investor group?

17

CHAPTER

DOES DEBT POLICY MATTER?

A firm's basic resource is the stream of cash flows produced by its assets. When the firm is financed entirely by common stock, all those cash flows belong to the stockholders. When it issues both debt and equity securities, it splits the cash flows into two streams, a relatively safe stream that goes to the debtholders and a riskier stream that goes to the stockholders.

The firm's mix of debt and equity financing is called its capital structure. Of course capital structure is not just "debt versus equity." There are many different flavors of debt, at least two flavors of equity (common versus preferred), plus hybrids such as convertible bonds. The firm can issue dozens of distinct securities in countless combinations. It attempts to find the particular combination that maximizes the overall market value of the firm.

Are such attempts worthwhile? We must consider the possibility that *no* combination has any greater appeal than any other. Perhaps the really important decisions concern the company's assets, and decisions about capital structure are mere details—matters to be attended to but not worried about.

Modigliani and Miller (MM), who showed that payout policy doesn't matter in perfect capital markets, also showed that financing decisions don't matter in perfect markets. Their famous "proposition 1" states that a firm cannot change the total value of its securities just by splitting its cash flows into different streams: The firm's value is determined by its real assets, not by the securities it issues. Thus capital structure is irrelevant as long as the firm's investment decisions are taken as given.

MM's proposition 1 allows complete separation of investment and financing decisions. It implies that any firm could use the capital budgeting procedures presented in Chapters 5 through 12 without worrying about where the money for capital expenditures comes from. In those chapters, we assumed all-equity financing without really thinking about it. If MM are right, that is exactly the right approach. If the firm uses a mix of debt and equity financing, its overall cost of capital will be exactly the same as its cost of equity with all-equity financing.

We believe that in practice capital structure does matter, but we nevertheless devote all of this chapter to MM's argument. If you don't fully understand the conditions under which MM's theory holds, you won't fully understand why one capital structure is better than another. The financial manager needs to know what kinds of market imperfection to look for.

For example, the firm may invent some new security that a particular clientele of investors is willing to buy at a premium price, thereby increasing the overall market value of the firm. (We argue, however, that such financial innovations are easily copied and that any gains in value will be confined to the first few issuers.)

In Chapter 18 we undertake a detailed analysis of the imperfections that are most likely to make a difference, including taxes, the costs of bankruptcy and financial distress, the costs of writing and enforcing complicated debt contracts, differences created by imperfect information, and the effects of debt on incentives for management. In Chapter 19 we show how such imperfections (especially taxes) affect the weighted-average cost of capital and the value of the firm.

17-1 THE EFFECT OF FINANCIAL LEVERAGE IN A COMPETITIVE TAX-FREE ECONOMY

Financial managers try to find the combination of securities that has the greatest overall appeal to investors—the combination that maximizes the market value of the firm. Before tackling this problem, we should check whether a policy that maximizes the total value of the firm's securities also maximizes the wealth of the shareholders.

Let D and E denote the market values of the outstanding debt and equity of the Wapshot Mining Company. Wapshot's 1,000 shares sell for ₹50 apiece. Thus

$$E = 1,000 \times 50 = ₹50,000$$

Wapshot has also borrowed ₹25,000, and so V, the aggregate market value of all Wapshot's outstanding securities, is

$$V = D + E = ₹75,000$$

Wapshot's stock is known as *levered equity*. Its stockholders face the benefits and costs of **financial leverage,** or *gearing*. Suppose that Wapshot "levers up" still further by borrowing an additional ₹10,000 and paying the proceeds out to shareholders as a special dividend of ₹10 per share. This substitutes debt for equity capital with no impact on Wapshot's assets.

What will Wapshot's equity be worth after the special dividend is paid? We have two unknowns, E and V:

Old debt	₹25,000 ⎫	₹35,000 = D
New debt	₹10,000 ⎭	
Equity		? = E
Firm value		? = V

If V is ₹75,000 as before, then E must be $V - D = 75,000 - 35,000 = ₹40,000$. Stockholders have suffered a capital loss that exactly offsets the ₹10,000 special dividend. But if V *increases* to, say, ₹80,000 as a result of the change in capital structure, then $E = ₹45,000$ and the stockholders are ₹5,000 ahead. In general, any increase or decrease in V caused by a shift in capital structure accrues to the firm's stockholders. We conclude that a policy that maximizes the market value of the firm is also best for the firm's stockholders.

This conclusion rests on two important assumptions: first, that Wapshot can ignore payout policy and, second, that after the change in capital structure the old and new debt are *worth* ₹35,000.

Payout policy may or may not be relevant, but there is no need to repeat the discussion of Chapter 16. We need only note that shifts in capital structure sometimes force important decisions about payout policy. Perhaps Wapshot's cash dividend has costs or benefits that should be considered in addition to any benefits achieved by its increased financial leverage.

Our second assumption that old and new debt ends up worth ₹35,000 seems innocuous. But it could be wrong. Perhaps the new borrowing has increased the risk of the old bonds. If the holders of old bonds cannot demand a higher rate of interest to compensate for the increased risk, the value of their investment is reduced. In this case Wapshot's stockholders gain at the expense of the holders of old bonds even though the overall value of the firm is unchanged.

But this anticipates issues better left to Chapter 18. In this chapter we assume that any new issue of debt has no effect on the market value of existing debt.

Enter Modigliani and Miller

Let us accept that the financial manager would like to find the combination of securities that maximizes the value of the firm. How is this done? MM's answer is that the financial manager should stop worrying: In a perfect market any combination of securities is as good as another. The value of the firm is unaffected by its choice of capital structure.[1]

You can see this by imagining two firms that generate the same stream of operating income and differ only in their capital structure. Firm U is unlevered. Therefore the total value of its equity E_U is the same as the total value of the firm V_U. Firm, L, on the other hand, is levered. The value of its stock is, therefore, equal to the value of the firm less the value of the debt: $E_L = V_L - D_L$.

Now think which of these firms you would prefer to invest in. If you don't want to take much risk, you can buy common stock in the unlevered firm U. For example, if you buy 1% of firm U's shares, your investment is $.01V_U$ and you are entitled to 1% of the gross profits:

Rupee Investment	Rupee Return
$.01V_U$	$.01 \times$ Profits

Now compare this with an alternative strategy. This is to purchase the same fraction of *both* the debt and the equity of firm L. Your investment and return would then be as follows:

---

[1] F. Modigliani and M. H. Miller, "The Cost of Capital, Corporation Finance and the Theory of Investment," *American Economic Review* 48 (June 1958), pp. 261–297. MM's basic argument was anticipated in 1938 by J. B. Williams and to some extent by David Durand. See J. B. Williams, *The Theory of Investment Value* (Cambridge, MA: Harvard University Press, 1938) and D. Durand, "Cost of Debt and Equity Funds for Business: Trends and Problems of Measurement," *Conference on Research in Business Finance* (New York: National Bureau of Economic Research, 1952).

	Rupee Investment	Rupee Return
Debt	$.01D_L$	$.01 \times$ Interest
Equity	$.01E_L$	$.01 \times$ (Profits $-$ interest)
Total	$.01\,(D_L + E_L)$	$.01 \times$ Profits
	$= .01V_L$	

Both strategies offer the same payoff: 1% of the firm's profits. The law of one price tells us that in well-functioning markets two investments that offer the same payoff must have the same price. Therefore, $.01V_U$ must equal $.01V_L$: the value of the unlevered firm must equal the value of the levered firm.

Suppose that you are willing to run a little more risk. You decide to buy 1% of the outstanding shares in the *levered* firm. Your investment and return are now as follows:

Rupee Investment	Rupee Return
$.01E_L$	$.01 \times$ (Profits $-$ interest)
$= .01(V_L - D_L)$	

But there is an alternative strategy. This is to borrow $.01D_L$ on your own account and purchase 1% of the stock of the *unlevered* firm. In this case, your borrowing gives you an immediate cash *inflow* of $.01D_L$, but you have to pay interest on your loan equal to 1% of the interest that is paid by firm L. Your total investment and return are, therefore, as follows:

	Rupee Investment	Rupee Return
Borrowing	$-.01D_L$	$-.01 \times$ Interest
Equity	$.01V_U$	$.01 \times$ Profits
Total	$.01(V_U - D_L)$	$.01 \times$ (Profits $-$ interest)

Again both strategies offer the same payoff: 1% of profits after interest. Therefore, both investments must have the same cost. The payoff $.01(V_U - D_L)$ must equal $.01(V_L - D_L)$ and V_U must equal V_L.

It does not matter whether the world is full of risk-averse chickens or venturesome lions. All would agree that the value of the unlevered firm U must be equal to the value of the levered firm L. As long as investors can borrow or lend on their own account on the same terms as the firm, they can "undo" the effect of any changes in the firm's capital structure. This is the basis for MM's famous proposition 1: "The market value of any firm is independent of its capital structure."

The Law of Conservation of Value

MM's argument that debt policy is irrelevant is an application of an astonishingly simple idea. If we have two streams of cash flow, A and B, then the present value of A + B is equal to the present value of A plus the present value of B. We met this principle of *value additivity* in our discussion of capital budgeting, where we saw that the present value of two assets combined is equal to the sum of their present values considered separately.

In the present context we are not combining assets but splitting them up. But value additivity works just as well in reverse. We can slice a cash flow into as many parts as we like; the values of the parts will always sum back to the value of the unsliced stream. (Of course, we have to make sure that none of the stream is lost in the slicing. We cannot say, "The value of a pie is independent of how it is sliced," if the slicer is also a nibbler.)

This is really a *law of conservation of value.* The value of an asset is preserved regardless of the nature of the claims against it. Thus proposition 1: Firm value is determined on the *left-hand* side of the balance sheet by real assets—not by the proportions of debt and equity securities issued to buy the assets.

The simplest ideas often have the widest application. For example, we could apply the law of conservation of value to the choice between issuing preferred stock, common stock, or some combination. The law implies that the choice is irrelevant, assuming perfect capital markets and providing that the choice does not affect the firm's investment and operating policies. If the total value of the equity "pie" (preferred and common combined) is fixed, the firm's owners (its common stockholders) do not care how this pie is sliced.

The law also applies to the *mix* of debt securities issued by the firm. The choices of long-term versus short-term, secured versus unsecured, senior versus subordinated, and convertible versus nonconvertible debt all should have no effect on the overall value of the firm.

Combining assets and splitting them up will not affect values as long as they do not affect an investor's choice. When we showed that capital structure does not affect choice, we implicitly assumed that both companies and individuals can borrow and lend at the same risk-free rate of interest. As long as this is so, individuals can undo the effect of any changes in the firm's capital structure.

In practice corporate debt is not risk-free and firms cannot escape with rates of interest appropriate to a government security. Some people's initial reaction is that this alone invalidates MM's proposition. It is a natural mistake, but capital structure can be irrelevant even when debt is risky.

If a company borrows money, it does not *guarantee* repayment: It repays the debt in full only if its assets are worth more than the debt obligation. The shareholders in the company, therefore, have limited liability.

Many individuals would like to borrow with limited liability. They might, therefore, be prepared to pay a small premium for levered shares *if the supply of levered shares were insufficient to meet their needs.*[2] But there are literally thousands of common stocks of companies that borrow. Therefore it is unlikely that an issue of debt would induce them to pay a premium for *your* shares.[3]

An Example of Proposition 1

Kavita Spot Removers is reviewing its capital structure. Table 17.1 shows its current position. The company has no leverage and all the operating income is paid as dividends to the common stockholders (we assume still that there are no taxes). The expected earnings and dividends per share are ₹1.50, but this figure is by no means certain—it could turn out to be more or less than ₹1.50. The price of each share is ₹10. Since the firm expects to produce a level stream of earnings in perpetuity, the expected return on the share is equal to the earnings–price ratio, 1.50/10.00 = .15, or 15%.

Ms. Kavita, the firm's president, has come to the conclusion that shareholders would be better off if the company had equal proportions of debt and equity. She, therefore, proposes to issue ₹5,000 of debt at an interest rate of 10% and use the proceeds to repurchase 500 shares. To support her proposal, Ms. Kavita has analyzed the situation under different assumptions about operating income. The results of her calculations are shown in Table 17.2.

---

[2] Of course, individuals could *create* limited liability if they chose. In other words, the lender could agree that borrowers need repay their debt in full only if the assets of company X are worth more than a certain amount. Presumably individuals don't enter into such arrangements because they can obtain limited liability more simply by investing in the stocks of levered companies.

[3] Capital structure is also irrelevant if each investor holds a fully diversified portfolio. In that case he or she owns *all* the risky securities offered by a company (both debt and equity). But anybody who owns *all* the risky securities doesn't care about how the cash flows are divided among different securities.

TABLE 17.1   Kavita Spot Removers is entirely equity-financed. Although it expects to have an income of ₹1,500 a year in perpetuity, this income is not certain. This table shows the return to the stockholder under different assumptions about operating income. We assume no taxes.

Data				
Number of shares	1,000			
Price per share	₹10			
Market value of shares	₹10,000			
Outcomes				
Operating income ($)	500	1,000	**1,500**	2,000
Earnings per share ($)	.50	1.00	**1.50**	2.00
Return on shares (%)	5	10	**15**	20
			Expected outcome	

TABLE 17.2   Kavita Spot Removers is wondering whether to issue ₹5,000 of debt at an interest rate of 10% and repurchase 500 shares. This table shows the return to the shareholder under different assumptions about operating income.

Data				
Number of shares	500			
Price per share	₹10			
Market value of shares	₹5,000			
Market value of debt	₹5,000			
Interest at 10%	₹500			
Outcomes				
Operating income (₹)	500	1,000	**1,500**	2,000
Interest (₹)	500	500	**500**	500
Equity earnings (₹)	0	500	**1,000**	1,500
Earnings per share (₹)	0	1	**2**	3
Return on shares (%)	0	10	**20**	30
			Expected outcome	

To see more clearly how leverage would affect earnings per share, Ms. Kavita has also produced Figure 17.1. The brown line shows how earnings per share would vary with operating income under the firm's current all-equity financing. It is, therefore, simply a plot of the data in Table 17.1. The green line shows how earnings per share would vary given equal proportions of debt and equity. It is, therefore, a plot of the data in Table 17.2.

Ms. Kavita reasons as follows: "It is clear that the effect of leverage depends on the company's income. If income is greater than ₹1,000, the return to the equityholder is *increased* by leverage. If it is

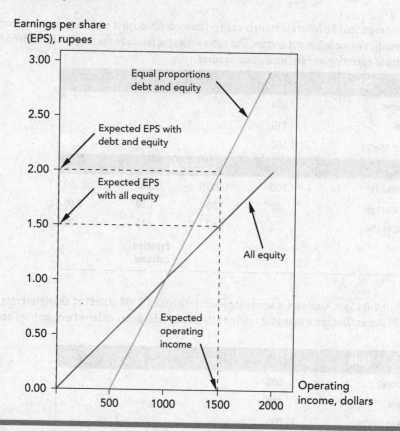

FIGURE 17.1

Borrowing increases Kavita's EPS (earnings per share) when operating income is greater than ₹1,000 and reduces EPS when operating income is less than ₹1,000. Expected EPS rises from ₹1.50 to ₹2.

less than ₹1,000, the return is *reduced* by leverage. The return is unaffected when operating income is exactly ₹1,000. At this point the return on the market value of the assets is 10%, which is exactly equal to the interest rate on the debt. Our capital structure decision, therefore, boils down to what we think about income prospects. Since we expect operating income to be above the ₹1,000 break-even point, I believe we can best help our shareholders by going ahead with the ₹5,000 debt issue."

As financial manager of Kavita Spot Removers, you reply as follows: "I agree that leverage will help the shareholder as long as our income is greater than ₹1,000. But your argument ignores the fact that Kavita shareholders have the alternative of borrowing on their own account. For example, suppose that an investor borrows ₹10 and then invests ₹20 in two unlevered Kavita shares. This person has to put up only ₹10 of his or her own money. The payoff on the investment varies with Kavita's operating income, as shown in Table 17.3. This is exactly the same set of payoffs as the investor would get by buying one share in the levered company. [Compare the last two lines of Tables 17.2 and 17.3.] Therefore, a share in the levered company must also sell for ₹10. If Kavita goes ahead and borrows, it will not allow investors to do anything that they could not do already, and so it will not increase value."

The argument that you are using is exactly the same as the one MM used to prove proposition 1.

TABLE 17.3 Individual investors can replicate Kavita's leverage.

	Operating Income (₹)			
	500	**1,000**	**1,500**	**2,000**
Earnings on two shares (₹)	1	2	3	4
Less interest at 10% (₹)	1	1	1	1
Net earnings on investment (₹)	0	1	2	3
Return on ₹10 investment (%)	0	10	20	30
			Expected outcome	

17-2 FINANCIAL RISK AND EXPECTED RETURNS

Consider now the implications of MM's proposition 1 for the expected returns on Kavita stock:

	Current Structure: All Equity	Proposed Structure: Equal Debt and Equity
Expected earnings per share (₹)	1.50	2.00
Price per share (₹)	10	10
Expected return on share (%)	15	20

Leverage increases the expected stream of earnings per share but *not* the share price. The reason is that the change in the expected earnings stream is exactly offset by a change in the rate at which the earnings are discounted. The expected return on the share (which for a perpetuity is equal to the earnings–price ratio) increases from 15% to 20%. We now show how this comes about.

The expected return on Kavita's assets r_A is equal to the expected operating income divided by the total market value of the firm's securities:

$$\text{Expected return on assets} = r_A = \frac{\text{expected operating income}}{\text{market value of all securities}}$$

We have seen that in perfect capital markets the company's borrowing decision does not affect *either* the firm's operating income *or* the total market value of its securities. Therefore the borrowing decision also does not affect the expected return on the firm's assets r_A.

Suppose that an investor holds all of a company's debt and all of its equity. This investor is entitled to all the firm's operating income; therefore, the expected return on the portfolio is just r_A.

The expected return on a portfolio is equal to a weighted average of the expected returns on the individual holdings. Therefore the expected return on a portfolio consisting of *all* the firm's securities is

$$\text{Expected return on assets} = (\text{proportion in debt} \times \text{expected return on debt})$$
$$+ (\text{proportion in equity} \times \text{expected return on equity})$$

$$r_A = \left(\frac{D}{D+E} \times r_D\right) + \left(\frac{E}{D+E} \times r_E\right)$$

This formula is of course an old friend from Chapter 9. The overall expected return r_A is called the *company cost of capital* or the *weighted-average cost of capital* (WACC).

We can turn the formula around to solve for r_E, the expected return to equity for a levered firm:

Expected return on equity = expected return on assets
+ (expected return on assets − expected return on debt)
× debt–equity ratio

$$r_E = r_A + (r_A - r_D)\frac{D}{E}$$

Proposition 2

This is MM's proposition 2: The expected rate of return on the common stock of a levered firm increases in proportion to the debt–equity ratio (D/E), expressed in market values; the rate of increase depends on the spread between r_A, the expected rate of return on a portfolio of all the firm's securities, and r_D, the expected return on the debt. Note that $r_E = r_A$ if the firm has no debt.

We can check out this formula for Kavita Spot Removers. Before the decision to borrow

$$r_E = r_A = \frac{\text{expected operating income}}{\text{market value of all securities}}$$

$$= \frac{1{,}500}{10{,}000} = .15, \text{ or } 15\%$$

If the firm goes ahead with its plan to borrow, the expected return on assets r_A is still 15%. The expected return on equity is

$$r_E = r_A + (r_A - r_D)\frac{D}{E}$$

$$= .15 + (.15 - .10)\frac{5{,}000}{5{,}000} = .20, \text{ or } 20\%$$

When the firm was unlevered, equity investors demanded a return of r_A. When the firm is levered, they require a premium of $(r_A - r_D)D/E$ to compensate for the extra risk.

MM's proposition 1 says that financial leverage has no effect on shareholders' wealth. Proposition 2 says that the rate of return they can expect to receive on their shares increases as the firm's debt–equity ratio increases. How can shareholders be indifferent to increased leverage when it increases expected return? The answer is that any increase in expected return is exactly offset by an increase in risk and therefore in shareholders' *required* rate of return.

Look at what happens to the risk of Kavita shares if it moves to equal debt–equity proportions. Table 17.4 shows how a shortfall in operating income affects the payoff to the shareholders.

The debt–equity proportion does not affect the *rupee* risk borne by equityholders. Suppose operating income drops from ₹1,500 to ₹500. Under all-equity financing, equity earnings drop by ₹1 per share. There are 1,000 outstanding shares, and so *total* equity earnings fall by ₹1 × 1,000 = ₹1,000. With 50% debt, the same drop in operating income reduces earnings per share by ₹2. But there are only 500 shares outstanding, and so total equity income drops by ₹2 × 500 = ₹1,000, just as in the all-equity case.

However, the debt–equity choice does amplify the spread of *percentage* returns. If the firm is all-equity-financed, a decline of ₹1,000 in the operating income reduces the return on the shares by 10%.

TABLE 17.4 Financial leverage increases the risk of Kavita shares. A ₹1,000 drop in operating income reduces earnings per share by ₹1 with all-equity financing, but by ₹2 with 50% debt.

If operating income falls from		₹1,500	to	₹500	Change
No debt:	Earnings per share	₹1.50		₹.50	−₹1.00
	Return	15%		5%	−10%
50% debt:	Earnings per share	₹2.00		0	−₹2.00
	Return	20%		0	−20%

If the firm issues risk-free debt with a fixed interest payment of ₹500 a year, then a decline of ₹1,000 in the operating income reduces the return on the shares by 20%. In other words, the effect of the proposed leverage is to double the amplitude of the swings in Kavita's shares. Whatever the beta of the firm's shares before the refinancing, it would be twice as high afterward.

Now you can see why investors require higher returns on levered equity. The required return simply rises to match the increased risk.

EXAMPLE 17.1 Leverage and the Cost of Equity

Let us revisit a numerical example from Chapter 9. We looked at a company with the following market-value balance sheet:

Asset value	100	Debt (D)	30	at $r_D = 7.5\%$
		Equity (E)	70	at $r_E = 15\%$
Asset value	100	Firm value (V)	100	

and an overall cost of capital of:

$$r_A = r_D \frac{D}{V} + r_E \frac{E}{V}$$

$$= \left(7.5 \times \frac{30}{100}\right) + \left(15 \times \frac{70}{100}\right) = 12.75\%$$

If the firm is contemplating investment in a project that has the same risk as the firm's existing business, the opportunity cost of capital for this project is the same as the firm's cost of capital; in other words, it is 12.75%.

What would happen if the firm issued an additional 10 of debt and used the cash to repurchase 10 of its equity? The revised market-value balance sheet is

Asset value	100	Debt (D)	40
		Equity (E)	60
Asset value	100	Firm value (V)	100

The change in financial structure does not affect the amount or risk of the cash flows on the total package of debt and equity. Therefore, if investors required a return of 12.75% on the total package before the refinancing, they must require a 12.75% return on the firm's assets afterward.

Although the required return on the *package* of debt and equity is unaffected, the change in financial structure does affect the required return on the individual securities. Since the company has more debt than before, the debtholders are likely to demand a higher interest rate. Suppose that the expected return on the debt rises to 7.875%. Now you can write down the basic equation for the return on assets

$$r_A = r_D \frac{D}{V} + r_E \frac{E}{V}$$

$$= \left(7.875 \times \frac{40}{100}\right) + \left(r_E \times \frac{60}{100}\right) = 12.75\%$$

and solve for the return on equity $r_E = 16.0\%$.

Increasing the amount of debt increased debtholder risk and led to a rise in the return that debtholders required (r_{debt} rose from 7.5 to 7.875%). The higher leverage also made the equity riskier and increased the return that shareholders required (r_E rose from 15% to 16%). The weighted-average return on debt and equity remained at 12.75%:

$$r_A = (r_D \times .4) + (r_E \times .6)$$

$$= (7.875 \times .4) + (16 \times 6) = 12.75\%$$

Suppose that the company decided instead to repay all its debt and to replace it with equity. In that case all the cash flows would go to the equityholders. The company cost of capital, r_A, would stay at 12.75%, and r_E would also be 12.75%.

How Changing Capital Structure Affects Beta

We have looked at how changes in financial structure affect expected return. Let us now look at the effect on beta.

The stockholders and debtholders both receive a share of the firm's cash flows, and both bear part of the risk. For example, if the firm's assets turn out to be worthless, there will be no cash to pay stockholders or debtholders. But debtholders usually bear much less risk than stockholders. Debt betas of large firms are typically in the range of .1 to .3.

If you owned a portfolio of all the firm's securities, you wouldn't share the cash flows with anyone. You wouldn't share the risks with anyone either; you would bear them all. Thus the firm's asset beta is equal to the beta of a portfolio of all the firm's debt and its equity.

The beta of this hypothetical portfolio is just a weighted average of the debt and equity betas:

$$\beta_A = \beta_{\text{portfolio}} = \beta_D \frac{D}{V} + \beta_E \frac{E}{V}$$

Think back to our example. If the debt before the refinancing has a beta of .1 and the equity has a beta of 1.1, then

$$\beta_A = \left(.1 \times \frac{30}{100}\right) + \left(1.1 \times \frac{70}{100}\right) = .8$$

What happens after the refinancing? The risk of the total package is unaffected, but both the debt and the equity are now more risky. Suppose that the debt beta increases to .2. We can work out the new equity beta:

$$\beta_A = \beta_{\text{portfolio}} = \beta_D \frac{D}{V} + \beta_E \frac{E}{V}$$

$$.8 = \left(.2 \times \frac{40}{100}\right) + \left(\beta_E \times \frac{60}{100}\right)$$

$$\beta_E = 1.2$$

Our example shows how borrowing creates financial leverage or gearing. Financial leverage does not affect the risk or the expected return on the firm's assets, but it does push up the risk of the common stock. Shareholders demand a correspondingly higher return because of this *financial risk*.

Now you can see how to *unlever* betas, that is, how to go from an observed β_E to β_A. You have the equity beta, say, 1.2. You also need the debt beta, say, .2, and the relative market values of debt (D/V) and equity (E/V). If debt accounts for 40% of overall value V, then the unlevered beta is

$$\beta_A = \left(.2 \times \frac{40}{100}\right) + \left(1.2 \times \frac{60}{100}\right) = .8$$

This runs the previous example in reverse. Just remember the basic relationship:

$$\beta_A = \beta_{\text{portfolio}} = \beta_D\left(\frac{D}{V}\right) + \beta_E\left(\frac{E}{V}\right)$$

MM's propositions warn us that higher leverage increases both expected equity returns and equity risk. It does *not* increase shareholder value. Having worked through the example of Kavita, this much should now seem obvious. But watch out for hidden changes in leverage, such as a decision to lease new equipment or to underfund the pension scheme. Do not interpret any resultant increase in the expected equity return as creating additional shareholder value.

17-3   The Weighted-Average Cost of Capital

What did financial experts think about debt policy before MM? It is not easy to say because with hindsight we see that they did not think too clearly. However, a "traditional" position emerged in response to MM. To understand it, we have to return to the weighted-average cost of capital.

Figure 17.2 sums up the implications of MM's propositions for the costs of debt and equity and the weighted-average cost of capital. The figure assumes that the firm's bonds are essentially risk-free at low debt levels. Thus r_D is independent of D/E, and r_E increases linearly as D/E increases. As the firm borrows more, the risk of default increases and the firm is required to pay higher rates of interest. Proposition 2 predicts that when this occurs the rate of increase in r_E slows down. This is also shown in Figure 17.2. The more debt the firm has, the less sensitive r_E is to further borrowing.

Why does the slope of the r_E line in Figure 17.2 taper off as D/E increases? Essentially because holders of risky debt bear some of the firm's business risk. As the firm borrows more, more of that risk is transferred from stockholders to bondholders.

Two Warnings

Sometimes the objective in financing decisions is stated not as "maximize overall market value" but as "minimize the weighted-average cost of capital." If MM's proposition 1 holds, then these are

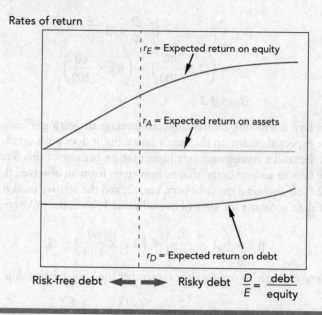

Rates of return

r_E = Expected return on equity

r_A = Expected return on assets

r_D = Expected return on debt

Risk-free debt ⟷ Risky debt $\dfrac{D}{E} = \dfrac{\text{debt}}{\text{equity}}$

FIGURE 17.2

MM's proposition 2. The expected return on equity r_E increases linearly with the debt–equity ratio so long as debt is risk-free. But if leverage increases the risk of the debt, debtholders demand a higher return on the debt. This causes the rate of increase in r_E to slow down.

equivalent objectives. If MM's proposition 1 does *not* hold, then the capital structure that maximizes the value of the firm also minimizes the weighted-average cost of capital, *provided* that operating income is independent of capital structure. Remember that the weighted-average cost of capital is the expected rate of return on the market value of all of the firm's securities. Anything that increases the value of the firm reduces the weighted-average cost of capital if operating income is constant. But if operating income is varying too, all bets are off.

In Chapter 18 we show that financial leverage can affect operating income in several ways. Therefore maximizing the value of the firm is *not* always equivalent to minimizing the weighted-average cost of capital.

Warning 1 Shareholders want management to increase the firm's value. They are more interested in being rich than in owning a firm with a low weighted-average cost of capital.

Warning 2 Trying to minimize the weighted-average cost of capital seems to encourage logical short circuits like the following. Suppose that someone says, "Shareholders demand—and deserve—higher expected rates of return than bondholders do. Therefore debt is the cheaper capital source. We can reduce the weighted-average cost of capital by borrowing more." But this doesn't follow if the extra borrowing leads stockholders to demand a still higher expected rate of return. According to MM's proposition 2 the cost of equity capital r_E increases by just enough to keep the weighted-average cost of capital constant.

This is not the only logical short circuit you are likely to encounter. We have cited two more in Problem 15 at the end of this chapter.

Rates of Return on Levered Equity—The Traditional Position

You may ask why we have even mentioned the aim of minimizing the weighted-average cost of capital if it is often wrong or confusing. We had to because the traditionalists accept this objective and argue their case in terms of it.

The logical short circuit we just described rested on the assumption that r_E, the expected rate of return demanded by stockholders, does not rise, or rises very slowly, as the firm borrows more. Suppose, just for the sake of argument, that this is true. Then r_A, the weighted-average cost of capital, must decline as the debt–equity ratio rises.

The traditionalists' position is shown in Figure 17.3. They say that a moderate degree of financial leverage may increase the expected equity return r_E, but not as much as predicted by MM's proposition 2. But irresponsible firms that borrow *excessively* find r_E shooting up *faster* than MM predict. Therefore the weighted-average cost of capital declines at first, then rises. It reaches a minimum at some intermediate debt ratio. Remember that minimizing the weighted-average cost of capital is equivalent to maximizing firm value if operating income is not affected by borrowing.

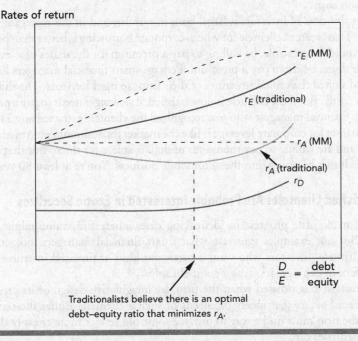

Traditionalists believe there is an optimal
debt–equity ratio that minimizes r_A.

FIGURE 17.3

The dashed lines show MM's view of the effect of leverage on the expected return on equity r_E and the weighted-average cost of capital r_A. (See Figure 17.2.) The solid lines show the traditional view. Traditionalists say that borrowing at first increases r_E more slowly than MM predict but that r_E shoots up with excessive borrowing. If so, the weighted-average cost of capital can be minimized if you use just the right amount of debt.

Two arguments could be advanced in support of this position. First, perhaps investors do not notice or appreciate the financial risk created by moderate borrowing, although they wake up when debt is "excessive." If so, stockholders in moderately leveraged firms may accept a lower rate of return than they really should.

That seems naive.[4] The second argument is better. It accepts MM's reasoning as applied to perfect capital markets but holds that actual markets are imperfect. Because of these imperfections, firms that borrow may provide a valuable service for investors. If so, levered shares might trade at premium prices compared to their theoretical values in perfect markets.

Suppose that corporations can borrow more cheaply than individuals. Then it would pay investors who want to borrow to do so indirectly by holding the stock of levered firms. They would be willing to live with expected rates of return that do not fully compensate them for the business and financial risk they bear.

Is corporate borrowing really cheaper? It's hard to say. Interest rates on home mortgages are not too different from rates on high-grade corporate bonds.[5] Rates on margin debt (borrowing from a stockbroker with the investor's shares tendered as security) are not too different from the rates firms pay banks for short-term loans.

There are some individuals who face relatively high interest rates, largely because of the costs lenders incur in making and servicing small loans. There are economies of scale in borrowing. A group of small investors could do better by borrowing via a corporation, in effect pooling their loans and saving transaction costs.[6]

Suppose that this class of investors is large, both in number and in the aggregate wealth it brings to capital markets. That creates a clientele for whom corporate borrowing is better than personal borrowing. That clientele would, in principle, be willing to pay a premium for the shares of a levered firm.

But maybe it doesn't *have* to pay a premium. Perhaps smart financial managers long ago recognized this clientele and shifted the capital structures of their firms to meet its needs. The shifts would not have been difficult or costly. But if the clientele is now satisfied, it no longer needs to pay a premium for levered shares. Only the financial managers who *first* recognized the clientele extracted any advantage from it.

Maybe the market for corporate leverage is like the market for automobiles. Americans need millions of automobiles and are willing to pay thousands of dollars apiece for them. But that doesn't mean that you could strike it rich by going into the automobile business. You're at least 80 years too late.

Today's Unsatisfied Clienteles Are Probably Interested in Exotic Securities

So far we have made little progress in identifying cases where firm value might plausibly depend on financing. But our examples illustrate what smart financial managers look for. They look for an *unsatisfied* clientele, investors who want a particular kind of financial instrument but because of market imperfections can't get it or can't get it cheaply.

MM's proposition 1 is violated when the firm, by imaginative design of its capital structure, can offer some *financial service* that meets the needs of such a clientele. Either the service must be new and unique or the firm must find a way to provide some old service more cheaply than other firms or financial intermediaries can.

Now, is there an unsatisfied clientele for garden-variety debt or levered equity? We doubt it. But perhaps you can invent an exotic security and uncover a latent demand for it.

---

[4] This first argument may reflect a confusion between financial risk and the risk of default. Default is not a serious threat when borrowing is moderate; stockholders worry about it only when the firm goes "too far." But stockholders bear financial risk—in the form of increased volatility of rates of return and a higher beta—even when the chance of default is nil.

[5] One of the authors once obtained a home mortgage at a rate 1/2 percentage point *less* than the contemporaneous yield on long-term AAA bonds.

[6] Even here there are alternatives to borrowing on personal account. Investors can draw down their savings accounts or sell a portion of their investment in bonds. The impact of reductions in lending on the investor's balance sheet and risk position is exactly the same as increases in borrowing.

In the next several chapters we will encounter a number of new securities that have been invented by companies and advisers. These securities take the company's basic cash flows and repackage them in ways that are thought to be more attractive to investors. However, while inventing these new securities is easy, it is more difficult to find investors who will rush to buy them.

Imperfections and Opportunities

The most serious capital market imperfections are often those created by government. An imperfection that supports a violation of MM's proposition 1 *also* creates a money-making opportunity. Firms and intermediaries will find some way to reach the clientele of investors frustrated by the imperfection.

For many years the U.S. government imposed a limit on the rate of interest that could be paid on savings accounts. It did so to protect savings institutions by limiting competition for their depositors' money. The fear was that depositors would run off in search of higher yields, causing a cash drain that savings institutions would not be able to meet.

These regulations created an opportunity for firms and financial institutions to design new savings schemes that were not subject to the interest-rate ceilings. One invention was the *floating-rate note*, first issued in 1974 by Citicorp, and with terms designed to appeal to individual investors. Floating-rate notes are medium-term debt securities whose interest payments "float" with short-term interest rates. On the Citicorp issue, for example, the coupon rate used to calculate each semiannual interest payment was set at 1 percentage point above the contemporaneous yield on Treasury bills. The holder of the Citicorp note was therefore protected against fluctuating interest rates, because Citicorp sent a larger check when interest rates rose (and, of course, a smaller check when rates fell).

In India, floating rate notes (or floaters as they are popularly known) were, however, introduced for entirely different reasons. The spread between the deposit rate and the borrowing rate in India was very high before 1994. The Governor of the RBI, therefore, proposed the banks to issue floating rate bonds to reduce the above spread. In 1994, SBI became the first company in India to issue floating rate bonds in India with an interest rate that was 3 percent higher than the maximum deposit rate ruling every six months.

Interest-rate regulation also provided financial institutions with an opportunity to create value by offering money-market funds. These are mutual funds invested in Treasury bills, commercial paper, and other high-grade, short-term debt instruments. Any saver with a few thousand dollars to invest can gain access to these instruments through a money-market fund and can withdraw money at any time by writing a check against his or her fund balance. Thus the fund resembles a checking or savings account that pays close to market interest rates. These money-market funds have become enormously popular. By 2009 their assets had risen to $3.7 trillion.[7]

Long before interest-rate ceilings were finally removed, most of the gains had gone out of issuing the new securities to individual investors. Once the clientele was finally satisfied, MM's proposition 1 was restored (until the government creates a new imperfection). The moral of the story is this: If you ever find an unsatisfied clientele, do something right away, or capital markets will evolve and steal it from you.

This is actually an encouraging message for the economy as a whole. If MM are right, investors' demands for different types of securities are satisfied at minimal cost. The cost of capital will reflect only business risk. Capital will flow to companies with positive-NPV investments, regardless of the companies' capital structures. This is the efficient outcome.

---

[7] Money-market funds are not totally safe. In 2008 the Reserve Primary Fund incurred heavy losses on its holdings of Lehman Brothers debt and became only the second money-market fund in history to "break the buck" by paying investors 97 cents in the dollar.

17-4   A FINAL WORD ON THE AFTER-TAX WEIGHTED-AVERAGE COST OF CAPITAL

MM left us a simple message. When the firm changes its mix of debt and equity securities, the risk and expected returns of these securities change, but the company's overall cost of capital does not change.

Now if you think that message is too neat and simple, you're right. The complications are spelled out in the next two chapters. But we must note one complication here: Interest paid on a firm's borrowing can be deducted from taxable income. Thus the *after-tax* cost of debt is $r_D(1 - T_c)$, where T_c is the marginal corporate tax rate. So, when companies discount an average-risk project, they do not use the company cost of capital as we have just computed it. Instead they use the after-tax cost of debt to compute the after-tax weighted-average cost of capital or WACC:

$$\text{After-tax WACC} = r_D(1 - T_c)\frac{D}{V} + r_E \frac{E}{V}$$

We briefly introduced this formula in Chapter 9, where we used it to estimate the weighted average cost of capital for Jet Airways. In 2011, Jet Airways' long-term borrowings rate was $r_D = 14\%$, and its estimated cost of equity was $r_E = 27.44\%$. With a 34% corporate tax rate, the after-tax cost of debt was $r_D(1 - T_c) = 14(1 - 0.34) = 9.24\%$. The ratio of debt to overall company value was $D/V = 77\%$. Therefore

$$\text{After-tax WACC} = r_D(1 - T_c)\frac{D}{V} + r_E \frac{E}{V}$$
$$= (1 - 0.34) \times 14 \times 0.77 + 27.44 \times 0.23 = 13.21\%$$

MM's proposition 2 states that *in the absence of taxes* the company cost of capital stays the same regardless of the amount of leverage. But, if companies receive a tax shield on their interest payments, then the after-tax WACC declines as debt increases. This is illustrated in Figure 17.4, which shows how Jet Airways' WACC changes as the debt–equity ratio changes.

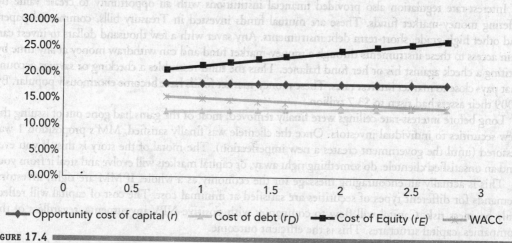

FIGURE 17.4

Estimated after-tax WACC for Jet Airways' at different debt–equity ratios. The figure assumes $r_E = 27.44\%$ at a 77% debt ratio and a borrowing rate of $r_D = 14\%$. Notice that the debt interest rate is assumed to increase with the debt–equity ratio.

SUMMARY

Think of the financial manager as taking all of the firm's real assets and selling them to investors as a package of securities. Some financial managers choose the simplest package possible: all-equity financing. Some end up issuing dozens of debt and equity securities. The problem is to find the particular combination that maximizes the market value of the firm.

Modigliani and Miller's (MM's) famous proposition 1 states that no combination is better than any other—that the firm's overall market value (the value of all its securities) is independent of capital structure. Firms that borrow do offer investors a more complex menu of securities, but investors yawn in response. The menu is redundant. Any shift in capital structure can be duplicated or "undone" by investors. Why should they pay extra for borrowing indirectly (by holding shares in a levered firm) when they can borrow just as easily and cheaply on their own accounts?

MM agree that borrowing raises the expected rate of return on shareholders' investments. But it also increases the risk of the firm's shares. MM show that the higher risk exactly offsets the increase in expected return, leaving stockholders no better or worse off.

Proposition 1 is an extremely general result. It applies not just to the debt–equity trade-off but to *any* choice of financing instruments. For example, MM would say that the choice between long-term and short-term debt has no effect on firm value.

The formal proofs of proposition 1 all depend on the assumption of perfect capital markets. MM's opponents, the "traditionalists," argue that market imperfections make personal borrowing excessively costly, risky, and inconvenient for some investors. This creates a natural clientele willing to pay a premium for shares of levered firms. The traditionalists say that firms should borrow to realize the premium.

But this argument is incomplete. There may be a clientele for levered equity, but that is not enough; the clientele has to be *unsatisfied*. There are already thousands of levered firms available for investment. Is there still an unsatiated clientele for garden-variety debt and equity? We doubt it.

Proposition 1 is violated when financial managers find an untapped demand and satisfy it by issuing something new and different. The argument between MM and the traditionalists finally boils down to whether this is difficult or easy. We lean toward MM's view: Finding unsatisfied clienteles and designing exotic securities to meet their needs is a game that's fun to play but hard to win.

If MM are right, the overall cost of capital—the expected rate of return on a portfolio of all the firm's outstanding securities—is the same regardless of the mix of securities issued to finance the firm. The overall cost of capital is usually called the company cost of capital or the weighted-average cost of capital (WACC). MM say that WACC doesn't depend on capital structure. But MM assume away lots of complications. The first complication is taxes. When we recognize that debt interest is tax-deductible, and compute WACC with the after-tax interest rate, WACC declines as the debt ratio increases. There is more—lots more—on taxes and other complications in the next two chapters.

FURTHER READING

The fall 1988 issue of the Journal of Economic Perspectives *contains a collection of articles, including one by Modigliani and Miller, which review and assess the MM propositions. The summer 1989 issue of* Financial Management *contains three more articles under the heading "Reflections on the MM Propositions 30 Years Later."*

Two surveys of financial innovation include:

K. A. Karow, G. R. Erwin, and J. J. McConnell, "Survey of U.S. Corporate Financing Innovations: 1970–1997," *Journal of Applied Corporate Finance* 12 (Spring 1999), pp. 55–69.

P. Tufano, "Financial Innovation," in G. M. Constantinides, M. Harris, and R. Stulz (eds.), *Handbook of the Economics of Finance,* Vol 1A (Amsterdam: Elsevier/North-Holland, 2003).

Miller reviews the MM propositions in:

M. H. Miller, "The Modigliani-Miller Propositions after Thirty Years," *Journal of Applied Corporate Finance* 2 (Spring 1989), pp. 6–18.

For a skeptic's view of MM's arguments see:

S. Titman, "The Modigliani-Miller Theorem and the Integration of Financial Markets," *Financial Management* 31 (Spring 2002), pp. 101–115.

BASIC

1. Ms. Pooja owns 50,000 shares of the common stock of Copper Corporation with a market value of ₹20 per share. The company is currently financed as follows:

	Book Value
Share Capital (8 million shares)	₹20 million
Short-term loans	₹20 million

Copper Corporation now announces that it is replacing ₹10 million of short-term debt with an issue of shares. What action can Ms. Pooja take to ensure that she is entitled to exactly the same proportion of profits as before?

2. Spam Corp. is financed entirely by equity and has a beta of 1.0. The firm is expected to generate a level, perpetual stream of earnings and dividends. The stock has a price–earnings ratio of 8 and a cost of equity of 12.5%. The company's stock is selling for ₹50. Now the firm decides to repurchase half of its shares and substitute an equal value of debt. The debt is risk-free, with a 5% interest rate. The company is exempt from corporate income taxes. Assuming MM are correct, calculate the following items after the refinancing:
   a. The cost of equity.
   b. The overall cost of capital (WACC).
   c. The price–earnings ratio.
   d. The stock price.
   e. The stock's beta.

3. The common stock and debt of NS Limited are valued at ₹50 million and ₹30 million, respectively. Investors currently require a 16% return on the common stock and an 8% return on the debt. If NS Limited issues an additional ₹10 million of common stock and uses this money to retire debt, what happens to the expected return on the stock? Assume that the change in capital structure does not affect the risk of the debt and that there are no taxes.

4. Suppose that Kavita Spot Removers issues only ₹2,500 of debt and uses the proceeds to repurchase 250 shares.
   a. Rework Table 17.2 to show how earnings per share and share return now vary with operating income.
   b. If the beta of Kavita's assets is .8 and its debt is risk-free, what would be the beta of the equity after the debt issue?

5. True or false?
   a. MM's propositions assume perfect financial markets, with no distorting taxes or other imperfections.
   b. MM's proposition 1 says that corporate borrowing increases earnings per share but reduces the price–earnings ratio.
   c. MM's proposition 2 says that the cost of equity increases with borrowing and that the increase is proportional to D/V, the ratio of debt to firm value.

d. MM's proposition 2 assumes that increased borrowing does not affect the interest rate on the firm's debt.

e. Borrowing does not increase financial risk and the cost of equity if there is no risk of bankruptcy.

f. Borrowing increases firm value if there is a clientele of investors with a reason to prefer debt.

6. Look back to Section 17.1. Suppose that Ms. Kavita's investment bankers have informed her that since the new issue of debt is risky, debtholders will demand a return of 12.5%, which is 2.5% above the risk-free interest rate.

   a. What are r_A and r_E?

   b. Suppose that the beta of the unlevered stock was .6. What will β_A, β_E, and β_D be after the change to the capital structure?

7. Note the two blank graphs in Figure 17.5 below. On graph (a), assume MM are right, and plot the relationship between financial leverage (debt-equity ratio) and (i) the rates of return on debt and equity and (ii) the weighted-average cost of capital. Then fill in graph (b), assuming the traditionalists are right.

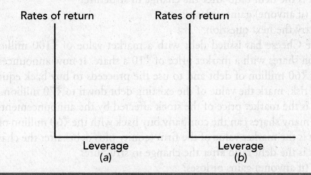

FIGURE 17.5
See Problem 7.

8. Gaucho Services starts life with all-equity financing and a cost of equity of 14%. Suppose it refinances to the following market-value capital structure:

Debt (D)	45%	at $r_D = 9.5\%$
Equity (E)	55%	

Use MM's proposition 2 to calculate the new cost of equity. Gaucho pays taxes at a marginal rate of $T_c = 40\%$. Calculate Gaucho's after-tax weighted-average cost of capital.

INTERMEDIATE

9. Companies A and B differ only in their capital structure. A is financed 30% debt and 70% equity; B is financed 10% debt and 90% equity. The debt of both companies is risk-free.

   a. Rosencrantz owns 1% of the common stock of A. What other investment package would produce identical cash flows for Rosencrantz?

   b. Guildenstern owns 2% of the common stock of B. What other investment package would produce identical cash flows for Guildenstern?

   c. Show that neither Rosencrantz nor Guildenstern would invest in the common stock of B if the *total* value of company A were less than that of B.

10. Here is a limerick:

There once was a man named Carruthers,
Who kept cows with miraculous udders.
He said, "Isn't this neat?
They give cream from one teat,
And skim milk from each of the others!"

What is the analogy between Mr. Carruthers's cows and firms' financing decisions? What would MM's proposition 1, suitably adapted, say about the value of Mr. Carruthers's cows? Explain.

11. Executive Chalk is financed solely by equity and has outstanding 25 million shares with a market price of ₹10 a share. It now announces that it intends to issue ₹160 million of debt and to use the proceeds to buy back equity.

a. How is the market price of the stock affected by the announcement?
b. How many shares can the company buy back with the ₹160 million of new debt that it issues?
c. What is the market value of the firm (equity plus debt) after the change in capital structure?
d. What is the debt ratio after the change in structure?
e. Who (if anyone) gains or loses?
Now try the next question.

12. Executive Cheese has issued debt with a market value of ₹100 million and has outstanding 15 million shares with a market price of ₹10 a share. It now announces that it intends to issue a further ₹60 million of debt and to use the proceeds to buy back equity. Debtholders, seeing the extra risk, mark the value of the existing debt down to ₹70 million.

a. How is the market price of the stock affected by the announcement?
b. How many shares can the company buy back with the ₹60 million of new debt that it issues?
c. What is the market value of the firm (equity plus debt) after the change in capital structure?
d. What is the debt ratio after the change in structure?
e. Who (if anyone) gains or loses?

13. Hubbard's Pet Foods is financed 80% by common stock and 20% by bonds. The expected return on the common stock is 12% and the rate of interest on the bonds is 6%. Assuming that the bonds are default-risk free, draw a graph that shows the expected return of Hubbard's common stock (r_E) and the expected return on the package of common stock and bonds (r_A) for different debt–equity ratios.

14. "MM totally ignore the fact that as you borrow more, you have to pay higher rates of interest." Explain carefully whether this is a valid objection.

15. Indicate what's wrong with the following arguments:

a. "As the firm borrows more and debt becomes risky, both stockholders and bondholders demand higher rates of return. Thus by *reducing* the debt ratio we can reduce *both* the cost of debt and the cost of equity, making everybody better off."
b. "Moderate borrowing doesn't significantly affect the probability of financial distress or bankruptcy. Consequently moderate borrowing won't increase the expected rate of return demanded by stockholders."

16. Each of the following statements is false or at least misleading. Explain why in each case.

a. "A capital investment opportunity offering a 10% DCF rate of return is an attractive project if it can be 100% debt-financed at an 8% interest rate."
b. "The more debt the firm issues, the higher the interest rate it must pay. That is one important reason why firms should operate at conservative debt levels."

17. Can you invent any new kinds of debt that might be attractive to investors? Why do you think they have not been issued?

18. Imagine a firm that is expected to produce a level stream of operating profits. As leverage is increased, what happens to:

a. The ratio of the market value of the equity to income after interest?

b. The ratio of the market value of the *firm* to income before interest if (i) MM are right and (ii) the traditionalists are right?

19. Archimedes Levers is financed by a mixture of debt and equity. You have the following information about its cost of capital:

$r_E =$ ___	$r_D = 12\%$	$r_A =$ ___
$\beta_E = 1.5$	$\beta_D =$ ___	$\beta_A =$ ___
$r_f = 10\%$	$r_m = 18\%$	$D/V = .5$

Can you fill in the blanks?

20. Look back to Problem 19. Suppose now that Archimedes repurchases debt and issues equity so that $D/V = .3$. The reduced borrowing causes r_D to fall to 11%. How do the other variables change?

21. Omega Corporation has 10 million shares outstanding, now trading at ₹55 per share. The firm has estimated the expected rate of return to shareholders at about 12%. It has also issued long-term bonds at an interest rate of 7%. It pays tax at a marginal rate of 35%.

a. What is Omega's after-tax WACC?

b. How much higher would WACC be if Omega used no debt at all? (*Hint:* For this problem you can assume that the firm's overall beta $[\beta_A]$ is not affected by its capital structure or the taxes saved because debt interest is tax-deductible.)

22. Gamma Airlines has an asset beta of 1.5. The risk-free interest rate is 6%, and the market risk premium is 8%. Assume the capital asset pricing model is correct. Gamma pays taxes at a marginal rate of 35%. Draw a graph plotting Gamma's cost of equity and after-tax WACC as a function of its debt-to-equity ratio D/E, from no debt to $D/E = 1.0$. Assume that Gamma's debt is risk-free up to $D/E = .25$. Then the interest rate increases to 6.5% at $D/E = .5$, 7% at $D/E = .8$, and 8% at $D/E = 1.0$. As in Problem 21, you can assume that the firm's overall beta (β_A) is not affected by its capital structure or the taxes saved because debt interest is tax-deductible.

CHALLENGE

23. Consider the following three tickets: ticket A pays ₹10 if _____ is elected as president, ticket B pays ₹10 if _____ is elected, and ticket C pays ₹10 if neither is elected. (Fill in the blanks yourself.) Could the three tickets sell for less than the present value of ₹10? Could they sell for more? Try auctioning off the tickets. What are the implications for MM's proposition 1?

24. People often convey the idea behind MM's proposition 1 by various supermarket analogies, for example, "The value of a pie should not depend on how it is sliced," or, "The cost of a whole chicken should equal the cost of assembling one by buying two drumsticks, two wings, two breasts, and so on."

Actually proposition 1 doesn't work in the supermarket. You'll pay less for an uncut whole pie than for a pie assembled from pieces purchased separately. Supermarkets charge more for chickens after they are cut up. Why? What costs or imperfections cause proposition 1 to fail in the supermarket? Are these costs or imperfections likely to be important for corporations issuing securities in India? Explain.

25. Suppose that new security designs could be patented.[8] The patent holder could restrict use of the new design or charge other firms royalties for using it. What effect would such patents have on MM's capital-structure irrelevance theory?

---

[8] So far security designs cannot be patented, but other financial applications have received patent protection. See J. Lerner, "Where Does State Street Lead? A First Look at Finance Patents," *Journal of Finance* 57 (April 2002), pp. 901–930.

18

CHAPTER

HOW MUCH SHOULD A CORPORATION BORROW?

In Chapter 17 we found that debt policy rarely matters in well-functioning capital markets with no frictions or imperfections. Few financial managers would accept that conclusion as a practical guideline. If debt policy doesn't matter, then they shouldn't worry about it—financing decisions could be routine or erratic—it wouldn't matter. Yet financial managers do worry about debt policy. This chapter explains why.

If debt policy were completely irrelevant, then actual debt ratios should vary randomly from firm to firm and industry to industry. Yet almost all airlines, utilities, banks, and real estate development companies rely heavily on debt. And so do many firms in capital-intensive industries such as steel, aluminum, chemicals, petroleum, and mining. On the other hand, it is rare to find a pharmaceutical company or advertising agency that is not predominantly equity-financed. Glamorous growth companies rarely use much debt despite rapid expansion and often heavy requirements for capital.

The explanation of these patterns lies partly in the things we left out of the last chapter. We mostly ignored taxes. We assumed bankruptcy was cheap, quick, and painless. It isn't, and there are costs associated with financial distress even if legal bankruptcy is ultimately avoided. We ignored potential conflicts of interest between the firm's security holders. For example, we did not consider what happens to the firm's "old" creditors when new debt is issued or when a shift in investment strategy takes the firm into a riskier business. We ignored the information problems that favor debt over equity when cash must be raised from new security issues. We ignored the incentive effects of financial leverage on management's investment and payout decisions.

Now we will put all these things back in: taxes first, then the costs of bankruptcy and financial distress. This will lead us to conflicts of interest and to information and incentive problems. In the end we will have to admit that debt policy does matter.

However, we will not throw away the MM theory we developed so carefully in Chapter 17. We're shooting for a theory combining MM's insights plus the effects of taxes, costs of bankruptcy and financial distress, and various other complications. We're not dropping back to a theory based on inefficiencies in the capital market. Instead, we want to see how well-functioning capital markets respond to taxes and the other things covered in this chapter.

18-1 CORPORATE TAXES

Debt financing has one important advantage under the corporate income tax system in India. The interest that the company pays is a tax-deductible expense. Thus the return to bondholders escapes taxation at the corporate level.

Table 18.1 shows simple income statements for firm U, which has no debt, and firm L, which has borrowed ₹1,000 at 8%. L's tax bill is ₹28 less than U's. This is the *tax shield* provided by the debt of L. In effect the government pays 35% of the interest expense of L. The total income that L can pay out to its bondholders and stockholders increases by that amount.

TABLE 18.1   The tax deductibility of interest increases the total income that can be paid out to bondholders and stockholders.

	Income Statement of Firm U	Income Statement of Firm L
Earnings before interest and taxes	₹1,000	₹1,000
Interest paid to bondholders	0	80
Pretax income	1,000	920
Tax at 35%	350	322
Net income to stockholders	₹ 650	₹ 598
Total income to both bondholders and stockholders	₹0 + 650 = ₹650	₹80 + 598 = ₹678
Interest tax shield (.35 × interest)	₹0	₹28

Tax shields can be valuable assets. Suppose that the debt of L is fixed and permanent. (That is, the company commits to refinance its present debt obligations when they mature and to keep rolling over its debt obligations indefinitely.) Then L can look forward to a permanent stream of cash flows of ₹28 per year. The risk of these flows is likely to be less than the risk of the operating assets of L. The tax shields depend only on the corporate tax rate[1] and on the ability of L to earn enough to cover interest payments. The corporate tax rate has been pretty stable. And the ability of L to earn its interest payments must be reasonably sure; otherwise it could not have borrowed at 8%. Therefore, we should discount the interest tax shields at a relatively low rate.

---

[1] Always use the marginal corporate tax rate, not the average rate. Average rates are often much lower than marginal rates because of difference in depreciation method (written down value method vis-a-vis straight line method) and other tax adjustments. For large corporations, the marginal rate is usually taken as the statutory rate, which was 33.99% for the Indian Companies when this chapter was written (2011). However, effective marginal rates can be less than the statutory rate, especially for smaller, riskier companies that cannot be sure that they will earn taxable income in the future.

But what rate? One common assumption is that the risk of the tax shields is the same as that of the interest payments generating them. Thus we discount at 8%, the expected rate of return demanded by investors who are holding the firm's debt:

$$PV(\text{tax shield}) = \frac{28}{.08} = ₹350$$

In effect the government assumes 35% of the ₹1,000 debt obligation of L.

Under these assumptions, the present value of the tax shield is independent of the return on the debt r_D. It equals the corporate tax rate T_c times the amount borrowed D:

$$\text{Interest payment} = \text{return on debt} \times \text{amount borrowed}$$
$$= r_D \times D$$

$$PV(\text{tax shield}) = \frac{\text{corporate tax rate} \times \text{interest payment}}{\text{expected return on debt}}$$
$$= \frac{T_c r_D D}{r_D} = T_c D$$

Of course, PV(tax shield) is less if the firm does not plan to borrow a permanent fixed amount,[2] or if it may not have enough taxable income to use the interest tax shields.[3]

How Do Interest Tax Shields Contribute to the Value of Stockholders' Equity?

MM's proposition 1 amounts to saying that the value of a pie does not depend on how it is sliced. The pie is the firm's assets, and the slices are the debt and equity claims. If we hold the pie constant, then a dollar more of debt means a dollar less of equity value.

But there is really a third slice, the government's. Look at Table 18.2. It shows an expanded balance sheet with *pretax* asset value on the left and the value of the government's tax claim recognized as a liability on the right. MM would still say that the value of the pie—in this case *pretax* asset value—is not changed by slicing. But anything the firm can do to reduce the size of the government's slice obviously makes stockholders better off. One thing it can do is borrow money, which reduces its tax bill and, as we saw in Table 18.1, increases the cash flows to debt and equity investors. The *after-tax* value of the firm (the sum of its debt and equity values as shown in a normal market value balance sheet) goes up by PV(tax shield).

Recasting Asian Paints' Capital Structure

Asian Paints is a large, successful firm that uses relatively little long-term debt. Table 18.3(*a*) shows simplified book and market value balance sheets for Asian Paints in March 2011.

Suppose that you were Asian Paints' financial manager with complete responsibility for its capital structure. You decide to borrow an additional ₹50 crores on a permanent basis and use the proceeds to repurchase shares.

---

[2] In this example, we assume that the amount of debt is fixed and stable over time. The natural alternative assumption is a fixed *ratio* of debt to firm value. If the ratio is fixed, then the level of debt and the amount of interest tax shields will fluctuate as firm value fluctuates. In that case projected interest tax shields can't be discounted at the cost of debt. We cover this point in detail in the next chapter.

[3] If the income of L does not cover interest in some future year, the tax shield is not necessarily lost. L can carry back the loss and receive a tax refund up to the amount of taxes paid in the previous two years. If L has a string of losses, and thus no prior tax payments that can be refunded, then losses can be carried forward and used to shield income in later years.

TABLE 18.2 Normal and expanded market value balance sheets. In a normal balance sheet, assets are valued after tax. In the expanded balance sheet, assets are valued pretax, and the value of the government's tax claim is recognized on the right-hand side. Interest tax shields are valuable because they reduce the government's claim.

Normal Balance Sheet (Market Values)	

Expanded Balance Sheet (Market Values)	
Pretax asset value (present value of pretax cash flows)	Debt
	Government's claim (present value of future taxes)

TABLE 18.3(A) Simplified balance sheets for Asian Paints Limited, March 2011 (figures in ₹ crores).

Book Values			
Secured and unsecured loans	₹64.13	₹–119.82	Net current assets
Equity	1975.32	1919.63	Long term assets
Total value	₹2039.45	₹2039.45	Total assets
Market Values			
Secured and unsecured loans	₹64.13	₹–119.82	Net current assets
		21.80	PV of interest tax shield
Equity	24987.1	24909.61	Long term assets
Total value	₹25051.23	₹25051.23	Total assets

Notes:
1. Market value is equal to book value for net current assets, secured and unsecured loans. Market value of equity = number of shares times closing price for March 2011. The difference between the market and book values of long-term assets is equal to the difference between the market and book value of equity.
2. PV of interest tax shield assumes fixed, perpetual debt, with a 33.99% tax rate.

TABLE 18.3(B) Balance Sheets for Asian Paints with additional ₹50 crores of long-term debt substituted for shareholders' equity (figures in crores).

Book Values			
Secured and unsecured loans	₹114.13	₹–119.82	Net current assets
Equity	1925.32	1919.63	Long term assets
Total value	₹2039.45	₹2039.45	Total assets
Market Values			
Secured and unsecured loans	₹114.13	₹–119.82	Net current assets
		38.79	PV of interest tax shield
Equity	24954.095	24909.62	Long term assets
Total value	₹25068.23	₹25068.23	Total assets

Table 18.3(*b*) shows the new balance sheets. The book version simply has ₹50 crores more long-term debt and ₹50 crores less equity. But we know that Asian Paints' assets must be worth more because its tax bill has been reduced by 33.99% of the interest on the new debt. In other words, Asian Paints has an increase in PV(interest tax shield), which is worth $T_cD = .3399 \times ₹50$ crores $= ₹16.83$ crores. If the MM theory holds *except* for taxes, firm value must increase by ₹16.995 crores to ₹25,068.23 crores. Asian Paints' equity ends up worth ₹24,954 crores.

Now you have repurchased ₹50 crores worth of shares, but Asian Paint's equity value has dropped by only ₹33.01 crores. Therefore, Asian Paints' stockholders must be ₹16.99 crores ahead. Not a bad day's work.[4]

MM and Taxes

We have just developed a version of MM's proposition 1 as corrected by them to reflect corporate income taxes.[5] The new proposition is

$$\text{Value of firm} = \text{value if all-equity-financed} + \text{PV(tax shield)}$$

In the special case of permanent debt,

$$\text{Value of firm} = \text{value if all-equity-financed} + T_cD$$

Our imaginary financial surgery on Asian Paints provides the perfect illustration of the problems inherent in this "corrected" theory. That ₹16.99 crores came too easily; it seems to violate the law that there is no such thing as a money machine. And if Asian Paints' shareholders would be richer with ₹50 crores of corporate debt, why not ₹60 crores or ₹100 crores? At what debt level should Asian Paints stop borrowing? Our formula implies that firm value and shareholders' wealth continue to go up as D increases. The optimal debt policy appears to be embarrassingly extreme. All firms should be 100% debt-financed.

MM were not that fanatical about it. No one would expect the formula to apply at extreme debt ratios. There are several reasons why our calculations overstate the value of interest tax shields. First, it's wrong to think of debt as fixed and perpetual; a firm's ability to carry debt changes over time as profits and firm value fluctuate. Second, many firms face marginal tax rates less than 33.99%. Third, you can't use interest tax shields unless there will be future profits to shield—and no firm can be absolutely sure of that.

But none of these qualifications explains why farms like Asian Paints not only exist but also thrive with scarcely any debt at all. It's hard to believe that Asian Paints' financial managers are simply missing the boat.

We seem to have argued ourselves into a blind alley. But there may be two ways out:

1. Perhaps a fuller examination of the Indian system of corporate *and personal* taxation will uncover a tax disadvantage of corporate borrowing, offsetting the present value of the interest tax shield.
2. Perhaps firms that borrow incur other costs—bankruptcy costs, for example.

We now explore these two escape routes.

---

[4] Notice that as long as the bonds are sold at a fair price, all the benefits from the tax shield must go to the shareholders.

[5] Interest tax shields are recognized in MM's original article, F. Modigliani and M. H. Miller, "The Cost of Capital, Corporation Finance and the Theory of Investment," *American Economic Review* 48 (June 1958), pp. 261–296. The valuation procedure used in Table 18.3(*b*) is presented in their 1963 article "Corporate Income Taxes and the Cost of Capital: A Correction," *American Economic Review* 53 (June 1963), pp. 433–443.

18-2 CORPORATE AND PERSONAL TAXES

When personal taxes are introduced, the firm's objective is no longer to minimize the *corporate* tax bill; the firm should try to minimize the present value of *all* taxes paid on corporate income. "All taxes" include *personal* taxes paid by bondholders and stockholders.

Figure 18.1 illustrates how corporate and personal taxes are affected by leverage. Depending on the firm's capital structure, a rupee of operating income will accrue to investors either as debt interest or equity income (dividends or capital gains). That is, the rupee can go down either branch of Figure 18.1.

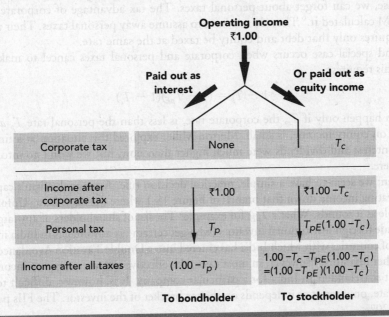

FIGURE 18.1
The firm's capital structure determines whether operating income is paid out as interest or equity income. Interest is taxed only at the personal level. Equity income is taxed at both the corporate and the personal levels. However, T_{pE}, the personal tax rate on equity income, can be less than T_p, the personal tax rate on interest income.

Notice that Figure 18.1 distinguishes between T_p, the personal tax rate on interest, and T_{pE}, the effective personal tax rate on equity income. As of now (2011), companies pay dividend distribution tax (effective rate = 16.609%) before distributing the dividends. The investors pay securities transaction tax of 0.125 percent on any purchase or sale of shares. The short term capital gains tax rate is 15 percent now and the long term capital gains tax rate is nil provided, securities transaction tax has been paid. So the effective personal tax rate on equity income is much lower than 16.609 percent. The personal tax rate on interest depends on the personal tax bracket of the tax payer and can be as high as 30.9 percent. T_{pE} can be well below T_p, depending on the mix of dividends and capital gains realized by shareholders. In fact, since the marginal tax rate is 20.6 percent for income exceeding ₹500,000, for most of the investors T_{pE} will be lower than T_p.

The firm's objective should be to arrange its capital structure to maximize after-tax income. You can see from Figure 18.1 that corporate borrowing is better if $(1 - T_p)$ is more than $(1 - T_{pE}) \times (1 - T_c)$; otherwise it is worse. The *relative tax* advantage of debt over equity is

$$\text{Relative tax advantage of debt} = \frac{1 - T_p}{(1 - T_{pE})(1 - T_c)}$$

This suggests two special cases. First, suppose that debt and equity income were taxed at the same effective personal rate. But with $T_{pE} = T_p$, the relative advantage depends only on the *corporate rate*:

$$\text{Relative advantage} = \frac{1 - T_p}{(1 - T_{pE})(1 - T_c)} = \frac{1}{1 - T_c}$$

In this case, we can forget about personal taxes. The tax advantage of corporate borrowing is exactly as MM calculated it.[6] They do not have to assume away personal taxes. Their theory of debt and taxes requires only that debt and equity be taxed at the same rate.

The second special case occurs when corporate and personal taxes cancel to make debt policy irrelevant. This requires

$$1 - T_p = (1 - T_{pE})(1 - T_c)$$

This case can happen only if T_c, the corporate rate, is less than the personal rate T_p *and* if T_{pE}, the effective rate on equity income, is small. Merton Miller explored this situation at a time when U.S. tax rates on interest and dividends were much higher than now, but we won't go into the details of his analysis here.[7]

In any event we seem to have a simple, practical decision rule. Arrange the firm's capital structure to shunt operating income down that branch of Figure 18.1 where the tax is least. Unfortunately that is not as simple as it sounds. What's T_{pE}, for example? The list of shareholders of any large company is likely to include foreign institutional investors (who get certain tax advantages in India in case they are tax residents of countries with which India has entered into a Double Taxation Avoidance Agreement), NRIs, and other investors. However, in most cases, the effective tax rate on equity income will be the same for most shareholders in India for a particular company. It is, however, difficult to find T_p, the personal tax rate, on interest as it depends on the tax bracket of the investor. The FIIs pay interest tax at the rate of 20%.

Some investors may be much happier to buy your debt than others. For example, you should have no problems inducing a tax resident of Cyprus to lend. But a high net worth investor in India may be more reluctant to hold debt and will be prepared to do so only if he is compensated by a high rate of interest. Investors paying tax at the top rate of 30.9% may be particularly reluctant to hold debt. They will prefer to hold common stock.

To determine the net tax advantage of debt, companies would need to know the tax rates faced by the *marginal* investor—that is, an investor who is equally happy to hold debt or equity. This makes it hard to put a precise figure on the tax benefit, but we can nevertheless provide a back-of-the-

---

[6] Personal taxes reduce the rupee amount of corporate interest tax shields, but the appropriate discount rate for cash flows after personal tax is also lower. If investors are willing to lend at a prospective return *before* personal taxes of r_D, then they must also be willing to accept a return *after* personal taxes of $r_D(1 - T_p)$, where T_p is the marginal rate of personal tax. Thus we can compute the value after personal taxes of the tax shield on permanent debt:

$$\text{PV(tax shield)} = \frac{T_c \times r_D D \times (1 - T_p)}{r_D \times (1 - T_p)} = T_c D$$

This brings us back to our previous formula for firm value:

$$\text{Value of firm} = \text{value if all-equity-financed} + T_c D$$

[7] M. H. Miller, "Debt and Taxes," *Journal of Finance* 32 (May 1977), pp. 261–276.

envelope calculation. Let's consider a large, dividend-paying company like Tata Steel. Tata Steel's dividend payout ratio is around 17 percent, so for each ₹1 of income, 17 paise is received as dividends and 83 paise as capital gains. Suppose that the marginal investor is in the top tax bracket paying 30.9 percent on interest income. Let's assume that the investor sells the shares after one year and hence pays only the securities transaction tax. Since he can defer the payment of the securities transaction tax, let's assume that the effective securities transaction tax rate is 0.10 percent. Therefore, if the investor invests in Tata Steel's shares, the tax on each ₹1 of equity income is $T_{pE} = (0.16609 \times 0.17) + (0.001 \times 0.83) = 2.91$ percent.

Now we can calculate the effect of shunting a dollar of income down each of the two branches in Figure 18.1:

	Interest	Equity Income
Income before tax	₹1.00	₹1.00
Less corporate tax at $T_c = .3399$	0	.34
Income after corporate tax	1.00	.66
Personal tax at $T_p = .309$ and $T_{pE} = .0291$	.34	.02
Income after all taxes	₹0.66	₹0.64
		Advantage to debt = ₹0.02

The advantage to debt financing appears to be about 2 paise on the rupee.

We should emphasize that our back-of-the-envelope calculation is just that. But it's interesting to see how debt's tax advantage shrinks when we account for the relatively low personal tax rate on equity. This reflects a tax-law change in this decade when the securities transaction tax was introduced. Before that change, the capital gains tax rate was 10 percent for the FIIs and NRIs and 20 percent for the most of the other investors. The advantage to debt is about 6 paise if we use these prior rates in our back-of-the envelope calculation.[8]

Most financial managers believe that there is a moderate tax advantage to corporate borrowing, at least for companies that are reasonably sure they can use the corporate tax shields. For companies that cannot benefit from corporate tax shields there is probably a moderate tax disadvantage.

Do companies make full use of interest tax shields? John Graham argues that they don't. His estimates suggest that a typical tax-paying corporation could add 7.5% to firm value by levering up to a still-conservative debt ratio.[9] This is hardly spare change. Therefore it still appears that financial managers have passed by some easy tax savings. Perhaps they saw some offsetting disadvantage to increased borrowing. We now explore this second escape route.

18-3 COSTS OF FINANCIAL DISTRESS

Financial distress occurs when promises to creditors are broken or honored with difficulty. Sometimes financial distress leads to bankruptcy. Sometimes it only means skating on thin ice.

[8] Here, we assume that 50 percent of the shares are controlled by the FIIs and NRIs. The actual benefit of debt will change for any different assumption.

[9] Graham's estimates for individual firms recognize both the uncertainty in future profits and the existence of noninterest tax shields. See J. R. Graham, "How Big Are the Tax Benefits of Debt?" *Journal of Finance* 55 (October 2000), pp. 1901–1941.

As we will see, financial distress is costly. Investors know that levered firms may fall into financial distress, and they worry about it. That worry is reflected in the current market value of the levered firm's securities. Thus, the value of the firm can be broken down into three parts:

$$\begin{array}{c} \text{Value} \\ \text{of firm} \end{array} = \begin{array}{c} \text{value if} \\ \text{all-equity-finaced} \end{array} + \text{PV(tax shield)} - \begin{array}{c} \text{PV(costs of} \\ \text{financial distress)} \end{array}$$

The costs of financial distress depend on the probability of distress and the magnitude of costs encountered if distress occurs.

Figure 18.2 shows how the trade-off between the tax benefits and the costs of distress could determine optimal capital structure. PV(tax shield) initially increases as the firm borrows more. At moderate debt levels the probability of financial distress is trivial, and so PV(cost of financial distress) is small and tax advantages dominate. But at some point the probability of financial distress increases rapidly with additional borrowing; the costs of distress begin to take a substantial bite out of firm value. Also, if the firm can't be sure of profiting from the corporate tax shield, the tax advantage of additional debt is likely to dwindle and eventually disappear. The theoretical optimum is reached when the present value of tax savings due to further borrowing is just offset by increases in the present value of costs of distress. This is called the *trade-off theory* of capital structure.

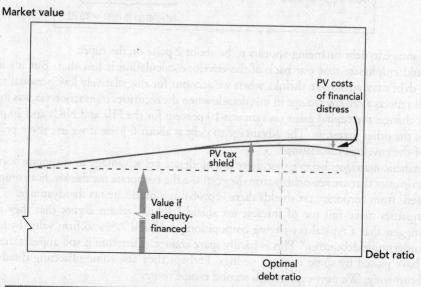

FIGURE 18.2

The value of the firm is equal to its value if all-equity-financed plus PV tax shield minus PV costs of financial distress. According to the trade-off theory of capital structure, the manager should choose the debt ratio that maximizes firm value.

Costs of financial distress cover several specific items. Now we identify these costs and try to understand what causes them.

Bankruptcy Costs

You rarely hear anything nice said about corporate bankruptcy. But there is some good in almost everything. Corporate bankruptcies occur when stockholders exercise their *right to default*. That right is valuable; when a firm gets into trouble, limited liability allows stockholders simply to walk away from it, leaving all its troubles to its creditors. The former creditors become the new stockholders, and the old stockholders are left with nothing.

Stockholders in corporations automatically get *limited liability*. But suppose that this were not so. Suppose that there are two firms with identical assets and operations. Each firm has debt outstanding, and each has promised to repay ₹1,000 (principal and interest) next year. But only one of the firms, Ace Limited, enjoys limited liability. The other firm, Ace Unlimited, does not; its stockholders are personally liable for its debt.[10]

Figure 18.3 compares next year's possible payoffs to the creditors and stockholders of these two firms. The only differences occur when next year's asset value turns out to be less than ₹1,000.

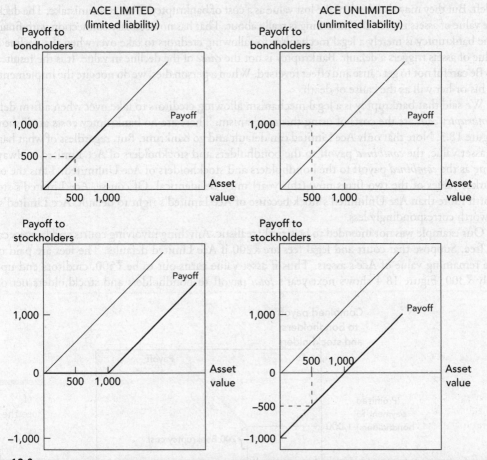

FIGURE 18.3

Comparison of limited and unlimited liability for two otherwise identical firms. If the two firms' asset values are less than ₹1,000, Ace Limited stockholders default and its bondholders take over the assets. Ace Unlimited stockholders keep the assets, but they must reach into their own pockets to pay off its bondholders. The total payoff to both stockholders and bondholders is the same for the two firms.

---

[10] Ace Unlimited could be a partnership or sole proprietorship, which do not provide limited liability.

Suppose that next year the assets of each company are worth only ₹500. In this case Ace Limited defaults. Its stockholders walk away; their payoff is zero. Bondholders get the assets worth ₹500. But Ace Unlimited's stockholders can't walk away. They have to cough up ₹500, the difference between asset value and the bondholders' claim. The debt is paid whatever happens.

Suppose that Ace Limited does go bankrupt. Of course, its stockholders are disappointed that their firm is worth so little, but that is an operating problem having nothing to do with financing. Given poor operating performance, the right to go bankrupt—the right to default—is a valuable privilege. As Figure 18.3 shows, Ace Limited's stockholders are in better shape than Unlimited's are.

The example illuminates a mistake people often make in thinking about the costs of bankruptcy. Bankruptcies are thought of as corporate funerals. The mourners (creditors and especially shareholders) look at their firm's present sad state. They think of how valuable their securities used to be and how little is left. But they may also think of the lost value as a cost of bankruptcy. That is the mistake. The decline in the value of assets is what the mourning is really about. That has no necessary connection with financing. The bankruptcy is merely a legal mechanism for allowing creditors to take over when the decline in the value of assets triggers a default. Bankruptcy is not the *cause* of the decline in value. It is the result.

Be careful not to get cause and effect reversed. When a person dies, we do not cite the implementation of his or her will as the cause of death.

We said that bankruptcy is a legal mechanism allowing creditors to take over when a firm defaults. *Bankruptcy costs* are the costs of using this mechanism. There are no bankruptcy costs at all shown in Figure 18.3. Note that only Ace Limited can default and go bankrupt. But, regardless of what happens to asset value, the *combined* payoff to the bondholders and stockholders of Ace Limited is always the same as the *combined* payoff to the bondholders and stockholders of Ace Unlimited. Thus the overall market values of the two firms now (this year) must be identical. Of course, Ace Limited's stock is worth more than Ace Unlimited's stock because of Ace Limited's right to default. Ace Limited's debt is worth correspondingly less.

Our example was not intended to be strictly realistic. Anything involving courts and lawyers cannot be free. Suppose that court and legal fees are ₹200 if Ace Limited defaults. The fees are paid out of the remaining value of Ace's assets. Thus if asset value turns out to be ₹500, creditors end up with only ₹300. Figure 18.4 shows next year's *total* payoff to bondholders and stockholders net of this

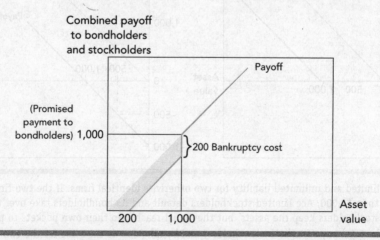

FIGURE 18.4

Total payoff to Ace Limited security holders. There is a ₹200 bankruptcy cost in the event of default (shaded area).

bankruptcy cost. Ace Limited, by issuing risky debt, has given lawyers and the court system a claim on the firm if it defaults. The market value of the firm is reduced by the present value of this claim.

It is easy to see how increased leverage affects the present value of the costs of financial distress. If Ace Limited borrows more, it increases the probability of default and the value of the lawyers' claim. It increases PV (costs of financial distress) and reduces Ace's present market value.

The costs of bankruptcy come out of stockholders' pockets. Creditors foresee the costs and foresee that *they* will pay them if default occurs. For this they demand compensation in advance in the form of higher payoffs when the firm does *not* default; that is, they demand a higher promised interest rate. This reduces the possible payoffs to stockholders and reduces the present market value of their shares.

Evidence on Bankruptcy Costs in the U.S.

Bankruptcy costs can add up fast. While United Airlines was in bankruptcy, it paid over $350 million to lawyers, accountants, and consultants.[11] Enron set a record with legal, accounting, and other professional costs of nearly $1 billion. Professional fees for another distressed energy company, Mirant Corp., were a bit more moderate. The "burn rate" of fees for the first year of Mirant's bankruptcy proceedings was $120 to $140 million.[12]

Daunting as such numbers may seem, they are not a large fraction of the companies' asset values. Lawrence Weiss, who studied 31 firms that went bankrupt between 1980 and 1986, found average costs of about 3% of total book assets and 20% of the market value of equity in the year prior to bankruptcy. A study by Andrade and Kaplan of a sample of troubled and highly leveraged firms estimated costs of financial distress amounting to 10% to 20% of predistress market value, although they found it hard to decide whether these costs were caused by financial distress or by the business setbacks that led to distress.[13]

Bankruptcy eats up a larger fraction of asset value for small companies than for large ones. There are significant economies of scale in going bankrupt. For example, a study of smaller U.K. bankruptcies by Franks and Sussman found that fees (legal and accounting) and other costs soaked up roughly 20% to 40% of the proceeds from liquidation of the companies.[14]

Direct versus Indirect Costs of Bankruptcy

So far we have discussed the *direct* (that is, legal and administrative) costs of bankruptcy. There are indirect costs too, which are nearly impossible to measure. But we have circumstantial evidence indicating their importance.

---

[11] "Bankruptcy Lawyers Flying High; Airlines' Woes Mean Big Paydays for Consultants and Law Firms; Partner's $177,000 Bill for August," *The Wall Street Journal*, October 21, 2005, p. C.1.

[12] "Enron Bankruptcy Specialist to File for Additional Payment; On Top of $63.4 Million, 'Success Fee' to Be Sought of Additional $25 Million," *The Wall Street Journal*, September 3, 2004, p. A.2; and "Mirant Bankruptcy Legal Fees Seen Topping $120 Million," Reuters, January 20, 2004.

[13] The pioneering study of bankruptcy costs is J. B. Warner, "Bankruptcy Costs: Some Evidence," *Journal of Finance* 26 (May 1977), pp. 337–348. See also L. A. Weiss, "Bankruptcy Resolution: Direct Costs and Violation of Priority of Claims," *Journal of Financial Economics* 27 (October 1990), pp. 285–314; E. I. Altman, "A Further Investigation of the Bankruptcy Cost Question," *Journal of Finance* 39 (September 1984), pp. 1067–1089; and G. Andrade and S. N. Kaplan, "How Costly Is Financial (not Economic) Distress? Evidence from Highly Leveraged Transactions That Became Distressed," *Journal of Finance* 53 (October 1998), pp. 1443–1493.

[14] J. Franks and O. Sussman, "Financial Distress and Bank Restructuring of Small to Medium Size UK Companies," *Review of Finance* 9 (2005), pp. 65–96. Karin Thornburg found that the Swedish bankruptcy system is reasonably efficient for smaller firms, however. See "Bankruptcy Auctions: Costs, Debt Recovery and Firm Survival," *Journal of Financial Economics* 58 (December 2000), pp. 337–368.

Managing a bankrupt firm is not easy. Consent of the bankruptcy court is required for many routine business decisions, such as the sale of assets or investment in new equipment. At best this involves time and effort; at worst proposals to reform and revive the firm are thwarted by impatient creditors, who stand first in line for cash from asset sales or liquidation of the entire firm.

Sometimes the problem is reversed: The bankruptcy court is so anxious to maintain the firm as a going concern that it allows the firm to engage in negative-NPV activities. When Eastern Airlines entered the "protection" of the bankruptcy court in 1989, it still had some valuable, profit-making routes and salable assets such as planes and terminal facilities. The creditors would have been best served by a prompt liquidation, which probably would have generated enough cash to pay off all debt and preferred stockholders. But the bankruptcy judge was keen to keep Eastern's planes flying at all costs, so he allowed the company to sell many of its assets to fund hefty operating losses. When Eastern finally closed down after two years, it was not just bankrupt, but *administratively* insolvent: There was almost nothing for creditors, and the company was running out of cash to pay legal expenses.[15]

We do not know what the sum of direct and indirect costs of bankruptcy amounts to. We suspect it is a significant number, particularly for large firms for which proceedings would be lengthy and complex. Perhaps the best evidence is the reluctance of creditors to force bankruptcy. In principle, they would be better off to end the agony and seize the assets as soon as possible. Instead, creditors often overlook defaults in the hope of nursing the firm over a difficult period. They do this in part to avoid costs of bankruptcy. There is an old financial saying, "Borrow $1,000 and you've got a banker. Borrow $10,000,000 and you've got a partner."

Creditors may also shy away from bankruptcy because they worry about violations of absolute priority. *Absolute priority* means that creditors are paid in full before stockholders receive a penny. But sometimes reorganizations provide something for everyone, including consolation prizes for stockholders. Sometimes other claimants move up in the queue. For example, after the Chrysler bankruptcy in 2009, the State of Indiana sued (unsuccessfully) on behalf of local pension funds that had invested in Chrysler bonds. The funds complained bitterly about the terms of sale of the bankrupt company's assets to Fiat, arguing that they would get only $.29 on the dollar, while other, more junior claimants fared better. The Chrysler bankruptcy was a special case, however. One of the key players in the proceedings was the U.S. government which was anxious to protect tens of thousands of jobs in the middle of a severe recession.

We cover bankruptcy procedures in more detail in Chapter 32.

Financial Distress without Bankruptcy

Not every firm that gets into trouble goes bankrupt. As long as the firm can scrape up enough cash to pay the interest on its debt, it may be able to postpone bankruptcy for many years. Eventually the firm may recover, pay off its debt, and escape bankruptcy altogether.

But the mere threat of financial distress can be costly to the threatened firm. Customers and suppliers are extra cautious about doing business with a firm that may not be around for long. Customers worry about resale value and the availability of service and replacement parts. (This was a serious drag on Chrysler's sales prebankruptcy, for example.) Suppliers are disinclined to put effort into servicing the distressed firm's account and may demand cash on the nail for their products. Potential employees are unwilling to sign on and existing staff keep slipping away from their desks for job interviews.

---

[15] See L. A. Weiss and K. H. Wruck, "Information Problems, Conflicts of Interest, and Asset Stripping: Chapter 11's Failure in the Case of Eastern Airlines," *Journal of Financial Economics* 48 (1998), pp. 55–97.

High debt, and thus high financial risk, also appear to reduce firms' appetites for business risk. For example, Luigi Zingales looked at the fortunes of U.S. trucking companies after the trucking industry was deregulated in the late 1970s.[16] The deregulation sparked a wave of competition and restructuring. Survival required new investment and improvements in operating efficiency. Zingales found that conservatively financed trucking companies were more likely to survive in the new competitive environment. High-debt firms were more likely to drop out of the game.

Debt and Incentives

When a firm is in trouble, both bondholders and stockholders want it to recover, but in other respects their interests may be in conflict. In times of financial distress the security holders are like many political parties—united on generalities but threatened by squabbling on any specific issue.

Financial distress is costly when these conflicts of interest get in the way of proper operating, investment, and financing decisions. Stockholders are tempted to forsake the usual objective of maximizing the overall market value of the firm and to pursue narrower self-interest instead. They are tempted to play games at the expense of their creditors. We now illustrate how such games can lead to costs of financial distress.

Here is the Circular File Company's book balance sheet:

Circular File Company (Book Values)

Net working capital	₹ 20	₹ 50	Bonds outstanding
Fixed assets	80	50	Shareholders' funds
Total assets	₹100	₹100	Total value

We will assume there is only one share and one bond outstanding. The stockholder is also the manager. The bondholder is somebody else.

Here is its balance sheet in market values—a clear case of financial distress, since the face value of Circular's debt (₹50) exceeds the firm's total market value (₹30):

Circular File Company (Market Values)

Net working capital	₹20	₹25	Bonds outstanding
Fixed assets	10	5	Shareholders' funds
Total assets	₹30	₹30	Total value

If the debt matured today, Circular's owner would default, leaving the firm bankrupt. But suppose that the bond actually matures one year hence, that there is enough cash for Circular to limp along for one year, and that the bondholder cannot "call the question" and force bankruptcy before then.

The one-year grace period explains why the Circular share still has value. Its owner is betting on a stroke of luck that will rescue the firm, allowing it to pay off the debt with something left over. The bet is a long shot—the owner wins only if firm value increases from ₹30 to more than ₹50.[17] But the owner has a secret weapon: He controls investment and operating strategy.

---

[16] L. Zingales, "Survival of the Fittest or the Fattest? Exit and Financing in the Trucking Industry," *Journal of Finance* 53 (June 1998), pp. 905–938.

[17] We are not concerned here with how to work out whether ₹5 is a fair price for stockholders to pay for the bet. We will come to that in Chapter 23 when we discuss risky debt.

Risk Shifting: The First Game

Suppose that Circular has ₹10 cash. The following investment opportunity comes up:

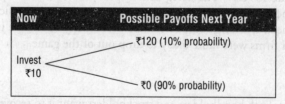

Now	Possible Payoffs Next Year
Invest ₹10	₹120 (10% probability)
	₹0 (90% probability)

This is a wild gamble and probably a lousy project. But you can see why the owner would be tempted to take it anyway. Why not go for broke? Circular will probably go under anyway, so the owner is essentially betting with the bondholder's money. But the owner gets most of the loot if the project pays off.

Suppose that the project's NPV is −₹2 but that it is undertaken anyway, thus depressing firm value by ₹2. Circular's new balance sheet might look like this:

Circular File Company (Market Values)

Net working capital	₹10	₹20	Bonds outstanding
Fixed assets	18	8	Shareholders' funds
Total assets	₹28	₹28	Total value

Firm value falls by ₹2, but the owner is ₹3 ahead because the bond's value has fallen by ₹5.[18] The ₹10 cash that used to stand behind the bond has been replaced by a very risky asset worth only ₹8.

Thus a game has been played at the expense of Circular's bondholder. The game illustrates the following general point: Stockholders of levered firms gain when business risk increases. Financial managers who act strictly in their shareholders' interests (and *against* the interests of creditors) will favor risky projects over safe ones. They may even take risky projects with negative NPVs.

This warped strategy for capital budgeting clearly is costly to the firm and to the economy as a whole. Why do we associate the costs with financial distress? Because the temptation to play is strongest when the odds of default are high. A blue-chip company like Exxon Mobil would never invest in our negative-NPV gamble. Its creditors are not vulnerable to one risky project.

Refusing to Contribute Equity Capital: The Second Game

We have seen how stockholders, acting in their immediate, narrow self-interest, may take projects that reduce the overall market value of their firm. These are errors of commission. Conflicts of interest may also lead to errors of omission.

Assume that Circular cannot scrape up any cash, and therefore cannot take that wild gamble. Instead a *good* opportunity comes up: a relatively safe asset costing ₹10 with a present value of ₹15 and NPV = +₹5.

This project will not in itself rescue Circular, but it is a step in the right direction. We might therefore expect Circular to issue ₹10 of new stock and to go ahead with the investment. Suppose that two new shares are issued to the original owner for ₹10 cash. The project is taken. The new balance sheet might look like this:

---

[18] We are not calculating this ₹5 drop. We are simply using it as a plausible assumption. The tools necessary for a calculation come in Chapters 21 and 23.

Circular File Company (Market Values)

Net working capital	₹20	₹33	Bonds outstanding
Fixed assets	25	12	Shareholders' funds
Total assets	₹45	₹45	Total value

The total value of the firm goes up by ₹15 (₹10 of new capital and ₹5 NPV). Notice that the Circular bond is no longer worth ₹25, but ₹33. The bondholder receives a capital gain of ₹8 because the firm's assets include a new, safe asset worth ₹15. The probability of default is less, and the payoff to the bondholder if default occurs is larger.

The stockholder loses what the bondholder gains. Equity value goes up not by ₹15 but by ₹15 − ₹8 = ₹7. The owner puts in ₹10 of fresh equity capital but gains only ₹7 in market value. Going ahead is in the firm's interest but not the owner's.

Again, our example illustrates a general point. If we hold business risk constant, any increase in firm value is shared among bondholders and stockholders. The value of any investment opportunity to the firm's *stockholders* is reduced because project benefits must be shared with bondholders. Thus it may not be in the stockholders' self-interest to contribute fresh equity capital even if that means forgoing positive-NPV investment opportunities.

This problem theoretically affects all levered firms, but it is most serious when firms land in financial distress. The greater the probability of default, the more bondholders have to gain from investments that increase firm value.

And Three More Games, Briefly

As with other games, the temptation to play the next three games is particularly strong in financial distress.

Cash In and Run   Stockholders may be reluctant to put money into a firm in financial distress, but they are happy to take the money out—in the form of a cash dividend, for example. The market value of the firm's stock goes down by less than the amount of the dividend paid, because the decline in *firm* value is shared with creditors. This game is just "refusing to contribute equity capital" run in reverse.[19]

Playing for Time   When the firm is in financial distress, creditors would like to salvage what they can by forcing the firm to settle up. Naturally, stockholders want to delay this as long as they can. There are various devious ways of doing this, for example, through accounting changes designed to conceal the true extent of trouble, by encouraging false hopes of spontaneous recovery, or by cutting corners on maintenance, research and development, and so on, in order to make this year's operating performance look better.

Bait and Switch   This game is not always played in financial distress, but it is a quick way to get *into* distress. You start with a conservative policy, issuing a limited amount of relatively safe debt. Then you suddenly switch and issue a lot more. That makes all your debt risky, imposing a capital loss on the "old" bondholders. Their capital loss is the stockholders' gain.

A dramatic example of bait and switch occurred in October 1988, when the management of RJR Nabisco announced its intention to acquire the company in a *leveraged buy-out* (LBO). This put the company "in play" for a transaction in which existing shareholders would be bought out and the

---

[19] If stockholders or managers take money out of the firm in anticipation of financial distress or bankruptcy, the bankruptcy court can treat the payout as *fraudulent conveyance* and claw back the money to the firm and its creditors.

company would be "taken private." The cost of the buy-out would be almost entirely debt-financed. The new private company would start life with an extremely high debt ratio.

RJR Nabisco had debt outstanding with a market value of about $2.4 billion. The announcement of the coming LBO drove down this market value by $298 million.[20]

What the Games Cost

Why should anyone object to these games so long as they are played by consenting adults? Because playing them means poor decisions about investments and operations. These poor decisions are *agency costs* of borrowing.

The more the firm borrows, the greater is the temptation to play the games (assuming the financial manager acts in the stockholders' interest). The increased odds of poor decisions in the future prompt investors to mark down the present market value of the firm. The fall in value comes out of the shareholders' pockets. Therefore it is ultimately in their interest to avoid temptation. The easiest way to do this is to limit borrowing to levels at which the firm's debt is safe or close to it.

Banks and other corporate lenders are also not financial innocents. They realize that games may be played at their expense and so protect themselves by rationing the amount that they will lend or by imposing restrictions on the company's actions.

EXAMPLE 18.1   Ms. Ketchup Faces Credit Rationing

Consider the case of Henrietta Ketchup, a budding entrepreneur with two possible investment projects that offer the following payoffs:

	Investment	Payoff	Probability of Payoff
Project 1	−12	+15	1.0
Project 2	−12	+24	.5
		0	.5

Project 1 is surefire and very profitable; project 2 is risky and a rotten project. Ms. Ketchup now approaches her bank and asks to borrow the present value of $10 (she will find the remaining money out of her own purse). The bank calculates that the payoff will be split as follows:

	Expected Payoff to Bank	Expected Payoff to Ms. Ketchup
Project 1	+10	+5
Project 2	(.5 × 10) + (.5 × 0) = +5	.5 × (24 − 10) = +7

If Ms. Ketchup accepts project 1, the bank's debt is certain to be paid in full; if she accepts project 2, there is only a 50% chance of payment and the expected payoff to the bank is only $5. Unfortunately, Ms. Ketchup will prefer to take project 2, for if things go well, she gets most of the profit, and

---

[20] We thank Paul Asquith for these figures. RJR Nabisco was finally taken private not by its management but by another LBO partnership. We discuss this LBO in Chapter 32.

if they go badly, the bank bears most of the loss. Unless Ms. Ketchup can convince the bank that she will not gamble with its money, the bank will limit the amount that it is prepared to lend.[21]

How can Ms. Ketchup in Example 18.1 reassure the bank of her intentions? The obvious answer is to give it veto power over potentially dangerous decisions. There we have the ultimate economic rationale for all that fine print backing up corporate debt. Debt contracts frequently limit dividends or equivalent transfers of wealth to stockholders; the firm may not be allowed to pay out more than it earns, for example. Additional borrowing is almost always limited. For example, many companies are prevented by existing bond indentures from issuing any additional long-term debt unless their ratio of earnings to interest charges exceeds 2.0.

Sometimes firms are restricted from selling assets or making major investment outlays except with the lenders' consent. The risks of playing for time are reduced by specifying accounting procedures and by giving lenders access to the firm's books and its financial forecasts.

Of course, fine print cannot be a complete solution for firms that insist on issuing risky debt. The fine print has its own costs; you have to spend money to save money. Obviously a complex debt contract costs more to negotiate than a simple one. Afterward it costs the lender more to monitor the firm's performance. Lenders anticipate monitoring costs and demand compensation in the form of higher interest rates; thus the monitoring costs—another agency cost of debt—are ultimately paid by stockholders.

Perhaps the most severe costs of the fine print stem from the constraints it places on operating and investment decisions. For example, an attempt to prevent the risk-shifting game may also prevent the firm from pursuing *good* investment opportunities. At the minimum there are delays in clearing major investments with lenders. In some cases lenders may veto high-risk investments even if net present value is positive. The lenders are tempted to play a game of their own, forcing the firm to stay in cash or low-risk assets even if good projects are forgone.

Debt contracts cannot cover every possible manifestation of the games we have just discussed. Any attempt to do so would be hopelessly expensive and doomed to failure in any event. Human imagination is insufficient to conceive of all the possible things that could go wrong. Therefore contracts are always *incomplete*. We will always find surprises coming at us on dimensions we never thought to think about.

We hope we have not left the impression that managers and stockholders always succumb to temptation unless restrained. Usually they refrain voluntarily, not only from a sense of fair play but also on pragmatic grounds: A firm or individual that makes a killing today at the expense of a creditor will be coldly received when the time comes to borrow again. Aggressive game playing is done only by out-and-out crooks and by firms in extreme financial distress. Firms limit borrowing precisely because they don't wish to land in distress and be exposed to the temptation to play.

Costs of Distress Vary with Type of Asset

Suppose your firm's only asset is a large downtown hotel, mortgaged to the hilt. The recession hits, occupancy rates fall, and the mortgage payments cannot be met. The lender takes over and sells the hotel to a new owner and operator. You use your firm's stock certificates for wallpaper.

---

[21] You might think that, if the bank suspects Ms. Ketchup will undertake project 2, it should just raise the interest rate on its loan. In this case Ms. Ketchup will not want to take on project 2 (they can't both be happy with a lousy project). But Ms. Ketchup also would not want to pay a high rate of interest if she is going to take on project 1 (she would do better to borrow less money at the risk-free rate). So simply raising the interest rate is not the answer.

What is the cost of bankruptcy? In this example, probably very little. The value of the hotel is, of course, much less than you hoped, but that is due to the lack of guests, not to the bankruptcy. Bankruptcy doesn't damage the hotel itself. The direct bankruptcy costs are restricted to items such as legal and court fees, real estate commissions, and the time the lender spends sorting things out.

Suppose we repeat the story of Heartbreak Hotel for Fledgling Electronics. Everything is the same, except for the underlying real assets—not real estate but a high-tech going concern, a growth company whose most valuable assets are technology, investment opportunities, and its employees' human capital.

If Fledgling gets into trouble, the stockholders may be reluctant to put up money to cash in on its growth opportunities. Failure to invest is likely to be much more serious for Fledgling than for the Heartbreak Hotel.

If Fledgling finally defaults on its debt, the lender will find it much more difficult to cash in by selling off the assets. Many of them are intangibles that have value only as a part of a going concern.

Could Fledgling be kept as a going concern through default and reorganization? It may not be as hopeless as putting a wedding cake through a car wash, but there are a number of serious difficulties. First, the odds of defections by key employees are higher than they would be if the firm had never gotten into financial trouble. Special guarantees may have to be given to customers who have doubts about whether the firm will be around to service its products. Aggressive investment in new products and technology will be difficult; each class of creditors will have to be convinced that it is in its interest for the firm to invest new money in risky ventures.

Some assets, like good commercial real estate, can pass through bankruptcy and reorganization largely unscathed;[22] the values of other assets are likely to be considerably diminished. The losses are greatest for the intangible assets that are linked to the health of the firm as a going concern—for example, technology, human capital, and brand image. That may be why debt ratios are low in the pharmaceutical industry, where value depends on continued success in research and development, and in many service industries where value depends on human capital. We can also understand why highly profitable growth companies, such as Infosys or HLL, use mostly equity finance.

The moral of these examples is this: *Do not think only about the probability that borrowing will bring trouble. Think also of the value that may be lost if trouble comes.*

Heartbreak Hotel for Enron?

Enron was one of the most glamorous, fast-growing, and (apparently) profitable companies of the 1990s. It played a lead role in the deregulation of electric power markets, both in the United States and internationally. It invested in electric power generation and distribution, gas pipelines, telecommunications networks, and various other ventures. It also built up an active energy trading business. At its peak the aggregate market value of Enron's common stock exceeded $60 billion. By the end of 2001, Enron was in bankruptcy and its shares were worthless.

With hindsight we see that Enron was playing many of the games that we described earlier in this section. It was borrowing aggressively and hiding the debt in "special purpose entities" (SPEs). The SPEs also allowed it to pump up its reported earnings, playing for time while making more and more risky investments. When the bubble burst, there was hardly any value left.

---

[22] In 1989 the Rockefeller family sold 80% of Rockefeller Center—several acres of extremely valuable Manhattan real estate—to Mitsubishi Estate Company for $1.4 billion. A REIT, Rockefeller Center Properties, held a $1.3 billion mortgage loan (the REIT's only asset) secured by this real estate. But rents and occupancy rates did not meet forecasts, and by 1995 Mitsubishi had incurred losses of about $600 million. Then Mitsubishi quit, and Rockefeller Center was bankrupt. That triggered a complicated series of maneuvers and negotiations. But did this damage the value of the Rockefeller Center properties? Was Radio City Music Hall, one of the properties, any less valuable because of the bankruptcy? We doubt it.

The collapse of Enron didn't really destroy $60 billion in value, because that $60 billion wasn't there in the first place. But there were genuine costs of financial distress. Let's focus on Enron's energy trading business. That business was not as profitable as it appeared, but it was nevertheless a valuable asset. It provided an important service for wholesale energy customers and suppliers who wanted to buy or sell contracts that locked in the future prices and quantities of electricity, natural gas, and other commodities.

What happened to this business when it became clear that Enron was in financial distress and probably headed for bankruptcy? It disappeared. Trading volume went to zero immediately. None of its customers were willing to make a new trade with Enron, because it was far from clear that Enron would be around to honor its side of the bargain. With no trading volume, there was no trading business. As it turned out, Enron's trading business more resembled Fledgling Electronics than a tangible asset like Heartbreak Hotel.

The value of Enron's trading business depended on Enron's creditworthiness. The value should have been protected by conservative financing. Most of the lost value can be traced back to Enron's aggressive borrowing. This loss of value was therefore a cost of financial distress.

The Trade-off Theory of Capital Structure

Financial managers often think of the firm's debt–equity decision as a trade-off between interest tax shields and the costs of financial distress. Of course, there is controversy about how valuable interest tax shields are and what kinds of financial trouble are most threatening, but these disagreements are only variations on a theme. Thus, Figure 18.2 illustrates the debt–equity trade-off.

This *trade-off theory* of capital structure recognizes that target debt ratios may vary from firm to firm. Companies with safe, tangible assets and plenty of taxable income to shield ought to have high target ratios. Unprofitable companies with risky, intangible assets ought to rely primarily on equity financing.

If there were no costs of adjusting capital structure, then each firm should always be at its target debt ratio. However, there are costs, and therefore delays, in adjusting to the optimum. Firms cannot immediately offset the random events that bump them away from their capital structure targets, so we should see random differences in actual debt ratios among firms having the same target debt ratio.

All in all, this trade-off theory of capital structure choice tells a comforting story. Unlike MM's theory, which seemed to say that firms should take on as much debt as possible, it avoids extreme predictions and rationalizes moderate debt ratios. Also, if you ask financial managers whether their firms have target debt ratios, they will usually say yes—although the target is often specified not as a debt ratio but as a debt rating. For example, the firm might manage its capital structure to maintain a single-A bond rating. Ratio or rating, a target is consistent with the trade-off theory.[23]

But what are the facts? Can the trade-off theory of capital structure explain how companies actually behave?

The answer is "yes and no." On the "yes" side, the trade-off theory successfully explains many industry differences in capital structure. High-tech growth companies, whose assets are risky and mostly intangible, normally use relatively little debt. Airlines can and do borrow heavily because their assets are tangible and relatively safe.[24]

---

[23] See J. Graham and C. Harvey, "The Theory and Practice of Corporate Finance: Evidence from the Field," *Journal of Financial Economics* 60 (May/June 2001), pp. 187–244.

[24] We are not suggesting that all airline companies are safe; many are not. But air*craft* can support debt where air*lines* cannot. If Fly-by-Night Airlines fails, its planes retain their value in another airline's operations. There's a good secondary market in used aircraft, so a loan secured by aircraft can be well protected even if made to an airline flying on thin ice (and in the dark).

On the "no" side, there are some things the trade-off theory cannot explain. It cannot explain why some of the most successful companies thrive with little debt. Think of Asian Paints, which as Table 18.3 (*a*) shows is basically all-equity-financed. Granted, Asian Paints' most valuable assets are intangible, its brand name and its distribution network. We know that intangible assets and conservative capital structures go together. But Asian Paints also has a very large corporate income tax bill (about ₹352 crores in 2011) and the highest possible credit rating (CRISIL rating: AAA). It could borrow enough to save crores of rupees without raising a whisker of concern about possible financial distress.

Asian Paints illustrates an odd fact about real-life capital structures: The most profitable companies commonly borrow the least.[25] Here the trade-off theory fails, for it predicts exactly the reverse. Under the trade-off theory, high profits should mean more debt-servicing capacity and more taxable income to shield and so should give a *higher* target debt ratio.[26]

In general it appears that public companies rarely make major shifts in capital structure just because of taxes,[27] and it is hard to detect the present value of interest tax shields in firms' market values.[28] Also, there are large, long-lived differences between debt ratios of firms in the same industry, even after controlling for attributes that the trade-off theory says should be important.[29]

A final point on the "no" side for the trade-off theory: The average debt ratio in India has remained stable at 60% in most of the last 21 years (1990-2011) despite huge declines in both corporate and personal tax rates. Similarly, in the U.S., the debt ratios have remained stable despite an increase in the income tax rates. Debt ratios in many other countries are equal to or higher than those in India. Many of these countries have imputation tax system, which should eliminate the value of the interest tax shields.[30]

None of this disproves the trade-off theory. As George Stigler emphasized, theories are not rejected by circumstantial evidence; it takes a theory to beat a theory. So we now turn to a completely different theory of financing.

18-4   THE PECKING ORDER OF FINANCING CHOICES

The pecking-order theory starts with *asymmetric information*—a fancy term indicating that managers know more about their companies' prospects, risks, and values than do outside investors.

---

[25] For example, in an international comparison Wald found that profitability was the single largest determinant of firm capital structure. See J. K. Wald, "How Firm Characteristics Affect Capital Structure: An International Comparison," *Journal of Financial Research* 22 (Summer 1999), pp. 161–187.

[26] Here we mean debt as a fraction of the book or replacement value of the company's assets. Profitable companies might not borrow a greater fraction of their market value. Higher profits imply higher market value as well as stronger incentives to borrow.

[27] Mackie-Mason found that taxpaying companies are more likely to issue debt (vs. equity) than nontaxpaying companies. This shows that taxes do affect financing choices. However, it is not necessarily evidence for the trade-off theory. Look back to Section 18.2, and note the special case where corporate and personal taxes cancel to make debt policy irrelevant. In that case, taxpaying firms would see no net tax advantage to debt: corporate interest tax shields would be offset by the taxes paid by investors in the firm's debt. But the balance would tip in favor of equity for a firm that was losing money and reaping no benefits from interest tax shields. See J. Mackie-Mason, "Do Taxes Affect Corporate Financing Decisions?" *Journal of Finance* 45 (December 1990), pp. 1471–1493.

[28] A study by E. F. Fama and K. R. French, covering over 2,000 firms from 1965 to 1992, failed to find any evidence that interest tax shields contributed to firm value. See "Taxes, Financing Decisions and Firm Value," *Journal of Finance* 53 (June 1998), pp. 819–843.

[29] M. L. Lemmon, M. R. Roberts, and J. F. Zender, "Back to the Beginning: Persistence and the Cross-Section of Corporate Capital Structure," *Journal of Finance* 63 (August 2008), pp. 1575–1608.

[30] We described the Australian imputation tax system in Section 16.7. Look again at Table 16.3, supposing that an Australian corporation pays A\$10 of interest. This reduces the corporate tax by A\$3.00; it also reduces the tax credit taken by the shareholders by A\$3.00. The final tax does not depend on whether the corporation or the shareholder borrows.

You can check this by redrawing Figure 18.1 for the Australian system. The corporate tax rate T_c will cancel out. Since income after all taxes depends only on investors' tax rates, there is no special advantage to corporate borrowing.

Managers obviously know more than investors. We can prove that by observing stock price changes caused by announcements by managers. For example, when a company announces an increased regular dividend, stock price typically rises, because investors interpret the increase as a sign of management's confidence in future earnings. In other words, the dividend increase transfers information from managers to investors. This can happen only if managers know more in the first place.

Asymmetric information affects the choice between internal and external financing and between new issues of debt and equity securities. This leads to a *pecking order,* in which investment is financed first with internal funds, reinvested earnings primarily; then by new issues of debt; and finally with new issues of equity. New equity issues are a last resort when the company runs out of debt capacity, that is, when the threat of costs of financial distress brings regular insomnia to existing creditors and to the financial manager.

We will take a closer look at the pecking order in a moment. First, you must appreciate how asymmetric information can force the financial manager to issue debt rather than common stock.

Debt and Equity Issues with Asymmetric Information

To the outside world Om & Company and Jai, Inc., our two example companies, are identical. Each runs a successful business with good growth opportunities. The two businesses are risky, however, and investors have learned from experience that current expectations are frequently bettered or disappointed. Current expectations price each company's stock at ₹100 per share, but the true values could be higher or lower:

	Om & Co.	Jai, Inc.
True value could be higher, say	₹120	₹120
Best current estimate	100	100
True value could be lower, say	80	80

Now suppose that both companies need to raise new money from investors to fund capital investment. They can do this either by issuing bonds or by issuing new shares of common stock. How would the choice be made? One financial manager—we will not tell you which one—might reason as follows:

Sell stock for ₹100 per share? Ridiculous! It's worth at least ₹120. A stock issue now would hand a free gift to new investors. I just wish those skeptical shareholders would appreciate the true value of this company. Our new factories will make us the world's lowest-cost producer. We've painted a rosy picture for the press and security analysts, but it just doesn't seem to be working. Oh well, the decision is obvious: we'll issue debt, not underpriced equity. A debt issue will save underwriting fees too.

The other financial manager is in a different mood:

Beefalo burgers were a hit for a while, but it looks like the fad is fading. The fast-food division's gotta find some good new products or it's all downhill from here. Export markets are OK for now, but how are we going to compete with those new Siberian ranches? Fortunately the stock price has held up pretty well—we've had some good short-run news for the press and security analysts. Now's the time to issue stock. We have major investments underway, and why add increased debt service to my other worries?

Of course, outside investors can't read the financial managers' minds. If they could, one stock might trade at ₹120 and the other at ₹80.

Why doesn't the optimistic financial manager simply educate investors? Then the company could sell stock on fair terms, and there would be no reason to favor debt over equity or vice versa.

This is not so easy. (Note that both companies are issuing upbeat press releases.) Investors can't be told what to think; they have to be convinced. That takes a detailed layout of the company's plans and prospects, including the inside scoop on new technology, product design, marketing plans, and so on. Getting this across is expensive for the company and also valuable to its competitors. Why go to the trouble? Investors will learn soon enough, as revenues and earnings evolve. In the meantime the optimistic financial manager can finance growth by issuing debt.

Now suppose there are two press releases:

Jai, Inc., will issue ₹120 million of five-year senior notes.

Om & Co. announced plans today to issue 1.2 million new shares of common stock. The company expects to raise ₹120 million.

As a rational investor, you immediately learn two things. First, Jai's financial manager is optimistic and Om's is pessimistic. Second, Om's financial manager is also naive to think that investors would pay ₹100 per share. The *attempt* to sell stock shows that it must be worth less. Om might sell stock at ₹80 per share, but certainly not at ₹100.[31]

Smart financial managers think this through ahead of time. The end result? Both Om and Jai end up issuing debt. Jai, Inc., issues debt because its financial manager is optimistic and doesn't want to issue undervalued equity. A smart, but pessimistic, financial manager at Om issues debt because an attempt to issue equity would force the stock price down and eliminate any advantage from doing so. (Issuing equity also reveals the manager's pessimism immediately. Most managers prefer to wait. A debt issue lets bad news come out later through other channels.)

The story of Om and Jai illustrates how asymmetric information favors debt issues over equity issues. If managers are better informed than investors and both groups are rational, then any company that can borrow will do so rather than issuing fresh equity. In other words, debt issues will be higher in the pecking order.

Taken literally this reasoning seems to rule out any issue of equity. That's not right, because asymmetric information is not always important and there are other forces at work. For example, if Om had already borrowed heavily, and would risk financial distress by borrowing more, then it would have a good reason to issue common stock. In this case announcement of a stock issue would not be entirely bad news. The announcement would still depress the stock price—it would highlight managers' concerns about financial distress—but the fall in price would not necessarily make the issue unwise or infeasible.

High-tech, high-growth companies can also be credible issuers of common stock. Such companies' assets are mostly intangible, and bankruptcy or financial distress would be especially costly. This calls for conservative financing. The only way to grow rapidly and keep a conservative debt ratio is to issue equity. If investors see equity issued for these reasons, problems of the sort encountered by Om's financial manager become much less serious.

With such exceptions noted, asymmetric information can explain the dominance of debt financing over new equity issues, at least for mature public corporations. Debt issues are frequent; equity issues, rare. The bulk of external financing comes from debt, even in the United States, where equity markets

---

[31] An Om stock issue might not succeed even at ₹80. Persistence in trying to sell at ₹80 could convince investors that the stock is worth even less!

are highly information-efficient. Equity issues are even more difficult in countries with less well developed stock markets.

None of this says that firms ought to strive for high debt ratios—just that it's better to raise equity by plowing back earnings than issuing stock. In fact, a firm with ample internally generated funds doesn't have to sell any kind of security and thus avoids issue costs and information problems completely.

Implications of the Pecking Order

The *pecking-order theory* of corporate financing goes like this.

1. Firms prefer internal finance.
2. They adapt their target dividend payout ratios to their investment opportunities, while trying to avoid sudden changes in dividends.
3. Sticky dividend policies, plus unpredictable fluctuations in profitability and investment opportunities, mean that internally generated cash flow is sometimes more than capital expenditures and other times less. If it is more, the firm pays off debt or invests in marketable securities. If it is less, the firm first draws down its cash balance or sells its marketable securities.
4. If external finance is required, firms issue the safest security first. That is, they start with debt, then possibly hybrid securities such as convertible bonds, then perhaps equity as a last resort.

In this theory, there is no well-defined target debt–equity mix, because there are two kinds of equity, internal and external, one at the top of the pecking order and one at the bottom. Each firm's observed debt ratio reflects its cumulative requirements for external finance.

The pecking order explains why the most profitable firms generally borrow less—not because they have low target debt ratios but because they don't need outside money. Less profitable firms issue debt because they do not have internal funds sufficient for their capital investment programs and because debt financing is first on the pecking order of *external* financing.

In the pecking-order theory, the attraction of interest tax shields is assumed to be second-order. Debt ratios change when there is an imbalance of internal cash flow, net of dividends, and real investment opportunities. Highly profitable firms with limited investment opportunities work down to low debt ratios. Firms whose investment opportunities outrun internally generated funds are driven to borrow more and more.

This theory explains the inverse intraindustry relationship between profitability and financial leverage. Suppose firms generally invest to keep up with the growth of their industries. Then rates of investment will be similar within an industry. Given sticky dividend payouts, the least profitable firms will have less internal funds and will end up borrowing more.

The Trade-off Theory vs. the Pecking-Order Theory—Some Recent Tests

In 1995 Rajan and Zingales published a study of debt versus equity choices by large firms in Canada, France, Germany, Italy, Japan, the U.K., and the U.S. Rajan and Zingales found that the debt ratios of individual companies seemed to depend on four main factors:[32]

1. *Size.* Large firms tend to have higher debt ratios.
2. *Tangible assets.* Firms with high ratios of fixed assets to total assets have higher debt ratios.

---

[32] R. G. Rajan and L. Zingales, "What Do We Know about Capital Structure? Some Evidence from International Data," *Journal of Finance* 50 (December 1995), pp. 1421–1460. The same four factors seem to work in developing economies. See L. Booth, V. Aivazian, A. Demirguc-Kunt, and V. Maksimovic, "Capital Structure in Developing Countries," *Journal of Finance* 56 (February 2001), pp. 87–130.

3. *Profitability.* More profitable firms have lower debt ratios.
4. *Market to book.* Firms with higher ratios of market-to-book value have lower debt ratios.

These results convey good news for both the trade-off and pecking-order theories. Trade-off enthusiasts note that large companies with tangible assets are less exposed to costs of financial distress and would be expected to borrow more. They interpret the market-to-book ratio as a measure of growth opportunities and argue that growth companies could face high costs of financial distress and would be expected to borrow less. Pecking-order advocates stress the importance of profitability, arguing that profitable firms use less debt because they can rely on internal financing. They interpret the market-to-book ratio as just another measure of profitability.

It seems that we have two competing theories, and they're both right! That's not a comfortable conclusion. So recent research has tried to run horse races between the two theories in order to find the circumstances in which one or the other wins. It seems that the pecking order works best for large, mature firms that have access to public bond markets. These firms rarely issue equity. They prefer internal financing, but turn to debt markets if needed to finance investment. Smaller, younger, growth firms are more likely to rely on equity issues when external financing is required.[33]

There is also some evidence that debt ratios incorporate the cumulative effects of *market timing.*[34] Market timing is an example of behavioral corporate finance. Suppose that investors are sometimes irrationally exuberant (as in the late 1990s) and sometimes irrationally despondent. If the financial manager's views are more stable than investors', then he or she can take advantage by issuing shares when the stock price is too high and switching to debt when the price is too low. Thus lucky companies with a history of buoyant stock prices will issue less debt and more shares, ending up with low debt ratios. Unfortunate and unpopular companies will avoid share issues and end up with high debt ratios.

Market timing could explain why companies tend to issue shares after run-ups in stock prices and also why aggregate stock issues are concentrated in bull markets and fall sharply in bear markets.

There are other behavioral explanations for corporate financing policies. For example, Bertrand and Schoar tracked the careers of individual CEOs, CFOs, and other top managers. Their individual "styles" persisted as they moved from firm to firm.[35] For example, older CEOs tended to be more conservative and pushed their firms to lower debt. CEOs with MBA degrees tended to be more aggressive. In general, financial decisions depended not just on the nature of the firm and its economic environment, but also on the personalities of the firm's top management.

The Bright Side and the Dark Side of Financial Slack

Other things equal, it's better to be at the top of the pecking order than at the bottom. Firms that have worked down the pecking order and need external equity may end up living with excessive debt or passing by good investments because shares can't be sold at what managers consider a fair price.

---

[33] L. Shyam-Sunder and S. C. Myers found that the pecking-order hypothesis outperformed the trade-off hypothesis for a sample of large companies in the 1980s. See "Testing Static Trade-off against Pecking-Order Theories of Capital Structure," *Journal of Financial Economics* 51 (February 1999), pp. 219–244. M. Frank and V. Goyal found that the performance of the pecking-order hypothesis deteriorated in the 1990s, especially for small growth firms. See "Testing the Pecking Order Theory of Capital Structure," *Journal of Financial Economics* 67 (February 2003), pp. 217–248. See also E. Fama and K. French, "Testing Trade-off and Pecking Order Predictions about Dividends and Debt," *Review of Financial Studies* 15 (Spring 2002), pp. 1–33; and M. L. Lemmon and J. F. Zender, "Debt Capacity and Tests of Capital Structure Theories," *Journal of Financial and Quantitative Analysis*, forthcoming.

[34] M. Baker and J. Wurgler, "Market Timing and Capital Structure," *Journal of Finance* 57 (February 2002), pp. 1–32.

[35] M. Bertrand and A. Schoar, "Managing with Style: The Effect of Managers on Firm Policies," *Quarterly Journal of Economics* 118 (November 2003), pp. 1169–1208.

Finance In Practice

Ford Cashes in All of its Financial Slack

In 2006, Ford Motor Company brought in a new CEO, Alan Mulally, who launched a thorough restructuring of the company. The company had to cut costs, improve efficiency, and renew its products. This was a massive investment, but debt financing was available. The company decided to borrow as much as it could, to maximize the amount of cash on hand to pay for the restructuring.

In December 2006, Ford issued $5 billion of senior convertible notes. It also arranged a $7 billion, seven-year term loan and an $11.5 billion, five-year revolving credit facility. The total was $23.5 billion.

Ford was able to get this money by pledging almost all of its assets as collateral, including its U.S. property, plant, and equipment; its equity investments in Ford Credit and Ford's foreign subsidiaries; and its trademarks, including the Ford brand name and logo.

Why did Ford decide to use up all of its financial slack in one gigantic gulp? First, debt financing was available on relatively easy terms in 2006. Second, Mulally must have been aware of the history of restructuring programs in the U.S. auto industry. Some of these initiatives were failures, some partial successes, but none solved Ford, GM, or Chrysler's competitive problems. The companies shrank but did not improve significantly.

So Mulally was in effect sending a wake-up call to Ford's managers and employees: "We've raised all the cash that we can get. This is our last chance to reform the company. If we don't make it, Ford is gone."

As we write in 2009 Ford has *not* followed GM and Chrysler into bankruptcy. It's losing money in a severe recession, but still launching new models. It looks like Ford is a survivor.

In other words, *financial slack* is valuable. Having financial slack means having cash, marketable securities, readily salable real assets, and ready access to debt markets or to bank financing. Ready access basically requires conservative financing so that potential lenders see the company's debt as a safe investment.

In the long run, a company's value rests more on its capital investment and operating decisions than on financing. Therefore, you want to make sure your firm has sufficient financial slack so that financing is quickly available for good investments. Financial slack is most valuable to firms with plenty of positive-NPV growth opportunities. That is another reason why growth companies usually aspire to conservative capital structures.

Of course financial slack is only valuable if you're willing to use it. Take a look at the nearby box, which describes how Ford used up all of its financial slack in one enormous debt issue.

There is also a dark side to financial slack. Too much of it may encourage managers to take it easy, expand their perks, or empire-build with cash that should be paid back to stockholders. In other words, slack can make agency problems worse.

Michael Jensen has stressed the tendency of managers with ample free cash flow (or unnecessary financial slack) to plow too much cash into mature businesses or ill-advised acquisitions. "The problem," Jensen says, "is how to motivate managers to disgorge the cash rather than investing it below the cost of capital or wasting it in organizational inefficiencies."[36]

If that's the problem, then maybe debt is an answer. Scheduled interest and principal payments are contractual obligations of the firm. Debt forces the firm to pay out cash. Perhaps the best debt level would leave just enough cash in the bank, after debt service, to finance all positive-NPV projects, with not a penny left over.

We do not recommend this degree of fine-tuning, but the idea is valid and important. Debt can discipline managers who are tempted to invest too much. It can also provide the pressure to force improvements in operating efficiency. We pick up this theme again in Chapter 32.

Is There a Theory of Optimal Capital Structure?

No. That is, there is no *one* theory that can capture everything that drives thousands of corporations' debt vs. equity choices. Instead there are several theories, each more or less helpful, depending on each particular corporation's assets, operations, and circumstances.

In other words, *relax:* Don't waste time searching for a magic formula for the optimal debt ratio. Remember too that most value comes from the left side of the balance sheet, that is, from the firm's operations, assets, and growth opportunities. Financing is less important. Of course, financing can subtract value rapidly if you screw it up, but you won't do that.

In practice, financing choices depend on the relative importance of the factors discussed in this chapter. In some cases, reducing taxes will be the primary objective. Thus high debt ratios are found in the lease-financing business (see Chapter 25). Long-term leases are often tax-driven transactions. High debt ratios are also found in developed commercial real estate. For example, modern downtown office buildings can be safe, cash-cow assets if the office space is rented to creditworthy tenants. Bankruptcy costs are small, so it makes sense to lever up and save taxes.

For smaller growth companies, interest tax shields are less important than preserving financial slack. Profitable growth opportunities are valuable only if financing is available when it comes time to invest. Costs of financial distress are high, so it's no surprise that growth companies try to use mostly equity financing.

Mature public corporations often end up following the pecking order. Information problems deter large equity issues, so such firms prefer to finance investment with retained earnings. They issue more debt when investments outrun retained earnings, and pay down debt when earnings outpace investment.

Sooner or later a corporation's operations age to the point where growth opportunities evaporate. In that case, the firm may issue large amounts of debt and retire equity, to constrain investment and force payout of cash to investors. The higher debt ratio may come voluntarily or be forced by a takeover.

These examples are not exhaustive, but they give some flavor of how a thoughtful CEO can set financing strategy.

---

[36] M. C. Jensen, "Agency Costs of Free Cash Flow, Corporate Finance and Takeovers," *American Economic Review* 26 (May 1986), pp. 323–329.

SUMMARY

Our task in this chapter was to show why capital structure matters. We did not throw away MM's proposition that capital structure is irrelevant; we added to it. However, we did not arrive at any simple, universal theory of optimal capital structure.

The trade-off theory emphasizes interest tax shields and the costs of financial distress. The value of the firm is broken down as

Value if all-equity-financed + PV(tax shield) − PV(costs of financial distress)

According to this theory, the firm should increase debt until the value from PV(tax shield) is just offset, at the margin, by increases in PV(costs of financial distress).

The costs of financial distress are:

1. Bankruptcy costs
   a. Direct costs such as legal and accounting fees.
   b. Indirect costs reflecting the difficulty of managing a company undergoing liquidation or reorganization.
2. Costs of financial distress short of bankruptcy
   a. Doubts about a firm's creditworthiness can hobble its operations. Customers and suppliers will be reluctant to deal with a firm that may not be around next year. Key employees will be tempted to leave. Highly leveraged firms seem to be less vigorous product-market competitors.
   b. Conflicts of interest between bondholders and stockholders of firms in financial distress may lead to poor operating and investment decisions. Stockholders acting in their narrow self-interest can gain at the expense of creditors by playing "games" that reduce the overall value of the firm.
   c. The fine print in debt contracts is designed to prevent these games. But fine print increases the costs of writing, monitoring, and enforcing the debt contract.

The value of the interest tax shield would be easy to compute if we had only corporate taxes to worry about. In that case the net tax saving from borrowing would be just the marginal corporate tax rate T_c times $r_D D$, the interest payment. If debt is fixed, the tax shield can be valued by discounting at the borrowing rate r_D. In the special case of fixed, permanent debt

$$PV(\text{tax shield}) = \frac{T_c r_D D}{r_D} = T_c D$$

However, corporate taxes are only part of the story. If investors pay higher taxes on interest income than on equity income (dividends and capital gains), then interest tax shields to the corporation will be partly offset by higher taxes paid by investors. The low (15% maximum) U.S. tax rates on dividends and capital gains have reduced the tax advantage to corporate borrowing.

The trade-off theory balances the tax advantages of borrowing against the costs of financial distress. Corporations are supposed to pick a target capital structure that maximizes firm value. Firms with safe, tangible assets and plenty of taxable income to shield ought to have high targets. Unprofitable companies with risky, intangible assets ought to rely more on equity financing.

This theory of capital structure successfully explains many industry differences in capital structure, but it does not explain why the most profitable firms *within* an industry generally have the most conservative capital structures. Under the trade-off theory, high profitability should mean high debt capacity *and* a strong tax incentive to use that capacity.

There is a competing, pecking-order theory, which states that firms use internal financing when available and choose debt over equity when external financing is required. This explains why the less profitable firms in an industry borrow more—not because they have higher target debt ratios but because they need more external financing and because debt is next on the pecking order when internal funds are exhausted.

The pecking order is a consequence of asymmetric information. Managers know more about their firms than outside investors do, and they are reluctant to issue stock when they believe the price is too low. They try to time issues when shares are fairly priced or overpriced. Investors understand this, and interpret a decision to issue shares as bad news. That explains why stock price usually falls when a stock issue is announced.

Debt is better than equity when these information problems are important. Optimistic managers will prefer debt to undervalued equity, and pessimistic managers will be pressed to follow suit. The pecking-order theory says that equity will be issued only when debt capacity is running out and financial distress threatens.

The pecking-order theory stresses the value of financial slack. Without sufficient slack, the firm may be caught at the bottom of the pecking order and be forced to choose between issuing undervalued shares, borrowing and risking financial distress, or passing up positive-NPV investment opportunities.

There is, however, a dark side to financial slack. Surplus cash or credit tempts managers to over-invest or to indulge an easy and glamorous corporate lifestyle. When temptation wins, or threatens to win, a high debt ratio can help: It forces the company to disgorge cash and prods managers and organizations to try harder to be more efficient.

FURTHER READING

The research literature on capital structure is enormous. We cite only a few of the most important and interesting articles. The following review articles give broader surveys.

M. Harris and A. Raviv, "The Theory of Capital Structure," *Journal of Finance* 46 (March 1991), pp. 297–355.

S. C. Myers, "Financing of Corporations," in G. M. Constantinides, M. Harris, and R. Stulz (eds.), *Handbook of the Economics of Finance* (Amsterdam: Elsevier North-Holland, 2003).

The Winter 2005 issue of the Journal of Applied Corporate Finance *contains several articles on capital structure decisions in practice.*

The following paper surveys chief financial officers' views about capital structure:

J. Graham and C. Harvey, "How Do CFOs Make Capital Budgeting and Capital Structure Decisions?" *Journal of Applied Corporate Finance* 15 (Spring 2002), pp. 8–23.

PROBLEM SETS

Basic

1. The present value of interest tax shields is often written as $T_c D$, where D is the amount of debt and T_c is the marginal corporate tax rate. Under what assumptions is this present value correct?
2. Here are book and market value balance sheets of the United Frypan Company (UF):

	Book				Market		
Net working capital	₹ 20	₹ 40	Debt	Net working capital	₹ 20	₹ 40	Debt
Long-term assets	80	60	Equity	Long-term assets	140	120	Equity
	₹100	₹100			₹160	₹160	

Assume that MM's theory holds with taxes. There is no growth, and the ₹40 of debt is expected to be permanent. Assume a 40% corporate tax rate.

a. How much of the firm's value is accounted for by the debt-generated tax shield?

b. How much better off will UF's shareholders be if the firm borrows ₹20 more and uses it to repurchase stock?

3. What is the relative tax advantage of corporate debt if the corporate tax rate is $T_c = .35$, the personal tax rate is $T_p = .35$, but all equity income is received as capital gains and escapes tax entirely $(T_{pE} = 0)$? How does the relative tax advantage change if the company decides to pay out all equity income as cash dividends that are taxed at 15%?

4. "The firm can't use interest tax shields unless it has (taxable) income to shield." What does this statement imply for debt policy? Explain briefly.

5. This question tests your understanding of financial distress.

   a. What are the costs of going bankrupt? Define these costs carefully.

   b. "A company can incur costs of financial distress without ever going bankrupt." Explain how this can happen.

   c. Explain how conflicts of interest between bondholders and stockholders can lead to costs of financial distress.

6. On February 29, 2009, when PDQ Computers announced bankruptcy, its share price fell from $3.00 to $.50 per share. There were 10 million shares outstanding. Does that imply bankruptcy costs of $10 \times (3.00 - .50) = \$25$ million? Explain.

7. The traditional theory of optimal capital structure states that firms trade off corporate interest tax shields against the possible costs of financial distress due to borrowing. What does this theory predict about the relationship between book profitability and target book debt ratios? Is the theory's prediction consistent with the facts?

8. Rajan and Zingales identified four variables that seemed to explain differences in debt ratios in several countries. What are the four variables?

9. Why does asymmetric information push companies to raise external funds by borrowing rather than by issuing common stock?

10. Fill in the blanks: According to the pecking-order theory,

    a. The firm's debt ratio is determined by _____.

    b. Debt ratios depend on past profitability, because _____.

11. For what kinds of companies is financial slack most valuable? Are there situations in which financial slack should be reduced by borrowing and paying out the proceeds to the stockholders? Explain.

INTERMEDIATE

12. Compute the present value of interest tax shields generated by these three debt issues. Consider corporate taxes only. The marginal tax rate is $T_c = .35$.

    a. A ₹1,000, one-year loan at 8%.

    b. A five-year loan of ₹1,000 at 8%. Assume no principal is repaid until maturity.

    c. A ₹1,000 perpetuity at 7%.

13. Suppose that, in an effort to increase the tax collections, the Finance Minister of India increases the top personal tax rate from 30 percent to 35 percent, but retains the securities transaction tax at its current level of 0.125 %. The corporate tax rate stays at 33.99 %. Compute the total corporate plus personal taxes paid on debt versus equity income if (a) all capital gains are realized immediately and the short-term capital gains tax (paid over and above the securities transaction tax) is 10 percent and (b) sell of shares is deferred forever. Assume capital gains are half of equity income.

14. "The trouble with MM's argument is that it ignores the fact that individuals can deduct interest for personal income tax." Show why this is not an objection if personal tax rates on interest and equity income are the same.

15. Look back at the Asian Paints example in Section 18.1. Suppose that Asian Paints moves to a 40 percent book debt ratio by issuing debt and using the proceeds to repurchase shares. Consider only corporate taxes. Now reconstruct Table 18.3(b) to reflect the new capital structure. How much additional value is created if the assumptions in the table are correct?

Visit the website of Asian Paints (http://www.apaints.com/AsianPaints.jsp).
a. Recalculate the book-and market-value balance sheets using the most recent available financial information.
b. Track Asian Paints' long-term debt and debt ratio over the last five years. How have they changed? Does it appear that Asian Paints has a stable target debt ratio? Do you see any incidence of pecking-order financing?
c. Would the trade-off theory predict share repurchases for a conservatively financed company like Asian Paints?

16. In Section 18-3, we briefly referred to three games: Playing for time, cash in and run, and bait and switch.

For each game, construct a simple numerical example (like the example for the risk-shifting game) showing how shareholders can gain at the expense of creditors. Then explain how the temptation to play these games could lead to costs of financial distress.

17. Look at some real companies with different types of assets. What operating problems would each encounter in the event of financial distress? How well would the assets keep their value?

18. Let us go back to Circular File's market value balance sheet:

Net working capital	₹20	₹25	Bonds outstanding
Fixed assets	10	5	Common stock
Total assets	₹30	₹30	Total value

Who gains and who loses from the following maneuvers?
a. Circular scrapes up ₹5 in cash and pays a cash dividend.
b. Circular halts operations, sells its fixed assets, and converts net working capital into ₹20 cash. Unfortunately the fixed assets fetch only $6 on the secondhand market. The ₹26 cash is invested in Treasury bills.
c. Circular encounters an acceptable investment opportunity, NPV = 0, requiring an investment of ₹10. The firm borrows to finance the project. The new debt has the same security, seniority, etc., as the old.
d. Suppose that the new project has NPV = +₹2 and is financed by an issue of preferred stock.
e. The lenders agree to extend the maturity of their loan from one year to two in order to give Circular a chance to recover.

19. The Salad Oil Storage (SOS) Company has financed a large part of its facilities with long-term debt. There is a significant risk of default, but the company is not on the ropes yet. Explain:
a. Why SOS stockholders could lose by investing in a positive-NPV project financed by an equity issue.
b. Why SOS stockholders could gain by investing in a negative-NPV project financed by cash.
c. Why SOS stockholders could gain from paying out a large cash dividend.

20. a. Who benefits from the fine print in bond contracts when the firm gets into financial trouble? Give a one-sentence answer.
b. Who benefits from the fine print when the bonds are issued? Suppose the firm is offered the choice of issuing (i) a bond with standard restrictions on dividend payout, additional borrowing, etc., and (ii) a bond with minimal restrictions but a much higher interest rate? Suppose the interest rates on both (i) and (ii) are fair from the viewpoint of lenders. Which bond would you expect the firm to issue? Why?

21. "I was amazed to find that the announcement of a stock issue drives down the value of the issuing firm by 30%, on average, of the proceeds of the issue. That issue cost dwarfs the underwriter's spread and the administrative costs of the issue. It makes common stock issues prohibitively expensive."

    a. You are contemplating a ₹100 million stock issue. On past evidence, you anticipate that announcement of this issue will drive down stock price by 3% and that the market value of your firm will fall by 30% of the amount to be raised. On the other hand, additional equity financing is required to fund an investment project that you believe has a positive NPV of ₹40 million. Should you proceed with the issue?

22. Ronald Masulis analyzed the stock price impact of *exchange offers* of debt for equity or vice versa.[37] In an exchange offer, the firm offers to trade freshly issued securities for seasoned securities in the hands of investors. Thus, a firm that wanted to move to a higher debt ratio could offer to trade new debt for outstanding shares. A firm that wanted to move to a more conservative capital structure could offer to trade new shares for outstanding debt securities.

    Masulis found that debt for equity exchanges were good news (stock price increased on announcement) and equity for debt exchanges were bad news.

    a. Are these results consistent with the trade-off theory of capital structure?
    b. Are the results consistent with the evidence that investors regard announcements of (i) stock issues as bad news, (ii) stock repurchases as good news, and (iii) debt issues as no news, or at most trifling disappointments?
    c. How could Masulis's results be explained?

23. The possible payoffs from Ms. Ketchup's projects (see Example 18.1, pages 455 & 456) have not changed but there is now a 40% chance that Project 2 will pay off ₹24 and a 60% chance that it will pay off ₹0.

    a. Recalculate the expected payoffs to the bank and Ms. Ketchup if the bank lends the present value of ₹10. Which project would Ms. Ketchup undertake?
    b. What is the maximum amount the bank could lend that would induce Ms. Ketchup to take Project 1?

24. Some corporations' debt–equity targets are expressed not as a debt ratio but as a target debt rating on the firm's outstanding bonds. What are the pros and cons of setting a target rating rather than a target ratio?

CHALLENGE

25. Most financial managers measure debt ratios from their companies' book balance sheets. Many financial economists emphasize ratios from market-value balance sheets. Which is the right measure in principle? Does the trade-off theory propose to explain book or market leverage? How about the pecking-order theory?

26. The trade-off theory relies on the threat of financial distress. But why should a public corporation ever have to land in financial distress? According to the theory, the firm should operate at the top of the curve in Figure 18.2. Of course market movements or business setbacks could bump it up to a higher debt ratio and put it on the declining, right-hand side of the curve. But in that case, why doesn't the firm just issue equity, retire debt, and move to back up to the optimal debt ratio?

    What are the reasons why companies don't issue stock—or enough stock—quickly enough to avoid financial distress?

[37] R. W. Masulis, "The Effects of Capital Structure Change on Security Prices: A Study of Exchange Offers," *Journal of Financial Economics* 8 (June 1980), pp. 139–177, and "The Impact of Capital Structure Change on Firm Value," *Journal of Finance* 38 (March 1983), pp. 107–126.

19

CHAPTER

FINANCING AND VALUATION

In Chapters 5 and 6 we showed how to value a capital investment project by a four-step procedure:

1. Forecast after-tax cash flows, assuming all-equity financing.
2. Assess the project's risk.
3. Estimate the opportunity cost of capital.
4. Calculate NPV, using the opportunity cost of capital as the discount rate.

There's nothing wrong with this procedure, but now we're going to extend it to include value contributed by financing decisions. There are two ways to do this:

1. *Adjust the discount rate.* The adjustment is typically downward, to account for the value of interest tax shields. This is the most common approach, which is usually implemented via the after-tax weighted-average cost of capital (WACC). We introduced the after-tax WACC in Chapters 9 and 17, but here we provide a lot more guidance on how it is calculated and used.
2. *Adjust the present value.* That is, start by estimating the firm or project's base-case value, assuming it is all-equity-financed, and then adjust this base-case value to account for financing.

> Adjusted present value (APV)
> = base-case value + value of financing side effects

Once you identify and value the financing side effects, calculating APV is no more than addition or subtraction.

This is a how-to-do-it chapter. In the first section, we explain and derive the after-tax WACC and use it to value a project and business. Then in Section 19-2 we work through a more complex and realistic valuation problem. Section 19-3 covers some tricks of the trade: helpful hints on how to estimate inputs and on how to adjust WACC when business risk or capital structure changes. Section 19-4 turns to the APV method.

The idea behind APV is simple enough, but tracing through all the financing side effects can be tricky. We conclude the chapter with a question-and-answer section designed to clarify points that managers and students often find confusing. The Appendix covers an important special case, namely, the after-tax valuation of safe cash flows.

19-1 THE AFTER-TAX WEIGHTED-AVERAGE COST OF CAPITAL

We first addressed problems of valuation and capital budgeting in Chapters 2 to 6. In those early chapters we said hardly a word about financing decisions. In fact we proceeded under the simplest possible financing assumption, namely, all-equity financing. We were really assuming a Modigliani–Miller (MM) world in which all financing decisions are irrelevant. In a strict MM world, firms can analyze real investments as if they are all-equity-financed; the actual financing plan is a mere detail to be worked out later.

Under MM assumptions, decisions to spend money can be separated from decisions to raise money. Now we reconsider the capital budgeting decision when investment and financing decisions interact and cannot be wholly separated.

One reason that financing and investment decisions interact is taxes. Interest is a tax-deductible expense. Think back to Chapters 9 and 17 where we introduced the *after-tax* weighted-average cost of capital:

$$\text{WACC} = r_D(1 - T_c)\frac{D}{V} + r_E\frac{E}{V}$$

Here D and E are the market values of the firm's debt and equity, $V = D + E$ is the total market value of the firm, r_D and r_E are the costs of debt and equity, and T_c is the marginal corporate tax rate.

Notice that the WACC formula uses the *after-tax* cost of debt $r_D(1 - T_c)$. That is how the after-tax WACC captures the value of interest tax shields. Notice too that all the variables in the WACC formula refer to the firm as a whole. As a result, the formula gives the right discount rate only for projects that are just like the firm undertaking them. The formula works for the "average" project. It is incorrect for projects that are safer or riskier than the average of the firm's existing assets. It is incorrect for projects whose acceptance would lead to an increase or decrease in the firm's target debt ratio.

The WACC is based on the firm's *current* characteristics, but managers use it to discount *future* cash flows. That's fine as long as the firm's business risk and debt ratio are expected to remain constant, but when the business risk and debt ratio are expected to change, discounting cash flows by the WACC is only approximately correct.

EXAMPLE 19.1 Calculating Sangria's WACC

Sangria is a India-based company whose products aim to promote happy, low-stress lifestyles. Let's calculate Sangria's WACC. Its book and market-value balance sheets are:

Sangria Corporation (Book Values, ₹ millions)

Asset value	₹1,000	₹ 500	Debt
		500	Equity
	₹1,000	₹1,000	

Sangria Corporation (Market Values, ₹ millions)

Asset value	₹1,250	₹ 500	Debt
		750	Equity
	₹1,250	₹1,250	

We calculated the market value of equity on Sangria's balance sheet by multiplying its current stock price (₹7.50) by 100 million, the number of its outstanding shares. The company's future prospects are good, so the stock is trading above book value (₹7.50 vs. ₹5.00 per share). However, interest rates have been stable since the firm's debt was issued and the book and market values of debt are in this case equal.

Sangria's cost of debt (the market interest rate on its existing debt and on any new borrowing[1]) is 6%. Its cost of equity (the expected rate of return demanded by investors in Sangria's stock) is 12.4%.

The market-value balance sheet shows assets worth ₹1,250 million. Of course we can't observe this value directly, because the assets themselves are not traded. But we know what they are worth to debt and equity investors (₹500 + 750 = ₹1,250 million). This value is entered on the left of the market-value balance sheet.

Why did we show the book balance sheet? Only so you could draw a big X through it. Do so now.

When estimating the weighted-average cost of capital, you are not interested in past investments but in current values and expectations for the future. Sangria's true debt ratio is not 50%, the book ratio, but 40%, because its assets are worth ₹1,250 million. The cost of equity, $r_E = .124$, is the expected rate of return from purchase of stock at ₹7.50 per share, the current market price. It is not the return on book value per share. You can't buy shares in Sangria for ₹5 anymore.

Sangria is consistently profitable and pays taxes at the marginal rate of 35%. This tax rate is the final input for Sangria's WACC. The inputs are summarized here:

Cost of debt (r_D)	.06
Cost of equity (r_E)	.124
Marginal tax rate (T_c)	.35
Debt ratio (D/V)	500/1,250 = .4
Equity ratio (E/V)	750/1,250 = .6

The company's after-tax WACC is:

$$\text{WACC} = .06 \times (1 - .35) \times .4 + .124 \times .6 = .090, \text{ or } 9.0\%$$

That's how you calculate the weighted-average cost of capital. Now let's see how Sangria would *use* it.

EXAMPLE 19.2   Using Sangria's WACC to value a project

Sangria's enologists have proposed investing ₹12.5 million in the construction of a perpetual crushing machine, which (conveniently for us) never depreciates and generates a perpetual stream of earnings

---

[1] Always use an up-to-date interest rate (yield to maturity), not the interest rate when the firm's debt was first issued and not the coupon rate on the debt's book value.

and cash flow of ₹1.731 million per year pretax. The project is average risk, so we can use WACC. The after-tax cash flow is:

Pretax cash flow	₹1.731 million
Tax at 35%	.606
After-tax cash flow	C = ₹1.125 million

Notice: This after-tax cash flow takes no account of interest tax shields on debt supported by the perpetual crusher project. As we explained in Chapter 6, standard capital budgeting practice calculates after-tax cash flows as if the project were all-equity-financed. However, the interest tax shields will not be ignored: We are about to discount the project's cash flows by Sangria's WACC, in which the cost of debt is entered after tax. The value of interest tax shields is picked up not as higher after-tax cash flows, but in a lower discount rate.

The crusher generates a perpetual after-tax cash flow of C = ₹1.125 million, so NPV is:

$$\text{NPV} = -12.5 + \frac{1.125}{0.09} = 0$$

NPV = 0 means a barely acceptable investment. The annual cash flow of ₹1.125 million per year amounts to a 9% rate of return on investment (1.125/12.5 = .09), exactly equal to Sangria's WACC.

If project NPV is exactly zero, the return to equity investors must exactly equal the cost of equity, 12.4%. Let's confirm that Sangria shareholders can actually look forward to a 12.4% return on their investment in the perpetual crusher project.

Suppose Sangria sets up this project as a mini-firm. Its market-value balance sheet looks like this:

Perpetual Crusher (Market Values, ₹ millions)

Asset value	₹ 12.5	₹ 5.0	Debt
		7.5	Equity
	₹ 12.5	₹ 12.5	

Calculate the expected dollar return to shareholders:

$$\text{After-tax interest} = r_D(1 - T_c)D = .06 \times (1 - .35) \times 5 = .195$$
$$\text{Expected equity income} = C - r_D(1 - T_c)D = 1.125 - .195 = .93$$

The project's earnings are level and perpetual, so the expected rate of return on equity is equal to the expected equity income divided by the equity value:

$$\text{Expected equity return} = r_E = \frac{\text{expected equity income}}{\text{equity value}}$$

$$= \frac{.93}{7.5} = .124, \text{ or } 12.4\%$$

The expected return on equity equals the cost of equity, so it makes sense that the project's NPV is zero.

Review of Assumptions

When discounting the perpetual crusher's cash flows at Sangria's WACC, we assume that:

- The project's business risks are the same as those of Sangria's other assets and remain so for the life of the project.

- The project supports the same fraction of debt to value as in Sangria's overall capital structure, which remains constant for the life of the project.

You can see the importance of these two assumptions: If the perpetual crusher had greater business risk than Sangria's other assets, or if the acceptance of the project would lead to a permanent, material change in Sangria's debt ratio,[2] then Sangria's shareholders would not be content with a 12.4% expected return on their equity investment in the project.

We have illustrated the WACC formula only for a project offering perpetual cash flows. But the formula works for any cash-flow pattern if the firm adjusts its borrowing to maintain a constant debt ratio over time.[3] When the firm departs from this borrowing policy, WACC is only approximately correct.

19-2 VALUING BUSINESSES

On most workdays the financial manager concentrates on valuing projects, arranging financing, and helping run the firm more effectively. The valuation of the business as a whole is left to investors and financial markets. But on some days the financial manager has to take a stand on what an entire business is worth. When this happens, a *big* decision is typically in the offing. For example:

- If firm A is about to make a takeover offer for firm B, then A's financial managers have to decide how much the combined business A + B is worth under A's management. This task is particularly difficult if B is a private company with no observable share price.

---

[2] Users of WACC need not worry about small or temporary fluctuations in debt-to-value ratios. Suppose that Sangria management decides for convenience to borrow ₹12.5 million to allow immediate construction of the crusher. This does not necessarily change Sangria's long-term financing policy. If the crusher supports only ₹5.0 million of debt, Sangria would have to pay down debt to restore its overall debt ratio to 40%. For example, it could fund later projects with less debt and more equity.

[3] We can prove this statement as follows. Denote expected after-tax cash flows (assuming all-equity financing) as $C_1, C_2, \ldots, C_T$. With all-equity financing, these flows would be discounted at the opportunity cost of capital r. But we need to value the cash flows for a firm that is financed partly with debt.

Start with value in the next to last period: $V_{T-1} = D_{T-1} + E_{T-1}$. The total cash payoff to debt and equity investors is the cash flow plus the interest tax shield. The expected total return to debt and equity investors is:

$$\text{Expected cash payoff in } T = C_T + T_c r_D D_{T-1} \tag{1}$$

$$= V_{T-1}\left(1 + r_D \frac{D_{T-1}}{V_{T-1}} + r_E \frac{E_{T-1}}{V_{T-1}}\right) \tag{2}$$

Assume the debt ratio is constant at $L = D/V$. Equate (1) and (2) and solve for V_{T-1}:

$$V_{T-1} = \frac{C_T}{1 + (1 - T_c)r_D L + r_E(1 - L)} = \frac{C_T}{1 + \text{WACC}}$$

The logic repeats for V_{T-2}. Note that the next period's payoff includes V_{T-1}:

$$\text{Expected cash payoff in } T - 1 = C_{T-1} + T_c r_D D_{T-2} + V_{T-1}$$

$$= V_{T-2}\left(1 + r_D \frac{D_{T-2}}{V_{T-2}} + r_E \frac{E_{T-2}}{V_{T-2}}\right)$$

$$V_{T-2} = \frac{C_{T-1} + V_{T-1}}{1 + (1 - T_c)r_D L + r_E(1 - L)} = \frac{C_{T-1} + V_{T-1}}{1 + \text{WACC}} = \frac{C_{T-1}}{1 + \text{WACC}} + \frac{C_T}{(1 + \text{WACC})^2}$$

We can continue all the way back to date 0:

$$V_0 = \sum_{t=1}^{T} \frac{C_t}{(1 + \text{WACC})^t}$$

- If firm C is considering the sale of one of its divisions, it has to decide what the division is worth in order to negotiate with potential buyers.
- When a firm goes public, the investment bank must evaluate how much the firm is worth in order to set the issue price.

In addition, thousands of analysts in stockbrokers' offices and investment firms spend every workday burrowing away in the hope of finding undervalued firms. Many of these analysts use the valuation tools we are about to cover.

In Chapter 4 we took a first pass at valuing an entire business. We assumed then that the business was financed solely by equity. Now we will show how WACC can be used to value a company that is financed by a mixture of debt and equity as long as the debt ratio is expected to remain approximately constant. You just treat the company as if it were one big project. You forecast the company's cash flows (the hardest part of the exercise) and discount back to present value. But be sure to remember three important points:

1. If you discount at WACC, cash flows have to be projected just as you would for a capital investment project. Do not deduct interest. Calculate taxes as if the company were all-equity-financed. (The value of interest tax shields is not ignored, because the after-tax cost of debt is used in the WACC formula.)
2. Unlike most projects, companies are potentially immortal. But that does not mean that you need to forecast every year's cash flow from now to eternity. Financial managers usually forecast to a medium-term horizon and add a terminal value to the cash flows in the horizon year. The terminal value is the present value at the horizon of all subsequent cash flows. Estimating the terminal value requires careful attention because it often accounts for the majority of the company's value.
3. Discounting at WACC values the assets and operations of the company. If the object is to value the company's equity, that is, its common stock, don't forget to subtract the value of the company's outstanding debt.

Here's an example.

Valuing Geo Corporation

Sangria is tempted to acquire the Geo Corporation, which is also in the business of promoting relaxed, happy lifestyles. Geo has developed a special weight-loss program called the Goa Diet, based on barbecues, red wine, and sunshine. The firm guarantees that within three months you will have a figure that will allow you to fit right in at Baga or Vagator beach in Goa. But before you head for the beach, you've got the job of working out how much Sangria should pay for Geo.

Geo is an Indian company. It is privately held, so Sangria has no stock-market price to rely on. Geo has 1.5 million shares outstanding and debt with a market and book value of ₹36 million. Geo is in the same line of business as Sangria, so we will assume that it has the same business risk as Sangria and can support the same proportion of debt. Therefore we can use Sangria's WACC.

Your first task is to forecast Geo's *free cash flow* (FCF). Free cash flow is the amount of cash that the firm can pay out to investors after making all investments necessary for growth. Free cash flow is calculated assuming the firm is all-equity-financed. Discounting the free cash flows at the after-tax WACC gives the total value of Geo (debt *plus* equity). To find the value of its equity, you will need to subtract the ₹36 million of debt.

We will forecast each year's free cash flow out to a *valuation horizon* (H) and predict the business's value at that horizon (PV$_H$). The cash flows and horizon value are then discounted back to the present:

$$PV = \underbrace{\frac{FCF_1}{1 + WACC} + \frac{FCF_2}{(1 + WACC)^2} + \cdots + \frac{FCF_H}{(1 + WACC)^H}}_{PV \text{ (free cash flow)}} + \underbrace{\frac{PV_H}{(1 + WACC)^H}}_{PV \text{ (horizon value)}}$$

Of course, the business will continue after the horizon, but it's not practical to forecast free cash flow year by year to infinity. PV_H stands in for the value in year H of free cash flow in periods $H + 1$, $H + 2$, etc.

Free cash flow and net income are not the same. They differ in several important ways:

- Income is the return to shareholders, calculated after interest expense. Free cash flow is calculated before interest.
- Income is calculated after various noncash expenses, including depreciation. Therefore we will add back depreciation when we calculate free cash flow.
- Capital expenditures and investments in working capital do not appear as expenses on the income statement, but they do reduce free cash flow.

Free cash flow can be negative for rapidly growing firms, even if the firms are profitable, because investment exceeds cash flow from operations. Negative free cash flow is normally temporary, fortunately for the firm and its stockholders. Free cash flow turns positive as growth slows down and the payoffs from prior investments start to roll in.

Table 19.1 sets out the information that you need to forecast Geo's free cash flows. We will follow common practice and start with a projection of sales. In the year just ended Geo had sales of ₹83.6 million. In recent years sales have grown by between 5% and 8% a year. You forecast that sales will grow by about 7% a year for the next three years. Growth will then slow to 4% for years 4 to 6 and to 3% starting in year 7.

The other components of cash flow in Table 19.1 are driven by these sales forecasts. For example, you can see that costs are forecasted at 74% of sales in the first year with a gradual increase to 76% of sales in later years, reflecting increased marketing costs as Geo's competitors gradually catch up.

Increasing sales are likely to require further investment in fixed assets and working capital. Geo's net fixed assets are currently about ₹.79 for each rupee of sales. Unless Geo has surplus capacity or can squeeze more output from its existing plant and equipment, its investment in fixed assets will need to grow along with sales. Therefore we assume that every rupee of sales growth requires an increase of ₹.79 in net fixed assets. We also assume that working capital grows in proportion to sales.

Geo's free cash flow is calculated in Table 19.1 as profit after tax, plus depreciation, minus investment. Investment is the change in the stock of (gross) fixed assets and working capital from the previous year. For example, in year 1:

$$\begin{aligned} \text{Free cash flow} &= \text{Profit after tax} + \text{depreciation} - \text{investment in fixed assets} \\ &\quad - \text{investment in working capital} \\ &= 8.7 + 9.9 - (109.6 - 95.0) - (11.6 - 11.1) = ₹3.5 \text{ million} \end{aligned}$$

Estimating Horizon Value

We will forecast cash flows for each of the first six years. After that, Geo's sales are expected to settle down to stable, long-term growth starting in year 7. To find the present value of the cash flows in years 1 to 6, we discount at the 9% WACC:

$$PV = \frac{3.5}{1.09} + \frac{3.2}{1.09^2} + \frac{3.4}{1.09^3} + \frac{5.9}{1.09^4} + \frac{6.1}{1.09^5} + \frac{6.0}{1.09^6} = ₹20.3 \text{ million}$$

Visit us at
www.mhhe.com/bmam10e

TABLE 19.1   Free-cash-flow projections and company value for Geo Corporation (₹ millions).

		Latest Year	Forecast						
		0	1	2	3	4	5	6	7
1	Sales	83.6	89.5	95.8	102.5	106.6	110.8	115.2	118.7
2	Cost of goods sold	63.1	66.2	71.3	76.3	79.9	83.1	87.0	90.2
3	EBITDA (1–2)	20.5	23.3	24.4	26.1	26.6	27.7	28.2	28.5
4	Depreciation	3.3	9.9	10.6	11.3	11.8	12.3	12.7	13.1
5	Profit before tax (EBIT) (3–4)	17.2	13.4	13.8	14.8	14.9	15.4	15.5	15.4
6	Tax	6.0	4.7	4.8	5.2	5.2	5.4	5.4	5.4
7	Profit after tax (5–6)	11.2	8.7	9.0	9.6	9.7	10.0	10.1	10.0
8	Investment in fixed assets	11.0	14.6	15.5	16.6	15.0	15.6	16.2	15.9
9	Investment in working capital	1.0	0.5	0.8	0.9	0.5	0.6	0.6	0.4
10	Free cash flow (7 + 4 − 8 − 9)	2.5	3.5	3.2	3.4	5.9	6.1	6.0	6.8
	PV free cash flow, years 1–6	20.3							
	PV horizon value	67.6			(Horizon value in year 6)			113.4	
	PV of company	87.9							
	Assumptions:								
	Sales growth, %	6.7	7.0	7.0	7.0	4.0	4.0	4.0	3.0
	Costs (percent of sales)	75.5	74.0	74.5	74.5	75.0	75.0	75.5	76.0
	Working capital (percent of sales)	13.3	13.0	13.0	13.0	13.0	13.0	13.0	13.0
	Net fixed assets (percent of sales)	79.2	79.0	79.0	79.0	79.0	79.0	79.0	79.0
	Depreciation (percent of net fixed assets)	5.0	14.0	14.0	14.0	14.0	14.0	14.0	14.0
	Tax rate, %	35.0							
	WACC, %	9.0							
	Long-term growth forecast, %	3.0							
	Fixed assets and working capital								
	Gross fixed assets	95.0	109.6	125.1	141.8	156.8	172.4	188.6	204.5
	Less accumulated depreciation	29.0	38.9	49.5	60.8	72.6	84.9	97.6	110.7
	Net fixed assets	66.0	70.7	75.6	80.9	84.2	87.5	91.0	93.8
	Net working capital	11.1	11.6	12.4	13.3	13.9	14.4	15.0	15.4

Now we need to find the value of the cash flows from year 7 onward. In Chapter 4 we looked at several ways to estimate horizon value. Here we will use the constant-growth DCF formula. This requires a forecast of the free cash flow for year 7, which we have worked out in the final column of Table 19.1, assuming a long-run growth rate of 3% per year.[4] The free cash flow is ₹6.8 million, so

$$PV_H = \frac{FCF_{H+1}}{WACC - g} = \frac{6.8}{.09 - .03} = ₹113.4 \text{ million}$$

$$PV \text{ at year } 0 = \frac{1}{1.09^6} \times 113.4 = ₹67.6 \text{ million}$$

---

[4] Notice that expected free cash flow increases by about 14% from year 6 to year 7 because the transition from 4% to 3% sales growth reduces required investment. But sales, investment, and free cash flow will all increase at 3% once the company settles into stable growth. Recall that the first cash flow in the constant-growth DCF formula occurs in the next year, year 7 in this case. Growth progresses at a steady-state 3% from year 7 onward. Therefore it's OK to use the 3% growth rate in the horizon-value formula.

We now have all we need to value the business:

$$PV(company) = PV(cash\ flow\ years\ 1–6) + PV(horizon\ value)$$
$$= ₹20.3 + 67.6 = ₹87.9\ million$$

This is the total value of Geo. To find the value of the equity, we simply subtract the value of the debt:

$$Total\ value\ of\ equity = ₹87.9 – 36.0 = ₹51.9\ million$$

And to find the value per share, we divide by the total number of shares outstanding:

$$Value\ per\ share = 51.9/1.5 = ₹34.60$$

Thus Sangria could afford to pay up to ₹34.60 per share for Geo.

You now have an estimate of the value of Geo Corporation. But how confident can you be in this figure? Notice that less than a quarter of Geo's value comes from cash flows in the first six years. The rest comes from the horizon value. Moreover, this horizon value can change in response to only minor changes in assumptions. For example, if the long-run growth rate is 4% rather than 3%, Geo needs to invest more to support this higher growth, but firm value increases from ₹87.9 million to ₹89.9 million.

In Chapter 4 we stressed that wise managers won't stop at this point. They will check their calculations by identifying comparable companies and comparing their price–earnings multiples and ratios of market to book value.[5]

When you forecast cash flows, it is easy to become mesmerized by the numbers and just do it mechanically. As we pointed out in Chapter 11, it is important to take a strategic view. Are the revenue figures consistent with what you expect your competitors to do? Are the costs you have predicted realistic? Probe the assumptions behind the numbers to make sure they are sensible. Be particularly careful about the growth rates and profitability assumptions that drive horizon values. Don't assume that the business you are valuing will grow and earn more than the cost of capital in perpetuity.[6] This would be a nice outcome for the business, but not an outcome that competition will tolerate.

You should also check whether the business is worth more dead than alive. Sometimes a company's *liquidation value* exceeds its value as a going concern. Smart financial analysts sometimes ferret out idle or underexploited assets that would be worth much more if sold to someone else. You may end up counting these assets at their likely sale price and valuing the rest of the business without them.

WACC vs. the Flow-to-Equity Method

When valuing Geo we forecast the cash flows assuming all-equity financing and we used the WACC to discount these cash flows. The WACC formula picked up the value of the interest tax shields. Then to find equity value, we subtracted the value of debt from the total value of the firm.

If our task is to value a firm's equity, there's an obvious alternative to discounting company cash flows at the firm's WACC: Discount cash flows to *equity,* after interest and after taxes, at the cost of equity capital. This is called the *flow-to-equity* method. If the company's debt ratio is constant over time, the flow-to equity method should give the same answer as discounting cash flows at the WACC and then subtracting debt.

[5] See Section 4-5.

[6] Table 19.1 is too optimistic in this respect, because the horizon value increases with the assumed long-run growth rate. This implies that Geo has valuable growth opportunities (PVGO) even after the horizon in year 6. A more sophisticated spreadsheet would add an intermediate growth stage, say from years 7 through 10, and gradually reduce profitability to competitive levels. See Problem 26 at the end of this chapter.

The flow-to-equity method seems simple, and it is simple if the proportions of debt and equity financing stay reasonably close to constant for the life of the company. But the cost of equity depends on financial leverage; in other words, it depends on financial risk as well as business risk. If financial leverage is expected to change significantly, discounting flows to equity at today's cost of equity will not give the right answer.

19-3   Using WACC In Practice

Some Tricks of the Trade

Sangria had just one asset and two sources of financing. A real company's market-value balance sheet has many more entries, for example:[7]

Current assets,
    including cash, inventory,
    and accounts receivable
	Current liabilities,
	    including accounts payable
	    and short-term debt

Property, plant, and equipment	Long-term debt (D)
	Preferred stock (P)
Growth opportunities	Equity (E)
Total assets	Total liabilities plus equity

Several questions immediately arise:

How does the formula change when there are more than two sources of financing? Easy: There is one cost for each element. The weight for each element is proportional to its market value. For example, if the capital structure includes both preferred and common shares,

$$\text{WACC} = r_D(1 - T_c)\frac{D}{V} + r_P\frac{P}{V} + r_E\frac{E}{V}$$

where r_P is investors' expected rate of return on the preferred stock, P is the amount of preferred stock outstanding, and $V = D + P + E$.

What about short-term debt? Many companies consider only long-term financing when calculating WACC. They leave out the cost of short-term debt. In principle this is incorrect. The lenders who hold short-term debt are investors who can claim their share of operating earnings. A company that ignores this claim will misstate the required return on capital investments.

But "zeroing out" short-term debt is not a serious error if the debt is only temporary, seasonal, or incidental financing or if it is offset by holdings of cash and marketable securities. Suppose, for

[7] This balance sheet is for exposition and should not be confused with a real company's books. It includes the value of growth opportunities, which accountants do not recognize, though investors do. It excludes certain accounting entries, for example, deferred taxes.

Deferred taxes arise when a company uses faster depreciation for tax purposes than it uses in reports to investors. That means the company reports more in taxes than it pays. The difference is accumulated as a liability for deferred taxes. In a sense there is a liability, because the Internal Revenue Service "catches up," collecting extra taxes, as assets age. But this is irrelevant in capital investment analysis, which focuses on actual after-tax cash flows and uses accelerated tax depreciation.

Deferred taxes should not be regarded as a source of financing or an element of the weighted-average cost of capital formula. The liability for deferred taxes is not a security held by investors. It is a balance sheet entry created for accounting purposes.

Deferred taxes can be important in regulated industries, however. Regulators take deferred taxes into account in calculating allowed rates of return and the time patterns of revenues and consumer prices.

example, that one of your foreign subsidiaries takes out a six-month loan to finance its inventory and accounts receivable. The dollar equivalent of this loan will show up as a short-term debt. At the same time headquarters may be lending money by investing surplus dollars in short-term securities. If this lending and borrowing offset, there is no point in including the cost of short-term debt in the weighted-average cost of capital, because the company is not a *net* short-term borrower.

What about other current liabilities? Current liabilities are usually "netted out" by subtracting them from current assets. The difference is entered as net working capital on the left-hand side of the balance sheet. The sum of long-term financing on the right is called *total capitalization*.

Net working capital
   = current assets
   − current liabilities
Property, plant, and equipment
Growth opportunities
	Long-term debt (*D*)
	
	Preferred stock (*P*)
	
	Equity (*E*)
	Total capitalization (*V*)

When net working capital is treated as an asset, forecasts of cash flows for capital investment projects must treat increases in net working capital as a cash outflow and decreases as an inflow. This is standard practice, which we followed in Section 6-2. We also did so when we estimated the future investments that Geo would need to make in working capital.

Since current liabilities include short-term debt, netting them out against current assets excludes the cost of short-term debt from the weighted-average cost of capital. We have just explained why this can be an acceptable approximation. But when short-term debt is an important, permanent source of financing—as is common for small firms and firms outside the United States—it should be shown explicitly on the right-hand side of the balance sheet, not netted out against current assets.[8] A quick glance at the financing pattern of 16,485 companies in India in 2010 shows that short-term borrowings constitute at least 50 percent of the total borrowings in 5724 companies (35 percent). Short-term borrowings constitute at least 25 percent of the total borrowings in 7859 companies (about 48 percent). The interest cost of short-term debt is then one element of the weighted-average cost of capital of such companies.

How are the costs of financing calculated? You can often use stock market data to get an estimate of r_E, the expected rate of return demanded by investors in the company's stock. With that estimate, WACC is not too hard to calculate, because the borrowing rate r_D and the debt and equity ratios D/V and E/V can be directly observed or estimated without too much trouble.[9] Estimating the value and required return for preferred shares is likewise usually not too complicated.

Estimating the required return on other security types can be troublesome. Convertible debt, where the investors' return comes partly from an option to exchange the debt for the company's stock, is one example. We leave convertibles to Chapter 24.

Junk debt, where the risk of default is high, is likewise difficult. The higher the odds of default, the lower the market price of the debt, and the higher is the *promised* rate of interest. But the weighted-average cost of capital is an *expected*, that is average, rate of return, not a promised one. For example, in

---

[8] Financial practitioners have rules of thumb for deciding whether short-term debt is worth including in WACC. One rule checks whether short-term debt is at least 10% of total liabilities and net working capital is negative. If so, then short-term debt is almost surely being used to finance long-term assets and is explicitly included in WACC.

[9] Most corporate debt is not actively traded, so its market value cannot be observed directly. But you can usually value a nontraded debt security by looking to securities that *are* traded and that have approximately the same default risk and maturity. See Chapter 23.

    For healthy firms the market value of debt is usually not too far from book value, so many managers and analysts use book value for *D* in the weighted-average cost of capital formula. However, be sure to use *market*, not book, values for *E*.

July 2009, MGM Mirage bonds maturing in 2015 sold at only 66% of face value and offered a 15% promised yield, nearly 13 percentage points above yields on the highest-quality debt issues maturing at the same time. The price and yield on the MGM bond demonstrated investors' concern about the company's chronic financial ill-health. But the 15% yield was not an expected return, because it did not average in the losses to be incurred if MGM were to default. Including 15% as a "cost of debt" in a calculation of WACC would therefore have overstated MGM's true cost of capital.

This is bad news: There is no easy or tractable way of estimating the expected rate of return on most junk debt issues.[10] The good news is that for most debt the odds of default are small. That means the promised and expected rates of return are close, and the promised rate can be used as an approximation in the weighted-average cost of capital.

Company vs. Industry WACCs   Of course you want to know what your company's WACC is. Yet industry WACCs are sometimes more useful. Here's an example. Grasim Industries Limited used to be a portfolio of Viscose Staple Fibre, Cement, and Sponge iron. Almost 94 percent of the total revenue of Grasim comes from these three business segments. Grasim's overall WACC is not right for any of the three business segments. The company will be well advised to use a VSF industry WACC for its VSF division, cement industry WACC for its cement division, and sponge iron WACC for its sponge iron division.

Grasim spun off the cement division and then merged it with its subsidiary company UltraTech Cements in 2009. But even now, when we find the cost of capital of UltraTech Cement, the company would be wise to check its WACC against a cement industry WACC. Industry WACCs are less exposed to random noise and estimation errors. Fortunately, for UltraTech, there are several large, pure-play (almost) Indian companies that are exclusively into the manufacturing of cement. Of course, use of an industry WACC for a particular company's investments assumes that the company and industry have approximately the same business risk and financing.

Mistakes People Make in Using the Weighted-Average Formula

The weighted-average formula is very useful but also dangerous. It tempts people to make logical errors. For example, manager Q, who is campaigning for a pet project, might look at the formula

$$\text{WACC} = r_D(1 - T_c)\frac{D}{V} + r_E\frac{E}{V}$$

and think, "Aha! My firm has a good credit rating. It could borrow, say, 90% of the project's cost if it likes. That means $D/V = .9$ and $E/V = .1$. My firm's borrowing rate r_D is 8%, and the required return on equity, r_E, is 15%. Therefore

$$\text{WACC} = .08(1 - .35)(.9) + .15(.1) = .062$$

or 6.2%. When I discount at that rate, my project looks great."

Manager Q is wrong on several counts. First, the weighted-average formula works only for projects that are carbon copies of the firm. The firm isn't 90% debt-financed.

Second, the immediate source of funds for a project has no necessary connection with the hurdle rate for the project. What matters is the project's overall contribution to the firm's borrowing power. A dollar invested in Q's pet project will not increase the firm's debt capacity by ₹.90. If the firm borrows

---

[10] When betas can be estimated for the junk issue or for a sample of similar issues, the expected return can be calculated from the capital asset pricing model. Otherwise the yield should be adjusted for the probability of default. Evidence on historical default rates on junk bonds is described in Chapter 23.

90% of the project's cost, it is really borrowing in part against its *existing* assets. Any advantage from financing the new project with more debt than normal should be attributed to the old projects, not to the new one.

Third, even if the firm were willing and able to lever up to 90% debt, its cost of capital would not decline to 6.2% (as Q's naive calculation predicts). You cannot increase the debt ratio without creating financial risk for stockholders and thereby increasing r_E, the expected rate of return they demand from the firm's common stock. Going to 90% debt would certainly increase the borrowing rate, too.

Adjusting WACC when Debt Ratios and Business Risks Differ

The WACC formula assumes that the project or business to be valued will be financed in the same debt–equity proportions as the company (or industry) as a whole. What if that is not true? For example, what if Sangria's perpetual crusher project supports only 20% debt, versus 40% for Sangria overall?

Moving from 40% to 20% debt may change all the inputs to the WACC formula.[11] Obviously the financing weights change. But the cost of equity r_E is less, because financial risk is reduced. The cost of debt may be lower too.

Take another look at Figure 17.4 which plots WACC and the costs of debt and equity as a function of the debt–equity ratio. The flat line is r, the opportunity cost of capital. Remember, this is the expected rate of return that investors would want from the project if it were all-equity-financed. The opportunity cost of capital depends only on business risk and is the natural reference point.

Suppose Sangria or the perpetual crusher project were all-equity-financed ($D/V = 0$). At that point WACC equals cost of equity, and both equal the opportunity cost of capital. Start from that point in Figure 19.1. As the debt ratio increases, the cost of equity increases, because of financial risk, but notice that WACC declines. The decline is *not* caused by use of "cheap" debt in place of "expensive" equity. It falls because of the tax shields on debt interest payments. If there were no corporate income taxes, the weighted-average cost of capital would be constant, and equal to the opportunity cost of capital, at all debt ratios. We showed this in Chapter 17.

Figure 19.1 shows the *shape* of the relationship between financing and WACC, but initially we have numbers only for Sangria's current 40% debt ratio. We want to recalculate WACC at a 20% ratio.

Here is the simplest way to do it. There are three steps.

Step 1   Calculate the opportunity cost of capital. In other words, calculate WACC and the cost of equity at zero debt. This step is called *unlevering* the WACC. The simplest unlevering formula is

$$\text{Opportunity cost of capital} = r = r_D D/V + r_E E/V$$

This formula comes directly from Modigliani and Miller's proposition 1 (see Section 17-1). If taxes are left out, the weighted-average cost of capital equals the opportunity cost of capital and is independent of leverage.

Step 2   Estimate the cost of debt, r_D, at the new debt ratio, and calculate the new cost of equity.

$$r_E = r + (r - r_D)D/E$$

This formula is Modigliani and Miller's proposition 2 (see Section 17-2). It calls for D/E, the ratio of debt to *equity*, not debt to value.

---

[11] Even the tax rate could change. For example, Sangria might have enough taxable income to cover interest payments at 20% debt but not at 40% debt. In that case the effective marginal tax rate would be higher at 20% than 40% debt.

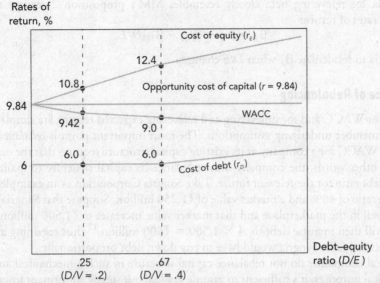

e**X**cel

Visit us at
www.mhhe.com/bmam10e

FIGURE 19.1

This plot shows WACC for the Sangria Corporation at debt-to-equity ratios of 25% and 67%. The corresponding debt-to-value ratios are 20% and 40%.

Step 3 Recalculate the weighted-average cost of capital at the new financing weights.

Let's do the numbers for Sangria at $D/V = .20$, or 20%.

Step 1. Sangria's current debt ratio is $D/V = .4$. So

$$r = .06(.4) + .124(.6) = .0984, \text{ or } 9.84\%$$

Step 2. We will assume that the debt cost stays at 6% when the debt ratio is 20%. Then

$$r_E = .0984 + (.0984 - .06)(.25) = .108, \text{ or } 10.8\%$$

Note that the debt–*equity* ratio is $.2/.8 = .25$.

Step 3. Recalculate WACC.

$$\text{WACC} = .06(1 - .35)(.2) + .108(.8) = .0942, \text{ or } 9.42\%$$

Figure 19.1 enters these numbers on the plot of WACC versus the debt–equity ratio.

Unlevering and Relevering Betas

Our three-step procedure (1) unlevers and then (2) relevers the cost of equity. Some financial managers find it convenient to (1) unlever and then (2) relever the equity beta. Given the beta of equity at the new debt ratio, the cost of equity is determined from the capital asset pricing model. Then WACC is recalculated.

The formula for unlevering beta was given in Section 17-2.

$$\beta_A = \beta_D (D/V) + \beta_E (E/V)$$

This equation says that the beta of a firm's assets is revealed by the beta of a portfolio of all of the firm's outstanding debt and equity securities. An investor who bought such a portfolio would own the assets free and clear and absorb only business risks.

The formula for relevering beta closely resembles MM's proposition 2, except that betas are substituted for rates of return:

$$\beta_E = \beta_A + (\beta_A - \beta_D)D/E$$

Use this formula to recalculate β_E when D/E changes.

The Importance of Rebalancing

The formulas for WACC and for unlevering and relevering expected returns are simple, but we must be careful to remember underlying assumptions. The most important point is *rebalancing*.

Calculating WACC for a company at its existing capital structure requires that the capital structure *not* change; in other words, the company must rebalance its capital structure to maintain the same market-value debt ratio for the relevant future. Take Sangria Corporation as an example. It starts with a debt-to-value ratio of 40% and a market value of ₹1,250 million. Suppose that Sangria's products do unexpectedly well in the marketplace and that market value increases to ₹1,500 million. Rebalancing means that it will then increase debt to $.4 \times 1,500 = ₹600$ million,[12] thus regaining a 40% ratio. If market value instead falls, Sangria would have to pay down debt proportionally.

Of course real companies do not rebalance capital structure in such a mechanical and compulsive way. For practical purposes, it's sufficient to assume gradual but steady adjustment toward a long-run target. But if the firm plans significant changes in capital structure (for example, if it plans to pay off its debt), the WACC formula won't work. In such cases, you should turn to the APV method, which we describe in the next section.

Our three-step procedure for recalculating WACC makes a similar rebalancing assumption.[13] Whatever the starting debt ratio, the firm is assumed to rebalance to maintain that ratio in the future.[14]

---

[12] The proceeds of the additional borrowing would be paid out to shareholders or used, along with additional equity investment, to finance Sangria's growth.

[13] Similar, but not identical. The basic WACC formula is correct whether rebalancing occurs at the end of each period or continuously. The unlevering and relevering formulas used in steps 1 and 2 of our three-step procedure are exact only if rebalancing is continuous so that the debt ratio stays constant day-to-day and week-to-week. However, the errors introduced from annual rebalancing are very small and can be ignored for practical purposes.

[14] Here's why the formulas work with continuous rebalancing. Think of a market-value balance sheet with assets and interest tax shields on the left and debt and equity on the right, with $D + E = PV(assets) + PV(tax\ shield)$. The total risk (beta) of the firm's debt and equity equals the blended risk of PV(assets) and PV(tax shield)

$$\beta_D\frac{D}{V} + \beta_E\frac{E}{V} = \alpha\beta_A + (1-\alpha)\beta_{tax\ shield} \tag{1}$$

where α is the proportion of the total firm value from its assets and $1 - \alpha$ is the proportion from interest tax shields. If the firm readjusts its capital structure to keep D/V constant, then the beta of the tax shield must be the same as the beta of the assets. With rebalancing, an $x\%$ change in firm value V changes debt D by $x\%$. So the interest tax shield $T_c r_D D$ will change by $x\%$ as well. Thus the risk of the tax shield must be the same as the risk of the firm as a whole:

$$\beta_{tax\ shield} = \beta_A = \beta_D\frac{D}{V} + \beta_E\frac{E}{V} \tag{2}$$

This is our unlevering formula expressed in terms of beta. Since expected returns depend on beta:

$$r_A = r_D\frac{D}{V} + r_E\frac{E}{V} \tag{3}$$

Rearrange formulas (2) and (3) to get the relevering formulas for β_E and r_E.

$$\beta_E = \beta_A + (\beta_A - \beta_D)D/E$$
$$r_E = r_A + (r_A - r_D)D/E$$

All this assumes continuous rebalancing. Suppose instead that the firm rebalances once a year, so that the next year's interest tax shield, which depends on this year's debt, is known. Then you can use a formula developed by Miles and Ezzell:

$$r_{Miles-Ezzell} = r_A - (D/V)r_D T_c\left(\frac{1+r_A}{1+r_D}\right)$$

See J. Miles and J. Ezzell, "The Weighted Average Cost of Capital, Perfect Capital Markets, and Project Life: A Clarification," *Journal of Financial and Quantitative Analysis* 15 (September 1980), pp. 719–730.

The Modigliani–Miller Formula, Plus Some Final Advice

What if the firm does not rebalance to keep its debt ratio constant? In this case the only general approach is adjusted present value, which we cover in the next section. But sometimes financial managers turn to other discount-rate formulas, including one derived by Modigliani and Miller (MM). MM considered a company or project generating a level, perpetual stream of cash flows financed with fixed, perpetual debt, and derived a simple after-tax discount rate:[15]

$$r_{MM} = r(1 - T_c D/V)$$

Here it's easy to unlever: just set the debt-capacity parameter (D/V) equal to zero.[16]

MM's formula is still used in practice, but the formula is exact only in the special case where there is a level, perpetual stream of cash flows and fixed, perpetual debt. However, the formula is not a bad approximation for shorter-lived projects when debt is issued in a fixed amount.[17]

So which team do you want to play with, the fixed-debt team or the rebalancers? If you join the fixed-debt team you will be outnumbered. Most financial managers use the plain, after-tax WACC, which assumes constant market-value debt ratios and therefore assumes rebalancing. That makes sense, because the debt *capacity* of a firm or project must depend on its future value, which will fluctuate.

At the same time, we must admit that the typical financial manager doesn't care much if his or her firm's debt ratio drifts up or down within a reasonable range of moderate financial leverage. The typical financial manager acts as if a plot of WACC against the debt ratio is "flat" (constant) over this range. This too makes sense, if we just remember that interest tax shields are the *only* reason why the after-tax WACC declines in Figure 17.4 or 19.1. The WACC formula doesn't explicitly capture costs of financial distress or any of the other nontax complications discussed in Chapter 18.[18] All these complications may roughly cancel the value added by interest tax shields (within a range of moderate leverage). If so, the financial manager is wise to focus on the firm's operating and investment decisions, rather than on fine-tuning its debt ratio.

---

[15] The formula first appeared in F. Modigliani and M. H. Miller, "Corporate Income Taxes and the Cost of Capital: A Correction," *American Economic Review* 53 (June 1963) pp. 433–443. It is explained more fully in M. H. Miller and F. Modigliani: "Some Estimates of the Cost of Capital to the Electric Utility Industry: 1954–1957," *American Economic Review* 56 (June 1966), pp. 333–391.

Given perpetual fixed debt,

$$V = \frac{C}{r} + T_c D$$

$$V = \frac{C}{r(1 - T_c D/V)} = \frac{C}{r_{MM}}$$

[16] In this case the relevering formula for the cost of equity is:

$$r_E = r_A + (1 - T_c)(r_A - r_D)D/E$$

The unlevering and relevering formulas for betas are

$$\beta_A = \frac{\beta_D(1 - T_c)D/E + \beta_E}{1 + (1 - T_c)D/E}$$

and

$$\beta_E = \beta_A + (1 - T_c)(\beta_A - \beta_D)D/E$$

See R. Hamada: "The Effect of a Firm's Capital Structure on the Systematic Risk of Common Stocks," *Journal of Finance* 27 (May 1972), pp. 435–452.

[17] See S. C. Myers, "Interactions of Corporate Financing and Investment Decisions—Implications for Capital Budgeting," *Journal of Finance* 29 (March 1974), pp. 1–25.

[18] Costs of financial distress can show up as rapidly increasing costs of debt and equity, especially at high debt ratios. The costs of financial distress could "flatten out" the WACC curve in Figures 17.4 and 19.1, and finally increase WACC as leverage climbs. Thus some practitioners calculate an industry WACC and take it as constant, at least within the range of debt ratios observed for healthy companies in the industry.

Personal taxes could also generate a flatter curve for after-tax WACC as a function of leverage. See Section 18-2.

19-4 ADJUSTED PRESENT VALUE

The idea behind **adjusted present value (APV)** is to divide and conquer. APV does not attempt to capture taxes or other effects of financing in a WACC or adjusted discount rate. A series of present value calculations is made instead. The first establishes a base-case value for the project or firm: its value as a separate, all-equity-financed venture. The discount rate for the base-case value is just the opportunity cost of capital. Once the base-case value is set, then each financing side effect is traced out, and the present value of its cost or benefit to the firm is calculated. Finally, all the present values are added together to estimate the project's total contribution to the value of the firm:

$$\text{APV} = \text{base-case NPV} + \text{sum of PVs of financing side effects}[19]$$

The most important financing side effect is the interest tax shield on the debt supported by the project (a plus). Other possible side effects are the issue costs of securities (a minus) or financing packages subsidized by a supplier or government (a plus).

APV gives the financial manager an explicit view of the factors that are adding or subtracting value. APV can prompt the manager to ask the right follow-up questions. For example, suppose that base-case NPV is positive but less than the costs of issuing shares to finance the project. That should prompt the manager to look around to see if the project can be rescued by an alternative financing plan.

APV for the Perpetual Crusher

APV is easiest to understand in simple numerical examples. Let's apply it to Sangria's perpetual crusher project. We start by showing that APV is equivalent to discounting at WACC if we make the same assumptions about debt policy.

We used Sangria's WACC (9%) as the discount rate for the crusher's projected cash flows. The WACC calculation assumed that debt will be maintained at a constant 40% of the future value of the project or firm. In this case, the risk of interest tax shields is the same as the risk of the project.[20] Therefore we will discount the tax shields at the opportunity cost of capital (r). We calculated the opportunity cost of capital in the last section by unlevering Sangria's WACC to obtain $r = 9.84\%$.

The first step is to calculate base-case NPV. We discount after-tax project cash flows of ₹1.125 million at the opportunity cost of capital of 9.84% and subtract the ₹12.5 million outlay. The cash flows are perpetual, so:

$$\text{Base-case NPV} = -12.5 + \frac{1.125}{.0984} = -₹1.067 \text{ million}$$

Thus the project would not be worthwhile with all-equity financing. But it actually supports debt of ₹5 million. At a 6% borrowing rate ($r_D = .06$) and a 35% tax rate ($T_c = .35$), annual tax shields are $.35 \times .06 \times 5 = .105$, or ₹105,000.

What are those tax shields worth? If the firm is constantly rebalancing its debt, we discount at $r = 9.84\%$:

$$\text{PV(interest tax shields, debt rebalanced)} = \frac{105,000}{.0984} = ₹1.067 \text{ million}$$

---

[19] "The adjusted-present-value rule was developed in S. C. Myers, "Interactions of Corporate Financing and Investment Decisions—Implications for Capital Budgeting," *Journal of Finance* 29 (March 1974), pp. 1–25.

[20] That is, $\beta_A = \beta_{\text{tax shields}}$. See footnote 15 above.

APV is the sum of base-case value and PV(interest tax shields)

$$\text{APV} = -1.067 \text{ million} + 1.067 \text{ million} = 0$$

This is exactly the same as we obtained by one-step discounting with WACC. The perpetual crusher is a break-even project by either valuation method.

But with APV, we don't have to hold debt at a constant proportion of value. Suppose Sangria plans to keep project debt fixed at ₹5 million. In this case we assume the risk of the tax shields is the same as the risk of the debt and we discount at the 6% rate on debt:

$$\text{PV(tax shields, debt fixed)} = \frac{105,000}{.06} = ₹1.75 \text{ million}$$

$$\text{APV} = -1.067 + 1.75 = ₹.683 \text{ million}$$

Now the project is more attractive. With fixed debt, the interest tax shields are safe and therefore worth more. (Whether the fixed debt is safer for Sangria is another matter. If the perpetual crusher project fails, the ₹5 million of fixed debt may end up as a burden on Sangria's other assets.)

Other Financing Side Effects

Suppose Sangria has to finance the perpetual crusher by issuing debt and equity. It issues ₹7.5 million of equity with issue costs of 7% (₹525,000) and ₹5 million of debt with issue costs of 2% (₹100,000). Assume the debt is fixed once issued, so that interest tax shields are worth ₹1.75 million. Now we can recalculate APV, taking care to subtract the issue costs:

$$\text{APV} = -1.067 + 1.75 - .525 - .100 = .058 \text{ million, or } ₹58,000$$

The issue costs would reduce APV to nearly zero.

Sometimes there are favorable financing side effects that have nothing to do with taxes. For example, suppose that a potential manufacturer of crusher machinery offers to sweeten the deal by leasing it to Sangria on favorable terms. Then you could calculate APV as the sum of base-case NPV plus the NPV of the lease. Or suppose that a local government offers to lend Sangria ₹5 million at a very low interest rate if the crusher is built and operated locally. The NPV of the subsidized loan could be added in to APV. (We cover leases in Chapter 25 and subsidized loans in the Appendix to this chapter.)

APV for Businesses

APV can also be used to value businesses. Let's take another look at the valuation of Geo. In Table 19.1, we assumed a constant 40% debt ratio and discounted free cash flow at Sangria's WACC. Table 19.2 runs the same analysis, but with a fixed debt schedule.

We'll suppose that Sangria has decided to make an offer for Geo. If successful, it plans to finance the purchase with ₹51 million of debt. It intends to pay down the debt to ₹45 million in year 6. Recall Geo's horizon value of ₹113.4 million, which is calculated in Table 19.1 and shown again in Table 19.2. The debt ratio at the horizon is therefore projected at 45/113.4 = .397, about 40%. Thus Sangria plans to take Geo back to a normal 40% debt ratio at the horizon.[21] But Geo will be carrying a heavier debt load before the horizon. For example, the ₹51 million of initial debt is about 58% of company value as calculated in Table 19.1.

---

[21] Therefore we still calculate the horizon value in year 6 by discounting subsequent free cash flows at WACC. The horizon value in year 6 is discounted back to year 0 at the opportunity cost of capital, however.

TABLE 19.2 APV valuation of Geo Corporation (₹ millions).

	Latest Year	Forecast						
	0	1	2	3	4	5	6	7
Free cash flow	2.5	3.5	3.2	3.4	5.9	6.1	6.0	6.8
PV free cash flow, years 1–6	19.7							
PV horizon value	64.6			(Horizon value in year 6)			113.4	
Base-case PV of company	84.3							
Debt	51.0	50.0	49.0	48.0	47.0	46.0	45.0	
Interest		3.06	3.00	2.94	2.88	2.82	2.76	
Interest tax shield		1.07	1.05	1.03	1.01	0.99	0.97	
PV Interest tax shields	5.0							
APV	89.3							
Tax rate, %	35.0							
Opportunity cost of capital, %	9.84							
WACC, % (to discount horizon value to year 6)	9.0							
Long-term growth forecast, %	3.0							
Interest rate, % (years 1–6)	6.0							
After-tax debt service		2.99	2.95	2.91	2.87	2.83	2.79	

Let's see how Geo's APV is affected by this more aggressive borrowing schedule. Table 19.2 shows projections of free cash flows from Table 19.1.[22] Now we need Geo's base-case value, so we discount these flows at the opportunity cost of capital (9.84%), not at WACC. The resulting base-case value for Geo is ₹84.3 million. Table 19.2 also projects debt levels, interest, and interest tax shields. If the debt levels are taken as fixed, then the tax shields should be discounted back at the 6% borrowing rate. The resulting PV of interest tax shields is ₹5.0 million. Thus,

$$\text{APV} = \text{base-case NPV} + \text{PV(interest tax shields)}$$
$$= ₹84.3 + 5.0 = ₹89.3 \text{ million}$$

an increase of ₹1.4 million from NPV in Table 19.1. The increase can be traced to the higher early debt levels and to the assumption that the debt levels and interest tax shields are fixed and relatively safe.[23]

Now a difference of ₹1.4 million is not a big deal, considering all the lurking risks and pitfalls in forecasting Geo's free cash flows. But you can see the advantage of the flexibility that APV provides. The APV spreadsheet allows you to explore the implications of different financing strategies without locking into a fixed debt ratio or having to calculate a new WACC for every scenario.

APV is particularly useful when the debt for a project or business is tied to book value or has to be repaid on a fixed schedule. For example, Kaplan and Ruback used APV to analyze the prices paid for

---

[22] Many of the assumptions and calculations in Table 19.1 have been hidden in Table 19.2. The hidden rows can be recalled in the "live" version of Table 19.2, which is available on this book's Web site (www.mhhe.com/bmam10e).

[23] But will Geo really *support* debt at the levels shown in Table 19.2? If not, then the debt must be partly supported by Sangria's other assets, and only part of the ₹5 million in PV(interest tax shields) can be attributed to Geo itself.

a sample of leveraged buyouts (LBOs). LBOs are takeovers, typically of mature companies, financed almost entirely with debt. However, the new debt is not intended to be permanent. LBO business plans call for generating extra cash by selling assets, shaving costs, and improving profit margins. The extra cash is used to pay down the LBO debt. Therefore you can't use WACC as a discount rate to evaluate an LBO because its debt ratio will not be constant.

APV works fine for LBOs. The company is first evaluated as if it were all-equity-financed. That means that cash flows are projected after tax, but without any interest tax shields generated by the LBO's debt. The tax shields are then valued separately and added to the all-equity value. Any other financing side effects are added also. The result is an APV valuation for the company.[24] Kaplan and Ruback found that APV did a pretty good job explaining prices paid in these hotly contested takeovers, considering that not all the information available to bidders had percolated into the public domain. Kaplan and Ruback were restricted to publicly available data.

APV for International Investments

APV is most useful when financing side effects are numerous and important. This is frequently the case for large international investments, which may have custom-tailored *project financing* and special contracts with suppliers, customers, and governments. Here are a few examples of financing side effects encountered in international finance.

We explain project finance in Chapter 24. It typically means very high debt ratios to start, with most or all of a project's early cash flows committed to debt service. Equity investors have to wait. Since the debt ratio will not be constant, you have to turn to APV.

Project financing may include debt available at favorable interest rates. Most governments subsidize exports by making special financing packages available, and manufacturers of industrial equipment may stand ready to lend money to help close a sale. Suppose, for example, that your project requires construction of an on-site electricity generating plant. You solicit bids from suppliers in various countries. Don't be surprised if the competing suppliers sweeten their bids with offers of low interest rate project loans or if they offer to lease the plant on favorable terms. You should then calculate the NPVs of these loans or leases and include them in your project analysis.

Sometimes international projects are supported by contracts with suppliers or customers. Suppose a manufacturer wants to line up a reliable supply of a crucial raw material—powdered magnoosium, say. The manufacturer could subsidize a new magnoosium smelter by agreeing to buy 75% of production and guaranteeing a minimum purchase price. The guarantee is clearly a valuable addition to project APV: if the world price of powdered magnoosium falls below the minimum, the project doesn't suffer. You would calculate the value of this guarantee (by the methods explained in Chapters 20 to 22) and add it to APV.

Sometimes local governments impose costs or restrictions on investment or disinvestment. For example, Chile, in an attempt to slow down a flood of short-term capital inflows in the 1990s, required investors to "park" part of their incoming money in non-interest-bearing accounts for a period of two years. An investor in Chile during this period would calculate the cost of this requirement and subtract it from APV.

---

[24] Kaplan and Ruback actually used "compressed" APV, in which all cash flows, including interest tax shields, are discounted at the opportunity cost of capital. S. N. Kaplan and R. S. Ruback, "The Valuation of Cash Flow Forecasts: An Empirical Analysis," *Journal of Finance* 50 (September 1995), pp. 1059–1093.

19-5 YOUR QUESTIONS ANSWERED

Question: All these cost of capital formulas—which ones do financial managers actually use?

Answer: The after-tax weighted-average cost of capital, most of the time. WACC is estimated for the company, or sometimes for an industry. We recommend industry WACCs when data are available for firms with similar assets, operations, business risks, and growth opportunities.

Of course, conglomerate companies, with divisions operating in two or more unrelated industries, should not use a single company or industry WACC. Such firms should try to estimate a different industry WACC for each operating division.

Question: But WACC is the correct discount rate only for "average" projects. What if the project's financing differs from the company's or industry's?

Answer: Remember, investment projects are usually not separately financed. Even when they are, you should focus on the project's contribution to the firm's overall debt capacity, not on its immediate financing. (Suppose it's convenient to raise all the money for a particular project with a bank loan. That doesn't mean the project itself supports 100% debt financing. The company is borrowing against its existing assets as well as the project.)

But if the project's debt capacity is materially different from the company's existing assets, or if the company's overall debt policy changes, WACC should be adjusted. The adjustment can be done by the three-step procedure explained in Section 19-3.

Question: Could we do one more numerical example?

Answer: Sure. Suppose that WACC has been estimated as follows at a 30% debt ratio:

$$\text{WACC} = r_D(1 - T_c)\frac{D}{V} + r_E\frac{E}{V}$$
$$= .09(1 - .35)(.3) + .15(.7) = .1226, \text{ or } 12.26\%$$

What is the correct discount rate at a 50% debt ratio?

Step 1. Calculate the opportunity cost of capital.

$$r = r_D D/V + r_E E/V$$
$$= .09(.3) + .15(.7) = .132, \text{ or } 13.2\%$$

Step 2. Calculate the new costs of debt and equity. The cost of debt will be higher at 50% debt than 30%. Say it is $r_D = .095$. The new cost of equity is:

$$r_E = r + (r - r_D)D/E$$
$$= .132 + (.132 - .095)50/50$$
$$= .169, \text{ or } 16.9\%$$

Step 3. Recalculate WACC.

$$\text{WACC} = r_D(1 - T_c)D/V + r_E E/V$$
$$= .095(1 - .35)(.5) + .169(.5) = .1154, \text{ or about } 11.5\%$$

Question: How do I use the capital asset pricing model to calculate the after-tax weighted-average cost of capital?

Answer: First plug the equity beta into the capital asset pricing formula to calculate r_E, the expected return to equity. Then use this figure, along with the after-tax cost of debt and the debt-to-value and equity-to-value ratios, in the WACC formula.

Of course the CAPM is not the only way to estimate the cost of equity. For example, you might be able to use the dividend-discount model (see Section 4-3).

Question: But suppose I do use the CAPM? What if I have to recalculate the equity beta for a different debt ratio?

Answer: The formula for the equity beta is:

$$\beta_E = \beta_A + (\beta_A - \beta_D)D/E$$

where β_E is the equity beta, β_A is the asset beta, and β_D is the beta of the company's debt. The asset beta is a weighted average of the debt and equity betas:

$$\beta_A = \beta_D\,(D/V) + \beta_E\,(E/V)$$

Suppose you needed the opportunity cost of capital r. You could calculate β_A and then r from the capital asset pricing model.

Question: I think I understand how to adjust for differences in debt capacity or debt policy. How about differences in business risk?

Answer: If business risk is different, then r, the opportunity cost of capital, is different.

Figuring out the right r for an unusually safe or risky project is never easy. Sometimes the financial manager can use estimates of risk and expected return for companies similar to the project. Suppose, for example, that a traditional pharmaceutical company is considering a major commitment to biotech research. The financial manager could pick a sample of biotech companies, estimate their average beta and cost of capital, and use these estimates as benchmarks for the biotech investment.

But in many cases it's difficult to find a good sample of matching companies for an unusually safe or risky project. Then the financial manager has to adjust the opportunity cost of capital by judgment. Section 9-3 may be helpful in such cases.

Question: When do I need adjusted present value (APV)?

Answer: The WACC formula picks up only one financing side effect: the value of interest tax shields on debt supported by a project. If there are other side effects—subsidized financing tied to a project, for example—you should use APV.

You can also use APV to break out the value of interest tax shields:

$$\text{APV} = \text{base-case NPV} + \text{PV(tax shield)}$$

Suppose, for example, that you are analyzing a company just after a leveraged buyout. The company has a very high initial debt level but plans to pay down the debt as rapidly as possible. APV could be used to obtain an accurate valuation.

Question: When should personal taxes be incorporated into the analysis?

Answer: Always use T_c, the marginal corporate tax rate, when calculating WACC as a weighted average of the costs of debt and equity. The discount rate is adjusted *only* for corporate taxes.

In principle, APV can be adjusted for personal taxes by replacing the marginal corporate rate T_c with an effective tax rate that combines corporate and personal taxes and reflects the net tax advantage per dollar of interest paid by the firm. We provided back-of-the-envelope calculations of this advantage in Section 18-2. The effective tax rate is almost surely less than T_c, but it is very difficult to pin down the numerical difference. Therefore, in practice T_c is almost always used as an approximation.

Question: Are taxes really that important? Do financial managers really fine-tune the debt ratio to minimize WACC?

Answer: As we saw in Chapter 18, financing decisions reflect many forces beyond taxes, including costs of financial distress, differences in information, and incentives for managers. There may not be a sharply defined optimal capital structure. Therefore most financial managers don't fine-tune their companies' debt ratios, and they don't rebalance financing to keep debt ratios strictly constant. In effect they assume that a plot of WACC for different debt ratios is "flat" over a reasonable range of moderate leverage.

SUMMARY

In this chapter we considered how financing can be incorporated into the valuation of projects and ongoing businesses. There are two ways to take financing into account. The first is to calculate NPV by discounting at an adjusted discount rate, usually the after-tax weighted-average cost of capital (WACC). The second approach discounts at the opportunity cost of capital and then adds or subtracts the present values of financing side effects. The second approach is called adjusted present value, or APV.

The formula for the after-tax WACC is:

$$\text{WACC} = r_D(1 - T_c)\frac{D}{V} + r_E\frac{E}{V}$$

where r_D and r_E are the expected rates of return demanded by investors in the firm's debt and equity securities, D and E are the current *market values* of debt and equity, and V is the total market value of the firm ($V = D + E$). Of course, the WACC formula expands if there are other sources of financing, for example, preferred stock.

Strictly speaking, discounting at WACC works only for projects that are carbon copies of the existing firm—projects with the same business risk that will be financed to maintain the firm's current, market debt ratio. But firms can use WACC as a benchmark rate to be adjusted for differences in business risk or financing. We gave a three-step procedure for adjusting WACC for different debt ratios.

Discounting cash flows at the WACC assumes that debt is rebalanced to keep a constant ratio of debt to market value. The amount of debt supported by a project is assumed to rise or fall with the project's after-the-fact success or failure. The WACC formula also assumes that financing matters *only* because of interest tax shields. When this or other assumptions are violated, only APV will give an absolutely correct answer.

APV is, in concept at least, simple. First calculate the base-case NPV of the project or business on the assumption that financing *doesn't* matter. (The discount rate is not WACC, but the opportunity cost of capital.) Then calculate the present values of any relevant financing side effects and add or subtract from base-case value. A capital investment project is worthwhile if

$$\text{APV} = \text{base-case NPV} + \text{PV(financing side effects)}$$

is positive. Common financing side effects include interest tax shields, issue costs, and special financing packages offered by suppliers or governments.

For firms or going-concern businesses, value depends on free cash flow. Free cash flow is the amount of cash that can be paid out to all investors, debt as well as equity, after deducting cash needed for new investment or increases in working capital. Free cash flow does not include the value of interest tax shields, however. The WACC formula accounts for interest tax shields by using the after-tax cost of debt. APV adds PV(interest tax shields) to base-case value.

Businesses are usually valued in two steps. First free cash flow is forecasted out to a valuation horizon and discounted back to present value. Then a horizon value is calculated and also discounted back. The horizon value is usually estimated by using the perpetual-growth DCF formula or by multiplying forecasted EBIT or EBITDA[25] by multiples observed for similar firms. Be particularly careful to avoid unrealistically high horizon values. By the time the horizon arrives, competitors will have had several years to catch up. Also, when you are done valuing the business, don't forget to subtract its debt to get the value of the firm's equity.

All of this chapter's examples reflect assumptions about the amount of debt supported by a project or business. Remember not to confuse "supported by" with the immediate source of funds for investment. For example, a firm might, as a matter of convenience, borrow ₹1 million for a ₹1 million research program. But the research is unlikely to contribute ₹1 million in debt capacity; a large part of the ₹1 million new debt would be supported by the firm's other assets.

Also remember that *debt capacity* is not meant to imply an absolute limit on how much the firm *can* borrow. The phrase refers to how much it *chooses* to borrow against a project or ongoing business.

---

[25] Recall that EBIT = earnings before interest and taxes and EBITDA = EBIT plus depreciation and amortization.

FURTHER READING

The Harvard Business Review *has published a popular account of APV:*

T. A. Luehrman, "Using APV: A Better Tool for Valuing Operations," *Harvard Business Review* 75 (May–June 1997), pp. 145–154.

There have been dozens of articles on the weighted-average cost of capital and other issues discussed in this chapter. Here are three:

J. Miles and R. Ezzell, "The Weighted Average Cost of Capital, Perfect Capital Markets, and Project Life: A Clarification," *Journal of Financial and Quantitative Analysis* 15 (September 1980), pp. 719–730.

R. A. Taggart, Jr., "Consistent Valuation and Cost of Capital Expressions with Corporate and Personal Taxes," *Financial Management* 20 (Autumn 1991), pp. 8–20.

R. S. Ruback, "Capital Cash Flows: A Simple Approach to Valuing Risky Cash Flows," *Financial Management* 31 (Summer 2002), pp. 85–103.

Two books that provide detailed explanations of how to value companies are:

T. Koller, M. Goedhart, and D. Wessels, *Valuation: Measuring and Managing the Value of Companies,* 4th ed. (New York: Wiley, 2005).

S. P. Pratt and A.V. Niculita, *Valuing a Business: The Analysis and Appraisal of Closely Held Companies,* 5th ed. (New York: McGraw-Hill, 2007).

The valuation rule for safe, nominal cash flows is developed in:

R. S. Ruback, "Calculating the Market Value of Risk-Free Cash Flows," *Journal of Financial Economics* 15 (March 1986), pp. 323–339.

PROBLEM SETS

BASIC

1. Calculate the weighted-average cost of capital (WACC) for Junkyards of India, using the following information:
   - Debt: ₹75,000,000 book value outstanding. The debt is trading at 90% of book value. The yield to maturity is 9%.
   - Equity: 2,500,000 shares selling at ₹42 per share. Assume the expected rate of return on Junkyards' stock is 18%.
   - Taxes: Junkyards' marginal tax rate is $T_c = 0.3399$.

2. Suppose Junkyards of India decides to move to a more conservative debt policy. A year later its debt ratio is down to 15% ($D/V = .15$). The interest rate has dropped to 8.6%. Recalculate Junkyards' WACC under these new assumptions. The company's business risk, opportunity cost of capital, and tax rate have not changed. Use the three-step procedure explained in Section 19-3.

3. True or false? Use of the WACC formula assumes
   a. A project supports a fixed amount of debt over the project's economic life.
   b. The *ratio* of the debt supported by a project to project value is constant over the project's economic life.
   c. The firm rebalances debt each period, keeping the debt-to-value ratio constant.

4. What is meant by the flow-to-equity valuation method? What discount rate is used in this method? What assumptions are necessary for this method to give an accurate valuation?

5. True or false? The APV method
   a. Starts with a base-case value for the project.
   b. Calculates the base-case value by discounting project cash flows, forecasted assuming all-equity financing, at the WACC for the project.
   c. Is especially useful when debt is to be paid down on a fixed schedule.

6. A project costs ₹1 million and has a base-case NPV of exactly zero (NPV = 0). What is the project's APV in the following cases?
   a. If the firm invests, it has to raise ₹500,000 by a stock issue. Issue costs are 15% of *net* proceeds.
   b. If the firm invests, its debt capacity increases by $500,000. The present value of interest tax shields on this debt is ₹76,000.

7. Whispering Pines Limited is all-equity-financed. The expected rate of return on the company's shares is 12%.
   a. What is the opportunity cost of capital for an average-risk Whispering Pines investment?
   b. Suppose the company issues debt, repurchases shares, and moves to a 30% debt-to-value ratio ($D/V = .30$). What will the company's weighted-average cost of capital be at the new capital structure? The borrowing rate is 7.5% and the tax rate is 35%.

8. Consider a project lasting one year only. The initial outlay is ₹1,000 and the expected inflow is ₹1,200. The opportunity cost of capital is $r = .20$. The borrowing rate is $r_D = .10$, and the tax shield per dollar of interest is $T_c = .35$.
   a. What is the project's base-case NPV?
   b. What is its APV if the firm borrows 30% of the project's required investment?

9. The WACC formula seems to imply that debt is "cheaper" than equity—that is, that a firm with more debt could use a lower discount rate. Does this make sense? Explain briefly.

10. Suppose Kolkata Motors Limited buys out Howrah Trucking, a privately owned business, for ₹50 million. Kolkata Motors has only ₹5 million cash in hand, so it arranges a ₹45 million bank loan. A normal debt-to-value ratio for a trucking company would be 50% at most, but the bank is satisfied with Kolkata Motor's credit rating.

    Suppose you were valuing Howrah Trucking by APV in the same format as Table 19.2. How much debt would you include? Explain briefly.

INTERMEDIATE

11. Table 19.3 shows a *book* balance sheet for the Wishing Well Motel chain. The company's long-term debt is secured by its real estate assets, but it also uses short-term bank financing. It pays 10% interest on the bank debt and 9% interest on the secured debt. Wishing Well

has 10 million shares of stock outstanding, trading at ₹90 per share. The expected return on Wishing Well's common stock is 18%.

Calculate Wishing Well's WACC. Assume that the book and market values of Wishing Well's debt are the same. The marginal tax rate is 35%.

TABLE 19.3 Balance sheet for Wishing Well Limited (figures in ₹ millions).

Cash and marketable securities	100	Bank loan	280
Accounts receivable	200	Accounts payable	120
Inventory	50	Current liabilities	400
Current assets	350		
Real estate	2,100	Long-term debt	1,800
Other assets	150	Equity	400
Total	2,600	Total	2,600

12. Suppose Wishing Well is evaluating a new motel and resort on a romantic site near Baga Beach, Goa. Explain how you would forecast the after-tax cash flows for this project. (*Hints:* How would you treat taxes? Interest expense? Changes in working capital?)

13. To finance the Baga Beach project, Wishing Well will have to arrange an additional ₹80 million of long-term debt and make a ₹20 million equity issue. Underwriting fees, spreads, and other costs of this financing will total ₹4 million. How would you take this into account in valuing the proposed investment?

14. Table 19.4 shows a simplified balance sheet for Divinity Felt. Calculate this company's weighted-average cost of capital. The debt has just been refinanced at an interest rate of 6% (short term) and 8% (long term). The expected rate of return on the company's shares is 15%. There are 7.46 million shares outstanding, and the shares are trading at ₹46. The tax rate is 35%.

TABLE 19.4 Simplified balance sheet for Divinity Felt (figures in ₹ thousands).

Cash and marketable securities	1,500	Short-term debt	75,600
Accounts receivable	120,000	Accounts payable	62,000
Inventories	125,000	Current liabilities	137,600
Current assets	246,500		
Fixed assets	302,000	Long-term debt	208,600
Other assets	89,000	Deferred taxes	45,000
		Shareholders' equity	246,300
Total	637,500	Total	637,500

15. How will Divinity Felt's WACC and cost of equity change if it issues ₹50 million in new equity and uses the proceeds to retire long-term debt? Assume the company's borrowing rates are unchanged. Use the three-step procedure from Section 19-3.

16. Digital Organics (DO) has the opportunity to invest ₹1 million now ($t = 0$) and expects after-tax returns of ₹600,000 in $t = 1$ and ₹700,000 in $t = 2$. The project will last for two years only. The appropriate cost of capital is 12% with all-equity financing, the borrowing rate is 8%, and DO will borrow $300,000 against the project. This debt must be repaid in two equal installments. Assume debt tax shields have a net value of $.30 per dollar of interest paid. Calculate the project's APV using the procedure followed in Table 19.2.

17. Consider another perpetual project like the crusher described in Section 19-1. Its initial investment is ₹1,000,000, and the expected cash inflow is ₹95,000 a year in perpetuity. The opportunity cost of capital with all-equity financing is 10%, and the project allows the firm to borrow at 7%. The tax rate is 35%.

    Use APV to calculate this project's value.
    a. Assume first that the project will be partly financed with ₹400,000 of debt and that the debt amount is to be fixed and perpetual.
    b. Then assume that the initial borrowing will be increased or reduced in proportion to changes in the market value of this project.

    Explain the difference between your answers to (a) and (b).

18. Suppose the project described in Problem 17 is to be undertaken by a university. Funds for the project will be withdrawn from the university's endowment, which is invested in a widely diversified portfolio of stocks and bonds. However, the university can also borrow at 7%. The university is tax exempt.

    The university treasurer proposes to finance the project by issuing ₹400,000 of perpetual bonds at 7% and by selling ₹600,000 worth of common stocks from the endowment. The expected return on the common stocks is 10%. He therefore proposes to evaluate the project by discounting at a weighted-average cost of capital, calculated as:

    $$r = r_D \frac{D}{V} + r_E \frac{E}{V}$$

    $$= .07\left(\frac{400,000}{1,000,000}\right) + .10\left(\frac{600,000}{1,000,000}\right)$$

    $$= .088, \text{ or } 8.8$$

    What's right or wrong with the treasurer's approach? Should the university invest? Should it borrow? Would the project's value to the university change if the treasurer financed the project entirely by selling common stocks from the endowment?

19. Consider a project to produce solar water heaters. It requires a ₹10 million investment and offers a level after-tax cash flow of ₹1.75 million per year for 10 years. The opportunity cost of capital is 12%, which reflects the project's business risk.
    a. Suppose the project is financed with ₹5 million of debt and ₹5 million of equity. The interest rate is 8% and the marginal tax rate is 35%. The debt will be paid off in equal annual installments over the project's 10-year life. Calculate APV.
    b. How does APV change if the firm incurs issue costs of ₹400,000 to raise the ₹5 million of required equity?

20. Take another look at the valuations of Geo in Tables 19.1 and 19.2. Use a spreadsheet to show how the valuation depends on:
    a. The forecasted long-term growth rate.
    b. The required amounts of investment in fixed assets and working capital.
    c. The opportunity cost of capital. Note you can also vary the opportunity cost of capital in Table 19.1.
    d. Profitability, that is, cost of goods sold as a percentage of sales.
    e. The assumed amount of debt financing.

21. The Bunsen Chemical Company is currently at its target debt ratio of 40%. It is contemplating a ₹1 million expansion of its existing business. This expansion is expected to produce a cash inflow of ₹130,000 a year in perpetuity.

    The company is uncertain whether to undertake this expansion and how to finance it. The two options are a ₹1 million issue of common stock or a ₹1 million issue of 20-year debt. Th flotation costs of a stock issue would be around 5% of the amount raised, and the flotation costs of a debt issue would be around 1½%.

Bunsen's financial manager, Ms. Polly Ethylene, estimates that the required return on the company's equity is 14%, but she argues that the flotation costs increase the cost of new equity to 19%. On this basis, the project does not appear viable.

On the other hand, she points out that the company can raise new debt on a 7% yield, which would make the cost of new debt 8½%. She therefore recommends that Bunsen should go ahead with the project and finance it with an issue of long-term debt.

Is Ms. Ethylene right? How would you evaluate the project?

22. Hyderabad Hydro is 40% debt-financed and has a weighted-average cost of capital of 9.7%:

$$\text{WACC} = (1 - T_c)r_D\frac{D}{V} + r_E\frac{E}{V}$$
$$= (1 - .35)(.085)(.40) + .125(.60) = .097$$

Goldensacks Company is advising Hyderabad Hydro to issue ₹75 million of preferred stock at a dividend yield of 9%. The proceeds would be used to repurchase and retire common stock. The preferred issue would account for 10% of the preissue market value of the firm.

Goldensacks argues that these transactions would reduce Hyderabad Hydro's WACC to 9.4%:

$$\text{WACC} = (1 - .35)(.085)(.40) + .09(.10) + .125(.50)$$
$$= .094, \text{ or } 9.4\%$$

Do you agree with this calculation? Explain.

23. Chiara Company's management has made the projections shown in Table 19.5. Use this Excel spreadsheet as a starting point to value the company as a whole. The WACC for Chiara is 12% and the long-run growth rate after year 5 is 4%. The company has ₹5 million debt and 865,000 shares outstanding. What is the value per share?

eXcel

Visit us at
www.mhhe.com/bmam10e

TABLE 19.5   Cash flow projections for Chiara Corp. (₹ thousands).

		Historical			Forecast				
Year:		−2	−1	0	1	2	3	4	5
1. Sales		35,348	39,357	40,123	36,351	30,155	28,345	29,982	30,450
2. Cost of goods sold		17,834	18,564	22,879	21,678	17,560	16,459	15,631	14,987
3. Other costs		6,968	7,645	8,025	6,797	5,078	4,678	4,987	5,134
4. EBITDA (1−2−3)		10,546	13,148	9,219	7,876	7,517	7,208	9,364	10,329
5. Depreciation		5,671	5,745	5,678	5,890	5,670	5,908	6,107	5,908
6. EBIT (Pretax profit) (4−5)		4,875	7,403	3,541	1,986	1,847	1,300	3,257	4,421
7. Tax at 35%		1,706	2,591	1,239	695	646	455	1,140	1,547
8. Profit after tax (6−7)		3,169	4,812	2,302	1,291	1,201	845	2,117	2,874
9. Change in working capital		325	566	784	−54	−342	−245	127	235
10. Investment (change in gross fixed assets)		5,235	6,467	6,547	7,345	5,398	5,470	6,420	6,598

CHALLENGE

2·4. In Footnote 15 we referred to the Miles–Ezzell discount rate formula, which assumes that debt is not rebalanced continuously, but at one-year intervals. Derive this formula. Then use it to unlever Sangria's WACC and calculate Sangria's opportunity cost of capital. Your answer will be slightly different from the opportunity cost that we calculated in Section 19-3. Can you explain why?

25. The WACC formula assumes that debt is rebalanced to maintain a constant debt ratio D/V. Rebalancing ties the level of future interest tax shields to the future value of the company. This makes the tax shields risky. Does that mean that fixed debt levels (no rebalancing) are better for stockholders?

26. Modify Table 19.1 on the assumption that competition eliminates any opportunities to earn more than WACC on new investment after year 7 (PVGO = 0). How does the valuation of Geo change?

REAL-TIME DATA ANALYSIS

Table 19.6 is a simplified book balance sheet for Jet Airways as on 31 March, 2011. Here is some further information:

Number of outstanding shares (N)	8.63 crores
Price per share (P)	₹174
Beta	1.74
Treasury bill rate	8.50%
20-year Treasury bond rate	8.83%
Cost of debt (r_D)	14%
Marginal tax rate	35%

a. Calculate Jet's WACC. Use the capital asset pricing model and the additional information given above. Make additional assumptions and approximations as necessary.

b. What is Jet's opportunity cost of capital?

c. Now, go to the websites of www.moneycontrol.com, www.nseindia.com and www. fimmda.org and get the relevant information to update your answers to questions (a) and (b).

TABLE 19.6 Simplified book balance sheet for Jet Airways, 31 March, 2011 (figures in ₹ Crores).

Current assets	5933.3	Current liabilities	5538.38
Fixed assets	13964.72	Long-term debt	13480.39
Investments	1725.09	Shareholders' equity	2604.34
Total	21623.11	Total	21623.11

Source: www.moneycontrol.com

APPENDIX

DISCOUNTING SAFE, NOMINAL CASH FLOWS

Suppose you're considering purchase of a ₹100,000 machine. The manufacturer sweetens the deal by offering to finance the purchase by lending you ₹100,000 for five years, with annual interest payments of 5%. You would have to pay 13% to borrow from a bank. Your marginal tax rate is 35% ($T_c = .35$).

How much is this loan worth? If you take it, the cash flows, in thousands of rupees, are:

	Period					
	0	**1**	**2**	**3**	**4**	**5**
Cash flow	100	−5	−5	−5	−5	−105
Tax shield		+1.75	+1.75	+1.75	+1.75	+1.75
After-tax cash flow	100	−3.25	−3.25	−3.25	−3.25	−103.25

What is the right discount rate?

Here you are discounting *safe, nominal* cash flows—safe because your company must commit to pay if it takes the loan,[26] and nominal because the payments would be fixed regardless of future inflation. Now, the correct discount rate for safe, nominal cash flows is your company's *after-tax*, unsubsidized borrowing rate,[27] which is $r_D(1 - T_c) = .13(1 - .35) = .0845$. Therefore,

$$NPV = +100 - \frac{3.25}{1.0845} - \frac{3.25}{(1.0845)^2} - \frac{3.25}{(1.0845)^3} - \frac{3.25}{(1.0845)^4} - \frac{103.25}{(1.0845)^5}$$

$$= +20.52, \text{ or } ₹20,520$$

The manufacturer has effectively cut the machine's purchase price from ₹100,000 to ₹100,000 − ₹20,520 = ₹79,480. You can now go back and recalculate the machine's NPV using this fire-sale price, or you can use the NPV of the subsidized loan as one element of the machine's adjusted present value.

General Rule   Clearly, we owe an explanation of why $r_D(1 - T_c)$ is the right discount rate for safe, nominal cash flows. It's no surprise that the rate depends on r_D, the unsubsidized borrowing rate, for that is investors' opportunity cost of capital, the rate they would demand from your company's debt. But why should r_D be converted to an *after-tax* figure?

Let's simplify by taking a *one-year* subsidized loan of ₹100,000 at 5%. The cash flows, in thousands of rupees are:

	Period 0	Period 1
Cash flow	100	−105
Tax shield		+1.75
After-tax cash flow	100	−103.25

---

[26] In theory, *safe* means literally "risk-free," like the cash returns on a Treasury bond. In practice, it means that the risk of not paying or receiving cash flow is small.

[27] In Section 13-1 we calculated the NPV of subsidized financing using the *pretax* borrowing rate. Now you can see that was a mistake. Using a pretax rate implicitly defines the loan in terms of its pretax cash flows, violating a rule promulgated way back in Section 6-1: *Always* estimate cash flows on an after-tax basis.

Now ask, What is the maximum amount X that could be borrowed for one year through regular channels if ₹103,250 is set aside to service the loan?

"Regular channels" means borrowing at 13% pretax and 8.45% after tax. Therefore you will need 108.45% of the amount borrowed to pay back principal plus after-tax interest charges. If $1.0845X = 103,250$, then $X = 95,205$. Now if you can borrow ₹100,000 by a subsidized loan, but only ₹95,205 through normal channels, the difference (₹4,795) is money in the bank. Therefore, it must also be the NPV of this one-period subsidized loan.

When you discount a safe, nominal cash flow at an after-tax borrowing rate, you are implicitly calculating the *equivalent loan,* the amount you could borrow through normal channels, using the cash flow as debt service. Note that:

$$\text{Equivalent loan} = \text{PV(cash flow available for debt service)} = \frac{103,250}{1.0845} = 95,205$$

In some cases, it may be easier to think of taking the lender's side of the equivalent loan rather than the borrower's. For example, you could ask, How much would my company have to invest today to cover next year's debt service on the subsidized loan? The answer is ₹95,205: If you lend that amount at 13%, you will earn 8.45% after tax, and therefore have $95,205(1.0845) = ₹103,250$. By this transaction, you can in effect cancel, or "zero out," the future obligation. If you can borrow ₹100,000 and then set aside only ₹95,205 to cover all the required debt service, you clearly have ₹4,795 to spend as you please. That amount is the NPV of the subsidized loan.

Therefore, regardless of whether it's easier to think of borrowing or lending, the correct discount rate for safe, nominal cash flows is an after-tax interest rate.[28]

In some ways, this is an obvious result once you think about it. Companies are free to borrow or lend money. If they *lend,* they receive the after-tax interest rate on their investment; if they *borrow* in the capital market, they pay the after-tax interest rate. Thus, the opportunity cost to companies of investing in debt-equivalent cash flows is the after-tax interest rate. This is the adjusted cost of capital for debt-equivalent cash flows.[29]

Some Further Examples

Here are some further examples of debt-equivalent cash flows.

Payout Fixed by Contract Suppose you sign a maintenance contract with a truck leasing firm, which agrees to keep your leased trucks in good working order for the next two years in exchange for 24 fixed monthly payments. These payments are debt-equivalent flows.

Depreciation Tax Shields Capital projects are normally valued by discounting the total after-tax cash flows they are expected to generate. Depreciation tax shields contribute to project cash flow, but they are not valued separately; they are just folded into project cash flows along with dozens, or hundreds, of other specific inflows and outflows. The project's opportunity cost of capital reflects the average risk of the resulting aggregate.

---

[28] Borrowing and lending rates should not differ by much if the cash flows are truly safe, that is, if the chance of default is small. Usually your decision will not hinge on the rate used. If it does, ask which offsetting transaction—borrowing or lending—seems most natural and reasonable for the problem at hand. Then use the corresponding interest rate.

[29] All the examples in this section are forward-looking; they call for the value today of a stream of future debt-equivalent cash flows. But similar issues arise in legal and contractual disputes when a *past* cash flow has to be brought forward in time to a present value today. Suppose it is determined that company A should have paid B ₹1 million 10 years ago. B clearly deserves more than ₹1 million today, because it has lost the time value of money. The time value of money should be expressed as an after-tax borrowing or lending rate, or if no risk enters, as the after-tax risk-free rate. The time value of money is *not* equal to B's overall cost of capital. Allowing B to "earn" its overall cost of capital on the payment allows it to earn a risk premium without bearing risk. For a broader discussion of these issues, see F. Fisher and C. Romaine, "Janis Joplin's Yearbook and Theory of Damages," *Journal of Accounting, Auditing & Finance* 5 (Winter/Spring 1990), pp. 145–157.

However, suppose we ask what depreciation tax shields are worth *by themselves*. For a firm that's sure to pay taxes, depreciation tax shields are a safe, nominal flow. Therefore, they should be discounted at the firm's after-tax borrowing rate.

Suppose we buy an asset with a depreciable basis of ₹200,000, which can be depreciated by the five-year tax depreciation schedule (see Table 6.4). The resulting tax shields are:

	Period					
	1	**2**	**3**	**4**	**5**	**6**
Percentage deductions	20	32	19.2	11.5	11.5	5.8
Dollar deductions (thousands)	₹40	₹64	₹38.4	₹23	₹23	₹11.6
Tax shields at T_c = .35 (thousands)	₹14	₹22.4	₹13.4	₹8.1	₹8.1	₹4.0

The after-tax discount rate is $r_D(1 - T_c) = .13(1 - .35) = .0845$. (We continue to assume a 13% pretax borrowing rate and a 35% marginal tax rate.) The present value of these shields is:

$$PV = \frac{14}{1.0845} + \frac{22.4}{(1.0845)^2} + \frac{13.4}{(1.0845)^3} + \frac{8.1}{(1.0845)^4} + \frac{8.1}{(1.0845)^5} + \frac{4.0}{(1.0845)^6}$$

$$= +56.2, \text{ or } ₹56,200$$

A Consistency Check   You may have wondered whether our procedure for valuing debt-equivalent cash flows is consistent with the WACC and APV approaches presented earlier in this chapter. Yes, it is consistent, as we will now illustrate.

Let's look at another very simple numerical example. You are asked to value a ₹1 million payment to be received from a blue-chip company one year hence. After taxes at 35%, the cash inflow is ₹650,000. The payment is fixed by contract.

Since the contract generates a debt-equivalent flow, the opportunity cost of capital is the rate investors would demand on a one-year note issued by the blue-chip company, which happens to be 8%. For simplicity, we'll assume this is your company's borrowing rate too. Our valuation rule for debt-equivalent flows is therefore to discount at $r_D(1 - T_c) = .08(1 - .35) = .052$:

$$PV = \frac{650,000}{1.052} = ₹617,900$$

What is the *debt capacity* of this ₹650,000 payment? Exactly ₹617,900. Your company could borrow that amount and pay off the loan completely—principal and after-tax interest—with the ₹650,000 cash inflow. The debt capacity is 100% of the PV of the debt-equivalent cash flow.

If you think of it that way, our discount rate $r_D(1 - T_c)$ is just a special case of WACC with a 100% debt ratio ($D/V = 1$).

$$WACC = r_D(1 - T_c)D/V + r_E E/V$$

$$= r_D(1 - T_c) \text{ if } D/V = 1 \text{ and } E/V = 0$$

Now let's try an APV calculation. This is a two-part valuation. First, the ₹650,000 inflow is discounted at the opportunity cost of capital, 8%. Second, we add the present value of interest tax shields on debt supported by the project. Since the firm can borrow 100% of the cash flow's value, the tax shield is $r_D T_c$ APV, and APV is:

$$APV = \frac{650,000}{1.08} + \frac{.08(.35)APV}{1.08}$$

Solving for APV, we get ₹617,900, the same answer we obtained by discounting at the after-tax borrowing rate. Thus our valuation rule for debt-equivalent flows is a special case of APV.

Questions

1. The U.S. government has settled a dispute with your company for $16 million. It is committed to pay this amount in exactly 12 months. However, your company will have to pay tax on the award at a marginal tax rate of 35%. What is the award worth? The one-year Treasury rate is 5.5%.

2. You are considering a five-year lease of office space for R&D personnel. Once signed, the lease cannot be canceled. It would commit your firm to six annual ₹100,000 payments, with the first payment due immediately. What is the present value of the lease if your company's borrowing rate is 9% and its tax rate is 35%? (*Note:* The lease payments would be tax-deductible.)

20

CHAPTER

UNDERSTANDING OPTIONS

Pop quiz: What do the following events have in common?

- The coffee roaster, Green Mountain, buys options that put a ceiling on the price that it will pay for its future purchases of beans.
- Flatiron offers its president a bonus if the company's stock price exceeds $120.
- Blitzen Computer dips a toe in the water and enters a new market.
- Malted Herring postpones investment in a positive-NPV plant.
- Hewlett-Packard exports partially assembled printers even though it would be cheaper to ship the finished product.
- Dominion installs a dual-fired unit at its Possum Point power station that can use either fuel oil or natural gas.
- In 2004 Air France acquires the Dutch airline, KLM, in exchange for a package of Air France shares and warrants. The warrants entitle KLM's shareholders to buy additional Air France shares for €20 each within then next 3.5 years.
- In February 2008 Chiquita Brands issues $200 million of 4.25% convertible bonds maturing in 2016. Each bond can be exchanged for 44.55 shares at any time before maturity.

Answers: (1) Each of these events involves an option, and (2) they illustrate why the financial manager of an industrial company needs to understand options.

Companies regularly use commodity, currency, and interest-rate options to reduce risk. For example, a meatpacking company that wishes to put a ceiling on the cost of beef might take out an option to buy live cattle at a fixed price. A company that wishes to limit its future borrowing costs might take out an option to sell long-term bonds at a fixed price. And so on. In Chapter 26 we explain how firms employ options to limit their risk.

Many capital investments include an embedded option to expand in the future. For instance, the company may invest in a patent that allows it to exploit a new technology or it may purchase adjoining land that gives it the option in the future to increase capacity. In each case the company is paying money today for the opportunity to make a further investment. To put it another way, the company is acquiring *growth opportunities.*

Here is another disguised option to invest: You are considering the purchase of a tract of desert land that is known to contain gold deposits. Unfortunately, the cost of extraction is higher than the current price of gold. Does this mean the land is almost worthless? Not at all. You are not obliged to mine the gold, but ownership of the land gives you the option to do so. Of course, if you know that the gold price will remain below the extraction cost, then the option is worthless. But if there is uncertainty about future gold prices, you could be lucky and make a killing.[1]

If the option to expand has value, what about the option to bail out? Projects don't usually go on until the equipment disintegrates. The decision to terminate a project is usually taken by management, not by nature. Once the project is no longer profitable, the company will cut its losses and exercise its option to abandon the project. Some projects have higher abandonment value than others. Those that use standardized equipment may offer a valuable abandonment option. Others may actually cost money to discontinue. For example, it is very costly to decommission an offshore oil platform.

We took a peek at investment options in Chapter 10, and we showed there how to use decision trees to analyze a pharmaceutical company's options to discontinue trials of a new drug. In Chapter 22 we take a more thorough look at these *real* options.

The other important reason why financial managers need to understand options is that they are often tacked on to an issue of corporate securities and so provide the investor or the company with the flexibility to change the terms of the issue. For example, in Chapter 24 we show how warrants or convertibles give their holders an option to buy common stock in exchange for cash or bonds.

In fact, we see in Chapter 23 that whenever a company borrows, it gains an option to walk away from its debts and surrender its assets to the bondholders. If the value of the company's assets is less than the amount of the debt, the company will choose to default on the payment and the bondholders will get to keep the company's assets. Thus, when the firm borrows, the lender effectively acquires the company and the shareholders obtain the option to buy it back by paying off the debt. This is an extremely important insight. It means that anything that we can learn about traded options applies equally to corporate liabilities.

In this chapter we use traded stock options to explain how options work, but we hope that our brief survey has convinced you that the interest of financial managers in options goes far beyond traded stock options. That is why we are asking you to invest here to acquire several important ideas for use later.

If you are unfamiliar with the wonderful world of options, it may seem baffling on first encounter. We therefore divide this chapter into three bite-sized pieces. Our first task is to introduce you to call and put options and to show you how the payoff on these options depends on the price of the underlying asset. We then show how financial alchemists can combine options to produce a variety of interesting strategies.

We conclude the chapter by identifying the variables that determine option values. There you encounter some surprising and counterintuitive effects. For example, investors are used to thinking that increased risk reduces present value. But for options it is the other way around.

---

[1] In Chapter 11 we valued Kingsley Solomon's gold mine by calculating the value of the gold in the ground and then subtracting the value of the extraction costs. That is correct only if we *know* that the gold will be mined. Otherwise, the value of the mine is increased by the value of the option to leave the gold in the ground if its price is less than the extraction cost.

20-1 CALLS, PUTS, AND SHARES

Investors regularly trade options on common stocks.[2] For example, Table 20.1 reproduces quotes from the National Stock Exchange of India (NSE) for options on the stock of Bombay Dyeing. You can see that there are two types of options—calls and puts. We will explain each in turn.

TABLE 20.1 Selected prices of put and call options on Bombay Dyeing stock in November 2011, when the closing stock price was about ₹420.

Maturity Date	Exercise Price	Price of Call Option	Price of Put Option
Nov-11	₹320	102.20	0.25
	340	82.90	0.85
	360	64.60	2.45
	380	48.20	5.90
	400	34.40	12.00
	420	23.75	21.25
	440	16.15	33.55
	460	11.25	48.55
Dec-11	₹320	107.50	2.60
	340	90.30	5.10
	360	74.50	9.00
	380	60.40	14.65
	400	48.25	22.20
	420	**38.10**	**31.75**
	440	29.80	43.15
	460	23.25	56.30
Jan-12	₹320	112.15	5.00
	340	96.00	8.45
	360	81.25	13.30
	380	68.05	19.60
	400	56.45	27.60
	420	46.45	37.20
	440	38.00	48.30
	460	31.00	60.90

Source: Settlement price as reported at the National Stock Exchange (www.nseindia.com).

Call Options and Position Diagrams

A **call option** gives its owner the right to buy stock at a specified *exercise* or *strike price* on or before a specified maturity date. If the option can be exercised only at maturity, it is conventionally known as a *European call;* in other cases (such as the Bombay Dyeing options shown in Table 20.1), the option can be exercised on or at any time before maturity, and it is then known as an *American call.*

---

[2] The two principal options exchanges in India are the National Stock Exchange of India and the Mumbai Stock Exchange.

The third column of Table 20.1 sets out the prices of Bombay Dyeing call options with different exercise prices and exercise dates. Look at the options maturing in December 2011.[3] The first entry says that for ₹107.50 you could acquire an option to buy one share[4] of Bombay Dyeing stock for ₹320 on or before December 2011. Moving down to the next row, you can see that an option to buy for ₹20 more (₹340 vs. ₹320) costs ₹17.20 less, that is ₹90.30. In general, the value of a call option goes down as the exercise price goes up.

Now look at the quotes for options maturing in November, 2011 and January 2012. Notice how the option price increases as option maturity is extended. For example, at an exercise price of ₹340, the November, 2011 call option costs ₹82.20, the December, 2011 option costs ₹90.30, and the January 2012 option costs ₹96.00.

In Chapter 13 we met Louis Bachelier, who in 1900 first suggested that security prices follow a random walk. Bachelier also devised a very convenient shorthand to illustrate the effects of investing in different options. We use this shorthand to compare a call option and a put option on Bombay Dyeing stock.

The *position diagram* in Figure 20.1(*a*) shows the possible consequences of investing in Bombay Dyeing December 2011 call options with an exercise price of ₹420 (boldfaced in Table 20.1). The outcome from investing in Bombay Dyeing calls depends on what happens to the stock price. If the stock price at the end of this two-month period turns out to be less than the ₹420 exercise price, nobody will pay ₹420 to obtain the share via the call option. On the other hand, if the stock price turns out to be greater than ₹420, it will pay to exercise your option to buy the share. In this case, when the call expires, it will be worth the market price of the share minus the ₹420 that you must pay to acquire it. For example, suppose Bombay Dyeing's stock price rises to ₹600. Your call will then be worth ₹600 − ₹420 = ₹180. That is your payoff, but of course it is not all profit. Table 20.1 shows that you had to pay ₹31.75 to buy the call.

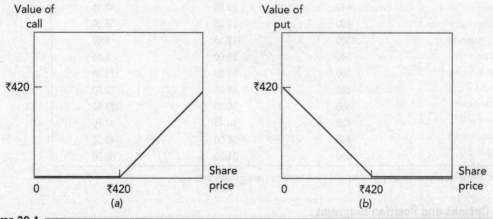

FIGURE 20.1

Position diagrams show how payoffs to owners of Bombay Dyeing calls and puts (shown by the colored lines) depend on the share price. (*a*) Result of buying Bombay Dyeing call exercisable at ₹420. (*b*) Result of buying Bombay Dyeing put exercisable at ₹420.

---

[3] In the NSE, options mature on the last Thursday of a month.

[4] You can't actually buy an option on a single share. Trades are in multiples of 1000. The minimum order would be for 1000 options on 1000 Bombay Dyeing shares. The lot size in the NSE is different for different underlying asset.

Put Options

Now let us look at the Bombay Dyeing **put options** in the right-hand column of Table 20.1. Whereas the call option gives you the right to *buy* a share for a specified exercise price, the comparable put gives you the right to *sell* the share. For example, the boldfaced entry in the right-hand column of Table 20.1 shows that for ₹31.75 you could acquire an option to sell Bombay Dyeing stock for a price of ₹420 anytime before December 2011. The circumstances in which the put turns out to be profitable are just the opposite of those in which the call is profitable. You can see this from the position diagram in Figure 20.1(*b*). If Bombay Dyeing's share price immediately before expiration turns out to be *greater* than ₹420, you won't want to sell stock at that price. You would do better to sell the share in the market, and your put option will be worthless. Conversely, if the share price turns out to be *less* than ₹420, it will pay to buy stock at the low price and then take advantage of the option to sell it for ₹420. In this case, the value of the put option on the exercise date is the difference between the ₹420 proceeds of the sale and the market price of the share. For example, if the share is worth ₹300, the put is worth ₹120:

$$\text{Value of put option at expiration} = \text{exercise price} - \text{market price of the share}$$
$$= ₹420 - ₹300 = ₹120$$

Selling Calls, Puts, and Shares

Let us now look at the position of an investor who *sells* these investments. If you sell, or "write," a call, you promise to deliver shares if asked to do so by the call buyer. In other words, the buyer's asset is the seller's liability. If the share price is below the exercise price when the option matures, the buyer will not exercise the call and the seller's liability will be zero. If it rises above the exercise price, the buyer will exercise and the seller must give up the shares. The seller loses the difference between the share price and the exercise price received from the buyer. Notice that it is the buyer who always has the option to exercise; option sellers simply do as they are told.

Suppose that the price of Bombay Dyeing stock turns out to be ₹500, which is above the option's exercise price of ₹420. In this case the buyer will exercise the call. The seller is forced to sell stock worth ₹500 for only ₹420 and so has a payoff of −₹80.[5] Of course, that ₹80 loss is the buyer's gain. Figure 20.2(*a*) shows how the payoffs to the seller of the Bombay Dyeing call option vary with the stock price. Notice that for every rupee the buyer makes, the seller loses a rupee. Figure 20.2(*a*) is just Figure 20.1(*a*) drawn upside down.

In just the same way we can depict the position of an investor who sells, or writes, a put by standing Figure 20.1(*b*) on its head. The seller of the put has agreed to pay ₹420 for the share if the buyer of the put should request it. Clearly the seller will be safe as long as the share price remains above ₹420 but will lose money if the share price falls below this figure. The worst thing that can happen is that the stock becomes worthless. The seller would then be obliged to pay ₹420 for a stock worth ₹0. The payoff to the option position would be −₹420.

Position Diagrams Are Not Profit Diagrams

Position diagrams show *only* the payoffs at option exercise; they do not account for the initial cost of buying the option or the initial proceeds from selling it.

---

[5] The seller has some consolation, for he or she was paid ₹38.10 in September for selling the call.

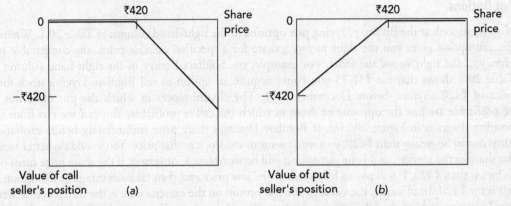

Value of call
seller's position   (a)   Value of put
seller's position   (b)

FIGURE 20.2

Payoffs to *sellers* of Bombay Dyeing calls and puts (shown by the colored lines) depend on the share price. (a) Result of selling Bombay Dyeing call exercisable at ₹420. (b) Result of selling Google put exercisable at ₹420.

This is a common point of confusion. For example, the position diagram in Figure 20.1(a) makes purchase of a call *look* like a sure thing—the payoff is at worst zero, with plenty of upside if Bombay Dyeing's stock price goes above ₹420 by December 2011. But compare the *profit diagram* in Figure 20.3(a), which subtracts the ₹38.10 *cost* of the call in September 2008 from the payoff at maturity. The call buyer loses money at all share prices less than ₹420 + 38.10 = ₹458.10. Take another example: The position diagram in Figure 20.2(b) makes selling a put *look* like a sure loss—the *best* payoff is zero. But the profit diagram in Figure 20.3(b), which recognizes the ₹31.75 received by the seller, shows that the seller gains at all prices above ₹420 − ₹31.75 = ₹388.25.[6]

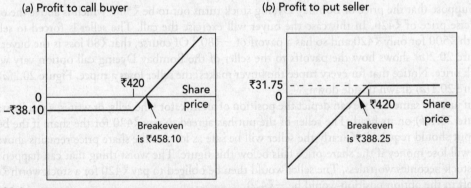

FIGURE 20.3

Profit diagrams incorporate the costs of buying an option or the proceeds from selling one. In panel (a), we subtract the ₹38.10 cost of the Bombay Dyeing call from the payoffs plotted in Figure 20.1(a). In panel (b), we add the ₹31.75 proceeds from selling the Bombay Dyeing put to the payoffs in Figure 20.2(b).

---

[6]The fact that you have made a profit on your position is not necessarily a cause for rejoicing. The profit needs to compensate you for the time value of money and the risk that you took.

Profit diagrams like those in Figure 20.3 may be helpful to the options beginner, but options experts rarely draw them.[7] Now that you've graduated from the first options class we won't draw them either. We stick to position diagrams, because you have to focus on payoffs at exercise to understand options and to value them properly.

20-2 FINANCIAL ALCHEMY WITH OPTIONS

Look now at Figure 20.4(a), which shows the payoff if you buy Bombay Dyeing stock at ₹420. You gain rupee-for-rupee if the stock price goes up and you lose rupee-for-rupee if it falls. That's trite; it doesn't take a genius to draw a 45-degree line.

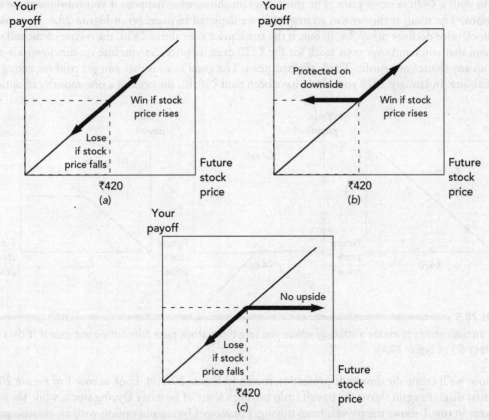

FIGURE 20.4

Payoffs at the end of six months to three investment strategies for Bombay Dyeing stock. (a) You buy one share for ₹420. (b) No downside. If stock price falls, your payoff stays at ₹420. (c) A strategy for masochists? You lose if stock price falls, but you don't gain if it rises.

---

[7] Profit diagrams such as Figure 20.3 deduct the initial cost of the option from the final payoff. They therefore ignore the first lesson of finance—"A rupee today is worth more than a rupee in the future."

Look now at panel (*b*), which shows the payoffs from an investment strategy that retains the upside potential of Bombay Dyeing stock but gives complete downside protection. In this case your payoff stays at ₹420 even if the Bombay Dyeing stock price falls to ₹400, ₹100, or zero. Panel (*b*)'s payoffs are clearly better than panel (*a*)'s. If a financial alchemist could turn panel (*a*) into panel (*b*), you'd be willing to pay for the service.

Of course alchemy has its dark side. Panel (*c*) shows an investment strategy for masochists. You lose if the stock price falls, but you give up any chance of profiting from a rise in the stock price. If you *like* to lose, or if someone pays you enough to take the strategy on, this is the investment for you.

Now, as you have probably suspected, all this financial alchemy is for real. You can do both the transmutations shown in Figure 20.4. You do them with options, and we will show you how.

Consider first the strategy for masochists. The first diagram in Figure 20.5 shows the payoffs from buying a share of Bombay Dyeing stock, while the second shows the payoffs from *selling* a call option with a ₹420 exercise price. The third diagram shows what happens if you combine these two positions. The result is the no-win strategy that we depicted in panel (*c*) of Figure 20.4. You lose if the stock price declines below ₹420, but, if the stock price rises above ₹420, the owner of the call will demand that you hand over your stock for the ₹420 exercise price. So you lose on the downside and give up any chance of a profit. That's the bad news. The good news is that you get paid for taking on this liability. In January 2012 you would have been paid ₹38.10, the price of a one-month call option.

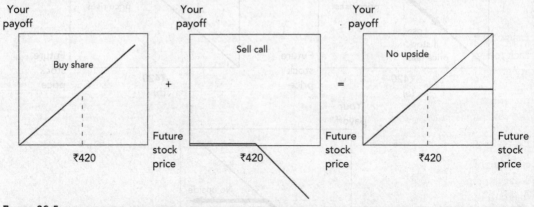

FIGURE 20.5

You can use options to create a strategy where you lose if the stock price falls but do not gain if it rises (strategy [c] in Figure 20.4).

Now, we'll create the downside protection shown in Figure 20.4(*b*). Look at row 1 of Figure 20.6. The first diagram again shows the payoff from buying a share of Bombay Dyeing stock, while the next diagram in row 1 shows the payoffs from buying a Bombay Dyeing put option with an exercise price of ₹420. The third diagram shows the effect of combining these two positions. You can see that, if Bombay Dyeing's stock price rises above ₹420, your put option is valueless, so you simply receive the gains from your investment in the share. However, if the stock price falls below ₹420, you can exercise your put option and sell your stock for ₹420. Thus, by adding a put option to your investment in the stock, you have protected yourself against loss.[8] This is the strategy that we depicted in panel (*b*) of Figure 20.4. Of course, there is no gain without pain. The *cost* of insuring yourself against loss is

---

[8] This combination of a stock and a put option is known as a *protective put.*

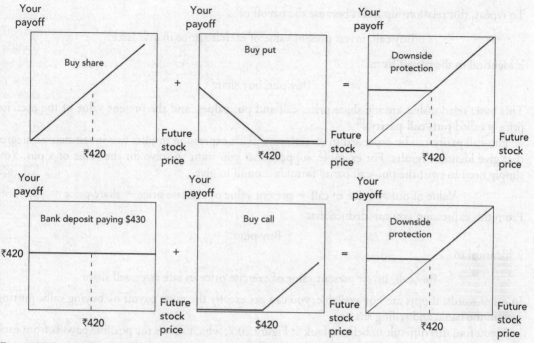

FIGURE 20.6

Each row in the figure shows a different way to create a strategy where you gain if the stock price rises but are protected on the downside (strategy [b] in Figure 20.4).

the amount that you pay for a put option on Bombay Dyeing stock with an exercise price of ₹420. In November 2011 the price of this put was ₹31.75. This was the going rate for financial alchemists.

We have just seen how put options can be used to provide downside protection. We now show you how call options can be used to get the same result. This is illustrated in row 2 of Figure 20.6. The first diagram shows the payoff from placing the present value of ₹420 in a bank deposit. Regardless of what happens to the price of Bombay Dyeing stock, your bank deposit will pay off ₹420. The second diagram in row 2 shows the payoff from a call option on Bombay Dyeing stock with an exercise price of ₹420, and the third diagram shows the effect of combining these two positions. Notice that, if the price of Bombay Dyeing stock falls, your call is worthless, but you still have your ₹420 in the bank. For every rupee that Bombay Dyeing stock price rises above ₹420, your investment in the call option pays off an extra rupee. For example, if the stock price rises to ₹500, you will have ₹420 in the bank and a call worth ₹80. Thus you participate fully in any rise in the price of the stock, while being fully protected against any fall! So we have just found another way to provide the downside protection depicted in panel (b) of Figure 20.4.

These two rows of Figure 20.6 tell us something about the relationship between a call option and a put option. Regardless of the future stock price, both investment strategies provide identical payoffs. In other words, if you buy the share and a put option to sell it for ₹420, you receive the same payoff as from buying a call option and setting enough money aside to pay the ₹420 exercise price. Therefore, if you are committed to holding the two packages until the options expire, the two packages should sell for the same price today. This gives us a fundamental relationship for European options:

$$\text{Value of call} + \text{present value of exercise price} = \text{value of put} + \text{share price}$$

To repeat, this relationship holds because the payoff of

Buy call, invest present value of exercise price in safe asset[9]

is identical to the payoff from

Buy put, buy share

This basic relationship among share price, call and put values, and the present value of the exercise price is called **put–call parity**.[10]

Put–call parity can be expressed in several ways. Each expression implies two investment strategies that give identical results. For example, suppose that you want to solve for the value of a put. You simply need to twist the put–call parity formula around to give

Value of put = value of call + present value of exercise price − share price

From this expression you can deduce that

Buy put

is identical to

Buy call, invest present value of exercise price in safe asset, sell share

In other words, if puts are not available, you can get exactly the same payoff by buying calls, putting cash in the bank, and selling shares.

If you find this difficult to believe, look at Figure 20.7, which shows the possible payoffs from each position. The diagram on the left shows the payoffs from a call option on Bombay Dyeing stock with an exercise price of ₹420. The second diagram shows the payoffs from placing the present value of ₹420 in the bank. Regardless of what happens to the share price, this investment will pay off ₹420. The third diagram shows the payoffs from selling Bombay Dyeing stock. When you sell a share that you don't own, you have a liability—you must sometime buy it back. As they say on Wall Street:

He who sells what isn't his'n

Buys it back or goes to pris'n

Therefore the best that can happen to you is that the share price falls to zero. In that case it costs you nothing to buy the share back. But for every extra rupee on the future share price, you will need to spend an extra rupee to buy the share. The final diagram in Figure 20.7 shows that the *total* payoff from these three positions is the same as if you had bought a put option. For example, suppose that when the option matures the stock price is ₹400. Your call will be worthless, your bank deposit will be worth ₹420, and it will cost you ₹400 to repurchase the share. Your total payoff is 0 + 420 − 400 = ₹20, exactly the same as the payoff from the put.

If two investments offer identical payoffs, then they should sell for the same price today. If the law of one price is violated, you have a potential arbitrage opportunity. So let's check whether there are any arbitrage profits to be made from our Bombay Dyeing calls and puts. In November 2011 the price

---

[9] The present value is calculated at the *risk-free* rate of interest. It is the amount that you would have to invest today in a bank deposit or Treasury bills to realize the exercise price on the option's expiration date.

[10] Put–call parity holds only if you are committed to holding the options until the final exercise date. It therefore does not hold for American options, which you can exercise *before* the final date. We discuss possible reasons for early exercise in Chapter 21. Also if the stock makes a dividend payment before the final exercise date, you need to recognize that the investor who buys the call misses out on this dividend. In this case the relationship is

Value of call + present value of exercise price = value of put + share price − present value of dividend

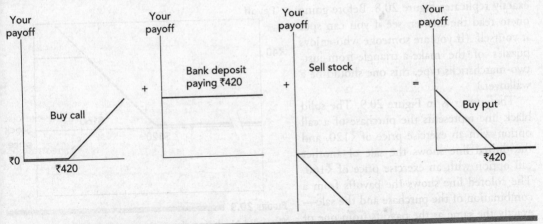

FIGURE 20.7
A strategy of buying a call, depositing the present value of the exercise price in the bank, and selling the stock is equivalent to buying a put.

of a six-month call with a ₹420 exercise price was ₹38.10, the interest rate was about 9.5%, and the price of Bombay Dyeing stock was ₹420. Therefore the cost of a homemade put was:

$$\text{Buy call} + \text{present value of exercise price} - \text{share price} = \text{cost of homemade put}$$
$$38.10 + 420/(1.095)^{1/6} - 420 = 31.75$$

This is almost exactly the same as it would have cost you to buy a put directly.

Spotting the Option

Options rarely come with a large label attached. Often the trickiest part of the problem is to identify the option. When you are not sure whether you are dealing with a put or a call or a complicated blend of the two, it is a good precaution to draw a position diagram. Here is an example.

OLP Limited has offered its president, Ms. Lakshmi, the following incentive scheme: At the end of the year Ms. Lakshmi will be paid a bonus of ₹50,000 for every rupee that the price of OLP stock exceeds its current figure of ₹120. However, the maximum bonus that she can receive is set at ₹2 million.

You can think of Ms. Lakhsmi as owning 50,000 tickets, each of which pays nothing if the stock price fails to beat ₹120. The value of each ticket then rises by ₹1 for each rupee rise in the stock price up to the maximum of ₹2,000,000/50,000 = ₹40. Figure 20.8 shows the payoffs from just one of these tickets. The payoffs are not the same as those of the simple put and call options that we drew in Figure 20.1, but it is possible to find a combination of options that

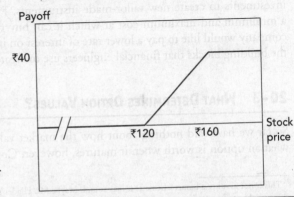

FIGURE 20.8
The payoff from one of Ms. Lakshmi's "tickets" depends on OLP Limited's stock price.

exactly replicates Figure 20.8. Before going on to read the answer, see if you can spot it yourself. (If you are someone who enjoys puzzles of the make-a-triangle-from-just-two-matchsticks type, this one should be a walkover.)

The answer is in Figure 20.9. The solid black line represents the purchase of a call option with an exercise price of ₹120, and the dotted line shows the sale of another call option with an exercise price of ₹160. The colored line shows the payoffs from a combination of the purchase and the sale—exactly the same as the payoffs from one of Ms. Lakshmi's tickets.

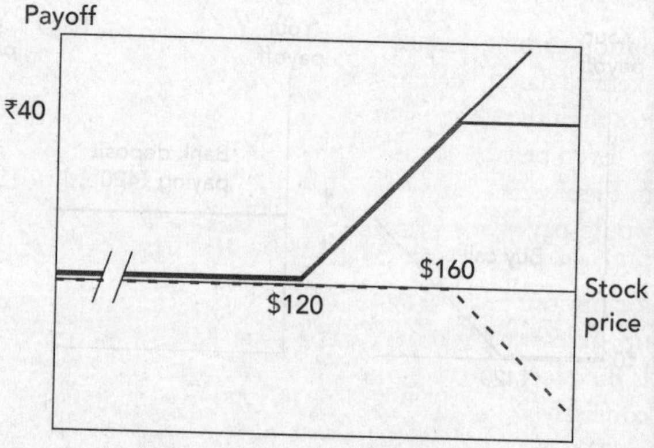

Thus, if we wish to know how much the incentive scheme is costing the company, we need to calculate the difference between the value of 50,000 call options with an exercise price of ₹120 and the value of 50,000 calls with an exercise price of ₹160.

FIGURE 20.9

The solid black line shows the payoff from buying a call with an exercise price of ₹120. The dotted line shows the sale of a call with an exercise price of ₹160. The combined purchase and sale (shown by the colored line) is identical to one of Ms. Lakshmi "tickets."

We could have made the incentive scheme depend in a much more complicated way on the stock price. For example, the bonus could peak at ₹2 million and then fall steadily back to zero as the stock price climbs above ₹160.[11] You could still have represented this scheme as a combination of options. In fact, we can state a general theorem:

Any set of contingent payoffs—that is, payoffs that depend on the value of some other asset—can be constructed with a mixture of simple options on that asset.

In other words, you can create any position diagram—with as many ups and downs or peaks and valleys as your imagination allows—by buying or selling the right combinations of puts and calls with different exercise prices.[12]

Finance pros often talk about **financial engineering,** which is the practice of packaging different investments to create new tailor-made instruments. Perhaps a German company would like to set a minimum and maximum cost at which it can buy rupees in six-months' time. Or perhaps an oil company would like to pay a lower rate of interest on its debt if the price of oil falls. Options provide the building blocks that financial engineers use to create these interesting payoff structures.

20-3 WHAT DETERMINES OPTION VALUES?

So far we have said nothing about how the market value of an option is determined. We do know what an option is worth when it matures, however. Consider, for instance, our earlier example of an

---

[11] This is not as nutty a bonus scheme as it may sound. Maybe Ms. Higden's hard work can lift the value of the stock by so much and the only way she can hope to increase it further is by taking on extra risk. You can deter her from doing this by making her bonus start to decline beyond some point. Too bad that the bonus schemes for some bank CEOs did not contain this feature.

[12] In some cases you may also have to borrow or lend money to generate a position diagram with your desired pattern. Lending raises the payoff line in position diagrams, as in the bottom row of Figure 20.6. Borrowing lowers the payoff line.

option to buy Bombay Dyeing stock at ₹420. If Bombay Dyeing's stock price is below ₹420 on the exercise date, the call will be worthless; if the stock price is above ₹420, the call will be worth ₹420 less than the value of the stock. This relationship is depicted by the heavy, lower line in Figure 20.10.

Even before maturity the price of the option can never remain *below* the heavy, lower-bound line in Figure 20.10. For example, if our option were priced at ₹10 and the stock were priced at ₹460, it would pay any investor to sell the stock and then buy it back by purchasing the option and exercising it for an additional ₹420. That would give an arbitrage opportunity with a profit of ₹30. The demand for options from investors seeking to exploit this opportunity would quickly force the option price up, at least to the heavy line in the figure. For options that still have some time to run, the heavy line is therefore a *lower bound* on the market price of the option. Option geeks express the same idea more concisely when they write Lower Bound = Max(stock price − exercise price, 0).

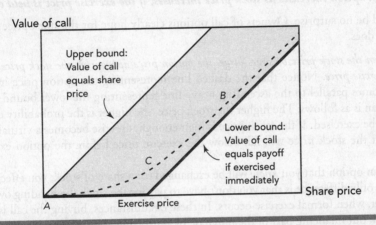

FIGURE 20.10
Value of a call before its expiration date (dashed line). The value depends on the stock price. It is always worth more than its value if exercised now (heavy line). It is never worth more than the stock price itself.

The diagonal line in Figure 20.10 is the *upper bound* to the option price. Why? Because the option cannot give a higher ultimate payoff than the stock. If at the option's expiration the stock price ends up *above* the exercise price, the option is worth the stock price *less* the exercise price. If the stock price ends up *below* the exercise price, the option is worthless, but the stock's owner still has a valuable security. For example, if the option's exercise price is ₹420, then the extra dollar returns realized by stockholders are shown in the following table:

	Stock Payoff	Option Payoff	Extra Payoff from Holding Stock Instead of Option
Option exercised (stock price greater than ₹420)	Stock price	Stock price −420	₹420
Option expires unexercised (stock price less than or equal to ₹420)	Stock price	0	Stock price

If the stock and the option have the same price, everyone will rush to sell the option and buy the stock. Therefore, the option price must be somewhere in the shaded region of Figure 20.10. In fact, it will lie on a curved, upward-sloping line like the dashed curve shown in the figure. This line begins its travels where the upper and lower bounds meet (at zero). Then it rises, gradually becoming parallel to the upward-sloping part of the lower bound.

But let us look more carefully at the shape and location of the dashed line. Three points, A, B, and C, are marked on the dashed line. As we explain each point you will see why the option price has to behave as the dashed line predicts.

Point A *When the stock is worthless, the option is worthless.* A stock price of zero means that there is no possibility the stock will ever have any future value.[13] If so, the option is sure to expire unexercised and worthless, and it is worthless today.

That brings us to our first important point about option value:

The value of an option increases as stock price increases, if the exercise price is held constant.

That should be no surprise. Owners of call options clearly hope for the stock price to rise and are happy when it does.

Point B *When the stock price becomes large, the option price approaches the stock price less the present value of the exercise price.* Notice that the dashed line representing the option price in Figure 20.10 eventually becomes parallel to the ascending heavy line representing the lower bound on the option price. The reason is as follows: The higher the stock price, the higher is the probability that the option will eventually be exercised. If the stock price is high enough, exercise becomes a virtual certainty; the probability that the stock price will fall below the exercise price before the option expires becomes trivially small.

If you own an option that you *know* will be exchanged for a share of stock, you effectively own the stock now. The only difference is that you don't have to pay for the stock (by handing over the exercise price) until later, when formal exercise occurs. In these circumstances, buying the call is equivalent to buying the stock but financing part of the purchase by borrowing. The amount implicitly borrowed is the present value of the exercise price. The value of the call is therefore equal to the stock price less the present value of the exercise price.

This brings us to another important point about options. Investors who acquire stock by way of a call option are buying on credit. They pay the purchase price of the option today, but they do not pay the exercise price until they actually take up the option. The delay in payment is particularly valuable if interest rates are high and the option has a long maturity.

Thus, the value of an option increases with both the rate of interest and the time to maturity.

Point C *The option price always exceeds its minimum value* (except when stock price is zero). We have seen that the dashed and heavy lines in Figure 20.10 coincide when stock price is zero (point A), but elsewhere the lines diverge; that is, the option price must exceed the minimum value given by the heavy line. The reason for this can be understood by examining point C.

At point C, the stock price exactly equals the exercise price. The option is therefore worthless if exercised today. However, suppose that the option will not expire until three months hence. Of course we do not know what the stock price will be at the expiration date. There is roughly a 50% chance that it will be higher than the exercise price and a 50% chance that it will be lower. The possible payoffs to the option are therefore:

---

[13] If a stock *can* be worth something in the future, then investors will pay *something* for it today, although possibly a very small amount.

Outcome	Payoff
Stock price rises (50% probability)	Stock price less exercise price (option is exercised)
Stock price falls (50% probability)	Zero (option expires worthless)

If there is a positive probability of a positive payoff, and if the worst payoff is zero, then the option must be valuable. That means the option price at point *C* exceeds its lower bound, which at point *C* is zero. In general, the option prices will exceed their lower-bound values as long as there is time left before expiration.

One of the most important determinants of the *height* of the dashed curve (i.e., of the difference between actual and lower-bound value) is the likelihood of substantial movements in the stock price. An option on a stock whose price is unlikely to change by more than 1% or 2% is not worth much; an option on a stock whose price may halve or double is very valuable.

As an option holder, you gain from volatility because the payoffs are not symmetric. If the stock price falls *below* the exercise price, your call option will be worthless, regardless of whether the shortfall is a few cents or many dollars. On the other hand, for every rupee that the stock price rises *above* the exercise price, your call will be worth an extra rupee. Therefore, the option holder gains from the increased volatility on the upside, but does not lose on the downside.

A simple example may help to illustrate the point. Consider two stocks, X and Y, each of which is priced at ₹100. The only difference is that the outlook for Y is much less easy to predict. There is a 50% chance that the price of Y will rise to ₹150 and a similar chance that it will fall to ₹70. By contrast, there is a 50-50 chance that the price of X will either rise to ₹130 or fall to ₹90.

Suppose that you are offered a call option on each of these stocks with an exercise price of ₹100. The following table compares the possible payoffs from these options:

	Stock Price Falls	Stock Price Rises
Payoff from option on X	₹0	₹130 − ₹100 = ₹30
Payoff from option on Y	₹0	₹150 − ₹100 = ₹50

In both cases there is a 50% chance that the stock price will decline and make the option worthless but, if the stock price rises, the option on Y will give the larger payoff. Since the chance of a zero payoff is the same, the option on Y is worth more than the option on X.

Of course, in practice future stock prices may take on a range of different values. We have recognized this in Figure 20.11, where the uncertain outlook for Y's stock price shows up in the wider probability distribution of future prices.[14] The greater spread of outcomes for stock Y again provides more upside potential and therefore increases the chance of a large payoff on the option.

Figure 20.12 shows how volatility affects the value of an option. The upper curved line depicts the value of the Bombay Dyeing call option assuming that Bombay Dyeing's stock price, like that of stock Y, is highly variable. The lower curved line assumes a lower (and more realistic) degree of volatility.[15]

---

[14] Figure 20.11 continues to assume that the exercise price on both options is equal to the current stock price. This is not a necessary assumption. Also in drawing Figure 20.11 we have assumed that the distribution of stock prices is symmetric. This also is not a necessary assumption, and we will look more carefully at the distribution of stock prices in the next chapter.

[15] The option values shown in Figure 20.12 were calculated by using the Black-Scholes option-valuation model. We explain this model in Chapter 21 and use it to value the Bombay Dyeing option.

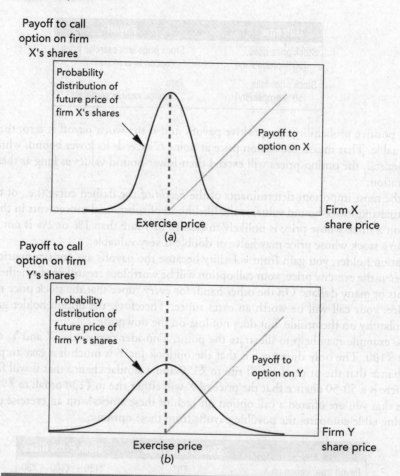

FIGURE 20.11

Call options on the shares of (a) firm X and (b) firm Y. In each case, the current share price equals the exercise price, so each option has a 50% chance of ending up worthless (if the share price falls) and a 50% chance of ending up "in the money" (if the share price rises). However, the chance of a large payoff is greater for the option on firm Y's shares because Y's stock price is more volatile and therefore has more upside potential.

The probability of large stock price changes during the remaining life of an option depends on two things: (1) the variance (i.e., volatility) of the stock price *per period* and (2) the number of periods until the option expires. If there are t remaining periods, and the variance per period is σ^2, the value of the option should depend on cumulative variability $\sigma^2 t$.[16] Other things equal, you would like to hold an option on a volatile stock (high σ^2). Given volatility, you would like to hold an option with a long life ahead of it (large t).

---

[16] Here is an intuitive explanation: If the stock price follows a random walk (see Section 13-2), successive price changes are statistically independent. The cumulative price change before expiration is the sum of t random variables. The variance of a sum of independent random variables is the sum of the variances of those variables. Thus, if σ^2 is the variance of the daily price change, and there are t days until expiration, the variance of the cumulative price change is $\sigma^2 t$.

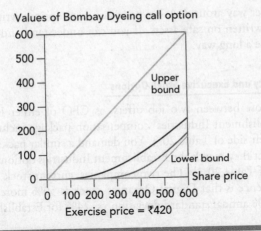

Values of Bombay Dyeing call option

Exercise price = ₹420

FIGURE 20.12

How the value of the Bombay Dyeing call option increases with the volatility of the stock price. Each of the curved lines shows the value of the option for different initial stock prices. The only difference is that the upper line assumes a much higher level of uncertainty about Bombay Dyeing's future stock price.

eXcel

Visit us at
www.mhhe.com/bmam10e

Thus the value of an option increases with both the volatility of the share price and the time to maturity.

It's a rare person who can keep all these properties straight at first reading. Therefore, we have summed them up in Table 20.2.

TABLE 20.2 What the price of a call option depends on.

1. If there is an *increase* in:	The change in the call option price is:
Stock price (P)	Positive
Exercise price (EX)	Negative
Interest rate (r_f)	Positive*
Time to expiration (t)	Positive
Volatility of stock price (σ)	Positive*

2. Other properties of call options:

a. *Upper bound.* The option price is always less than the stock price.

b. *Lower bound.* The call price never falls below the payoff to immediate exercise ($P - EX$ or zero, whichever is larger).

c. If the stock is worthless, the call is worthless.

d. As the stock price becomes very large, the call price approaches the stock price less the present value of the exercise price.

* The direct effect of increases in r_f or σ on option price, *given* the stock price. There may also be *indirect* effects. For example, an increase in r_f could reduce stock price P. This in turn could affect option price.

Risk and Option Values

In most financial settings, risk is a bad thing; you have to be paid to bear it. Investors in risky (high-beta) stocks demand higher expected rates of return. High-risk capital investment projects have correspondingly high costs of capital and have to beat higher hurdle rates to achieve positive NPV.

For options it's the other way around. As we have just seen, options written on volatile assets are worth *more* than options written on safe assets. If you can understand and remember that one fact about options, you've come a long way.

EXAMPLE 20.1   Volatility and Executive Stock Options

Suppose you have to choose between two job offers, as CFO of either Establishment Industries or Digital Organics. Establishment Industries' compensation package includes a grant of the stock options described on the left side of Table 20.3. You demand a similar package from Digital Organics, and they comply. In fact they match the Establishment Industries options in every respect, as you can see on the right side of Table 20.3. (The two companies' current stock prices just happen to be the same.) The only difference is that Digital Organics' stock is 50% more volatile than Establishment Industries' stock (36% annual standard deviation vs. 24% for Establishment Industries).

TABLE 20.3   Which package of executive stock options would you choose? The package offered by Digital Organics is more valuable, because the volatility of that company's stock is higher.

	Establishment Industries	Digital Organics
Number of options	100,000	100,000
Exercise price	₹25	₹25
Maturity	5 years	5 years
Current stock price	₹22	₹22
Stock price volatility (standard deviation of return)	24%	36%

If your job choice hinges on the value of the executive stock options, you should take the Digital Organics offer. The Digital Organics options are written on the more volatile asset and therefore are worth more.

We value the two stock-option packages in the next chapter.

SUMMARY

If you have managed to reach this point, you are probably in need of a rest and a stiff gin and tonic. So we will summarize what we have learned so far and take up the subject of options again in the next chapter when you are rested (or drunk).

There are two types of option. An American call is an option to buy an asset at a specified exercise price on or before a specified maturity date. Similarly, an American put is an option to sell the asset at a specified price on or before a specified date. European calls and puts are exactly the same except that they cannot be exercised before the specified maturity date. Calls and puts are the basic building blocks that can be combined to give any pattern of payoffs.

What determines the value of a call option? Common sense tells us that it ought to depend on three things:

1. To exercise an option you have to pay the exercise price. Other things being equal, the less you are obliged to pay, the better. Therefore, the value of a call option increases with the ratio of the asset price to the exercise price.

2. You do not have to pay the exercise price until you decide to exercise the option. Therefore, a call option gives you a free loan. The higher the rate of interest and the longer the time to maturity, the more this free loan is worth. So the value of a call option increases with the interest rate and time to maturity.

3. If the price of the asset falls short of the exercise price, you won't exercise the call option. You will, therefore, lose 100% of your investment in the option no matter how far the asset depreciates below the exercise price. On the other hand, the more the price rises *above* the exercise price, the more profit you will make. Therefore the option holder does not lose from increased volatility if things go wrong, but gains if they go right. The value of an option increases with the variance per period of the stock return multiplied by the number of periods to maturity.

Always remember that an option written on a risky (high-variance) asset is worth more than an option on a safe asset. It's easy to forget, because in most other financial contexts increases in risk reduce present value.

FURTHER READING

See Further Readings for Chapter 21.

PROBLEM SETS

BASIC

1. Complete the following passage:
   A _____ option gives its owner the opportunity to buy a stock at a specified price that is generally called the _____ price. A _____ option gives its owner the opportunity to sell stock at a specified price. Options that can be exercised only at maturity are called _____ options.

2. Note Figure 20.13 on the next page. Match each diagram, (*a*) and (*b*), with one of the following positions:
   - Call buyer
   - Call seller
   - Put buyer
   - Put seller

3. Suppose that you hold a share of stock and a put option on that share. What is the payoff when the option expires if (a) the stock price is below the exercise price? (b) the stock price is above the exercise price?

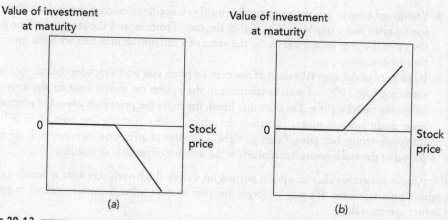

Figure 20.13

See Problem 2.

4. What is put–call parity and why does it hold? Could you apply the parity formula to a call and put with different exercise prices?

5. There is another strategy involving calls and borrowing or lending that gives the same payoffs as the strategy described in Problem 3. What is the alternative strategy?

6. Dr. Livingstone I. Presume holds £600,000 in East African gold stocks. Bullish as he is on gold mining, he requires absolute assurance that at least £500,000 will be available in six months to fund an expedition. Describe two ways for Dr. Presume to achieve this goal. There is an active market for puts and calls on East African gold stocks, and the rate of interest is 6% per year.

7. Suppose you buy a one-year European call option on Wombat stock with an exercise price of ₹100 and sell a one-year European put option with the same exercise price. The current stock price is ₹100, and the interest rate is 10%.
   a. Draw a position diagram showing the payoffs from your investments.
   b. How much will the combined position cost you? Explain.

8. Look again at Figure 20.13. It appears that the investor in panel (b) can't lose and the investor in panel (a) can't win. Is that correct? Explain. (*Hint:* Draw a profit diagram for each panel.)

9. What is a call option worth if (a) the stock price is zero? (b) the stock price is extremely high relative to the exercise price?

10. How does the price of a call option respond to the following changes, other things equal? Does the call price go up or down?
    a. Stock price increases.
    b. Exercise price is increased.
    c. Risk-free rate increases.
    d. Expiration date of the option is extended.
    e. Volatility of the stock price falls.
    f. Time passes, so the option's expiration date comes closer.

11. Respond to the following statements.
    a. "I'm a conservative investor. I'd much rather hold a call option on a safe stock like Hindustan Unilever than a volatile stock like Bharti Airtel."
    b. "I bought an American call option on Fava Farms stock, with an exercise price of ₹45 per share and three more months to maturity. Fava Farms' stock has skyrocketed from ₹35 to ₹55 per share, but I'm afraid it will fall back below ₹45. I'm going to lock in my gain and exercise my call right now."

INTERMEDIATE

12. Discuss briefly the risks and payoffs of the following positions:
    a. Buy stock and a put option on the stock.
    b. Buy stock.
    c. Buy call.
    d. Buy stock and sell call option on the stock.
    e. Buy bond.
    f. Buy stock, buy put, and sell call.
    g. Sell put.

13. "The buyer of the call and the seller of the put both hope that the stock price will rise. Therefore the two positions are identical." Is the speaker correct? Illustrate with a position diagram.

14. Pintail's stock price is currently ₹200. A one-year *American* call option has an exercise price of ₹50 and is priced at ₹75. How would you take advantage of this great opportunity? Now suppose the option is a *European* call. What would you do?

15. It is possible to buy three-month call options and three-month puts on stock Q. Both options have an exercise price of ₹60 and both are worth ₹10. If the interest rate is 5% a year, what is the stock price? (*Hint:* Use put–call parity.)

16. In January 2009, a one-year call on the stock of Amazon.com, with an exercise price of $45.00, sold for $19.55. The stock price was $55. The risk-free interest rate was 2.5%. How much would you be willing to pay for a put on Amazon stock with the same maturity and exercise price? Assume that the Amazon options are European options. (*Note:* Amazon does not pay a dividend.)

17. FX Bank has succeeded in hiring ace foreign exchange trader Lucinda Cable. Her remuneration package reportedly includes an annual bonus of 20% of the profits that she generates in excess of ₹100 million. Does Ms. Cable have an option? Does it provide her with the appropriate incentives?

18. Suppose that Mr. Vishnu borrows the present value of ₹100, buys a six-month put option on stock Y with an exercise price of ₹150, and sells a six-month put option on Y with an exercise price of ₹50.
    a. Draw a position diagram showing the payoffs when the options expire.
    b. Suggest two other combinations of loans, options, and the underlying stock that would give Mr. Vishnu the same payoffs.

19. Which *one* of the following statements is correct?
    a. Value of put + present value of exercise price = value of call + share price.
    b. Value of put + share price = value of call + present value of exercise price.
    c. Value of put − share price = present value of exercise price − value of call.
    d. Value of put + value of call = share price − present value of exercise price.
    The correct statement equates the value of two investment strategies. Plot the payoffs to each strategy as a function of the stock price. Show that the two strategies give identical payoffs.

20. Test the formula linking put and call prices by using it to explain the relative prices of actual traded puts and calls. (*Note:* The formula is exact only for European options. Most traded puts and calls are American.)

21. a. If you can't sell a share short, you can achieve exactly the same final payoff by a combination of options and borrowing or lending. What is this combination?
    b. Now work out the mixture of stock and options that gives the same final payoff as investment in a risk-free loan.

22. The common stock of Triangular File Company is selling at ₹90. A 26-week call option written on Triangular File's stock is selling for ₹8. The call's exercise price is ₹100. The risk-free interest rate is 10% per year.

a. Suppose that puts on Triangular stock are not traded, but you want to buy one. How would you do it?

b. Suppose that puts *are* traded. What should a 26-week put with an exercise price of ₹100 sell for?

23. Ms. Lakshmi has been offered yet another incentive scheme (see Section 20-2). She will receive a bonus of ₹500,000 if the stock price at the end of the year is ₹120 or more; otherwise she will receive nothing. (Don't ask why anyone should want to offer such an arrangement. Maybe there's some tax angle.)

a. Draw a position diagram illustrating the payoffs from such a scheme.

b. What combination of options would provide these payoffs? (*Hint:* You need to buy a large number of options with one exercise price and sell a similar number with a different exercise price.)

24. Option traders often refer to "straddles" and "butterflies." Here is an example of each:
- *Straddle:* Buy call with exercise price of ₹100 and simultaneously buy put with exercise price of ₹100.
- *Butterfly:* Simultaneously buy one call with exercise price of ₹100, sell two calls with exercise price of ₹110, and buy one call with exercise price of ₹120.

    Draw position diagrams for the straddle and butterfly, showing the payoffs from the investor's net position. Each strategy is a bet on variability. Explain briefly the nature of each bet.

25. Look at actual trading prices of call options on stocks to check whether they behave as the theory presented in this chapter predicts. For example,

a. Follow several options as they approach maturity. How would you expect their prices to behave? Do they actually behave that way?

b. Compare two call options written on the same stock with the same maturity but different exercise prices.

c. Compare two call options written on the same stock with the same exercise price but different maturities.

26. Is it more valuable to own an option to buy a portfolio of stocks or to own a portfolio of options to buy each of the individual stocks? Say briefly why.

27. Table 20.4 lists some prices of options on common stocks (prices are quoted to the nearest dollar). The interest rate is 10% a year. Can you spot any mispricing? What would you do to take advantage of it?

TABLE 20.4   Prices of options on common stocks (in dollars). See Problem 27.

Stock	Time to Exercise (months)	Exercise Price	Stock Price	Put Price	Call Price
Drongo Corp.	6	$ 50	$80	$20	$52
Ragwort, Inc.	6	100	80	10	15
Wombat Corp.	3	40	50	7	18
	6	40	50	5	17
	6	50	50	8	10

28. You've just completed a month-long study of energy markets and conclude that energy prices will be *much* more volatile in the next year than historically. Assuming you're right, what types of option strategies should you undertake? (*Note:* You can buy or sell options on oil-company stocks or on the price of future deliveries of crude oil, natural gas, fuel oil, etc.)

CHALLENGE

29. Figure 20.14 below shows some complicated position diagrams. Work out the combination of stocks, bonds, and options that produces each of these positions.

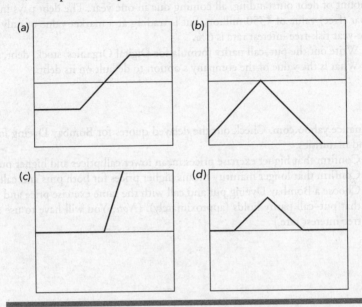

FIGURE 20.14

Some complicated position diagrams. See Problem 29.

30. Some years ago the Australian firm Bond Corporation sold a share in some land that it owned near Rome for $110 million and as a result boosted its annual earnings by $74 million. A television program subsequently revealed that the buyer was given a put option to sell its share in the land back to Bond for $110 million and that Bond had paid $20 million for a call option to repurchase the share in the land for the same price.
    a. What happens if the land is worth more than $110 million when the options expire? What if it is worth less than $110 million?
    b. Use position diagrams to show the net effect of the land sale and the option transactions.
    c. Assume a one-year maturity on the options. Can you deduce the interest rate?
    d. The television program argued that it was misleading to record a profit on the sale of land. What do you think?

31. Three six-month call options are traded on Hogswill stock:

Exercise Price	Call Option Price
$ 90	$ 5
100	11
110	15

How would you make money by trading in Hogswill options? (*Hint:* Draw a graph with the option price on the vertical axis and the ratio of stock price to exercise price on the horizontal axis. Plot the three Hogswill options on your graph. Does this fit with what you know about how option prices should vary with the ratio of stock price to exercise price?) Now look in the newspaper at options with the same maturity but different exercise prices. Can you find any money-making opportunities?

32. Digital Organics has 10 million outstanding shares trading at ₹25 per share. It also has a large amount of debt outstanding, all coming due in one year. The debt pays interest at 8%. It has a par (face) value of ₹350 million, but is trading at a market value of only ₹280 million. The one-year risk-free interest rate is 6%.
   a. Write out the put–call parity formula for Digital Organics' stock, debt, and assets.
   b. What is the value of the company's option to default on its debt?

Go to **finance.yahoo.com**. Check out the delayed quotes for Bombay Dyeing for different exercise prices and maturities.
   a. Confirm that higher exercise prices mean lower call prices and higher put prices.
   b. Confirm that longer maturity means higher prices for both puts and calls.
   c. Choose a Bombay Dyeing put and call with the same exercise price and maturity. Confirm that put–call parity holds (approximately). (*Note:* You will have to use an up-to-date risk-free interest rate.)

21

CHAPTER

VALUING OPTIONS

In the last chapter we introduced you to call and put options. Call options give the owner the right to buy an asset at a specified exercise price; put options give the right to sell. We also took the first step toward understanding how options are valued. The value of a call option depends on five variables:

1. The higher the price of the asset, the more valuable an option to buy it.
2. The lower the price that you must pay to exercise the call, the more valuable the option.
3. You do not need to pay the exercise price until the option expires. This delay is most valuable when the interest rate is high.
4. If the stock price is below the exercise price at maturity, the call is valueless regardless of whether the price is ₹1 below or ₹100 below. However, for every dollar that the stock price rises above the exercise price, the option holder gains an additional dollar. Thus, the value of the call option increases with the volatility of the stock price.
5. Finally, a long-term option is more valuable than a short-term option. A distant maturity delays the point at which the holder needs to pay the exercise price and increases the chance of a large jump in the stock price before the option matures.

In this chapter we show how these variables can be combined into an exact option-valuation model—a formula we can plug numbers into to get a definite answer. We first describe a simple way to value options, known as the binomial model. We then introduce the Black–Scholes formula for valuing options. Finally, we provide a checklist showing how these two methods can be used to solve a number of practical option problems.

The most efficient way to value most options is to use a computer. But in this chapter we will work through some simple examples by hand. We do so because unless you understand the basic principles behind option valuation, you are likely to make mistakes in setting up an option problem and you won't know how to interpret the computer's answer and explain it to others.

In the last chapter we looked at the put and call options on Bombay Dyeing stock. In this chapter we stick with that example and show you how to value the Bombay Dyeing options. But remember *why* you need to understand option valuation. It is not to make a quick buck trading on an options exchange. It is because many capital budgeting and financing decisions have options embedded in them. We discuss a variety of these options in subsequent chapters.

21-1 A SIMPLE OPTION-VALUATION MODEL

Why Discounted Cash Flow Won't Work for Options

For many years economists searched for a practical formula to value options until Fischer Black and Myron Scholes finally hit upon the solution. Later we will show you what they found, but first we should explain why the search was so difficult.

Our standard procedure for valuing an asset is to (1) figure out expected cash flows and (2) discount them at the opportunity cost of capital. Unfortunately, this is not practical for options. The first step is messy but feasible, but finding *the* opportunity cost of capital is impossible, because the risk of an option changes every time the stock price moves.

When you buy a call, you are taking a position in the stock but putting up less of your own money than if you had bought the stock directly. Thus, an option is always riskier than the underlying stock. It has a higher beta and a higher standard deviation of return.

How much riskier the option is depends on the stock price relative to the exercise price. A call option that is in the money (stock price greater than exercise price) is safer than one that is out of the money (stock price less than exercise price). Thus a stock price increase raises the option's price *and* reduces its risk. When the stock price falls, the option's price falls *and* its risk increases. That is why the expected rate of return investors demand from an option changes day by day, or hour by hour, every time the stock price moves.

We repeat the general rule: The higher the stock price is relative to the exercise price, the safer is the call option, although the option is always riskier than the stock. The option's risk changes every time the stock price changes.

Constructing Option Equivalents from Common Stocks and Borrowing

If you've digested what we've said so far, you can appreciate why options are hard to value by standard discounted-cash-flow formulas and why a rigorous option-valuation technique eluded economists for many years. The breakthrough came when Black and Scholes exclaimed, "Eureka! We have found it![1] The trick is to set up an *option equivalent* by combining common stock investment and borrowing. The net cost of buying the option equivalent must equal the value of the option."

We'll show you how this works with a simple numerical example. We'll travel back to November 2011 and consider a six-month call option on Bombay Dyeing stock with an exercise price of ₹420. We'll pick a day when Bombay Dyeing stock was also trading at ₹420, so that this option is *at the money*. The short-term, risk-free interest rate was 9% per year, or about 1.5% for two months.

To keep the example as simple as possible, we assume that Bombay Dyeing stock can do only two things over the option's six-month life: either the price will fall by a quarter to ₹322.5 or rise by one-third to ₹573.33.

---

[1] We do not know whether Black and Scholes, like Archimedes, were sitting in bathtubs at the time.

If Bombay Dyeing's stock price falls to ₹350, the call option will be worthless, but if the price rises to ₹504, the option will be worth $504 - 420 = ₹84$. The possible payoffs to the option are therefore:

	Stock Price = ₹350	Stock Price = ₹504
1 call option	₹0	₹84

Now compare these payoffs with what you would get if you bought 4/7 Bombay Dyeing shares and borrowed ₹188.09 from the bank:[2]

	Stock Price = ₹350	Stock Price = ₹504
6/11 shares	₹190.90	₹274.90
Repayment of loan + interest	−190.90	−190.90
Total payoff	₹0	₹84.00

Notice that the payoffs from the levered investment in the stock are identical to the payoffs from the call option. Therefore, the law of one price tells us that both investments must have the same value:

$$\text{Value of call} = \text{value of (6/11) shares} - ₹188.09 \text{ bank loan}$$
$$= 420 \times (6/11) - 188.09 = ₹41.00$$

Presto! You've valued a call option.

To value the Bombay Dyeing option, we borrowed money and bought stock in such a way that we exactly replicated the payoff from a call option. This is called a **replicating portfolio.** The number of shares needed to replicate one call is called the **hedge ratio** or **option delta.** In our Bombay Dyeing example one call is replicated by a levered position in 6/11 shares. The option delta is, therefore, 6/11, or about .545.

How did we know that Bombay Dyeing's call option was equivalent to a levered position in 6/11 shares? We used a simple formula that says:

$$\text{Option delta} = \frac{\text{spread of possible option prices}}{\text{spread of possible share prices}} = \frac{84 - 0}{504 - 350} = \frac{84}{154} = \frac{6}{11}$$

You have learned not only to value a simple option but also that you can replicate an investment in the option by a levered investment in the underlying asset. Thus, if you can't buy or sell a call option on an asset, you can create a homemade option by a replicating strategy—that is, you buy or sell delta shares and borrow or lend the balance.

Risk-Neutral Valuation Notice why the Bombay Dyeing call option should sell for ₹41. If the option price is higher than ₹41, you could make a certain profit by buying 6/11 shares of stock, selling a call option, and borrowing ₹188.09. Similarly, if the option price is less than ₹41, you could make an equally certain profit by selling 6/11 shares, buying a call, and lending the balance. In either case there would be an arbitrage opportunity.[3]

If there's a possible arbitrage profit, everyone scurries to take advantage of it. So when we said that the option price had to be ₹41 or there would be an arbitrage opportunity, we did not have to know

---

[2] The amount that you need to borrow from the bank is simply the present value of the difference between the payoffs from the option and the payoffs from 6/11 shares. In our example, amount borrowed = $((6/11) \times ₹350.00 - 0)/1.015 = ((6/11) \times 504 - 84)/1.015 = ₹188.09$.

[3] Of course, you don't get seriously rich by dealing in 6/11 shares. But if you multiply each of our transactions by a million, it begins to look like real money.

anything about investor attitudes to risk. The option price cannot depend on whether investors detest risk or do not care a jot.

This suggests an alternative way to value the option. We can *pretend* that all investors are *indifferent* about risk, work out the expected future value of the option in such a world, and discount it back at the risk-free interest rate to give the current value. Let us check that this method gives the same answer.

If investors are indifferent to risk, the expected return on the stock must be equal to the risk-free rate of interest:

Expected return on Bombay Dyeing stock = 1.5% per two months

We know that Bombay Dyeing stock can either rise by 20% to ₹504 or fall by 16.67% to ₹350. We can, therefore, calculate the probability of a price rise in our hypothetical risk-neutral world:

Expected return = [probability of rise × 20]
$$+ [(1 - \text{probability of rise}) \times (-16.67)]$$
$$= 1.5\%$$

Therefore,

Probability of rise = .4955, or 49.55%

Notice that this is *not* the *true* probability that Bombay Dyeing stock will rise. Since investors dislike risk, they will almost surely require a higher expected return than the risk-free interest rate from Bombay Dyeing stock. Therefore the true probability is greater than .4955.

The general formula for calculating the risk-neutral probability of a rise in value is:

$$p = \frac{\text{interest rate} - \text{downside change}}{\text{upside change} - \text{downside change}}$$

In the case of Bombay Dyeing stock:

$$p = \frac{.015 - (-.1667)}{.2 - (-.1667)} = .4955$$

We know that if the stock price rises, the call option will be worth ₹84; if it falls, the call will be worth nothing. Therefore, if investors are risk-neutral, the expected value of the call option is:

[Probability of rise × 84] + [(1 - probability of rise) × 0]
$$= (.4955 \times 84) + (.5045 \times 0)$$
$$= ₹41.62$$

And the *current* value of the call is:

$$\frac{\text{Expected future value}}{1 + \text{interest rate}} = \frac{41.62}{1.015} = ₹41.00$$

Exactly the same answer that we got earlier!

We now have two ways to calculate the value of an option:

1. Find the combination of stock and loan that replicates an investment in the option. Since the two strategies give identical payoffs in the future, they must sell for the same price today.

2. Pretend that investors do not care about risk, so that the expected return on the stock is equal to the interest rate. Calculate the expected future value of the option in this hypothetical *risk-neutral* world and discount it at the risk-free interest rate. This idea may seem familiar to you. In Chapter 9 we showed how you can value an investment either by discounting the expected cash flows at a risk-adjusted discount rate or by adjusting the expected cash flows for risk and then discounting these *certainty-equivalent* flows at the risk-free interest rate. We have just used this second method to value the Bombay Dyeing option. The certainty-equivalent cash flows on the stock and option are the cash flows that would be expected in a risk-neutral world.

Valuing the Bombay Dyeing Put Option

Valuing the Bombay Dyeing call option may well have seemed like pulling a rabbit out of a hat. To give you a second chance to watch how it is done, we will use the same method to value another option—this time, the two-month Bombay Dyeing put option with a ₹420 strike price.[4] We continue to assume that the stock price will either rise to ₹504 or fall to ₹350.

If Bombay Dyeing's stock price rises to ₹504, the option to sell for ₹420 will be worthless. If the price falls to ₹350, the put option will be worth ₹420 − 350 = ₹70. Thus the payoffs to the put are:

	Stock Price = ₹350	Stock Price = ₹504.00
1 put option	₹70	₹0

We start by calculating the option delta using the formula that we presented above:[5]

$$\text{Option delta} = \frac{\text{spread of possible option prices}}{\text{spread of possible stock prices}} = \frac{0 - 70}{504 - 350} = \frac{-70}{154}$$

$$= -\frac{5}{11}$$

Notice that the delta of a put option is always negative; that is, you need to *sell* delta shares of stock to replicate the put. In the case of the Bombay Dyeing stock put you can replicate the option payoffs by *selling* 5/11 Bombay Dyeing stock and *lending* ₹225.71. Since you have sold the share short, you will need to lay out money at the end of six months to buy it back, but you will have money coming in from the loan. Your net payoffs are exactly the same as the payoffs you would get if you bought the put option:

	Stock Price = ₹350	Stock Price = ₹504
Sale of 5/11 shares	− ₹159.09	− ₹229.09
Repayment of loan + interest	+229.09	+229.09
Total payoff	₹70	₹ 0

Since the two investments have the same payoffs, they must have the same value:

$$\text{Value of put} = - (5/11)\ \text{shares} + ₹225.71\ \text{bank loan}$$

$$= - (5/11) \times 420 + ₹225.71 = ₹34.80$$

---

[4] When valuing *American* put options, you need to recognize the possibility that it will pay to exercise early. We discuss this complication later in the chapter, but it is unimportant for valuing the Bombay Dyeing put and we ignore it here.

[5] The delta of a put option is always equal to the delta of a call option with the same exercise price minus one. In our example, delta of put = (6/11) − 1 = − 5/11.

Valuing the Put Option by the Risk-Neutral Method Valuing the Bombay Dyeing put option with the risk-neutral method is a cinch. We already know that the probability of a rise in the stock price is .4955. Therefore the expected value of the put option in a risk-neutral world is:

$$[\text{Probability of rise} \times 0] + [(1 - \text{probability of rise}) \times 70]$$
$$= (.4955 \times 0) + (.5045 \times 70)$$
$$= ₹35.31$$

And therefore the *current* value of the put is:

$$\frac{\text{Expected future value}}{1 + \text{interest rate}} = \frac{35.31}{1.015} = ₹34.80$$

The Relationship between Call and Put Prices We pointed out earlier that for European options there is a simple relationship between the value of the call and that of the put.[6]

$$\text{Value of put} = \text{value of call} + \text{present value of exercise price} - \text{share price}$$

Since we had already calculated the value of the Bombay Dyeing call, we could also have used this relationship to find the value of the put:

$$\text{Value of put} = 41 + \frac{420}{1.015} - 420 = ₹34.80$$

Everything checks.

21-2 THE BINOMIAL METHOD FOR VALUING OPTIONS

The essential trick in pricing any option is to set up a package of investments in the stock and the loan that will exactly replicate the payoffs from the option. If we can price the stock and the loan, then we can also price the option. Equivalently, we can pretend that investors are risk-neutral, calculate the expected payoff on the option in this fictitious risk-neutral world, and discount by the rate of interest to find the option's present value.

These *concepts* are completely general, but there are several ways to find the replicating package of investments. The example in the last section used a simplified version of what is known as the **binomial method.** The method starts by reducing the possible changes in next period's stock price to two, an "up" move and a "down" move. This assumption that there are just two possible prices for Bombay Dyeing stock at the end of three months is clearly fanciful.

We could make the Bombay Dyeing problem a trifle more realistic by assuming that there are two possible price changes in each one-month period. This would give a wider variety of two-month prices. And there is no reason to stop at one-month periods. We could go on to take shorter and shorter intervals, with each interval showing two possible changes in Bombay Dyeing's stock price and giving an even wider selection of two-month prices.

This is illustrated in Figure 21.1. The two left hand diagram show our starting assumption: just two possible prices at the end of six months. Moving down, you can see what happens when there are two possible price changes every month. This gives three possible stock prices when the option matures. In Figure 21.1(*c*) we have gone on to divide the two-month period into 26 shorter periods

---

[6] *Reminder:* This formula applies only when the two options have the same exercise price and exercise date.

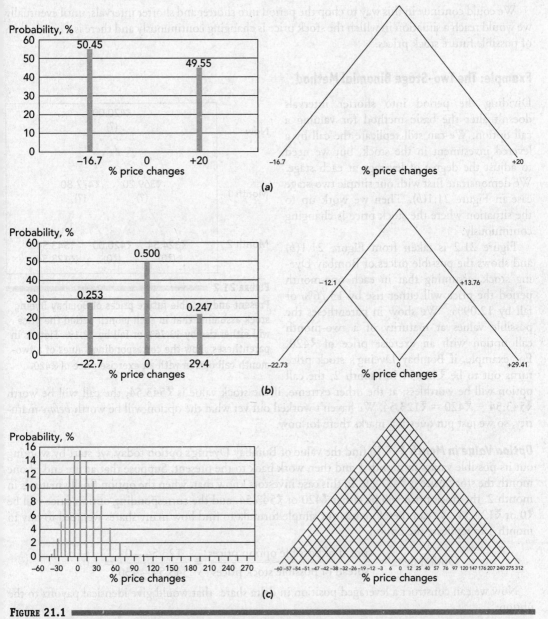

FIGURE 21.1

This figure shows the possible two-month price changes for Bombay Dyeing stock assuming that the stock makes a single up or down move each two months (Fig. 21.1[a]), 2 moves, one every month (Fig. 21.1[b]), or 26 moves, one every week (Fig. 21.1[c]). Beside each tree we show a histogram of the possible two-month price changes, assuming investors are risk-neutral.

(around 2.3 days to be exact), in each of which the price can make one of two small moves. The distribution of prices at the end of two months is now looking much more realistic.

We could continue in this way to chop the period into shorter and shorter intervals, until eventually we would reach a situation in which the stock price is changing continuously and there is a continuum of possible future stock prices.

Example: The Two-Stage Binomial Method

Dividing the period into shorter intervals doesn't alter the basic method for valuing a call option. We can still replicate the call by a levered investment in the stock, but we need to adjust the degree of leverage at each stage. We demonstrate first with our simple two-stage case in Figure 21.1(*b*). Then we work up to the situation where the stock price is changing continuously.

Figure 21.2 is taken from Figure 21.1(*b*) and shows the possible prices of Bombay Dyeing stock, assuming that in each one-month period the price will either rise by 13.76% or fall by 12.09%.[7] We show in parentheses the possible values at maturity of a two-month call option with an exercise price of ₹420. For example, if Bombay Dyeing's stock price turns out to be ₹324.54 in month 2, the call

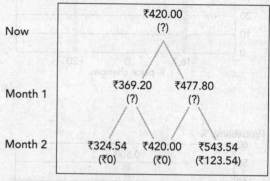

FIGURE 21.2

Present and possible future prices of Bombay Dyeing stock assuming that in each month period the price will either rise by 13.76% or fall by 12.1%. Figures in parentheses show the corresponding values of a two-month call option with an exercise price of ₹420.

option will be worthless; at the other extreme, if the stock value is ₹543.54, the call will be worth ₹543.54 − ₹420 = ₹123.54. We haven't worked out yet what the option will be worth *before* maturity, so we just put question marks there for now.

Option Value in Month 1   To find the value of Bombay Dyeing's option today, we start by working out its possible values in month 1 and then work back to the present. Suppose that at the end of one month the stock price is ₹477.80. In this case investors know that, when the option finally matures in month 2, the stock price will be either ₹420 or ₹543.54, and the corresponding option price will be ₹0 or ₹123.54. We can therefore use our simple formula to find how many shares we need to buy in month 1 to replicate the option:

$$\text{Option delta} = \frac{\text{spread of possible option prices}}{\text{spread of possible stock prices}} = \frac{123.54 - 0}{543.54 - 430} = 1.0$$

Now we can construct a leveraged position in delta shares that would give identical payoffs to the option:

	Month 6 Stock Price = ₹420	Month 2 Stock Price = ₹543.54
Buy 1 shares	₹420	₹543.54
Borrow PV(420)	−420	−420
Total payoff	₹0	₹123.54

---

[7] We explain shortly why we picked these figures.

Since this portfolio provides identical payoffs to the option, we know that the value of the option in month 1 must be equal to the price of one share less the ₹420 loan discounted for three months at 9% per year, about .75% for one month:

$$\text{Value of call in month 1} = ₹477.80 - ₹420/1.0075 = ₹60.92$$

Therefore, if the share price rises in the first three months, the option will be worth ₹60.92. But what if the share price falls to ₹369.20? In that case the most that you can hope for is that the share price will recover to ₹420. Therefore the option is bound to be worthless when it matures and must be worthless at month 1.

Option Value Today We can now get rid of two of the question marks in Figure 21.2. Figure 21.3 shows that if the stock price in month 1 is ₹477.80, the option value is ₹60.92 and, if the stock price is ₹369.20, the option value is zero. It only remains to work back to the option value today.

We again begin by calculating the option delta:

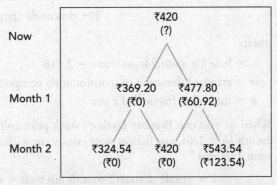

Figure 21.3

Present and possible future prices of Bombay Dyeing stock. Figures in parentheses show the corresponding values of a six-month call option with an exercise price of ₹420.

$$\text{Option delta} = \frac{\text{spread of possible option prices}}{\text{spread of possible stock prices}} = \frac{60.92 - 0}{477.80 - 369.20} = .561$$

We can now find the leveraged position in delta shares that would give identical payoffs to the option:

	Month 1 Stock Price = ₹420	Month 1 Stock Price = ₹543.54
Buy 0.561 shares	₹207.11	₹268.03
Borrow PV(207.11)	−207.11	−207.11
Total payoff	₹0	₹60.92

The value of the Bombay Dyeing option today is equal to the value of this leveraged position:

$$\text{PV option} = 0.561 \times \text{Share price} - \text{PV}(₹207.11)$$
$$= 0.561 \times ₹420 - ₹207.11/1.0075 = ₹30.04$$

The General Binomial Method

Moving to two steps when valuing the Bombay Dyeing call probably added extra realism. But there is no reason to stop there. We could go on, as in Figure 21.1, to chop the period into smaller and smaller intervals. We could still use the binomial method to work back from the final date to the present. Of course, it would be tedious to do the calculations by hand, but simple to do so with a computer.

Since a stock can usually take on an almost limitless number of future values, the binomial method gives a more realistic and accurate measure of the option's value if we work with a large number of subperiods. But that raises an important question. How do we pick sensible figures for the up and down changes in value? For example, why did we pick figures of $+13.76\%$ and -12.1% when we revalued Bombay Dyeing's option with two subperiods? Fortunately, there is a neat little formula that relates the up and down changes to the standard deviation of stock returns:

$$1 + \text{upside change} = u = e^{\sigma\sqrt{h}}$$

$$1 + \text{downside change} = d = 1/u$$

where,

e = base for natural logarithms = 2.718

σ = standard deviation of (continuously compounded) stock returns

h = interval as fraction of a year

When we said that Bombay Dyeing's stock price could either rise by 20% or fall by 16.17% over two month ($h = 1/6$), our figures were consistent with a figure of 44.66% for the standard deviation of annual returns:[8]

$$1 + \text{upside change(2-month interval)} = u = e^{.4466\sqrt{1/6}} = 1.2$$

$$1 + \text{downside change} = d = 1/u = 1/1.2 = 0.833$$

To work out the equivalent upside and downside changes when we divide the period into two one-month intervals ($h = 1/12$), we use the same formula:

$$1 + \text{upside change(1-month interval)} = u = e^{.4466\sqrt{1/12}} = 1.1376$$

$$1 + \text{downside change} = d = 1/u = 1/1.1376 = 0.8790$$

The center columns in Table 21.1 show the equivalent up and down moves in the value of the firm if we chop the period into six monthly or 26 weekly periods, and the final column shows the effect on the estimated option value.

TABLE 21.1 As the number of steps is increased, you must adjust the range of possible changes in the value of the asset to keep the same standard deviation. But you will get increasingly close to the Black–Scholes value of the Bombay Dyeing call option.

Number of Steps	Change per Interval (%)		Estimated Option Value
	Upside	Downside	
1	+20	−16.67	₹41.02
2	+13.76	−12.1	30.05
6	+7.73	−7.17	32.28
26	+3.64	−3.51	33.22
		Black–Scholes value =	33.51

(*Note:* The standard deviation is σ = .4466)

---

[8] To find the standard deviation given u, we turn the formula around:

$$\sigma = \log(u)/\sqrt{h}$$

where log = natural logarithm. In our example:

$$\sigma = \ln(1.2)/\sqrt{1/6} = 0.4466$$

The Binomial Method and Decision Trees

Calculating option values by the binomial method is basically a process of solving decision trees. You start at some future date and work back through the tree to the present. Eventually the possible cash flows generated by future events and actions are folded back to a present value.

Is the binomial method *merely* another application of decision trees, a tool of analysis that you learned about in Chapter 10? The answer is no, for at least two reasons. First, option pricing theory is absolutely essential for discounting within decision trees. Discounting expected cash flows doesn't work within decision trees for the same reason that it doesn't work for puts and calls. As we pointed out in Section 21-1, there is no single, constant discount rate for options because the risk of the option changes as time and the price of the underlying asset change. There is no single discount rate inside a decision tree, because if the tree contains meaningful future decisions, it also contains options. The market value of the future cash flows described by the decision tree has to be calculated by option pricing methods.

Second, option theory gives a simple, powerful framework for describing complex decision trees. For example, suppose that you have the option to abandon an investment. The complete decision tree would overflow the largest classroom chalkboard. But now that you know about options, the opportunity to abandon can be summarized as "an American put." Of course, not all real problems have such easy option analogies, but we can often approximate complex decision trees by some simple package of assets and options. A custom decision tree may get closer to reality, but the time and expense may not be worth it. Most men buy their suits off the rack even though a custom-made Armani suit would fit better and look nicer.

21-3 THE BLACK–SCHOLES FORMULA

Look back at Figure 21.1, which showed what happens to the distribution of possible Bombay Dyeing stock price changes as we divide the option's life into a larger and larger number of increasingly small subperiods. You can see that the distribution of price changes becomes increasingly smooth.

If we continued to chop up the option's life in this way, we would eventually reach the situation shown in Figure 21.4, where there is a continuum of possible stock price changes at maturity. Figure 21.4 is an example of a lognormal distribution. The lognormal distribution is often used to summarize the probability of different stock price changes.[9] It has a number of good commonsense features. For example, it recognizes the fact that the stock price can never fall by more than 100%, but that there is some, perhaps small, chance that it could rise by much more than 100%.

Subdividing the option life into indefinitely small slices does not affect the principle of option valuation. We could still replicate the call option by a levered investment in the stock, but we would need to adjust the degree of leverage continuously as time went by. Calculating option value when there is an infinite number of subperiods may sound a hopeless task. Fortunately, Black and Scholes derived a formula that does the trick.[10] It is an unpleasant-looking formula, but on closer acquaintance you will find it exceptionally elegant and useful. The formula is:

---

[9] When we first looked at the distribution of stock price changes in Chapter 8, we depicted these changes as normally distributed. We pointed out at the time that this is an acceptable approximation for very short intervals, but the distribution of changes over longer intervals is better approximated by the lognormal.

[10] The pioneering articles on options are F. Black and M. Scholes, "The Pricing of Options and Corporate Liabilities," *Journal of Political Economy* 81 (May–June 1973), pp. 637–654; and R. C. Merton, "Theory of Rational Option Pricing," *Bell Journal of Economics and Management Science* 4 (Spring 1973), pp. 141–183.

$$\text{Value of call option} = [\text{delta} \times \text{share price}] - [\text{bank loan}]$$

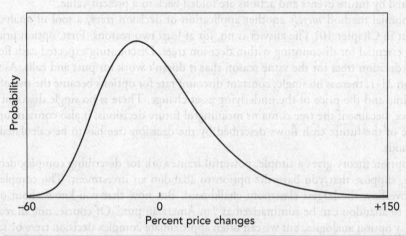

$$[N(d_1) \times P] - [N(d_2) \times \text{PV(EX)}]$$

FIGURE 21.4

As the option's life is divided into more and more subperiods, the distribution of possible stock price changes approaches a lognormal distribution.

where,

$$d_1 = \frac{\log[P/\text{PV(EX)}]}{\sigma\sqrt{t}} + \frac{\sigma\sqrt{t}}{2}$$

$$d_2 = d_1 - \sigma\sqrt{t}$$

$N(d)$ = cumulative normal probability density function[11]

EX = exercise price of option; PV(EX) is calculated by discounting at the risk-free interest rate r_f

t = number of periods to exercise date

P = price of stock now

σ = standard deviation per period of (continuously compounded) rate of return on stock

Notice that the value of the call in the Black–Scholes formula has the same properties that we identified earlier. It increases with the level of the stock price P and decreases with the present value of the exercise price PV(EX), which in turn depends on the interest rate and time to maturity. It also increases with the time to maturity and the stock's variability ($\sigma\sqrt{t}$).

To derive their formula Black and Scholes assumed that there is a continuum of stock prices, and therefore to replicate an option investors must continuously adjust their holding in the stock.[12] Of course this is not literally possible, but even so the formula performs remarkably well in the real world,

---

[11] That is, $N(d)$ is the probability that a normally distributed random variable x̃ will be less than or equal to d. $N(d_1)$ in the Black–Scholes formula is the option delta. Thus the formula tells us that the value of a call is equal to an investment of $N(d_1)$ in the common stock less borrowing of $N(d_2) \times \text{PV(EX)}$.

[12] The important assumptions of the Black-Scholes formula are that (a) the price of the underlying asset follows a lognormal random walk, (b) investors can adjust their hedge continuously and costlessly, (c) the risk-free rate is known, and (d) the underlying asset does not pay dividends.

where stocks trade only intermittently and prices jump from one level to another. The Black–Scholes model has also proved very flexible; it can be adapted to value options on a variety of assets such as foreign currencies, bonds, and commodities. It is not surprising, therefore, that it has been extremely influential and has become the standard model for valuing options. Every day dealers on the options exchanges use this formula to make huge trades. These dealers are not for the most part trained in the formula's mathematical derivation; they just use a computer or a specially programmed calculator to find the value of the option.

Using the Black–Scholes Formula

The Black–Scholes formula may look difficult, but it is very straightforward to apply. Let us practice using it to value the Bombay Dyeing call.

Here are the data that you need:

- Price of stock now $= P = 420$
- Exercise price $=$ EX $= 420$
- Standard deviation of continuously compounded annual returns $= \sigma = .4466$
- Years to maturity $= t = 1/6$
- Interest rate per annum $= r_f = 9\%$ (about 1.5% for two months).[13]

Remember that the Black–Scholes formula for the value of a call is

$$[N(d_1) \times P] - [N(d_2) \times PV(EX)]$$

where,

$$d_1 = \log[P/PV(EX)]/\sigma\sqrt{t} + \sigma\sqrt{t}/2$$
$$d_2 = d_1 - \sigma\sqrt{t}$$
$$N(d) = \text{cumulative normal probability function}$$

There are three steps to using the formula to value the Bombay Dyeing call:

Step 1 Calculate d_1 and d_2. This is just a matter of plugging numbers into the formula (noting that "log" means *natural* log):

$$d_1 = \log[P/PV(EX)]/\sigma\sqrt{t} + \sigma\sqrt{t}/2$$
$$= \log[420/(420/1.015)]/(.4466 \times \sqrt{1/6}) + .4466 \times \sqrt{1/6}$$
$$= .1734$$
$$d_2 = d_1 - \sigma\sqrt{t} = .1734 - .4466 \times \sqrt{1/6} = -.0089$$

Step 2 Find $N(d_1)$ and $N(d_2)$. $N(d_1)$ is the probability that a normally distributed variable will be less than d_1 standard deviations above the mean. If d_1 is large, $N(d_1)$ is close to 1.0 (i.e., you can be

---

[13] More precisely, an annually compounded interest rate of 9% is equivalent to a two-month rate of $1.09^{1/6} - 1 = .014467$, or 1.4467%. Thus PV(EX) $= 420/1.014467 = ₹414.01$.

While valuing options, it is more common to use continuously compounded rates (see Section 2-4). If the annually compounded rate is 9%, the equivalent continuously compounded rate is 8.6178%. (The natural log of 1.09 is .086178. Using continuous compounding, PV(EX) $= 420 \times e^{-(1/6) \times .086178} = ₹414.01$.

If both methods give the same answer, why do we bother to mention the subject here? It is simply because most computer programs for valuing options call for a continuously compounded rate. If you enter an annually compounded rate by mistake, the error will usually be small, but you can waste a lot of time trying to trace it.

almost certain that the variable will be less than d_1 standard deviations above the mean). If d_1 is zero, $N(d_1)$ is .5 (i.e., there is a 50% chance that a normally distributed variable will be below the average).

The simplest way to find $N(d_1)$ is to use the Excel function NORMSDIST. For example, if you enter NORMSDIST(.1734) into an Excel spreadsheet, you will see that there is a .5688 probability that a normally distributed variable will be less than .1734 standard deviations above the mean. Alternatively, you can use a set of normal probability tables such as the present value tables (Appendix Table 6) located on the book Web site at **www.mhhe.com/bmam10e**.

Again you can use the Excel function to find $N(d_2)$. If you enter NORMSDIST(−.0089) into an Excel spreadsheet, you should get the answer .4964. In other words, there is a probability of .4964 that a normally distributed variable will be less than .0089 standard deviations *below* the mean. Alternatively, if you use Appendix Table 6 (again located at **www.mhhe.com/bmam10e** under the Present Value Tables heading), you need to look up the value for +.0921 and subtract it from 1.0:

$$N(d_2) = N(-.0089) = 1 - N(+.0089)$$
$$= 1 - .5036 = .4964$$

Step 3 Plug these numbers into the Black–Scholes formula. You can now calculate the value of the Bombay Dyeing call:

$$[\text{Delta} \times \text{price}] - [\text{bank loan}]$$
$$= [N(d_1) \times P] - [N(d_2) \times \text{PV(EX)}]$$
$$= [.5688 \times 420] - [.4964 \times 420/1.015] = 238.9 - 205.4 = 33.5$$

In other words, you can replicate the Bombay Dyeing call option by investing ₹238.90 in the company's stock and borrowing ₹205.40. Subsequently, as time passes and the stock price changes, you may need to borrow a little more to invest in the stock or you may need to sell some of your stock to reduce your borrowing.

The Risk of an Option

How risky is the Bombay Dyeing call option? We have seen that you can exactly replicate a call by a combination of risk-free borrowing and an investment in the stock. So the risk of the option must be the same as the risk of this replicating portfolio. We know that the beta of any portfolio is simply a weighted average of the betas of the separate holdings. So the risk of the option is just a weighted average of the betas of the investments in the loan and the stock.

On past evidence the beta of Bombay Dyeing stock is $\beta_{stock} = 1.86$; the beta of a risk-free loan is $\beta_{loan} = 0$. You are investing ₹238.90 in the stock and −₹205.40 in the loan. (Notice that the investment in the loan is negative—you are *borrowing* money.) Therefore the beta of the option is $\beta_{option} = (-205.40 \times 0 + 238.90 \times 1.86)/(-205.40 + 238.90) = 13.26$. Notice that, because a call option is equivalent to a levered position in the stock, it is always riskier than the stock itself. In Bombay Dyeing's case the option is nearly five times as risky as the stock. As time passes and the price of Bombay Dyeing stock changes, the risk of the option will also change.

Some More Practice Suppose you repeat the calculations for the Bombay Dyeing call for a wide range of stock prices. The result is shown in Figure 21.5. You can see that the option values lie along an upward-sloping curve that starts its travels in the bottom left-hand corner of the diagram. As the stock price increases, the option value rises and gradually becomes parallel to the lower bound for the option value. This is exactly the shape we deduced in Chapter 20 (see Figure 20.10).

The height of this curve of course depends on risk and time to maturity. For example, if the risk of Bombay Dyeing stock had suddenly decreased, the curve shown in Figure 21.5 would drop at every possible stock price.

The Black–Scholes Formula and the Binomial Method

Look back at Table 21.1 where we used the binomial method to calculate the value of the Bombay Dyeing call. Notice that, as the number of intervals is increased, the values that you obtain from the binomial method begin to snuggle up to the Black–Scholes value of ₹33.51.

The Black–Scholes formula recognizes a continuum of possible outcomes. This is usually more realistic than the limited number of outcomes assumed

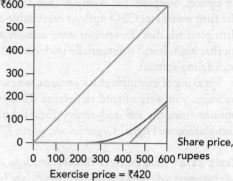

Values of Bombay Dyeing call option, rupees

Exercise price = ₹420

FIGURE 21.5

The curved line shows how the value of the Bombay Dyeing call option changes as the price of Bombay Dyeing stock changes.

Visit us at www.mhhe.com/bmam10e

in the binomial method. The formula is also more accurate and quicker to use than the binomial method. So why use the binomial method at all? The answer is that there are many circumstances in which you cannot use the Black–Scholes formula but the binomial method will still give you a good measure of the option's value. We will look at several such cases in Section 21-5.

21-4 BLACK–SCHOLES IN ACTION

To illustrate the principles of option valuation, we focused on the example of Bombay Dyeing's options. But financial managers turn to the Black–Scholes model to estimate the value of a variety of different options. Here are four examples.

Executive Stock Options

The 2007 winner in *Forbes*'s annual list of the most highly paid executives was Larry Ellison, the CEO of Oracle Corporation. His salary was just $1 million, but he also pocketed another $182 million from the exercise of stock options.

The example highlights that executive stock options are often an important part of compensation. For many years companies were able to avoid reporting the cost of these options in their annual statements. However, they must now treat options as an expense just like salaries and wages, so they need to estimate the value of all new options that they have granted. For example, Oracle's financial statements show that in fiscal 2008 the company issued a total of 69 million options with an average life of five years and an exercise price of $20.49. Oracle calculated that the average value of these options was $7.53. How did it come up with this figure? It just used the Black–Scholes model assuming a standard deviation of 29% and an interest rate of 4.6%.[14]

---

[14] Many of the recipients of these options may not have agreed with Oracle's valuation. First, the options were less valuable to their owners if they created substantial undiversifiable risk. Second, if the holders planned to quit the company in the next few years, they were liable to forfeit the options. For a discussion of these issues see J. I. Bulow and J. B. Shoven, "Accounting for Stock Options," *Journal of Economic Perspectives* 19 (Fall 2005), pp. 115–134.

Some companies have disguised how much their management is paid by backdating the grant of an option. Suppose, for example, that a firm's stock price has risen from $20 to $40. At that point the firm awards its CEO options exercisable at $20. That is generous but not illegal. However, if the firm pretends that the options were *actually* awarded when the stock price was $20 and values them on that basis, it will substantially understate the CEO's compensation.[15] The nearby box discusses the backdating scandal.

Speaking of executive stock options, we can now use the Black–Scholes formula to value the option packages you were offered in Section 20-3 (see Table 20.3). Table 21.2 calculates the value of the options from the safe-and-stodgy Establishment Industries at ₹5.26 each. The options from risky-and-glamorous Digital Organics are worth ₹7.40 each. Congratulations.

TABLE 21.2 Using the Black–Scholes formula to value the executive stock options for Establishment Industries and Digital Organics (see Table 20.3).

Visit us at
www.mhhe.com/bmam10e

	Establishment Industries	Digital Organics
Stock price (P)	₹22	₹22
Exercise price (EX)	₹25	₹25
Interest rate (r_f)	.04	.04
Maturity in years (t)	5	5
Standard deviation (σ)	.24	.36
$d_1 = \log[P/PV(EX)]/\sigma\sqrt{t} + \sigma\sqrt{t}/2$	0.3955	0.4873
$d_2 = d_1 - \sigma\sqrt{t}$	−0.1411	−0.3177
Call value = $[N(d_1) \times P] - [N(d_2) \times PV(EX)]$	₹5.26	₹7.40

Warrants

When Owens Corning emerged from bankruptcy in 2006, the debtholders became the sole owners of the company. But the old stockholders were not left entirely empty handed. They were given warrants to buy the new common stock at any point in the next seven years for $45.25 a share. Because the stock in the restructured firm was worth about $30 a share, the stock needed to appreciate by 50% before the warrants would be worth exercising. However, this option to buy Owens Corning stock was clearly valuable and shortly after the warrants started trading they were selling for $6 each. You can be sure that before shareholders were handed this bone, all the parties calculated the value of the warrants under different assumptions about the stock's volatility. The Black–Scholes model is tailor-made for this purpose.

Portfolio Insurance

Your company's pension fund owns an $800 million diversified portfolio of common stocks that moves closely in line with the market index. The pension fund is currently fully funded, but you are concerned that if it falls by more than 20% it will start to be underfunded. Suppose that your bank offers to insure you for one year against this possibility. What would you be prepared to pay for this insurance? Think back to Section 20-2 (Figure 20.6), where we showed that you can shield against a

---

[15] Until 2005 companies were obliged to record as an expense any difference between the stock price when the options were granted and the exercise price. Thus, as long as the options were granted at-the-money (exercise price equals stock price), the company was not obliged to show any expense.

Finance In Practice

The Perfect Payday[*]

On an October day in 1999 the shares of the giant insurer United Health Group sank to their lowest level of the year. That may have been bad news for investors but it was good news for William McGuire, the chief executive, for the company granted him options to buy the stock in the future at that low price. If the options had been dated a month later when the stock price was 40% higher, those options would have been far less valuable. Lucky coincidence? Possibly, but the following year also Mr. McGuire was granted options on the day that the stock price hit the year's low. And in 2001 the grant came near the bottom of a sharp dip in the stock price.

Over the following years evidence began to accumulate that in other companies too executives were being granted options at unusually favorable prices. It seemed that these firms were using hindsight to choose the date on which the options were granted. Such backdating is not necessarily illegal, but most options are granted under a shareholder-approved plan that typically requires the exercise price to be equal to the fair market value of the company's stock at the time of the grant. Also backdating may result in an underestimate of the amount of compensation paid and therefore to a misstatement of earnings and an underpayment of taxes.

Investigations by the SEC and prosecutions by disgruntled shareholders led to the resignation of a number of directors and officers of major corporations that were found to have backdated options. William McGuire was among those who fell on their sword. He subsequently agreed to pay $39 million and forfeit another 3.7 million compensatory stock options to settle a class-action suit headed by the California Public Employee Retirement System (Calpers).

[*] "The Perfect Payday" is the title of an article in *The Wall Street Journal* that drew attention to the practice of backdating. See C. Forelle and J. Bandler, "The Perfect Payday; Some CEOs Reap Millions by Landing Stock Options When They Are Most Valuable; Luck—or Something Else?" *The Wall Street Journal*, March 18, 2006, p. A1. Earlier evidence of backdating appeared in D. Yermack, "Good Timing: CEO Stock Option Awards and Company News Announcements," *Journal of Finance* 52 (1997), pp. 449–476, and in E. Lie, "On the Timing of CEO Stock Option Awards," *Management Science* 51 (2005), pp. 802–812.

fall in asset prices by buying a protective put option. In the present case the bank would be selling you a one-year put option on U.S. stock prices with an exercise price 20% below their current level. You can get the value of that option in two steps. First use the Black–Scholes formula to value a call with the same exercise price and maturity. Then back out the put value from put–call parity. (You will have to adjust for dividends, but we'll leave that to the next section.)

Calculating Implied Volatilities

So far we have used our option pricing model to calculate the value of an option given the standard deviation of the asset's returns. Sometimes it is useful to turn the problem around and ask what the option price is telling us about the asset's volatility. For example, the National Stock Exchange (NSE) trades options on several market indexes. As we write this, S&P CNX Nifty is at 5923, while a three-month call with a strike of 5300 on the index is priced at 236. If the Black–Scholes formula is correct,

Finance In Practice

The Fear Index[*]

The Market Volatility Index or VIX measures the volatility that is implied by near-term Standard & Poor's 500 Index options and is therefore an estimate of expected *future* market volatility over the next 30 calendar days. Implied market volatilities have been calculated by the Chicago Board Options Exchange (CBOE) since January 1986, though in its current form the VIX dates back only to 2003.

Investors regularly trade volatility. They do so by buying or selling VIX futures and options contracts. Since these were introduced by the Chicago Board Options Exchange (CBOE), combined trading activity in the two contracts has grown to more than 100,000 contracts per day, making them two of the most successful innovations ever introduced by the exchange.

Because VIX measures investor uncertainty, it has been dubbed the "fear index." The market for index options tends to be dominated by equity investors who buy index puts when they are concerned about a potential drop in the stock market. Any subsequent decline in the value of their portfolio is then offset by the increase in the value of the put option. The more that investors demand such insurance, the higher the price of index put options. Thus VIX is an indicator that reflects the price of portfolio insurance.

Between January 1986 and April 2009 the VIX has averaged 20.5%, almost identical to the long-term level of market volatility that we cited in Chapter 7. The high point for the index was in October 1987 when the VIX closed the month at 61%,[**] but there have been several other short-lived spikes, for example, at the time of Iraq's invasion of Kuwait and the subsequent response by U.N. forces.

Although the VIX is the most widely quoted measure of volatility, volatility measures are also available for several other U.S. and overseas stock market indexes (such as the FTSE 100 Index in the U.K. and the CAC 40 in France), as well as for gold, oil, and the euro.

---

[*]For a review of the VIX index see R. E. Whaley, "Understanding the VIX," *Journal of Portfolio Management* 35 (Spring 2009), pp. 98–105.

[**]On October 19, 1987 (Black Monday), the VIX closed at 150. Fortunately, the market volatility returned fairly rapidly to less exciting levels.

---

then an option value of 236 makes sense only if investors believe that the standard deviation of index returns is about 19.6% a year.[16]

The NSE regularly publishes the implied volatility on the Nifty index, which it terms the VIX (see the nearby box to read about volatility index in the U.S.). There is an active market in the India VIX. For example, suppose you feel that the implied volatility is implausibly low. Then you can "buy" the India VIX at the current low price and hope to "sell" it at a profit when implied volatility has increased.

---

[16] In calculating the implied volatility we need to allow for the dividends paid on the shares. We explain how to take these into account in the next section.

You may be interested to compare the current implied volatility that we calculated earlier with Figure 21.6, which shows past measures of implied volatility for the S&P CNX Nifty. Notice the decrease in investor volatility between 2009 and 2011.

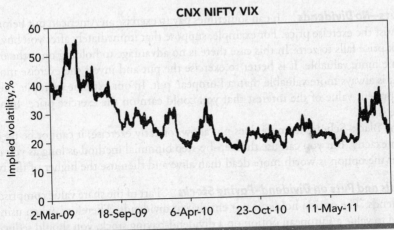

FIGURE 21.6

Standard deviations of market returns implied by prices of options on S&P CNX Nifty.

Source: Data from the National Stock Exchange **www.nseindia.com**.

21-5 OPTION VALUES AT A GLANCE

So far our discussion of option values has assumed that investors hold the option until maturity. That is certainly the case with European options that *cannot* be exercised before maturity but may not be the case with American options that can be exercised at any time. Also, when we valued the Bombay Dyeing Shares, we ignored dividends, because Bombay Dyeing has already paid the dividend for 2011 and the next dividend is not expected to be paid in the next two months.[17] Can the same valuation methods be extended to American options and to stocks that pay dividends?

Another question concerns dilution. When investors buy and then exercise traded options, there is no effect on the number of shares issued by the company. But sometimes the company itself may give options to key employees or sell them to investors. When these options are exercised, the number of outstanding shares *does* increase, and therefore the stake of existing stockholders is diluted. Can standard option-valuation models cope with the effect of dilution?

In this section we look at how the possibility of early exercise and dividends affect option value. We hold over the problem of dilution to the Appendix to this chapter.

American Calls—No Dividends Unlike European options, American options can be exercised anytime. However, we know that in the absence of dividends the value of a call option increases with time to maturity. So, if you exercised an American call option early, you would needlessly reduce its value. Since an American call should not be exercised before maturity, its value is the same as that of a European call, and the Black–Scholes model applies to both options.

---

[17] After March 2000, Bombay Dyeing never paid any interim dividend.

European Puts—No Dividends
If we wish to value a European put, we can use the put–call parity formula from Chapter 20:

$$\text{Value of put} = \text{value of call} - \text{value of stock} + \text{PV(exercise price)}$$

American Puts—No Dividends
It can sometimes pay to exercise an American put before maturity in order to reinvest the exercise price. For example, suppose that immediately after you buy an American put, the stock price falls to zero. In this case there is no advantage to holding onto the option since it *cannot* become more valuable. It is better to exercise the put and invest the exercise money. Thus an American put is always more valuable than a European put. In our extreme example, the difference is equal to the present value of the interest that you could earn on the exercise price. In all other cases the difference is less.

Because the Black–Scholes formula does not allow for early exercise, it cannot be used to value an American put exactly. But you can use the step-by-step binomial method as long as you check at each point whether the option is worth more dead than alive and then use the higher of the two values.

European Calls and Puts on Dividend-Paying Stocks
Part of the share value comprises the present value of dividends. The option holder is not entitled to dividends. Therefore, when using the Black–Scholes model to value a European option on a dividend-paying stock, you should reduce the price of the stock by the present value of the dividends to be paid before the option's maturity.

Dividends don't always come with a big label attached, so look out for instances where the asset holder gets a benefit and the option holder does not. For example, when you buy foreign currency, you can invest it to earn interest; but if you own an option to buy foreign currency, you miss out on this income. Therefore, when valuing an option to buy foreign currency, you need to deduct the present value of this foreign interest from the current price of the currency.[18]

American Calls on Dividend-Paying Stocks
We have seen that when the stock does not pay dividends, an American call option is *always* worth more alive than dead. By holding onto the option, you not only keep your option open but also earn interest on the exercise money. Even when there are dividends, you should never exercise early if the dividend you gain is less than the interest you lose by having to pay the exercise price early. However, if the dividend is sufficiently large, you might want to capture it by exercising the option just before the ex-dividend date.

The only general method for valuing an American call on a dividend-paying stock is to use the step-by-step binomial method. In this case you must check at each stage to see whether the option is more valuable if exercised just before the ex-dividend date than if held for at least one more period.

21-6 THE OPTION MENAGERIE

Our focus in the past two chapters has been on plain-vanilla puts and calls or combinations of them. An understanding of these options and how they are valued will allow you to handle most of the option problems that you are likely to encounter in corporate finance. However, you may occasionally

---

[18] For example, suppose that it currently costs $2 to buy £1 and that this pound can be invested to earn interest of 5%. The option holder misses out on interest of $.05 \times \$2 = \$.10$. So, before using the Black–Scholes formula to value an option to buy sterling, you must adjust the current price of sterling:

$$\text{Adjusted price of sterling} = \text{current price} - \text{PV(interest)}$$
$$= \$2 - .10/1.05 = \$1.905$$

encounter some more unusual options. We are not going to be looking at them in this book, but just for fun and to help you hold your own in conversations with your investment banker friends, here is a crib sheet that summarizes a few of these exotic options:

Asian (or average) option	The exercise price is equal to the *average* of the asset's price during the life of the option.
Barrier option	Option where the payoff depends on whether the asset price reaches a specified level. A knock-in option (up-and-in call or down-and-in put) comes into existence only when the underlying asset reaches the barrier. Knock-out options (down-and-out call or up-and-out put) *cease* to exist if the asset price reaches the barrier.
Bermuda option	The option is exercisable on discrete dates before maturity.
Caput option	Call option on a put option.
Chooser (as-you-like-it) option	The holder must decide before maturity whether the option is a call or a put.
Compound option	An option on an option.
Digital (binary or cash-or-nothing) option	The option payoff is zero if the asset price is the wrong side of the exercise price and otherwise is a fixed sum.
Lookback option	The option holder chooses as the exercise price any of the asset prices that occurred before the final date.
Rainbow option	Call (put) option on the best (worst) of a basket of assets.

SUMMARY

In this chapter we introduced the basic principles of option valuation by considering a call option on a stock that could take on one of two possible values at the option's maturity. We showed that it is possible to construct a package of the stock and a loan that would provide exactly the same payoff as the option *regardless* of whether the stock price rises or falls. Therefore the value of the option must be the same as the value of this replicating portfolio.

We arrived at the same answer by pretending that investors are risk-neutral, so that the expected return on every asset is equal to the interest rate. We calculated the expected future value of the option in this imaginary risk-neutral world and then discounted this figure at the interest rate to find the option's present value.

The general binomial method adds realism by dividing the option's life into a number of subperiods in each of which the stock price can make one of two possible moves. Chopping the period into these shorter intervals doesn't alter the basic method for valuing a call option. We can still replicate the call by a package of the stock and a loan, but the package changes at each stage.

Finally, we introduced the Black–Scholes formula. This calculates the option's value when the stock price is constantly changing and takes on a continuum of possible future values.

An option can be replicated by a package of the underlying asset and a risk-free loan. Therefore, we can measure the risk of any option by calculating the risk of this portfolio. Naked options are often substantially more risky than the asset itself.

When valuing options in practical situations there are a number of features to look out for. For example, you may need to recognize that the option value is reduced by the fact that the holder is not entitled to any dividends.

Three readable articles about the Black–Scholes model are:

F. Black, "How We Came up with the Option Formula," *Journal of Portfolio Management* 15 (1989), pp. 4–8.

F. Black, "The Holes in Black–Scholes," *RISK Magazine* 1 (1988), pp. 27–29.

F. Black, "How to use the Holes in Black–Scholes," *Journal of Applied Corporate Finance* 1 (Winter 1989), pp. 67–73.

There are a number of good books on option valuation. They include:

J. Hull, *Options, Futures and Other Derivatives,* 7th ed. (Englewood Cliffs, NJ: Prentice-Hall, Inc., 2008).

R. L. McDonald, *Derivatives Markets,* 2nd ed. (Reading, MA: Pearson Addison Wesley, 2005).

P. Wilmott, *Paul Wilmott on Quantitative Finance,* 2nd ed. (New York: John Wiley & Sons, 2006).

BASIC

1. The stock price of Heavy Metal (HM) changes only once a month: either it goes up by 20% or it falls by 16.7%. Its price now is ₹40. The interest rate is 12.7% per year, or about 1% per month.
   a. What is the value of a one-month call option with an exercise price of ₹40?
   b. What is the option delta?
   c. Show how the payoffs of this call option can be replicated by buying HM's stock and borrowing.
   d. What is the value of a two-month call option with an exercise price of ₹40?
   e. What is the option delta of the two-month call over the first one-month period?

2. a. Can the delta of a call option be greater than 1.0? Explain.
   b. Can it be less than zero?
   c. How does the delta of a call change if the stock price rises?
   d. How does it change if the risk of the stock increases?

3. Take another look at our two-step binomial trees for Bombay Dyeing, for example, in Figure 21.2. Use the replicating-portfolio or risk-neutral method to value six-month call and put options with an exercise price of ₹400. Assume the Bombay Dyeing stock price is ₹420.

4. Imagine that Bombay Dyeing's stock price will either rise by 25% or fall by 20% over the next three months (see Section 21-1). Recalculate the value of the call option (exercise price = ₹420) using (a) the replicating portfolio method and (b) the risk-neutral method. Explain intuitively why the option value falls from the value computed in Section 21-1.

5. Over the coming year OLP's stock price will halve to ₹50 from its current level of ₹100 or it will rise to ₹200. The one-year interest rate is 10%.
   a. What is the delta of a one-year call option on OLP stock with an exercise price of ₹100?
   b. Use the replicating-portfolio method to value this call.
   c. In a risk-neutral world what is the probability that OLP stock will rise in price?
   d. Use the risk-neutral method to check your valuation of the OLP option.
   e. If someone told you that in reality there is a 60% chance that OLP's stock price will rise to ₹200, would you change your view about the value of the option? Explain.

6. Use the Black–Scholes formula to value the following options:

   a. A call option written on a stock selling for ₹60 per share with a ₹60 exercise price. The stock's standard deviation is 6% per month. The option matures in three months. The risk-free interest rate is 1% per month.

   b. A put option written on the same stock at the same time, with the same exercise price and expiration date.

   Now for each of these options find the combination of stock and risk-free asset that would replicate the option.

7. "An option is always riskier than the stock it is written on." True or false? How does the risk of an option change when the stock price changes?

8. For which of the following options *might* it be rational to exercise before maturity? Explain briefly why or why not.

   a. American put on a non-dividend-paying stock.

   b. American call—the dividend payment is ₹5 per annum, the exercise price is ₹100, and the interest rate is 10%.

   c. American call—the interest rate is 10%, and the dividend payment is 5% of future stock price. (*Hint:* The dividend depends on the stock price, which could either rise or fall.)

INTERMEDIATE

9. Johnny Jones's high school derivatives homework asks for a binomial valuation of a 12-month call option on the common stock of the Overland Railroad. The stock is now selling for $45 per share and has an annual standard deviation of 24%. Johnny first constructs a binomial tree like Figure 21.2, in which stock price moves up or down every six months. Then he constructs a more realistic tree, assuming that the stock price moves up or down once every three months, or four times per year.

   a. Construct these two binomial trees.

   b. How would these trees change if Overland's standard deviation were 30%? (*Hint:* Make sure to specify the right up and down percentage changes.)

10. Suppose a stock price can go up by 15% or down by 13% over the next year. You own a one-year put on the stock. The interest rate is 10%, and the current stock price is ₹60.

    a. What exercise price leaves you indifferent between holding the put or exercising it now?

    b. How does this break-even exercise price change if the interest rate is increased?

11. The price of Rakha Mining stock is ₹100. During each of the next two six-month periods the price may either rise by 25% or fall by 20% (equivalent to a standard deviation of 31.5% a year). At month 6 the company will pay a dividend of ₹20. The interest rate is 10% per six-month period. What is the value of a one-year American call option with an exercise price of ₹80? Now recalculate the option value, assuming that the dividend is equal to 20% of the with-dividend stock price.

12. Buffelhead's stock price is ₹220 and could halve or double in each six-month period (equivalent to a standard deviation of 98%). A one-year call option on Buffelhead has an exercise price of ₹165. The interest rate is 21% a year.

    a. What is the value of the Buffelhead call?

    b. Now calculate the option delta for the second six months if (i) the stock price rises to ₹440 and (ii) the stock price falls to ₹110.

    c. How does the call option delta vary with the level of the stock price? Explain intuitively why.

d. Suppose that in month 6 the Buffelhead stock price is ₹110. How at that point could you replicate an investment in the stock by a combination of call options and risk-free lending? Show that your strategy does indeed produce the same returns as those from an investment in the stock.

13. Suppose that you own an American put option on Buffelhead stock (see Problem 12) with an exercise price of ₹220.

   a. Would you ever want to exercise the put early?

   b. Calculate the value of the put.

   c. Now compare the value with that of an equivalent European put option.

14. Recalculate the value of the Buffelhead call option (see Problem 12), assuming that the option is American and that at the end of the first six months the company pays a dividend of ₹25. (Thus the price at the end of the year is either double or half the *ex*-dividend price in month 6.) How would your answer change if the option were European?

15. Suppose that you have an option that allows you to sell Buffelhead stock (see Problem 12) in month 6 for ₹165 *or* to buy it in month 12 for ₹165. What is the value of this unusual option?

16. The current price of the stock of Mont Tremblant Air is C$100. During each six-month period it will either rise by 11.1% or fall by 10% (equivalent to an annual standard deviation of 14.9%). The interest rate is 5% per six-month period.

   a. Calculate the value of a one-year European put option on Mont Tremblant's stock with an exercise price of C$102.

   b. Recalculate the value of the Mont Tremblant put option, assuming that it is an American option.

17. The current price of United Carbon (UC) stock is ₹200. The standard deviation is 22.3% a year, and the interest rate is 21% a year. A one-year call option on UC has an exercise price of ₹180.

Visit us at
www.mhhe.com/bmam10e

   a. Use the Black–Scholes model to value the call option on UC. You may find it helpful to use the "live" spreadsheet in Table 21.2 on the book's Web site, www.mhhe.com/bmam10e.

   b. Use the formula given in Section 21-2 to calculate the up and down moves that you would use if you valued the UC option with the one-period binomial method. Now value the option by using that method.

   c. Recalculate the up and down moves and revalue the option by using the two-period binomial method.

   d. Use your answer to part (c) to calculate the option delta (i) today; (ii) next period if the stock price rises; and (iii) next period if the stock price falls. Show at each point how you would replicate a call option with a levered investment in the company's stock.

18. Suppose you construct an option hedge by buying a levered position in delta shares of stock and selling one call option. As the share price changes, the option delta changes, and you will need to adjust your hedge. You can minimize the cost of adjustments if changes in the stock price have only a small effect on the option delta. Construct an example to show whether the option delta is likely to vary more if you hedge with an in-the-money option, an at-the-money option, or an out-of-the-money option.

19. a. In Section 21-3 we calculated the risk (beta) of a two-month call option on Bombay Dyeing stock with an exercise price of ₹420. Now repeat the exercise for a similar option with an exercise price of ₹400. Does the risk rise or fall as the exercise price is reduced?

   b. Now calculate the risk of a three-month call on Bombay Dyeing stock with an exercise price of ₹420. Does the risk rise or fall as the maturity of the option lengthens?

20. Other things equal, which of these American options are you most likely to want to exercise early?
    a. A put option on a stock with a large dividend or a call on the same stock.
    b. A put option on a stock that is selling below exercise price or a call on the same stock.
    c. A put option when the interest rate is high or the same put option when the interest rate is low.
       Illustrate your answer with examples.

21. Is it better to exercise a call option on the with-dividend date or on the ex-dividend date? How about a put option? Explain.

22. Use the "live" Black–Scholes program on this book's Web site, **www.mhhe. com/bmam10e**, to value the Owens Corning warrants described in Section 21-4. The standard deviation of Owens Corning stock was 41% a year and the interest rate when the warrants were issued was 5%. Owens Corning did not pay a dividend. Ignore the problem of dilution.

Visit us at
www.mhhe.com/bmam10e

23. Use the "live" Black–Scholes program at **www.mhhe.com/bmam10e** to estimate how much you should be prepared to pay to insure the value of your pension fund portfolio for the coming year. Make reasonable assumptions about the volatility of the market and use current interest rates. Remember to subtract the present value of likely dividend payments from the current level of the market index.

Visit us at
www.mhhe.com/bmam10e

CHALLENGE

24. Use the formula that relates the value of the call and the put (see Section 20-2) and the one-period binomial model to show that the option delta for a put option is equal to the option delta for a call option minus 1.

25. Show how the option delta changes as the stock price rises relative to the exercise price. Explain intuitively why this is the case. (What happens to the option delta if the exercise price of an option is zero? What happens if the exercise price becomes indefinitely large?)

26. Your company has just awarded you a generous stock option scheme. You suspect that the board will either decide to increase the dividend or announce a stock repurchase program. Which do you secretly hope they will decide? Explain. (You may find it helpful to refer back to Chapter 16.)

27. Calculate and compare the risk (betas) of the following investments: (a) a share of Bombay Dyeing stock; (b) a one-year call option on Bombay Dyeing; (c) a one-year put option; (d) a portfolio consisting of a share of Bombay Dyeing stock and a one-year put option; (e) a portfolio consisting of a share of Bombay Dyeing stock, a one-year put option, and the sale of a one-year call. In each case assume that the exercise price of the option is ₹420, which is also the current price of Bombay Dyeing stock.

28. Some corporations have issued *perpetual* warrants. Warrants are call options issued by a firm, allowing the warrant holder to buy the firm's stock.
    a. What does the Black–Scholes formula predict for the value of an infinite-lived call option on a non-dividend-paying stock? Explain the value you obtain. (*Hint:* What happens to the present value of the exercise price of a long-maturity option?)
    b. Do you think this prediction is realistic? If not, explain carefully why. (*Hints:* What about dividends? What about bankruptcy?)

REAL-TIME DATA ANALYSIS

Look back at the companies listed in Table 7.3. Download the daily stock price data from the website of NSE (www.nseindia.com). For each company, compute the monthly adjusted prices and save it in an Excel spreadsheet. Calculate each company's standard deviation from the monthly returns given on the spreadsheet. The Excel function is STDEV. Convert the standard deviations from monthly to annual units by multiplying by the square root of 12.

a. Use the Black-Scholes formula to value 1,2, and 3 month call options on each stock. Assume the exercise price equals the current stock price, and use a current risk-free annual interest rate. If the stock pays dividends, remember to subtract from the stock price the present value of any dividends that the option holder will miss out on. How close is your calculated value to the traded price of the option?

b. Your answer to part (a) will not exactly match the traded price. Experiment with different values for the standard deviation until your calculated values match the prices of the traded options as closely as possible. What are these implied volatilities? What do the implied volatilities say about investors' forecasts of future volatility?

BRUCE HONIBALL'S INVENTION

It was another disappointing year for Bruce Honiball, the manager of retail services at the Gibb River Bank. Sure, the retail side of Gibb River was making money, but it didn't grow at all in 2009. Gibb River had plenty of loyal depositors, but few new ones. Bruce had to figure out some new product or financial service—something that would generate some excitement and attention.

Bruce had been musing on one idea for some time. How about making it easy *and safe* for Gibb River's customers to put money in the stock market? How about giving them the upside of investing in equities—at least *some* of the upside—but none of the downside?

Bruce could see the advertisements now:

How would you like to invest in Australian stocks completely risk-free? You can with the new Gibb River Bank *Equity-Linked Deposit*. You share in the good years; we take care of the bad ones.

Here's how it works. Deposit A$100 with us for one year. At the end of that period you get back your A$100 *plus* A$5 for every 10% rise in the value of the Australian All Ordinaries stock index. But, if the market index falls during this period, the Bank will still refund your A$100 deposit in full.

There's no risk of loss. Gibb River Bank is your safety net.

Bruce had floated the idea before and encountered immediate skepticism, even derision: "Heads they win, tails we lose—is that what you're proposing, Mr. Honiball?" Bruce had no ready answer. Could the bank really afford to make such an attractive offer? How should it invest the money that would come in from customers? The bank had no appetite for major new risks.

Bruce has puzzled over these questions for the past two weeks but has been unable to come up with a satisfactory answer. He believes that the Australian equity market is currently fully valued, but he realizes that some of his colleagues are more bullish than he is about equity prices.

Fortunately, the bank had just recruited a smart new MBA graduate, Sheila Liu. Sheila was sure that she could find the answers to Bruce Honiball's questions. First she collected data on the Australian market to get a preliminary idea of whether equity-linked deposits could work. These data are shown in Table 21.3. She was just about to undertake some quick calculations when she received the following further memo from Bruce:

Sheila, I've got another idea. A lot of our customers probably share my view that the market is overvalued. Why don't we also give them a chance to make some money by offering a "bear market deposit"? If the market goes up, they would just get back their A$100 deposit. If it goes down, they get their A$100 back plus $5 for each 10% that the market falls. Can you figure out whether we could do something like this? Bruce.

TABLE 21.3   Australian interest rates and equity returns, 1989–2008.

Year	Interest Rate	Market Return	End-Year Dividend Yield	Year	Interest Rate	Market Return	End-Year Dividend Yield
1989	17.3%	17.4%	5.7%	1999	4.9%	16.1%	3.2%
1990	15.9	−17.5	6.8	2000	4.9	5.2	3.4
1991	11.1	34.2	3.8	2001	4.8	10.4	3.3
1992	6.8	−2.3	3.8	2002	4.8	−8.8	4.0
1993	5.3	45.4	3.0	2003	4.8	14.6	3.9
1994	5.4	−8.7	4.0	2004	5.4	28.0	3.5
1995	8.0	20.2	4.0	2005	5.6	22.8	3.7
1996	7.4	14.6	3.6	2006	5.9	24.2	3.7
1997	5.5	12.2	3.9	2007	6.4	11.8	3.7
1998	5.0	11.6	3.5	2008	7.16	−40.38	6.8

QUESTION

1. What kinds of options is Bruce proposing? How much would the options be worth? Would the equity-linked and bear-market deposits generate positive NPV for Gibb River Bank?

APPENDIX

HOW DILUTION AFFECTS OPTION VALUE

If you buy a call option on an options exchange and then exercise it, you have no effect on the number of outstanding shares. The investor who sold the call simply hands over to you his or her shares. However, sometimes the company itself may issue options to buy its own shares. For example, we saw in Section 21-4 that in 2008 Oracle Corporation issued a total of 69 million executive stock options.

Companies also issue convertible bonds, which give investors the option to exchange their bonds in the future for common stock. Therefore, a convertible bond resembles a package of a straight bond and an option to buy the stock. Alternatively, the company may sell a package of bonds and warrants. These warrants are long-term call options to buy the company's stock. Presumably the company hopes that the warrants will serve as a "sweetener," so that by including options in the package investors will be induced to pay a much higher price. If the holders of the convertible bonds or the warrants decide to exercise their option, the company must issue the additional shares to them.

Options that are issued by the company are somewhat trickier to value than exchange-traded options. When these options are exercised, the firm's assets and profits are spread over a larger number of shares. Sometimes this dilution is negligible and can safely be ignored. But, if the number of shares can increase substantially, you need to take it into account when valuing the options. To illustrate how you can do so, we will work through the example of United Glue's warrants.

Example: Valuing United Glue's Warrants United Glue has just issued a ₹2 million package of debt and warrants. Here are some basic data that we can use to value the warrants:

Number of shares outstanding (N)	1 million
Current stock price (P)	₹12
Number of warrants issued per share outstanding (q)	.10
Total number of warrants issued (Nq)	100,000
Exercise price of warrants (EX)	₹10
Time to expiration of warrants (t)	4 years
Annual standard deviation of stock price changes (σ)	.40
Rate of interest (r)	10%
United stock pays no dividends	

Suppose that without the warrants the debt is worth ₹1.5 million. Then investors must be paying ₹.5 million for the warrants:

$$\text{Cost of warrants} = \text{total amount of financing} - \text{value of loan without warrants}$$
$$₹500,000 \quad = \quad ₹2,000,000 \quad - \quad ₹1,500,000$$

$$\text{Each warrant costs investors } \frac{500,000}{100,000} = ₹5$$

Table 21A.1 shows the market value of United's assets and liabilities both before and after the issue.

TABLE 21A.1 United Glue's market value balance sheet (in ₹ millions).

Before the Issue

Existing assets	₹16	₹ 4	Existing loans
		12	Common stock
			(1 million shares at
			₹12 a share)
Total	₹16	₹16	Total

After the Issue

Existing assets	₹16	₹ 4	Existing loans
New assets financed		1.5	New loan without warrants
by debt and warrants	2	5.5	Total debt
		.5	Warrants
		12	Common stock
		12.5	Total equity
Total	₹18	₹18.0	Total

Now let us take a stab at checking whether the warrants are really worth the ₹500,000 that investors are paying for them. Since the warrant is a call option to buy the United stock, we can use the Black–Scholes formula to value the warrant. It turns out that a four-year call to buy United stock at ₹10 is worth ₹6.15.[19] Thus the warrant issue looks like a good deal for investors and a bad deal for United. Investors are paying ₹5 a share for warrants that are worth ₹6.15.

How the Value of United Warrants Is Affected by Dilution Unfortunately, our calculations for United warrants do not tell the whole story. Remember that when investors exercise a traded call or put option, there is no change in either the company's assets or the number of shares outstanding. But, if United's warrants are exercised, the number of shares outstanding will increase by $Nq = 100,000$. Also the assets will increase by the amount of the exercise money ($Nq \times EX = 100,000 \times ₹10 = ₹1$ million). In other words, there will be dilution. We need to allow for this dilution when we value the warrants.

Let us call the value of United's equity V:

$$\text{Value of equity} = V = \text{value of United's total assets} - \text{value of debt}$$

If the warrants are exercised, equity value will increase by the amount of the exercise money to $V + NqEX$. At the same time the number of shares will increase to $N + Nq$. So the share price after the warrants are exercised will be:

$$\text{Share price after exercise} = \frac{V + NqEX}{N + Nq}$$

At maturity the warrant holder can choose to let the warrants lapse or to exercise them and receive the share price less the exercise price. Thus the value of the warrants will be the share price minus the exercise

---

[19] Plugging the data for United into the Black–Scholes formula gives

$$d_1 = \log[12/(10/1.1^4)]/(.40 \times \sqrt{4}) + .40 \times \sqrt{4}/2 = 1.104 \text{ and } d_2 = 1.104 - .40 \times \sqrt{4} = .304$$

The Excel NORMSDIST function tells us that $N(d_1) = .865$, and $N(d_2) = .620$. Therefore, estimated warrant value = $.865 \times 12 - .620 \times (10/1.1^4) = ₹6.15$.

price or zero, whichever is the higher. Another way to write this is:

$$\text{Warrant value at maturity} = \text{maximum}(\text{share price} - \text{exercise price, zero})$$

$$= \text{maximum}\left(\frac{V + Nq\text{EX}}{N + Nq} - \text{EX}, 0\right)$$

$$= \text{maximum}\left(\frac{V/N - \text{EX}}{1 + q}, 0\right)$$

$$= \frac{1}{1 + q}\text{maximum}\left(\frac{V}{N} - \text{EX}, 0\right)$$

This tells us the effect of dilution on the value of United's warrants. The warrant value is the value of $1/(1 + q)$ call options written on the stock of an alternative firm with the same total equity value V, *but with no outstanding warrants*. The alternative firm's stock price would be equal to V/N—that is, the total value of United's equity (V) divided by the number of shares outstanding (N). The stock price of this alternative firm is more variable than United's stock price. So when we value the call option on the alternative firm, we must remember to use the standard deviation of the changes in V/N.

Now we can recalculate the value of United's warrants allowing for dilution. First we find the stock price of the alternative firm:

$$\text{Current equity value of alternative firm} = V = \text{value of United's total assets} - \text{value of loans}$$

$$= 18 - 5.5 = ₹12.5 \text{ millon}$$

$$\text{Current share price of alternative firm} = \frac{V}{N} = \frac{12.5 \text{ millon}}{1 \text{ millon}} = ₹12.50$$

Also, suppose the standard deviation of the share price changes of this alternative firm is $\sigma^* = .41$.[20]

The Black–Scholes formula gives a value of ₹6.64 for a call option on a stock with a price of ₹12.50 and a standard deviation of .41. The value of United warrants is equal to the value of $1/(1 + q)$ call options on the stock of this alternative firm. Thus warrant value is:

$$\frac{1}{1 + q} \times \text{value of call on alternative firm} = \frac{1}{1.1} \times 6.64 = ₹6.04$$

---

[20] How in practice could we compute σ^*? It would be easy if we could wait until the warrants had been trading for some time. In that case σ^* could be computed from the returns on a package of *all* the company's shares and warrants. In the present case we need to value the warrants *before* they start trading. We argue as follows: The standard deviation of the *assets* before the issue is equal to the standard deviation of a package of the common stock and the existing loans. For example, suppose that the company's debt is risk-free and that the standard deviation of stock returns *before* the bond-warrant issue is 38%. Then we calculate the standard deviation of the initial assets as follows:

$$\begin{array}{c}\text{Standard deviation} \\ \text{of initial assets}\end{array} = \begin{array}{c}\text{proportion in} \\ \text{common stock}\end{array} \times \begin{array}{c}\text{standard deviation} \\ \text{of common stock}\end{array}$$

$$= \frac{12}{16} \times 38 = 28.5\%$$

Now suppose that the assets after the issue are equally risky. Then,

$$\begin{array}{c}\text{Standard deviation} \\ \text{of assets after issue}\end{array} = \begin{array}{c}\text{proportion of equity} \\ \text{after issue}\end{array} \times \begin{array}{c}\text{standard deviation} \\ \text{of equity}(\sigma^*)\end{array}$$

$$28.5 = \frac{12.5}{18} \times \text{standard deviation of equity}(\sigma^*)$$

$$\text{Standard deviation of equity } (\sigma^*) = 41\%$$

Notice that in our example the standard deviation of the stock returns *before* the warrant issue was slightly lower than the standard deviation of the package of stock and warrants. However, the warrant holders bear proportionately more of this risk than do the stockholders; so the bond-warrant package could either increase or reduce the risk of the stock.

This is a somewhat lower value than the one we computed when we ignored dilution but still a bad deal for United.

It may sound from all this as if you need to know the value of United warrants to compute their value. This is not so. The formula does not call for warrant value but for V, the value of United's equity (that is, the shares *plus* warrants). Given equity value, the formula calculates how the overall value of equity should be split up between stock and warrants. Thus, suppose that United's underwriter advises that ₹500,000 extra can be raised by issuing a package of bonds and warrants rather than bonds alone. Is this a fair price? You can check using the Black–Scholes formula with the adjustment for dilution.

Finally, notice that these modifications are necessary to apply the Black–Scholes formula to value a warrant. They are not needed by the warrant holder, who must decide whether to exercise at maturity. If at maturity the price of the stock exceeds the exercise price of the warrant, the warrant holder will of course exercise.

Question

1. Here is a question about dilution. The Electric Bassoon Company has outstanding 2,000 shares with a total market value of ₹20,000 *plus* 1,000 warrants with a total market value of ₹5,000. Each warrant gives its holder the option to buy one share at ₹20.
   a. To value the warrants, you first need to value a call option on an alternative share. How might you calculate its standard deviation?
   b. Suppose that the value of a call option on this alternative share was ₹6. Calculate whether the Electric Bassoon warrants were undervalued or overvalued.

22

REAL OPTIONS

When you use discounted cash flow (DCF) to value a project, you implicitly assume that your firm will hold the project passively. In other words, you are ignoring the *real options* attached to the project—options that sophisticated managers can take advantage of. You could say that DCF does not reflect the value of management. Managers who hold real options do not have to be passive; they can make decisions to capitalize on good fortune or to mitigate loss. The opportunity to make such decisions clearly adds value whenever project outcomes are uncertain.

Chapter 10 introduced the four main types of real options:

- The option to expand if the immediate investment project succeeds.
- The option to wait (and learn) before investing.
- The option to shrink or abandon a project.
- The option to vary the mix of output or the firm's production methods.

Chapter 10 gave several simple examples of real options. We also showed you how to use decision trees to set out possible future outcomes and decisions. But we did not show you how to value real options. That is our task in this chapter. We apply the concepts and valuation principles you learned in Chapter 21.

For the most part we work with simple numerical examples. The art and science of valuing real options are illustrated just as well with simple calculations as complex ones. But we also describe several more realistic examples, including:

- A strategic investment in the computer business.
- The valuation of an aircraft purchase option.
- The option to develop commercial real estate.
- The decision to operate or mothball an oil tanker.

These examples show how financial managers can value real options in real life. We also show how managers can *create* real options, adding value by adding flexibility to the firm's investments and operations.

We should start with a warning. Setting out the possible future choices that the firm may encounter usually calls for a strong dose of judgment. Therefore, do not expect precision when valuing real options. Often managers do not even try to put a figure on the value of the option, but simply draw on their experience to decide whether it is worth paying for additional flexibility. Thus they might say, "We just don't know whether gargle blasters will catch on, but it probably makes sense to spend an extra ₹200,000 now to allow for an extra production line in the future."

22-1 THE VALUE OF FOLLOW-ON INVESTMENT OPPORTUNITIES

It is 1982. You are assistant to the chief financial officer (CFO) of Blitzen Computers, an established computer manufacturer casting a profit-hungry eye on the rapidly developing personal computer market. You are helping the CFO evaluate the proposed introduction of the Blitzen Mark I Micro.

The Mark I's forecasted cash flows and NPV are shown in Table 22.1. Unfortunately the Mark I can't meet Blitzen's customary 20% hurdle rate and has a ₹46 million negative NPV, contrary to top management's strong gut feeling that Blitzen ought to be in the personal computer market.

TABLE 22.1 Summary of cash flows and financial analysis of the Mark I microcomputer (₹ millions).

	Year					
	1982	**1983**	**1984**	**1985**	**1986**	**1987**
After-tax operating cash flow (1)		+110	+159	+295	+185	0
Capital investment (2)	450	0	0	0	0	0
Increase in working capital (3)	0	50	100	100	−125	−125
Net cash flow (1) − (2) − (3)	−450	+ 60	+ 59	+195	+310	+125
NPV at 20% = − ₹46.45, or about − ₹46 million						

The CFO has called you in to discuss the project:

"The Mark I just can't make it on financial grounds," the CFO says. "But we've got to do it for strategic reasons. I'm recommending we go ahead."

"But you're missing the all-important financial advantage, Chief," you reply.

"Don't call me 'Chief.' What financial advantage?"

"If we don't launch the Mark I, it will probably be too expensive to enter the micro market later, when Apple, IBM, and others are firmly established. If we go ahead, we have the opportunity to make follow-on investments that could be extremely profitable. The Mark I gives not only its own cash flows but also a call option to go on with a Mark II micro. That call option is the real source of strategic value."

"So it's strategic value by another name. That doesn't tell me what the Mark II investment's worth. The Mark II could be a great investment or a lousy one—we haven't got a clue."

"That's exactly when a call option is worth the most," you point out perceptively. "The call lets us invest in the Mark II if it's great and walk away from it if it's lousy."

"So what's it worth?"

"Hard to say precisely, but I've done a back-of-the-envelope calculation, which suggests that the value of the option to invest in the Mark II could more than offset the Mark I's ₹46 million negative NPV. [The calculations are shown in Table 22.2.] If the option to invest is worth ₹55 million, the total value of the Mark I is its own NPV, −₹46 million, plus the ₹55 million option attached to it, or +₹9 million."

TABLE 22.2 Valuing the option to invest in the Mark II microcomputer.

Assumptions

1. The decision to invest in the Mark II must be made after three years, in 1985.

2. The Mark II investment is double the scale of the Mark I (note the expected rapid growth of the industry). Investment required is ₹900 million (the exercise price), which is taken as fixed.

3. Forecasted cash inflows of the Mark II are also double those of the Mark I, with present value of ₹807 million in 1985 and $807/(1.2)^3 = ₹467$ million in 1982.

4. The future value of the Mark II cash flows is highly uncertain. This value evolves as a stock price does with a standard deviation of 35% per year. (Many high-technology stocks have standard deviations higher than 35%.)

5. The annual interest rate is 10%.

Interpretation

The opportunity to invest in the Mark II is a three-year call option on an asset worth ₹467 million with a ₹900 million exercise price.

Valuation

$$PV(\text{exercise price}) = \frac{900}{(1.1)^3} = 676$$

$$\text{Call value} = [N(d_1) \times P] - [N(d_2) \times PV(EX)]$$

$$d_1 = \log[P/PV(EX)]/\sigma\sqrt{t} + \sigma\sqrt{t}/2$$

$$= \log[.691]/.606 + .606/2 = -.3072$$

$$d_2 = d_1 - \sigma\sqrt{t} = -.3072 - .606 = -.9134$$

$$N(d_1) = .3793, N(d_2) = .1805$$

$$\text{Call value} = [.3793 \times 467] - [.1805 \times 676] = ₹55.1 \text{ million}$$

"You're just overestimating the Mark II," the CFO says gruffly. "It's easy to be optimistic when an investment is three years away."

"No, no," you reply patiently. "The Mark II is expected to be no more profitable than the Mark I—just twice as big and therefore twice as bad in terms of discounted cash flow. I'm forecasting it to have a negative NPV of about ₹100 million. But there's a chance the Mark II could be extremely valuable. The call option allows Blitzen to cash in on those upside outcomes. The chance to cash in could be worth ₹55 million.

"Of course, the ₹55 million is only a trial calculation, but it illustrates how valuable follow-on investment opportunities can be, especially when uncertainty is high and the product market is growing rapidly. Moreover, the Mark II will give us a call on the Mark III, the Mark III on the Mark IV, and so on. My calculations don't take subsequent calls into account."

"I think I'm beginning to understand a little bit of corporate strategy," mumbles the CFO.

Questions and Answers about Blitzen's Mark II

Question: I know how to use the Black–Scholes formula to value traded call options, but this case seems harder. What number do I use for the stock price? I don't see any traded shares.

Answer: With traded call options, you can see the value of the *underlying asset* that the call is written on. Here the option is to buy a nontraded real asset, the Mark II. We can't observe the Mark II's value; we have to compute it.

The Mark II's forecasted cash flows are set out in Table 22.3. The project involves an initial outlay of ₹900 million in 1985. The cash inflows start in the following year and have a present value of ₹807 million in 1985, equivalent to ₹467 million in 1982 as shown in Table 22.3. So the real option to invest in the Mark II amounts to a three-year call on an underlying asset worth ₹467 million, with a ₹900 million exercise price.

TABLE 22.3   Cash flows of the Mark II microcomputer, as forecasted from 1982 (₹ millions).

	1982	1985	1986	1987	1988	1989	1990
After-tax operating cash flow			+220	+318	+590	+370	0
Increase in working capital			100	200	200	−250	−250
Net cash flow			+120	+118	+390	+620	+250
Present value at 20%	+467	⟵ +807					
Investment, PV at 10%	676	⟵ 900					
	(PV in 1982)						
Forecasted NPV in 1985		− 93					

Notice that real options analysis does *not* replace DCF. You typically need DCF to value the underlying asset.

Question: Table 22.2 uses a standard deviation of 35% per year. Where does that number come from?

Answer: We recommend you look for *comparables,* that is, traded stocks with business risks similar to the investment opportunity.[1] For the Mark II, the ideal comparables would be growth stocks in the personal computer business, or perhaps a broader sample of high-tech growth stocks. Use the average standard deviation of the comparable companies' returns as the benchmark for judging the risk of the investment opportunity.[2]

---

[1] You could also use scenario analysis, which we described in Chapter 10. Work out "best" and "worst" scenarios to establish a range of possible future values. Then find the annual standard deviation that would generate this range over the life of the option. For the Mark II, a range from ₹300 million to ₹2 billion would cover about 90% of the possible outcomes. This range, shown in Figure 22.1, is consistent with an annual standard deviation of 35%.

[2] Be sure to "unlever" the standard deviations, thereby eliminating volatility created by debt financing. Chapter 17 covered unlevering procedures for beta. The same principles apply for standard deviation: You want the standard deviation of a portfolio of all the debt and equity securities issued by the comparable firm.

Question: Table 22.3 discounts the Mark II's cash flows at 20%. I understand the high discount rate, because the Mark II is risky. But why is the ₹900 million investment discounted at the risk-free interest rate of 10%? Table 22.3 shows the present value of the investment in 1982 of ₹676 million.

Answer: Black and Scholes assumed that the exercise price is a fixed, certain amount. We wanted to stick with their basic formula. If the exercise price is uncertain, you can switch to a slightly more complicated valuation formula.[3]

Question: Nevertheless, if I had to decide in 1982, once and for all, whether to invest in the Mark II, I wouldn't do it. Right?

Answer: Right. The NPV of a commitment to invest in the Mark II is negative:

$$\text{NPV(1982)} = \text{PV(cash inflows)} - \text{PV(investment)} = ₹467 - 676 = -₹209 \text{ million}$$

The option to invest in the Mark II is "out of the money" because the Mark II's value is far less than the required investment. Nevertheless, the option is worth +₹55 million. It is especially valuable because the Mark II is a risky project with lots of upside potential. Figure 22.1 shows the probability distribution of the possible present values of the Mark II in 1985. The expected (mean or average) outcome is our forecast of ₹807,[4] but the actual value could exceed ₹2 billion.

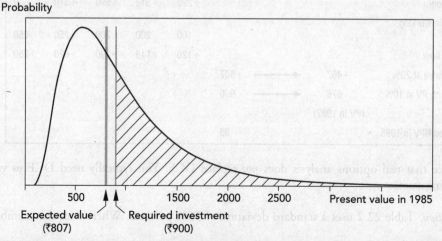

FIGURE 22.1

This distribution shows the range of possible present values for the Mark II project in 1985. The expected value is about ₹800 million, less than the required investment of ₹900 million. The option to invest pays off in the shaded area above ₹900 million.

Question: Could it also be far below ₹807 million—₹500 million or less?

Answer: The downside is irrelevant, because Blitzen won't invest unless the Mark II's actual value turns out higher than ₹900 million. The net option payoffs for all values less than ₹900 million are zero.

---

[3] If the required investment is uncertain, you have, in effect, an option to exchange one risky asset (the future value of the exercise price) for another (the future value of the Mark II's cash inflows). See W. Margrabe, "The Value of an Option to Exchange One Asset for Another," *Journal of Finance* 33 (March 1978), pp. 177–186.

[4] We have drawn the future values of the Mark II as a lognormal distribution, consistent with the assumptions of the Black–Scholes formula. Lognormal distributions are skewed to the right, so the average outcome is greater than the most likely outcome. The most likely outcome is the highest point on the probability distribution.

In a DCF analysis, you discount the expected outcome (₹807 million), which averages the downside against the upside, the bad outcomes against the good. The value of a call option depends only on the upside. You can see the danger of trying to value a future investment option with DCF.

Question: What's the decision rule?

Answer: Adjusted present value. The Mark I project costs ₹46 million (NPV = − ₹46 million), but accepting it creates the expansion option for the Mark II. The expansion option is worth ₹55 million, so:

$$APV = -46 + 55 = +₹9 \text{ million}$$

Of course we haven't counted other follow-on opportunities. If the Mark I and Mark II are successes, there will be an option to invest in the Mark III, possibly the Mark IV, and so on.

Other Expansion Options

You can probably think of many other cases where companies spend money today to create opportunities to expand in the future. A mining company may acquire rights to an ore body that is not worth developing today but could be very profitable if product prices increase. A real estate developer may invest in worn-out farmland that could be turned into a shopping mall if a new highway is built. A pharmaceutical company may acquire a patent that gives the right but not the obligation to market a new drug. In each case the company is acquiring a real option to expand.

22-2 The Timing Option

The fact that a project has a positive NPV does not mean that you should go ahead today. It may be better to wait and see how the market develops.

Suppose that you are contemplating a now-or-never opportunity to build a malted herring factory. In this case you have an about-to-expire call option on the present value of the factory's future cash flows. If the present value exceeds the cost of the factory, the call option's payoff is the project's NPV. But if NPV is negative, the call option's payoff is zero, because in that case the firm will not make the investment.

Now suppose that you can delay construction of the plant. You still have the call option, but you face a trade-off. If the outlook is highly uncertain, it is tempting to wait and see whether the malted herring market takes off or decays. On the other hand, if the project is truly profitable, the sooner you can capture the project's cash flows, the better. If the cash flows are high enough, you will want to exercise your option right away.

The cash flows from an investment project play the same role as dividend payments on a stock. When a stock pays no dividends, an American call is always worth more alive than dead and should never be exercised early. But payment of a dividend before the option matures reduces the ex-dividend price and the possible payoffs to the call option at maturity. Think of the extreme case: If a company pays out all its assets in one bumper dividend, the stock price must be zero and the call worthless. Therefore, any in-the-money call would be exercised just before this liquidating dividend.

Dividends do not always prompt early exercise, but if they are sufficiently large, call option holders capture them by exercising just before the ex-dividend date. We see managers acting in the same way: When a project's forecasted cash flows are sufficiently large, managers capture the cash flows by investing right away. But when forecasted cash flows are small, managers are inclined to hold on to their call rather than to invest, even when project NPV is positive.[5] This explains why managers are sometimes reluctant to commit to positive-NPV projects. This caution is rational as long as the option to wait is open and sufficiently valuable.

Valuing the Malted Herring Option

Figure 22.2 shows the possible cash flows and end-of-year values for the malted herring project. If you commit and invest $180 million, you have a project worth $200 million. If demand turns out to be low in year 1, the cash flow is only $16 million and the value of the project falls to $160 million. But if demand is high in year 1, the cash flow is $25 million and value rises to $250 million. Although the project lasts indefinitely, we assume that investment cannot be postponed beyond the end of the first year, and therefore we show only the cash flows for the first year and the possible values at the end of the year. Notice that if you undertake the investment right away, you capture the first year's cash flow ($16 million or $25 million); if you delay, you miss out on this cash flow, but you will have more information on how the project is likely to work out.

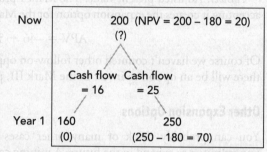

FIGURE 22.2

Possible cash flows and end-of-period values for the malted herring project are shown in black. The project costs $180 million, either now or later. The red figures in parentheses show payoffs from the option to wait and to invest later if the project is positive-NPV at year 1. Waiting means loss of the first year's cash flows. The problem is to figure out the current value of the option.

We can use the binomial method to value this option. The first step is to pretend that investors are risk neutral and to calculate the probabilities of high and low demand in this risk-neutral world. If demand is high in the first year, the malted herring plant has a cash flow of $25 million and a year-end value of $250 million. The total return is $(25 + 250)/200 - 1 = .375$, or 37.5%. If demand is low, the plant has a cash flow of $16 million and a year-end value of $160 million. Total return is $(16 + 160)/200 - 1 = -.12$, or −12%. In a *risk-neutral* world, the expected return would be equal to the interest rate, which we assume is 5%:

$$\text{Expected return} = \left(\begin{array}{c}\text{Probability of}\\ \text{high demand}\end{array}\right) \times 37.5 + \left(\begin{array}{c}1 - \text{probability of}\\ \text{high demand}\end{array}\right) \times (-12) = 5\%$$

Therefore the (pretend) probability of high demand is 34.3%.

We want to value a call option on the malted herring project with an exercise price of $180 million. We begin as usual at the end and work backward. The bottom row of Figure 22.2 shows the possible values of this option at the end of the year. If project value is $160 million, the option to invest is worthless. At the other extreme, if project value is $250 million, option value is $250 − 180 = $70 million.

To calculate the value of the option today, we work out the expected payoffs in a risk-neutral world and discount at the interest rate of 5%. Thus, the value of your option to invest in the malted herring

---

[5] We have been a bit vague about forecasted project cash flows. If competitors can enter and take away cash that you could have earned, the meaning is clear. But what about the decision to, say, develop an oil well? Here delay doesn't waste barrels of oil in the ground; it simply postpones production and the associated cash flow. The cost of waiting is the decline in today's *present value* of revenues from production. Present value declines if the cash flow from production increases more slowly than the cost of capital.

plant is:

$$\frac{(.343 \times 70) + (.657 \times 0)}{1.05} = \$22.9 \text{ million}$$

But here is where we need to recognize the opportunity to exercise the option immediately. The option is worth $22.9 million if you keep it open, and it is worth the project's immediate NPV (200 − 180 = $20 million) if exercised now. Therefore we decide to wait, and then to invest next year only if demand turns out high.

We have of course simplified the malted herring calculations. You won't find many actual investment-timing problems that fit into a one-step binomial tree. (We work through a more realistic, 8-step tree in the next section.) But the example delivers an important practical point: A positive NPV is not a sufficient reason for investing. It may be better to wait and see.

Optimal Timing for Real Estate Development

Sometimes it pays to wait for a long time, even for projects with large positive NPVs. Suppose you own a plot of vacant land in the suburbs.[6] The land can be used for a hotel or an office building, but not for both. A hotel could be later converted to an office building, or an office building to a hotel, but only at significant cost. You are therefore reluctant to invest, even if both investments have positive NPVs.

In this case you have two options to invest, but only one can be exercised. You therefore learn two things by waiting. First, you learn about the general *level* of cash flows from development, for example, by observing changes in the value of developed properties near your land. Second, you can update your estimates of the *relative* size of the hotel's future cash flows versus the office building's.

Figure 22.3 shows the conditions in which you would finally commit to build either the hotel or the office building. The horizontal axis shows the current cash flows that a hotel would generate. The vertical axis shows current cash flows for an office building. For simplicity, we assume that each investment would have an NPV of exactly zero at a current cash flow of 100. Thus, if you were forced to invest today, you would choose the building with the higher cash flow, assuming the cash flow is

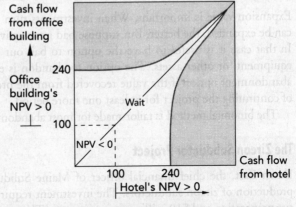

FIGURE 22.3

Development option for vacant land, assuming two mutually exclusive uses, either hotel or office building. The developer should "wait and see" unless the hotel's and office building's cash flows end up in one of the shaded areas.

Source: Adapted from Figure 1 in P. D. Childs, T. J. Riddiough, and A. J. Triantis, "Mixed Uses and the Redevelopment Option," *Real Estate Economics* 24 (Fall 1996), pp. 317–339. © 1996 Blackwell Publishers.

---

[6] The following example is based on P. D. Childs, T. J. Riddiough, and A. J. Triantis, "Mixed Uses and the Redevelopment Option," *Real Estate Economics* 24 (Fall 1996), pp. 317–339.

greater than 100. (What if you were forced to decide today and each building could generate the same cash flow, say, 150? You would flip a coin.)

If the two buildings' cash flows plot in the colored area at the lower right of Figure 22.3, you build the hotel. To fall in this area, the hotel's cash flows have to beat two hurdles. First, they must exceed a minimum level of about 240. Second, they must exceed the office building's cash flows by a sufficient amount. If the situation is reversed, with office building cash flows above the minimum level of 240, and also sufficiently above the hotel's, then you build the office building. In this case, the cash flows plot in the colored area at the top left of the figure.

Notice how the "Wait and see" region extends upward along the 45-degree line in Figure 22.3. When the cash flows from the hotel and office building are nearly the same, you become *very* cautious before choosing one over the other.

You may be surprised at how high cash flows have to be in Figure 22.3 to justify investment. There are three reasons. First, building the office building means not building the hotel, and vice versa. Second, the calculations underlying Figure 22.3 assumed cash flows that were small, but growing; therefore, the costs of waiting to invest were small. Third, the calculations did not consider the threat that someone might build a competing hotel or office building right next door. In that case the "relax and wait" area of Figure 22.3 would shrink dramatically.

22-3 THE ABANDONMENT OPTION

Expansion value is important. When investments turn out well, the quicker and easier the business can be expanded, the better. But suppose bad news arrives, and cash flows are far below expectations. In that case it is useful to have the option to bail out and recover the value of the project's plant, equipment, or other assets. The option to abandon is equivalent to a put option. You exercise that abandonment option if the value recovered from the project's assets is greater than the present value of continuing the project for at least one more period.

The binomial method is tailor-made for most abandonment options. Here is an example.

The Zircon Subductor Project

Dawn East, the chief financial officer of Maine Subductor Corp., has to decide whether to start production of zircon subductors. The investment required is $12 million—$2 million for roads and site preparation and $10 million for equipment. The equipment costs $700,000 per year ($.7 million) to operate (a fixed cost). For simplicity, we ignore other costs and taxes.

At today's prices, the project would generate revenues of $2.5 million per year. Annual output will be constant, so revenue is proportional to price. If the mine were operating today, cash flow would be $2.5 − .7 = $1.8 million.

Calculate the Present Value of the Project The first step in a real options analysis is to value the underlying asset, that is, the project if it had no options attached. Usually this is done by discounted cash flow (DCF). In this case the chief source of uncertainty is the future selling price of zircon subductors. Therefore Ms. East starts by calculating the present value of future revenues. She perceives no upward trend in subductor prices, and ends up forecasting stable prices for the next 8 years. Fixed costs are constant at $.7 million. The top panel of Figure 22.4 shows these cash-flow forecasts and calculates present values: about $13.8 million for revenues, after discounting at a risk-adjusted rate

YEAR	0	1	2	3	4	5	6	7	8
Forecasted revenues		2.50	2.50	2.50	2.50	2.50	2.50	2.50	2.50
Present value	13.837								
Fixed costs		0.70	0.70	0.70	0.70	0.70	0.70	0.70	0.70
Present value	4.347								
NPV	−2.510								

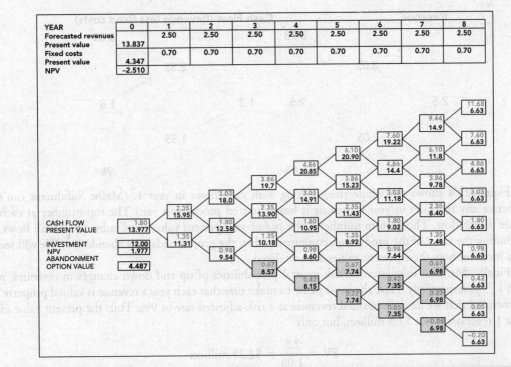

FIGURE 22.4

Binomial tree for the Subductor project. Cash flow (top number) and end-of-period present value are shown for each node in millions of dollars. Abandonment occurs if cash flows drop into the shaded boxes. Beginning present value is about $14 million.

Visit us at
www.mhhe.com/bmam10e

of 9%, and $4.3 million for fixed costs, after discounting at a risk-free rate of 6%.[7] The NPV of the project, assuming no salvage value or abandonment over its 10-year life, is:

$$NPV = PV(\text{revenues}) - PV(\text{fixed costs}) - \text{investment required}$$
$$= \$13.84 - 4.35 - 12.00 = -\$2.51 \text{ million}$$

This NPV is slightly negative, but Ms. East has so far made no provision for abandonment.

Build a Binomial Tree   Now Ms. East constructs a binomial tree for revenues and PV(revenues). She notes that subductor prices have followed a random walk with an annual standard deviation of about 20%. She constructs a binomial tree with one step per year. The "up" values for revenues are 122% of the prior year's revenues. The "down" values are 82% of prior revenues.[8] Thus, the up and down revenues for year 1 are $2.5 × 1.22 = $3.05 and $2.5 × .82 = $2.05 million, respectively. After deduction of fixed costs, the up and down cash flows are $2.35 and $1.35 million, respectively. The first two years of the resulting tree are shown below (figures in millions of dollars).

---

[7] Why calculate present values for revenues and fixed costs separately? Because it's easier to construct a binomial tree for revenues, which can be assumed to follow a random walk with constant standard deviation. We will subtract fixed costs after the binomial tree is constructed.

[8] The formula (given in Section 21-2) for the up percentage is $u = e^{\sigma\sqrt{h}}$ where σ is the standard deviation per year and h is the interval as a fraction of a year. In this case, $h = 1$ and $e^{\sigma} = e^{.2} = 1.22$. The down value is $d = 1/u = .82$.

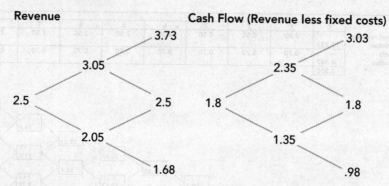

Revenue   Cash Flow (Revenue less fixed costs)

Figure 22.4 shows the whole tree, starting with cash flows in year 1. (Maine Subductor can't generate any revenues in year 0 because it hasn't started production yet.) The top number at each node is cash flow. The bottom number is the *end*-of-year present value of *all* subsequent cash flows, including the value of the production equipment when the project ends or is abandoned. We will see in a moment how these present values are calculated.

Finally, Ms. East calculates the risk-neutral probabilities of up and down changes in revenues, p and $1 - p$, respectively. Here she must pause to make sure that each year's revenue is valued properly. Remember that we have discounted revenues at a risk-adjusted rate of 9%. Thus the present value of year 1 revenues is not $2.5 million, but only

$$PV = \frac{2.5}{1.09} = \$2.29 \text{ million}$$

Therefore, Ms. East needs to calculate the risk-neutral probabilities that generate an expected return equal to the 6% risk-free rate.[9]

$$\text{Expected return} = \frac{[3.05p + 2.05(1 - p)]}{2.29} - 1 = .06$$

$$\text{Probability of up change} = .382$$
$$\text{Probability of down change} = .618$$

Ms. East can use these probabilities at every node of the binomial tree, because the proportional up and down moves are the same at each node.

Solve for Optimal Abandonment and Project Value

Ms. East has assumed a project life of 8 years. At that time the production equipment, which normally depreciates by about 5% per year, should be worth $6.63 million. This salvage value represents what the equipment could be sold for, or its value to Maine Subductor if shifted to another use.

Now let's calculate this project's value in the binomial tree. We start at the far right of Figure 22.4 (year 8) and work back to the present. The company will abandon for sure in year 8, when the ore body is exhausted. Thus we enter the ending salvage value ($6.63 million) as the end-of-year value in year 8. Then we step back to year 7.

Suppose that Maine Subductor ends up in the best possible place in that year, where cash flow is $9.44 million. The upside payoff if the company does not abandon is the "up" node in year 8:

---

[9] Notice that the "up" revenues are 122% of today's revenue level, but 133% of the present value of next year's forecasted revenues. Thus the "up" probability required to generate a 6% average return is relatively small.

.68 + 6.63 = $18.31 million. The downside payoff is 7.60 + 6.63 = $14.23 million. The present value, using the risk-neutral probabilities, is:

$$PV = \frac{(.382 \times 18.31) + (.618 \times 14.23)}{1.06} = \$14.90 \text{ million}$$

The company could abandon at the end of year 7, realizing salvage value of $6.98 million, but continuing is better. We therefore enter $14.90 million as the end-of-year value at the top node for year 7 in Figure 22.4.

We can fill in the end-of-period values for the other nodes in year 7 by the same procedure. But at some point, as we step down to lower and lower cash flows, there will come a node where it's better to bail out than continue. This occurs when cash flow is $.67 million. The present value of continuing is only:

$$PV = \frac{.382 \times (.98 + 6.63) + .618 \times (.42 + 6.63)}{1.06} = \$6.85 \text{ million}$$

The payoff to abandonment is $6.98 million, so that payoff is entered as the value in year 7 at all nodes with cash flows equal to or less than $.67 million.

The cash flows and end-of-year values for year 7 are the payoffs to continuing from year 6. We then calculate values in year 6, checking at each node whether to abandon. Repeat this drill for year 5, then year 4, and so on back to year 0. In this example, Maine Subductor should abandon the project if cash flows drop to $.67 million or less in each year. We have colored the nodes in Figure 22.4 where abandonment occurs.

Solving back through the binomial tree, we get a present value of $13.977 million at year 0, and net present value of $13.977 − 12.0 = $1.977 million.[10] If there were no option to abandon, the DCF valuation would be − $2.51 million. Therefore the option to abandon is worth 1.977 + 2.510 = $4.487 million.[11] In an APV format,

$$APV = NPV \text{ with no abandonment} + \text{abandonment option value}$$
$$= -2.51 + 4.487 = +\$1.977 \text{ million}$$

The project looks good, although Ms. East may wish to check out the timing option. She could decide to wait.

Abandonment Value and Project Life

Ms. East assumed that the zircon subductor project had a definite 8-year life. But most projects' economic lives are not known at the start. Cash flows from a new product may last only a year or so if the product fails in the marketplace. But if it succeeds, that product, or variations or improvements of it, could be produced for decades.

A project's economic life can be just as hard to predict as the project's cash flows. Yet in standard DCF capital-budgeting analysis, that life is assumed to end at a fixed future date. Real options analysis allows us to relax that assumption. Here is the procedure.[12]

We will spare you the calculations. You can check them, however. The "live" spreadsheet for Figure 22.4 is on this book's Web site (**www.mhhe.com/bmam10e**).

It turns out, however, that the value of *early* abandonment in this example is relatively small. Suppose that Maine Subductor could recover salvage value of $6.63 million in year 8, but not before. The present value of this recovery in year 0, using a 6% discount rate, is $4.16 million. APV in this case is −2.51 + 4.16 = $1.65 million, a little less than the APV of $1.977 million if early abandonment is allowed.

See S. C. Myers and S. Majd, "Abandonment Value and Project Life," in *Advances in Futures and Options Research*, ed. F. J. Fabozzi (Greenwich, CT: JAI Press, 1990).

1. Forecast the range of possible cash flows well beyond your best guess of the project's econom life. Suppose, for example, that your guess is 8 years. You could prepare a binomial tree li Figure 22.4 stretching out 20 years into the future.

2. Then value the project, including its abandonment value. In the best upside scenarios, proje life will be 20 years—it will never make sense to abandon before year 20. In the worst downsi scenarios, project life will be much shorter, because the project will be more valuable dead th alive. If your original guess about project life is right, then in intermediate scenarios, where actu cash flows match expectations, abandonment will occur around year 8.

This procedure links project life to the performance of the project. It does not impose an arbitra ending date, except in the far distant future.

Temporary Abandonment

Companies are often faced with complex options that allow them to abandon a project *temporari* that is, to mothball it until conditions improve. Suppose you own an oil tanker operating in the sho term spot market. (In other words, you charter the tanker voyage by voyage, at whatever short-ter charter rates prevail at the start of the voyage.) The tanker costs $50 million a year to operate and current tanker rates it produces charter revenues of $52.5 million per year. The tanker is therefo profitable but scarcely cause for celebration. Now tanker rates dip by about 10%, forcing revenu down to $47 million. Do you immediately lay off the crew and mothball the tanker until pric recover? The answer is clearly yes if the tanker business can be turned on and off like a faucet. B that is unrealistic. There is a fixed cost to mothballing the tanker. You don't want to incur this co only to regret your decision next month if rates rebound to their earlier level. The higher the co of mothballing and the more variable the level of charter rates, the greater the loss that you will prepared to bear before you call it quits and lay up the boat.

Suppose that eventually you do decide to take the boat off the market. You lay up the tank temporarily.[13] Two years later your faith is rewarded; charter rates rise, and the revenues fro operating the tanker creep above the operating cost of $50 million. Do you reactivate immediatel Not if there are costs to doing so. It makes more sense to wait until the project is well in the black a you can be fairly confident that you will not regret the cost of bringing the tanker back into operatio

These choices are illustrated in Figure 22.5. The blue line shows how the value of an operatin tanker varies with the level of charter rates. The black line shows the value of the tanker whe mothballed.[14] The level of rates at which it pays to mothball is given by M and the level at which pays to reactivate is given by R. The higher the costs of mothballing and reactivating and the great the variability in tanker rates, the further apart these points will be. You can see that it will pay f you to mothball as soon as the value of a mothballed tanker reaches the value of an operating tank plus the costs of mothballing. It will pay to reactivate as soon as the value of a tanker that is operatin in the spot market reaches the value of a mothballed tanker plus the costs of reactivating. If the lev of rates falls below M, the value of the tanker is given by the black line; if the level is greater than value is given by the blue line. If rates lie between M and R, the tanker's value depends on whether happens to be mothballed or operating.

---

[13] We assume it makes sense to keep the tanker in mothballs. If rates fall sufficiently, it will pay to scrap the tanker.

[14] Dixit and Pindyck estimate these thresholds for a medium-sized tanker and show how they depend on costs and the volatility of freight rat See A. K. Dixit and R. S. Pindyck, *Investment under Uncertainty* (Princeton, NJ: Princeton University Press, 1994), Chapter 7. Brennan a Schwartz provide an analysis of a mining investment that also includes an option to shut down temporarily. See M. Brennan and E. Schwar "Evaluating Natural Resource Investments," *Journal of Business* 58 (April 1985), pp. 135–157.

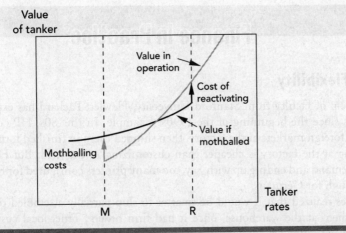

oil tanker should be mothballed when tanker rates fall to M, where the tanker's value if mothballed is enough
ove its value in operation to cover mothballing costs. The tanker is reactivated when rates recover to R.

2-4 FLEXIBLE PRODUCTION

exible production means the ability to vary production inputs or outputs in response to fluctuating
:mand or prices. Take the case of CT (combustion-turbine) generating plants, which are designed
) deliver short bursts of peak-load electrical power. CTs can't match the thermal efficiency of coal or
.iclear power plants, but CTs can be turned on or off on short notice. The coal plants and "nukes"
:e efficient only if operated on "base load" for long periods.

The profits from operating a CT depend on the *spark spread,* that is, on the difference between
.ie price of electricity and the cost of the natural gas used as fuel. CTs are money-losers at average
)ark spreads, but the spreads are volatile and can spike to very high levels when demand is high and
:nerating capacity tight. Thus a CT delivers a series of call options that can be exercised day by day
ven hour by hour) when spark spreads are sufficiently high. The call options are normally out-of-
.e-money (CTs typically operate only about 5% of the time), but the money made at peak prices
.akes investment in the CTs worthwhile.

The volatility of spark spreads depends on the correlation between the price of electricity and the
rice of natural gas used as fuel. If the correlation were 1.0, so that electricity and natural gas prices
noved together dollar for dollar, the spark spread would barely move from its average value, and the
ptions to operate the gas turbine would be worthless. But in fact the correlation is less than 1.0, so
ie options are valuable. In addition, some CTs are set up to give a further option, because they can
e run on oil as well as natural gas.[15]

In this example, the output is the same (electricity); option value comes from the ability to vary
ie amount produced and the raw materials used (natural gas or oil). In other cases, option value
omes from the flexibility to switch from product to product using the same production facilities. For
xample, textile firms have invested heavily in computer-controlled knitting machines, which allow
roduction to shift from product to product, or from design to design, as demand and fashion dictate.

Industrial steam and heating systems can also be designed to switch between fuels, depending on relative fuel costs. See N. Kulatilaka, "The
alue of Flexibility: The Case of a Dual-Fuel Industrial Steam Boiler," *Financial Management* 22 (Autumn 1993), pp. 271–280.

Finance In Practice

Valuing Flexibility

With the help of faculty from Stanford University, Hewlett-Packard has experimented with real options since the beginning of the 1990s. Example: In the '80s, HP customized inkjet printers for foreign markets at the factory, then shipped them in finished form to warehouses. Customizing at the factory is cheaper than customizing in the field. But HP kept guessing wrong on demand and ending up with, say, too many printers configured for French customers but not enough for Germans.

Executives realized that it would be smarter to ship partially assembled printers and then customize them at the warehouse, once it had firm orders. True, local customization costs more. But even though production costs rose, HP saved $3 million a month by more effectively matching supply to demand, says Corey A. Billington, a former Stanford professor who directs HP's Strategic Planning & Modeling group.

Common sense? Sure. But you can also view it as a neat solution of a real-options problem. Increasing the cost of production—anathema to your average engineer—was in effect the price HP paid for the option to delay configuration choices until the optimal time.

Source: P. Coy, "Exploiting Uncertainty." Reprinted from June 7, 1999 issue of *Business Week* by special premission, © 1999 by The McGraw-Hill Companies, Inc.

Flexibility in *procurement* can also have option value. For example, a computer manufacturer planning next year's production must also plan to buy components, such as disk drives and microprocessors, in large quantities. Should it strike a deal today with the component manufacturer? This locks in the quantity, price, and delivery dates. But it also gives up flexibility, for example, the ability to switch suppliers next year or buy at a "spot" price if next year's prices are lower.

The Finance in Practice box features another example of the value of flexibility in production or procurement.

22-5 Aircraft Purchase Options

For our final example, we turn to the problem confronting airlines that order new airplanes for future use. In this industry lead times between an order and delivery can extend to several years. Long lead times mean that airlines that order planes today may end up not needing them. You can see why an airline might negotiate for an aircraft purchase *option.*

In Section 10-3, we used aircraft purchase options to illustrate the option to expand. What we said there was the truth, but not the whole truth. Let's take another look. Suppose an airline forecasts a need for a new Airbus A320 four years hence.[16] It has at least three choices.

---

[16] The following example is based on J. E. Stonier, "What Is an Aircraft Purchase Option Worth? Quantifying Asset Flexibility Created through Manufacturer Lead-Time Reductions and Product Commonality," in *Handbook of Airline Finance,* ed. G. F. Butler and M. R. Keller. © 1999 Aviation Week Books.

Commit now. It can commit now to buy the plane, in exchange for Airbus's offer of locked-in price and delivery date.

Acquire option. It can seek a purchase option from Airbus, allowing the airline to decide later whether to buy. A purchase option fixes the price and delivery date if the option is exercised.

Wait and decide later. Airbus will be happy to sell another A320 at any time in the future if the airline wants to buy one. However, the airline may have to pay a higher price and wait longer for delivery, especially if the airline industry is flying high and many planes are on order.

The top half of Figure 22.6 shows the terms of a typical purchase option for an Airbus A320. The option must be exercised at year 3, when final assembly of the plane will begin. The option fixes the purchase price and the delivery date in year 4. The bottom half of the figure shows the consequences of "wait and decide later." We assume that the decision will come at year 3. If the decision is "buy," the airline pays the year-3 price and joins the queue for delivery in year 5 or later.

	Year 0	Year 3	Year 4	Year 5 or later
Buy option	Airline and manufacturer set price and delivery date	Exercise? (Yes or no)	Aircraft delivered if option exercised	
Wait	Wait and decide later	Buy now? If yes, negotiate price and wait for delivery.		Aircraft delivered if purchased at year 3.

FIGURE 22.6

This aircraft purchase option, if exercised at year 3, guarantees delivery at year 4 at a fixed price. Without the option, the airline can still order the plane at year 3, but the price is uncertain and the wait for delivery longer.

Source: Adapted from Figure 17–17 in J. Stonier, "What Is an Aircraft Purchase Option Worth? Quantifying Asset Flexibility Created through Manufacturer Lead-Time Reductions and Product Commonality," *Handbook of Airline Finance,* ed. G.F. Butler and M.R. Keller. Copyright 1999 Aviation Week Books; Reprinted with permission from The McGraw-Hill Companies, Inc.

The payoffs from "wait and decide later" can never be better than the payoffs from an aircraft purchase option, since the airline can discard the option and negotiate afresh with Airbus if it wishes. In most cases, however, the airline will be better off in the future with the option than without it; the airline is at least guaranteed a place in the production line, and it may have locked in a favorable purchase price. But how much are these advantages worth today, compared to the wait-and-see strategy?

Figure 22.7 illustrates Airbus's answers to this problem. It assumes a three-year purchase option with an exercise price equal to the current A320 price of $45 million. The present value of the purchase option depends on both the NPV of purchasing an A320 at that price and on the forecasted wait for delivery if the airline does *not* have a purchase option but nevertheless decides to place an order in year 3. The longer the wait in year 3, the more valuable it is to have the purchase option today. (Remember that the purchase option holds a place in the A320 production line and guarantees delivery in year 4.)

If the NPV of buying an A320 today is very high (the right-hand side of Figure 22.7), future NPV will probably be high as well, and the airline will want to buy regardless of whether it has a purchase option. In this case the value of the purchase option comes mostly from the value of guaranteed delivery

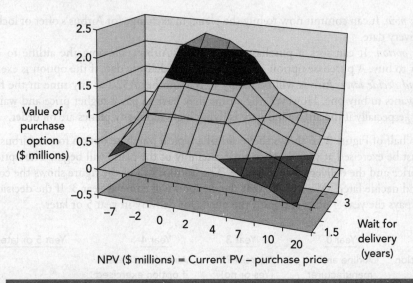

FIGURE 22.7

Value of aircraft purchase option—the extra value of the option versus waiting and possibly negotiating purchase later. (See Figure 22.6.) The purchase option is worth most when NPV of purchase now is about zero and the forecasted wait for delivery is long.

Source: Adapted from Fig. 17–20 in J. Stonier, "What Is an Aircraft Purchase Option Worth? Quantifying Asset Flexibility Created Through Manufacturer Lead-Time Reductions and Product Commonality," in *Handbook of Aviation Finance.*, ed. G. F. Butler and M. R. Keller. © 1999 Aviation Week Books; Reprinted with permission from The McGraw-Hill Companies, Inc.

in year 4.[17] If the NPV is very low, then the option has low value because the airline is unlikely exercise it. (Low NPV today probably means low NPV in year 3.) The purchase option is worth t most, compared to the wait-and-decide-later strategy, when NPV is around zero. In this case the airli can exercise the option, getting a good price and early delivery, if future NPV is higher than expecte alternatively, it can walk away from the option if NPV disappoints. Of course, if it walks away, it m still wish to negotiate with Airbus for delivery at a price lower than the option's exercise price.

We have cruised by many of the technical details of Airbus's valuation model for purchase optio But the example does illustrate how real-options models are being built and used. By the way, Airb offers more than just plain-vanilla purchase options. Airlines can negotiate "rolling options," whi lock in price but do not guarantee a place on the production line. (Exercise of the rolling option mea that the airline joins the end of the queue.) Airbus also offers a purchase option that includes the ri to switch from delivery of an A320 to an A319, a somewhat smaller plane.

22-6 A CONCEPTUAL PROBLEM?

In this chapter we have suggested that option pricing models can help to value the real options capital investment decisions. But that raises a question.

---

[17] The Airbus real-options model assumes that future A320 prices will be increased when demand is high, but only to an upper bound. T the airline that waits and decides later may still have a positive-NPV investment opportunity if future demand and NPV are high. Figure 2 plots the *difference* between the value of the purchase option and this wait-and-see opportunity. This difference can shrink when NPV is h especially if forecasted waiting times are short.

When we introduced option pricing models in Chapter 21, we suggested that the trick is to nstruct a package of the underlying asset and a loan that would give exactly the same payoffs as the tion. If the two investments do not sell for the same price, then there are arbitrage possibilities. But any assets are not freely traded. This means that we can no longer rely on arbitrage arguments to stify the use of option models.

The risk-neutral method still makes practical sense, however. It's really just an application of the *tainty-equivalent* method introduced in Chapter 9.[18] The key assumption—implicit till now—is at the company's *shareholders* have access to assets with the same risk characteristics (e.g., the same ta) as the capital investments being evaluated by the firm.

Think of each real investment opportunity as having a "double," a security or portfolio with entical risk. Then the expected rate of return offered by the double is also the cost of capital for the al investment and the discount rate for a DCF valuation of the investment project. Now what would vestors pay for a real *option* based on the project? The same as for an identical traded option written the double. This traded option does not have to exist; it is enough to know how it would be valued investors, who could employ either the arbitrage or the risk-neutral method. The two methods give e same answer, of course.

When we value a real option by the risk-neutral method, we are calculating the option's value it could be traded. This exactly parallels standard capital budgeting. Shareholders would vote nanimously to accept any capital investment whose market value *if traded* exceeds its cost, as long as ey can buy traded securities with the same risk characteristics as the project. This key assumption pports the use of both DCF and real-option valuation methods.

actical Challenges

ne challenges in applying real-options analysis are not conceptual but practical. It isn't always easy. e can tick off some of the reasons why.

First, real options can be complex, and valuing them can absorb a lot of analytical and computational rsepower. Whether you want to invest in that horsepower is a matter for business judgment. metimes an approximate answer now is more useful than a "perfect" answer later, particularly if the rfect answer comes from a complicated model that other managers will regard as a black box. One vantage of real options analysis, if you keep it simple, is that it's relatively easy to explain. Complex cision trees can often be described as the payoffs to one or two simple call or put options.

The second problem is lack of *structure*. To quantify the value of a real option, you have to specify possible payoffs, which depend on the range of possible values of the underlying asset, exercise ices, timing of exercise, etc. In this chapter we have taken well-structured examples where it is easy see the road map of possible outcomes. In other cases you may not have a road map. For example, ading this book can enhance your personal call option to work in financial management, yet we spect that you would find it hard to write down how that option would change the binomial tree your entire future career.

A third problem can arise when your *competitors* have real options. This is not a problem in dustries where products are standardized and no single competitor can shift demand and prices. But hen you face just a few key competitors, all with real options, then the options can interact. If so, u can't value your options without thinking of your competitors' moves. Your competitors will be inking in the same fashion.

Jse of risk-neutral probabilities converts future cash flows to certainty equivalents, which are then discounted to present value at a risk-free e.

An analysis of competitive interactions would take us into other branches of economics, includir game theory. But you can see the danger of assuming passive competitors. Think of the timing optior A simple real-options analysis will often tell you to wait and learn before investing in a new marke Be careful that you don't wait and learn that a competitor has moved first.[19]

Given these hurdles, you can understand why systematic, quantitative valuation of real optior is restricted mostly to well-structured problems like the examples in this chapter. The qualitativ implications of real options are widely appreciated, however. Real options give the financial manage a conceptual framework for strategic planning and thinking about capital investments. If you ca identify and understand real options, you will be a more sophisticated consumer of DCF analysis an better equipped to invest your company's money wisely.

Understanding real options also pays off when you can *create* real options, adding value by addin flexibility to the company's investments and operations. For example, it may be better to desig and build a series of modular production plants, each with capacity of 50,000 tons per year c magnoosium alloy, than to commit to one large plant with capacity of 150,000 tons per year. Th larger plant will probably be more efficient because of economies of scale. But with the smaller plant, you retain the flexibility to expand in step with demand and to defer investment when demand growt is disappointing.

Sometimes valuable options can be created simply by "overbuilding" in the initial round c investment. For example, oil-production platforms are typically built with vacant deck space to reduc the cost of adding equipment later. Undersea oil pipelines from the platforms to shore are often buil with larger diameters and capacity than production from the platform will require. The addition; capacity is then available at low cost if additional oil is found nearby. The extra cost of a larger diameter pipeline is much less than the cost of building a second pipeline later.

SUMMARY

In Chapter 21 you learned the basics of option valuation. In this chapter we described four importan real options:

1. *The option to make follow-on investments.* Companies often cite "strategic" value when takin; on negative-NPV projects. A close look at the projects' payoffs reveals call options on follow-o; projects in addition to the immediate projects' cash flows. Today's investments can generat tomorrow's opportunities.

2. *The option to wait (and learn) before investing.* This is equivalent to owning a call option on th investment project. The call is exercised when the firm commits to the project. But rather than exercising the call immediately, it's often better to defer a positive-NPV project in order to keep the call alive. Deferral is most attractive when uncertainty is great and immediate project cash flows—which are lost or postponed by waiting—are small.

3. *The option to abandon.* The option to abandon a project provides partial insurance against failure. This is a put option; the put's exercise price is the value of the project's assets if sold o shifted to a more valuable use.

4. *The option to vary the firm's output or its production methods.* Firms often build flexibility into thei production facilities so that they can use the cheapest raw materials or produce the most valuabl set of outputs. In this case they effectively acquire the option to exchange one asset for another.

[19] Being the first mover into a new market is not always the best strategy, of course. Sometimes later movers win. For a survey of real option and product-market competition, see H. Smit and L. Trigeorgis, *Strategic Investment, Real Options and Games* (Princeton, NJ: Princeton University Press, 2004).

We should offer here a healthy warning: The real options encountered in practice are often complex. Each real option brings its own issues and trade-offs. Nevertheless the tools that you have learned in this and previous chapters can be used in practice. The Black–Scholes formula often suffices to value expansion options. Problems of investment timing and optimal abandonment can be tackled with binomial trees.

Binomial trees are cousins of decision trees. You work back through binomial trees from future payoffs to present value. Whenever a future decision needs to be made, you figure out the value-maximizing choice, using the principles of option pricing theory, and record the resulting value at the appropriate node of the tree.

Don't jump to the conclusion that real-option-valuation methods can replace discounted cash flow (DCF). First, DCF works fine for safe cash flows. It also works for "cash cow" assets—that is, for assets or businesses whose value depends primarily on forecasted cash flows, not on real options. Second, the starting point in most real-option analyses is the present value of an underlying asset. To value the underlying asset, you typically have to use DCF.

Real options are rarely traded assets. When we value a real option, we are estimating its value if it could be traded. This is the standard approach in corporate finance, the same approach taken in DCF valuations. The key assumption is that shareholders can buy traded securities or portfolios with the same risk characteristics as the real investments being evaluated by the firm. If so, they would vote unanimously for any real investment whose market value if traded would exceed the investment required. This key assumption supports the use of both DCF and real-option valuation methods.

FURTHER READING

The Further Reading for Chapter 10 lists several introductory articles on real options. The Spring 2005 and 2007 issues of the Journal of Applied Corporate Finance *contain additional articles.*

The Spring 2006 issue contains two further articles:

R. L. McDonald, "The Role of Real Options in Capital Budgeting: Theory and Practice," *Journal of Applied Corporate Finance* 18 (Spring 2006), pp. 28–39.

M. Amram, F. Li, and C. A. Perkins, "How Kimberly-Clark Uses Real Options," *Journal of Applied Corporate Finance* 18 (Spring 2006), pp. 40–47.

The standard texts on real options include:

M. Amran and N. Kulatilaka, *Real Options: Managing Strategic Investments in an Uncertain World* (Boston: Harvard Business School Press, 1999).

T. Copeland and V. Antikarov, *Real Options: A Practitioner's Guide* (New York: Texere, 2001).

A. K. Dixit and R. S. Pindyck, *Investment under Uncertainty* (Princeton, NJ: Princeton University Press, 1994).

H. Smit and L. Trigeorgis, *Strategic Investment, Real Options and Games* (Princeton, NJ: Princeton University Press, 2004).

L. Trigeorgis, *Real Options* (Cambridge, MA: MIT Press, 1996).

Mason and Merton review a range of option applications to corporate finance:

S. P. Mason and R. C. Merton, "The Role of Contingent Claims Analysis in Corporate Finance," in E. I. Altman and M. G. Subrahmanyan (eds.), *Recent Advances in Corporate Finance* (Homewood, IL: Richard D. Irwin, Inc., 1985).

Brennan and Schwartz have worked out an interesting application to natural resource investments:

M. J. Brennan and E. S. Schwartz, "Evaluating Natural Resource Investments," *Journal of Business* 58 (April 1985), pp. 135–157.

BASIC

1. Look again at the valuation in Table 22.2 of the option to invest in the Mark II project. Consider a change in each of the following inputs. Would the change increase or decrease the value of the expansion option?
   a. Increased uncertainty (higher standard deviation).
   b. More optimistic forecast (higher expected value) of the Mark II in 1985.
   c. Increase in the required investment in 1985.

2. A start-up company is moving into its first offices and needs desks, chairs, filing cabinets, and other furniture. It can buy the furniture for $25,000 or rent it for $1,500 per month. The founders are of course confident in their new venture, but nevertheless they rent. Why? What's the option?

3. Flip back to Tables 6.2 and 6.6, where we assumed an economic life of seven years for IM&C's guano plant. What's wrong with that assumption? How would you undertake a more complete analysis?

4. You own a parcel of vacant land. You can develop it now, or wait.
   a. What is the advantage of waiting?
   b. Why might you decide to develop the property immediately?

5. Gas turbines are among the least efficient ways to produce electricity, much less thermally efficient than coal or nuclear plants. Why do gas-turbine generating stations exist? What's the option?

6. Why is quantitative valuation of real options often difficult in practice? List the reasons briefly.

7. True or false?
   a. Real-options analysis sometimes tells firms to make negative-NPV investments to secure future growth opportunities.
   b. Using the Black–Scholes formula to value options to invest is dangerous when the investment project would generate significant immediate cash flows.
   c. Binomial trees can be used to evaluate options to acquire or abandon an asset. It's OK to use risk-neutral probabilities in the trees even when the asset beta is 1.0 or higher.
   d. It's OK to use the Black–Scholes formula or binomial trees to value real options, even though the options are not traded.
   e. A real-options valuation will sometimes reveal that it's better to invest in a single large plant than a series of smaller plants.

8. Alert financial managers can *create* real options. Give three or four possible examples.

INTERMEDIATE

9. Describe each of the following situations in the language of options:
   a. Drilling rights to undeveloped heavy crude oil in Bombay High. Development and production of the oil is a negative-NPV endeavor. (The break-even oil price is ₹3,000 per barrel, versus a spot price of ₹2,500.) However, the decision to develop can be put off for up to five years. Development costs are expected to increase by 5% per year.
   b. A restaurant is producing net cash flows, after all out-of-pocket expenses, of ₹700,000 per year. There is no upward or downward trend in the cash flows, but they fluctuate as a random walk, with an annual standard deviation of 15%. The real estate occupied by the restaurant is owned, not leased, and could be sold for ₹5 million. Ignore taxes.

c. A variation on part (b): Assume the restaurant faces known fixed costs of ₹300,000 per year, incurred as long as the restaurant is operating. Thus,

$$\text{Net cash flow} = \text{revenue less variable costs} - \text{fixed costs}$$
$$₹700,000 = 1,000,000 - 300,000$$

The annual standard deviation of the forecast error of revenue less variable costs is 10.5%. The interest rate is 10%. Ignore taxes.

d. A paper mill can be shut down in periods of low demand and restarted if demand improves sufficiently. The costs of closing and reopening the mill are fixed.

e. A real estate developer uses a parcel of urban land as a parking lot, although construction of either a hotel or an apartment building on the land would be a positive-NPV investment.

f. Air India negotiates a purchase option for 10 Dreamliners produced by Boeing. Air India must confirm its order in 2018. Otherwise, Boeing will be free to sell the aircraft to other airlines.

10. Look again at Table 22.2. How does the value in 1982 of the option to invest in the Mark II change if:

   Visit us at
   www.mhhe.com/bmam10e

   a. The investment required for the Mark II is ₹800 million (vs. ₹900 million)?
   b. The present value of the Mark II in 1982 is ₹500 million (vs. ₹467 million)?
   c. The standard deviation of the Mark II's present value is only 20% (vs. 35%)?

11. You own a one-year call option on one acre of Mumbai real estate. The exercise price is ₹200 crores, and the current, appraised market value of the land is ₹170 crores. The land is currently used as a parking lot, generating just enough money to cover real estate taxes. The annual standard deviation is 20% and the interest rate 8%. How much is your call worth?

   Visit us at
   www.mhhe.com/bmam10e

12. A variation on Problem 11: Suppose the land is occupied by a warehouse generating rents of ₹150,000 after real estate taxes and all other out-of-pocket costs. The present value of the land plus warehouse is again ₹1.7 million. Other facts are as in Problem 11. You have a European call option. What is it worth?

   Visit us at
   www.mhhe.com/bmam10e

13. You have an option to purchase all of the assets of the Overland Railroad for $2.5 billion. The option expires in nine months. You estimate Overland's current (month 0) present value (PV) as $2.7 billion. Overland generates after-tax free cash flow (FCF) of $50 million at the end of each quarter (i.e., at the end of each three-month period). If you exercise your option at the start of the quarter, that quarter's cash flow is paid out to you. If you do not exercise, the cash flow goes to Overland's current owners.

   Visit us at
   www.mhhe.com/bmam10e

   In each quarter, Overland's PV either increases by 10% or decreases by 9.09%. This PV includes the quarterly FCF of $50 million. After the $50 million is paid out, PV drops by $50 million. Thus the binomial tree for the first quarter is (figures in millions):

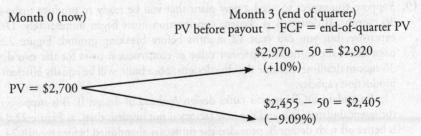

The risk-free interest rate is 2% per quarter.

a. Build a binomial tree for Overland, with one up or down change for each three-month period (three steps to cover your nine-month option).

b. Suppose you can only exercise your option now, or after nine months (not at month 3 or 6). Would you exercise now?

c. Suppose you can exercise now, or at month 3, 6, or 9. What is your option worth today? Should you exercise today, or wait?

14. In Section 10-4 we considered two production technologies for a new Wankel-engined outboard motor. Technology A was the most efficient but had no salvage value if the new outboards failed to sell. Technology B was less efficient but offered a salvage value of $17 million.

Visit us at
www.mhhe.com/bmam10e

Figure 10.5 shows the present value of the project as either $24 or $16 million in year 1 if Technology A is used. Assume that the present value of these payoffs is $18 million at year 0.

a. With Technology B, the payoffs at year 1 are $22.5 or $15 million. What is the present value of these payoffs in year 0 if Technology B is used? (*Hint:* The payoffs with Technology B are 93.75% of the payoffs from Technology A.)

b. Technology B allows abandonment in year 1 for $17 million salvage value. You also get cash flow of $1.5 million, for a total of $18.5 million. Calculate abandonment value, assuming a risk-free rate of 7%.

15. Respond to the following comments.

a. "You don't need option pricing theories to value flexibility. Just use a decision tree. Discount the cash flows in the tree at the company cost of capital."

b. "These option pricing methods are just plain nutty. They say that real options on risky assets are worth more than options on safe assets."

c. " Real-options methods eliminate the need for DCF valuation of investment projects."

16. We mentioned that combustion-turbine (CT) generators can be set up to burn either oil or natural gas. How will the value of this option be affected by the correlation between oil and natural gas prices? Explain briefly.

17. Ravi Jacob, who has only read part of Chapter 10, decides to value a real option by (1) setting out a decision tree, with cash flows and probabilities forecasted for each future outcome; (2) deciding what to do at each decision point in the tree; and (3) discounting the resulting expected cash flows at the company cost of capital. Will this procedure give the right answer? Why or why not?

18. In binomial trees, risk-neutral probabilities are set to generate an expected rate of return equal to the risk-free interest rate in each branch of the tree. What do you think of the following statement: "The value of an option to acquire an asset increases with the difference between the risk-free rate of interest and the weighted-average cost of capital for the asset"?

CHALLENGE

19. Suppose you expect to need a new plant that will be ready to produce turbo-encabulators in 36 months. If design A is chosen, construction must begin immediately. Design B is more expensive, but you can wait 12 months before breaking ground. Figure 22.8 on the next page shows the cumulative present value of construction costs for the two designs up to the 36-month deadline. Assume that the designs, once built, will be equally efficient and have equal production capacity.

A standard DCF analysis ranks design A ahead of design B. But suppose the demand for turbo-encabulators falls and the new factory is not needed; then, as Figure 22.8 shows, the firm is better off with design B, provided the project is abandoned before month 24.

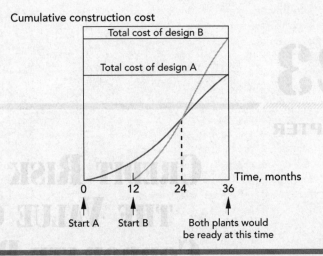

Cumulative construction cost of the two plant designs. Plant A takes 36 months to build; plant B, only 24. But plant B costs more.

Describe this situation as the choice between two (complex) call options. Then describe the same situation in terms of (complex) abandonment options. The two descriptions should imply identical payoffs, given optimal exercise strategies.

20. In Chapter 4, we expressed the value of a share of stock as:

$$P_0 = \frac{EPS_1}{r} + PVGO$$

where EPS_1 is earnings per share from existing assets, r is the expected rate of return required by investors, and PVGO is the present value of growth opportunities. PVGO really consists of a portfolio of expansion options.[20]

a. What is the effect of an increase in PVGO on the standard deviation or beta of the stock's rate of return?

b. Suppose the CAPM is used to calculate the cost of capital for a growth (high-PVGO) firm. Assume all-equity financing. Will this cost of capital be the correct hurdle rate for investments to expand the firm's plant and equipment, or to introduce new products?

---

[20] If this challenge problem intrigues you, check out two articles by Eduardo Schwartz and Mark Moon, who attempt to use real-options theory to value Internet companies: "Rational Valuation of Internet Companies," *Financial Analysts Journal* 56 (May/June 2000), pp. 62–65, and "Rational Pricing of Internet Companies Revisited," *The Financial Review* 36 (November 2001), pp. 7–25.

23

CHAPTER

CREDIT RISK AND THE VALUE OF CORPORATE DEBT

We first looked at how to value bonds way back in Chapter 3. We explained in that chapter what bond dealers mean when they refer to spot rates of interest and yields to maturity. We discussed why long-term and short-term bonds may offer different rates of interest and why prices of long-term bonds are affected more by a change in rates. We looked at the difference between nominal and real (inflation-adjusted) interest rates, and we saw how interest rates respond to changes in the prospects for inflation.

All the lessons of Chapter 3 hold good for both government and corporate bonds, but there is also a fundamental distinction between government and corporate issues. When the U.S. Treasury borrows money, you can be confident that the debt will be repaid in full and on time. This is not true of corporate borrowing. Look, for example, at Figure 23.1. You can see that in 2008 companies defaulted on a record $430 billion of debt. Bondholders are aware of the danger that they will not get their money back and so demand a higher rate of interest.

The extra yield on corporate bonds is the annual payment that investors demand for taking on the possibility of default. We begin our review of corporate bonds by looking at how this yield spread varies with the likelihood of default. Then in Section 23-2 we look more carefully at the company's decision to default. We show that default is an *option;* if the going becomes too tough, the company has the option to stop payments on its bonds and hand over the business to the debtholders. We know what determines the value of options; therefore, we know the basic variables that must enter into the valuation of corporate bonds.

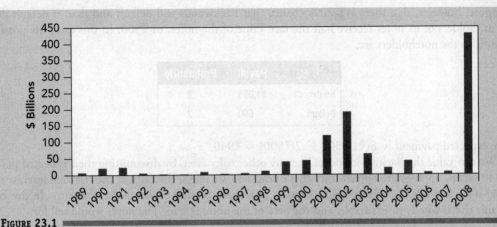

FIGURE 23.1

Global face value of defaulting debt, 1989–2008, in billions of dollars.

Source: Standard & Poor's, *Default, Transition and Recovery: 2008 Annual Global Corporate Default Study and Rating Transitions*, April 2, 2009.

Our next step is to look at bond ratings and some of the techniques that are used by banks and bond investors to estimate the probability that the borrower will not be able to repay its debts. As a company's prospects deteriorate, bondholders worry increasingly about this risk, and their worries are reflected in lower bond prices. Therefore, in the final section we describe some of the ways that financial managers measure the risk of loss from investment in corporate bonds.

23-1 YIELDS ON CORPORATE DEBT

Six Flags is known for the roller-coaster rides at its theme parks, but the company itself has also experienced a white-knuckle ride of its own. By early 2009 the price of its 9.625% bonds of 2014 had fallen to 19.5% of face value and offered a yield to maturity of 64%. A naïve investor who compared this yield with the 2% yield on Treasury bonds might have concluded that the Six Flags debt was a wonderful investment. But the owner would earn a return of 64% on the debt only if the company repaid the bonds in full. That was looking increasingly doubtful. Over the previous decade the company had recorded a series of losses, and it entered 2009 with over $2 billion of debt and negative book equity. Because there was a considerable risk that the company would default on its bonds, the *expected* return was much less than 64%.

Corporate bonds, such as the Six Flags bond, offer a higher *promised* yield than government bonds, but do they necessarily offer a higher *expected* yield? We can answer this question with a simple numerical example. Suppose that the interest rate on one-year *risk-free* bonds is 5%. Backwoods Chemical Company has issued 5% notes with a face value of ₹1,000, maturing in one year. What will the Backwoods notes sell for?

If the notes are risk-free, the answer is easy—just discount principal (₹1,000) and interest (₹50) at 5%:

$$\text{PV of notes} = \frac{₹1,000 + 50}{1.05} = ₹1,000$$

Suppose, however, that there is a 20% chance that Backwoods will default and that, if default does occur, holders of its notes receive half the face value of the notes, or ₹500. In this case, the possible payoffs to the noteholders are:

	Payoff	Probability
No default	₹1,050	.8
Default	500	.2

The expected payment is $.8(₹1,050) + .2(₹500) = ₹940$.

We can value the Backwoods notes like any other risky asset, by discounting their expected payoff (₹940) at the appropriate opportunity cost of capital. We might discount at the risk-free interest rate (5%) if Backwoods's possible default is totally unrelated to other events in the economy. In this case default risk is wholly diversifiable, and the beta of the notes is zero. The notes would sell for:

$$\text{PV of notes} = \frac{₹940}{1.05} = ₹895$$

An investor who purchased the notes for ₹895 would receive a *promised* yield of 17.3%:

$$\text{Promised yield} = \frac{₹1050}{₹895} - 1 = .173$$

That is, an investor who purchased the notes for ₹895 would earn a return of 17.3% if Backwoods does not default. Bond traders therefore might say that the Backwoods notes "yield 17.3%." But the smart investor would realize that the notes' *expected* yield is only 5%, the same as on risk-free bonds.

This of course assumes that the risk of default with these notes is wholly diversifiable, so that they have no market risk. In general, risky bonds do have market risk (that is, positive betas) because default is more likely to occur in recessions when all businesses are doing poorly. Suppose that investors demand a 3% risk premium and an 8% expected rate of return. Then the Backwoods notes will sell for $940/1.08 = ₹870$ and offer a promised yield of $(1,050/870) - 1 = .207$, or 20.7%.

What Determines the Yield Spread?

Figure 23.2 shows how the yield spread on U.S. corporate bonds varies with the bond's risk. Bonds rated Aaa by Moody's are the highest-grade bonds and are issued only by blue-chip companies. The promised yield on these bonds has on average been 1% higher than the yield on Treasuries. Baa bonds are rated three notches lower; the yield spread on these bonds has averaged over 2%. At the bottom of the heap are high-yield or "junk" bonds. There is considerable variation in the yield spreads on junk bonds; a typical spread might be about 5% over Treasuries, but, as we saw in the case of the Six Flags bond, spreads can go skyward as companies approach distress.

Remember these are promised yields and companies don't always keep their promises. Many high-yielding bonds have defaulted, while some of the more successful issuers have called their debt, thus depriving their holders of the prospect of a continuing stream of high coupon payments. So while the *promised yield* on junk bonds has averaged 5% more than yields on Treasuries, the annual *return* since 1980 has been less than 2% higher.

Figure 23.2 also shows that yield spreads can vary quite sharply from one year to the next. For example, they were unusually high in 1990–1991, 2000–2002, and 2008. Why is this? The main reason is that these were periods when profits were poor and defaults more likely. (Figure 23.1 shows

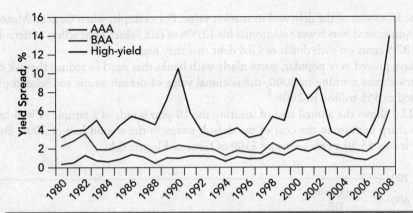

FIGURE 23.2

End-year yield spreads between corporate and 10-year Treasury bonds, 1980–2008.

Source: The Federal Reserve, **www.federalreserve.gov**, and Datastream.

how default rates jumped in these years.) However, the fluctuations in spreads appear to be too large to be due simply to changing probabilities of default. It seems that there are occasions when investors are particularly reluctant to bear the risk of low-grade bonds and so scurry to the safe haven of government debt.[1]

To understand more precisely what the yield spread measures, compare these two strategies:

Strategy 1: Invest $1,000 in a floating-rate default-free bond yielding 9%.[2]

Strategy 2: Invest $1,000 in a comparable floating-rate corporate bond yielding 10%. At the same time take out an insurance policy to protect yourself against the possibility of default. You pay an insurance premium of 1% a year, but in the event of default you are compensated for any loss in the bond's value.

Both strategies provide exactly the same payoff. In the case of Strategy 2 you gain a 1% higher yield but this is exactly offset by the 1% annual premium on the insurance policy. Why does the insurance premium have to be equal to the spread? Because, if it weren't, one strategy would dominate the other and there would be an arbitrage opportunity. The law of one price tells us that two equivalent risk-free investments must cost the same.

Our example tells us how to interpret the spread on corporate bonds. It is equal to the annual premium that would be needed to insure the bond against default.[3]

By the way, you *can* insure corporate bonds; you do so with an arrangement called a *credit default swap* (CDS). If you buy a default swap, you commit to pay a regular insurance premium (or *spread*).[4] In return, if the company subsequently defaults on its debt, the seller of the swap pays you the difference

---

[1] For evidence on the effect of changing risk aversion on bond spreads, see A. Berndt, R. Douglas, D. Duffie, M. Ferguson, and D. Schranzk, "Measuring Default Risk Premia from Default Swap Rates and EDFs," unpublished paper, Graduate School of Business, Stanford University, November 2005.

[2] The interest payment on floating-rate bonds goes up and down as the general level of interest rates changes. Thus a floating-rate default-free bond will sell at close to face value on each coupon date. Many governments issue "floaters." The U.S. Treasury does not do so, though some U.S. government agencies do.

[3] For illustration, we have used the example of a floating-rate bond to demonstrate the equivalence between the yield spread and the cost of default insurance. But the spread on a fixed-rate corporate bond should be effectively identical to that on a floater.

[4] In the case of low-grade bonds, when the regular spread does not sufficiently protect the seller against the possibility of an early default, the buyer of the default swap may also be asked to pay an up-front fee.

between the face value of the debt and its market value. For example, when General Motors defaulted in 2009, its unsecured bonds were auctioned for 12.5% of face value. Thus sellers of default swaps had to pay out 87.5 cents on each dollar of GM debt that they had insured.

CDSs have proved very popular, particularly with banks that need to reduce the risk of their loan books. From almost nothing in 2000, the notional value of default swaps and related products had mushroomed to $55 trillion in 2008.[5]

Figure 23.3 shows the annual cost of insuring the 10-year bonds of a sample of well-known firms. Notice the sharp increase in the cost of the default swaps in the second half of 2008. By the end of September it cost $5.50 a year to insure $100 of General Electric debt.

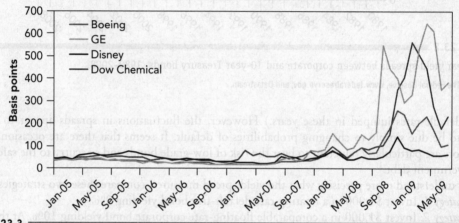

FIGURE 23.3

Credit default swaps insure the holders of corporate bonds against default. This figure shows the cost of default swaps on the 10-year senior debt of four companies.

Source: Datastream

Many of these default swaps were sold by *monoline insurers,* which specialize in providing services to the capital markets. The monolines had traditionally concentrated on insuring relatively safe municipal debt but had been increasingly prepared to underwrite corporate debt, as well as many securities that were backed by subprime mortgages. By 2008 insurance companies had sold protection on $2.4 trillion of bonds. As the outlook for many of these bonds deteriorated, investors began to question whether the insurance companies had sufficient capital to make good on their guarantees.

One of the largest providers of credit protection was AIG Financial Products, part of the giant insurance group, AIG, with a portfolio of over $440 billion of credit guarantees. AIG's clients never dreamt that the company would be unable to pay up: not only was AIG triple-A rated, but it had promised to post generous collateral if the value of the insured securities dropped or if its own credit rating fell. So confident was AIG of its strategy that the head of its financial products group claimed that it was hard "to even see a scenario within any kind of realm of reason that would see us losing one dollar in any of these transactions." But in September 2008 this unthinkable scenario occurred, when the credit rating agencies downgraded AIG's debt, and the company found itself obliged to provide $32 billion of additional collateral within the next 15 days. Had AIG defaulted, everyone who had

---

[5] Related credit derivatives include credit-linked notes, total return swaps, and credit options. For a useful survey of the credit-derivative market, see J. P. Morgan, "The J. P. Morgan Guide to Credit Derivatives," at **www.investinginbonds.com/assets/files/intro_to_credit_derivatives.pdf.**

ought a CDS contract from the company would have suffered large losses on these contracts. To ave AIG from imminent collapse, the Federal Reserve stepped in with an $85 billion rescue package.

The Reserve Bank of India (RBI) allowed banks to hedge their bond portfolios using CDS in November 2011. The first CDS deal in India took place in early December 2011, when IDBI nderwrote ₹100 million of AAA rated bonds of Rural Electrification Corporation and Indian Railway inance Corporation. The CDS spread was 90 basis points.

3-2 THE OPTION TO DEFAULT

The difference between a corporate bond and a comparable Government security is that the company as the option to default whereas the government supposedly doesn't.[6] That is a valuable option. If ou don't believe us think about whether (other things equal) you would prefer to be a shareholder n a company with limited liability or in a company with unlimited liability. Of course, you would refer to have the option to walk away from your company's debts. Unfortunately, every silver lining as its cloud, and the drawback to having a default option is that corporate bondholders expect to be ompensated for giving it to you. That is why corporate bonds sell at lower prices and offer higher ields than government bonds.

We can illustrate the nature of the default option by returning to the plight of Circular File Company, which we discussed in Chapter 18. Circular File borrowed ₹50 per share, but then the firm ell on hard times and the market value of its assets fell to ₹30. Circular's bond and stock prices fell to ₹25 and ₹5, respectively. Thus Circular's *market-value* balance sheet is:

Circular File Company (Market Values)

Asset value	₹30	₹25	Bonds
		5	Stock
	₹30	₹30	Firm value

If Circular's debt were due and payable now, the firm could not repay the ₹50 it originally borrowed. It would default, leaving bondholders with assets worth ₹30 and shareholders with nothing. The reason that Circular stock has a market value of ₹5 is that the debt is *not* due now, but rather a year from now. A stroke of good fortune could increase firm value enough to pay off the bondholders in full, with something left over for the stockholders.

When Circular File borrowed, it acquired an option to default. In other words, it is not compelled to repay the debt at maturity. If the value of its assets is less than the ₹50 that it owes, it will choose to default on the debt and the bondholders will get to keep the assets. To put it another way, when Circular borrowed, the bondholders effectively acquired the company's assets and the shareholders gained an option to buy them back by paying off the debt. In effect, the stockholders purchased a call option on the assets of the firm. Thus the balance sheet of Circular File can be expressed as follows:

Circular File Company (Market Values)

Asset value	₹30	₹25	Bond value = asset value − value of call
		5	Stock value = value of call
	₹30	₹30	Firm value = asset value

---

[6] But governments cannot print the currencies of other countries. Therefore, they may be forced into default on their foreign currency debt. For example, in 2008 Ecuador defaulted on ₹3.9 billion of foreign currency debt. Very occasionally governments have even defaulted on their own currency's debt. For example, in 1998 the Russian government defaulted on ₹36 billion of ruble debt.

Figure 23.4 shows the possible payoffs to Circular File's shareholders when the bonds mature at the end of the year. If the future value of the assets is less than ₹50, Circular will default and the stock will be worthless. If the value of the assets exceeds ₹50, the stockholders will receive asset value *less* the ₹50 paid over to the bondholders. Does Figure 23.4 look familiar to you? It should if you have read Chapter 20 on options. The payoffs in Figure 23.4 are identical to those of a call option on the firm's assets with an exercise price of ₹50.

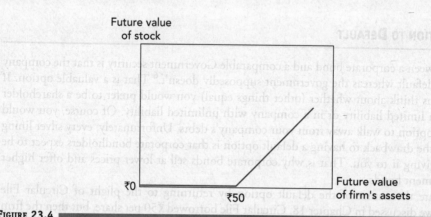

FIGURE 23.4

The value of Circular's common stock is the value of a call option on the firm's assets with an exercise price of ₹50.

In Chapter 20 we also set out the basic relationship between calls and puts:

$$\text{Value of call} + \text{present value of exercise price} = \text{value of put} + \text{value of share}$$

To apply this to Circular File, we need to interpret "value of share" as "asset value," because the common stock is a call option on the firm's assets. Also "present value of exercise price" is the present value of receiving the promised payment of ₹50 to bondholders *for sure* next year. Thus,

$$\text{Value of call} + \text{present value of promised payment to bondholders}$$
$$= \text{value of put} + \text{asset value}$$

Now we can solve for the value of Circular's bonds. This is equal to the firm's asset value less the value of the shareholders' call option on these assets:

$$\text{Bond value} = \text{asset value} - \text{value of call}$$
$$= \text{present value of promised payment to bondholders} - \text{value of put}$$

Circular's bondholders have in effect bought a safe bond, but at the same time given the shareholders a put option to sell them the firm's assets for the amount of the debt.

Now you can see why bond traders, investors, and financial managers refer to *default puts*. When a firm defaults, its stockholders are in effect exercising their default put. The put's value is the value of limited liability—the value of the stockholders' right to walk away from their firm's debts in exchange for handing over the firm's assets to its creditors. In the case of Circular File this option to default is extremely valuable because default is likely to occur. At the other extreme, the value of Asian Paints' option to default is trivial compared with the value of Asian Paints' assets. Default on Asian Paints bonds is possible but extremely unlikely. Option traders would say that for Circular File the put option is "deep in the money" because today's asset value (₹30) is well below the exercise price (₹50). For Asian Paints the put option is far "out of the money" because the value of Asian Paints' assets substantially exceeds the amount of Asian Paints' debt.

Valuing corporate bonds should be a two-step process:

$$\text{Bond value} = \frac{\text{bond value assuming}}{\text{no chance of default}} - \frac{\text{value of put}}{\text{option on assets}}$$

The first step is easy: Calculate the bond's value assuming no default risk. (Discount promised interest and principal payments at the rates offered by Treasury issues.) Second, calculate the value of a put written on the firm's assets, where the maturity of the put equals the maturity of the bond and the exercise price of the put equals the promised payment to bondholders.

Owning a corporate bond is also equivalent to owning the firm's assets but giving a call option on these assets to the firm's stockholders:

$$\text{Bond value} = \text{asset value} - \text{value of call option on assets}$$

Thus you can also calculate a bond's value, given the value of the firm's assets, by valuing a call option on these assets and subtracting the value of this call from that of the assets. (Remember: The call value is just the value of the firm's common stock.) Therefore, if you can value puts and calls on the firm's assets, you can value its debt.[7]

How the Default Option Affects a Bond's Risk and Yield

If the firm's debt is risk-free, the equityholders bear all the risk of the underlying assets. But when the firm has limited liability, the debtholders share this risk with the equityholders. We have seen that the equity of a firm with limited liability is equivalent to a call option on the firm's assets. So, if we can calculate the risk of this call, we can find how the firm's risk is shared between the equityholders and the debtholders.[8]

Think back to Chapter 21 where you learned how to calculate the risk of a call option. This involved two steps:

Step 1: Find the combination of the underlying asset and risk-free borrowing that provides the same payoffs as the call option (in the present case, the call option is the leveraged equity).

Step 2: Calculate the beta of this replicating portfolio.

Figure 23.5 takes a hypothetical company whose underlying assets have a beta of 1.0 and shows how the beta of these assets is shared between the equityholders and the debtholders. If the company had unlimited liability, the equityholders would bear all the risk of the assets and the debt would be risk-free. But with *limited* liability, the debtholders bear part of the risk. The higher the leverage and the longer the maturity of the debt, the greater the proportion of the risk that is assumed by the debtholders. For example, suppose that our hypothetical company is financed 60% by 25-year debt.

---

[7] However, option-valuation procedures cannot value the *assets* of the firm. Puts and calls must be valued as a proportion of asset value. For example, note that the Black–Scholes formula (Section 21-3) requires stock price to compute the value of a call option.

[8] The classic paper on the valuation of the option to default is R. Merton, "On the Pricing of Corporate Debt: The Risk Structure of Interest Rates," *Journal of Finance* 29 (May 1974), pp. 449–470.

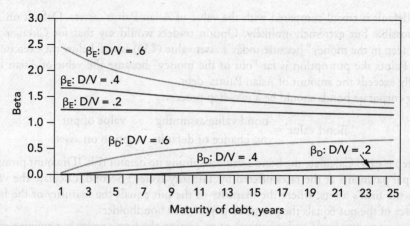

FIGURE 23.5

How the betas of the debt and equity vary with the degree of leverage and the maturity of the debt. These curves are calculated using option pricing theory under the following simplified assumptions: (1) the risk-free interest rate is constant for all maturities; (2) the standard deviation of the returns on the company's assets is 25% per annum; (3) the asset beta is 1.0; (4) debt is in the form of zero-coupon bonds; and (5) leverage is the ratio D/V, where D is the face value of the debt discounted at the risk-free interest rate and V is the market value of the assets.

eXcel

Visit us at
www.mhhe.com/bmam1(

With *unlimited* liability the debt would have a beta of zero and the equity would have a beta of 2.5. But, when the risk of the assets is shared, the debt has a beta of .7 and the equity a beta of 1.4.

Figure 23.6 stays with the same hypothetical company and shows how the promised yield on its deb varies with leverage and bond maturity. For example, you can see that if a company has a 20% debt rati and all its debt matures in 25 years, then it should pay about .50 percentage point above the governmen rate to compensate for default risk. Notice that just as risk increases with maturity, so generally does th promised yield. This makes sense, for the longer you have to wait for repayment, the greater the chanc that things will go wrong.[10]

Notice that in constructing Figure 23.6 we made several artificial assumptions. One assumption i that the company does not pay dividends or repurchase stock. If it does regularly pay out part of it assets to stockholders, there will be fewer assets to protect the bondholder in the event of trouble. I this case, the market will justifiably require a higher yield on the company's bonds.

There are other complications that make the valuation of corporate debt a good bit more difficul than it sounds. For example, Figure 23.6 assumes that the company makes only a single issue o zero-coupon debt. But suppose instead that it issues a 10-year bond that pays interest annually. W can still think of the company's stock as a call option that can be exercised by making the promised

---

[9] Remember that the beta of the assets is a weighted average of the beta of the debt and that of the equity:

$$\beta_{assets} = (D/V)\beta_{debt} + (E/V)\beta_{equity}$$

If $\beta_{assets} = 1.0$ and $\beta_{debt} = 0$, then with 60% leverage:

$$1.0 = (.6 \times 0) + (.4 \times \beta_{equity})$$
$$\beta_{equity} = 2.5$$

[10] The *price* of the bond always declines with maturity and leverage. (Remember the value of a put option increases with maturity and with th exercise price.) However, with very long maturities and high leverage the bond's *yield per annum* will start to decline.

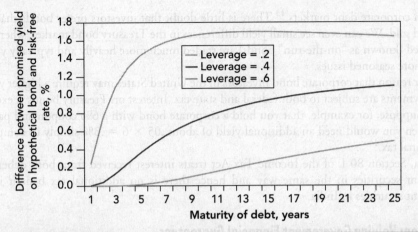

Visit us at
www.mhhe.com/bmam10e

FIGURE 23.6

How the interest rate on risky corporate debt changes with leverage and maturity.

payments. But in this case there are 10 payments rather than just one. To value the stock, we would need to value 10 sequential call options. The first option can be exercised by making the first interest payment when it comes due. By exercising, the stockholders obtain a second call option, which can be exercised by making the second interest payment. The reward to exercising is that the stockholders get a third call option, and so on. Finally, in year 10 the stockholders can exercise the tenth option. By paying off both the principal and the last year's interest, the stockholders regain unencumbered ownership of the company's assets.

Of course, if the firm does not make any of these payments when due, bondholders take over and stockholders are left with nothing. In other words, by not exercising one call option, stockholders give up all subsequent call options.

Valuing the equity when the 10-year bond is issued is equivalent to valuing the first of the 10 call options. But you cannot value the first option without valuing the nine that follow.[11] Even this example understates the practical difficulties, because large firms may have dozens of outstanding debt issues with different interest rates and maturities, and before the current debt matures they may make further issues. Consequently, when bond traders evaluate a corporate bond, they do not immediately reach for their option calculator. They are more likely to start by identifying bonds with a similar risk of default and look at the yield spreads offered by these bonds.

In practice, interest rate differentials tend to be much greater than those shown in Figure 23.6. The highest-grade corporate bonds typically offer promised yields about 1.5 percentage point higher than Indian Government securities. It is very difficult to justify differentials of this magnitude simply in terms of default risk.[12] So what is going on? It could be that companies are paying too much for their debt, but it seems likely that the high yields on corporate bonds stem in part from some other drawback. One possibility is that investors demand the additional yield to compensate for the lack of

---

[11] The other approach to valuing the company's debt (subtracting the value of a put option from risk-free bond value) is no easier. The analyst would be confronted by not one simple put option but a package of 10 sequential puts.

[12] See, for example, J. Huang and M. Huang, "How Much of the Corporate-Treasury Yield Spread Is Due to Credit Risk? Results from a New Calibration Approach," working paper, Pennsylvania State University, May 2003.

liquidity in corporate debt markets.[13] There is little doubt that investors prefer bonds that are easily bought and sold. We can even see small yield differences in the Treasury bond market, where the latest bonds issued (known as "on-the-run" bonds) are traded much more heavily and typically yield a little less than more seasoned issues.

Another reason that corporate bond investors in the United States may require a higher yield is that interest payments are subject to both federal and state tax. Interest on Treasury bonds is exempt from state tax. Suppose, for example, that you hold a corporate bond with a 6% coupon and pay state tax of 5%. Then you would need an additional yield of about $.05 \times 6 = .3\%$ simply to compensate for the additional tax.[14]

In India, Section 80 L of the Income Tax Act treats interest received from both debentures and Government securities in the same way and hence there is no additional tax benefit in holding Government securities in India.

A Digression: Valuing Government Financial Guarantees

When Bethlehem Steel declared bankruptcy in 2003, its pension plan had liabilities of $7 billion and assets of just $3 billion. But the 97,000 workers and retirees did not face a destitute old age. Their pensions were largely guaranteed by the Pension Benefit Guaranty Corporation (PBGC).[15]

Pension promises don't always appear on the company's balance sheet, but they are a long-term liability just like the promises to bondholders. The guarantee by the PBGC changes the pension promises from a risky liability to a safe one. If the company goes belly-up and there are insufficient assets to cover the pensions, the PBGC makes up the difference.

The government recognizes that the guarantee provided by the PBGC is costly. Thus shortly after assuming the liability for the Bethlehem Steel plan, the PBGC calculated that the discounted value of payments on defaulted plans and those close to default amounted to $23 billion.

Unfortunately, these calculations ignore the risk that other firms in the future may fail and hand over their pension liability to the PBGC. To calculate the cost of the guarantee, we need to think about what the value of company pension promises would be without any guarantee:

$$\text{Value of guarantee} = \text{value of guaranteed pensions}$$
$$- \text{ value of pension promises without a guarantee}$$

With the guarantee the pensions are as safe as a promise by the U.S. government;[16] *without* the guarantee the pensions are like an ordinary debt obligation of the firm. We already know what the difference is between the value of safe government debt and risky corporate debt. It is the value of the firm's right to hand over the assets of the firm and to walk away from its obligations. Thus the value of the pension guarantee is the value of this put option.

In a paper prepared for the Congressional Budget Office, Wendy Kiska, Deborah Lucas, and Marvin Phaup show how option pricing models can help to give a better measure of the cost to the

---

[13] For evidence that the more liquid corporate bonds have lower yields than less liquid bonds, see E. J. Elton, M. J. Gruber, D. Agrawal, and C. Mann, "Factors Affecting the Valuation of Corporate Bonds," *Journal of Banking and Finance* 28 (November 2006), pp. 2747–2767.

[14] See E. J. Elton, M. J. Gruber, D. Agrawal, and C. Mann, "Explaining the Rate Spread on Corporate Bonds," *Journal of Finance* 56 (February 2001), pp. 247–277. Since state taxes are deductible when calculating federal taxes, our calculation slightly overstates the effect of state tax.

[15] An even more costly failure occurred when United Airlines declared bankruptcy, leaving the PBGC with a liability of $6.6 billion.

[16] The pension guarantee is not ironclad. If the PBGC cannot meet its obligations, the government is not committed to providing the extra cash. But few doubt that it would do so.

BGC of pension guarantees.[17] Their estimates suggest that the true cost is in excess of $87 billion, or 54 billion more than the published figure.

The PBGC is not the only government body to provide financial guarantees. For example, the ederal Deposit Insurance Corporation (FDIC) guarantees bank deposit accounts; the Federal Family ducation Loan (FFEL) program guarantees loans to students; the Small Business Administration BA) provides partial guarantees for loans to small businesses, and so on. The government's liability nder these programs is enormous. Fortunately, option pricing is leading to a better way to calculate eir cost.

3-3 BOND RATINGS AND THE PROBABILITY OF DEFAULT

anks and other financial institutions not only want to know the value of the loans that they have made. hey also need to know the risk that they are incurring. Some rely on the judgments of specialized ond rating services. Others have developed their own models for measuring the probability that the orrower will default. We describe bond ratings first, and then discuss two models for predicting efault.

The relative quality of most traded bonds can be dged by bond ratings. There are three principal rating rvices in India—Credit Rating Information Services f India Limited (CRISIL), Investment Information d Credit Rating Agency of India Limited (ICRA), d Credit Analysis and Research Limited (CARE)[18]. able 23.1 summarizes these ratings. For example, e highest-quality bonds are rated triple-A (AAA) by RISIL then come double-A (AA) bonds, and so on. onds rated BBB or above are known as *investment- rade* bonds.[19] As per IRDA regulations, insurance ompanies are not allowed to invest in any bonds with rating below AA.

Bonds rated below BBB are termed **high-yield, or unk, bonds.** Most junk bonds in the U.S. used to e *fallen angels,* that is, bonds of companies that had llen on hard times. But during the 1980s new issues f junk bonds multiplied tenfold as more and more ompanies issued large quantities of low-grade debt to nance takeovers. The result was that for the first time corporate midgets were able to take control of orporate giants.

TABLE 23.1 Key to bond ratings. The highest-quality bonds are rated triple-A. Investment-grade bonds have to be the equivalent of triple-B or higher. Bonds that don't make this cut are called "high-yield" or "junk" bonds.

CRISIL	ICRA
Investment-grade bonds:	
AAA	LAAA
AA	LAA
A	LA
BBB	LBBB
Junk bonds:	
BB	LBB
B	LB
C	LC
D	LD

Bond ratings are judgments about firms' financial and business prospects. There is no fixed formula y which ratings are calculated. Nevertheless, investment bankers, bond portfolio managers, and thers who follow the bond market closely can get a fairly good idea of how a bond will be rated by ooking at a few key numbers such as the firm's debt ratio, the ratio of earnings to interest, and book

---

Congressional Budget Office, "The Risk Exposure of the Pension Benefit Guaranty Corporation," Washington, DC, September 2005.

As per Indianfolix.com survey, these three rating agencies enjoy a combined market share of 96 percent in India.

Rating services also provide a finer breakdown. Thus a bond might be rated AA+, AA, or AA– (the lowest AA rating). In addition, the rating rvice may announce that it has put an issue on its watch list for a possible upgrade or downgrade.

value of total assets, the return on assets, retained earnings to total assets, etc. Table 23.2 shows how these ratios vary with the firm's bond rating (as rated by CRISIL).

TABLE 23.2 How financial ratios differ according to a firm's bond rating.

Ratio	AAA	AA	A	BBB	BB	B	C	D
Retained earnings to total assets	0.06	0.04	0.04	0.03	0.01	−0.01	0.00	−0.02
Total assets (natural logarithm of)*	7.71	5.69	4.71	4.88	4.74	5.12	4.74	4.97
Market value of equity to book debt	4.51	1.95	1.19	0.58	0.51	0.24	0.26	0.18

*Total assets measured in ₹ crores

Source: Sahoo, B.K., and P Mohanty, 2002, "An Alternative to CRISIL Credit rating using Discriminant Analysis", The ICFAI Journal of Applied Finance, January.

Table 23.3 shows that bond ratings do reflect the probability of default. Since 1988, no bond that was initially rated triple-A by CRISIL has defaulted in the next three years after issue. At the other extreme, about 60% of the speculative-grade bonds defaulted within three years of the issue. Of course, bonds do not usually fall suddenly from grace. As time passes and the company becomes progressively more shaky, the agencies revise downward the bond's rating to reflect the increasing probability of default.

TABLE 23.3 Default rates of corporate bonds, 1988–2010, by CRISIL rating at time of issue.

CRISIL's Average Cumulative Default Rates between 1988 and 2010			
Rating	One-Year	Two-Year	Three-Year
AAA	0.00%	0.00%	0.00%
AA	0.04%	0.44%	1.19%
A	0.93%	3.98%	8.39%
BBB	2.82%	8.57%	16.24%
BB	8.90%	18.75%	29.93%
B	9.18%	33.05%	61.19%
C	24.98%	46.25%	59.99%

Source: CRISIL Default Study 2010, May 2011.

Rating agencies don't always get it right. When Enron went belly-up in 2001, investors protested that only two months earlier the company's debt had an investment-grade rating. And when agencies *do* downgrade a company's debt, they are often accused of precipitate action that increases the cost of borrowing.

23-4 PREDICTING THE PROBABILITY OF DEFAULT

Credit Scoring

If you apply for a credit card or a bank loan, you will probably be asked to complete a questionnaire that provides details about your job, home, and financial health. This information is then used to calculate an overall credit score. If you do not make the grade on the score, you are likely to be refused credit or subjected to a more detailed analysis. In a similar way, mechanical credit scoring systems re used by banks to assess the risk of their corporate loans and by firms when they extend credit to customers.

Suppose that you are given the task of developing a credit scoring system that will help to decide whether to extend credit to businesses. You start by comparing the financial statements of companies that went bankrupt over a 40-year period with those of surviving firms. Figure 23.7 shows what you find. Panel (*a*) illustrates that, as early as four years before they went bankrupt, failing firms were earning a much lower return on assets (ROA) than firms that survived. Panel (*b*) shows that on average they also had a high ratio of liabilities to assets, and Panel (*c*) shows that EBITDA (earnings before interest, taxes, and depreciation) was low relative to the firms' total liabilities. Thus bankrupt firms were less profitable (low ROA), were more highly leveraged (high ratio of liabilities to assets), and generated relatively little cash (low ratio of EBITDA to liabilities). In each case these indicators of the firms' financial health steadily deteriorated as bankruptcy approached.

William Beaver, Maureen McNichols, and Jung-Wu Rhie, who studied these firms, concluded that the chance of failing during the next year relative to the chance of not failing was best estimated by the following equation:[20]

Log(relative chance of failure)

$$= -6.445 - 1.192\,\text{ROA} + 2.307\,\text{liabilities/assets} - .346\,\text{EBITDA/liabilities}$$

As we write this in early 2009, Eastman Kodak is struggling with declining sales and huge debts. Its bonds are rated B. But what are the odds that Kodak will fail over the coming year? Let's use the above equation to check. Based on the latest annual statements, Kodak's return on assets was -4.5%, its total liabilities were 89.5% of its assets, and its EBITDA was -2.5% of liabilities. Plugging these figures into the equation gives Kodak's relative odds of failing as:

Log(relative chance of failure)

$$= -6.445 - 1.192(-.045) + 2.307(.895) - .346(-.025) = -4.32$$

Relative chance of failure $= e^{(-4.32)} = .013$, or 1.3%

A variety of techniques have been used to develop credit scoring systems. The model that we described just above uses the technique of *hazard analysis*. An early, and still widely used model, the famous Z-score model developed by Edward Altman, uses *multiple discriminant analysis* to separate the creditworthy sheep from the impecunious goats.[21]

Credit scoring systems should carry a health warning. When you construct a risk index, it is tempting to experiment with many different combinations of variables until you find the equation that would have worked best in the past. Unfortunately, if you "mine" the data in this way, you are likely to find that the system works less well in the future than it did previously. If you are misled by the past successes into placing too much faith in your model, you may refuse credit to a number of potentially good customers. The profits that you lose by turning away these customers could more than offset the gains that you make by avoiding a few bad eggs. As a result, you could be worse off than if you had pretended that you could not tell one would-be borrower from another and extended credit to all of them.

Does this mean that firms should not use credit scoring systems? Not a bit. It merely implies that it is not sufficient to have a good system; you also need to know how much to rely on it.

---

[20] See W. H. Beaver, M. F. McNichols, and J-W. Rhie, "Have Financial Statements Become Less Informative? Evidence from the Ability of Financial Ratios to Predict Bankruptcy," *Review of Accounting Studies* 10 (2005), pp. 93–122.

[21] For a description of the Z-score model, see E. I. Altman, *Corporate Financial Distress and Bankruptcy*, 3rd ed. (New York: John Wiley, 2005).

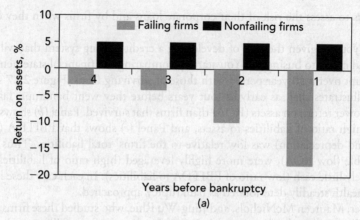

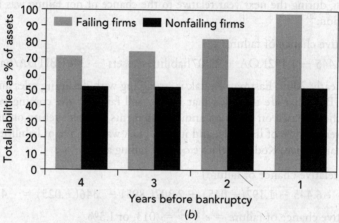

FIGURE 23.7

Financial ratios of 544 failing and nonfailing firms.

Source: W. H. Beaver, M. F. McNichols, and J-W. Rhie, "Have Financial Statements Become Less Informative? Evidence from the Ability of Financial Ratios to Predict Bankruptcy," *Review of Accounting Studies* 10 (2005), pp. 93–122. © 2005 Springer Verlag.

Market-Based Risk Models

Credit scoring systems rely primarily on the companies' financial statements to estimate which firms are most likely to become bankrupt and default on their debts. For small businesses there may be little alternative to the use of accounting data, but for large, publicly traded firms it is also possible to take advantage of the information in security prices. These techniques build on the idea that stockholders will exercise their option to default if the market value of the assets falls below the payments that must be made on the debt.

Suppose that the assets of Sanjeev Chemical have a current market value of ₹100 and its debt has a face value of ₹60 (i.e., 60% leverage), all of which is due to be repaid at the end of five years. Figure 23.8 shows the range of possible values of Sanjeev's assets when the loan becomes due. The expected value of the assets is ₹120, but this value is by no means certain. There is a probability of 20% that the asset value could fall below ₹60, in which case the company will default on its debt. This probability is shown by the shaded area in Figure 23.8.

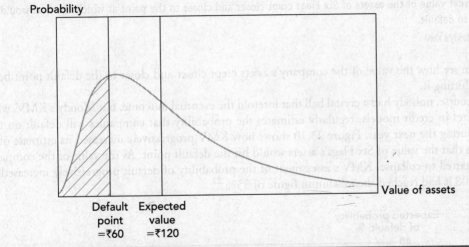

FIGURE 23.8

Sanjeev Chemical has issued five-year debt with a face value of ₹60. The shaded area shows that there is a 20% probability that the value of the company's assets in year 5 will be less than ₹60, in which case the company will choose to default.

To calculate the probability that Sanjeev will default, we need to know the expected growth in the market value of its assets, the face value and maturity of the debt, and the variability of future asset values. Real-world cases are likely to be more complex than our Sanjeev example. For example, firms may have several classes of debt maturing on different dates. If so, it may pay the stockholders to put up more money to pay off the short-term debt and thus keep alive the chance that the firm's fortunes will recover before the rest of the debt becomes due.

However, banks and consulting firms are now finding that they can use these ideas to measure the risk of actual loans. For example, in Section 23-1 we encountered the troubled theme-park operator, Six Flags. In June 2009, Six Flags finally succumbed and filed for bankruptcy.

The black line in Figure 23.9 shows the market value that investors placed on Six Flags's assets, and the red line shows the asset value at which the company would choose to default on its debts.

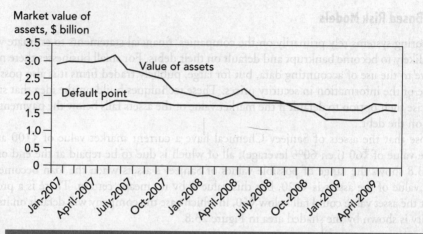

FIGURE 23.9

The market value of the assets of Six Flags crept closer and closer to the point at which the firm would choose to default.

Source: Moody's KMV.

You can see how the value of the company's assets crept closer and closer to the default point before finally hitting it.

Of course, nobody had a crystal ball that foretold the eventual outcome, but Moody's KMV, which specializes in credit models, regularly estimates the probability that companies will default on their debts during the next year. Figure 23.10 shows how KMV progressively increased its estimate of the chances that the value of Six Flags's assets would hit the default point. As the value of the company's assets started to collapse, KMV's assessment of the probability of default progressively increased. By July 2008 it had reached the maximum figure of 35%.[22]

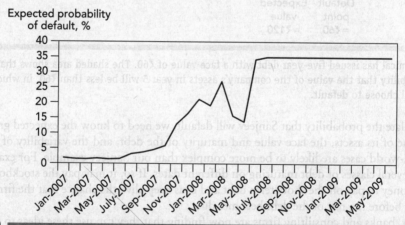

FIGURE 23.10

Estimates by Moody's KMV of the probability that Six Flags would default on its debt within a year.

Note: The probabilities reported by Moody's KMV are limited to a range from .01% to 35%.

---

[22] The probabilities provided by Moody's KMV are kept within the range of .01% to 35%.

3-5   VALUE AT RISK

t is January 2012 and you own Pantaloon Retail 12.1% debentures maturing in 2017. The bonds are ated A by CRISIL and are currently priced to offer a promised yield of 12.25%. If you plan to hold his bond for the next 12 months, how much risk are you taking?

You may be tempted to look back at past default rates for A-rated bonds and conclude that there is nly a negligible chance that the bonds will default during the next year and therefore your investment s almost as safe as Indian Government securities. But of course this ignores the possibility that, lthough default is unlikely in the short-term, Pantaloon's prospects may not be as good at the end of he year as they are now. If so, the bonds could be downrated and their value would fall.

Banks and consulting firms have developed a variety of ways to measure the risk of a deterioration n credit quality. For example, one of the most popular, the *CreditMetrics* system, looks at the possible mpact of changes in the bond rating.[23] Table 23.4 shows how frequently bonds were rerated in the ears 1998–2010 by CRISIL. Since your Pantaloon bonds are A-rated, we will focus on the third row of the table. You can see that in the past 84.63% of A-bonds were still rated A after one year and a few were even upgraded to AA. However, the bad news is that after one year over 5% of A-rated bonds had moved into the junk bond category of BB or below.

TABLE 23.4   Average One-Year Transition Rates of CRISIL Ratings, 1998-2010, showing the percentage change debentures changing from one rating to another

Rating at Start of Year	Rating at Year-end							
	AAA	AA	A	BBB	BB	B	C	D
AAA	96.36%	3.64%	0.00%	0.00%	0.00%	0.00%	0.00%	0.00%
AA	1.98%	91.29%	5.58%	0.73%	0.29%	0.05%	0.04%	40.00%
A	0.00%	3.61%	84.63%	6.76%	3.32%	0.24%	0.49%	0.93%
BBB	0.00%	0.27%	3.98%	81.59%	8.75%	1.50%	1.09%	2.82%
BB	0.00%	0.27%	0.00%	2.97%	81.23%	3.58%	3.05%	8.90%
B	0.00%	0.00%	0.03%	0.47%	7.74%	80.73%	1.85%	9.18%
C	0.00%	0.00%	0.00%	0.83%	0.96%	11.56%	61.67%	24.98%

Source: CRISIL Default Study, 2010. May 2011.

If Pantaloon debt were to be downgraded to BB, investors would undoubtedly demand a higher yield. For example, in 2012 the yield on BB bonds was about 3% higher than that of A. If the yield on your Pantaloon bonds rose by this amount, the price would fall by about 10% or more over the coming year. Bankers refer to this as the **value at risk** (or **VAR**) on the Pantaloon debenture.

There are a number of ways to improve this back-of-the-envelope estimate of the value at risk. For example, we assumed that the yield spreads on corporate bonds are constant. But, if investors become more reluctant to take on credit risk, you could lose much more than 10% on your investment. Notice

[23] *CreditMetrics* was originally developed by J.P. Morgan. For a description of *CreditMetrics*, see the manuals provided by **www.riskmetrics. com**.

also that when we calculated the risk from investing in Pantaloon bonds, we looked at how the pri[c]e of the bonds would be affected by a change in credit rating. If we wanted a comprehensive measu[re] of value at risk, we would need to recognize that risk-free interest rates, too, may change over th[e] year.

Banks and bond investors are not just interested in the risk of individual loans; they would also li[ke] to know the risk of their entire portfolio. Therefore, specialists in credit risk need to worry about th[e] correlation between the outcomes. A portfolio of loans, all of which are to factory outlets in suburba[n] Jaipur, is likely to be more risky than a portfolio with a variety of different borrowers.

SUMMARY

Corporations have limited liability. If companies are unable to pay their debts, they can file f[or] bankruptcy. Lenders are aware that they may receive less than they are owed, and that the *expecte[d]* yield on a corporate bond is less than the *promised yield*.

Because of the possibility of default, the promised yield on a corporate bond is higher than o[n] a government bond. You can think of this extra yield as the amount that you would need to pa[y] to insure the bond against default. There is an active market for insurance policies that protect th[e] debtholder against default. These policies are called credit default swaps. There are no free lunche[s] in financial markets. So the extra yield you get for buying a corporate bond is eaten up by the co[st] of insuring against default.

The company's option to default is equivalent to a put option. If the value of the firm's asse[ts] is less than the amount of the debt, it will pay for the company to default and to allow the lende[r] to take over the assets in settlement of the debt. This insight tells us what we need to think abo[ut] when valuing corporate debt—the current value of the firm relative to the point at which it woul[d] default, the volatility of the assets, the maturity of the debt payments, and the risk-free intere[st] rate. Unfortunately, most companies have several loans outstanding with payments due at differe[nt] times. This considerably complicates the task of valuing the put option.

Because of these complications, bond investors do not regularly use option models to value th[e] default option that is attached to a corporate bond. More commonly, they rely on their experienc[e] to judge whether the spread between the yield on a corporate bond and the yield on a comparabl[e] government issue compensates for the possibility of default. Spreads can change rapidly as investo[rs] reassess the chances of default or become more or less risk-averse.

When investors want a measure of the risk of a company's bonds, they usually look at the ratin[g] that has been assigned by CRISIL's, CARE's, or ICRA. They know that bonds with a triple-A ratin[g] are much less likely to default than bonds with a junk rating.

Banks, rating services, and consulting firms have also developed a number of models fo[r] estimating the likelihood of default. Credit scoring systems take accounting ratios or other indicato[rs] of corporate health and weight them to produce a single measure of default. Moody's KMV takes [a] different tack and seeks to measure the probability that the market value of the firm's assets will fall t[o] the point at which the firm will choose to default rather than try to keep up with its debt payment[s].

Don't assume that there is no risk just because there is no immediate prospect of default. If th[e] quality of the bonds deteriorates, investors will demand a higher yield and the bond price will fal[l]. One way to calculate the value at risk is to look at the probability of possible ratings changes and t[o] estimate the likely effect of these changes for the bond's price.

FURTHER READING

The Web sites of the main credit rating agencies and of Moody's KMV contain a variety of useful reports on credit risk. (See in particular **www.moodys.com**, **www.standardandpoors.com**, **www.fitch.com**, and **www.moodyskmv.com**.)

Altman provides a review of credit scoring models in:

E. I. Altman, *Corporate Financial Distress and Bankruptcy,* 3rd ed. (New York: John Wiley, 2005).

There are a number of books that discuss corporate bonds and credit risk. Look, for example, at:

A. Saunders and L. Allen, *Credit Risk Measurement,* 2nd ed. (New York: John Wiley, 2002).

J. B. Caouette, E. I. Altman, P. Narayanan, and R. Nimmo, *Managing Credit Risk* (New York: John Wiley, 2008).

D. Duffie and K. J. Singleton, *Credit Risk: Pricing, Measurement and Management* (Princeton, NJ: Princeton University Press, 2003).

PROBLEM SETS

BASIC

1. You own a 5% bond maturing in two years and priced at 87%. Suppose that there is a 10% chance that at maturity the bond will default and you will receive only 40% of the promised payment. What is the bond's promised yield to maturity? What is its expected yield?

2. Other things equal, would you expect the difference between the price of a G-Sec and a corporate bond to increase or decrease with
   a. The company's business risk?
   b. The degree of leverage?

3. The difference between the value of a G-Sec and a simple corporate bond is equal to the value of an option. What is this option and what is its exercise price?

4. The following table shows some financial data for two companies:

	A	B
Total assets	₹1,552.1	₹1,565.7
EBITDA	−60	70
Net income + interest	−80	24
Total liabilities	814.0	1,537.1

   Use the formula shown in Section 23-4 to calculate which has the higher probability of default.

5. What variables are required to use a market-based approach to calculate the probability that a company will default on its debt?

6. You have a AAA-rated bond. On past evidence, what is the probability that it will continue to be rated AAA in one year's time? What is the probability that it will have a lower rating?

7. You have an A-rated bond. Is a rise in rating more likely than a fall? Would your answer be the same if the bond were B-rated?

8. Why is it more difficult to estimate the value at risk for a portfolio of loans rather than for a single loan?

INTERMEDIATE

9. Company A has issued a single zero-coupon bond maturing in 10 years. Company B has issued a coupon bond maturing in 10 years. Explain why it is more complicated to value B's debt than A's.

10. Company X has borrowed ₹150 maturing this year and ₹50 maturing in 10 years. Company Y has borrowed ₹200 maturing in five years. In both cases asset value is ₹140. Sketch a scenario in which X does not default but Y does.

11. Discuss the problems with developing a numerical credit scoring system for evaluating personal loans. You can only test your system using data for applicants who have in the past been granted credit. Is this a potential problem?

12. What problems are you likely to encounter when using a market-based approach for estimating the probability that a company will default?

13. How much would it cost you to insure the bonds of Backwoods Chemical against default? (See Section 23-1.)

CHALLENGE

14. Look back to the first Backwoods Chemical example at the start of Section 23-1. Suppose that the firm's book balance sheet is:

Backwoods Chemical Company (Book Values)

Net working capital	₹ 400	₹1,000	Debt
Net fixed assets	1,600	1,000	Equity (net worth)
Total assets	₹2,000	₹2,000	Total value

The debt has a one-year maturity and a promised interest payment of 9%. Thus, the promised payment to Backwoods's creditors is ₹1,090. The market value of the assets is ₹1,200 and the standard deviation of asset value is 45% per year. The risk-free interest rate is 9%. Calculate the value of Backwoods debt and equity.

15. Use the Black–Scholes model and redraw Figures 23.5 and 23.6 assuming that the standard deviation of the return on the firm's assets is 40% a year. Do the calculations for 60% leverage only. (*Hint:* It is simplest to assume that the risk-free interest rate is zero.) What does this tell you about the effect of changing risk on the spread between high-grade and low-grade corporate bonds? (You may find it helpful to use the Black–Scholes program on the "live" spreadsheet for Chapter 21 at **www.mhhe.com/bmam10e**.)

eXcel
Visit us at
www.mhhe.com/bmam10e

REAL-TIME DATA ANALYSIS

Use data from the Standard & Poor's Market Insight Database at www.mhhe.com/edumarketinsight to answer the following question.

1. Select any three industrial companies. Calculate Z-score for each, using the formula shown in Section 23.4. Now look at each company's bond rating. Do these two measures provide consistent message?

2. Suppose that in 2012 you owned a 10-year A- rated bond with a coupon of 9.08 percent and a price of ₹100. Use the data in Tables 24.3 to measure the value at risk.

24

CHAPTER

THE MANY DIFFERENT KINDS OF DEBT

In Chapters 17 and 18 we discussed how much a company should borrow. But companies also need to think about what *type* of debt to issue. They can choose to issue short- or long-term debt, straight or convertible bonds; they can issue in the United States or in the international debt market; and they can sell the debt publicly or place it privately with a few large investors.

As a financial manager, you need to choose the type of debt that makes sense for your company. For example, if a firm has only a temporary need for funds, it should generally issue short-term debt. Firms with a substantial overseas business may prefer to issue foreign currency debt. Sometimes competition between lenders opens a window of opportunity in a particular sector of the debt market. The effect may be only a few basis points reduction in yield, but on a large issue that can translate into savings of several million dollars. Remember the saying, "A million dollars here and a million there—pretty soon it begins to add up to real money."[1]

Our focus in this chapter is on long-term debt.[2] We begin our discussion by looking at different types of bonds. We examine the differences between senior and junior bonds and between secured and unsecured bonds. Then we describe how bonds may be repaid by means of a sinking fund and how the borrower or the lender may have an option for early repayment. In Section 24-6 we look at convertible bonds and at their close relative, the package of bonds and warrants.

Debt may be sold to the public or placed privately with large financial institutions. Because privately placed bonds are broadly similar to public issues, we do not discuss them at length. However, we do discuss another form of private placement known as project finance. This is the glamorous part of the debt

---

[1] The remark was made by the late Senator Everett Dirksen. However, he was talking billions.

[2] Short-term debt is discussed in Chapter 30.

market. The words *project finance* conjure up images of multi-million-dollar loans to finance huge ventures in exotic parts of the world. You'll find there's something to the popular image, but it's not the whole story.

We conclude with a look at a few unusual bonds and consider the reasons for innovation in the debt market.

As we look at these different features of corporate debt, we try to explain why sinking funds, repayment options, convertible securities, and the like exist. They are not simply matters of custom or neutral mutations; there are generally good reasons for their use.

We should point out that many debts are not shown on the company's balance sheet. For example, companies may be able to disguise the debt by establishing *special purpose entities (SPEs),* which raise cash by a mixture of equity and debt and then use that cash to help fund the parent company. By making use of SPEs, Enron kept a large amount of its debt off-balance-sheet, but that did not stop the company from going bankrupt. Since the Enron scandal accountants have moved to tighten up the rules on disclosing SPE debt.

Companies have other important long-term liabilities that we do *not* discuss in this chapter. For instance, long-term leases are very similar to debt. The user of the equipment agrees to make a series of lease payments and, if it defaults, it may be forced into bankruptcy. We discuss leases in Chapter 25.

Postretirement health benefits and pension promises can also be huge liabilities. For example, in 2003 General Motors had a pension deficit of $19 billion. To reduce this deficit, GM made a large issue of bonds and invested the majority of the proceeds in its pension fund. You could say that the effect was to increase the company's debt, but the economic reality was that it substituted one long-term obligation (the new debt) for another (its pension obligation). Management of pension plans is outside the scope of this book, but financial managers spend a good deal of time worrying about the pension "debt."

24-1 DOMESTIC BONDS, FOREIGN BONDS, AND EUROBONDS

A firm can issue a bond either in its home country or in another country. Bonds that are sold to local investors in another country's bond market are known as *foreign bonds*. The United States is by far the largest market for foreign bonds, but Japan and Switzerland are also substantial markets. Foreign bonds have a variety of nicknames: A bond sold by a foreign company in the United States is known as a *yankee bond;* a bond sold by a foreign firm in Japan is a *samurai.*

Of course, any firm that raises money in a foreign country is subject to the rules of that country. For example, any issue in the United States of publicly traded bonds needs to be registered with the SEC. However, foreign firms commonly avoid registration by complying with the SEC's Rule 144A for bond issues in the United States. Rule 144A bonds can be bought and sold only by large financial institutions.[3]

We have seen that a firm may issue a bond in its home country or in another country. In each case the offer is subject to local laws governing the sale and is overseen by the country's financial regulator. Instead of issuing a bond in a particular country's market, a bond issue may also be sold internationally. For example, IBM could issue a dollar bond to investors outside the United States. Because the issue is not marketed to U.S. investors, it does not need to be registered with the SEC.

---

[3] We described Rule 144A in Section 15-5.

International issues that are marketed outside any domestic jurisdiction are known as *eurobonds,* and are usually made in one of the major currencies, such as the U.S. dollar, the euro, or the yen. Eurobond issues are marketed by international syndicates of underwriters, such as the London branches of large U.S., European, and Japanese banks and security dealers. Be careful not to confuse a eurobond (which is outside the jurisdiction of any domestic market and may be in any currency) with a bond that is marketed in a European country and denominated in euros.

The eurobond market arose during the 1960s because the U.S. government imposed a tax on the purchase of foreign securities and discouraged American corporations from exporting capital. Therefore both European and American multinationals were forced to tap an international market for capital.

The tax was removed in 1974. Since firms can now choose whether to borrow in New York or London, the interest rates in the two markets are usually similar. However, the eurobond market is not directly subject to regulation by the U.S. authorities, and therefore the financial manager needs to be alert to small differences in the cost of borrowing in one market rather than another.

These days very large bond issues are often marketed both internationally (that is, in the eurobond market) and in individual domestic markets. For example, IBM could sell its dollar bonds internationally and also register the issue for sale in the United States. Such bonds are called *global bonds.*

24-2   THE BOND CONTRACT

To give you some feel for the bond contract (and for some of the language in which it is couched), we have summarized in Table 24.1 the terms of an issue of 5-year bonds by India Infoline Investment Services Limited. We will look at the principal items in turn.

TABLE 24.1   Summary of terms of 11.7% debenture issued by India Infoline Investment Services

Trustee	IDBI Trusteeship Services Limited
Denomination	₹1,000
Rights on Default	The Debenture Trustee will protect the interest of the debenture holders in the event of default by India Infoline and the trustee will take necessary action at the cost of India Infoline.
Amount Issued	₹750 crores
Issue Date	4 August 2011
Interest	11.7% payable per annum, payable on 1st April of every year
Seniority	Ranks pari passu with other secured creditors and priority over unsecured creditors
Security	The principal payments with all interest due are secured by way of first pari passu charge in favor of the Debenture Trustee on an identified immovable property and over all the current assets, book debts, receivables (present and future) upto the extent of 1.1 times the amount outstanding at any time.
Debenture Redemption Reserve	The company is required to create a debenture redemption reserve of 50% (since it is an NBFC) of the value of the debentures issued through the public issue. The amounts credited shall not be used for any purpose other than redemption of the debentures.
Rating	AA – (both CARE and ICRA assigned the same rating)

Trust Deed

The India Infoline bond offering was a public issue of bonds, which was registered with the SEBI. In the case of a public issue, the bond agreement is in the form of an **indenture,** or **trust deed,** between the bondholders and a trust company.[4] IDBI Trusteeship Services Limited, which is the debenture trustee for the issue, represents the bondholders. It must see that the terms of the trust deed are observed and look after the bondholders in the event of default.

Most of the bonds in India are issued in registered form, but in many countries, bonds may be issued in bearer form. In this case, the certificate constitutes the primary evidence of ownership, so the bondholder must send the certificate itself to claim the final payment of principal. Eurobonds almost invariably allow the owner to hold them in bearer form.

The Bond Terms

The India Infoline debentures have a face value of ₹1,000. The annual interest payment on each debenture is 11.7% of ₹1,000, or ₹117. The interest is payable annually and will be paid on the 1st of April of each year. Since the debentures issue closed on August, 8, 2011, the first interest was paid on April 1, 2012 for the period commencing from the deemed date of allotment till March 31, 2012. The last interest payment will be made at the time of redemption of the debenture on a pro-rata basis.

The India Infoline interest payment is fixed for the life of the debenture, but in some issues the payment varies with the general level of interest rates. For example, the payment may be set at 1% of the 364-day. Treasury bill rate or (more commonly) over the **London interbank offered rate (LIBOR),** which is the rate at which international banks lend to one another. Sometimes these *floating-rate notes* specify a minimum (or floor) interest rate or they may specify a maximum (or cap) on the rate.[5] You may also come across "collars," which stipulate both a maximum and a minimum payment.

24-3 SECURITY AND SENIORITY

Almost all debt issues by Government of India, state governments, undertakings owned by governments, and development financial institutions are generally unsecured obligations and are called bonds. All debt issues made by private entities are usually secured obligations and are called debentures.[6] This means that if a company defaults on its debt, the trustee or lender may take possession of the relevant assets. If these are insufficient to satisfy them, the remaining debt will have a general claim, alongside any unsecured debt, on the other assets of the firm.

In the case of secured debt issue (debentures), the issuing company will provides security in the form of a first mortgage or charge on the fixed assets on a pari-passu basis with other fixed charge holders. Usually the charge is created on behalf of all the debenture holders by a trustee appointed for this purpose by the issuing company.

Under Section 117C of the Companies Act (introduced through the Companies Amendment Act, 2000), all companies that have issued debentures and are making profits must mandatorily create a debenture redemption reserve out of the profits. This fund is created to protect the interests of the

[4] In the case of a eurobond issue, there is a *fiscal agent,* who carries out some of the same functions as the bond trustee.

[5] Instead of issuing a capped floating-rate loan, a company sometimes issues an uncapped loan and at the same time buys a cap from a bank. The bank pays the interest in excess of the specified level.

[6] Another important difference between bond and debenture in India is that the stamp duty on debentures is a state subject, whereas the stamp duties on bonds come under Indian Stamp Act, 1899.

debenture holders and is to be maintained by the company till the debentures are redeemed. However, financial institutions and the non-banking financial institutions are not required to create this reserve.[7]

Bonds may be senior claims or they may be subordinated to the senior bonds or to *all* other creditors.[8] If the firm defaults, the senior bonds come first in the pecking order. The subordinated lender gets in line behind the general creditors but ahead of the preferred stockholders and the common stockholders.

As you can see from Figure 24.1 (that is based on U.S. research), if default does occur, it pays to hold senior secured bonds. On average, investors in these bonds can expect to recover nearly two-thirds of the amount of the loan. At the other extreme, recovery rates for junior unsecured bondholders are only 15% of the face value of the debt.

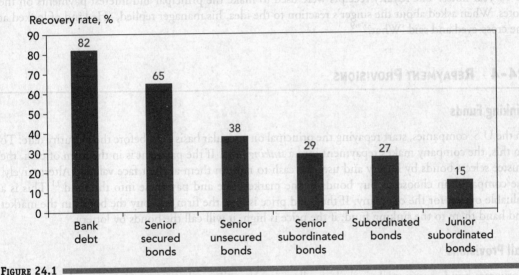

FIGURE 24.1

Ultimate percentage recovery rates on defaulting debt by seniority and security, 1987–2006.

Source: Moody's, "Moody's Ultimate Recovery Database."

Asset-Backed Securities

Instead of borrowing money directly, companies sometimes bundle up a group of assets and then sell the cash flows from these assets. This issue is known as an *asset-backed security,* or *ABS.*

Suppose your company has made a large number of mortgage loans to buyers of homes or commercial real estate. However, you don't want to wait until the loans are paid off; you would like to get your hands on the money now. Here is what you do. You establish a separate company that buys a package of the mortgage loans. To finance this purchase, the company sells *mortgage pass-through certificates.* The holders of these certificates simply receive a share of the mortgage payments. For example, if interest rates fall and the mortgages are repaid early, holders of the pass-through certificates are also repaid early. That is not generally popular with these holders, for they get their money back just when they don't want it—when interest rates are low.

---

[7] The Government of India, Ministry of Company Affairs has vide General Circular No. 9/2002 No.6/3/2001-CL.V dated April 18,2002 clarified that banks need not create Debenture Redemption Reserve as specified under section 117C of the Companies Act, 1956.

[8] If a bond does not specifically state that it is junior, you can assume that it is senior.

Sometimes, instead of issuing one class of pass-through certificates, the company will issue several different classes of security, known as *collateralized mortgage obligations* or *CMOs*. For example, any mortgage payments might be used first to pay off one class of security holders and only then will other classes start to be repaid. As we will see in Chapter 30, these CMOs ran into heavy weather during the credit crisis of 2007–2009.

Real estate companies are not unique in wanting to turn future cash receipts into up-front cash. Automobile loans, student loans, and credit card receivables are also often bundled and remarketed as an asset-backed security. Indeed, investment bankers seem able to repackage any set of cash flows into a loan. In 1997 David Bowie, the British rock star, established a company that then purchased the royalties from his current albums. The company financed the purchase by selling $55 million of 10-year notes. The royalty receipts were used to make the principal and interest payments on the notes. When asked about the singer's reaction to the idea, his manager replied, "He kind of looked at me cross-eyed and said 'What?' "[9]

24-4 REPAYMENT PROVISIONS

Sinking Funds

In the U.S. companies, start repaying the principal on a regular basis even before the maturity date. To do this, the company makes repayment into a *sinking fund*. If the payment is in the form of cash, the trustee selects bonds by lottery and uses the cash to redeem them at their face value.[10] Alternatively, the company can choose to buy bonds in the marketplace and pay these into the fund.[11] This is a valuable option for the company. If the bond price is low, the firm will buy the bonds in the market and hand them to the sinking fund; if the price is high, it will call the bonds by lottery.

Call Provisions

Corporate bonds occasionally include a call option that allows the company to repay the debt early. Sometimes you come across bonds that give the *investor* the repayment option. Retractable (or puttable) bonds give investors the right to demand early repayment; extendible bonds give them the option to extend the bond's life.

For some companies callable bonds offer a natural form of insurance. For example, Fannie Mae and Freddie Mac of the U.S. are federal agencies that offer fixed-rate mortgages to home buyers. When interest rates fall, home owners are likely to repay their fixed-rate mortgage and take out a new mortgage at the lower interest rate. This can severely dent the income of the two agencies. Therefore, to protect themselves against the effect of falling interest rates, they have traditionally issued large quantities of long-term callable debt. When interest rates fall, the agencies can reduce their funding costs by calling their bonds and replacing them with new bonds at a lower rate. Ideally, the fall in bond interest payments should exactly offset the reduction in mortgage income.

How does a company know when to call its bonds? The answer is simple: Other things equal, if it wishes to maximize the value of its stock, it must minimize the value of its bonds. Therefore, a

[9] See J. Matthews, "David Bowie Reinvents Himself, This Time as a Bond Issue," *Washington Post*, February 7, 1997.

[10] Every investor dreams of buying up the entire supply of a sinking-fund bond that is selling way below face value and then forcing the company to buy the bonds back at face value. Cornering the market in this way is fun to dream about but difficult to do.

[11] If the bonds are privately placed, the company cannot repurchase them in the marketplace; it must call them at their face value.

company should never call the bonds if their market value is less than the call price, for that would just be giving a present to the bondholders. Equally, a company *should* call the bond if it is worth *more* than the call price.

Of course, investors take the call option into account when they buy or sell the bond. They know that the company will call the bond as soon as it is worth more than the call price, so no investor will be willing to pay more than the call price for the bond. The market price of the bond may, therefore, reach the call price, but it will not rise above it. This gives the company the following rule for calling its bonds: *Call the bond when, and only when, the market price reaches the call price.*[12]

If we know how bond prices behave over time, we can modify the basic option-valuation model of Chapter 21 to find the value of the callable bond, *given* that investors know that the company will call the issue as soon as the market price reaches the call price. For example, look at Figure 24.2. It illustrates the relationship between the value of a straight 8% five-year bond and the value of a comparable callable bond. Suppose that the value of the straight bond is very low. In this case there is little likelihood that the company will ever wish to call its bonds. (Remember that it will call the bonds only when their price equals the call price.) Therefore the value of the callable bond will be almost identical to the value of the straight bond. Now suppose that the straight bond is worth exactly 100. In this case there is a good chance that at some time the company will

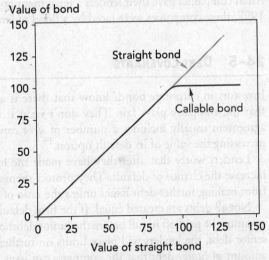

FIGURE 24.2

Relationship between the value of a callable bond and that of a straight (noncallable) bond. Assumptions: (1) Both bonds have an 8% coupon and a five-year maturity; (2) the callable bond may be called at face value any time before maturity; (3) the short-term interest rate follows a random walk, and the expected returns on bonds of all maturities are equal.

Source: M. J. Brennan and E. S. Schwartz, "Savings Bonds, Retractable Bonds, and Callable Bonds," *Journal of Financial Economics* 5 (1977), pp. 67–88. © 1977 Elsevier Science, with permission.

wish to call its bonds. Therefore the value of our callable bond will be slightly less than that of the straight bond. If interest rates decline further, the price of the straight bond will continue to rise, but nobody will ever pay more than the call price for the callable bond.

A call provision is not a free lunch. It provides the issuer with a valuable option, but that is recognized in a lower issue price. So why do companies bother with a call provision? One reason is that bond indentures often place a number of restrictions on what the company can do. Companies are happy to agree to these restrictions as long as they know that they can escape from them if the restrictions prove too inhibiting. The call provision provides the escape route.

We mentioned earlier that some bonds also provide the *investor* with an option to demand early repayment. *Puttable* bonds exist largely because bond indentures cannot anticipate every action the

---

[12] Of course, this assumes that the bond is correctly priced, that investors are behaving rationally, and that investors expect the *firm* to behave rationally. Also we ignore some complications. First, you may not wish to call a bond if you are prevented by a nonrefunding clause from issuing new debt. Second, the call premium is a tax-deductible expense for the company but is taxed as a capital gain to the bondholder. Third, there are other possible tax consequences to both the company and the investor from replacing a high-coupon bond with a lower-coupon bond. Fourth, there are costs and delays to calling and reissuing debt.

company may take that could harm the bondholder. If the value of the bonds is reduced, the put option allows the bondholders to demand repayment.

Puttable loans can sometimes get their issuers into BIG trouble. During the 1990s many loans to Asian companies gave their lenders a repayment option. Consequently, when the Asian crisis struck in 1997, these companies were faced by a flood of lenders demanding their money back.

24-5   DEBT COVENANTS

Investors in corporate bonds know that there is a risk of default. But they still want to make sure that the company plays fair. They don't want it to gamble with their money. Therefore, the loan agreement usually includes a number of *debt covenants* that prevent the company from purposely increasing the value of its default option.[13]

Lenders worry that after they have made the loan, the company may pile up more debt and so increase the chance of default. They protect themselves against this risk by prohibiting the company from making further debt issues unless the ratio of debt to equity is below a specified limit.

Not all debts are created equal. If the firm defaults, the senior debt comes first in the pecking order and must be paid off in full before the junior debtholders get a cent. Therefore, when a company issues senior debt, the lenders will place limits on further issues of senior debt. But they won't restrict the amount of *junior* debt that the company can issue. Because the senior lenders are at the front of the queue, they view the junior debt in the same way that they view equity: They would be happy to see an issue of either. Of course, the converse is not true. Holders of the junior debt *do* care both about the total amount of debt and the proportion that is senior to their claim. As a result, an issue of junior debt generally includes a restriction on both total debt and senior debt.

All bondholders worry that the company may issue more secured debt. An issue of mortgage bonds often imposes a limit on the amount of secured debt. This is not necessary when you are issuing unsecured debentures. As long as the debenture holders are given an equal claim, they don't care how much you mortgage your assets. Therefore, unsecured bonds usually include a so-called negative-pledge clause, in which the unsecured holders simply say, "Me too."[14]

Instead of borrowing money to buy an asset, companies may enter into a long-term agreement to rent or lease it. For the debtholder this is very similar to secured borrowing. Therefore debt agreements also include limitations on leasing.

We have talked about how an unscrupulous borrower can try to increase the value of the default option by issuing more debt. But this is not the only way that such a company can exploit its existing bondholders. For example, we know that the value of an option is reduced when the company pays out some of its assets to stockholders. In the extreme case a company could sell all its assets and distribute the proceeds to shareholders as a bumper dividend. That would leave nothing for the lenders. To guard against such dangers, debt issues may restrict the amount that the company may pay out in the form of dividends or repurchases of stock.[15]

Take a look at Table 24.2, which summarizes the principal covenants in a large sample of senior bond issues. Notice that investment-grade bonds tend to have fewer restrictions than high-yield

---

[13] We described in Section 18-3 some of the games that managers can play at the expense of bondholders.

[14] "Me too" is not acceptable legal jargon. Instead the bond agreement may state that the company "will not consent to any lien on its assets without securing the existing bonds equally and ratably."

[15] A dividend restriction might typically prohibit the company from paying dividends if their cumulative amount would exceed the sum of (1) cumulative net income, (2) the proceeds from the sale of stock or conversion of debt, and (3) a dollar amount equal to one year's dividend.

TABLE 24.2 Percentage of sample of bonds with covenant restrictions. Sample consists of 4,478 senior bonds issued between 1993 and 2007.

Type of Covenant	Percentage of Bonds with Covenants	
	Investment-Grade Bonds	Other Bonds
Merger restrictions	92%	93%
Dividends or other payment restrictions	6	44
Debt covenants	74	67
Default-related events[a]	52	71
Change in control	24	74

[a] For example, default on other loans, rating changes, or declining net worth.

Source: S. Chava, P. Kumar, and A. Warga, "Managerial Agency and Bond Covenants," *Review of Financial Studies,* forthcoming.

Finance In Practice

U.S. Shoe's Owner Riles Bondholders with Its Debt Moves

Imagine a company trying to push its bonds into technical default just so it can redeem them before maturity. Some bond analysts assert that this is exactly what Luxottica Group SpA of Italy—the new owner of U.S. Shoe Corp.—is doing with U.S. Shoe's 8 5/8% note issue.

Luxottica's strategy, which the company asserts wasn't deliberately designed to hurt bondholders, is shaping to be the newest wrinkle in corporate America's scramble to pry high-interest-bearing bonds from the hands of investors before they mature, some analysts say. As interest rates have fallen, a host of corporate issuers—from stodgy utilities to fleet-footed finance companies—have rushed to redeem their high-interest bonds with lower coupon issues. As long as the bonds are "callable," or redeemable, there is usually no problem. Increasingly, however, corporate issuers are trying to redeem noncallable bonds—securities that can't be wrested from investors before maturity—using unusual tactics.

Bond analysts say Luxottica has been trying to put U.S. Shoe's 8 5/8% note issue, maturing in 2002, in technical default by piling $1.4 billion of secured debt onto the company earlier this year. That's because a little-noticed covenant in U.S. Shoe's bond indenture says its bonds are in technical default if it adds secured debt to its financial ledger without simultaneously adding collateral to back the 8 5/8% securities so they're on the same level as the bank debt.

What's riling bondholders is that Luxottica hasn't been willing to secure its 8 5/8% notes even though it took on a load of secured debt earlier this year. Now Luxottica is trying to redeem its bonds early, which the company says it can do under the covenants when the issue is in technical default.

"This action is 10 times worse than Marriott on its worst day, because Marriott never violated an explicit covenant," contends Max Holmes, a securities analyst.

bonds. For example, restrictions on the amount of any dividends or repurchases are less common in the case of investment-grade bonds.

These debt covenants *do* matter. Asquith and Wizman, who studied the effect of leveraged buyouts on the value of the company's debt, found that when there were no restrictions on further debt issues, dividend payments, or mergers, the buyout led to a 5.2% fall in the value of existing bonds.[16] Those bonds that were protected by strong covenants against excessive borrowing increased in price by 2.6%.

Unfortunately, it is not always easy to cover all loopholes, as the bondholders of Marriott Corporation discovered in 1992. They hit the roof when the company announced plans to divide its operations into two separate businesses. One business, Marriott International, would manage Marriott's hotel chain and receive most of the revenues, while the other, Host Marriott, would own all the company's real estate and be responsible for servicing essentially all of the old company's $3 billion of debt. As a result the price of Marriott's bonds plunged nearly 30%, and investors began to think about how they could protect themselves against such *event risks*. As you can see from Table 24.2 it is now more common for bondholders to insist on *poison-put* clauses that oblige the borrower to repay the debt if there is a change of control and the bonds are downrated.

However, there are always nasty surprises round the next corner. The above box describes one such surprise for bond investors of U.S. Shoe.

24-6 CONVERTIBLE BONDS AND WARRANTS

Unlike the common bonds, a convertible security may change its spots. It starts life as a bond (or preferred stock), but subsequently may turn into common stock. For example, in February 2007, Reliance Communications (RCOM) issued $1.27 billion of five-year zero-coupon foreign currency convertible bonds (FCCB) at a conversion price of ₹661 per share. The face value of each bond was $100,000 each. The number of shares into which each bond can be converted is called the bond's **conversion ratio**. The rupee-dollar exchange rate in February 2007 was approximately ₹44/$. So, the conversion ratio for this bond was 6657 shares.

The 52-week high of RCOM was ₹592 and the 52-week low was ₹264. The stock of RCOM is trading at about ₹73 in January 2012. It seems very unlikely that the stock price of RCOM will reach ₹661 before the expiry of the bond in March 2012. So the bondholders would get $100,000 in cash and RCOM will not have to issue any additional shares.

You can think of a convertible bond as equivalent to a straight bond plus an option to acquire common stock. When convertible bondholders exercise this option, they do not pay cash; instead they give up their bonds in exchange for shares. The difference between the price of a convertible bond and the price of an equivalent straight bond (zero-coupon bond in case of RCOM) represents the value that investors place on the conversion option.

The Value of a Convertible at Maturity

By the time that the company convertible matures, investors need to choose whether to stay with the bond or convert to common stock. Figure 24.3(*a*) shows the possible bond values at maturity.[17]

---

[16] P. Asquith and T. Wizman "Event Risk, Covenants, and Bondholder Returns in Leveraged Buyouts," *Journal of Financial Economics* 27 (September 1990), pp. 195–213. Leveraged buyouts (LBOs) are company acquisitions that are financed by large issues of (usually unsecured) debt. We describe LBOs in Chapter 32.

[17] You may recognize this as the position diagram for a default-free bond *minus* a put option on the assets with an exercise price equal to the face value of the bonds. See Section 23-2.

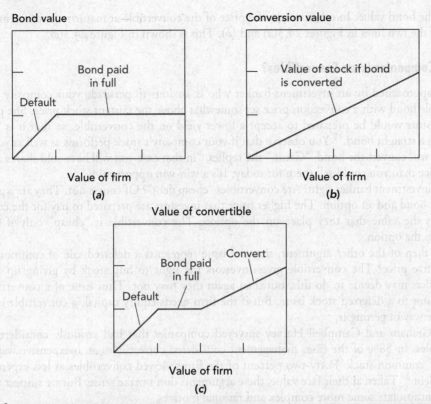

FIGURE 24.3

(*a*) The bond value when the company's convertible bond matures. If firm value is at least equal to the face value of the company's debt, the bond is paid off at face value.

(*b*) The conversion value at maturity. If converted, the value of the convertible rises in proportion to firm value.

(*c*) At maturity the convertible bondholder can choose to receive the payment on the bond or convert to common stock. The value of the convertible bond is therefore the higher of its bond value and its conversion value.

Notice that the bond value is simply the face value as long as the company does not default. However, if the value of company's assets is sufficiently low, the bondholders will receive *less* than the face value and, in the extreme case that the assets are worthless, they will receive nothing. You can think of the bond value as a lower bound, or "floor," to the price of the convertible. But that floor has a nasty slope and, when the company falls on hard times, the bond may not be worth much.

Figure 24.3(*b*) shows the value of the shares that investors receive if they choose to convert. If the company's assets at that point are worthless, the shares into which the convertible can be exchanged are also worthless. But, as the value of the assets rises, so does the conversion value.

The company's convertible cannot sell for less than its conversion value. If it did, investors would buy the convertible, exchange it rapidly for stock, and sell the stock. Their profit would be equal to the difference between the conversion value and the price of the convertible. Therefore, there are two lower bounds to the price of the convertible: its bond value and its conversion value. Investors will not convert if the convertible is worth more as a bond; they *will* do so if the conversion value at maturity exceeds the bond value. In other words, the price of the convertible at maturity is represented by the higher of the two lines in Figures 24.3(a) and (b). This is shown in Figure 24.3(c).

Why Do Companies Issue Convertibles?

You are approached by an investment banker who is anxious to persuade your company to issue a convertible bond with a conversion price set somewhat above the current stock price. She points out that investors would be prepared to accept a lower yield on the convertible, so that it is "cheaper" debt than a straight bond.[18] You observe that if your company's stock performs as well as you expect, investors will convert the bond. "Great," she replies, "in that case you will have sold shares at a much better price than you could sell them for today. It's a win-win opportunity."

Is the investment banker right? Are convertibles "cheap debt"? Of course not. They are a package of a straight bond and an option. The higher price that investors are prepared to pay for the convertible represents the value that they place on the option. The convertible is "cheap" only if this price overvalues the option.

What then of the other argument, that the issue represents a deferred sale of common stock at an attractive price? The convertible gives investors the right to buy stock by giving up a bond.[19] Bondholders may decide to do this, but then again they may not. Thus issue of a convertible bond *may* amount to a deferred stock issue. But if the firm needs equity capital, a convertible issue is an unreliable way of getting it.

John Graham and Campbell Harvey surveyed companies that had seriously considered issuing convertibles. In 58% of the cases management considered convertibles an inexpensive way to issue "delayed" common stock. Forty-two percent of the firms viewed convertibles as less expensive than straight debt.[20] Taken at their face value, these arguments don't make sense. But we suspect that these phrases encapsulate some more complex and rational motives.

Notice that convertibles tend to be issued by the smaller and more speculative firms. They are almost invariably unsecured and generally subordinated. Now put yourself in the position of a potential investor. You are approached by a firm with an untried product line that wants to issue some junior unsecured debt. You know that if things go well, you will get your money back, but if they do not, you could easily be left with nothing. Since the firm is in a new line of business, it is difficult to assess the chances of trouble. Therefore you don't know what the fair rate of interest is. Also, you may be worried that once you have made the loan, management will be tempted to run extra risks. It may take on additional senior debt, or it may decide to expand its operations and go for broke on your money. In fact, if you charge a very high rate of interest, you could be encouraging this to happen.

What can management do to protect you against a wrong estimate of the risk and to assure you that its intentions are honorable? In crude terms, it can give you a piece of the action. You don't mind the company running unanticipated risks as long as you share in the gains as well as the losses.[21]

---

[18] She might even point out to you that in 2002 several Japanese companies issued convertible bonds at a negative yield. Investors actually *paid* the companies to hold their debt.

[19] That is much the same as already having the stock together with the right to sell it for the convertible's bond value. In other words, instead of thinking of a convertible as a bond plus a call option, you could think of it as the stock plus a put option. Now you can see why it is wrong to think of a convertible as equivalent to the sale of stock; it is equivalent to the sale of both stock and a put option. If there is any possibility that investors will want to hold onto their bond, that put option has value.

[20] See J. R. Graham and C. R. Harvey, "The Theory and Practice of Finance: Evidence from the Field," *Journal of Financial Economics* 61 (2001), pp. 187–243.

[21] In the survey referred to above a further 44% of the respondents reported that an important factor in their decision was the fact that convertibles were attractive to investors who were unsure about the riskiness of the company.

Convertible securities make sense whenever it is unusually costly to assess the risk of debt or whenever investors are worried that management may not act in the bondholders' interest.[22]

The relatively low coupon rate on convertible bonds may also be a convenience for rapidly growing firms facing heavy capital expenditures.[23] They may be willing to provide the conversion option to reduce immediate cash requirements for debt service. Without that option, lenders might demand extremely high (promised) interest rates to compensate for the probability of default. This would not only force the firm to raise still more capital for debt service but also increase the risk of financial distress. Paradoxically, lenders' attempts to protect themselves against default may actually increase the probability of financial distress by increasing the burden of debt service on the firm.

Valuing Convertible Bonds

We have seen that a convertible bond is equivalent to a package of a bond and an option to buy stock. This means that the option-valuation models that we described in Chapter 21 can also be used to value the option to convert. We don't want to repeat that material here, but we should note three wrinkles that you need to look out for when valuing a convertible:

1. *Dividends.* If you hold the common stock, you may receive dividends. The investor who holds an option to convert into common stock misses out on these dividends. In fact the convertible holder loses out every time a cash dividend is paid because the dividend reduces the stock price and thus reduces the value of the conversion option. If the dividends are high enough, it may even pay to convert before maturity to capture the extra income. We showed how dividend payments affect option value in Section 21-5.

2. *Dilution.* The second complication arises because conversion increases the number of outstanding shares. Therefore, exercise means that each shareholder is entitled to a smaller proportion of the firm's assets and profits.[24] This problem of *dilution* never arises with traded options. If you buy an option through an option exchange and subsequently exercise it, you have no effect on the number of shares outstanding. We showed how dilution affects option value in the Appendix to Chapter 21.

3. *Changing bond value.* When investors convert to shares, they give up their bond. The exercise price of the option is therefore the value of the bond that they are relinquishing. But this bond value is not constant. If the bond value at issue is less than the face value (and it usually is less), it is likely to change as maturity approaches. Also the bond value varies as interest rates change and as the company's credit standing changes. If there is some possibility of default, investors cannot even be certain of what the bond will be worth at maturity. In Chapter 21 we did not get into the complication of uncertain exercise prices.

---

[22] Changes in risk are more likely when the firm is small and its debt is low-grade. Therefore, we should find that convertible bonds of such firms offer their holders a larger potential ownership share. This is indeed the case. See C. M. Lewis, R. J. Rogalski, and J. K. Seward, "Understanding the Design of Convertible Debt," *Journal of Applied Corporate Finance* 11 (Spring 1998), pp. 45–53.

[23] Of course, the firm could also make an equity issue rather than an issue of straight debt or convertibles. However, a convertible issue sends a better signal to investors than an issue of common stock. As we explained in Chapter 15, announcement of a stock issue prompts worries of overvaluation and usually depresses the stock price. Convertibles are hybrids of debt and equity and send a less negative signal. If the company is likely to need equity, its willingness to issue a convertible and take the chance that the stock price will rise enough to lead to conversion also signals management's confidence in the future. See J. Stein, "Convertible Bonds as Backdoor Equity Financing," *Journal of Financial Economics* 32 (1992), pp. 3–21.

[24] In their financial statements companies recognize the possibility of dilution by showing how earnings would be affected by the issue of the extra shares.

A Variation on Convertible Bonds: The Bond–Warrant Package

Instead of issuing a convertible bond, companies sometimes sell a package of straight bonds and warrants. Warrants are simply long-term call options that give the investor the right to buy the firm's common stock. For example, each warrant might allow the holder to buy a share of stock for $50 at any time during the next five years. Obviously, the warrant holders hope that the company's stock will zoom up, so that they can exercise their warrants at a profit. But, if the company's stock price remains below $50, holders will choose not to exercise, and the warrants will expire worthless.

24-7 PRIVATE PLACEMENTS AND PROJECT FINANCE

India Infoline debentures were registered with the SEC and sold to the public. However, debt is often placed privately with a small number of financial institutions. As we saw in Section 15-5, it costs less to arrange a private placement than to make a public debt issue. But there are three other differences between a privately placed bond and its public counterpart.

First, if you place an issue privately with one or two financial institutions, it may be necessary to sign only a simple promissory note. This is just an IOU that lays down certain conditions that the borrower must observe. However, when you make a public issue of debt, you must worry about who is supposed to represent the bondholders in any subsequent negotiations and what procedures are needed for paying interest and principal. Therefore, the contract has to be somewhat more complicated.

The second characteristic of publicly issued bonds is that they are somewhat standardized products. They *have* to be—investors are constantly buying and selling without checking the fine print in the agreement. This is not so necessary in private placements and so the debt can be custom-tailored for firms with special problems or opportunities. The relationship between borrower and lender is much more intimate. Imagine a $200 million debt issue privately placed with an insurance company, and compare it with an equivalent public issue held by 200 anonymous investors. The insurance company can justify a more thorough investigation of the company's prospects and therefore may be more willing to accept unusual terms or conditions.[25]

As we saw earlier, all bond agreements seek to protect the lender by imposing conditions on the borrower. Because covenants are more easily renegotiated in the case of privately placed debt, the conditions tend to be more severe. For example, the loan agreement may state that the borrower will be in default if interest payments ever exceed a certain multiple of earnings or if the company fails to maintain a minimum level of liquid assets. In many cases the loan contains restrictions on the firm's capital expenditures. Since privately placed debt keeps the borrower on a fairly short leash, it is quite common for a covenant to be breached.[26] This is not as calamitous as it may sound. As long as the borrower is in good financial health, the bank may simply readjust the terms of the covenant. Only if covenants continue to be violated will the lender choose to take more drastic action.

These features of private placements give them a particular niche in the corporate debt market, namely, loans to small- and medium-sized firms. These are the firms that face the highest costs in public issues, that require the most detailed investigation, and that may require specialized, flexible loan arrangements. However, many large companies also use private placements.

---

[25] Of course debt with the same terms could be offered publicly, but then 200 separate investigations would be required—a much more expensive proposition.

[26] In a study of large, private placements, Dichev and Skinner found that 30% of the loans resulted in covenant violations. See I. D. Dichev and D. J. Skinner, "Large-Sample Evidence on the Debt Covenant Hypothesis," *Journal of Accounting Research* 40 (2002), pp. 1091–1123.

Of course, the advantages of private placements are not free, for the lenders demand a higher rate of interest to compensate them for holding an illiquid asset. It is difficult to generalize about the difference in interest rates between private placements and public issues, but a typical differential is 50 basis points, or .50 percentage points.

Project Finance

We are not going to dwell further on the topic of private placement bonds, because the greater part of what we have had to say about public issues is also true of private placements. However, we do need to discuss a different form of private loan, one that is tied as closely as possible to the fortunes of a particular project and that minimizes the exposure of the parent. Such a loan is usually referred to as **project finance** and is a specialty of large international banks.

Project finance means debt supported by the project, not by the project's sponsoring companies. Debt ratios are nevertheless very high for most project financings. They can be high because the debt is supported not just by the project's assets but also by a variety of contracts and guarantees provided by customers, suppliers, and local governments as well as by the project's owners.

EXAMPLE 24.1   Project Finance for a Power Station

Here is how project finance was used to construct a $1.8 billion oil-fired power plant in Pakistan. First, a separate firm, the Hub Power Company (Hubco) was established to own the power station. Hubco then engaged a consortium of companies, headed by the Japanese company Mitsui & Co., to build the power station, while the British company International Power became responsible for managing and running it for an initial period of 12 years. Hubco agreed to buy the fuel from the Pakistan State Oil Company and to sell the power station's output to another government body, the Water and Power Development Authority (WAPDA).

Hubco's lawyers drew up a complex series of contracts to make certain that each of these parties came up to scratch. For example, the contractors agreed to deliver the plant on time and to ensure that it would operate to specifications. International Power, the plant manager, agreed to maintain the plant and operate it efficiently. Pakistan State Oil Company entered into a long-term contract to supply oil to Hubco, and WAPDA agreed to buy Hubco's output for the next 30 years.[27] Since WAPDA would pay for the electricity with rupees, Hubco was concerned about the possibility of a fall in the value of the rupee. The State Bank of Pakistan therefore arranged to provide Hubco with foreign exchange for debt service at guaranteed exchange rates. The Pakistan government guaranteed that WAPDA, Pakistan State Oil, and the State Bank would honor their agreements.

The effect of these contracts was to ensure that each risk was borne by the party that was best able to measure and control it. For example, the contractors were best placed to ensure that the plant was completed on time, so it made sense to ask them to bear the risk of construction delays. Similarly, the plant operator was best placed to operate the plant efficiently and would be penalized if it failed to do so. The contractors and the plant manager were prepared to take on these risks because the project involved an established technology and there was relatively little chance of unpleasant surprises.

---

[27] WAPDA entered into a *take-or-pay* agreement with Hubco; if it did not take the electricity, it still had to pay for it. In the case of pipeline projects the contract with the customer is often in the form of a *throughput* agreement, whereby the customer agrees to make a minimum use of the pipeline. Another arrangement for transferring revenue risk to a customer is the *tolling contract,* whereby the customer agrees to deliver to the project company materials that the company is to process and return to the customer. One purpose of transferring revenue risk to customers is to encourage them to estimate their demand for the project's output thoroughly.

While these contracts sought to be as precise as possible about each party's responsibilities, they could not cover every eventuality; inevitably the contracts were incomplete. Therefore, to buttress the formal legal agreements, the contractors and the plant manager became major shareholders in Hubco. This meant that if they cut corners in building and running the plant, they would share in the losses.

The equity in Hubco was highly levered. Over 75% of the $1.8 billion investment in the project was financed by debt. Just under $600 million was junior debt provided by a fund that was set up by the World Bank and the export credit agencies of France, Italy, and Japan. The remainder was senior debt provided in seven different currencies by 58 local and international banks.[28] The banks were encouraged to invest because they knew that the World Bank and several governments were in the front line and would take a hit if the project were to fail. But they were still concerned that the government of Pakistan might prevent Hubco from paying out foreign currency or it might impose a special tax or prevent the company from bringing in the specialist staff it needed. Therefore, to protect Hubco against these political risks, the government promised to pay compensation if it interfered in such ways with the operation of the project. Of course, the government could not be prevented from tearing up that agreement, but, if it did, Hubco could call on a $360 million guarantee by the World Bank and the Japan Bank for International Cooperation. This was supposed to keep the Pakistan government honest once the plant was built and operating. Governments can be surprisingly relaxed when faced with the wrath of a private corporation but are usually reluctant to break an agreement that lands the World Bank with a large bill.

The arrangements for the Hubco project were complex, costly, and time-consuming. Over 200 person-years were spent in setting up the project. Not everything was plain sailing. The project was suspended for over a year by a Pakistani court ruling that the interest on the loans contravened Islamic law. Ten years after the start of the discussions the final agreement on financing the project was signed and within a short time Hubco was producing a fifth of all Pakistan's electricity.

That was not the end of the Hubco story. WAPDA was obliged by its contract to make regular payments to Hubco regardless of whether it took the electricity, and as a result found itself on the brink of collapse. After the fall of Benazir Bhutto's government in Pakistan, the new government terminated the contract with Hubco and announced a 30% cut in electricity tariffs. After three years of painful dispute, which threatened Pakistan's relationships with the World Bank, Hubco finally agreed to a new tariff. The feud with the government was finally over, and by 2006 Hubco had fully repaid its senior debts.

Project Finance—Some Common Features

No two project financings are alike, but they have some common features:

- The project is established as a separate company.
- Equity ownership is privately held by a small group of investors. These usually include the contractors and the plant manager, who therefore share in the risk of the project's failure.
- The project company enters into a complex series of contracts that distribute risk among the contractors, the plant manager, the suppliers, and the customers.

---

[28] Notice that, although most of Hubco's debt had a maturity of about 12 years, the project was not financed by a public bond issue. The concentrated ownership of bank debt induces the lenders to evaluate the project carefully and to monitor its subsequent progress. It also facilitates the renegotiation of the debt if the project company runs into difficulties.

- The government may guarantee that it will provide the necessary permits, allow the purchase of foreign exchange, and so on.
- The detailed contractual arrangements and the government guarantees typically allow about 70% of the capital for the project to be provided in the form of bank debt or other privately placed borrowing. This debt is supported by the project cash flows; if these flows are insufficient, the lenders do not have any recourse against the parent companies.

The Role of Project Finance

Project finance is widely used in developing countries to fund power, telecommunications, and transportation projects, but it is also used in the major industrialized countries. In the United States project finance has been most commonly used to fund power plants. For example, an electric utility company may get together with an industrial company to construct a cogeneration plant that provides electricity to the utility and waste heat to a nearby industrial plant. The utility stands behind the cogeneration project and guarantees its revenue stream. Banks are happy to lend a high proportion of the cost of the project because they know that once the project is up and running, the cash flow is insulated from most of the risks facing normal businesses.[29]

Project financing is costly to arrange[30] and the project debt usually carries a relatively high interest rate. So why don't companies simply finance the projects by borrowing against their existing assets? Notice that most of the projects have limited lives and employ established technologies. They generate substantial free cash flow, and there are few options to make profitable follow-on investments. If such investments are funded with project finance, management has little discretion over how the cash flows are used. Instead, the debt-service requirements ensure that the cash must be returned to investors rather than frittered away on unprofitable future ventures.[31]

Our example of the Hubco power station illustrates another important motivation for project finance. The success of the project depends on the performance of a number of different parties. For example, Hubco had only one source of fuel and one customer. To prevent any of the parties from changing the rules of the game after the project has begun, all of them need to enter into a complex set of contracts that are designed to ensure that risks are borne by those best able to control them. And because project viability is often dependent on the goodwill of the government, the government is also often a party to these contracts and the financing is structured to reduce the chance of punitive government action.

24-8   INNOVATION IN THE BOND MARKET

Domestic bonds and eurobonds, fixed- and floating-rate bonds, coupon bonds and zeros, callable and puttable bonds, privately placed bonds and project finance—you might think that this would give you as much choice as you need. Yet almost every day some new type of bond seems to be issued.

---

[29] There are some interesting regulatory implications to this arrangement. When a utility builds a power plant, it is entitled to a fair return on its investment: Regulators are supposed to set customer charges that will allow the utility to earn its cost of capital. Unfortunately, the cost of capital is not easily measured and is a natural focus for argument in regulatory hearings. But when a utility buys electric power, the cost of capital is rolled into the contract price and treated as an operating cost. In this case the pass-through to the customer may be less controversial.

[30] Total transaction costs for infrastructure projects average 3% to 5% of the amount invested. See M. Klein, J. So, and B. Shin, "Transaction Costs in Private Infrastructure Projects—Are They Too High?" The World Bank Group, October 1996.

[31] Because the project is an independent company, it cannot drag down the parent company if something does go badly wrong with the project.

Table 24.3 lists some of the more interesting bonds that have been invented in recent years.[32] Earlier in the chapter we cited the "Bowie bonds" as an example of asset-backed securities, and in Chapter 26 we discuss catastrophe bonds whose payoffs are linked to the occurrence of natural disasters.

TABLE 24.3   Some examples of innovation in bond design.

Liquid yield option notes (LYONs)	Puttable, callable, convertible, zero-coupon debt.
Floating-price (death-spiral) convertibles	Convertible debt where the bondholder can convert into a fixed *value* of shares.
Asset-backed securities	Many small loans are packaged together and resold as a bond.
Catastrophe (CAT) bonds	Payments are reduced in the event of a specified natural disaster.
Reverse floaters (yield-curve notes)	Floating-rate bonds that pay a higher rate of interest when other interest rates fall and a lower rate when other rates rise.
Equity-linked bonds	Payments are linked to the performance of a stock market index.
Pay-in-kind bonds (PIKs)	Issuer can choose to make interest payments either in cash or in more bonds with an equivalent face value.
Rate-sensitive bonds	Coupon rate changes as company's credit rating changes.
Mortality bonds	Bonds whose payments are reduced or eliminated if there is a jump in mortality rates.

Some financial innovations appear to serve little or no economic purpose; they may flower briefly but then wither. For example, toward the end of the 1990s in the United States there was a bout of new issues of *floating-price convertibles,* or, as they were more commonly called, death-spiral, or toxic, convertibles. When death-spiral convertibles are issued, the conversion price is set below the current stock price. Moreover, each bond is convertible not into a fixed *number* of shares but into shares with a fixed *value.* Therefore, the more the share price falls, the more shares that the convertible bondholder is entitled to. With a normal convertible, the value of the conversion option falls whenever the value of the firm's assets falls; so the convertible holder shares some of the pain with the stockholders. With a death-spiral convertible, the holder is entitled to shares with a fixed value, so the entire effect of the decrease in the asset price falls on the common stockholders. Death-spiral convertibles were issued largely by companies that were already in desperate straits, and, when the issuers failed to recover, the toxic chicken came home to roost. After the initial flurry of issues in the United States, death-spiral convertibles seem now to have been consigned to the garbage heap of unsuccessful innovations.

Many other innovations seem to have a more obvious purpose. Here are some important motives for creating new securities:

1. *Investor choice.* Sometimes new financial instruments are created to widen investor choice. Economists refer to such securities as helping to "complete the market." This was the idea behind the 2006 issue of nearly €350 million of *mortality bonds* by the French insurance company Axa. One of the big risks for a life insurance company is a pandemic or other disaster that results in a sharp increase in the death rate. Axa's bond, therefore, offers investors a higher interest rate for taking on some of that risk. Holders of the bond will lose their entire investment if death rates for two consecutive years are 10% or more above expectations.

---

[32] For a more comprehensive list of innovations, see K. A. Carrow and J. J. McConnell, "A Survey of U.S. Corporate Financing Innovations: 1970–1997," *Journal of Applied Corporate Finance* 12 (Spring 1999), pp. 55–69.

Pension funds are in the opposite position to insurance companies. Their worry is that the scheme's members will continue to draw their pensions into a ripe old age. Investment bankers have therefore been working to design *longevity bonds* that pay a higher rate of interest if an unusually high proportion of the population survives to a particular age. A pension fund that held these bonds would be protected against an unexpected increase in longevity.[33]

Both mortality and longevity bonds widen investor choice. They allow insurance companies and pension funds to protect themselves against adverse changes in mortality and they spread the risk widely around the market.

2. *Government regulation and tax.* Merton Miller has described new government regulations and taxes as the sand in the oyster that stimulates the design of new types of security. For example, we have already seen how the eurobond market was a response to the U.S. government's imposition of a tax on purchases of foreign securities.

Asset-backed securities provide another instance of a market that has been encouraged by regulation. To reduce the likelihood of failure, banks are obliged to finance part of their loan portfolio with equity capital. Many banks have sought to reduce the amount of capital that they need to hold by packaging up their loans or credit card receivables and selling them off as bonds. Bank regulators worry about this. They think that banks may be tempted to sell off their riskiest loans and to keep their safest ones. They have therefore introduced new regulations that will link the capital requirement to the riskiness of the loans.

3. *Reducing agency costs.* At the turn of the century investors were worried by the huge spending plans of telecom companies. So when BT, the British telecom giant, decided to sell $10 billion of bonds in 2000, it offered a *step-up* provision to reassure investors. Under this arrangement, BT was required to increase the coupon rate on the bonds by 25 basis points if ever its bonds were downgraded a notch by Moody's or Standard & Poor's. BT's rate-sensitive bonds protected investors against possible future attempts by the company to exploit existing bondholders by loading on more debt.

Dreaming up new financial instruments is only half the battle. The other problem is to produce them efficiently. Think, for example, of the problems of packaging together several hundred million dollars' worth of credit card receivables and allocating the cash flows to a diverse group of investors. That requires good computer systems. The deal also needs to be structured so that, if the issuer goes bankrupt, the receivables will not be part of the bankruptcy estate. That depends on the development of legal structures that will stand up in the event of a dispute.

SUMMARY

You should now have a fair idea of what you are letting yourself in for when you make an issue of bonds. You can issue bonds in the domestic U.S. market, in a foreign bond market, or in the eurobond market. Eurobonds are marketed simultaneously in a number of foreign countries, usually by the London branches of international banks and security dealers.

The detailed bond agreement is set out in the indenture between your company and a trustee, but the main provisions are summarized in the prospectus to the issue. The indenture states whether the bonds are senior or subordinated, and whether they are secured or unsecured. Most bonds are unsecured debentures or notes. This means that they are general claims on the corporation. The principal exceptions are utility mortgage bonds, collateral trust bonds, and equipment trust

---

[33] The French bank BNP Paribas attempted to launch a $1 billion issue of longevity bonds in 2004, but had difficulty attracting buyers.

certificates. In the event of default, the trustee to these issues can repossess the company's assets to pay off the debt.

Some long-term bond issues have a sinking fund. This means that the company must set aside enough money each year to retire a specified number of bonds. A sinking fund reduces the average life of the bond, and it provides a yearly test of the company's ability to service its debt. It therefore helps to protect the bondholders against the risk of default.

Long-dated bonds may be callable before maturity. The option to call the bond may be very valuable. If interest rates decline and bond value rises, you may be able to call a bond that would be worth substantially more than the call price. Of course, if investors know that you may call the bond, the call price will act as a ceiling on the market price. Your best strategy, therefore, is to call the bond as soon as the market price hits the call price. You are unlikely to do better than that.

Lenders usually seek to prevent the borrower from taking actions that would damage the value of their loans. Here are some examples of debt covenants:

1. The loan agreement may limit the amount of additional borrowing by the company.
2. Unsecured loans may incorporate a negative pledge clause, which prohibits the company from securing additional debt without giving equal treatment to the existing unsecured bonds.
3. Lenders may place a limit on the company's dividend payments or repurchases of stock.

Bank loans and other privately placed debt tend to impose more restrictive conditions, but these conditions are more easily changed if it makes sense to do so.

Most bonds start and finish their lives as bonds, but convertible bonds give their owner the option to exchange the bond for common stock. The *conversion ratio* measures the number of shares into which each bond can be exchanged. You can think of a convertible bond as equivalent to a straight bond plus a call option on the stock. Sometimes, instead of issuing a convertible, companies may decide to issue a package of bonds and options (or *warrants*) to buy the stock. If the stock price rises above the exercise price, the investor may then keep the bond and exercise the warrants for cash.

Private placements are less standardized than public issues, but otherwise they are generally close counterparts of publicly issued bonds. Sometimes private debt takes the form of project finance. In this case the loan is tied to the fortunes of a particular project.

There is an enormous variety of bond issues and new forms of bonds are spawned almost daily. By a process of natural selection, some of these new instruments become popular and may even replace existing species. Others are ephemeral curiosities. Some innovations succeed because they widen investor choice or reduce agency costs. Others owe their origin to tax rules and government regulation.

FURTHER READING

A useful general work on debt securities is:

F. J. Fabozzi (ed.), *The Handbook of Fixed Income Securities,* 6th ed. (New York: McGraw-Hill, 2005).

For nontechnical discussions of the pricing of convertible bonds and the reasons for their use, see:

M. J. Brennan and E. S. Schwartz, "The Case for Convertibles," *Journal of Applied Corporate Finance* 1 (Summer 1988), pp. 55–64.

C. M. Lewis, R. J. Rogalski, and J. K. Seward, "Understanding the Design of Convertible Debt," *Journal of Applied Corporate Finance* 11 (Spring 1998), pp. 45–53.

Discussions of project finance include:

B. C. Esty, *Modern Project Finance: A Casebook* (New York: John Wiley, 2003).

B. C. Esty, "Returns on Project-Financed Investments: Evolution and Managerial Implications," *Journal of Applied Corporate Finance* 15 (Spring 2002), pp. 71–86.

R. A. Brealey, I. A. Cooper, and M. Habib, "Using Project Finance to Fund Infrastructure Investments," *Journal of Applied Corporate Finance* 9 (Fall 1996), pp. 25–38.

The readings listed at the end of Chapter 17 include several articles on financial innovation.

PROBLEM SETS

BASIC

1. Select the most appropriate term from within the parentheses:
   a. (Bonds/debentures) are usually unsecured debt instruments.
   b. Public Sector Units in India raise debt capital by issue of (bonds/debentures).
   c. Mortgage pass-through certificate is an example of (an asset-backed security/project finance).
   d. Dhabol Power Project is an example of (project finance/private placement).

2. a. As a senior bondholder, would you like the company to issue more junior debt to finance its investment program, would you prefer it not to do so, or would you not care?
   b. You hold debt secured on the company's existing property. Would you like the company to issue more unsecured debt to finance its investments, would you prefer it not to do so, or would you not care?

3. Use Table 24.1 (but not the text) to answer the following questions:
   a. Who is the trustee for the issue?
   b. Is the debenture "bearer" or "registered"?
   c. What is the maximum interest that India Infoline has to pay to the bond-holders every year?

5. Look at Table 24.1:
   a. When is the first interest payment on the bond, and what is the amount of the payment?
   b. On what date do the bonds finally mature? Assume that India Infoline does not pay any interest to the bondholders. It rather reinvests the interest in the bond itself. How much money will the bondholders get from India Infoline on the maturity date for every bond held?
   c. Suppose that the bond is callable and that the market price of the bond rises to ₹1100 and thereafter does not change. When should the company call the issue? Assume that the bank has the right to call back the bond at ₹1200 in March 2013, at ₹1150 in March 2014, at ₹1100 in March 2015, and at ₹1000 in March 2016.

6. Explain the three principal ways in which the terms of private placement bonds commonly differ from those of public issues.

7. True or false? Briefly explain in each case.
   a. Lenders in project financings rarely have any recourse against the project's owners if the project fails.
   b. Many new and exotic debt securities are triggered by government policies or regulations.
   c. Call provisions give a valuable option to debt investors.
   d. Restrictive covenants have been shown to protect debt investors when takeovers are financed with large amounts of debt.
   e. Privately placed debt issues often include stricter covenants than public debt. However, public debt covenants are more difficult and expensive to renegotiate.

8. Maple Aircraft has issued a 4 ¾% convertible subordinated debenture due 2014. The conversion price is ₹47.00 and the debenture is callable at 102.75% of face value. The market price of the convertible is 91% of face value, and the price of the share is ₹41.50. Assume that the value of the bond in the absence of a conversion feature is about 65% of face value.
   a. What is the conversion ratio of the debenture?
   b. If the conversion ratio were 50, what would be the conversion price?
   c. What is the conversion value?
   d. At what stock price is the conversion value equal to the bond value?
   e. Can the market price be less than the conversion value?
   f. How much is the convertible holder paying for the option to buy one share of share stock?
   g. By how much does the common have to rise by 2014 to justify conversion?
   h. When should Maple call the debenture?
9. True or false?
   a. Convertible bonds are usually senior claims on the firm.
   b. The higher the conversion ratio, the more valuable the convertible.
   c. The higher the conversion price, the more valuable the convertible.
   d. Convertible bonds do not share fully in the price of the common stock, but they provide some protection against a decline.

INTERMEDIATE

10. Suppose that the India Infoline bond was issued at ₹900 (discount to the face value). Sketch what you think would happen to the bond price as the first interest payment date approaches and then passes. What about the price of the bond plus accrued interest?
11. Visit the website of SEBI (www.sebi.gov.in) and find out the terms and conditions of a recent bond issue and compare them with those of the India Infoline bond issue.
12. Bond prices can fall either because of a change in the general level of interest rates or because of an increased risk of default. To what extent do floating-rate bonds and puttable bonds protect the investor against each of these risks?
13. Proctor Power has fixed assets worth ₹200 million and net working capital worth ₹100 million. It is financed partly by equity and partly by three issues of debt. These consist of ₹250 million of First Mortgage Bonds secured only on the company's fixed assets, ₹100 million of senior debentures, and ₹120 million of subordinated debentures. If the debt were due today, how much would each debtholder be entitled to receive?
14. Elixir Corporation has just filed for bankruptcy. Elixir is a holding company whose assets consist of real estate worth ₹80 million and 100% of the equity of its two operating subsidiaries. It is financed partly by equity and partly by an issue of ₹400 million of senior collateral trust bonds that are just about to mature. Subsidiary A has issued directly ₹320 million of debentures and ₹15 million of preferred stock. Subsidiary B has issued ₹180 million of senior debentures and ₹60 million of subordinated debentures. A's assets have a market value of ₹500 million and B's have a value of ₹220 million. How much will each security holder receive if the assets are sold and distributed strictly according to precedence?
15. a. Residential mortgages may stipulate either a fixed rate or a variable rate. As a *borrower*, what considerations might cause you to prefer one rather than the other?
   b. Why might holders of mortgage pass-through certificates wish the mortgages to have a floating rate?
16. After a sharp change in interest rates, newly issued bonds generally sell at yields different from those of outstanding bonds of the same quality. One suggested explanation is that there is a difference in the value of the call provisions. Explain how this could arise.

17. Suppose that a company simultaneously issues a zero-coupon bond and a coupon bond with identical maturities. Both are callable at any time at their face values. Other things equal, which is likely to offer the higher yield? Why?

18. a. If interest rates rise, will callable or noncallable bonds fall more in price?
    b. Sometimes you encounter bonds that can be repaid after a fixed interval at the option of *either* the issuer or the bondholder. If the exercise price of each option is the same and both the issuer and bondholder act rationally, what will happen when the options can be exercised? (Ignore refinements such as transactions or issue costs.)

19. A puttable bond is a bond that may be repaid before maturity at the investor's option. Sketch a diagram similar to Figure 24.2 showing the relationship between the value of a straight bond and that of a puttable bond.

20. Alpha Corp. is prohibited from issuing more senior debt unless net tangible assets exceed 200% of senior debt. Currently the company has outstanding ₹100 million of senior debt and has net tangible assets of ₹250 million. How much more senior debt can Alpha Corp. issue?

21. Explain carefully why bond indentures may place limitations on the following actions:
    a. Sale of the company's assets.
    b. Payment of dividends to shareholders.
    c. Issue of additional senior debt.

22. Explain when it makes sense to use project finance rather than a direct debt issue by the parent company.

23. The Surplus Value Company had ₹10 million (face value) of convertible bonds outstanding in 2010. Each bond has the following features.

Face value	₹1000
Conversion price	₹25
Current call price	105 (percent of face value)
Current trading price	130 (percent of face value)
Maturity	2017
Current stock price	₹30 (per share)
Interest rate	10% (coupon as percent of face value)

   a. What is the bond's conversion value?
   b. Can you explain why the bond is selling above conversion value?
   c. Should Surplus call? What will happen if it does so?

24. Piglet Pies has issued a zero-coupon 10-year bond that can be converted into 10 Piglet shares. Comparable straight bonds are yielding 8%. Piglet stock is priced at $50 a share.
   a. Suppose that you had to make a now-or-never decision on whether to convert or to stay with the bond. Which would you do?
   b. If the convertible bond is priced at $550, how much are investors paying for the option to buy Piglet shares?
   c. If after one year the value of the conversion option is unchanged, what is the value of the convertible bond?

25. Iota Microsystems' 10% convertible is about to mature. The conversion ratio is 27.
   a. What is the conversion price?
   b. The stock price is ₹47. What is the conversion value?
   c. Should you convert?

26. In 1996 Marriott International made an issue of unusual bonds called Liquid Yield Option Notes, or LYONS. The bond matures in 2011, has a zero coupon, and was issued at $532.15. It

could be converted into 8.76 shares. Beginning in 1999 the bonds could be called by Marriott. The call price was $603.71 in 1999 and increased by 4.3% a year thereafter. Holders had an option to put the bond back to Marriott in 1999 at $603.71 and in 2006 at $810.36. At the time of issue the price of the common stock was about $50.50.

a. What was the yield to maturity on the bond?

b. Assuming that comparable nonconvertible bonds yielded 10%, how much were investors paying for the conversion option?

c. What was the conversion value of the bonds at the time of issue?

d. What was the initial conversion price of the bonds?

e. What was the conversion price in 2005? Why did it change?

f. If the price of the bond in 2006 was less than $810.36, would you have put the bond back to Marriott?

g. At what price could Marriott have called the bonds in 2006? If the price of the bond in 2006 was more than this, should Marriott have called them?

CHALLENGE

27. Dorlcote Milling has outstanding a $1 million 3% mortgage bond maturing in 10 years. The coupon on any new debt issued by the company is 10%. The finance director, Mr. Tulliver, cannot decide whether there is a tax benefit to repurchasing the existing bonds in the marketplace and replacing them with new 10% bonds. What do you think? Does it matter whether bond investors are taxed?

28. Refer back to the Hub Power project in Section 24-7. There were many other ways that the Hubco project could have been financed. For example, a government agency could have invested in the power plant and hired National Power to run it. Alternatively, National Power could have owned the power plant directly and funded its cost by a mixture of new borrowing and the sale of shares. What do you think were the advantages of setting up a separately financed company to undertake the project?

29. This question illustrates that when there is scope for the firm to vary its risk, lenders may be more prepared to lend if they are offered a piece of the action through the issue of a convertible bond. Ms. Blavatsky is proposing to form a new start-up firm with initial assets of $10 million. She can invest this money in one of two projects. Each has the same expected payoff, but one has more risk than the other. The relatively safe project offers a 40% chance of a $12.5 million payoff and a 60% chance of an $8 million payoff. The risky project offers a 40% chance of a $20 million payoff and a 60% chance of a $5 million payoff.

Ms. Blavatsky initially proposes to finance the firm by an issue of straight debt with a promised payoff of $7 million. Ms. Blavatsky will receive any remaining payoff. Show the possible payoffs to the lender and to Ms. Blavatsky if (a) she chooses the safe project and (b) she chooses the risky project. Which project is Ms. Blavatsky likely to choose? Which will the lender want her to choose?

Suppose now that Ms. Blavatsky offers to make the debt convertible into 50% of the value of the firm. Show that in this case the lender receives the same expected payoff from the two projects.

30. Occasionally it is said that issuing convertible bonds is better than issuing stock when the firm's shares are undervalued. Suppose that the financial manager of the Butternut Furniture Company does have inside information indicating that the Butternut stock price is too low. Butternut's future earnings will in fact be higher than investors expect. Suppose further that the inside information cannot be released without giving away a valuable competitive secret.

Clearly, selling shares at the present low price would harm Butternut's existing shareholders. Will they also lose if convertible bonds are issued? If they do lose in this case, is the loss more or less than it would be if common stock were issued?

Now suppose that investors forecast earnings accurately, but still undervalue the stock because they overestimate Butternut's actual business risk. Does this change your answers to the questions posed in the preceding paragraph? Explain.

THE SHOCKING DEMISE OF MR. THORNDIKE

It was one of Morse's most puzzling cases. That morning Rupert Thorndike, the autocratic CEO of Thorndike Oil, was found dead in a pool of blood on his bedroom floor. He had been shot through the head, but the door and windows were bolted on the inside and there was no sign of the murder weapon.

Morse looked in vain for clues in Thorndike's bedroom and office. He had to take another tack. He decided to investigate the financial circumstances surrounding Thorndike's demise. The company's capital structure was as follows:

- 5% debentures: $250 million face value. The bonds mature in 10 years and offer a yield of 12%.
- Stock: 30 million shares, which closed at $9 a share the day before the murder.
- 10% subordinated convertible notes: The notes mature in one year and are convertible at any time at a conversion ratio of 110. The day before the murder these notes were priced at 5% more than their conversion value.

Yesterday Thorndike had flatly rejected an offer by T. Spoone Dickens to buy all of the common stock for $10 a share. With Thorndike out of the way, it appeared that Dickens's offer would be accepted, much to the profit of Thorndike Oil's other shareholders.[34]

Thorndike's two nieces, Doris and Patsy, and his nephew John all had substantial investments in Thorndike Oil and had bitterly disagreed with Thorndike's dismissal of Dickens's offer. Their stakes are shown in the following table:

	5% Debentures (Face Value)	Shares of Stock	10% Convertible Notes (Face Value)
Doris	$4 million	1.2 million	$0 million
John	0	.5	5
Patsy	0	1.5	3

All debt issued by Thorndike Oil would be paid off at face value if Dickens's offer went through. Holders of the convertible notes could choose to convert and tender their shares to Dickens.

Morse kept coming back to the problem of motive. Which niece or nephew, he wondered, stood to gain most by eliminating Thorndike and allowing Dickens's offer to succeed?

QUESTION

1. Help Morse solve the case. Which of Thorndike's relatives stood to gain most from his death?

---

[43] Rupert Thorndike's shares would go to a charitable foundation formed to advance the study of financial engineering and its crucial role in world peace and progress. The managers of the foundation's endowment were not expected to oppose the takeover.

25

CHAPTER

LEASING

Most of us occasionally rent a car, bicycle, or boat. Usually such personal rentals are short-lived; we may rent a car for a day or week. But in corporate finance longer-term rentals are common. A rental agreement that extends for a year or more and involves a series of fixed payments is called a lease.

Firms lease as an alternative to buying capital equipment. In the U.S., about 30% of new capital equipment is leased. Trucks and farm machinery are often leased; so are railroad cars, aircraft, and ships. Just about every kind of asset can be leased. Many of the pandas in American zoos are leased, with the proceeds going to panda conservation.

Every lease involves two parties. The *user* of the asset is called the *lessee*. The lessee makes periodic payments to the *owner* of the asset, who is called the *lessor*. For example, if you sign an agreement to rent an apartment for a year, you are the lessee and the owner is the lessor.

You often see references to the *leasing industry*. This refers to lessors. (Almost all firms are lessees to at least a minor extent.) Who are the lessors?

Some of the largest lessors are equipment manufacturers. For example, IBM is a large lessor of computers, and Deere is a large lessor of agricultural and construction equipment.

The other two major groups of lessors are banks and independent leasing companies. Leasing companies play an enormous role in the airline business. For example, in 2008 GE Capital Aviation Services, a subsidiary of GE Capital, owned and leased out nearly 1,500 commercial aircraft. The world's airlines rely largely on leasing to finance their fleets.

Leasing companies offer a variety of services. Some act as lease brokers (arranging lease deals) as well as being lessors. Others specialize in leasing automobiles, trucks, and standardized industrial equipment; they succeed because they can buy equipment in quantity, service it efficiently, and if necessary resell it at a good price.

We begin this chapter by cataloging the different kinds of leases and some of the reasons for their use. Then we show how short-term, or cancelable, lease payments can be interpreted as equivalent annual costs. The remainder of the chapter analyzes long-term leases used as alternatives to debt financing.

25-1 WHAT IS A LEASE?

Leases come in many forms, but in all cases the lessee (user) promises to make a series of payments to the lessor (owner). The lease contract specifies the monthly or semiannual payments, with the first payment usually due as soon as the contract is signed. The payments are usually level, but their time pattern can be tailored to the user's needs. For example, suppose that a manufacturer leases a machine to produce a complex new product. There will be a year's "shakedown" period before volume production starts. In this case, it might be possible to arrange for lower payments during the first year of the lease.

When a lease is terminated, the leased equipment reverts to the lessor. However, the lease agreement often gives the user the option to purchase the equipment or take out a new lease.

Some leases are short-term or cancelable during the contract period at the option of the lessee. These are generally known as *operating leases*. Others extend over most of the estimated economic life of the asset and cannot be canceled or can be canceled only if the lessor is reimbursed for any losses. These are called *capital, financial,* or *full-payout leases*.

Financial leases are a *source of financing*. Signing a financial lease contract is like borrowing money. There is an immediate cash inflow because the lessee is relieved of having to pay for the asset. But the lessee also assumes a binding obligation to make the payments specified in the lease contract. The user could have borrowed the full purchase price of the asset by accepting a binding obligation to make interest and principal payments to the lender. Thus the cash-flow consequences of leasing and borrowing are similar. In either case, the firm raises cash now and pays it back later. Later in this chapter we compare leasing and borrowing as financing alternatives.

Leases also differ in the services provided by the lessor. Under a *full-service*, or *rental*, lease, the lessor promises to maintain and insure the equipment and to pay any property taxes due on it. In a *net* lease, the lessee agrees to maintain the asset, insure it, and pay any property taxes. Financial leases are usually net leases.

Most financial leases are arranged for brand new assets. The lessee identifies the equipment, arranges for the leasing company to buy it from the manufacturer, and signs a contract with the leasing company. This is called a *direct* lease. In other cases, the firm sells an asset it already owns and leases it back from the buyer. These *sale and lease-back* arrangements are common in real estate. For example, firm X may wish to raise cash by selling an office or factory but still retain use of the building. It could do this by selling the building for cash to a leasing company and simultaneously signing a long-term lease contract. For example, in 2007 HSBC sold its head office building in London for £1.09 billion, or about $2 billion. HSBC then leased the building back at an annual rent of £43.5 million. Thus legal ownership of the building passed to the new owner, but the right to use it remained with HSBC. Back in India, Jet Airways sold and leased back aircrafts it owned in 2012 to raise $300 million to reduce its debt.

You may also encounter *leveraged* leases. These are financial leases in which the lessor borrows part of the purchase price of the leased asset, using the lease contract as security for the loan. This does not change the lessee's obligations, but it can complicate the lessor's analysis considerably.

25-2 WHY LEASE?

You hear many suggestions about why companies should lease equipment rather than buy it. Let us look at some sensible reasons and then at four more dubious ones.

Sensible Reasons for Leasing

Short-Term Leases Are Convenient Suppose you want the use of a car for a week. You could buy one and sell it seven days later, but that would be silly. Quite apart from the fact that registering ownership is a nuisance, you would spend some time selecting a car, negotiating purchase, and arranging insurance. Then at the end of the week you would negotiate resale and cancel the registration and insurance. When you need a car only for a short time, it clearly makes sense to rent it. You save the trouble of registering ownership, and you know the effective cost. In the same way, it pays a company to lease equipment that it needs for only a year or two. Of course, this kind of lease is always an operating lease.

Sometimes the cost of short-term rentals may seem prohibitively high, or you may find it difficult to rent at any price. This can happen for equipment that is easily damaged by careless use. The owner knows that short-term users are unlikely to take the same care they would with their own equipment. When the danger of abuse becomes too high, short-term rental markets do not survive. Thus, it is easy enough to buy a Lamborghini Gallardo, provided your pockets are deep enough, but nearly impossible to rent one.

Cancellation Options Are Valuable Some leases that *appear* expensive really are fairly priced once the option to cancel is recognized. We return to this point in the next section.

Maintenance Is Provided Under a full-service lease, the user receives maintenance and other services. Many lessors are well equipped to provide efficient maintenance. However, bear in mind that these benefits will be reflected in higher lease payments.

Standardization Leads to Low Administrative and Transaction Costs Suppose that you operate a leasing company that specializes in financial leases for trucks. You are effectively lending money to a large number of firms (the lessees) that may differ considerably in size and risk. But, because the underlying asset is in each case the same salable item (a truck), you can safely "lend" the money (lease the truck) without conducting a detailed analysis of each firm's business. You can also use a simple, standard lease contract. This standardization makes it possible to "lend" small sums of money without incurring large investigative, administrative, or legal costs.

For these reasons leasing is often a relatively cheap source of cash for the small company. It offers secure financing on a flexible, piecemeal basis, with lower transaction costs than in a bond or stock issue.

Tax Shields Can Be Used The lessor owns the leased asset and deducts its depreciation from taxable income. If the lessor can make better use of depreciation tax shields than an asset's user can, it may make sense for the leasing company to own the equipment and pass on some of the tax benefits to the lessee in the form of low lease payments.

Leasing and Financial Distress Lessors in financial leases are in many ways similar to secured lenders, but lessors may fare better in bankruptcy. If a lessee defaults on a lease payment, you might think that the lessor could pick up the leased asset and take it home. But if the bankruptcy court decides that the asset is "essential" to the lessee's business, it *affirms* the lease. Then the bankrupt firm can continue to use the asset. It must continue to make the lease payments, however. This can be good news for the lessor, who is paid while other creditors cool their heels. Even secured creditors are not paid until the bankruptcy process works itself out.

If the lease is not affirmed but *rejected*, the lessor can recover the leased asset. If it is worth less than the present value of the remaining lease payments, the lessor can try to recoup this loss. But in this case the lender must get in line with unsecured creditors.

Unfortunately for lessors, there is a third possibility. A lessee in financial distress may be able to renegotiate the lease, forcing the lessor to accept lower lease payments. For example, in 2001 American Airlines (AA) acquired most of the assets of Trans World Airlines (TWA). TWA was bankrupt, and AA's purchase contract was structured so that AA could decide whether to affirm or reject TWA's aircraft leases. AA contacted the lessors and threatened to reject. The lessors realized that rejection would put about 100 leased aircraft back in their laps to sell or re-lease, probably at fire-sale prices. (The market for used aircraft was not strong at the time.) The lessors ended up accepting renegotiated lease rates that were about half what TWA had been paying.[1]

Avoiding the Alternative Minimum Tax

Red-blooded financial managers want to earn lots of money for their shareholders but *report* low profits to the tax authorities. Tax law in the United States allows this. A firm may use straight-line depreciation in its annual report but choose accelerated depreciation (and the shortest possible asset life) for its tax books. By this and other perfectly legal and ethical devices, profitable companies have occasionally managed to escape tax entirely. Almost all companies pay less tax than their public income statements suggest.[2]

But there is a trap for U.S. companies that shield too much income: the alternative minimum tax (*AMT*). Corporations must pay the AMT whenever it is higher than their tax computed in the regular way.

Here is how the AMT works: It requires a second calculation of taxable income, in which part of the benefit of accelerated depreciation and other tax-reducing items[3] is added back. The AMT is 20% of the result.

Suppose Yuppytech Services would have $10 million in taxable income but for the AMT, which forces it to add back $9 million of tax privileges:

	Regular Tax	Alternative Minimum Tax
Income	$10	10 + 9 = 19
Tax rate	.35	.20
Tax	$ 3.5	$3.8

---

[1] If the leases had been rejected, the lessors would have had a claim only on TWA's assets and cash flows, not AA's. The renegotiation of the TWA leases is described in E. Benmelech and N. K. Bergman, "Liquidation Values and the Credibility of Financial Contract Renegotiation: Evidence from U.S. Airlines," *Quarterly Journal of Economics* 123 (2008), pp. 1635–1677.

[2] Year-by-year differences between reported tax expense and taxes actually paid are explained in footnotes to the financial statements. The cumulative difference is shown on the balance sheet as a deferred tax liability. (Note that accelerated depreciation *postpones* taxes; it does not eliminate taxes.)

[3] Other items include some interest receipts from tax-exempt municipal securities and taxes deferred by use of completed contract accounting. (The completed contract method allows a manufacturer to postpone reporting taxable profits until a production contract is completed. Since contracts may span several years, this deferral can have a substantial positive NPV.)

Yuppytech must pay $3.8 million, not $3.5.[4]

How can this painful payment be avoided? How about leasing? Lease payments are *not* on the list of items added back in calculating the AMT. If you lease rather than buy, tax depreciation is less and the AMT is less. There is a net gain if the *lessor* is not subject to the AMT and can pass back depreciation tax shields in the form of lower lease payments.

In India, however, only the excess depreciation relating to the revalued assets is added back to the book profit. Secondly, the lessee deducts lease rentals while calculating taxable income, whereas it deducts apportioned interest (on lease rentals) and depreciation while calculating the book profit (following AS 19 issued by the ICAI). If lease rental is equal to the apportioned interest plus depreciation, then the difference between book profit and taxable income will be entirely due to factors not related to the leasing transaction. So minimum alternative tax (MAT) cannot be a sensible reason for leasing in India.

Some Dubious Reasons for Leasing

Leasing Avoids Capital Expenditure Controls

In many companies lease proposals are scrutinized as carefully as capital expenditure proposals, but in others leasing may enable an operating manager to avoid the approval procedures needed to buy an asset. Although this is a dubious reason for leasing, it may be influential, particularly in the public sector. For example, city hospitals have sometimes found it politically more convenient to lease their medical equipment than to ask the city government to provide funds for purchase.

Leasing Preserves Capital

Leasing companies provide "100% financing"; they advance the full cost of the leased asset. Consequently, they often claim that leasing preserves capital, allowing the firm to save its cash for other things.

But the firm can also "preserve capital" by borrowing money. If Blueline Bus Lines leases a ₹800,000 bus rather than buying it, it does conserve ₹800,000 cash. It could also (1) buy the bus for cash and (2) borrow ₹800,000, using the bus as security. Its bank balance ends up the same whether it leases or buys and borrows. It has the bus in either case, and it incurs a ₹800,000 liability in either case. What's so special about leasing?

Leases May Be Off-Balance-Sheet Financing

In some countries financial leases are off-balance-sheet financing; that is, a firm can acquire an asset, finance it through a financial lease, and show neither the asset nor the lease contract on its balance sheet.

In India, Accounting Standard 19 issued by ICAI requires that all financial leases (capital leases) be capitalized. This means that the present value of the lease payments must be calculated and shown alongside debt on the right-hand side of the balance sheet. The same amount must be shown as an asset on the left-hand side and written off over the life of the lease.

The AS19 defines financial leases as leases which meet *any one* of the following requirements:

1. The lease agreement transfers ownership to the lessee before the lease expires.
2. The lessee can purchase the asset for a bargain price when the lease expires.
3. The lease lasts for at least 75% of the asset's estimated economic life.
4. The present value of the lease payments is at least 90% of the asset's value.

---

[4] But Yuppytech can carry forward the $.3 million difference. If later years' AMTs are *lower* than regular taxes, the difference can be used as a tax credit. Suppose the AMT next year is $4 million and the regular tax is $5 million. Then Yuppytech pays only 5 − .3 = $4.7 million.

ll other leases are operating leases as far as the accountants are concerned.[5]

Many financial managers have tried to take advantage of this arbitrary boundary between operating nd financial leases. Suppose that you want to finance a computer-controlled machine tool costing ₹1 million. The machine tool's life is expected to be 12 years. You could sign a lease contract for 8 years 1 months (just missing requirement 3), with lease payments having a present value of ₹899,000 (just missing requirement 4). You could also make sure the lease contract avoids requirements 1 and 2. Result? You have off-balance-sheet financing. This lease would not have to be capitalized, although it s clearly a long-term, fixed obligation.

Now we come to the ₹64,000 question: Why should anyone *care* whether financing is off balance heet or on balance sheet? Shouldn't the financial manager worry about substance rather than appearance?

When a firm obtains off-balance-sheet financing, the conventional measures of financial leverage, uch as the debt–equity ratio, understate the true degree of financial leverage. Some believe that financial analysts do not always notice off-balance-sheet lease obligations (which are still referred to in footnotes) or the greater volatility of earnings that results from the fixed lease payments. They may be right if off-balance-sheet lease obligations are moderate and "lost in the noise" of all the firm's other activities. But we would not expect investors, security analysts, and debt-rating agencies to miss large hidden obligations unless they were systematically misled by management.

Leasing Affects Book Income   Leasing can make the firm's balance sheet and income statement *look* better by increasing book income or decreasing book asset value, or both.

A lease that qualifies as off-balance-sheet financing affects book income in only one way: The lease payments are an expense. If the firm buys the asset instead and borrows to finance it, both depreciation and interest expense are deducted. Leases are usually set up so that payments in the early years are less than depreciation plus interest under the buy-and-borrow alternative. Consequently, leasing increases book income in the early years of an asset's life. The book rate of return can increase even more dramatically, because the book value of assets (the denominator in the book-rate-of-return calculation) is understated if the leased asset never appears on the firm's balance sheet.

Leasing's impact on book income should in itself have no effect on firm value. In efficient capital markets investors will look through the firm's accounting results to the true value of the asset and the liability incurred to finance it.

25-3   OPERATING LEASES

Remember our discussion of *equivalent annual* costs in Chapter 6? We defined the equivalent annual cost of, say, a machine as the annual rental payment sufficient to cover the present value of all the costs of owning and operating it.

In Chapter 6's examples, the rental payments were hypothetical—just a way of converting a present value to an annual cost. But in the leasing business the payments are real. Suppose you decide to lease a machine tool for one year. What will the rental payment be in a competitive leasing industry? The lessor's equivalent annual cost, of course.

---

[5] In March 2009 the FASB and the International Accounting Standards Board (IASB) published a discussion paper entitled *Leases: Preliminary Views*. This set out some possible changes to accounting rules that would lead to more leasing activity being shown on the balance sheet.

Example of an Operating Lease

The boyfriend of the daughter of the CEO of Establishment Industries takes her to the college par[t] in a pearly white stretch limo. The CEO is impressed. He decides Establishment Industries oug[ht] to have one for VIP transportation. Establishment's CFO prudently suggests a one-year operatin[g] lease instead and approaches Sriram Limolease for a quote.

Table 25.1 shows Sriram's analysis. Suppose it buys a new limo for ₹40.50 lakhs which it plan[s] to lease out for seven years (years 0 through 6). The table gives Sriram's forecasts of operating maintenance, and administrative costs, the latter including the costs of negotiating the lease, keepin[g] track of payments and paperwork, and finding a replacement lessee when Establishment's year is up For simplicity we assume zero inflation and use a 7% real cost of capital. We also assume that the lim[o] will have zero salvage value at the end of year 6. The present value of all costs, partially offset by the value of depreciation tax shields,[6] is ₹54.68 lakhs. Now, how much does Sriram have to charge to break even?

TABLE 25.1   Calculating the zero-NPV rental value (or equivalent annual cost) for Establishment Industries' pearly white stretch limo (figures in ₹ thousands)

eXcel
Visit us at
www.mhhe.com/bmam10e

	0	1	2	3	4	5	6
Initial cost	−4050						
Maintenance costs, etc	−648	−648	−648	−648	−648	−648	−648
Tax shield on costs	+220.26	+220.26	+220.26	+220.26	+220.26	+220.26	+220.26
Depreciation		607.5	516.375	438.9188	373.0809	317.1188	1797.007
Depreciation tax shield[a]		+206.49	+175.52	+149.19	+126.81	+107.79	+610.80
Total	−4,477.74	−221.26	−252.23	−278.56	−300.93	−319.96	183.06
PV at 7% = −5467.94[b]							
Break−even rent (level)	−1,436.48	−1,436.48	−1,436.48	−1,436.48	−1,436.48	−1,436.48	−1,436.48
Tax	+488.26	+488.26	+488.26	+488.26	+488.26	+488.26	+488.26
Breakeven rent after tax	−948.22	−948.22	−948.22	−948.22	−948.22	−948.22	−948.22
PV at 7% = −5467.94[b]							

Note: We assume no inflation and a 7 percent real cost of capital. The tax rate is 33.99%
[a] Depreciation tax shields are calculated using 15 percent written down value rate and by assuming that scrap value of limo is zero.
[b] Note that the first payment of these annuities comes immediately. The standard annuity factor must be multiplied by 1 + r = 1.07.

Sriram can afford to buy and lease out the limo only if the rental payments forecasted over six years have a present value of at least ₹54.68 lakhs. The problem, then, is to calculate a six-year annuity with a present value of ₹54.68 lakhs. We will follow common leasing practice and assume rental payments in advance.[7]

As Table 25.1 shows, the required annuity is ₹1,436.48 thousands, that is, about ₹14.36 lakhs.[8] This annuity's present value (after taxes) exactly equals the present value of the after-tax costs of

[6] The depreciation tax shields are safe cash flows if the tax rate does not change and Sriram is sure to pay taxes. If 7% is the right discount rate for the other flows in Table 25.1, the depreciation tax shields deserve a lower rate. A more refined analysis would discount safe depreciation tax shields at an after-tax borrowing or lending rate. See the Appendix to Chapter 19 or the next section of this chapter.
[7] In Section 6-4 the hypothetical rentals were paid *in arrears*.
[8] This is a level annuity because we are assuming that (1) there is no inflation and (2) the services of a six-year-old limo are no different from a brand-new limo's. If users of aging limos see them as obsolete or unfashionable, or if purchase costs of new limos are declining, then lease rates have to decline as limos age. This means that rents follow a *declining* annuity. Early users have to pay more to make up for declining rents later.

owning and operating the limo. The annuity provides Sriram with a competitive expected rate of return (7%) on its investment. Sriram could try to charge Establishment Industries more than ₹14.36 lakhs, but if the CFO is smart enough to ask for bids from Sriram's competitors, the winning lessor will end up receiving this amount.

Remember that Establishment Industries is not obligated to continue using the limo for more than one year. Sriram may have to find several new lessees over the limo's economic life. Even if Establishment continues, it can renegotiate a new lease at whatever rates prevail in the future. Thus Sriram does not know what it can charge in year 1 or afterward. If pearly white falls out of favor with teenagers and CEOs, Sriram is probably out of luck.

In real life Sriram would have several further things to worry about. For example, how long will the limo stand idle when it is returned at year 1? If idle time is likely before a new lessee is found, then lease rates have to be higher to compensate.[9]

In an operating lease, the *lessor* absorbs these risks, not the lessee. The discount rate used by the lessor must include a premium sufficient to compensate its shareholders for the risks of buying and holding the leased asset. In other words, Sriram's 7% real discount rate must cover the risks of investing in stretch limos. (As we see in the next section, risk bearing in *financial* leases is fundamentally different.)

Lease or Buy?

If you need a car or limo for only a day or a week you will surely rent it; if you need one for five years you will probably buy it. In between there is a gray region in which the choice of lease or buy is not obvious. The decision rule should be clear in concept, however: If you need an asset for your business, *buy it if the equivalent annual cost of ownership and operation is less than the best lease rate you can get from an outsider.* In other words, buy if you can "rent to yourself" cheaper than you can rent from others. (Again we stress that this rule applies to *operating* leases.)

If you plan to use the asset for an extended period, your equivalent annual cost of owning the asset will usually be less than the operating lease rate. The lessor has to mark up the lease rate to cover the costs of negotiating and administering the lease, the foregone revenues when the asset is off-lease and idle, and so on. These costs are avoided when the company buys and rents to itself.

There are two cases in which operating leases may make sense even when the company plans to use an asset for an extended period. First, the lessor may be able to buy and manage the asset at less expense than the lessee. For example, the major truck leasing companies buy thousands of new vehicles every year. That puts them in an excellent bargaining position with truck manufacturers. These companies also run very efficient service operations, and they know how to extract the most salvage value when trucks wear out and it is time to sell them. A small business, or a small division of a larger one, cannot achieve these economies and often finds it cheaper to lease trucks than to buy them.

Second, operating leases often contain useful options. Suppose Sriram offers Establishment Industries the following two leases:

1. A one-year lease for ₹14.32 lakhs.
2. A six-year lease for ₹15.00 lakhs, *with the option to cancel the lease* at any time from year 1 on.[10]

The second lease has obvious attractions. Suppose Establishment's CEO becomes fond of the limo and wants to use it for a second year. If rates increase, lease 2 allows Establishment to continue at the

---

[9] If, say, limos were off-lease and idle 20% of the time, lease rates would have to be 25% above those shown in Table 25.1.

[10] Sriram might also offer a one-year lease for $28,000 but give the lessee an option to *extend* the lease on the same terms for up to five additional years. This is, of course, identical to lease 2. It doesn't matter whether the lessee has the (put) option to cancel or the (call) option to continue.

old rate. If rates decrease, Establishment can cancel lease 2 and negotiate a lower rate with Sriram or one of its competitors.

Of course, lease 2 is a more costly proposition for Sriram: In effect it gives Establishment an insurance policy protecting it from increases in future lease rates. The difference between the costs of leases 1 and 2 is the annual insurance premium. But lessees may happily pay for insurance if they have no special knowledge of future asset values or lease rates. A leasing company acquires such knowledge in the course of its business and can generally sell such insurance at a profit.

Airlines face fluctuating demand for their services and the mix of planes that they need is constantly changing. Most airlines, therefore, lease a proportion of their fleet on a short-term, cancelable basis and are willing to pay a premium to lessors for bearing the cancelation risk. Specialist aircraft lessors are prepared to bear this risk, for they are well-placed to find new customers for any aircraft that are returned to them. Aircraft owned by specialist lessors spend less time parked and more time flying than aircraft owned by airlines.[11]

Be sure to check out the options before you sign (or reject) an operating lease.[12]

25-4 VALUING FINANCIAL LEASES

For operating leases the decision centers on "lease versus buy." For *financial* leases the decision amounts to "lease versus borrow." Financial leases extend over most of the economic life of the leased equipment. They are *not* cancelable. The lease payments are fixed obligations equivalent to debt service.

Financial leases make sense when the company is prepared to take on the business risks of owning and operating the leased asset. If Establishment Industries signs a *financial* lease for the stretch limo, it is stuck with that asset. The financial lease is just another way of borrowing money to pay for the limo.

Financial leases do offer special advantages to some firms in some circumstances. However, there is no point in further discussion of these advantages until you know how to value financial lease contracts.

Example of a Financial Lease

Imagine yourself in the position of Haridas Pai, president of Blueline Bus. Your firm was established by your grandfather, who was quick to capitalize on the growing demand for transportation between Mangalore and Mumbai. The company has owned all its vehicles from the time the company was formed; you are now reconsidering that policy. Your operating manager wants to buy a new bus costing ₹46 lakhs. The bus will last only eight years before going to the scrap yard. You are convinced that investment in the additional equipment is worthwhile. However, the representative of the bus manufacturer has pointed out that her firm would also be willing to lease the bus to you for eight annual payments of ₹7.82 lakhs each. Blueline would remain responsible for all maintenance, insurance, and operating expenses.

Table 25.2 shows the direct cash-flow consequences of signing the lease contract. (An important indirect effect is considered later.) The consequences are:

1. Blueline does not have to pay for the bus. This is equivalent to a cash inflow of ₹46 lakhs.

---

[11] A. Gavazza, "Leasing and Secondary Markets: Theory and Evidence from Commercial Aviation," Working paper, Yale School of Management, March 2007.

[12] McConnell and Schallheim calculate the value of options in operating leases under various assumptions about asset risk, depreciation rates, etc. See J. J. McConnell and J. S. Schallheim, "Valuation of Asset Leasing Contracts," *Journal of Financial Economics* 12 (August 1983), pp. 237–261.

2. Blueline no longer owns the bus, and so it cannot depreciate it. Therefore it gives up a valuable depreciation tax shield. In Table 25.2, we have assumed depreciation would be calculated using written down value method. The WDV rate is 25%. The net book value of the bus at the end of year 6 has been written off in year 7.
3. Blueline must pay ₹7.82 lakhs per year for eight years to the lessor. The first payment is due immediately.
4. However, these lease payments are fully tax-deductible. At a 33.99% marginal tax rate, the lease payments generate tax shields of about ₹2.66 lakhs per year. You would say that the after-tax cost of the lease payment is ₹7.82 − ₹2.66 = ₹5.16 lakhs.

eXcel

Visit us at
www.mhhe.com/bmam10e

TABLE 25.2   Cash-flow consequences of the lease contract offered to Blueline Bus (figures in ₹ thousands; some columns do not add due to rounding).

	Year							
	0	1	2	3	4	5	6	7
Cost of new bus	+4600.00							
lost depreciation		+1150.00	+862.50	+646.88	+485.16	+363.87	+272.90	818.70
Lost depreciation tax shield		−390.89	−293.16	−219.87	−164.90	−123.68	−92.76	−278.28
Lease payments	−782.00	−782.00	−782.00	−782.00	−782.00	−782.00	−782.00	−782.00
Tax shield on lease payments	+265.80	+265.80	+265.80	+265.80	+265.80	+265.80	+265.80	+265.80
cash flow from lease	+4083.80	−907.08	−809.36	−736.07	−681.10	−639.88	−608.96	−794.47

We must emphasize that Table 25.2 assumes that Blueline will pay taxes at the full 33.99% marginal tax rate. If the firm were sure to lose money, and therefore pay no taxes, lines 2 and 4 would be left blank. The depreciation tax shields are worth nothing to a firm that pays no taxes, for example.

Table 25.2 also assumes the bus will be worthless when it goes to the scrap yard at the end of year 7. Otherwise there would be an entry for salvage value lost.

Who Really Owns the Leased Asset?

To a lawyer or a tax accountant, that would be a silly question: The lessor is clearly the *legal* owner of the leased asset. That is why the lessor is allowed to deduct depreciation from taxable income.

From an *economic* point of view, you might say that the *user* is the real owner, because in a *financial* lease, the user faces the risks and receives the rewards of ownership. Blueline cannot cancel a financial lease. If the new bus turns out to be hopelessly costly and unsuited for Blueline's routes, that is Blueline's problem, not the lessor's. If it turns out to be a great success, the profit goes to Blueline, not the lessor. The success or failure of the firm's business operations does not depend on whether the buses are financed by leasing or some other financial instrument.

In many respects, a financial lease is equivalent to a secured loan. The lessee must make a series of fixed payments; if the lessee fails to do so, the lessor can repossess the asset. Thus we can think of a balance sheet like this:

Blueline Bus (Figures in ₹ Thousands)

Bus	4,600	4,600	Loan secured by bus
All other assets	46,000	20,700	Other loans
		25,300	Equity
Total assets	50,600	50,600	Total liabilities

as being economically equivalent to a balance sheet like this:

Blueline Bus (Figures in ₹ Thousands)

Bus	4,600	4,600	Financial lease	
All other assets	46,000	20,700	Other loans	
		25,300	Equity	
Total assets	50,600	50,600	Total liabilities	

Having said this, we must immediately qualify. Legal ownership can make a big difference when a financial lease expires because the lessor gets the asset. Once a secured loan is paid off, the user owns the asset free and clear.

Leasing and the Income Tax Act

We have already noted that the lessee loses the tax depreciation of the leased asset but can deduct the lease payment in full. The *lessor,* as legal owner, uses the depreciation tax shield but must report the lease payments as taxable rental income.

However, the Income Tax department is suspicious by nature and will not allow the lessor to charge the entire depreciation expenses unless it is satisfied that the arrangement is a genuine lease. The Central Board of Direct Taxes (CBDT) in a circular issued on February 9, 2001 raised concerns about leases on assets that do not exist, and sale and leaseback transactions. Some companies, for example, show a water purifier as a pollution preventing equipment and claim 100 percent depreciation on such assets in the very first year of its purchase. The CBDT circular has asked the assessing officers to be very careful before granting depreciation benefits to the lessor on such assets. In case of a sale and lease back transaction, the depreciation is estimated at the depreciated book value of the asset and not on the sale price. Thus, for example, if Come Airlines sells an aircraft valued at ₹10 crores to a leasing company at ₹15 crores and leases it back, then the leasing company can claim depreciation only on ₹10 crores and not on ₹15 crores.

A First Pass at Valuing a Lease Contract

When we left Haridas Pai, president of Blueline Bus, he had just set down in Table 25.2 the cash flows of the financial lease proposed by the bus manufacturer.

These cash flows are typically assumed to be about as safe as the interest and principal payments on a secured loan issued by the lessee. This assumption is reasonable for the lease payments because the lessor is effectively lending money to the lessee. But the various tax shields might carry enough risk to deserve a higher discount rate. For example, Blueline might be confident that it could make the lease payments but not confident that it could earn enough taxable income to use these tax shields. In that case the cash flows generated by the tax shields would probably deserve a higher discount rate than the borrowing rate used for the lease payments.

A lessee might, in principle, end up using a separate discount rate for each line of Table 25.2, each rate chosen to fit the risk of that line's cash flow. But established, profitable firms usually find it reasonable to simplify by discounting the types of flows shown in Table 25.2 at a single rate based on the rate of interest the firm would pay if it borrowed rather than leased. We assume Bluelines' borrowing rate is 10%.

At this point we must go back to our discussion in the Appendix to Chapter 19 of debt-equivalent flows. When a company lends money, it pays tax on the interest it receives. Its net return is the after-tax

terest rate. When a company borrows money, it can deduct interest payments from its taxable
income. The net cost of borrowing is the after-tax interest rate. Thus the after-tax interest rate is the
effective rate at which a company can transfer debt-equivalent flows from one time period to another.
Therefore, to value the incremental cash flows stemming from the lease, we need to discount them at
the after-tax interest rate.

Since Blueline can borrow at 10%, we should discount the lease cash flows at $r_D (1 - T_c)$
$= .10(1 - .3399) = .6601$, or 6.601%. This gives:

$$NPV \text{ Lease} = +4083.8 - \frac{907.08}{1.06601} - \frac{809.36}{(1.06601)^2} - \frac{736.07}{(1.06601)^3} - \frac{681.10}{(1.06601)^4}$$

$$- \frac{639.88}{(1.06601)^5} - \frac{608.96}{(1.06601)^6} - \frac{794.47}{(1.06601)^7}$$

$$= -2.07$$

Since the lease has a negative NPV, Blueline is better off buying the bus.

A positive or negative NPV is not an abstract concept; in this case Bluelines' shareholders really
are $2.07 thousands poorer if the company leases. Let us now check how this situation comes about.
Look once more at Table 25.2. The lease cash flows are:

	Year							
	0	1	2	3	4	5	6	7
Cash flow from lease Rs. thousands	+4083.80	(907.08)	(809.36)	(736.07)	(681.10)	(639.88)	(608.96)	(794.47)

The lease payments are contractual obligations like the principal and interest payments on secured
debt. Thus you can think of the incremental lease cash flows in years 1 through 7 as the "debt service"
of the lease. Table 25.3 shows a loan with *exactly* the same debt service as the lease. The initial amount
of the loan is ₹40.86 lakhs. If Blueline borrowed this sum, it would need to pay interest in the first
year of .1 × 40.86 = 4.086 and would *receive* a tax shield on this interest of 0.3399 × 4.086 = 1.39.
Blueline could then repay 6.37 of the loan, leaving a net cash outflow of 9.07 (exactly the same as for
the lease) in year 1 and an outstanding debt at the start of year 2 of 34.48.

TABLE 25.3 Details of the equivalent loan to the lease offered to Blueline Bus (figures in
₹ thousands; cash outflows shown with negative sign).

eXcel
Visit us at
www.mhhe.com/bmam10e

	Year							
	0	1	2	3	4	5	6	7
Amount borrowed at year–end	4085.87	3448.49	2866.77	2319.93	1791.97	1270.38	745.28	0.00
Interest paid at 10%		−408.59	−344.85	−286.68	−231.99	−179.20	−127.04	−74.53
Interest tax shield at 33.66%		138.88	117.21	97.44	78.85	60.91	43.18	25.33
Interest paid after tax		−269.71	−227.64	−189.24	−153.14	−118.29	−83.86	−49.20
Principal repaid		−637.37	−581.73	−546.84	−527.96	−521.59	−525.10	−745.28
Net cash flow of equivalent loan	4085.87	−907.08	−809.36	−736.07	−681.10	−639.88	−608.96	−794.47

As you walk through the calculations in Table 25.3, you see that it costs exactly the same to service
a loan that brings an immediate flow of ₹40.86 lakhs as it does to service the lease, which brings

₹40.84 lakhs. That is why we say that the lease has a net present value of 40.84 − 40.86 = −.2, or −₹0.0 lakhs. If Blueline leases the bus rather than raising an *equivalent loan,*[13] there will be ₹2.07 thousand less in the Blueline's bank account.

Our example illustrates two general points about leases and equivalent loans. First, if you can devise a borrowing plan that gives the same cash flow as the lease in every future period but a higher immediate cash flow, then you should not lease. If, however, the equivalent loan provides the same future cash outflows as the lease but a lower immediate inflow, then leasing is the better choice.

Second, our example suggests two ways to value a lease:

1. *Hard way.* Construct a table like Table 25.3 showing the equivalent loan.
2. *Easy way.* Discount the lease cash flows at the *after-tax* interest rate that the firm would pay on an equivalent loan. Both methods give the same answer—in our case an NPV of −₹0.02 lakhs.

The Story So Far

We concluded that the lease contract offered to Blueline Bus was *not* attractive because the lease provided ₹0.02 lakhs less financing than the equivalent loan. The underlying principle is as follows: A financial lease is superior to buying and borrowing if the financing provided by the lease exceeds the financing generated by the equivalent loan.

The principle implies this formula:

$$\text{Net value of lease} = \text{initial financing provided} - \sum_{t=1}^{N} \frac{\text{lease cash flow}}{[1 + r_D(1 - T_c)]^t}$$

where N is the length of the lease. Initial financing provided equals the cost of the leased asset minus any immediate lease payment or other cash outflow attributable to the lease.[14]

Notice that the value of the lease is its incremental value relative to borrowing via an equivalent loan. A positive lease value means that *if* you acquire the asset, lease financing is advantageous. It does not prove you should acquire the asset.

Sometimes favorable lease terms rescue a capital investment project. Suppose that Blueline had decided *against* buying a new bus because the NPV of the ₹46 lakhs investment was −₹1 lakh assuming normal financing. The bus manufacturer could rescue the deal by offering a lease with a value of, say, +₹2 lakhs. By offering such a lease, the manufacturer would in effect cut the price of the bus to ₹44 lakhs, giving the bus-lease package a positive value to Blueline. We could express this more formally by treating the lease's NPV as a favorable financing side effect that adds to project adjusted present value (APV):[15]

$$\text{APV} = \text{NPV of project} + \text{NPV of lease}$$
$$= -1 + 2 = ₹1 \text{ lakhs}$$

Notice also that our formula applies to net financial leases. Any insurance, maintenance, and other operating costs picked up by the lessor have to be evaluated separately and added to the value of the lease. If the asset has salvage value at the end of the lease, that value should be taken into account also.

---

[13] When we compare the lease to its equivalent loan, we do not mean to imply that the bus alone could support all of that loan. Some part of the loan would be supported by Blueline's other assets. Some part of the lease obligation would likewise be supported by the other assets.

[14] The principles behind lease valuation were originally set out in S. C. Myers, D. A. Dill, and A. J. Bautista, "Valuation of Financial Lease Contracts," *Journal of Finance* 31 (June 1976), pp. 799–819; and J. R. Franks and S. D. Hodges, "Valuation of Financial Lease Contracts: A Note," *Journal of Finance* 33 (May 1978), pp. 647–669.

[15] See Chapter 19 for the general definition and description of APV.

Suppose, for example, that the bus manufacturer offers to provide routine maintenance that would otherwise cost ₹92,000 per year after tax. However, Mr. Haridas Pai reconsiders and decides that the bus will probably be worth ₹4.6 lakhs after eight years. (Previously he assumed the bus would be worthless at the end of the lease.) Then the value of the lease increases by the present value of the maintenance savings and decreases by the present value of the lost salvage value.

Maintenance and salvage value are harder to predict than the cash flows shown in Table 25.2, and normally deserve a higher discount rate. Suppose that Mr. Pai uses 12%. Then the maintenance savings are worth:

$$\sum_{t=0}^{7} \frac{92,000}{(1.12)^t} = ₹5.12 \text{ lakhs}$$

The lost salvage value is worth ₹460,000/$(1.12)^8$ = ₹1.86 lakhs.[16] Remember that we previously calculated the value of the lease as −₹1.22 lakhs. The revised value is therefore −0.02 +5.12 − 1.86 = ₹3.24 lakhs. Now the lease looks like a good deal.

25-5 WHEN DO FINANCIAL LEASES PAY?

We have examined the value of a lease from the viewpoint of the lessee. However, the lessor's criterion is simply the reverse. As long as lessor and lessee are in the same tax bracket, every cash outflow to the lessee is an inflow to the lessor, and vice versa. In our numerical example, the bus manufacturer would project cash flows in a table like Table 25.2, but with the signs reversed. The value of the lease to the bus manufacturer would be:

$$NPV \text{ Lease} = -4083.8 + \frac{907.08}{1.06601} + \frac{809.36}{(1.06601)^2} + \frac{736.07}{(1.06601)^3} + \frac{681.10}{(1.06601)^4}$$
$$+ \frac{639.88}{(1.06601)^5} + \frac{608.96}{(1.06601)^6} + \frac{794.47}{(1.06601)^7}$$
$$= 2.07$$

In this case, the values to lessee and lessor exactly offset (−₹0.02 + ₹0.02 = 0). The lessor can win only at the lessee's expense.

But both lessee and lessor can win if their tax rates differ. Suppose that Blueline paid no tax (T_c = 0). Then the only cash flows of the bus lease would be:

	Year							
	0	1	2	3	4	5	6	7
Cost of new bus	+4600.00							
Lease payments	−782.00	−782.00	−782.00	−782.00	−782.00	−782.00	−782.00	−782.00
Cash flow from lease	+3818.00	−782.00	−782.00	−782.00	−782.00	−782.00	−782.00	−782.00

---

[16] For simplicity, we have assumed that maintenance expenses are paid at the start of the year and that salvage value is measured at the *end* of year 8.

These flows would be discounted at 10%, because $r_D(1 - T_c) = r_D$ when $T_c = 0$. The value of the lease is:

$$\text{Value of Lease} = +4{,}600 - \sum_{t=0}^{7} \frac{782}{(1.1)^t}$$
$$= +10.9.$$

In this case there is a net gain of ₹0.02 lakh to the lessor (who has the 33.99% tax rate) *and* a net gain of ₹0.11 thousand to the lessee (who pays zero tax). This mutual gain is at the expense of the government. On the one hand, the government gains from the lease contract because it can tax the lease payments. On the other hand, the contract allows the lessor to take advantage of depreciation and interest tax shields that are of no use to the lessee. However, because the depreciation is accelerated and the interest rate is positive, the government suffers a net loss in the present value of its tax receipts as a result of the lease.

Now you should begin to understand the circumstances in which the government incurs a loss on the lease and the other two parties gain. Other things being equal, the combined gains to lessor and lessee are highest when

- The lessor's tax rate is substantially higher than the lessee's.
- The depreciation tax shield is received early in the lease period.
- The lease period is long and the lease payments are concentrated toward the end of the period.
- The interest rate r_D is high—if it were zero, there would be no advantage in present value terms to postponing tax.

Leasing around the World

In most developed economies, leasing is widely used to finance investment in plant and equipment.[17] But there are important differences in the treatment of long-term financial leases for tax and accounting purposes. For example, France, Italy, and the U.K. allow the lessor to use depreciation tax shields, just as in the U.S. In Germany, the Netherlands, and Sweden it is the other way around; the lessee claims depreciation deductions. Accounting usually follows suit. Thus in France the leased equipment shows up on the books of the lessor, while in Germany it moves to the books of the lessee.

A number of *big-ticket* leases are cross-border deals. Cross-border leasing can be attractive when the lessor is located in a country that offers generous depreciation allowances. The ultimate cross-border transaction occurs when *both* the lessor *and* the lessee can claim depreciation deductions. Ingenious leasing companies look for such opportunities to *double-dip*. Tax authorities look for ways to stop them.[18]

25-6 LEVERAGED LEASES

Big-ticket leases are usually *leveraged leases*. The structure of a leveraged lease is summarized in Figure 25.1. In this example, the leasing company (or a syndicate of several leasing companies) sets up

---

[17] For example, in 2008 leasing accounted for 22.8% of all European investments in industrial equipment (**www.leaseurope.org**).

[18] Currently in the U.S. the tax authorities seem to be winning. The American Jobs Creation Act (JOBS) of 2004 eliminated much of the profit from cross-border leases.

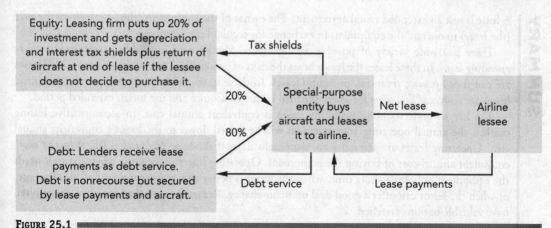

FIGURE 25.1

Structure of a leveraged lease for commercial aircraft.

a special-purpose entity (SPE) to buy and lease a commercial aircraft. The SPE raises up to 80% of the cost of the aircraft by borrowing, usually from insurance companies or other financial institutions. The leasing company puts up the remaining 20% as the equity investment in the lease.

Once the lease is up and running, lease payments begin and depreciation and interest tax shields are generated. All (or almost all) of the lease payments go to debt service. The leasing company gets no cash inflows until the debt is paid off, but does get all depreciation and interest deductions, which generate tax losses that can be used to shield other income.

By the end of the lease, the debt is paid off and the tax shields exhausted. At this point the lessee has the option to purchase the aircraft. The leasing company gets the purchase price if the lessee's purchase option is exercised, and takes back the aircraft otherwise. (In some cases the lessee also has an early buyout option partway through the term of the lease.)

The debt in a leveraged lease is *nonrecourse*. The lenders have first claim on the lease payments and on the aircraft if the lessee can't make scheduled payments, but no claim on the leasing company. Thus the lenders must depend solely on the airline lessee's credit and on the airplane as collateral.

So the leasing company puts up only 20% of the money, gets 100% of the tax shields, but is not on the hook if the lease transaction falls apart. Does this sound like a great deal? Don't jump to that conclusion, because the lenders will demand a higher interest rate in exchange for giving up recourse. In efficient debt markets, paying extra interest to avoid recourse should be a zero-NPV transaction—otherwise one side of the deal would get a free ride at the expense of the other. Nevertheless, nonrecourse debt, as part of the overall structure shown in Figure 25.1, is a customary and convenient financing method.[19]

---

[19] Leveraged leases have special tax and accounting requirements, which we won't go into here. Also, the equity investment in leveraged leases can be tricky to value, because the stream of after-tax cash flows changes sign more than once, and there can be two or more internal rates of return (IRRs). This requires use of modified internal rates of return, if you insist on using IRRs. We discussed multiple IRRs and modified IRRs in Section 5-3. Also take a look at Problem 23 at the end of this chapter.

SUMMARY

A lease is just an extended rental agreement. The owner of the equipment (the *lessor*) allows the user (the *lessee*) to operate the equipment in exchange for regular lease payments.

There is a wide variety of possible arrangements. Short-term, cancelable leases are known as *operating leases*. In these leases the lessor bears the risks of ownership. Long-term, noncancelable leases are called *full-payout, financial,* or *capital* leases. In these leases the lessee bears the risks. Financial leases are *sources of financing* for assets the firm wishes to acquire and use for an extended period.

The key to understanding operating leases is equivalent annual cost. In a competitive leasing market, the annual operating lease payment will be forced down to the lessor's equivalent annual cost. Operating leases are attractive to equipment users if the lease payment is less than the *user's* equivalent annual cost of buying the equipment. Operating leases make sense when the user needs the equipment only for a short time, when the lessor is better able to bear the risks of obsolescence, or when the lessor can offer a good deal on maintenance. Remember too that operating leases often have valuable options attached.

A financial lease extends over most of the economic life of the leased asset and cannot be canceled by the lessee. Signing a financial lease is like signing a secured loan to finance purchase of the leased asset. With financial leases, the choice is not "lease versus buy" but "lease versus borrow."

Many companies have sound reasons for financing via leases. For example, companies that are not paying taxes can usually strike a favorable deal with a tax-paying lessor. Also, it may be less costly and time-consuming to sign a standardized lease contract than to negotiate a long-term secured loan.

When a firm borrows money, it pays the after-tax rate of interest on its debt. Therefore, the opportunity cost of lease financing is the after-tax rate of interest on the firm's bonds. To value a financial lease, we need to discount the incremental cash flows from leasing by the after-tax interest rate.

An equivalent loan is one that commits the firm to exactly the same future cash flows as a financial lease. When we calculate the net present value of the lease, we are measuring the difference between the amount of financing provided by the lease and the financing provided by the equivalent loan:

$$\text{Value of lease} = \text{financing provided by lease} - \text{value of equivalent loan}$$

We can also analyze leases from the lessor's side of the transaction, using the same approaches we developed for the lessee. If lessee and lessor are in the same tax bracket, they will receive exactly the same cash flows but with signs reversed. Thus, the lessee can gain only at the lessor's expense, and vice versa. However, if the lessee's tax rate is lower than the lessor's, then both can gain at the federal government's expense. This is a tax timing advantage, because the lessor gets interest and depreciation tax shields early in the lease.

Leveraged leases are three-way transactions that include lenders as well as the lessor and lessee. Lenders advance up to 80% of the cost of the leased equipment and lessors put in the rest as an equity investment. The lenders get first claim on the lease payments and on the asset but have no recourse to the equity lessors if the lessee can't pay. The lessor's return comes mostly from interest and depreciation tax shields early in the lease and the value of the leased asset at the end of the lease. Leveraged leases are common in big-ticket, cross-border lease-financing transactions.

Two useful general references on leasing are:

J. S. Schallheim, *Lease or Buy? Principles for Sound Decision Making* (Boston: Harvard Business School Press, 1994).

P. K. Nevitt and F. J. Fabozzi, *Equipment Leasing,* 4th ed. (New Hope, PA: Frank Fabozzi Associates, 2000).

Smith and Wakeman discuss the economic motives for leasing:

C. W. Smith, Jr., and L. M. Wakeman, "Determinants of Corporate Leasing Policy," *Journal of Finance* 40 (July 1985), pp. 895–908.

The options embedded in many operating leases are discussed in:

J. J. McConnell and J. S. Schallheim, "Valuation of Asset Leasing Contracts," *Journal of Financial Economics* 12 (August 1983), pp. 237–261.

S. R. Grenadier, "Valuing Lease Contracts: A Real Options Approach," *Journal of Financial Economics* 38 (July 1995), pp. 297–331.

FURTHER READING

PROBLEM SETS

BASIC

1. The following terms are often used to describe leases:
   a. Direct
   b. Full-service
   c. Operating
   d. Financial
   e. Rental
   f. Net
   g. Leveraged
   h. Sale and lease-back
   i. Full-payout

   Match one or more of these terms with each of the following statements:
   A. The initial lease period is shorter than the economic life of the asset.
   B. The initial lease period is long enough for the lessor to recover the cost of the asset.
   C. The lessor provides maintenance and insurance.
   D. The lessee provides maintenance and insurance.
   E. The lessor buys the equipment from the manufacturer.
   F. The lessor buys the equipment from the prospective lessee.
   G. The lessor finances the lease contract by issuing debt and equity claims against it.

2. Some of the following reasons for leasing are rational. Others are irrational or assume imperfect or inefficient capital markets. Which of the following reasons are the rational ones?
   a. The lessee's need for the leased asset is only temporary.
   b. Specialized lessors are better able to bear the risk of obsolescence.
   c. Leasing provides 100% financing and thus preserves capital.
   d. Leasing allows firms with low marginal tax rates to "sell" depreciation tax shields.
   e. Leasing increases earnings per share.
   f. Leasing reduces the transaction cost of obtaining external financing.
   g. Leasing avoids restrictions on capital expenditures.
   h. Leasing can reduce the alternative minimum tax.

3. Explain why the following statements are *true:*
   a. In a competitive leasing market, the annual operating lease payment equals the lessor's equivalent annual cost.
   b. Operating leases are attractive to equipment users if the lease payment is less than the *user's* equivalent annual cost.

4. True or false?
   a. Lease payments are usually made at the start of each period. Thus the first payment is usually made as soon as the lease contract is signed.
   b. Some financial leases can provide off-balance-sheet financing.
   c. The cost of capital for a financial lease is the interest rate the company would pay on a bank loan.
   d. An equivalent loan's principal plus after-tax interest payments exactly match the after-tax cash flows of the lease.
   e. A financial lease should not be undertaken unless it provides more financing than the equivalent loan.
   f. It makes sense for firms that pay no taxes to lease from firms that do.
   g. Other things equal, the net tax advantage of leasing increases as nominal interest rates increase.

5. What happens if a bankrupt lessee affirms the lease? What happens if the lease is rejected?

6. How does a leveraged lease differ from an ordinary, long-term financial lease? List the key differences.

7. Lenders to leveraged leases hold nonrecourse debt. What does "nonrecourse" mean? What are the benefits and costs of nonrecourse debt to the equity investors in the lease?

INTERMEDIATE

8. Sriram has branched out to rentals of office furniture to start-up companies. Consider a ₹75,000 desk. Desks last for six years and can be depreciated over a six year period using the WDV rate of 20%. What is the break-even operating lease rate for a new desk? Assume that lease rates for old and new desks are the same and that Sriram's pretax administrative costs are ₹1,000 per desk per year. The cost of capital is 9% and the tax rate is 35%. Lease payments are made in advance, that is, at the start of each year. The inflation rate is zero.

9. Refer again to Problem 8. Suppose a blue-chip company requests a six-year *financial* lease for a ₹75,000 desk. The company has just issued five-year debentures at an interest rate of 6% per year. What is the break-even rate in this case? Assume administrative costs drop to ₹500 per year. Explain why your answers to Problem 8 and this question differ.

10. In Problem 8 we assumed identical lease rates for old and new desks.
    a. How does the initial break-even lease rate change if the expected inflation rate is 5% per year? Assume that the *real* cost of capital does not change. (*Hint:* Look at the discussion of equivalent annual costs in Chapter 6.)
    b. How does your answer to part (a) change if wear and tear force Sriram to cut lease rates by 10% in real terms for every year of a desk's age?

11. Look at Table 25.1. How would the initial break-even operating lease rate change if rapid technological change in limo manufacturing reduces the costs of new limos by 5% per year? (*Hint:* We discussed technological change and equivalent annual costs in Chapter 6.)

12. Suppose that National Waferonics has before it a proposal for a four-year financial lease. The firm constructs a table like Table 25.2. The bottom line of its table shows the lease cash flows:

	Year 0	Year 1	Year 2	Year 3
Lease cash flow	+62,000	−26,800	−22,200	−17,600

These flows reflect the cost of the machine, depreciation tax shields, and the after-tax lease payments. Ignore salvage value. Assume the firm could borrow at 10% and faces a 35% marginal tax rate.

a. What is the value of the equivalent loan?

b. What is the value of the lease?

c. Suppose the machine's NPV under normal financing is −₹5,000. Should National Waferonics invest? Should it sign the lease?

The following questions all apply to financial leases. To answer Problems 13 to 17 you may find it helpful to use the "live" Excel spreadsheets at **www.mhhe.com/bmam10e.**

13. Look again at the bus lease described in Table 25.2.

    a. What is the value of the lease if Bluelines' marginal tax rate is $T_c = .20$?

    b. What would the lease value be if Blueline had to use 15% WDV rate to depreciate the bus?

Visit us at
www.mhhe.com/bmam10e

14. In Section 25-4 we showed that the lease offered to Blueline Bus had a positive NPV of ₹0.11 lakhs if Blueline paid no tax *and* a +₹0.02 lakh to a lessor paying 33.99% tax. What is the minimum lease payment the lessor could accept under these assumptions? What is the maximum amount that Blueline could pay?

Visit us at
www.mhhe.com/bmam10e

15. In Section 25-5 we listed four circumstances in which there are potential gains from leasing. Check them out by conducting a sensitivity analysis on the Blueline Bus lease, assuming that Blueline does not pay tax. Try, in turn, (a) a lessor tax rate of 40% (rather than 33.99%), (b) immediate 100% depreciation in year 0 (rather than 25% WDV), (c) a three-year lease with four annual rentals (rather than an eight-year lease), and (d) an interest rate of 20% (rather than 10%). In each case, find the minimum rental that would satisfy the lessor and calculate the NPV to the lessee.

Visit us at
www.mhhe.com/bmam10e

16. In Section 25-5 we stated that if the interest rate were zero, there would be no advantage in postponing tax and therefore no advantage in leasing. Value the Blueline Bus lease with an interest rate of zero. Assume that Blueline does not pay tax. Can you devise any lease terms that would make both a lessee and a lessor happy? (If you can, we would like to hear from you.)

Visit us at
www.mhhe.com/bmam10e

17. A lease with a varying rental schedule is known as a *structured lease.* Try structuring the Blueline Bus lease to increase value to the lessee while preserving the value to the lessor. Assume that Blueline does not pay tax.

Visit us at
www.mhhe.com/bmam10e

18. Nodhead College needs a new computer. It can either buy it for $250,000 or lease it from Compulease. The lease terms require Nodhead to make six annual payments (prepaid) of $62,000. Nodhead pays no tax. Compulease pays tax at 35%. Compulease can depreciate the computer for tax purposes over five years. The computer will have no residual value at the end of year 5. The interest rate is 8%.

    a. What is the NPV of the lease for Nodhead College?

    b. What is the NPV for Compulease?

    c. What is the overall gain from leasing?

19. The Safety Razor Company has a large tax-loss carryforward and does not expect to pay taxes for another 10 years. The company is therefore

Visit us at
www.mhhe.com/bmam10e

proposing to lease ₹50 lakhs of new machinery. The lease terms consist of eight equal lease payments prepaid annually. The lessor can write the machinery off over seven years using 20% WDV method. There is no salvage value at the end of the machinery's economic life. The tax rate is 33.99%, and the rate of interest is 10%. Mr. Rahul Birani, the president of Safety Razor, wants to know the maximum lease payment that his company should be willing to make and the minimum payment that the lessor is likely to accept. Can you help him? How would your answer differ, if the lessor was allowed to use straight-line depreciation for tax purpose? Assume that it is allowed in India.

20. How does the position of an equipment lessor differ from the position of a secured lender when a firm falls into bankruptcy? Assume that the secured loan would have the leased equipment as collateral. Which is better protected, the lease or the loan? Does your answer depend on the value of the leased equipment if it were sold or re-leased?

21. How would the *lessee* in Figure 25.1 evaluate the NPV of the lease? Sketch the correct valuation procedure. Then suppose that the equity lessor wants to evaluate the lease. Again sketch the correct procedure. (*Hint:* APV. How would you calculate the *combined* value of the lease to lessee and lessor?)

Challenge

22. Pooja Charter has been asked to operate a Beaver bush plane for a mining company exploring north and west of Odisha. Pooja will have a firm one-year contract with the mining company and expects that the contract will be renewed for the five-year duration of the exploration program. If the mining company renews at year 1, it will commit to use the plane for four more years.

    Pooja Charter has the following choices.
    • Buy the plane for ₹2.5 crores.
    • Take a one-year operating lease for the plane. The lease rate is ₹59 lakhs, paid in advance.
    • Arrange a five-year, noncancelable financial lease at a rate of ₹37.5 lakhs per year, paid in advance.
    These are net leases: all operating costs are absorbed by Pooja Charter.

    How would you advise Pooja Varma, the charter company's CEO? For simplicity assume 25% WDV depreciation for tax purposes. The company's tax rate is 33.99%. The weighted-average cost of capital for the bush-plane business is 14%, but Pooja can borrow at 9%. The expected inflation rate is 4%.

    Ms. Pooja thinks the plane will be worth ₹1.5 crores after five years. But if the contract with the mining company is not renewed (there is a 20% probability of this outcome at year 1), the plane will have to be sold on short notice for ₹2 crores.

    If Pooja Charter takes the five-year financial lease and the mining company cancels at year 1, Pooja can sublet the plane, that is, rent it out to another user.

    Make additional assumptions as necessary.

23. Reconstruct Table 25.2 as a leveraged lease, assuming that the lessor borrows ₹36.8 lakhs, 80% of the cost of the bus, nonrecourse at an interest rate of 11%. All lease payments are devoted to debt service (interest and principal) until the loan is paid off. Assume that the bus is worth ₹10 lakhs at the end of lease. Calculate after-tax cash flows on the lessor's equity investment of ₹9.2 lakhs. What is the IRR of the equity cash flows? Is there more than one IRR? How would you value the lessor's equity investment?

26

MANAGING RISK

Most of the time we take risk as God-given. A project has its beta, and that's that. Its cash flow is exposed to changes in demand, raw material costs, technology, and a seemingly endless list of other uncertainties. There's nothing the manager can do about it.

That's not wholly true. The manager can avoid some risks. We have already come across one way to do so: firms use *real options* to provide flexibility. For example, a petrochemical plant that is designed to use either oil or natural gas as a feedstock reduces the risk of an unfavorable shift in the price of raw materials. As another example, think of a company that employs standard machine tools rather than custom machinery and thereby lowers the cost of bailing out if its products do not sell. In other words, the standard machinery provides the firm with a valuable abandonment option.

We covered real options in Chapter 22. This chapter explains how companies also use financial contracts to protect against various hazards. We discuss the pros and cons of corporate insurance policies that protect against specific risks, such as fire, floods, or environmental damage. We describe forward and futures contracts, which can be used to lock in the future price of commodities such as oil, copper, or soybeans. *Financial* forward and futures contracts allow the firm to lock in the prices of financial assets such as interest rates or foreign exchange rates. We also describe swaps, which are packages of forward contracts.

Most of this chapter describes how financial contracts may be used to reduce business risks. But why bother? Why should *shareholders* care whether the company's future profits are linked to future changes in interest rates, exchange rates, or commodity prices? We start the chapter with that question.

26-1 WHY MANAGE RISK?

Financial transactions undertaken *solely* to reduce risk do not add value in perfect markets. Why not? There are two basic reasons.

- *Reason 1: Hedging is a zero-sum game.* A corporation that insures or hedges a risk does not eliminate it. It simply passes the risk to someone else. For example, suppose that a heating-oil distributor contracts with a refiner to buy all of next winter's heating-oil deliveries at a fixed price. This contract is a *zero-sum game,* because the refiner loses what the distributor gains, and vice versa.[1] If next winter's price of heating oil turns out to be unusually high, the distributor wins from having locked in a below-market price, but the refiner is forced to sell below the market. Conversely, if the price of heating oil is unusually *low,* the refiner wins, because the distributor is forced to buy at the high fixed price. Of course, neither party knows next winter's price at the time that the deal is struck, but they consider the range of possible prices, and in an efficient market they negotiate terms that are fair (zero-NPV) on both sides of the bargain.

- *Reason 2: Investors' do-it-yourself alternative.* Corporations cannot increase the value of their shares by undertaking transactions that investors can easily do on their own. When the shareholders in the heating-oil distributor made their investment, they were presumably aware of the risks of the business. If they did not want to be exposed to the ups and downs of energy prices, they could have protected themselves in several ways. Perhaps they bought shares in both the distributor and refiner, and do not care whether one wins next winter at the other's expense.

Of course, shareholders can adjust their exposure only when companies keep investors fully informed of the transactions that they have made. For example, when a group of European central banks announced in 1999 that they would limit their sales of gold, the gold price immediately shot up. Investors in gold-mining shares rubbed their hands at the prospect of rising profits. But when they discovered that some mining companies had protected themselves against price fluctuations and would *not* benefit from the price rise, the hand-rubbing by investors turned to hand-wringing.[2]

Some stockholders of these gold-mining companies wanted to make a bet on rising gold prices; others didn't. But all of them gave the same message to management. The first group said, "Don't hedge! I'm happy to bear the risk of fluctuating gold prices, because I think gold prices will increase." The second group said, "Don't hedge! I'd rather do it myself." We have seen this do-it-yourself principle before. Think of other ways that the firm could reduce risk. It could do so by diversifying, for example, by acquiring another firm in an unrelated industry. But we know that investors can diversify on their own, and so diversification by corporations is redundant.[3]

Corporations can also lessen risk by borrowing less. But we showed in Chapter 17 that just reducing financial leverage does not make shareholders any better or worse off, because they can instead reduce financial risk by borrowing less (or lending more) in their personal accounts. Modigliani and Miller (MM) proved that a corporation's debt policy is irrelevant in perfect financial markets. We could extend their proof to say that risk management is also irrelevant in perfect financial markets.

Of course, in Chapter 18 we decided that debt policy *is* relevant, not because MM were wrong, but because of other things, such as taxes, agency problems, and costs of financial distress. The same

---

[1] In game theory, "zero-sum" means that the payoffs to all players add up to zero, so that one player can win only at the others' expense.

[2] The news was worst for the shareholders of Ashanti Goldfields, the huge Ghanaian mining company. Ashanti had gone to the opposite extreme and placed a bet that gold prices would fall. The 1999 price rise nearly drove Ashanti into bankruptcy.

[3] See Section 7-5 and also our discussion of diversifying mergers in Chapter 31. Note that diversification reduces overall risk, but not necessarily market risk.

line of argument applies here. If risk management affects the value of the firm, it must be because of "other things," not because risk shifting is inherently valuable.

Let's review the reasons that risk-reducing transactions can make sense in practice.[4]

Reducing the Risk of Cash Shortfalls or Financial Distress

Transactions that reduce risk make financial planning simpler and reduce the odds of an embarrassing cash shortfall. This shortfall might mean only an unexpected trip to the bank, but a financial manager's worst nightmare is landing in a financial pickle and having to pass up a valuable investment opportunity for lack of funds. In extreme cases an unhedged setback could trigger financial distress or even bankruptcy.

Banks and bondholders recognize these dangers. They try to keep track of the firm's risks, and before lending they may require the firm to carry insurance or to implement hedging programs. Risk management and conservative financing are therefore substitutes, not complements. Thus a firm might hedge part of its risk in order to operate safely at a higher debt ratio.

Smart financial managers make sure that cash (or ready financing) will be available if investment opportunities expand. That happy match of cash and investment opportunities does not necessarily require hedging, however. Let's contrast two examples.

Cirrus Oil produces from several oil fields and also invests to find and develop new fields. Should it lock in future revenues from its existing fields by hedging oil prices? Probably not, because its investment opportunities expand when oil prices rise and contract when they fall. Locking in oil prices could leave it with too much cash when oil prices fall and too little, relative to its investment opportunities, when prices rise.

Ranbaxy Pharmaceuticals sells worldwide and half of its revenues are received in foreign currencies. Most of its R&D is done in India. Should it hedge at least some of its foreign exchange exposure? Probably yes, because pharmaceutical R&D programs are very expensive, long-term investments. Ranbaxy can't turn its R&D program on or off depending on a particular year's earnings, so it may wish to stabilize cash flows by hedging against fluctuations in exchange rates.

Agency Costs May Be Mitigated by Risk Management

In some cases hedging can make it easier to monitor and motivate managers. Suppose your confectionery division delivers a 60% profit increase in a year when cocoa prices fall by 12%. Does the division manager deserve a stern lecture or a pat on the back? How much of the profit increase is due to good management and how much to lower cocoa prices? If the cocoa prices were hedged, it's probably good management. If they were not hedged, you will have to sort things out with hindsight, probably by asking, What would profits have been if cocoa prices had been hedged?

The fluctuations in cocoa prices are outside the manager's control. But she will surely worry about cocoa prices if her bottom line and bonus depend on them. Hedging prices ties her bonus more closely to risks that she can control and allows her to spend worrying time on these risks.

Hedging external risks that would affect individual managers does not necessarily mean that the *firm* ends up hedging. Some large firms allow their operating divisions to hedge away risks in an

---

[4]There may be other, special reasons not covered here. For example, governments are quick to tax profits, but may be slow to rebate taxes when there are losses. In the United States, losses can only be set against tax payments in the last two years. Any losses that cannot be offset in this way can be carried forward and used to shield future profits. Thus a firm with volatile income and more frequent losses has a higher effective tax rate. A firm can reduce the fluctuations in its income by hedging. For most firms this motive for risk reduction is not a big deal. See J. R. Graham and C. W. Smith, Jr., "Tax Incentives to Hedge," *Journal of Finance* 54 (December 1999), pp. 2241–2262.

internal "market." The internal market operates with real (external) market prices, transferring risks from the division to the central treasurer's office. The treasurer then decides whether to hedge the firm's aggregate exposure.

This sort of internal market makes sense for two reasons. First, divisional risks may cancel out. For example, your refining division may benefit from an increase in heating-oil prices at the same time that your distribution division suffers. Second, because operating managers do not trade actual financial contracts, there is no danger that the managers will cause the firm to take speculative positions. For example, suppose that profits are down late in the year, and hope for end-year bonuses is fading. Could you be tempted to make up the shortfall with a quick score in the cocoa futures market? Well . . . not you, of course, but you can probably think of some acquaintances who would try just one speculative fling.

The dangers of permitting operating managers to make real speculative trades should be obvious. The manager of your confectionery division is an amateur in the cocoa futures market. If she were a skilled professional trader, she would probably not be running chocolate factories.[5]

Risk management requires some degree of centralization. These days many companies appoint a chief risk officer to develop a risk strategy for the company as a whole. The risk manager needs to come up with answers to the following questions:

1. *What are the major risks that the company is facing and what are the possible consequences?* Some risks are scarcely worth a thought, but there are others that might cause a serious setback or even bankrupt the company.

2. *Is the company being paid for taking these risks?* Managers are not paid to avoid all risks, but if they can reduce their exposure to risks for which there are no corresponding rewards, they can afford to place larger bets when the odds are stacked in their favor.

3. *How should risks be controlled?* Should the company reduce risk by building extra flexibility into its operations? Should it change its operating or financial leverage? Or should it insure or hedge against particular hazards?

The Evidence on Risk Management

Which firms use financial contracts to manage risk? Almost all do to some extent. For example, they may have contracts that fix prices of raw materials or output, at least for the near future. Most take out insurance policies against fire, accidents, and theft. In addition, as we shall see, managers employ a variety of specialized tools for hedging risk. These are known collectively as *derivatives*. A survey of the world's 500 largest companies found that most of them use derivatives to manage their risk.[6] Eighty-five percent of the companies employ derivatives to control interest rate risk. Seventy-eight percent use them to manage currency risk, and 24% to manage commodity price risk.

Risk policies differ. For example, some natural resource companies work hard to hedge their exposure to price fluctuations; others shrug their shoulders and let prices wander as they may. Explaining why some hedge and others don't is not easy. Peter Tufano's study of the gold-mining industry suggests that managers' personal risk aversion may have something to do with it. Hedging of gold prices appears to be more common when top management has large personal shareholdings in the company. It is less common when top management holds lots of stock options. (Remember that

---

[5] Amateur speculation is doubly dangerous when the manager's initial trades are losers. At that point the manager is already in deep trouble and has nothing more to lose by going for broke.

[6] International Swap Dealers Association (ISDA), "2003 Derivatives Usage Survey," www.isda.org.

the value of an option falls when the risk of the underlying security is reduced.) David Haushalter's study of oil and gas producers found the firms that hedged the most had high debt ratios, no debt ratings, and low dividend payouts. It seems that for these firms hedging programs were designed to improve the firms' access to debt finance and to reduce the likelihood of financial distress.[7]

26-2 INSURANCE

Most businesses buy insurance against a variety of hazards—the risk that their plants will be damaged by fire; that their ships, planes, or vehicles will be involved in accidents; that the firm will be held liable for environmental damage; and so on.

When a firm takes out insurance, it is simply transferring the risk to the insurance company. Insurance companies have some advantages in bearing risk. First, they may have considerable experience in insuring similar risks, so they are well placed to estimate the probability of loss and price the risk accurately. Second, they may be skilled at providing advice on measures that the firm can take to reduce the risk, and they may offer lower premiums to firms that take this advice. Third, an insurance company can *pool* risks by holding a large, diversified portfolio of policies. The claims on any individual policy can be highly uncertain, yet the claims on a portfolio of policies may be very stable. Of course, insurance companies cannot diversify away market or macroeconomic risks; firms use insurance policies to reduce their specific risk, and they find other ways to avoid macro risks.

Insurance companies also suffer some *disadvantages* in bearing risk, and these are reflected in the prices they charge. Suppose your firm owns a ₹1 billion offshore oil platform. A meteorologist has advised you that there is a 1-in-10,000 chance that in any year the platform will be destroyed as a result of a storm. Thus the *expected* loss from storm damage is ₹1 billion/10,000 = ₹100,000.

The risk of storm damage is almost certainly not a macroeconomic risk and can potentially be diversified away. So you might expect that an insurance company would be prepared to insure the platform against such destruction as long as the premium was sufficient to cover the expected loss. In other words, a fair premium for insuring the platform should be ₹100,000 a year.[8] Such a premium would make insurance a zero-NPV deal for your company. Unfortunately, no insurance company would offer a policy for only ₹100,000. Why not?

- *Reason 1: Administrative costs.* An insurance company, like any other business, incurs a variety of costs in arranging the insurance and handling any claims. For example, disputes about the liability for environmental damage can eat up millions of dollars in legal fees. Insurance companies need to recognize these costs when they set their premiums.
- *Reason 2: Adverse selection.* Suppose that an insurer offers life insurance policies with "no medical exam needed, no questions asked." There are no prizes for guessing who will be most tempted to buy this insurance. Our example is an extreme case of the problem of *adverse selection.* Unless the insurance company can distinguish between good and bad risks, the latter will always be most eager to take out insurance. Insurers increase premiums to compensate or require the owners to share any losses.

---

[7] See P. Tufano, "The Determinants of Stock Price Exposure: Financial Engineering and the Gold Mining Industry," *Journal of Finance* 53 (June 1998), pp. 1014–1052; and G. D. Haushalter, "Financing Policy, Basis Risk and Corporate Hedging," *Journal of Finance* 55 (February 2000), pp. 107–152.

[8] If the premium is paid at the beginning of the year and the claim is not settled until the end, then the zero-NPV premium equals the discounted value of the expected claim or ₹100,000/$(1 + r)$.

- *Reason 3: Moral hazard.* Two farmers met on the road to town. "George," said one, "I was sorry to hear about your barn burning down." "Shh," replied the other, "that's tomorrow night." The story is an example of another problem for insurers, known as *moral hazard*. Once a risk has been insured, the owner may be less careful to take proper precautions against damage. Insurance companies are aware of this and factor it into their pricing.

The extreme forms of adverse selection and moral hazard (like the fire in the farmer's barn) are rarely encountered in professional corporate finance. But these problems arise in more subtle ways. That oil platform may not be a "bad risk," but the oil company knows more about the platform's weaknesses than the insurance company does. The oil company will not purposely scuttle the platform, but once insured it could be tempted to save on maintenance or structural reinforcements. Thus, the insurance company may end up paying for engineering studies or for a program to monitor maintenance. All these costs are rolled into the insurance premium.

When the costs of administration, adverse selection, and moral hazard are small, insurance may be close to a zero-NPV transaction. When they are large, insurance is a costly way to protect against risk.

Many insurance risks are *jump risks;* one day there is not a cloud on the horizon and the next day the hurricane hits. The risks can also be huge. For example, Hurricane Andrew, which devastated Florida, cost insurance companies $17 billion; the attack on the World Trade Center on September 11, 2001, involved payments of about $36 billion, while Hurricane Katrina cost insurers a record $66 billion.

If the losses from such disasters can be spread more widely, the cost of insuring them should decline. Therefore, insurance companies have been looking for ways to share catastrophic risks with investors. One solution is for the companies to issue *catastrophe bonds* (or *Cat bonds*). If a catastrophe occurs, the payment on a Cat bond is reduced or eliminated.[9] For example, in 2009 Chubb Corporation issued $150 million worth of Cat bonds. The bonds cover Chubb against any losses in excess of $850 million resulting from Florida hurricanes. For taking on this risk investors receive a tempting interest rate of 10.25% over LIBOR.

How BP Changed Its Insurance Strategy[10]

Major public companies typically buy insurance against large potential losses and self-insure against routine ones. The idea is that large losses can trigger financial distress. On the other hand, routine losses for a corporation are predictable, so there is little point paying premiums to an insurance company and receiving back a fairly constant proportion as claims.

BP has challenged this conventional wisdom. Like all oil companies, BP is exposed to a variety of potential losses. Some arise from routine events such as vehicle accidents and industrial injuries. At the other extreme, they may result from catastrophes such as a major oil spill or the loss of an offshore oil rig. In the past BP purchased considerable external insurance.[11] During the 1980s it paid out an average of $115 million a year in insurance premiums and recovered $25 million a year in claims.

---

[9] For a discussion of Cat bonds and other techniques to spread insurance risk, see N. A. Doherty, "Financial Innovation in the Management of Catastrophe Risk," *Journal of Applied Corporate Finance* 10 (Fall 1997), pp. 84–95; and K. Froot, "The Market for Catastrophe Risk: A Clinical Examination," *Journal of Financial Economics* 60 (2001), pp. 529–571.

[10] Our description of BP's insurance strategy draws heavily on N. A. Doherty and C. W. Smith, Jr., "Corporate Insurance Strategy: The Case of British Petroleum," *Journal of Applied Corporate Finance* 6 (Fall 1993), pp. 4–15.

[11] However, with one or two exceptions insurance has not been available for the very largest losses of $500 million or more.

BP then took a hard look at its insurance strategy. It decided to allow local managers to insure against routine risks, where insurance companies have an advantage in assessing and pricing risk and compete vigorously against one another. BP considered that the insurance companies could do these tasks more efficiently than its own managers. But BP decided not to insure against most losses over $10 million. For these larger, more specialized risks BP felt that insurance companies had less ability to assess risk and were less well placed to advise on safety measures. As a result, BP concluded, insurance against large risks was not competitively priced.

How much extra risk did BP assume by its decision not to insure against major losses? BP estimated that large losses of above $500 million could be expected to occur once in 30 years. But BP is a huge company with equity worth about $150 billion. So even a $500 million loss, which could throw most companies into bankruptcy, would translate after tax into a fall of less than 1% in the value of BP's equity. BP concluded that this was a risk worth taking. In other words, it concluded that for large, low-probability risks the stock market was a more efficient risk-absorber than the insurance industry.

26-3   REDUCING RISK WITH OPTIONS

Managers regularly buy options on currencies, interest rates, and commodities to limit downside risk. Consider, for example, the problem faced by the Mexican government. Forty percent of its revenue comes from Pemex, the state-owned oil company. So, if oil prices fall, the government may be compelled to reduce its planned spending. That is always an unwelcome outcome, but it was particularly so in 2008 when the country faced recession.

The Mexican government's solution was to establish a floor on the price at which it could sell 330 million barrels of oil, equivalent to the country's total expected net oil exports in 2009. To do this, the government bought *put* options that gave it the right to sell oil at an exercise price of $70 per barrel. If oil prices rose above this figure, Mexico would reap the benefit. But if oil prices fell below $70 a barrel, the payoff to the put options would exactly offset the revenue shortfall. Of course, you don't get something for nothing. The price that the government paid for insurance against a fall in the price of oil was the estimated $1.5 billion cost of the put options.

Figure 26.1 illustrates the nature of Mexico's insurance strategy. Panel (a) shows the revenue derived from selling 330 million barrels of oil. If the price of oil falls, so do the government's revenues. But, as panel (b) illustrates, the payoff on the option to sell 330 million barrels rises as oil prices fall below $70 a barrel. This payoff exactly offsets the decline in oil revenues. Panel (c) shows the government's total revenues after buying the put options. For prices below $70 per barrel, revenues are fixed at $70 \times 330 = \$23,100$ million. But for every dollar that oil prices rise above $70, revenues increase by $330 million. The profile in panel (c) should be familiar to you as the protective put strategy that we encountered in Section 20-2.

26-4   FORWARD AND FUTURES CONTRACTS

Hedging involves taking on one risk to offset another. It potentially removes all uncertainty, eliminating the chance of both happy and unhappy surprises. We explain shortly how to set up a hedge, but first we give some examples and describe some tools that are specially designed for hedging. These are forwards, futures, and swaps. Together with options, they are known as *derivative instruments* or *derivatives* because their value depends on the value of another asset.

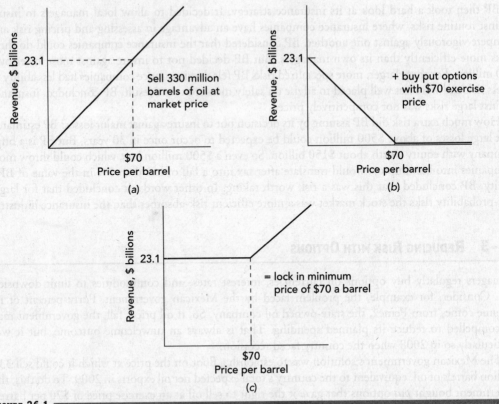

FIGURE 26.1

How put options protected Mexico against a fall in oil prices.

A Simple Forward Contract

We start with an example of a simple **forward contract**. Agarwal Jewellery, a leading gold ornament designer from India, requires 100 kilogram of gold to deliver gold jewellery to the Duty-Free Shopping Arcade of Dubai before next Christmas. Agarwal worries about high gold prices and wants to lock in the cost of buying its supply. Shah Gold Mines of Kollar is in the opposite position. It will extract gold before next Christmas, but does not know what the gold can be sold for. So the two firms strike a deal: Agarwal Jewellery agrees in August to buy 100 kg gold from Shah Gold Mines at ₹28,000 per 10 grams, to be paid on delivery in November. Shah Gold Mines agrees to sell and deliver 100 kg gold to Agarwal Jewellery in November at ₹28,000 per 10 grams.

Agarwal and Shah are now the two counterparties in a forward contract. The **forward price** is ₹28,000 per 10 grams. This price is fixed today, in August in our example, but payment and delivery occur later. (The price for immediate delivery is called the **spot price**). Agarwal Jewellery, which has agreed to buy in November, has the long position in the contract. Shah Gold Mines, which has agreed to sell in November, has the short position. Both companies have eliminated a business risk: Agarwal has locked in its costs, and Shah has locked in its revenues for 100 kg of output.[12]

---

[12] For now we are ignoring several complications. Suppose, for example, that retail gold prices move up and down with wholesale prices. In that case the gold distributor is naturally hedged, because costs and revenues move together. Locking in costs with a forward contract could actually make the distributor's profits more volatile

Do not confuse this forward contract with an option. Agarwal does not have the option to buy. It has committed to buy, even if spot prices in November turn out to be much lower than ₹28,000 per 10 grams. Shah does not have the option to sell. It cannot back away from the deal, even if spot prices in November turn out to be much higher than ₹28,000 per 10 grams. Note, however, that both Agarwal and Shah have to worry about *counterparty risk*, that is, the risk that the other party will not perform as promised.

We confess that our gold example glossed over several complications. For example, we assumed that the risk of both companies is reduced by locking in the price of gold. But suppose that the retail price of gold jewellery moves up and down with the wholesale price. In that case, the jewellery distributor is naturally hedged because costs and revenues move together. Locking in costs with a futures contract could actually make the distributor's profits more volatile. The nearby box illustrates that hedging decisions are not always straightforward.

Futures Exchanges

Agarwal Jewellery and Shah Gold Mines do not have to negotiate a one-off bilateral contract. Each can go to an exchange where standardized contracts on gold are traded. Agarwal would buy contracts and Shah would sell.

Here we encounter some tricky vocabulary. When a standardized forward contract is traded on an exchange, it is called a **futures contract**—same contract, but a different label. The exchange is called a **futures exchange.** The distinction between "futures" and "forward" does not apply to the contract, but to how the contract is traded. We describe futures trading in a moment.

Table 26.1 lists the most important commodity futures contracts and the exchanges on which they are traded in India. Agarwal and Shah can trade on the Multi Commodity Exchange of India Limited (MCX). A wheat farmer and a miller can trade wheat futures on the National Multi-Commodity Exchange of India Limited (NMCE). A chilli farmer and a chilli powder manufacturer can trade on the National Commodity & Derivatives Exchange Limited.

TABLE 26.1   Some commodity futures in India and some of the exchanges in which they are traded.

Future	Exchange	Future	Exchange
Aluminium	MCX, NCDEX	Cardamom	NMCE
Cashew	NCDEX	Coffee	NMCE, NCDEX
Coconut Oil Cake	MCX, NMCE	Castor Seed	NMCE, NCDEX
Chana	MCX, NCDEX, NMCE	Chilli	NCDEX
Gold	MCX, NCDEX	Jeera	MCX, NCDEX, NMCE
Masoor	MCX, NCDEX	Pepper	MCX, NCDEX, NMCE
Potato	MCX, NCDEX	PVC	MCX
Raw Jute	NMCE, NCDEX	Rubber	NMCE, NCDEX
Sponge Iron	NCDEX	Sugar	MCX, NCDEX, NMCE
Turmeric	NCDEX	Urad Dal	MCX, NCDEX
Wheat	MCX, NCDEX, NMCE	Zinc	MCX, NCDEX

Key to abbreviations:

NCDEX   National Commodity & Derivatives Exchange Limited
MCX   Multi Commodity Exchange of India Limited
NMCE   National Multi-Commodity Exchange of India Limited

Finance In Practice

The Pros and Cons of Hedging Airline Fuel Costs

Jet fuel is a major cost of running an airline. For example, in 2008 purchases of kerosene accounted for about 20% of the operating costs of the German airline, Lufthansa. Jet fuel costs are notoriously volatile, rising by over 150% between January 2007 and May 2008, before falling by more than 70% over the following 12 months. Therefore, Lufthansa like many airlines uses a variety of market instruments, such as forward contracts and options, to hedge against unexpected fluctuations in fuel prices. In early 2009 it had hedged 63% of its fuel requirements for that year and 26% of its requirements for the following year.

Carter, Rogers, and Simkins, who conducted a study of hedging by U.S. airlines, concluded that investors placed a premium on airlines, such as Lufthansa, that hedged their fuel costs. The reason for this premium, they suggested, was that airlines may be led to cut back on profitable investments when fuel prices are high and operating cash flows values are low. An airline that is protected against rising fuel prices is better placed to take advantage of investment opportunities.

Hedging has its advantages for airlines, but there are also dangers. One problem is that if fuel prices fall, those airlines that have entered into contracts to cover their future fuel needs will suffer losses on these contracts. If they bought the contracts on a futures exchange, they will need to put up cash as collateral to cover these losses. This was the case for many airlines when fuel prices plunged in the second half of 2008. Writing in *Aviation Week*, Adrian Schofield noted that at the end of 2008 Delta and United Airlines each had about $1 billion in cash tied up as hedge collateral, while American had to put up $575 million. These were large amounts of cash to find when the skies were far from friendly for U.S. airlines.

Schofield added an additional caution for would-be hedgers: "Competition among airlines paying lower jet-fuel prices should lead to lower fares. When that happens, lower fuel costs are offset by lower revenues, and losses on hedging contracts fall straight down to bottom-line income. Costs that are passed through to customers are naturally hedged." Usually, only a portion of any increase in costs is passed through, so the natural hedge is partial. However, a firm needs to be careful when adding a financial hedge transaction to a natural hedge. It could overshoot and increase risk, not reduce it.

Sources: D. A. Carter, D. A. Rogers, and B. J. Simkins, "Hedging and Value in the U.S. Airline Industry," *Journal of Applied Corporate Finance* 18 (Fall 2006), pp. 21–33; and A. Schofield, "High Anxiety," *Aviation Week & Space Technology*, February 2, 2009, pp. 24–25.

For many firms the wide fluctuations in interest rates and exchange rates have become at least as important a source of risk as changes in commodity prices. Financial futures are similar to commodity futures, but instead of placing an order to buy or sell a commodity at a future date, you place an order to buy or sell a financial asset at a future date. Table 26.2 lists some important financial futures. Like Table 26.1 it is far from complete. For example, you can also trade futures on the Thai stock market index, the Hungarian forint, Finnish government bonds, and many other financial assets.

TABLE 26.2   Some financial futures and some of the exchanges on which they are traded.

Future	Exchange	Future	Exchange
U.S. Treasury bonds	CBOT	Euroyen deposits	CME, SGX, TFX
U.S. Treasury notes	CBOT		
German government bonds (bunds)	Eurex	S&P 500 Index	CME
Japanese government bonds (JGBs)	CME, SGX, TSE	French equity index (CAC)	LIFFE
British government bonds (gilts)	LIFFE	German equity index (DAX)	Eurex
BSE Sensex	BSE	BSE PSU Index	BSE
U.S. Treasury bills	CME	Japanese equity index (Nikkei)	CME, OSE, SGX
S&P CNX Nifty	NSE		
Swaps	CBOT	U.K. equity index (FTSE)	LIFFE
Credit default swaps	CBOT	Chinese renminbi	CME
LIBOR	CME	Euro	CME
EURIBOR	LIFFE	Japanese yen	CME
Eurodollar deposits	CME		

Key to abbreviations:

BSE	Mumbai Stock Exchange	OSE	Osaka Securities Exchange
CBOT	Chicago Board of Trade	SGX	Singapore Exchange
CME	Chicago Mercantile Exchange	TFX	Tokyo Financial Futures Exchange
LIFFE	Euronext LIFFE	TSE	Tokyo Stock Exchange
NSE	National Stock Exchange		

Almost every day some new futures contract seems to be invented. At first there may be just a few private deals between a bank and its customers, but if the idea proves popular, one of the futures exchanges will try to muscle in on the business. For example, in the last few years the Chicago Mercantile Exchange has offered futures contracts on the weather in 18 U.S. cities and on house prices in 10 cities.

The Mechanics of Futures Trading

When you buy or sell futures contract, the price is fixed today but payment is not made until later. You will, however, be asked to put up **margin** in the form of (a) cash, or (b) bank guarantee issued by any of the approved commercial banks, or (c) fixed deposits issued by any one or more of the approved commercial banks, or (d) deposit of approved securities in dematerialized form to demonstrate that you have the money to honor your side of the bargain. As long as you earn interest on the margined securities, there is no cost to you.

In addition, futures contract are marked to market. This means that each day any profits or losses on the contract are calculated; you pay the exchange any losses and receive any profits. For example, suppose that in August Agarwal Jewellery buys 100 November gold futures contract at a futures price of ₹28,000 per 10 gram of gold.[13] The next day the price of the November contract increases to ₹28,200. Agarwal now has a profit of ₹0.2 lakhs × 100 = ₹2 lakhs. The exchange's clearing house therefore pays ₹2 lakhs into Agarwal's margin account. If the price then drops back to ₹28,100,

---

[13] In NCDEX, the unit of trading for gold futures is 1 kg. However, the price is quoted in rupees per 10 grams of gold with 995 fineness. So when one buys one gold futures contract, one effectively agrees to buy 1 kg of gold at some future date. So when Agarwal Jewellery buys 100 kg gold futures contract, it agrees to buy 100 kg of gold. In NCDEX, the maximum order size is for 50 kgs of gold. In this example, we ignore this.

Agarwal's margin account pays ₹1 lakhs back to the clearing house. It is as if Agarwal closes out its position every day and then opens a new position at the new futures price.

Of course Shah Gold Mines is in the opposite position. Suppose it sells 100 November gold futures contract at a futures price of ₹28 lakhs per kg (₹28,000 per 10 grams of gold). If the price increases to ₹28.2 lakhs per kg, it loses ₹0.2 lakhs × 100 = ₹2 lakhs and must pay this amount into the clearinghouse. In effect the goldmine closes out its position at a loss of ₹0.2 lakhs per kg and opens a new contract to deliver in November at ₹28.2 lakhs per kg. Notice that neither Agarwal nor Shah has to worry about whether the other party will honor the other side of the bargain. The futures exchange guarantees the contracts and protects itself by setting up profits and losses each day. Futures trading eliminates counterparty risk.

Now consider what happens over the life of the futures contract. We're assuming that Agarwal and Shah take offsetting short and long positions in the November contract (not directly with each other, but with the exchange). Suppose that a sudden increase in demand of gold pushes the spot price of gold in November to ₹30 lakhs per kg. Then the futures price at the end of the contract will also be ₹30 lakhs per kg.[14] So Agarwal gets a cumulative profit of (30 – 28) × 100 = ₹200 lakhs. It can take delivery of 100 kg of gold, paying ₹30 lakhs per kg, or ₹3000 lakhs. Its net cost, counting the profits on the futures contract is ₹3,000 lakhs – ₹200 lakhs = ₹2,800 lakhs, or ₹28 lakhs per kg of gold. Thus, it has locked in the ₹28 lakhs per kg price quoted in August when it first brought the futures contract. You can easily check that Agarwal's net cost always ends up at ₹28 lakhs per kg, regardless of the spot price at the ending futures price in November.

Shah Gold Mines suffers a cumulative loss of ₹200 lakhs, if the November price is ₹30 lakhs. That's bad news; the good news is that it can sell and deliver gold for ₹30 lakhs per kg. Its net revenues are ₹3,000 lakhs – ₹200 lakhs = ₹2,800 lakhs, or ₹28 lakhs per kg, the futures price in August. Again you can easily check that Shah's net selling price always ends up at ₹28 lakhs per 1 kg.

Agarwal does not have to take delivery directly from the futures exchange, and Shah does not have to deliver to the exchange. They will probably close out their futures positions just before the end of the contract, take their profits and losses, and buy or sell in the spot market.[15] In the previous two paragraphs, this is what we have assumed.

Taking delivery directly from an exchange can be costly and inconvenient. For example, the NCDEX gold futures contract calls for delivery in Mumbai or Ahmedabad. Agarwal will be better off taking delivery from a local source such as Jaipur. Shah will likewise be better off delivering gold locally rather than sending it to Mumbai from Karnataka. Both parties can nevertheless use the NCDEX futures contract to hedge their risk.

The effectiveness of this hedge depends on the correlation between changes in gold prices locally and in Mumbai or Ahmedabad. Prices in both locations will be highly positively correlated because of a common dependence on world gold prices. But the correlation need not be perfect. In that case the hedging will not be perfect. This is an example of what is known as **basis risk**. We return to the problems created by basis risk later in this chapter.

Trading and Pricing Financial Futures Contracts

Financial futures trade in the same way as commodity futures. Suppose that you work with a U.S. firm in New York after your MBA from India. Your firm's pension fund manager thinks that the German

---

[14] Recall that the spot price is the price for immediate delivery. The futures contract also calls for immediate delivery when the contract ends in January. Therefore, the ending price of a futures or forward contract must converge to the spot price at the end of the contract.

[15] Some financial futures contracts *prohibit* delivery. All positions are closed out at the spot price at contract maturity.

stock market will outperform other European markets over the next six months. She forecasts a 10% six-month return. How can she place a bet? She can buy German stocks, of course. But she could also buy futures contracts on the DAX index of German stocks, which are traded on the Eurex exchange. Suppose she buys 10 six-month futures contracts at 4,000. Each contract pays off 25 times the level of the index, so she has a long position of $10 \times 25 \times 4,000 = €1,000,000$. This position is marked to market daily. If the DAX goes up, Eurex puts the profits into your fund's margin account; if the DAX falls, the margin account falls too. If your pension manager is right about the German market, and the DAX ends up at 4,400 after six months, then your fund's cumulative profit on the futures position is $10 \times (4,400 - 4,000) \times 25 = €100,000$.

If you want to buy a security, you have a choice. You can buy for immediate delivery at the spot price or you can "buy forward" by placing an order for future delivery at the futures price. You end up with the same security either way, but there are two differences. First, if you buy forward, you don't pay up front, and so you can earn interest on the purchase price. Second, you miss out on any interest or dividend that is paid in the meantime. This tells us the relationship between spot and futures prices:

$$F_t = S_0(1 + r_f - y)^t$$

where F_t is the futures price for a contract lasting t periods, S_0 is today's spot price, r_f is the risk-free interest rate, and y is the dividend yield or interest rate.[16] The following example shows how and why this formula works.

EXAMPLE 26.1 **Valuing Index Futures**

Suppose the six-month DAX futures contract trades at 4,000 when the current (spot) DAX index is 3,980.10. The interest rate is 3% per year (about 1.5% over six months) and the dividend yield on the index is 2% (about 1% over six months). These numbers fit the formula because

$$F_t = 3,980.10 \times (1 + .015 - .01) = 4,000$$

but why are the numbers consistent?

Suppose you just buy the DAX index for 3,980.10 today. Then in six months you will own the index and also have dividends of $.01 \times 3,980.10 = 39.80$. But you decide to buy a futures contract for 4,000 instead, and you put €3,980.10 in the bank. After six months, the bank account has earned interest at 1.5%, so you have $3,980.10 \times 1.015 = €4,039.80$, enough to buy the index for 4,000 with €39.80 left over, just enough to cover the dividend you missed by buying futures rather than spot. You get what you pay for.[17]

---

[16] This formula is strictly true only for forward contracts that are not marked to market. Otherwise the value of the future depends on the path of interest rates over the life of the contract. In practice this qualification is usually not important, and the formula works for futures as well as forward contracts.

[17] We can derive our formula as follows. Let S_6 be the value of the index after six months. Today S_6 is unknown. You can invest S_0 in the index today and get $S_6 + yS_0$ after six months. You can also buy the futures contract, put S_0 in the bank, and use your bank balance to pay the futures price F_6 in six months. In the latter strategy you get $S_6 - F_6 + S_0(1 + r_f)$ after six months. Since the investment is the same, and you get S_6 with either strategy, the payoffs must be the same:

$$S_6 + yS_0 = S_6 - F_6 + S_0(1 + r_f)$$
$$F_6 = S_0(1 + r_f - y)$$

Here we assume that r_f and y are six-month rates. If they are monthly rates, the general formula is $F_t = S_0(1 + r_f - y)^t$, where t is the number of months. If they are annual rates, the formula is $F_t = S_0(1 + r_f - y)^{t/12}$.

Financial futures have been a remarkably successful innovation. They were invented in 1972 in the U.S. Within a few years, trading in financial futures far outspaced trading in commodity futures. In India, trading in futures started in 2000-01. Within a span of five years, the total turnover in Index futures in NSE alone has increased by more than 639 times.

Spot and Futures Prices—Commodities

The difference between buying *commodities* today and buying commodity futures is more complicated. First, because payment is again delayed, the buyer of the future earns interest on her money. Second, she does not need to store the commodities and, therefore, saves warehouse costs, wastage, and so on. On the other hand, the futures contract gives no *convenience yield,* which is the value of being able to get your hands on the real thing. The manager of a supermarket can't burn heating oil futures if there's a sudden cold snap, and he can't stock the shelves with orange juice futures if he runs out of inventory at 1 p.m. on a Saturday.

Let's express storage costs and convenience yield as fractions of the spot price. For commodities, the futures price for t periods ahead is[18]

$$F_t = S_0(1 + r_f + \text{storage costs} - \text{convenience yield})^t$$

It's interesting to compare this formula with the formula for a financial future. Convenience yield plays the same role as dividends or interest foregone (y) on securities. But financial assets cost nothing to store, and storage costs do not appear in the formula for financial futures.

Usually you can't observe storage cost or convenience yield, but you can infer the difference between them by comparing spot and futures prices. This difference—that is, convenience yield less storage cost—is called *net convenience yield* (net convenience yield = convenience yield − storage costs).

EXAMPLE 26.2   Calculating Net Convenience Yield

In January 2012, the spot price of gold was ₹27,219.50 per 10 gram and the 4-month futures price was ₹27,721 per 10 gram in NCDEX. The interest rate was about 8.8 percent, or 2.93 percent over 4 months. Thus

$$F_t = S_0 (1 + r_f + \text{storage costs} - \text{convenience yield})$$
$$27,721 = 27,219.50 (1.0293 - \text{net convenience yield})$$

So net convenience yield was negative, that is, net convenience yield = convenience yield − storage costs = 0.011, or 4.4 percent over 4 months. Evidently the cost of holding coffee inventories was greater than the convenience yield provided by those inventories.

Figure 26.2 plots the annualized net convenience yield for crude oil in the U.S. over a 10-year period. Notice how much the spread between the spot and futures price can bounce around. When there are shortages or fears of an interruption of supply, traders may be prepared to pay a hefty premium for the convenience of having inventories of crude oil rather than the promise of future delivery.

---

[18] This formula could overstate the futures price if no one is willing to hold the commodity, that is, if inventories fall to zero or some absolute minimum.

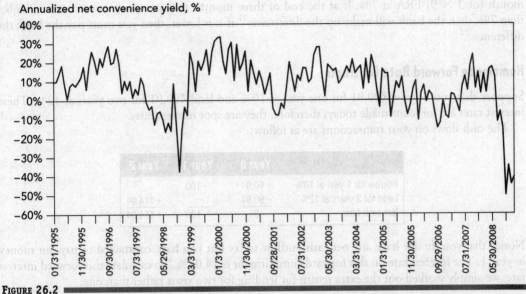

FIGURE 26.2

Annualized percentage net convenience yield (convenience yield *less* storage costs) for crude oil.

There is one further complication that we should note. There are some commodities that cannot be stored at all. You can't store electricity, for example. As a result, electricity supplied in, say, six-months' time is effectively a different commodity from electricity available now, and there is no simple link between today's price and that of a futures contract to buy or sell at the end of six months. Of course, generators and electricity users will have their own views of what the spot price is likely to be, and the futures price will reveal these views to some extent.[19]

More about Forward Contracts

Each day billions of dollars of futures contracts are bought and sold. This liquidity is possible only because futures contracts are standardized and mature on a limited number of dates each year.

Fortunately there is usually more than one way to skin a financial cat. If the terms of futures contracts do not suit your particular needs, you may be able to buy or sell a tailor-made forward contract. The main forward market is in foreign currency. We discuss forward exchange rates in the next chapter.

It is also possible to enter into a forward interest rate contract. For example, suppose you know that at the end of three months you are going to need a six-month loan. If you are worried that interest rates will rise over the three-month period, you can lock in the interest rate on the loan by buying a *forward rate agreement (FRA)* from a bank.[20] For example, the bank might sell you a 3-against-9

---

[19] Critics and proponents of futures markets sometimes argue about whether the markets provide "price discovery." That is, they argue about whether futures prices reveal traders' forecasts of spot prices when the futures contract matures. If one of these fractious personalities comes your way, we suggest that you respond with a different question: Do futures prices reveal information about spot prices that is not already in *today's* spot price? Our formulas reveal the answer to this question. There is useful information in futures prices, but it is information about convenience yields and storage costs, or about dividend or interest payments in the case of financial futures. Futures prices reveal information about spot prices only when a commodity is not stored or cannot be stored. Then the link between spot and futures prices is broken, and futures prices can assist with price discovery.

[20] Note that the party that profits from a rise in rates is described as the "buyer." In our example you would be said to "buy three against nine months" money, meaning that the forward rate agreement is for a six-month loan in three months' time.

month (or 3 × 9) FRA at 7%. If at the end of three months the six-month interest rate is higher than 7%, then the bank will make up the difference;[21] if it is lower, then you must pay the bank the difference.[22]

Homemade Forward Rate Contracts

Suppose that you borrow ₹90.91 for one year at 10% and lend ₹90.91 for two years at 12%. These interest rates are for loans made today; therefore, they are spot interest rates.

The cash flows on your transactions are as follows:

	Year 0	Year 1	Year 2
Borrow for 1 year at 10%	+90.91	−100	
Lend for 2 years at 12%	−90.91		+114.04
Net cash flow	0	−100	+114.04

Notice that you do not have any net cash outflow today but you have contracted to pay out money in year 1. The interest rate on this forward commitment is 14.04%. To calculate this forward interest rate, we simply worked out the extra return for lending for two years rather than one:

$$\text{Forward interest rate} = \frac{(1 + 2\text{-year spot rate})^2}{1 + 1\text{-year spot rate}} - 1$$

$$= \frac{(1.12)^2}{1.10} - 1 = .1404, \text{ or } 14.04\%$$

In our example you manufactured a forward loan by borrowing short term and lending long. But you can also run the process in reverse. If you wish to fix today the rate at which you borrow next year, you borrow long and lend the money until you need it next year.

26-5 SWAPS

Some company cash flows are fixed. Others vary with the level of interest rates, rates of exchange, prices of commodities, and so on. These characteristics may not always result in the desired risk profile. For example, a company that pays a fixed rate of interest on its debt might prefer to pay a floating rate, while another company that receives cash flows in euros might prefer to receive them in yen. Swaps allow them to change their risk in these ways.

The market for swaps is huge. In 2008 the total notional amount of swaps outstanding was over ₹370 trillion. By far the major part of this figure consisted of interest rate swaps.[23] We therefore show first how interest rate swaps work, and then describe a currency swap. We conclude with a brief look at total return swaps.

---

[21] The interest rate is usually measured by LIBOR. LIBOR (London interbank offered rate) is the interest rate at which major international banks in London lend each other dollars (or euros, yen, etc.).

[22] These payments would be made when the loan matures nine months from now.

[23] Data on swaps are provided by the International Swaps and Derivatives Association (www.isda.org) and the Bank for International Settlements (www.bis.org).

Interest Rate Swaps

Friendly Bancorp has made a five-year, ₹50 million loan to fund part of the construction cost of a large cogeneration project. The loan carries a fixed interest rate of 8%. Annual interest payments are therefore ₹4 million. Interest payments are made annually, and all the principal will be repaid at year 5.

Suppose that instead of receiving fixed interest payments of ₹4 million a year, the bank would prefer to receive floating-rate payments. It can do so by swapping the ₹4 million, five-year annuity (the fixed interest payments) into a five-year floating-rate annuity. We show first how Friendly Bancorp can make its own homemade swap. Then we describe a simpler procedure.

The bank (we assume) can borrow at a 6% fixed rate for five years.[24] Therefore, the ₹4 million interest it receives can support a fixed-rate loan of $4/.06 = ₹66.67$ million. The bank can now construct the homemade swap as follows: It borrows ₹66.67 million at a fixed interest rate of 6% for five years and simultaneously lends the same amount at MIBOR. We assume that MIBOR is initially 5%.[25] MIBOR is a short-term interest rate, so future interest receipts will fluctuate as the bank's investment is rolled over.

The net cash flows to this strategy are shown in the top portion of Table 26.3. Notice that there is no net cash flow in year 0 and that in year 5 the principal amount of the short-term investment is used to pay off the ₹66.67 million loan. What's left? A cash flow equal to the *difference* between the interest earned (MIBOR × 66.67) and the ₹4 million outlay on the fixed loan. The bank also has ₹4 million per year coming in from the project financing, so it has transformed that fixed payment into a floating payment keyed to MIBOR.

TABLE 26.3 The top panel shows the cash flows in millions of rupees to a homemade fixed-to-floating interest rate swap. The bottom panel shows the cash flows to a standard swap transaction.

	Year					
	0	**1**	**2**	**3**	**4**	**5**
Homemade swap:						
1. Borrow ₹66.67 at 6% fixed rate	+66.67	−4	−4	−4	−4	−(4 + 66.67)
2. Lend ₹66.67 at MIBOR floating rate	−66.67	+.05 × 66.67	+MIBOR$_1$ ×66.67	+MIBOR$_2$ ×66.67	+MIBOR$_3$ ×66.67	+MIBOR$_4$ × 66.67 + 66.67
Net cash flow	0	−4 +.05 × 66.67	−4 +MIBOR$_1$ ×66.67	−4 +MIBOR$_2$ ×66.67	−4 +MIBOR$_3$ ×66.67	−4 +MIBOR$_4$ ×66.67
Standard fixed-to-floating swap:						
Net cash flow	0	−4 +.05 × 66.67	−4 +MIBOR$_1$ ×66.67	−4 +MIBOR$_2$ ×66.67	−4 +MIBOR$_3$ ×66.67	−4 +MIBOR$_4$ ×66.67

Of course, there's an easier way to do this, shown in the bottom portion of Table 26.3. The bank can just enter into a five-year swap.[26] Naturally, Friendly Bancorp takes this easier route. Let's see what happens.

---

[24] The spread between the bank's 6% borrowing rate and the 8% lending rate is the bank's profit on the project financing.

[25] Maybe the short-term interest rate is below the five-year interest rate because investors expect interest rates to rise.

[26] Both strategies are equivalent to a series of forward contracts on MIBOR. The forward prices are ₹4 million each for MIBOR$_1$ × ₹66.67, MIBOR$_2$ × ₹66.67, and so on. Separately negotiated forward prices would not be ₹4 million for any one year, but the PVs of the "annuities" of forward prices would be identical.

Friendly Bancorp calls a swap dealer, which is typically a large commercial or investment bank, and agrees to *swap* the payments on a ₹66.67 million fixed-rate loan for the payments on an equivalent floating-rate loan. The swap is known as a fixed-to-floating interest rate swap and the ₹66.67 million is termed the *notional principal* amount of the swap. Friendly Bancorp and the dealer are the counterparties to the swap.

The dealer is quoting a rate for five-year swaps of 6% against MIBOR.[27] This figure is sometimes quoted as a spread over the yield on U.S. Treasuries. For example, if the yield on five-year Treasury notes is 5.25%, the swap spread is .75%.

The first payment on the swap occurs at the end of year 1 and is based on the starting MIBOR rate of 5%.[28] The dealer (who pays floating) owes the bank 5% of ₹66.67 million, while the bank (which pays fixed) owes the dealer ₹4 million (6% of ₹66.67 million). The bank therefore makes a net payment to the dealer of $4 - (.05 \times 66.67) = ₹.67$ million:

Bank	←	.05 × ₹66.67 = ₹3.33	←	Counterparty
Bank		₹4	→	Counterparty
Bank	→	Net = ₹.67		Counterparty

The second payment is based on MIBOR at year 1. Suppose it increases to 6%. Then the net payment is zero:

Bank	←	.06 × ₹66.67 = ₹4	←	Counterparty
Bank		₹4	→	Counterparty
Bank	→	Net = 0		Counterparty

The third payment depends on MIBOR at year 2, and so on.

Notice that, when the two counterparties entered into the swap, the deal was fairly valued. In other words, the net cash flows had zero present value. What happens to the value of the swap as time passes? That depends on long-term interest rates. For example, suppose that after two years interest rates are unchanged, so a 6% note issued by the bank would continue to trade at its face value. In this case the swap still has zero value. (You can confirm this by checking that the NPV of a new three-year homemade swap is zero.) But if long rates increase over the two years to 7% (say), the value of a three-year note falls to

$$PV = \frac{4}{1.07} + \frac{4}{(1.07)^2} + \frac{4 + 66.67}{(1.07)^3} = ₹64.92 \text{ million}$$

Now the fixed payments that the bank has agreed to make are less valuable and the swap is worth $66.67 - 64.92 = ₹1.75$ million.

How do we know the swap is worth ₹1.75 million? Consider the following strategy:

1. The bank can enter a new three-year swap deal in which it agrees to *pay* MIBOR on the same notional principal of ₹66.67 million.

2. In return it receives fixed payments at the new 7% interest rate, that is, $.07 \times 66.67 = ₹4.67$ per year.

---

[27] Notice that the swap rate always refers to the interest rate on the fixed leg of the swap. Rates are generally quoted against MIBOR, though dealers will also be prepared to quote rates against other short-term debt.

[28] More commonly, interest rate swaps are based on three-month MIBOR and involve quarterly cash payments.

The new swap cancels the cash flows of the old one, but it generates an extra ₹.67 million for three years. This extra cash flow is worth

$$PV = \sum_{t=1}^{3} \frac{.67}{(1.07)^t} = ₹1.75 \text{ million}$$

Remember, ordinary interest rate swaps have no initial cost or value (NPV = 0), but their value drifts away from zero as time passes and long-term interest rates change. One counterparty wins as the other loses.

In our example, the swap dealer loses from the rise in interest rates. Dealers will try to hedge the risk of interest rate movements by engaging in a series of futures or forward contracts or by entering into an offsetting swap with a third party. As long as Friendly Bancorp and the other counterparty honor their promises, the dealer is fully protected against risk. The recurring nightmare for swap managers is that one party will default, leaving the dealer with a large unmatched position. This is another example of counterparty risk.

The market for interest rate swaps is large and liquid. Consequently, financial analysts often look at swap rates when they want to know how interest rates vary with maturity. For example, Figure 26.3 shows swap curves in March 2009 for the Indian rupees, the euro, and the yen. You can see that in each country long-term interest rates are much higher than short-term rates, though the level of swap rates varies from one country to another.

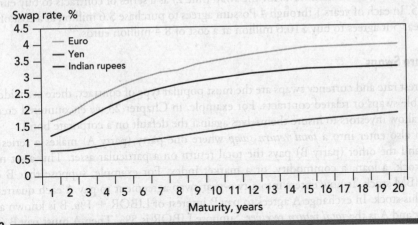

FIGURE 26.3

Swap curves for three currencies, March 2009.

Currency Swaps

We now look briefly at an example of a currency swap.

Suppose that the Possum Company of the United States needs 11 million euros to help finance its European operations. We assume that the euro interest rate is about 5%, whereas the dollar rate is about 6%. Since Possum is better known in the United States, the financial manager decides not to borrow euros directly. Instead, the company issues $10 million of five-year 6% notes in the United States. Then it arranges with a counterparty to swap this dollar loan into euros. Under this arrangement the counterparty agrees to pay Possum sufficient dollars to service its dollar loan, and in exchange Possum agrees to make a series of annual payments in euros to the counterparty.

Here are Possum's cash flows (in millions):

	Year 0		Years 1–4		Year 5	
	Dollars	Euros	Dollars	Euros	Dollars	Euros
1. Issue dollar loan	+10		−.6		−10.6	
2. Swap dollars for euros	−10	+8	+.6	−.4	+10.6	−8.4
3. Net cash flow	0	+8	0	−.4	0	−8.4

Look first at the cash flows in year 0. Possum receives $10 million from its issue of dollar notes, which it then pays over to the swap counterparty. In return the counterparty sends Possum a check for €8 million. (We assume that at current rates of exchange $10 million is worth €8 million.)

Now move to years 1 through 4. Possum needs to pay interest of 6% on its debt issue, which works out at $.06 \times 10 = \$.6$ million. The swap counterparty agrees to provide Possum each year with sufficient cash to pay this interest and in return Possum makes an annual payment to the counterparty of 5% of €8 million, or €.4 million. Finally, in year 5 the swap counterparty pays Possum enough to make the final payment of interest and principal on its dollar notes ($10.6 million), while Possum pays the counterparty €8.4 million.

The combined effect of Possum's two steps (line 3) is to convert a 6% dollar loan into a 5% euro loan. You can think of the cash flows for the swap (line 2) as a series of contracts to buy euros in years 1 through 5. In each of years 1 through 4 Possum agrees to purchase $.6 million at a cost of .4 million euros; in year 5 it agrees to buy $10.6 million at a cost of 8.4 million euros.[29]

Total Return Swaps

While interest rate and currency swaps are the most popular type of contract, there is a wide variety of other possible swaps or related contracts. For example, in Chapter 23 we encountered credit default swaps that allow investors to insure themselves against the default on a corporate bond.

You can also enter into a *total return swap* where one party (party A) makes a series of agreed payments and the other (party B) pays the total return on a particular asset. This asset might be a common stock, a loan, a commodity, or a market index. For example, suppose that B owns $10 million of IBM stock. It now enters into a two-year swap agreement to pay A each quarter the total return on this stock. In exchange A agrees to pay B interest of LIBOR + 1%. B is known as the *total return payer* and A is the *total return receiver*. Suppose LIBOR is 5%. Then A must pay B 6% of $10 million, or about 1.5% a quarter. If IBM stock returns more than this, there will be a net payment from B to A; if the return is less than 1.5%, A must make a net payment to B. Although ownership of the IBM stock does not change hands, the effect of this total return swap is the same as if B had sold the asset to A and bought it back at an agreed future date.

26-6 HOW TO SET UP A HEDGE

To hedge risk the firm buys one asset and sells an equal amount of another asset. Suppose a farmer owns 100 metric tons (MT) of potato and sells 10 potato futures in NCDEX (The unit of trading

---

[29] Usually in a currency swap the two parties make an initial payment to each other (i.e., Possum pays the bank $10 million and receives €8 million). However, this is not necessary and Possum might prefer to buy the €8 million from another bank.

for potato futures in NCDEX is 10 MT). As long as the potato that the farmer owns is identical to the potato that he has promised to deliver, this strategy minimizes risk.

In practice, the potato that the farmer owns and the potato that he sells in the futures market are unlikely to be identical. For example, if he sells potato futures on the NCDEX, he agrees to deliver potatoes with width between 40mm and 75mm, potatoes with a maximum of 2 kg soil in a 51 kg bag, and a maximum of 15 percent damaged potatoes (dull, skin blemishes, black scars, cut, cracked, and green potatoes). If the potatoes he grows are different then the prices of the two potatoes will not exactly move together.

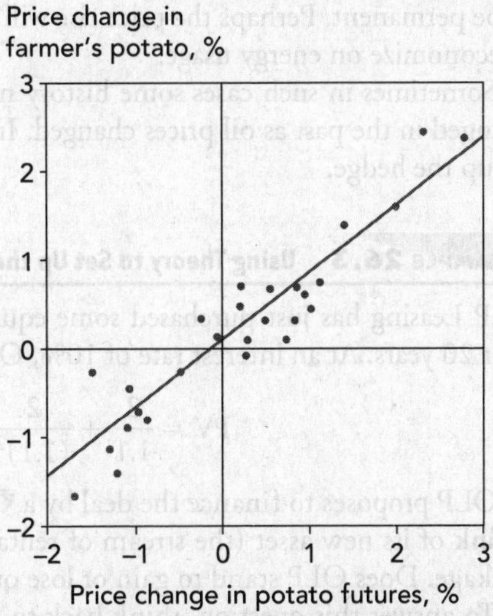

Figure 26.4 shows how changes in the prices of the two types of potatoes may have been related in the past. Notice two things about this figure. First, the scatter of points suggests that the price changes are imperfectly related. If so, it is not possible to construct a hedge that eliminates all risk. Some basis risk will remain. Second, the slope of the fitted line shows that a 1% change in the price of potatoes

FIGURE 26.4

Hypothetical plot of past changes in the price of the farmer's potato against changes in the price of NCDEX-specified potato futures. A 1% change in the futures price implies, on average, an .8% change in the price of the farmer's potato.

specified by NCDEX was on average associated with an .8% change in the price of the farmer's potato. Because the price of the farmer's potato is relatively insensitive to changes in NCDEX-specified potato prices, he needs to sell .8 × 10 = 8 potato futures to minimize risk.

Let us generalize. Suppose that you already own an asset, A (e.g., potato), and that you wish to hedge against changes in the value of A by making an offsetting sale of another asset, B (e.g., potato futures). Suppose also that percentage changes in the value of A are related in the following way to percentage changes in the value of B:

$$\text{Expected change in value of A} = a + \delta \, (\text{change in value of B})$$

Delta (δ) measures the sensitivity of A to changes in the value of B. It is also equal to the *hedge ratio*—that is, the number of units of B that should be sold to hedge the purchase of A. You minimize risk if you offset your position in A by the sale of delta units of B.[30]

The trick in setting up a hedge is to estimate the delta or hedge ratio. This often calls for a strong dose of judgment. For example, suppose that Antarctic Air would like to protect itself against a hike in oil prices. As the financial manager, you need to decide how much a rise in oil prices would affect firm value. Suppose the company spent $200 million on fuel last year. Other things equal, a 10% increase in the price of oil will cost the company an extra .1 × 200 = $20 million. But perhaps you can partially offset the higher costs by higher ticket prices, in which case earnings will fall by *less* than $20 million. Or perhaps an oil price rise will lead to a slowdown in business activity and therefore lower passenger numbers. In that case earnings will decline by *more* than $20 million. Working out the likely effect on firm *value* is even more tricky, because that depends on whether the rise is likely

---

[30] Notice that A, the item that you wish to hedge, is the dependent variable. Delta measures the sensitivity of A to changes in B.

to be permanent. Perhaps the price rise will induce an increase in production or encourage consumers to economize on energy usage.

Sometimes in such cases some history may help. For example, you could look at how firm value changed in the past as oil prices changed. In other cases it may be possible to call on a little theory to set up the hedge.

EXAMPLE 26.3   Using Theory to Set Up the Hedge

OLP Leasing has just purchased some equipment and arranged to rent it out for ₹2 million a year over 20 years. At an interest rate of 10%, OLP's rental income has a present value of ₹17.0 million:[31]

$$PV = \frac{2}{1.1} + \frac{2}{(1.1)^2} + \cdots + \frac{2}{(1.1)^{20}} = 17.0 \text{ million}$$

OLP proposes to finance the deal by a ₹17 million issue of 12-year bonds with a coupon of 10%. Think of its new asset (the stream of rental income) and the new liability (the issue of bonds) as a package. Does OLP stand to gain or lose on this package if interest rates change?

To answer this question, think back to Chapter 3 where we introduced the concept of duration. Duration, you may remember, is the weighted-average time to each cash flow. It is important because it is directly related to volatility. If two assets have the same duration, their prices will be equally affected by a general change in interest rates. If we call the total value of OLP's rental income V, then the duration of the rental income is calculated as follows:

$$Duration = \frac{1}{V}\{[PV(C_1) \times 1] + [PV(C_2) \times 2] + [PV(C_3) \times 3] + \cdots\}$$

$$= \frac{1}{17.0}\left\{\left[\frac{2}{1.10} \times 1\right] + \left[\frac{2}{1.10^2} \times 2\right] + \cdots + \left[\frac{2}{1.10^{20}} \times 20\right]\right\}$$

$$= 7.51 \text{ years}$$

We can also calculate the duration of OLP's bond in the same way. It turns out that it is 7.50 years, which is almost identical to the duration of the rental income. Therefore, the values of both the rental income and the bond are more or less equally affected by a change in interest rates. If rates rise, the present value of Potterton's rental income will decline, but the value of its debt obligation will also decline by the same amount. By equalizing the duration of the asset and that of the liability, Potterton has *immunized* itself against any change in interest rates. It looks as if Potterton's financial manager knows a thing or two about hedging.

The issue of a 12-year bond is not the only way for Potterton to hedge its income stream. For example, the company could issue a package of a 1-year bond and a 20-year bond that together had the same duration as the rental income. Again the values of the asset and the liability would be equally affected by a change in interest rates.

An important feature of these duration hedges is that they are dynamic. As interest rates change and time passes, the duration of Potterton's asset may no longer be the same as that of its liability. Thus to remain hedged against interest rate changes, Potterton must be prepared to keep adjusting the duration of its debt.

---

[31] We ignore taxes in this example.

26-7 IS "DERIVATIVE" A FOUR-LETTER WORD?

A wheat farmer can sell wheat futures to reduce business risk. But if you were to copy the farmer and sell futures without an offsetting holding of wheat, you would increase risk, not reduce it. You would be *speculating.*

Speculators in search of large profits (and prepared to tolerate large losses) are attracted by the leverage that derivatives provide. By this we mean that it is not necessary to lay out much money up front and the profits or losses may be many times the initial outlay. "Speculation" has an ugly ring, but a successful derivatives market needs speculators who are prepared to take on risk and provide more cautious people such as farmers or millers with the protection they need. For example, if an excess of farmers wishes to sell wheat futures, the price of futures will be forced down until enough speculators are tempted to buy in the hope of a profit. If there is a surplus of millers wishing to buy wheat futures, the reverse will happen. The price of wheat futures will be forced *up* until speculators are drawn in to sell.

Speculation may be necessary to a thriving derivatives market, but it can get companies into serious trouble. The nearby Finance in Practice box describes how the German metals and oil trading company, Metallgesellschaft, took a $1 billion bath on its positions in oil futures.[32] Metallgesellschaft had plenty of company. The Japanese company, Showa Shell, reported a loss of $1.5 billion on positions in foreign exchange futures. And in 1995 Baring Brothers, a blue-chip British merchant bank with a 200-year history, became insolvent. The reason: Nick Leeson, a trader in Baring's Singapore office, had placed very large bets on the Japanese stock market index that resulted in losses of $1.4 billion.

These tales of woe have some cautionary messages for corporations. During the 1970s and 1980s many firms turned their treasury operations into profit centers and proudly announced their profits from trading in financial instruments. But it is not possible to make large profits in financial markets without also taking large risks, so these profits should have served as a warning rather than a matter for congratulation.

A Boeing 747 weighs 400 tons, flies at nearly 600 miles per hour, and is inherently very dangerous. But we don't ground 747s; we just take precautions to ensure that they are flown with care. Similarly, it is foolish to suggest that firms should ban the use of derivatives, but it makes obvious sense to take precautions against their misuse. Here are two bits of horse sense:

• *Precaution 1: Don't be taken by surprise.* By this we mean that senior management needs to monitor regularly the value of the firm's derivatives positions and to know what bets the firm has placed. At its simplest, this might involve asking what would happen if interest rates or exchange rates were to change by 1%. But large banks and consultants have also developed sophisticated models for measuring the risk of derivatives positions.

• *Precaution 2: Place bets only when you have some comparative advantage that ensures the odds are in your favor.* If a bank were to announce that it was drilling for oil or launching a new soap powder, you would rightly be suspicious about whether it had what it takes to succeed.

Imprudent speculation in derivatives is undoubtedly an issue of concern for the company's shareholders, but is it a matter for more general concern? Some people believe, like Warren Buffett, that derivatives are "financial weapons of mass destruction." They point to the huge volume of trading in derivatives and argue that speculative losses could lead to major defaults that might threaten the whole financial system. These worries have led to calls for increased regulation of derivatives markets.

[32] The Metallgesellschaft debacle makes fascinating reading. See, for example, F. Edwards, "The Collapse of Metallgesellschaft: Unhedgeable Risks, Poor Hedging Strategy, or Just Bad Luck?" *Journal of Future Markets* 15 (May 1995), pp. 211–264.

Finance In Practice

The Debacle at Metallgesellschaft

In January 1994 the German industrial giant Metallgesellschaft shocked investors with news of huge losses in its U.S. oil subsidiary, MGRM. These losses, later estimated at over $1 billion, brought the firm to the brink of bankruptcy and it was saved only by a $1.9 billion rescue package from 120 banks.

The previous year MGRM had embarked on what looked like a sure-fire way to make money. It offered its customers forward contracts on deliveries of gasoline, heating oil, and diesel fuel for up to 10 years. These price guarantees proved extremely popular. By September 1993, MGRM had sold forward over 150 million barrels of oil at prices that were $3 to $5 a barrel over the prevailing spot prices.

As long as oil prices did not rise appreciably, MGRM stood to make a handsome profit from its forward sales, but if oil prices did return to their level of earlier years the result would be a calamitous loss. MGRM therefore sought to avoid such an outcome by buying energy futures. Unfortunately, the long-term futures contracts that were needed to offset MGRM's price guarantees did not exist. MGRM's solution was to enter into what is known as a "stack-and-roll" hedge. In other words, it bought a stack of short-dated futures contracts and, as these were about to expire, it rolled them over into a fresh stack of short-dated contracts.

MGRM was relaxed about the mismatch between the long-term maturity of its price guarantees and the much shorter maturity of its futures contracts. It could point to past history to justify its confidence, for in most years energy traders have placed a high value on owning the oil rather than having a promise of future delivery. In other words, the net convenience yield on oil has generally been positive. As long as that continued to be the case, then each time that MGRM rolled over its futures contracts, it would be selling its maturing contracts at a higher price than it would need to pay for the stack of new contracts. However, if the net convenience yield were to become negative, the maturing futures contracts would sell for *less* than more distant ones. Unfortunately, this is what occurred in 1993. In that year there was a glut of oil, the storage tanks were full, and nobody was prepared to pay extra to get his hands on oil. The result was that MGRM was forced to pay a premium to roll over each stack of maturing contracts.

The fall in oil prices had another unfortunate consequence for MGRM. Futures contracts are marked to market. This means that the investor settles up the profits and losses on each contract as they arise. Therefore, as oil prices continued to fall in 1993, MGRM incurred losses on its purchases of oil futures. This resulted in huge margin calls.* The offsetting good news was that the fall in oil prices meant that its long-term forward contracts were looking increasingly profitable, but this profit was not money in the bank.

When Metallgesellschaft's board learned of these problems, it fired the chief executive and instructed the company to cease all hedging activities and to start negotiations with customers to cancel the long-term contracts. Almost immediately the fall in oil prices reversed. Within eight months the price had risen about 40%. If only MGRM had been able to hold on, it would have enjoyed a huge cash inflow.

Observers have continued to argue about the Metallgesellschaft debacle. Was the company's belief that the net convenience yield would remain positive a reasonable assumption or a gigantic speculation? How much did the company anticipate its cash needs and could it have financed them by borrowing on the strength of its long-term forward contracts? Did senior management mistake the margin calls for losses and just lose its nerve when it decided to liquidate the company's positions?

---

* In addition to buying futures contracts, MGRM also bought short-term over-the-counter forward contracts and commodity swaps. As these matured, MGRM had to make good the loss on them, even though it did not receive the gains on the price guarantees.

Now, this is not the place for a discussion of regulation, but we should warn you about careless measures of the size of the derivatives markets and the possible losses. In mid- 2008 the notional value of outstanding derivative contracts was about $684 trillion.[33] This is a very large sum, but it tells you *nothing* about the money that was being put at risk. For example, suppose that a bank enters into a $10 million interest rate swap and the other party goes bankrupt the next day. How much has the bank lost? Nothing. It hasn't paid anything up front; the two parties simply promised to pay sums to each other in the future. Now the deal is off.

Suppose that the other party does not go bankrupt until a year after the bank entered into the swap. In the meantime interest rates have moved in the bank's favor, so it should be receiving more money from the swap than it is paying out. When the other side defaults on the deal, the bank loses the difference between the interest that it is due to receive and the interest that it should pay. But it doesn't lose $10 million.[34]

The only meaningful measure of the potential loss from default is the amount that it would cost firms showing a profit to replace their swap positions. This figure is only about 1% of the principal amount of swaps outstanding.

SUMMARY

As a manager, you are paid to take risks, but you are not paid to take just any risks. Some risks are simply bad bets, and others could jeopardize the value of the firm. Hedging risks, when it is practical to do so, can make sense if it reduces the chance of cash shortfalls or financial distress. In some cases, hedging can also make it easier to monitor and motivate operating managers. Relieving managers of risk outside their control helps them concentrate on what can be controlled.

Most businesses insure against possible losses. Insurance companies specialize in assessing risks and can pool risks by holding a diversified portfolio of policies. Insurance works less well when policies are taken up by companies that are most at risk (*adverse selection*) or when the insured company is tempted to skip on maintenance or safety procedures (*moral hazard*).

Firms can also hedge with options and with forward and futures contracts. A forward contract is an advance order to buy or sell an asset. The forward price is fixed today, but payment is not made until the delivery date at the end of the contract. Forward contracts traded on organized futures exchanges are called futures contracts. Futures contracts are standardized and traded in huge volumes. The futures markets allow firms to lock in future prices for dozens of different commodities, securities, and currencies.

---

[32] Bank of International Settlements, *Derivatives Statistics* (www.bis.org/statistics/derstats.htm).

[33] This does not mean that firms don't worry about the possibility of default, and there are a variety of ways that they try to protect themselves. In the case of swaps, firms are reluctant to deal with banks that do not have the highest credit rating.

Instead of buying or selling a standardized futures contract, you may be able to arrange a tailor-made forward contract with a bank. Firms can protect against changes in foreign exchange rates by buying or selling forward currency contracts. Forward rate agreements (FRAs) provide protection against changes in interest rates. You can also construct homemade forward contracts. For example, if you borrow for two years and at the same time lend for one year, you have effectively taken out a forward loan.

Firms also hedge with swap contracts. For example, a firm can make a deal to pay interest to a bank at a fixed long-term rate and receive interest from the bank at a floating short-term rate. The firm swaps a fixed for a floating rate. Such a swap could make sense if the firm has relatively easy access to short-term borrowing but dislikes the exposure to fluctuating short-term interest rates.

The theory of hedging is straightforward. You find two closely related assets. You then buy one and sell the other in proportions that minimize the risk of your net position. If the assets are *perfectly* correlated, you can make the net position risk-free. If they are less than perfectly correlated, you will have to absorb some basis risk.

The trick is to find the hedge ratio or delta—that is, the number of units of one asset that is needed to offset changes in the value of the other asset. Sometimes the best solution is to look at how the prices of the two assets have moved together in the past. For example, suppose you observe that a 1% change in the value of B has been accompanied on average by a 2% change in the value of A. Then delta equals 2.0; to hedge each dollar invested in A, you need to sell two dollars of B.

On other occasions theory can help to set up the hedge. For example, the effect of a change in interest rates on an asset's value depends on the asset's duration. If two assets have the same duration, they will be equally affected by fluctuations in interest rates.

Many of the hedges described in this chapter are static. Once you have set up the hedge, you can take a long vacation, confident that the firm is well protected. However, some hedges, such as those that match durations, are dynamic. As time passes and prices change, you need to rebalance your position to maintain the hedge.

Hedging and risk reduction sound as wholesome as mom's apple pie. But remember that hedging solely to reduce risk, with no other business purpose, cannot add value. It is a zero-sum game: risks aren't eliminated, just shifted to some counterparty. And remember that your shareholders can also hedge by adjusting the composition of their portfolios or by trading in futures or other derivatives. Investors won't reward the firm for doing something that they can do perfectly well for themselves.

Some companies have decided that speculation is much more fun than hedging. This view can lead to serious trouble. We do not believe that speculation makes sense for an industrial company, but we caution against the view that derivatives are a threat to the financial system.

FURTHER READING

Three general articles on corporate risk management are:

K. A. Froot, D. Scharfstein, and J. C. Stein, "A Framework for Risk Management," *Harvard Business Review* 72 (November–December 1994), pp. 59–71.

B. W. Nocco and R. M. Stulz, "Enterprise Risk Management: Theory and Practice," *Journal of Applied Corporate Finance* 18 (Fall 2006), pp. 8–20.

C. H. Smithson and B. Simkins, "Does Risk Management Add Value? A Survey of the Evidence," *Journal of Applied Corporate Finance* 17 (Summer 2005), pp. 8–17.

The Summer 2005 and Fall 2006 issues of the Journal of Applied Corporate Finance *are devoted to risk management, and current news and developments are discussed in* Risk *magazine. You may also wish to refer to the following texts:*

J. C. Hull, *Options, Futures, and other Derivatives,* 7th ed. (Englewood Cliffs, NJ: Prentice Hall, 2008).

C. H. Smithson, *Managing Financial Risk,* 3rd ed. (New York: McGraw-Hill, 1998).

R. M. Stulz, *Risk Management and Derivatives* (Cincinnati, OH: Thomson-Southwestern Publishing, 2003).

Schaefer's paper is a useful review of how duration measures are used to immunize fixed liabilities:

S. M. Schaefer, "Immunisation and Duration: A Review of Theory, Performance and Applications," *Midland Corporate Finance Journal* 3 (Autumn 1984), pp. 41–58.

PROBLEM SETS

BASIC

1. Vocabulary check. Define the following terms:
   a. Spot price
   b. Forward vs. futures contract
   c. Long vs. short position
   d. Basis risk
   e. Mark to market
   f. Net convenience yield

2. True or false?
   a. Hedging transactions in an active futures market have zero or slightly negative NPVs.
   b. When you buy a futures contract, you pay now for delivery at a future date.
   c. The holder of a financial futures contract misses out on any dividend or interest payments made on the underlying security.
   d. The holder of a commodities futures contract does not have to pay for storage costs, but foregoes convenience yield.

3. Yesterday you sold six-month futures contract on the Nifty index at a price of ₹5,250. Today the Nifty closed at 5,255 and Nifty futures closed at 5,260. You get a call from your broker, who reminds you that your futures position is marked to market each day. Is she asking you to pay money, or is she about to offer to pay you?

4. Calculate the value of a six-month futures contract on a G-Sec. You have the following information:
   • Six-month interest rate: 10% per year, or 4.9% for six months.
   • Spot price of bond: 95.
   • The bond pays an 8% coupon, 4% every six months.

5. "The farmer does not avoid risk by selling wheat futures. If spot wheat prices stay about ₹1021 per quintal (100 kg), then it will actually have lost by selling wheat futures at ₹1,000 per quintal." Is this a fair comment?

6. Calculate convenience yield for magnoosium scrap from the following information:
   • Spot price: ₹116 per kg.
   • Futures price: ₹110 for a six month contract.
   • Interest rate: 6%.
   • Storage costs: ₹1 per year.

7. Residents of the northeastern United States suffered record-setting low temperatures throughout November and December 2021. Spot prices of heating oil rose 25%, to over $2 a gallon.
   a. What effect did this have on the net convenience yield and on the relationship between futures and spot prices?
   b. In late 2022 refiners and distributors were surprised by record-setting *high* temperatures. What was the effect on net convenience yield and spot and futures prices for heating oil?

8. After a record harvest, grain silos are full to the brim. Are storage costs likely to be high or low? What does this imply for the *net* convenience yield?

9. A year ago a bank entered into a $50 million five-year interest rate swap. It agreed to pay company A each year a fixed rate of 6% and to receive in return MIBOR. When the bank entered into this swap, MIBOR was 5%, but now interest rates have risen, so on a four-year interest rate swap the bank could expect to pay 6½% and receive MIBOR.
    a. Is the swap showing a profit or loss to the bank?
    b. Suppose that at this point company A approaches the bank and asks to terminate the swap. If there are four annual payments still remaining, how much should the bank charge A to terminate?

10. What is basis risk? In which of the following cases would you expect basis risk to be most serious?
    a. A broker owning a large block of Tata Motors common stock hedges by selling index futures.
    b. A Kerala farmer hedges the selling price of her crop by selling MCX Basmati rice futures.
    c. An importer must pay 900 million euros in six months. He hedges by buying euros forward.

11. You own a ₹1 million portfolio of software stocks with a beta of 1.2. You are very enthusiastic about IT but uncertain about the prospects for the overall stock market. Explain how you could hedge out your market exposure by selling the market short. How much would you sell? How in practice would you go about "selling the market"?

12. a. Marshall Arts has just invested ₹1 million in long-term Government securities. Marshall is concerned about increasing volatility in interest rates. He decides to hedge using bond futures contracts. Should he buy or sell such contracts?
    b. The treasurer of Zeta Corporation plans to issue bonds in three months. She is also concerned about interest rate volatility and wants to lock in the price at which her company could sell 5% coupon bonds. How would she use bond futures contracts to hedge?

INTERMEDIATE

13. Large businesses spend millions of dollars annually on insurance. Why? Should they insure against all risks or does insurance make more sense for some risks than others?

14. On some catastrophe bonds, payments are reduced if the claims against the issuer exceed a specified sum. In other cases payments are reduced only if claims against the entire industry exceed some sum. What are the advantages and disadvantages of the two structures? Which involves more basis risk? Which may create a problem of moral hazard?

15. List some of the commodity futures contracts that are traded on exchanges. Who do you think could usefully reduce risk by buying each of these contracts? Who do you think might wish to sell each contract?

16. Bata Motors wants to lock in the cost of 2,000 kg of aluminum to be used in next quarter's production of Mindica cars. It buys three-month futures contracts for 2,000 kg of aluminum at a price of ₹115 per kg.
    a. Suppose the spot price of platinum falls to ₹110 in three months' time. Does Bata have a profit or loss on the futures contract? Has it locked in the cost of purchasing the aluminum it needs?
    b. How do your answers change if the spot price of aluminum increases to ₹150 per kg after three months?

17. In March 2009, nine-month futures on the Brazilian Ibovespa stock index traded at 44,439. Spot was 41,908. The interest rate was 11.25% and the dividend yield was about 3%. Were the futures fairly priced?

18. If you buy a nine-month T-bill future, you undertake to buy a three-month bill in nine months' time. Suppose that Treasury bills and notes currently offer the following yields:

Months to Maturity	Annual Yield
3	6%
6	6.5
9	7
12	8

What is the value of a nine-month bill future?

19. Table 26.4 contains spot and six-month futures prices for several commodities and financial instruments. There may be some money-making opportunities. See if you can find them, and explain how you would trade to take advantage of them. The interest rate is 14.5%, or 7% over the six-month life of the contracts.

TABLE 26.4 Spot and six-month futures prices for selected commodities and securities. See Problem 19.

Commodity	Spot Price	Futures Price	Comments
Magnoosium	$2,550 per ton	$2,728.50 per ton	Monthly storage cost = monthly convenience yield
Frozen quiche	$.50 per pound	$.514 per pound	Six months' storage costs = $.10 per pound; six months' convenience yield = $.05 per pound.
Nevada Hydro 8s of 2002	77	78.39	4% semiannual coupon payment is due just before futures contract expires.
Costaguanan pulgas (currency)	9,300 pulgas = $1	6,900 pulgas = $1	Costaguanan interest rate is 95% per year.
Establishment Industries common stock	$95	$97.54	Establishment pays dividends of $2 per quarter. Next dividend is paid two months from now.
Cheap white wine	$12,500 per 10,000-gal. tank	$14,200 per 10,000-gal. tank	Six months' convenience yield = $250 per tank. Your company has surplus storage and can store 50,000 gallons at no cost.

20. The following table shows 2009 gold futures prices for varying contract lengths. Gold is predominantly an investment good, not an industrial commodity. Investors hold gold because it diversifies their portfolios and because they hope its price will rise. They do not hold it for its convenience yield.

   Calculate the interest rate faced by traders in gold futures for each of the contract lengths shown below. The spot price is $915.50 per ounce.

	Contract Length (months)		
	3	**6**	**9**
Futures price	$917.90	$920.85	$923.30

21. In September 2014 swap dealers were quoting a rate for five-year euro interest-rate swaps of 4.5% against Euribor (the short-term interest rate for euro loans). Euribor at the time was 4.1%. Suppose that A arranges with a dealer to swap a €10 million five-year fixed-rate loan for an equivalent floating-rate loan in euros.

   a. What is the value of this swap at the time that it is entered into?

   b. Suppose that immediately after A has entered into the swap, the long-term interest rate rises by 1%. Who gains and who loses?

   c. What is now the value of the swap?

22. Securities A, B, and C have the following cash flows:

	Period 1	Period 2	Period 3
A	₹ 40	₹40	₹ 40
B	₹120	—	—
C	₹ 10	₹10	₹110

   a. Calculate their durations if the interest rate is 8%.

   b. Suppose that you have an investment of ₹10 million in A. What combination of B and C would immunize this investment against interest rate changes?

   c. Now suppose that you have a ₹10 million investment in B. How would you immunize?

23. What is meant by "delta" (δ) in the context of hedging? Give examples of how delta can be estimated or calculated.

24. A gold-mining firm is concerned about short-term volatility in its revenues. Gold currently sells for ₹27,500 per 10 gm, but the price is extremely volatile and could fall as low as ₹16,000 or rise as high as ₹41,000 in the next month. The company will bring 10,000 kg of gold to the market next month.

   a. What will be total revenues if the firm remains unhedged for gold prices of ₹22,000, ₹28,000, and ₹30,000 per 10 gm?

   b. The futures price of gold for delivery one month ahead is ₹28,000. What will be the firm's total revenues at each gold price if the firm enters into a one-month futures contract to deliver 10,000 kg of gold?

   c. What will total revenues be if the firm buys a one-month put option to sell gold for ₹27,500 per 10 gm? The put option costs ₹400 per 10 gm.

25. Legs Diamond owns shares in a Vanguard Index 500 mutual fund worth $1 million on July 15. (This is an index fund that tracks the Standard and Poor's 500 Index.) He wants to cash in now, but his accountant advises him to wait six months so as to defer a large capital gains tax. Explain to Legs how he can use stock index futures to hedge out his exposure to market movements over the next six months. Could Legs "cash in" without actually selling his shares?

26. Price changes of two gold-mining stocks have shown strong positive correlation. Their historical relationship is

$$\text{Average percentage change in A} = .001 + .75 \text{ (percentage change in B)}$$

Changes in B explain 60% of the variation of the changes in A ($R^2 = .6$).

   a. Suppose you own ₹100,000 of A. How much of B should you sell to minimize the risk of your net position?

   b. What is the hedge ratio?

   c. Here is the historical relationship between stock A and gold prices.

$$\text{Average percentage change in A} = -.002 + 1.2 \text{ (percentage change in gold price)}$$

If $R^2 = .5$, can you lower the risk of your net position by hedging with gold (or gold futures) rather than with stock B? Explain.

27. In Section 26-6, we stated that the duration of OLP's lease equals the duration of its debt.
    a. Show that this is so.
    b. Now suppose that the interest rate falls to 3%. Show how the value of the lease and the debt are now affected by a .5% rise or fall in the interest rate. What would OLP need to do to reestablish the interest rate hedge?

28. Petrochemical Parfum (PP) is concerned about a possible increase in the price of heavy fuel oil, which is one of its major inputs. Show how PP can use either options or futures contracts to protect itself against a rise in the price of crude oil. Show how the payoffs in each case would vary if the oil price were $70, $80, or $90 a barrel. What are the advantages and disadvantages for PP of using futures rather than options to reduce risk?

29. Consider the commodities and financial assets listed in Table 26.5. The risk-free interest rate is 6% a year, and the term structure is flat.
    a. Calculate the six-month futures price for each case.
    b. Explain how a magnoosium producer would use a futures market to lock in the selling price of a planned shipment of 1,000 tons of magnoosium six months from now.
    c. Suppose the producer takes the actions recommended in your answer to (b), but after one month magnoosium prices have fallen to $2,200. What happens? Will the producer have to undertake additional futures market trades to restore its hedged position?
    d. Does the biotech index futures price provide useful information about the expected future performance of biotech stocks?
    e. Suppose Allen Wrench stock falls suddenly by $10 per share. Investors are confident that the cash dividend will not be reduced. What happens to the futures price?
    f. Suppose interest rates suddenly fall to 4%. The term structure remains flat. What happens to the six-month futures price on the five-year Treasury note? What happens to a trader who shorted 100 notes at the futures price calculated in part (a)?
    g. An importer must make a payment of one million ruples three months from now. Explain *two* strategies the importer could use to hedge against unfavorable shifts in the ruple–dollar exchange rate.

TABLE 26.5 Spot prices for selected commodities and financial assets. See Problem 29.

Asset	Spot Price	Comments
Magnoosium	$2,800 per ton	Net convenience yield = 4% per year
Oat bran	$.44 per bushel	Net convenience yield = .5% per month
Biotech stock index	140.2	Dividend = 0
Allen Wrench Co. common stock	$58.00	Cash dividend = $2.4 per year
5-year Treasury note	108.93	8% coupon
Westonian ruple	3.1 ruples = $1	12% interest rate in ruples

30. Is a total return swap on a bond the same as a credit default swap (see Section 23-1)? Why or why not?

31. "Speculators want futures contracts to be incorrectly priced; hedgers want them to be correctly priced." Why?

32. Your investment bank has an investment of $100 million in the stock of the Swiss Roll Corporation and a short position in the stock of the Frankfurter Sausage Company. Here is the recent price history of the two stocks:

Percentage Price Change		
Month	Frankfurter Sausage	Swiss Roll
January	−10	−10
February	−10	−5
March	−10	0
April	+10	0
May	+10	+5
June	+10	+10

On the evidence of these six months, how large would your short position in Frankfurter Sausage need to be to hedge you as far as possible against movements in the price of Swiss Roll?

CHALLENGE

33. Phillip's Screwdriver Company has borrowed $20 million from a bank at a floating interest rate of 2 percentage points above three-month Treasury bills, which now yield 5%. Assume that interest payments are made quarterly and that the entire principal of the loan is repaid after five years.

Phillip's wants to convert the bank loan to fixed-rate debt. It could have issued a fixed-rate five-year note at a yield to maturity of 9%. Such a note would now trade at par. The five-year Treasury note's yield to maturity is 7%.

a. Is Phillip's stupid to want long-term debt at an interest rate of 9%? It is borrowing from the bank at 7%.

b. Explain how the conversion could be carried out by an interest rate swap. What will be the initial terms of the swap? (Ignore transaction costs and the swap dealer's profit.)

One year from now short and medium-term Treasury yields *decrease* to 6%, so the term structure then is flat. (The changes actually occur in month 5.) Phillip's credit standing is unchanged; it can still borrow at 2 percentage points over Treasury rates.

c. What net swap payment will Phillip's make or receive?

d. Suppose that Phillip's now wants to cancel the swap. How much would it need to pay the swap dealer? Or would the dealer pay Phillip's? Explain.

34. Har-Jeet Securities owns shares in UTI's Sensex fund worth ₹10 millions on September 15 (This is an index that tracks the BSE Sensitivity Index). It wants to cash in now, but his accountant advises him to wait six months so as to defer a large capital gains tax. Explain to Har-Jeet how he can use stock index futures to hedge out his exposure to market movements over the next six months. Could Har-Jeet 'cash in' without actually selling his shares?

REAL-TIME DATA ANALYSIS

1. The Web sites of the major commodities exchanges provide futures prices. Calculate and plot (as in Figure 26.2) the *annualized* net convenience yield for a commodity of your choice. (*Note:* You may need to use the futures price of a contract that is about to mature as your estimate of the current spot price.)

2. You can find swap rates for the U.S. dollar and the euro on www.ft.com. Plot the current swap curves as in Figure 26.3.

3. You can find spot and futures prices for a variety of equity indexes on www.nseindia.com. Pick one and check whether it is fairly priced. You will need to do some detective work to find the dividend yield on the index and the interest rate.

27

CHAPTER

MANAGING INTERNATIONAL RISKS

The last chapter grappled with risks from changing interest rates and volatile commodity prices. Corporations that operate internationally face still more hazards from currency fluctuations and political risks.

To understand currency risk, you first have to understand how the foreign exchange market works and how currency exchange rates are determined. We cover those topics first, with special emphasis on the linkages between exchange rates and cross-country differences in interest rates and inflation. Then we describe how corporations assess and hedge their currency exposures.

We also review international capital investment decisions. Cash flows for an investment project in Germany, say, must be forecasted in euros, with attention to German inflation rates and taxes. But euro cash flows require a euro discount rate. How should that rate be estimated? Should it depend on whether the investing company is located in the U.S., Germany, or another country? Should the discount rate be adjusted for the risk that the euro may fall relative to other currencies? (The answer to the last question is no. The answers to the preceding questions are not so clear-cut.)

We conclude the chapter with a discussion of political risk. Political risk means possible adverse acts by a hostile foreign government, for example, discriminatory taxes or limits on the profits that can be taken out of the country. Sometimes governments expropriate businesses with minimal compensation. We explain how companies structure their operations and financing to reduce their exposure to political risks.

27-1 THE FOREIGN EXCHANGE MARKET

An Indian company that imports goods from the U.S. may need to buy dollars to pay for the purchase. An Indian company exporting to the U.S. may receive dollars, which it sells in exchange for rupees. Both firms make use of the foreign exchange market.

The foreign exchange market has no central marketplace. Business is conducted electronically. The principal dealers are the larger commercial banks and investment banks. A corporation that wants to buy or sell currency usually does so through a commercial bank. Turnover in the foreign exchange market is huge. In London in 2007 $1,359 billion of currency changed hands each day. That is equivalent to an annual turnover of about $340 trillion ($340,000,000,000,000). New York and Tokyo together accounted for a further $400 billion of turnover per day.[1] The total turnover in India in 2007 was $32 billion per day. This is equivalent to an annual turnover of $11,680 billion per annum.[2]

Table 27.1 is adapted from the table of exchange rates in the *Business Line*. Exchange rates are generally expressed in terms of Indian rupees needed to buy one unit of foreign currency. This is named a *direct quote*. In the first column of Table 27.1, the direct quote for the Euro shows you can buy 1 Euro (€) for ₹65.91. This is often written as ₹65.91/€.

TABLE 27.1   Spot and Forward Exchange rates, January 13, 2012

	Spot Rate*	Forward Rate		
		1 Month	3 Months	6 Months
US Dollar	51.51	51.92	52.53	53.27
Euro	65.91	66.42	67.2	68.16
Pound Sterling	78.96	79.57	80.48	81.56
Japanese Yen**	67.12	67.68	68.49	69.51
Singapore Dollar	39.97	40.3	40.77	41.36
Hong Kong Dollar	6.63	6.68	6.76	6.86
Canadian Dollar	50.62	51.03	51.59	52.25
Chinese Yuan	8.16	—	—	—
Arab Emirates Dirham	14.02	—	—	—

* Rates show number of Indian rupees per unit of foreign currency, except for Yen, which show the number of Indian rupees per 100 Japanese Yen. Rates mentioned above are the averages of bid and ask rates.

Source: Business Line, January 14, 2012

An *indirect* exchange quote states the number of units of foreign currency needed to buy one Indian rupee. In the U.S., currency rates are usually quoted as indirect quotes. For example, Table 27.1 shows that 1$ is equivalent to ₹51.51 or, more concisely, ₹51.51/$. It can also be stated as an indirect quote: $0.0194/₹.

The exchange rates in the first column of Table 27.1 are the prices of currency for immediate delivery. They are known as **spot rates of exchange**. The spot rate for Singapore dollar is ₹39.97/SG$, and the spot rate for Japanese Yen is ₹67.12/100Yen.

In addition to the spot exchange market, there is a *forward market*. In the forward market you buy and sell currency for future delivery. If you know that you are going to pay out or receive foreign

---

[1]The results of the triennial survey of foreign exchange business are published on **www.bis.org/forum/research.htm**.

[2] *Source:* www.rbi.org.in

currency at some future date, you can insure yourself against loss by buying or selling forward. Thus, if you need one million U.S. dollars in three months, you can enter into a three-month *forward contract*. The **forward rate** on this contract is the price you agree to pay in three months when the one million U.S. dollars are delivered. If you look again at Table 27.1, you will see that the three-month forward rate for the U.S. dollar is quoted at ₹52.53/$. If you buy U.S. dollars for three months' delivery, you get fewer U.S. dollar for your rupee than if you buy them spot. In this case the dollar is said to trade at a forward *premium* relative to the rupee, because forward rates are expensive than spot ones. Expressed as an annual rate, the forward premium is[3]

$$4 \times \left(\frac{52.53}{51.51} - 1 \right) = +0.0792, \text{ or } +7.92\%$$

You could also say that the *rupee* was selling at a *forward discount*.

A forward purchase or sale is a made-to-measure transaction between you and the bank. It can be for any currency, any amount, and any delivery day. You could buy, say, 99,999 Vietnamese dong or Haitian gourdes for a year and a day forward as long as you can find a bank ready to deal. Most forward transactions are for six months or less, but the long-term currency swaps that we described in Chapter 26 are equivalent to a bundle of forward transactions. When firms want to enter into long-term forward contracts, they usually do so through a currency swap.[4]

There is also an organized market for currency for future delivery known as the currency *futures* market. Futures contracts are highly standardized; they are for specified amounts and for a limited choice of delivery dates.[5]

When you buy a forward or futures contract, you are committed to taking delivery of the currency. As an alternative, you can take out an *option* to buy or sell currency in the future at a price that is fixed today. Made-to-measure currency options can be bought from the major banks, and standardized options are traded on the options exchanges.

27-2 SOME BASIC RELATIONSHIPS

You can't develop a consistent international financial policy until you understand the reasons for the differences in exchange rates and interest rates. We consider the following four problems:

- *Problem 1.* Why is the dollar rate of interest ($r_\$$) different from, say, the peso rate (r_{peso})?
- *Problem 2.* Why is the forward rate of exchange ($f_{peso/\$}$) different from the spot rate ($s_{peso/\$}$)?
- *Problem 3.* What determines next year's expected spot rate of exchange between dollars and pesos [$E(s_{peso/\$})$]?
- *Problem 4.* What is the relationship between the inflation rate in the United States ($i_\$$) and the inflation rate in Mexico (i_{peso})?

---

[3] Here is an occasional point of confusion. Since the quote is a direct quote, we calculate the premium by taking the ratio of the forward rate to the spot rate. If it is a *direct* quote, then we need to calculate the ratio of the spot rate to the forward rate. In the case of the U.S. dollar, the forward premium with direct quotes is $4 \times [(1/51.51)/(1/52.53) - 1] = +0.0792$, or +7.92%.

[4] Notice that spot and short-term forward trades are sometimes undertaken together. For example, a company might need the use of Mexican pesos for one month. In this case it would buy pesos spot and simultaneously sell them forward. Dealers refer to this as a *swap* trade. But do not confuse it with the longer term currency swaps that we described in Chapter 26.

[5] See Chapter 26 for a further discussion of the difference between forward and futures contracts.

Suppose that individuals were not worried about risk and that there were no barriers or costs to international trade on capital flows. In that case the spot exchange rates, forward exchange rates, interest rates, and inflation rates would stand in the following simple relationship to one another:

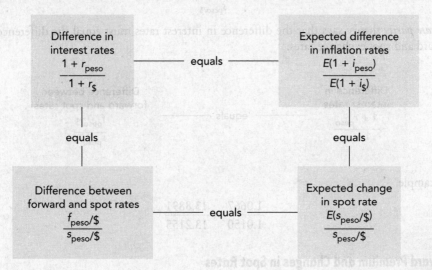

Why should this be so?

Interest Rates and Exchange Rates

It is July 2009 and you have $1 million to invest for one year. U.S. dollar deposits are offering an interest rate of about 1.50%; Mexican peso deposits are offering an (attractive?) 6.67%. Where should you put your money? Does the answer sound obvious? Let's check:

- *Dollar loan.* The rate of interest on one-year dollar deposits is 1.50%. Therefore at the end of the year you get $1,000,000 \times 1.0150 = \$1,015,000$.
- *Peso loan.* The current exchange rate is 13.2155/$. For $1 million, you can buy $1,000,000 \times 13.2155 = $ peso 13,215,500. The rate of interest on a one-year peso deposit is 6.67%. Therefore at the end of the year you get $13,215,500 \times 1.0667 = $ peso 14,096,974. Of course, you don't know what the exchange rate is going to be in one year's time. But that doesn't matter. You can fix today the price at which you sell your pesos. The one-year forward rate is peso 13.8891/$. Therefore, by selling forward, you can make sure that you will receive $14,096,974/13.8891 = \$1,014,967$ at the end of the year.

Thus, the two investments offer almost exactly the same rate of return. They have to—they are both risk-free. If the domestic interest rate were different from the *covered* foreign rate, you would have a money machine.

When you make the peso loan, you receive a higher interest rate. But you get an offsetting loss because you sell pesos forward at a lower price than you pay for them today. The interest rate differential is

$$\frac{1 + r_{peso}}{1 + r_\$}$$

And the differential between the forward and spot exchange rates is

$$\frac{f_{peso/\$}}{s_{peso/\$}}$$

Interest rate parity theory says that the difference in interest rates must equal the difference between the forward and spot exchange rates:

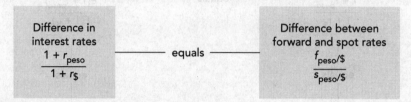

$$\begin{array}{ccc}
\boxed{\begin{array}{c}\text{Difference in} \\ \text{interest rates} \\ \dfrac{1 + r_{peso}}{1 + r_{\$}}\end{array}} & \text{equals} & \boxed{\begin{array}{c}\text{Difference between} \\ \text{forward and spot rates} \\ \dfrac{f_{peso/\$}}{s_{peso/\$}}\end{array}}
\end{array}$$

In our example,

$$\frac{1.0667}{1.0150} \approx \frac{13.8891}{13.2155}$$

The Forward Premium and Changes in Spot Rates

Now let's consider how the forward premium is related to changes in spot rates of exchange. If people didn't care about risk, the forward rate of exchange would depend solely on what people expected the spot rate to be. For example, if the one-year forward rate on pesos is peso 13.8891/$, that could only be because traders expect the spot rate in one year's time to be peso 13.8891/$. If they expected it to be, say, peso 14.0/$, nobody would be willing to buy pesos forward. They could get more pesos for their dollar by waiting and buying spot.

Therefore the *expectations theory* of exchange rates tells us that the percentage difference between the forward rate and today's spot rate is equal to the expected change in the spot rate:

$$\begin{array}{ccc}
\boxed{\begin{array}{c}\text{Difference between} \\ \text{forward and spot rates} \\ \dfrac{f_{peso/\$}}{s_{peso/\$}}\end{array}} & \text{equals} & \boxed{\begin{array}{c}\text{Expected change} \\ \text{in spot rate} \\ \dfrac{E(s_{peso/\$})}{s_{peso/\$}}\end{array}}
\end{array}$$

Of course, this assumes that traders don't care about risk. If they do care, the forward rate can be either higher or lower than the expected spot rate. For example, suppose that you have contracted to receive one million pesos in three months. You can wait until you receive the money before you change it into dollars, but this leaves you open to the risk that the price of the peso may fall over the next three months. Your alternative is to sell the peso forward. In this case, you are fixing today the price at which you will sell your pesos. Since you avoid risk by selling forward, you may be willing to do so even if the forward price of pesos is a little *lower* than the expected spot price.

Other companies may be in the opposite position. They may have contracted to pay out pesos in three months. They can wait until the end of the three months and then buy pesos, but this leaves them open to the risk that the price of the peso may rise. It is safer for these companies to fix the price today by *buying* pesos forward. These companies may, therefore, be willing to buy forward even if the forward price of the peso is a little *higher* than the expected spot price.

Thus some companies find it safer to *sell* the peso forward, while others find it safer to *buy* the peso forward. When the first group predominates, the forward price of pesos is likely to be less than the expected spot price. When the second group predominates, the forward price is likely to be greater than the expected spot price. On average you would expect the forward price to underestimate the expected spot price just about as often as it overestimates it.

Changes in the Exchange Rate and Inflation Rates

Now we come to the third side of our quadrilateral—the relationship between changes in the spot exchange rate and inflation rates. Suppose that you notice that silver can be bought in Mexico for 120 pesos a troy ounce and sold in the United States for $15.00. You think you may be on to a good thing. You take $9,080 and exchange it for $9,080 × peso 13.2155/$ = peso 120,000. That's enough to buy 1,000 ounces of silver. You put this silver on the first plane to the United States, where you sell it for $15,000. You have made a gross profit of just under $6,000. Of course, you have to pay transportation and insurance costs out of this, but there should still be something left over for you.

Money machines don't exist—not for long, anyway. As others notice the disparity between the price of silver in Mexico and the price in the United States, the price will be forced up in Mexico and down in the United States until the profit opportunity disappears. Arbitrage ensures that the dollar price of silver is about the same in the two countries. Of course, silver is a standard and easily transportable commodity, but the same forces should act to equalize the domestic and foreign prices of other goods. Those goods that can be bought more cheaply abroad will be imported, and that will force down the price of domestic products. Similarly, those goods that can be bought more cheaply in the United States will be exported, and that will force down the price of the foreign products.

This is often called *purchasing power parity*.[6] Just as the price of goods in Safeway supermarkets must be roughly the same as the price of goods in A&P, so the price of goods in Mexico when converted into dollars must be roughly the same as the price in the United States:

$$\text{Dollar price of goods in the USA} = \frac{\text{peso price of goods in Mexico}}{\text{number of pesos per dollar}}$$

Purchasing power parity implies that any differences in the rates of inflation will be offset by a change in the exchange rate. For example, if prices are rising by 1.0% in the United States and by 6.0% in Mexico, the number of pesos that you can buy for $1 must rise by 1.06/1.01 − 1, or about 5.0%. Therefore purchasing power parity says that to estimate changes in the spot rate of exchange, you need to estimate differences in inflation rates:[7]

$$\underbrace{\frac{E(1 + i_{peso})}{E(1 + i_{\$})}}_{\substack{\text{Expected difference} \\ \text{in inflation rates}}} \quad \text{equals} \quad \underbrace{\frac{E(s_{peso/\$})}{s_{peso/\$}}}_{\substack{\text{Expected change} \\ \text{in spot rate}}}$$

---

[6] Economists use the term *purchasing power parity* to refer to the notion that the level of prices of goods in general must be the same in the two countries. They tend to use the phrase *law of one price* when they are talking about the price of a single good.

[7] In other words, the *expected* difference in inflation rates equals the *expected* change in the exchange rate. Strictly interpreted, purchasing power parity also implies that the *actual* difference in the inflation rates always equals the *actual* change in the exchange rate.

In our example,

$$\text{Current spot rate} \times \text{expected difference in inflation rates} = \text{expected spot rate}$$

$$13.2155 \times \frac{1.060}{1.010} = 13.87$$

Interest Rates and Inflation Rates

Now for the fourth leg! Just as water always flows downhill, so capital tends to flow where returns are greatest. But investors are not interested in *nominal* returns; they care about what their money will buy. So, if investors notice that real interest rates are higher in Mexico than in the United States, they will shift their savings into Mexico until the expected real returns are the same in the two countries. If the expected real interest rates are equal, then the difference in money rates must be equal to the difference in the expected inflation rates:[8]

$$
\begin{array}{ccc}
\begin{array}{c}\text{Difference in} \\ \text{interest rates} \\ \dfrac{1 + r_{peso}}{1 + r_{\$}}\end{array}
& \text{equals} &
\begin{array}{c}\text{Expected difference} \\ \text{in inflation rates} \\ \dfrac{E(1 + i_{peso})}{E(1 + i_{\$})}\end{array}
\end{array}
$$

In Mexico the real one-year interest rate is .6%:

$$r_{peso}(\text{real}) = \frac{1 + r_{peso}}{E(1 + i_{peso})} - 1 = \frac{1.0667}{1.060} - 1 = .006$$

In the United States it is close at .5%:

$$r_{\$}(\text{real}) = \frac{1 + r_{\$}}{E(1 + i_{\$})} - 1 = \frac{1.015}{1.010} - 1 = .005$$

Is Life Really That Simple?

We have described above four theories that link interest rates, forward rates, spot exchange rates, and inflation rates. Of course, such simple economic theories are not going to provide an exact description of reality. We need to know how well they predict actual behavior. Let's check.

1. Interest Rate Parity Theory   Interest rate parity theory says that the peso rate of interest covered for exchange risk should be the same as the dollar rate. As long as money can be moved easily between deposits in different currencies, interest rate parity almost always holds. In fact, dealers *set* the forward price of pesos by looking at the difference between the interest rates on deposits of dollars and pesos.

2. The Expectations Theory of Forward Rates   How well does the expectations theory explain the level of forward rates? Scholars who have studied exchange rates have found that forward rates

---

[8] In Section 3-5 we discussed Irving Fisher's theory that over time money interest rates change to reflect changes in anticipated inflation. Here we argue that international differences in money interest rates also reflect differences in anticipated inflation. This theory is sometimes known as the *international Fisher effect*.

ypically exaggerate the likely change in the spot rate. When the forward rate appears to predict a sharp ise in the spot rate (a forward premium), the forward rate tends to overestimate the rise in the spot ate. Conversely, when the forward rate appears to predict a fall in the currency (a forward discount), t tends to overestimate this fall.[9]

This finding is *not* consistent with the expectations theory. Instead it looks as if sometimes companies re prepared to give up return to *buy* forward currency and other times they are prepared to give up eturn to *sell* forward currency. In other words, forward rates seem to contain a risk premium, but the ign of this premium swings backward and forward.[10] You can see this from Figure 27.1. Almost half he time the forward rate for the Swiss franc *overstates* the likely future spot rate and half the time it *nderstates* the likely spot rate. *On average* the forward rate and future spot rate are almost identical. This is important news for the financial manager; it means that a company that always uses the orward market to protect against exchange rate movements does not pay any extra for this insurance.

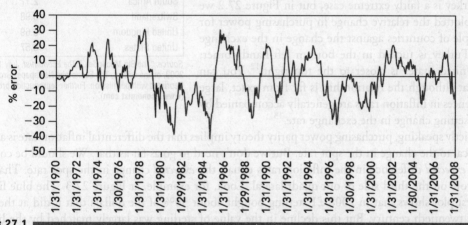

IGURE 27.1

Percentage error from using the one-year forward rate for Swiss francs to forecast next year's spot rate. Note that the forward rate overestimates and underestimates the spot rate with about equal frequency.

5. Purchasing Power Parity Theory What about the third side of our quadrilateral—purchasing power parity theory? No one who has compared prices in foreign stores with prices at home really believes that prices are the same throughout the world. Look, for example, at Table 27.2, which hows the price of a Big Mac in different countries. Notice that at current rates of exchange a Big Mac costs $5.98 in Switzerland but only $3.57 in the United States. To equalize prices in the two ountries, the number of Swiss francs that you could buy for your dollar would need to increase by 5.98/3.57 − 1 = .68, or 68%.

This suggests a possible way to make a quick buck. Why don't you buy a hamburger-to-go in (say) China for the equivalent of $1.83 and take it for resale in Switzerland, where the price in dollars is $5.98? The answer, of course, is that the gain would not cover the costs. The same good can be sold for different

Many researchers have even found that, when the forward rate predicts a rise, the spot rate is more likely to fall, and vice versa. For a readable iscussion of this puzzling finding, see K. A. Froot and R. H. Thaler, "Anomalies: Foreign Exchange," *Journal of Economic Perspectives* 4 (1990), p. 179–192.

) For evidence that forward exchange rates contain risk premiums that are sometimes positive and sometimes negative, see, for example, E. F. ama, "Forward and Spot Exchange Rates," *Journal of Monetary Economics* 14 (1984), pp. 319–338.

prices in different countries because transportation is costly and inconvenient.[11]

On the other hand, there is clearly some relationship between inflation and changes in exchange rates. For example, between the beginning of 2000 and the end of 2007 prices in Turkey rose 5.9 times. Or, to put it another way, you could say that the purchasing power of money in Turkey declined by about 83%. If exchange rates had not adjusted, Turkish exporters would have found it impossible to sell their goods. But, of course, exchange rates did adjust. In fact, the value of the Turkish currency declined by 52% relative to the U.S. dollar.

Turkey is a fairly extreme case, but in Figure 27.2 we have plotted the relative change in purchasing power for a sample of countries against the change in the exchange rate. Turkey is tucked in the bottom left-hand corner; the United States is closer to the top right.[12] You can see that although the relationship is far from exact, large differences in inflation rates are generally accompanied by an offsetting change in the exchange rate.[13]

TABLE 27.2 Price of Big Mac hamburgers in different countries.

Country	Local Price Converted to U.S. Dollars
Canada	3.35
China	1.83
Denmark	5.53
Euro area	4.62
Japan	3.46
Mexico	2.39
Philippines	2.05
Russia	2.04
South Africa	2.17
Switzerland	5.98
United Kingdom	3.69
United States	3.57

Source: "The Big Mac Index," *The Economist*, July 16, 2009, online edition, The Economist Newspaper Group, Inc. Reprinted with permission. Further reproduction prohibited (**www.economist.com**).

Strictly speaking, purchasing power parity theory implies that the differential inflation rate is always identical to the change in the spot rate. But we don't need to go as far as that. We should be content if the *expected* difference in the inflation rates equals the *expected* change in the spot rate. That's all we wrote on the third side of our quadrilateral. Look, for example, at Figure 27.3. The blue line in the first plot shows that in 2008 £1 sterling bought about 30% of the dollars that it did at the start of the twentieth century. But this decline in the value of sterling was largely matched by the higher inflation rate in the U.K. The red line shows that the inflation-adjusted, or *real*, exchange rate ended the century at roughly the same level as it began.[14] The second and third plots show the experiences of France and Italy, respectively. The fall in nominal exchange rates for both countries is much greater. Adjusting for changes in currency units, the equivalent of one French franc in 2008 bought about 1% of the dollars that it did at the start of 1900. The equivalent of one Italian lira bought about .4% of the number of dollars. In both cases the real exchange rates in 2008 are not much different from those at the beginning of the twentieth century. Of course, real exchange rates *do* change, sometimes quite sharply. For example, the real value of sterling rose by about 40% between the end of 2001 and the end of 2007. However, if you were a financial manager called on to make a long-term forecast of the

---

[11] Of course, even within a currency area there may be considerable price variations. The price of a Big Mac, for example, differs substantially from one part of the United States to another.

[12] Turkey did not have the highest inflation rate or the most rapidly depreciating currency. That honor belonged to Angola, followed closely by Belarus. These are shown by the two points in the extreme bottom left of Figure 27.2.

[13] Note that some of the countries represented in Figure 27.2 have highly controlled economies, so that their exchange rates are not those that would exist in an unrestricted market. The interest rates shown in Figure 27.4 are subject to a similar caveat.

[14] The real exchange rate is equal to the nominal exchange rate multiplied by the inflation differential. For example, suppose that the value of sterling falls from $1.65 = £1 to $1.50 = £1 at the same time that the price of goods rises 10% faster in the United Kingdom than in the United States. The inflation-adjusted, or real, exchange rate is unchanged at

$$\text{Nominal exchange rate} \times (1 + i_\pounds)/(1 + i_\$) = 1.5 \times 1.1 = \$1.65/\pounds$$

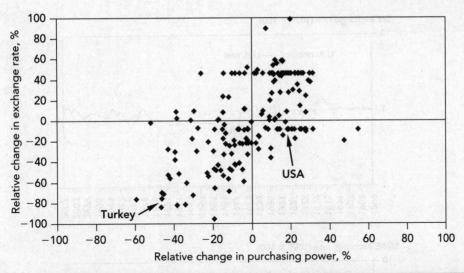

FIGURE 27.2

A decline in the exchange rate and a decline in a currency's purchasing power tend to go hand in hand. In this diagram each of the 179 points represents the experience of a different country in the eight years to 2007. The vertical axis shows the change in the value of the foreign currency relative to the average. The horizontal axis shows the change in the purchasing power relative to the average. The point in the lower left is Turkey. The plot for the USA shows that the dollar did not fully reflect the relatively low inflation rate in the USA.

exchange rate, you could not have done much better than to assume that changes in the value of the currency would offset the difference in inflation rates.

4. Equal Real Interest Rates   Finally we come to the relationship between interest rates in different countries. Do we have a single world capital market with the same *real* rate of interest in all countries? Does the difference in money interest rates equal the difference in the expected inflation rates?

This is not an easy question to answer since we cannot observe *expected* inflation. However, in Figure 27.4 we have plotted the average interest rate in each of 55 countries against the inflation that subsequently occurred. Japan is tucked into the bottom-left corner of the chart, while Turkey is represented by the dot in the top-right corner. You can see that, in general, the countries with the highest interest rates also had the highest inflation rates. There were much smaller differences between the real rates of interest than between the nominal (or money) rates.[15]

Interest Rate Parity in India

Prof. J R Varma observed that the theoretical linkage between interest rates and the foreign exchange markets were observed for the first time in India after September 1995. As Figure 27.5 shows, there was no relationship between the two markets prior to September 1995. Bhatt and Virmani similarly

---

[15] In Chapter 3 we saw that in some countries the government has issued indexed bonds promising a fixed real return. The annual interest payment and the amount repaid at maturity increase with the rate of inflation. In these cases, therefore, we can observe and compare the real rate of interest. As we write this, real interest rates in Australia, Canada, France, Sweden, the U.K., and the United States cluster within the range of 0% to 2.5%.

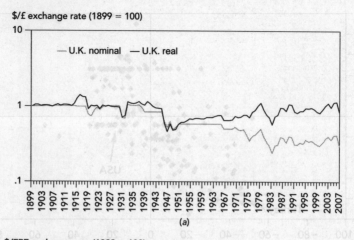

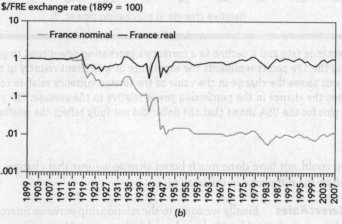

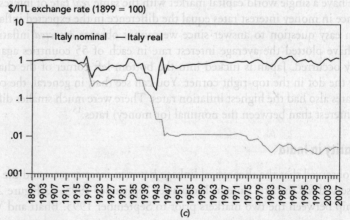

Figure 27.3

Nominal versus real exchange rates in the U.K., France, and Italy. December 1899 = 1. (Values are shown on log scale.)

Source: E. Dimson, P. R. Marsh, and M. Staunton, *Triumph of the Optimist: 101 Years of Global Investment Returns* (Princeton, NJ: Princeton University Press, 2002). Reprinted by permission of Princeton University Press, with updates provided by the authors.

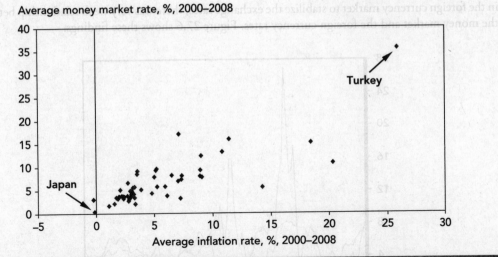

Average money market rate, %, 2000–2008

FIGURE 27.4

Countries with the highest interest rates generally have the highest inflation. In this diagram each of the 55 points represents the experience of a different country.

Source: Global Insight, WRDS (Wharton Research Data Services), **http://wrds.wharton.upenn.edu**

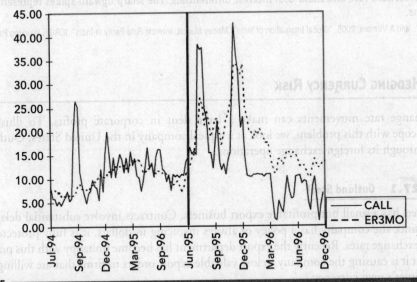

FIGURE 27.5

Relationship between the implicit euro-rupee rate (estimated by Prof. J R Varma) and the call market interest rate in India. After September 1995, the two rates track each other fairly well.

Source: Varma, J. R., 1997, "Indian Money Market: Market Structure, Covered Parity, and Term Structure", *ICFAI Journal of Applied Finance.* Pp1-10

report linkage between the money market and the foreign currency market between 1993 and 2003. However, during periods of crisis (like Cargil war or Pokhran sanctions) when the RBI has intervened in the foreign currency market to stabilize the exchange rates, there was very weak relationship between the money market and the foreign currency rates. Figure 27.6 shows these findings.

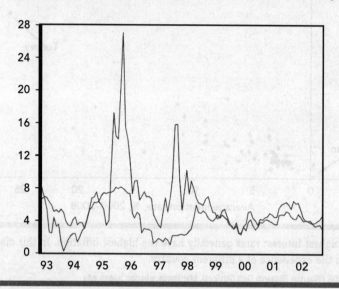

FIGURE 27.6

Three-Month forward rate and India-U.S. interest differentials. The sharp upward spikes represent RBI interventions.

Source: Bhatt, V., and A Virmani, 2005, "Global Integration of India's Money Market: Interest Rate Parity in India", ICRIER Working Paper, no 164, July 2005.

27-3   HEDGING CURRENCY RISK

Sharp exchange rate movements can make a large dent in corporate profits. To illustrate how companies cope with this problem, we look at a typical company in the United States, Outland Steel, and walk through its foreign exchange operations.

EXAMPLE 27.1   Outland Steel

Outland Steel has a small but profitable export business. Contracts involve substantial delays in payment, but since the company has a policy of always invoicing in dollars, it is fully protected against changes in exchange rates. Recently the export department has become unhappy with this practice and believes that it is causing the company to lose valuable export orders to firms that are willing to quote in the customer's own currency.

You sympathize with these arguments, but you are worried about how the firm should price long-term export contracts when payment is to be made in foreign currency. If the value of that currency declines before payment is made, the company may suffer a large loss. You want to take the currency risk into account, but you also want to give the sales force as much freedom of action as possible.

Notice that Outland can insure against its currency risk by selling the foreign currency forward. This means that it can separate the problem of negotiating sales contracts from that of managing the company's foreign exchange exposure. The sales force can allow for currency risk by pricing on the basis of the forward exchange rate. And you, as financial manager, can decide whether the company *ought* to hedge.

What is the cost of hedging? You sometimes hear managers say that it is equal to the difference between the forward rate and *today's* spot rate. That is wrong. If Outland does not hedge, it will receive the spot rate at the time that the customer pays for the steel. Therefore, the cost of insurance is the difference between the forward rate and the expected spot rate when payment is received.

Insure or speculate? We generally vote for insurance. First, it makes life simpler for the firm and allows it to concentrate on its main business. Second, it does not cost much. (In fact, the cost is zero on average if the forward rate equals the expected spot rate, as the expectations theory of forward rates implies.) Third, the foreign currency market seems reasonably efficient, at least for the major currencies. Speculation should be a zero-NPV game, unless financial managers have information that is not available to the pros who make the market.

Is there any other way that Outland can protect itself against exchange loss? Of course. It can borrow foreign currency against its foreign receivables, sell the currency spot, and invest the proceeds in the United States. Interest rate parity theory tells us that in free markets the difference between selling forward and selling spot should be equal to the difference between the interest that you have to pay overseas and the interest that you can earn at home.

Our discussion of Outland's export business illustrates four practical implications of our simple theories about forward exchange rates. First, you can use forward rates to adjust for exchange risk in contract pricing. Second, the expectations theory suggests that protection against exchange risk is usually worth having. Third, interest rate parity theory reminds us that you can hedge either by selling forward or by borrowing foreign currency and selling spot. Fourth, the cost of forward cover is not the difference between the forward rate and *today's* spot rate; it is the difference between the forward rate and the expected spot rate when the forward contract matures.

Perhaps we should add a fifth implication. You don't make money simply by buying currencies that go up in value and selling those that go down. For example, suppose that you buy Narnian leos and sell them after a year for 2% more than you paid for them. Should you give yourself a pat on the back? That depends on the interest that you have earned on your leos. If the interest rate on leos is 2 percentage points less than the interest rate on dollars, the profit on the currency is exactly canceled out by the reduction in interest income. Thus you make money from currency speculation only if you can predict whether the exchange rate will change by more or less than the interest rate differential. In other words, you must be able to predict whether the exchange rate will change by more or less than the forward premium or discount.

Transaction Exposure and Economic Exposure

The exchange risk from Outland Steel's export business is due to delays in foreign currency payments and is therefore referred to as *transaction exposure*. Transaction exposure can be easily identified and hedged. Since a 1% fall in the value of the foreign currency results in a 1% fall in Outland's dollar receipts, for every euro or yen that Outland is owed by its customers, it needs to sell forward one euro or one yen.[16]

However, Outland may still be affected by currency fluctuations even if its customers do not owe it a cent. For example, Outland may be in competition with Swedish steel producers. If the value of

[16] To put it another way, the hedge ratio is 1.0.

the Swedish krona falls, Outland will need to cut its prices in order to compete.[17] Outland can protect itself against such an eventuality by selling the krona forward. In this case the loss on Outland's steel business will be offset by the profit on its forward sale.

Notice that Outland's exposure to the krona is not limited to specific transactions that have already been entered into. Financial managers often refer to this broader type of exposure as *economic exposure.*[18] Economic exposure is less easy to measure than transaction exposure. For example, it is clear that the value of Outland Steel is positively related to the value of the krona, so to hedge its position it needs to sell kronor forward. But in practice it may be hard to say exactly how many kronor Outland needs to sell.

The automobile industry provides a good example of an industry with significant economic exposure. Table 27.3 shows global automotive sales and production in 2003.[19] Panel A shows sales and panel B production. Notice that most manufacturers have significant sales in more than one market and are therefore potentially exposed to the risk of exchange rate fluctuations.

One solution is for the company to undertake *operational hedging* by balancing production closely with sales. Look, for example, at Ford. Thirty-eight percent of its sales are outside North America, but so is 44% of its production. Because its costs and revenues in each currency are reasonably closely balanced, exchange rate changes do not affect its profits nearly as much as would be the case if its production were concentrated in one country.

Other manufacturers, particularly the Japanese firms, have less operational hedging. For example, Toyota produces 63% of its output in Japan, but only 37% is sold there. Exchange rate fluctuations are potentially a more serious risk for Toyota. On the other hand, the Japanese companies operate in a wider range of markets than U.S. firms. They have therefore diversified away a good part of their currency risk.

Operational hedging rarely eliminates all exchange risk. Look again at Ford. It is a net importer of autos and components into North America and is therefore exposed to a decline in the value of the dollar. Of course, Ford could try to pass some of the higher dollar cost of imported autos on to the customer, but competition limits the extent to which this is possible. Thus Ford's 2006 Annual Report commented as follows on the effect of the dollar's depreciation:

> The U.S. dollar has depreciated against most major currencies since 2002. This created downward margin pressure on auto manufacturers that have U.S. dollar revenue with foreign currency cost. Because we produce vehicles in Europe . . . for sale in the United States and produce components in Europe (e.g., engines) for use in some of our North American vehicles, we experienced margin pressure. . . . We, like any other automotive manufacturers with sales in the United States, are not always able to price for depreciation of the U.S. dollar due to the extremely competitive pricing environment in the United States.

In addition to operational hedging, Ford and other automobile companies also control exchange rate risk by using *financial hedges.* They do this by borrowing in foreign currencies, selling currency forward, or using foreign currency derivatives such as swaps and options. Ford's Annual Report describes how its financing subsidiary minimizes currency risk:

> To meet funding objectives, Ford Credit issues debt or, for its international affiliates, draws on local credit lines in a variety of currencies. Ford Credit faces exposure to currency exchange rate

---

[17] Of course, if purchasing power parity always held, the fall in the value of the krona would be matched by higher inflation in Sweden. The risk for Outland is that the *real* value of the krona may decline, so that when measured in dollars Swedish costs are lower than previously. Unfortunately, it is much easier to hedge against a change in the *nominal* exchange rate than against a change in the *real* rate.

[18] Financial managers also refer to *translation exposure,* which measures the effect of an exchange rate change on the company's financial statements.

[19] See S. M. Bartram, G. W. Brown, and B. A. Minton, "Resolving the Exposure Puzzle: The Many Facets of Exchange Rate Exposure," *Journal of Financial Economics,* forthcoming.

TABLE 27.3 Percentage sales and production of major automotive companies by geographic region for 2003.

	Home Country	Europe	North America	Japan	Other
Panel A: Sales, %					
Ford	United States	30.3%	62.3%	0.0%	7.4%
General Motors	United States	20.2	67.6	0.0	12.2
Hyundai	South Korea	17.5	31.1	0.0	51.4
Honda	Japan	7.5	54.8	25.6	12.1
Isuzu	Japan	1.8	14.0	27.8	56.4
Mazda	Japan	23.5	34.6	29.7	12.2
Mitsubishi	Japan	14.5	22.8	37.1	25.7
Nissan	Japan	18.8	40.2	31.5	9.5
Suzuki	Japan	14.2	4.5	41.9	39.4
Toyota	Japan	13.2	32.8	36.8	17.2
Fiat	Italy	80.1	0.0	0.0	19.8
BMW	Germany	64.6	30.6	0.0	4.9
DaimlerChrysler	Germany	28.4	68.4	0.0	3.2
Volkswagen	Germany	62.9	13.4	0.0	23.7
Peugeot	France	92.8	0.5	0.0	6.7
Renault	France	90.6	0.8	0.0	8.6
Panel B: Production, %					
Ford	United States	35.2%	56.1%	0.0%	8.7%
General Motors	United States	24.2	64.5	0.0	11.3
Hyundai	South Korea	1.3	0.0	0.0	98.7
Honda	Japan	6.7	43.2	40.2	9.9
Isuzu	Japan	1.0	7.2	56.2	35.6
Mazda	Japan	0.0	16.9	80.2	2.9
Mitsubishi	Japan	6.0	10.7	64.6	18.6
Nissan	Japan	15.3	27.8	51.5	5.4
Suzuki	Japan	6.7	0.5	59.3	33.5
Toyota	Japan	6.9	18.8	62.6	11.6
Fiat	Italy	79.4	0.0	0.0	20.6
BMW	Germany	80.3	14.8	0.0	4.9
DaimlerChrysler	Germany	34.6	63.0	0.0	2.4
Volkswagen	Germany	68.1	5.8	0.0	26.1
Peugeot	France	94.3	0.0	0.0	5.7
Renault	France	95.7	0.8	0.0	3.6

Source: Adapted from Table 1 in S. M. Bartram, G. W. Brown, and B. A. Minton, "Resolving the Exposure Puzzle: The Many Facets of Exchange Rate Exposure," Working paper, *Journal of Financial Economics*, forthcoming, with original data from WARD'S *World Motor Vehicle Data Book* (2003).

changes if a mismatch exists between the currency of its receivables and the currency of the debt funding those receivables. When possible, receivables are funded with debt in the same currency, minimizing exposure to exchange rate movements. When a different currency is used, Ford Credit seeks to minimize its exposure to changes in currency exchange rates by executing foreign currency derivatives. These derivatives convert substantially all of its foreign currency debt obligations to the local country currency of the receivables. As a result, Ford Credit's market risk exposure relating to currency exchange rates is believed to be immaterial.

Bartram, Brown, and Minton estimate that financial hedges allow the automobile industry to reduce its exchange rate risk by 45–50%. Operational hedges provide a 10–15% risk reduction and a further 10–15% of the risk is passed through to the customer in the form of price adjustments. In total auto manufacturers are able to reduce their currency exposure by about three-quarters.

Many of the Software companies in India face similar problems as does Ford. A large part of the revenue comes from their international clients. However, their software testing centres are located mostly in India and hence, their expenses are in Indian rupees. So they suffer revenue losses whenever rupee appreciates against the major international currencies. Thus, for example, in the first quarter of 2006, Wipro suffered a revenue loss of ₹27 crores because of the appreciation of rupee. In the quarter ending December 2011, however, many software companies reported decent increase in their rupee revenue because of the huge depreciation in Indian rupee.

27-4   EXCHANGE RISK AND INTERNATIONAL INVESTMENT DECISIONS

Suppose that the Swiss pharmaceutical company, Roche, is evaluating a proposal to build a new plant in India. To calculate the project's net present value, Roche forecasts the following rupee cash flows from the project:

Cash Flows (₹ millions)					
C_0	C_1	C_2	C_3	C_4	C_5
−1,300	400	450	510	575	650

These cash flows are stated in rupees. So to calculate their net present value Roche discounts them at the rupee cost of capital. (Remember rupees need to be discounted at a *rupee* rate, not the Swiss franc rate.) Suppose this cost of capital is 12%. Then

$$\text{NPV} = -1,300 + \frac{400}{1.12} + \frac{450}{1.12^2} + \frac{510}{1.12^3} + \frac{575}{1.12^4} + \frac{650}{1.12^5} = ₹513 \text{ million}$$

To convert this net present value to Swiss francs, the manager can simply divide the rupee NPV by the spot rate of exchange. For example, if the spot rate is ₹54.3/SFr, then the NPV in Swiss francs is

$$\text{NPV in francs} = \text{NPV in rupees/SFr} = 513/54.3 = 9.45 \text{ million francs}$$

Notice one very important feature of this calculation. Roche does not need to forecast whether the rupee is likely to strengthen or weaken against the Swiss franc. No currency forecast is needed, because the company can hedge its foreign exchange exposure. In that case, the decision to accept or reject the pharmaceutical project in India is totally separate from the decision to bet on the outlook for the rupee. For example, it would be foolish for Roche to accept a poor project in India just because management is optimistic about the outlook for the rupee; if Roche wishes to speculate in this way t can simply buy rupees forward. Equally, it would be foolish for Roche to reject a good project just because management is pessimistic about the rupee. The company would do much better to go ahead with the project and sell rupees forward. In that way, it would get the best of both worlds.[20]

When Roche ignores currency risk and discounts the rupee cash flows at a rupee cost of capital, it is implicitly assuming that the currency risk is hedged. Let us check this by calculating the number of Swiss francs that Roche would receive if it hedged the currency risk by selling forward each future dollar cash flow.

We need first to calculate the forward rate of exchange between rupees and francs. This depends on the interest rates in India and Switzerland. For example, suppose that the rupee interest rate is 6% and the Swiss franc interest rate is 4%. Then interest rate parity theory tells us that the one-year forward exchange rate is

$$s_{₹/SFr} \times (1 + r_₹)/(1 + r_{SFr}) = \frac{54.3 \times 1.06}{1.04} = 55.34$$

Similarly, the two-year forward rate is

$$s_{₹/SFr} \times (1 + r_₹)^2/(1 + r_{SFr})^2 = \frac{54.3 \times 1.06^2}{1.04^2} = 56.41$$

So, if Roche hedges its cash flows against exchange rate risk, the number of Swiss francs it will receive in each year is equal to the rupee cash flow times the forward rate of exchange:

Cash Flows (Millions of Swiss francs)					
C_0	C_1	C_2	C_3	C_4	C_5
−1300	400	450	510	575	650
−1300 / 54.3	400 / 55.344	450 / 56.409	510 / 57.493	575 / 58.599	650 / 59.726
= −23.94	= 7.23	= 7.98	= 8.87	= 9.81	= 10.88

These cash flows are in Swiss francs and therefore they need to be discounted at the risk-adjusted Swiss franc discount rate. Since the Swiss rate of interest is lower than the rupee rate, the risk-adjusted discount rate must also be correspondingly lower. The formula for converting from the required rupee return to the required Swiss franc return is[21]

$$(1 + \text{Swiss franc return}) = (1 + \text{rupee return}) \times \frac{(1 + \text{Swiss franc interest rate})}{(1 + \text{rupee interest rate})}$$

In our example,

$$(1 + \text{Swiss franc return}) = 1.12 \times \frac{1.04}{1.06} = 1.099$$

---

[20] There is a general point here that is not confined to currency hedging. Whenever you face an investment that appears to have a positive NPV, decide what it is that you are betting on and then think whether there is a more direct way to place the bet. For example, if a copper mine looks profitable only because you are unusually optimistic about the price of copper, then maybe you would do better to buy copper futures or the shares of other copper producers rather than opening a copper mine.

[21] The following example should give you a feel for the idea behind this formula. Suppose the spot rate for Swiss francs is ₹38/SFr. Interest rate parity tells us that the forward rate must be 38 × 1.06/1.04 = ₹38.73/SFr. Now suppose that a share costs ₹100 and will pay an expected ₹112 at the end of the year. The cost to the Swiss investors of buying the share is 100/38 = SFr 2.63. If the Swiss investors sell forward the expected payoff, they will receive an expected 112/38,73 = SFr2.89. The expected return in Swiss francs is 2.89/2.63 − 1 = .099, or 9.99%. More simply, the Swiss franc return is 1.12 × 1.04/1.06 − 1 = 0.099.

Thus the risk-adjusted discount rate in rupees is 12%, but the discount rate in Swiss francs is only 9.9%.

All that remains is to discount the Swiss franc cash flows at the 9.9% risk-adjusted discount rate:

$$NPV = -23.94 + \frac{7.23}{1.099} + \frac{7.98}{1.099^2} + \frac{8.87}{1.099^3} + \frac{9.81}{1.099^4} + \frac{10.88}{1.099^5}$$

$$= 9.45 \text{ million francs}$$

Everything checks. We obtain exactly the same net present value by (a) ignoring currency risk and discounting Roche's rupee cash flows at the rupee cost of capital and (b) calculating the cash flows in francs on the assumption that Roche hedges the currency risk and then discounting these Swiss franc cash flows at the franc cost of capital.

To repeat: When deciding whether to invest overseas, separate out the investment decision from the decision to take on currency risk. This means that your views about future exchange rates should NOT enter into the investment decision. The simplest way to calculate the NPV of an overseas investment is to forecast the cash flows in the foreign currency and discount them at the foreign currency cost of capital. The alternative is to calculate the cash flows that you would receive if you hedged the foreign currency risk. In this case you need to translate the foreign currency cash flows into your own currency *using the forward exchange rate* and then discount these domestic currency cash flows at the domestic cost of capital. If the two methods don't give the same answer, you have made a mistake.

When Roche analyzes the proposal to build a plant in India, it is able to ignore the outlook for the rupee *only because it is free to hedge the currency risk.* Because investment in a pharmaceutical plant does not come packaged with an investment in rupee, the opportunity for firms to hedge allows for better investment decisions.

The Cost of Capital for International Investments

Roche should discount dollar cash flows at a rupee cost of capital. But how should a Swiss company like Roche calculate a cost of capital in rupees for an investment in India? There is no simple, consensus procedure for answering this question, but we suggest the following procedure as a start.

First you need to decide on the risk of an Indian pharmaceutical investment to a Swiss investor. You could look at the betas of a sample of Indian pharmaceutical companies *relative to the Swiss market index.*

Why measure betas relative to the Swiss index, while an Indian counterpart such as Ranbaxy would measure betas relative to the Indian index? The answer lies in Section 7-4, where we explained that risk cannot be considered in isolation; it depends on the other securities in the investor's portfolio. Beta measures risk *relative to the investor's portfolio.* If Indian investors already hold the Indian market, an additional rupee invested at home is just more of the same. But if Swiss investors hold the Swiss market, an investment in the India can reduce their risk because the Swiss and Indian markets are not perfectly correlated. That explains why an investment in India can be lower risk for Roche's shareholders than for Ranbaxy's shareholders. It also explains why Roche's shareholders may be willing to accept a relatively low expected return from an Indian investment.[22]

Suppose that you decide that the investment's beta relative to the Swiss market is .8 and that the market risk premium in Switzerland is 7.4%. Then the required return on the project can be estimated as

---

[22] When an investor holds an efficient portfolio, the expected reward for risk on each stock in the portfolio is proportional to its beta *relative to the portfolio.* So if the Swiss market index is an efficient portfolio for Swiss investors, then these investors will want Roche to invest in India. if the expected rate of return more than compensates for the investment's beta relative to the Swiss index.

$$\text{Required return} = \text{Swiss interest rate} + (\text{beta} \times \text{Swiss market risk premium})$$
$$= 4 + (.8 \times 7.4) = 9.9$$

This is the project's cost of capital measured in Swiss francs. We used it above to discount the expected *Swiss franc* cash flows if Roche hedged the project against currency risk. We cannot use it to discount the *rupee* cash flows from the project.

To discount the expected *rupee* cash flows, we need to convert the Swiss franc cost of capital to a rupee cost of capital. This means running our earlier calculation in reverse:

$$(1 + \text{rupee return}) = (1 + \text{Swiss franc return}) \times \frac{(1 + \text{rupee interest rate})}{(1 + \text{Swiss franc interest rate})}$$

In our example,

$$(1 + \text{rupee return}) = 1.099 \times \frac{1.06}{1.04} = 1.12$$

We used this 12% rupee cost of capital to discount the forecasted rupee cash flows from the project.

When a company measures risk relative to its domestic market as in our example, its managers are implicitly assuming that shareholders hold simply domestic stocks. That is not a bad approximation, particularly in India. Although Indian investors generally invest only in the stocks of Indian companies.

The world is getting smaller and "flatter," however, and investors everywhere are increasing their holdings of foreign securities. Pension funds and other institutional investors have diversified internationally, and dozens of mutual funds have been set up for people who want to invest abroad. If investors throughout the world held the world portfolio, then costs of capital would converge. The cost of capital would still depend on the risk of the investment, but not on the domicile of the investing company. There is some evidence that for large U.S. firms it does not make much difference whether a U.S. or global beta is used. For smaller countries the evidence is not so clear-cut and sometimes a global beta may be more appropriate.[23]

Do Some Countries Have a Lower Interest Rate?

Some countries enjoy much lower interest rates than others. For example, in early 2007, before the recent financial crisis, the long-term interest rate in Japan was about 1.4% and in Australia it was 5.9%. People often conclude from this kind of comparison that Japan has a low cost of capital.

This view is one part confusion and one part probable truth. The confusion arises because the interest rate in Japan is measured in yen and the rate in Australia is measured in Australian dollars. You would not say that a 10-inch-high rabbit was taller than a 9-foot elephant. In the same way it makes no sense to compare interest rates for different currencies.

But suppose that you measure the interest rate in real terms. Then you are comparing like with like, and it does make sense to ask whether the *real* cost of capital is lower in Japan. Real interest rates do sometimes diverge and, when that happens, investors may see a profit opportunity. For example, in early 2007, financial institutions had borrowed an estimated $200 billion in Japan and reinvested it at higher rates in other countries such as Australia.[24] These trades are known as *carry trades*. This huge

---

[23] See R. M. Stulz, "The Cost of Capital in Internationally Integrated Markets: The Case of Nestlé," *European Financial Management* 1, no. 1 (1995), pp. 11–22; R. S. Harris, F. C. Marston, D. R. Mishra, and T. J. O'Brien, "Ex Ante Cost of Capital Estimates of S&P 500 Firms: The Choice Between Global and Domestic CAPM," *Financial Management* (Autumn 2003), pp. 51–66; and Standard & Poor's, "Domestic vs Global CAPM," *Global Cost of Capital Report*, 4th Quarter 2003.

[24] See "Yen Low Sparks Carry Trade Alert," *Financial Times*, January 30, 2007. This carry trade proved profitable until August 2008, but in the following three months it went very sour, as the Australian dollar slumped by over 40% against the yen.

volume of carry trades suggested that investors believed that the real cost of capital was indeed lower in Japan than in Australia and some other countries.

27-5   POLITICAL RISK

So far we have focused on the management of exchange rate risk, but managers also worry about political risk. By this they mean the threat that a government will change the rules of the game—that is, break a promise or understanding—*after* the investment is made. Of course political risks are not confined to overseas investments. Businesses in every country are exposed to the risk of unanticipated actions by governments or the courts. But in some parts of the world foreign companies are particularly vulnerable.

A number of consultancy services offer analyses of political and economic risks and draw up country rankings.[25] For example, Table 27.4 is an extract from the 2008 political risk rankings provided by the PRS Group. You can see that each country is scored on 12 separate dimensions. Finland comes top of the class overall, while Somalia languishes at the bottom.

TABLE 27.4   Political risk scores for a sample of countries, January 2008.

	A	B	C	D	E	F	G	H	I	J	K	L	Total
Maximum	12	12	12	12	12	6	6	6	6	6	6	4	100
Finland	9.5	9.5	12.0	11.0	11.5	6.0	6.0	6.0	6.0	6.0	6.0	4.0	93.5
Sweden	7.5	9.0	12.0	11.5	11.0	5.0	5.5	6.0	6.0	5.0	6.0	4.0	88.5
Switzerland	9.0	10.5	12.0	12.0	11.0	4.5	6.0	4.5	5.0	4.0	6.0	4.0	88.5
Australia	10.0	10.5	12.0	10.0	9.5	4.5	6.0	6.0	5.5	4.0	6.0	4.0	88.0
Germany	10.0	8.0	12.0	11.0	10.5	5.0	6.0	5.0	5.0	4.0	6.0	4.0	86.5
Singapore	11.0	9.5	12.0	10.5	10.5	4.5	5.0	4.5	5.0	6.0	2.0	4.0	84.5
U.K.	8.0	9.5	12.0	9.5	7.0	4.0	6.0	6.0	5.5	4.0	6.0	4.0	81.5
France	9.5	8.0	12.0	10.0	10.0	5.0	5.5	4.0	5.0	2.5	6.0	3.0	80.5
Japan	6.5	8.0	11.5	10.5	9.5	3.0	5.0	5.5	5.0	5.5	5.0	4.0	79.0
U.S.	6.0	8.0	12.0	10.0	7.0	4.0	4.0	5.5	5.0	5.0	6.0	4.0	76.5
China, P.R.	11.0	9.0	7.0	10.0	10.0	2.5	3.0	5.0	4.5	4.5	1.5	2.0	70.0
Russian Fed.	11.5	7.0	9.5	8.0	8.5	2.0	4.5	5.5	4.0	3.0	2.5	1.0	67.0
Brazil	8.5	6.0	7.5	10.0	10.5	2.0	4.0	6.0	2.0	3.0	5.0	2.0	66.5
Turkey	9.0	6.5	8.0	8.0	7.5	2.5	2.0	4.5	4.5	2.5	5.0	2.0	62.0
India	6.0	5.5	8.5	6.5	10.0	2.5	4.0	2.5	4.0	2.5	6.0	3.0	61.0
Pakistan	4.0	5.0	7.5	5.5	8.5	2.0	1.0	1.0	3.0	1.0	1.0	2.0	41.5
Somalia	5.5	0.0	2.0	4.0	4.0	1.0	1.0	3.0	0.5	2.0	1.0	0.0	24.0

Key:
A Government stability   D Internal conflict   G Military in politics   J Ethnic tensions
B Socioeconomic conditions   E External conflict   H Religious tensions   K Democratic accountability
C Investment profile   F Corruption   I Law and order   L Bureaucracy quality

Source: *International Country Risk Guide*, a publication of The PRS Group, Inc. (**www.prsgroup.com**), 2008.

---

[25] For a discussion of these services see C. Erb, C. R. Harvey, and T. Viskanta, "Political Risk, Financial Risk, and Economic Risk," *Financial Analysts Journal* 52 (1996), pp. 28–46. Also, Campbell Harvey's Web page (**www.duke.edu/~charvey**) is a useful source of information on political risk.

Some managers dismiss political risk as an act of God, like a hurricane or earthquake. But the most successful multinational companies structure their business to reduce political risk. Foreign governments are not likely to expropriate a local business if it cannot operate without the support of its parent. For example, the foreign subsidiaries of American computer manufacturers or pharmaceutical companies would have relatively little value if they were cut off from the know-how of their parents. Such operations are much less likely to be expropriated than, say, a mining operation that can be operated as a stand-alone venture.

We are not recommending that you turn your silver mine into a pharmaceutical company, but you may be able to plan your overseas manufacturing operations to improve your bargaining position with foreign governments. For example, Ford has integrated its overseas operations so that the manufacture of components, subassemblies, and complete automobiles is spread across plants in a number of countries. None of these plants would have much value on its own, and Ford can switch production between plants if the political climate in one country deteriorates.

Multinational corporations have also devised financing arrangements to help keep foreign governments honest. For example, suppose your firm is contemplating an investment of $500 million to reopen the San Tomé silver mine in Costaguana with modern machinery, smelting equipment, and shipping facilities.[26] The Costaguanan government agrees to invest in roads and other infrastructure and to take 20% of the silver produced by the mine in lieu of taxes. The agreement is to run for 25 years.

The project's NPV on these assumptions is quite attractive. But what happens if a new government comes into power five years from now and imposes a 50% tax on "any precious metals exported from the Republic of Costaguana"? Or changes the government's share of output from 20% to 50%? Or simply takes over the mine "with fair compensation to be determined in due course by the Minister of Natural Resources of the Republic of Costaguana"?

No contract can absolutely restrain sovereign power. But you can arrange project financing to make these acts as painful as possible for the foreign government. For example, you might set up the mine as a subsidiary corporation, which then borrows a large fraction of the required investment from a consortium of major international banks. If your firm guarantees the loan, make sure the guarantee stands only if the Costaguanan government honors its contract. The government will be reluctant to break the contract if that causes a default on the loans and undercuts the country's credit standing with the international banking system.

If possible, you should arrange for the World Bank (or one of its affiliates) to finance part of the project or to guarantee your loans against political risk.[27] Few governments have the guts to take on the World Bank. Here is another variation on the same theme. Arrange to borrow, say, $450 million through the Costaguanan Development Agency. In other words, the development agency borrows in international capital markets and relends to the San Tomé mine. Your firm agrees to stand behind the loan as long as the government keeps its promises. If it does keep them, the loan is your liability. If not, the loan is *its* liability.

Political risk is not confined to the risk of expropriation. Multinational companies are always exposed to the criticism that they siphon funds out of countries in which they do business, and, therefore, governments are tempted to limit their freedom to repatriate profits. This is most likely to happen when there is considerable uncertainty about the rate of exchange, which is usually when you would most like to get your money out. Here again a little forethought can help. For example, there

---

[26] The early history of the San Tomé mine is described in Joseph Conrad's *Nostromo*.

[27] In Section 24-7 we described how the World Bank provided the Hubco power project with a guarantee against political risk.

are often more onerous restrictions on the payment of dividends to the parent than on the payment of interest or principal on debt. Royalty payments and management fees are less sensitive than dividends, particularly if they are levied equally on all foreign operations. A company can also, within limits, alter the price of goods that are bought or sold within the group, and it can require more or less prompt payment for such goods.

Calculating NPVs for investment projects becomes exceptionally difficult when political risks are significant. You have to estimate cash flows and project life with extra caution. You may want to take a peek at the discounted payback period (see Chapter 5), on the theory that quick-payback projects are less exposed to political risks. But do not try to compensate for political risks by adding casual fudge factors to discount rates. Fudge factors spawn bias and confusion, as we explained in Chapter 9.

SUMMARY

The international financial manager has to cope with different currencies, interest rates, and inflation rates. To produce order out of chaos, the manager needs some model of how they are related. We described four very simple but useful theories.

Interest rate parity theory states that the interest differential between two countries must be equal to the difference between the forward and spot exchange rates. In the international markets, arbitrage ensures that parity almost always holds. There are two ways to hedge against exchange risk: One is to take out forward cover; the other is to borrow or lend abroad. Interest rate parity tells us that the costs of the two methods should be the same.

The expectations theory of exchange rates tells us that the forward rate equals the expected spot rate. In practice forward rates seem to incorporate a risk premium, but this premium is about equally likely to be negative as positive.

In its strict form, purchasing power parity states that $1 must have the same purchasing power in every country. That doesn't square well with the facts, for differences in inflation rates are not perfectly related to changes in exchange rates. This means that there may be some genuine exchange risks in doing business overseas. On the other hand, the difference in inflation rates is just as likely to be above as below the change in the exchange rate.

Finally, we saw that in an integrated world capital market real rates of interest would have to be the same. In practice government regulation and taxes can cause differences in real interest rates. But do not simply borrow where interest rates are lowest. Those countries are also likely to have the lowest inflation rates and the strongest currencies.

With these precepts in mind we showed how you can use forward markets or the loan markets to hedge transactions exposure, which arises from delays in foreign currency payments and receipts. But the company's financing choices also need to reflect the impact of a change in the exchange rate on the value of the entire business. This is known as economic exposure. Companies protect themselves against economic exposure either by hedging in the financial markets or by building plants overseas.

Because companies can hedge their currency risk, the decision to invest overseas does not involve currency forecasts. There are two ways for a company to calculate the NPV of an overseas project. The first is to forecast the foreign currency cash flows and to discount them at the foreign currency cost of capital. The second is to translate the foreign currency cash flows into domestic currency assuming that they are hedged against exchange rate risk. These domestic currency flows can then be discounted at the domestic cost of capital. The answers should be identical.

In addition to currency risk, overseas operations may be exposed to extra political risk. However, firms may be able to structure the financing to reduce the chances that government will change the rules of the game.

There are a number of useful textbooks in international finance. Here is a small selection:

P. Sercu, *International Finance: Theory into Practice* (Princeton: Princeton University Press, 2009).

D. K. Eiteman, A. I. Stonehill, and M. H. Moffett, *Multinational Business Finance,* 11th ed. (Reading, MA: Pearson Addison Wesley, 2007).

A. C. Shapiro, *Multinational Financial Management,* 8th ed. (New York: John Wiley & Sons, 2006).

Here are some general discussions of international investment decisions and associated exchange risks:

G. Allayanis, J. Ihrig, and J. P. Weston, "Exchange-Rate Hedging: Financial versus Operational Strategies," *American Economic Review* 91 (May 2001), pp. 391–395.

D. R. Lessard, "Global Competition and Corporate Finance in the 1990s," *Journal of Applied Corporate Finance* 3 (Winter 1991), pp. 59–72.

M. D. Levi and P. Sercu, "Erroneous and Valid Reasons for Hedging Foreign Exchange Exposure," *Journal of Multinational Financial Management* 1 (1991), pp. 25–37.

Listed below are a few of the articles on the relationship between interest rates, exchange rates, and inflation:

Forward and spot exchange rates

M. D. Evans and K. K. Lewis, "Do Long-Term Swings in the Dollar Affect Estimates of the Risk Premia?" *Review of Financial Studies* 8 (1995), pp. 709–742.

Interest rate parity

K. Clinton, "Transaction Costs and Covered Interest Arbitrage: Theory and Evidence," *Journal of Political Economy* 96 (April 1988), pp. 358–370.

Purchasing power parity

K. Froot and K. Rogoff, "Perspectives on PPP and Long-run Real Exchange Rates," in G. Grossman and K. Rogoff (eds.), *Handbook of International Economics* (Amsterdam: North-Holland Publishing Company, 1995):

K. Rogoff, "The Purchasing Power Parity Puzzle," *Review of Economic Literature* 34 (June 1996), pp. 667–668.

A. M. Taylor and M. P. Taylor, "The Purchasing Power Parity Debate," *Journal of Economic Perspectives* 18 (Autumn 2004), pp. 135–158.

FURTHER READING (side)

PROBLEM SETS (side)

BASIC

1. Look at Table 27.1.
   a. How many Singapore dollars do you get for your rupee?
   b. What is the one-month forward rate for Singapore dollars?
   c. Is the Singapore dollar at a forward discount or premium on the rupee?
   d. Use the six-month forward rate to calculate the six-month percentage discount or premium on yen.
   e. If the six-month interest rate on rupees is 4.25% (about 8.5% per annum), what do you think is the six-month interest rate on Singapore dollar?
   f. According to the expectations theory, what is the expected spot rate for Singapore dollar in three months' time?

g. According to law of one price, what then is the expected difference in the three-month rate of price inflation in India and Singapore?

2. Define each of the following theories in a sentence or simple equation:
   a. Interest rate parity.
   b. Expectations of forward rates.
   c. Purchasing power parity.
   d. International capital market equilibrium (relationship of real and nominal interest rates in different countries).

3. In January 2011, the exchange rate between U.S. dollar and Indian rupee was ₹47/$. Inflation in the year to December 2011 was about 11% in India and 2% in the United States.
   a. If purchasing power parity held, what should have been the nominal exchange rate in January 2012?
   b. The actual exchange rate in January 2012 was ₹52/$. What was the change in the *real* exchange rate?

4. The following table shows interest rates and exchange rates for the U.S. dollar and the Philippine peso in 2007. The spot exchange rate is 47.46 pesos = $1. Complete the missing entries:

	1 Month	3 Months	1 Year
Dollar interest rate (annually compounded)	5.3	5.3	?
Peso interest rate (annually compounded)	4.15	?	4.95
Forward pesos per dollar	?	?	47.482
Forward premium on peso (% per year)	?	+0.19	?

5. An importer in India is due to take delivery of clothing from Mexico in six months. The price is fixed in Mexican pesos. Which of the following transactions could eliminate the importer's exchange risk?
   a. Sell six-month call options on pesos.
   b. Buy pesos forward.
   c. Sell pesos forward.
   d. Sell pesos in the currency futures market.
   e. Borrow pesos; buy rupees at the spot exchange rate.
   f. Sell pesos at the spot exchange rate; lend rupees.

6. An Indian company has committed to pay 10 million Hong Kong dollars to a Chinese company. What is the cost (in present value) of covering this liability by buying HK$ forward? The Hong Kong interest rate is 4.25%, and exchange rates are shown in Table 27.1. Briefly explain.

7. A firm in the United States is due to receive payment of €1 million in eight years' time. It would like to protect itself against a decline in the value of the euro, but finds it difficult to get forward cover for such a long period. Is there any other way in which it can protect itself?

8. Suppose that two-year interest rates are 8% in India and 0.06% in Japan. The spot exchange rate is ₹60/100 yens. Suppose that one year later interest rates are 5% in both the countries, while the value of the yen has appreciated to ₹65/100 yens.
   a. Sanjay Dutt from Mumbai invested in an Indian two-year zero-coupon bond at the start of the period and sold it after one year. What was his return?
   b. Madame Butterfly from Tokyo bought some rupees. She also invested in the two-year Indian zero-coupon bond and sold it after one year. What was her return *in yen*?

c. Suppose that Ms. Butterfly had correctly forecasted the price at which she sold her bond and that she hedged her investment against currency risk. How could she have done so? What would have been her return in yen?

9. It is the year 2018 and Indian Pork Barrels Company is considering construction of a new barrel plant in Spain. The forecasted cash flows in millions of euros are as follows:

C_0	C_1	C_2	C_3	C_4	C_5
−80	+10	+20	+23	+27	+25

The spot exchange rate is ₹66 = €1. The interest rate in India is 8% and the euro interest rate is 4%. You can assume that pork barrel production is effectively risk-free.

a. Calculate the NPV of the euro cash flows from the project. What is the NPV in rupees?

b. What are the rupee cash flows from the project if the company hedges against exchange rate changes?

c. Suppose that the company expects the euro to depreciate by 5% a year. How does this affect the value of the project?

INTERMEDIATE

10. Table 27.1 shows the six-month forward rate on the Hong Kong dollar.
    a. Is rupee at a forward discount or premium on the Hong Kong dollar?
    b. What is the annual *percentage* discount or premium?
    c. If you have no other information about the two currencies, what is your best guess about the spot rate on the Hong Kong dollar six months hence?
    d. Suppose that you expect to receive 100,000 Hong Kong dollar in six months. How many rupees is this likely to be worth?

11. Look at Table 27.1. If the three-month interest rate on rupees is 2%, what do you think is the three-month interest rate on Singapore dollar? Explain what would happen if the rate were substantially above your figure.

12. Ms. Rosetta Stone, the treasurer of International Reprints, Inc., has noticed that the interest rate in Japan is below the rates in most other countries. She is, therefore, suggesting that the company should make an issue of Japanese yen bonds. Does this make sense?

13. Suppose you are the treasurer of Lufthansa, the German international airline. How is company value likely to be affected by exchange rate changes? What policies would you adopt to reduce exchange rate risk?

14. Companies may be affected by changes in the nominal exchange rate or in the real exchange rate. Explain how this can occur. Which risks are easiest to hedge against?

15. A Ford dealer in the United States may be exposed to a devaluation of the yen if this leads to a cut in the price of Japanese cars. Suppose that the dealer estimates that a 1% decline in the value of the yen would result in a permanent decline of 5% in the dealer's profits. How should she hedge against this risk, and how should she calculate the size of the hedge position? (*Hint:* You may find it helpful to refer back to Section 26-6.)

16. You have bid for a possible export order that would provide a cash inflow of €1 million in six months. The spot exchange rate is ₹66 = €1 and the six-month forward rate is ₹68 = €1. There are two sources of uncertainty: (1) the euro could appreciate or depreciate and (2) you may or may not receive the export order. Illustrate in each case the final payoffs if (a) you sell one million euros forward, and (b) you buy a six-month option to sell euros with an exercise price of ₹66/€.

17. In March 2012, an American investor buys 1,000 shares in an Indian company at a price of ₹500 each. The share does not pay any dividend. A year later she sells the shares for ₹550 each. The exchange rates when she buys the stock are shown in Table 27.1. Suppose that the exchange rate at the time of sale is ₹55/$.
    a. How many dollars does she invest?
    b. What is her total return in Indian rupees? In dollars?
    c. Do you think that she has made an exchange rate profit or loss? Explain.

18. Table 27.5 above shows the annual interest rate (annually compounded) and exchange rates against the dollar for different currencies. Are there any arbitrage opportunities? If so, how would you secure a positive cash flow today, while zeroing out all future cash flows?

TABLE 27.5 Interest rates and exchange rates.

	Interest Rate (%)	Spot Exchange Rate*	1-Year Forward Exchange Rate*
United States (dollar)	3	—	—
Costaguana (pulga)	23	10,000	11,942
Westonia (ruple)	5	2.6	2.65
Gloccamorra (pint)	8	17.1	18.2
Anglosaxophonia (wasp)	4.1	2.3	2.28

*Number of units of foreign currency that can be exchanged for $1.

19. "Last year we had a substantial income in sterling, which we hedged by selling sterling forward. In the event sterling appreciated. So our decision to sell forward cost us a lot of money. I think that in the future we should either stop hedging our currency exposure or just hedge when we think sterling is overvalued." As financial manager, how would you respond to your chief executive's comment?

20. Carpet Baggers, Inc., of the U.S. is proposing to construct a new bagging plant in a country in Europe. The two prime candidates are Germany and Switzerland. The forecasted cash flows from the proposed plants are as follows:

eXcel

Visit us at
www.mhhe.com/bmam10e

	C_0	C_1	C_2	C_3	C_4	C_5	C_6	IRR(%)
Germany (millions of euros)	−60	+10	+15	+15	+20	+20	+20	18.8
Switzerland (millions of Swiss francs)	−120	+20	+30	+30	+35	+35	+35	12.8

The spot exchange rate for euros is $1.3/€, while the rate for Swiss francs is SFr 1.5/$. The interest rate is 5% in the United States, 4% in Switzerland, and 6% in the euro countries. The financial manager has suggested that, if the cash flows were stated in dollars, a return in excess of 10% would be acceptable.

Should the company go ahead with either project? If it must choose between them, which should it take?

CHALLENGE

21. If investors recognize the impact of inflation and exchange rate changes on a firm's cash flows, changes in exchange rates should be reflected in stock prices. How would the stock price of each of the following Swiss companies be affected by an unanticipated appreciation of the Swiss franc of 10%? Assume that only 2% of the appreciation can be attributed to increased inflation in the rest of the world (relative to the Swiss inflation rate).

   a. *A Swiss airline:* More than two-thirds of its employees are Swiss. Most revenues come from international fares set in U.S. dollars.

   b. *Nestlé:* Fewer than 5% of its employees are Swiss. Most revenues are derived from sales of consumer goods in a wide range of countries with competition from local producers.

   c. *UBS:* Forty percent of the employees work in Switzerland. The bank's Group Treasury periodically hedges any non-Swiss franc monetary positions.

22. Alpha and Omega are Indian corporations. Alpha has a plant in Dubai that imports components from India, assembles them, and then sells the finished product in Thailand. Omega is at the opposite extreme. It also has a plant in Dubai, but it buys its raw material in Thailand and exports its output back to India. How is each firm likely to be affected by a fall in the value of the dirham? How could each firm hedge itself against exchange risk?

REAL-TIME DATA ANALYSIS

1. Find the foreign exchange rate tables in the online versions of *The Wall Street Journal* (**www.wsj.com**) or the *Financial Times* (**www.ft.com**).

   a. How many U.S. dollars are worth one Canadian dollar today?

   b. How many Canadian dollars are worth one U.S. dollar today?

   c. Suppose that you arrange today to buy Canadian dollars in 90 days. How many Canadian dollars could you buy for each U.S. dollar?

   d. If forward rates simply reflect market expectations, what is the likely spot exchange rate for the Canadian dollar in 90 days' time?

   e. Look at the table of money rates in the same issue. What is the three-month interest rate on dollars?

   f. Can you deduce the likely three-month interest rate for the Canadian dollar?

   g. You can also buy currency for future delivery in the financial futures market. Look at the table of futures prices. What is the rate of exchange for Canadian dollars to be delivered in approximately six months' time?

2. Find the foreign exchange rate tables in the online versions of *The Wall Street Journal* (**www.wsj.com**) or the *Financial Times* (**www.ft.com**). How many Swiss francs can you buy for $1? How many Hong Kong dollars can you buy? What rate do you think a Swiss bank would quote for buying or selling Hong Kong dollars? Explain what would happen if it quoted a rate that was substantially above your figure.

MINI-CASE

EXACTA, S.A.

Exacta, s.a., is a major French producer, based in Lyons, of precision machine tools. About two-thirds of its output is exported. The majority of these sales is within the European Union. However, the company also has a thriving business in the United States, despite strong competition from several U.S. firms. Exacta usually receives payment for exported goods within two months of the invoice date, so that at any point in time only about one-sixth of annual exports to the United States is exposed to currency risk.

The company believes that its North American business is now large enough to justify a local manufacturing operation, and it has recently decided to establish a plant in South Carolina. Most of the output from this plant will be sold in the United States, but the company believes that there should also be opportunities for future sales in Canada and Mexico.

The South Carolina plant will involve a total investment of $380 million and is expected to be in operation by the year 2012. Annual revenues from the plant are expected to be about $420 million and the company forecasts net profits of $52 million a year. Once the plant is up and running, it should be able to operate for several years without substantial additional investment.

Although there is widespread enthusiasm for the project, several members of the management team have expressed anxiety about possible currency risk. M. Pangloss, the finance director, reassured them that the company was not a stranger to currency risk; after all, the company is already exporting about $320 million of machine tools each year to the United States and has managed to exchange its dollar revenue for euros without any major losses. But not everybody was convinced by this argument. For example, the CEO, M. B. Bardot, pointed out that the $380 million to be invested would substantially increase the amount of money at risk if the dollar fell relative to the euro. M. Bardot was notoriously risk-averse on financial matters and would push for complete hedging if practical.

M. Pangloss attempted to reassure the CEO. At the same time, he secretly shared some of the anxieties about exchange rate risk. Nearly all the revenues from the South Carolina plant would be in U.S. dollars and the bulk of the $380 million investment would likewise be incurred in the United States. About two-thirds of the operating costs would be in dollars, but the remaining one-third would represent payment for components brought in from Lyons plus the charge by the head office for management services and use of patents. The company has yet to decide whether to invoice its U.S. operation in dollars or euros for these purchases from the parent company.

M. Pangloss is optimistic that the company can hedge itself against currency risk. His favored solution is for Exacta to finance the plant by a $380 million issue of dollar bonds. That way the dollar investment would be offset by a matching dollar liability. An alternative is for the company to sell forward at the beginning of each year the expected revenues from the U.S. plant. But he realizes from experience that these simple solutions might carry hidden dangers. He decides to slow down and think more systematically about the additional exchange risk from the U.S. operation.

QUESTIONS

1. What would Exacta's true exposure be from its new U.S. operations, and how would it change from the company's current exposure?

2. Given that exposure, what would be the most effective and inexpensive approach to hedging?

28-1 FINANCIAL STATEMENTS

PART 9 FINANCIAL PLANNING AND WORKING CAPITAL MANAGEMENT

28

CHAPTER

FINANCIAL ANALYSIS

Good financial managers plan for the future. They check that they will have enough cash to pay the upcoming tax bill or dividend payment. They think about how much investment the firm will need to make over the next few years and about how they might finance that investment. They reflect on whether they are well placed to ride out an unexpected downturn in demand or an increase in the cost of materials.

In Chapter 29 we will describe how the financial manager develops both short- and long-term financial plans. But knowing where you stand today is a necessary prelude to contemplating where you might be in the future. Therefore, in this chapter we show how the firm's financial statements help you to understand the firm's overall performance and how some key financial ratios may alert senior management to potential problem areas. For example, when the firm needs a loan from the bank, the financial manager can expect some searching questions about the firm's debt ratio and the proportion of profits that is absorbed by interest. Likewise, if a division is earning a low return on its capital or its profit margins are under pressure, you can be sure that management will demand an explanation.

You have probably heard stories of whizzes who can take a company's accounts apart in minutes, calculate some financial ratios, and divine the company's future. Such people are like abominable snowmen: often spoken of but never truly seen. Financial ratios are no substitute for a crystal ball. They are just a convenient way to summarize large quantities of financial data and to compare firms' performance. The ratios help you to ask the right questions; they seldom answer them.

28-1   FINANCIAL STATEMENTS

Public companies have a variety of stakeholders, such as shareholders, bondholders, bankers, suppliers, employees, and management. All these stakeholders need to monitor the firm and to ensure that their interests are being served. They rely on the company's financial statements to provide the necessary information. Public companies report to their shareholders quarterly and annually. The annual financial statements are filed with the Ministry of Corporate Affairs in format prescribed in Schedule VI of the Companies Act.

Finance in Practice

Speaking in Tongues

Forget Esperanto. Too straightforward. The *lingua franca* that is increasingly spanning the globe is a tongue-twisting accounting-speak that is forcing even Americans to rethink some precious notions of financial sovereignty.

International Financial Reporting Standards (IFRS), which aim to harmonize financial reporting in a world of cross-border trade and investment, have made great strides since they were adopted by 7,000 or so listed companies in the European Union. To date, over 100 countries from Canada to China have adopted the rules or say they plan to adopt them. The London-based International Accounting Standards Board (IASB) expects that to swell to 150 in the next four years.

Even America, no ardent internationalist, is working with the IASB to narrow the gap between its own accounting standards and IFRS, which rules foreign companies listed in America could choose by 2009 or possibly sooner. Today such companies must "reconcile" their accounts with American rules—a costly exercise that some believe is driving foreign listings away from the United States.

In 2007 America's Securities and Exchange Commission (SEC) unexpectedly floated the idea of giving American, and not just foreign, companies the choice of using IFRS. Critics of the idea claim that this will give companies the option of shopping around for whichever regime best suits their business. Inevitably, however, by opening the door (if only a crack), America's own accounting regime would be in jeopardy.

Whether pure IFRS or not, all countries are prone to interpret the rules in ways that reflect their old accounting standards. Regulators are working through IOSCO, an international body of securities regulators, to attempt to whittle down these differences. The task is further complicated by the fact that international accounting rules tend to be "principles based," which means there are no hard-and-fast codes to follow. This is different from America, where accounting principles are accompanied by thousands of pages of prescriptive regulatory guidance and interpretations from auditors and accounting groups, some of it gleaned from SEC speeches. IFRS have no such baggage, leaving more room for judgment.

Source: Adapted from "Speaking in Tongues," *The Economist,* May 19, 2007, p. 83.

When reviewing a company's financial statements, it is important to remember that accountants still have a fair degree of leeway in reporting earnings and book values. For example, they have discretion in the choice of depreciation method and the speed at which the firm's assets are written off.

Although accountants around the world are working toward common practices, there are still considerable variations in the accounting rules of different countries. In Anglo-Saxon countries such as India, the U.S. or the U.K., which have large and active equity markets, the rules have been designed largely with the shareholder in mind. By contrast, in Germany the focus of accounting standards is to verify that the creditors are properly protected.

Another difference is the way that taxes are shown in the income statement. For example, in Germany taxes are paid on the published profits, and the depreciation method must therefore be approved by the revenue service. That is not the case in Anglo-Saxon countries, where the numbers shown in the published accounts are generally *not* the basis for calculating the company's tax payments. For instance, the depreciation method used to calculate the published profits usually differs from the depreciation method used by the tax authorities.

For investors and multinational companies these variations in accounting rules can be irksome. Accounting bodies have therefore been getting together to see whether they can iron out some of the differences. It is not a simple task, as the nearby box illustrates.

28-2 ACC's FINANCIAL STATEMENTS

Your task is to assess the financial standing of ACC Limited, the cement company from India. Perhaps you are a mutual fund manager trying to decide whether to allocate ₹10 crores of new money to ACC's stock. Perhaps you are a major shareholder pondering a sellout. You could be an investment banker seeking business from the company or a bondholder concerned with its credit standing. You could be the financial manager of ACC's or of one of its competitors.

In each case your first step is to assess the company's *current* condition. You have before you the latest balance sheet and income statement.

The Balance Sheet

Table 28.1 sets out a simplified balance sheet for ACC for its fiscal year 2010. It provides a snapshot of the company's assets at the end of that year and the sources of the money that was used to buy those assets.

The assets are listed in declining order of liquidity. For example, the accountant lists first those assets that are most likely to be turned into cash in the near future. They include cash itself, marketable securities and receivables (that is, bills to be paid by the firm's customers), and inventories of raw materials, work in process, and finished goods. These assets are all known as *current assets*.

The remaining assets on the balance sheet consist of long-term assets such as land, building, plant, machinery, investments in shares, debentures, etc. The balance sheet does not show up-to-date market values of the fixed assets. Instead, the accountant records the amount that each asset originally cost and deducts a fixed annual amount for depreciation. Indian companies, however, report the aggregate market value of company's quoted investments.[1] The balance sheet does not include all the company's assets. Some of the most valuable ones are intangible, such as patents, reputation, a skilled

---

[1] However, while finding the total value of all the assets, companies include only the book value of the Investments.

TABLE 28.1   Balance sheet of ACC Limited, fiscal 2009 and 2010 (figures in ₹ crores)

	2010	2009
Assets		
Current assets:		
Cash and marketable securities	94.96	95.64
Accounts receivable	178.28	203.7
Inventories	914.98	778.98
Other current assets	1737.48	1365.29
Total current assets	2925.7	2443.61
Fixed assets:		
Net fixed assets	9,639.75	8,982.48
Less accumulated depreciation	2,994.51	2,667.98
Net fixed assets	6,645.24	6,314.50
Investments	1,702.67	1,475.64
Total assets	11,273.61	10,233.75
Liabilities and Shareholders' Equity		
Current liabilities:		
Accounts payable	2,627.84	2,558.73
Other current liabilities	1,652.46	1,091.88
Total current liabilities	4,280.30	3,650.61
Long-term debt	523.82	566.92
Share capital	187.95	187.94
Reserves & surpluses	6,281.54	5,828.20
Total shareholders' equity	6469.49	6016.14
Total liabilities and shareholders' equity	11,273.61	10,233.67

management, and a well-trained labor force. Accountants are generally reluctant to record these assets in the balance sheet unless they can be readily identified and valued.

Now look at the bottom portion of ACC's balance sheet, which shows where the money to buy the assets came from. We start by looking at the liabilities, that is, the money owed by the company. First come those liabilities that need to be paid off in the near future. These current liabilities include sundry creditors (or accounts payable), provisions. One should include the debts that are due to be repaid within the next year.[2]

---

[2] Indian companies, however, include these debts under the head 'Secured and Unsecured Liabilities'.

The difference between the current assets and current liabilities is known as the *net current assets* or *net working capital* (or simply working capital). It roughly measures the company's potential reservoir of cash. For ACC in 2010

$$\text{Net working capital} = \text{current assets} - \text{current liabilities}$$
$$= 2,925.7 - 4,280.3 = -₹1,354.60 \text{ crores}$$

The bottom portion of the balance sheet shows the sources of the cash that was used to acquire the net working capital, investments and fixed assets. Some of the cash has come from the issue of bonds that will not be paid for many years. After all these long-term liabilities have been paid off, the remaining assets belong to the common stockholders. The company's equity is simply the net working capital, investments and fixed assets less the long-term liabilities. Part of this equity has come from the sale of shares to investors, and the remainder has come from earnings that the company has retained and invested on behalf of the shareholders.

The Profit and Loss Account Statement

If ACC's balance sheet resembles a snapshot of the firm at a particular point in time, its profit and loss account is like a video. It shows how profitable the firm has been over the past year.

Look at the summary of profit and loss account in Table 28.2. You can see that during 2010, ACC sold goods worth ₹7,647.77 crores and that the total raw material costs were ₹1,520.68 crores. The total selling, general and administrative expenses were ₹4,320.74 crores. In addition to these out-of-pocket expenses, ACC also made a deduction of ₹392.68 crores for the value of the fixed assets used up in producing the goods. ACC also earned revenue from other sources amounting to ₹226.57 crores. Thus ACC's earnings before interest and taxes (EBIT) were

$$\text{EBIT} = \text{total revenues} - \text{costs} - \text{depreciation}$$
$$= 7,874.34 - 5,841.42 - 392.68$$
$$= ₹1,640.24 \text{ crores}$$

Of this sum ₹56.78 crores went to pay the interest on the short- and long-term debt (remember debt interest is paid out of pretax income) and a further ₹424.15 crores to the government in the form of taxes. The ₹1,59.31 crores that was left out belonged to the shareholders. ACC's paid out ₹667.73 crores as dividends and dividend tax, and reinvested the remaining ₹491.58 crores in the business.

TABLE 28.2 Profit and Loss account of ACC Limited for the year ending December 31, 2010. Figures in ₹ crores.

Visit us at www.mhhe.com/bmam10e

	₹ Crores
Net Sales	7,647.77
Other income	226.57
Raw Material	1,520.68
Selling, general, and administrative expenses	4,320.74
Depreciation	392.68
Earnings before interest and taxes (EBIT)	1,640.24
Interest expense	56.78
Taxable income	1,583.46
Tax	424.15
Net income	1,159.31
Dividends (including dividend tax)	667.73
Addition to reserves and surpluses	491.58

28-3 MEASURING ACC's PERFORMANCE

You want to use ACC's financial statements to assess its financial performance and current standing. Where do you start?

At the close of fiscal 2010, ACC's common stock was priced at ₹1070 per share.[3] There were 18,77,45,356 shares (approximately 18.77 crores) outstanding, so total **market capitalization** was 18.77 × 1070 = ₹20,084 crores. This is a big number, of course, but ACC is a sizeable company. Its shareholders have, over the years, invested hundreds of crores of rupees in the company. Therefore, you decide to compare ACC's market capitalization with the book value of equity. The book value measures shareholders' cumulative investment in the company.

At the end of fiscal 2010 the book value of ACC's equity was ₹6,469.49 crores. Therefore, the **market value added,** the difference between the market value of the firm's shares and the amount of money that shareholders have invested in the firm, was ₹20,084 − ₹6,469.49 = ₹13,614.51 crores. In other words, the shareholders have contributed about ₹13,500 crores and ended up with shares worth about ₹20,000 crores. They have accumulated about ₹13,500 crores in market value added.

In Table 28.3, we show the market value added of a few large Indian companies. Reliance Industries heads the group. It has created ₹2,239,802 crores of wealth for its shareholders. Jet Airways is at the bottom of the class; the market value of Jet Airways is ₹799 crores less than the amount of shareholders' money invested in the firm.

TABLE 28.3 Stock market measures of company performance in 2011 (Rupee values in mullions)

	Market Value Added	Market-to-Book Ratio		Market Value Added	Market-to-Book Ratio
Reliance Industries	2,239,803	15.23	Infosys	1,455,322	50.58
Coal India	2,145,246	86.61	NTPC	1,295,940	18.90
ONGC	2,117,398	21.19	ICICI Bank	852,199	15.71
TCS	2,103,161	90.29	Tata Power	216,455	19.29
ITC	1,593,106	85.97	Jet Airways	-799	0.69

Source: Prowess Database

Reliance Industries is a large firm. Its managers have lots of assets to work with. A small firm could not hope to create so much value. Therefore, financial managers and analysts also like to calculate how much value has been added *for each rupee that the shareholders have invested*. To do this, they compute the ratio of market value to book value. For example, ACC's **market-to-book ratio** is[4]

$$\text{Market-to-book ratio} = \text{Market value of equity} / \text{book value of equity}$$
$$= 20215.9/6469.49 = 3.12$$

In other words, ACC has multiplied the value of its shareholders' investment 3 times.

Table 28.3 also shows market-to-book ratios for our sample Indian companies. Notice that TCS has a much higher market-to-book ratio than Reliance Industries. But Reliance's market value added is higher because of its larger scale.

The market value performance measures in Table 28.3 have two drawbacks. First, the market value of the company's shares reflects investors' expectations about *future* performance. Investors pay attention to current profits and investment, of course, but market-value measures can nevertheless be noisy measures of current performance.

---

[3] ACC's fiscal year ended on December 31, 2010.

[4] The market-to-book ratio can also be calculated by dividing stock price by book value per share.

Second, you can't look up the market value of privately owned companies whose shares are not traded. Nor can you observe the market value of divisions or plants that are parts of larger companies. You may use market values to satisfy yourself that ICICI Bank as a whole has performed well, but you can't use them to drill down to look at the performance of, say, its branch in Bangalore. To do this, you need accounting measures of profitability. We start with economic value added (EVA).

Economic Value Added (EVA)

When accountants draw up an income statement, they start with revenues and then deduct operating and other costs. But one important cost is *not* included: the cost of the capital that the company has raised from investors. Therefore, to see whether the firm has truly created value, we need to measure whether it has earned a profit after deducting *all* costs, including its cost of capital.

The cost of capital is the minimum acceptable rate of return on capital investment. It is an *opportunity* cost of capital, because it equals the expected rate of return on investment opportunities open to investors in financial markets. The firm creates value for investors only if it can earn more than its cost of capital, that is, more than its investors can earn by investing on their own.

The profit after deducting all costs, *including the cost of capital,* is called the company's **economic value added** or **EVA**. We encountered EVA in Chapter 12, where we looked at how firms often link executive compensation to accounting measures of performance. Let's calculate EVA for ACC.

Total long-term capital, sometimes called *total capitalization,* is the sum of long-term debt and shareholders' equity. At the end of December 2009, ACC's total capitalization amounted to ₹6,583.14 crores, which was made up of ₹566.92 crores of debt and ₹6,016.22 crores of equity. This is the cumulative amount that has been invested in the past by the debt and equityholders. ACC's weighted-average cost of capital was about 16%. Therefore, investors who provided the ₹6,583.14 crores required the company in 2011 to earn at least $.16 \times 6,583.14 = ₹1,053.30$ crores for its debt and equityholders.

In 2010, ACC's after-tax interest and net income totaled $(1 - 0.34) \times 56.78 + 1,159.31 = ₹1,196.78$ crores (we assume 34% tax rate). If you deduct the total cost of ACC's capital from this figure, you can see that the company earned $₹1196.78 - 1,053.3 = ₹143.48$ crores more than investors required. This was ACC's residual income, or EVA.

$$EVA = (\text{after-tax interest} + \text{net income}) - (\text{cost of capital} \times \text{capital})$$
$$= 1196.78 - 1053.3 = ₹143.48 \text{ crores.}$$

Sometimes it is helpful to re-express EVA as follows:

$$EVA = \left(\frac{\text{after-tax interest} + \text{net income}}{\text{total capital}} - \text{cost of capital}\right) \times \text{total capital}$$

$$= (\text{return on capital} - \text{cost of capital}) \times \text{total capital}$$

The **return on capital** (or **ROC**) is equal to the total profits that the company has earned for its debt and equityholders, divided by the amount of money that they have contributed. If the company earns a higher return on its capital than investors require, EVA is positive.

In the case of ACC's, the return on capital was

$$\frac{\text{after-tax interest} + \text{net income}}{\text{total capital}} = \frac{(1 - 0.34) \times 56.78 + 1159.31}{6583.14} = 0.1818, \text{about } 18.18\%$$

ACC's cost of capital was about 16%. So,

$$EVA = (\text{return on capital} - \text{cost of capital}) \times \text{total capital}$$
$$= (0.1818 - 0.16) \times 6583.14 = ₹143.48 \text{ crores.}$$

The first four columns on Table 28.4 show measures of EVA for our sample of large companies. This time TCS heads the list. In 2011, it earned around ₹50,600 crores more than what was needed to satisfy the investors. By contrast, Reliance was a laggard. Although it earned an accounting profit of nearly ₹218,000 crores, this figure was calculated before deducting the cost of the capital that was employed. After deducting the cost of capital, Reliance made an EVA loss of nearly ₹119,000 crores.

TABLE 28.4 Accounting measures of company performance, 2011 (rupee values in millions).

	1. After-tax interest + net income	2. Cost of capital (WACC) %	3. Total long-term capital	4. EVA = 1 – (2 × 3)	5. Return on Capital (ROC) % (¹⁄₃)
RIL	218,096	15.4	2,189,370	– 119,749	9.96
Coal India	49,299	15.3	208,078	+ 17,378	23.7
ONGC	189,406	16.8	975,044	+ 25,598	19.4
TCS	75,832	12.9	195,206	+ 50,653	38.8
ITC	50,267	12.8	160,525	+29,727	31.3
Infosys	64,430	12.6	245,010	+ 33,559	26.3
NTPC	99,125	12.8	1,110,846	– 43,369	8.9
ICICI Bank	163,431	13.7	1,646,451	– 62,525	9.9
Tata Power	11,829	15.2	182,292	– 15,830	6.5
Jet Airways	1,246	12.7	16,085	– 645	7.7

Note: EVAs do not compute exactly because of rounding in column 2.
Source: We are grateful to EVA Dimensions for providing these statistics.

Accounting Rates of Return

EVA measures how many rupees a business is earning after deducting the cost of capital. Other things equal, the more assets the manager has to work with, the greater the opportunity to generate a large EVA. The manager of a small division may be highly competent, but if that division has few assets, she is unlikely to rank high in the EVA stakes. Therefore, when comparing managers, it can also be helpful to measure the firm's return *per dollar of investment.*

Three common return measures are the return on capital (ROC), the return on equity (ROE), and the return on assets (ROA). All are based on accounting information and are therefore known as *book rates of return.*

Return on Capital (ROC)[5]   We have already calculated ACC's return on capital in 2010:

$$\text{ROC} = \frac{\text{after-tax interest} + \text{net income}}{\text{total capital}} = \frac{(1 - .34) \times 56.78 + 1159.31}{6583.14} = .1818, \text{ or } 18.18\%$$

---

[5] The expression, *return on capital,* is commonly used when calculating the profitability of an entire firm. When measuring the profitability of an individual plant, the equivalent measure is generally called *return on investment* (or *ROI*).

You will encounter a variety of alternative ways to calculate any book rate of return. For example, a company may have issued new capital during the year and invested the proceeds. If that is the case, it may be better to use the average of the capital at the beginning and end of the year.[6] If we do so, ACC's ROC changes to

$$ROC = \frac{\text{after-tax interest} + \text{net income}}{\text{average total capital}} = \frac{(1-0.34)\times 56.78 + 1159.31}{(6583.14 + 6993.31)/2} = 0.1763, \text{ or } 17.63\%$$

Here is another technical point. When we calculated ACC's return on capital we summed the company's *after-tax* interest and net income.[7] The reason that we subtracted the tax shield on debt interest was that we wished to calculate the income that the company would have earned with all-equity financing. The tax advantages of debt financing are picked up when we compare the company's return on capital with its weighted-average cost of capital (WACC).[8] WACC already includes an adjustment for the interest tax shield.[9] More often than not, financial analysts ignore this refinement and use the gross interest payment to calculate ROC. It is only approximately correct to compare this measure with the weightedaverage cost of capital.

The last column in Table 28.4 shows the return on capital for our sample of well-known companies. Notice that Coal India's return on capital was 23.7%, about 8 percentage points above its cost of capital. Although Coal India had a higher return on capital than ONGC, another public sector company, it had a lower EVA. This was partly because it had fewer rupees invested than ONGC.

Return on Equity (ROE)   We measure the **return on equity (ROE)** as the income to shareholders per dollar invested. ACC's had net income of ₹1,159.31 crores in 2010 and stockholders' equity of ₹6,016.14 crore at the start of the year. So its return on equity was

$$ROE = \frac{\text{net income}}{\text{equity}} = \frac{1159.31}{6016.14} = 0.1927 \text{ or } 19.27\%$$

If we recalculate ROE using average equity, then the return was

$$ROE = \frac{\text{net income}}{\text{average equity}} = \frac{1159.31}{(6016.14 + 6469.49)/2} = 0.1857 \text{ or } 18.57\%$$

Return on Assets (ROA)   **Return on assets** measures the income available to debt and equity investors per dollar of the firm's *total* assets. Total assets (which equal total liabilities plus shareholders' equity) are greater than total capital because total capital does not include current liabilities. For ACC's, return on assets was

$$ROA = \frac{(\text{after-tax interest} + \text{net income})}{\text{total assets}} = \frac{(1-0.34)\times 56.78 + 1159.31}{10233.67} = 0.117 \text{ or } 11.7\%$$

---

[6] Averages are used when a flow figure (in this case, income) that builds up over the course of the year is compared with a snapshot figure of assets or liabilities (in this case, capital). Sometimes it's convenient to use a snapshot figure at the end of the year, although this procedure is not strictly correct.

[7] This figure is called the company's Net Operating Profit After Tax or NOPAT:

$$NOPAT = \text{after-tax interest} + \text{net income}$$

In the case of ACC's

$$NOPAT = (1 - .34) \times 56.78 + 1159.31 = ₹1196.78 \text{ crores.}$$

[8] For the same reason we used the after-tax interest payment when we calculated ACC's EVA.

[9] Remember WACC is a weighted average of the *after-tax* rate of interest and the cost of equity.

When we subtract the tax shield on ACC's interest payments, we are asking how much the company would have earned if all-equity-financed. This adjustment is helpful when comparing the profitability of firms with very different capital structures. Again, this refinement is ignored more often than not, and ROA is calculated using the gross interest payment.[10] Sometimes analysts take no account of interest payments and measure ROA as the income for equityholders divided by total assets. This measure ignores entirely the income that the assets have generated for debtholders.

We see shortly how ACC's return on assets is determined by the sales that these assets generate and the profit margin that the company earns on its sales.

Problems with EVA and Accounting Rates of Return

Rate of return and economic value added have some obvious attractions as measures of performance. Unlike market-value-based measures, they show current performance and are not affected by the expectations about future events that are reflected in today's stock market prices. Rate of return and economic value added can also be calculated for an entire company or for a particular plant or division. However, remember that both measures are based on book (balance sheet) values for assets. Debt and equity are also book values. Accountants do not show every asset on the balance sheet, yet our calculations take accounting data at face value. For example, we ignored the fact that ACC's has invested large sums in marketing to establish its brand name. This brand name is an important asset, but its value is not shown on the balance sheet. If it were shown, the book values of assets, capital, and equity would increase, and ACC's would not appear to earn such high returns.

In Table 28.4, we showed the return on assets and EVA figure for a sample of Indian companies. It is, however, impossible to include the value of all assets or judge how rapidly they depreciate. For example, did Infosys really earn a return of 26.3%? It is difficult to say, because its investment in its human resources (one of its key resource) is not shown on the balance sheet and cannot be measured exactly.

Remember also that the balance sheet does not show the current market values of the firm's assets. The assets in a company's books are valued at their original cost less any depreciation. Older assets may be grossly undervalued in today's market conditions and prices. So a high return on assets indicates that the business has performed well by making profitable investments in the past, but it does not necessarily mean that you could buy the same assets today at their reported book values. Conversely a low return suggests some poor decisions in the past, but it does not always mean that today the assets could be employed better elsewhere.

28-4 MEASURING EFFICIENCY

We began our analysis of ACC's by calculating how much value the company has added for its shareholders and how much profit it is earning after deducting the cost of the capital that it employs. We examined ACC's rates of return on capital, equity, and total assets and found that its return has been higher than the cost of capital. Our next task is to probe a little deeper to understand the reasons for the company's success. What factors contribute to a firm's overall profitability? One factor clearly must be the efficiency with which it uses its many types of assets.

---

[10] Again, when calculating ROA, financial analysts sometimes use an average of the assets at the start and end of the year.

Asset Turnover Ratio   The asset turnover, or sales-to-assets, ratio shows how much sales are generated by each dollar of total assets, and therefore it measures how hard the firm's assets are working. For ACC's, each rupee of assets produced ₹.75 of sales:

$$\text{Asset turnover} = \frac{\text{sales}}{\text{total assets at start of year}} = \frac{7,647.77}{10,233.67} = .75$$

Like some of our profitability ratios, the sales-to-assets ratio compares a flow measure (sales over the entire year) to a snapshot measure (assets on one day). Therefore, financial managers and analysts often calculate the ratio of sales over the entire year to the *average* level of assets over the same period. In this case,

$$\text{Asset turnover} = \frac{\text{sales}}{\text{average total assets}} = \frac{7,647.77}{(10,233.67 + 11,273.61)/2} = 0.71$$

The asset turnover ratio measures how efficiently the business is using its entire asset base. But you also might be interested in how hard *particular types* of assets are being put to use. Below are a couple of examples.

Inventory Turnover   Efficient firms don't tie up more capital than they need in raw materials and finished goods. They hold only a relatively small level of inventories of raw materials and finished goods, and they turn over those inventories rapidly. The balance sheet shows the cost of inventories rather than the amount that the finished goods will eventually sell for. So it is usual to compare the average level of inventories with the cost of goods sold rather than with sales. In ACC's case,

$$\text{Inventory turnover} = \frac{\text{sales}}{\text{inventory at start of year}} = \frac{7,647.77}{778.98} = 9.82$$

Receivables Turnover   Receivables are sales for which the company has not yet been paid. The receivables turnover ratio measures the firm's sales as a proportion of its receivables. For ACC's,

$$\text{Receivables turnover} = \frac{\text{sales}}{\text{receivables at start of year}} = \frac{7,647.77}{203.7} = 37.54$$

If customers are quick to pay, unpaid bills will be a relatively small proportion of sales and the receivables turnover will be high. Therefore, a comparatively high ratio often indicates an efficient credit department that is quick to follow up on late payers. Sometimes, however, a high ratio indicates that the firm has an unduly restrictive credit policy and offers credit only to customers who can be relied on to pay promptly.[11]

Another way to measure the efficiency of the credit operation is by calculating the average length of time for customers to pay their bills. The faster the firm turns over its receivables, the shorter the collection period. ACC's customers pay their bills in about 9.7 days:

$$\text{Average collection period} = \frac{\text{receivables at start of year}}{\text{average daily sales}} = \frac{203.7}{(7647.77/365)} = 9.72 \text{ days}$$

The receivables turnover ratio and the inventory turnover ratio may help to highlight particular areas of inefficiency, but they are not the only possible indicators. For example, ACC's might compare

---

[11] Where possible, it makes sense to look only at *credit* sales. Otherwise a high ratio might simply indicate that a small proportion of sales is made on credit.

its sales per ton of current capacity with those of its competitors, a steel producer might calculate the cost per ton of steel produced, an airline might look at revenues per passenger-mile, and a law firm might look at revenues per partner. A little thought and common sense should suggest which measures are likely to produce the most helpful insights into your company's efficiency.

28-5 ANALYZING THE RETURN ON ASSETS: THE DU PONT SYSTEM

We have seen that every rupee of ACC's assets generates ₹.75 of sales. But a company's success depends not only on the volume of its sales but also on how profitable those sales are. This is measured by the profit margin.

Profit Margin The profit margin measures the proportion of sales that finds its way into profits. It is sometimes defined as

$$\text{Profit margin} = \frac{\text{net income}}{\text{sales}} = \frac{1159.31}{7647.77} = .1516, \text{ or } 15.16\%$$

This definition can be misleading. When companies are partly financed by debt, a portion of the profits from the sales must be paid as interest to the firm's lenders. We would not want to say that a firm is less profitable than its rivals simply because it employs debt finance and pays out part of its profits as interest. Therefore, when we are calculating the profit margin, it is useful to add back the debt interest to net income. This gives an alternative measure of profit margin, which is called the **operating profit margin:**[12]

$$\text{Operating profit margin} = \frac{\text{after-tax interest} + \text{net income}}{\text{sales}}$$

$$= \frac{56.78 \times (1 - .34) + 1159.31}{7647.77}$$

$$= .1565, \text{ or } 15.65\%$$

The Du Pont System

We calculated earlier that ACC's has earned a return of 18.18% on its assets. The following equation shows that this return depends on two factors—the sales that the company generates from its assets (asset turnover) and the profit that it earns on each rupee of sales (operating profit margin):

$$\text{Return on assets} = \frac{\text{after-tax interest} + \text{net income}}{\text{assets}} = \underbrace{\frac{\text{sales}}{\text{assets}}}_{\text{asset turnover}} \times \underbrace{\frac{\text{after-tax interest} + \text{net income}}{\text{sales}}}_{\text{operating profit margin}}$$

---

[12] If a firm pays out most of its profits as interest, it will pay less tax and have a higher operating profit margin than one that is financed solely by equity. To obtain a measure of the profit margin that is unaffected by the firm's financial structure, we need to subtract the tax savings on the interest.

This breakdown of ROA into the product of turnover and margin is often called the **Du Pont formula,** after the chemical company that popularized the procedure. In ACC's case the formula gives the following breakdown of ROA:

$$\text{ROA} = \text{asset turnover} \times \text{operating profit margin} = .75 \times .1565 = .117$$

All firms would like to earn a higher return on their assets, but their ability to do so is limited by competition. The Du Pont formula helps to identify the constraints that firms face. Fast-food chains, which have high asset turnover, tend to operate on low margins. Classy hotels have relatively low turnover ratios but tend to compensate with higher margins.

Firms often seek to improve their profit margins by acquiring a supplier. The idea is to capture the supplier's profit as well as their own. Unfortunately, unless they have some special skill in running the new business, they are likely to find that any gain in profit margin is offset by a decline in asset turnover.

A few numbers may help to illustrate this point. Table 28.5 shows the sales, profits, and assets of Admiral Motors and its components supplier, Diana Corporation. Both earn a 10% return on assets, though Admiral has a lower operating profit margin (20% versus Diana's 25%). Since all of Diana's output goes to Admiral, Admiral's management reasons that it would be better to merge the two companies. That way, the merged company would capture the profit margin on both the auto components and the assembled car.

TABLE 28.5 Merging with suppliers or customers generally increases the profit margin, but this increase is offset by a reduction in asset turnover.

	Sales	Profits	Assets	Asset Turnover	Profit Margin	ROA
Admiral Motors	₹20	₹4	₹40	.50	20%	10%
Diana Corporation	8	2	20	.40	25	10
Diana Motors (the merged firm)	20	6	60	.33	30	10

The bottom row of Table 28.5 shows the effect of the merger. The merged firm does indeed earn the combined profits. Total sales remain at ₹20 million, however, because all the components produced by Diana are used within the company. With higher profits and unchanged sales, the profit margin increases. Unfortunately, the asset turnover is *reduced* by the merger since the merged firm has more assets. This exactly offsets the benefit of the higher profit margin. The return on assets is unchanged.

28-6 MEASURING LEVERAGE

When a firm borrows money, it promises to make a series of interest payments and then to repay the amount that it has borrowed. If profits rise, the debtholders continue to receive only the fixed interest payment, so all the gains go to the shareholders. Of course, the reverse happens if profits fall. In this case shareholders bear the greater part of the pain. If times are sufficiently hard, a firm that has borrowed heavily may not be able to pay its debts. The firm is then bankrupt, and shareholders lose most or all of their investment.

Because debt increases the returns to shareholders in good times and reduces them in bad times, it is said to create *financial leverage.* Leverage ratios measure how much financial leverage the firm has taken on. CFOs keep an eye on leverage ratios to ensure that lenders are happy to continue to take on the firm's debt.

Debt Ratio   Financial leverage is usually measured by the ratio of long-term debt to total long-term capital. (Here "long-term debt" should include not just bonds or other borrowing but also financing from long-term leases.)[13] For ACC's,

$$\text{Long-term debt ratio} = \frac{\text{long-term debt}}{\text{long-term debt} + \text{equity}} = \frac{566.92}{566.92 + 6{,}016.14} = .086, \text{ or } 8.6\%$$

This means that 9 paise of every rupee of long-term capital is in the form of debt.

Notice that debt ratios make use of book (i.e., accounting) values rather than market values.[14] The market value of the company finally determines whether the debtholders get their money back, so you might expect analysts to look at the face amount of the debt as a proportion of the total market value of debt and equity. On the other hand, the market value includes the value of intangible assets generated by research and development, advertising, staff training, and so on. These assets are not readily salable and, if the company falls on hard times, their value may disappear altogether. For some purposes, it may be just as good to follow the accountant and ignore these intangible assets. This is what lenders do when they insist that the borrower should not allow the book debt ratio to exceed a specified limit.

Notice also that these measures of leverage ignore short-term debt. That probably makes sense if the short-term debt is temporary or is matched by similar holdings of cash, but if the company is a regular short-term borrower, it may be preferable to widen the definition of debt to include all liabilities. In this case,

$$\text{Total debt ratio} = \frac{\text{total liabilities}}{\text{total assets}} = \frac{4{,}217.53}{10{,}233.67} = .41, \text{ or } 41\%$$

Therefore, ACC's is financed 41% with long- and short-term debt and 59% with equity.[15] We could also say that its ratio of total debt to equity is $4{,}217.53/6{,}016.14 = .70$.

Managers sometimes refer loosely to a company's debt ratio, but we have just seen that the debt ratio may be measured in several different ways. For example, ACC's has a debt ratio of .086 (the long-term debt ratio) and also .41 (the total debt ratio). This is not the first time we have come across several ways to define a financial ratio. There is no law stating how a ratio should be defined. So be warned: do not use a ratio without understanding how it has been calculated.

Times-Interest-Earned Ratio   Another measure of financial leverage is the extent to which interest obligations are covered by earnings. Banks prefer to lend to firms whose earnings cover interest payments with room to spare. *Interest coverage* is measured by the ratio of earnings before interest and taxes (EBIT) to interest payments. For ACC's,[16]

---

[13] A finance lease is a long-term rental agreement that commits the firm to make regular payments. This commitment is just like the obligation to make payments on an outstanding loan. See Chapter 25.

[14] In the case of leased assets, accountants estimate the value of the lease commitments. In the case of long-term debt, they simply show the face value, which can be very different from market value. For example, the present value of low-coupon debt may be only a fraction of its face value. The difference between the book value of equity and its market value can be even more dramatic.

[15] In this case, the debt consists of all liabilities, including current liabilities.

[16] The numerator of times-interest-earned can be defined in several ways. Sometimes depreciation is excluded. Sometimes it is just earnings plus interest, that is, earnings before interest but *after* tax. This last definition seems nutty to us, because the point of times-interest-earned is to assess the risk that the firm won't have enough money to pay interest. If EBIT falls below interest obligations, the firm won't have to worry about taxes. Interest is paid before the firm pays taxes.

$$\text{Times-interest-earned} = \frac{\text{EBIT}}{\text{interest payments}} = \frac{1,640.24}{56.78} = 28.89$$

ACC's enjoys a comfortable interest coverage or *times-interest-earned* ratio. Sometimes lenders are content with coverage ratios as low as 2 or 3.

The regular interest payment is a hurdle that companies must keep jumping if they are to avoid default. Times-interest-earned measures how much clear air there is between hurdle and hurdler. The ratio is only part of the story, however. For example, it doesn't tell us whether ACC's is generating enough cash to repay its debt as it comes due.

Cash Coverage Ratio In the previous chapter we pointed out that depreciation is deducted when calculating the firm's earnings, even though no cash goes out the door. Suppose we add back depreciation to EBIT to calculate operating cash flow. We can then calculate a *cash* coverage ratio. For ACC's,

$$\text{Cash coverage} = \frac{\text{EBIT} + \text{depreciation}}{\text{interest payments}} = \frac{1,640.24 + 392.68}{56.78} = 35.8$$

Leverage and the Return on Equity

When the firm raises cash by borrowing, it must make interest payments to its lenders. This reduces net profits. On the other hand, if a firm borrows instead of issuing equity, it has fewer equityholders to share the remaining profits. Which effect dominates? An extended version of the Du Pont formula helps us answer this question. It breaks down the return on equity (ROE) into four parts:

$$\text{ROE} = \frac{\text{net income}}{\text{equity}}$$

$$= \underbrace{\frac{\text{assets}}{\text{equity}}}_{\substack{\text{leverage} \\ \text{ratio}}} \times \underbrace{\frac{\text{sales}}{\text{assets}}}_{\substack{\text{asset} \\ \text{turnover}}} \times \underbrace{\frac{\text{after-tax interest} + \text{net income}}{\text{sales}}}_{\substack{\text{operating profit} \\ \text{margin}}} \times \underbrace{\frac{\text{net income}}{\text{after-tax interest} + \text{net income}}}_{\substack{\text{"debt} \\ \text{burden"}}}$$

Notice that the product of the two middle terms is the return on assets. It depends on the firm's production and marketing skills and is unaffected by the firm's financing mix. However, the first and fourth terms do depend on the debt–equity mix. The first term, assets/equity, which we call the *leverage ratio,* can be expressed as (equity + liabilities)/equity, which equals 1 + total-debt-to-equity ratio. The last term, which we call the "debt burden," measures the proportion by which interest expense reduces net income.

Suppose that the firm is financed entirely by equity. In this case, both the leverage ratio and the debt burden are equal to 1, and the return on equity is identical to the return on assets. If the firm borrows, however, the leverage ratio is greater than 1 (assets are greater than equity) and the debt burden is less than 1 (part of the profits is absorbed by interest). Thus leverage can either increase or reduce return on equity.

28-7 MEASURING LIQUIDITY

If you are extending credit to a customer or making a short-term bank loan, you are interested in more than the company's leverage. You want to know whether the company can lay its hands on the cash to repay you. That is why credit analysts and bankers look at several measures of **liquidity.** Liquid assets can be converted into cash quickly and cheaply.

Think, for example, what you would do to meet a large unexpected bill. You might have some money in the bank or some investments that are easily sold, but you would not find it so easy to turn your old sweaters into cash. Companies, likewise, own assets with different degrees of liquidity. For example, accounts receivable and inventories of finished goods are generally quite liquid. As inventories are sold off and customers pay their bills, money flows into the firm. At the other extreme, real estate may be very *illiquid.* It can be hard to find a buyer, negotiate a fair price, and close a deal on short notice.

Managers have another reason to focus on liquid assets: Their book (balance sheet) values are usually reliable. The book value of a catalytic cracker may be a poor guide to its true value, but at least you know what cash in the bank is worth. Liquidity ratios also have some *less* desirable characteristics. Because short-term assets and liabilities are easily changed, measures of liquidity can rapidly become outdated. You might not know what the catalytic cracker is worth, but you can be fairly sure that it won't disappear overnight. Cash in the bank can disappear in seconds.

Also, assets that seem liquid sometimes have a nasty habit of becoming illiquid. This happened during the subprime mortgage crisis in 2007. Some financial institutions had set up funds known as *structured investment vehicles (SIVs)* that issued short-term debt backed by residential mortgages. As mortgage default rates began to climb, the market in this debt dried up and dealers became very reluctant to quote a price. Investors, who were forced to sell, found that the prices that they received were less than half the debt's estimated value.

Bankers and other short-term lenders applaud firms that have plenty of liquid assets. They know that when they are due to be repaid, the firm will be able to get its hands on the cash. But more liquidity is not always a good thing. For example, efficient firms do not leave excess cash in their bank accounts. They don't allow customers to postpone paying their bills, and they don't leave stocks of raw materials and finished goods littering the warehouse floor. In other words, high levels of liquidity may indicate sloppy use of capital. Here, EVA can help, because it penalizes managers who keep more liquid assets than they really need.

Net-Working-Capital-to-Total-Assets Ratio Current assets include cash, marketable securities, inventories, and accounts receivable. Current assets are mostly liquid. The difference between current assets and current liabilities is known as *net working capital.* Since current assets usually exceed current liabilities, net working capital is generally positive. For ACC's,

$$\text{Net working capital} = ₹2,925.7 - 3,650.61 = -₹724.91 \text{ crores}$$

For ACC, the net working capital is negative. Many large and profitable Indian companies exhibit this trend these days. Since the net working capital is negative, we do not compute the working-capital-to-total-assets ratio here as it would be meaningless number.

Current Ratio The current ratio is just the ratio of current assets to current liabilities:

$$\text{Current ratio} = \frac{\text{current assets}}{\text{current liabilities}} = \frac{2,925.7}{3,650.6} = .80$$

ACC has ₹.80 in current assets for every rupee in current liabilities.

Changes in the current ratio can be misleading. For example, suppose that a company borrows a large sum from the bank and invests it in marketable securities. Current liabilities rise and so do current assets. If nothing else changes, net working capital is unaffected but the current ratio changes. For this reason it is sometimes preferable to net short-term investments against short-term debt when calculating the current ratio.

Quick (Acid-Test) Ratio   Some current assets are closer to cash than others. If trouble comes, inventory may not sell at anything above fire-sale prices. (Trouble typically comes *because* the firm can't sell its inventory of finished products for more than production cost.) Thus managers often exclude inventories and other less liquid components of current assets when comparing current assets to current liabilities. They focus instead on cash, marketable securities, and bills that customers have not yet paid. This results in the quick ratio:

$$\text{Quick ratio} = \frac{\text{cash} + \text{marketable securities} + \text{receivables}}{\text{current liabilities}} = \frac{94.96 + 178.28}{3{,}650.61} = .07$$

Cash Ratio   A company's most liquid assets are its holdings of cash and marketable securities. That is why analysts also look at the cash ratio:

$$\text{Cash ratio} = \frac{\text{Cash} + \text{marketable securities}}{\text{current liabilities}} = \frac{94.96}{3{,}650.61} = .03$$

A low cash ratio may not matter if the firm can borrow on short notice. Who cares whether the firm has actually borrowed from the bank or whether it has a guaranteed line of credit so it can borrow whenever it chooses? None of the standard measures of liquidity takes the firm's "reserve borrowing power" into account.

28-8   INTERPRETING FINANCIAL RATIOS

We have shown how to calculate some common summary measures of ACC's performance and financial condition. These are summarized in Table 28.6.[17] Now that you have calculated these measures, you need some way to judge whether they are high or low. In some cases there may be a natural benchmark. For example, if a firm has negative economic value added or a return on capital less than the cost of that capital, it is not creating wealth for its shareholders.

But what about some of our other measures? There is no right level for, say, the asset turnover or profit margin, and if there were, it would almost certainly vary from industry to industry and company to company. For example, you would not expect a soft-drink manufacturer to have the same profit margin as a jeweler or the same leverage as a finance company.

The alternative is to confine your comparison to companies that are in a similar business. A good starting point is to prepare *common-size financial statements* for each of these firms. In this case all items in the balance sheet are expressed as a percentage of total assets and all items in the income statement are expressed as a percentage of revenues.

---

[17] If you would like to see how we calculated these ratios or to calculate your own, you can use the live Excel spreadsheet available on our Web site at www.mhhe.com/bmam10e.

Visit us at
www.mhhe.com/bmam10e

TABLE 28.6   Summary of ACC's financial ratios.

Performance Measures:		
Market Value Added (Rs. Crores)	Market value of equity - book value of equity	13614.51
Market-to-book ratio	Market value of equity / book value of equity	3.12
EVA (Rs. Crores)	(after-tax interest + net income) − (cost of capital × capital)	143.48
Return on Capital (ROC)	(after-tax interest + net income)/total capital	18.18%
Return on Equity (ROE)	net income/equity	19.27%
Return on Assets (ROA)	(after-tax interest + net income)/(total assets)	11.70%
Efficiency Ratios:		
Asset Turnover	Sales/total assets at start of year	0.75
Inventory Turnover	Sales/inventory at start of year	9.82
Receivables Turnover	Sales/receivables at start of year	37.54
Average collection period (days)	Receivables at start of year/ daily sales	9.72
Profit Margin	net income/sales	15.16%
Operating profit margin	(after-tax interest + net income)/sales	15.65%
Leverage Ratios:		
Long-term debt ratio	Long-term debt/(long-term debt + equity)	0.086
Long-term debt-equity ratio	long-term debt/equity	0.094
Total debt ratio	total liabilities/total assets	0.41
Times interest earned	EBIT/interest payments	28.89
Cash coverage ratio	(EBIT + depreciation)/interest payments	35.8
Liquidity Ratios:		
Net-working-capital-to-total assets	(Current asset − current liabilities)/total assets	NA
Current ratio	Current assets/current liabilities	0.80
Quick ratio	(Cash + receivables + marketable securities)/current liabilities	0.07
Cash ratio	(Cash + marketable securities)/current liabilities	0.03

We have not calculated here common-size statements for ACC, but Tables 28.7 and 28.8 provide summary common-size statements for a sample of Indian industries. Notice the large variations. For example, retail firms have a major investment in inventory; software companies have almost none. High-tech businesses, such as semiconductors, hold huge amounts of cash; utilities hold very little.[18] Oil companies and utilities invest principally in fixed assets; software companies and computer manufacturers have mainly current assets.

Table 28.9 lists some financial ratios for these companies. The variation between industries also shows up in many of the ratios. The differences arise partly from chance; sometimes the sun shines more kindly on some industries than on others. But the differences also reflect some fundamental industry factors. For example, notice the high debt ratios of utilities. By contrast, computer companies scarcely borrow at all. We pointed out earlier that some businesses are able to generate a high level of

---

[18] We return to this difference in Chapter 30.

eXcel
Visit us at
www.mhhe.com/bmam10e

TABLE 28.7 Common-size balance sheets for Indian companies in CMIE sector indices, 2011. Entries for each company are expressed as a percentage of total assets and averaged by industry

Industry	Manu-facturing	Airlines	Auto-mobiles	Chemicals	Computer Software	Oil & Gas	Food	Hotels	Machinery	Metals	Minerals	Paper	Real Estate	Media	Retail	Telecom	Textiles
Cash	7	3	6	8	18	7	6	5	11	6	6	2	4	9	9	3	3
Receivables	15	14	15	22	27	10	20	8	31	9	18	12	28	16	28	11	19
Inventories	12	3	11	14	1	14	14	3	16	12	22	10	30	7	20	1	20
Other current assets	10	7	10	14	11	9	14	7	8	8	8	5	22	14	11	12	5
Total current assets	44	27	42	58	58	40	54	23	67	36	54	29	84	45	68	28	46
Net fixed assets	42	71	40	30	19	45	35	59	23	49	41	52	4	31	16	57	46
Investments	15	2	17	13	24	14	11	18	10	15	4	18	11	24	16	15	8
Total assets	100	100	100	100	100	100	100	100	100	100	100	100	100	100	100	100	100
Current liabilities	26	25	31	24	23	28	26	16	43	19	29	16	43	28	31	25	16
Secured & unsecured loan	32	77	27	28	13	23	34	37	20	38	37	55	30	23	40	32	62
Total liabilities	58	102	57	52	36	52	60	53	63	57	66	70	72	51	71	57	78
Shareholders' equity	42	-2	43	48	64	48	40	47	37	43	34	30	28	49	29	43	22
Total liabilities & equity	100	100	100	100	100	100	100	100	100	100	100	100	100	100	100	100	100

Note: Some columns do not add up because of rounding.
Source: Data compiled using data from Prowess database

TABLE 28.8   Common-size income statements for Indian companies in CMIE sector indices, 2011. Entries for each company are expressed as a percentage of revenues and averaged by industry

	Airlines	Auto- mobile	Chemicals	Computer software	Oil & Gas	Food	Hotels	Machinery	Manu- facturing	Metals	Minerals	Paper	Real estate	Media	Retail	Telecom	Textiles
Sales	100%	100%	100%	100%	100%	100%	100%	100%	100%	100%	100%	100%	100%	100%	100%	100%	100%
Raw material	1%	63%	51%	2%	3%	49%	4%	50%	51%	55%	9%	52%	11%	1%	0%	0%	57%
Power & fuel	32%	1%	2%	1%	0%	2%	6%	1%	3%	7%	2%	14%	1%	2%	2%	8%	7%
Wages & salaries	17%	5%	3%	42%	9%	4%	19%	8%	4%	5%	5%	6%	4%	11%	6%	13%	7%
Selling & distribution expenses	5%	4%	4%	1%	4%	5%	4%	4%	4%	3%	10%	4%	2%	8%	4%	7%	3%
Repairs & maintenance	5%	1%	1%	1%	1%	1%	4%	1%	1%	2%	2%	2%	1%	2%	1%	3%	1%
Other expenses	31%	14%	29%	27%	27%	29%	37%	22%	24%	13%	18%	9%	38%	56%	85%	48%	11%
EBITDA	7%	13%	11%	26%	56%	10%	25%	14%	13%	17%	54%	13%	44%	21%	2%	22%	14%
Depreciation	8%	3%	2%	4%	16%	2%	6%	2%	3%	3%	2%	5%	2%	11%	3%	18%	4%
EBIT	-1%	10%	9%	23%	40%	8%	19%	12%	10%	14%	52%	8%	42%	10%	-1%	4%	10%
Interest expenses	10%	1%	2%	2%	1%	3%	7%	3%	3%	4%	2%	5%	19%	7%	4%	7%	6%
PBT	-11%	9%	7%	21%	39%	6%	12%	9%	7%	10%	49%	3%	23%	3%	-5%	-2%	4%
Tax	0%	3%	2%	4%	14%	2%	5%	3%	2%	3%	18%	1%	7%	5%	0%	1%	2%
Profit after tax	-11%	6%	5%	17%	25%	4%	7%	6%	5%	7%	32%	2%	16%	-2%	-5%	-4%	2%

Note: Some columns do not add up because of rounding

Source: Data compiled using data from Prowess database

Visit us at
www.mhhe.com/bmam10e

TABLE 28.9 Financial ratios for Indian companies in CMIE sector indices, 2011.

	Airlines	Automobile	Chemicals	Computer software	Oil & Gas	Food	Hotels	Machinery	Manufacturing	Metals	Minerals	Paper	Real estate	Media	Retail	Telecom	Textiles
Return on equity*	-1.78	0.18	0.17	0.21	0.15	0.13	0.05	0.15	0.14	0.10	0.25	0.04	0.08	-0.02	-0.27	-0.03	0.09
Retrn on assets*	0.06	0.21	0.18	0.24	0.20	0.17	0.09	0.21	0.16	0.13	0.34	0.09	0.13	0.01	0.04	0.06	0.14
Sales-to-assets ratio*	0.56	1.22	1.69	0.78	0.38	1.67	0.34	1.07	1.31	0.92	0.51	0.73	0.24	0.49	1.26	0.35	1.09
Operating profit margin	0.09	0.11	0.10	0.24	0.38	0.10	0.23	0.13	0.11	0.16	0.51	0.11	0.55	0.02	0.04	0.13	0.13
Sales to net working capital*	-8.28	-6.54	100.61	2.26	3.74	30.89	4.52	8.05	28.91	11.84	1.27	15.63	0.90	2.81	210.88	18.30	8.33
Receivables turnover*	4.08	6.50	8.02	2.69	7.18	7.74	2.89	2.58	5.72	5.55	6.96	5.02	0.70	2.37	14.97	2.85	4.27
Long-term debt ratio	0.96	0.35	0.44	0.16	0.13	0.52	0.45	0.40	0.47	0.48	0.13	0.68	0.51	0.42	0.77	0.44	0.78
Current ratio	0.80	0.71	1.05	2.41	1.30	1.15	1.37	1.24	1.12	1.27	2.43	1.25	1.59	1.65	1.02	1.07	1.57
Quick ratio	0.51	0.56	0.80	1.95	0.60	0.84	0.95	1.01	0.86	0.89	1.58	0.91	0.89	1.10	0.52	0.58	1.31
Cash ratio	0.11	0.27	0.22	0.77	0.44	0.24	0.37	0.25	0.25	0.32	1.32	0.13	0.14	0.33	0.20	0.14	0.18

* Computed using end-year balance sheet data (see footnote 6)
Source: Data compiled using data from Prowess database

sales from relatively few assets. For example, you can see that the sales-to-assets ratio for retailers is more than three times that for pharmaceutical companies. But competition ensures that retailers earn a correspondingly lower margin on their sales.

SUMMARY

Managers use financial statements to monitor their own company's performance, to help understand the policies of a competitor, and to check on the financial health of customers. But there is a danger of being overwhelmed by the sheer volume of data in the company's Annual Report.[19] That is why managers use a few salient ratios to summarize the firm's market valuation, profitability, efficiency, capital structure, and liquidity. We have described some of the more popular financial ratios.

We offer the following general advice to users of these ratios:

1. Financial ratios seldom provide answers, but they do help you to ask the right questions.
2. There is no international standard for financial ratios. A little thought and common sense are worth far more than blind application of formulas.
3. You need a benchmark for assessing a company's financial position. It is generally useful to compare the company's current financial ratios with the equivalent ratios in the past and with the ratios of other firms in the same business.

FURTHER READING

There are some good general texts on financial statement analysis. See, for example:

K. G. Palepu, V. L. Bernard, and P. M. Healy, *Business Analysis and Valuation,* 4th ed. (Cincinnati, OH: South-Western Publishing, 2008).

L. Revsine, D. Collins, B. Johnson, and F. Mittelstaedt, *Financial Reporting and Analysis,* 4th ed. (New York: McGraw-Hill/Irwin, 2008).

S. Penman, *Financial Statement Analysis and Security Valuation,* 4th ed. (New York: McGraw-Hill/Irwin, 2009).

PROBLEM SETS

BASIC

1. Construct a balance sheet for Galactic Enterprises given the following data:

Cash balances	₹25,000
Inventories	₹30,000
Net plant and equipment	₹140,000
Accounts receivable	₹35,000
Accounts payable	₹24,000
Long-term debt	₹130,000

What is shareholders' equity?

---

[19] HSBC's 2007 *Annual Report* totaled 454 pages. The *Financial Times* reported that Britain's postal service was obliged to limit the number that its postmen carried in order to prevent back injuries.

2. Table 28.10 on the following page gives abbreviated balance sheets and income statements for Colgate Palmolive (India) Limited. Calculate the following ratios:
   a. Debt ratio.
   b. Operating profit margin.
   c. Sales-to-assets ratio.
   d. Inventory turnover.

TABLE 28.10 Balance sheets and income statement for Colgate Palmolive Limited, 2011 (figures in ₹ crores).

Visit us at
www.mhhe.com/bmam10e

Assets	2011	2010
Net block	**255.04**	**246.95**
Capital work in progress	12.26	6.19
Investments	**38.74**	**21**
Inventories	153.7	110.55
Sundry debtors	42.96	9.77
Cash and bank balance	13.74	19.52
Other current assets	528.8	486.87
Total current assets	**210.4**	**139.84**
Current liabilities	491.84	445.33
Provisions	169.31	124.82
Total CL & provisions	**661.15**	**570.15**
Net current assets	**78.05**	**56.56**
Total assets	**384.09**	**330.7**
Liabilities and shareholders' equity		
Total share capital	13.6	13.6
Reserves	370.45	312.51
Shareholders' equity	**384.05**	**326.11**
Secured Loans	0	0
Unsecured Loans	0.05	4.59
Total debt	**0.05**	**4.59**
Total liabilities	**384.1**	**330.7**
Net sales	2,284.46	
Other income	36.48	
Total income	**2,351.00**	
Raw materials	881.17	
Power & fuel cost	14.46	
Employee cost	193.22	
Other manufacturing Expenses	124.87	
Selling and admin expenses	469.76	
Miscellaneous expenses	80.79	
PBDIT	**556.67**	
Interest	8.61	
Depreciation	34.25	
Profit before tax	513.81	
Tax	117.37	
Net profit	396.44	

  e. Debt–equity ratio.
  f. Current ratio.
  g. Quick ratio
3. Look again at Table 28.10. Calculate a common-size balance sheet and income statement for Colgate Palmolive Limited.
4. Look again at Table 28.10. At the end of fiscal 2011, Colgate had 1.36 crore shares outstanding with a share price of ₹960. The company's weighted-average cost of capital was about 12%. Calculate
  a. Market value added.
  b. Market-to-book ratio.
  c. Economic value added.
  d. Return on capital.
5. There are no universally accepted definitions of financial ratios, but five of the following ratios are clearly incorrect. Substitute the correct definitions.
  a. Debt–equity ratio = (long-term debt + value of leases)/(long-term debt + value of leases + equity)
  b. Return on equity = (EBIT−tax)/average equity
  c. Profit margin = net income/sales
  d. Days in inventory = sales/(inventory/365)
  e. Current ratio = current liabilities/current assets
  f. Sales-to-net-working-capital = average sales/average net working capital
  g. Quick ratio = (current assets − inventories)/current liabilities
  h. Times-interest-earned = interest earned × long-term debt
6. True or false?
  a. A company's debt–equity ratio is always less than 1.
  b. The quick ratio is always less than the current ratio.
  c. The return on equity is always less than the return on assets.
7. Bindu Cosmetics maintains an operating profit margin of 4% and a sales-to-assets ratio of 3. It has assets of ₹500,000 and equity of ₹300,000. Interest payments are ₹30,000 and the tax rate is 35%.
  a. What is the return on assets?
  b. What is the return on equity?
8. A firm has a long-term debt–equity ratio of .4. Shareholders' equity is ₹1 million. Current assets are ₹200,000, and total assets are ₹1.5 million. If the current ratio is 2.0, what is the ratio of debt to total long-term capital?
9. Magic Flutes has total receivables of ₹3,000, which represent 20 days' sales. Total assets are ₹75,000. The firm's operating profit margin is 5%. Find the firm's sales-to-assets ratio and return on assets.
10. Consider this simplified balance sheet for Geomorph Trading:

Current assets	₹100	₹ 60	Current liabilities
Long-term assets	500	280	Long-term debt
		70	Other liabilities
		190	Equity
	₹600	₹600	

  a. Calculate the ratio of debt to equity.

    b. What are Geomorph's net working capital and total long-term capital? Calculate the ratio of debt to total long-term capital.

11. Look again at the balance sheet for Geomorph in Problem 10. Suppose that at year-end Geomorph had ₹30 in cash and marketable securities. Immediately after the year-end it used a line of credit to borrow ₹20 for one year, which it invested in additional marketable securities. Would the company appear to be (a) more or less liquid, (b) more or less highly leveraged? Make any additional assumptions that you need.

12. Airlux Antarctica has current assets of ₹300 million, current liabilities of ₹200 million and a crash—sorry—*cash* ratio of .05. How much cash and marketable securities does it hold?

13. On average, it takes Microlimp's customers 60 days to pay their bills. If Microlimp has annual sales of ₹500 million, what is the average value of unpaid bills?

INTERMEDIATE

14. This question reviews some of the difficulties encountered in interpreting accounting numbers.
    a. Give four examples of important assets, liabilities, or transactions that may not be shown on the company's books.
    b. How does investment in intangible assets, such as research and development, distort accounting ratios? Give at least two examples.

15. Describe some alternative measures of a firm's overall performance. What are their advantages and disadvantages? In each case discuss what benchmarks you might use to judge whether performance is satisfactory.

16. Discuss alternative measures of financial leverage. Should the market value of equity be used or the book value? Is it better to use the market value of debt, the book value, or the book value discounted at the risk-free interest rate? How should you treat off-balance-sheet obligations such as pension liabilities? How would you treat preferred stock?

17. Suppose that a firm has both fixed-rate and floating-rate debt outstanding. What effect will a decline in interest rates have on the firm's times-interest-earned ratio? What about the ratio of the market value of debt to that of equity? Would you judge that leverage has increased or decreased?

18. How would the following actions affect a firm's current ratio?
    a. Inventory is sold.
    b. The firm takes out a bank loan to pay its suppliers.
    c. The firm arranges a line of credit with a bank that allows it to borrow at any time to pay its suppliers.
    d. A customer pays its overdue bills.
    e. The firm uses cash to purchase additional inventories.

19. Aditi Drugs sells all its output to OLP Stores. The following table shows selected financial data, in millions, for the two firms:

	Sales	Interest Payment	Net Income	Assets at Start of Year
OLP Stores	₹100	₹4	₹10	₹50
Aditi Drugs	20	1	4	20

Calculate the sales-to-assets ratio, the operating profit margin, and the return on assets for the two firms. Now assume that the two companies merge. If OLP continues to sell goods worth ₹100 million, how will the three ratios change?

20. As you can see, someone has spilled ink over some of the entries in the balance sheet and income statement of Transylvania Railroad (Table 28.11). Can you use the following information to work out the missing entries?

- Debt ratio: .4.
- Times-interest-earned: 6.25.
- Current ratio: 1.4.
- Quick ratio: 1.0.
- Cash ratio: .2.
- Return on equity: 24%.
- Inventory turnover: 5.0.
- Receivables collection period: 71.2 days.

TABLE 28.11 Balance sheet and income statement of Transylvania Railroad (figures in $ millions).

	December 2009	December 2008
Balance Sheet		
Cash	▪✱✚	20
Accounts receivable	▪✱✚	34
Inventory	▪✱✚	26
Total current assets	✱▪✚	80
Fixed assets, net	▪✚▪	110
Total	▪✚▪	190
Notes payable	30	20
Accounts payable	25	15
Total current liabilities	▪✱✚	35
Long-term debt	▪✚▪	55
Equity	▪✱✚	100
Total	235	190
Income Statement		
Sales	▪✚▪	
Cost of goods sold	✚▪▪	
Selling, general, and administrative expenses	10	
Depreciation	20	
EBIT	▪✱✚	
Interest	▪✚▪	
Earnings before tax	▪✱✚	
Tax	▪✚▪	
Earnings available for common stock	▪✚▪	

21. Here are some data for five companies in the same industry:

	Company Code				
	A	**B**	**C**	**D**	**E**
EBIT	10	30	100	−3	80
Interest expense	5	15	50	2	1

You have been asked to calculate a measure of times-interest-earned for the industry. Discuss the possible ways that you might calculate such a measure. Does changing the method of calculation make a significant difference to the end result?

22. How would rapid inflation affect the accuracy and relevance of a manufacturing company's balance sheet and income statement? Does your answer depend on how much debt the firm has issued?

23. Suppose that you wish to use financial ratios to estimate the risk of a company's stock. Which of those that we have described in this chapter are likely to be helpful? Can you think of other accounting measures of risk?

24. Look up some firms that have been in trouble. Plot the changes over the preceding years in the principal financial ratios. Are there any patterns?

CHALLENGE

25. We noted that, when calculating EVA, you should calculate income as the sum of the after-tax interest payment and net income. Why do you need to deduct the tax shield? Would an alternative be to use a different measure of the cost of capital? Or would you get the same result if you simply deducted the cost of equity from net income (as is often done)?

26. Sometimes analysts use the average of capital at the start and end of the year to calculate return on capital. Provide some examples to illustrate when this does and does not make sense. (*Hint:* Start by assuming that capital increases solely as a result of retained earnings.)

27. Take another look at Geomorph Trading's balance sheet in Problem 10 and consider the following additional information:

Current Assets		Current Liabilities		Other Liabilities	
Cash	₹15	Payables	₹35	Deferred tax	₹32
Inventories	35	Taxes due	10	Unfunded pensions	22
Receivables	50	Bank loan	15	R&R reserve	16
	₹100		₹60		₹70

The "R&R reserve" covers the future costs of removal of an oil pipeline and environmental restoration of the pipeline route.

There are many ways to calculate a debt ratio for Geomorph. Suppose you are evaluating the safety of Geomorph's debt and want a debt ratio for comparison with the ratios of other companies in the same industry. Would you calculate the ratio in terms of total liabilities or total capitalization? What would you include in debt—the bank loan, the deferred tax account, the R&R reserve, the unfunded pension liability? Explain the pros and cons of these choices.

REAL-TIME DATA ANALYSIS

Use data from the Standard & Poor's Market Insight Database (www.mhhe.com/edumarket insight) or Yahoo! Finance (http://finance.yahoo.com) to answer the following questions.

1. Find financial ratios for five different industries. Can you account for some of the differences between industries?   **STANDARD &POOR'S**

2. Select two companies that are in a similar line of business and find their simplified balance sheets and income statements. Then draw up common-size statements for each company and compute the principal financial ratios. Compare and contrast the companies based on these data.   **STANDARD &POOR'S**

3. Look up the latest financial statements for a company of your choice and calculate the following ratios for the latest year:
   a. Return on capital.
   b. Return on equity.
   c. Operating profit margin.
   d. Days in inventory.
   e. Debt ratio.
   f. Times-interest-earned.
   g. Current ratio.
   h. Quick ratio.   **STANDARD &POOR'S**

4. Select five companies and, using their financial statements, compare the days in inventory and average collection period for receivables. Can you explain the differences between the companies?   **STANDARD &POOR'S**

29

CHAPTER

FINANCIAL PLANNING

This chapter is concerned with financial planning. We look first at short-term planning where the focus is on ensuring that the firm does not run out of cash. Short-term planning is, therefore, often termed *cash budgeting*. In the second half of the chapter we look at how firms also use financial planning models to develop a coherent *long-term* strategy.

In the last chapter we introduced you to the principal short-term assets—inventory, accounts receivable, cash, and marketable securities. Decisions on these assets cannot be made in isolation. For example, suppose that the marketing manager wishes to give customers more time to pay for their purchases. This reduces the firm's future cash balances. Or perhaps the production manager adopts a just-in-time system for ordering from suppliers. That allows the firm to get by on smaller inventories and frees up cash.

Managers concerned with short-term financial decisions can avoid many of the difficult conceptual issues encountered elsewhere in this book. In that respect short-term decisions are easier than long-term decisions, but they are not less important. A firm can identify extremely valuable capital investment opportunities, find the precise optimal debt ratio, follow the perfect dividend policy, and yet founder because no one bothers to raise the cash to pay this year's bills. Hence the need for short-term planning.

Short-term planning rarely looks further ahead than the next 12 months. It seeks to ensure that the firm has enough cash to pay its bills and makes sensible short-term borrowing and lending decisions. But the financial manager also needs to think about the investments that will be needed to meet the firm's *long-term* goals and the financing that must be arranged. Long-term financial planning focuses on the implications of alternative financial strategies. It allows managers to avoid some surprises and consider how they should react to surprises that *cannot* be avoided. And it helps to establish goals for the firm and to provide standards for measuring performance.

29-1 LINKS BETWEEN SHORT-TERM AND LONG-TERM FINANCING DECISIONS

Short-term financial decisions differ in two ways from long-term decisions such as the purchase of plant and equipment or the choice of capital structure. First, they generally involve short-lived assets and liabilities, and, second, they are usually easily reversed. Compare, for example, a 60-day bank loan with an issue of 20-year bonds. The bank loan is clearly a short-term decision. The firm can repay it two months later and be right back where it started. A firm might conceivably issue a 20-year bond in January and retire it in March, but it would be extremely inconvenient and expensive to do so. In practice, the bond issue is a long-term decision, not only because of the bond's 20-year maturity but also because the decision to issue it cannot be reversed on short notice.

Short-term financing needs are nevertheless tied to the firm's long-term decisions. All businesses require capital—that is, money invested in plant, machinery, inventories, accounts receivable, and all the other assets it takes to run a business. These assets can be financed by either long-term or short-term sources of capital.

Let us call the total investment the firm's *cumulative capital requirement*. For most firms the cumulative capital requirement grows irregularly, like the wavy line in Figure 29.1. This line shows a clear upward trend as the firm's business grows. But the figure also shows seasonal variation around the trend, with the capital requirement peaking late in each year. In addition, there would be unpredictable week-to-week and month-to-month fluctuations, but we have not attempted to show these in Figure 29.1.

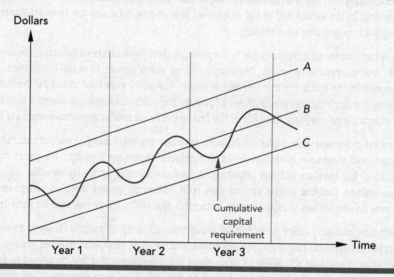

FIGURE 29.1

The firm's cumulative capital requirement (red line) is the cumulative investment in all the assets needed for the business. This figure shows that the requirement grows year by year, but there is some seasonal fluctuation within each year. The requirement for short-term financing is the difference between long-term financing (lines *A*, *B*, and *C*) and the cumulative capital requirement. If long-term financing follows line *C*, the firm always needs short-term financing. At line *B*, the need is seasonal. At line *A*, the firm never needs short-term financing. There is always extra cash to invest.

When long-term financing does not cover the cumulative capital requirement, the firm must raise short-term capital to make up the difference. When long-term financing *more* than covers the cumulative capital requirement, the firm has surplus cash available. Thus the amount of long-term financing raised, given the capital requirement, determines whether the firm is a short-term borrower or lender.

Lines *A*, *B*, and *C* in Figure 29.1 illustrate this. Each depicts a different long-term financing strategy. Strategy *A* implies a permanent cash surplus, which can be invested in short-term securities. Strategy *C* implies a permanent need for short-term borrowing. Under *B*, which is probably the most common strategy, the firm is a short-term lender during part of the year and a borrower during the rest.

What is the *best* level of long-term financing relative to the cumulative capital requirement? It is hard to say. There is no convincing theoretical analysis of this question. We can make practical observations, however. First, most financial managers attempt to "match maturities" of assets and liabilities.[1] That is, they largely finance long-lived assets like plant and machinery with long-term borrowing and equity. Second, most firms make a permanent investment in net working capital (current assets less current liabilities). This investment is financed from long-term sources.

Current assets can be converted into cash more easily than long-term assets. So firms with large holdings of current assets enjoy greater liquidity. Of course, some of these assets are more liquid than others. Inventories are converted into cash only when the goods are produced, sold, and paid for. Receivables are more liquid; they become cash as customers pay their outstanding bills. Short-term securities can generally be sold if the firm needs cash on short notice and are therefore more liquid still.

Some firms choose to hold more liquidity than others. For example, many high-tech companies, such as Intel and Cisco, hold huge amounts of short-term securities. On the other hand, firms in old-line manufacturing industries—such as chemicals, paper, or steel—manage with a far smaller reserve of liquidity. Why is this? One reason is that companies with rapidly growing profits may generate cash faster than they can redeploy it in new positive-NPV investments. This produces a surplus of cash that can be invested in short-term securities. Of course, companies faced with a growing mountain of cash may eventually respond by adjusting their payout policies. In Chapter 16 we saw how Microsoft reduced its cash mountain by paying a special dividend and repurchasing its stock.

There are some advantages to holding a large reservoir of cash, particularly for smaller firms that face relatively high costs to raising funds on short notice. For example, biotech firms require large amounts of cash to develop new drugs. Therefore, these firms generally have substantial cash holdings to fund their R&D programs. If these precautionary reasons for holding liquid assets are important, we should find that small companies in relatively high-risk industries are more likely to hold large cash surpluses. A study by Tim Opler and others confirms that this is in fact the case.[2]

Financial managers of firms with a surplus of long-term financing and with cash in the bank don't have to worry about finding the money to pay next month's bills. The cash can help to protect the firm against a rainy day and give it the breathing space to make changes to operations. However, there are also drawbacks to surplus cash. Holdings of marketable securities are at best a zero-NPV investment for a taxpaying firm.[3] Also managers of firms with large cash surpluses may be tempted to run a less tight ship and may simply allow the cash to seep away in a succession of operating losses.

---

[1] A survey by Graham and Harvey found that managers considered that the desire to match the maturity of the debt with that of the assets was the single most important factor in their choice between short- and long-term debt. See J. R. Graham and C. R. Harvey, "The Theory and Practice of Finance: Evidence from the Field," *Journal of Financial Economics* 61 (May 2001), pp. 187–243. Stohs and Mauer confirm that firms with a preponderance of short-term assets do indeed tend to issue short-term debt. See M. H. Stohs and D. C. Mauer, "The Determinants of Corporate Debt Maturity Structure," *Journal of Business* 69 (July 1996), pp. 279–312.

[2] T. Opler, L. Pinkowitz, R. Stulz, and R. Williamson, "The Determinants and Implications of Corporate Cash Holdings," *Journal of Financial Economics* 52 (April 1999), pp. 3–46.

[3] If, as most people believe, there is a tax advantage to borrowing there must be a corresponding tax disadvantage to lending, since the firm must pay tax at the corporate rate on the interest that it receives from Treasury bills. In this case investment in Treasury bills has a negative NPV. See Section 18-1.

For example, at the end of 2007 General Motors held $27 billion in cash and short-term investments. But shareholders valued GM stock at less than $14 billion. It seemed that shareholders realized that the cash would be used to support ongoing losses and to service GM's huge debts.

Pinkowitz and Williamson looked at the value that investors place on a firm's cash and found that on average shareholders valued a dollar of cash at $1.20.[4] They placed a particularly high value on liquidity in the case of firms with plenty of growth opportunities. At the other extreme, they found that, when a firm was likely to face financial distress, a dollar of cash within the firm was often worth less than a dollar to the shareholders.[5]

29-2 TRACING CHANGES IN CASH

Table 29.1 shows the 2009 income statement for Dynamic Mattress Company, and Table 29.2 compares the firm's 2008 and 2009 year-end balance sheets. You can see that in 2009 Dynamic's cash balance increased from ₹20 million to ₹25 million.

TABLE 29.1 Income statement for Dynamic Mattress Company, 2009 (figures in ₹ millions).

eXcel
Visit us at
www.mhhe.com/bmam10e

1	Sales	2,200
2	Cost of goods sold	1,644
3	Other expenses	411
4	Depreciation	20
5	EBIT (1−2−3−4)	125
6	Interest	5
7	Pretax income (5−6)	120
8	Tax at 50%	60
9	Net income (7−8)	60
	Dividend	30
	Earnings retained in the business	30

What caused this increase? Did the extra cash come from Dynamic's issue of long-term debt, from reinvested earnings, from cash released by reducing inventory, or from extra credit extended by Dynamic's suppliers? (Note the increase in accounts payable.) The answer is provided in the company's cash flow statement shown in Table 29.3.

Cash flow statements classify cash flows into those from operating activities, investing activities, and financing activities. Sources of cash are shown as positive numbers; uses of cash are shown as negative numbers. Dynamic's cash flow statement shows that Dynamic *generated* cash from the following sources:

1. It earned ₹60 million of net income (*operating activity*).
2. It set aside ₹20 million as depreciation. Remember that depreciation is *not* a cash outlay. Thus, it must be added back to obtain Dynamic's cash flow (*operating activity*).
3. It reduced inventory, releasing ₹5 million (*operating activity*).
4. It increased its accounts payable, in effect borrowing an additional ₹25 million from its suppliers (*operating activity*).
5. It issued ₹30 million of long-term debt (*financing activity*).

Dynamic's cash flow statement shows that it *used* cash for the following purposes:

1. It allowed accounts receivable to expand by ₹25 million (*operating activity*). In effect, it lent this additional amount to its customers.
2. It invested ₹30 million (*investing activity*). This shows up as the increase in gross fixed assets in Table 29.2.

---

[4] L. Pinkowitz and R. Williamson. "The Market Value of Cash," *Journal of Applied Corporate Finance* 19 (2007), pp. 74–81.

[5] The apparent implication is that the firm should distribute the cash to shareholders. However, debtholders may place restrictions on dividend payments to the shareholders.

3. It paid a ₹30 million dividend (*financing activity*). (*Note:* The ₹30 million increase in Dynamic's equity in Table 29.2 is due to retained earnings: ₹60 million of equity income, less the ₹30 million dividend.)

4. It purchased ₹25 million of marketable securities (*financing activity*).

5. It repaid ₹25 million of short-term bank debt (*financing activity*).[6]

Look again at Table 29.3. Notice that to calculate cash flows from operating activities, we start with net income and then make two adjustments. First, since depreciation is *not* a cash outlay, we must add it back to net income.[7] Second, we need to recognize the fact that the income statement shows sales and expenditures when they are made, rather than when cash changes hands. For example, think of what happens when Dynamic sells goods on credit. The company records a profit at the time of sale, but there is no cash inflow until the bills are paid. Since there is no cash inflow, there is no change in the company's cash balance, although there is an increase in working capital in the form of an increase in accounts receivable. No net addition to cash would be shown in a cash flow statement like Table 29.3. The increase in cash from operations would be offset by an increase in accounts receivable. Later, when the bills are paid, there is an increase in the cash balance. However, there is no further profit at this point and no increase in working capital. The increase in the cash balance is exactly matched by a decrease in accounts receivable.

Table 29.3 adjusts the cash flow from operating activities *downward* by ₹25 million to reflect the additional credit that Dynamic has extended to its customers. On the other hand, in 2009 Dynamic reduced its inventories and increased the amount

TABLE 29.2 Year-end balance sheets for 2009 and 2008 for Dynamic Mattress Company (figures in ₹ millions).

e**X**cel
Visit us at
www.mhhe.com/bmam10e

	2009	2008
Current assets:		
Cash	25	20
Marketable securities	25	0
Accounts receivable	150	125
Inventory	125	130
Total current assets	325	275
Fixed assets:		
Gross investment	350	320
Less depreciation	100	80
Net fixed assets	250	240
Total assets	575	515
Current liabilities:		
Bank loans	0	25
Accounts payable	135	110
Total current liabilities	135	135
Long-term debt	90	60
Net worth (equity and retained earnings)	350	320
Total liabilities and net worth	575	515

TABLE 29.3 Statement of cash flows for Dynamic Mattress Company, 2009 (figures in ₹ millions).

e**X**cel
Visit us at
www.mhhe.com/bmam10e

Cash flows from operating activities:	
Net income	60
Depreciation	20
Decrease (increase) in accounts receivable	−25
Decrease (increase) in inventories	5
Increase (decrease) in accounts payable	25
Net cash flow from operating activities	85
Cash flows from investing activities:	
Investment in fixed assets	−30
Cash flows from financing activities:	
Dividends	−30
Sale (purchase) of marketable securities	−25
Increase (decrease) in long-term debt	30
Increase (decrease) in short-term debt	−25
Net cash flow from financing activities	−50
Increase (decrease) in cash balance	5

---

[6] This is principal repayment, not interest. Sometimes interest payments are explicitly recognized as a use of funds. If so, cash flow from operations would be defined *before* interest, that is, as net income plus interest plus depreciation.

[7] There is a potential complication here, for the depreciation figure shown in the company's report to shareholders is rarely the same as the depreciation figure used to calculate tax. The reason is that firms can minimize their current tax payments by using *accelerated* depreciation when computing their taxable income. As a result, the shareholder books (which generally use straight-line depreciation) overstate the firm's current tax liability. Accelerated depreciation does not eliminate taxes; it only delays them. Since the ultimate liability has to be recognized, the additional taxes that will need to be paid are shown on the balance sheet as a deferred tax liability. In the statement of cash flows any increase in deferred taxes is treated as a source of funds. In the Dynamic Mattress example we ignore deferred taxes.

that is owed to its suppliers. The cash flow from operating activities is adjusted *upward* to reflect these changes.

That brings up an interesting characteristic of working capital. Imagine a company that conducts a very simple business. It buys raw materials for cash, processes them into finished goods, and then sells these goods on credit. The whole cycle of operations looks like this:

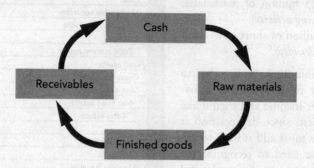

If you draw up a balance sheet at the beginning of the process, you see cash. If you delay a little, you find the cash replaced by inventories of raw materials and, still later, by inventories of finished goods. When the goods are sold, the inventories give way to accounts receivable, and, finally, when the customers pay their bills, the firm draws out its profit and replenishes the cash balance.

There is only one constant in this process, namely, working capital. That is one reason why (net) working capital is a useful summary measure of current assets and liabilities. The strength of the working-capital measure is that it is unaffected by seasonal or other temporary movements between different current assets or liabilities. But the strength is also its weakness, for the working-capital figure hides a lot of interesting information. In our example cash was transformed into inventory, then into receivables, and back into cash again. But these assets have different degrees of risk and liquidity. You can't pay bills with inventory or with receivables, you must pay with cash.

The Cash Cycle

In Chapter 28 we showed how to calculate the average time that materials remain in inventory and the average time that it takes for customers to pay their bills. In the case of Dynamic:

$$\text{Average days in inventory} = \frac{\text{inventory at start of year}}{\text{daily cost of goods sold}} = \frac{130}{1,644/365} = 29 \text{ days}$$

$$\text{Average collection period} = \frac{\text{receivables at start of year}}{\text{average daily sales}} = \frac{125}{2,200/365} = 21 \text{ days}$$

We can also calculate the average time that it takes *Dynamic* to pay its bills:[8]

$$\text{Average payment period} = \frac{\text{payables at start of year}}{\text{daily cost of goods sold}} = \frac{110}{1,644/365} = 24 \text{ days}$$

---

[8] Since the balance sheet shows the cost of materials rather than the amount that the finished goods will eventually sell for, it makes sense to compare the level of inventories and payables with the cost of goods sold rather than with sales.

Think what this implies for the financing that is needed to maintain regular operations. Suppose that Dynamic purchases materials on day 0. It pays for these materials on day 24 (average payment period = 24 days). By day 29 Dynamic has converted the raw materials into finished mattresses that are then sold (days in inventory = 29). Twenty-one days later on day 50 Dynamic's customers pay for their purchases (collection period = 21). Thus, cash went out the door on day 24; it did not come back in again until day 50. This 26-day interval is called the *cash cycle* or *cash conversion period:*[9]

Cash cycle (days)	=	average days in inventory	+	average collection period	−	average payment period
26	=	29	+	21	−	24

The cash cycle affects the amount of working capital that the firm needs. For example, major machinery manufacturers typically hold large inventories and offer long payment periods. Their cash cycle is nearly six months and they need to make a substantial investment in net working capital. By contrast, utilities with their low investment in inventory have a cash cycle of only about one and a half months. Utilities often have negative working capital.

29-3 CASH BUDGETING

The past is interesting for what one can learn from it. The financial manager's problem is to forecast *future* sources and uses of cash. These forecasts serve two purposes. First, they provide a standard, or budget, against which subsequent performance can be judged. Second, they alert the manager to future cash-flow needs. Cash, as we all know, has a habit of disappearing fast.

Preparing the Cash Budget: Inflows

We illustrate the preparation of the capital budget by continuing the example of Dynamic Mattress.

Most of Dynamic's cash inflow comes from the sale of mattresses. We therefore start with a sales forecast by quarter for 2010:[10]

	First Quarter	Second Quarter	Third Quarter	Fourth Quarter
Sales (₹ millions)	560	502	742	836

But sales become accounts receivable before they become cash. Cash flow comes from *collections* on accounts receivable.

Most firms keep track of the average time it takes customers to pay their bills. From this they can forecast what proportion of a quarter's sales is likely to be converted into cash in that quarter and what proportion is likely to be carried over to the next quarter as accounts receivable. Suppose that 70% of sales are "cashed in" in the immediate quarter and 30% are cashed in the following quarter. Table 29.4 shows forecasted collections under this assumption. For example, you can see that in the first quarter collections from current sales are 70% of ₹560, or ₹392 million. But the firm also collects 30% of the previous quarter's sales, or .3(₹397) = ₹119 million. Therefore total collections are ₹392 + ₹119 = ₹511 million.

---

[9] The total length of time from the purchase of raw materials until the final payment by the customer is termed the *operating cycle*.

[10] Most firms would forecast by month instead of by quarter. Sometimes weekly or even daily forecasts are made. But presenting a monthly forecast would triple the number of entries in Table 29.4 and subsequent tables. We wanted to keep the examples as simple as possible.

TABLE 29.4 To forecast Dynamic Mattress's collections on accounts receivable, you have to forecast sales and collection rates in 2010 (figures in ₹ millions).

		First Quarter	Second Quarter	Third Quarter	Fourth Quarter
1	Receivables at start of period	150	199	181.6	253.6
2	Sales	560	502	742	836
	Collections:				
	Sales in current period (70%)	392	351.4	519.4	585.2
	Sales in last period (30%)	119*	168	150.6	222.6
3	Total collections	511	519.4	670	807.8
4	Receivables at end of period 1+2−3	199	181.6	253.6	281.8

*We assume that sales in the last quarter of the previous year were ₹397 million.

Dynamic started the first quarter with ₹150 million of accounts receivable. The quarter's sales of ₹560 million were *added* to accounts receivable, but collections of ₹511 million were *subtracted*. Therefore, Table 29.4 shows that Dynamic ended the quarter with accounts receivable of ₹150 + 560 − 511 = ₹199 million. The general formula is

$$\text{Ending accounts receivable} = \text{beginning accounts receivable} + \text{sales} - \text{collections}$$

The top section of Table 29.5 shows forecasted sources of cash for Dynamic Mattress. Collection of receivables is the main source, but it is not the only one. Perhaps the firm plans to dispose of some land or expects a tax refund or payment of an insurance claim. All such items are included as "other"

TABLE 29.5 Dynamic Mattress's cash budget for 2010 (figures in ₹ millions)

	First Quarter	Second Quarter	Third Quarter	Fourth Quarter
Sources of cash:				
Collections on accounts receivable	511	519.4	670	807.8
Other	0	0	77	0
Total sources	511	519.4	747	807.8
Uses of cash:				
Payments on accounts payable	250	250	267	261
Increase in inventory	150	150	170	180
Labor and other expenses	136	136	136	136
Capital expenditures	70	10	8	14.5
Taxes, interest, and dividends	46	46	46	46
Total uses	652	592	627	637.5
Sources minus uses	−141	−72.6	120	170.3
Calculation of short-term borrowing requirement:				
Cash at start of period	25	−116	−188.6	−68.6
Change in cash balance	−141	−72.6	120	170.3
Cash at end of period	−116	−188.6	−68.6	101.7
Minimum operating balance	25	25	25	25
Cumulative financing required	141	213.6	93.6	−76.7

sources. It is also possible that you may raise additional capital by borrowing or selling stock, but we don't want to prejudge that question. Therefore, for the moment we just assume that Dynamic will not raise further long-term finance.

Preparing the Cash Budget: Outflows

So much for the incoming cash. Now for the outgoing. There always seem to be many more uses for cash than there are sources. For simplicity, we have condensed the uses into five categories in Table 29.5.

1. *Payments on accounts payable.* The firm has to pay its bills for raw materials, parts, electricity, etc. The cash-flow forecast assumes all these bills are paid on time, although Dynamic could probably delay payment to some extent. Delaying payment is sometimes called *stretching payables*. Stretching is one source of short-term financing, but for most firms it is an expensive source, because by stretching they lose discounts given to firms that pay promptly.
2. *Increase in inventories.* The expected increase in sales in 2010 requires additional investment in inventories.
3. *Labor, administrative, and other expenses.* This category includes all other regular business expenses.
4. *Capital expenditures.* Note that Dynamic Mattress plans a major capital outlay in the first quarter.
5. *Taxes, interest, and dividend payments.* This includes interest on presently outstanding long-term debt but does not include interest on any additional borrowing to meet cash requirements in 2010. At this stage in the analysis, Dynamic does not know how much it will have to borrow, or whether it will have to borrow at all.

The forecasted net inflow of cash (sources *minus* uses) is shown by the shaded line in Table 29.5. Note the large negative figure for the first quarter: a ₹141 million forecasted *outflow*. There is a smaller forecasted outflow in the second quarter, and then substantial cash inflows in the third and fourth quarters.

The bottom part of Table 29.5 calculates how much financing Dynamic will have to raise if its cash-flow forecasts are right. It starts the year with ₹25 million in cash. There is a ₹141 million cash outflow in the first quarter, and so Dynamic will have to obtain at least ₹141 − 25 = ₹116 million of additional financing. This would leave the firm with a forecasted cash balance of exactly zero at the start of the second quarter.

Most financial managers regard a planned cash balance of zero as driving too close to the edge of the cliff. They establish a *minimum operating cash balance* to absorb unexpected cash inflows and outflows. We assume that Dynamic's minimum operating cash balance is ₹25 million. This means it will have to raise the full ₹141 million in the first quarter and ₹72.6 million more in the second quarter. Thus its *cumulative* financing requirement is ₹213.6 million by the second quarter. Fortunately, this is the peak: the cumulative requirement declines in the third quarter by ₹120 million to ₹93.6 million. In the final quarter Dynamic is out of the woods: its cash balance is ₹101.7 million, well clear of its minimum operating balance.

The next step is to develop a *short-term financing plan* that covers the forecasted requirements in the most economical way. We move on to that topic after two general observations:

1. The large cash outflows in the first two quarters do not necessarily spell trouble for Dynamic Mattress. In part, they reflect the capital investment made in the first quarter: Dynamic is spending ₹70 million, but it should be acquiring an asset worth that much or more. In part, the cash

outflows reflect low sales in the first half of the year; sales recover in the second half.[11] If this is a predictable seasonal pattern, the firm should have no trouble borrowing to tide it over the slow months.

2. Table 29.5 is only a best guess about future cash flows. It is a good idea to think about the *uncertainty* in your estimates. For example, you could undertake a sensitivity analysis, in which you inspect how Dynamic's cash requirements would be affected by a shortfall in sales or by a delay in collections. The trouble with such sensitivity analyses is that you are changing only one item at a time, whereas in practice a downturn in the economy might affect, say, sales levels *and* collection rates. An alternative but more complicated solution is to build a model of the cash budget and then to simulate possible alternative cash requirements. If cash requirements are difficult to predict, you may wish to hold additional cash or marketable securities to cover a possible unexpected cash outflow.

29-4   THE SHORT-TERM FINANCING PLAN

Dynamic's cash budget defines its problem: its financial manager must find short-term financing to cover the firm's forecasted cash requirements. There are dozens of sources of short-term financing, but for simplicity we assume that Dynamic has just two options.

Options for Short-Term Financing

1. *Bank loan:* Dynamic has an existing arrangement with its bank allowing it to borrow up to ₹100 million at an interest cost of 10% a year or 2.5% per quarter. The firm can borrow and repay whenever it wants to do so, as long as it does not exceed its credit limit.
2. *Stretching payables:* Dynamic can also raise capital by putting off paying its bills. The financial manager believes that Dynamic can defer up to ₹100 million of payables each quarter. Thus, ₹100 million can be saved in the first quarter by *not* paying bills in that quarter. (Note that the cash-flow forecasts in Table 29.5 assumed that these bills *will* be paid in the first quarter.) If deferred, these payments *must* be made in the second quarter, but a further ₹100 million of the second quarter bills can be deferred to the third quarter, and so on.

Stretching payables is often costly, even if no ill will is incurred. The reason is that suppliers may offer discounts for prompt payment. Dynamic loses this discount if it pays late. In this example we assume the lost discount is 5% of the amount deferred. In other words, if a ₹100 payment is delayed, the firm must pay ₹105 in the next quarter.

Dynamic's Financing Plan

With these two options, the short-term financing strategy is obvious. Use the bank loan first, if necessary up to the ₹100 million limit. If there is still a shortage of cash, stretch payables.

Table 29.6 shows the resulting plan. In the first quarter the plan calls for borrowing the full amount from the bank (₹100 million) and stretching ₹16 million of payables (see lines 1 and 2 in the table). In addition the company sells the ₹25 million of marketable securities it held at the end of 2009 (line 8). Thus it raises 100 + 16 + 25 = ₹141 million of cash in the first quarter (line 10).

---

[11] Maybe people buy more mattresses late in the year when the nights are longer.

TABLE 29.6 Dynamic Mattress's financing plan (figures in ₹ millions).

		First Quarter	Second Quarter	Third Quarter	Fourth Quarter
	New borrowing:				
1	Bank loan	100.0	0.0	0.0	0.0
2	Stretching payables	16.0	92.4	0.0	0.0
3	Total	116.0	92.4	0.0	0.0
	Repayments:				
4	Bank loan	0.0	0.0	20.0	80.0
5	Stretching payables	0.0	16.0	92.4	0.0
6	Total	0.0	16.0	112.4	80.0
7	Net new borrowing	116.0	76.4	−112.4	−80.0
8	Plus securities sold	25.0	0.0	0.0	0.0
9	Less securities bought	0.0	0.0	0.0	87.8
10	Total cash raised	141.0	76.4	−112.4	−167.8
	Note: Cumulative borrowing and security sales				
	Bank loan	100.0	100.0	80.0	0.0
	Stretching payables	16.0	92.4	0.0	0.0
	Net securities sold	25.0	25.0	25.0	−62.8
	Interest payments:				
11	Bank loan	0.0	2.5	2.5	2.0
12	Stretching payables	0.0	0.8	4.6	0.0
13	Interest on securities sold	0.0	0.5	0.5	0.5
14	Net interest paid	0.0	3.8	7.6	2.5
15	Cash required for operations	141.0	72.6	−120.0	−170.3
16	Total cash required	141.0	76.4	−112.4	−167.8

In the second quarter, the plan calls for Dynamic to continue to borrow ₹100 million from the bank and to stretch ₹92.4 million of payables. This raises ₹76.4 million after paying off the ₹16 million of bills deferred from the first quarter.

Why raise ₹76.4 million when Dynamic needs only an additional ₹72.6 million to finance its operations? The answer is that the company must pay interest on the borrowings that it undertook in the first quarter and it forgoes interest on the marketable securities that were sold.[12]

In the third and fourth quarters the plan calls for Dynamic to pay off its debt and to make a purchase of marketable securities.

Evaluating the Plan

Does the plan shown in Table 29.6 solve Dynamic's short-term financing problem? No: the plan is feasible, but Dynamic can probably do better. The most glaring weakness is its reliance on stretching payables, an extremely expensive financing device. Remember that it costs Dynamic 5% *per quarter* to delay paying bills—an effective interest rate of over 20% per year. The first plan would merely stimulate the financial manager to search for cheaper sources of short-term borrowing.

---

[12] The bank loan calls for quarterly interest of .025 × 100 = ₹2.5 million; the lost discount on the payables amounts to .05 × 16 = ₹.8 million, and the interest lost on the marketable securities is .02 × 25 = ₹.5 million.

The financial manager would ask several other questions as well. For example:

1. Does the plan yield satisfactory current and quick ratios?[13] Its bankers may be worried if these ratios deteriorate.[14]
2. Are there intangible costs of stretching payables? Will suppliers begin to doubt Dynamic's creditworthiness?
3. Does the plan for 2010 leave Dynamic in good financial shape for 2011? (Here the answer is yes, since Dynamic will have paid off its short-term borrowing by the end of the year.)
4. Should Dynamic try to arrange long-term financing for the major capital expenditure in the first quarter? This seems sensible, following the rule of thumb that long-term assets deserve long-term financing. It would also reduce the need for short-term borrowing dramatically. A counterargument is that Dynamic is financing the capital investment only temporarily by short-term borrowing. By year-end, the investment is paid for by cash from operations. Thus Dynamic's initial decision not to seek immediate long-term financing may reflect a preference for ultimately financing the investment with retained earnings.
5. Is it possible to adjust the firm's operating and investment plans to make the short-term financing problem easier. Perhaps there is a way to defer the first quarter's large cash outflow? For example, suppose that the large capital investment in the first quarter is for new mattress-stuffing machines to be delivered and installed in the first half of the year. The new machines are not scheduled to be ready for full-scale use until August. Perhaps the machine manufacturer could be persuaded to accept 60% of the purchase price on delivery and 40% when the machines are installed and operating satisfactorily.
6. Should Dynamic release cash by reducing the level of other current assets? For example, it could reduce receivables by getting tough with customers who are late paying their bills. (The cost is that in the future these customers may take their business elsewhere.) Or it may be able to get by with lower inventories of mattresses. (The cost is that it may lose business if there is a rush of orders that it cannot supply.)

Short-term financing plans are developed by trial and error. You lay out one plan, think about it, and then try again with different assumptions on financing and investment alternatives. You continue until you can think of no further improvements.

Trial and error is important because it helps you understand the real nature of the problem the firm faces. Here we can draw a useful analogy between the *process* of planning and Chapter 10, "Project Analysis." In Chapter 10 we described sensitivity analysis and other tools used by firms to find out what makes capital investment projects tick and what can go wrong with them. Dynamic's financial manager faces the same kind of task here: not just to choose a plan but to understand what can go wrong and what will be done if conditions change unexpectedly.[15]

A Note on Short-Term Financial Planning Models

Working out a consistent short-term plan requires burdensome calculations.[16] Fortunately much of the arithmetic can be delegated to a computer. Many large firms have built *short-term financial*

[13] These ratios were discussed in Chapter 28.

[14] We have not worked out these ratios explicitly, but you can infer from Table 29.6 that they would be fine at the end of the year but relatively low midyear, when Dynamic's borrowing is high.

[15] This point is even more important in *long-term* financial planning.

[16] If you doubt that, look again at Table 29.6. Notice that the cash requirements in each quarter depend on borrowing in the previous quarter, because borrowing creates an obligation to pay interest. Moreover, the problem's complexity would have been tripled had we not simplified by forecasting per quarter rather than by month.

planning models to do this. Smaller companies do not face so much detail and complexity and find it easier to work with a spreadsheet program on a personal computer. In either case the financial manager specifies forecasted cash requirements or surpluses, interest rates, credit limits, etc., and the model grinds out a plan like the one shown in Table 29.6.

The computer also produces balance sheets, income statements, and whatever special reports the financial manager may require. Smaller firms that do not want custom-built models can rent general-purpose models offered by banks, accounting firms, management consultants, or specialized computer software firms.

Most of these models simply work out the consequences of the assumptions and policies specified by the financial manager. *Optimization* models for short-term financial planning are also available. These models are usually linear programming models. They search for the *best* plan from a range of alternative policies identified by the financial manager. Optimization helps when the firm faces complex problems where trial and error might never identify the *best* combination of alternatives.

Of course the best plan for one set of assumptions may prove disastrous if the assumptions are wrong. Thus the financial manager has to explore the implications of alternative assumptions about future cash flows, interest rates, and so on.

29-5 LONG-TERM FINANCIAL PLANNING

It's been said that a camel looks like a horse designed by a committee. If a firm made every decision piecemeal, it would end up with a financial camel. That is why smart financial managers also need to plan for the long term and to consider the financial actions that will be needed to support the company's long-term growth. Here is where finance and strategy come together. A coherent long-term plan demands an understanding of how the firm can generate superior returns by its choice of industry and by the way that it positions itself within that industry.

Long-term planning involves capital budgeting on a grand scale. It focuses on the investment by each line of business and avoids getting bogged down in details. Of course, some individual projects may be large enough to have significant individual impact. For example, the telecom giant Verizon recently began implementing a project to spend billions of rupees to deploy fiber-optic-based broadband technology to its residential customers. You can bet that this project was explicitly analyzed as part of its long-range financial plan. Normally, however, planners do not work on a project-by-project basis. Instead, they are content with rules of thumb that relate average levels of fixed and short-term assets to annual sales, and do not worry so much about seasonal variations in these relationships. In such cases, the likelihood that accounts receivable may rise as sales peak in the holiday season would be a needless detail that would distract from more important strategic decisions.

Why Build Financial Plans?

Firms spend considerable time and resources in long-term planning. What do they get for this investment?

Contingency Planning Planning is not just forecasting. Forecasting concentrates on the most likely outcomes, but planners worry about unlikely events as well as likely ones. If you think ahead about what could go wrong, then you are less likely to ignore the danger signals and you can respond faster to trouble.

Companies have developed a number of ways of asking "what-if" questions about both individual projects and the overall firm. For example, managers often work through the consequences of their decisions under different scenarios. One scenario might envisage high interest rates contributing to a slowdown in world economic growth and lower commodity prices. A second scenario might involve a buoyant domestic economy, high inflation, and a weak currency. The idea is to formulate responses to inevitable surprises. What will you do, for example, if sales in the first year turn out to be 10% below forecast? A good financial plan should help you adapt as events unfold.

Considering Options Planners need to think whether there are opportunities for the company to exploit its existing strengths by moving into a wholly new area. Often they may recommend entering a market for "strategic" reasons—that is, not because the immediate investment has a positive net present value but because it establishes the firm in a new market and creates options for possibly valuable follow-on investments.

For example, Verizon's costly fiber-optic initiative gives the company the *real option* to offer additional services that may be highly valuable in the future, such as the rapid delivery of an array of home entertainment services. The justification for the huge investment lies in these potential growth options.

Forcing Consistency Financial plans draw out the connections between the firm's plans for growth and the financing requirements. For example, a forecast of 25% growth might require the firm to issue securities to pay for necessary capital expenditures, while a 5% growth rate might enable the firm to finance these expenditures by using only reinvested profits.

Financial plans should help to ensure that the firm's goals are mutually consistent. For example, the chief executive might say that she is shooting for a profit margin of 10% and sales growth of 20%, but financial planners need to think about whether the higher sales growth may require price cuts that will reduce profit margin.

Moreover, a goal that is stated in terms of accounting ratios is not operational unless it is translated back into what that means for business decisions. For example, a higher profit margin can result from higher prices, lower costs, or a move into new, high-margin products. Why then do managers define objectives in this way? In part, such goals may be a code to communicate real concerns. For example, a target profit margin may be a way of saying that in pursuing sales growth, the firm has allowed costs to get out of control. The danger is that everyone may forget the code and the accounting targets may be seen as goals in themselves. No one should be surprised when lower-level managers focus on the goals for which they are rewarded. For example, when Volkswagen set a goal of a 6.5% profit margin, some VW groups responded by developing and promoting expensive, high-margin cars. Less attention was paid to marketing cheaper models, which had lower profit margins but higher sales volume. As soon as this became apparent, Volkswagen announced that it would de-emphasize its profit margin goal and would instead focus on return on investment. It hoped that this would encourage managers to get the most profit out of every rupee of invested capital.

A Long-Term Financial Planning Model for Dynamic Mattress

Financial planners often use a financial planning model to help them explore the consequences of alternative strategies. We will drop in again on the financial manager of Dynamic Mattress to see how he uses a simple spreadsheet program to draw up the firm's long-term plan.

Long-term planning is concerned with the big picture. Therefore, when constructing long-term planning models it is generally acceptable to collapse all current assets and liabilities into a single figure or net working capital. Table 29.7 replaces Dynamic's latest balance sheets with condensed versions that report only net working capital rather than individual current assets or liabilities.

TABLE 29.7 Condensed year-end balance sheets for 2009 and 2008 for Dynamic Mattress Company (figures in ₹ millions).

	2009	2008
Net working capital	190	140
Fixed assets:		
Gross investment	350	320
Less depreciation	100	80
Net fixed assests	250	240
Total net assets	440	380
Long-term debt	90	60
Net worth (equity and retained earnings)	350	320
Long-term liabilities and net worth*	440	380

*When only net working capital appears on a firm's balance sheet, this figure (the sum of long-term liabilities and net worth) is often referred to as total capitalization.

Suppose that Dynamic's analysis of the industry leads it to forecast a 20% annual growth in the company's sales and profits over the next five years. Can the company realistically expect to finance this out of retained earnings and borrowing, or should it plan for an issue of equity? Spreadsheet programs are tailor-made for such questions. Let's investigate.

The basic sources and uses relationship tells us that

External capital required = investment in net working capital + investment in fixed assets
+ dividends − cash flow from operations

Thus there are three steps to finding how much extra capital Dynamic will need and the implications for its debt ratio.

Step 1 Project next year's net income plus depreciation, assuming the planned 20% increase in revenues. The first column of Table 29.8 shows this figure for Dynamic in the latest year (2009) and is taken from Table 29.1. The remaining columns show the forecasted values for the following five years.

TABLE 29.8 Actual (2009) and forecasted operating cash flows for Dynamic Mattress Company (figures in ₹ millions).

		2009	2010	2011	2012	2013	2014
1	Revenues	2200.0	2640.0	3168.0	3801.6	4561.9	5474.3
2	Costs (92% of revenues)	2055.0	2428.8	2914.6	3497.5	4197.0	5036.4
3	Depreciation (9% of net fixed assets at start of year)	20.0	22.5	29.7	35.6	42.8	51.3
4	EBIT (1−2−3)	125.0	188.7	223.7	268.5	322.2	386.6
5	Interest (10% of long-term debt at start of year)	5.0	9.0	23.4	31.8	42.0	54.3
6	Tax at 50%	60.0	89.8	100.1	118.3	140.1	166.2
7	Net income (4−5−6)	60.0	89.8	100.1	118.3	140.1	166.2
8	Operating cash flow (3+7)	80.0	112.4	129.8	154.0	182.9	217.5

Step 2 Project what additional investment in net working capital and fixed assets will be needed to support this increased activity and how much of the net income will be paid out as dividends. The sum

of these expenditures gives you the total *uses* of capital. If the total uses of capital exceed the cash flow generated by operations, Dynamic will need to raise additional long-term capital. The first column of Table 29.9 shows that in 2009 Dynamic needed to raise ₹30 million of new capital. The remaining columns forecast its capital needs for the following five years. For example, you can see that Dynamic will need to issue ₹144.5 million of debt in 2010 if it is to expand at the planned rate and not sell more shares.

TABLE 29.9 Actual (2009) and forecasted amounts of external capital required for Dynamic Mattress Company (figures in ₹ millions).

Visit us at
www.mhhe.com/bmam10e

		2009	2010	2011	2012	2013	2014
	Sources of capital:						
1	Net income plus depreciation	80.0	112.4	129.8	154.0	182.9	217.5
	Uses of capital:						
2	Increase in net working capital (NWC) assuming NWC = 11% of revenues	50.0	100.4	58.1	69.7	83.6	100.4
3	Investment in fixed assets (FA) assuming net FA = 12.5% of revenues	30.0	102.5	95.7	114.8	137.8	165.4
4	Dividend (60% of net income)	30.0	53.9	60.1	71.0	84.1	99.7
5	Total uses of funds (2 + 3 + 4)	110.0	256.8	213.9	255.5	305.5	365.4
6	External capital required (1 − 5)	30.0	144.5	84.0	101.6	122.6	147.9

Step 3   Finally, construct a forecast, or pro forma, balance sheet that incorporates the additional assets and the new levels of debt and equity. For example, the first column in Table 29.10 shows the latest condensed balance sheet for Dynamic Mattress. The remaining columns show that the company's equity grows by the additional retained earnings (net income less dividends), while long-term debt increases steadily to ₹691 million.

TABLE 29.10 Actual (2009) and pro forma balance sheets for Dynamic Mattress Company (figures in ₹ millions).

Visit us at
www.mhhe.com/bmam10e

	2009	2010	2011	2012	2013	2014
Net working capital	190	290.4	348.5	418.2	501.8	602.2
Net fixed assets	250	330.0	396.0	475.2	570.2	684.3
Total net assets	440	620.4	744.5	893.4	1072.1	1286.5
Long-term debt	90	234.5	318.5	420.0	542.7	690.6
Equity	350	385.9	426.0	473.3	529.4	595.8
Total long-term liabilities and equity	440	620.4	744.5	893.4	1072.1	1286.5

Over the five-year period Dynamic Mattress is forecasted to borrow an additional ₹601 million, and by year 2014 its debt ratio will have risen from 20% to 54%. The interest payments would still be comfortably covered by earnings and most financial managers could just about live with this amount of debt. However, the company could not continue to borrow at that rate beyond five years, and the debt ratio might be close to the limit set by the company's banks and bondholders.

An obvious alternative is for Dynamic to issue a mix of debt and equity, but there are other possibilities that the financial manager may want to explore. One option may be to hold back dividends during this period of rapid growth. An alternative might be to investigate whether the company could cut back on net working capital. For example, it may be able to economize on inventories or speed up the collection of receivables. The model makes it easy to examine these alternatives.

We stated earlier that financial planning is not just about exploring how to cope with the most likely outcomes. It also needs to ensure that the firm is prepared for unlikely or unexpected ones. For example, management would certainly wish to check that Dynamic Mattress could cope with a cyclical decline in sales and profit margins. Sensitivity analysis or scenario analysis can help to do this.

Pitfalls in Model Design

The Dynamic Mattress model that we have developed is too simple for practical application. You probably have already thought of several ways to improve it—by keeping track of the outstanding shares, for example, and printing out earnings and dividends per share. Or you might want to distinguish between short-term lending and borrowing opportunities, now buried in working capital.

The model that we developed for Dynamic Mattress is known as a *percentage of sales model.* Almost all the forecasts for the company are proportional to the forecasted level of sales. However, in reality many variables will *not* be proportional to sales. For example, important components of working capital such as inventory and cash balances will generally rise less rapidly than sales. In addition, fixed assets such as plant and equipment are not usually added in small increments as sales increase. The Dynamic Mattress plant may well be operating at less than full capacity, so that the company can initially increase output without *any* additions to capacity. Eventually, however, if sales continue to increase, the firm may need to make a large new investment in plant and equipment.

But beware of adding too much complexity: There is always the temptation to make a model bigger and more detailed. You may end up with an exhaustive model that is too cumbersome for routine use. The fascination of detail, if you give in to it, distracts attention from crucial decisions like stock issues and payout policy.

Choosing a Plan

Financial planning models help the manager to develop consistent forecasts of crucial financial variables. For example, if you wish to value Dynamic Mattress, you need forecasts of future free cash flows. These are easily derived up to the end of the planning period from our financial planning model.[17] However, a planning model does not tell you whether the plan is optimal. It does not even tell you which alternatives are worth examining. For example, we saw that Dynamic Mattress is planning for a rapid growth in sales and earnings per share. But is that good news for the shareholders? Well, not necessarily; it depends on the opportunity cost of the capital that Dynamic Mattress needs to invest. If the new investment earns more than the cost of capital, it will have a positive NPV and add to shareholder wealth. If the investment earns less than the cost of capital, shareholders will be worse off, even though the company expects steady growth in earnings.

The capital that Dynamic Mattress needs to raise depends on its decision to pay out 60% of its earnings as a dividend. But the financial planning model does not tell us whether this dividend payment makes sense or what mixture of equity or debt the company should issue. In the end the management has to decide. We would like to tell you exactly how to make the choice, but we can't. There is no model that encompasses all the complexities encountered in financial planning and decision making.

---

[17] Look back at Table 19.1, where we set out the free cash flows for Rio Corporation. A financial planning model would be a natural tool for deriving these figures.

As a matter of fact, there never will be one. This bold statement is based on Brealey, Myers, and Allen's Third Law:[18]

Axiom: The number of unsolved problems is infinite.

Axiom: The number of unsolved problems that humans can hold in their minds is at any time limited to 10.

Law: Therefore in any field there will always be 10 problems that can be addressed but that have no formal solution.

BMA's Third Law implies that no model can find the best of all financial strategies.[19]

29-6 GROWTH AND EXTERNAL FINANCING

We started this chapter by noting that financial plans force managers to be consistent in their goals for growth, investment, and financing. Before leaving the topic of financial planning, we should look at some general relationships between a firm's growth objectives and its financing needs.

Recall that Dynamic Mattress ended 2009 with fixed assets and net working capital of ₹440 million. In 2010 it plans to plow back retained earnings of ₹35.9 million, so net assets will increase by 35.9/440, or 8.16%. Thus Dynamic Mattress can grow by 8.16% without needing to raise additional capital. The maximum growth rate that a company can achieve without external funds is known as the **internal growth rate.** For Dynamic Mattress

$$\text{Internal growth rate} = \frac{\text{retained earnings}}{\text{net assets}} = 8.16\%$$

We can gain more insight into what determines this growth rate by multiplying the top and bottom of the expression for internal growth rate by *net income* and *equity* as follows:

$$\text{Internal growth rate} = \frac{\text{retained earnings}}{\text{net income}} \times \frac{\text{net income}}{\text{equity}} \times \frac{\text{equity}}{\text{net assets}}$$

In 2010 Dynamic Mattress expects to plow back 40% of net income and to earn a return of 25.66% on the equity with which it began the year. At the start of the year equity finances 79.55% of Dynamic Mattress's net assets. Therefore

$$\text{Internal growth rate} = .40 \times .2566 \times .7955 = .0816 \text{ or } 8.16\%$$

Notice that if Dynamic Mattress wishes to grow faster than this without raising equity capital, it would need to (1) plow back a higher proportion of its earnings, (2) earn a higher return on equity (ROE), or (3) have a lower debt-to-equity ratio.[20]

Instead of focusing on how rapidly the company can grow without *any* external financing, Dynamic Mattress's financial manager may be interested in the growth rate that can be sustained without additional *equity* issues. Of course, if the firm is able to raise enough debt, virtually any growth rate can

---

[18] The Second Law is presented in Section 10-1.

[19] It is possible to build linear programming models that help search for the best strategy subject to specified assumptions and conditions. These models can be more effective in screening alternative financial strategies.

[20] Notice, however, that if assets grow by only 8.16%, either the sales-to-assets ratio or the profit margin must increase to maintain a 25.66% return on equity.

be financed. It makes more sense to assume that the firm has settled on an optimal capital structure that it will maintain as equity is increased by the retained earnings. Thus the firm issues only enough debt to keep the debt–equity ratio constant. The **sustainable growth rate** is the highest growth rate the firm can maintain without increasing its financial leverage. It turns out that the sustainable growth rate depends only on the plowback rate and the return on equity:

$$\text{Sustainable growth rate} = \text{plowback ratio} \times \text{return on equity}$$

For Dynamic Mattress,

$$\text{Sustainable growth rate} = .40 \times .2566 = .1026, \text{ or } 10.26\%$$

We first encountered this formula in Chapter 4, where we used it to value common stocks.

These simple formulas remind us that firms may grow rapidly in the short term by relying on debt finance, but such growth can rarely be maintained without incurring excessive debt levels.

SUMMARY

Short-term financial planning is concerned with the management of the firm's short-term, or current, assets and liabilities. The most important current assets are cash, marketable securities, accounts receivable, and inventory. The most important current liabilities are short-term loans and accounts payable. The difference between current assets and current liabilities is called (net) working capital.

The nature of the firm's short-term financial planning problem is determined by the amount of long-term capital it raises. A firm that issues large amounts of long-term debt or common stock, or that retains a large part of its earnings, may find it has permanent excess cash. In such cases there is never any problem paying bills, and short-term financial planning consists of managing the firm's portfolio of marketable securities. A firm holding a reserve of cash is able to buy itself time to react to a short-term crisis. This may be important for growth firms that find it difficult to raise cash on short notice. However, large cash holdings can lead to complacency. We suggest that firms with permanent cash surpluses ought to consider returning the excess cash to their stockholders.

Other firms raise relatively little long-term capital and end up as permanent short-term debtors. Most firms attempt to find a golden mean by financing all fixed assets and part of current assets with equity and long-term debt. Such firms may invest cash surpluses during part of the year and borrow during the rest of the year.

The starting point for short-term financial planning is an understanding of sources and uses of cash. Firms forecast their net cash requirements by estimating collections on accounts receivable, adding other cash inflows, and subtracting all cash outlays. If the forecasted cash balance is insufficient to cover day-to-day operations and to provide a buffer against contingencies, the company will need to find additional finance. The search for the best short-term financial plan inevitably proceeds by trial and error. The financial manager must explore the consequences of different assumptions about cash requirements, interest rates, sources of finance, and so on. Firms use computerized financial models to help in this process. These models range from simple spreadsheet programs that merely help with the arithmetic to linear programming models that search for the best financial plan.

Short-term financial planning focuses on the firm's cash flow over the coming year. But the financial manager also needs to consider what financial actions will be needed to support the firm's plans for growth over the next 5 or 10 years. Most firms, therefore, prepare a long-term financial plan that describes the firm's strategy and projects its financial consequences. The plan establishes financial goals and is a benchmark for evaluating subsequent performance.

The process that produces this plan is valuable in its own right. First, planning forces the financial manager to consider the combined effects of all the firm's investment and financing decisions. This is important because these decisions interact and should not be made independently. Second, planning requires the manager to consider events that could upset the firm's progress and to devise strategies to be held in reserve for counterattack when unhappy surprises occur.

There is no theory or model that leads straight to *the* optimal financial strategy. As in the case of short-term planning, many different strategies may be projected under a range of assumptions about the future. The dozens of separate projections that may need to be made generate a heavy load of arithmetic. We showed how you can use a simple spreadsheet model to analyze Dynamic Mattress's long-term strategy.

FURTHER READING

The following text is concerned with liquidity management and short-term planning:

J. G. Kallberg and K. Parkinson, *Corporate Liquidity Management and Measurement,* (Burr Ridge, IL: Irwin/McGraw-Hill, 1996).

Long-term financial models are discussed in:

J. R. Morris and J. P Daley, *Introduction to Financial Models for Management and Planning* (Boca Raton, FL: Chapman & Hall/CRC Finance Series, 2009).

PROBLEM SETS

BASIC

1. Listed below are six transactions that Dynamic Mattress might make. Indicate how each transaction would affect (a) cash and (b) working capital.
   The transactions are
   i. Pay out an extra ₹10 million cash dividend.
   ii. Receive ₹2,500 from a customer who pays a bill resulting from a previous sale.
   iii. Pay ₹50,000 previously owed to one of its suppliers.
   iv. Borrow ₹10 million long term and invest the proceeds in inventory.
   v. Borrow ₹10 million short term and invest the proceeds in inventory.
   vi. Sell ₹5 million of marketable securities for cash.

2. State how each of the following events would affect the firm's balance sheet. State whether each change is a source or use of cash.
   a. An automobile manufacturer increases production in response to a forecasted increase in demand. Unfortunately, the demand does not increase.
   b. Competition forces the firm to give customers more time to pay for their purchases.
   c. Rising commodity prices increase the value of raw material inventories by 20%.
   d. The firm sells a parcel of land for ₹100,000. The land was purchased five years earlier for ₹200,000.
   e. The firm repurchases its own common stock.
   f. The firm doubles its quarterly dividend.
   g. The firm issues ₹1 million of long-term debt and uses the proceeds to repay a short-term bank loan.

3. Here is a forecast of sales by National Bromide for the first four months of 2010 (figures in ₹ thousands):

	Month 1	Month 2	Month 3	Month 4
Cash sales	15	24	18	14
Sales on credit	100	120	90	70

On the average 50% of credit sales are paid for in the current month, 30% are paid in the next month, and the remainder are paid in the month after that. What is the expected cash inflow from operations in months 3 and 4?

4. Dynamic Futon forecasts the following purchases from suppliers:

	Jan.	Feb.	Mar.	Apr.	May	Jun.
Value of goods (₹ millions)	32	28	25	22	20	20

   a. Forty percent of goods are supplied cash-on-delivery. The remainder are paid with an average delay of one month. If Dynamic Futon starts the year with payables of ₹22 million, what is the forecasted level of payables for each month?
   b. Suppose that from the start of the year the company stretches payables by paying 40% after one month and 20% after two months. (The remainder continue to be paid cash on delivery.) Recalculate payables for each month assuming that there are no cash penalties for late payment.

5. Each of the following events affects one or more tables in Sections 29-2 to 29-3. Show the effects of each event by adjusting the tables listed in parentheses:
   a. Dynamic repays only ₹10 million of short-term debt in 2009. (Tables 29.2 and 29.3)
   b. Dynamic issues an additional ₹40 million of long-term debt in 2009 and invests ₹25 million in a new warehouse. (Tables 29.1–29.3)
   c. In 2009 Dynamic reduces the quantity of stuffing in each mattress. Customers don't notice, but operating costs fall by 10%. (Tables 29.1–29.3)
   d. Starting in the third quarter of 2010, Dynamic employs new staff members who prove very effective in persuading customers to pay more promptly. As a result, 90% of sales are paid for immediately and 10% are paid in the following quarter. (Tables 29.4 and 29.5)
   e. Starting in the first quarter of 2010, Dynamic cuts wages by ₹20 million a quarter. (Table 29.5)
   f. In the second quarter of 2010 a disused warehouse catches fire mysteriously. Dynamic receives a ₹50 million check from the insurance company. (Table 29.5)
   g. Dynamic's treasurer decides he can scrape by on a ₹10 million operating cash balance. (Table 29.5)

6. True or false?
   a. Financial planning should attempt to minimize risk.
   b. The primary aim of financial planning is to obtain better forecasts of future cash flows and earnings.
   c. Financial planning is necessary because financing and investment decisions interact and should not be made independently.
   d. Firms' planning horizons rarely exceed three years.
   e. Financial planning requires accurate forecasting.
   f. Financial planning models should include as much detail as possible.

7. Table 29.11 on the next page summarizes the 2011 income statement and end-year balance sheet of Koromongala Bowling, Bangalore. Koromongala's financial manager forecasts a 10% increase in sales and costs in 2009. The ratio of sales to *average* assets is expected to remain a .40. Interest is forecasted at 5% of debt at the start of the year.
   a. What is the implied level of assets at the end of 2012?
   b. If the company pays out 50% of net income as dividends, how much cash will Koromongala need to raise in the capital markets in 2012?
   c. If Koromongala is unwilling to make an equity issue, what will be the debt ratio at the end of 2012?

TABLE 29.11 Financial statements for Koromongala's Bowling, Bangalore, 2011 (figures in thousands). See Problem 7.

Income Statement		
Sales	₹1,000	(40% of average assets)*
Costs	750	(75% of sales)
Interest	25	(5% of debt at start of year)**
Pretax profit	225	
Tax	90	(40% of pretax profit)
Net income	₹135	
Balance Sheet		
Assets	₹2,600	Debt	₹500
		Equity	2,100
Total	₹2,600	Total	₹2,600

*Assets at the end of 2010 were ₹2,400,000.
**Debt at the end of 2010 was ₹500,000.

8. Abbreviated financial statements for Archimedes Levers are shown in Table 29.12 on the next page. If sales increase by 10% in 2011 and all other items, including debt, increase correspondingly, what must be the balancing item? What will be its value?

TABLE 29.12 Financial statements for Archimedes Levers, 2010. See Problem 8 and 9.

Income Statement					
Sales		$4,000			
Costs, including interest		3,500			
Net income		$500			
Balance Sheet, Year-end					
	2010	**2009**		**2010**	**2009**
Assets	$3,200	$2,700	Debt	$1,200	$1,033
			Equity	2,000	1,667
Total	$3,200	$2,700	Total	$3,200	$2,700

9. What is the maximum possible growth rate for Archimedes (see Problem 8) if the payout ratio is set at 50% and (a) no external debt or equity is to be issued? (b) the firm maintains a fixed debt ratio but issues no equity?

INTERMEDIATE

10. Table 29.13 (on the next page) lists data from the budget of Ritewell Publishers. Half the company's sales are for cash on the nail; the other half are paid for with a one-month delay. The company pays all its credit purchases with a one-month delay. Credit purchases in January were ₹30, and total sales in January were ₹180. Complete the cash budget in Table 29.14

TABLE 29.13 Selected budget data for Ritewell Publishers. See Problems 10.

	February	March	April
Total sales	₹200	₹220	₹180
Purchases of materials			
For cash	70	80	60
For credit	40	30	40
Other expenses	30	30	30
Taxes, interest, and dividends	10	10	10
Capital investment	100	0	0

TABLE 29.14 Cash budget for Ritewell Publishers. See Problems 10.

	February	March	April
Sources of cash:			
Collections on cash sales			
Collections on accounts receivables			
Total sources of cash			
Uses of cash:			
Payments of accounts payable			
Cash purchases of materials			
Other expenses			
Capital expenditures			
Taxes, interest, and dividends			
Total uses of cash			
Net cash inflow			
Cash at start of period	100		
+ Net cash inflow			
= Cash at end of period			
+ Minimum operating cash balance	100	100	100
= Cumulative short-term financing required			

11. If a firm pays its bills with a 30-day delay, what fraction of its purchases will be paid in the current quarter? In the following quarter? What if the delay is 60 days?

12. Which items in Table 29.6 would be affected by the following events?
    a. There is a rise in interest rates.
    b. Suppliers demand interest for late payment.
    c. Dynamic receives an unexpected bill in the third quarter from the Income Tax Department for underpayment of taxes in previous years.

13. Table 29.15 shows Dynamic Mattress's year-end 2007 balance sheet, and Table 29.16 shows its income statement for 2008. Work out the statement of cash flows for 2008. Group these items into sources of cash and uses of cash.

eXcel
Visit us at
www.mhhe.com/bmam10e

TABLE 29.15   Year-end balance sheet for Dynamic Mattress for 2007 (figures in ₹ millions). See Problems 13.

Current Assets:		Current Liabilities:	
Cash	₹ 20	Bank loans	₹ 20
Marketable securities	10	Accounts payable	75
Accounts receivable	110	Total current liabilities	95
Inventory	100		
Total current assets	240	Long-term debt	25
		Net worth (equity and retained earnings)	300
Fixed assets:			
Gross investment	250		
Less depreciation	70		
Net fixed assets	180		
Total assets	420	Total liabilities and net worth	420

14. Work out a short-term financing plan for Dynamic Mattress Company, assu-ming the limit on the line of credit is raised from ₹100 to ₹120 million. Otherwise keep to the assumptions used in developing Table 29.6.

eXcel
Visit us at
www.mhhe.com/bmam10e

TABLE 29.16   Income statement for Dynamic Mattress for 2008 (figures in ₹ millions).

Sales	₹1,500
Operating costs	1,405
	95
Depreciation	10
	85
Interest	5
Pretax income	80
Tax at 50%	40
Net income	40

Note: Dividend = ₹30.
Retained earnings = ₹10.

15. Dynamic Mattress decides to lease its new mattress-stuffing machines rather than buy them. As a result, capital expenditure in the first quarter is reduced by ₹50 million, but the company must make lease payments of ₹2.5 million for each of the four quarters. Assume that the lease has no effect on tax payments until after the fourth quarter. Construct two tables like Tables 29.5 and 29.6 showing Dynamic's cumulative financing requirement and a new financing plan. Check your answer using the "live" spreadsheet on the book's Web site, www.mhhe.com/bmam10e.

16. Our long-term planning model of Dynamic Mattress is an example of a top-down planning model. Some firms use a bottom-up financial planning model, which incorporates forecasts of revenues and costs for particular products, advertising plans, major investment projects, and so on. What sort of firms would you expect to use each type, and what would they use them for?

17. Corporate financial plans are often used as a basis for judging subsequent performance. What do you think can be learned from such comparisons? What problems are likely to arise, and how might you cope with these problems?

18. The balancing item in the Dynamic long-term planning model is borrowing. What is meant by *balancing item?* How would the model change if dividends were made the balancing item instead? In that case how would you suggest that planned borrowing be determined?

19. Construct a new model for Dynamic Mattress based on your answer to Problem 18. Does your model generate a feasible financial plan for 2010? (*Hint:* If it doesn't, you may have to allow the firm to issue stock.)

20. a. Use the Dynamic Mattress model (Tables 29.8–29.10) and the "live" spreadsheets on the book's Web site at www.mhhe.com/bmam10e to produce pro forma income statements, balance sheets, and statements of cash flows for 2010 and 2011. Assume business as usual except that now sales and costs are planned to expand by 30% per year, as are fixed assets and net working capital. The interest rate is forecasted to remain at 10% and stock issues are ruled out. Dynamic also sticks to its 60% dividend payout ratio.

   b. What are the firm's debt ratio and interest coverage under this plan?
   c. Can the company continue to finance expansion by borrowing?

21. The financial statements of Eagle Sport Supply are shown in Table 29.17 (on the next page). For simplicity, "Costs" include interest. Assume that Eagle's assets are proportional to its sales.
   a. Find Eagle's required external funds if it maintains a dividend payout ratio of 60% and plans a growth rate of 15% in 2012.
   b. If Eagle chooses not to issue new shares of stock, what variable must be the balancing item? What will its value be?
   c. Now suppose that the firm plans instead to increase long-term debt only to $1,100 and does not wish to issue any new shares of stock. Why must the dividend payment now be the balancing item? What will its value be?

TABLE 29.17 Financial statements for Eagle Sport Supply, 2011. See Problem 21.

Income Statement				
Sales	₹950			
Costs	250			
Pretax income	700			
Taxes (at 28.6%)	200			
Net income	₹500			

Balance Sheet, Year-end				
	2011	**2010**	**2011**	**2010**
Assets	₹3,000	₹2,700	Debt	₹1,000	₹900
			Equity	2,000	1,800
Total	₹3,000	₹2,700	Total	₹3,000	₹2,700

22. a. What is the internal growth rate of Eagle Sport (see Problem 21) if the dividend payout ratio is fixed at 60% and the equity-to-asset ratio is fixed at two-thirds?
   b. What is the sustainable growth rate?

23. Bio-Plasma Corp. is growing at 30% per year. It is all-equity-financed and has total assets of ₹1 million. Its return on equity is 20%. Its plowback ratio is 40%.

a. What is the internal growth rate?

b. What is the firm's need for external financing this year?

c. By how much would the firm increase its internal growth rate if it reduced its payout rate to zero?

d. By how much would such a move reduce the need for external financing? What do you conclude about the relationship between dividend policy and requirements for external financing?

CHALLENGE

24. Table 29.18 shows the 2010 financial statements for the Executive Cheese Company. Annual depreciation is 10% of fixed assets at the beginning of the year, plus 10% of new investment.

TABLE 29.18 Financial statements for Executive Cheese Company, 2010 (figures in thousands).

Income Statement	
Revenue	₹1,785
Fixed costs	53
Variable costs (80% of revenue)	1,428
Depreciation	80
Interest (at 11.8%)	24
Taxes (at 40%)	80
Net income	₹ 120

Balance Sheet, Year-end		
	2010	**2009**
Assets:		
Net working capital	₹ 400	₹ 340
Fixed assets	800	680
Total assets	₹1,200	₹1,020
Liabilities:		
Debt	₹ 240	₹ 204
Book equity	960	816
Total liabilities	₹1,200	₹1,020

Sources and Uses	
Sources:	
Net income	₹120
Depreciation	80
Borrowing	36
Stock issues	104
Total sources	₹340
Uses:	
Increase in net working capital	₹ 60
Investment	200
Dividends	80
Total uses	₹340

The company plans to invest a further ₹200,000 per year in fixed assets for the next five years and net working capital is expected to remain a constant proportion of fixed assets. The company forecasts that the ratio of revenues to total assets at the start of each year will remain at 1.75. Fixed costs are expected to remain at ₹53, and variable costs at 80% of revenue. The company's policy is to pay out two-thirds of net income as dividends and to maintain a book debt ratio of 20%.

a. Construct a model for Executive Cheese like the one in Tables 29.8–29.10.

b. Use your model to produce a set of financial statements for 2011.

REAL-TIME DATA ANALYSIS

Look up the financial statements for any company either on http://finance. yahoo.com or on the Market Insight Database (www.mhhe.com/edumarketinsight). Make some plausible forecasts for future growth and the asset base needed to support that growth. Then use a spreadsheet program to develop a five-year financial plan. What financing is needed to support the planned growth? How vulnerable is the company to an error in your forecasts?

STANDARD & POOR'S

30

CHAPTER

WORKING CAPITAL
MANAGEMENT

Most of this book is devoted to long-term financial decisions such as capital budgeting and the choice of
capital structure. It is now time to look at the management of short-term assets and liabilities. Short-term,
or *current,* assets and liabilities are collectively known as **working capital.** Table 30.1 gives a breakdown
of working capital for all manufacturing corporations in India in 2011. Note that current assets are larger
than current liabilities. **Net working capital** (current assets *less* current liabilities) is positive.

TABLE 30.1   Current assets and liabilities for Indian corporations, March 31, 20115
(figures in ₹ crores)

Current Assets		Current Liabilities	
Cash	14,699,243	Current liabilities	27,571,609
Sundry debtors	16,908,767		
Inventories	9,718,010		
Other current assets	8,795,801		
Total	50,121,821	Total	27,571,609

Source: Compiled from Prowess database

Look also at Figure 30.1, which shows the relative importance of different items in current assets in
different industries in India in 2011. Cash and receivables constitute about 75% of the total current assets
in power generation and distribution companies. For some companies, current assets means principally
inventory. For example, you can see that inventories constitute more than 50% of the total current assets
in the retail firms.

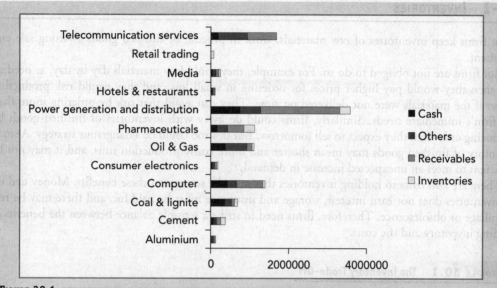

FIGURE 30.1

Break-up of current assets in different industries in India in 2011.

Source: Compiled from Prowess database

We begin our discussion of working capital management by focusing on the four principal types of current asset. We look first at the management of inventory. To do business, firms need reserves of raw materials, work in process, and finished goods. But these inventories can be expensive to store and they tie up capital. Therefore, inventory management involves a trade-off between the advantages of holding large inventories and the costs. In manufacturing companies the production manager is best placed to make this judgment, and the financial manager is not usually directly involved in inventory management. So we spend less time on this topic than on the management of other current assets.

Our second task is to look at **accounts receivable.** Companies frequently sell goods on credit, so that it may be weeks or even months before the company is paid. These unpaid bills are shown in the accounts as receivables. We explain how the company's credit manager sets the terms for payment, decides which customers should be offered credit, and ensures that they pay promptly.

Our next task is to discuss the firm's cash balances. The cash manager faces two principal problems. The first is to decide how much cash the firm needs to retain and therefore how much can be invested in interest-bearing securities. The second is to ensure that cash payments are handled efficiently. You don't want to stuff incoming checks into your desk drawer until you can walk them round to the bank; you want to get the money into your bank account as quickly as possible. We describe some of the techniques that firms use to move money around efficiently.

Cash that is not required immediately is usually invested in a variety of short-term securities. Some of these literally pay off the next day; others may mature in a few months. In Section 30-4 we describe the different features of these securities and show how to compare their yields.

For many firms the problem is not where to invest surplus cash, but how to make good a cash shortfall. In Chapter 24 we reviewed some of the types of long-term debt. In the final section of this chapter we review short-term loans. Many of these are provided by banks, but large companies can also sell their short-term debt directly to investors.

30-1 INVENTORIES

Most firms keep inventories of raw materials, work in process, or finished goods awaiting sale and shipment.

But firms are not obliged to do so. For example, they could buy materials day by day, as needed. But then they would pay higher prices for ordering in small lots, and they would risk production delays if the materials were not delivered on time. They can avoid that risk by ordering more than the firm's immediate needs. Similarly, firms could do away with inventories of finished goods by producing only what they expect to sell tomorrow. But this too could be a dangerous strategy. A small inventory of finished goods may mean shorter and more costly production runs, and it may not be sufficient to meet an unexpected increase in demand.

There are also costs to holding inventories that must be set against these benefits. Money tied up in inventories does not earn interest, storage and insurance must be paid for, and there may be risk of spillage or obsolescence. Therefore, firms need to strike a sensible balance between the benefits of holding inventory and the costs.

EXAMPLE 30.1 The Inventory Trade-Off

Allahabad Wire Products uses 255,000 tons a year of wire rod. Suppose that it orders Q tons at a time from the manufacturer. Just before delivery, Allahabad has effectively no inventories. Just *after* delivery it has an inventory of Q tons. Thus Allahabad's inventory of wire rod roughly follows the sawtooth pattern in Figure 30.2.

There are two costs to this inventory. First, each order that Allahabad places involves a handling and delivery cost. Second, there are carrying costs, such as the cost of storage and the opportunity cost of the capital that is invested in inventory. Allahabad can reduce the order costs by placing fewer and larger orders. On the other hand, a larger order size increases the average quantity held in inventory, so that the carrying costs rise. Good inventory management requires a trade-off between these two types of cost.

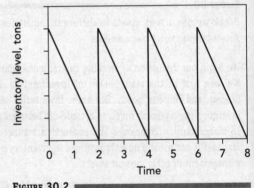

FIGURE 30.2

A simple inventory rule. The company waits until inventories of materials are about to be exhausted and then reorders a constant quantity.

This is illustrated in Figure 30.3. We assume here that each order that Allahabad places involves a fixed order cost of ₹450, while the annual carrying cost of the inventory works out at about ₹55 a ton. You can see how a larger order size results in lower order costs but higher carrying costs. The sum of the two costs is minimized when the size of each order is $Q = 2,043$ tons.

The optimal order size (2,043 tons in our example) is termed the *economic order quantity,* or *EOQ.*[1] Our example was not wholly realistic. For instance, most firms do not use up their inventory

---

[1] Where the firm uses up materials at a constant rate as in our example, there is a simple formula for calculating the economic order quantity (or EOQ). Its optimal size = $Q = \sqrt{(2 \times \text{sales} \times \text{cost per order}/\text{carrying cost})}$. In our example $Q = \sqrt{(2 \times 255,000 \times 450/55)} = 2,043$ tons.

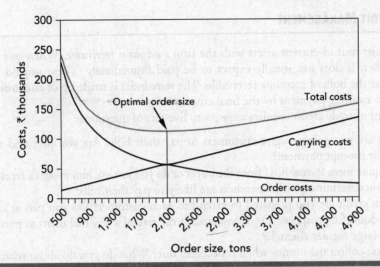

Visit us at
www.mhhe.com/bmam10e

FIGURE 30.3

As the inventory order size is increased, order costs fall and inventory carrying costs rise. Total costs are minimized when the saving in order costs is equal to the increase in carrying costs.

of raw material at a constant rate, and they would not wait until stocks had completely run out before they were replenished. But this simple model does capture some essential features of inventory management:

- Optimal inventory levels involve a trade-off between carrying costs and order costs.
- Carrying costs include the cost of storing goods as well as the cost of capital tied up in inventory.
- A firm can manage its inventories by waiting until they reach some minimum level and then replenish them by ordering a predetermined quantity.[2]
- When carrying costs are high and order costs are low, it makes sense to place more frequent orders and maintain higher levels of inventory.
- Inventory levels do not rise in direct proportion to sales. As sales increase, the optimal inventory level rises, but less than proportionately.

It seems that corporations in the U.S. today get by with lower levels of inventory than they used to. Thirty years ago, inventories held by U.S. companies accounted for 12% of firm assets. Today the figure is little more than half of that. The ratio of inventory to total assets for a sample of about 11,000 manufacturing companies in India also show similar trend. It has come down from 21% in 1991 to 16% in 2011.

Firms are finding that they can also reduce their inventories of finished goods by producing their goods to order. For example, Dell Computer discovered that it did not need to keep a large stock of finished machines. Its customers are able to use the Internet to specify what features they want on their PCs. The computer is then assembled to order and shipped to the customer.[3]

---

[2] This is known as a *reorder point* (or *two-bin*) *system.* Some firms use instead a *periodic review system,* where the firm reviews inventory levels periodically and tops the inventory up to the desired amount.

[3] These examples of just-in-time and build-to-order production are taken from T. Murphy, "JIT When ASAP Isn't Good Enough," *Ward's Auto World* (May 1999), pp. 67–73; R. Schreffler, "Alive and Well," *Ward's Auto World* (May 1999), pp. 73–77; "A Long March: Mass Customization," *The Economist,* July 14, 2001, pp. 63–65.

30-2 CREDIT MANAGEMENT

We continue our tour of current assets with the firm's *accounts receivable.* When one company sells goods to another, it does not usually expect to be paid immediately. These unpaid bills, or **trade credit,** compose the bulk of accounts receivable. The remainder is made up of **consumer credit,** that is, bills that are awaiting payment by the final customer.

Management of trade credit requires answers to five sets of questions:

1. How long are you going to give customers to pay their bills? Are you prepared to offer a cash discount for prompt payment?
2. Do you require some formal IOU from the buyer or do you just ask him to sign a receipt?
3. How do you determine which customers are likely to pay their bills?
4. How much credit are you prepared to extend to each customer? Do you play it safe by turning down any doubtful prospects? Or do you accept the risk of a few bad debts as part of the cost of building a large regular clientele?
5. How do you collect the money when it becomes due? What do you do about reluctant payers or deadbeats?

We discuss each of these topics in turn.

Terms of Sale

Not all sales involve credit. For example, if you are supplying goods to a wide variety of irregular customers, you may demand cash on delivery (COD). And, if your product is custom-designed, it may be sensible to ask for cash before delivery (CBD) or to ask for progress payments as the work is carried out.

When we look at transactions that do involve credit, we find that each industry seems to have its own particular practices.[4] These norms have a rough logic. For example, firms selling consumer durables may allow the buyer a month to pay, while those selling perishable goods, such as cheese or fresh fruit, typically demand payment in a week. Similarly, a seller may allow more extended payment if its customers are in a low-risk business, if their accounts are large, if they need time to check the quality of the goods, or if the goods are not quickly resold.

To encourage customers to pay before the final date, it is common to offer a cash discount for prompt settlement. For example, pharmaceutical companies commonly require payment within 30 days but may offer a 2% discount to customers who pay within 10 days. These terms are referred to as "2/10, net 30."

If goods are bought on a recurrent basis, it may be inconvenient to require separate payment for each delivery. A common solution is to pretend that all sales during the month in fact occur at the end of the month (EOM). Thus goods may be sold on terms of 8/10 EOM, net 60. This arrangement allows the customer a cash discount of 8% if the bill is paid within 10 days of the end of the month; otherwise the full payment is due within 60 days of the invoice date.

Cash discounts are often very large. For example, a customer who buys on terms of 2/10, net 30 may decide to forgo the cash discount and pay on the thirtieth day. This means that the customer obtains an extra 20 days' credit but pays about 2% more for the goods. This is equivalent to borrowing

---

[4] Standard credit terms in different industries are reported in O. K. Ng, J. K. Smith, and R. L. Smith, "Evidence on the Determinants of Credit Terms Used in Interfirm Trade," *Journal of Finance* 54 (June 1999), pp. 1109–1129.

money at a rate of 44.6% per annum.[5] Of course, any firm that delays payment beyond the due date gains a cheaper loan but damages its reputation.

The Promise to Pay

Repetitive sales to domestic customers are almost always made on *open account*. The only evidence of the customer's debt is the record in the seller's books and a receipt signed by the buyer.

If you want a clear commitment from the buyer before you deliver the goods, you can arrange a **commercial draft.**[6] This works as follows: You draw a draft ordering payment by the customer and send this to the customer's bank together with the shipping documents. If immediate payment is required, the draft is termed a *sight draft;* otherwise it is known as a *time draft.* Depending on whether it is a sight draft or a time draft, the customer either pays up or acknowledges the debt by signing it and adding the word *accepted.* The bank then hands the shipping documents to the customer and forwards the money or **trade acceptance** to you, the seller.

If your customer's credit is shaky, you can ask the customer to arrange for a bank to *accept* the time draft and thereby guarantee the customer's debt. These **bankers' acceptances** are often used in overseas trade. The bank guarantee makes the debt easily marketable. If you don't want to wait for your money, you can sell the acceptance to a bank or to another firm that has surplus cash to invest.

An alternative when you are selling goods overseas is to ask the customer to arrange for an *irrevocable letter of credit.* In this case the customer's bank sends you a letter stating that it has established a credit in your favor at a bank in India. You then know that the money is available and already in the country. You therefore draw a draft on the customer's bank and present it to your bank together with the letter of credit and the shipping documents. Your bank arranges for this draft to be either accepted or paid, and forwards the documents to the customer's bank.

If you sell your goods to a customer who proves unable to pay, you cannot get your goods back. You simply become a general creditor of the company together with many other unfortunates. You may be able to avoid this situation by making a *conditional sale,* so that you remain the owner of the goods until payment has been made. The conditional sale is common practice in Europe. In the United States it is used only for goods that are bought on an installment basis. So, if you buy a new car and fail to make all the payments, the dealer can repossess the car.

Credit Analysis

There are a number of ways to find out whether customers are likely to pay their debts. For existing customers an obvious indication is whether they have paid promptly in the past. For new customers you can use the firm's financial statements to make your own assessment, or you may be able to look at how highly investors value the firm.[7] However, the simplest way to assess a customer's credit standing is to seek the views of a specialist in credit assessment. For example, in Chapter 23 we described how bond rating agencies, such as CRISIL and ICRA, provide a useful guide to the riskiness of the firm's bonds.

---

[5] The cash discount allows you to pay $98 rather than ₹100. If you do not take the discount, you get a 20-day loan, but you pay 2/98 = 2.04% more for your goods. The number of 20-day periods in a year is 365/20 = 18.25. A rupee invested for 18.25 periods at 2.04% per period grows to $(1.0204)^{18.25} = ₹1.446$, a 44.6% return on the original investment. If a customer is happy to borrow at this rate, it's a good bet that he or she is desperate for cash (or can't work out compound interest). For a discussion of this issue, see J. K. Smith, "Trade Credit and Information Asymmetry," *Journal of Finance* 42 (September 1987), pp. 863–872.

[6] Commercial drafts are sometimes known by the general term *bills of exchange.*

[7] We discussed how you can use these sources of information in Section 23-4.

Bond ratings are usually available only for relatively large firms. However, you can obtain information on many smaller companies from a credit agency. Dun and Bradstreet is by far the largest of these agencies and its database contains credit information on millions of businesses worldwide. In the U.S., credit bureaus are another source of data on a customer's credit standing. In addition to providing data on small businesses, they can also provide an overall credit score for individuals.[8]

Finally, firms can also ask their bank to undertake a credit check. It will contact the customer's bank and ask for information on the customer's average balance, access to bank credit, and general reputation.

Of course you don't want to subject each order to the same credit analysis. It makes sense to concentrate your attention on the large and doubtful orders.

The Credit Decision

Let us suppose that you have taken the first three steps toward an effective credit operation. In other words, you have fixed your terms of sale; you have decided on the contract that customers must sign; and you have established a procedure for estimating the probability that they will pay up. Your next step is to work out which of your customers should be offered credit.

If there is no possibility of repeat orders, the decision is relatively simple. Figure 30.4 summarizes your choice. On one hand, you can refuse credit. In this case you make neither profit nor loss. The alternative is to offer credit. Suppose that the probability that the customer will pay up is p. If the customer does pay, you receive additional revenues (REV) and you incur additional costs; your net gain is the present value of

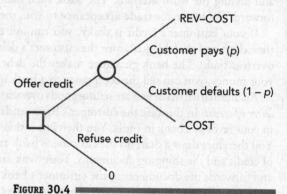

FIGURE 30.4

If you refuse credit, you make neither profit nor loss. If you offer credit, there is a probability p that the customer will pay and you will make REV − COST; there is a probability $(1 - p)$ that the customer will default and you will lose COST.

REV − COST. Unfortunately, you can't be certain that the customer will pay; there is a probability $(1 - p)$ of default. Default means that you receive nothing and incur the additional costs. The *expected* profit from each course of action is therefore as follows:

	Expected Profit
Refuse credit	0
Grant credit	$p\,\mathrm{PV(REV - COST)} - (1 - p)\,\mathrm{PV(COST)}$

You should grant credit if the expected gain from doing so is positive.

Consider, for example, the case of the Cast Iron Company. On each nondelinquent sale Cast Iron receives revenues with a present value of ₹1,200 and incurs costs with a value of ₹1,000. Therefore the company's expected profit if it offers credit is

$$p\,\mathrm{PV(REV - COST)} - (1 - p)\mathrm{PV(COST)} = p \times 200 - (1 - p) \times 1{,}000$$

[8] We discussed credit scoring models in Section 23-4. Credit bureau scores are often called "FICO scores" because most credit bureaus use a credit scoring model developed by Fair Isaac and Company. FICO scores are provided by the three major credit bureaus—Equifax, Experian, and TransUnion.

If the probability of collection is 5/6, Cast Iron can expect to break even:

$$\text{Expected profit} = \frac{5}{6} \times 200 - \left(1 - \frac{5}{6}\right) \times 1{,}000 = 0$$

Therefore Cast Iron's policy should be to grant credit whenever the chances of collection are better than 5 out of 6.

So far we have ignored the possibility of repeat orders. But one of the reasons for offering credit today is that it may help to get yourself a good, regular customer. Figure 30.5 illustrates the problem. Cast Iron has been asked to extend credit to a new customer. You can find little information on the firm, and you believe that the probability of payment is no better than .8. If you grant credit, the expected profit on this customer's order is

$$\text{Expected profit on initial order} = p_1 PV(REV - COST) - (1 - p_1) PV(COST)$$
$$= (.8 \times 200) - (.2 \times 1{,}000) = -₹40$$

You decide to refuse credit.

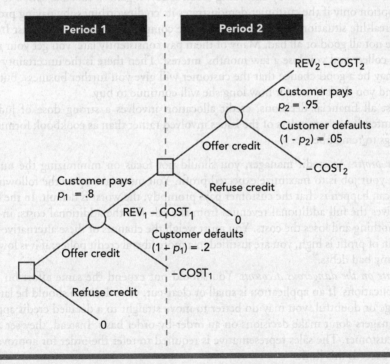

FIGURE 30.5

In this example there is only a .8 probability that your customer will pay in period 1; but if payment is made, there will be another order in period 2. The probability that the customer will pay for the second order is .95. The possibility of this good repeat order more than compensates for the expected loss in period 1.

This is the correct decision if there is no chance of a repeat order. But look again at the decision tree in Figure 30.5. If the customer does pay up, there will be a repeat order next year. Because the customer has paid once, you can be 95% sure that he or she will pay again. For this reason any repeat order is very profitable:

$$\text{Next year's expected profit on repeat order} = p_2 \text{PV(REV} - \text{COST)}$$
$$- (1 - p_1)\text{PV(COST)}$$
$$= (.95 \times 200) - (.05 \times 1,000) = ₹140$$

Now you can reexamine today's credit decision. If you grant credit today, you receive the expected profit on the initial order *plus* the possible opportunity to extend credit next year:

$$\text{Total expected profit} = \text{expected profit on initial order}$$
$$+ \text{ probability of payment and repeat order}$$
$$\times \text{ PV (next year's expected profit on repeat order)}$$
$$= -40 + .80 \times \text{PV(140)}$$

At any reasonable discount rate, you ought to extend credit. Notice that you should do so even though you expect to take a loss on the initial order. The expected loss is more than outweighed by the possibility that you will secure a reliable and regular customer. Cast Iron is not committed to making further sales to the customer, but by extending credit today, it gains a valuable *option* to do so. It will exercise this option only if the customer demonstrates its creditworthiness by paying promptly.

Of course real-life situations are generally far more complex than our simple Cast Iron examples. Customers are not all good or all bad. Many of them pay consistently late; you get your money, but it costs more to collect and you lose a few months' interest. Then there is the uncertainty about repeat sales. There may be a good chance that the customer will give you further business, but you can't be sure of that and you don't know for how long she will continue to buy.

Like almost all financial decisions, credit allocation involves a strong dose of judgment. Our examples are intended as reminders of the issues involved rather than as cookbook formulas. Here are the basic things to remember.

1. *Maximize profit.* As credit manager, you should not focus on minimizing the number of bad accounts; your job is to maximize expected profit. You must face up to the following facts: The best that can happen is that the customer pays promptly; the worst is default. In the best case, the firm receives the full additional revenues from the sale less the additional costs; in the worst, it receives nothing and loses the costs. You must weigh the chances of these alternative outcomes. If the margin of profit is high, you are justified in a more liberal credit policy; if it is low, you cannot afford many bad debts.[9]

2. *Concentrate on the dangerous accounts.* You should not expend the same effort on analyzing all credit applications. If an application is small or clear-cut, your decision should be largely routine; if it is large or doubtful, you may do better to move straight to a detailed credit appraisal. Most credit managers don't make decisions on an order-by-order basis. Instead, they set a credit limit for each customer. The sales representative is required to refer the order for approval only if the customer exceeds this limit.

3. *Look beyond the immediate order.* The credit decision is a dynamic problem. You cannot look only at the present. Sometimes it may be worth accepting a relatively poor risk as long as there is a good chance that the customer will become a regular and reliable buyer. New businesses must,

---

[9] Look back at our Cast Iron example, where we concluded that the company is justified in granting credit if the probability of collection is greater than 5/6. If the customer pays, Cast Iron will earn a profit margin of 200/1200 = 1/6. In other words, the company is justified in granting credit if the probability of payment exceeds 1 − profit margin.

therefore, be prepared to incur more bad debts than established businesses. This is part of the cost of building a good customer list.

Collection Policy

The final step in credit management is to collect payment. When a customer is in arrears, the usual procedure is to send a statement of account and to follow this at intervals with increasingly insistent letters or telephone calls. If none of these has any effect, most companies turn the debt over to a collection agent or an attorney.

Large firms can reap economies of scale in record keeping, billing, and so on, but the small firm may not be able to support a fully fledged credit operation. However, the small firm may be able to obtain some scale economies by farming out part of the job to a **factor.** This arrangement is known as **factoring.**

Factoring typically works as follows. The factor and the client agree on a credit limit for each customer. The client then notifies the customer that the factor has purchased the debt. Thereafter, whenever the client makes a sale to an approved customer, it sends a copy of the invoice to the factor, and the customer makes payment directly to the factor. Most commonly the factor does not have any recourse to the client if the customer fails to pay, but sometimes the client assumes the risk of bad debts. There are, of course, costs to factoring, and the factor typically charges a fee of 1% or 2% for administration and a roughly similar sum for assuming the risk of nonpayment. In addition to taking over the task of debt collection, most factoring agreements also provide financing for receivables. In these cases the factor pays the client 70% to 80% of the value of the invoice in advance at an agreed interest rate. Of course, factoring is not the only way to finance receivables; firms can also raise money by borrowing against their receivables.

Factoring is slowly becoming very popular among the small and medium firms in India. The total size of funds deployed by the factoring companies in India was a little more than € 5 billion in 2007. Canbank Factors and SBI Factors are two of the leading players in the factoring market in India. They mostly cater to the requirements of the small and medium sized firms in India. Because a factor may be employed by a number of manufacturers, it sees a larger proportion of the transactions that any single firm and therefore is better placed to judge the creditworthiness of each customer.[10]

If you don't want help with collection but do want protection against bad debts, you can obtain credit insurance. For example, most governments have established agencies to insure export business. In India, the Export Credit Guarantee Corporation of India provides credit risk insurance covers to exporters against payment risks. It also offers guarantees to banks and financial institutions to enable exporters to obtain better facilities from them.

There is always a potential conflict of interest between the collection operation and the sales department. Sales representatives commonly complain that they no sooner win new customers than the collection department frightens them off with threatening letters. The collection manager, on the other hand, bemoans the fact that the sales force is concerned only with winning orders and does not care whether the goods are subsequently paid for.

There are also many instances of cooperation between the sales force and the collection department. For example, the specialty chemical division of a major pharmaceutical company actually made a business loan to an important customer that had been suddenly cut off by its bank. The pharmaceutical company bet that it knew its customer better than the customer's bank did. The bet paid off. The

---

[10] This point is made in S. L. Mian and C. W. Smith, Jr., "Accounts Receivable Management Policy: Theory and Evidence," *Journal of Finance* 47 (March 1992), pp. 169–200.

customer arranged alternative bank financing, paid back the pharmaceutical company, and became an even more loyal customer. It was a nice example of financial management supporting sales.

It is not common for suppliers to make business loans in this way, but they lend money indirectly whenever they allow a delay in payment. Trade credit can be an important source of funds for indigent customers that cannot obtain a bank loan. But that raises an important question: if the bank is unwilling to lend, does it make sense for you, the supplier, to continue to extend trade credit? Here are two possible reasons that it may make sense: First, as in the case of our pharmaceutical company, you may have more information than the bank about the customer's business. Second, you need to look beyond the immediate transaction and recognize that your firm may stand to lose some profitable future sales if the customer goes out of business.[11]

30-3 CASH

Short-term securities pay interest, cash doesn't. So why do corporations and individuals hold billions of dollars in cash and demand deposits? Why, for example, don't you take all *your* cash and invest it in interest-bearing securities? The answer of course is that cash gives you more *liquidity* than do securities. You can use it to buy things. It is hard enough to get Mumbai taxi drivers to give you change for a ₹1,000 note, but try asking them to split a Treasury bill.

In equilibrium all assets in the same risk class are priced to give the same expected marginal benefit. The benefit from holding Treasury bills is the interest that you receive; the benefit from holding cash is that it gives you a convenient store of liquidity. In equilibrium the marginal value of this liquidity is equal to the marginal value of the interest on Treasury bills. This is just another way of saying that Treasury bills have zero net present value; they are fair value relative to cash.

Does this mean that it does not matter how much cash you hold? Of course not. The marginal value of liquidity declines as you hold increasing amounts of cash. When you have only a small proportion of your wealth in cash, a little extra can be extremely useful; when you have a substantial holding, any additional liquidity is not worth much. Therefore, as financial manager you want to hold cash balances up to the point where the marginal value of the liquidity is equal to the value of the interest foregone.

In choosing between cash and short-term securities, the financial manager faces a task like that of the production manager. After all, cash is just another raw material that you need to do business, and there are costs and benefits to holding large "inventories" of cash. If the cash were invested in securities, it would earn interest. On the other hand, you can't use those securities to pay the firm's bills. If you had to sell them every time you needed to pay a bill, you could incur heavy transactions costs. The financial manager must trade off the cost of keeping an inventory of cash (the lost interest) against the benefits (the saving on transactions costs).

For small firms this trade-off can be important. But for very large firms the transactions costs of buying and selling securities become trivial compared with the opportunity cost of holding idle cash balances. Suppose that the interest rate is 5% a year, or roughly 5/365 = .0137% per day. Then the daily interest earned by ₹1 million is .000137 × 1,000,000 = ₹137. Even at a cost of ₹50 per transaction, which is generously high, it pays to buy Treasury bills today and sell them tomorrow rather than to leave ₹1 million idle overnight. Consider Wal-Mart, which has annual sales of about

---

[11] Of course, banks also need to recognize the possibility of continuing business from the firm. The question therefore is whether suppliers have a *greater* stake in the firm's continuing prosperity. For some evidence on the determinants of the supply and demand for trade credit, see M. A. Petersen and R. G. Rajan, "Trade Credit: Theories and Evidence," *Review of Financial Studies* 10 (Fall 1997), pp. 661–692.

₹400 billion and an average daily cash flow of ₹400,000,000,000/365, or ₹1.1 billion. Firms of this size generally end up buying or selling securities once a day every day.

Banks have developed ways to help firms to invest idle cash. For example, they may provide **sweep programs,** where the bank automatically "sweeps" surplus funds into an interest-bearing investment, such as a money-market mutual fund.

Why then do large firms hold any significant amounts of cash? There are basically two reasons. First, cash may be left in non-interest-bearing accounts to compensate banks for the services they provide. Second, large corporations may have literally hundreds of accounts with dozens of different banks. It is often better to leave idle cash in these accounts than to monitor each account daily and make daily transfers among them.

One major reason for this proliferation of bank accounts is decentralized management. You cannot give a subsidiary operating autonomy without giving its managers the right to spend and receive cash. Good cash management nevertheless implies some degree of centralization. It is impossible to maintain your desired cash inventory if all the subsidiaries in the group are responsible for their own private pools of cash. And you certainly want to avoid situations in which one subsidiary is investing its spare cash at 5% while another is borrowing at 8%. It is not surprising, therefore, that even in highly decentralized companies there is generally central control over cash balances and bank relations.

How Purchases Are Paid For

Most small, face-to-face purchases are made with rupee notes. But you probably would not want to use cash to buy a new car, and you can't use cash to make a purchase over the Internet. There are a variety of ways that you can pay for larger purchases or send payments to another location. Some of the more important ways are set out in Table 30.2.

TABLE 30.2 Small, face-to-face purchases are commonly paid for with cash, but here are some of the other ways to pay your bills.

Check When you write a check, you are instructing your bank to pay a specified sum on demand to the particular firm or person named on the check.
Credit card A credit card, such as a Visa card or MasterCard, gives you a line of credit that allows you to make purchases up to a specified limit. At the end of each month, either you pay the credit card company in full for these purchases or you make a specified minimum payment and are charged interest on the outstanding balance.
Charge card A charge card may look like a credit card and you can spend money with it as with a credit card. But with a charge card the day of reckoning comes at the end of each month, when you must pay for all purchases that you have made. In other words, you must pay off the entire balance each month.
Debit card A debit card allows you to have your purchases from a store charged directly to your bank account. The deduction is usually made electronically and is immediate. Often, debit cards may be used to make withdrawals from a cash machine (ATM).
Credit transfer With a credit transfer you ask your bank to set up a standing order to make a regular set payment to a supplier. For example, standing orders are often used to make regular fixed mortgage payments.
Direct payment A direct payment (or debit) is an instruction to your bank to allow a company to collect varying amounts from your account, as long as you have been given advance notice of the amount and date. For example, an electric utility company may ask you to arrange an automatic payment of your electricity bills from your bank account.

Look now at Figure 30.6. You can see that there are large differences in the ways that people around the world pay for their purchases. For example, checks are almost unknown in Germany, the Netherlands, and Sweden.[12] Most payments in these countries are by debit card or credit transfer. By contrast, Americans love to write checks. Each year individuals and firms in the United States write about 31 billion checks. India presents a mixed picture. Check payments (or cheques, as they are written in India) constitute 24.6% of the total non-cash transactions in India (as of 2010). Indians also love to pay by cards (both debit and credit) as the share of card payments in the total non-cash transactions in India is more than 66% in 2010.

But throughout the world the use of checks is on the decline. For one-off purchases they are being replaced by credit or debit cards. In addition mobile phone technology and the Internet are encouraging the development of new infant payment systems. For example,

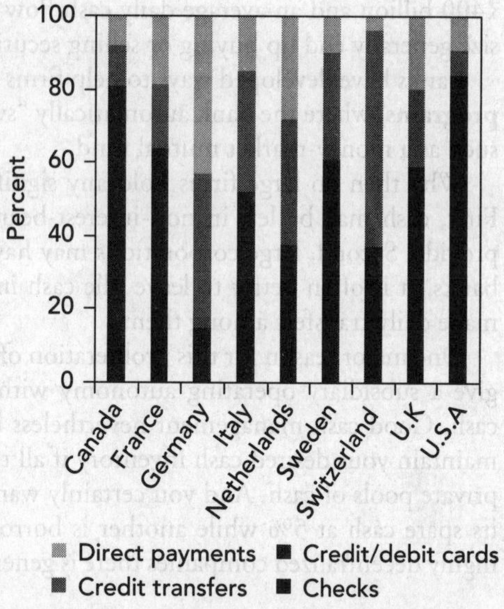

- Electronic bill presentment and payment (or EBPP) allows companies to bill customers and receive payments via the Internet. EBPP is forecasted to grow rapidly. Already in Finland two out of three people regard the Internet as the most typical medium for paying bills.
- Stored-value cards (or e-money) let you transfer cash value to a card that can be used to buy a variety of goods and services. For example, Hong

- Direct payments   ■ Credit/debit cards
- Credit transfers   ■ Checks

FIGURE 30.6

How purchases are paid for. Percentage of total *volume* of cashless transactions, 2007. (Data exclude small usage of card-based e-money.)

Source: Bank for International Settlements, "Statistics on Payment and Settlement Systems in Selected Countries," March 2009, **www.bis.org/publ/cpss86.htm.**

Kong's Octopus card system, which was developed to pay for travel fares, has become a widely used electronic cash system throughout the territory.

There are three main ways that firms send and receive money electronically. These are direct payments, direct deposits, and wire transfers.

Recurring expenditures, such as utility bills, mortgage payments, and insurance premiums, are increasingly settled by *direct payment* (also called *automatic debit* or *direct debit*). In this case the firm's customers simply authorize it to debit their bank account for the amount due. The company provides its bank with a file showing details of each customer, the amount to be debited, and the date. The payment then travels electronically through the **Automated Clearing House (ACH)** system. The firm knows exactly when the cash is coming in and avoids the labor-intensive process of handling thousands of checks.

The ACH system also allows money to flow in the reverse direction. Thus while a *direct payment* transaction provides an automatic debit, a *direct deposit* constitutes an automatic credit. Direct deposits are used to make bulk payments such as wages or dividends. Again the company provides its bank with a file of instructions. The bank then debits the company's account and transfers the cash via the ACH to the bank accounts of the firm's employees or shareholders.

The volume of direct payments and deposits has increased rapidly. Over 50% of U.S. households now use direct payment for recurring expenditures and nearly three-quarters of employees are paid by

---

[12] For a discussion of the reasons for these international differences in payment methods, see "Retail Payments in Selected Countries: A Comparative Study," Committee on Payment and Settlement Systems, Bank for International Settlements, Basel, Switzerland, September 1999.

direct deposit. You can see from Table 30.3 that the total value of ACH transactions is approaching that of checks.[13]

TABLE 30.3   Use of Payment Systems in the United States, 2008.

	Volume (millions)	Value ($ trillions)
Checks (2007)	29,000	$ 42
ACH direct payments and deposits	15,000	30
Fedwire	190	986
Chips	92	509

Sources: **www.federalreserve.gov, www.nacha.org,** and **www.chips.org.**

Large-value payments between companies are usually made electronically through Fedwire or CHIPS. Fedwire is operated by the Federal Reserve system, and connects nearly 9,000 financial institutions to the Fed and thereby to each other.[14] CHIPS is a bank-owned system serving more than 1,400 U.S. financial institutions and hundreds of international participants. It mainly handles eurodollar payments and foreign exchange transactions, and is used for over 95% of cross-border payments in dollars.

Table 30.3 shows that the *number* of payments by Fedwire and CHIPS is relatively small, but the sums involved are huge. Both systems are fast and low risk, but they are also relatively expensive. For example, a Fedwire transaction might cost $20 for each party, whereas an ACH payment might cost 10 to 20 cents. Consequently, where urgency is not an issue, companies sometimes turn to ACH for large-value payments.

The Reserve Bank of India introduced the RBI Electronic Funds Transfer (EFT) scheme to help the banks offer electronic funds transfer facilities to their customers. As of now, this facility is available in all the branches of the 27 public sector banks and 55 scheduled commercial banks at 15 centres. Under this system, money gets transferred on the same day or next day depending on when the transfer order has been placed. Prior to the introduction of the RBI EFT system, banks used to offer electronic money transfer facilities under the telegraphic transfer (TT) scheme. However, both the remitter and beneficiary need to have accounts with the same bank under the telegraphic transfer system. A lot of paper work was required when the two companies used to have different banks. We explain the details of operation of RBI EFT in Table 30.4.

Electronic funds transfer system has at least three advantages:

- Record keeping and routine transactions are easy to automate when money moves electronically.
- The marginal cost of transaction is very low. In fact, the RBI had waived the processing charges till March 31, 2007.
- Because companies do not need to wait for cheques to clear, they may get earlier access to their funds.

---

[13] The Automated Clearing House also handles the growing number of check conversion transactions (see below) and nonrecurring transactions made by telephone or over the Internet.

[14] Fedwire is a *real-time, gross settlement system,* which means that each transaction over Fedwire is settled individually and immediately. With a net settlement system transactions are put into a pot and periodically netted off before being settled. CHIPS is an example of a net system that settles at frequent intervals.

TABLE 30.4   Details of operation of RBI EFT.

Steps in RBI EFT System
Step-1: The remitter fills in the EFT application form giving the particulars of the beneficiary (city, bank, branch, beneficiary's name, account type and account number) and authorizes the branch to remit a specified amount to the beneficiary by raising a debit to the remitter's account.
Step-2: The remitting branch prepares a schedule and sends the duplicate of the EFT application form to its Service branch for EFT data preparation. If the branch is equipped with a computer system, data preparation can be done at the branch level in the specified format.
Step-3: The service branch prepares the EFT data file by using a software package supplied by RBI and transmits the same to the local RBI (National Clearing Cell) to be included for the settlement of 12 noon, 2 pm and 4 pm.
Step-4: The RBI at the remitting centre consolidates the files received from all banks, sorts the transactions city-wise and prepares vouchers for debiting the remitting banks on Day-1 itself. City-wise files are transmitted to the RBI offices at the respective destination centres.
Step-5: RBI at the destination centre receives the files from the originating centres, consolidates them and sorts them bank-wise. Thereafter, bank-wise remittance data files are transmitted to banks on Day 1 itself. Bank-wise vouchers are prepared for crediting the receiving banks' accounts the same day or next day.
Step-6: On Day 1/2 morning the receiving banks at the destination centres process the remittance files transmitted by RBI and forward credit reports to the destination branches for crediting the beneficiaries' accounts.

Source: www.rbi.org.in

Speeding Up Check Collections

Although checks are rarely used for large-value payments, they continue to be the most common method of payment for smaller nonrecurring transactions. About three-quarters of business-to-business (B2B) transactions in the United States are still made by check.

Check handling is a cumbersome and labor-intensive task. However, recent changes to legislation in the United States have helped to reduce costs and speed up collections. The Check Clearing for the 21st Century Act, usually known as Check 21, allows banks to send digital images of checks to one another rather than sending the checks themselves. As the new technology becomes more widespread, there will be fewer cargo planes crisscrossing the country to take bundles of checks from one bank to another. The cost of processing checks is also being reduced by a technological innovation known as check conversion. In this case, when you write a check, the details of your bank account and the amount of the payment are automatically captured at the point of sale, your check is handed back to you, and your bank account is immediately debited.

Firms that receive a large volume of checks have devised a number of ways to ensure that the cash becomes available as quickly as possible. For example, a retail chain may arrange for each branch to deposit receipts in a collection account at a local bank. Surplus funds are then periodically transferred electronically to a **concentration account** at one of the company's principal banks. There are two reasons that concentration banking allows the company to gain quicker use of its funds. First, because the store is nearer to the bank, transfer times are reduced. Second, because the customer's check is likely to be drawn on a local bank, the time taken to clear the check is also reduced.

The Reserve Bank of India introduced the Cheque Truncation System (CTS) in February 2008 in the National Capital region (NCR) in a pilot project. Subsequently, the CTS was introduced in Chennai in September 2011. Under this system, the collecting bank sends the data (on the MICR band) and the image of the cheque to the central processing location for onward transmission to the paying bank. For this purpose, the presenting and the drawee banks are provided with an interface called the Clearing House Interface (CHI) that enables them to connect and transmit data and captured images in a safe and secure manner. The clearing house processes the data and routes the images and data to the drawee bank.[15]

International Cash Management

Cash management in domestic firms is child's play compared with cash management in large multinational corporations operating in dozens of countries, each with its own currency, banking system, and legal structure.

A single centralized cash management system is an unattainable ideal for these companies, although they are edging toward it. For example, suppose that you are treasurer of a large multinational company with operations throughout Europe. You could allow the separate businesses to manage their own cash, but that would be costly and would almost certainly result in each one accumulating little hoards of cash. The solution is to set up a regional system. In this case the company establishes a local concentration account with a bank in each country. Any surplus cash is swept daily into a central multicurrency account in London or another European banking center. This cash is then invested in marketable securities or used to finance any subsidiaries that have a cash shortage.

Payments can also be made out of the regional center. For example, to pay wages in each European country, the company just needs to send its principal bank a computer file of the payments to be made. The bank then finds the least costly way to transfer the cash from the company's central accounts and arranges for the funds to be credited on the correct day to the employees in each country.

Rather than physically moving funds between local bank accounts and a regional concentration account, the company may employ a multinational bank with branches in each country and then arrange for the bank to *pool* all the cash surpluses and shortages. In this case no money is transferred between accounts. Instead, the bank just adds together the credit and debit balances, and pays the firm interest at its lending rate on any surplus.

When a company's international branches trade with each other, the number of cross-border transactions can multiply rapidly. Rather than having payments flowing in all directions, the company can set up a netting system. Each branch can then calculate its net position and undertake a single transaction with the netting center. Several industries have set up netting systems for their members. For example, over 200 airlines have come together to establish a netting system for the foreign currency payments that they must make to each other.

Paying for Bank Services

Much of the work of cash management—processing checks, transferring funds, running lockboxes, helping keep track of the company's accounts—is done by banks. And banks provide many other services not so directly linked to cash management, such as handling payments and receipts in foreign currency, or acting as custodian for securities.

All these services need to be paid for. Usually payment is in the form of a monthly fee, but banks may agree to waive the fee as long as the firm maintains a minimum average balance in an interest-free deposit. Banks are prepared to do this, because, after setting aside a portion of the money in a reserve account with the Fed, they can relend the money to earn interest. Demand deposits earmarked to pay for bank services are termed *compensating balances*. They used to be a very common way to pay for bank services, but since banks have been permitted to pay interest on demand deposits there has been a steady trend away from using compensating balances and toward direct fees.

---

[15] Source: www.rbi.org.in/scripts/FAOView.apex?id=63.

30-4 MARKETABLE SECURITIES

At the end of March 2011, Bajaj Auto was sitting on a ₹1236.70 crores mountain of cash, amounting to about half of the company's total assets[16]. The company kept ₹156.47 crores in the bank to support day-to-day operations and invested the surplus as follows:

Investments	Amount (₹ in crores)
Government securities	108.83
Certificates of deposits	571.38
Fixed deposits	400.02
Cash and bank balances	156.97
Total	1236.70

Most companies do not have the luxury of such huge cash surpluses, but they also park any cash that is not immediately needed in short-term investments. The market for these investments is known as the **money market.** The money market has no physical marketplace. It consists of a loose collection of banks and dealers linked together by telephones or through the Web. But a huge volume of securities is regularly traded on the money market, and competition is vigorous.

Most large corporations manage their own money-market investments, but small companies sometimes find it more convenient to hire a professional investment management firm or to put their cash into a money-market fund. This is a mutual fund that invests only in low-risk, short-term securities.[17]

The relative safety of money-market funds has made them particularly popular at times of financial stress. During the credit crunch of 2008 fund assets mushroomed as investors fled from plunging stock markets. Then it was revealed that one fund, the Reserve Primary Fund, had incurred heavy losses on its holdings of Lehman Brothers' commercial paper. The fund became only the second money-market fund in history to "break the buck," by offering just 97 cents on the dollar to investors who cashed in their holdings. That week investors pulled nearly $200 billion out of money-market funds, prompting the government to offer emergency insurance to investors.

Calculating the Yield on Money-Market Investments

Many money-market investments are pure discount securities. This means that they don't pay interest. The return consists of the difference between the amount you pay and the amount you receive at maturity. Unfortunately, it is no good trying to persuade the Income Tax Department that this difference represents capital gain. The Income Tax Department is wise to that one and will tax your return as interest income.

Interest rates on money-market investments are often quoted on a discount basis. For example, suppose that three-month bills are issued at a discount of 5%. This is a rather complicated way of saying that the price of a three-month bill is $100 - (3/12) \times 5 = 98.75$. Therefore, for every ₹98.75 that you invest today, you receive ₹100 at the end of three months. The return over three months is

---

[16] In fact, in 2008, more than a third- of the total assets of Microsoft was in the form of cash. As we explained in Chapter 16, in July 2004, Microsoft decided to pay out a large part of its surplus cash to shareholders.

[17] We discussed money-market funds in Section 17-3.

1.25/98.75 = .0127, or 1.27%. This is equivalent to an annual yield of 5.18%. Note that the return is always higher than the discount. When you read that an investment is selling at a discount of 5%, it is very easy to slip into the mistake of thinking that this is its return.[18]

Yields on Money-Market Investments

When we value long-term debt, it is important to take account of default risk. Almost anything may happen in 30 years, and even today's most respectable company may get into trouble eventually. Therefore, corporate bonds offer higher yields than Treasury bonds.

Short-term debt is not risk-free either. When California was mired in the energy crisis of 2001, Southern California Edison and Pacific Gas and Electric were forced to suspend payments on nearly $1 billion of maturing commercial paper.[19] However, such examples are exceptions; in general, the danger of default is less for money-market securities issued by corporations than for corporate bonds. There are two reasons for this. First, the range of possible outcomes is smaller for short-term investments. Even though the distant future may be clouded, you can usually be confident that a particular company will survive for at least the next month. Second, for the most part only well-established companies can borrow in the money market. If you are going to lend money for just a few days, you can't afford to spend too much time in evaluating the loan. Thus, you will consider only blue-chip borrowers.

Despite the high quality of money-market investments, there are often significant differences in yield between corporate and government securities. Why is this? One answer is the risk of default. Another is that the investments have different degrees of liquidity or "moneyness." Investors like Treasury bills because they are easily turned into cash on short notice. Securities that cannot be converted so quickly and cheaply into cash need to offer relatively high yields. During times of market turmoil investors may place a particularly high value on having ready access to cash. On these occasions the yield on illiquid securities can increase dramatically.

The International Money Market

In Chapter 24 we pointed out that there are two main markets for dollar bonds. There is the domestic market in the United States and there is the eurobond market centered in London. Similarly, in addition to the domestic money market, there is also an international market for short-term dollar investments, which is known as the *eurodollar* market.

Eurodollars have nothing to do with the euro, the currency of the European Monetary Union (EMU). They are simply dollars deposited in a bank in Europe. For example, suppose that an American oil company buys crude oil from an Arab sheik and pays for it with a $1 million check drawn on JP Morgan Chase. The sheik then deposits the check with his account at Barclays Bank in London. As a result, Barclays has an asset in the form of a $1 million credit in its account with JP Morgan Chase. It also has an offsetting liability in the form of a dollar deposit. Since that dollar deposit is placed in Europe, it is called a eurodollar deposit.[20]

Just as there is both a domestic U.S. money market and a eurodollar market, so there is both a domestic Japanese money market and a market in London for euroyen. So, if a U.S. corporation

---

[18] To confuse things even more, dealers in the money market often quote rates as if there were only 360 days in a year. So a discount of 5% on a bill maturing in 91 days translates into a price of $100 - 5 \times (91/360) = 98.74\%$.

[19] Commercial paper is short-term debt issued by corporations. We describe it in Section 30-5.

[20] The sheik could equally well deposit the check with the London branch of a U.S. bank or a Japanese bank. He would still have made a eurodollar deposit.

wishes to make a short-term investment in yen, it can deposit the yen with a bank in Tokyo or it can make a euroyen deposit in London. Similarly, there is both a domestic money market in the euro area as well as a money market for euros in London.[21] And so on.

Major international banks in London lend dollars to one another at the *London interbank offered rate* (LIBOR). Similarly, they lend yen to each other at the yen LIBOR interest rate, and they lend euros at the **euro interbank offered rate,** or **Euribor.** These interest rates are used as a benchmark for pricing many types of short-term loans in the United States and in other countries. For example, a corporation in the United States may issue a floating-rate note with interest payments tied to dollar LIBOR.

If we lived in a world without regulation and taxes, the interest rate on a eurodollar loan would have to be the same as the rate on an equivalent domestic dollar loan. However, the international debt markets thrive because governments attempt to regulate domestic bank lending. When the U.S. government limited the rate of interest that banks in the United States could pay on domestic deposits, companies could earn a higher rate of interest by keeping their dollars on deposit in Europe. As these restrictions have been removed, differences in interest rates have largely disappeared.

In the late 1970s the U.S. government was concerned that its regulations were driving business overseas to foreign banks and the overseas branches of American banks. To attract some of this business back to the States, the government in 1981 allowed U.S. and foreign banks to establish **international banking facilities (IBFs).** An IBF is the financial equivalent of a free-trade zone; it is physically located in the United States, but it is not required to maintain reserves with the Federal Reserve and depositors are not subject to any U.S. tax.[22] However, there are tight restrictions on what business an IBF can conduct. In particular, it cannot accept deposits from domestic U.S. corporations or make loans to them.

Money-Market Instruments

The principal money-market instruments are summarized in Table 30.5. We describe each in turn.

Government of India Treasury Bills The first item in Table 30.5 is Government of India treasury bills. These are issued by the RBI on behalf of the Government of India. The RBI auctions 91-day T-bills on a weekly basis (every Wednesdays) and 182-day and 364-day T-bills on a fortnightly basis (every alternative Wednesdays).[23] Before November 1998, all auctions were based on the multiple-price auction system (same as French auction). In case of multiple-price auctions, successful bidders pay their own bid prices. However, after November 6, 1998, auction of 91-day T-bills are conducted based on uniform-price auction (same as Dutch auction) method. Under the uniform-price auction system, all bidders pay the same price, i.e., the cut-off price. Non-competitive bids (allowed only for specific entities like State Governments and certain other statutory bodies) are filled-in at the same price as the successful competitive bids.

Bank Time Deposits and Certificates of Deposit If you make a time deposit with a bank, you are lending money to the bank for a fixed period. If you need the money before maturity, the bank usually allows you to withdraw it but exacts a penalty in the form of a reduced rate of interest.

---

[21] Occasionally (but only occasionally) referred to as "euroeuros."

[22] For these reasons dollars held on deposit in an IBF are classed as eurodollars.

[23] A small proportion of bills is sold to *noncompetitive* bidders. Noncompetitive bids are filled at the same price as the successful competitive bids.

TABLE 30.5 Money-market investments in India

Investment	Borrower	Maturities When Issued	Marketability	Basis for Calculating Interest	Comments
Treasury bills	Government of India	91-days, 182-days, or 364 days	Good secondary market	Discount	14-day and 91-day T-Bills are auctioned weekly. The 182-days and 364-days T-Bills are auctioned fortnightly.
Certificates of deposit	Banks	14 days to 1 year	Fair secondary market	Discount	The CDs are negotiable instruments
Commercial papers	Industrial firms, financial institutions apart from primary dealers and satellite dealers	15 days to 1 year	Fair secondary market	Discount	Only companies with a CRISIL rating of P2 and above or equivalent rating can issue CPs
Repurchase agreements (repos)	Banks and primary dealers, and all entities having SGL and current account with RBI	1 day (2 to 3 days if issued on Fridays or holidays)	Excellent Secondary market	Repurchase price set higher than selling price; difference quoted as repo interest rate (adjusted for coupon)	Since June 2000, RBI is conducting Repo transactions every day under the Liquidity Adjustment Scheme

In June 1989, banks in India introduced the certificates of deposit (CD) with maturity value of ₹ 1 lakh. The certificates of deposit are issued at a discount to the face value and have a maturity period ranging from 15 days to 1 year. In this case, when a bank borrows, it issues a certificate of deposit, which is simply evidence of a time deposit with that bank. The CDs are negotiable instruments. That means if a lender needs the money before maturity, it can sell the CD to another investor. When the CD matures, the new owner of the CD presents it to the bank and receives payment.[24]

Commercial Paper and Medium-Term Notes   These consist of unsecured, short- and medium-term debt issued by companies on a fairly regular basis. We discuss both in more detail later in the chapter.

Bankers' Acceptances   We saw earlier in the chapter how bankers' acceptances (BAs) may be used to finance exports or imports. An acceptance begins life as a written demand for the bank to pay a given sum at a future date. Once the bank accepts this demand, it becomes a negotiable security that can be bought or sold through money-market dealers. Acceptances by the large U.S. banks generally mature in one to six months and involve very low credit risk.

Repurchase Agreements   Repurchase agreements, or *repos,* are effectively secured loans that are typically made to a government security dealer. They work as follows: The investor buys part of the dealer's holding of Treasury securities and simultaneously arranges to sell them back again at a later date at a specified higher price.[25] The borrower (the dealer) is said to have entered into a *repo;* the lender (who buys the securities) is said to have a *reverse repo.*

---

[24] Some CDs are not negotiable and are simply identical to time deposits. For example, banks may sell low-value nonnegotiable CDs to individuals.

[25] To reduce the risk of repos, it is common to value the security at less than its market value. This difference is known as a *haircut.*

Under the Liquidity Adjustment Scheme (LAF), RBI is conducting repo and reverse-repo auctions daily (excepting on Saturdays and Sundays) since 5 June, 2000. Excepting for the intervening holidays and Fridays, the repo tenure is 1 day. On Fridays, repo auctions are held for three days maturity to cover the following Saturday and Sunday.

30-5 SOURCES OF SHORT-TERM BORROWING

We have looked at how firms can invest any excess cash. But, if your firm is in the opposite position and has a temporary cash shortage, it will probably need to take out a short-term loan. Banks are the principal supplier of these loans, but finance companies are also a major source of cash, particularly for financing receivables and inventories.[26] In addition to borrowing from an intermediary such as a bank or finance company, firms also sell short-term commercial paper or medium-term notes directly to investors. It is time to look more closely at these sources of short-term funds.

Bank Loans

Bank loans come in a variety of flavors. Here are a few of the ways that they differ.

Commitment Companies sometimes wait until they need the money before they apply for a bank loan, but nearly three-quarters of commercial loans are made under commitment. In this case, the company establishes a line of credit that allows it to borrow from the bank up to an established unit. This line of credit is usually in the form of cash credit in India, where the firms withdraw funds from the banks up to the sanctioned credit limit. Banks charge interest only on the actual balance utilized by the company. The cash credit advances are given on the security of current assets. Usually, the stocks of inventory remain with the borrowing company and a floating charge over the inventory is created in favor of the bank. This type of cash credit facility is popularly known as the **cash credit hypothecation (CCH)**.

Such credit lines give guaranteed access to the bank's money at a given interest rate. This amounts to a put option, because the firm can sell its debt to the bank on fixed terms, even if its creditworthiness deteriorates or the cost of credit rises. The growth in the use of credit lines is changing the role of banks. They are no longer simply lenders; they are also in the business of providing companies with liquidity insurance.

Maturity Many bank loans are for only a few months. For example, a company may need a short-term **bridge loan** to finance the purchase of new equipment or the acquisition of another firm. In this case the loan serves as interim financing until the purchase is completed and long-term financing arranged. Often a short-term loan is needed to finance a temporary increase in inventory. Such a loan is described as **self-liquidating;** in other words, the sale of goods provides the cash to repay the loan.

Banks also provide longer-maturity loans, known as **term loans.** A term loan typically has a maturity of four to five years. Usually the loan is repaid in level amounts over this period, though there is sometimes a large final *balloon* payment or just a single *bullet* payment at maturity. Banks can accommodate the repayment pattern to the anticipated cash flows of the borrower. For example, the first repayment might be delayed a year until the new factory is completed. Term loans are often

[26] *Finance companies* are firms that specialize in lending to businesses or individuals. They include independent firms.

Finance In Practice

Libor

Each day at around 11 a.m. in London, some 16 major banks provide estimates of the interest rate at which they could borrow funds from another bank in reasonable market size. They produce these estimates for 15 maturities that range from overnight to one year. In each case the top and bottom quarter of the estimates are dropped, and the remainder are averaged to provide the set of London Interbank Offered Rates or LIBOR.

The most commonly quoted LIBOR rates are for borrowing U.S. dollars, but similar sets of LIBOR rates are also produced for nine other currencies—the euro; the Japanese yen; the pound sterling; the Swiss franc; the Danish kroner; the Swedish krona; and the Canadian, Australian, and New Zealand dollars. The British Bankers' Association, which publishes these rates, estimates that the payments on about $10 trillion of loans and $300 trillion of swaps are tied to LIBOR.[27]

Figure 30.7 plots the three-month dollar LIBOR rate against the rate on Treasury bills. The spread between the two rates is known as the TED spread. For many years the TED spread was typically less than 50 basis points (.5%), but in 2008 it widened dramatically, at one point reaching 460 basis points (4.6%). Suddenly the choice of benchmark for bank loans began to be very important.

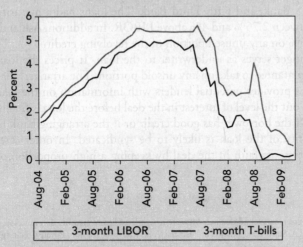

FIGURE 30.7

Month-end values for three-month dollar LIBOR and three-month Treasury bills, August 2004 to July 2009.

Source: British Bankers' Association and the Federal Reserve Board.

---

[27] In the case of euro deposits, the European Banking Federation calculates an alternative measure, known as Euribor. You can find historical LIBOR rates on www.bbalibor.com and Euribor rates on www.euribor.org.

renegotiated before maturity. Banks are willing to do this if the borrower is an established customer, remains creditworthy, and has a sound business reason for making the change.[28]

Rate of Interest   Most short-term bank loans are made at a fixed rate of interest, which is often quoted as a discount in the U.S. For example, if the interest rate on a one-year loan is stated as a discount of 5%, the borrower receives $100 - $5 = $95 and undertakes to pay $100 at the end of the year. The return on such a loan is not 5%, but $5/95 = .0526$, or 5.26%.

In July 2010, banks in India shifted to the Base Rate system from the earlier Benchmark Prime Lending Rate system. Banks now decide their actual lending rates on loans with reference to this Base Rate. The State Bank of India, for example, used 10% as its Base Rate in early 2012. Punjab National Bank, on the other hand, was using 10.75% as the Base Rate. The Base Rate is the minimum rate at which the banks can lend to their customers.

It is standard practice in the U.S. to link the interest rate to LIBOR.[29] Thus, if the rate is set at "1 percent above LIBOR," the borrower may pay 5 percent for the first three months when LIBOR is 4 percent, 6 percent in the next three months when LIBOR is 5 percent, and so on.[30]

Syndicated Loans   Some bank loans and credit lines are too large for a single lender. In these cases the borrower may pay an arrangement fee to one or more lead banks, which then parcels out the loan or credit line among a syndicate of banks.[31] For example, in 2008 the chemical company Ashland needed to borrow $1.65 billion to finance its purchase of Hercules. It did so by means of a package of term loans and a revolving credit facility. The package was arranged by BankAmerica and the Bank of Nova Scotia, and other members of the syndicate reportedly included Citibank, SunTrust Banks, Wells Fargo Bank, US Bank, and Fifth Third Bank. The loans had a maturity of around five years and were priced at between 2.75% and 4% above LIBOR. In addition, Ashland was required to pay a commitment fee of .5% on any unused portion of the revolving credit.

The syndicate arranger serves as underwriter to the loan. It prices the loan, markets it to other banks, and may also guarantee to take on any unsold portion. The arranger's first step is to prepare an *information memo* that provides potential lenders with information on the loan. The syndicate desk will then try to sound out the level of interest in the deal before the loan is finally priced and marketed to interested buyers. If the borrower has good credit or if the arranging bank has a particularly good reputation, the majority of the loan is likely to be syndicated. In other cases the arranging bank may need to demonstrate its faith in the deal by keeping a high proportion of the loan on its own books.[32]

---

[28] One study of private debt agreements found that over 90% are renegotiated before maturity. In most cases this is not because of financial distress. See M. R. Roberts and A. Sufi, "Renegotiation of Financial Contracts: Evidence from Private Credit Agreements," *Journal of Financial Economics*, forthcoming.

[29] Three-month bills actually mature 91 days after issue, six-month bills mature in 182 days, and one-year bills mature in 364 days. For information on bill auctions, see www.publicdebt.treas.gov.

[30] Exceptions are the Government National Mortgage Association (Ginnie Mae), the Small Business Administration, the General Services Administration (GSA), the Financial Assistance Corporation, the Agency for International Development, and the Private Export Funding Corporation. Their debts are backed by the "full faith and credit" of the U.S. government.

[31] For a standard loan to a blue-chip company the fee for arranging a syndicated loan may be as low as 10 basis points, while a complex deal with a highly leveraged firm may carry a fee of up to 250 basis points. For good reviews of the syndicated loan market see S. C. Miller, "A Guide to the Syndicated Loan Market," Standard & Poor's, September 2005 (www.standardandpoors.com); and B. Gadanecz, "The Syndicated Loan Market: Structure, Development and Implications," *BIS Quarterly Review*, December 2004, pp. 75–89 (www.bis.org).

[32] See A. Sufi, "Information Asymmetry and Financing Arrangements: Evidence from Syndicated Loans," *Journal of Finance* 62 (April 2007), pp. 629–668.

Loan Sales and Collateralized Debt Obligations   Bank loans used to be illiquid; once the bank had made a loan, it was stuck with it. This is no longer the case, so that banks with an excess demand for loans may solve the problem by selling a portion of their existing loans to other institutions. For example, about 20% of syndicated loans are subsequently resold, and these sales are reported weekly in *The Wall Street Journal.*

Loan sales generally take one of two forms: *assignments* or *participations*. In the former case a portion of the loan is transferred with the agreement of the borrower. In the second case the lead bank maintains its relationship with the borrower but agrees to pay over to the buyer a portion of the cash flows that it receives.

Loan sales often involve a single loan, but sometimes they can be huge deals involving a portfolio of several hundred loans. The buyer is then entitled to a share of the cash flows on this portfolio. In the early years of the century many banks repackaged the cash flows from a portfolio of loans and sold off separate slices (or *tranches*) known as *collateralized debt obligations* (or *CDOs*).[33] The senior tranches had first claim on the cash flows and therefore proved attractive to conservative investors such as insurance companies or pension funds. The riskiest (or *equity*) tranche was retained by the bank or bought by hedge funds or mutual funds that specialized in low-quality debt.[34]

By 2007 over half of the new issues of CDOs involved exposure to subprime mortgages. Because the mortgages were packaged together, investors in these CDOs were protected against the risk of default on an individual mortgage. However, even the senior tranches were exposed to the risk of an economy-wide slump in the housing market. For this reason the debt has been termed "economic catastrophe debt."[35]

Economic catastrophe struck in the summer of 2007, when the investment bank, Bear Stearns, revealed that two of its hedge funds had invested heavily in nearly worthless CDOs. Bear Stearns was rescued with help from the Federal Reserve, but it signalled the start of the credit crunch and the collapse of the CDO market. In 2008 issues of CDOs fell by nearly 90%.[36]

Security   If a bank is concerned about a firm's credit risk, it will ask the firm to provide security for the loan. This is most common for longer-term bank loans, over half of which are secured.[37] The collateral usually consists of liquid assets such as receivables, inventories, or securities. Sometimes the bank will take a *floating charge*. This gives it a general claim if the firm defaults. However, it does not specify the assets in detail, and it sets few restrictions on what the company can do with the assets.

More commonly, banks require specific collateral. For example, suppose that there is a significant delay between the time that you ship your goods and when your customers pay you. If you need the money up front, you can borrow by using these receivables as collateral. First, you must send the bank a copy of each invoice and provide it with a claim against the money that you receive from your customers. The bank will then lend up to 80% of the value of the receivables.

---

[33] CDOs comprise collateralized loan obligations (CLOs), together with collateralized bond obligations (CBOs) and collateralized mortgage obligations (CMOs).

[34] Rather than backing the CLO with a package of risky loans, banks often created *synthetic CLOs.* In this case the bank kept the loans on its books. The cash flows on the CLO came from the purchase of high-grade bonds and the sale of a default swap on a package of the bank's loans. (We described default swaps in Chapter 23.) If none of the bank loans defaults, the CLO receives a series of fixed cash flows. If there is a default, the seller of the default swap must compensate the buyer for the amount of the loss. This loss would be borne first by the equity tranche of the CLO.

[35] J. D. Coval, J. Jurek, and E. Stafford, "Economic Catastrophe Bonds," *American Economic Review* 3 (June 2009), pp. 628–666.

[36] www.sifma.org.

[37] The results of a survey of the terms of business lending by banks in the United States are published quarterly in the *Federal Reserve Bulletin* (see www.federalreserve.gov/releases/E2).

Each day, as you make more sales, your collateral increases and you can borrow more money. Each day also some customers pay their bills. This money is placed in a special collateral account under the bank's control and is periodically used to reduce the size of the loan. Therefore, as the firm's business fluctuates, so does the amount of the collateral and the size of the loan.

You can also use inventories as security for a loan. For example, if your goods are stored in a warehouse, you need to arrange for an independent warehouse company to provide the bank with a receipt showing that the goods are held on the bank's behalf. The bank will generally be prepared to lend up to 50% of the value of the inventories. When the loan is repaid, the bank returns the warehouse receipt and you are free to remove the goods.[38]

Banks are naturally choosey about the security that they will accept. They want to make sure that they can identify and sell the collateral if you default. They may be happy to lend against a warehouse full of a standard nonperishable commodity, but they would turn up their nose at a warehouse of ripe Camemberts.

Banks also need to ensure that the collateral is safe and the borrower doesn't sell the assets and run off with the money. This is what happened in the great salad oil swindle. Fifty-one banks and companies made loans of nearly $200 million to the Allied Crude Vegetable Oil Refining Corporation. In return the company agreed to provide security in the form of storage tanks full of valuable salad oil. Unfortunately, cursory inspections failed to notice that the tanks contained seawater and sludge. When the fraud was discovered, the president of Allied went to jail and the 51 lenders were left out in the cold, looking for their $200 million.

Commercial Paper

Banks borrow money from one group of firms or individuals and relend the money to another group. They make their profit by charging the borrowers a higher rate of interest than they offer the lender.

Sometimes it is convenient to have a bank in the middle. It saves the lenders the trouble of looking for borrowers and assessing their creditworthiness, and it saves the borrowers the trouble of looking for lenders. Depositors do not care to whom the bank lends: they need only satisfy themselves that the bank as a whole is safe.

There are also occasions on which it is *not* worth paying an intermediary to perform these functions. Large well-known companies can bypass the banking system by issuing their own short-term unsecured notes. These notes are known as **commercial paper (CP).** Financial institutions, such as bank holding companies and finance companies,[39] also issue commercial paper, sometimes in very large quantities. For example, at one point GE Capital Corporation had over $100 billion of commercial paper in issue.[40] The major issuers of commercial paper have set up their own marketing departments and sell their paper directly to investors, often using the Web to do so. Smaller companies sell through dealers who receive a fee for marketing the issue.

Commercial paper in the United States has a maximum maturity of nine months, though most paper is for 60 days or less. Buyers of commercial paper generally hold it to maturity, but the company or dealer that sells the paper is usually prepared to repurchase it earlier.

---

[38] It is not always practicable to keep inventory in a warehouse. For example, automobile dealers need to display their cars in a showroom. One solution is to enter into a floor-planning arrangement in which the finance company buys the cars and the dealer holds them in trust. When the cars are sold, the proceeds are used to redeem the cars from the finance company. The interest or "flooring charge," depends on how long the cars have been in the showroom.

[39] A *bank holding company* is a firm that owns both a bank and nonbanking subsidiaries.

[40] GE reduced its reliance on commercial paper in 2008.

The majority of commercial paper is issued by high-grade, nationally known companies.[41] Issuers generally support their commercial paper by arranging a backup line of credit with a bank, which guarantees that they can find the money to repay the paper.[42] The risk of default is, therefore, small.

Because investors are reluctant to buy commercial paper that does not have the highest credit rating, companies cannot rely on the commercial paper market to provide them always with the short-term capital that they need. For example, when the rating services downgraded the commercial paper of Ford and General Motors, both companies were forced to reduce sharply their sales of paper. Ford Credit had $45 billion of unsecured commercial paper outstanding at the end of 2000; five years later it had cut the amount to $1.0 billion.

Recent years have not been kind to the commercial paper market. In addition to Ford and GM, a number of other major companies have had their commercial paper downgraded. An even bigger shock occurred in 2007, when Lehman Brothers defaulted on its commercial paper. This led to a sharp fall in the volume of issues until the Fed announced plans to buy large volumes of high-grade paper.

In addition to unsecured commercial paper, there is also a market for *asset-backed commercial paper*. In this case the company sells its assets to a special-purpose vehicle that then issues the paper. For example, as the auto companies reduced their sales of unsecured commercial paper, they increasingly relied on asset-backed paper secured by the firm's receivables. As the customers paid their bills, the cash was passed through to the holders of this paper.

Weaknesses in this market surfaced when a number of banks set up structured investment vehicles (SIVs) that invested in mortgage-backed securities financed by asset-backed paper. Because the buyers of the commercial paper bore the credit risk, the banks had less incentive to worry about the quality of the underlying mortgages. Many of the SIVs found it impossible to refinance the maturing paper and went into default.

The Reserve Bank of India introduced commercial papers in India following the recommendations of the Vagul working group in 1989. Highly rated companies (with a CRISIL rating of P2 and above or an equivalent rating from other rating agencies) can issue commercial papers in India. Initial issue of commercial papers is done primarily to the banks because of the differences in the stamp duties. The stamp duty on the primary issue of commercial papers is 0.25 percent for all investors, while it is only 0.05 percent for the banks. However, since the secondary market transactions do not attract stamp duties, other investors find it attractive to buy commercial papers in the secondary market. The secondary market transactions are usually done over the counter. The maturities of the commercial papers range between 15 days and 1 year.

Medium-Term Notes

New issues of securities do not need to be registered with the SEC as long as they mature within 270 days. So by limiting the maturity of commercial paper issues, companies can avoid the delays and expense of registration. However, large blue-chip companies also make regular issues of unsecured **medium-term notes (MTNs).**

---

[41] Moody's, Standard and Poor's, and Fitch publish quality ratings for commercial paper. For example, Moody's provides three ratings, from P-1 (that is, Prime 1, the highest-grade paper) to P-3. Most investors are reluctant to buy low-rated paper. For example, money-market funds are largely limited to holding P-1 paper.

[42] For top-tier issuers the credit line is generally 75% of the amount of paper; for lower-grade issuers it is 100%. The company may not be able to draw on this line of credit if it does not satisfy bank covenants. Therefore, lower-rated companies may need to back their paper with an irrevocable line of credit.

You can think of MTNs as a hybrid between corporate bonds and commercial paper. Like bonds they are relatively long-term instruments; their maturity is never less than 270 days, though it is typically less than 10 years.[43] On the other hand, like commercial paper, MTNs are not underwritten but are sold on a regular basis either through dealers or, occasionally, directly to investors. Dealers support a secondary market in these MTNs and are prepared to buy the notes back before maturity.

Borrowers such as finance companies, which always need cash, welcome the flexibility of MTNs. For example, a company may tell its dealers the amount of money that it needs to raise that week, the range of maturities that it can offer, and the maximum interest that it is prepared to pay. It is then up to the dealers to find the buyers. Investors may also suggest their own terms to one of the dealers, and, if these terms are acceptable, the deal is done.

SUMMARY

Companies invest in four principal short-term assets—inventories, accounts receivable, cash, and short-term securities. Each of these investments needs to be managed.

Inventories consist of raw materials, work in process, and finished goods. Inventories have benefits. For example, a stock of raw materials reduces the risk that the firm will be forced to shut down production because of an unexpected shortage. But inventories also tie up capital and are expensive to store. The task of the production manager is to strike a sensible balance between these benefits and costs. In recent years many companies have decided that they can get by on lower inventories than before. For example, some have adopted *just-in-time* systems that allow the firm to keep inventories to a minimum by receiving a regular flow of components and raw materials throughout the day.

Credit management (the management of receivables) involves five steps:

1. Establish the length of the payment period and the size of any cash discounts for customers who pay promptly.
2. Decide the form of the contract with your customer. For example, if your customer's credit is somewhat shaky, you can ask the customer to arrange for a banker's acceptance. In this case payment is guaranteed by the customer's bank.
3. Assess your customer's creditworthiness. You can either do your own homework or rely on a credit agency or credit bureau that specializes in gathering information about the credit standing of firms or individuals.
4. Establish sensible credit limits. Remember your aim is not to minimize the number of bad debts, it is to maximize profits. Remember also not to be too shortsighted in reckoning the expected profit. It may be worth accepting marginal applicants if there is a chance that they may become regular and reliable customers.
5. Collect. You need to be resolute with the truly delinquent customers, but you do not want to offend the good ones by writing demanding letters just because their check has been delayed in the mail.

You can think of cash as just another raw material that the firm needs to do business. There are always advantages to holding large "inventories" of cash. They reduce the risk of a sudden shortage and having to raise more at short notice. On the other hand, there is a cost to holding idle cash balances rather than putting the money to work in marketable securities. In balancing these benefits and costs the cash manager faces a task similar to that of the production manager. This trade-off is more important for small firms, for whom the costs of continually buying and selling securities are relatively large compared with the opportunity cost of holding idle cash balances.

---

[43] Occasionally, an MTN registration may be used to issue much longer term bonds. For example, Disney has even used its MTN program to issue a 100-year bond.

Good cash management involves moving cash around efficiently. For example, if the firm receives a large number of small checks, it needs to ensure that they are not left lying about. We described how concentration banking and lockbox systems are used to speed up collections. Most large payments are made electronically by wire transfer. This allows companies to economize on the use of cash by transferring funds rapidly from local bank accounts to the firm's main *concentration* bank. Electronic funds transfer also speeds up payments and makes it possible to automate more of the cash management process.

If you have more cash than is currently needed, you can invest it in the money market. There is a wide choice of money-market investments, with different degrees of liquidity and risk. Remember that the interest rate on these investments is often quoted as a discount. The compound return is always higher than the rate of discount. The principal money-market investments in India are

- Government of India Treasury bills
- Certificates of Deposit
- Commercial paper
- Repurchase agreements

When long-term finance does not cover the capital requirement, firms must raise short- or medium-term capital. Often they arrange a *revolving line of credit* with a bank that allows them to borrow up to an agreed amount whenever they need financing. This is often intended to tide the firm over a temporary shortage of cash and is therefore repaid in only a few months. However, banks also make *term loans* that sometimes extend for five years or more.

The interest rate on very short-term bank loans is generally fixed for the life of the loan, but in other cases the rate floats with the general level of short-term interest rates. For example, it might be set at 1% over MIBOR (the London Interbank Offered Rate).

The interest rate that the bank charges must be sufficient to cover not only the opportunity cost of capital for the loan but also the costs of running the loan department. Large regular borrowers have found it cheaper to bypass the banking system and issue their own short-term unsecured debt. This is called *commercial paper.* Longer-term loans that are marketed on a regular basis are known as *medium-term notes.*

Generally, markets for short-term capital work smoothly, but in the credit crunch of 2008 many of these sources of funds dried up. It remains to be seen whether in each case this was a temporary hiccup or whether the events that year revealed a fatal weakness in security design.

FURTHER READING

Here are some general textbooks on working capital management:

G. W. Gallinger and B. P. Healey, *Liquidity Analysis and Management,* 2nd ed. (Reading, MA: Addison-Wesley, 1991).

N. C. Hill and W. L. Sartoris, *Short-Term Financial Management: Text and Cases,* 3rd ed. (Englewood Cliffs, NJ: Prentice-Hall, Inc., 1994).

K. V. Smith and G. W. Gallinger, *Readings on Short-Term Financial Management,* 3rd. ed. (New York: West, 1988).

F. C. Scherr, *Modern Working Capital Management: Text and Cases* (Englewood Cliffs, NJ: Prentice-Hall, Inc., 1989).

A standard text on the practice and institutional background of credit management is:

R. H. Cole and L. Mishler, *Consumer and Business Credit Management,* 11th ed. (New York: McGraw-Hill, 1998).

For a more analytical discussion of credit policy, see:

S. Mian and C. W. Smith, "Extending Trade Credit and Financing," *Journal of Applied Corporate Finance* 7 (Spring 1994), pp. 75–84.

M. A. Petersen and R. G. Rajan, "Trade Credit: Theories and Evidence," *Review of Financial Studies* 10 (Fall 1997), pp. 661–692.

Two useful books on cash management are:

M. Allman-Ward and J. Sagner, *Essentials of Managing Corporate Cash* (New York: Wiley, 2003).

R. Bort, *Corporate Cash Management Handbook* (New York: Warren Gorham and Lamont, 2004).

Two readable discussions of why some companies maintain more liquidity than others are:

A. Dittmar, "Corporate Cash Policy and How to Manage It with Stock Repurchases," *Journal of Applied Corporate Finance* 20 (Summer 2008), pp. 22–34.

L. Pinkowitz and R. Williamson, "What Is the Market Value of a Dollar of Corporate Cash?" *Journal of Applied Corporate Finance* 19 (Summer 2007), pp. 74–81.

For descriptions of the money-market and short-term borrowing and lending opportunities, see:

F. J. Fabozzi, *The Handbook of Fixed Income Securities,* 6th ed. (New York: McGraw-Hill, 2000).

F. J. Fabozzi, S. V. Mann, and M. Choudhry, *The Global Money Markets* (New York: John Wiley, 2002).

Chapter 4 of *U.S. Monetary Policy and Financial Markets,* available on the New York Federal Reserve Web site, www.ny.frb.org.

PROBLEM SETS

BASIC

1. What are the trade-offs involved in the decision of how much inventory the firm should carry? In what way does the cash manager face a similar trade-off?
2. Company X sells on a 1/30, net 60 basis. Customer Y buys goods invoiced at ₹1,000.
   a. How much can Y deduct from the bill if Y pays on day 30?
   b. What is the effective annual rate of interest if Y pays on the due date rather than on day 30?
   c. How would you expect payment terms to change if
   i. The goods are perishable.
   ii. The goods are not rapidly resold.
   iii. The goods are sold to high-risk firms.
3. The lag between the purchase date and the date on which payment is due is known as the *terms lag.* The lag between the due date and the date on which the buyer actually pays is the *due lag,* and the lag between the purchase and actual payment dates is the *pay lag.* Thus,

$$\text{Pay lag} = \text{terms lag} + \text{due lag}$$

State how you would expect the following events to affect each type of lag:
   a. The company imposes a service charge on late payers.
   b. A recession causes customers to be short of cash.
   c. The company changes its terms from net 10 to net 20.
4. The Branding Iron Company sells its irons for ₹2,500 apiece wholesale. Production cost is ₹2,000 per iron. There is a 25% chance that wholesaler Q will go bankrupt within the next year. Q orders 1,000 irons and asks for six months' credit. Should you accept the order? Assume that the discount rate is 10% per year, there is no chance of a repeat order, and Q will pay either in full or not at all.

5. Look back at Section 30-2. Cast Iron's costs have increased from ₹1,000 to ₹1,050. Assuming there is no possibility of repeat orders, answer the following:
   a. When should Cast Iron grant or refuse credit?
   b. If it costs ₹12 to determine whether a customer has been a prompt or slow payer in the past, when should Cast Iron undertake such a check?

6. Look back at the discussion in Section 30-2 of credit decisions with repeat orders. If $p_1 = .8$, what is the minimum level of p_2 at which Cast Iron is justified in extending credit?

7. True or False?
   a. Exporters who require greater certainty of payment arrange for the customers to sign a bill of lading in exchange for a sight draft.
   b. It makes sense to monitor the credit manager's performance by looking at the proportion of bad debts.
   c. If a customer refuses to pay despite repeated reminders, the company usually turns the debt over to a factor or an attorney.

8. How should your willingness to grant credit be affected by differences in (a) the profit margin, (b) the interest rate, (c) the probability of repeat orders? In each case illustrate your answer with a simple example.

9. How would you expect a firm's cash balance to respond to the following changes?
   a. Interest rates increase.
   b. The volatility of daily cash flow decreases.
   c. The transaction cost of buying or selling marketable securities goes up.

10. Suppose that you can hold cash that pays no interest or invest in securities that pay interest at 8%. The securities are not easily sold on short notice; therefore, you must make up any cash deficiency by drawing on a bank line of credit that charges interest at 10%. Should you invest more or less in securities under each of the following circumstances?
    a. You are unusually uncertain about future cash flows.
    b. The interest rate on bank loans rises to 11%.
    c. The interest rates on securities and on bank loans both rise by the same proportion.
    d. You revise downward your forecast of future cash needs.

11. In January 2012, 91-day T-bills were issued at a discount of 8.3%. What is the annual yield?

12. For each item below, choose the investment that best fits the accompanying description:
    a. Maturity often overnight (repurchase agreements/bankers' acceptances).
    b. Maturity never more than 1 year (debentures/commercial paper).
    c. Issued by RBI on behalf of Government of India (Municipal bonds/Treasury bills).
    d. Sold by auction (Treasury bills/Certificates of deposit).
    e. Quoted on a discount basis (certificates of deposit/Treasury bills).

13. Consider three securities:
    a. A floating-rate bond.
    b. A preferred share paying a fixed dividend.
    c. A floating-rate preferred.
    If you were responsible for short-term investment of your firm's excess cash, which security would you probably prefer to hold? Why? Explain briefly.

14. True or false?
    a. Most commercial bank loans are made under commitment.
    b. A line of credit provides the lender with a put option.
    c. Bank term loans typically have a maturity of several years.
    d. If the interest rate on a one-year bank loan is stated as a discount of 10%, the actual yield on the loan is less than 10%.

e. The interest rate on term loans is usually linked to MIBOR, the federal funds rate, or the bank's prime rate.

15. Complete the passage below by selecting the most appropriate terms from the following list: *floating charge, syndicated, commercial paper, warehouse receipt, arranger, collateral, commitment fee, line of credit, medium-term notes, collateralized loan obligations (CLOs).*

   Companies with fluctuating capital needs often arrange a _____ with their bank. This is relatively expensive because companies need to pay a _____ on any unused amount.

   Secured short-term loans are sometimes covered by a _____ on all receivables and inventory. Generally, however, the borrower pledges specific assets as _____. For example, if goods are stored in a warehouse, an independent warehouse company may issue a _____ to the lender. The goods can then only be released with the lender's consent.

   Very large bank loans are often _____. In this case the lead bank acts as the _____ and will parcel out the loan among a group of banks.

   Banks also often sell loans. Sometimes they put together a portfolio of loans and sell separate slices (or tranches). These are known as _____.

   Banks are not the only source of short-term debt. Many large companies issue their own unsecured debt directly to investors, often on a regular basis. If the maturity is less than nine months, this debt is generally known as _____. Companies also make regular issues of longer-term debt to investors. These are called _____.

INTERMEDIATE

16. Listed below are some common terms of sale. Can you explain what each means?
   a. 2/30, net 60.
   b. 2/5, EOM, net 30.
   c. COD.

17. Some of the items in Problem 17 involve a cash discount. For each of these, calculate the rate of interest paid by customers who pay on the due date instead of taking the cash discount.

18. Phoenix Lambert currently sells its goods cash-on-delivery. However, the financial manager believes that by offering credit terms of 2/10 net 30 the company can increase sales by 4%, without significant additional costs. If the interest rate is 6% and the profit margin is 5%, would you recommend offering credit? Assume first that all customers take the cash discount. Then assume that they all pay on day 30.

19. As treasurer of the Universal Bed Corporation, Aristotle Procrustes is worried about his bad debt ratio, which is currently running at 6%. He believes that imposing a more stringent credit policy might reduce sales by 5% and reduce the bad debt ratio to 4%. If the cost of goods sold is 80% of the selling price, should Mr. Procrustes adopt the more stringent policy?

20. Jim Khana, the credit manager of Velcro Saddles, is reappraising the company's credit policy. Velcro sells on terms of net 30. Cost of goods sold is 85% of sales, and fixed costs are a further 5% of sales. Velcro classifies customers on a scale of 1 to 4. During the past five years, the collection experience was as follows:

Classification	Defaults as Percent of Sales	Average Collection Period in Days for Nondefaulting Accounts
1	.0	45
2	2.0	42
3	10.0	40
4	20.0	80

The average interest rate was 15%.

What conclusions (if any) can you draw about Velcro's credit policy? What other factors should be taken into account before changing this policy?

21. Look again at Problem 21. Suppose (a) that it costs $95 to classify each new credit applicant and (b) that an almost equal proportion of new applicants falls into each of the four categories. In what circumstances should Mr. Khana not bother to undertake a credit check?

22. Until recently, Augean Cleaning Products sold its products on terms of net 60, with an average collection period of 75 days. In an attempt to induce customers to pay more promptly, it has changed its terms to 2/10, EOM, net 60. The initial effect of the changed terms is as follows:

| | Average Collection Periods, Days | |
Percent of Sales with Cash Discount	Cash Discount	Net
60	30*	80

* Some customers deduct the cash discount even though they pay after the specified date.

Calculate the effect of the changed terms. Assume
- Sales volume is unchanged.
- The interest rate is 12%.
- There are no defaults.
- Cost of goods sold is 80% of sales.

23. Look back at Problem 23. Assume that the change in credit terms results in a 2% increase in sales. Recalculate the effect of the changed credit terms.

24. Knob, Inc., is a nationwide distributor of furniture hardware. The company now uses a central billing system for credit sales of ₹180 million annually. First National, Knob's principal bank, offers to establish a new concentration banking system for a flat fee of ₹100,000 per year. The bank estimates that mailing and collection time can be reduced by three days. By how much will Knob's cash balances be increased under the new system? How much extra interest income will the new system generate if the extra funds are used to reduce borrowing under Knob's line of credit with First National? Assume that the borrowing rate is 12%. Finally, should Knob accept First National's offer if collection costs under the old system are ₹40,000 per year?

25. Anne Teak, the financial manager of a furniture manufacturer, is considering operating a lockbox system. She forecasts that 300 payments a day will be made to lockboxes, with an average payment size of ₹1,500. The bank's charge for operating the lockboxes is *either* ₹.40 a check *or* compensating balances of ₹800,000.
   a. If the interest rate is 9%, which method of payment is cheaper?
   b. What reduction in the time to collect and process each check is needed to justify use of the lockbox system?

26. A parent company settles the collection account balances of its subsidiaries once a week. (That is, each week it transfers any balances in the accounts to a central account.) The cost of a wire transfer is $10. A check costs $.80. Cash transferred by wire is available the same day, but the parent must wait three days for checks to clear. Cash can be invested at 12% per year. How much money must be in a collection account before it pays to use a wire transfer?

27. A three-month Treasury bill and a six-month bill both sell at a discount of 10%. Which offers the higher annual yield?

28. In Section 30-4 we described a three-month bill that was issued on an annually compounded yield of 5.18%. Suppose that one month has passed and the investment still offers the same annually compounded return. What is the percentage discount? What was your return over the month?

29. Look again at Problem 30. Suppose another month has passed, so the bill has only one month left to run. It is now selling at a discount of 3%. What is the yield? What was your realized return over the two months?

30. Look up current interest rates offered by short-term investment alternatives. Suppose that your firm has ₹1 million excess cash to invest for the next two months. How would you invest this cash? How would your answer change if the excess cash were ₹5,000, ₹20,000, ₹100,000, or ₹100 million?

31. In 2006 agency corporates in theU.S. sold at a yield of 5.32%, while high-grade tax-exempts of comparable maturity offered 3.7% annually. If an investor receives the same *after-tax* return from corporates and tax-exempts, what is that investor's marginal rate of tax? What other factors might affect an investor's choice between the two types of securities?

32. The IRS in the U.S. prohibits companies from borrowing money to buy tax-exempts and deducting the interest payments on the borrowing from taxable income. Should the IRS prohibit such activity? If it didn't, would you advise the company to borrow to buy tax-exempts?

33. Suppose you are a wealthy individual paying 35% tax on income. What is the expected after-tax yield on each of the following investments?
    a. A municipal note yielding 7.0% pretax.
    b. A Treasury bill yielding 10% pretax.
    c. A floating-rate preferred stock yielding 7.5% pretax.
    How would your answer change if the investor is a corporation paying tax at 35%? What other factors would you need to take into account when deciding where to invest the corporation's spare cash?

34. You need to borrow ₹10 crore for 90 days. You have the following alternatives:
    a. Issue high-grade commercial paper, with a backup line of credit costing .3% a year.
    b. Borrow from First Cookham Bank at an interest rate of .25% over MIBOR.
    c. Borrow from the Test Bank at prime.
    Given the rates currently prevailing in the market (see, for example, *The Business Line*), which alternative would you choose?

35. Suppose that you are a banker responsible for approving corporate loans. Nine firms are seeking secured loans. They offer the following assets as collateral:
    a. Firm A, a heating oil distributor, offers a tanker load of fuel in transit from the Middle East.
    b. Firm B, a wine wholesaler, offers 1,000 cases of Beaujolais Nouveau, located in a warehouse.
    c. Firm C, a stationer, offers an account receivable for office supplies sold to the City of New York.
    d. Firm D, a bookstore, offers its entire inventory of 15,000 used books.
    e. Firm E, a wholesale grocer, offers a boxcar full of bananas.
    f. Firm F, an appliance dealer, offers its inventory of electric typewriters.
    g. Firm G, a jeweler, offers 100 ounces of gold.
    h. Firm H, a government securities dealer, offers its portfolio of Treasury bills.
    i. Firm I, a boat builder, offers a half-completed luxury yacht. The yacht will take four months more to complete.
    Which of these assets are most likely to be good collateral? Which are likely to be bad collateral? Explain.

CHALLENGE

36. Reliant Umbrellas has been approached by Plumpton Variety Stores of Nevada. Plumpton has expressed interest in an initial purchase of 5,000 umbrellas at $10 each on Reliant's standard terms of 2/30, net 60. Plumpton estimates that if the umbrellas prove popular with customers, its purchases could be in the region of 30,000 umbrellas a year. After deductions for variable cos ;, this account would add $47,000 per year to Reliant's profits.

Reliant has been anxious for some time to break into the lucrative Nevada market, but its credit manager has some doubts about Plumpton. In the past five years, Plumpton had embarked on an aggressive program of store openings. In 2007, however, it went into reverse. The recession, combined with aggressive price competition, caused a cash shortage. Plumpton laid off employees, closed one store, and deferred store openings. The company's Dun and Bradstreet rating is only fair, and a check with Plumpton's other suppliers reveals that, although Plumpton traditionally took cash discounts, it has recently been paying 30 days slow. A check through Reliant's bank indicates that Plumpton has unused credit lines of $350,000 but has entered into discussions with the banks for a renewal of a $1,500,000 term loan due at the end of the year. Table 30.5 summarizes Plumpton's latest financial statements.

TABLE 30.5 Plumpton Variety Stores: summary financial statements (figures in millions).

	2010	2009		2010	2009
Cash	$ 1.0	$ 1.2	Payables	$ 2.3	$ 2.5
Receivables	1.5	1.6	Short-term loans	3.9	1.9
Inventory	10.9	11.6	Long-term debt	1.8	2.6
Fixed assets	5.1	4.3	Equity	10.5	11.7
Total assets	$18.5	$18.7	Total liabilities	$18.5	$18.7

	2010	2009
Sales	$55.0	$59.0
Cost of goods sold	32.6	35.9
Selling, general, and administrative expenses	20.8	20.2
Interest	.5	.3
Tax	.5	1.3
Net income	$ .6	$ 1.3

As credit manager of Reliant, how do you feel about extending credit to Plumpton?

37. Galenic, Inc., is a wholesaler for a range of pharmaceutical products. Before deducting any losses from bad debts, Galenic operates on a profit margin of 5%. For a long time the firm has employed a numerical credit scoring system based on a small number of key ratios. This has resulted in a bad debt ratio of 1%.

Galenic has recently commissioned a detailed statistical study of the payment record of its customers over the past eight years and, after considerable experimentation, has identified five variables that could form the basis of a new credit scoring system. On the evidence of the past eight years, Galenic calculates that for every 10,000 accounts it would have experienced the following default rates:

	Number of Accounts		
Credit Score under Proposed System	Defaulting	Paying	Total
Greater than 80	60	9,100	9,160
Less than 80	40	800	840
Total	100	9,900	10,000

By refusing credit to firms with a low credit score (less than 80), Galenic calculates that it would reduce its bad debt ratio to 60/9,160, or just under .7%. While this may not seem like a big deal, Galenic's credit manager reasons that this is equivalent to a decrease of one-third in the bad debt ratio and would result in a significant improvement in the profit margin.

a. What is Galenic's current profit margin, allowing for bad debts?

b. Assuming that the firm's estimates of default rates are right, how would the new credit scoring system affect profits?

c. Why might you suspect that Galenic's estimates of default rates will not be realized in practice? What are the likely consequences of overestimating the accuracy of such a credit scoring scheme?

d. Suppose that one of the variables in the proposed scoring system is whether the customer has an existing account with Galenic (new customers are more likely to default). How would this affect your assessment of the proposal?

38. Axle Chemical Corporation's treasurer has forecasted a $1 million cash deficit for the next quarter. However, there is only a 50% chance this deficit will actually occur. The treasurer estimates that there is a 20% probability the company will have no deficit at all and a 30% probability that it will actually need $2 million in short-term financing. The company can either take out a 90-day unsecured loan for $2 million at 1% per month or establish a line of credit, costing 1% per month on the amount borrowed plus a commitment fee of $20,000. If excess cash can be reinvested at 9%, which source of financing gives the lower expected cost?

39. Term loans usually require firms to pay a fluctuating interest rate. For example, the interest rate may be set at "1% above prime." The prime rate sometimes varies by several percentage points within a single year. Suppose that your firm has decided to borrow $40 million for five years. It has three alternatives. It can (a) borrow from a bank at the prime rate, currently 10%. The proposed loan agreement requires no principal repayments until the loan matures in five years. It can (b) issue 26-week commercial paper, currently yielding 9%. Since funds are required for five years, the commercial paper will have to be rolled over semiannually. That is, financing the $40 million requirement for five years will require 10 successive commercial paper sales. Or, finally, it can (c) borrow from an insurance company at a fixed rate of 11%. As in the bank loan, no principal has to be repaid until the end of the five-year period. What factors would you consider in analyzing these alternatives? Under what circumstances would you choose (a)? Under what circumstances would you choose (b) or (c)? (*Hint:* Don't forget Chapters 3 and 23.)

REAL-TIME DATA ANALYSIS

1. The Dun and Bradstreet Web site (www.dnb.com) contains a sample comprehensive report on a small business. Would you extend credit to the firm? Why or why not?

2. The three main credit bureaus maintain useful Web sites with examples of their business and consumer reports. Log on to www.equifax.com and look at the sample report on a small business. What information do you think would be most useful if you were considering granting credit to the firm?

3. Log on to the Federal Reserve site at www.federalreserve.gov and look up current money-market interest rates. Suppose your business has $7 million set aside for an expenditure in three months. How would you choose to invest it in the meantime? Would your decision be different if there were some chance that you might need the money earlier?

4. The Federal Reserve Bulletin publishes the results of a quarterly survey of bank lending (see **www.federalreserve.gov/releases/E2**). Use the latest survey to describe the pattern of lending by domestic banks. Examine, for example, whether most loans are secured and whether they are made under commitment. What are the different characteristics of small and large loans? Now compare the results of this survey with an earlier one. Have there been any important changes?

31

CHAPTER

MERGERS

The scale and pace of merger activity in India have been remarkable. In 2011, a total of 1,026 deals were struck in India (including PE deals) with total value exceeding $54 billion.[1] During such periods of intense merger activity, management spends significant amounts of time either searching for firms to acquire or worrying about whether some other firm will acquire them.

A merger adds value only if the two companies are worth more together than apart. This chapter covers why two companies could be worth more together and how to get the merger deal done if they are. Many marriages between companies are amicable, but sometimes one party is dragged unwillingly to the altar. So we also look at what is involved in hostile takeovers.

We proceed as follows.

- *Motives.* Sources of value added.
- *Dubious motives.* Don't be tempted.
- *Benefits and costs.* It's important to estimate them consistently.
- *Mechanics.* Legal, tax, and accounting issues.
- *Takeover battles and tactics.* We look at merger tactics and show some of the economic forces driving merger activity.
- *Mergers and the economy.* How can we explain merger waves? Who gains and who loses as a result of mergers?

Mergers are partly about economies from combining two firms, but they are also about who gets to run the company. Pick a merger, and you'll almost always find that one firm is the protagonist and the other is the target.

---

[1] Source: Business Line, January 20, 2012.

Financial economists now view mergers as part of a broader *market for corporate control*. The activity in this market goes far beyond ordinary mergers. It includes leveraged buyouts (LBOs), spin-offs and divestitures, and also nationalizations and privatizations where the government acquires or sells a business. These are the subject of the next chapter.

31-1 SENSIBLE MOTIVES FOR MERGERS

Table 31.1 lists a few recent mergers. Notice that most of these are **horizontal mergers,** that is, combinations of two firms in the same line of business[2]. Two recent headline-grabbing examples are the acquisition of MTN Group by Bharti Airtel for a consideration of ₹53,000 million in May 2009 and Quipo Telecom Infrastructure's takeover of 49% stake in Tata Teleservices' telecom and infrastructure arm for a consideration of $49 million.

TABLE 31.1 Some important recent mergers.

Industry	Acquiring Company	Selling Company	Payment (₹ Millions)	% stake acquired
Retail Trade	Sujana Universal Industries	Vijaya Home Appliances	100	100%
Telecom	Bharti Airtel	MTN Group (South Africa)	23000	49%
Petroleum	Reliance Industries	Reliance Petroleum	1691	24.62%
Petroleum & Coal	Reliance Industries	Indian Petrochemicals Corporation	995	100%
Pharmaceuticals	Pfizer	Pharmacia Healthcare	457	100%

Source: ISI Emerging Markets Database.

A **vertical merger** involves companies at different stages of production. The buyer expands back toward the source of raw materials or forward in the direction of the ultimate consumer. An example of a vertical merger is the 2008 acquisition of Tele Atlas by its fellow Dutch firm, TomTom. TomTom, the world's largest maker of car navigation devices, plans to use Tele Atlas's digital map data to provide real-time updates to its sat-nav systems. Other recent vertical mergers include that between Google and Double-Click and the proposed tie-up between Live Nation and Ticketmaster.

A **conglomerate merger** involves companies in unrelated lines of businesses. The principal mergers of the 1960s and 1970s were mostly conglomerate. Conglomerates are much less popular now, at least in the United States and other developed economies. Much of the action in the 1980s and 1990s has come from breaking up the conglomerates that had been formed 10 to 20 years earlier. Most of the mergers and acquisitions that have taken place in India between 2000-05 are actually horizontal mergers. In 1994, Bombay Dyeing made an unsuccessful bid for Union Carbide. Similarly, in 1995, it made another unsuccessful bid for Ahmedabad Electricity Corporation. Had these bids succeeded, Bombay Dyeing would have been a larger conglomerate today.

With these distinctions in mind, we are about to consider motives for mergers, that is, reasons why two firms may be worth more together than apart. We proceed with some trepidation. The motives,

---

[2] In India, sometimes a finance company makes a bid for a manufacturing company, thereby giving us the false impression that this is a conglomerate merger. However, quite often another company (from the same industry as that of the target) makes a bid indirectly through the finance company (in which it has substantial stake). So for all practical purposes, we can consider such mergers as horizontal mergers.

though they often lead the way to real benefits, are sometimes just mirages that tempt unwary or overconfident managers into takeover disasters. This was the case for AOL, which spent a record-breaking $156 billion to acquire Time Warner. The aim was to create a company that could offer consumers a comprehensive package of media and information products. It didn't work. Even more embarrassing (on a smaller scale) was the acquisition of Apex One, a sporting apparel company, by Converse Inc. The purchase was made on May 18, 1995. Apex One was closed down on August 11, after Converse failed to produce new designs quickly enough to satisfy retailers. Converse lost an investment of over $40 million in 85 days.[3]

The importance of managing the merger becomes more important when the bidding and the target companies belong to different countries and different cultures. Thus, for example, when Tata Motors took over Daewoo in Korea, they used the locals in Korea to do most of the work. In fact, when Tata Chemicals took over Brunner Mond with operations in the tribal areas of Masai, Kenya, its management made sure to be in good terms with the chiefs of the tribe.[4]

The value of most businesses depends on *human* assets—managers, skilled workers, scientists, and engineers. If these people are not happy in their new roles in the merged firm, the best of them will leave. Beware of paying too much for assets that go down in the elevator and out to the parking lot at the close of each business day. They may drive into the sunset and never return.

Consider the $38 billion merger between Daimler-Benz and Chrysler. Although it was hailed as a model for consolidation in the auto industry, the early years were rife with conflicts between two very different cultures:

> German management-board members had executive assistants who prepared detailed position papers on any number of issues. The Americans didn't have assigned aides and formulated their decisions by talking directly to engineers or other specialists. A German decision worked its way through the bureaucracy for final approval at the top. Then it was set in stone. The Americans allowed midlevel employees to proceed on their own initiative, sometimes without waiting for executive-level approval.
>
> . . .
>
> Cultural integration also was proving to be a slippery commodity. The yawning gap in pay scales fueled an undercurrent of tension. The Americans earned two, three, and, in some cases, four times as much as their German counterparts. But the expenses of U.S. workers were tightly controlled compared with the German system. Daimler-side employees thought nothing of flying to Paris or New York for a half-day meeting, then capping the visit with a fancy dinner and a night in an expensive hotel. The Americans blanched at the extravagance.[5]

Nine years after acquiring Chrysler, Daimler threw in the towel and announced that it was offloading an 80% stake in Chrysler to a leveraged-buyout firm, Cerberus Capital Management. Daimler actually paid Cerberus $677 million to take Chrysler off its hands. Cerberus in return assumed about $18 billion in pension and employee health care liabilities and agreed to invest $6 billion in Chrysler and its finance subsidiary.

There are also occasions when the merger does achieve gains but the buyer nevertheless loses because it pays too much. For example, the buyer may overestimate the value of stale inventory or underestimate the costs of renovating old plant and equipment, or it may overlook the warranties on

---

[3] Mark Maremount, "How Converse Got Its Laces All Tangled," *BusinessWeek,* September 4, 1995, p. 37.

[4] "For Corporate India, it's no longer a culture shock", *Economic Times,* June 29, 2006.

[5] Bill Vlasic and Bradley A. Stertz, "Taken for a Ride," *BusinessWeek,* June 5, 2000. Reprinted with special permission © The McGraw-Hill Companies, Inc.

Finance In Practice

Those Elusive Synergies

When three of Japan's largest banks combined to form Mizuho Bank the result was a bank with assets of $1.5 trillion, more than twice those of the world leader Deutsche Bank. The name "Mizuho" means "rich rice harvest" and the bank's management forecasted that the merger would yield a rich harvest of synergies. In a message to shareholders, the bank president claimed that the merger would create "a comprehensive financial services group that will surge forward in the 21st century." He predicted that the bank would "lead the new era through cutting-edge comprehensive financial services . . . by exploiting to the fullest extent the Group's enormous strengths, which are backed by a powerful customer base and state-of-the-art financial and information technologies." The cost of putting the banks together was forecasted at ¥130 billion, but management predicted future benefits of ¥466 billion a year.

Within a few months of the announcement, reports began to emerge of squabbles among the three partners. One problem area was IT. Each of the three merging banks had a different supplier for its computer system. At first it was proposed to use just one of these three systems, but then the banks decided to connect the three different systems together using "relay" computers.

Three years after the initial announcement the new company opened for business on April 1, 2002. Five days later, computer glitches resulted in a spectacular foul-up. Some 7,000 of the bank's cash machines did not work, 60,000 accounts were debited twice for the same transaction, and millions of bills went unpaid. *The Economist* reported that two weeks later Tokyo Gas, the biggest gas company, was still missing ¥2.2 billion in payments, and the top telephone company, NTT, which was looking for ¥12.7 billion, was forced to send its customers receipts marked with asterisks in place of figures, since it did not know which of about 760,000 bills had been paid.

One of the objectives behind the formation of Mizuho was to exploit economies in its IT systems. The launch fiasco illustrated dramatically that it is easier to predict such merger synergies than to realize them.

Sources: The creation of Mizuho Bank and its launch problems are described in "Undispensable: A Fine Merger Yields One Fine Mess," *The Economist*, April 27, 2002, p. 72; "Big, Bold, but . . .", *Euromoney*, December 2000, pp. 30–35; and "Godzilla Bank," *Forbes*, March 20, 2000, pp. 132–133.

a defective product. Buyers need to be particularly careful about environmental liabilities. If there is pollution from the seller's operations or toxic waste on its property, the costs of cleaning up will probably fall on the buyer.

Now we turn to the possible sources of merger *synergies*, that is, the possible sources of added value.

Economies of Scale

Many mergers are intended to reduce costs and achieve economies of scale. For example, when Bank of New York and Mellon Financial Corporation merged in 2007, management forecasted annual cost savings of $700 million or over 8% of the current combined costs. They anticipated that the merger would allow the two companies to share services and technology, and would permit a reduction in staff from 40,000 to about 36,000. (Some of these savings involved senior management. For example, there were two chief financial officers before the merger and only one afterward.)

Achieving these *economies of scale* is the natural goal of horizontal mergers. But such economies have been claimed in conglomerate mergers, too. The architects of these mergers have pointed to the economies that come from sharing central services such as office management and accounting, financial control, executive development, and top-level management.[6]

Economies of Vertical Integration

Vertical mergers seek economies in vertical integration. Some companies try to gain control over the production process by expanding back toward the output of the raw material or forward to the ultimate consumer. One way to achieve this is to merge with a supplier or a customer.

Vertical integration facilitates coordination and administration. We illustrate via an extreme example. Think of an airline that does not own any planes. If it schedules a flight from Boston to San Francisco, it sells tickets and then rents a plane for that flight from a separate company. This strategy might work on a small scale, but it would be an administrative nightmare for a major carrier, which would have to coordinate hundreds of rental agreements daily. In view of these difficulties, it is not surprising that all major airlines have integrated backward, away from the consumer, by buying and flying airplanes rather than simply patronizing rent-a-plane companies.

Do not assume that more vertical integration is better than less. Carried to extremes, it is absurdly inefficient, as in the case of LOT, the Polish state airline, which in the late 1980s found itself raising pigs to make sure that its employees had fresh meat on their tables. (Of course, in a centrally managed economy it may be necessary to raise your own cattle or pigs, since you can't be sure you'll be able to buy meat.)

Here is an example of vertical merger from India. Reliance Industries Limited was procuring naphtha and propane from Reliance Petroleum, a group company prior to their merger in 2002[7]. Prior to the merger, the Gujarat Government granted sales tax waiver to Reliance Petroleum. Since Indian Oil (IOL) was the distribution agent of RIL, the sales tax incidence was falling on IOL. However, with the dismantling of the Administered Price Mechanism (APM) and after the renegotiation of the marketing deal, RIL was required to pay the sales tax. After the merger between RIL and RPL, the sales tax waiver granted to RPL would automatically come to the merged entity and hence RIL would not be required to pay any sales tax on the petroleum products sold out of Jamnagar in Gujarat.

Nowadays the tide of vertical integration seems to be flowing out. Companies are finding it more efficient to *outsource* the provision of many services and various types of production. For example, back in the 1950s and 1960s, General Motors was deemed to have a cost advantage over its main competitors, Ford and Chrysler, because a greater fraction of the parts used in GM's automobiles were produced in-house. By the 1990s, Ford and Chrysler had the advantage: they could buy the parts cheaper from outside suppliers. This was partly because the outside suppliers tended to use nonunion labor at lower wages. But it also appears that manufacturers have more bargaining power versus independent suppliers than versus a production facility that's part of the corporate family. In 1998 GM decided to spin off Delphi, its automotive parts division, as a separate company. After the

---

[6] Economies of scale are enjoyed when the average unit cost of production goes down as production increases. One way to achieve economies of scale is to spread fixed costs over a larger volume of production.

[7] "RIL – RPL Merger: Smartly Timed", *Business Line*, March 10, 2002.

spin-off, GM can continue to buy parts from Delphi in large volumes, but it negotiates the purchases at arm's length.

Complementary Resources

Many small firms are acquired by large ones that can provide the missing ingredients necessary for the small firms' success. The small firm may have a unique product but lack the engineering and sales organization required to produce and market it on a large scale. The firm could develop engineering and sales talent from scratch, but it may be quicker and cheaper to merge with a firm that already has ample talent. The two firms have *complementary resources*—each has what the other needs—and so it may make sense for them to merge. Also, the merger may open up opportunities that neither firm would pursue otherwise.

Of course, two large firms may also merge because they have complementary resources. Consider the 1999 merger between two banks, HDFC Bank and Times Bank. HDFC Bank had branches mostly in the metros, whereas Times Bank was predominantly present in the non-metro urban areas. Similarly, when ICICI Bank and Bank of Madura (present mostly in the rural areas of South India) merged in 2000, ICICI Bank got a strong hold on the lucrative South Indian market. These two mergers enabled the merged banks to enlarge the branch network in places in which they did not have a significant presence.

In recent years many of the major pharmaceutical firms have faced the loss of patent protection on their more profitable products and have not had an offsetting pipeline of promising new compounds. This has prompted an increasing number of acquisitions of biotech firms. For example, in 2008 Eli Lilly acquired ImClone Systems. Lilly paid $6.5 billion for ImClone, a premium of some 50% over the company's earlier market value. But Lilly's CEO claimed that the acquisition would "broaden Lilly's portfolio of marketed cancer therapies and boost Lilly's oncology pipeline with up to three promising targeted therapies in Phase III in 2009." At the same time ImClone obtained the resources necessary to bring its products to market.

Surplus Funds

Here's another argument for mergers: Suppose that your firm is in a mature industry. It is generating a substantial amount of cash, but it has few profitable investment opportunities. Ideally such a firm should distribute the surplus cash to shareholders by increasing its dividend payment or repurchasing stock. Unfortunately, energetic managers are often reluctant to adopt a policy of shrinking their firm in this way. If the firm is not willing to purchase its own shares, it can instead purchase another company's shares. Firms with a surplus of cash and a shortage of good investment opportunities often turn to mergers *financed by cash* as a way of redeploying their capital.

Hindustan Levers Limited (HLL) and Brooke Bond Lipton India Limited (BBLIL), for example, justified their merger in 1996 by arguing that the surplus cash of HLL can be "gainfully deployed to seek accelerated growth in processed foods".[8]

Some firms have excess cash and do not pay it out to stockholders or redeploy it by wise acquisitions. Such firms often find themselves targeted for takeover by other firms that propose to redeploy the cash for them. During the oil price slump of the early 1980s, many cash-rich oil companies found themselves threatened by takeover. This was not because their cash was a unique asset. The acquirers wanted to capture the companies' cash flow to make sure it was not frittered away on negative-NPV oil exploration projects. We return to this *free-cash-flow* motive for takeovers later in this chapter.

---

[8] See the Directors' Report, Annual Report of Brooke Bond Lipton India Limited, 1995.

Eliminating Inefficiencies

Cash is not the only asset that can be wasted by poor management. There are always firms with unexploited opportunities to cut costs and increase sales and earnings. Such firms are natural candidates for acquisition by other firms with better management. In some instances "better management" may simply mean the determination to force painful cuts or realign the company's operations. Notice that the motive for such acquisitions has nothing to do with benefits from combining two firms. Acquisition is simply the mechanism by which a new management team replaces the old one.

A merger is not the only way to improve management, but sometimes it is the only simple and practical way. Managers are naturally reluctant to fire or demote themselves, and stockholders of large public firms do not usually have much *direct* influence on how the firm is run or who runs it.[9]

If this motive for merger is important, one would expect to observe that acquisitions often precede a change in the management of the target firm. This seems to be the case. For example, Martin and McConnell found that the chief executive is four times more likely to be replaced in the year after a takeover than during earlier years.[10] The firms they studied had generally been poor performers; in the four years before acquisition their stock prices had lagged behind those of other firms in the same industry by 15%. Apparently many of these firms fell on bad times and were rescued, or reformed, by merger.

Industry Consolidation

The biggest opportunities to improve efficiency seem to come in industries with too many firms and too much capacity. These conditions seem to trigger a wave of mergers and acquisitions, which then force companies to cut capacity and employment and release capital for reinvestment elsewhere in the economy. For example, when U.S. defense budgets fell after the end of the Cold War, a round of consolidating takeovers followed in the defense industry. The consolidation was inevitable, but the takeovers accelerated it.

The banking industry is another example. Most of the banking mergers in Table 31.1 have involved rescues of failing banks by larger and stronger rivals. But many earlier bank mergers involved successful banks that sought to achieve economies of scale. The United States entered the 1980s with far too many banks, largely as a result of outdated restrictions on interstate banking. As these restrictions eroded and communications and technology improved, hundreds of small banks were swept up into regional or "super-regional" banks. For example, look at Figure 31.1, which shows the dozens of acquisitions by Bank of America and its predecessor companies. The main motive of these mergers was to reduce costs.[11]

In Europe also during the past 20 years there has been a wave of bank mergers as companies have sought to gain the financial muscle to compete in a Europe-wide banking market. These include the mergers of UBS and Swiss Bank Corp (1997), BNP and Banque Paribas (1998), Hypobank and Bayerische Vereinsbank (1998), Banco Santander and Banco Central Hispanico (1999), Unicredit and Capitalia (2007), and Commerzbank and Dresdner Bank (2009).

---

[9] It is difficult to assemble a large-enough block of stockholders to effectively challenge management and the incumbent board of directors. Stockholders can have enormous indirect influence, however. Their displeasure shows up in the firm's stock price. A low stock price may encourage a takeover bid by another firm.

[10] K. J. Martin and J. J. McConnell, "Corporate Performance, Corporate Takeovers, and Management Turnover," *Journal of Finance* 46 (June 1991), pp. 671–687.

[11] A study of 41 large bank mergers estimated cost savings with present value averaging 12% of the combined market values of the merging banks. See J. F. Houston, C. M. James, and M. D. Ryngaert, "Where Do Merger Gains Come From? Bank Mergers from the Perspective of Insiders and Outsiders," *Journal of Financial Economics* 60 (May/June 2001), pp. 285–331.

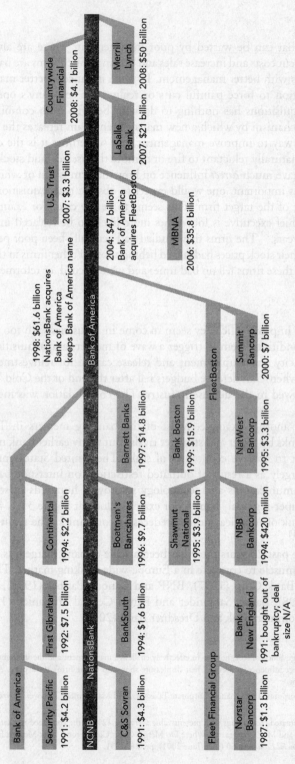

FIGURE 31.1

Part of Bank of America's family tree.

Sources: Thomson Financial SDC M&A Database and Bank of America annual reports.

In India, consolidation (via mergers and acquisitions) is taking in certain industries because of certain regulatory changes. The Industries (Development and Regulation) Act, 1951 has been changed now and the number of industries that require license now has been brought down to less than 10. The licensing regime determined the entry and exit of firms as well as the level of production capacity. The MRTP Act that effectively restricted the growth of large businesses was diluted in the early 1980s removing licensing restrictions, and allowing big businesses to expand in core areas like chemicals, drugs, ceramics and drugs[12]. The licensing policy was responsible for the industry becoming fragmented. In the cement industry, for example, more than 50 players were controlling 110 million ton capacity and out of these as many as 40 were marginal players controlling 1 million ton capacity each.[13] However, a number of the cement manufacturing firms have been merged with (taken over by) other cement firms in the last 20 years after the removal of the outdated licensing policy.

31-2 SOME DUBIOUS REASONS FOR MERGERS

The benefits that we have described so far all make economic sense. Other arguments sometimes given for mergers are dubious. Here are a few of the dubious ones.

Diversification

We have suggested that the managers of a cash-rich company may prefer to see it use that cash for acquisitions rather than distribute it as extra dividends. That is why we often see cash-rich firms in stagnant industries merging their way into fresh woods and pastures new.

What about diversification as an end in itself? It is obvious that diversification reduces risk. Isn't that a gain from merging?

The trouble with this argument is that diversification is easier and cheaper for the stockholder than for the corporation. There is little evidence that investors pay a premium for diversified firms; in fact, as we will explain in Chapter 32, discounts are more common. The Appendix to this chapter provides a simple proof that corporate diversification does not increase value in perfect markets as long as investors' diversification opportunities are unrestricted. This is the *value-additivity* principle introduced in Chapter 7.

Increasing Earnings per Share: The Bootstrap Game

Some acquisitions that offer no evident economic gains nevertheless produce several years of rising earnings per share. To see how this can happen, let us look at the acquisition of Muck and Slurry by the well-known conglomerate World Enterprises.

The position before the merger is set out in the first two columns of Table 31.2. Because Muck and Slurry has relatively poor growth prospects, its stock's price–earnings ratio is lower than World Enterprises' (line 3). The merger, we assume, produces no economic benefits, and so the firms should be worth exactly the same together as they are apart. The market value of World Enterprises after the merger should be equal to the sum of the separate values of the two firms (line 6).

Since World Enterprises' stock is selling for double the price of Muck and Slurry stock (line 2), World Enterprises can acquire the 100,000 Muck and Slurry shares for 50,000 of its own shares. Thus World will have 150,000 shares outstanding after the merger.

[12] Kohli, A., 2006, "Politics of Economic Growth in India, 1980-2005", Economic and Political Weekly, April 1. pp 1361 – 1370.

[13] See Mergers and Acquisitions, International Financial Law Review, http://www.iflr.com/?Page=17&ISS=16166&SID=508005.

TABLE 31.2   Impact of merger on market value and earnings per share of World Enterprises.

	World Enterprises before Merger	Muck and Slurry	World Enterprises after Merger
1. Earnings per share	$2.00	$2.00	$2.67
2. Price per share	$40	$20	$40
3. Price–earnings ratio	20	10	15
4. Number of shares	100,000	100,000	150,000
5. Total earnings	$200,000	$200,000	$400,000
6. Total market value	$4,000,000	$2,000,000	$6,000,000
7. Current earnings per dollar invested in stock (line 1 ÷ line 2)	$.05	$.10	$.067

Note: When World Enterprises purchases Muck and Slurry, there are no gains. Therefore, total earnings and total market value should be unaffected by the merger. But earnings per share increase. World Enterprises issues only 50,000 of its shares (priced at $40) to acquire the 100,000 Muck and Slurry shares (priced at $20).

Total earnings double as a result of the merger (line 5), but the number of shares increases by only 50%. Earnings *per share* rise from $2.00 to $2.67. We call this the *bootstrap effect* because there is no real gain created by the merger and no increase in the two firms' combined value. Since the stock price is unchanged, the price–earnings ratio falls (line 3).

Figure 31.2 illustrates what is going on here. Before the merger $1 invested in World Enterprises bought 5 cents of current earnings and rapid growth prospects. On the other hand, $1 invested in Muck and Slurry bought 10 cents of current earnings but slower growth prospects. If the *total* market value is not altered by the merger, then $1 invested in the merged firm gives 6.7 cents of immediate earnings but slower growth than World Enterprises offered alone. Muck and Slurry shareholders get lower immediate earnings but faster growth. Neither side gains or loses provided everybody understands the deal.

Financial manipulators sometimes try to ensure that the market does *not* understand the deal. Suppose that investors are fooled by the exuberance of the president of World Enterprises and by plans to introduce modern management techniques into its new Earth Sciences Division (formerly known as Muck and Slurry). They could easily mistake the 33% postmerger increase in earnings per share for real growth. If they do, the price of World Enterprises stock rises and the shareholders of both companies receive something for nothing.

This is a "bootstrap" or "chain letter" game. It generates earnings growth not from capital investment or improved profitability, but from purchase of slowly growing firms with low price–earnings ratios. If this fools investors, the financial manager may be able to puff up stock price artificially. But to keep fooling investors, the firm has to continue to expand by merger *at the same compound rate*. Clearly this cannot go on forever; one day expansion must slow down or stop. At this point earnings growth falls dramatically and the house of cards collapses.

This game is not often played these days, but you may still encounter managers who would rather acquire firms with low price–earnings ratios. Beware of false prophets who suggest that you can appraise mergers just by looking at their immediate impact on earnings per share.

Lower Financing Costs

You often hear it said that a merged firm is able to borrow more cheaply than its separate units could. In part this is true. We have already seen (in Section 15-4) that there are significant economies of scale

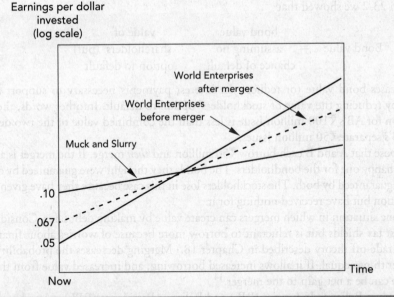

Earnings per dollar
invested
(log scale)

World Enterprises
after merger

World Enterprises
before merger

Muck and Slurry

.10
.067
.05

Time

Now

FIGURE 31.2

Effects of merger on earnings growth. By merging with Muck and Slurry, World Enterprises increases current earnings but accepts a slower rate of future growth. Its stockholders should be no better or worse off unless investors are fooled by the bootstrap effect.

Source: S. C. Myers, "A Framework for Evaluating Mergers," in *Modern Developments in Financial Management,* ed. S. C. Myers (New York: Frederick A. Praeger, Inc., 1976), Figure 1, p. 639. Copyright © 1976 Praeger. Reprinted by permission of Greenwood Publishing Group Inc., Westport, CT.

in making new issues. Therefore, if firms can make fewer, larger security issues by merging, there are genuine savings.

But when people say that borrowing costs are lower for the merged firm, they usually mean something more than lower issue costs. They mean that when two firms merge, the combined company can borrow at lower interest rates than either firm could separately. This, of course, is exactly what we should expect in a well-functioning bond market. While the two firms are separate, they do not guarantee each other's debt; if one fails, the bondholder cannot ask the other for money. But after the merger each enterprise effectively does guarantee the other's debt; if one part of the business fails, the bondholders can still take their money out of the other part. Because these mutual guarantees make the debt less risky, lenders demand a lower interest rate.

Does the lower interest rate mean a net gain to the merger? Not necessarily. Compare the following two situations:

- *Separate issues.* Firm A and firm B each make a ₹50 million bond issue.
- *Single issue.* Firms A and B merge, and the new firm AB makes a single ₹100 million issue.

Of course AB would pay a lower interest rate, other things being equal. But it does not make sense for A and B to merge just to get that lower rate. Although AB's shareholders do gain from the lower rate, they lose by having to guarantee each other's debt. In other words, they get the lower interest rate only by giving bondholders better protection. There is no *net* gain.

In Section 23-2 we showed that

$$\begin{array}{ccc} \text{Bond value} & = & \text{bond value} \\ & & \text{assuming no} \\ & & \text{chance of default} \end{array} - \begin{array}{c} \text{value of} \\ \text{shareholders' (put)} \\ \text{option to default} \end{array}$$

Merger increases bond value (or reduces the interest payments necessary to support a *given* bond value) only by reducing the value of stockholders' option to default. In other words, the value of the default option for AB's ₹100 million issue is less than the combined value of the two default options on A's and B's separate ₹50 million issues.

Now suppose that A and B each borrow ₹50 million and *then* merge. If the merger is a surprise, it is likely to be a happy one for the bondholders. The bonds they thought were guaranteed by one of the two firms end up guaranteed by both. The stockholders lose in this case because they have given bondholders better protection but have received nothing for it.

There is one situation in which mergers can create value by making debt safer. Consider a firm that covets interest tax shields but is reluctant to borrow more because of worries about financial distress. (This is the trade-off theory described in Chapter 18.) Merging decreases the probability of financial distress, other things equal. If it allows increased borrowing, and increased value from the interest tax shields, there can be a net gain to the merger.[14]

In India, when Reliance Industries (RIL) and Reliance Petroleum (RPL) merged with each other, they could manage to reduce the financing costs by ₹0.45 billion because of the difference in the rating of the bonds issued by RIL and RPL. Prior to the merger, the non-convertible debentures of RPL of face value of about ₹60 billions had AA+ rating. After the merger, the rating of the bonds of RIL (the merged firm) was AAA (same as the pre-merger rating of the bonds of RIL), and this implied savings of about 75 basis points.

31-3 ESTIMATING MERGER GAINS AND COSTS

Suppose that you are the financial manager of firm A and you want to analyze the possible purchase of firm B.[15] The first thing to think about is whether there is an *economic gain* from the merger. There is an economic gain *only if the two firms are worth more together than apart.* For example, if you think that the combined firm would be worth PV_{AB} and that the separate firms are worth PV_A and PV_B, then

$$\text{Gain} = PV_{AB} - (PV_A + PV_B) = \Delta PV_{AB}$$

If this gain is positive, there is an economic justification for merger. But you also have to think about the *cost* of acquiring firm B. Take the easy case in which payment is made in cash. Then the cost of acquiring B is equal to the cash payment minus B's value as a separate entity. Thus

$$\text{Cost} = \text{cash paid} - PV_B$$

---

[14] This merger rationale was first suggested by W. G. Lewellen, "A Pure Financial Rationale for the Conglomerate Merger," *Journal of Finance* 26 (May 1971), pp. 521–537. If you want to see some of the controversy and discussion that this idea led to, look at R. C. Higgins and L. D. Schall, "Corporate Bankruptcy and Conglomerate Merger," *Journal of Finance* 30 (March 1975), pp. 93–114; and D. Galai and R. W. Masulis, "The Option Pricing Model and the Risk Factor of Stock," *Journal of Financial Economics* 3 (January–March 1976), especially pp. 66–69.

[15] This chapter's definitions and interpretations of the gains and costs of merger follow those set out in S. C. Myers, "A Framework for Evaluating Mergers," in *Modern Developments in Financial Management*, ed. S. C. Myers (New York: Praeger, 1976).

The net present value to A of a merger with B is measured by the difference between the gain and the cost. Therefore, you should go ahead with the merger if its net present value, defined as

$$NPV = gain - cost$$
$$= \Delta PV_{AB} - (cash - PV_B)$$

is positive.

We like to write the merger criterion in this way because it focuses attention on two distinct questions. When you estimate the benefit, you concentrate on whether there are any gains to be made from the merger. When you estimate cost, you are concerned with the division of these gains between the two companies.

An example may help make this clear. Firm A has a value of ₹200 million, and B has a value of ₹50 million. Merging the two would allow cost savings with a present value of ₹25 million. This is the gain from the merger. Thus,

$$PV_A = ₹200$$
$$PV_B = ₹50$$
$$Gain = \Delta PV_{AB} = +₹25$$
$$PV_{AB} = ₹275 \text{ million}$$

Suppose that B is bought for cash, say, for ₹65 million. The cost of the merger is

$$Cost = cash \; paid - PV_B$$
$$= 65 - 50 = ₹15 \text{ million}$$

Note that the stockholders of firm B—the people on the other side of the transaction—are ahead by ₹15 million. *Their* gain is *your* cost. They have captured ₹15 million of the ₹25 million merger gain. Thus when we write down the NPV of the merger from A's viewpoint, we are really calculating the part of the gain that A's stockholders get to keep. The NPV to A's stockholders equals the overall gain from the merger less that part of the gain captured by B's stockholders:

$$NPV = 25 - 15 = +₹10 \text{ million}$$

Just as a check, let's confirm that A's stockholders really come out ₹10 million ahead. They start with a firm worth $PV_A = ₹200$ million. They end up with a firm worth ₹275 million and then have to pay out $65 million to B's stockholders.[16] Thus their net gain is

$$NPV = wealth \; with \; merger - wealth \; without \; merger$$
$$= (PV_{AB} - cash) - PV_A$$
$$= (₹275 - ₹65) - ₹200 = +₹10 \text{ million}$$

Suppose investors do not anticipate the merger between A and B. The announcement will cause the value of B's stock to rise from ₹50 million to ₹65 million, a 30% increase. If investors share management's assessment of the merger gains, the market value of A's stock will increase by ₹10 million, only a 5% increase.

It makes sense to keep an eye on what investors think the gains from merging are. If A's stock price falls when the deal is announced, then investors are sending the message that the merger benefits are doubtful or that A is paying too much for them.

---

[16] We are assuming that PV_A includes enough cash to finance the deal, or that the cash can be borrowed at a market interest rate. Notice that the value to A's stockholders after the deal is done and paid for is $275 - 65 = $210 million—a gain of $10 million.

Right and Wrong Ways to Estimate the Benefits of Mergers

Some companies begin their merger analyses with a forecast of the target firm's future cash flows. Any revenue increases or cost reductions attributable to the merger are included in the forecasts, which are then discounted back to the present and compared with the purchase price:

$$\begin{matrix} \text{Estimated} \\ \text{net gain} \end{matrix} = \begin{matrix} \text{DCF valuation} \\ \text{of target, including} \\ \text{merger benefits} \end{matrix} - \begin{matrix} \text{cash required} \\ \text{for acquisition} \end{matrix}$$

This is a dangerous procedure. Even the brightest and best-trained analyst can make large errors in valuing a business. The estimated net gain may come up positive not because the merger makes sense but simply because the analyst's cash-flow forecasts are too optimistic. On the other hand, a good merger may not be pursued if the analyst fails to recognize the target's potential as a stand-alone business.

Our procedure *starts* with the target's stand-alone market value (PV_B) and concentrates on the *changes* in cash flow that would result from the merger. *Ask yourself why the two firms should be worth more together than apart.*

The same advice holds when you are contemplating the sale of part of your business. There is no point in saying to yourself, This is an unprofitable business and should be sold. Unless the buyer can run the business better than you can, the price you receive will reflect the poor prospects.

Sometimes you may come across managers who believe that there are simple rules for identifying good acquisitions. They may say, for example, that they always try to buy into growth industries or that they have a policy of acquiring companies that are selling below book value. But our comments in Chapter 11 about the characteristics of a good investment decision also hold true when you are buying a whole company. *You add value only if you can generate additional economic rents*—some competitive edge that other firms can't match and the target firm's managers can't achieve on their own.

One final piece of horse sense: Often two companies bid against each other to acquire the same target firm. In effect, the target firm puts itself up for auction. In such cases, ask yourself whether the target is worth more to you than to the other bidder. If the answer is no, you should be cautious about getting into a bidding contest. Winning such a contest may be more expensive than losing it. If you lose, you have simply wasted your time; if you win, you have probably paid too much.

More on Estimating Costs—What If the Target's Stock Price Anticipates the Merger?

The cost of a merger is the premium that the buyer pays over the seller's stand-alone value. How can that value be determined? If the target is a public company, you can start with its market value; just observe price per share and multiply by the number of shares outstanding. But bear in mind that if investors *expect* A to acquire B, or if they expect *somebody* to acquire B, the market value of B may overstate its stand-alone value.

This is one of the few places in this book where we draw an important distinction between market value (MV) and the true, or "intrinsic," value (PV) of the firm as a separate entity. The problem here is not that the market value of B is wrong but that it may not be the value of firm B as a separate entity. Potential investors in B's stock will see two possible outcomes and two possible values:

Outcome	Market Value of B's Stock
1. No merger	PV_B: Value of B as a separate firm
2. Merger occurs	PV_B *plus* some part of the benefits of the merger

If the second outcome is possible, MV_B, the stock market value we observe for B, will overstate PV_B. This is exactly what *should* happen in a competitive capital market. Unfortunately, it complicates the task of a financial manager who is evaluating a merger.

Here is an example: Suppose that just before A and B's merger announcement we observe the following:

	Firm A	Firm B
Market price per share	₹200	₹100
Number of shares	1,000,000	500,000
Market value of firm	₹200 million	₹50 million

Firm A intends to pay $65 million cash for B. If B's market price reflects only its value as a separate entity, then

$$\text{Cost} = (\text{cash paid} - PV_B)$$
$$= (65 - 50) = ₹15 \text{ million}$$

However, suppose that B's share price has *already* risen ₹12 because of rumors that B might get a favorable merger offer. That means that its intrinsic value is overstated by $12 \times 500,000 = ₹6$ million. Its true value, PV_B, is only ₹44 million. Then

$$\text{Cost} = (65 - 44) = ₹21 \text{ million}$$

Since the merger gain is ₹25 million, this deal still makes A's stockholders better off, but B's stockholders are now capturing the lion's share of the gain.

Notice that if the market made a mistake, and the market value of B was *less* than B's true value as a separate entity, the cost could be negative. In other words, B would be a *bargain* and the merger would be worthwhile from A's point of view, even if the two firms were worth no more together than apart. Of course, A's stockholders' gain would be B's stockholders' loss, because B would be sold for less than its true value.

Firms have made acquisitions just because their managers believed they had spotted a company whose intrinsic value was not fully appreciated by the stock market. However, we know from the evidence on market efficiency that "cheap" stocks often turn out to be expensive. It is not easy for outsiders, whether investors or managers, to find firms that are truly undervalued by the market. Moreover, if the shares are bargain-priced, A doesn't need a merger to profit by its special knowledge. It can just buy up B's shares on the open market and hold them passively, waiting for other investors to wake up to B's true value.

If firm A is wise, it will not go ahead with a merger if the cost exceeds the gain. Firm B will not consent if A's gain is so big that B loses. This gives us a range of possible cash payments that would allow the merger to take place. Whether the payment is at the top or the bottom of this range depends on the relative bargaining power of the two participants.

Estimating Cost When the Merger Is Financed by Stock

Many mergers involve payment wholly or partly in the form of the acquirer's stock. When a merger is financed by stock, cost depends on the value of the shares in the new company received by the shareholders of the selling company. If the sellers receive N shares, each worth P_{AB}, the cost is

$$\text{Cost} = N \times P_{AB} - PV_B$$

Just be sure to use the price per share *after the merger is announced* and its benefits are appreciated by investors.

Suppose that A offers 325,000 (.325 million) shares instead of ₹65 million in cash. A's share price before the deal is announced is ₹200. If B is worth ₹50 million stand-alone,[17] the cost of the merger *appears* to be

$$\text{Apparent cost} = .325 \times 200 - 50 = ₹15 \text{ million}$$

However, the apparent cost may not be the true cost. A's stock price is ₹200 before the merger announcement. At the announcement it ought to go up.

Given the gain and the terms of the deal, we can calculate share prices and market values after the deal. The new firm will have 1.325 million shares outstanding and will be worth ₹275 million.[18] The new share price is 275/1.325 = ₹207.55. The true cost is

$$\text{Cost} = .325 \times 207.55 - 50 = ₹17.45 \text{ million}$$

This cost can also be calculated by figuring out the gain to B's shareholders. They end up with .325 million shares, or 24.5% of the new firm AB. Their gain is

$$.245(275) - 50 = ₹17.45 \text{ million}$$

In general, if B's shareholders are given the fraction x of the combined firms,

$$\text{Cost} = x\text{PV}_{AB} - \text{PV}_B$$

We can now understand the first key distinction between cash and stock as financing instruments. If cash is offered, the cost of the merger is unaffected by the merger gains. If stock is offered, the cost depends on the gains because the gains show up in the postmerger share price.

Stock financing also mitigates the effect of overvaluation or undervaluation of either firm. Suppose, for example, that A overestimates B's value as a separate entity, perhaps because it has overlooked some hidden liability. Thus A makes too generous an offer. Other things being equal, A's stockholders are better off if it is a stock offer rather than a cash offer. With a stock offer, the inevitable bad news about B's value will fall partly on the shoulders of B's stockholders.

Asymmetric Information

There is a second key difference between cash and stock financing for mergers. A's managers will usually have access to information about A's prospects that is not available to outsiders. Economists call this *asymmetric information*.

Suppose A's managers are more optimistic than outside investors. They may think that A's shares will really be worth ₹215 after the merger, ₹7.45 higher than the ₹207.55 market price we just calculated. If they are right, the true cost of a stock-financed merger with B is

$$\text{Cost} = .325 \times 215 - 50 = ₹19.88$$

B's shareholders would get a "free gift" of ₹7.45 for every A share they receive—an extra gain of ₹7.45 × .325 = 2.42, that is, ₹2.42 million.

---

[17] In this case we assume that B's stock price has *not* risen on merger rumors and accurately reflects B's stand-alone value.

[18] In this case no cash is leaving the firm to finance the merger. In our example of a cash offer, $65 million would be paid out to B's stockholders, leaving the final value of the firm at 275 − 65 = $210 million. There would only be one million shares outstanding, so share price would be $210. The cash deal is better for A's shareholders in this example.

Of course, if A's managers were really this optimistic, they would strongly prefer to finance the merger with cash. Financing with stock would be favored by *pessimistic* managers who think their company's shares are *over*valued.

Does this sound like "win-win" for A—just issue shares when overvalued, cash otherwise? No, it's not that easy, because B's shareholders, and outside investors generally, understand what's going on. Suppose you are negotiating on behalf of B. You find that A's managers keep suggesting stock rather than cash financing. You quickly infer A's managers' pessimism, mark down your own opinion of what the shares are worth, and drive a harder bargain.

This asymmetric-information story explains why buying-firms' share prices generally fall when stock-financed mergers are announced.[19] Andrade, Mitchell, and Stafford found an average market-adjusted fall of 1.5% on the announcement of stock-financed mergers between 1973 and 1998. There was a small *gain* (.4%) for a sample of cash-financed deals.[20]

31-4 THE MECHANICS OF A MERGER

Buying a company is a much more complicated affair than buying a piece of machinery. Thus we should look at some of the problems encountered in arranging mergers. In practice, these arrangements are often *extremely* complex, and specialists must be consulted. We are not trying to replace those specialists; we simply want to alert you to the kinds of legal, tax, and accounting issues they deal with.

Mergers, Antitrust Law, and Popular Opposition

Prior to 1991, pre-entry scrutiny of the mergers in India was required under the MRTP Act, 1969. However, after the amendment of the MRTP Act, there was no provision under which mergers that give rise to monopoly situations are scrutinized and cleared by any legal authority. In June 2011, the Competition Commission of India (CCI) made it mandatory to get prior approval of the CCI in mergers that satisfy certain criteria.[21]

In the U.S., mergers can get bogged down in the federal antitrust laws. The most important statute here is the Clayton Act of 1914, which forbids an acquisition whenever "in any line of commerce or in any section of the country" the effect "*may be* substantially to lessen competition, or to *tend* to create a monopoly."

Antitrust law can be enforced by the federal government in either of two ways: by a civil suit brought by the Justice Department or by a proceeding initiated by the Federal Trade Commission (FTC).[22] The Hart–Scott–Rodino Antitrust Act of 1976 requires that these agencies be informed of all acquisitions of stock amounting to $15 million or 15% of the target's stock, whichever is less. Thus, almost all large mergers are reviewed at an early stage.[23] Both the Justice Department and the

---

[19] The same reasoning applies to stock issues. See Sections 15-4 and 18-4.

[20] See G. Andrade, M. Mitchell, and E. Stafford, "New Evidence and Perspectives on Mergers," *Journal of Economic Perspectives* 15 (Spring 2001), pp. 103–120. This result confirms earlier work, including N. Travlos, "Corporate Takeover Bids, Methods of Payment, and Bidding Firms' Stock Returns," *Journal of Finance* 42 (September 1987), pp. 943–963; and J. R. Franks, R. S. Harris, and S. Titman, "The Postmerger Share-Price Performance of Acquiring Firms," *Journal of Financial Economics* 29 (March 1991), pp. 81–96.

[21] Thus for example, mergers that result in combined assets of ₹1,500 crores or combined turnover of ₹4,500 crore require the prior approval of the CCI.

[22] Competitors or third parties who think they will be injured by the merger can also bring antitrust suits.

[23] The target has to be notified also, and it in turn informs investors. Thus the Hart–Scott–Rodino Act effectively forces an acquiring company to "go public" with its bid.

FTC then have the right to seek injunctions delaying a merger. An injunction is often enough to scupper the companies' plans.

Both the FTC and the Justice Department have been flexing their muscles in recent years. Here is an example. After the end of the Cold War, sharp declines in defense budgets triggered consolidation in the U.S. aerospace industry. By 1998 there remained just three giant companies—Boeing, Lockheed Martin, and Raytheon—plus several smaller ones, including Northrup Grumman. Thus, when Lockheed Martin and Northrup Grumman announced plans to get together, the Departments of Justice and Defense decided that this was a merger too far. In the face of this opposition, the two companies broke off their engagement.

Other industries in which large mergers have been blocked on antitrust grounds include aluminum (Reynolds and Alcoa), telecoms (WorldCom and Sprint), supermarkets (Kroger and WinnDixie), video rentals (Hollywood Entertainment and Blockbuster), and office equipment (Office Depot and Staples).

Companies that do business outside the U.S. also have to worry about foreign antitrust laws. For example, GE's $46 billion takeover bid for Honeywell was blocked by the European Commission, which argued that the combined company would have too much power in the aircraft industry.

Sometimes trustbusters will object to a merger, but then relent if the companies agree to divest certain assets and operations. For example, when the organic grocer Whole Foods Market acquired its closest rival, Wild Oats Markets, the FTC required the company to sell the Wild Oats brand and 13 stores.

Mergers may also be stymied by political pressures and popular resentment even when no formal antitrust issues arise. The news in 2005 that PepsiCo might bid for Danone aroused considerable hostility in France. The prime minister added his support to opponents of the merger and announced that the French government was drawing up a list of strategic industries that should be protected from foreign ownership. It was unclear whether yogurt production would be one of these strategic industries.

Economic nationalism is not confined to Europe. In 2005 China National Offshore Oil Corporation (CNOOC) felt obliged to withdraw its bid for Unocal, after what it described as "unprecedented political opposition" in Congress. The following year Congress voiced its opposition to the takeover of Britain's P&O by the Dubai company DP World. The acquisition went ahead only after P&O's ports in the United States were excluded from the deal.

The Form of Acquisition

Next you will want to consider the form of the acquisition. One possibility is literally to *merge* the two companies, in which case one company automatically assumes *all* the assets and *all* the liabilities of the other. Such a merger must have the approval of at least 75% of the stockholders (present and voting, is value terms) of each firm.[24]

Section 395 of the Companies Act in India further stipulates that the shareholding of the dissenting shareholders can be purchased provided at least 90 percent of the shareholders (present and voting, in value terms) agree to the scheme of the merger. In the U.S. a merger must have the approval of at least 50 percent of the shareholders of each firm.[25]

---

[24] Corporate charters and state laws sometimes specify a higher percentage.

[25] As per the SEBI (Substantial Acquisition of Shares and Takeovers) Regulations, 1997, the offer price shall be payable in (a) cash, (b) shares of the buying company, (c) secured instruments of the buying company with a minimum 'A' grade rating, (d) or any combination of (a), (b), (c). However, most acquisitions are financed with cash only.

An alternative is simply to buy the seller's stock in exchange for cash, shares, or other securities.[25] In this case the buyer can deal individually with the shareholders of the selling company. The seller's managers may not be involved at all. Their approval and cooperation are generally sought, but if they resist, the buyer will attempt to acquire an effective majority of the outstanding shares. If successful, the buyer has control and can complete the merger and, if necessary, toss out the incumbent management. It is not necessary to buy 100 percent of the shares of the selling company to obtain effective management control over the selling company. In fact, in India, one rarely finds the buying company buying all the 100 percent of the shares of the target company. With 51 percent stake in the selling company, a buying company can effectively control the management decision making of the selling company. However, in the U.S., it is often a common practice to buy all the 100 percent of the shares of the selling company.

The third approach is to buy some or all of the seller's assets. In this case ownership of the assets needs to be transferred, and payment is made to the selling firm rather than directly to its stockholders.

Merger Accounting

When one company buys another, its management worries about how the purchase will show up in its financial statements. According to Accounting Standard 14 (AS 14) issued by the Institute of Chartered Accountants of India (ICAI), an amalgamation (same as merger) can be in the nature of pooling of interests (referred to as amalgamation in the nature of merger) or acquisition. AS 14 lays down five conditions that must be satisfied for an amalgamation to be in the nature of merger. The five conditions are:

1. All assets and liabilities of the "Transferor Company"[26] before amalgamation should become assets and liabilities of the "Transferee Company".
2. Shareholders holding not less than 90% of shares (in value terms) of the "Transferor Company" should become the shareholders of the "Transferee Company".
3. The consideration payable to the shareholders of the "Transferor Company" should be in the form of shares of the "Transferee Company" only; cash can however, be paid in respect of fractional shares.
4. Business of the "Transferor Company" is intended to be carried on by the "Transferee Company."
5. The "Transferee Company" incorporates, in its balance sheet, the book values of assets and liabilities of the "Transferor Company" without any adjustment except to the extent needed to ensure uniformity of accounting policies.

An amalgamation which does not satisfy all the conditions stated above will be regarded as an "Acquisition". For a merger, the 'pooling of interests' method is used and for an acquisition, the 'purchase method' is used. The U.S. GAAP, however, allows only the purchase method.

We illustrate the difference between the two methods in Table 31.3, which shows what happens when A Corporation buys B Corporation, leading to a new AB Corporation. The two firms' initial balance sheets are shown at the top of the table. Below this we show what happens to the balance sheet when the two firms merge under the two different methods. We assume (under Purchase Method) that B Corporation has been purchased for ₹18 million, 180 percent of the book value. Similarly, we assume that A Corporation issues shares to the shareholders of the B Corporation (under the Pooling of Interests Method).

---

[26] Here, the term 'transferor company' refers to the merging company or the selling company. The term 'transferee company' refers to the buying company or the merged company.

TABLE 31.3 Accounting for the merger of A Corporation and B Corporation assuming that (**a**) A Corporation issues shares to the shareholders of B Corporation (under the pooling of interest method) and (**b**) A Corporation pays ₹18 million for B Corporation (Figures in ₹ millions)

Initial Balance Sheets							
A Corporation				**B Corporation**			
NWC	20	30	D	NWC	1	0	D
FA	80	70	E	FA	9	10	E
	100	100			10	10	
Balance Sheet of AB Corporation (Pooling of Interests Method)							
NWC	21	30	D				
FA	89	80	E				
	110	110					
Balance Sheet of AB Corporation (Purchase Method)							
NWC	21	30	D				
FA	89	88	E				
Goodwill	8						
	110	110					

Key: NWC = Net working capital (or net current assets)
FA: Net book value of fixed assets
D: Debt
E: Book value of equity

Under the pooling of interest method, the balance sheet of AB Corporation is arrived at by a line-by-line addition of the corresponding line items of the balance sheets of both the companies. Under the purchase method, the A Corporation will treat B Corporation as an acquisition investment and hence reports the assets (wherever possible) at the market values.

We assume that A Corporation pays ₹18 million to the shareholders of B Corporation under 'Purchase Method'. Why did A Corporation pay an ₹8 million premium over B's book value? There are two possible reasons. First, the true values of B's *tangible assets*—its working capital, plant, and equipment—may be greater than ₹10 million. We will assume that this is *not* the reason; that is, we assume that the assets listed on its balance sheet are valued there correctly.[27] Second, A Corporation may be paying for an *intangible asset* that is not listed on B Corporation's balance sheet. For example, the intangible asset may be a promising product or technology. Or it may be no more than B Corporation's share of the expected economic gains from the merger.

A Corporation is buying an asset worth ₹18 million. The problem is to show that asset on the left-hand side[28] of AB Corporation's balance sheet. B Corporation's tangible assets are worth only ₹10 million. This leaves ₹8 million. Under the purchase method, the accountant takes care of this by creating a new asset category called goodwill and assigning ₹8 million to it.[29] As long as the goodwill continues to be worth at least ₹8 million, it stays on the balance sheet and the company's earnings

---

[27] If B's tangible assets are worth more than their previous book values, they would be reappraised and their current values entered on AB Corporation's balance sheet.

[28] A die-hard fan of accounting in India may raise an objection to our showing assets on the left hand side. But how does it matter?

[29] If part of the $8 million consisted of payment for identifiable intangible assets such as patents, the accountant would place these under a separate category of assets. Identifiable intangible assets that have a finite life need to be written off over their life.

are unaffected.[30] Goodwill amortization can have a substantial impact on the reported net income if the premium paid is an acquisition is very large.

Some Tax Considerations[31]

In order to understand the tax implications of mergers under the Income Tax Act, 1961, we need to divide the mergers into two categories. Under Section 2(1B) of the IT Act, mergers satisfying the following conditions get different tax benefits mentioned under the various sections (Section 35, for example):

"All the property and liabilities of the amalgamating company (same as merging company) or companies immediately before the amalgamation (same as merger) must become part of the amalgamated company (same as merged company) by virtue of the amalgamation. Shareholders holding not less than nine-tenths in value of the shares in the amalgamating company or companies (other than shares already held therein immediately before the amalgamation by, or by a nominee for, the amalgamated company or its subsidiary) become shareholders of the amalgamated company by virtue of the amalgamation procedure."

Mergers that do not satisfy the above conditions do not get the tax benefits. It is therefore very important to design the merger transaction in such a way that the above conditions are satisfied. In most cases, when a merger is financed by the exchange of shares of the buying company, all the conditions will automatically get satisfied. However, special care needs to be taken when the buying company does not want to buy the entire business of the selling company. Let's assume that the selling company is into the manufacturing of cements and construction. The buying company is into cements only. Let's also assume that the buying company is not interested in acquiring the construction business of the selling company. However, in order to satisfy the requirements of Sec 2 (1B) of the Act, it needs to buy all the properties of the selling company, including the construction division. In India, companies usually follow one of the two approaches to directly avoid the provisions of the above section. The buying company can, for example, first buy all the properties of the selling company and then sell the constriction division to some other company. It can alternatively ask the selling company to spin off the cements division into a separate company and then merge with the newly-created cement company.

The merging company loses its identity after a merger, and this has a great significance for the estimation of tax benefits arising out of mergers. Under the provisions of the Income Tax Act, only the loss-making company can carry-forward the loss. The right to carry-forward is attached to the company and not to the assets of the company. Thus, for example, prior to the merger with Godrej Soaps Limited (GSL), Gujarat Godrej Innovative Chemicals Limited (GGICL) had accumulated losses of ₹95 crores in 1994. However, as per the IT Act in India, only GGICL could carry forward these losses. So Godrej Soaps got merged with GGICL to ensure that the identity of the loss-making company remains intact after the merger. And the merged entity (that is GGICL) changed its name to Godrej Soaps Limited with effect from January 6, 1995. This way, Godrej Soaps managed to retain its brand name and at the same time managed to set off the accumulated losses of GGICL against its own profit. Of course, Godrej Soaps could have obtained an approval under Sec 72A of the IT Act to carry forward the business losses of GGICL. However, the reverse merger route (where GGICL and *not* GSL is the merged company) is a preferred route because the merged entity can carry forward both

---

[30] In India, the goodwill arising out of such deals needs to be amortized by the buyer for tax purposes over a period of five years.

[31] For a detailed discussion on the tax considerations in case of mergers, refer to "Mergers et al" by S Ramanujam (2006), Chapter 20. Wadha Publication, Nagpur.

the business and capital losses and secondly, the merged entity does not have to face the bureaucratic hassles associated with managing BIFR.

Apart from income tax, one has also to consider stamp duties to be paid in case of mergers in India. Certain states like Maharashtra, Gujarat, Karnataka, Chhattisgarh, Madhya Pradesh, Andhra Pradesh and Rajasthan have made mergers under Section 391-394 of the Companies Act stampable. However, many other states have not. In Table 31.4, we mention the tax laws that one needs to keep in mind in the case of mergers in India.

TABLE 31.4 A brief description of some of the sections under the Income Tax Act of India that affect mergers.

Income Tax Act	Mergers
Sec 2 (1B)	Explains which mergers will get some tax benefits under Section 35
Sec 35 (5), 35A(6), 35D(5), 35E(7)	Benefits under these acts (which the merging company was getting prior to the merger) will continue to be available to the merged company, when merger satisfies the conditions laid down under Section 2(1B)
Sec 72A	If a profit making company acquires a loss making company, then it can continue to carry forward the business losses subject to certain conditions (including Section 32 of SICA)
Section 47	Explains when the exchange of shares in case of mergers will not be treated as capital gains

31-5 PROXY FIGHTS, TAKEOVERS, AND THE MARKET FOR CORPORATE CONTROL

The shareholders are the owners of the firm. But most shareholders do not feel like the boss, and with good reason. Try buying a share of IBM stock and marching into the boardroom for a chat with your employee, the chief executive officer.

The *ownership* and *management* of large corporations are separated. Shareholders elect the board of directors but have little direct say in most management decisions. Agency costs arise when managers or directors are tempted to make decisions that are not in the shareholders' interests.

As we pointed out in Chapter 1, there are many forces and constraints working to keep managers' and shareholders' interests in line. But what can be done to ensure that the board has engaged the most talented managers? What happens if managers are inadequate? What if the board is derelict in monitoring the performance of managers? Or what if the firm's managers are fine but the resources of the firm could be used more efficiently by merging with another firm? Can we count on managers to pursue policies that might put them out of a job?

These are all questions about the *market for corporate control,* the mechanism by which firms are matched up with owners and management teams, who can make the most of the firm's resources. You should not take a firm's current ownership and management for granted. If it is possible for the value of the firm to be enhanced by changing management or by reorganizing under new owners, there will be incentives for someone to make the change.

There are three ways to change the management of a firm: (1) a successful proxy contest in which a group of shareholders votes in a new board of directors who then pick a new management team, (2) a takeover of one company by another, and (3) a leveraged buyout of the firm by a private group of investors. We focus here on the first two methods and postpone discussion of buyouts until the next chapter.

Proxy Contests

Shareholders elect the board of directors to keep watch on management and replace unsatisfactory managers. If the board is lax, shareholders are free to elect a different board.

When a group of investors believes that the board and its management should be replaced, they can launch a proxy contest at the next annual meeting. A *proxy* is the right to vote another shareholder's shares. In a proxy contest, the dissident shareholders attempt to obtain enough proxies to elect their own slate to the board of directors. Once the new board is in control, management can be replaced and company policy changed. A proxy fight is therefore a direct contest for control of the corporation. Many proxy fights are initiated by major shareholders who consider the firm poorly managed. In other cases a fight may be a prelude to the merger of two firms. The proponent of the merger may believe that a new board will better appreciate the advantages of combining the two firms.

Proxy contests are expensive and difficult to win. Dissidents who engage in proxy fights must use their own money, but management can use the corporation's funds and lines of communications with shareholders to defend itself. To level the playing field somewhat, the SEC has proposed new rules to make it easier to mount a proxy fight. In the meantime, shareholders have found that simply voting against the reelection of existing directors can send a powerful signal. When Disney shareholders voted 43% of the shares against the reelection of Michael Eisner, the company's autocratic chairman, he heard the message and resigned the next day.

The threat of a proxy fight may also encourage management to change company policy. For example, in 2008 shareholder activist Carl Icahn indicated his intention to put himself forward for nomination to the board of Motorola. However, Icahn controlled less than 7% of the votes and failed to prevent the reelection of the existing board. Nevertheless the pressure from Icahn had an effect: Motorola agreed to nominate two new board members and to consult with Icahn about a possible spin off of the company's handset division.[32]

Takeovers

The alternative to a proxy fight is for the would-be acquirer to make a *tender offer* directly to the shareholders. If the offer is successful, the new owner is free to make any management changes. The management of the target firm may advise its shareholders to accept the offer, or it may fight the bid in the hope that the acquirer will either raise its offer or throw in the towel.

Tender offers in India are regulated by the SEBI (Substantial Acquisition of Shares and Takeovers) Regulations, 1997. Tender offers in India can be made by a hostile bidder, by a friendly outside bidder, or by the promoters of the company. The promoters of a company can, for example, make a tender offer to the public shareholders of a company to increase their stake in the company.

Most mergers in India are negotiated by the two firms' top management and boards of directors. And in most cases, the top management will be under the same business groups in India. From a list of 190 mergers that were announced between 1993 and 2001, we find that as many as 177 were mergers where both the merged and the merging companies were controlled by the same business group or management. In only 13 cases, the merged and the merging companies were controlled by unrelated management. Hostile takeovers are rare events in India.

In the United States the rules for tender offers are set largely by the Williams Act of 1968 and by state laws. The courts act as a referee to see that contests are conducted fairly. The problem in setting these rules is that it is unclear who requires protection. Should the management of the target firm be

---

[32] In Chapter 1 we also saw how in the same year Carl Icahn used the threat of a proxy fight to gain seats on the board of Yahoo! Inc.

given more weapons to defend itself against unwelcome predators? Or should it simply be encouraged to sit the game out? Or should it be obliged to conduct an auction to obtain the highest price for its shareholders? And what about would-be acquirers? Should they be forced to reveal their intentions at an early stage, or would that allow other firms to piggyback on their good ideas by entering bids of their own?[33] Keep these questions in mind as we review a recent takeover battle.

Oracle Bids for PeopleSoft

Hostile takeover bids tend to be less common in high-tech industries where an acrimonious takeover battle may cause many of the target's most valued staff to leave. Investors were therefore startled in June 2003 when the software giant, Oracle Corp, announced a $5.1 billion cash tender offer for its rival PeopleSoft. The offer price of $16 a share was only a modest 6% above the recent price of PeopleSoft stock. PeopleSoft's CEO angrily rejected the bid as dramatically undervaluing the business and accused Oracle of trying to disrupt PeopleSoft's business and to thwart its recently announced plan to merge with its smaller rival J.D. Edwards & Co. PeopleSoft immediately filed a suit claiming that Oracle's management had engaged in "acts of unfair trade practices" and had "disrupted PeopleSoft's customer relationships." In another suit J.D. Edwards claimed that Oracle had wrongly "interfered with its proposed merger with PeopleSoft" and demanded $1.7 billion in compensatory damages.

Oracle's bid was the opening salvo in a battle that was to last 18 months. Some of the key dates in this battle are set out in Table 31.5. PeopleSoft had several defenses at its disposal. First, it had in place a **poison pill** that would allow it to flood the market with additional shares if a predator acquired 20% of the stock. Second, the company instituted a customer-assurance program that offered customers money-back guarantees if an acquirer were to reduce customer support. At one point in the takeover battle the potential liability under this program reached nearly $1.6 billion. Third, elections to the PeopleSoft board were staggered, so that different directors came up for re-election in different years. This meant that it would take two annual meetings to replace a majority of PeopleSoft's board.

TABLE 31.5 Some key dates in the Oracle/PeopleSoft takeover battle.

Date	Event
June 6, 2003	Oracle offers cash of $16 a share for PeopleSoft stock, a premium of 6%.
June 18, 2003	Oracle increases offer to $19.50 a share.
February 4, 2004	Oracle raises offer to $26 a share.
February 26, 2004	Justice Department files suit to block deal. Oracle announces plans to appeal.
May 16, 2004	Oracle *reduces* offer to $21 a share.
September 9, 2004	Oracle wins appeal in a federal court against Department of Justice antitrust ruling.
September 27, 2004	Hearing begins in Delaware court of Oracle's request to overturn PeopleSoft's poison pill.
November 1, 2004	Oracle raises offer to $24 a share. Accepted in respect of 61% of PeopleSoft shares.
November 23, 2004	Oracle announces plans to mount a proxy fight by naming four nominees for PeopleSoft's board.
December 13, 2004	Oracle raises offer to $26.50 a share. Accepted by PeopleSoft's board.

Oracle not only had to overcome PeopleSoft's defenses, but it also had to clear possible antitrust roadblocks. Connecticut's attorney general instituted an antitrust action to block Oracle's bid, in

---

[33] The Williams Act obliges firms who own 5% or more of another company's shares to tip their hand by reporting their holding in a Schedule 13(d) filing with the SEC.

part to protect his state's considerable investment in PeopleSoft software. Then an investigation of the deal by the U.S. Department of Justice ruled that the deal was anticompetitive. Normally such an objection is enough to kill a deal, but Oracle was persistent and successfully appealed the ruling in a federal court.

While these battles were being fought out, Oracle revised its offer four times. It upped its offer first to $19.50 and then to $26 a share. Then, in an effort to put pressure on PeopleSoft shareholders, Oracle *reduced* its offer to $21 a share, citing a drop of 28% in the price of PeopleSoft's shares. Six months later it raised the offer again to $24 a share, warning investors that it would walk away if the offer was not accepted by PeopleSoft's board or a majority of PeopleSoft shareholders.

Sixty percent of PeopleSoft's shareholders indicated that they wished to accept this last offer, but before Oracle could gain control of PeopleSoft, it still needed the company to get rid of the poison pill and customer-assurance scheme. That meant putting pressure on PeopleSoft's management, which had continued to reject every approach. Oracle tried two tactics. First it initiated a proxy fight to change the composition of PeopleSoft's board. Second, it filed a suit in a Delaware court alleging that PeopleSoft's management breached its fiduciary duty by trying to thwart Oracle's offer and not giving it "due consideration." The lawsuit asked the court to require PeopleSoft to dismantle its takeover defenses, including the poison-pill plan and the customer-assurance program.

PeopleSoft's CEO had at one point said that he "could imagine no price nor combination of price and other conditions to recommend accepting the offer." But with 60% of PeopleSoft's shareholders in favor of taking Oracle's latest offer, it was becoming less easy for the company to keep saying no, and many observers were starting to question whether PeopleSoft's management was acting in shareholders' interest. If management showed itself deaf to shareholders' interests, the court could well rule in favor of Oracle, or disgruntled shareholders might vote to change the composition of the PeopleSoft board. PeopleSoft's directors therefore decided to be less intransigent and testified at the Delaware trial that they would consider negotiating with Oracle if it were to offer $26.50 or $27 a share. This was the breakthrough that Oracle was looking for. It upped its offer immediately to $26.50 a share, PeopleSoft lifted its defenses, and within a month 97% of PeopleSoft's shareholders had agreed to the bid. After 18 months of punch and counterpunch the battle for PeopleSoft was over.

Takeover Defenses

What are the lessons from the battle for PeopleSoft? First, the example illustrates some of the stratagems of modern merger warfare. Firms like PeopleSoft that are worried about being taken over usually prepare their defenses in advance. Often they persuade shareholders to agree to **shark-repellent** changes to the corporate charter. For example, the charter may be amended to require that any merger must be approved by a *supermajority* of 80% of the shares rather than the normal 50%. Although shareholders are generally prepared to go along with management's proposals, it is doubtful whether such shark-repellent defenses are truly in their interest. Managers who are protected from takeover appear to enjoy higher remuneration and to generate less wealth for their shareholders.[34]

Many firms follow PeopleSoft's example and deter potential bidders by devising poison pills that make the company unappetizing. For example, the poison pill may give existing shareholders the right to buy the company's shares at half price as soon as a bidder acquires more than 15% of the shares. The bidder is not entitled to the discount. Thus the bidder resembles Tantalus—as soon as it has

---

[34] A. Agarwal and C. R. Knoeber, "Managerial Compensation and the Threat of Takeover," *Journal of Financial Economics* 47 (February 1998), pp. 219–239; and P. A. Gompers, J. L. Ishii, and A. Metrick, "Corporate Governance and Equity Prices," *Quarterly Journal of Economics* 118 (2003), pp. 107–155.

acquired 15% of the shares, control is lifted away from its reach. These and other lines of defense are summarized in Table 31.6.

TABLE 31.6 A summary of takeover defenses.

Preoffer Defenses	Description
Shark-repellent charter amendments:	
Staggered board	The board is classified into three equal groups. Only one group is elected each year. Therefore the bidder cannot gain control of the target immediately.
Supermajority	A high percentage of shares, typically 80%, is needed to approve a merger.
Fair price	Mergers are restricted unless a fair price (determined by formula or appraisal) is paid.
Restricted voting rights	Shareholders who acquire more than a specified proportion of the target have no voting rights unless approved by the target's board.
Waiting period	Unwelcome acquirers must wait for a specified number of years before they can complete the merger.
Other:	
Poison pill	Existing shareholders are issued rights that, if there is a significant purchase of shares by a bidder, can be used to purchase additional stock in the company at a bargain price.
Poison put	Existing bondholders can demand repayment if there is a change of control as a result of a hostile takeover.
Postoffer Defenses	
Litigation	Target files suit against bidder for violating antitrust or securities laws.
Asset restructuring	Target buys assets that bidder does not want or that will create an antitrust problem.
Liability restructuring	Target issues shares to a friendly third party, increases the number of shareholders, or repurchases shares from existing shareholders at a premium.

Why did PeopleSoft's management contest the takeover bid? One possible reason was to extract a higher price for the stock, for Oracle was ultimately forced to pay 66% more than its original offer. But the comment by PeopleSoft's CEO that he could imagine no price at which the merger would be welcome suggests that the defensive tactics may have been intended to defeat the bid and protect managers' positions with the firm.

Companies sometimes reduce these conflicts of interest by offering their managers **golden parachutes,** that is, generous payoffs if the managers lose their jobs as a result of a takeover. It may seem odd to reward managers for being taken over. However, if a soft landing overcomes their opposition to takeover bids, a few million may be a small price to pay.

Any management team that tries to develop improved weapons of defense must expect challenge in the courts. In the early 1980s the courts tended to give managers the benefit of the doubt and respect their business judgment about whether a takeover should be resisted. But the courts' attitudes to takeover battles have changed. For example, in 1993 a court blocked Viacom's agreed takeover of Paramount on the grounds that Paramount directors did not do their homework before turning down a higher offer from QVC. Paramount was forced to give up its poison-pill defense and the stock options that it had offered to Viacom. Such decisions have led managers to become more careful in opposing bids, and they do not throw themselves blindly into the arms of any white knight.[35]

At the same time governments have provided some new defensive weapons. In 1987 the Supreme Court upheld state laws that allow companies to deprive an investor of voting rights as soon as the investor's share in the company exceeds a certain level. Since then state antitakeover laws have proliferated. Many allow boards of directors to block mergers with hostile bidders for several years and to consider the interests of employees, customers, suppliers, and their communities in deciding whether to try to block a hostile bid.

Anglo-Saxon countries used to have a near-monopoly on hostile takeovers. That is no longer the case. Takeover activity in Europe now exceeds that in the United States, and in recent years some of the most bitterly contested takeovers have involved European companies. For example, Mittal's $27 billion takeover of Arcelor resulted from a fierce and highly politicized five-month battle. Arcelor used every defense in the book—including inviting a Russian company to become a leading shareholder.

Mittal is now based in Europe, but it began operations in Indonesia. This illustrates another change in the merger market: Acquirers are no longer confined to the major industrialized countries. They now include Brazilian, Russian, Indian, and Chinese companies. For example, Tetley Tea, Anglo-Dutch steelmaker Corus, and Jaguar and Land Rover have all been acquired by Indian conglomerate Tata Group. IBM's personal computer business has been bought by the Chinese company Lenovo, and Inco, the Canadian nickel producer, is now owned by Brazil's Vale.

Who Gains Most in Mergers?

As our brief history illustrates, in mergers sellers generally do better than buyers. Andrade, Mitchell, and Stafford found that following the announcement of the bid, selling shareholders received a healthy gain averaging 16%.[36] The overall value of the merging firms, buyer and seller combined, increases by about 2% on average. Thus the merging firms are worth more together than apart. But it seems that the stock prices of the acquiring firms *decline* on average.[37]

Why do so many firms make acquisitions that appear to destroy value? One explanation appeals to behavioral traits; the managers of acquiring firms may be driven by hubris or overconfidence in their ability to run the target firm better than its existing management. This may well be so, but we should not dismiss more charitable explanations. For example, McCardle and Viswanathan have pointed out that firms can enter a market either by building a new plant or by buying an existing business. If the market is not growing, it makes more sense for the firm to expand by acquisition. Hence, when it announces the acquisition, firm value may drop simply because investors conclude that the market is no longer growing. The acquisition in this case does not destroy value; it just signals the stagnant state of the market.[38]

Why do sellers earn higher returns? There are two reasons. First, buying firms are typically larger than selling firms. In many mergers the buyer is so much larger that even substantial net benefits would not show up clearly in the buyer's share price. Suppose, for example, that company A buys

---

[35] In 1985 a shiver ran through many boardrooms when the directors of Trans Union Corporation were held personally liable for being too hasty in accepting a takeover bid.

[36] G. Andrade, M. Mitchell, and E. Stafford, "New Evidence and Pespectives on Mergers," *Journal of Economics Perspectives* 15 (Spring 2001), pp. 103–120.

[37] One recent study found that the losers were mainly the largest acquirers; the stockholders of the other acquirers appeared to gain. See S. B. Moeller, F. P. Schlingemann, and R. Stulz, "Firm Size and the Gains from Acquisitions," *Journal of Financial Economics* 73 (August 2004), pp. 201–228.

[38] K. F. McCardle and S. Viswanathan, "The Direct Entry versus Takeover Decision and Stock Price Performance around Takeovers," *Journal of Business* 67 (January 1994), pp. 1–43.

company B, which is only one-tenth A's size. Suppose the dollar value of the net gain from the merger is split equally between A and B.[39] Each company's shareholders receive the same *dollar* profit, but B's receive 10 times A's *percentage* return.

The second, and more important, reason is the competition among potential bidders. Once the first bidder puts the target company "in play," one or more additional suitors often jump in, sometimes as white knights at the invitation of the target firm's management. Every time one suitor tops another's bid, more of the merger gain slides toward the target. At the same time, the target firm's management may mount various legal and financial counterattacks, ensuring that capitulation, if and when it comes, is at the highest attainable price.

Of course, bidders and targets are not the only possible winners. Unsuccessful bidders often win, too, by selling off their holdings in target companies at substantial profits.

Other winners include investment bankers, lawyers, accountants, and in some cases arbitrageurs such as hedge funds, which speculate on the likely success of takeover bids.[40] "Speculate" has a negative ring, but it can be a useful social service. A tender offer may present shareholders with a difficult decision. Should they accept, should they wait to see if someone else produces a better offer, or should they sell their stock in the market? This dilemma presents an opportunity for hedge funds, which specialize in answering such questions. In other words, they buy from the target's shareholders and take on the risk that the deal will not go through.

31-6 MERGERS AND THE ECONOMY

Merger Waves

Figure 31.3 shows the number of mergers in the United States for each year from 1962 to 2008. Notice that mergers come in waves. There was an upsurge in merger activity from 1967 to 1969 and then again in the late 1980s and 1990s. Another merger boom got under way in 2003, only to peter out with the onset of the credit crisis.

We don't really understand why merger activity is so volatile. If mergers are prompted by economic motives, at least one of these motives must be "here today and gone tomorrow," and it must somehow be associated with high stock prices. But none of the economic motives that we review in this chapter has anything to do with the general level of the stock market. None burst on the scene in 1967, departed in 1970, and reappeared for most of the 1980s and again in the mid-1990s and early 2000s.

Some mergers may result from mistakes in valuation on the part of the stock market. In other words, the buyer may believe that investors have underestimated the value of the seller or may hope that they *will* overestimate the value of the combined firm. But we see (with hindsight) that mistakes are made in bear markets as well as bull markets. Why don't we see just as many firms hunting for bargain acquisitions when the stock market is low? It is possible that "suckers are born every minute," but it is difficult to believe that they can be harvested only in bull markets.

Merger activity tends to be concentrated in a relatively small number of industries and is often prompted by deregulation and by changes in technology or the pattern of demand. For example, deregulation of telecoms and banking in the 1990s led to a spate of mergers in both industries. Andrade, Mitchell, and Stafford found that about half of the value of all U.S. mergers between 1988

---

[39] In other words, the *cost* of the merger to A is one-half the gain ΔPV_{AB}.

[40] Strictly speaking, an arbitrageur is an investor who takes a fully hedged, that is, riskless, position. But arbitrageurs in merger battles often take very large risks indeed. Their activities are known as "risk arbitrage."

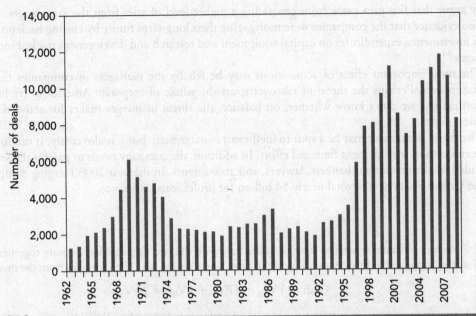

FIGURE 31.3

The number of mergers in the United States, 1962–2008.

Source: Mergerstat, **www.mergerstat.com**.

and 1998 occurred in industries that had been deregulated.[41]

Do Mergers Generate Net Benefits?

There are undoubtedly good acquisitions and bad acquisitions, but economists find it hard to agree on whether acquisitions are beneficial *on balance.* Indeed, since there seem to be transient fashions in mergers, it would be surprising if economists could come up with simple generalizations.

We do know that mergers generate substantial gains to acquired firms' stockholders and overall gains in the value of the two merging firms. But not everybody is convinced. Some believe that investors react to mergers with short-run enthusiasm and don't give enough critical attention to long-term prospects.

Since we can't observe how companies would have fared in the absence of a merger, it is difficult to measure the long-run effects on profitability. Ravenscroft and Scherer, who looked at mergers during the 1960s and early 1970s, argued that productivity declined in the years following a merger.[42] But studies of subsequent merger activity suggest that mergers *do* seem to improve real productivity. For example, Paul Healy, Krishna Palepu, and Richard Ruback examined 50 large mergers between 1979 and 1983 and found an average increase of 2.4 percentage points in the companies' pretax returns.[43]

[41] See Footnote 24. See also J. Harford, "What Drives Merger Waves?" *Journal of Financial Economics* 77 (September 2005), pp. 529–560.

[42] See D. J. Ravenscroft and F. M. Scherer, "Mergers and Managerial Performance," in *Knights, Raiders, and Targets: The Impact of the Hostile Takeover* ed. J. C. Coffee, Jr., L. Lowenstein, and S. Rose-Ackerman (New York: Oxford University Press, 1988).

[43] See P. Healy, K. Palepu, and R. Ruback, "Does Corporate Performance Improve after Mergers?" *Journal of Financial Economics* 31 (April 1992), pp. 135–175. The study examined the pretax returns of the merged companies relative to industry averages. A study by Lichtenberg and Siegel came to similar conclusions. Before merger, acquired companies had lower levels of productivity than did other firms in their industries, but by seven years after the control change, two-thirds of the productivity gap had been eliminated. See F. Lichtenberg and D. Siegel, "The Effect of Control Changes on the Productivity of U.S. Manufacturing Plants," *Journal of Applied Corporate Finance* 2 (Summer 1989), pp. 60–67.

They argue that this gain came from generating a higher level of sales from the same assets. There was no evidence that the companies were mortgaging their long-term future by cutting back on long-term investments; expenditures on capital equipment and research and development tracked industry averages.[44]

The most important effect of acquisitions may be felt by the managers of companies that are *not* taken over. Perhaps the threat of takeover spurs the whole of corporate America to try harder. Unfortunately, we don't know whether, on balance, the threat of merger makes for active days or sleepless nights.

The threat of takeover may be a spur to inefficient management, but it is also costly. It can soak up large amounts of management time and effort. In addition, the company needs to pay for the services provided by the investment bankers, lawyers, and accountants. In the year 2006 merging companies in the United States paid in total nearly $4 billion for professional assistance.

SUMMARY

A merger generates synergies—that is, added value—if the two firms are worth more together than apart. Suppose that firms A and B merge to form a new entity, AB. Then the gain from the merger is

$$\text{Gain} = PV_{AB} - (PV_A + PV_B) = \Delta PV_{AB}$$

Gains from mergers may reflect economies of scale, economies of vertical integration, improved efficiency, the combination of complementary resources, or redeployment of surplus funds. In some cases the object is to install a more efficient management team or to force shrinkage and consolidation in an industry with excess capacity or too many small, inefficient companies. There are also dubious reasons for mergers. There is no value added by merging just to diversify risks, to reduce borrowing costs, or to pump up earnings per share.

You should go ahead with the acquisition if the gain exceeds the cost. Cost is the premium that the buyer pays for the selling firm over its value as a separate entity. It is easy to estimate when the merger is financed by cash. In that case,

$$\text{Cost} = \text{cash paid} - PV_B$$

When payment is in the form of shares, the cost naturally depends on what those shares are worth after the merger is complete. If the merger is a success, B's stockholders will share the merger gains.

The mechanics of buying a firm are much more complex than those of buying a machine. First, you have to make sure that the purchase does not fall afoul of the antitrust laws. Second, you have a choice of procedures: You can merge all the assets and liabilities of the seller into those of your own company; you can buy the stock of the seller rather than the company itself; or you can buy the individual assets of the seller. Third, you have to worry about the tax status of the merger.

Mergers are often amicably negotiated between the management and directors of the two companies; but if the seller is reluctant, the would-be buyer can decide to make a tender offer. We sketched some of the offensive and defensive tactics used in takeover battles. We also observed that when the target firm loses, its shareholders typically win: selling shareholders earn large abnormal returns, while the bidding firm's shareholders roughly break even. The typical merger appears to

[44] Maintained levels of capital spending and R&D are also observed by Lichtenberg and Siegel, "The Effect of Control Changes on the Productivity of U.S. Manufacturing Plants," *Journal of Applied Corporate Finance* 2 (Summer 1989), pp. 60-67; and B. H. Hall, "The Effect of Takeover Activity on Corporate Research and Development," in *Corporate Takeover: Causes and Consequences* ed. A. J. Auerbach (Chicago: University of Chicago Press, 1988).

generate positive net benefits for investors, but competition among bidders, plus active defense by target management, pushes most of the gains toward the selling shareholders.

Mergers come and go in waves. The most recent wave, which peaked in 2006, consisted mostly of horizontal mergers. Merger activity thrives in periods of economic expansion and buoyant stock prices. Mergers are most frequent in industries that are coping with change, for example, changes in technology or regulation. The wave of mergers in banking and telecoms, for instance, can be traced to deregulation of these industries in the 1990s.

FURTHER READING

Here are three general works on mergers:

R. Bruner, *Applied Mergers and Acquisitions* (Hoboken, NJ: John Wiley & Sons, 2004).

J. F. Weston, M. L. Mitchell, and J. H. Mulherin, *Takeovers, Restructuring and Corporate Governance,* 4th ed. (Upper Saddle River, NJ: Prentice-Hall 2000).

S. Betton, B. E. Eckbo, and K. S. Thorburn, "Corporate Takeovers," in B. E. Eckbo (ed.), *Handbook of Empirical Corporate Finance* (Amsterdam: Elsevier/North-Holland, 2007), chapter 15.

Recent merger waves are reviewed in:

G. Andrade, M. Mitchell, and E. Stafford, "New Evidence and Perspectives on Mergers," *Journal of Economic Perspectives* 15 (Spring 2001), pp. 103–120.

S. J. Everett, "The Cross-Border Mergers and Acquisitions Wave of the Late 1990s," in R. E. Baldwin and L. A. Winters (eds.), *Challenges to Globalization* (Chicago: University of Chicago Press, 2004).

J. Harford, "What Drives Merger Waves?" *Journal of Financial Economics* 77 (September 2005), pp. 529–560.

B. Holmstrom and S. N. Kaplan, "Corporate Governance and Merger Activity in the U.S.: Making Sense of the 1980s and 1990s," *Journal of Economic Perspectives* 15 (Spring 2001), pp. 121–144.

Finally, here are some informative case studies:

S. N. Kaplan (ed.), *Mergers and Productivity* (Chicago: University of Chicago Press, 2000). This is a collection of case studies.

R. Bruner, "An Analysis of Value Destruction and Recovery in the Alliance and Proposed Merger of Volvo and Renault," *Journal of Financial Economics* 51 (1999), pp. 125–166.

PROBLEM SETS

BASIC

1. Are the following hypothetical mergers horizontal, vertical, or conglomerate?
   a. Infosys acquires TCS.
   b. Wipro acquires Pritish Nandy Communications.
   c. Tata Motors acquires Shriram Transport Finance Company.
   d. Maruti Udyog Limited acquires MRF Tyres.
2. Which of the following motives for mergers make economic sense?
   a. Merging to achieve economies of scale.
   b. Merging to reduce risk by diversification.
   c. Merging to redeploy cash generated by a firm with ample profits but limited growth opportunities.

    d. Merging to combine complementary resources.

    e. Merging just to increase earnings per share.

3. Velcro Saddles is contemplating the acquisition of Pogo Ski Sticks, Inc. The values of the two companies as separate entities are ₹20 million and ₹10 million, respectively. Velcro Saddles estimates that by combining the two companies, it will reduce marketing and administrative costs by ₹500,000 per year in perpetuity. Velcro Saddles can either pay ₹14 million cash for Pogo or offer Pogo a 50% holding in Velcro Saddles. The opportunity cost of capital is 10%.

    a. What is the gain from merger?

    b. What is the cost of the cash offer?

    c. What is the cost of the stock alternative?

    d. What is the NPV of the acquisition under the cash offer?

    e. What is its NPV under the stock offer?

4. In which of the following mergers, the merged company will not get Sec 2(1B) benefits of the Income Tax Act of India?

    a. The merged company acquires the merging company by exchanging preference shares for the equity shares of the merging company.

    b. The merged company acquires the merging company by exchanging zero-coupon bonds for the equity shares of the merging company.

5. True or false?

    a. Sellers almost always gain in mergers.

    b. Buyers usually gain more than sellers.

    c. Firms that do unusually well tend to be acquisition targets.

    d. Merger activity in the United States varies dramatically from year to year.

    e. On the average, mergers produce large economic gains.

    f. Tender offers require the approval of the selling firm's management.

    g. The cost of a merger to the buyer equals the gain realized by the seller.

6. Briefly define the following terms:

    a. Purchase accounting

    b. Tender offer

    c. Poison pill

    d. Golden parachute

    e. Synergy

INTERMEDIATE

7. Tata Steel acquired acquired NatSteel of Singapore in August 2004, 40% stake in Millennium Steel of Thailand in 2005 and Corus, an Anglo-Dutch company, in 2006. Download the background material for these three acquisitions and identify the principal motive for acquisition in each case.

8. Examine a recent merger in which at least part of the payment made to the seller was in the form of stock. Use stock market prices to obtain an estimate of the gain from the merger and the cost of the merger.

9. Respond to the following comments.

    a. "Our cost of debt is too darn high, but our banks won't reduce interest rates as long as we're stuck in this volatile widget-trading business. We've got to acquire other companies with safer income streams."

    b. "Merge with Fledgling Electronics? No way! Their P/E's too high. That deal would knock 20% off our earnings per share."

c. "Our stock's at an all-time high. It's time to make our offer for Digital Organics. Sure, we'll have to offer a hefty premium to Digital stockholders, but we don't have to pay in cash. We'll give them new shares of our stock."

10. Sometimes the stock price of a possible target company rises in anticipation of a merger bid. Explain how this complicates the bidder's evaluation of the target company.

11. Suppose you obtain special information—information unavailable to investors—indicating that L&T's stock price is 40% undervalued. Is that a reason to launch a takeover bid for L&T? Explain carefully.

12. As treasurer of Leisure Products, Inc., you are investigating the possible acquisition of Plastitoys. You have the following basic data:

	Leisure Products	Plastitoys
Earnings per share	₹5.00	₹1.50
Dividend per share	₹3.00	₹.80
Number of shares	1,000,000	600,000
Stock price	₹90	₹20

You estimate that investors currently expect a steady growth of about 6% in Plastitoys' earnings and dividends. Under new management this growth rate would be increased to 8% per year, without any additional capital investment required.

a. What is the gain from the acquisition?

b. What is the cost of the acquisition if Leisure Products pays ₹25 in cash for each share of Plastitoys?

c. What is the cost of the acquisition if Leisure Products offers one share of Leisure Products for every three shares of Plastitoys?

d. How would the cost of the cash offer and the share offer alter if the expected growth rate of Plastitoys were not changed by the merger?

13. The Muck and Slurry merger has fallen through (see Section 31-2). But World Enterprises is determined to report earnings per share of $2.67. It therefore acquires the Wheelrim and Axle Company. You are given the following facts:

	World Enterprises	Wheelrim and Axle	Merged Firm
Earnings per share	$2.00	$2.50	$2.67
Price per share	$40	$25	?
Price–earnings ratio	20	10	?
Number of shares	100,000	200,000	?
Total earnings	$200,000	$500,000	?
Total market value	$4,000,000	$5,000,000	?

Once again there are no gains from merging. In exchange for Wheelrim and Axle shares, World Enterprises issues just enough of its own shares to ensure its $2.67 earnings per share objective.

a. Complete the above table for the merged firm.

b. How many shares of World Enterprises are exchanged for each share of Wheelrim and Axle?

c. What is the cost of the merger to World Enterprises?

d. What is the change in the total market value of the World Enterprises shares that were outstanding before the merger?

14. Explain the difference between merger and reverse merger. If you are the CFO of a company that plans to acquire a sick company, what factors (pertaining to the Income Tax Act of India) should you take into consideration?

15. Look again at Table 31.3. Suppose that B Corporation's fixed assets are reexamined and found to be worth ₹12 million instead of ₹9 million. How would this affect the AB Corporation's balance sheet under purchase accounting? How about pooling of interest accounting? How would the value of AB Corporation change under the purchase method? Would your answer depend on whether the merger is taxable?

CHALLENGE

16. Examine a hostile acquisition is the U.S. and discuss the tactics employed by both the predator and the target companies. Do you think that the management of the target firm was trying to defeat the bid or to secure the highest price for its stockholders? How did each announcement by the protagonists affect their stock prices?

17. How do you think mergers should be regulated? For example, what defenses should target companies be allowed to employ? Should managers of target firms be compelled to seek out the highest bids? Should they simply be passive and watch from the sidelines?

APPENDIX

CONGLOMERATE MERGERS AND VALUE ADDITIVITY

A pure conglomerate merger is one that has no effect on the operations or profitability of either firm. If corporate diversification is in stockholders' interests, a conglomerate merger would give a clear demonstration of its benefits. But if present values add up, the conglomerate merger would not make stockholders better or worse off.

In this appendix we examine more carefully our assertion that present values add. It turns out that values *do* add as long as capital markets are perfect and investors' diversification opportunities are unrestricted.

Call the merging firms A and B. Value additivity implies

$$PV_{AB} = PV_A + PV_B$$

where

$$PV_{AB} = \text{market value of combined firms just after merger}$$

$$PV_A, PV_B = \text{separate market values of A and B just before merger}$$

For example, we might have

$$PV_A = ₹100 \text{ million } (₹200 \text{ per share} \times 500{,}000 \text{ shares outstanding})$$

and

$$PV_B = ₹200 \text{ million } (₹200 \text{ per share} \times 1{,}000{,}000 \text{ shares outstanding})$$

Suppose A and B are merged into a new firm, AB, with one share in AB exchanged for each share of A or B. Thus there are 1,500,000 AB shares issued. *If* value additivity holds, then PV_{AB} must equal the sum of the separate values of A and B just before the merger, that is, ₹300 million. That would imply a price of ₹200 per share of AB stock.

But note that the AB shares represent a portfolio of the assets of A and B. Before the merger investors could have bought one share of A and two of B for ₹600. Afterward they can obtain a claim on *exactly* the same real assets by buying three shares of AB.

Suppose that the opening price of AB shares just after the merger is ₹200, so that $PV_{AB} = PV_A + PV_B$. Our problem is to determine if this is an equilibrium price, that is, whether we can rule out excess demand or supply at this price.

For there to be excess demand, there must be some investors who are willing to increase their holdings of A and B as a consequence of the merger. Who could they be? The only thing new created by the merger is diversification, but those investors who want to hold assets of A *and* B will have purchased A's and B's stock before the merger. The diversification is redundant and consequently won't attract new investment demand.

Is there a possibility of excess supply? The answer is yes. For example, there will be some shareholders in A who did not invest in B. After the merger they cannot invest solely in A, but only in a fixed combination of A and B. Their AB shares will be less attractive to them than the pure A shares, so they will sell part of or all their AB stock. In fact, the only AB shareholders who will *not* wish to sell are those who happened to hold A and B in exactly a 1:2 ratio in their premerger portfolios!

Since there is no possibility of excess demand but a definite possibility of excess supply, we seem to have

$$PV_{AB} \leq PV_A + PV_B$$

That is, corporate diversification can't help, but it may hurt investors by restricting the types of portfolios they can hold. This is not the whole story, however, since investment demand for AB shares might be attracted from other sources if PV_{AB} drops below $PV_A + PV_B$. To illustrate, suppose there are two other firms, A^* and B^*, which are judged by investors to have the same risk characteristics as A and B, respectively. Then before the merger,

$$r_A = r_{A^*} \quad \text{and} \quad r_B = r_{B^*}$$

where r is the rate of return expected by investors. We'll assume $r_A = r_{A^*} = .08$ and $r_B = r_{B^*} = .20$.

Consider a portfolio invested one-third in A^* and two-thirds in B^*. This portfolio offers an expected return of 16%:

$$r = x_{A^*}r_{A^*} + x_{B^*}r_{B^*}$$
$$= \tfrac{1}{3}(.08) + \tfrac{2}{3}(.20) = .16$$

A similar portfolio of A and B before their merger also offered a 16% return.

As we have noted, a new firm AB is really a portfolio of firms A and B, with portfolio weights of $\tfrac{1}{3}$ and $\tfrac{2}{3}$. It is therefore equivalent in risk to the portfolio of A^* and B^*. Thus the price of AB shares must adjust so that it likewise offers a 16% return.

What if AB shares drop below ₹200, so that PV_{AB} is less than $PV_A + PV_B$? Since the assets and earnings of firms A and B are the same, the price drop means that the expected rate of return on AB shares has risen above the return offered by the A^*B^* portfolio. That is, if r_{AB} exceeds $\tfrac{1}{3}r_A + \tfrac{2}{3}r_B$, then r_{AB} must also exceed $\tfrac{1}{3}r_{A^*} + \tfrac{2}{3}r_{B^*}$. But this is untenable: Investors A^* and B^* could sell part of their holdings (in a 1:2 ratio), buy AB, and obtain a higher expected rate of return with no increase in risk.

On the other hand, if PV_{AB} rises above $PV_A + PV_B$, the AB shares will offer an expected return less than that offered by the A^*B^* portfolio. Investors will unload the AB shares, forcing their price down.

A stable result occurs only if AB shares stick at ₹200. Thus, value additivity will hold exactly in a perfect-market equilibrium if there are ample substitutes for the A and B assets. If A and B have unique risk characteristics, however, then PV_{AB} can fall below $PV_A + PV_B$. The reason is that the merger curtails investors' opportunity to tailor their portfolios to their own needs and preferences. This makes investors worse off, reducing the attractiveness of holding the shares of firm AB.

In general, the condition for value additivity is that investors' opportunity set—that is, the range of risk characteristics attainable by investors through their portfolio choices—is independent of the particular portfolio of real assets held by the firm. Diversification per se can never expand the opportunity set given perfect security markets. Corporate diversification may reduce the investors' opportunity set, but only if the real assets the corporations hold lack substitutes among traded securities or portfolios.

In a few cases the firm may be able to expand the opportunity set. It can do so if it finds an investment opportunity that is unique—a real asset with risk characteristics shared by few or no other financial assets. In this lucky event the firm should not diversify, however. It should set up the unique asset as a separate firm so as to expand investors' opportunity set to the maximum extent. If Gallo by chance discovered that a small portion of its vineyards produced wine comparable to Chateau Margaux, it would not throw that wine into the Hearty Burgundy vat.

32

CHAPTER

CORPORATE RESTRUCTURING

In the last chapter we described how mergers and acquisitions enable companies to change their ownership and management teams, and often force major shifts in corporate strategy. But this is not the only way that company structure can be altered. In this chapter we look at a variety of other mechanisms for changing ownership and control, including leveraged buyouts (LBOs), spin-offs and carve-outs, nationalizations and privatizations, workouts, and bankruptcy.

The first section starts with a famous takeover battle, the leveraged buyout of RJR Nabisco. The rest of Sections 32-1 and 32-2 offers a general review of LBOs, spin-offs, and privatizations. The main point of these transactions is not just to change control, although existing management is often booted out, but also to change incentives for managers and improve financial performance.

RJR Nabisco was an early example of a **private-equity** deal. Section 32-3 takes a closer look at how private-equity investment funds are structured and how the private-equity business has developed since the 1980s.

Private-equity funds usually end up holding a portfolio of companies in different industries. In this respect they resemble the conglomerates that dominated takeover activity in the 1960s and 1970s. These conglomerates are mostly gone—it seems that private equity is a superior financial technology for doing the tasks that conglomerates used to do. Our review of conglomerates' weaknesses helps us to understand the strengths of private equity.

Some companies choose to restructure but others have it thrust upon them. None more so than those that fall on hard times and can no longer service their debts. The chapter therefore concludes by looking at how distressed companies either work out a solution with their debtors or go through a formal bankruptcy process.

32-1 LEVERAGED BUYOUTS

Leveraged buyouts (LBOs) differ from ordinary acquisitions in two immediately obvious ways. First, a large fraction of the purchase price is financed by debt. Some, if not all, of its debt is usually junk, that is, below investment-grade. Thus, for example, when Tata Steel acquired Corus in 2007, $5.6 billion of the total acquisition cost of $11.3 billion was financed through debt (including $2.6 billion of below investment grade loan). Second, usually after the LBO, the company goes private and its shares no longer trade on the open market. The LBO's stock is held by partnership of (usually institutional) investors and is often referred to as **private equity.** When the group is led by the company's management, the transaction is called a **management buyout (MBO).**

In the 1970s and 1980s many MBOs were arranged for unwanted divisions of large diversified companies. Smaller divisions outside the companies' main line of business sometimes failed to attract top management's interest and commitment, and divisional management chafed under corporate bureaucracy. Many such divisions flowered when spun off as MBOs. Their managers, pushed by the need to generate cash for debt service and encouraged by a substantial personal stake in the business, found ways to cut costs and compete more effectively.

In the 1980s, LBO activity shifted to buyouts of entire businesses, including large, mature, public corporations. Table 32.1 lists the largest LBOs of the 1980s, plus a sample of more-recent transactions.

Table 32.1 starts with the largest, most dramatic, and best documented LBO of the 1980s, the $25 billion takeover of RJR Nabisco by Kohlberg, Kravis, Roberts (KKR). The players, tactics, and controversies of LBOs are writ large in this case.

TABLE 32.1 The 10 largest LBOs of the 1980s, plus examples of more-recent deals (values in $ millions).

Industry	Acquirer	Target	Year	Value ($ billions)
Food, tobacco	KKR	RJR Nabisco	1989	$24.7
Food	KKR	Beatrice	1986	6.3
Glass	KKR	Owens-Illinois	1987	4.7
Supermarkets	KKR	Safeway	1986	4.2
Convenience stores	Thompson Co.	Southland (7-11)	1987	4.0
Airlines	Wings Holdings	NWA, Inc.	1989	3.7
Utilities	TPG, KKR	TXU	2007	45.0
Real estate	Blackstone Gp	Equity Office Properties	2007	38.9
Entertainment	Apollo Management Texas Pacific Group	Harrah's Entertainment	2008	31.3
Credit card processing	KKR	First Data	2007	29.0
Hotels	Blackstone	Hilton	2007	26.9
Pipelines	Management, several private-equity groups.	Kinder Morgan	2007	21.6
Radio	Thomas Lee, Bain Capital	Clear Channel Communications	2007	19.4

Source: Mergers and Acquisitions, various issues.

RJR Nabisco

In October 1988 the board of directors of RJR Nabisco revealed that Ross Johnson, the company's chief executive officer, had formed a group of investors that proposed to buy all RJR's stock for $75 per share in cash and take the company private. RJR's share price immediately moved to about $75, handing shareholders a 36% gain over the previous day's price of $56. At the same time RJR's bonds fell, since it was clear that existing bondholders would soon have a lot more company.[1]

Johnson's offer lifted RJR onto the auction block. Once the company was in play, its board of directors was obliged to consider other offers, which were not long in coming. Four days later, KKR bid $90 per share, $79 in cash plus PIK preferred stock valued at $11. (PIK means "pay in kind." The company could choose to pay preferred dividends with more preferred shares rather than cash.)

The resulting bidding contest had as many turns and surprises as a Dickens novel. In the end it was Johnson's group against KKR. KKR bid $109 per share, after adding $1 per share (roughly $230 million) in the last hour.[2] The KKR bid was $81 in cash, convertible subordinated bonds valued at about $10, and PIK preferred shares valued at about $18. Johnson's group bid $112 in cash and securities.

But the RJR board chose KKR. Although Johnson's group had offered $3 a share more, its security valuations were viewed as "softer" and perhaps overstated. The Johnson group's proposal also contained a management compensation package that seemed extremely generous and had generated an avalanche of bad press.

But where did the merger benefits come from? What could justify offering $109 per share, about $25 billion in all, for a company that only 33 days previously was selling for $56 per share? KKR and other bidders were betting on two things. First, they expected to generate billions in additional cash from interest tax shields, reduced capital expenditures, and sales of assets that were not strictly necessary to RJR's core businesses. Asset sales alone were projected to generate $5 billion. Second, they expected to make the core businesses significantly more profitable, mainly by cutting back on expenses and bureaucracy. Apparently, there was plenty to cut, including the RJR "Air Force," which at one point included 10 corporate jets.

In the year after KKR took over, a new management team set out to sell assets and cut back operating expenses and capital spending. There were also layoffs. As expected, high interest charges meant a net loss of nearly a billion dollars in the first year, but pretax operating income actually increased, despite extensive asset sales.

Inside the firm, things were going well. But outside there was confusion and prices in the junk bond market were declining rapidly, implying much higher future interest charges for RJR and stricter terms on any refinancing. In 1990 KKR made an additional equity investment in the firm and the company retired some of its junk bonds. RJR's chief financial officer described the move as "one further step in the deleveraging of the company."[3] For RJR, the world's largest LBO, it seemed that high debt was a temporary, not a permanent, virtue.

RJR, like many other firms that were taken private through LBOs, enjoyed only a short period as a private company. In 1991 it went public again with the sale of $1.1 billion of stock. KKR progressively sold off its investment, and its last remaining stake in the company was sold in 1995 at roughly the original purchase price.

---

[1] N. Mohan and C. R. Chen track the abnormal returns of RJR securities in "A Review of the RJR Nabisco Buyout," *Journal of Applied Corporate Finance* 3 (Summer 1990), pp. 102–108.

[2] The whole story is reconstructed by B. Burrough and J. Helyar in *Barbarians at the Gate: The Fall of RJR Nabisco* (New York: Harper & Row 1990)—see especially Chapter 18—and in a movie with the same title.

[3] C. Andress, "RJR Swallows Hard, Offers $5-a-Share Stock," *The Wall Street Journal*, December 18, 1990, pp. C1–C2.

Barbarians at the Gate?

The RJR Nabisco LBO crystallized views on LBOs, the junk bond market, and the takeover business. For many it exemplified all that was wrong with finance in the late 1980s, especially the willingness of "raiders" to carve up established companies, leaving them with enormous debt burdens, basically in order to get rich quick.[4]

There was plenty of confusion, stupidity, and greed in the LBO business. Not all the people involved were nice. On the other hand, LBOs generated large increases in market value, and most of the gains went to the selling shareholders, not to the raiders. For example, the biggest winners in the RJR Nabisco LBO were the company's stockholders.

The most important sources of added value came from making RJR Nabisco leaner and meaner. The company's new management was obliged to pay out massive amounts of cash to service the LBO debt. It also had an equity stake in the business and therefore strong incentives to sell off nonessential assets, cut costs, and improve operating profits.

LBOs are almost by definition *diet deals*. But there were other motives. Here are some of them.

The Junk Bond Markets   LBOs and debt-financed takeovers may have been driven by artificially cheap funding from the junk bond markets. With hindsight, it seems that investors underestimated the risks of default in junk bonds. Default rates climbed painfully, reaching 10.3% in 1991.[5] The market also became temporarily much less liquid after the demise in 1990 of Drexel Burnham, the investment banking firm that was the chief market maker in junk bonds.

Leverage and Taxes   Borrowing money saves taxes, as we explained in Chapter 18. But taxes were not the main driving force behind LBOs. The value of interest tax shields was simply not big enough to explain the observed gains in market value.[6] For example, Richard Ruback estimated the present value of additional interest tax shields generated by the RJR LBO at $1.8 billion.[7] But the gain in market value to RJR stockholders was about $8 billion.

Of course, if interest tax shields were the main motive for LBOs' high debt, then LBO managers would not be so concerned to pay down debt. We saw that this was one of the first tasks facing RJR Nabisco's new management.

Other Stakeholders   We should look at the total gain to all investors in an LBO, not just to the selling stockholders. It's possible that the latter's gain is just someone else's loss and that no value is generated overall.

Bondholders are the obvious losers. The debt that they thought was secure can turn into junk when the borrower goes through an LBO. We noted how market prices of RJR debt fell sharply when Ross Johnson's first LBO offer was announced. But again, the losses suffered by bondholders in LBOs are not nearly large enough to explain stockholder gains. For example, Mohan and Chen's estimate of losses to RJR bondholders was at most $575 million[8]—painful to the bondholders, but far below the stockholders' gain.

---

[4] This view persists in some quarters: in April 2005, Franz Müntefering, Chairman of the German Social Democratic Party, branded private-equity investors as a plague of "locusts" bent on devouring German industry. Try an Internet search on "private equity" with "locusts."

[5] See E. I. Altman and G. Fanjul, "Defaults and Returns in the High Yield Bond Market: The Year 2003 in Review and Market Outlook," Monograph, Salomon Center, Leonard N. Stern School of Business, New York University, 2004.

[6] There are some tax *costs* to LBOs. For example, selling shareholders realize capital gains and pay taxes that otherwise would be deferred. See L. Stiglin, S. N. Kaplan, and M. C. Jensen, "Effects of LBOs on Tax Revenues of the U.S. Treasury," *Tax Notes* 42 (February 6, 1989), pp. 727–733.

[7] R. J. Ruback, "RJR Nabisco," case study, Harvard Business School, Cambridge, MA, 1989.

[8] Mohan and Chen, 1990. "A Review of the RJR Nabisco Buyout," *Journal of Applied Corporate Finance*, 3(2) pp. 102–108.

Leverage and Incentives   Managers and employees of LBOs work harder and often smarter. They have to generate cash for debt service. Moreover, managers' personal fortunes are riding on the LBO's success. They become owners rather than organization men and women.

It's hard to measure the payoff from better incentives, but there is some evidence of improved operating efficiency in LBOs. Kaplan, who studied 48 MBOs during the 1980s, found average increases in operating income of 24% three years after the buyouts. Ratios of operating income and net cash flow to assets and sales increased dramatically. He observed cutbacks in capital expenditures but not in employment. Kaplan concludes that these "operating changes are due to improved incentives rather than layoffs."[9]

We have reviewed several motives for LBOs. We do not say that all LBOs are good. On the contrary, there have been many mistakes, and even soundly motivated LBOs are risky, as the bankruptcies of a number of highly leveraged transactions have demonstrated. Yet, we do quarrel with those who portray LBOs solely as undertaken by Wall Street barbarians breaking up the traditional strengths of corporate America.

Leveraged Restructurings

The essence of a leveraged buyout is of course leverage. So why not take on the leverage and dispense with the buyout? Here is one well-documented success story of a *leveraged restructuring*.[10]

In 1989 Sealed Air was a very profitable company. The problem was that its profits were coming too easily because its main products were protected by patents. When the patents expired, strong competition was inevitable, and the company was not ready for it. The years of relatively easy profits had resulted in too much slack:

> We didn't need to manufacture efficiently; we didn't need to worry about cash. At Sealed Air, capital tended to have limited value attached to it—cash was perceived as being free and abundant.

The company's solution was to borrow the money to pay a $328 million special cash dividend. In one stroke the company's debt increased 10 times. Its book equity went from $162 million to *minus* $161 million. Debt went from 13% of total book assets to 136%. The company hoped that this leveraged restructuring would "disrupt the status quo, promote internal change," and simulate "the pressures of Sealed Air's more competitive future." The shakeup was reinforced by new performance measures and incentives, including increases in stock ownership by employees.

It worked. Sales and operating profits increased steadily without major new capital investments, and net working capital *fell* by half, releasing cash to help service the company's debt. The stock price quadrupled in the five years following the restructuring.

Sealed Air's restructuring was not typical. It is an exemplar chosen with hindsight. It was also undertaken by a successful firm under no outside pressure. But it clearly shows the motive for most leveraged restructurings. They are designed to force mature, successful, but overweight companies to disgorge cash, reduce operating costs, and use assets more efficiently.

---

[9] S. Kaplan, "The Effects of Management Buyouts on Operating Performance and Value," *Journal of Financial Economics* 24 (October 1989), pp. 217–254. For more recent evidence on changes in employment, see S. J. Davis, J. Haltiwanger, R. S. Jarmin, J. Lerner, and J. Miranda, "Private Equity and Employment," U.S. Census Bureau Center for Economic Studies Paper No. CES-WP-08-07, January 2009.

[10] K. H. Wruck, "Financial Policy as a Catalyst for Organizational Change: Sealed Air's Leveraged Special Dividend," *Journal of Applied Corporate Finance* 7 (Winter 1995), pp. 20–37.

LBOs and Leveraged Restructurings

The financial characteristics of LBOs and leveraged restructurings are similar. The three main characteristics of LBOs are

1. *High debt.* The debt is not intended to be permanent. It is designed to be paid down. The requirement to generate cash for debt service is intended to curb wasteful investment and force improvements in operating efficiency. Of course, this solution only makes sense in the case of companies that are generating lots of cash and have few investment opportunities.
2. *Incentives.* Managers are given a greater stake in the business via stock options or direct ownership of shares.
3. *Private ownership.* The LBO goes private. It is owned by a partnership of private investors who monitor performance and can act right away if something goes awry. But private ownership is not intended to be permanent. The most successful LBOs go public again as soon as debt has been paid down sufficiently and improvements in operating performance have been demonstrated.

Leveraged restructurings share the first two characteristics but continue as public companies.

32-2 FUSION AND FISSION IN CORPORATE FINANCE

Figure 32.1 shows some of AT&T's acquisitions and divestitures. Before 1984, AT&T controlled most of the local and virtually all of the long-distance telephone service in the United States. (Customers used to speak of the ubiquitous "Ma Bell.") Then in 1984 the company accepted an antitrust settlement requiring local telephone services to be spun off to seven new, independent companies. AT&T was left with its long-distance business plus Bell Laboratories, Western Electric (telecommunications manufacturing), and various other assets. As the communications industry became increasingly competitive, AT&T acquired several other businesses, notably in computers, cellular telephone service, and cable television. Some of these acquisitions are shown as the green incoming arrows in Figure 32.1.

AT&T was an unusually active acquirer. It was a giant company trying to respond to rapidly changing technologies and markets. But AT&T was simultaneously *divesting* dozens of other businesses. For example, its credit card operations (the AT&T Universal Card) were sold to Citicorp. AT&T also created several new companies by spinning off parts of its business. For example, in 1996 it spun off Lucent (incorporating Bell Laboratories and Western Electric) and its computer business (NCR). Only six years earlier AT&T had paid $7.5 billion to acquire NCR. These and several other important divestitures are shown as the green outgoing arrows in Figure 32.1.

Figure 32.1 is not the end of AT&T's story. In 2004, AT&T was acquired by Cingular Wireless, which retained the AT&T name. In 2005, that company in turn merged with SBC Communications, Inc., a descendant of Southwestern Bell. In 2006, that company merged with BellSouth. There's not much left of the original AT&T, but the name survives.[11]

In the market for corporate control, fusion—that is, mergers and acquisitions—gets most of the attention and publicity. But fission—the sale or distribution of assets or operating businesses—can be just as important, as the top half of Figure 32.1 illustrates. In many cases businesses are sold in LBOs or MBOs. But other transactions are common, including spin-offs, carve-outs, divestitures, asset sales, and privatizations. We start with spin-offs.

---

[11] The merger with BellSouth did not signal the end of the acquisitions. In 2007 AT&T undertook a series of acquisitions to expand its wireless services.

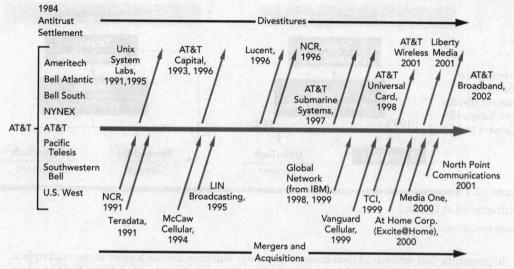

FIGURE 32.1

The effects of AT&T's antitrust settlement in 1984, and a few of AT&T's acquisitions and divestitures from 1991 to 2003. Divestitures are shown by the outgoing green arrows. When two years are given, the transaction was completed in two steps.

Spin-offs

A **spin-off** (or *split-up*) is a new, independent company created by detaching part of a parent company's assets and operations. Shares in the new company are distributed to the parent company's shareholders. For example, in Novermber 2009, Grasim spun off its cement division into a company called Samruddhi, which in turn got merged with Ultra Tech, another group company. (See Fig. 32.2). Similarly, in December 2009, Time Warner spun off its investment in AOL. Time Warner's shareholders received shares in the new company and could trade their AOL shares as well as those of the slimmed down Time Warner.[12]

Spin-offs widen investor choice by allowing them to invest in just one part of the business. More important, they can improve incentives for managers. Companies sometimes refer to divisions or lines of business as "poor fits." By spinning these businesses off, management of the parent company can concentrate on its main activity. If the businesses are independent, it is easier to see the value and performance of each and to reward managers by giving them stock or stock options in their company. Also, spin-offs relieve investors of the worry that funds will be siphoned from one business to support unprofitable capital investments in another.

When AT&T announced its planned spin-offs of Lucent and NCR, the chairman commented that the

> three independent corporations will be able to go after the exploding opportunities of the industry faster than they could as parts of a much larger corporation. The three new companies . . . will be free

---

[12] Instead of undertaking a spin-off, some companies have given their shareholders *tracking stock* tied to the performance of particular divisions. For example, in 2000 AT&T distributed a special class of shares tied to the performance of its wireless business. But tracking stocks did not prove popular with investors, and a year later AT&T went whole hog and spun off AT&T Wireless into a separate company.

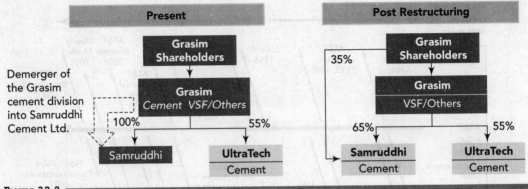

FIGURE 32.2

Restructuring at Grasim.

Source: Company website

to pursue the best interests of their customers without bumping into each other in the marketplace. They are designed to be fast and focused, with a capital structure suited to their individual industries.

Investors were apparently convinced, for the announcement of the spin-offs added $10 billion to the value of the stock overnight.

AT&T's spin-off of Lucent and NCR was unusual in many respects. But scholars who have studied the topic have found that investors generally greet the announcement of a spin-off as good news.[13] Their enthusiasm appears to be justified, for spin-offs seem to bring about more efficient capital investment decisions by each company and improved operating performance.[14]

Carve-outs

Carve-outs are similar to spin-offs, except that shares in the new company are not given to existing shareholders but are sold in a public offering. An example of a recent carve-out was the sale in 2009 by Bristol Myers Squibb of 17% of the shares of Mead Johnson Nutrition. The initial public offering raised $720 million for Bristol Myers.

Most carve-outs leave the parent with majority control of the subsidiary, usually about 80% ownership.[15] This may not reassure investors who are worried about lack of focus or a poor fit, but it does allow the parent to set the manager's compensation based on the performance of the subsidiary's stock price. Sometimes companies carve out a small proportion of the shares to establish the market in the subsidiary and subsequently spin off the remainder of the shares. The nearby box describes how the computer company, Palm, was first carved and then spun.

---

[13] For example, P. J. Cusatis, J. A. Miles, and J. R. Woolridge, "Restructuring Through Spin-offs: The Stock-Market Evidence," *Journal of Financial Economics* 33 (Summer 1994), pp. 293–311.

[14] See R. Gertner, E. Powers, and D. Scharfstein, "Learning about Internal Capital Markets from Corporate Spin-offs," *Journal of Finance* 57 (December 2003), pp. 2479–2506; L. V. Daley, V. Mehrotra, and R. Sivakumar, "Corporate Focus and Value Creation: Evidence from Spin-offs," *Journal of Financial Economics* 45 (August 1997), pp. 257–281; T. R. Burch and V. Nanda, "Divisional Diversity and the Conglomerate Discount: Evidence from Spin-offs," *Journal of Financial Economics* 70 (October 2003), pp. 69–78; and A. K. Dittmar and A. Shivdasani, "Divestitures and Divisional Investment Policies," *Journal of Finance* 58 (December 2003), pp. 2711–2744. But G. Colak and T. M. Whited argue that apparent increases in value are due to econometric problems rather than actual increases in investment efficiency. See "Spin-offs, Divestitures and Conglomerate Investment," *Review of Economic Studies* 20 (May 2007), pp. 557–595.

[15] The parent must retain an 80% interest to consolidate the subsidiary with the parent's tax accounts. Otherwise the subsidiary is taxed as a freestanding corporation.

Finance In Practice

How Palm was Carved and Spun

When 3Com acquired U.S. Robotics in 1997, it also became the owner of Palm, a small start-up business developing handheld computers. It was a lucky purchase, for over the next three years the Palm Pilot came to dominate the market for handheld computers. But as Palm began to take up an increasing amount of management time, 3Com concluded that it needed to return to its knitting and focus on its basic business of selling computer network systems. In 2000 it announced that it would carve out 5% of its holding of Palm through an initial public offering, and then spin off the remaining 95% of Palm shares by giving 3Com shareholders about 1.5 Palm shares for each 3Com share that they owned.

The Palm carve-out occurred at close to the peak of the high-tech boom and got off to a dazzling start. The shares were issued in the IPO at $38 each. On the first day of trading the stock price touched $165 before closing at $95. Therefore, anyone owning a share of 3Com stock could look forward later in the year to receiving about 1.5 shares of Palm worth $1.5 \times 95 = \$142.50$. But apparently 3Com's shareholders were not fully convinced that their newfound wealth was for real, for on the same day 3Com's stock price closed at $82, or more than $60 a share *less* than the market value of the shares in Palm that they were due to receive.*

Three years after 3Com spun off its holding in Palm, Palm itself entered the spin-off business by giving shareholders stock in PalmSource, a subsidiary that was responsible for developing and licensing the Palm™ operating system. The remaining business, renamed palmOne, would focus on making mobile gadgets. The company gave three reasons for its decision to split into two. First, like 3Com's management, Palm's management believed that the company would benefit from clarity of focus and mission. Second, it argued that shareholder value could "be enhanced if investors could evaluate and choose between both businesses separately, thereby attracting new and different investors." Finally, it seemed that Palm's rivals were reluctant to buy software from a company that competed with them in making handheld hardware.

---

* This difference would seem to present an arbitrage opportunity. An investor who bought 1 share of 3Com and sold short 1.5 shares of Palm would earn a profit of $60 and own 3Com's other assets for free. The difficulty in executing this arbitrage is explored in O. A. Lamont and R. H. Thaler, "Can the Market Add and Subtract? Mispricing in Tech Stock Carve-Outs," *Journal of Political Economy* 111 (April 2003), pp. 227–268.

Perhaps the most enthusiastic carver-outer of the 1980s and 1990s was Thermo Electron, with operations in health care, power generation equipment, instrumentation, environmental protection, and various other areas. By 1997 it had carved out stakes in seven publicly traded subsidiaries, which in turn had carved out 15 further public companies. The 15 were grandchildren of the ultimate parent, Thermo Electron. The company's management reasoned that the carve-outs would give each company's managers responsibility for their own decisions and expose their actions to the scrutiny of the capital markets. For a while the strategy seemed to work, and Thermo Electron's stock was a star performer. But the complex structure began to lead to inefficiencies, and in 2000 Thermo Electron went into reverse. It reacquired many of the subsidiaries that the company had carved out only a few years earlier, and it spun off several of its progeny, including Viasis Health Care and Kadant Corp., a manufacturer of papermaking and paper-recycling equipment. Then in November 2006 Thermo Electron merged with Fisher Scientific.

Asset Sales

The simplest way to divest an asset is to sell it. An *asset sale* or *divestiture* means sale of a part of one firm to another. This may consist of an odd factory or warehouse, but sometimes whole divisions are sold. Asset sales are another way of getting rid of "poor fits." Such sales are frequent. For example, one study found that over 30% of assets acquired in a sample of hostile takeovers were subsequently sold.[16]

Maksimovic and Phillips examined a sample of about 50,000 U.S. manufacturing plants each year from 1974 to 1992. About 35,000 plants in the sample changed hands during that period. One-half of the ownership changes were the result of mergers or acquisitions of entire firms, but the other half resulted from asset sales, that is, sale of part or all of a division.[17] Asset sales sometimes raise huge sums of money. For example, in 2009 mining giant Rio Tinto announced that it had sold its potash deposits to the Brazilian company Vale for $850 million. The deal was part of a package of asset sales that raised more than $4.5 billion for Rio Tinto in two years.

Announcements of asset sales are good news for investors in the selling firm and on average the assets are employed more productively after the sale.[18] It appears that asset sales transfer business units to the companies that can manage them most effectively.

Demerger

A demerger is very similar to an asset sale. The parent company sells off a division to another company and the buying company issues shares (instead of paying cash to the parent company) to the shareholders of the parent company. Thus, for example, in September 1998, the Aditya Birla group, as part of its restructuring exercise, transferred the cement division of Indian Rayon to Grasim in a share-swap transaction. The shareholders of Indian Rayon received 3 shares of Grasim for every 10 shares in Indian Rayon held by them. This transaction is very similar to a spin off or equity carve out. The parent company that transfers the division becomes more focused after the transaction and hence can focus on its core competency.

In India, often companies resort to spin-offs, demergers or asset sales just before (or sometimes after) a merger for some tax-related reasons. Let's assume that Company B wants to acquire Company A in a share-swap transaction. 'A' manufactures steel and cement and 'B' manufacturers cement only. Here, B may not be interested in the steel division of A. As per Sec 2 (1B) of the Income Tax Act in India, a merged company gets some of the tax benefits (like carrying forward expenditure on acquisition of patent rights, preliminary expenses, etc) only if, among other things, all the assets of the merging company become assets of the merged company by virtue of the amalgamation. So here, B has the choice of either asking A to spin off the cement division into a cement company before the merger. Alternatively, B can first takeover A and then demerge the steel division. Thus, for example, in 1993, Voltas first got Hyderabad Allwyn Limited (HAL) merged with itself and then transferred the watch division of HAL to Allwyn Watches Limited.

---

[16] See S. Bhagat, A. Shleifer, and R. Vishny, "Hostile Takeovers in the 1980s: The Return to Corporate Specialization," *Brookings Papers on Economic Activity: Microeconomics*, 1990, pp. 1–12.

[17] V. Maksimovic and G. Phillips, "The Market for Corporate Assets: Who Engages in Mergers and Asset Sales and Are There Efficiency Gains?" *Journal of Finance* 56 (December 2001), Table 1, p. 2000.

[18] Ibid.

Privatization and Nationalization

A **privatization** is a sale of a government-owned company to private investors. In recent years almost every government in the world seems to have a privatization program. Here are some examples of recent privatization news:

- Pakistan sells a majority stake in Habib Bank (February 2004).
- Japan sells the West Japan Railway Company (March 2004).
- India sells a stake in ONGC, an oil exploration and production company (March 2004).
- Ukraine sells the steel company Kryvorizhstal (June 2004).
- Germany privatizes Postbank, the country's largest retail bank (June 2004).
- Turkey sells a 55% stake in Türk Telecom (November 2005).
- France sells 30% of EDF (Electricité de France; December 2005).
- China sells Industrial and Commercial Bank of China (October 2006).
- Poland announces plans to sell Tauron Polska Energia (July 2009).

Most privatizations are more like carve-outs than spin-offs, because shares are sold for cash rather than distributed to the ultimate "shareholders," that is, the citizens of the selling country. But several former Communist countries, including Russia, Poland, and the Czech Republic, privatized by means of vouchers distributed to citizens. The vouchers could be used to bid for shares in the companies that were being privatized. Thus the companies were not sold for cash, but for vouchers.[19]

Privatizations have raised enormous sums for selling governments. China raised $22 billion from the privatization of the Industrial and Commercial Bank of China. The Japanese government's successive sales of its holding of NTT (Nippon Telegraph and Telephone) brought in $100 billion.

The motives for privatization seem to boil down to the following three points:

1. *Increased efficiency.* Through privatization, the enterprise is exposed to the discipline of competition and insulated from political influence on investment and operating decisions. Managers and employees can be given stronger incentives to cut costs and add value.
2. *Share ownership.* Privatizations encourage share ownership. Many privatizations give special terms or allotments to employees or small investors.
3. *Revenue for the government.* Last but not least.

There were fears that privatizations would lead to massive layoffs and unemployment, but that does not appear to be the case. While it is true that privatized companies operate more efficiently and thus reduce employment, they also grow faster as privatized companies, which increases employment. In many cases the net effect on employment is positive.

On other dimensions, the impact of privatization is almost always positive. A review of research on privatization concludes that the firms "almost always become more efficient, more profitable, . . . financially healthier and increase their capital investment spending."[20]

The process of privatization is not a one-way street. It can sometimes go into reverse and publicly owned firms may be taken over by the government. For example, as part of his aim to construct a Socialist republic in Venezuela, Hugo Chavez has nationalized firms in the banking, oil, power, telecom, steel, and cement sectors.

---

[19] There is extensive research on voucher privatizations. See, for example, M. Boyco, A. Shleifer, and R. Vishny, "Voucher Privatizations," *Journal of Financial Economics* 35 (April 1994), pp. 249–266; and R. Aggarwal and J. T. Harper, "Equity Valuation in the Czech Voucher Privatization Auctions," *Financial Management* 29 (Winter 2000), pp. 77–100.

[20] W. L. Megginson and J. M. Netter, "From State to Market: A Survey of Empirical Studies on Privatization," *Journal of Economic Literature* 39 (June 2001), p. 381.

In some other countries temporary nationalization has been a pragmatic last resort for governments rather than part of a long-term strategy. So, when the giant mortgage companies Fannie Mae and Freddie Mac were threatened with bankruptcy in 2008, the U.S. government stepped in and took over the two firms. The following year, GM's bankruptcy resulted in the U.S. Treasury acquiring a 60% holding in the equity of the restructured firm.[21]

32-3   PRIVATE EQUITY

The years 2006 and 2007 witnessed an exceptional volume of private-equity deals. For example, in April 2007 one of the largest private-equity firms, Blackstone, won a $39 billion bidding contest for Equity Office Properties, the largest owner of office buildings in the United States. In July it invested nearly $12 billion in Biomet, a manufacturer of medical equipment. Three months later Blackstone announced the $27 billion purchase of Hilton, the hotel operator.

Perhaps the most interesting news of 2007 was DaimlerChrysler's announcement that it was selling an 80% stake in Chrysler to Cerberus Capital Management. Chrysler, one of Detroit's original Big Three automakers, merged into DaimlerChrysler in 1998, but the expected synergies between the Chrysler and Mercedes-Benz product lines were hard to grasp. The Chrysler division had some profitable years, but lost $1.5 billion in 2006. Prospects looked grim. DaimlerChrysler (now Daimler A. G.) *paid* Cerberus $677 million to take Chrysler off its hands. Cerberus assumed about $18 billion in pension and employee health-care liabilities, however, and agreed to invest $6 billion in Chrysler and its finance subsidiary.[22] Two years later, Chrysler filed for bankruptcy, wiping out Cerberus's investment.

Private equity was "hot" in many other countries in 2007. For example, Australia's largest retailers, Coles and Myer, went private. An investment consortium including the Australian Macquarie Bank and the Texas Pacific Group came within a gnat's eyelash of taking over Qantas, Australia's largest airline. (Macquarie also makes private-equity investments around the world, for example, in toll highways and shipping ports.)

With the onset of the credit crisis the LBO boom of 2007 withered rapidly. Although buyout firms entered 2008 with large amounts of equity, the debt market for leveraged buyouts dried up and the volume of deals fell by more than 70%. (You probably noticed that only one of the buyouts listed in Table 32.1 took place in 2008 or 2009.)

Private-Equity Partnerships

Figure 32.3 shows how a private-equity investment fund is organized. The fund is a partnership, not a corporation. The *general partner* sets up and manages the partnership. The *limited partners* put up almost all of the money. Limited partners are generally institutional investors, such as pension funds, endowments, and insurance companies. Wealthy individuals may also participate. The limited partners have limited liability, like shareholders in a corporation, but do not participate in management.

Once the partnership is formed, the general partners seek out companies to invest in. Venture capital partnerships look for high-tech startups or adolescent companies that need capital to grow. LBO funds look for mature businesses with ample free cash flow that need restructuring. Some funds

---

[21] The credit crisis prompted a number of company nationalizations throughout the world, such as that of Northern Rock in the U.K., Hypo Real Estate in Germany, Landsbanki in Iceland, and Anglo-Irish Bank in Ireland.

[22] Cerberus had previously purchased a controlling stake in GMAC, General Motors' finance subsidiary.

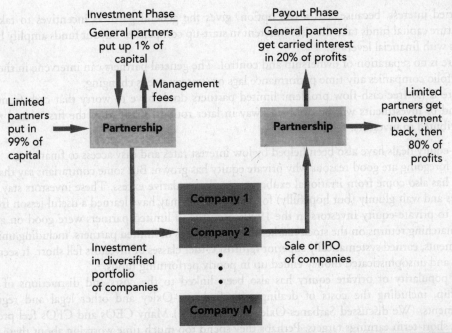

Investment Phase

General partners put up 1% of capital

Management fees

Limited partners put in 99% of capital

Partnership

Investment in diversified portfolio of companies

Company 1

Company 2

•
•
•

Company N

Payout Phase

General partners get carried interest in 20% of profits

Partnership

Sale or IPO of companies

Limited partners get investment back, then 80% of profits

FIGURE 32.3

Organization of a typical private-equity partnership. The limited partners, having put up almost all of the money, get first crack at the proceeds from sale or IPO of the portfolio companies. Once their investment is returned, they get 80% of any profits. The general partners, who organize and manage the partnership, get a 20% carried interest in profits.

specialize in particular industries, for example, biotech, real estate, or energy. However, buyout funds like Blackstone's and Cerberus's look for opportunities almost anywhere.

The partnership agreement has a limited term, which is typically 10 years. The portfolio companies must then be sold and the proceeds distributed. So the general partners cannot reinvest the limited partners' money. Of course, once a fund is proved successful, the general partners can usually go back to the limited partners, or to other institutional investors, and form another one. (We mentioned three of Blackstone's 2007 deals earlier in this section. These buyouts were funded from Blackstone's existing investment partnerships. At the same time it was raising $20 billion for a *new* buyout fund and $10 billion for a new real estate fund.)

The general partners get a management fee, usually 1% or 2% of capital committed,[23] plus a *carried interest* in 20% of any profits earned by the partnership. In other words, the limited partners get paid off first, but then get only 80% of any further returns. The general partners therefore have a call option on 20% of the partnership's total future payoff, with an exercise price set by the limited partners' investment.[24]

You can see some of the advantages of private-equity partnerships:

• Carried interest gives the general partners plenty of upside. They are strongly motivated to earn back the limited partners' investment and deliver a profit.

---

[23] LBO and buyout funds also extract fees for arranging financing for their takeover transactions.

[24] The structure and compensation of private-equity partnerships are described in A. Metrick and A. Yasuda, "The Economics of Private Equity Funds," *Review of Financial Studies*, forthcoming.

- Carried interest, because it is a call option, gives the general partners incentives to take risks. Venture capital funds take the risks inherent in start-up companies. Buyout funds amplify business risks with financial leverage.
- There is no separation of ownership and control. The general partners can intervene in the fund's portfolio companies any time performance lags or strategy needs changing.
- There is no free-cash-flow problem: limited partners don't have to worry that cash from a first round of investments will be dribbled away in later rounds. Cash from the first round *must* be distributed to investors.

Private-equity deals have also been helped by low interest rates and easy access to financing.

The foregoing are good reasons why private equity has grown. But some contrarians say that rapid growth has also come from irrational exuberance and speculative excess. These investors stay on the sidelines and wait glumly (but hopefully) for a crash. They may have learned a useful lesson from the returns to private-equity investors in the 1990s. Returns to limited partners were good on average, about matching returns on the stock market. But some types of limited partners, including university endowments, earned systematically superior returns. Other classes of investors fell short. It seems that the late and unsophisticated money ended up in poorly performing funds.[25]

The popularity of private equity has also been linked to the costs and distractions of public ownership, including the costs of dealing with Sarbanes-Oxley and other legal and regulatory requirements. (We discussed Sarbanes-Oxley in Chapter 1.) Many CEOs and CFOs feel pressured to meet short-term earnings targets. Perhaps they spend too much time worrying about these targets and about day-to-day changes in stock price. Perhaps going private avoids public investors' "short-termism" and makes it easier to invest for the long run. But recall that for private equity, the long run is the life of the partnership, 8 or 10 years at most. General partners *must* find a way to cash out of the companies in the partnership's portfolio. There are only two ways to cash out: an IPO or a *trade sale* to another company. Many of today's private-equity deals will be future IPOs, thus private-equity investors need public markets. The firms that seek divorce from public shareholders may well have to remarry them later.

Are Private-Equity Funds Today's Conglomerates?

A *conglomerate* is a firm that diversifies across several unrelated businesses. Is Blackstone a conglomerate? Table 32.2, which lists some of the companies held by Blackstone funds, suggests that it is. Blackstone funds have invested in dozens of industries.

At the start of this chapter, we suggested that private equity today does some of the tasks that public conglomerates used to do. Let's take a brief look at the history of U.S. conglomerates.

The merger boom of the 1960s created more than a dozen sprawling conglomerates. Table 32.3 shows that by the 1970s some of these conglomerates had achieved amazing spans of activity. The largest conglomerate, ITT, was operating in 38 different industries and ranked eighth in sales among U.S. corporations.

Most of these conglomerates were broken up in the 1980s and 1990s. In 1995 ITT, which had already sold or spun off several businesses, split what was left into three separate firms. One acquired ITT's interests in hotels and gambling; the second took over ITT's automotive parts, defense, and electronics businesses, and the third specialized in insurance and financial services.

---

[25] J. Lerner, A. Schoar, and W. Wongsunwai, "Smart Institutions, Foolish Choices: The Limited Partner Performance Puzzle," *Journal of Finance* 62 (April 2007), pp. 731–764.

TABLE 32.2 The Blackstone Group invests in many different industries. Here are some of its portfolio holdings in 2009.

Company	Business	Company	Business
Alliant	Insurance	Nielsen	Media, publishing
Biomet	Medical equipment	Orangina	Soft drinks
Catalent	Pharmaceutical and health services	Pinnacle Foods	Convenience foods
Centerparcs	U.K. holiday villages	SunGard	Software
Freescale	Semiconductors for telecommunications	TDC	Danish telecom operator
Health Markets	Health insurance	Travelport	Travel agent
Hilton	Hospitality	United Biscuits	Biscuits, cookies, snacks
Michaels	Arts and crafts retailer	Weather Channel	Media

Source: The Blackstone Group, **www.blackstone.com**.

TABLE 32.3 The largest conglomerates of 1979, ranked by sales compared with U.S. industrial corporations. Most of these companies have been broken up.

Sales Rank	Company	Number of Industries
8	International Telephone & Telegraph (ITT)	38
15	Tenneco	28
42	Gulf & Western Industries	4
51	Litton Industries	19
66	LTV	18

Source: A. Chandler and R. S. Tetlow (eds.), *The Coming of Managerial Capitalism* (Homewood, IL: Richard D. Irwin, Inc., 1985), p. 772. © 1985 Richard D. Irwin. See also J. Baskin and P. J. Miranti, Jr., *A History of Corporate Finance* (Cambridge, U.K.: Cambridge University Press, 1997), ch. 7.

What advantages were claimed for the conglomerates of the 1960s and 1970s? First, diversification across industries was supposed to stabilize earnings and reduce risk. That's hardly compelling, because shareholders can diversify much more efficiently on their own.

Second, a widely diversified firm can operate an *internal capital market*. Free cash flow generated by divisions in mature industries (*cash cows*) can be funneled within the company to those divisions (*stars*) with plenty of profitable growth opportunities. Consequently, there is no need for fast-growing divisions to raise finance from outside investors.

There are some good arguments for internal capital markets. The company's managers probably know more about its investment opportunities than outside investors do, and transaction costs of issuing securities are avoided. Nevertheless, it appears that attempts by conglomerates to allocate capital investment across many unrelated industries were more likely to subtract value than add it. Trouble is, internal capital markets are not really markets but combinations of central planning (by the conglomerate's top management and financial staff) and intracompany bargaining. Divisional capital budgets depend on politics as well as pure economics. Large, profitable divisions with plenty of free cash flow may have the most bargaining power; they may get generous capital budgets while smaller divisions with good growth opportunities are reined in.

Internal Capital Markets in the Oil Business Misallocation in internal capital markets is not restricted to pure conglomerates. For example, Lamont found that, when oil prices fell by half in 1986, diversified oil companies cut back capital investment in their *non-oil* divisions. The non-oil divisions were forced to "share the pain," even though the drop in oil prices did not diminish their investment opportunities. *The Wall Street Journal* reported one example:[26]

> Chevron Corp. cut its planned 1986 capital and exploratory budget by about 30% because of the plunge in oil prices. . . . A Chevron spokesman said that the spending cuts would be across the board and that no particular operations will bear the brunt.
>
> About 65% of the $3.5 billion budget will be spent on oil and gas exploration and production—about the same proportion as before the budget revision.
>
> Chevron also will cut spending for refining and marketing, oil and natural gas pipelines, minerals, chemicals, and shipping operations.

Why cut back on capital outlays for minerals, say, or chemicals? Low oil prices are generally good news, not bad, for chemical manufacturing, because oil distillates are an important raw material.

By the way, most of the oil companies in Lamont's sample were large, blue-chip companies. They could have raised additional capital from investors to maintain spending in their non-oil divisions. They chose not to. We do not understand why.

All large companies must allocate capital among divisions or lines of business. Therefore, they all have internal capital markets and must worry about mistakes and misallocations. But the danger probably increases as the company moves from a focus on one, or a few related industries, to unrelated conglomerate diversification. Look again at Table 32.3: how could top management of ITT keep accurate track of investment opportunities in 38 different industries?

Conglomerates face further problems. Their divisions' market values can't be observed independently, and it is difficult to set incentives for divisional managers. This is particularly serious when managers are asked to commit to risky ventures. For example, how would a biotech startup fare as a division of a traditional conglomerate? Would the conglomerate be as patient and risk-tolerant as investors in the stock market? How are the scientists and clinicians doing the biotech R&D rewarded if they succeed? We don't mean to say that high-tech innovation and risk-taking are impossible in public conglomerates, but the difficulties are evident.

The third argument for traditional conglomerates came from the idea that good managers were fungible; in other words, it was argued that modern management would work as well in the manufacture of auto parts as in running a hotel chain. Thus conglomerates were supposed to add value by removing old-fashioned managers and replacing them with ones trained in the new management science.

There was some truth in this claim. The best of the conglomerates did add value by targeting companies that needed fixing—companies with slack management, surplus assets, or excess cash that was not being invested in positive-NPV projects. These conglomerates targeted the same types of companies that LBO and private-equity funds would target later. The difference is that conglomerates would buy companies, try to improve them, and then manage for the long run. The long-run management was the most difficult part of the game. Conglomerates would buy, fix, and hold. Private equity buys, fixes, and sells. By selling (cashing out), private equity avoids the problems of managing

---

[26] O. Lamont, "Cash Flow and Investment: Evidence from Internal Capital Markets," *Journal of Finance* 52 (March 1997), pp. 83–109. *The Wall Street Journal* quotation appears on pp. 89–90. © 1997 Dow Jones & Company, Inc.

the conglomerate firm and running internal capital markets.[27] You could say that private-equity partnerships are *temporary conglomerates.*

Table 32.4 summarizes a comparison by Baker and Montgomery of the financial structure of a private-equity fund and of a typical public conglomerate. Both are diversified, but the fund's limited partners do not have to worry that free cash flow will be plowed back into unprofitable investments. The fund has no internal capital market. Monitoring and compensation of management also differ. In the fund, each company is run as a separate business. The managers report directly to the owners, the fund's partners. Each company's managers own shares or stock options in that company, not in the fund. Their compensation depends on their firm's market value in a trade sale or IPO.

TABLE 32.4 Private-equity fund vs. public conglomerate. Both diversify, investing in a portfolio of unrelated businesses, but their financial structures are otherwise fundamentally different.

Private-Equity Fund	Public Conglomerate
Widely diversified, investment in unrelated industries	Widely diversified, investment in unrelated industries.
Limited-life partnership forces sale of portfolio companies.	Public corporations designed to operate divisions for the long run.
No financial links or transfers between portfolio companies.	Internal capital market.
General partners "do the deal," then monitor; lenders also monitor.	Hierarchy of corporate staff evaluates divisions' plans and performance.
Managers' compensation depends on exit value of company.	Divisional managers' compensation depends mostly on earnings—"smaller upside, softer downside."

Source: Adapted from G. Baker and C. Montgomery, "Conglomerates and LBO Associations: A Comparison of Organizational Forms," working paper, Harvard Business School, Cambridge, MA, July 1996. Used by permission of the authors.

In a public conglomerate, these businesses would be divisions, not freestanding companies. Ownership of the conglomerate would be dispersed, not concentrated. The divisions would not be valued separately by investors in the stock market, but by the conglomerate's corporate staff, the very people who run the internal capital market. Managers' compensation wouldn't depend on divisions' market values because no shares in the divisions would be traded and the conglomerate would not be committed to selling the divisions or spinning them off.

You can see the arguments for focus and against corporate diversification. But we must be careful not to push the arguments too far. For example, GE, a very successful company, operates in a wide range of unrelated industries. Also, in the next chapter we will find that conglomerates, though rare in the U.S., are common, and apparently successful, in many parts of the world.

Group Diversification in India

Unlike in the U.S., we see a different type of diversification in India. The Indian business groups (e.g., Tatas and Birlas) are diversified across a wide range of businesses and hence are not focused

---

[27] Economists have tried to measure whether corporate diversification adds or subtracts value. Berger and Ofek estimate an average conglomerate discount of 12% to 15%. That is, the estimated market value of the whole is 12% to 15% less than the sum of the values of the parts. The chief cause of the discount seems to be overinvestment and misallocation of investment. See P. Berger and E. Ofek, "Diversification's Effect on Firm Value," *Journal of Financial Economics* 37 (January 1995), pp. 39–65. But not everyone is convinced that the conglomerate discount is real. Other researchers have found smaller discounts or pointed out statistical problems that make the discount hard to measure. See, for example, J. M. Campa and S. Kedia, "Explaining the Diversification Discount," *Journal of Finance* 57 (August 2002), pp. 1731–1762; and B. Villalonga, "Diversification Discount or Premium? Evidence from the Business Information Tracking Service," *Journal of Finance* 59 (April 2004), pp. 479–506.

business groups.[28] Thus, for example, the Tata Group has interests in engineering, automobiles, steel, software, etc. Khanna and Palepu argue that diversification makes sense in emerging countries like India where the different institutions like product market, capital market, etc are ill-developed.[29] The business groups add value by effectively mediating between the group companies and the rest of the economy. In this sense, the business groups serve the functions of the different institutions that are not well developed.

Khanna and Palepu argue that the different institutions like the capital market, the labor market, the product market, government regulation and contract enforcement are not well-developed in the emerging countries. Successful business groups can fill the void created by the lack of good institutions and hence can create value for the investors. Thus for example, the capital markets are illiquid and underdeveloped. This creates problems for companies from raising equity capital from the primary market. However, the business groups can serve the role of a venture capital company and provide necessary funds to the group companies. Similarly, despite underdeveloped labor market, the business groups can serve management competency to the different groups companies. Many of the Tata Group companies, for example, benefit by borrowing skilled managers from Tata Administrative Service.

32-4 BANKRUPTCY

Some firms are forced to reorganize by the onset of financial distress. At this point they need to agree to a reorganization plan with their creditors or file for bankruptcy. We list the largest nonfinancial U.S. bankruptcies in Table 32.5. The credit crunch also ensured a good dose of very large financial bankruptcies. Lehman Brothers tops the list. It failed in September 2008 with assets of $691.1 billion. Two weeks later Washington Mutual went the same way with assets of $327.9 billion.

TABLE 32.5 The largest nonfinancial bankruptcies.

Company	Bankruptcy Date	Total Assets Prebankruptcy ($ billions)
WorldCom	July 2002	103.9
General Motors	July 2009	91.0
Enron	December 2001	65.5
Conseco	December 2002	61.4
Chrysler	April 2009	39.3
Pacific Gas and Electric	April 2001	36.2
Texaco	April 1987	34.9
Refco	October 2005	33.3
Global Crossing	January 2002	30.2
Calpine	December 2005	27.2
UAL	December 2002	25.2

Source: New Generation Research, Inc., **www.bankruptcydata.com**.

---

[28] It is possible that the different companies operating under the banner of a particular business group are all focused companies.

[29] See Khanna, T., and K Palepu (1997), "Why Focused Strategies May be Wrong for Emerging Markets", *Harvard Business Review*, July-August.

Bankruptcy proceedings in the United States may be initiated by the creditors, but in the case of public corporations it is usually the firm itself that decides to file. It can choose one of two procedures, which are set out in Chapters 7 and 11 of the 1978 Bankruptcy Reform Act. The purpose of **Chapter 7** is to oversee the firm's death and dismemberment, while **Chapter 11** seeks to nurse the firm back to health.

Most small firms make use of Chapter 7. In this case the bankruptcy judge appoints a trustee, who then closes the firm down and auctions off the assets. The proceeds from the auction are used to pay off the creditors. Secured creditors can recover the value of their collateral. Whatever is left over goes to the unsecured creditors, who take assigned places in a queue. The court and the trustee are first in line. Wages come next, followed by federal and state taxes and debts to some government agencies such as the Pension Benefit Guarantee Corporation. The remaining unsecured creditors mop up any remaining crumbs from the table.[30] Frequently the trustee needs to prevent some creditors from trying to jump the gun and collect on their debts, and sometimes the trustee retrieves property that a creditor has recently seized.

Managers of small firms that are in trouble know that Chapter 7 bankruptcy means the end of the road and, therefore, try to put off filing as long as possible. For this reason, Chapter 7 proceedings are often launched not by the firm but by its creditors.

When large public companies can't pay their debts, they generally attempt to rehabilitate the business. This is in the shareholders' interests; they have nothing to lose if things deteriorate further and everything to gain if the firm recovers. The procedures for rehabilitation are set out in Chapter 11. Most companies find themselves in Chapter 11 because they can't pay their debts. But sometimes companies have filed for Chapter 11 not because they run out of cash, but to deal with burdensome labor contracts or lawsuits. For example, Delphi, the automotive parts manufacturer, filed for bankruptcy in 2005. Delphi's North American operations were running at a loss, partly because of high-cost labor contracts with the United Auto Workers (UAW) and partly because of the terms of its supply contract with GM, its largest customer. Delphi sought the protection of Chapter 11 to restructure its operations and to negotiate better terms with the UAW and GM.

The aim of Chapter 11 is to keep the firm alive and operating while a plan of reorganization is worked out.[31] During this period, other proceedings against the firm are halted, and the company usually continues to be run by its existing management.[32] The responsibility for developing the plan falls on the debtor firm but, if it cannot devise an acceptable plan, the court may invite anyone to do so—for example, a committee of creditors.

The plan goes into effect if it is accepted by the creditors and confirmed by the court. Each *class* of creditors votes separately on the plan. Acceptance requires approval by at least one-half of votes cast in each class, and those voting "aye" must represent two-thirds of the value of the creditors' aggregate claim against the firm. The plan also needs to be approved by two-thirds of the shareholders. Once the creditors and the shareholders have accepted the plan, the court normally approves it, provided that each class of creditors is in favor and that the creditors will be no worse off under the plan than they would be if the firm's assets were liquidated and the proceeds distributed. Under certain conditions

---

[30] On average there isn't much left. See M. J. White, "Survey Evidence on Business Bankruptcy," in *Corporate Bankruptcy*, ed. J. S. Bhandari and L. A. Weiss (Cambridge, U.K.: Cambridge University Press, 1996).

[31] To keep the firm alive, it may be necessary to continue to use assets that were offered as collateral, but this denies secured creditors access to their collateral. To resolve this problem, the Bankruptcy Reform Act makes it possible for a firm operating under Chapter 11 to keep such assets as long as the creditors who have a claim on them are compensated for any decline in their value. Thus, the firm might make cash payments to the secured creditors to cover economic depreciation of the assets.

[32] Occasionally the court appoints a trustee to manage the firm.

the court may confirm a plan even if one or more classes of creditors votes against it,[33] but the rules for a "cram-down" are complicated and we will not attempt to cover them here.

The reorganization plan is basically a statement of who gets what; each class of creditors gives up its claim in exchange for new securities or a mixture of new securities and cash. The problem is to design a new capital structure for the firm that will (1) satisfy the creditors and (2) allow the firm to solve the *business* problems that got the firm into trouble in the first place.[34] Sometimes satisfying these two conditions requires a plan of baroque complexity, involving the creation of a dozen or more new securities.

The Securities and Exchange Commission (SEC) plays a role in many reorganizations, particularly for large, public companies. Its interest is to ensure that all relevant and material information is disclosed to the creditors before they vote on the proposed plan of reorganization.

Chapter 11 proceedings are often successful, and the patient emerges fit and healthy. But in other cases rehabilitation proves impossible, and the assets are liquidated under Chapter 7. Sometimes the firm may emerge from Chapter 11 for a brief period before it is once again submerged by disaster and back in the bankruptcy court. For example, TWA came out of Chapter 11 bankruptcy at the end of 1993, was back again less than two years later, and then for a third time in 2001, prompting jokes about "Chapter 22" and "Chapter 33."[35]

Is Chapter 11 Efficient?

Here is a simple view of the bankruptcy decision: Whenever a payment is due to creditors, management checks the value of the equity. If the value is positive, the firm makes the payment (if necessary, raising the cash by an issue of shares). If the equity is valueless, the firm defaults on its debt and files for bankruptcy. If the assets of the bankrupt firm can be put to better use elsewhere, the firm is liquidated and the proceeds are used to pay off the creditors; otherwise the creditors become the new owners and the firm continues to operate.[36]

In practice, matters are rarely so simple. For example, we observe that firms often petition for bankruptcy even when the equity has a positive value. And firms often continue to operate even when the assets could be used more efficiently elsewhere. The problems in Chapter 11 usually arise because the goal of paying off the creditors conflicts with the goal of maintaining the business as a going concern. We described in Chapter 18 how the assets of Eastern Airlines seeped away in bankruptcy. When the company filed for Chapter 11, its assets were more than sufficient to repay in full its liabilities of $3.7 billion. But the bankruptcy judge was determined to keep Eastern flying. When it finally became clear that Eastern was a terminal case, the assets were sold off and the creditors received less than $.9 billion. The creditors would clearly have been better off if Eastern had been liquidated immediately; the unsuccessful attempt at resuscitation cost the creditors $2.8 billion.[37]

Here are some further reasons that Chapter 11 proceedings do not always achieve an efficient solution:

---

[33] But at least one class of creditors must vote for the plan; otherwise the court cannot approve it.

[34] Although Chapter 11 is designed to keep the firm in business, the reorganization plan often involves the sale or closure of large parts of the business.

[35] One study found that after emerging from Chapter 11, about one in three firms reentered bankruptcy or privately restructured their debt. See E. S. Hotchkiss, "Postbankruptcy Reform and Management Turnover," *Journal of Finance* 50 (March 1995), pp. 3–21.

[36] If there are several classes of creditors in this simplistic model, the junior creditors initially become the owners of the company and are responsible for paying off the senior debt. They now face exactly the same decision as the original owners. If their newly acquired equity is valueless, they will also default and turn over ownership to the next class of creditors.

[37] These estimates of creditor losses are taken from L. A. Weiss and K. H. Wruck, "Information Problems, Conflicts of Interest, and Asset Stripping: Chapter 11's Failure in the Case of Eastern Airlines," *Journal of Financial Economics* 48 (April 1998), pp. 55–97.

1. Although the reorganized firm is legally a new entity, it is entitled to the tax-loss carryforwards belonging to the old firm. If the firm is liquidated rather than reorganized, the tax-loss carryforwards disappear. Thus there is a tax incentive to continue operating the firm even when its assets could be sold and put to better use elsewhere.
2. If the firm's assets are sold, it is easy to determine what is available to pay creditors. However, when the company is reorganized, it needs to conserve cash. Therefore, claimants are often paid off with a mixture of cash and securities. This makes it less easy to judge whether they receive a fair shake.
3. Senior creditors who know they are likely to get a raw deal in a reorganization may press for a liquidation. Shareholders and junior creditors prefer a reorganization. They hope that the court will not interpret the creditors' pecking order too strictly and that they will receive consolation prizes when the firm's remaining value is sliced up.
4. Although shareholders and junior creditors are at the bottom of the pecking order, they have a secret weapon—they can play for time. When they use delaying tactics, the junior creditors are betting on a stroke of luck that will rescue their investment. On the other hand, the senior claimants know that time is working against them, so they may be prepared to settle for a lower payoff as part of the price for getting the plan accepted. Also, prolonged bankruptcy cases are costly, as we pointed out in Chapter 18. Senior claimants may see their money seeping into lawyers' pockets and decide to settle quickly.

But bankruptcy practices do change and in recent years Chapter 11 proceedings have become more creditor-friendly.[38] For example, equity investors and junior debtholders used to find that managers were willing allies in dragging out a settlement, but these days the managers of bankrupt firms often receive a key employee retention plan, which provides them with a large bonus if the reorganization proceeds quickly and a smaller one if the company lingers on in Chapter 11. This has contributed to a reduction in the time spent in bankruptcy from nearly two years before 1990 to about 16 months today.

While a reorganization plan is being drawn up, the company is likely to need additional working capital. It has, therefore, become increasingly common to allow the firm to buy goods on credit and to borrow money (known as *debtor in possession*, or *DIP*, debt). The lenders, who frequently comprise the firm's existing creditors, are liable to insist on stringent conditions and so have considerable influence on the outcome of the bankruptcy proceedings.

As creditors have gained more influence, shareholders of the bankrupt firms have received fewer and fewer crumbs. In recent years the court has faithfully observed the pecking order in about 90% of Chapter 11 settlements.

In 2009 GM and Chrysler both filed for bankruptcy. They were not only two of the largest bankruptcies ever, but they were also extraordinary legal events. With the help of billions of fresh money from the U.S. Treasury, the companies were in and out of bankruptcy court with blinding speed, compared with the normal placid pace of Chapter 11. The U.S. government was deeply involved in the rescue and the financing of New GM and New Chrysler. The nearby box explains some of the financial issues raised by the Chrysler bankruptcy. The GM bankruptcy raised similar issues.

Workouts

If Chapter 11 reorganizations are not efficient, why don't firms bypass the bankruptcy courts and get together with their creditors to work out a solution? Many firms that are in distress *do* first seek a

---

[38] For a discussion of these changes see S. T. Bharath, V. Panchapegesan, and I. Werner, "The Changing Nature of Chapter 11," working paper, Ohio State University, October 2007.

Finance In Practice

The Controversial Chrysler Bankruptcy

Chrysler was the weakest of the Big Three U.S. auto manufacturers. We have noted its purchase in 2007 by the private-equity fund Cerberus. By 2009, in the midst of the financial crisis and recession, Chrysler was headed for the dustbin unless it could arrange a rescue from the U.S. government. The rescue came *after* Chrysler's bankruptcy, however. Cerberus's stake was wiped out.

Chrysler filed for bankruptcy on April 30, 2009. It owed $6.9 billion to secured lenders, $5.3 billion to trade creditors (parts suppliers, for example), and $10 billion to a Voluntary Employees' Beneficiary Association (VEBA) trust set up to fund health and other benefits promised to retired employees. It also had unfunded pension liabilities, obligations to dealers, and warranty obligations to customers.

Just six weeks later on June 11 the bankruptcy was resolved, when all of Chrysler's assets and operations were sold to a new corporation for $2 billion. The $2 billion gave secured creditors 29 cents on the dollar. Fiat agreed to take over management of New Chrysler and received a 35% equity stake. New Chrysler received $6 billion in fresh loans from the U.S. Treasury and the Canadian government, in addition to $9.5 billion lent earlier. The Treasury and Canadian government also got 8% and 2% equity stakes, respectively.

The secured bondholders were of course unhappy. The court and government did not pause to see if Chrysler was really worth only $2 billion or if a higher value could have been achieved by breaking up the company. But the unsecured creditors must have been unhappier still, right? The sale for $2 billion left nothing to them.

Wrong! The trade creditors got a $5.3 billion debt claim on New Chrysler, 100 cents on the dollar. The unfunded pension liabilities and dealer and warranty obligations were likewise carried over dollar-for-dollar to New Chrysler. The VEBA trust got a $4.6 billion claim and a 55% equity stake.

We noted that junior creditors and stockholders sometimes get small slices of reorganized companies that emerge from bankruptcy. These consolation prizes are referred to as *violations of absolute priority,* because absolute priority pays senior creditors in full before junior creditors or stockholders get anything. But the Chrysler bankruptcy was resolved with *reverse* priority: junior claims were honored and senior claims mostly wiped out.

What this means for U.S. bankruptcy law and practice is not clear. Perhaps Chrysler's 42-day bankruptcy was a one-off deal never to be repeated, except by GM. But now secured investors worry that "junior creditors might leapfrog them if things don't work out."*

---

* George J. Schultze, quoted in M. Roe and D. Skeel, "Assessing the Chrysler Bankruptcy," http://ssrn.com/abstract=1426530. This article reviews the legal issues created by the reverse priority of creditors in the sale to New Chrysler.

---

negotiated settlement, or **workout.** For example, they can seek to delay payment of the debt or negotiate an interest rate holiday. However, shareholders and junior creditors know that senior creditors are anxious to avoid formal bankruptcy proceedings. So they are likely to be tough negotiators, and senior creditors generally need to make concessions to reach agreement.[39] The larger the firm, and the more complicated its capital structure, the less likely it is that everyone will agree to any proposal.

Sometimes the firm does agree to an informal workout with its creditors and then files under Chapter 11 to obtain the approval of the bankruptcy court. Such *prepackaged or prenegotiated bankruptcies* reduce the likelihood of subsequent litigation and allow the firm to gain the special tax advantages of Chapter 11.[40] For example, in 2004 Trump Hotels & Casino Resorts arranged a *prepack* after reaching agreement with its creditors. Since 1980 about 25% of U.S. bankruptcies have been prepackaged or prenegotiated.[41]

Alternative Bankruptcy Procedures

The United States bankruptcy system is often described as a debtor-friendly system. Its principal focus is on rescuing firms in distress. But this comes at a cost, for there are many instances in which the firm's assets would be better deployed in other uses. Michael Jensen, a critic of Chapter 11, has argued that "the U.S. bankruptcy code is fundamentally flawed. It is expensive, it exacerbates conflicts of interest among different classes of creditors, and it often takes years to resolve individual cases." Jensen's proposed solution is to require that any bankrupt company be put immediately on the auction block and the proceeds distributed to claimants in accordance with the priority of their claims.[42]

In some countries the bankruptcy system is even more friendly to debtors. For example, in France the primary duties of the bankruptcy court are to keep the firm in business and preserve employment. Only once these duties have been performed does the court have a responsibility to creditors. Creditors have minimal control over the process, and it is the court that decides whether the firm should be liquidated or preserved. If the court chooses liquidation, it may select a bidder who offers a lower price but better prospects for employment.

The U.K. is just about at the other end of the scale. When a British firm is unable to pay its debts, the control rights pass to the creditors. Most commonly, a designated secured creditor appoints a *receiver,* who assumes direction of the firm, sells sufficient assets to repay the secured creditors, and ensures that any excess funds are used to pay off the other creditors according to the priority of their claims.

Franks and Davydenko, who have examined alternative bankruptcy systems, found that banks responded to these differences in the bankruptcy code by adjusting their lending practices. Nevertheless, as you would expect, lenders recover a smaller proportion of their money in those countries that have a debtor-friendly bankruptcy system. For example, in France the banks recover on average only 47% of the money owed by bankrupt firms, while in the U.K. the corresponding figure is 69%.[43]

---

[39] Franks and Torous show that creditors make even greater concessions to junior creditors in informal workouts than in Chapter 11. See J. R. Franks and W. N. Torous, "How Shareholders and Creditors Fare in Workouts and Chapter 11 Reorganizations," *Journal of Financial Economics* 35 (May 1994), pp. 13–33.

[40] In a prepackaged bankruptcy the debtor gains agreement to the reorganization plan before the filing. In a prenegotiated bankruptcy the debtor negotiates the terms of the plan only with the principal creditors.

[41] Data from Lynn LoPucki's Bankruptcy Research Database at http://lopucki.law.ucla.edu.

[42] M. C. Jensen, "Corporate Control and the Politics of Finance," *Journal of Applied Corporate Finance* 4 (Summer 1991), pp. 13–33. An ingenious alternative set of bankruptcy procedures is proposed in L. Bebchuk, "A New Approach to Corporate Reorganizations," *Harvard Law Review* 101 (1988), pp. 775–804; and P. Aghion, O. Hart, and J. Moore, "The Economics of Bankruptcy Reform," *Journal of Law, Economics and Organization* 8 (1992), pp. 523–546.

[43] S. A. Davydenko and J. R. Franks, "Do Bankruptcy Codes Matter? A Study of Defaults in France, Germany and the U.K.," *Journal of Finance* 63 (2008), pp. 565–608. For descriptions of bankruptcy in Sweden and Finland, see P. Stromberg, "Conflicts of Interest and Market Illiquidity in Bankruptcy Auctions: Theory and Tests," *Journal of Finance* 55 (December 2000), pp. 2641–2692; and S. A. Ravid and S. Sundgren, "The Comparative Efficiency of Small-Firm Bankruptcies: A Study of the U.S. and Finnish Bankruptcy Codes," *Financial Management* 27 (Winter 1998), pp. 28–40.

Of course, the grass is always greener elsewhere. In the United States and France, critics complain about the costs of trying to save businesses that are no longer viable. By contrast, in countries such as the U.K., bankruptcy laws are blamed for the demise of healthy businesses and Chapter 11 is held up as a model of an efficient bankruptcy system.

Bankruptcy Regulations in India

Unlike in the U.S., India did not have one law dealing with bankruptcy of companies. The Sick Industries Companies Act, 1985 (SICA) was dealing with revival and rehabilitation of sick companies. The Companies Act, 1956 was dealing with the winding up (or liquidation) of the companies. Following the recommendation of the Eradi Committee (Justice V B Eradi Committee, set up in 1999), the Bill to Repeal SICA was passed in the Parliament in 2003. It also got the President's assent in 2004. However, due to a delay in setting up an alternative mechanism, i.e., the National Company Law Tribunal (NCLT), the Ministry of Finance has asked BIFR (under SICA) to continue in its existing form.

Under SICA, a sick industrial company was defined as one with negative net worth. Therefore under SICA, it was possible that a company had defaulted in its debt payments and still was not defined as a sick company simply because its net worth was positive. Once a firm was referred to BIFR, the creditors could not take any action against the company to recover their dues because all claims against the firm were automatically stayed. This provision enabled many unscrupulous managers to manipulate its accounts and show negative net worth and refer the company to BIFR. This ens ed that the creditors of the firm could no longer seize the assets of the company. This virtually made any debt covenant meaningless.

Under the SICA, a company had to register with BIFR within 60 days after its net worth became negative. Then BIFR used to decide in another 60 days whether the firm registered with it was indeed sick. Then BIFR would appoint an Operating Agency (OA) to investigate into the matter and recommend a suitable rehabilitation scheme. The OA would design an appropriate rehabilitation scheme in another 90 days' time. Once a plan was proposed, it required a lot of time in implementing it.

In 2002, the Government of India enacted the Securitisation and Reconstruction of Financial Assets and Enforcement of Security Interest Act.[44] This Act gave some leeway to the creditors. Chapter III of the Act, for example, says that "...*any security interest created in favor of any secured creditor may be enforced without the intervention of the court or tribunal, by such creditor in accordance with the provisions of this Act*".

The new Act allows for the creation of **Asset Reconstruction Companies (ARCs)** with the objective to acquire the non-performing assets from banks and financial institutions and try maximizing the recovery through improved management. The banks and financial institutions can transfer all financial assets (loans issued to the defaulting company) to an ARC and the ARC, in turn, will issue debentures and bonds to the banks and financial institutions. This way the ARC takes the responsibility of recovering the dues from the defaulting companies. The ARC can takeover the management of the borrowing company, can sale or lease its assets, can reschedule the payments to be made to the borrowers, can take possession of secured assets, etc. ICICI bank, State Bank of India, IDBI Bank, etc set up the first asset reconstruction company, namely the Asset Reconstruction Company of India Limited (ARCIL). Thus, for example, in January 2005, the Asset Reconstruction Company of India took over the assets of the ailing company Kumar Metallurgical Corporation Limited of Hyderabad.

---

[44] Downloadable from www.arcil.co.in.

A corporation's structure is not immutable. Companies frequently reorganize by adding new businesses or disposing of existing ones. They may alter their capital structure and they may change their ownership and control. In this chapter we looked at some of the mechanisms by which companies transform themselves.

We started with leveraged buyouts (LBOs). An LBO is a takeover or buyout of a company or division that is financed mostly with debt. The LBO is owned privately, usually by an investment partnership. Debt financing is not the objective of most LBOs; it is a means to an end. Most LBOs are diet deals. The cash requirements for debt service force managers to shed unneeded assets, improve operating efficiency, and forego wasteful expenditure. The managers and employees are given a significant stake in the business, so they have strong incentives to make these improvements.

A leveraged restructuring is in many ways similar to an LBO. In this case the company puts *itself* on a diet. Large amounts of debt are added and the proceeds are paid out to shareholders. The company is forced to generate cash to service the debt, but there is no change in control and the company stays public.

Most investments in LBOs are made by private-equity partnerships. The limited partners, who put up most of the money, are mostly institutional investors, including pension funds, endowments, and insurance companies. The general partners, who organize and manage the funds, receive a management fee and get a carried interest in the fund's profits. We called these partnerships "temporary conglomerates." They are conglomerates because they create a portfolio of companies in unrelated industries. They are temporary because the partnership has a limited life, usually about 10 years. At the end of this period, the partnership's investments must be sold or taken public again in IPOs. Private-equity funds do not buy and hold; they buy, fix, and sell. Investors in the partnership therefore do not have to worry about wasteful reinvestment of free cash flow.

The private-equity market has been growing steadily. In contrast to these temporary conglomerates, public conglomerates have been declining in the United States. In public companies, unrelated diversification seems to destroy value—the whole is worth less than the sum of its parts. There are two possible reasons for this. First, since the value of the parts can't be observed separately, it is harder to set incentives for divisional managers. Second, conglomerates' internal capital markets are inefficient. It is difficult for management to appreciate investment opportunities in many different industries, and internal capital markets are prone to overinvestment and cross-subsidies.

Of course, companies shed assets as well as acquire them. Assets may be divested by spin-offs, carve-outs, or asset sales. In a spin-off the parent firm splits off part of its business into a separate public company and gives its shareholders stock in the company. In a carve-out the parent raises cash by separating off part of its business and selling shares in this business through an IPO. These divestitures are generally good news to investors; it appears that the divisions are moving to better homes, where they can be well managed and more profitable. The same improvements in efficiency and profitability are observed in privatizations, which are spin-offs or carve-outs of businesses owned by governments.

Companies in distress may reorganize by getting together with their creditors to arrange a workout. For example, they may agree to a delay in repayment. If a workout proves impossible, the company needs to file for bankruptcy. Chapter 11 of the Bankruptcy Act, which is used by most large public companies, seeks to reorganize the company and put it back on its feet again. However, the goal of paying off the company's creditors often conflicts with the aim of keeping the business going. As a result, Chapter 11 sometimes allows a firm to continue to operate when its assets could be better used elsewhere and the proceeds used to pay off creditors.

Chapter 11 tends to favor the debtor. But in some other countries the bankruptcy system is designed almost exclusively to recover as much cash as possible for the lenders. While U.S. critics of Chapter 11 complain about the costs of saving businesses that are not worth saving, commentators elsewhere bemoan the fact that their bankruptcy laws are causing the breakup of potentially healthy businesses.

FURTHER READING

The following paper provides a general overview of corporate restructuring:

B. E. Eckbo and K. S. Thorburn, "Corporate Restructurings: Breakups and LBOs," in B. E. Eckbo (ed.), *Handbook of Empirical Corporate Finance* (Amsterdam: Elsevier/North-Holland, 2007), Chapter 16.

The papers by Kaplan and Stein, and Kaplan and Stromberg, provide evidence on the evolution and performance of LBOs. Jensen, the chief proponent of the free-cash-flow theory of takeovers, gives a spirited and controversial defense of LBOs:

S. N. Kaplan and J. C. Stein, "The Evolution of Buyout Pricing and Financial Structure (Or What Went Wrong) in the 1980s," *Journal of Applied Corporate Finance* 6 (Spring 1993), pp. 72–88.

S. N. Kaplan and P. Stromberg, "Leveraged Buyouts and Private Equity," *Journal of Economic Perspectives* 23 (2009), pp. 121–146.

M. C. Jensen, "The Eclipse of the Public Corporation," *Harvard Business Review* 67 (September/October 1989), pp. 61–74.

The Summer 2006 issue of the Journal of Applied Corporate Finance *includes a panel discussion and several articles on private equity. Privatization is surveyed in:*

W. L. Megginson, *The Financial Economics of Privatization* (Oxford: Oxford University Press, 2005).

The following books and articles survey the bankruptcy process. Bris, Welch, and Zhu give a detailed comparison of bankrupt firms' experience in Chapter 7 versus Chapter 11.

E. I. Altman, *Corporate Financial Distress and Bankruptcy: A Complete Guide to Predicting and Avoiding Distress and Profiting from Bankruptcy,* 3rd ed. (New York: John Wiley & Sons, 2005).

E. S. Hotchkiss, K. John, R. M. Mooradian, and K. S. Thorburn, "Bankruptcy and the Resolution of Financial Distress," in B. E. Eckbo (ed.), *Handbook of Empirical Corporate Finance* (Amsterdam: Elsevier/North-Holland, 2007), Chapter 14.

L. Senbet and J. Seward, "Financial Distress, Bankruptcy and Reorganization," in R. A. Jarrow, V. Maksimovic, and W. T. Ziemba (eds.), *North-Holland Handbooks of Operations Research and Management Science: Finance,* vol. 9 (New York: Elsevier, 1995), pp. 921–961.

J. S. Bhandari, L. A. Weiss, and B. E. Adler (eds.), *Corporate Bankruptcy: Economic and Legal Perspectives* (Cambridge, U.K.: Cambridge University Press, 1996).

A. Bris, I. Welch, and N. Zhu, "The Costs of Bankruptcy: Chapter 7 Liquidation versus Chapter 11 Reorganization," *Journal of Finance* 61 (June 2006), pp. 1253–1303.

Here are several good case studies on topics covered in this chapter:

B. Burrough and J. Helyar, *Barbarians at the Gate: The Fall of RJR Nabisco* (New York: Harper & Row, 1990).

G. P. Baker, "Beatrice: A Study in the Creation and Destruction of Value," *Journal of Finance* 47 (July 1992), pp. 1081–1120.

K. H. Wruck, "Financial Policy as a Catalyst for Organizational Change: Sealed Air's Leveraged Special Dividend," *Journal of Applied Corporate Finance* 7 (Winter 1995), pp. 20–37.

J. Allen, "Reinventing the Corporation: The Satellite Structure of Thermo Electron," *Journal of Applied Corporate Finance* 11 (Summer 1998), pp. 38–47.

R. Parrino, "Spinoffs and Wealth Transfers: The Marriott Case," *Journal of Financial Economics* 43 (February 1997), pp. 241–274.

C. Eckel, D. Eckel, and V. Singal, "Privatization and Efficiency: Industry Effects of the Sale of British Airways," *Journal of Financial Economics* 43 (February 1997), pp. 275–298.

L. A. Weiss and K. H. Wruck, "Information Problems, Conflicts of Interest, and Asset Stripping: Chapter 11's Failure in the Case of Eastern Airlines," *Journal of Financial Economics* 48 (April 1998), pp. 55–97.

W. Megginson and D. Scannapieco, "The Financial and Economic Lessons of Italy's Privatization Program," *Journal of Applied Corporate Finance* 18 (Summer 2006), pp. 56–65.

PROBLEM SETS

BASIC

1. Define the following terms:
   a. LBO
   b. MBO
   c. Spin-off
   d. Carve-out
   e. Asset sale
   f. Privatization
   g. Leveraged restructuring

2. True or false?
   a. One of the first tasks of an LBO's financial manager is to pay down debt.
   b. Once an LBO or MBO goes private, it almost always stays private.
   c. Targets for LBOs in the 1980s tended to be profitable companies in mature industries.
   d. "Carried interest" refers to the deferral of interest payments on LBO debt.
   e. By 2008 new LBO and private-equity transactions were extremely rare.
   f. The announcement of a spin-off is generally followed by a sharp fall in the stock price.
   g. Privatizations are generally followed by massive layoffs.
   h. On average, privatization seems to improve efficiency and add value.

3. What are the government's motives in a privatization?

4. What *advantages* have been claimed for public conglomerates?

5. List the *disadvantages* of traditional U.S. conglomerates.

6. Private-equity partnerships have a limited term. What are the advantages of this arrangement?

7. What is the difference between Chapter 7 and Chapter 11 bankruptcies?

8. True or false?
   a. When a company becomes bankrupt, it is usually in the interests of stockholders to seek a liquidation rather than a reorganization.
   b. In Chapter 11 a reorganization plan must be presented for approval by each class of creditor.
   c. In a reorganization, creditors may be paid off with a mixture of cash and securities.
   d. When a company is liquidated, one of the most valuable assets to be sold off is the tax-loss carryforward.

9. Explain why equity can sometimes have a positive value even when companies file for bankruptcy.

INTERMEDIATE

10. True, false, or "It depends on . . ."?
    a. Carve-out or spin-off of a division improves incentives for the division's managers.
    b. Private-equity partnerships have limited lives. The main purpose is to force the general partners to seek out quick payback investments.
    c. Managers of private-equity partnerships have an incentive to make risky investments.

11. For what kinds of firm would an LBO or MBO transaction *not* be productive?

12. Outline the similarities and differences between the RJR Nabisco LBO and the Sealed Air leveraged restructuring. Were the economic motives the same? Were the results the same? Do you think it was an advantage for Sealed Air to remain a public company?

13. Examine some recent examples of divestitures. What do you think were the underlying reason for them? How did investors react to the news?

14. Read *Barbarians at the Gate* (Further Reading). What agency costs can you identify? (*Hint:* Se Chapter 12.) Do you think the LBO was well-designed to reduce these costs?

15. Explain the structure of a private-equity partnership. Pay particular attention to incentives and compensation. What types of investment were such partnerships designed to make?

16. We described carried interest as an option. What kind of option? How does this option chang incentives in a private-equity partnership? Can you think of circumstances where these incentiv changes would be perverse, that is, potentially value-destroying? Explain.

17. "Privatization appears to bring efficiency gains because public companies are better able t reduce agency costs." Why do you think this may (or may not) be true?

18. We described several problems with Chapter 11 bankruptcy. Which of these problems could b mitigated by negotiating a prepackaged bankruptcy?

33

CHAPTER

GOVERNANCE AND CORPORATE CONTROL AROUND THE WORLD

Much of corporate finance (and much of this book) assumes a particular financial structure—-public corporations with actively traded shares and relatively easy access to financial markets. But there are other ways to organize and finance business ventures. The arrangements for ownership, control, and financing vary greatly around the world. In this chapter we consider some of these differences.

Corporations raise cash from financial markets and also from financial institutions. Markets are relatively more important in the United States, United Kingdom, and other "Anglo-Saxon" economies. Financial institutions, particularly banks, are relatively more important in many other countries, including Germany and Japan. In bank-based systems, individual investors are less likely to hold corporate debt and equity directly. Instead ownership passes through banks, insurance companies, and other financial intermediaries.

This chapter starts with an overview of financial markets, financial institutions, and sources of financing. We contrast Europe, Japan, and the rest of Asia to the United States and United Kingdom. Then Section 33-2 looks more closely at ownership, control, and governance. Here we start with the United States and United Kingdom and then turn to Japan, Germany, and the rest of the world. Section 33-3 asks whether these differences matter. For example, do well-functioning financial markets and institutions contribute to economic development and growth? What are the advantages and disadvantages of market-based versus bank-based systems?

Before starting on this worldwide tour, remember that the principles of financial management apply throughout the journey. The concepts and basic tools of the trade do not vary. For example, all companies in all countries should recognize the opportunity cost of capital (although the cost of capital is even harder to measure where stock markets are small or erratic). Discounted cash flow still makes sense. Real options are encountered everywhere. And even in bank-based financial systems, corporations participate in world financial markets—by trading foreign exchange or hedging risks in futures markets, for instance.

33-1 FINANCIAL MARKETS AND INSTITUTIONS

In most of this book we have assumed that a large part of debt financing comes from public bond markets. Nothing in principle changes when a firm borrows from a bank instead. But in some countries bond markets are stunted and bank financing is more important. Figure 33.1 shows the total values of bank loans, private (nongovernment) bonds, and stock markets in different parts of the world in 2007. To measure these financial claims on a comparable basis, the amounts are scaled by gross domestic product (GDP).[1]

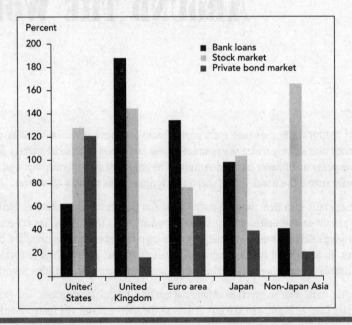

FIGURE 33.1

Value of financial claims in 2007, percentage of GDP.

Sources: Bloomberg, IMF, World Federation of Exchanges, and BIS. We are grateful to Michael Chui for this figure.

Company financing in the United States is different from that in most other countries. The United States not only has a large amount of bank loans outstanding, but there is also a large stock market *and* a large corporate bond market. Thus the United States is said to have a market-based financial

[1] For more detailed data and discussion of the material in this section, see F. Allen, M. Chui, and A. Maddaloni, "Financial Structure and Corporate Governance in Europe, the USA, and Asia," in *Handbook of European Financial Markets and Institutions,* ed. X. Freixas, P. Hartmann, and C. Mayer (Oxford: Oxford University Press, 2008), pp. 31–67.

system. Stock market value is also high in the United Kingdom and Asia,[2] but bank loans are much more important than the bond market in these countries. In Europe[3] and Japan, bank financing again outpaces bond markets, but the stock market is relatively small. Most countries in Europe, including Germany, France, Italy, and Spain, have bank-based financial systems. So does Japan.

Let's look at these regions from a different perspective. Figure 33.2 shows the financial investments made by households, again scaled by GDP.[4] ("Households" means individual investors.) Household portfolios are divided into four categories: bank deposits, insurance policies and mutual and pension funds, equity securities, and "other." Notice in Figure 33.2 the differences in the total amounts of financial assets. Summing the columns for each country and region, the amount of financial assets is 275% of GDP in the United States, 288% in the United Kingdom, 286% in Japan, and 185% in Europe. This does not mean that European investors are poor, just that they hold less wealth in the form of financial assets. Figure 33.2 excludes other important investment categories, such as real estate or privately owned businesses. It also excludes the value of pensions provided by governments.

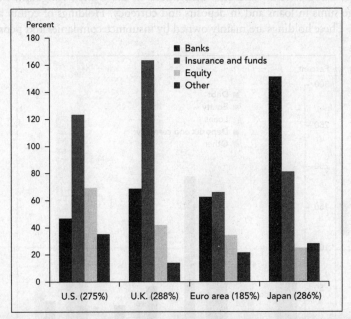

FIGURE 33.2

Household portfolio allocations, 1995–2007, percentage of GDP.

Sources: Bank of Japan, EUROSTAT, Federal Reserve Board, and the U.K. Office for National Statistics. We are grateful to Michael Chui for this figure.

In the United States, a large fraction of households' portfolios is held directly in equity securities, mostly common stocks. Therefore individual investors can potentially play an important role in corporate governance. Direct equity holdings are smaller in the United Kingdom, smaller still in Europe, and smallest in Japan. Japanese households could not play a significant direct role in corporate governance even if they wanted to. They can't vote shares that they don't own.

---

[2] Asia here includes Hong Kong, Indonesia, Korea, Malaysia, the Philippines, Singapore, Taiwan, and Thailand.

[3] Europe here includes: Austria, Belgium, Finland, France, Germany, Greece, Italy, the Netherlands, Portugal, Slovenia, and Spain.

[4] Data for Asia are not available for this and the following figures that summarize portfolio allocations.

Where direct equity investment is small, household investments in bank deposits, insurance policies, and mutual and pension funds are correspondingly large. In the United Kingdom, the insurance and funds category dominates, with bank deposits in second place. In Europe, bank deposits and insurance and funds run a close race for first. In Japan, bank deposits win by a mile, with insurance and funds in second place and equities a distant third.

Figure 33.2 tells us that in many parts of the world there are relatively few individual stockholders. Most individuals don't invest directly in equity markets, but indirectly, through insurance companies, mutual funds, banks, and other financial intermediaries. Of course the thread of ownership traces back through these intermediaries to individual investors. All assets are ultimately owned by individuals. There are no Martian or extraterrestrial investors that we know of.[5]

Now let's look at financial institutions. Figure 33.3 shows the financial assets held by financial institutions, including banks, mutual funds, insurance companies, pension funds, and other intermediaries. These investments are smaller in the United States, relative to GDP, than in other countries (as expected in the U.S. market-based system). Financial institutions in the United Kingdom, Europe, and Japan have invested large sums in loans and in deposits and currency. Holdings of equity are highest in the United Kingdom. These holdings are mainly owned by insurance companies and pension funds.

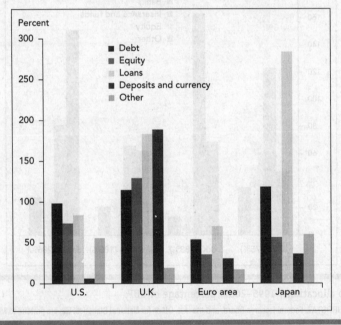

FIGURE 33.3

Financial institutions' portfolio allocations, 1995–2007, percentage of GDP.

Sources: Bank of Japan, EUROSTAT, Federal Reserve Board, and the U.K. Office for National Statistics. We are grateful to Michael Chui for this figure.

We've covered households and financial institutions. Is there any other source for corporate financing? Yes, financing can come from other corporations. Take a look at Figure 33.4, which shows the

---

[5] There may be owners not yet present on this planet, however. For example, endowments of educational, charitable, and religious organizations are partly held in trust for future generations.

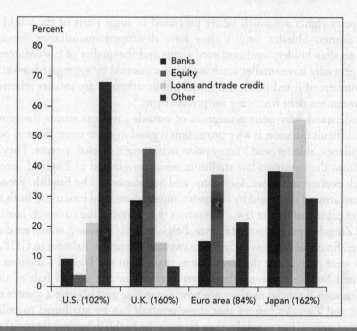

FIGURE 33.4

Nonfinancial corporations' portfolio allocations, 1995–2007, Percentage of GDP.

Sources: Bank of Japan, EUROSTAT, Federal Reserve Board, and the U.K. Office for National Statistics. We are grateful to Michael Chui for this figure.

financial assets held by nonfinancial corporations. Perhaps the most striking feature is the large amount of equity held by firms in Europe. The amount of equity held in Japan and the United Kingdom is also large. In the United States it is relatively small. As we will see, these holdings of shares by other nonfinancial corporations have important implications for corporate ownership and governance.

Another interesting aspect of Figure 33.4 is the large amount of intercompany loans and trade credit (mostly trade credit) in Japan. Many Japanese firms rely heavily on trade-credit financing, that is, on accounts payable to other firms. Of course the other firms see the reverse side of trade credit: They are providing financing in the form of accounts receivable.

Figures 33.1 to 33.4 show that just drawing a line between market-based, "Anglo-Saxon" financial systems and bank-based financial systems is simplistic. We need to dig a little deeper when comparing financial systems. For example, more equity is held directly by households in the United States than in the United Kingdom and the portfolio allocations of households, nonfinancial corporations, and financial institutions are also significantly different. In addition, we noted the large cross-holdings of shares among European corporations. Finally, Japanese households put significantly more of their savings in banks and Japanese corporations use trade credit much more than in other advanced economies.

Investor Protection and the Development of Financial Markets

What explains the importance of financial markets in some countries, while other countries rely less on markets and more on banks and other financial institutions? One answer is investor protection. Stock and bond markets thrive where investors in these markets are protected reasonably well.

Investors' property rights are much better protected in some parts of the world than others. La Porta, Lopez-de-Silanes, Shleifer, and Vishny have developed quantitative measures of investor protection based on shareholders' and creditors' rights and the quality of law enforcement. Countries with poor scores generally have smaller stock markets, measured by aggregate market value relative to GDP, and the numbers of listed firms and initial public offerings are smaller relative to population. Poor scores also mean less debt financing for private firms.[6]

It's easy to understand why poor protection of outside investors stunts the growth of financial markets. A more difficult question is why protection is good in some countries and poor in others. La Porta, Lopez-de-Silanes, Shleifer, and Vishny point to the origin of legal systems. They distinguish legal systems derived from the common-law tradition, which originated in England, from systems based on civil law, which evolved in France, Germany, and Scandinavia. The English, French, and German systems have spread around the world by conquest, imperialism, and imitation. Both shareholders and creditors are better protected by the law in countries that adopted the common-law tradition.

But Rajan and Zingales[7] point out that France, Belgium, and Germany, which are civil-law countries, had well-developed financial markets early in the twentieth century. Relative to GDP, these countries' financial markets were then about the same size as markets in the United Kingdom and bigger than those in the United States. These rankings were reversed in the second half of the century, after World War II, although financial markets are now expanding and playing a greater role in European economies. Rajan and Zingales believe that these reversals can be attributed to political trends and shifts in government policy. For example, they recount the backlash against financial markets after the stock market crash of 1929 and the expansion of government regulation and ownership in the Great Depression and after World War II.

33-2   Ownership, Control, and Governance

Who owns the corporation? In the United States and United Kingdom, we just say "the stockholders." There is usually just one class of common stock, and each share has one vote. Some stockholders may have more influence than others, but only because they own more shares. In other countries, ownership is not so simple, as we see later in this section.

What is the corporation's financial objective? Normally we just say "to maximize stockholder value." According to U.S. and U.K. corporation law, managers have a *fiduciary duty* to the shareholders. In other words, they are legally required to act in the interests of shareholders. Consider the classic illustration provided by an early case involving the Ford Motor Company. Henry Ford announced a special dividend, but then reneged, saying that the cash earmarked for the dividend would be spent for the benefit of employees. A shareholder sued on the grounds that corporations existed for the benefit of shareholders and the management did not have the right to improve the lot of workers at shareholders' expense. Ford lost the case.[8]

The idea that the corporation should be run in the interests of the shareholders is thus embedded in the law in the United States and United Kingdom. The board of directors is supposed to represent shareholders' interests. But laws and customs differ in other countries. Now we look at some of these differences. We start with Japan.

---

[6] R. La Porta, F. Lopez-de-Silanes, A. Shleifer, and R. Vishny, "Legal Determinants of External Finance," *Journal of Finance* 52 (July 1997) pp. 1131–1150, and "Law and Finance," *Journal of Political Economy* 106 (December 1998), pp. 1113–1155.

[7] R. Rajan and L. Zingales, *Saving Capitalism from the Capitalists* (New York: Crown Business, 2003).

[8] Subsequently it appeared that Henry Ford reneged on the dividend so that he could purchase blocks of shares at depressed prices!

Ownership and Control in India

One notable feature about corporate ownership in India is the concentration of control in the hands of the promoters. One can divide the companies in India into the following four broad categories:

- Companies controlled by the Indian Business Groups
- Companies controlled by Government of India and the different state governments
- Companies controlled by MNCs and NRIs
- Other companies

Ninety-three percent of the total corporate assets are controlled by the first three categories of companies, leaving aside only 7 percent of the assets for the non-promoter controlled companies. A quick survey of about 19,500 companies from the Prowess database shows that in October 2011, the Indian Business Groups controlled 53 percent of the total corporate assets, the government controlled companies (both Central and State governments) controlled another 27 percent of the total corporate assets. We show the results in Table 33.1 below.

TABLE 33.1 Types of Indian companies and assets controlled by them

Groups	No of Companies	Total Assets (₹ Crores)	ROA
Indian business groups	5,565 (28%)	3,917,455 (53%)	2%
Foreign business groups	172 (1%)	141,629 (2%)	8%
Government	536 (3%)	1,991,522 (27%)	3%
Private Indian	12,516 (64%)	985,982 (13%)	2%
Private foreign	748 (4%)	342,420 (5%)	7%
Total	19537	₹7,379,008 Crores	

Source: Compiled from Prowess database

TABLE 33.2 Shareholding pattern in Indian companies

Shareholders	%Stake
Promoters	45.97%
Financial institutions	12.83%
Corporate bodies	22.84%
Individuals	15.20%
Others	3.16%
Total	100.00%

Source: Compiled from Prowess database

From Table 33.2, we can see that promoters control a little less than half of the shares in the companies managed by them. The average stake of the promoters in an Indian company used to be around 20% in 1997. It increased after 1997 and got more than doubled to 47% in 2001 after SEBI accepted the Substantial Acquisition of Shares and Takeovers Regulations in 1997.

A higher equity stake gives tremendous power to the promoters as they can pass any ordinary resolution in the company irrespective of whether the other shareholders agree to it or not. This also makes the market for corporate control virtually ineffective in disciplining the management. That is why, we normally observe mergers taking place between companies belonging to the same business groups in India. In only about 6 percent of the mergers that have taken place between 1991 and 2000, the promoters of the merged and merging companies are different.

Though the average stake of the Indian promoters is about 46 percent, in about 15 percent of the companies, the promoters control less than 30 percent of the total shares. In about 30 percent of the companies, the promoters control less than 40 percent of the shares. The promoters in such companies, however, manage to maintain their control over such company because of the tacit support they receive from the financial institutions. The Indian business groups also manage to control the different group companies by effectively using the concept of **cross-holdings**. This way the promoter can increase its stake in the different companies indirectly without having to spend anything while acquiring the shares. Thus, for example, in 2006, Tata Sons had 20.04 percent stake in Tata Steel and 21.98 percent stake in Tata Motors. Tata Steel had 8.46 percent stake in Tata Motors and Tata Motors in turn had 4.66 percent stake in Tata Steel. We show this cross-holding pattern here.

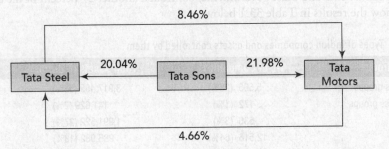

In emerging markets like India, some of the institutions like capital market or labor market are not well-developed. As we discussed in Chapter 33, the successful business groups have managed to create shareholders' wealth by performing the role of these institutions. It has a negative side also. As we discussed in Chapter 1, there is always a conflict of interest between the minority shareholders and the promoters and hence the promoters may take investment decisions that are not in the overall interest of the company.

Ownership and Control in Japan

Traditionally the most notable feature of Japanese corporate finance has been the **keiretsu.** A keiretsu is a network of companies, usually organized around a major bank. Japan is said to have a *main bank* system, with long-standing relationships between banks and firms. There are also long-standing business relationships between a keiretsu's companies. For example, a manufacturing company might buy most of its raw materials from group suppliers and in turn sell much of its output to other group companies.

The bank and other financial institutions at the keiretsu's center own shares in most of the group companies (though a commercial bank in Japan is limited to 5% ownership of each company). Those companies may in turn hold the bank's shares or each others' shares. For example, as of March 2009, Sumitomo Corporation held about 10% of Sumitomo Metal Industries, which in turn held about 2% of the shares of Sumitomo Corporation. Because of the cross-holdings, the number of shares available for purchase by outside investors is much lower than the total number outstanding.

The keiretsu is tied together in other ways. Most debt financing comes from the keiretsu's main bank or from affiliated financial institutions. Managers may sit on the boards of directors of other group companies, and a "presidents' council" of the CEOs of the most important group companies meets regularly.

Think of the keiretsu as a system of corporate governance, where power is divided among the main bank, the group's largest companies, and the group as a whole. This confers certain financial advantages. First, firms have access to additional "internal" financing—internal to the group, that is. Thus a company with a capital budget exceeding operating cash flows can turn to the main bank or other keiretsu companies for financing. This avoids the cost or possible bad-news signal of a public sale of securities. Second, when a keiretsu firm falls into financial distress, with insufficient cash to pay its bills or fund necessary capital investments, a workout can usually be arranged. New management can be brought in from elsewhere in the group, and financing can be obtained, again "internally."

Hoshi, Kashyap, and Scharfstein tracked capital expenditure programs of a large sample of Japanese firms—many, but not all, members of keiretsus. The keiretsu companies' investments were more stable and less exposed to the ups and downs of operating cash flows or to episodes of financial distress.[9] It seems that the financial support of the keiretsus enabled members to invest for the long run, regardless of temporary setbacks.

Corporation law in Japan resembles that in the United States, but there are some important differences. For example, in Japan it is easier for shareholders to nominate and elect directors. Also, management remuneration must be approved at general meetings of shareholders.[10] Nevertheless, ordinary shareholders do not in fact have much influence. Japanese boards traditionally have 40 or 50 members, with only a handful who are potentially independent of management.[11] The CEO effectively controls nominations to the board. As long as the financial position of a Japanese corporation is sound, the CEO and senior management control the corporation. Outside stockholders have very little influence.

Given this control, plus the cross-holdings within industrial groups, it's no surprise that hostile takeovers are exceedingly rare in Japan. Also, Japanese corporations have been stingy with dividends, which probably reflects the relative lack of influence of outside shareholders. On the other hand, Japanese CEOs do not use their power to generate large sums of personal wealth. They are not well paid, compared to CEOs in most other developed countries. (Look back to Figure 12.1 for average top-management compensation levels for Japan and other countries.)

Cross-holdings reached a peak around 1990 when about 50% of corporations' shares were held by other Japanese companies and financial institutions. Starting in the mid-1990s a banking crisis began to emerge in Japan. This led firms to sell off bank shares because they viewed them as bad investments. Banks and firms in financial distress, including Nissan, sold off other companies' shares to raise funds. By 2004 the level of cross-holdings had fallen to 20%. In the next few years, however, cross-holdings rose again as companies in the steel and other industries began to worry about hostile takeovers, which was the original motivation for acquisition of cross-holdings in the 1950s and 1960s.[12]

Ownership and Control in Germany

Traditionally banks in Germany played a significant role in corporate governance. This involved providing loans, owning large amounts of equity directly, and the proxy voting of shares held on

---

[9] T. Hoshi, A. Kashyap, and D. Scharfstein, "Corporate Structure, Liquidity and Investment: Evidence from Japanese Industrial Groups," *Quarterly Journal of Economics* 106 (February 1991), pp. 33–60, and "The Role of Banks in Reducing the Costs of Financial Distress in Japan," *Journal of Financial Economics* 27 (September 1990), pp. 67–88.

[10] These requirements have led to a unique feature of Japanese corporate life, the *sokaiya*, who are racketeers who demand payment in exchange for not disrupting shareholders' meetings.

[11] In recent years some Japanese companies such as Sony have changed to U.S.-style boards with fewer members and more independent directors.

[12] See H. Miyajima and F. Kuroki, "The Unwinding of Cross-Shareholding in Japan: Causes, Effects and Implications," in *Corporate Governance in Japan: Institutional Change and Organizational Diversity,* ed. M. Aoki, G. Jackson, and H. Miyajima (Oxford and New York: Oxford University Press, 2007), pp. 79–124. Also see "Criss-Crossed Capitalism," *The Economist* print edition, November 6, 2008.

behalf of customers. Over time this role has changed significantly. The relationship between the largest German bank, Deutsche Bank, and one of the largest German companies, Daimler AG, provides a good illustration.

Panel *a* of Figure 33.5 shows the 1990 ownership structure of Daimler, or as it was known then, Daimler-Benz. The immediate owners were Deutsche Bank with 28%, Mercedes Automobil Holding with 25%, and the Kuwait Government with 14%. The remaining 32% of the shares were widely held by about 300,000 individual and institutional investors. But this was only the top layer. Mercedes Automobil's holding was half owned by holding companies "Stella" and "Stern," for short. The rest of its shares were widely held. Stella's shares were in turn split four ways: between two banks; Robert Bosch, an industrial company; and another holding company, "Komet." Stern's ownership was split five ways but we ran out of space.[13]

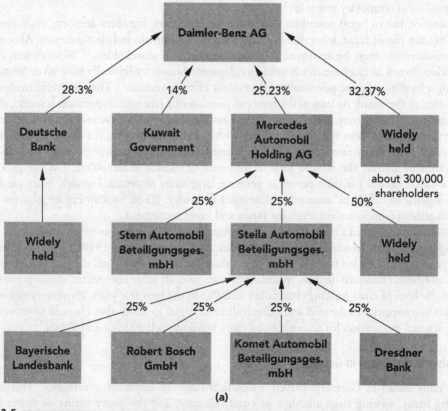

(a)

FIGURE 33.5

Panel a: Ownership of Daimler-Benz, 1990; *Panel b:* Ownership of Daimler, 2009. *(see next page)*

Sources: Panel a: J. Franks and C. Mayer, "The Ownership and Control of German Corporations," *Review of Financial Studies* 14 (Winter 2001), Figure 1, p. 949. © 2001 Oxford University Press. Used with permission. *Panel* b: OSIRIS Database (Bureau van Dijk Electronic publishing). We are grateful to Pedro Matos for providing this figure.

---

[13] A five-layer ownership tree for Daimler-Benz is given in S. Prowse, "Corporate Governance in an International Perspective: A Survey of Corporate Control Mechanisms among Large Firms in the U.S., U.K., Japan and Germany," *Financial Markets, Institutions, and Instruments* 4 (February 1995), Table 16.

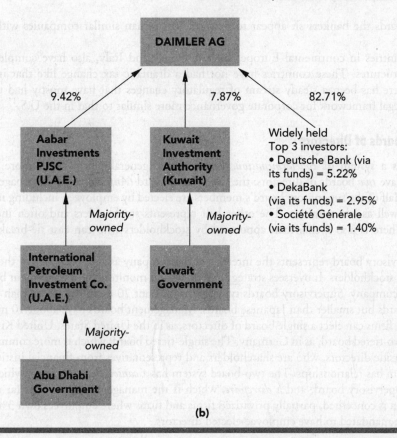

(b)

FIGURE 33.5
(Continued)

Panel *b* shows the ownership structure in 2009. It is quite different. Deutsche Bank does not have a direct stake anymore. Its holdings of 5% are now via its investment funds. The Kuwait government still owns a substantial stake of about 8%, but considerably less than the 14% it owned in 1990. The only other large investor is Aabar Investments, which owns 9%. Aabar is itself majority-owned by International Petroleum Investment Company, which is in turn majority-owned by the Abu Dhabi government. In stark contrast to the situation in 1990 when only 32% was widely held, in 2009 82% was widely held. The ownership structure has moved a long way toward the U.S. ownership pattern, where many large companies are entirely widely held.

An important reason for this dramatic change in ownership structure was a tax change that took effect in 2002. This exempted capital gains on shares held for more than one year from corporate taxation. Prior to that, the corporate capital gains rate had been 52%, which made selling shares very costly for corporations.

Daimler was not the only company to experience a significant drop in bank ownership. Dittman, Maug, and Schneider point out that average bank ownership of equity fell from 4.1% in 1994 to .4% in 2005. Board seats held by bank representatives fell from 9.6% to 5.6% of the total. Dittman, Maug, and Schneider's evidence suggests that banks are now primarily interested in using their board representation to promote their lending and investment banking activities. However, the companies on whose boards the bankers sit appear to perform worse than similar companies without such a presence.[14]

Other countries in continental Europe, such as France and Italy, also have complex corporate ownership structures. These countries have not had a dramatic tax change like that in Germany. However, there has been a steady stream of regulatory changes that have mostly had the effect of making the legal framework for corporate governance more similar to that in the U.S.[15]

European Boards of Directors

Germany has a system of *codetermination.* Larger firms (generally firms with more than 2,000 employees) have *two* boards of directors: the supervisory board *(Aufsichtsrat)* and management board *(Vorstand).* Half of the supervisory board's members are elected by employees, including management and staff as well as labor unions. The other half represents stockholders and often includes bank executives. There is also a chairman appointed by stockholders who can cast tie-breaking votes if necessary.

The supervisory board represents the interests of the company as a whole, not just the interests of employees or stockholders. It oversees strategy and elects and monitors the management board, which operates the company. Supervisory boards typically have about 20 members, more than typical U.S. and U.K. boards but smaller than Japanese boards. Management boards have about 10 members.

In France, firms can elect a single board of directors, as in the United States, United Kingdom, and Japan, or a two-tiered board, as in Germany. The single-tiered board, which is more common, consists mostly of outside directors, who are shareholders and representatives from financial institutions with which the firm has relationships. The two-board system has a *conseil de surveillance,* which resembles a German supervisory board, and a *directoire,* which is the management board. As far as employee representation is concerned, partially privatized firms and firms where employees own 3% or more of the shares are mandated to have employee-elected directors.

Ownership and Control in Other Countries

La Porta, Lopez-de-Silanes, and Shleifer surveyed corporate ownership in 27 developed economies.[16] They found relatively few firms with actively traded shares and dispersed ownership. The German pattern of significant ownership by banks and other financial institutions is also uncommon. Instead, firms are typically controlled by wealthy families or the state. The ultimate controlling shareholders typically have secure voting control even when they do not have the majority stake in earnings, dividends, or asset values.

Family control is common in Europe and also in Asia. Table 33.3 summarizes a study by Claessens, Djankov, and Lang, who traced ownership in 1996 for a sample of nearly 3,000 Asian companies. Except in Japan, a high proportion of public firms were family controlled. Thus wealthy families control large fractions of many Asian economies. For example, in Hong Kong, the 10 largest family groups control 32% of the assets of all listed firms. In Thailand, the top 10 families control 46% of assets. In Indonesia, they control nearly 58% of assets.

---

[14] See I. Dittmann, E. Maug, and C. Schneider, "Bankers on the Boards of German Firms: What They Do, What They Are Worth, and Why They Are (Still) There," *Review of Finance,* forthcoming.

[15] See L. Enriques and P. Volpin, "Corporate Governance Reforms in Continental Europe," *Journal of Economic Perspectives* 21 (2007), pp. 117–140.

[16] R. La Porta, F. Lopez-de-Silanes, and A. Shleifer, "Corporate Ownership around the World," *Journal of Finance* 54 (1999), pp. 471–517.

TABLE 33.3 Family control in Asia.

	Number of Firms in Sample	Control [a]			Percentage of Assets [b] Controlled by Top 10 Families
		Family	State	Widely Held	
Hong Kong	330	66.7%	1.4%	7.0%	32.1%
Indonesia	178	71.5	8.2	5.1	57.7
Japan	1,240	9.7	0.8	79.8	2.4
Korea	345	48.4	1.6	43.2	36.8
Malaysia	238	67.2	13.4	10.3	24.8
Philippines	120	44.6	2.1	19.2	52.5
Singapore	221	55.4	23.5	5.4	26.6
Taiwan	141	48.2	2.8	26.2	18.4
Thailand	167	61.6	8.0	6.6	46.2

[a] "Control" means ownership of shares with at least 20% of voting rights. Percentages controlled by financial institutions or corporations are not reported.
[b] Percentage of total assets of all sample firms in each country.
Source: S. Claessens, S. Djankov, and L. H. P. Lang, "The Separation of Ownership and Control in East Asian Corporations," *Journal of Financial Economics* 58 (October/November 2000), Table 6, p. 103, and Table 9, p. 108. © 2000 Elsevier, used with permission.

Family control does not usually mean a direct majority stake in the public firm. Control is usually exercised by cross-shareholdings, pyramids, and dual-class shares. We have already seen an example of cross-holdings with Sumitomo. Pyramids and dual-class shares need further explanation.

Pyramids Pyramids are common in Asian countries as well as several European countries.[17] In a pyramid, control is exercised through a sequence of controlling positions in several layers of companies. The actual operating companies are at the bottom of the pyramid. Above each operating company is a first holding company, then a second one, then perhaps others still higher in the pyramid.[18] Consider a three-tier pyramid and a single operating company. Assume that 51% of the votes confer control at each tier. Suppose that the second holding company—the highest one in the pyramid—holds a 51% controlling stake in a lower holding company, which in turn holds a 51% controlling stake in the operating company. A 51% stake in the highest holding company is really only a 26% stake in the operating company ($.51 \times .51 = .26$, or 26%). Thus an investor in the top holding company could control an operating company worth $100 million with an investment of only $26 million. By adding another layer, the required investment falls to $.51 \times 26 = \$13$ million.

Usually less than 51% of shares are needed for effective control, so the shareholders of the topmost holding company may be able to maintain control with an even smaller investment. Figure 33.6 shows how the Wallenberg family controls ABB, one of Sweden's largest companies. ABB, the operating company, is shown at the right of the diagram. ABB is controlled by Incentive, which holds 24% of ABB's shares but controls about 33% of the shareholder votes. Incentive is in turn controlled by

---

[17] L. A. Bebchuk, R. Kraakman, and G. R. Triantis, "Stock Pyramids, Cross-Ownership, and Dual Class Equity," in *Concentrated Corporate Ownership,* ed. R. Morck (Chicago: University of Chicago Press, 2000), pp. 295–318.

[18] A holding company is a firm whose only assets are controlling blocks of shares in other companies.

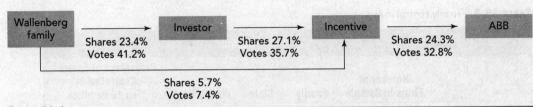

FIGURE 33.6

The pyramid that controls ABB, one of Sweden's largest companies.

Source: R. La Porta, F. Lopez-Silanes, and A. Shleifer, "Corporate Ownership Around the World," *Journal of Finance* 54 (April 1999), Figure 8, p. 488. Reprinted by permission from Blackwell Publishers Journal Rights.

Investor, an investment holding company, and by the Wallenberg family directly. The family also holds about 41% of Investor's votes. At each stage the family's voting control is at least 33%, which is amply sufficient to control the next layer of the pyramid.[19]

Dual-Class Equity Another way to maintain control is to hold stock with extra voting rights. (Note the extra voting rights at each level of the pyramid in Figure 33.6.) Extra votes can be attached to a special class of shares. For example, a firm's Class A shares could have 10 votes and the Class B shares only 1. *Dual-class equity* occurs frequently in many countries, including Brazil, Canada, Denmark, Finland, Germany, Italy, Mexico, Norway, South Korea, Sweden, and Switzerland. Stocks with different voting rights also occur (but less frequently) in Australia, Chile, France, Hong Kong, South Africa, the United Kingdom, and the United States. For example, the Ford Motor Company is still controlled by the Ford family, who hold a special class of shares with 40% of the voting power. Dual-class equity is forbidden in Belgium, China, Japan, Singapore, and Spain.

As we briefly discussed in Chapter 14, there is a wide variation in the value of votes across countries. Table 33.4 shows Tatiana Nenova's estimates of the value of controlling blocks in different countries, calculated as a fraction of firms' market values. These values are calculated from the differences in prices between ordinary shares and shares with extra votes. The range of values is large. For example,

TABLE 33.4 The value of control-block votes as a proportion of firm value.

Australia	.23	Italy	.29
Brazil	.23	Korea	.48
Canada	.03	Mexico	.36
Chile	.23	Norway	.06
Denmark	.01	South Africa	.07
Finland	.00	Sweden	.01
France	.28	Switzerland	.06
Germany	.09	U.K.	.10
Hong Kong	−.03	U.S.	.02

Source: T. Nenova, "The Value of Corporate Voting Rights and Control: A Cross-Country Analysis," *Journal of Financial Economics* 68 (June 2003), Table 4, p. 336. © 2003 Elsevier, used with permission.

[19] Figure 33.6 shows only part of the Wallenberg holdings. The Wallenbergs control companies whose shares account for about 50% of the value of the Stockholm Stock Exchange. See J. Agnblad, E. Berglof, P. Hogfeld, and H. Svancar, "Ownership and Control in Sweden: Strong Owners, Weak Minorities and Social Control," in *The Control of Corporate Europe* ed. F. Barca and M. Becht (Oxford: Oxford University Press, 2001).

the Scandinavian countries have uniformly low premiums for control. South Korea and Mexico have very high control premiums.

Why is shareholder control valuable? For two reasons, one positive and one negative. The controlling shareholder may maximize value by monitoring management and making sure that the firm pursues the best operating and investment strategies. On the other hand, a controlling shareholder may be tempted to *capture* value by extracting private benefits at other shareholders' expense. In this case the control premium is really a discount on the shares with inferior voting rights, a discount reflecting the value that these shareholders can*not* expect to receive.

Conglomerates Revisited

Of course there are also examples of U.S. companies that are controlled by families or by investors holding large blocks of stock. But in these cases control is exercised for a single firm, not a group of firms. Elsewhere in the world, and particularly in countries without fully developed financial markets, control extends to groups of firms in several different industries. These industrial groups are really conglomerates.

In Korea, for example, the 10 largest conglomerates control roughly two-thirds of the corporate economy. These *chaebols* are also strong exporters: names like Samsung and Hyundai are recognized worldwide. Conglomerates are also common in Latin America. One of the more successful, the Chilean holding company Quinenco, is a dizzying variety of businesses, including hotels and brewing, mobile telephone services, banking, and the manufacture of copper cable. Widely diversified groups are also common in India. The largest, the Tata Group, spans 80 companies in various industries, including steel, electric power, real estate, telecommunications, and financial services. All of these companies are public, but control rests with the group and ultimately with the Tata family.

The United States had a conglomerate merger wave in the 1960s and 1970s, but diversification didn't deliver value in the longer run, and most of the conglomerates of that era have dissolved. But conglomerates survive and grow in developing economies. Why?

Family ownership is part of the answer. A wealthy family can reduce risk, while maintaining control and expanding the family business into new industries. Of course the family could also diversify by buying shares of other companies. But where financial markets are limited and investor protection is poor, internal diversification can beat out financial diversification. Internal diversification means running an internal capital market, but if a country's financial markets and institutions are substandard, an internal capital market may not be so bad after all.

"Substandard" does not just mean lack of scale or trading activity. It may mean government regulations limiting access to bank financing or requiring government approval before bonds or shares are issued.[20] It may mean poor information. If accounting standards are loose and companies are secretive, monitoring by outside investors becomes especially costly and difficult, and agency costs proliferate.

Internal diversification may also be the only practical way to grow. You can't be big *and* focused in a small, closed economy, because the scale of one-industry companies is limited by the local market. Size can be an advantage if larger companies have easier access to international financial markets. This is important if local financial markets are inefficient.

Size also means political power, which is especially important in managed economies or in countries where the government economic policy is unpredictable. In Korea, for example, the government has

---

[20] In the United States, the SEC does *not* have the power to deny share issues. Its mandate is only to assure that investors are given adequate information.

controlled access to bank loans. Bank lending has been directed to government-approved uses. The Korean conglomerate chaebols have usually been first in line.

Many widely diversified business groups have been efficient and successful, particularly in countries like Korea that have grown rapidly. But there is also a dark side. Sometimes conglomerate business groups *tunnel* resources between the group companies at the expense of outside minority shareholders. Group company X can transfer value to Y by lending it money at a low interest rate, buying some of Y's output at high prices or selling X's assets to Y at low prices. Bertrand, Mehta, and Mullainathan found evidence of widespread tunneling in India.[21] Johnson, Boone, Breach, and Friedman note that the temptation to tunnel is stronger during a recession or financial crisis and argue that tunneling—and poor corporate governance in general—contributed to the Asian crisis of 1997–1998.[22]

33-3 DO THESE DIFFERENCES MATTER?

A good financial system appears to accelerate economic growth.[23] In fact, at least rudimentary finance may be necessary for any growth at all. Raghu Rajan and Luigi Zingales give the example of a bamboo-stool maker in Bangladesh, who needed 22 cents to buy the raw materials for each stool. Unfortunately, she did not have the 22 cents and had to borrow it from middlemen. She was forced to sell the stools back to the lenders in repayment for the loans and was left with only 2 cents' profit. Because of a lack of finance, she was never able to break out of this cycle of poverty. In contrast, they give the example of Kevin Taweel and Jim Ellis, two Stanford MBAs, who were able to purchase their own business soon after graduating. They had insufficient capital of their own but were able to raise seed funding to search for the right acquisition, and then additional funding to complete it.[24] Taweel and Ellis were the beneficiaries of a modern financial system, including a sophisticated private-equity market.

It is easy to understand the connection between financial and economic development by considering a very simple financial decision. Suppose you need to decide whether to extend credit to a small business. If you are in the United States, you can almost instantaneously pull down a Dun and Bradstreet report via the Internet on any one of several million businesses. This report will show the company's financial statements, the average size of its bank balances, and whether it pays its bills on time. You will also receive an overall credit score for the company. Such widely available credit information reduces the cost of lending and increases the availability of credit. It also means that no one lender has a monopoly of information, which increases competition among suppliers of credit and reduces the costs to borrowers. In contrast, good credit information is not readily available in most developing economies, and lenders to small businesses are both few and expensive.

Of course finance matters. But does the nature of a country's financial system matter as long as it is advanced? Does it matter whether a developed country has a market-based or bank-based system? Both types are effective, but each has potential advantages.

---

[21] M. Bertrand, P. Mehta, and S. Mullainathan, "Ferreting out Tunneling: An Application to Indian Business Groups," *Quarterly Journal of Economics* 117 (February 2002), pp. 121–148.

[22] S. Johnson, P. Boone, A. Breach, and E. Friedman, "Corporate Governance in the Asian Financial Crisis," *Journal of Financial Economics* 58 (October/November 2000), pp. 141–186.

[23] R. Levine, "Financial Development and Economic Growth: Views and Agenda," *Journal of Economic Literature* 35 (1997), pp. 688–726; and R. Rajan and L. Zingales, "Financial Dependence and Growth," *American Economic Review* 88 (1998), pp. 559–586.

[24] R. Rajan and L. Zingales, *Saving Capitalism from the Capitalists* (New York: Crown Business, 2003), pp. 4–8.

Risk and Short-termism

If you look back to Figure 33.2, you will see that in different countries the amount of risk borne by households in their financial portfolios varies significantly. At one extreme is Japan, where households hold over half of their financial assets in bank accounts. Much of the remainder is in insurance and pension funds, which in Japan mainly make fixed payments and are not linked to the stock market. Only a small proportion of household portfolios are linked to the stock market and to the business risk of Japanese corporations. European households also have relatively little direct exposure to the risks of the corporate sector. At the other extreme, households in the United States have large investments in shares and mutual funds.

Of course someone has to bear business risks. The risks that are not borne directly by households are passed on to banks and other financial institutions, and finally to the government. In most countries, the government guarantees bank deposits either explicitly or implicitly. If the banks get into trouble, the government steps in and society as a whole bears the burden. This is what happened in the crisis of 2007–2009.[25]

Some people argue that firms are free to "invest for the long run" in bank-based systems where financial institutions absorb business risks and few individuals invest directly in the stock market. The close ties of Japanese and German companies to banks are supposed to prevent the dreaded disease of *short-termism*. Firms in the United States and United Kingdom are supposedly held captive by shareholders' demands for quick payoffs and therefore have to deliver quick earnings growth at the expense of long-term competitive advantage. Many found this argument persuasive in the late 1980s when the Japanese and German economies were especially robust.[26] But market-based economies surged ahead in the 1990s, and views have changed accordingly.

Growth Industries and Declining Industries

Market-based systems seem to be particularly successful in developing brand-new industries. For example, railways were first developed in the United Kingdom in the nineteenth century, financed largely through the London Stock Exchange. In the twentieth century, the United States led development of mass production in the automobile industry, even though the automobile was invented in Germany. The commercial aircraft industry was also mainly developed in the United States, as was the computer industry after World War II, and more recently the biotechnology and Internet industries.[27] On the other hand, Germany and Japan, two countries with bank-based financial systems, have sustained their competitive advantages in established industries, such as automobiles.

Why are financial markets better at fostering innovative industries?[28] When new products or processes are discovered, there is a wide diversity of opinion about the prospects for a new industry and the best way to develop it. Financial markets accommodate this diversity, allowing young, ambitious

---

[25] Another possibility is that banks that take a long-run view and are not subject to intense competition can smooth risk across different generations by building up reserves when returns are high and running them down when returns are low. Competition from financial markets prevents this type of intergenerational risk sharing. Generations with high returns want to receive their full returns and will not be willing to have reserves built up. See F. Allen and D. Gale, "Financial Markets, Intermediaries, and Intertemporal Smoothing," *Journal of Political Economy* 105 (June 1997), pp. 523–546.

[26] See M. Porter, "Capital Disadvantage: America's Failing Capital Investment System," *Harvard Business Review*, September/October 1992, pp. 65–82.

[27] There are counterexamples, such as the development of the chemical industry on a large scale in nineteenth-century Germany.

[28] See F. Allen and D. Gale, "Diversity of Opinion and the Financing of New Technologies," *Journal of Financial Intermediation* 8 (April 1999), pp. 68–89.

companies to search out like-minded investors to fund their growth. This is less likely when financing has to come through a few major banks.

Market-based systems also seem to be more effective at forcing companies in declining industries to shrink and release capital.[29] When a company cannot earn its cost of capital and further growth would destroy value, stock price drops, and the drop sends a clear negative signal. But in bank-based financial systems, uneconomic firms are often bailed out. When Mazda faltered in the 1970s, Sumitomo Bank guaranteed Mazda's debts and orchestrated a rescue, in part by exhorting employees within its keiretsu to purchase Mazda cars. Sumitomo Bank had an incentive to undertake the rescue, because it knew that it would keep Mazda's business when it recovered. In the 1990s, Japanese banks continued to lend to "zombie" firms long after it became clear that prospects for their recovery were hopeless. For example, a coalition of banks kept the Japanese retailer Sogo afloat for years, despite clear evidence of insolvency. When Sogo finally failed in 2000, its debts had accumulated to ¥1.9 trillion.[30]

Transparency and Governance

Despite all the advantages of market-based systems, serious accidents happen. Think of the many sudden, costly corporate meltdowns after the telecom and dot.com boom of the late 1990s. In the last chapter we noted the $100 billion bankruptcy of WorldCom (now reorganized as MCI). But the most notorious meltdown was Enron, which failed in late 2001.

Enron started as a gas pipeline company, but expanded rapidly into trading energy and commodities, and made large investments in electricity generation, broadband communications, and water companies. By the end of 2000, its total stock market value was about $60 billion. A year later, it was bankrupt. But that $60 billion wasn't really lost when Enron failed, because most of that value wasn't there in the first place. By late 2001, Enron was in many ways an empty shell. Its stock price was supported more by investors' enthusiasm than by profitable operating businesses. The company had also accumulated large hidden debts. For example, Enron borrowed aggressively through *special-purpose entities* (SPEs). The SPE debts were not reported on its balance sheet, even though many of the SPEs did not meet the requirements for off-balance-sheet accounting. (The fall of Enron also brought down its accounting firm, Arthur Andersen.)

The bad news started to leak out in the last months of 2001. In October, Enron announced a $1 billion write-down of its water and broadband businesses. In November, it consolidated its SPEs retroactively, which increased the debt on its balance sheet by $658 million and reduced past earnings by $591 million.[31] Its public debt was downgraded to junk ratings on November 28 and on December 2 it filed for bankruptcy.

Enron demonstrated the importance of *transparency* in market-based financial systems. If a firm is transparent to outside investors—if the investors can see its true profitability and prospects—then problems will show up right away in a falling stock price. That in turn generates extra scrutiny from security analysts, bond rating agencies, and investors. It may also lead to a takeover.

---

[29] See R. Rajan and L. Zingales, "Banks and Markets: The Changing Character of European Finance," in V. Gaspar, P. Hartmann, O. Sleijpen (eds.), *The Transformation of the European Financial System*, Second ECB Central Banking Conference, October 2002, Frankfurt, Germany, (Frankfurt: European Central Bank, 2003), pp. 123–167.

[30] T. Hoshi and A. Kashyap, "Japan's Financial Crisis and Economic Stagnation," *Journal of Economic Perspectives* 18 (Winter 2004), pp. 3–26.

[31] Enron faced many further financial problems. For example, it told investors that it had hedged business risks in SPE transactions, but failed to say that many of the SPEs were backed up by pledges of Enron shares. When Enron's stock price fell, the hedges unraveled. See P. Healy and K. Palepu, "The Fall of Enron," *Journal of Economic Perspectives* 17 (Spring 2003), pp. 3–26.

With transparency, corporate troubles generally lead to corrective action. But the top management of a troubled opaque company may be able to maintain its stock price and postpone the discipline of the market. Market discipline caught up with Enron only a month or two before bankruptcy.

Opaqueness is not so dangerous in a bank-based system. Firms will have long-standing relationships with banks, which can monitor the firm closely and urge it to staunch losses or to cancel excessively risky strategies. But no financial system can avoid occasional corporate meltdowns.

Parmalat, the Italian food company, appeared to be a solidly profitable firm with good growth prospects. It had expanded around the world, and by 2003 was operating in 30 countries with 36,000 employees. It reported about €2 billion in debt but also claimed to hold large portfolios of cash and short-term liquid securities. But doubts about the company's financial strength began to accumulate. On December 19, 2003, it was revealed that a €3.9 billion bank deposit reported by Parmalat had never existed. Parmalat's stock price fell by 80% in two weeks, and it was placed in administration (the Italian bankruptcy process) on December 24. Investors learned later that Parmalat's true debts exceeded €14 billion, that additional billions of euros of asset value had disappeared into a black hole, and that its sales and earnings had been overstated.

It's nice to dream of a financial system that would completely protect investors against nasty surprises like Enron and Parmalat. Complete protection of investors is impossible, however. In fact, complete protection would be unwise and inefficient even if it were feasible. Why? Because outside investors cannot know everything that managers are doing or why they are doing it. Laws and regulations can specify what managers can't do but can't tell them what they should do. Therefore managers have to be given discretion to act in response to unanticipated problems and opportunities.

Once managers have discretion, they will consider their self-interest as well as investors' interests. Agency problems are inevitable. The best a financial system can do is to protect investors reasonably well and to try to keep managers' and investors' interests congruent. We have discussed agency problems at several points in this book, but it won't hurt to reiterate the mechanisms that keep these problems under control:

- Laws and regulations that protect outside investors from self-dealing by insiders.
- Disclosure requirements and accounting standards that keep public firms reasonably transparent.
- Monitoring by banks and other financial intermediaries.
- Monitoring by boards of directors.
- The threat of takeover (although takeovers are very rare in some countries).
- Compensation tied to earnings and stock price.

In this chapter we have stressed the importance of investor protection for the development of financial markets. But don't assume that more protection for investors is always a good thing. A corporation is a kind of partnership between outside investors and the managers and employees who operate the firm. The managers and employees are investors too: they commit human capital instead of financial capital. A successful firm requires co-investment of human and financial capital. If you give the financial capital too much power, the human capital won't show up—or if it does show up, it won't be properly motivated.[32]

---

[32] It is difficult to observe effort and the value of human capital, and therefore difficult to set up compensation schemes that reward effort and human capital appropriately. Thus it can be better to allow managers some leeway to act in their own interests to preserve their incentives. Stockholders can provide this leeway by relaxing some of their rights and committing not to interfere if managers and employees capture private benefits when the firm is successful. How to commit? One way is to take the firm public. Direct intervention by public stockholders in the operation of the firm is difficult and therefore rare. See M. Burkart, D. Gromb, and F. Panunzi, "Large Shareholders, Monitoring and the Value of the Firm," *Quarterly Journal of Economics* 112 (1997), pp. 693–728; S. C. Myers, "Outside Equity," *Journal of Finance* 55 (June 2000), pp. 1005–1037; and S. C. Myers, "Financial Architecture," *European Financial Management* 5 (July 1999), pp. 133–142.

SUMMARY

It's customary to distinguish market-based and bank-based financial systems. The United States has a market-based system, because it has large stock and bond markets. The United Kingdom also has a market-based system: its bond market is less important, but the U.K. stock market still plays a crucial role in corporate finance and governance. Germany and Japan have bank-based systems, because most debt financing comes from banks and these countries' stock markets are less important.

Of course the simple distinction between banks and markets is far from the end of the story. For example:

- U.K. households tend to hold shares indirectly, through equity-linked insurance and pensions. Direct investment in shares is much less common than in the United States.
- Japanese households bear relatively little equity risk. Most of their savings goes into bank accounts and insurance policies.
- In Europe, large blocks of a company's stock are often held by other corporations.
- In Japan, companies rely heavily on trade-credit financing, that is, on accounts payable to other companies.

In Japan and Germany, the role of banks goes beyond just lending money. The largest Japanese banks are the hubs of *keiretsus*, large, cooperative groups of firms. Each keiretsu is held together by long-standing ties to the main bank and by extensive cross-shareholdings within group companies. German banks also have traditionally had long-standing ties to their corporate customers (the *hausbank* system). The banks end up voting shares held for other investors.

Ownership of large, public corporations in the United States and United Kingdom is pretty simple: there is one class of shares, which trade actively, and ownership is dispersed. In Japan, there is usually one class of shares, but a significant fraction of the shares is locked up in cross-shareholdings within keiretsus, although this fraction has decreased since the mid-1990s. Japanese stockholders have little say in corporate governance. European stockholders likewise have little say, given the concentration of ownership by banks and other corporations.

In the United States and United Kingdom, the law puts shareholders' interests first. Managers and boards of directors have a fiduciary duty to shareholders. But in Germany, the management board, which runs the business, answers to a supervisory board, which represents all employees as well as investors. The company as a whole is supposed to come first.

Outside the largest developed economies, a different pattern of ownership emerges. Groups of companies are controlled by families and sometimes by the state. Control is maintained by cross-shareholdings, pyramids, and issues of shares with extra voting rights to the controlling investors.

Wealthy families control large fractions of the corporate sector in many developing economies. These family groups operate as conglomerates. Conglomerates are a declining species in the United States, but a conglomerate's internal capital market can make sense where financial markets and institutions are not well-developed. The conglomerates' scale and scope may also provide political power, which can add value in countries where the government tries to manage the economy or where laws and regulations are enforced erratically.

Concentrated family control can be a good thing, if it is used to force managers to run a tight ship and focus on value-maximizing investments. But concentration of control can also open the door to tunneling of resources out of the firm at the expense of minority investors.

Protection for outside investors varies greatly around the world. Where protection is good, market-based systems flourish. These systems have certain advantages: they appear to foster innovation and to encourage the release of capital from declining industries. On the other hand, market-based systems may end up investing too much in trendy innovations, as the collapse of the dot.com and telecom boom has illustrated. Bank-based systems may be better-suited to established industries. These systems also help shield individuals from direct exposure to stock market risk.

Market-based systems work only when public firms are reasonably transparent to investors. When they are opaque, like Enron, occasional meltdowns can be expected. Bank-based financial systems may have an advantage in monitoring and controlling opaque firms. The banks have long-standing relationships with their corporate customers, and therefore have better information than outside investors.

FURTHER READING

The following studies survey or compare financial systems:

F. Allen and D. Gale, *Comparing Financial Systems* (Cambridge, MA: MIT Press, 2000).

T. Hoshi and A. Kashyap, *Corporate Financing and Governance in Japan: The Road to the Future* (Cambridge, MA: MIT Press, 2001).

J. P. Krahnen and R. H. Schmidt (eds.), *The German Financial System* (Oxford: Oxford University Press, 2004).

R. La Porta, F. Lopez-de-Silanes, and A. Shleifer, "Corporate Ownership around the World," *Journal of Finance* 54 (April 1999), pp. 471–517.

For excellent discussions of corporate governance, see:

M. Becht, P. Bolton, and A. Röell, "Corporate Governance and Control" in G. Constantinides, M. Harris, and R. Stulz (eds.), *Handbook of the Economics of Finance* (Amsterdam: North-Holland, 2003), pp. 1–109.

R. Morck and B. Yeung, "Never Waste a Good Crisis: An Historical Perspective on Comparative Corporate Governance," *Review of Financial Economics 1* (November 2009), forthcoming.

A. Shleifer and R. W. Vishny, "A Survey of Corporate Governance," *Journal of Finance* 52 (June 1997), pp. 737–783.

For discussions of the role of law, politics, and finance see:

R. LaPorta, F. Lopez-de-Silanes, and A. Shleifer, "The Economic Consequences of Legal Origins," *Journal of Economic Literature* 46 (2008), pp. 285–332.

R. Rajan and L. Zingales, *Saving Capitalism from the Capitalists* (New York: Crown Business, 2003).

For the evidence on why finance matters for growth, see:

R. Levine, "Financial Development and Economic Growth: Views and Agenda," *Journal of Economic Literature* 35 (1997), pp. 688–726.

R. Rajan and L. Zingales, "Financial Dependence and Growth," *American Economic Review* 88 (June 1998), pp. 559–586.

Finally, if you'd like to read about corporate governance gone wrong . . .

P. Healy and K. Palepu, "The Fall of Enron," *Journal of Economic Perspectives* 17 (Spring 2003), pp. 3–26.

S. Johnson, R. La Porta, F. Lopez-de-Silanes, and A. Shleifer, "Tunneling," *American Economic Review* 90 (May 2000), pp. 22–27.

PROBLEM SETS

BASIC

1. Which countries have:
   a. The largest stock markets?
   b. The largest bond markets?
   c. The smallest direct holdings of shares by individual investors?
   d. The largest holdings of bank deposits by individual investors?
   e. The largest holdings of shares by other corporations?
   f. The largest use of trade credit for financing?
   In each case, define "largest" or "smallest" as total value relative to GDP.

2. What is a keiretsu? Give a brief description.

3. Do Japanese investors play an important role in corporate financial policy and governance? If not, could they?

4. German banks often control a large fraction of the shareholder votes for German businesses. How do they get that voting power?

5. What is meant by the German system of *codetermination?*

6. What is the most common form of ownership of corporations worldwide?

7. Suppose that a shareholder can gain effective control of a company with 30% of the shares. Explain how a shareholder might gain control of company Z by setting up a holding company X^2 that holds shares in a second holding company X, which in turn holds shares in Z.

8. Why may market-based financial systems be better in supporting innovation and in releasing capital from declining industries?

9. What is tunneling? Why does the threat of tunneling impede the development of financial markets?

INTERMEDIATE

10. Agency problems are inevitable. That is, we can never expect managers to give 100% weight to shareholders' interests and none to their own.
    a. Why not?
    b. List the mechanisms that are used around the world to keep agency problems under control.

11. Banks are not the only financial intermediary from which corporations can obtain financing. What are the other intermediaries? How much financing do they supply, relative to banks, in the United Kingdom, Germany, and Japan?

12. Why is transparency important in a market-based financial system? Why is it less important in a bank-based system?

13. What is meant by dual-class equity? Do you think it should be allowed or outlawed?

14. What kind of industries do you think should thrive in a market-based financial system? In a bank-based system?

15. Why are pyramids common in many countries but not in the United States or United Kingdom?

16. What are some of the advantages and disadvantages of Indian Business Groups?

34

CHAPTER

CONCLUSION: WHAT WE DO AND DO NOT KNOW ABOUT FINANCE

It is time to sign off. Let us finish by thinking about some of the things that we do and do not know about finance.

34-1   WHAT WE DO KNOW: THE SEVEN MOST IMPORTANT IDEAS IN FINANCE

What would you say if you were asked to name the seven most important ideas in finance? Here is our list.

1. Net Present Value

When you wish to know the value of a used car, you look at prices in the secondhand car market. Similarly, when you wish to know the value of a future cash flow, you look at prices quoted in the capital markets, where claims to future cash flows are traded (remember, those highly paid investment bankers are just secondhand cash-flow dealers). If you can buy cash flows for your shareholders at a cheaper price than they would have to pay in the capital market, you have increased the value of their investment.

This is the simple idea behind *net present value* (NPV). When we calculate an investment project's NPV, we are asking whether the project is worth more than it costs. We are estimating its value by calculating what its cash flows would be worth if a claim on them were offered separately to investors and traded in the capital markets.

That is why we calculate NPV by discounting future cash flows at the opportunity cost of capital—that is, at the expected rate of return offered by securities having the same degree of risk as the project. In well-functioning capital markets, all equivalent-risk assets are priced to offer the same expected return. By discounting at the opportunity cost of capital, we calculate the price at which investors in the project could expect to earn that rate of return.

Like most good ideas, the net present value rule is "obvious when you think about it." But notice what an important idea it is. The NPV rule allows thousands of shareholders, who may have vastly different levels of wealth and attitudes toward risk, to participate in the same enterprise and to delegate its operation to a professional manager. They give the manager one simple instruction: "Maximize net present value."

2. The Capital Asset Pricing Model

Some people say that modern finance is all about the capital asset pricing model. That's nonsense. If the capital asset pricing model had never been invented, our advice to financial managers would be essentially the same. The attraction of the model is that it gives us a manageable way of thinking about the required return on a risky investment.

Again, it is an attractively simple idea. There are two kinds of risk: risks that you can diversify away and those that you can't. You can measure the *nondiversifiable,* or *market,* risk of an investment by the extent to which the value of the investment is affected by a change in the *aggregate* value of all the assets in the economy. This is called the *beta* of the investment. The only risks that people care about are the ones that they can't get rid of—the nondiversifiable ones. This is why the required return on an asset increases in line with its beta.

Many people are worried by some of the rather strong assumptions behind the capital asset pricing model, or they are concerned about the difficulties of estimating a project's beta. They are right to be worried about these things. In 10 or 20 years' time we may have much better theories than we do now. But we will be extremely surprised if those future theories do not still insist on the crucial distinction between diversifiable and nondiversifiable risks—and that, after all, is the main idea underlying the capital asset pricing model.

3. Efficient Capital Markets

The third fundamental idea is that security prices accurately reflect available information and respond rapidly to new information as soon as it becomes available. This *efficient-market theory* comes in three flavors, corresponding to different definitions of "available information." The weak form (or random-walk theory) says that prices reflect all the information in past prices. The semistrong form says that prices reflect all publicly available information, and the strong form holds that prices reflect all acquirable information.

Don't misunderstand the efficient-market idea. It doesn't say that there are no taxes or costs; it doesn't say that there aren't some clever people and some stupid ones. It merely implies that competition in capital markets is very tough—there are no money machines or arbitrage opportunities, and security prices reflect the true underlying values of assets.

Extensive empirical testing of the efficient-market hypothesis began around 1970. By 2009, after almost 40 years of work, the tests have uncovered dozens of statistically significant anomalies. Sorry, but this work does *not* translate into dozens of ways to make easy money. Superior returns are elusive. For example, only a few mutual fund managers can generate superior returns for a few years in a row, and then only in small amounts.[1] Statisticians can beat the market, but real investors have a much harder time of it.

4. Value Additivity and the Law of Conservation of Value

The principle of *value additivity* states that the value of the whole is equal to the sum of the values of the parts. It is sometimes called the *law of the conservation of value*.

When we appraise a project that produces a succession of cash flows, we always assume that values add up. In other words, we assume

$$PV(\text{project}) = PV(C_1) + PV(C_2) + \cdots + PV(C_t)$$

$$= \frac{C_1}{1 + r} + \frac{C_2}{(1 + r)^2} + \cdots + \frac{C_t}{(1 + r)^t}$$

We similarly assume that the sum of the present values of projects A and B equals the present value of a composite project AB.[2] But value additivity also means that you can't increase value by putting two whole companies together unless you thereby increase the total cash flow. In other words, there are no benefits to mergers solely for diversification.

5. Capital Structure Theory

If the law of the conservation of value works when you add up cash flows, it must also work when you subtract them.[3] Therefore, financing decisions that simply divide up operating cash flows don't increase overall firm value. This is the basic idea behind Modigliani and Miller's famous proposition 1: In perfect markets changes in capital structure do not affect value. As long as the *total* cash flow generated by the firm's assets is unchanged by capital structure, value is independent of capital structure. The value of the whole pie does not depend on how it is sliced.

Of course, MM's proposition is not The Answer, but it does tell us where to look for reasons why capital structure decisions may matter. Taxes are one possibility. Debt provides a corporate interest tax shield, and this tax shield may more than compensate for any extra personal tax that the investor has to pay on debt interest. Also, high debt levels may spur managers to work harder and to run a tighter ship. But debt has its drawbacks if it leads to costly financial distress.

6. Option Theory

In everyday conversation we often use the word "option" as synonymous with "choice" or "alternative;" thus we speak of someone as "having a number of options." In finance *option* refers specifically to the

---

[1] See, for example, R. Kosowski, A. Timmerman, R. Werners, and H. White, "Can Mutual Fund 'Stars' Really Pick Stocks? New Evidence from a Bootstrap Analysis," *Journal of Finance* 61 (December 2006), pp. 2551–2595.

[2] That is, if

$$PV(A) = PV[C_1(A)] + PV[C_2(A)] + \cdots + PV[C_t(A)]$$
$$PV(B) = PV[C_1(B)] + PV[C_2(B)] + \cdots + PV[C_t(B)]$$

and if for each period t, $C_t(AB) = C_t(A) + C_t(B)$, then

$$PV(AB) = PV(A) + PV(B)$$

[3] If you *start* with the cash flow $C_t(AB)$ and split it into two pieces, $C_t(A)$ and $C_t(B)$, then total value is unchanged. That is, $PV[C_t(A)] + PV[C_t(B)] = PV[C_t(AB)]$. See Footnote 2.

opportunity to trade in the future on terms that are fixed today. Smart managers know that it is often worth paying today for the option to buy or sell an asset tomorrow.

Since options are so important, the financial manager needs to know how to value them. Finance experts always knew the relevant variables—the exercise price and the exercise date of the option, the risk of the underlying asset, and the rate of interest. But it was Black and Scholes who first showed how these can be put together in a usable formula.

The Black–Scholes formula was developed for simple call options and does not directly apply to the more complicated options often encountered in corporate finance. But Black and Scholes's most basic ideas—for example, the risk-neutral valuation method implied by their formula—work even where the formula doesn't. Valuing the real options described in Chapter 22 may require extra number crunching but no extra concepts.

7. Agency Theory

A modern corporation is a team effort involving a number of players, such as managers, employees, shareholders, and bondholders. For a long time economists used to assume without question that all these players acted for the common good, but in the last 30 years they have had a lot more to say about the possible conflicts of interest and how companies attempt to overcome such conflicts. These ideas are known collectively as *agency theory*.

Consider, for example, the relationship between the shareholders and the managers. The shareholders (the *principals*) want managers (their *agents*) to maximize firm value. In the United States the ownership of many major corporations is widely dispersed and no single shareholder can check on the managers or reprimand those who are slacking. So, to encourage managers to pull their weight, firms seek to tie the managers' compensation to the value that they have added. For those managers who persistently neglect shareholders' interests, there is the threat that their firm will be taken over and they will be turfed out.

Some corporations are owned by a few major shareholders and therefore there is less distance between ownership and control. For example, the families, companies, and banks that hold or control large stakes in many German companies can review top management's plans and decisions as insiders. In most cases they have the power to force changes as necessary. However, hostile takeovers in Germany are rare.

We discussed the problems of management incentives and corporate control in Chapters 12, 14, 32, and 33, but they were not the only places in the book where agency issues arose. For example, in Chapters 18 and 24 we looked at some of the conflicts that arise between shareholders and bondholders, and we described how loan agreements try to anticipate and minimize these conflicts.

Are these seven ideas exciting theories or plain common sense? Call them what you will, they are basic to the financial manager's job. If by reading this book you really understand these ideas and know how to apply them, you have learned a great deal.

34-2 What We Do Not Know: 10 Unsolved Problems in Finance

Since the unknown is never exhausted, the list of what we do not know about finance could go on forever. But, following Brealey, Myers, and Allen's Third Law (see Section 29.5), we list and briefly discuss 10 unsolved problems that seem ripe for productive research.

1. What Determines Project Risk and Present Value?

A good capital investment is one that has a positive NPV. We have talked at some length about how to calculate NPV, but we have given you very little guidance about how to find positive-NPV projects, except to say in Section 11.2 that projects have positive NPVs when the firm can earn economic rents. But why do some companies earn economic rents while others in the same industry do not? Are the rents merely windfall gains, or can they be anticipated and planned for? What is their source, and how long do they persist before competition destroys them? Very little is known about any of these important questions.

Here is a related question: Why are some real assets risky and others relatively safe? In Section 9.3 we suggested a few reasons for differences in project betas—differences in operating leverage, for example, or in the extent to which a project's cash flows respond to the performance of the national economy. These are useful clues, but we have as yet no general procedure for estimating project betas. Assessing project risk is therefore still largely a seat-of-the-pants matter.

2. Risk and Return—What Have We Missed?

In 1848 John Stuart Mill wrote, "Happily there is nothing in the laws of value which remains for the present or any future writer to clear up; the theory is complete." Economists today are not so sure about that. For example, the capital asset pricing model is an enormous step toward understanding the effect of risk on the value of an asset, but there are many puzzles left, some statistical and some theoretical.

The statistical problems arise because the capital asset pricing model is hard to prove or disprove conclusively. It appears that average returns from low-beta stocks are too high (that is, higher than the capital asset pricing model predicts) and that those from high-beta stocks are too low; but this could be a problem with the way that the tests are conducted and not with the model itself.[4] We also described the puzzling discovery by Fama and French that expected returns appear to be related to the firm's size and to the ratio of the book value of the stock to its market value. Nobody understands why this should be so; perhaps these variables are related to variable x, that mysterious second risk variable that investors may rationally take into account in pricing shares.[5]

Meanwhile scholars toil on the theoretical front. We discussed some of their work in Section 8.4. But just for fun, here is another example: Suppose that you love fine wine. It may make sense for you to buy shares in a grand cru chateau, even if doing so soaks up a large fraction of your personal wealth and leaves you with a relatively undiversified portfolio. However, you are *hedged* against a rise in the price of fine wine: Your hobby will cost you more in a bull market for wine, but your stake in the chateau will make you correspondingly richer. Thus you are holding a relatively undiversified portfolio for a good reason. We would not expect you to demand a premium for bearing that portfolio's undiversifiable risk.

In general, if two people have different tastes, it may make sense for them to hold different portfolios. You may hedge your consumption needs with an investment in wine making, whereas somebody else may do better to invest in a chain of ice cream parlors. The capital asset pricing model

[4] See R. Roll, "A Critique of the Asset Pricing Theory's Tests: Part 1: On Past and Potential Testability of the Theory," *Journal of Financial Economics* 4 (March 1977), pp. 129–176; and, for a critique of the critique, see D. Mayers and E. M. Rice, "Measuring Portfolio Performance and the Empirical Content of Asset Pricing Models," *Journal of Financial Economics* 7 (March 1979), pp. 3–28.

[5] Fama and French point out that small firms, and firms with high book-to-market ratios, are also low-profitability firms. Such firms may suffer more in downturns in the economy. Thus size and book-to-market measures may be proxies for exposure to business-cycle risk. See E. F. Fama and K. R. French, "Size and Book-to-Market Factors in Earnings and Returns," *Journal of Finance* 50 (March 1995), pp. 131–155.

isn't rich enough to deal with such a world. It assumes that all investors have similar tastes: The hedging motive does not enter, and therefore they hold the same portfolio of risky assets.

Merton has extended the capital asset pricing model to accommodate the hedging motive.[6] If enough investors are attempting to hedge against the same thing, the model implies a more complicated risk–return relationship. However, it is not yet clear who is hedging against what, and so the model remains difficult to test.

So the capital asset pricing model survives not from a lack of competition but from a surfeit. There are too many plausible alternative risk measures, and so far no consensus exists on the right course to plot if we abandon beta.

In the meantime we must recognize the capital asset pricing model for what it is: an incomplete but extremely useful way of linking risk and return. Recognize too that the model's most basic message, that diversifiable risk doesn't matter, is accepted by nearly everyone.

3. How Important Are the Exceptions to the Efficient-Market Theory?

The efficient-market theory is strong, but no theory is perfect; there must be exceptions.

Now some of the apparent exceptions could simply be coincidences, for the more that researchers study stock performance, the more strange coincidences they are likely to find. For example, there is evidence that daily returns around new moons have been roughly double those around full moons.[7] It seems difficult to believe that this is anything other than a chance relationship—fun to read about but not a concern for serious investors or financial managers. But not all exceptions can be dismissed so easily. We saw that the stocks of firms that announce unexpectedly good earnings continue to perform well for a couple of months after the announcement date. Some scholars believe that this may mean that the stock market is inefficient and investors have consistently been slow to react to earnings announcements. Of course, we can't expect investors never to make mistakes. If they have been slow to react in the past, perhaps they will learn from this mistake and price the stocks more efficiently in the future.

Some researchers believe that the efficient-market hypothesis ignores important aspects of human behavior. For example, psychologists find that people tend to place too much emphasis on recent events when they are predicting the future. If so, we may find that investors are liable to overreact to new information. It will be interesting to see how far such behavioral observations can help us to understand apparent anomalies.

During the dot.com boom of the late 1990s stock prices rose to astronomic levels. The Nasdaq Composite Index rose 580% from the beginning of 1995 to its peak in March 2000 and then fell by nearly 80%. Such gyrations were not confined to the United States. For example, stock prices on Germany's Neuer Markt rose 1,600% in the three years from its foundation in 1997, before falling by 95% by October 2002.

This is not the only occasion that asset prices have reached unsustainable levels. In the late 1980s there was a surge in the prices of Japanese stock and real estate. In 1989 at the peak of the real estate boom, choice properties in Tokyo's Ginza district were selling for about $1 million a square foot. Over the next 17 years Japanese real estate prices fell by 70%.[8]

Maybe such extreme price movements can be explained by standard valuation techniques. However, others argue that stock prices are liable to speculative bubbles, where investors are caught up in a scatty

---

[6] See R. Merton, "An Intertemporal Capital Asset Pricing Model," *Econometrica* 41 (1973), pp. 867–887.

[7] K. Yuan, L. Zheng, and Q. Zhu, "Are Investors Moonstruck? Lunar Phases and Stock Returns," *Journal of Empirical Finance* 13 (January 2006), pp. 1–23.

[8] See W. Ziemba and S. Schwartz, *Invest Japan* (Chicago, IL: Probus, 1992), p. 109.

whirl of irrational exuberance.[9] Now that may be true of your Uncle Harry or Aunt Hetty, but why don't hard-headed professional investors bail out of the overpriced stocks? Perhaps they would do so if it was their money at stake, but maybe there is an agency problem that stems from the way that their performance is measured and rewarded that encourages them to run with the herd.[10]

These are important questions. Much more research is needed before we have a full understanding of why asset prices sometimes get so out of line with what appears to be their discounted future payoffs.

4. Is Management an Off-Balance-Sheet Liability?

Closed-end funds are firms whose only asset is a portfolio of common stocks. One might think that if you knew the value of these common stocks, you would also know the value of the firm. However, this is not the case. The stock of the closed-end fund often sells for substantially less than the value of the fund's portfolio.[11]

All this might not matter much except that it could be just the tip of the iceberg. For example, real estate stocks appear to sell for less than the market values of the firms' net assets. In the late 1970s and early 1980s the market values of many large oil companies were less than the market values of their oil reserves. Analysts joked that you could buy oil cheaper on Wall Street than in West Texas.

All these are special cases in which it was possible to compare the market value of the whole firm with the values of its separate assets. But perhaps if we could observe the values of other firms' separate parts, we might find that the value of the whole was often less than the sum of the values of the parts.

Whenever firms calculate the net present value of a project, they implicitly assume that the value of the whole project is simply the sum of the values of all the years' cash flows. We referred to this earlier as the law of the conservation of value. If we cannot rely on that law, the tip of the iceberg could turn out to be a hot potato.

We don't understand why closed-end investment companies or any of the other firms sell at a discount on the market values of their assets. One explanation is that the value added by the firm's management is less than the cost of the management. That is why we suggest that management may be an off-balance-sheet liability. For example, the discount of oil company shares from oil-in-the-ground value can be explained if investors expected the profits from oil production to be frittered away in negative-NPV investments and bureaucratic excess. The present value of growth opportunities (PVGO) was negative!

We do not mean to portray managers as leeches soaking up cash flows meant for investors. Managers commit their human capital to the firm and rightfully expect a reasonable cash return on these personal investments. If investors extract too great a share of the firm's cash flow, the personal investments are discouraged, and the long-run health and growth of the firm can be damaged.

In most firms, managers and employees coinvest with stockholders and creditors—human capital from the insiders and financial capital from outside investors. So far we know very little about how this coinvestment works.

---

[9] See C. Kindleberger, *Manias, Panics, and Crashes: A History of Financial Crises*, 4th ed. (New York: Wiley, 2000); and R. Shiller, *Irrational Exuberance* (Princeton, NJ: Princeton University Press, 2000).

[10] Investment managers may reason that if the stocks continue to do well, they will benefit from increased business in the future; on the other hand, if the stocks do badly, it is the customers who incur the losses and the worst that can happen to the managers is that they have to find new jobs. See F. Allen, "Do Financial Institutions Matter?" *Journal of Finance* 56 (August 2001), pp. 1165–1174.

[11] There are relatively few closed-end funds. Most mutual funds are *open-end*. This means that they stand ready to buy or sell additional shares at a price equal to the fund's net asset value per share. Therefore the share price of an open-end fund always equals net asset value.

5. How Can We Explain the Success of New Securities and New Markets?

In the last 30 years companies and the securities exchanges have created an enormous number of new securities: options, futures, options on futures; zero-coupon bonds, floating-rate bonds; bonds with collars and caps, asset-backed bonds; catastrophe bonds, . . . the list is endless. In some cases, it is easy to explain the success of new markets or securities; perhaps they allow investors to insure themselves against new risks or they result from a change in tax or in regulation. Sometimes a market develops because of a change in the costs of issuing or trading different securities. But there are many successful innovations that cannot be explained so easily. Why do investment bankers continue to invent, and successfully sell, complex new securities that outstrip our ability to value them? The truth is we don't understand why some innovations in markets succeed and others never get off the ground.

And then there are the innovations that do get off the ground but crash later, including many of the complex and over-rated securities backed by subprime mortgages. Subprime mortgages are not intrinsically bad, of course: they may be the only route to home ownership for some worthy people. But subprime loans also put many homeowners in nasty traps when house prices fell and jobs were lost. Securities based on subprime mortgages caused enormous losses in the banking industry. A number of new securities and derivatives went out of favor during the crisis. It will be interesting to see which will remain permanently consigned to the dustbin, and which will be dusted off and recover their usefulness.

6. How Can We Resolve the Payout Controversy?

We spent all of Chapter 16 on payout policy without being able to resolve the payout controversy. Many people believe dividends are good; others point out that dividends attract more tax and therefore it is better for firms to repurchase stock; and still others believe that, as long as the firm's investment decisions are unaffected, the payout decision is irrelevant.

Perhaps the problem is that we are asking the wrong question. Instead of inquiring whether dividends are good or bad, perhaps we should be asking *when* it makes sense to pay high or low dividends. For example, investors in mature firms with few investment opportunities may welcome the financial discipline imposed by a high dividend payout. For younger firms or firms with a temporary cash surplus, the tax advantage of stock repurchase may be more influential. But we don't know enough yet about how payout policy should vary from firm to firm.

The way that companies distribute cash has been changing. An increasing number of companies do not pay any dividends, while the volume of stock repurchases has mushroomed. This may partly reflect the growth in the proportion of small high-growth firms with lots of investment opportunities, but this does not appear to be the complete explanation. Understanding these shifts in company payout policy may also help us to understand how that policy affects firm value.

7. What Risks Should a Firm Take?

Financial managers end up managing risk. For example,

- When a firm expands production, managers often reduce the cost of failure by building in the option to alter the product mix or to bail out of the project altogether.
- By reducing the firm's borrowing, managers can spread operating risks over a larger equity base.
- Most businesses take out insurance against a variety of specific hazards.
- Managers often use futures or other derivatives to protect against adverse movements in commodity prices, interest rates, and exchange rates.

All these actions reduce risk. But less risk can't always be better. The point of risk management is not to reduce risk but to add value. We wish we could give general guidance on what bets the firm should place and what the *appropriate* level of risk is.

In practice, risk management decisions interact in complicated ways. For example, firms that are hedged against commodity price fluctuations may be able to afford more debt than those that are not hedged. Hedging can make sense if it allows the firm to take greater advantage of interest tax shields, provided the costs of hedging are sufficiently low.

How can a company set a risk management strategy that adds up to a sensible whole?

8. What Is the Value of Liquidity?

Unlike Treasury bills, cash pays no interest. On the other hand, cash provides more liquidity than Treasury bills. People who hold cash must believe that this additional liquidity offsets the loss of interest. In equilibrium, the marginal value of the additional liquidity must equal the interest rate on bills.

Now what can we say about corporate holdings of cash? It is wrong to ignore the liquidity gain and to say that the cost of holding cash is the lost interest. This would imply that cash always has a *negative* NPV. It is equally foolish to say that, because the marginal value of liquidity is equal to the loss of interest, it doesn't matter how much cash the firm holds. This would imply that cash always has a *zero* NPV. We know that the marginal value of cash to a holder declines with the size of the cash holding, but we don't really understand how to value the liquidity service of cash and therefore we can't say how much cash is enough or how readily the firm should be able to raise it. To complicate matters further, we note that cash can be raised on short notice by borrowing, or by issuing other new securities, as well as by selling assets. The financial manager with a $100 million unused line of credit may sleep just as soundly as one whose firm holds $100 million in marketable securities. In our chapters on working-capital management we largely finessed these questions by presenting models that are really too simple or by speaking vaguely of the need to ensure an "adequate" liquidity reserve.

A better knowledge of liquidity would also help us to understand better how corporate bonds are priced. We already know part of the reason that corporate bonds sell for lower prices than Treasury bonds—companies in distress have the option to walk away from their debts. However, the differences between the prices of corporate bonds and Treasury bonds are too large to be explained just by the company's default option. It seems likely that the price difference is partly due to the fact that corporate bonds are less liquid than Treasury bonds. But until we know how to price differences in liquidity, we can't really say much more than this.

The crisis of 2007–2009 has again demonstrated that investors seem to value liquidity much more highly at some times than at others. Despite massive injections of liquidity by central banks, many financial markets effectively dried up. For example, banks became increasingly reluctant to lend to one another on an unsecured basis, and would do so only at a large premium. In the spring of 2007 the spread between LIBOR and the interest rate on Treasury bills (known as the TED spread) was .4%. By October 2008 the market for unsecured lending between banks had largely disappeared and LIBOR was being quoted at more than 4.6% above the Treasury bill rate.[12]

Financial markets work well most of the time, but we don't understand well why they sometimes shut down or clog up, and we can offer relatively little advice to managers as to how to respond.

---

[12] See M. Brunnermeier, "Deciphering the Liquidity and Credit Crunch 2007–2008," *Journal of Economic Perspectives* 23 (Winter 2009), pp. 77–100.

9. How Can We Explain Merger Waves?

Of course there are many plausible motives for merging. If you single out a *particular* merger, it is usually possible to think up a reason why that merger could make sense. But that leaves us with a special hypothesis for each merger. What we need is a general hypothesis to explain merger waves. For example, everybody seemed to be merging in 1998–2000 and again in 2006–2007, but in the intervening years mergers went out of fashion.

There are other instances of apparent financial fashions. For example, from time to time there are hot new-issue periods when there seem to be an insatiable supply of speculative new issues and an equally insatiable demand for them. We don't understand why hard-headed businessmen sometimes seem to behave like a flock of sheep, but the following story may contain the seeds of an explanation.

It is early evening and George is trying to decide between two restaurants, the Hungry Horse and the Golden Trough. Both are empty and, since there seems to be little reason to prefer one to the other, George tosses a coin and opts for the Hungry Horse. Shortly afterward Georgina pauses outside the two restaurants. She somewhat prefers the Golden Trough, but observing George inside the Hungry Horse while the other restaurant is empty, she decides that George may know something that she doesn't and therefore the rational decision is to copy George. Fred is the third person to arrive. He sees that George and Georgina have both chosen the Hungry Horse, and, putting aside his own judgment, decides to go with the flow. And so it is with subsequent diners, who simply look at the packed tables in the one restaurant and the empty tables elsewhere and draw the obvious conclusions. Each diner behaves fully rationally in balancing his or her own views with the revealed preferences of the other diners. Yet the popularity of the Hungry Horse owed much to the toss of George's coin. If Georgina had been the first to arrive or if all diners could have pooled their information before coming to a decision, the Hungry Horse might not have scooped the jackpot.

Economists refer to this imitative behavior as a *cascade*.[13] It remains to be seen how far cascades or some alternative theory can help to explain financial fashions.

10. Why Are Financial Systems So Prone to Crisis?

The crisis that started in 2007 was an unwelcome reminder of the fragility of financial systems. One moment everything seems to be going fine; the next moment markets crash, banks fail, and before long the economy is in recession. Carmen Reinhart and Kenneth Rogoff have documented the effects of banking crises in many countries.[14] They find that systemic banking crises are typically preceded by credit booms and asset price bubbles. When the bubbles burst, housing prices drop on average by 35% and stock prices fall by 55%. Output falls by 9% over the following two years and unemployment rises by 7% over a period of four years. Central government debt nearly doubles compared with its precrisis level.

Our understanding of these financial crises is limited. We need to know what causes them, how they can be prevented, and how they can be managed when they do occur. We reviewed the roots of the latest crisis in Chapter 14. But crisis prevention will have to incorporate principles and practices that we discussed in other chapters, such as the importance of good governance systems, well-constructed compensation schemes, and efficient risk management. Understanding financial crises will occupy

---

[13] For an introduction to cascades, see S. Bikhchandani, D. Hirshleifer, and I. Welch, "Learning from the Behavior of Others: Conformity, Fads, and Informational Cascades," *Journal of Economic Perspectives* 12 (Summer 1998), pp. 151–170.

[14] See C. Reinhart and K. Rogoff, "The Aftermath of Financial Crises," *American Economic Review* 99 (May 2009), pp. 466–472.

economists and financial regulators for many years to come.[15] Let's hope they figure out the last one before the next one knocks on the door.

34-3   A FINAL WORD

That concludes our list of unsolved problems. We have given you the 10 uppermost in our minds. If there are others that you find more interesting and challenging, by all means construct your own list and start thinking about it.

It will take years for our 10 problems to be finally solved and replaced with a fresh list. In the meantime, we invite you to go on to further study of what we *already* know about finance. We also invite you to apply what you have learned from reading this book.

Now that the book is done, we sympathize with Huckleberry Finn. At the end of his book he says:

> So there ain't nothing more to write, and I am rotten glad of it, because if I'd a' knowed what a trouble it was to make a book I wouldn't a' tackled it, and I ain't a'going to no more.

---

[15] For a review of the current literature on financial crises see F. Allen, A. Babus, and E. Carletti, "Financial Crises: Theory and Evidence," *Annual Review of Financial Economics* 1, forthcoming.

APPENDIX

ANSWERS TO SELECT BASIC PROBLEMS

CHAPTER 1

1. (a) Real; (b) executive airplanes; (c) brand names;
   (d) financial; (e) bonds; (f) investment; (g) capital budgeting; (h) financing.
3. a. Financial assets, such as stocks or bank loans, are claims held by investors. Corporations sell financial assets to raise the cash to invest in real assets such as plant and equipment. Some real assets are intangible.
   b. Capital budgeting means investment in real assets. Financing means raising the cash for this investment.
   c. The shares of public corporations are traded on stock exchanges and can be purchased by a wide range of investors. The shares of closely held corporations are not traded and are not generally available to investors.
   d. Unlimited liability: investors are responsible for all the firm's debts. A sole proprietor has unlimited liability. Investors in corporations have limited liability. They can lose their investment, but no more.
5. *b, c.*

CHAPTER 2

1. ₹1.00.
3. $374/(1.09)^9 = ₹172$.
5. $100 \times (1.15)^8 = ₹305.90$.
7. $PV = 4/(.14 - .04) = ₹40$.
9. a. $600,000/1.05^5 = ₹470,115.7$
   b. You need to set aside (600,000 × 6-year Annuity factor) = 600,000 × 4.623 = ₹2,773,800
   c. At the end of 6 years you would have $1.08^6 \times (3,000,000 - 2,773,800) = ₹358,951$.
11. (a) ₹12.625 million; (b) ₹12.705 million; (c) ₹12.712 million.

CHAPTER 3

1. (a) Does not change; (b) Price falls; (c) Yield rises.
3. The yield over 6 months is $3.965/2 = 1.79825\%$. Therefore, $PV = 3/1.0179825 + 3/1.0179825^2 + \ldots + 103/1.0179825^{34} = 130.37$.
5. a. Fall (e.g., 1-year 10% bond is worth $110/1.1 = 100$ if $r = 10\%$ and is worth $110/1.15 = 95.65$ if $r = 15\%$).
   b. Less (e.g., see 5a).
   c. Less (e.g., with $r = 5\%$, 1-year 10% bond is worth $110/1.05 = 104.76$).
   d. Higher (e.g., if $r = 10\%$, 1-year 10% bond is worth $110/1.1 = 100$, while 1-year 8% bond is worth $108/1.1 = 98.18$).
   e. No, low-coupon bonds have longer durations (unless there is only one period to maturity) and are therefore more volatile (e.g., if r falls from 10% to 5%, the value of a 2-year 10% bond rises from 100 to 109.3 (a rise of 9.3%). The value of a 2-year 5% bond rises from 91.3 to 100 (a rise of 9.5%).
7. (a) 4%; (b) $PV = \$1,075.44$.
9. a. $r_1 = 100/99.423 - 1 = .58\%$; $r_2 = (100/97.546)^{.5} - 1 = 1.25\%$; $r_3 = (100/94.510)^{.33} - .1 = 1.90\%$; $r_4 = (100/90.524)^{.25} - 1 = 2.52\%$.
   b. Upward-sloping.
   c. Lower. (The yield on the bond is a complicated average of the separate spot rates.)
11. a. False. Duration depends on the coupon as well as the maturity.
    b. False. Given the yield to maturity, volatility is proportional to duration.
    c. True. A lower coupon rate means longer duration and therefore higher volatility.
    d. False. A higher interest rate reduces the relative present value of (distant) principal repayments.
13. 7.01%. (The extra return that you earn for investing for 2 years rather than 1 is $1.06^2/1.05 - 1 = .0701$.)

CHAPTER 4

1. (a) True; (b) true.
3. $P_0 = (5 + 110)/1.08 = ₹106.48$
5. $P_0 = 10/(.08 - .05) = ₹333.33$.
7. $15/.08 + PVGO = 333.33$; therefore $PVGO = ₹145.83$.
9. (a) False; (b) true.
11. Free cash flow is the amount of cash thrown off by a business after all investments necessary for growth. In our simple examples, free cash flow equals operating cash flow minus capital expenditure. Free cash flow can be negative if investments are large.
13. If $PVGO = 0$ at the horizon date H, horizon value $=$ earnings forecasted for $H + 1$ divided by r.

CHAPTER 5

1. (a) A = 3 years, B = 2 years, C = 3 years; (b) B;
   (c) A, B, and C; (d) B and C ($NPV_B = \$3,378$; $NPV_C = ₹2,405$); (e) true; (f) It will accept no negative-NPV projects but will turn down some with positive NPVs. A project can have positive NPV if all future cash flows are considered but still do not meet the stated cutoff period.
3. (a) $15,750; $4,250; $0; (b) 100%.
5. (a) Two; (b) -50% and $+50\%$; (c) yes, $NPV = +14.6$.
7. 1, 2, 4, and 6.

CHAPTER 6

1. *a, b, d, g, h.*

3. (a) False; (b) false; (c) false; (d) false.

5.

	2010	2011	2012	2013	2014
Working capital	50,000	230,000	305,000	250,000	0
Cash flows	+50,000	+180,000	+75,000	−55,000	−250,000

7. PV cost = 1.5 + .2 × 14.09 = ₹4.319 million. Equivalent annual cost = 4.319/14.09 = .306, or ₹306,000.

9. Replace at end of 5 years (₹80,000 > ₹72,376).

CHAPTER 7

1. Expected payoff is ₹100 and expected return is zero. Variance is 20,000 (% squared) and standard deviation is 141%.

3. The fund had an average return of 6.47 percent and a standard deviation of 23.4 percent. The market had a lower return (0.69 percent) and a higher standard deviation (24.36 percent). Mr. Sabharwal's fund performed better than the market.

5. *d*

7. (a) 35.1%, (b) zero, (c) 0.56, (d) less than 1.0 (the portfolio's risk is the same as the market, but some of this risk is unique risk).

9. A, 1.0; B, 2.0; C, 1.5; D, 0; E, − 1.0.

CHAPTER 8

1. (a) 7%; (b) 27% with perfect positive correlation; 1% with perfect negative correlation; 19.1% with no correlation; (c) See Figure 1; (d) No, measure risk by beta, not by standard deviation.

3. Sharpe ratio = 7.1/20.2 = .351.

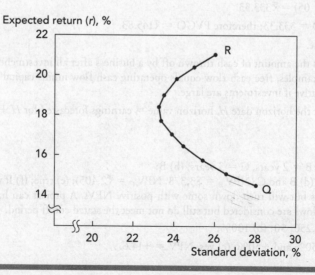

FIGURE 1

Chapter 8, Problem 1(*c*).

5. (a) See Figure 2; (b) A, D, G; (c) F; (d) 15% in C.

(e) Put 25/32 of your money in F and lend 7/32 at 12%: Expected return = 7/32 × 12 + 25/32 × 18 = 16.7%; standard deviation = 7/32 × 0 + (25/32) × 32 = 25%. If you could borrow without limit, you would achieve as high an expected return as you'd like, with correspondingly high risk, of course.

7. (a) True; (b) false (it offers twice the market *risk premium*); (c) false.

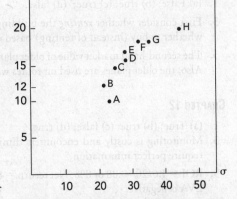

FIGURE 2
Chapter 8, Problem 5(*a*).

CHAPTER 9

1. Overestimate.

3. 36 percent was explained by market movements, 64 percent by unique risk. Unique risk shows up as scatter of points around the fitted line. The standard error is 0.07, so plus or minus two standard errors gives us a range of 0.63 to 0.91.

5. Beta of assets = .5 × .15 + .5 × 1.25 = .7.

7. Suppose that the expected cash flow in year 1 is 100, but the project proposer provides an estimate of 100 × 115/108 = 106.5. Discounting this figure at 15% gives the same result as discounting the true expected cash flow at 8%. Adjusting the discount rate, therefore, works for the first cash flow but it does not do so for later cash flows (e.g., discounting a 2-year cash flow of 106.5 by 15% is *not* equivalent to discounting a 2-year flow of 100 by 8%).

9. (a) False; (b) false; (c) true.

CHAPTER 10

1. (a) False; (b) true; (c) true.

3. a. Analysis of how project profitability and NPV change if different assumptions are made about sales, cost, and other key variables.

b. Project NPV is recalculated by changing several inputs to new, but consistent, values.

c. Determines the level of future sales at which project profitability or NPV equals zero.

d. An extension of sensitivity analysis that explores all possible outcomes and weights each by its probability.

e. A graphical technique for displaying possible future events and decisions taken in response to those events.

f. Option to modify a project at a future date.

g. The additional present value created by the option to bail out of a project, and recover part of the initial investment, if the project performs poorly.

h. The additional present value created by the option to invest more and expand output, if a project performs well.

5. a. Describe how project cash flow depends on the underlying variables.

b. Specify probability distributions for forecast errors for these cash flows.

c. Draw from the probability distributions to simulate the cash flows.

7. Adding a fudge factor to the discount rate pushes project analysts to submit more optimistic forecasts.

CHAPTER 11

1. (a) False; (b) true; (c) true; (d) false.

3. First consider whether *renting* the building and opening the Taco Palace is positive NPV. Then consider whether to buy (instead of renting) based on your optimistic view of local real estate.

5. The second-hand market value of older planes falls by enough to make up for their higher fuel consumption. Also, the older planes are used on routes where fuel efficiency is relatively less important.

CHAPTER 12

1. (a) True; (b) true; (c) false; (d) true.
3. Monitoring is costly and encounters diminishing returns. Also, completely effective monitoring would require perfect information.
5. ROI = 1.6/20 = .08 or 8%. Net return = 8 − 11.5 = − 3.5%. EVA = 1.6 − (.115 × 20) = − ₹.7 million. EVA is negative.
7. Not usually by creative accounting, but by reducing or delaying discretionary advertising, maintenance, R&D, or other expenses.

CHAPTER 13

1. *c*
3. (a) False; (b) false; (c) true; (d) false; (e) false; (f) true.
5. 6 − (1.49 + .83 × 5) = 0.36
7. Decrease. The stock price already reflects an expected 25% increase. The 20% increase conveys bad news relative to expectations.
9. a. Evidence that two securities with identical cash flows (e.g., Royal Dutch Shell and Shell Transport & Trading) can sell at different prices.
   b. Small-cap stocks and high book-to-market stocks appear to have given above-average returns for their level of risk.
   c. IPOs provide relatively low returns after their first few days of trading.
   d. Stocks of firms that announce unexpectedly good earnings perform well over the coming months.

   In each case there appear to have been opportunities for earning superior profits.

CHAPTER 14

1. (a) True; (b) true; (c) False.
3. a. 80 votes; (b) 10 × 80 = 800 votes.
5. a. False; (b) true

CHAPTER 15

1. a. Further sale of an already publicly traded stock;
   b. U.S. bond issue by foreign corporation;
   c. Bond issue by industrial company;
   d. Bond issue by large financial institution.
3. a. Financing of start-up companies.
   b. Underwriters gather nonbinding indications of demand for a new issue.

c. The difference between the price at which the underwriter buys the security from the company and resells it to investors.

d. Winning bidders for a new issue tend to overpay.

5. (a) False; (b) false; (c) true.

7. a. Number of new shares, 50,000;

b. Amount of new investment, ₹500,000;

c. Total value of company after issue, ₹4,500,000;

d. Total number of shares after issue, 150,000;

e. Stock price after issue, ₹4,500,000/150,000 = ₹30;

f. The opportunity to buy one share is worth ₹20.

CHAPTER 16

1. a. A1, B5; A2, B4; A3, B3; A4, B1; A5, B2;

b. On August 12, the ex-dividend date;

c. $(.35 \times 4)/52 = .027$, or 2.7%;

d. $(.35 \times 4)/4.56 = .31$, or 3.1%;

e. The price would fall to $52/1.10 = ₹47.27$.

3. a. Reinvest $1,000 \times ₹.50 = ₹500$ in the stock. If the ex-dividend price is $₹150 - ₹2.50$, this should involve the purchase of 500/147.50, or about 3.4 shares.

b. Sell shares worth $1,000 \times ₹3 = ₹3,000$. If the ex-dividend price is $₹200 - ₹5$, this should involve the sale of 3,000/195, or about 15 shares.

5. a. Company value is unchanged at $5,000 \times 140 = \$700,000$. Share price stays at \$140.

b. The discount rate $r = (DIV_1/P_0) + g = (20/140) + .05 = .193$. The price at which shares are repurchased in year 1 is $140 \times (1 + r) = 140 \times 1.193 = \$167$. Therefore the firm repurchases $50,000/167 = 299$ shares. Total dividend payments in year 1 fall to $5,000 \times 10 = \$50,000$, which is equivalent to $50,000/(5000 - 299) = \$10.64$ a share. Similarly, in year 2 the firm repurchases 281 shares at \$186.52 and the dividend per share increases by 11.7% to \$11.88. In each subsequent year, total dividends increase by 5%, the number of shares declines by 6% and, therefore, dividends per share increase by 11.7%. The constant-growth model gives PV share = $10.64/(.193 - .117) = \$140$.

7. Current tax law (assuming dividend distribution tax rate of 16.65% and securities transaction tax of 0.125%): All will prefer 'Lo'.

Alternative tax law (assuming dividends are taxed in the hands of investors at a rate of 30 percent and capital gains tax of 20%): All will prefer 'Lo' again.

CHAPTER 17

1. Note the market value of Copper Corporation is far in excess of its book value:

	Market Value
Equity (8 million shares at ₹20)	₹160 million
Short-term loans	₹20 million

Ms. Pooja owns 0.625% of the firm, which proposes to increase equity to ₹170 million and cut short-term debt. Ms. Pooja can offset this by (a) borrowing $0.00625 \times 10,000,000 = ₹62,500$, and (b) buying that much more Copper stock.

3. Expected return on assets is $r_A = .08 \times 30/80 + .16 \times 50/80 = .13$. The new return on equity will be $r_E = .13 + (20/60)(.13 - .08) = .147$.

5. a. True;

   b. True (as long as the return earned by the company is greater than the interest payment, earnings per share increase, but the P/E falls to reflect the higher risk);

   c. False (the cost of equity increases with the ratio D/E);

   d. False (the formula $r_E = r_A + (D/E)(r_A - r_D)$ does not require r_D to be constant);

   e. False (debt amplifies variations in equity income);

   f. False (value increases only if clientele is not satisfied).

7. See Figure 17.3.

CHAPTER 18

1. The calculation assumes that the tax rate is fixed, that debt is fixed and perpetual, and that investors' personal tax rates on interest and equity income are the same.

3. Relative advantage of debt $= \dfrac{1 - T_p}{(1 - T_{pE})(1 - T_c)}$

$$= \frac{.65}{(1)(.65)} = 1.00$$

Relative advantage $= \dfrac{.65}{(.85)(.65)} = 1.18$

5. a. Direct costs of financial distress are the legal and administrative costs of bankruptcy. Indirect costs include possible delays in liquidation (Eastern Airlines) or poor investment or operating decisions while bankruptcy is being resolved. Also the *threat* of bankruptcy can lead to costs.

   b. If financial distress increases odds of default, managers' and shareholders' incentives change. This can lead to poor investment or financing decisions.

   c. See the answer to 5(*b*). Examples are the "games" described in Section 18-3.

7. More profitable firms have more taxable income to shield and are less likely to incur the costs of distress. Therefore the trade-off theory predicts high (book) debt ratios. In practice the more profitable companies borrow least.

9. When a company issues securities, outside investors worry that management may have unfavorable information. If so the securities can be overpriced. This worry is much less with debt than equity. Debt securities are safer than equity, and their price is less affected if unfavorable news comes out later.

   A company that can borrow (without incurring substantial costs of financial distress) usually does so. An issue of equity would be read as "bad news" by investors, and the new stock could be sold only at a discount to the previous market price.

11. Financial slack is most valuable to growth companies with good but uncertain investment opportunities. Slack means that financing can be raised quickly for positive-NPV investments. But too much financial slack can tempt mature companies to overinvest. Increased borrowing can force such firms to pay out cash to investors.

CHAPTER 19

1. Market values of debt and equity are: $D = 0.9 \times 75 = ₹67.5$ million and $E = 42 \times 2.5 = ₹105$ million. $D/V = 0.39$

   WACC $= 0.09 \times (1 - 0.3399) \times 0.39 + 0.18 \times 0.61 = 0.1333$, or 13.33 percent

3. (a) False; (b) true; (c) true.

5. (a) True; (b) false, if interest tax shields are valued separately; (c) true.

7. a. 12%, of course.

  b. $r_E = .12 + (.12 - .075)(30/70) = .139$; WACC $= .075(1 - .35)(.30) + .139(.70) = .112$, or 11.2%.

9. No. The more debt you use, the higher rate of return equity investors will require. (Lenders may demand more also.) Thus there is a hidden cost of the "cheap" debt: it makes equity more expensive.

CHAPTER 20

1. Call; exercise; put; European.

3. a. The exercise price of the put option (i.e., you'd sell stock for the exercise price).

  b. The value of the stock (i.e., you would throw away the put and keep the stock).

5. Buy a call and lend the present value of the exercise price.

7. (a) See Figure 3; (b) stock price $-$ PV(EX) $= 100 - 100/1.1 = ₹9.09$.

9. (a) Zero; (b) Stock price less the present value of the exercise price.

11. a. All investors, however risk-averse, should value more highly an option on a volatile stock. For both Hindustan Unilevers and Bharati Airtel the option is valueless if final stock price is below the exercise price, but the option on Bharati Airtel has more upside potential.

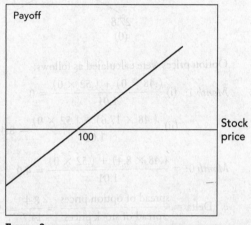

FIGURE 3

Chapter 20, Problem 7.

  b. Other things equal, stockholders lose and debtholders gain if the company shifts to safer assets. When the assets are risky, the option to default is more valuable. Debtholders bear much of the losses if asset value declines, but shareholders get the gains if asset value increases.

CHAPTER 21

1. a. Using risk-neutral method, $(p \times 20) + (1 - p)(-16.7) = 1$, $p = .48$.

$$\text{Value of call} = \frac{(.48 \times 8) + (.52 \times 0)}{1.01} = 3.8$$

  b. Delta $= \dfrac{\text{spread of option prices}}{\text{spread of stock prices}}$

    $= \dfrac{8}{14.7} = .544$.

c.

	Current Cash Flow	Possible Future Cash Flows	
Buy call equals	−3.8	0	+8.0
Buy .544 shares	−21.8	−18.2	+26.2
Borrow 18.0	+18.0	−18.2	−18.2
	−3.8	0	+8.0

d. Possible stock prices with call option prices in parentheses:

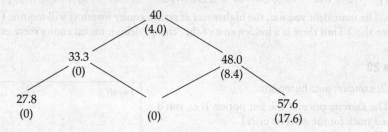

Option prices were calculated as follows:

Month 1: (i) $\dfrac{(.48 \times 0) + (.52 \times 0)}{1.01} = 0$

(ii) $\dfrac{(.48 \times 17.6) + (.52 \times 0)}{1.01} = 8.4.$

Month 0: $= \dfrac{(.48 \times 8.4) + (.52 \times 0)}{1.01} = 4.0$

e. Delta $= \dfrac{\text{spread of option prices}}{\text{spread of stock prices}} = \dfrac{8.4}{14.7} = .57$

3. Using the replicating-portfolio method:
If month 1 stock price = 369.2, delta = (20 − 0)/(420 − 324.54) = 0.209.
To replicate call, buy 0.209 shares, and borrow PV(67.97).
Option Value = 0.209 × 369.18 − 67.97/1.0075 = 9.86.
If month 1 stock price = 477.8, delta = (123.54 − 0)/(543.54 − 420) = 1
To replicate call, buy 1 share and borrow PV(400).
Option Value = 1 × 477.8 − 400/1.0075 = 80.77
At month 0, delta = (80.77 − 9.86)/(477.8 − 369.2) = 0.653
To replicate option, buy 0.653 share, and borrow PV(231.16)
Option Value = 0.653 × 420 − 231.16/1.0075 = 44.76
Using the risk-neutral method:
p × 13.76 + (1 − p) × 12.1 = 0.0075: p = 0.4969
If month 1 stock price = 369.2, option value = (0.4969 × 20 + 0.5031 × 0)/1.0075 = 9.86
If month 1 sock price = 477.8, option value = (0.4969 × 123.54 + 0.5031 × 20)/1.0075 = 80.77
At month 0 option value = (0.4969 × 80.77 + 0.5031 × 80.77)/1.0075 = 44.76
The put option can be valued using put-call parity:
Value of put = 80.77 + 400/1.0075 − 420 = 57.79

5. a. Delta = 100/(200 − 50) = .667.

b.

	Current Cash Flow	Possible Future Cash Flows	
Buy call equals	−36.36	0	+100
Buy .667 shares	−66.67	+33.33	+133.33
Borrow 30.30	+30.30	−33.33	−33.33
	−36.36	0	+100

c. $(p \times 100) + (1 - p)(- 50) = 10, p = .4.$

d. Value of call $= \dfrac{(.4 \times 100) + (.6 \times 0)}{1.10} = 36.36.$

e. No. The true probability of a price rise is almost certainly higher than the risk-neutral probability, but it does not help to value the option.

7. True; as the stock price rises, the risk of the option falls.

CHAPTER 22

1. a. Increase value (unless the cash flows from the Mark II needed to be discounted at a higher rate).
   b. Increase value.
   c. Reduce value.

3. The life of a project is not fixed ahead of time. IM&C has the option to abandon the guano project after 2 or 3 years if performance is poor. If performance is great, exercise of the abandonment option could be delayed well beyond the estimated 7-year life.

5. Gas turbines can be started up on short notice when spark spreads are high. The turbines' value comes from flexibility in production.

7. (a) True; (b) true; (c) true; (d) true; (e) true—the series of smaller plants generates real options, but the large plant may nevertheless be more efficient.

CHAPTER 23

1. Promised yield = 12.72%; expected yield = 9.37%.

3. Put option on company's assets with an exercise price equal to the face value of the bond.

5. The expected growth in the market value of the assets, the face value and maturity of the debt, and the variability of future asset values. (In practice, compromises need to be made if, for example, the company has issued bonds with different maturities.)

7. Both bonds are more likely to be downrated.

CHAPTER 24

1. (a) Bonds; (b) bonds; (c) an asset backed security; (d) project finance.

2. a. You would like an issue of junior debt.
   b. You prefer it not to do so (unless it is also junior debt). The existing property may not be sufficient to pay off your debt.

4. (a) 4 August 2012; ₹117, (b) 4 August, 2017; ₹1942.31, (c) 2016 (but see footnote 20 for some possible complications)

6. a. False. Lenders usually retain some recourse; e.g., they may demand a completion guarantee.
   b. True, but some new securities (e.g., eurobonds) survive even when the original motive for issuing them disappears.
   c. False. The borrower has the option.
   d. True. But debt issues with weak covenants suffered in such takeovers.
   e. True. The costs of renegotiation are less for private placements.

8. (a) False; (b) true; (c) false; (d) true.

CHAPTER 25

1. *A, c; B, d* or *i; C, b* or *e; D, f; E, a; F, h; G, g.*

3. a. The lessor must charge enough to cover the present value of the costs of owning and operating the asset over its expected economic life. In a competitive leasing market the present value of rentals cannot exceed the present value of costs. The competitive rental payment ends up equal to the lessor's equivalent annual cost.

   b. The user's equivalent annual cost is the annual cost to the user of owning and operating the asset. If the operating lease rate is less than this cost, it pays to lease.

5. If the lease is affirmed, the lessee continues to use the leased asset and must make the full lease payments. If the lease is rejected, the leased asset is returned to the lessor. If the value of the returned asset is not enough to cover the remaining lease payments, the lessor's loss becomes an unsecured claim on the bankrupt firm.

7. Lenders have no claim on the lessor if the lessee defaults. The lessor avoids liability in this case. But lenders will demand better terms, for example, a higher interest rate, as compensation for lack of recourse.

CHAPTER 26

1. a. Price paid for immediate delivery.

   b. Forward contracts are contracts to buy or sell at a specified future date at a specified price. Futures differ from forwards in two main ways. They are traded on an exchange and they are marked to market.

   c. Investors who are long have agreed to buy the asset. Investors who are short have contracted to sell.

   d. The risk that arises because the price of the asset used to hedge is not perfectly correlated with that of the asset that is being hedged.

   e. Profits and losses on a position are settled on a regular basis (e.g., daily).

   f. The advantage from owning the commodity rather than the promise of future delivery *less* the cost of storing the commodity.

3. She is asking you to pay money, because your sale is showing a loss.

5. The farmer has fixed the price that he will receive for his wheat (we ignore possible basis risk). Because it now has a certain income, it gives up the possibility of pleasant surprises as well as unpleasant ones.

7. a. A shortage of heating oil increases net convenience yield and reduces the futures price relative to spot price.

   b. Spot and futures prices decrease. The futures price rises relative to spot because convenience yield falls and storage costs rise.

9. (a) Profit;

   (b) If the bank took out a new 4-year swap, it would need to pay an extra ₹.25 million a year. At the new interest rate of 6.5%, the extra payment has a present value of ₹856,000. This is the amount that the bank should charge to terminate.

11. Sell short ₹1.2 million of the market portfolio. In practice rather than "sell the market" you would sell futures on ₹1.2 million of the market index.

CHAPTER 27

1. a. 0.0250;
   b. ₹40.3 per 1 S$;
   c. Singapore $ is at a premium. Rupee is at a discount;
   d. Premium = 41.36/39.97 − 1 = 0.0348 or 3.48%;
   e. From interest rate parity, 41.36/39.97 = $(1+r_{S\$})/(1+0.0425)$. $r_{S\$}$ = 0.75%;

f. ₹40.77/1 S$;

g. If the real exchange rate is expected to be constant, expected difference in inflation is 40.77/39.97 – 1 = 0.0200, i.e., inflation in Indian over the three months is expected to be 2% less than in Singapore.

3. a. $47 \times 1.11 / 1.02 = ₹51.15 = 1$$. b. Real value of rupee fell by 51.15/52 – 1 = 0.016, or 1.6%.

5. *b.*

7. It can borrow the present value of €1 million, sell the euros in the spot market, and invest the proceeds in an 8-year dollar loan.

9. a. NPV = $12.18 \times 66 = ₹803.97$

Year	0	1	2	3	4	5
Forward rate	66.00	68.54	71.17	73.91	76.75	79.71
₹ million	−5,280.00	685.38	1,423.49	1,699.98	2,072.38	1,992.67

c. It doesn't. The company can always hedge against a fall in the euro.

CHAPTER 28

1.

₹ Thousands		₹ Thousands	
Cash	₹25	₹ 24	Accounts payable
Accounts receivable	35	24	Total current liabilities
Inventories	30	130	Long-term debt
Total current assets	90	76	Equity
Net plant & equipment	140		
Total assets	230	230	Total liabilities & equity

3.

Common-size Balance Sheet, 2011			
Cash	1%	Current Liabilities	47%
Accounts receivable	4%	Provisions	16%
Inventories	15%	Total current liabilities	63%
Other current assets	51%	Long-term debt	0%
Total current assets	71%	Total shareholders equity	37%
Net fixed assets	24%		
Long term investments	4%		
Other long-term assets	1%		
Total assets	100%	Total Liabilities & equity	100%

Common Size Income Stetement, 2012	
Sales	100%
Other Income	2%
Total Income	102%
Raw Materials	39%
Employee Cost	8%
Other Manufacturing Expenses	6%
Selling, General, and Administraive Expenses	21%
Depreciation	1%
Interest	0%
Tax	5%
Net Income	17%

5. The illogical ratios are *a, b, c, f,* and *i.* The correct definitions are

$$\text{Debt-equity ratio} = \frac{\text{long-term debt} + \text{value of leases}}{\text{equity}}$$

$$\text{Return on equity} = \frac{\text{net income}}{\text{equity at start of year}}$$

$$\text{Payout ratio} = \frac{\text{dividend per share}}{\text{earnings per share}}$$

$$\text{Current ratio} = \frac{\text{current assets}}{\text{current liabilities}}$$

$$\text{Average collection period} = \frac{\text{receivables at start of year}}{\text{daily sales}}$$

7. a. Sales = $3 \times 500,000 = 1,500,000$; after-tax interest + net income = $.08 \times 1,500,000 = 120,000$; ROA = $120,000/500,000 = 24\%$;

b. Net income = $.08 \times 3 \times 500,000 - (1 - .35) \times 30,000 = 100,500$. ROE = net income/equity = $100,500/300,000 = .34$.

9. .73.; 3.65%

11. Assume that new debt is a current liability.

a. Current ratio goes from $100/60 = 1.67$ to $120/80 = 1.50$; cash ratio goes from $30/60 = .5$ to $50/80 = .63$;

b. Long-term debt ratio is unchanged; total liabilities/total assets goes from $410/600 = .6833$ to $430/620 = .6935$.

13. ₹82 million.

CHAPTER 29

1.

	Cash	Working Capital
1.	₹2 million decline	₹2 million decline
2.	₹2,500 increase	Unchanged
3.	₹50,000 decline	Unchanged
4.	Unchanged	₹10 million increase
5.	Unchanged	Unchanged
6.	₹5 million increase	Unchanged

3. Month 3: $18 + (.5 \times 90) + (.3 \times 120) + (.2 \times 100) = ₹119,000$.

Month 4: $14 + (.5 \times 70) + (.3 \times 90) + (.2 \times 120) = ₹100,000$.

5. a. Table 29.2: Cash = 40, Total current assets = 340; Bank loans = 15; Current liabilities = 150; and Total assets = Total liabilities and net worth = 590.

Table 29.3: Increase (decrease) in short-term debt = -10; net cash flow from financing activities = -35; Increase in cash balance = 20.

b. Table 29.2: Long-term debt = 130; Gross investment = 375; Net fixed assets = 275; Cash = 40; Current assets = 340; and Total assets = Total liabilities and net worth = 615.

Table 29.3: Increase (decrease) in long-term debt = $30 + 40 = 70$; Net cash flow from financing activities = $-50 + 40 = -10$; Investment in fixed assets = $-(25 + 30) = -55$; Increase in cash balance = 20.

c. Table 29.1: Operating cost (cost of goods sold + other expenses) = $(1,644 + 411) \times .9 = 1,850$; Pretax income = $2,200 - 1,850 - 20 - 5 = 325$; Net income = $325 \times .5 = 162.5$. If dividend is unchanged, earnings retained in the business = $162.5 - 30 = 132.5$.

Table 29.2: assuming inventories are unchanged, Cash = $25 + 132.5 - 30 = 127.5$; Current assets = 427.5; Net worth = 452.5; total assets = total liabilities and net worth = 677.5.

Table 29.3: Net income = 162.5; Net cash flow from operating activities = $85 + 102.5 = 187.5$; Increase (decrease) in cash balance = 107.5

d. Table 29.4 changes as follows:

	Q3	Q4
Receivables at start	181.6	105.2
Sales	742	836
Collections:		
Current sales	667.8	752.4
Last period sales	150.6	74.2
Total collections	818.4	826.6
Receivables at end	105.2	114.6

Table 29.5 changes as follows:

	Q3	Q4
Collections on accounts receivable	818.4	826.6
Total sources	895.4	826.6
Sources minus uses	268.4	189.1
Cash at start	−188.6	79.8
Change in cash balance	268.4	189.1
Cash at end	79.8	268.9
Cumulative financing required	−54.8	243.9

e. Table 29.5 changes as follows:

	Q1	Q2	Q3	Q4
Labor and other expenses	116	116	116	116
Total sources	531	539.4	767	827.8
Sources minus uses	121	−52.6	140	190.3
Short-term borrowing requirement:				
Cash at start	25	−96	−148.6	−8.6
Change in cash balance	−121	−52.6	140	190.3
Cash at end	−96	−148.6	−8.6	181.7
Cumulative financing required	121	173.6	33.6	−156.7

f. Table 29.5 changes as follows:

	Q2	Q3	Q4
Other	50	77	
Total sources	569.4	747	807.8
Sources minus uses	−22.6	120	170.3
Short-term borrowing requirement:			
Cash at start	−116	−138.6	−18.6
Change in cash balance	−22.6	120	170.3
Cash at end	−138.6	−18.6	151.7
Cumulative financing required	163.6	43.6	−126.7

g. Table 29.5 changes as follows:

	Q1	Q2	Q3	Q4
Minimum operating balance	10	10	10	10
Cumulative financing required	126	198.6	78.6	−91.7

7. (a) ₹ 2,900,000; (b) ₹ 225,000; (c) .25.
9. (a) 8.6%; (b) 13.75%.

CHAPTER 30

1. By holding large inventories, the firm avoids the risk of running out of materials and finished goods. It can order materials in larger quantities and arrange longer production runs. On the other hand, inventories tie up capital, must be stored and insured, and may be subject to damage.

   Similarly, large cash inventories reduce the risk of running out of cash or having to sell securities at short notice. The firm needs to make less frequent sales of securities and therefore minimize the fixed costs of such sales. On the other hand, inventories of cash tie up capital.

3. a. Due lag decreases, therefore pay lag decreases.
   b. Due lag increases, therefore pay lag increases.
   c. Terms lag increases, therefore pay lag increases.

5. a. Expected profit = $p(1,200 - 1,050) - 1,050 (1 - p) = 0$

$$p = .875$$

   Therefore, grant credit if probability of payment exceeds 87.5%.

   b. Expected profit from selling to slow payer: $.8(150) - .2(1,050) = -90$. Break-even point for credit check: $(.05 \times 90 \times units) - 12 = 0$. Units = 2.67.

7. (a) False; (b) false; (c) false—should be collection agency or attorney.

9. a. The $.40 per check fee is cheaper at $300 \times .40 = \$120$ per day. The cost of putting up $800,000 of compensating balances is $.09 \times 800,000 = \$72,000$ per year, or 72,000/365 = $197 per day.

   b. The lockbox system costs $120 per day, or $43,800 per year. You would need $486,700 additional cash to generate this much interest. Thus the lockbox system must generate at least this much cash. The cash flow is $300 \times 1,500 = \$450,000$ per day. Thus the lockbox must speed up average collection time by 486,700/450,000 = 1.08 days.

10. (a) Less; (b) less; (c) invest the same amount; (d) more.

12. (a) Repurchase agreements; (b) commercial paper;
(c) finance company commercial paper; (d) 3-month bills; (e) Treasury bills; (f) Treasury bills.

14. (a) True; (b) false (borrower has a call); (c) true; (d) false ($100/90 - 1 = .111$, or 11.1%); (e) true.

CHAPTER 31

1. (a) Horizontal; (b) conglomerate; (c) vertical;
(d) vertical.

3. (a) ₹5 million (We assume that the ₹500,000 saving is an after-tax figure.); (b) ₹4 million; (c) ₹7.5 million; (d) +₹1 million; (e) − ₹2.5 million.

5. (a) True; (b) false; (c) false; (d) true; (e) false (They may produce gains, but "large" is stretching it.);
(f) false; (g) true.

CHAPTER 32

1. a. Purchase of a business using mostly debt financing. The company goes private. Management is given a substantial equity stake.
   b. An LBO undertaken by management.
   c. A parent company creates a new company with part of its assets and operations. Shares in the new business are distributed to the parent's stockholders.
   d. Like a spin-off, but shares in the new business are sold to investors.
   e. Sale of specific assets rather than entire firm.
   f. A government-owned business is sold to private investors.
   g. A company moves to a much higher debt ratio. Proceeds of additional borrowing are paid out to stockholders.

3. Increased efficiency, broader share ownership, and revenue for the government.

5. Internal capital markets often misallocate capital. The market values of the conglomerate's divisions can't be observed separately, so it's hard to set incentives and to reward risk-taking.

7. Chapter 7 usually leads to liquidation. Chapter 11 protects the firm from its creditors while a reorganization plan is developed.

9. There is always a chance that the company can recover, allowing creditors to be paid off and leaving something for shareholders. Also, the court may not observe *absolute priority*, so shareholders may be given some crumbs in a Chapter 11 reorganization.

CHAPTER 33

1. (a) USA and UK; (b) USA; (c) Japan and Europe;
(d) Japan; (e) UK; (f) Japan. (*Note:* Answers exclude countries not separately shown in Figures 33.1–33.4.)

3. No. Individual investors hold relatively little common stock directly. Also the cross-holdings of stock by Japanese companies limit the opportunities for individuals to play an important role in governance.

5. German firms have two boards of directors: a management board and a supervisory board, half of whose members are elected by employees. The supervisory board represents the interests of the company as a whole, not just the interests of employees or stockholders.

7. The shareholder has a .3 holding in x_2. x_2 has a .3 holding in x, which has a .3 holding in z. The shareholder really has only a $.3^3$ or .027 holding in z.

9. If firm y has a large stake in x, it may be able to transfer value from x by borrowing from x at a low interest rate, selling materials to x at excessive prices, or buying x's output at low prices.

GLOSSARY

Note:
1. *Italicized* words are listed elsewhere in the glossary.
2. A number of Web sites contain comprehensive financial glossaries. See, for example, **www.finance-glossary.com** and **www.duke.edu/~ charvey/ Classes/wpg/glossary.htm**.

A

Abnormal return   Part of return that is not due to marketwide price movements.

Absolute priority   Rule in bankruptcy proceedings whereby senior creditors are required to be paid in full before junior creditors receive any payment.

Accelerated depreciation   Any *depreciation* method that produces larger deductions for depreciation in the early years of a project's life.

Accounts payable (payables, trade debt)   Money owed to suppliers.

Accounts receivable (receivables, trade credit)   Money owed by customers.

Accrued interest   Interest that has been earned but not yet paid.

ACH   *Automated Clearing House*.

Acid-test ratio   *Quick ratio*.

Adjusted present value (APV)   *Net present value* of an asset if financed solely by equity plus the *present value* of any financing side effects.

ADR   *American depository receipt*.

Adverse selection   A situation in which a pricing policy causes only the less desirable customers to do business, e.g., a rise in insurance prices that leads only the worst risks to buy insurance.

Affirmative covenant   Loan *covenant* specifying certain actions that the borrower must take.

Agency costs   Losses that arise when an agent (e.g., a manager) does not act solely in the interests of the principal (e.g., the shareholder).

Agency theory   Theory of the relationship between a principal, e.g., a shareholder, and an agent of the principal, e.g., the company's manager.

Aging schedule   Summary of age of *receivables* that are outstanding from each customer.

AIBD   Association of International Bond Dealers.

All-or-none underwriting   An arrangement whereby a security issue is canceled if the *underwriter* is unable to resell the entire issue.

Alpha   Measure of portfolio return adjusted for effect of market.

Alternative minimum tax (AMT)   A separately calculated minimum amount of tax that must be paid by corporations or individuals.

American depository receipt (ADR)   A certificate issued in the United States to represent shares of a foreign company.

American option   *Option* that can be exercised any time before the final exercise date (cf. *European option*).

Amex   American Stock Exchange.

Amortization   (1) Repayment of a loan by installments; (2) allowance for *depreciation*.

AMT   *Alternative minimum tax*.

Angel investor   Wealthy individual who provides capital for small start-up businesses.

Annual percentage rate (APR)   The interest rate per period (e.g., per month) multiplied by the number of periods in a year.

Annuity   Investment that produces a level stream of cash flows for a limited number of periods.

Annuity due   *Annuity* whose payments occur at the start of each period.

Annuity factor   *Present value* of $1 paid for each of *t* periods.

Anticipation   Arrangement whereby customers who pay before the final date may be entitled to deduct a normal rate of interest.

Appraisal rights   A right of shareholders in a *merger* to demand the payment of a fair price for their shares, as determined independently.

Appropriation request   Formal request for funds for a capital investment project.

APR   *Annual percentage rate.*

APT   *Arbitrage pricing theory.*

APV   *Adjusted present value.*

Arbitrage   Purchase of one security and simultaneous sale of another to give a risk-free profit.

"Arbitrage" or "risk arbitrage"   Often used loosely to describe the taking of offsetting positions in related securities, e.g., at the time of a takeover bid.

Arbitrage pricing theory (APT)   Model in which expected returns increase linearly with an asset's sensitivity to a small number of pervasive factors.

Arranger   Lead *underwriter* to a *syndicated loan.*

Articles of incorporation   Legal document establishing a corporation and its structure and purpose.

Asian currency units   Dollar deposits held in Singapore or other Asian centers.

Asian option   *Option* based on the average price of the asset during the life of the option.

Asked price (offered price)   Price at which a dealer is willing to sell (cf. *bid price*).

Asset-backed securities   Securities issued by a special-purpose company that holds a package of assets whose cash flows are sufficient to service the *bonds.*

Asset stripper   Acquirer who takes over firms in order to sell off a large part of their assets.

Asymmetric information   Difference in information available to two parties, e.g., a manager and investors.

At-the-money option   Option whose exercise price equals the current asset price (cf. *in-the-money option, out-of-the-money option*).

Auction market   Securities exchange in which prices are determined by an auction process, e.g., *NYSE* (cf. *dealer market*).

Auction-rate preferred   A variant of *floating-rate preferred* stock where the dividend is reset every 49 days by auction.

Authorized share capital   Maximum number of shares that a company can issue, as specified in the firm's *articles of incorporation.*

Automated Clearing House (ACH)   Private electronic system run by banks for high-volume, low-value payments.

Automatic debit   *Direct payment.*

Availability float   Checks deposited by a company that have not yet been cleared.

Aval   Bank guarantee for debt purchased by *forfaiter.*

B

BA   *Banker's acceptance.*

Backdating   Discredited practice of using hindsight to select a grant date for at-the-money executive stock *options* when the stock price (and therefore *exercise price*) were unusually low.

Backwardation   Condition in which *spot price* of commodity exceeds price of *future* (cf. *contango*).

Balloon payment   Large final payment (e.g., when a loan is repaid in installments).

Bank discount   Interest deducted from the initial amount of a loan.

Banker's acceptance (BA)   Written demand that has been accepted by a bank to pay a given sum at a future date (cf. *trade acceptance*).

Barrier option   *Option* whose existence depends on asset price hitting some specified barrier (cf. *down-and-out option, down-and-in option*).

Basel Accord   International agreement on the amount of capital to be maintained by large banks to support their risky loans.

Basis point (bp)   .01%.

Basis risk   Residual risk that results when the two sides of a hedge do not move exactly together.

Bearer security Security for which primary evidence of ownership is possession of the certificate (cf. *registered security*).

Bear market Widespread decline in security prices (cf. *bull market*).

Behavioral finance Branch of finance that stresses aspects of investor irrationality.

Benchmark maturity Maturity of a newly issued Treasury bond.

Benefit–cost ratio One plus *profitability index*.

Bermuda option *Option* that is exercisable on discrete dates before maturity.

Best-efforts underwriting An arrangement whereby *underwriters* do not commit themselves to selling a security issue but promise only to use best efforts.

Beta Measure of *market risk*.

Bid price Price at which a dealer is willing to buy (cf. *asked price*).

Big Board Colloquial term for the New York Stock Exchange.

Bill of exchange General term for a document demanding payment.

Bill of lading Document establishing ownership of goods in transit.

Binomial method Method for valuing *options* that assumes there are only two possible changes in the asset price in any one period.

Blue-chip company Large and creditworthy company.

Blue-sky laws State laws covering the issue and trading of securities.

Boilerplate Standard terms and conditions, e.g., in a debt contract.

Bond Long-term debt.

Bond rating Rating of the likelihood of bond's default.

Bookbuilding The procedure whereby *underwriters* gather nonbinding indications of demand for a new issue.

Book entry Registered ownership of stock without issue of stock certificate.

Book runner The managing *underwriter* for a new issue. The book runner maintains the book of securities sold.

Bought deal Security issue where one or two *underwriters* buy the entire issue.

BP *Basis point.*

Bracket A term signifying the extent of an *underwriter's* commitment in a new issue, e.g., major bracket, minor bracket.

Break-even analysis Analysis of the level of sales at which a project would just break even.

Bridge loan Short-term loan to provide temporary financing until more permanent financing is arranged.

Bull–bear bond *Bond* whose *principal* repayment is linked to the price of another security. The bonds are issued in two *tranches:* In the first the repayment increases with the price of the other security; in the second the repayment decreases with the price of the other security.

Bulldog bond *Foreign bond* issue made in London.

Bullet payment Single final payment, e.g., of a loan (in contrast to payment in installments).

Bull market Widespread rise in security prices (cf. *bear market*).

Butterfly spread The purchase of two *call options* with different *exercise prices* and simultaneous sale of two calls exercisable at the average of these two exercise prices. Provides a bet that the share price will stay within a narrow range.

Bund Long-term German government *bond*.

Buyback *Repurchase agreement.*

C

Cable The exchange rate between U.S. dollars and sterling.

Call option Option to buy an asset at a specified exercise price on or before a specified exercise date (cf. *put option*).

Call premium (1) Difference between the price at which a company can call its *bonds* and their *face value;* (2) price of a call *option*.

Call provision Provision that allows an issuer to buy back the *bond* issue at a stated price.

Cap An upper limit on the interest rate on a *floating-rate note*.

CAPEX Capital expenditure.

Capital asset pricing model (CAPM) Model in which expected returns increase linearly with an asset's *beta*.

Capital budget List of planned investment projects, usually prepared annually.

Capitalization Long-term debt plus *preferred stock* plus *net worth*.

Capital lease *Financial lease*.

Capital market Financial market (particularly the market for long-term securities).

Capital market line A plot of the set of portfolios with the highest *Sharpe ratio*. The line passes through the risk-free interest rate and the *tangent efficient portfolio* of risky assets.

Capital rationing Shortage of funds that forces a company to choose between worthwhile projects.

Capital structure Mix of different securities issued by a firm.

CAPM *Capital asset pricing model*.

Captive finance company Subsidiary whose function is to provide finance for purchases from the parent company.

Caput option *Call option* on a *put option*.

CAR Cumulative *abnormal return*.

CARDs (Certificates for Amortizing Revolving Debt) *Pass-through securities* backed by credit card *receivables*.

Carried interest A proportion of the profits to which *private equity* partnerships, etc. are entitled.

Carry trade Borrowing in country with low interest rate to relend in another country with a higher rate.

CARs (Certificates of Automobile Receivables) *Pass-through securities* backed by automobile *receivables*.

Carve-out Public offering of shares in a subsidiary.

Cascade Rational herding in which each individual deduces that previous decisions by others may have been based on extra information.

Cash and carry Purchase of a security and simultaneous sale of a *future*, with the balance being financed with a loan or *repo*.

Cash budget Forecast of sources and uses of cash.

Cash cow Mature company producing a large *free cash flow*.

Cash cycle The time from a firm's payment for raw materials until the payment for the finished product from the customer.

Cash-deficiency arrangement Arrangement whereby a project's shareholders agree to provide the operating company with sufficient *net working capital*.

Catastrophe bond (CAT bond) *Bond* whose payoffs are linked to a measure of catastrophe losses such as insurance claims.

CAT bond *Catastrophe bond*.

CBD Cash before delivery.

CD *Certificate of deposit*.

CDS *Credit default swap*.

CEO Chief executive officer.

Certainty equivalent A certain cash flow that has the same present value as a specified risky cash flow.

Certificate of deposit (CD) A certificate providing evidence of a bank time deposit.

CFTC Commodity Futures Trading Commission.

CFO Chief financial officer.

Chaebol A Korean conglomerate.

Chapter 7 Bankruptcy procedure whereby a debtor's assets are sold and the proceeds are used to repay creditors.

Chapter 11 Bankruptcy procedure designed to reorganize and rehabilitate defaulting firm.

Check conversion When customer writes a check, information is automatically captured and his bank account immediately debited.

Check 21 Check Clearing for the 21st Century Act allows banks to process checks electronically.

CHIPS *Clearinghouse Interbank Payments System*.

Chooser option Holder decides whether it is a *call option* or *put option*.

Clean price (flat price) *Bond* price excluding *accrued interest* (cf. *dirty price*).

Clearinghouse Interbank Payments System (CHIPS) An international wire transfer system operated by a group of major banks for high-value dollar payments.

CLO *Collateralized loan obligation*. Also CDO (collateralized debt obligation) and CMO (collateralized mortgage obligation).

Closed-end fund Company whose assets consist of investments in a number of industrial and commercial companies.

Closed-end mortgage Mortgage against which no additional debt may be issued (cf. *open-end mortgage*).

CMOs *Collateralized mortgage obligations*.

COD Cash on delivery.

Collar An upper and lower limit on the interest rate on a *floating-rate note*.

Collateral Assets that are given as security for a loan.

Collateralized loan obligation (CLO) A security backed by a pool of loans and issued in *tranches* with different levels of seniority.

Collateralized mortgage obligations (CMOs) A variation on the mortgage *pass-through security* in which the cash flows from a pool of mortgages are repackaged into several *tranches* of *bonds* with different maturities.

Collateral trust bonds *Bonds* secured by *common stocks* or other securities that are owned by the borrower.

Collection float Customer-written checks that have not been received, deposited, and added to the company's available balance (cf. *payment float*).

Commercial draft (bill of exchange) Demand for payment.

Commercial paper Unsecured *notes* issued by companies and maturing within nine months.

Commitment fee Fee charged by bank on an unused *line of credit*.

Common-size financial statements Balance sheet where entries are expressed as proportion of total assets and income statement where entries are expressed as a proportion of revenues.

Common stock Security representing ownership of a *corporation*.

Company cost of capital The expected return on a portfolio of all the firm's securities.

Compensating balance Non-interest-bearing demand deposits to compensate banks for bank loans or services.

Competitive bidding Means by which public utility *holding companies* are required to choose their underwriter (cf. *negotiated underwriting*).

Completion bonding Insurance that a construction contract will be successfully completed.

Composition Voluntary agreement to reduce payments on a firm's debt.

Compound interest Reinvestment of each interest payment on money invested to earn more interest (cf. *simple interest*).

Compound option Option on an *option*.

Concentration banking System whereby customers make payments to a regional collection center. The collection center pays the funds into a regional bank account and surplus money is transferred to the company's principal bank.

Conditional sale Sale in which ownership does not pass to the buyer until payment is completed.

Conglomerate merger *Merger* between two companies in unrelated businesses (cf. *horizontal merger, vertical merger*).

Consol Name of a perpetual *bond* issued by the British government. Sometimes used as a general term for *perpetuity*.

Contango Condition in which spot price of a commodity is below that of the *future* (cf. *backwardation*).

Contingent claim Claim whose value depends on the value of another asset.

Contingent project Project that cannot be undertaken unless another project is also undertaken.

Continuous compounding Interest compounded continuously rather than at fixed intervals.

Controller Officer responsible for budgeting, accounting, and auditing in a firm (cf. *treasurer*).

Convenience yield The extra advantage that firms derive from holding the commodity rather than the *future*.

Conversion price *Par value* of a *convertible bond* divided by the number of shares into which it may be exchanged.

Conversion ratio Number of shares for which a *convertible bond* may be exchanged.

Convertible bond *Bond* that may be converted into another security at the holder's option. Similarly convertible *preferred stock*.

Convexity In a plot of a *bond*'s price against the interest rate, convexity measures the curvature of the line.

Corporate venturing Practice by which a large manufacturer provides financial support to new companies.

Corporation A business that is legally separate from its owners.

Correlation coefficient Measure of the closeness of the relationship between two variables.

Cost company arrangement Arrangement whereby the shareholders of a project receive output free of charge but agree to pay all operating and financing charges of the project.

Cost of (equity) capital *Opportunity cost of capital*.

Counterparty Party on the other side of a *derivative* contract.

Coupon (1) Specifically, an attachment to the certificate of a *bearer security* that must be surrendered to collect interest payment; (2) more generally, interest payment on debt.

Covariance Measure of the co-movement between two variables.

Covenant Clause in a loan agreement.

Covered option *Option* position with an offsetting position in the underlying asset.

Cramdown Action by a bankruptcy court to enforce a plan of reorganization.

Credit default swap (CDS) *Credit derivative* in which one party makes fixed payments while the payments by the other party depend on the occurrence of a loan default.

Credit derivative Contract for *hedging* against loan default or changes in credit risk (e.g., *credit default swap*).

Credit rating Debt rating assigned by a rating agency such as Moody's or Standard & Poor's.

Credit scoring A procedure for assigning scores to borrowers on the basis of the risk of default.

Cross-default clause Clause in a loan agreement stating that the company is in default if it fails to meet its obligation on any other debt issue.

Cum dividend *With dividend.*

Cum rights *With rights.*

Cumulative preferred stock Stock that takes priority over *common stock* in regard to dividend payments. Dividends may not be paid on the common stock until all past *dividends* on the *preferred stock* have been paid.

Cumulative voting Voting system under which a stockholder may cast all of his or her votes for one candidate for the board of directors (cf. *majority voting*).

Current asset Asset that will normally be turned into cash within a year.

Current liability Liability that will normally be repaid within a year.

Current ratio *Current assets* divided by *current liabilities*—a measure of liquidity.

Current yield *Bond coupon* divided by price.

D

Data mining (data snooping) Excessive search to find interesting (but probably coincidental) behavior in a body of data.

DCF *Discounted cash flow.*

DDM *Dividend discount model.*

Dealer market Securities exchange in which dealers post offers to buy or sell, e.g., *Nasdaq* (cf. *auction market*).

Dealer paper *Commercial paper* sold through a dealer rather than directly by the company.

Death spiral convertible *Convertible bond* exchangeable for shares with a specified market value.

Debenture Unsecured *bond.*

Debtor-in-possession financing (DIP financing) Debt issued by a company in *Chapter 11 bankruptcy.*

Decision tree Method of representing alternative sequential decisions and the possible outcomes from these decisions.

Defeasance Practice whereby the borrower sets aside cash or *bonds* sufficient to service the borrower's debt. Both the borrower's debt and the offsetting cash or bonds are removed from the balance sheet.

Degree of operating leverage (DOL) The percentage change in profits for a 1% change in sales.

Delta *Hedge ratio.*

Depository transfer check (DTC) Check made out directly by a local bank to a particular company.

Depreciation (1) Reduction in the book or market value of an asset; (2) portion of an investment that can be deducted from taxable income.

Derivative Asset whose value derives from that of some other asset (e.g., a *future* or an *option*).

Designated market maker Member of *NYSE* responsible for market in specified securities (formerly called "specialist").

Diff *Differential swap.*

Differential swap (diff, quanto swap) Swap between two *LIBOR* rates of interest, e.g., yen LIBOR for dollar LIBOR. Payments are in one currency.

Digital option *Option* paying fixed sum if asset price is the right side of *exercise price*, otherwise zero.

Dilution Diminution in the proportion of income to which each share is entitled.

DIP financing *Debtor-in-possession financing.*

Direct deposit The firm authorizes its bank to deposit money in the accounts of its employees or shareholders.

Direct lease *Lease* in which the *lessor* purchases new equipment from the manufacturer and leases it to the *lessee* (cf. *sale and lease-back*).

Direct payment (automatic debit, direct debit) The firm's customers authorize it to debit their bank accounts for the amounts due (cf. *direct deposit*).

Direct quote For foreign exchange, the number of U.S. dollars needed to buy one unit of a foreign currency (cf. *indirect quote*).

Dirty price *Bond* price including *accrued interest*, i.e., the price paid by the bond buyer (cf. *clean price*).

Discount bond Debt sold for less than its *principal* value. If a discount bond pays no interest, it is called a "pure" discount, or *zero-coupon*, bond.

Discounted cash flow (DCF) Future cash flows multiplied by *discount factors* to obtain *present value*.

Discount factor *Present value* of $1 received at a stated future date.

Discount rate Rate used to calculate the *present value* of future cash flows.

Discounted payback rule Requirement that discounted values of cash flows should be sufficient to pay back initial investment within a specified time.

Discriminatory price auction Auction in which successful bidders pay the price that they bid (cf. *uniform price auction*).

Disintermediation Withdrawal of funds from a financial institution in order to invest them directly (cf. *intermediation*).

Dividend Payment by a company to its stockholders.

Dividend discount model Model showing that the value of a share is equal to the discounted value of future *dividends*.

Dividend reinvestment plan (DRIP) Plan that allows shareholders to reinvest dividends automatically.

Dividend yield Annual *dividend* divided by share price.

DOL *Degree of operating leverage.*

Double-declining-balance depreciation Method of *accelerated depreciation*.

Double-tax agreement Agreement between two countries that taxes paid abroad can be offset against domestic taxes levied on foreign *dividends*.

Down-and-in option *Barrier option* that comes into existence if asset price hits a barrier.

Down-and-out option *Barrier option* that expires if asset price hits a barrier.

DRIP *Dividend reinvestment plan.*

Drop lock An arrangement whereby the interest rate on a *floating-rate note* or *preferred stock* becomes fixed if it falls to a specified level.

DTC *Depository transfer check.*

Dual-class equity Shares with different voting rights.

Dual-currency bond *Bond* with interest paid in one currency and *principal* paid in another.

DuPont formula Formula expressing relationship between return on assets, sales-to-assets, profit margin, and measures of leverage.

Duration The average number of years to an asset's *discounted cash flows*.

Dutch auction In a Dutch auction investors submit the prices at which they are prepared to buy (or sell) the security. The purchase price is the lowest price that allows the firm to sell (or buy) the specified amount of the security.

E

EBIT Earnings before interest and taxes.

EBITDA Earnings before interest, taxes, depreciation, and *amortization*.

EBPP *Electronic bill presentment and payment.*

Economic depreciation Decline in *present value* of an asset.

Economic exposure Risk that arises from changes in real exchange rates (cf. *transaction exposure, translation exposure*).

Economic income Cash flow plus change in *present value*.

Economic rents Profits in excess of the competitive level.

Economic value added (EVA) A measure of *residual income* implemented by the consulting firm Stern Stewart.

Efficient market Market in which security prices reflect information instantaneously.

Efficient portfolio Portfolio that offers the lowest risk (*standard deviation*) for its *expected return* and the highest expected return for its level of risk.

EFT *Electronic funds transfer.*

Electronic bill presentment and payment (EBPP) Allows companies to bill customers and receive payments via the Internet.

Electronic funds transfer (EFT) Transfer of money electronically (e.g., by *Fedwire*).

Employee stock ownership plan (ESOP)   A company contributes to a trust fund that buys stock on behalf of employees.

Entrenching investment   An investment that makes particular use of the skills of existing management.

EPS   Earnings per share.

Equipment trust certificate   Form of *secured debt* generally used to finance railroad equipment. The trustee retains ownership of the equipment until the debt is repaid.

Equity   (1) *Common stock* and *preferred stock*. Often used to refer to common stock only. (2) *Net worth.*

Equity-linked bond   *Bond* whose payments are linked to a stock market index.

Equivalent annual cash flow (or cost)   *Annuity* with the same *present value* as the company's proposed investment.

ESOP   *Employee stock ownership plan.*

ETF   *Exchange-traded fund.*

Euribor   *Euro interbank offered rate.*

Euro interbank offered rate (Euribor)   The interest rate at which major international banks in Europe lend euros to each other.

Eurobond   *Bond* that is marketed internationally.

Eurocurrency   Deposit held outside the currency's issuing country (e.g., euroyen, or *eurodollar deposit*)

Eurodollar deposit   Dollar deposit with a bank outside the United States.

European option   *Option* that can be exercised only on final exercise date (cf. *American option*).

EVA   *Economic value added.*

Event risk   The risk that an unanticipated event (e.g., a takeover) will lead to a debt default.

Evergreen credit   *Revolving credit* without maturity.

Exchange of assets   Acquisition of another company by purchase of its assets in exchange for cash or shares.

Exchange of stock   Acquisition of another company by purchase of its stock in exchange for cash or shares.

Exchange-traded fund (ETF)   A stock designed to track a stock market index.

Ex dividend   Purchase of shares in which the buyer is not entitled to the forthcoming *dividend* (cf. *with dividend, cum dividend*).

Exercise price (strike price)   Price at which a *call option* or *put option* may be exercised.

Expectations theory   Theory that *forward interest rate* (*forward exchange rate*) equals expected *spot rate.*

Expected return   Average of possible returns weighted by their probabilities.

Ex rights   Purchase of shares that do not entitle the owner to buy shares in the company's *rights issue* (cf. *with rights, cum rights, rights on*).

Extendable bond   *Bond* whose maturity can be extended at the option of the lender (or issuer).

External finance   Finance that is not generated by the firm: new borrowing or an issue of stock (cf. *internal finance*).

Extra dividend   *Dividend* that may or may not be repeated (cf. *regular dividend*).

F

Face value   *Par value.*

Factoring   Arrangement whereby a financial institution buys a company's *accounts receivable* and collects the debt.

Fair price provision   *Appraisal rights.*

Fallen angel   *Junk bond* that was formerly *investment grade.*

FASB   Financial Accounting Standards Board.

FCIA   Foreign Credit Insurance Association.

FDIC   Federal Deposit Insurance Corporation.

Federal funds   Non-interest-bearing deposits by banks at the Federal Reserve. Excess reserves are lent by banks to each other.

Fedwire   A wire transfer system for high-value payments operated by the Federal Reserve System (cf. *CHIPS*).

Field warehouse   Warehouse rented by a warehouse company on another firm's premises (cf. *public warehouse*).

Financial assets   Claims on *real assets.*

Financial engineering   Combining or dividing existing instruments to create new financial products.

Financial lease (capital lease, full-payout lease)   Long-term, noncancelable lease (cf. *operating lease*).

Financial leverage (gearing)   Use of debt to increase the *expected return* on *equity*. Financial leverage is measured by the ratio of debt to debt plus equity (cf. *operating leverage*).

Firm commitment   Arrangement whereby the *underwriter* guarantees to sell the entire issue.

Fiscal agency agreement   An alternative to a bond *trust deed*. Unlike the trustee, the fiscal agent acts as an agent of the borrower.

Flat price   *Clean price.*

Flipping   Buying shares in an *IPO* and selling immediately.

Float   *See availability float, collection float, payment float.*

Floating lien   General *lien* against a company's assets or against a particular class of assets.

Floating-price convertible   *Death spiral convertible.*

Floating-rate note (FRN)   *Note* whose interest payment varies with the short-term interest rate.

Floating-rate preferred   *Preferred stock* paying dividends that vary with short-term interest rates.

Floor planning   Arrangement used to finance inventory. A finance company buys the inventory, which is then held in trust by the user.

Flow-to-equity method   Discounted value of cash flows to equityholders.

Foreign bond   A *bond* issued on the domestic *capital market* of another country.

Forex   Foreign exchange.

Forfaiter   Purchaser of promises to pay (e.g., *bills of exchange* or *promissory notes*) issued by importers.

Forward cover   Purchase or sale of forward foreign currency in order to offset a known future cash flow.

Forward exchange rate   Exchange rate fixed today for exchanging currency at some future date (cf. *spot exchange rate*).

Forward interest rate   Interest rate fixed today on a loan to be made at some future date (cf. *spot interest rate*).

Forward rate agreement (FRA)   Agreement to borrow or lend at a specified future date at an interest rate that is fixed today.

FRA   *Forward rate agreement.*

Free cash flow   Cash not required for operations or for reinvestment.

Free-rider problem   The temptation not to incur the costs of participating in a decision when one's influence on that decision is small.

FRN   *Floating-rate note.*

Full-payout lease   *Financial lease.*

Full-service lease (rental lease)   *Lease* in which the *lessor* promises to maintain and insure the equipment (cf. *net lease*).

Fundamental analysis   Security analysis that seeks to detect misvalued securities by an analysis of the firm's business prospects (cf. *technical analysis*).

Funded debt   Debt maturing after more than one year (cf. *unfunded debt*).

Futures contract   A contract to buy a commodity or security on a future date at a price that is fixed today. Unlike forward contracts, futures are traded on organized exchanges and are *marked to market* daily.

G

GAAP   Generally accepted accounting principles.

Gamma   A measure of how the *option delta* changes as the asset price changes.

Gearing   *Financial leverage.*

General cash offer   Issue of securities offered to all investors (cf. *rights issue*).

Gilt   A British government *bond*.

Golden parachute   A large termination payment due to a company's officers if they lose their jobs as a result of a *merger*.

Goodwill   The difference between the amount paid for a firm in a *merger* and its book value.

Governance   The oversight of a firm's management.

Gray market   Purchases and sales of securities that occur before the issue price is set.

Greenmail   Situation in which a large block of stock is held by an unfriendly company, forcing the target company to repurchase the stock at a substantial premium to prevent a takeover.

Greenshoe option   *Option* that allows the *underwriter* for a new issue to buy and resell additional shares.

Growth stock   *Common stock* of a company that has an opportunity to invest money to earn more than the *opportunity cost of capital* (cf. *income stock*).

H

Haircut   An additional margin of *collateral* for a loan.

Hedge fund   An investment fund charging a performance fee and open to a limited range of investors. Funds often follow complex strategies including *short sales*.

Hedge ratio (delta, option delta)   The number of shares to buy for each *option* sold to create a safe position;

more generally, the number of units of an asset that should be bought to hedge one unit of a liability.

Hedging Buying one security and selling another to reduce risk. A perfect hedge produces a riskless portfolio.

Hell-or-high-water clause Clause in a *lease* agreement that obligates the *lessee* to make payments regardless of what happens to the *lessor* or the equipment.

Highly leveraged transaction (HLT) Bank loan to a highly leveraged firm (formerly needed to be separately reported to the Federal Reserve Board).

High-yield bond *Junk bond.*

HLT *Highly leveraged transaction.*

Holding company Company whose sole function is to hold stock in the firm's subsidiaries.

Horizontal merger *Merger* between two companies that manufacture similar products (cf. *vertical merger, conglomerate merger*).

Horizontal spread The simultaneous purchase and sale of two *options* that differ only in their exercise date (cf. *vertical spread*).

Hurdle rate Minimum acceptable rate of return on a project.

I

IBF *International banking facility.*

IMM *International Monetary Market.*

Immunization The construction of an asset and a liability that have offsetting changes in value.

Implied volatility The volatility implied by *option* prices.

Imputation tax system Arrangement by which investors who receive a *dividend* also receive a tax credit for corporate taxes that the firm has paid.

Income bond *Bond* on which interest is payable only if earned.

Income stock *Common stock* with high *dividend yield* and few profitable investment opportunities (cf. *growth stock*).

Indenture Formal agreement, e.g., establishing the terms of a *bond* issue.

Indexed bond *Bond* whose payments are linked to an index, e.g., a consumer price index (see *TIPS*).

Index fund Investment fund designed to match the returns on a stock market index.

Indirect quote For foreign exchange, the number of units of a foreign currency needed to buy one U.S. dollar (cf. *direct quote*).

Industrial revenue bond (IRB) Bond issued by local government agencies on behalf of *corporations.*

Initial public offering (IPO) A company's first public issue of *common stock.*

Inside director Director who is also employed by the company.

In-substance defeasance *Defeasance* whereby debt is removed from the balance sheet but not canceled (cf. *novation*).

Intangible asset Nonmaterial asset, such as technical expertise, a trademark, or a patent (cf. *tangible asset*).

Integer programming Variant of *linear programming* whereby the solution values must be integers.

Interest cover *Times interest earned.*

Interest rate parity Theory that the differential between the *forward exchange rate* and the *spot exchange rate* is equal to the differential between the foreign and domestic interest rates.

Intermediation Investment through a financial institution (cf. *disintermediation*).

Internal finance Finance generated within a firm by *retained earnings* and *depreciation* (cf. *external finance*).

Internal growth rate The maximum rate of firm growth without *external finance* (cf. *sustainable growth rate*).

Internal rate of return (IRR) *Discount rate* at which investment has zero *net present value.*

International banking facility (IBF) A branch that an American bank establishes in the United States to do eurocurrency business.

International Monetary Market (IMM) The financial futures market within the Chicago Mercantile Exchange.

Interval measure The number of days that a firm can finance operations without additional cash income.

In-the-money option An *option* that would be worth exercising if it expired immediately (cf. *out-of-the-money option*).

Investment-grade bond *Bond* rated at least Baa by Moody's or BBB by Standard and Poor's or Fitch.

IOSCO International Organization of Securities Commissions.

IPO *Initial public offering.*

IRB *Industrial revenue bond.*

IRR *Internal rate of return.*

IRS Internal Revenue Service.

ISDA International Swap and Derivatives Association.

ISMA International Securities Market Association.

Issued share capital Total amount of shares that are in issue (cf. *outstanding share capital*).

J

Junior debt *Subordinated debt.*

Junk bond (high-yield bond) Debt that is rated below an *investment-grade bond.*

Just-in-time System of inventory management that requires minimum inventories of materials and very frequent deliveries by suppliers.

K

Keiretsu A network of Japanese companies organized around a major bank.

L

LBO *Leveraged buyout.*

Lease Long-term rental agreement.

Legal capital Value at which a company's shares are recorded in its books.

Legal defeasance *Novation.*

Lessee User of a leased asset (cf. *lessor*).

Lessor Owner of a leased asset (cf. *lessee*).

Letter of credit Letter from a bank stating that it has established a credit in the company's favor.

Letter stock Privately placed *common stock,* so called because the *SEC* requires a letter from the purchaser that the stock is not intended for resale.

Leverage See *financial leverage, operating leverage.*

Leveraged buyout (LBO) Acquisition in which (1) a large part of the purchase price is debt-financed and (2) the remaining *equity* is privately held by a small group of investors.

Leveraged lease *Lease* in which the *lessor* finances part of the cost of the asset by an issue of debt secured by the asset and the lease payments.

Liabilities, total liabilities Total value of financial claims on a firm's assets. Equals (1) total assets or (2) total assets minus *net worth.*

LIBOR *London interbank offered rate.*

Lien Lender's claims on specified assets.

Limited liability Limitation of a shareholder's losses to the amount invested.

Limited partnership *Partnership* in which some partners have *limited liability* and general partners have unlimited liability.

Limit order Order to buy (sell) securities within a maximum (minimum) price (cf. *market order*).

Linear programming (LP) Technique for finding the maximum value of some objective function subject to stated linear constraints.

Line of credit Agreement by a bank that a company may borrow at any time up to an established limit.

Liquid asset Asset that is easily and cheaply turned into cash—notably cash itself and short-term securities.

Liquidating dividend *Dividend* that represents a return of capital.

Liquidator Person appointed by unsecured creditors in the United Kingdom to oversee the sale of an insolvent firm's assets and the repayment of debts.

Liquidity-preference theory Theory that investors demand a higher yield to compensate for the extra risk of long-term *bonds.*

Liquidity premium (1) Additional return for investing in a security that cannot easily be turned into cash; (2) difference between the *forward interest rate* and the expected *spot interest rate.*

Liquid yield option note (LYON) *Zero-coupon,* callable, puttable, *convertible bond.*

Loan origination fee Up-front fee charged by the lending bank.

Lockbox system Form of *concentration banking.* Customers send payments to a post office box. A local bank collects and processes the checks and transfers surplus funds to the company's principal bank.

London interbank offered rate (LIBOR) The interest rate at which major international banks in London lend to each other. (LIBID is London interbank bid rate; LIMEAN is mean of bid and offered rate.)

Long hedge Purchase of a *hedging* instrument (e.g., a *future*) to hedge a short position in the underlying asset (cf. *short hedge*).

Longevity bonds *Bonds* that pay a higher rate of interest if a high proportion of the population survives to a particular age.

Lookback option   *Option* whose payoff depends on the highest asset price recorded over the life of the option.

LP   *Linear programming.*

LYON   *Liquid yield option note.*

M

MACRS   *Modified accelerated cost recovery system.*

Maintenance margin   Minimum margin that must be maintained on a *futures* contract.

Majority voting   Voting system under which each director is voted upon separately (cf. *cumulative voting*).

Management buyout (MBO)   *Leveraged buyout* whereby the acquiring group is led by the firm's management.

Mandatory convertible   *Bond* automatically convertible into equity, usually with a limit on the value of stock received.

Margin   Cash or securities set aside by an investor as evidence that he or she can honor a commitment.

Marked to market   An arrangement whereby the profits or losses on a *futures* contract are settled up each day.

Market capitalization   Market value of *outstanding share capital.*

Market capitalization rate   *Expected return* on a security.

Market model   Model suggesting a linear relationship between actual returns on a stock and on the market portfolio.

Market order   Order to buy or sell securities at the prevailing market price (cf. *limit order*).

Market risk (systematic risk)   Risk that cannot be diversified away.

Market-to-book ratio   Ratio of market value to book value of firm's *equity.*

Market value added   Difference between market value and book value of firm's *equity.*

Maturity factoring   *Factoring* arrangement that provides collection and insurance of *accounts receivable.*

MBO   *Management buyout.*

MDA   *Multiple-discriminant analysis.*

Medium-term note (MTN)   Debt with a typical maturity of 1 to 10 years offered regularly by a company using the same procedure as *commercial paper.*

Merger   (1) Acquisition in which all assets and liabilities are absorbed by the buyer (cf. *exchange of assets, exchange of stock*); (2) more generally, any combination of two companies.

MIP (Monthly income preferred security)   *Preferred stock* issued by a subsidiary located in a tax haven. The subsidiary relends the money to the parent.

Mismatch bond   *Floating-rate note* whose interest rate is reset at more frequent intervals than the rollover period (e.g., a note whose payments are set quarterly on the basis of the one-year interest rate).

Modified accelerated cost recovery system (MACRS)   Schedule of *depreciation* deductions allowed for tax purposes.

Modified IRR   *Internal rate of return* calculated by first discounting later cash flows back to earlier periods so that there remains only one change in the sign of the cash flows.

Momentum   Characteristic of stocks showing persistent recent high returns.

Money center bank   A major U.S. bank that undertakes a wide range of banking activities.

Money market   Market for short-term safe investments.

Money-market deposit account (MMDA)   A bank account paying *money-market* interest rate.

Money-market fund   *Mutual fund* that invests solely in short-term safe securities.

Monoline   Insurance company that insures debtholders against the risk of default.

Monte Carlo simulation   Method for calculating the probability distribution of possible outcomes, e.g., from a project.

Moral hazard   The risk that the existence of a contract will change the behavior of one or both parties to the contract; e.g., an insured firm may take fewer fire precautions.

Mortality bonds   *Bonds* that pay a higher rate of interest if there is a sharp rise in the death rate.

Mortgage bond   *Bond* secured against plant and equipment.

MTN   *Medium-term note.*

Multiple-discriminant analysis (MDA)   Statistical technique for distinguishing between two groups on the basis of their observed characteristics.

Mutual fund   Managed investment fund whose shares are sold to investors.

Mutually exclusive projects Two projects that cannot both be undertaken.

N

Naked option *Option* held on its own, i.e., not used for *hedging* a holding in the asset or other options.

Nasdaq National Association of Security Dealers Automated Quote System. A U.S. stock exchange whose dealers tend to specialize in high-tech stocks.

Negative pledge clause Clause under which the borrower agrees not to permit an exclusive *lien* on any of its assets.

Negotiated underwriting Method of choosing an *underwriter.* Most firms may choose their *underwriter* by negotiation (cf. *competitive bidding*).

Net lease *Lease* in which the *lessee* promises to maintain and insure the equipment (cf. *full-service lease*).

Net present value (NPV) A project's net contribution to wealth—*present value* minus initial investment.

Net working capital *Current assets* minus *current liabilities.*

Net worth Book value of a company's *common stock,* surplus, and *retained earnings.*

Nominal interest rate Interest rate expressed in money terms (cf. *real interest rate*).

Nonrefundable debt Debt that may not be called in order to replace it with another issue at a lower interest cost.

NOPAT Net operating profit after tax.

Normal distribution Symmetric bell-shaped distribution that can be completely defined by its mean and *standard deviation.*

Note Unsecured debt with a maturity of up to 10 years.

Novation (legal defeasance) *Defeasance* whereby the firm's debt is canceled (cf. *in-substance defeasance*).

NPV *Net present value.*

NYSE New York Stock Exchange.

O

OAT (Obligation assimilable du Trésor) French government *bond.*

Odd lot A trade of less than 100 shares (cf. *round lot*).

Off-balance-sheet financing Financing that is not shown as a liability in a company's balance sheet.

Offer price *Asked price.*

OID debt *Original issue discount debt.*

Old-line factoring *Factoring* arrangement that provides collection, insurance, and finance for *accounts receivable.*

On the run The most recently issued (and, therefore, typically the most liquid) government *bond* in a particular maturity range.

Open account Arrangement whereby sales are made with no formal debt contract. The buyer signs a receipt, and the seller records the sale in the sales ledger.

Open-end mortgage Mortgage against which additional debt may be issued (cf. *closed-end mortgage*).

Open interest The number of currently outstanding *futures* contracts.

Operating cycle The time from a firm's initial purchase of raw materials until the payment from the customer for the finished product.

Operating lease Short-term, cancelable *lease* (cf. *financial lease*).

Operating leverage Fixed operating costs, so called because they accentuate variations in profits (cf. *financial leverage*).

Opportunity cost of capital (hurdle rate, cost of capital) *Expected return* that is foregone by investing in a project rather than in comparable financial securities.

Option See *call option, put option.*

Option delta *Hedge ratio.*

Original issue discount debt (OID debt) Debt that is initially offered at a price below *face value.*

OTC *Over-the-counter.*

Out-of-the-money option An *option* that would not be worth exercising if it matured immediately (cf. *in-the-money option*).

Outstanding share capital *Issued share capital* less the *par value* of shares that are held in the company's treasury.

Oversubscription privilege In a *rights issue,* arrangement by which shareholders are given the right to apply for any shares that are not taken up.

Over-the-counter (OTC) Informal market that does not involve a securities exchange.

P

Partnership Joint ownership of business whereby general partners have unlimited liability.

Par value (face value) Value of a security shown on the certificate.

Pass-through securities *Notes* or *bonds* backed by a package of assets (e.g., mortgage pass-throughs, *CARs, CARDs*).

Path-dependent option *Option* whose value depends on the sequence of prices of the underlying asset rather than just the final price of the asset.

Payables *Accounts payable.*

Payback rule Requirement that project should recover its initial investment within a specified time.

Pay-in-kind bond (PIK) *Bond* that allows the issuer to choose to make interest payments in the form of additional bonds.

Payment float Company-written checks that have not yet cleared (cf. *availability float*).

Payout ratio *Dividend* as a proportion of earnings per share.

PBGC Pension Benefit Guarantee Corporation.

P/E ratio Share price divided by earnings per share.

PERC (Preferred equity redemption cumulative stock) *Preferred stock* that converts automatically into equity at a stated date. A limit is placed on the value of the shares that the investor receives.

Perpetuity Investment offering a level stream of cash flows in perpetuity (cf. *consol*).

PIK *Pay-in-kind bond.*

PN *Project note.*

Poison pill Includes a variety of takeover defenses, notably the right of existing shareholders to acquire stock at a discount if a bidder acquires a minimum number of shares.

Poison put A *covenant* allowing the *bond*holder to demand repayment in the event of a hostile *merger*.

Pooling of interest Method of accounting for *mergers* (no longer available in the USA). The consolidated balance sheet of the merged firm is obtained by combining the balance sheets of the separate firms (cf. *purchase accounting*).

Position diagram Diagram showing the possible payoffs from a *derivative* investment.

Postaudit Evaluation of an investment project after it has been undertaken.

Praecipium Arrangement fee for *syndicated loan*.

Preemptive right Common stockholder's right to anything of value distributed by the company.

Preferred stock Stock that takes priority over common stock in regard to *dividends*. Dividends may not be paid on *common stock* unless the dividend is paid on all preferred stock (cf. *cumulative preferred stock*). The dividend rate on preferred is usually fixed at time of issue.

Prenegotiated bankruptcy *Chapter 11* bankruptcy where only principal creditors have agreed to the reorganization plan before filing (cf. *prepackaged bankruptcy*).

Prepack *Prepackaged bankruptcy.*

Prepackaged bankruptcy (prepack) Bankruptcy proceedings intended to confirm a reorganization plan that has already been agreed to informally.

Present value Discounted value of future cash flows.

Present value of growth opportunities (PVGO) *Net present value* of investments the firm is expected to make in the future.

PRIDE Similar to a *PERC* except that as the equity price rises beyond a specified point, the investor shares in the stock appreciation.

Primary issue Issue of new securities by a firm (cf. *secondary issue*).

Prime rate Benchmark lending rate set by U.S. banks.

Principal Amount of debt that must be repaid.

Principal–agent problem Problem faced by a principal (e.g., shareholder) in ensuring that an agent (e.g., manager) acts on his or her behalf.

Private equity *Equity* that is not publicly traded and that is used to finance business start-ups, *leveraged buyouts*, etc.

Private placement Issue of *bonds* or *stock* that is placed privately with a few investors and is not then publicly traded.

Privileged subscription issue *Rights issue.*

Production payment Loan in the form of advance payment for future delivery of a product.

Profitability index Ratio of a project's *NPV* to the initial investment.

Pro forma Projected.

Project finance Debt that is largely a claim against the cash flows from a particular project rather than against the firm as a whole.

Project note (PN) *Note* issued by public housing or urban renewal agencies.

Promissory note Promise to pay.

Prospect theory A theory of asset pricing suggested by the observation of behavioral psychologists that investors have a particular aversion to losses even if very small.

Prospectus Summary of the *registration* statement providing information on an issue of securities.

Protective put *Put option* that is combined with holding in the underlying asset.

Proxy vote Vote cast by one person on behalf of another.

Public warehouse (terminal warehouse) Warehouse operated by an independent warehouse company on its own premises (cf. *field warehouse*).

Purchase accounting Method of accounting for *mergers*. The assets of the acquired firm are shown at market value on the balance sheet of the acquirer (cf. *pooling of interest*).

Purchase fund Resembles a *sinking fund* except that money is used only to purchase bonds if they are selling below their *par value*.

Put–call parity The relationship between the prices of European *put* and *call options*.

Put option *Option* to sell an asset at a specified *exercise price* on or before a specified exercise date (cf. *call option*).

PVGO *Present value of growth opportunities.*

Pyramid Created by forming a *holding company* whose only asset is a controlling interest in a second holding company, which in turn has a controlling interest in an operating company.

Q

q Ratio of the market value of an asset to its replacement cost.

QIBs *Qualified institutional buyers.*

Quadratic programming Variant of *linear programming* whereby the equations are quadratic rather than linear.

Qualified Institutional buyers (QIBs) Institutions that are allowed to trade unregistered stock among themselves.

Quanto swap *Differential swap.*

Quick ratio (acid-test ratio) Measure of liquidity: (cash + marketable securities + *receivables*) divided by *current liabilities*.

R

Range forward A *forward exchange rate* contract that places upper and lower bounds on the cost of foreign exchange.

Ratchet bonds Floating-rate *bonds* whose coupon can only be reset downward.

Rate-sensitive bonds *Bonds* whose coupon rate changes as issuer's credit-rating changes.

Real assets *Tangible assets* and *intangible assets* used to carry on business (cf. *financial assets*).

Real estate investment trust (REIT) Trust company formed to invest in real estate.

Real interest rate Interest rate expressed in terms of real goods, i.e., *nominal interest rate* adjusted for inflation.

Real option The flexibility to modify, postpone, expand, or abandon a project.

Receivables *Accounts receivable.*

Receiver A bankruptcy practitioner appointed by secured creditors in the United Kingdom to oversee the repayment of debts.

Record date Date set by directors when making dividend payment. *Dividends* are sent to stockholders who are registered on the record date.

Recourse Term describing a type of loan. If a loan is with recourse, the lender has a general claim against the parent company if the *collateral* is insufficient to repay the debt.

Red herring Preliminary *prospectus*.

Refunding Replacement of existing debt with a new issue of debt.

Registered security Security whose ownership is recorded by the company's *registrar* (cf. *bearer security*).

Registrar Financial institution appointed to record issue and ownership of company securities.

Registration Process of obtaining *SEC* approval for a public issue of securities.

Regression analysis In statistics, a technique for finding the line of best fit.

Regular dividend *Dividend* that the company expects to maintain in the future.

Regulation A issue Small security issues that are partially exempt from *SEC registration* requirements.

REIT *Real estate investment trust.*

Rental lease *Full-service lease.*

Replicating portfolio Package of assets whose returns exactly replicate those of an *option*.

Repo *Repurchase agreement.*

Repurchase agreement (RP, repo, buy-back) Purchase of Treasury securities from a securities dealer with an agreement that the dealer will repurchase them at a specified price.

Residual income After-tax profit less the *opportunity cost of capital* employed by the business (see also *Economic Value Added*).

Residual risk *Specific risk.*

Retained earnings Earnings not paid out as *dividends*.

Return on equity Usually, equity earnings as a proportion of the book value of equity.

Return on investment (ROI) Generally, book income as a proportion of net book value.

Revenue bond Municipal *bond* that is serviced out of the revenues from a particular project.

Reverse convertible Bond that gives the issuer the right to convert it into common stock.

Reverse FRN (yield curve note) *Floating-rate note* whose payments rise as the general level of interest rates falls and vice versa.

Reverse split Action by the company to reduce the number of outstanding shares by replacing two or more of its shares with a single, more valuable share.

Revolving credit Legally assured *line of credit* with a bank.

Rights issue (privileged subscription issue) Issue of securities offered to current stockholders (cf. *general cash offer*).

Rights on *With rights.*

Risk premium Expected additional return for making a risky investment rather than a safe one.

Road show Series of meetings between a company and potential investors before the company decides on the terms of a new issue.

ROI *Return on investment.*

Roll-over CD A package of successive *certificates of deposit*.

Round lot A trade of 100 shares (cf. *odd lot*).

RP *Repurchase agreement.*

R squared (R^2) Square of the *correlation coefficient*—the proportion of the variability in one series that can be explained by the variability of one or more other series.

Rule 144a *SEC* rule allowing *qualified institutional buyers* to buy and trade unregistered securities.

S

Sale and lease-back Sale of an existing asset to a financial institution that then *leases* it back to the user (cf. *direct lease*).

Salvage value Scrap or resale value of plant and equipment.

Samurai bond A yen *bond* issued in Tokyo by a non-Japanese borrower (cf. *bulldog bond, Yankee bond*).

SBIC Small Business Investment Company.

Scenario analysis Analysis of the profitability of a project under alternative economic scenarios.

Season datings Extended credit for customers who order goods out of the peak season.

Seasoned issue Issue of a security for which there is an existing market (cf. *unseasoned issue*).

SEC Securities and Exchange Commission.

Secondary issue (1) Procedure for selling blocks of *seasoned issues* of stock; (2) more generally, sale of already issued stock.

Secondary market Market in which one can buy or sell *seasoned issues* of securities.

Secured debt Debt that, in the event of default, has first claim on specified assets.

Securitization Substitution of tradable securities for privately negotiated instruments.

Security market line Line representing the relationship between *expected return* and *market risk*.

Self-liquidating loan Loan to finance *current assets*. The sale of the current assets provides the cash to repay the loan.

Self-selection Consequence of a contract that induces only one group (e.g., low-risk individuals) to participate.

Semistrong-form efficient market Market in which security prices reflect all publicly available information (cf. *weak-form efficient market* and *strong-form efficient market*).

Senior debt   Debt that, in the event of bankruptcy, must be repaid before *subordinated debt* receives any payment.

Sensitivity analysis   Analysis of the effect on project profitability of possible changes in sales, costs, and so on.

Serial bonds   Package of *bonds* that mature in successive years.

Series bond   *Bond* that may be issued in several series under the same *indenture*.

Shark repellant   Amendment to company charter intended to protect against takeover.

Sharpe ratio   Ratio of portfolio's *risk premium* to its risk (*standard deviation*).

Shelf registration   A procedure that allows firms to file one *registration* statement covering several issues of the same security.

Shogun bond   Dollar *bond* issued in Japan by a nonresident.

Short hedge   Sale of a *hedging* instrument (e.g., a *future*) to *hedge* a long position in the underlying asset (cf. *long hedge*).

Short sale   Sale of a security the investor does not own.

Sight draft   Demand for immediate payment (cf. *time draft*).

Signal   Action that demonstrates an individual's unobservable characteristics (because it would be unduly costly for someone without those characteristics to take the action).

Simple interest   Interest calculated only on the initial investment (cf. *compound interest*).

Simulation   *Monte Carlo simulation.*

Sinker   *Sinking fund.*

Sinking fund (sinker)   Fund established by a company to retire debt before maturity.

SIV (structured investment vehicle)   A fund that typically invested in mortgage-backed securities, which it financed by issuing senior and junior *tranches* of *asset-backed commercial paper* and longer-term *notes*.

Skewed distribution   Probability distribution in which an unequal number of observations lie below and above the mean.

SPE   *Special-purpose entity.*

Special dividend (extra dividend)   *Dividend* that is unlikely to be repeated.

Specialist   *Designated market maker.*

Special-purpose entity   *Partnerships* established by companies to hold certain assets and obtain funding. May be used to obtain off-balance-sheet debt for the parent.

Specific risk (residual risk, unique risk, unsystematic risk)   Risk that can be eliminated by diversification.

Spinning   The *underwriter* of an *IPO* unethically allots a portion of offering to senior management of a client company.

Spin-off   Distribution of shares in a subsidiary to the company's shareholders so that they hold shares separately in the two firms.

Spot exchange rate   Exchange rate on currency for immediate delivery (cf. *forward exchange rate*).

Spot price   Price of asset for immediate delivery (in contrast to forward or futures price).

Spot rate   Interest rate fixed today on a loan that is made today (cf. *forward interest rate*).

Spread   Difference between the price at which an *underwriter* buys an issue from a firm and the price at which the underwriter sells it to the public.

Staggered board   Board whose directors are elected periodically, instead of at one time.

Standard deviation   Square root of the *variance*—a measure of variability.

Standard error   In statistics, a measure of the possible error in an estimate.

Standby agreement   In a *rights issue,* agreement that the *underwriter* will purchase any stock not purchased by investors.

Step-up bond   *Bond* whose *coupon* is stepped up over time (also step-down bond).

Stock dividend   *Dividend* in the form of stock rather than cash.

Stock split   "Free" issue of shares to existing shareholders.

Straddle   The combination of a *put option* and a *call option* with the same *exercise price*.

Straight-line depreciation   An equal dollar amount of *depreciation* in each period.

Strike price   *Exercise price* of an *option*.

Stripped bond (strip)   *Bond* that is subdivided into a series of *zero-coupon bonds*.

Strong-form efficient market Market in which security prices reflect instantaneously all information available to investors (cf. *weak-form efficient market* and *semistrong-form efficient market*).

Structured debt Debt that has been customized for the buyer, often by incorporating unusual *options*.

Subordinated debt (junior debt) Debt over which *senior debt* takes priority. In the event of bankruptcy, subordinated debtholders receive payment only after senior debt is paid off in full.

Subprime loans The most risky category of loans.

Sum-of-the-years'-digits depreciation Method of *accelerated depreciation*.

Sunk costs Costs that have been incurred and cannot be reversed.

Supermajority Provision in a company's charter requiring a majority of, say, 80% of shareholders to approve certain changes, such as a *merger*.

Sushi bond A *eurobond* issued by a Japanese corporation.

Sustainable growth rate Maximum rate of firm growth without increasing financial leverage (cf. *internal growth rate*).

Swap An arrangement whereby two companies lend to each other on different terms, e.g., in different currencies, or one at a fixed rate and the other at a floating rate.

Swaption *Option* on a *swap*.

Sweep program Arrangement whereby bank invests a company's available cash at the end of each day.

Swingline facility Bank borrowing facility to provide finance while the firm replaces U.S. *commercial paper* with eurocommercial paper.

Syndicated loan A large loan provided by a group of banks.

Systematic risk *Market risk.*

T

Take-or-pay In *project finance*, arrangement where parent company agrees to pay for output of project even if it chooses not to take delivery.

Take-up fee Fee paid to *underwriters* of a *rights issue* on any stock they are obliged to purchase.

Tangent efficient portfolio The portfolio of risky assets offering the highest risk premium per unit of risk (*standard deviation*).

Tangible asset Physical asset, such as plant, machinery, and offices (cf. *intangible asset*).

Tax-anticipation bill Short-term bill issued by the U.S. Treasury that can be surrendered at *face value* in payment of taxes.

T-bill *Treasury bill.*

Technical analysis Security analysis that seeks to detect and interpret patterns in past security prices (cf. *fundamental analysis*).

TED spread Difference between *LIBOR* and U.S. *Treasury bill* rate.

Tender offer General offer made directly to a firm's shareholders to buy their stock.

10-K Annual financial statements as filed with the *SEC*.

10-Q Quarterly financial statements as filed with the *SEC*.

Tenor Maturity of a loan.

Terminal warehouse *Public warehouse.*

Term loan Medium-term, privately placed loan, usually made by a bank.

Term structure of interest rates Relationship between interest rates on loans of different maturities (cf. *yield curve*).

Throughput arrangement Arrangement by which shareholders of a pipeline company agree to make sufficient use of pipeline to enable the pipeline company to service its debt.

Tick Minimum amount the price of a security may change.

Time draft Demand for payment at a stated future date (cf. *sight draft*).

Times-interest-earned (interest cover) Earnings before interest and tax, divided by interest payments.

TIPS (Treasury Inflation Protected Securities) U.S. Treasury *bonds* whose *coupon* and *principal* payments are linked to the Consumer Price Index.

Toehold Small investment by a company in the shares of a potential takeover target.

Tolling contract In *project finance*, arrangement whereby parent company promises to deliver materials to project for processing and then to repurchase them.

Tombstone Advertisement listing the *underwriters* to a security issue.

Trade acceptance   Written demand that has been accepted by an industrial company to pay a given sum at a future date (cf. *banker's acceptance*).

Trade credit   *Accounts receivable.*

Trade debt   *Accounts payable.*

Tranche   Portion of a new issue sold at a point in time different from the remainder or that has different terms.

Transaction exposure   Risk to a firm with known future cash flows in a foreign currency that arises from possible changes in the exchange rate (cf. *economic exposure, translation exposure*).

Transfer agent   Individual or institution appointed by a company to look after the transfer of securities.

Translation exposure   Risk of adverse effects on a firm's financial statements that may arise from changes in exchange rates (cf. *economic exposure, transaction exposure*).

Treasurer   Principal financial manager (cf. *controller*).

Treasury bill (T-bill)   Short-term discount debt maturing in less than one year, issued regularly by the government.

Treasury stock   *Common stock* that has been repurchased by the company and held in the company's treasury.

Trust deed   Agreement between trustee and borrower setting out terms of a *bond*.

Trust receipt   Receipt for goods that are to be held in trust for the lender.

Tunneling   Actions by a controlling shareholder to transfer wealth out of the firm (e.g., by supplying goods at an inflated price).

U

Underpricing   Issue of securities below their market value.

Underwriter   Firm that buys an issue of securities from a company and resells it to investors.

Unfunded debt   Debt maturing within one year (cf. *funded debt*).

Uniform price auction   Auction in which all successful bidders pay the same price (cf. *discriminatory price auction*).

Unique risk   *Specific risk.*

Unseasoned issue   Issue of a security for which there is no existing market (cf. *seasoned issue*).

Unsystematic risk   *Specific risk.*

V

Value additivity   Rule that the value of the whole must equal the sum of the values of the parts.

Value at risk (VAR)   The probability of portfolio losses exceeding some specified proportion.

Value stock   A stock that is expected to provide steady income but relatively low growth (often refers to stocks with a low ratio of market-to-book value).

Vanilla issue   Issue without unusual features.

VAR   *Value at risk.*

Variable-rate demand bond (VRDB)   Floating-rate *bond* that can be sold back periodically to the issuer.

Variance   Mean squared deviation from the expected value; a measure of variability.

Variation margin   The daily gains or losses on a *futures* contract credited to the investor's margin account.

Vega   A measure of how the *option* price changes as the asset's volatility changes.

Venture capital   Capital to finance a new firm.

Vertical merger   *Merger* between a supplier and its customer (cf. *horizontal merger, conglomerate merger*).

Vertical spread   Simultaneous purchase and sale of two options that differ only in their *exercise price* (cf. *horizontal spread*).

VIX   A measure of the *implied volatility* of stocks in the S&P 500 Index.

VRDB   *Variable rate demand bond.*

W

WACC   *Weighted-average cost of capital.*

Warehouse receipt   Evidence that a firm owns goods stored in a warehouse.

Warrant   Long-term *call option* issued by a company.

Weak-form efficient market   Market in which security prices instantaneously reflect the information in the history of security prices. In such a market security prices follow a random walk (cf. *semistrong-form efficient market* and *strong-form efficient market*).

Weighted-average cost of capital (WACC)   *Expected return* on a portfolio of all the firm's securities. Used as *hurdle rate* for capital investment.

White knight   A friendly potential acquirer sought out by a target company threatened by a less welcome suitor.

Wi.   When issued.

Winner's curse   Problem faced by uninformed bidders. For example, in an *initial public offering* uninformed participants are likely to receive larger allotments of issues that informed participants know are overpriced.

With dividend (cum dividend)   Purchase of shares in which the buyer is entitled to the forthcoming *dividend* (cf. *ex dividend*).

Withholding tax   Tax levied on *dividends* paid abroad.

With rights (cum rights, rights on)   Purchase of shares in which the buyer is entitled to the rights to buy shares in the company's *rights issue* (cf. *ex rights*).

Working capital   *Current assets* and *current liabilities*. The term is commonly used as synonymous with *net working capital*.

Workout   Informal arrangement between a borrower and creditors.

Writer   *Option* seller.

X

xd   *Ex dividend.*

xr   *Ex rights.*

Y

Yankee bond   A dollar *bond* issued in the United States by a non-U.S. borrower (cf. *bulldog bond, Samurai bond*).

Yield curve   *Term structure of interest rates.*

Yield curve note   *Reverse FRN.*

Yield to maturity   *Internal rate of return* on a bond.

Z

Zero-coupon bond   *Discount bond* making no *coupon* payments.

Z-score   Measure of the likelihood of bankruptcy.

INDEX

Note: Page numbers followed by *n* indicate notes.